BELCH BELCH GUOLLA

ADVERTISING & PROMOTION

THIRD CANADIAN EDITION

AN INTEGRATED MARKETING COMMUNICATIONS PERSPECTIVE

George E. Belch
San Diego State University

Michael A. Belch
San Diego State University

Michael A. Guolla
University of Ottawa

Toronto Montréal Boston Burr Ridge, IL Dubuque, IA Madison, WI New York
San Francisco St. Louis Bangkok Bogotá Caracas Kuala Lumpur Lisbon London
Madrid Mexico City Milan New Delhi Santiago Seoul Singapore Sydney Taipei

The McGraw·Hill Companies

Advertising & Promotion
An Integrated Marketing Communications Perspective
Third Canadian Edition

ISBN-13: 978-0-07-097428-9
ISBN-10: 0-07-097428-4

2 3 4 5 6 7 8 9 10 CTP 0 9

Printed in China

Editorial Director: Joanna Cotton
Executive Sponsoring Editor: Leanna MacLean
Senior Marketing Manager: Joy Armitage Taylor
Senior Developmental Editor: Denise Foote
Editorial Associate: Stephanie Hess
Permissions Editor: Alison Derry
Photo/Permissions Research: Tracey Haggert
Supervising Editor: Elizabeth Priest
Copy Editor: Kelli Howey
Senior Production Coordinator: Jennifer Hall
Cover and Interior Design: Greg Devitt
Cover Image: © First Light
Page Layout: SR Nova Pvt Ltd., Bangalore, India
Printer: China Translation & Printing Services Limited

Library and Archives Canada Cataloguing in Publication

Belch, George E. (George Eugene)
Advertising & Promotion: an integrated marketing communications perspective / George E. Belch, Michael A. Belch, Michael A. Guolla. -- 3rd Canadian ed.

Includes bibliographical references and index.
ISBN 978-0-07-097428-9
1. Advertising--Textbooks. 2. Sales promotion--Textbooks. 3. Communication in marketing--Textbooks. I. Belch, Michael A. II. Guolla, Michael Angelo III. Title. IV. Title: Advertising and Promotion.

HF5823.B38 2008 659.1 C2008-900093-5

Dedicated to my wonderful family,
Teresa, Louise, Daniel, and Nicolas.

BRIEF CONTENTS

CONTENTS

Contents

Contents

PREFACE

ADVERTISING AND PROMOTION

Nearly everyone in the modern world is influenced to some degree by advertising and other forms of promotion. Organizations in both the private and public sectors have learned that communicating effectively and efficiently with their target audiences is critical to their success. Advertising and other types of promotional messages are used to sell goods and services as well as to promote causes and individuals, and to influence societal problems. The field of advertising and promotion has changed tremendously with recent advancements in technology coupled with adaptations of organizations and their agencies to meet the needs of many different target audiences.

For decades, the advertising strategy for a national brand involved creating one or two commercials that could be run on network television, a few print ads that would run in general interest magazines, and some sales promotion support such as coupons or premium offers. However, in today's world there are myriad media outlets—print, radio, specialty TV channels on cable and satellite delivery services, and the Internet—competing for consumers' attention. Marketers are also communicating with their customers and potential customers, along with various stakeholders through additional means like events, sponsorships, public relations, and innovative digital applications.

This text introduces students to the field of advertising and promotion. While advertising is its primary focus, it goes beyond an introductory advertising text because there is more to most organizations' promotional programs than just advertising. Currently marketers and their agencies to approach advertising and promotion from an integrated marketing communications (IMC) perspective, which calls for a "big picture" approach to planning promotion programs and coordinating the various communication functions. To understand the role of advertising and promotion in today's business world, one must recognize how a firm can use all the promotional tools to communicate.

OVERVIEW OF THE THIRD CANADIAN EDITION

- **A Continuing Emphasis on Integrated Marketing Communications** This edition emphasizes on approaching the field of advertising and promotion from an integrated marketing communications perspective to attain communication and behavioural objectives for multiple target audiences. The importance of specific communication objectives for each target audience and the importance of unique messages that resonate for each target audience are developed in many chapters. This approach helps establish a unique brand position for each target audience while maintaining the overall market position of the brand.
- **New Chapter Opening Vignettes** All of the chapter opening vignettes are new and were chosen for their currency and relevance to Canadian students. They demonstrate how various companies and advertising agencies use advertising and other IMC tools and provide interesting insights regarding trends and developments occurring throughout Canada.
- **New and Updated Perspectives** All of the boxed items focusing on specific examples of how companies are using integrated marketing communications are new or updated, and provide insight into many of the most current and popular advertising and promotional campaigns. The IMC, Ethical, and Global Perspectives address interesting issues related to IMC tools in a variety of contexts.
- **Canadian Examples** Wherever possible, the statistical information presented in tables, charts, and figures throughout the text has been updated. The most current Canadian trade literature was reviewed to ensure that this text reflects the most current perspectives. Many new Canadian examples and ads throughout the book have been added.
- **Clear Decision Focus** Chapter 1 features a clear planning framework and identifies the content of an IMC plan. This framework is followed more closely throughout the text as major parts are organized and given a title that corresponds to the steps in the IMC plan. A clear distinction is made between the type of decisions that a marketer or advertiser makes versus the information they use to formulate the decision. This approach makes it easier for students to understand the key decisions that need to be made for a successful IMC plan.
- **IMC Planning** This new and revised section has been placed at the conclusion of each chapter to

indicate how managers can use the concepts of the chapter while making decisions for an IMC plan, offering a consistent theme of planning integration throughout the text.

Organization of this Text

This book is divided into five major parts. In Part 1, "Understand Integrated Marketing Communications," we provide students with a solid background in the areas of IMC planning, consumer behaviour, and communication. Chapter 1 provides an overview of advertising and promotion and an IMC planning model shows the steps in the promotional planning process. This model provides a framework for developing the IMC program and is followed throughout the text. In Chapter 2, we describe how firms organize for advertising and promotion and examine the role of ad agencies and other firms that deliver promotional services. Chapter 3 explains how managers can use an understanding of buyer behaviour to develop effective communication that is directed to specific target audiences. Chapter 4 examines various communication theories and models of how consumers respond to advertising messages and other forms of marketing communication.

In Part 2, "Articulate the Message," we consider how firms develop objectives for their IMC programs and how to translate those objectives into meaningful messages. Chapter 5 stresses the importance of knowing what to expect from advertising and promotion, the different types of communication objectives, characteristics of good objectives, and problems in setting objectives. Chapter 6 explores various ways advertisers try to position their brands through effective communication. Chapter 7 discusses the planning and development of the creative strategy and advertising campaign. In Chapter 8 we turn our attention to ways to execute the creative strategy and some criteria for evaluating creative work. Chapter 9 discusses ways to measure the effectiveness of promotional messages from an IMC program, including methods for pretesting and posttesting advertising messages and campaigns.

In Part 3, "Deliver the Message," we explore the various ways of getting the message to the target audience. Chapters 10 through 13 cover media strategy and planning and advertising media. Chapter 10 introduces the key principles of media planning and strategy, and examines how a media plan is developed. We have also included methods for determining and allocating the promotional budget into this chapter. Chapter 11 discusses the strengths and limitations of broadcast media, as well as issues regarding the purchase of radio and TV time and audience measurement. Chapter 12 considers the same issues for the print media (magazines and newspapers). Chapter 13 examines the role of out-of-home and support media.

In Part 4, "Strengthen the Message," we continue the IMC emphasis by examining other promotional tools. Chapter 14 examines the area of sales promotion, including both consumer-promotions and programs targeted to the trade (retailers, wholesalers, and other intermediaries). Chapter 15 covers the role of public relations in IMC. Chapter 16 looks at direct marketing and database marketing allowing companies communicate directly with target audiences through various media. Chapter 17 describes how Internet media delivers promotional messages and other IMC tools.

The text concludes with Part 5, "Advertising and Society," and contains Chapter 18, which discusses the regulatory, social, ethical, and economic issues advertising and promotion.

Chapter Features

The following features in each chapter enhance students' understanding of the material as well as their reading enjoyment.

Chapter Objectives

Objectives are provided at the beginning of each chapter to identify the major areas and points covered in the chapter and guide the learning effort.

Chapter Objectives

- To understand how companies organize for advertising and other aspects of integrated marketing communications.
- To examine methods for selecting, compensating, and evaluating advertising agencies.
- To explain the role and functions of specialized marketing communications organizations.
- To examine various perspectives on the use of integrated services and responsibilities of advertisers versus agencies.

Chapter Opening Vignettes

Each chapter begins with a vignette that shows the effective use of integrated marketing communications by a company or ad agency or discusses an interesting issue that is relevant to the chapter. These opening vignettes are designed to draw the students into the chapter by presenting an interesting example, development, or issue that relates to the material covered in the chapter.

IMC, Ethical, and Global Perspectives

These boxed items feature in-depth discussions of interesting issues related to the chapter material and the practical application of integrated marketing communications and ethical and global marketing. Each chapter contains insights into the world of integrated marketing communications.

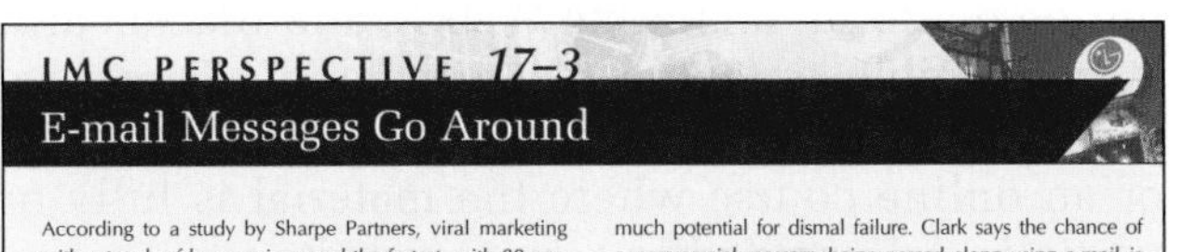

IMC PERSPECTIVE 17–3
E-mail Messages Go Around

According to a study by Sharpe Partners, viral marketing with a touch of humour is spread the fastest, with 88 percent of respondents to the study saying they send along jokes or cartoons. The second most popular category was news, with a 56 percent pass-along rate, and health care and health information at 32 percent. Business and personal finance and sports and hobbies were found to be least popular, at 24 percent for each category.

"Humour is completely subjective, but we usually know most of the time, or believe we know, that when we think something is funny [we know others who] would find that humour funny," says Sharpe Partners CEO Kathy Sharpe.

Overall, the Sharpe study found that 89 percent of U.S. adult Internet users share content with others via e-mail. It also reported that 63 percent share content at least once a week, and a whopping 75 percent forward content to as many as six others. Those with no college education were only slightly more likely much potential for dismal failure. Clark says the chance of a commercial message being passed along using e-mail is extremely low. "Viral [marketing] doesn't often perform," she says, though there are steps marketers can take to give their viral campaigns a better shot at success.

Apart from humour, one tactic that will help is incentives, says Clark. She notes a big trend in viral marketing today is giving consumers a little something to persuade them to pass along a marketer's message, such as an extra entry in a sweepstakes contest. A third factor is recognizing the consumer is in charge with an optional "send to a friend" feature in any viral e-mail and a chance for recipients to personalize the message before they forward it.

Virgin Mobile used humour and consumer involvement (viewers could choose different plot lines) for its "Billy the Finger" campaign. James Powell, senior manager, brand and communications, says Virgin Mobile worked with Helios Design and Lowe Roche, both in Toronto, to come up with Billy the Finger to promote new

IMC Planning

Each chapter now includes an IMC Planning section illustrating how chapter content relates to integrated marketing communication.

IMC Planning: Program for Measuring Effectiveness

Our discussion of what should be tested, when, and where was general and designed to establish a basic understanding of the overall process of evaluative research. Many research methods discussed in the last section showed the complexities of good research. In this section, we offer some prescriptions for managers planning for evaluative research. In a significant industry move, 21 of the largest U.S. ad agencies endorsed a set of principles aimed at "improving the research used in preparing and testing ads, providing a better creative product for clients, and controlling the cost of TV commercials."[24] This set of nine principles, called PACT (Positioning Advertising Copy Testing), defines *copy testing* as research "which is undertaken when a decision is to be made about whether advertising should run in the marketplace. Whether this stage utilizes a single test or a combination of tests, its purpose is to aid in the judgment of specific advertising executions."[25] The nine principles of good copy testing are shown in Figure 9–16 on page 266.

Key Terms

Important terms are highlighted in boldface and listed at the end of each chapter with a page reference. These terms help call students' attention to important ideas, concepts, and definitions and help them review their learning progress.

KEY TERMS

benchmark measures, *131*
brand attitude, *141*
brand awareness, *140*
brand purchase facilitation, *142*
brand purchase intention, *141*
brand re-trial objective, *135*
brand re-trial purchase, *135*
brand-switching objective, *135*
brand-switching purchase, *135*
brand trial objective, *135*
brand trial purchase, *134*
carryover effect, *126*
category need, *138*
category trial objective, *135*
category trial purchase, *135*
communication objectives, *127*
communication task, *130*
DAGMAR, *130*
marketing objectives, *123*
purchase-related behaviour, *136*
repeat consumption, *136*
repeat-consumption objective, *136*
repeat purchase, *135*
repeat-purchase objective, *135*

Chapter Summaries

These synopses serve as a quick review of important topics covered and a very helpful study guide.

SUMMARY

This chapter has examined the role of objectives in the planning and evaluation of the IMC. Specific objectives are needed to guide the development of the promotional program, as well as to provide a benchmark against which performance can be measured and evaluated. Objectives serve important functions as communications devices, as a guide to planning the IMC program and deciding on various alternatives, and for measurement and evaluation.

Many of the principles used in setting advertising objectives can be applied to other elements in the promotional mix.

We presented a comprehensive framework for setting behaviour objectives and communication objectives for all levels: IMC plans, individual IMC tools (i.e., advertising), and specific elements (i.e., print ad). The framework identified options for behaviour objectives to guide the formation of communication objectives. It also

ting objectives. However, many promotional planners believe the role of advertising and other promotional mix elements is to communicate because of the various problems associated with sales-based objectives. They use communications-based objectives like those in the response hierarchy as the basis for setting goals. The first approach for this was DAGMAR, which outlined four principles for setting communication objectives for advertising: well-defined target

Discussion Questions

Questions at the end of each chapter give students an opportunity to test their understanding of the material and to apply it. These questions can also serve as a basis for class discussion or assignments.

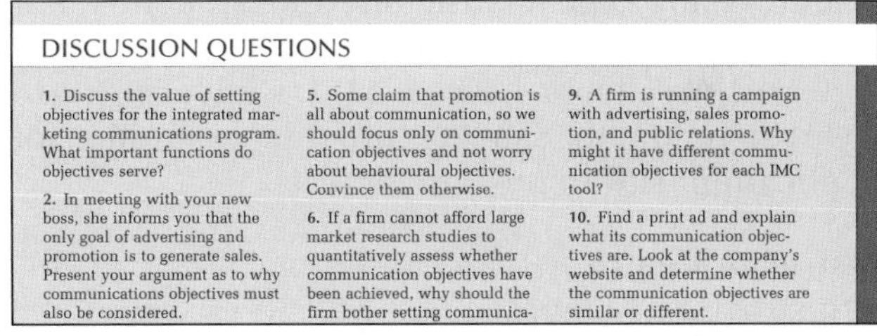
DISCUSSION QUESTIONS

1. Discuss the value of setting objectives for the integrated marketing communications program. What important functions do objectives serve?

2. In meeting with your new boss, she informs you that the only goal of advertising and promotion is to generate sales. Present your argument as to why communications objectives must also be considered.

5. Some claim that promotion is all about communication, so we should focus only on communication objectives and not worry about behavioural objectives. Convince them otherwise.

6. If a firm cannot afford large market research studies to quantitatively assess whether communication objectives have been achieved, why should the firm bother setting communica-

9. A firm is running a campaign with advertising, sales promotion, and public relations. Why might it have different communication objectives for each IMC tool?

10. Find a print ad and explain what its communication objectives are. Look at the company's website and determine whether the communication objectives are similar or different.

Support Material

With this support package, you and your students receive everything from the basic supplements to the latest in educational technologies. Check it out for yourself.

Lecture Preparation, Assessment, and Presentation Tools

Instructor's CD-ROM. The CD-ROM includes all of the necessary instructor supplements, including:

- *Instructor's Manual.* The Instructor's Manual includes Chapter Overviews, Chapter Objectives, Chapter and Lecture Outlines, Teaching Suggestions, Answers to Discussion Questions, and Additional Discussion Questions and Answers (not shown in text).
- *PowerPoint® Presentation and Digital Assets.* These incorporate a high-quality photo and art program, including figure slides, product shots, and advertisements.
- *Computerized Test Bank.* This test bank contains 3,000 questions categorized by topic and level of learning (definitional, conceptual, or application).

The instructor-friendly format allows easy selection of questions from any part of the text, boxed materials, and cases. The program allows you to select any of the questions, make changes if desired, or add new questions—and quickly print out a finished set customized to your course.

Video Case Studies. A unique series of contemporary advertising cases (both Canadian and international) is available on DVD and from the Online Learning Centre. A DVD will also include the Bessies Showreel (Canadian Television Commercial Festival).

Online Technology

Online Learning Centre

This robust, book-specific website, at www.mcgrawhill.ca/olc/belch, includes resources for both instructors and students. For the instructor, we offer downloadable supplement materials. Students have a 24/7 study centre to keep them up to date, to provide examples for application, and to prepare for tests.

Instructor Centre

- Instructor's Manual
- PowerPoint®—Includes concept screens, art from the text, and notes on other digital assets available in the PowerPoint® Presentations.
- CBC Videos
- Video Case Solutions
- *Marketing Horizons* Newsletter
- Notes for Using the Advertising Campaign Planner

Student Centre

- Chapter Objectives
- Multiple Choice Quizzes
- Internet Exercises
- Video Cases
- Web Links
- Glossary
- Access to *Marketing Magazine*
- Marketing Plan
- Σ-STAT
- *Globe and Mail* Headlines
- Career Profiles & Planning
- Advertising Campaign Planner

New Online IMC Campaign Builder

An online template demonstrates how to build and design a comprehensive Integrated Marketing Communications (IMC) plan, enabling students to understand the decisions, issues, and activities involved in developing such a plan. In the creation of their own first-rate IMC plan, students will apply the fundamental concepts they have learned and gain an appreciation for the complexity of a complete IMC plan.

Online Course Options

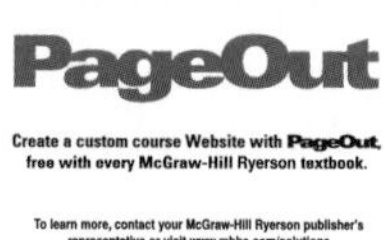

The material in *Advertising & Promotion* can be used with instructor-generated online learning sites. Any online platform, including WebCT and Blackboard, is compatible with the text's material. There are two basic options here: a course companion website or an online course where the material is fully or partially delivered via a course website.

McGraw-Hill's PageOut course website tool enables you to create a course website where you can post your syllabus, case solutions, course information updates, test results, and other key material. You can include links to McGraw-Hill's Online Learning Centre content, add links to important resources, and maintain student results in the online gradebook.

Superior Service

Service takes on a whole new meaning with McGraw-Hill Ryerson and *Advertising & Promotion*. More than just bringing you the textbook, we have consistently raised the bar in terms of innovation and educational research—both in marketing and in education in general. These investments in learning and the education community have helped us to understand the needs of students and educators across the country, and allowed us to foster the growth of truly innovative, integrated learning.

Integrated Learning

Your Integrated Learning Sales Specialist is a McGraw-Hill Ryerson representative who has the experience, product knowledge, training, and support to help you assess and integrate any of our products, technology, and services into your course for optimum teaching and learning performance. Whether it's using our test bank software, helping your students improve their grades, or putting your entire course online, your *i*Learning Sales Specialist is there to help you do it. Contact your local *i*Learning Sales Specialist today to learn how to maximize all of McGraw-Hill Ryerson's resources!

iLearning Services Program

McGraw-Hill Ryerson offers a unique *i*Services package designed for Canadian faculty. Our mission is to equip providers of higher education with superior tools and resources required for excellence in teaching. For additional information, visit www.mcgrawhill.ca/highereducation/iservices.

Teaching, Learning & Technology Conference Series

The educational environment has changed tremendously in recent years, and McGraw-Hill Ryerson continues to be committed to helping you acquire the skills you need to succeed in this new milieu. Our innovative Teaching, Learning & Technology Conference Series brings faculty together from across Canada with 3M Teaching Excellence award winners to share teaching and learning best practices in a collaborative and stimulating environment.

Acknowledgements

A number of colleagues provided detailed, thoughtful reviews that were immensely helpful. I would like to thank the following reviewers who provided valuable feedback to guide the content of the third Canadian edition:

Judith Nash, Southern Alberta Institute of Technology; Bev Holoboff, Northern Alberta Institute of Technology; Ron Smith, Ryerson Polytechnic University; Dwight Dyson, Centennial College; John Pracejus, University of Alberta; Janice Shearer, Mohawk College; Harold Simpkins, Concordia University; Harvey Skolnick, Sheridan College; Albert Mastromartino, Sir Sandford Fleming College; Steve Finlay, Conestoga College; Beth Pett, Niagara College; Lillian Tepera, Georgian College; Brad Davis, Wilfrid Laurier University; Joe Freeburn, British Columbia Institute of Technology; Marianne Marando, Seneca College. I would like to recognize and extend my appreciation to Harvey Skolnick of Sheridan College, who contributed to many Perspectives boxes.

I would also like to acknowledge the cooperation I received from many people in the business, advertising, and media communities. The third Canadian edition contains several additional ads, illustrations, charts, and tables that have been provided by advertisers and/or their agencies, various publications, and other advertising and industry organizations. Many individuals took time from their busy schedules to provide us with requested materials and gave us permission to use them. A special thanks to all of you.

A manuscript does not become a book without a great deal of work on the part of a publisher. Various individuals at McGraw-Hill Ryerson have been involved with this project over the past 18 months. My sponsoring editor, Leanna Maclean, provided valuable guidance and encouragement to complete the revision successfully. A special thanks goes to Emma Gain and Denise Foote, my developmental editors, for their continuous hard work and appropriate reminders to stay on schedule. I want to acknowledge the outstanding work of Alison Derry and Tracey Haggert for obtaining permissions for the Canadian content that appears throughout the book. I'd also like to recognize Kelli Howey for her splendid editing and attention to detail that improve the text immensely. Thank you to Elizabeth Priest for managing the production process. Thanks to the other members of the production team for all of their hard work on this edition.

Many thanks to my current and previous students who have given me the opportunity to develop my ideas. It is very gratifying to know that you enjoy my teaching and are using your newfound knowledge in the business world.

On a personal note, my kids, Louise, Daniel, and Nicholas, have been very supportive during this time-consuming and hectic process of working on the text. Their interest and encouragement have been very inspiring. All my love and gratitude goes to my wife, Teresa, who has helped me tremendously during this and all my academic pursuits.

Michael Guolla

About the Author

Michael Guolla is an assistant professor at the Telfer School of Management of the University of Ottawa. He completed his Ph.D. in Business Administration with a concentration in Marketing at the University of Michigan (Ann Arbor) and received his Honours in Business Administration from the Richard Ivey School of Business at the University of Western Ontario. Dr. Guolla has published articles in academic journals, proceedings of scholarly conferences, and management journals.

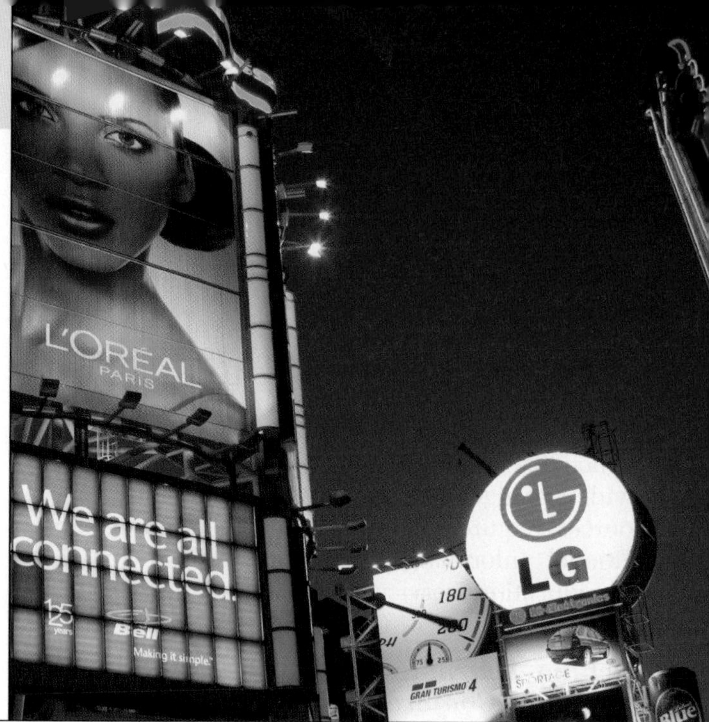

CHAPTER 1

INTEGRATED MARKETING COMMUNICATIONS

Chapter Objectives

- To review the marketing mix decisions to illustrate the content of marketing communication.
- To highlight the elements of the promotional mix: advertising, sales promotion, public relations, direct marketing, Internet marketing, and personal selling.
- To introduce the concept of integrated marketing communications (IMC) by considering its evolution, renewed perspective, growth, and importance.
- To examine how the promotional elements must be coordinated to communicate effectively with the IMC perspective.
- To summarize a model of the IMC planning process and examine the steps in developing a marketing communications program.

Healthy Returns for CV Technologies' Cold-fX

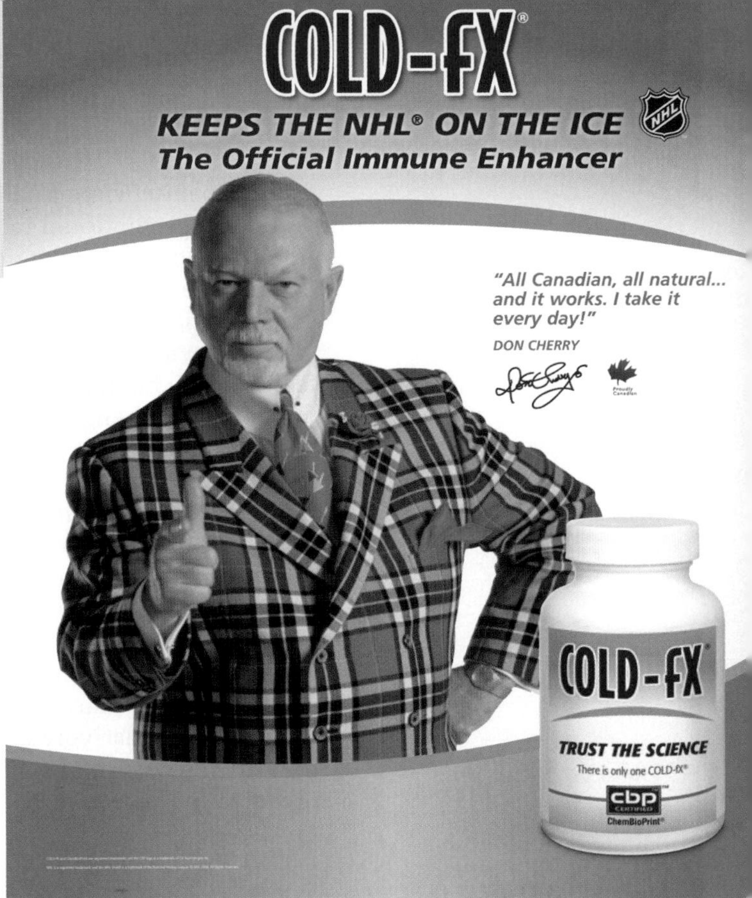

Cold-fX, the cold and flu prevention and remedy brand, propelled CV Technologies to unprecedented success in the over-the-counter treatment market in 2005, and earned the young firm the distinction of Marketer of the Year from *Marketing Magazine.* Careful deployment of advertising, public relations, athletic endorsements, sales promotion, and Internet marketing allowed CV Technologies—nearly bankrupt in 2003—to achieve significant growth beyond its local Alberta market and initial niche audience of professional and Olympic athletes to national distribution, reaching health-conscious Canadians seeking an alternative to drugs or prescription medicines.

While Cold-fX achieved some notoriety in the 1990s with professional hockey players and Olympic athletes using the product in clinical trials, the brand faced the common problem of being a very good product requiring effective marketing communication to establish itself. Starting with a front-page story in the *National Post,* Canadians learned the remarkable story of CV's co-founder, Jacqueline Shan, and CV's primary brand Cold-fX. Shan immigrated to Canada, received her doctorate in physiology and pharmacology from the University of Alberta, and started the company leading with the Cold-fX brand that could prevent colds and flu or reduce the length of these ailments with natural, ginseng-based ingredients.

Extensive follow-up publicity through other print and television media convinced Shan that Cold-fX needed additional marketing communication. Enter the avid user Don Cherry, a former NHL coach and commentator on the CBC's *Hockey Night in Canada,* who emerged as a spokesperson for Cold-fX in lieu of a percentage of profits directed to charity. Despite Cherry's sometimes-controversial opinions and persona Canadians in general tend to believe what he says, and his endorsement of Cold-fX in television, print, and radio ads provided a clear national message as the brand expanded beyond Alberta. Point-of-sale promotion convinced national retailers to stock Cold-fX, with Shoppers Drug Mart and Wal-Mart leading the way and other major pharmacies joining later. An informative Internet site explained to Canadians the scientific studies demonstrating the medicinal superiority of Cold-fX.

By November 2005, ACNielsen reported Cold-fX as the number-one brand for solving or preventing a cold or flu, consistent with the growing trend of 55 percent of all Canadians buying alternative medicines. Extensive profits resulting from Cold-fX allowed CV to extend its communication to build other "fX" brands: Remember-fX for memory enhancement; Ad-fX for improved cognition; Menta-fX for mood normalization; Cell-fX for bone and joint pain; and Pressure-fX for better-functioning blood pressure and cardiovascular systems. The success in Canada of Cold-fX helped CV to build its launch to other countries including the United States.

Source: Norma Ramage, "As Good as Their Word," *Marketing Magazine,* February 27, 2006.

Questions

1. Why is Don Cherry a good spokesperson for Cold-fX?
2. What other IMC tools might Cold-fX consider in the future?

As the opening vignette illustrates, companies like CV Technologies use advertising and other promotional techniques such as websites, direct marketing, sales promotion, public relations, and event sponsorship to effectively communicate. In fact, finding the right combination of marketing communication tools is a critical decision for small and large firms, private and public organizations, and those marketing goods, services, or ideas. Complicating this decision is an uncertain environment featuring niche markets, new communication technology, the emergence of global markets, and changes in consumer buying behaviour.

In response, many companies link or connect their promotional tools to effectively communicate with their current and prospective customers. This emerging trend is known as *integrated marketing communications*. Companies develop their promotional plans knowing that each communication tool retains its unique communication effect and that the combination of communication tools contributes to the overall communication effect of the brand or organization.

This opening chapter highlights the marketing context for promotion and introduces the topic of marketing communications. It briefly describes the different promotional or marketing communication tools available for marketers. Next, we illustrate the relatively new idea of integrated marketing communications. We then identify the contents of a promotional plan as a way of orienting the perspective and organization of this text.

Marketing

For nearly two decades, the American Marketing Association (AMA), the organization that represents marketing professionals in the United States and Canada, defined marketing as *the process of planning and executing the conception, pricing, promotion, and distribution of ideas, goods, and services to create exchanges that satisfy individual and organizational objectives.*[1] This definition of marketing focused on **exchange** as a central concept in marketing and the use of the basic marketing activities to create and sustain relationships with customers.[2] For exchange to occur there must be two or more parties with something of value to one another, a desire and ability to give up that something to the other party, and a way to communicate with each other. Advertising and promotion play an important role in the exchange process by informing customers of an organization's product and convincing them of its ability to satisfy their needs or wants.

The marketing function in an organization facilitates the exchange process by carefully examining the needs and wants of consumers, developing a product or service that satisfies these needs, offering it at a certain price, making it available through a particular place or channel of distribution, and developing a program of promotion or communication. These four Ps—product, price, place (distribution), and promotion (marketing communications)—are elements of the **marketing mix**. The basic task of marketing is combining these four elements into a marketing program to facilitate the potential for exchange with consumers in the marketplace. This initial section will review the product, price, and distribution decisions of the marketing mix (Figure 1–1), as these elements are often the content of promotional messages.

Product Decisions

An organization exists because it offers a product to consumers, generally in exchange for money. This offering may come in the form of a physical good (such as a soft drink, pair of jeans, or car), a service (banking, airlines, or legal assistance), a cause (United Way, March of Dimes), an idea (no drinking and driving), or even a person (a political candidate). The product is anything that can be marketed and that, when used or supported, gives satisfaction to the individual. And these

Product Decisions	Price Decisions	Distribution Decisions
Product Type	Price Level	Channel Type
Features or Attributes	Price Policy	Channel Policy
Benefits	Discount	Type of Intermediary or Reseller
Corporate Name/Identification	Allowance	Type of Location/Store
Brand Name/Identification	Flexibility	Service Level
Package Design		

FIGURE *1–1*

Examples of typical marketing decisions

different product types are not always independent. When going to a restaurant, consumers enjoy the service of not having to prepare the meal as well as the food itself. Thus, when we refer to "product" in this text, we use the term as a general reference to the overall offering directed to an identifiable group of consumers. Product planning involves many other decisions beyond this basic distinction.

All products have fairly obvious features or attributes that characterize what it is. A chocolate bar can have varying types of chocolate (e.g., milk, dark) and different kinds of ingredients (e.g., nuts, wafers). However, a product does not comprise physical characteristics only. Consumers typically view a product as a bundle of benefits signifying what the attributes can do. Benefits can be functional (the performance of the product), experiential (what it feels like to use the product), and/or psychological (feelings such as self-esteem or status that result from owning a particular brand). Advertising and all other marketing communication tools draw attention toward these product characteristics. Manager often have to decide which characteristics to emphasize in a message and the best way to deliver that message.

The term **product symbolism** refers to what a product or brand means to consumers and what they experience in purchasing and using it.[3] For products with strong symbolic features, the social and psychological meaning may be more important than functional utility.[4] For example, designer clothing such as Versace, Gucci, and Prada is often purchased on the basis of its symbolic meaning, particularly by teenagers and young adults. Advertising plays an important role in developing and maintaining the symbolism of these brands (Exhibit 1–1).

Exhibit 1–1
Advertising for designer clothing

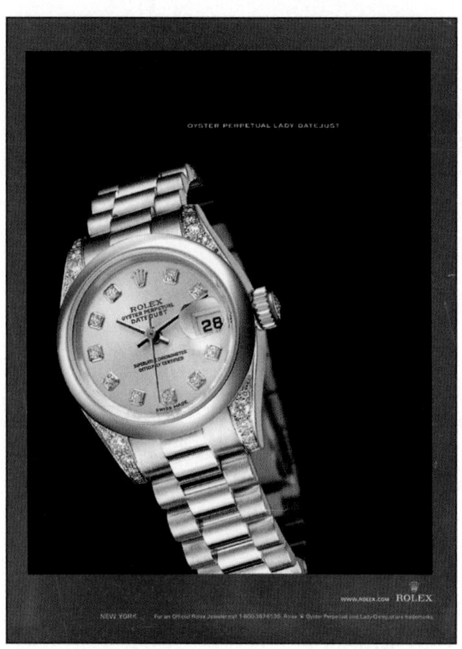

Exhibit 1–2 Rolex creates strong brand equity through advertising

A brand or corporate name and its identification through its logo, symbol, or trademark represent critical product decisions. Marketers use brand names that can communicate product concepts clearly, such as Air Canada (airlines) and Seadoo (water craft). The importance of selecting an appropriate visual representation of the brand can be seen every day when we look at virtually any automobile and notice the symbol used to convey the brand or company. One important role of advertising for a brand is creating and maintaining **brand equity**, which can be thought of as an intangible asset of added value or goodwill that results from the favourable image, impressions of differentiation, and/or the strength of consumer attachment to a company name, brand name, or trademark. Brand equity allows a brand to earn greater sales volume and/or higher margins than it could without the name, providing the company with a competitive advantage. The strong equity position a company and/or its brand enjoys is often reinforced through advertising. For example, Rolex watches command a premium price because of their high quality as well as the strong brand equity they have developed through advertising (Exhibit 1–2).

Packaging is another aspect of product strategy that has become increasingly important. Traditionally, the package provided functional benefits such as economy, protection, and storage, and these aspects can be the main message of an ad. For example, the new package for M&M's protects the candy and makes it easy to dispense (Exhibit 1–3). However, the role and function of the package have changed because of the self-service emphasis of many stores and the fact that many buying decisions are made at the point of purchase. The package is often the consumer's first exposure to the product, so it must make a favourable impression and communicate information on how to use the product, divulge its composition and content, and satisfy any legal requirements regarding disclosure.

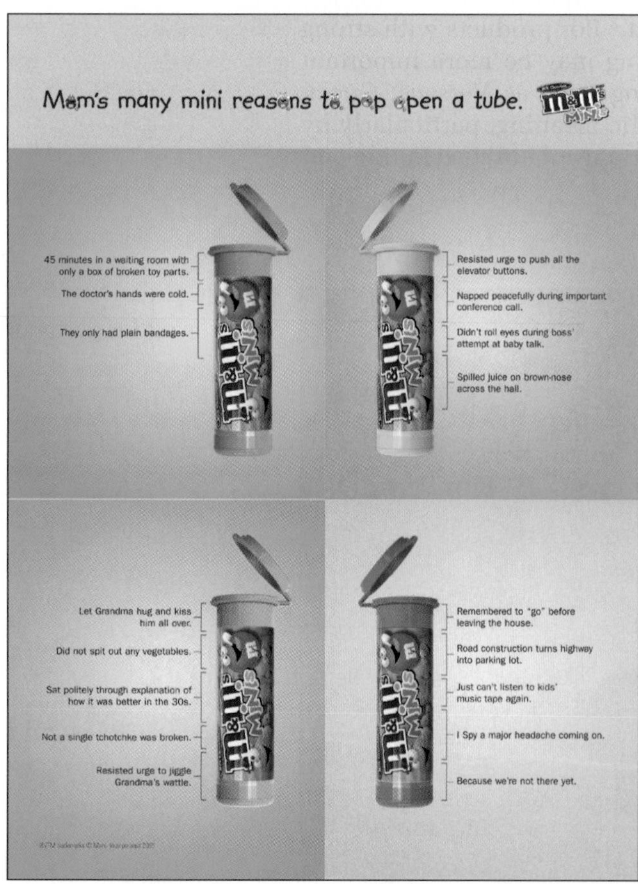

Exhibit 1–3 Packaging may also add product benefits

Many companies view the package as an important way to communicate with consumers. Notice the effective use of the instructions on the Listerine package shown in Exhibit 1–4. Besides offering value-added attributes beyond the product itself, the packaging gives Listerine a unique way to convey the claim that its oral care strips dissolve instantly. Design factors such as size, shape, colour, and lettering all contribute to the appeal of a package and can be as important as a commercial in determining what goes from the store shelf to the consumer's shopping cart. Many products use packaging to create a distinctive look for the brand (see Exhibit 1–5).

Price Decisions

The *price* refers to what the consumer must give up to purchase a product. While price is discussed in terms of the dollar amount exchanged for an item, the cost of a product to the consumer includes time, mental activity, and behavioural effort.[5] Price planning involves decisions concerning the level, policy, adjustments through discounts or allowances, and flexibility when facing competition. Moreover, it also communicates the economic cost to consumers for all of the product benefits combined. Advertising and promotion play a key role in reinforcing a consumer's belief that the product's benefit or quality accurately indicates the price decisions (Exhibit 1–6). Moreover, price is often a key aspect of the product conveyed in a promotional offer. The relationship among price, product quality, and advertising was examined in one study using information on 227 consumer businesses from the PIMS (Profit Impact of Marketing Strategies) project of the Strategic Planning Institute.[6] The study concluded that pricing and advertising strategies go together. High relative ad expenditures should accompany premium prices, and low relative ad expenditures should be tailored to low prices.

Exhibit 1–4 Listerine communicates through effective packaging

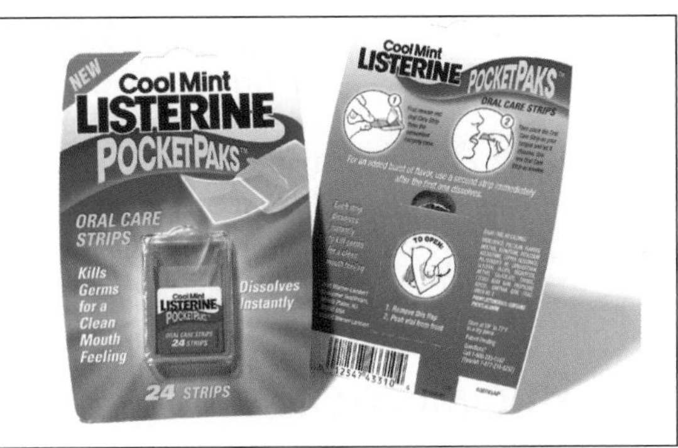

Distribution Channel Decisions

One of a marketer's most important marketing decisions involves the way it makes its products and services available for purchase. A firm can have an excellent product at a great price, but it will be of little value unless it is available where the customer wants it, when the customer wants it, and with the proper support and service. Marketing channels, the place element of the marketing mix, are "sets of

Exhibit 1–5 The packaging creates product image

Exhibit 1–6 Some products compete on the basis of quality rather than price

interdependent organizations involved in the process of making a product or service available for use or consumption."[7] Most consumer-product companies distribute through **indirect channels**, usually using a network of wholesalers (institutions that sell to other resellers) and/or retailers (which sell primarily to the final consumer). Advertising and other promotional communications often provide information as to where a product can be purchased or what kinds of service might be available in various locations. Channel decisions involve selecting and managing intermediaries such as wholesalers, distributors, brokers, and retailers that help a firm make a product or service available to customers. Policies are critical to motivate resellers and ensure the success of a company's marketing program. Marketers are also concerned with the service level resellers provide. Placing a product in an upscale or discount location influences the degree of assistance consumers receive.

A company can choose not to use any channel intermediaries, but rather to sell to its customers through **direct channels**. This type of channel arrangement is sometimes used in the consumer market by firms using direct-selling programs, or firms that use direct-response advertising, telemarketing, or the Internet to sell their products. Direct channels are also frequently used by manufacturers of industrial products and services, which are often selling expensive and complex products that require extensive negotiations and sales efforts, as well as service and follow-up calls after the sale.

The Promotional Mix

The primary focus of this book is one element of the marketing mix: promotion, or marketing communications. **Promotion** is defined as the coordination of all seller-initiated efforts to set up channels of information and persuasion to sell goods and services or promote an idea.[8] While implicit communication occurs through the other elements of the marketing mix, most of an organization's communication with the marketplace occurs as part of a carefully planned and controlled promotional program. The basic tools an organization uses in a promotional program are often referred to as the **promotional mix** (Figure 1–2).

Traditionally the promotional mix has included four elements: advertising, sales promotion, public relations, and personal selling. However, we view direct marketing and interactive media as major promotional-mix elements that marketers use to communicate with their target audiences. Furthermore, while either term is suitable, promotion or marketing communication, many marketers are using the latter since the tools are often connected. For example, a television commercial can direct

FIGURE 1–2 Tools of the promotional mix

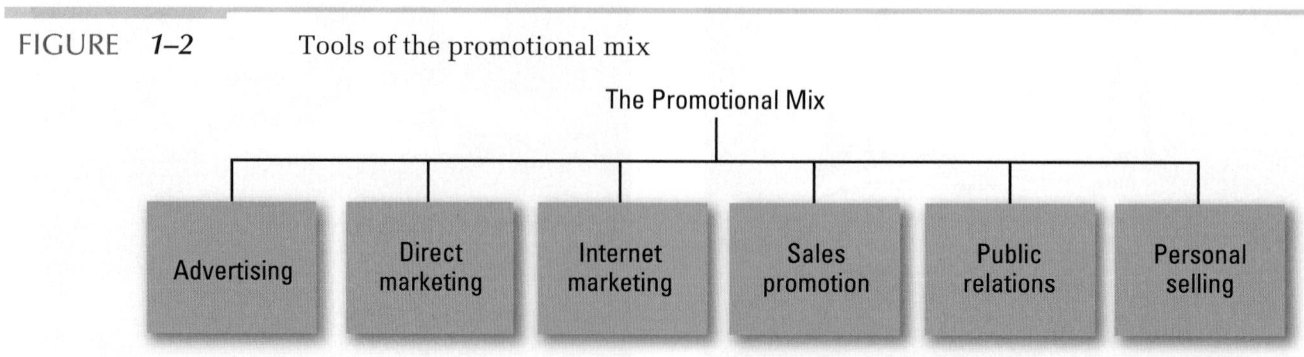

viewers to a website. Or, a brand may use the same type of message in its radio and print ads. We now review the definition of each tool and summarize its role more clearly.

Advertising

Advertising is defined as any paid form of nonpersonal communication about an organization, product, service, or idea by an identified sponsor.[9] The *paid* aspect of this definition reflects the fact that the space or time for an advertising message generally must be bought. An occasional exception to this is the public service announcement (PSA), whose advertising space or time is donated by the media.

The *nonpersonal* component means advertising involves mass media (e.g., TV, radio, magazines, newspapers) that can transmit a message to large groups of individuals, often at the same time. The nonpersonal nature of advertising means there is generally no opportunity for immediate feedback from the message recipient (except in direct-response advertising). Therefore, before the message is sent, the advertiser must consider how the audience will interpret and respond to it.

Advertising is the best-known and most widely discussed form of promotion, probably because of its pervasiveness. It is also a very important promotional tool, particularly for companies whose products and services are targeted at mass consumer markets. In fact, Canadian advertisers spend over $11 billion annually to reach their audiences.

There are several reasons why advertising is such an important part of many marketers' promotional mixes. First, it can be a very cost-effective method for communicating with large audiences. For example, during a television season, prime-time network television reached 85 percent of Canadians on a daily basis. The most-watched TV show each week attracts an audience of about two million viewers. A recent cost per thousand households reached was estimated to be approximately $18.00.[10]

Second, advertising is also a valuable tool for building company or brand equity as it is a powerful way to provide consumers with information as well as to influence their perceptions. Advertising can be used to create favourable and unique images and associations for a brand, which can be very important for companies selling products or services that are difficult to differentiate on the basis of functional attributes. Brand image plays an important role in the purchase of many products and services, and advertising is still recognized as one of the best ways to build a brand.

Finally, advertising is a flexible tool that can be used for many industries (e.g., cars versus soft drinks), situations (e.g., new products versus established products, as in Exhibit 1–7 on page 10), and target audiences (e.g., new customers versus loyal customers). Furthermore, marketers advertise to the consumer market with national and retail/local advertising, which may stimulate primary or selective demand. For other markets, they use business-to-business (Exhibit 1–8 on page 10), professional, and trade advertising. Figure 1–3 on page 11 describes the most common types of advertising.

Sales Promotion

Sales promotion is defined as those marketing activities that provide extra value or incentives to the sales force, distributors, or the ultimate consumer and can stimulate immediate sales. Sales promotion is generally broken into two major categories: consumer-oriented and trade-oriented activities.

Exhibit 1–7 The goals of this milk campaign are to change the image of milk and increase sales of the product

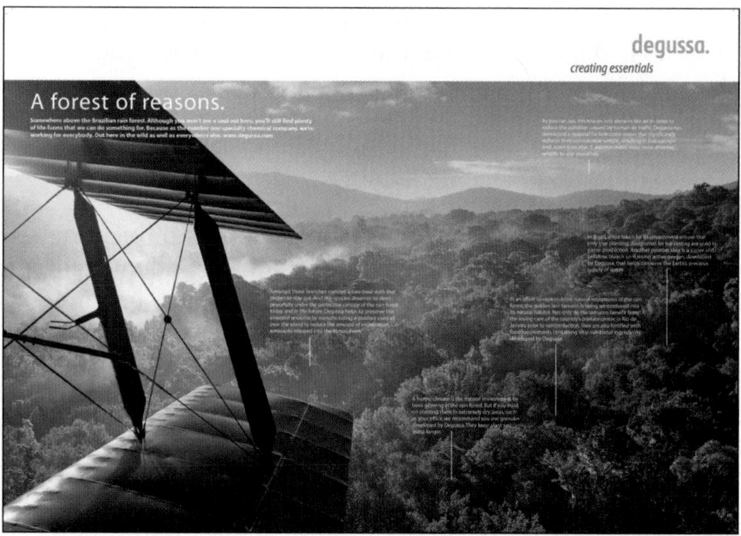

Exhibit 1–8 Business-to-business marketers use advertising to build awareness and brand identity

Consumer sales promotion is targeted to the ultimate user of a product or service and includes couponing, sampling, premiums, rebates, contests, sweepstakes, and various point-of-purchase mate-rials. These promotional tools encourage consumers to make an immediate purchase and thus can stimulate short-term sales. *Trade sales promotion* is targeted toward marketing intermediaries such as wholesalers, distributors, and retailers. Promotional and merchandising allowances, price deals, sales contests, and trade shows are some of the promotional tools used to encourage the trade to stock and promote a company's products.

Promotion and *sales promotion* are two terms that often create confusion in advertising and marketing. As noted, promotion is an element of marketing by which firms communicate with their customers; it is a term that is synonymous with all the marketing communication tools outlined in Figure 1–2. However, many practitioners use the term sales promotion to mean the incentives directed toward either consumers or the trade (retailers, wholesalers) to stimulate sales. Therefore, promotion is used in the broader sense to refer to the various marketing communication activities of an organization.

Public Relations

Another important component of an organization's promotional mix is public relations. When an organization systematically plans and distributes information in an attempt to control and manage its image, it is engaging in a function known as public relations. **Public relations** is defined as "the management function which evaluates public attitudes, identifies the policies and procedures of an individual or organization with the public interest, and executes a program of action to earn public understanding and acceptance."[11] Public relations uses a variety of tools—including special publications, participation in community activities, fundraising, sponsorship of special events, and various public affairs activities—to enhance an organization's image. Organizations also use advertising as a public relations tool.

FIGURE 1–3

Classifications of advertising

ADVERTISING TO CONSUMER MARKETS

National Advertising

Advertising done by large companies on a nationwide basis or in most regions of the country. Most of the ads for well-known companies and brands that are seen on prime-time TV or in other major national or regional media are examples of national advertising. The goals of national advertisers are to inform or remind consumers of the company or brand and its features, benefits, advantages, or uses and to create or reinforce its image so that consumers will be predisposed to purchase it.

Retail/Local Advertising

Advertising done by retailers or local merchants to encourage consumers to shop at a specific store, use a local service, or patronize a particular establishment. Retail or local advertising tends to emphasize specific partronage motives such as price, hours of operation, service, atmosphere, image, or merchandise assortment. Retailers are concerned with building store traffic, so their promotions often take the form of direct action advertising designed to produce immediate store traffic and sales.

Primary versus Selective Demand Advertising

Primary demand advertising is designed to stimulate demand for the general product class or entire industry. Selective demand advertising focuses on creating demand for a specific company's brands. Most advertising for various products and services is concerned with stimluating selective demand and emphasizes reasons for purchasing a particular brand.

An advertiser might concentrate on stimulating primary demand when, for example, its brand dominates a market and will benefit the most from overall market growth. Primary demand advertising is often used as part of a promotional strategy to help a new product gain market acceptance, since the challenge is to sell customers on the product concept as much as to sell a particular brand. Industry trade associations also try to stimulate primary demand for their members' products, among them cotton, milk, orange juice, pork, and beef.

ADVERTISING TO BUSINESS AND PROFESSIONAL MARKETS

Business-to-Business Advertising

Advertising targeted at individuals who buy or influence the purchase of industrial goods or services for their companies. Industrial goods are products that either become a physical part of another product (raw material or component parts), are used in manufacturing other goods (machinery), or are used to help a company conduct its business (e.g., office supplies, computers). Business services such as insurance, travel services, and health care are also included in this category.

Professional Advertising

Advertising targeted to professionals such as doctors, lawyers, dentists, engineers, or professors to encourage them to use a company's product in their business operations. It might also be used to encourage professionals to recommend or specify the use of a company's product by end-users.

Trade Advertising

Advertising targeted to marketing channel members such as wholesalers, distributors, and retailers. The goal is to encourage channel members to stock, promote, and resell the manufacturer's branded products to their customers.

Publicity refers to nonpersonal communications regarding an organization, product, service, or idea not directly paid for or run under identified sponsorship. The message reaches the public in the form of a news story, editorial, or announcement about an organization and/or its products and services. Like advertising, publicity involves nonpersonal communication to a mass audience, but unlike advertising, publicity is not directly paid for by the company. The company or organization attempts to get the media to cover or run a favourable story on a product, service, cause, or event. Tools used to gain publicity include news releases, press conferences, feature articles, photographs, films, and videotapes.

An advantage of publicity over other forms of promotion is its credibility. Consumers generally tend to be less skeptical toward favourable information about a product or service when it comes from a source they perceive as unbiased. For example, the success (or failure) of a new movie is often determined by the reviews it receives from film critics, who are viewed by many moviegoers as objective evaluators. Another advantage of publicity is its low cost, since the company is not paying for time or space in a mass medium such as TV, radio, or newspapers. While an organization may incur some costs in developing publicity items or maintaining a staff to do so, these expenses will be far less than those for the other promotional programs.

Traditionally, public relations and publicity have been considered more supportive than primary to the marketing and promotional process. However, many firms have begun making PR an integral part of their predetermined marketing and promotional strategies. PR firms are increasingly touting public relations as a communications tool that supports many of the functions of conventional advertising and marketing.[12]

Direct Marketing

One of the fastest-growing sectors of the Canadian economy is **direct marketing**, in which organizations communicate directly with target customers to generate a response and/or a transaction. Direct marketing includes telemarketing and call centres, direct mail, mail-order catalogues, and direct-response ads in various broadcast and print media. Traditionally, direct marketing has not been considered a part of the promotional mix since it had distinct objectives, strategies, and tactics. However, we view direct marketing as an important component of a firm's marketing communication program since it is connected to many other communication tools.

Direct-marketing tools are used by companies that distribute their products to consumers directly and by companies that distribute their products through traditional distribution channels or their own sales force. Companies spend large amounts of money each year developing and maintaining databases containing the addresses and/or phone numbers of present and prospective customers. They use telemarketing to call customers directly and attempt to sell them products and services or qualify them as sales leads. Call centres are used to respond to customer inquiries or concerns. Marketers also send out direct-mail pieces ranging from simple letters and flyers to detailed brochures, catalogues, and DVDs to give potential customers information about their products or services. Direct-marketing techniques are also used to distribute product samples and other promotional items. In addition, marketers use **direct-response advertising**, whereby a product is promoted through an ad (e.g., television or print) that encourages the consumer to purchase directly from the manufacturer (Exhibit 1–9).

Direct marketing has become very popular over the past two decades, owing primarily to changing lifestyles, particularly the increase in two-income households. This has meant more discretionary income but less time for in-store shopping. The availability of credit cards, toll-free phone numbers, and reliable delivery services has facilitated the purchase of products from direct marketing tools. This evolution has made shopping more convenient for consumers and has led to a tremendous growth of direct marketing.

Internet Marketing

We are currently experiencing a dynamic and revolutionary change in marketing. This change is being driven by advances in technology and developments that have led to dramatic growth of communication through interactive media, delivered via the Internet. **Interactive media** allow for a back-and-forth flow of information whereby users can participate in and modify the form and content of the information they receive in real time. Unlike traditional forms of marketing communication such as advertising, which are one-way in nature, these new media allow users to perform a variety of functions such as receive and alter information and images, make inquiries, respond to questions, and, of course, make purchases.

Exhibit 1–9 Energy uses direct advertising to promote its product line

While the Internet is changing the ways companies design and implement their entire business and marketing strategies, it is also a marketing communications tool in its own right. Thousands of companies, ranging from large multinational corporations to small local firms, have developed websites to promote their products by providing current and potential customers with information. Other firms develop websites to entertain or communicate more emotionally with their clientele. In fact, as part of a complete IMC program that included advertising, sales promotion, events, and public relations, Guinness beer used the Internet to help initiate the Guinness Party of Canada, a pseudo-political organization dedicated to making St. Patrick's Day a national holiday. Interested drinkers could join via the website and keep track of the results of Guinness's efforts.[13] The Internet is a medium that can be used to execute all the elements of the promotional mix. In addition to advertising on the Web, marketers offer sales promotion incentives such as coupons, contests, and sweepstakes online, and they use the Internet to conduct direct marketing, personal selling, and public relations activities more effectively and efficiently. For example, Exhibit 1–10 shows how consumers can shop and purchase interactively through the Lee Valley Tools website.

Exhibit 1–10 Lee Valley Tools uses a website as part of its direct marketing efforts

Personal Selling

The final element of an organization's promotional mix is **personal selling**, a form of person-to-person communication in which a seller attempts to assist and/or persuade prospective buyers to purchase the company's product or service or to act on an idea. Personal selling involves direct contact between buyer and seller, either face-to-face or through some form of telecommunications such as a telephone. This interaction gives the marketer communication flexibility; and the seller can see or hear the potential buyer's reactions and tailor the message to the customer's specific needs or situation. In this book, we do not devote any material to personal selling as many decisions pertaining to this topic are the responsibility of a sales manager.

Participants in the Promotional Process

Thus far we have identified the major promotional tools that marketers use. To understand the context in which promotional decisions are made, we identify the participants of the promotional process (Figure 1–4). Overall, there are five major groups: the advertiser (or client), advertising agencies, media organizations, specialized marketing communication services, and collateral services. Each group has specific roles in the promotional process.

The advertisers, or **clients**, have the products, services, or causes to be marketed, and they provide the funds that pay for advertising and promotions. The advertisers also assume major responsibility for developing the marketing program and making the final decisions regarding the advertising and promotional program to be employed. The organization may perform most of these efforts itself, either through its own advertising department or by setting up an in-house agency.

However, many organizations use an **advertising agency**, an outside firm that specializes in the creation, production, and/or placement of promotional messages. The agency may also provide other services like research to facilitate the promotional process. Many large advertisers retain the services of a number of agencies, particularly when they have multiple products. Often, an ad agency will act as a partner with an advertiser and assume more responsibility for developing the marketing and promotional programs.

The primary function of **media organizations** is to provide information or entertainment to their subscribers, viewers, or readers. But from the perspective of the promotional planner, the purpose of media is to provide an environment for the firm's marketing communication message. The media must have editorial or program content that attracts consumers so advertisers and their agencies will want to buy time or space with them. While the media perform many other functions that

FIGURE 1–4 Participants in the promotional process

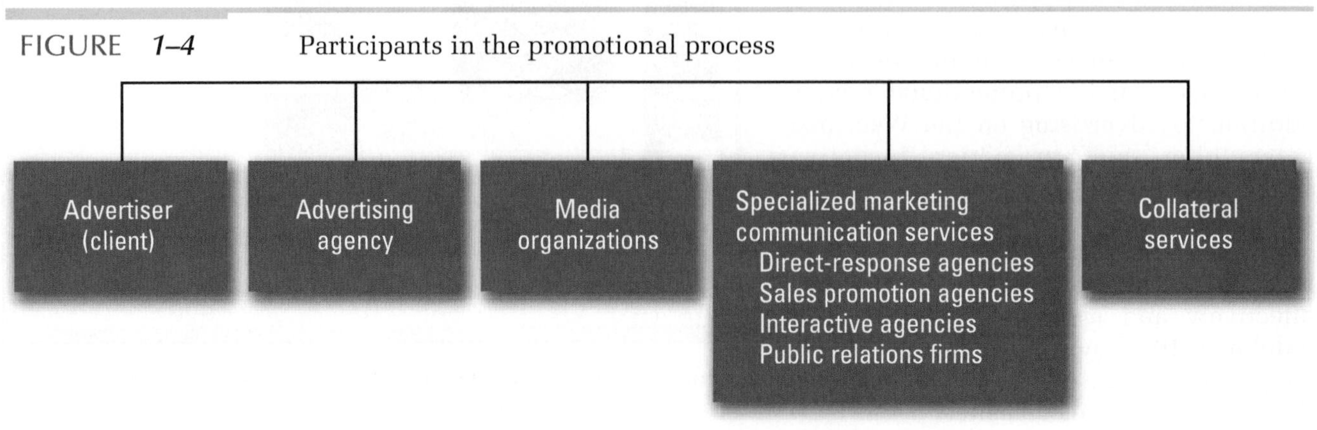

help advertisers understand their markets and their customers, a medium's primary objective is to sell itself as a way for companies to reach their target audiences with their messages effectively.

Specialized marketing communication services include direct marketing agencies, sales promotion agencies, interactive agencies, and public relations firms. These organizations provide services in their areas of expertise. A direct-response agency develops and implements direct-marketing programs, while sales promotion agencies develop contests and sweepstakes, premium offers, or sampling programs. Interactive agencies are being retained to develop websites for the Internet. Public relations firms are used to generate and manage publicity for a company and its products and services as well as to focus on its relationships with its relevant publics.

Other firms provide **collateral services**, the wide range of support functions used by advertisers, agencies, media organizations, and specialized marketing communication firms. These individuals and companies perform specialized functions the other participants use in planning and executing advertising and other promotional functions. They include marketing research companies, package design firms, consultants, media buying services, photographers, printers, video production houses, and event marketing services companies.

Integrated Marketing Communications

For many years, the promotional function in most companies was dominated by mass media advertising. Companies relied primarily on their advertising agencies for guidance in nearly all areas of marketing communication. Most marketers did use additional promotional tools, but sales promotion and direct marketing agencies as well as package design firms were generally viewed as auxiliary services and often used on a per-project basis. Public relations agencies were used to manage the organization's publicity, image, and affairs with relevant publics on an ongoing basis but were not viewed as integral participants in the marketing communications process.

Consequently, many marketers planned and managed the different promotional tools as separate practices, with different budgets, different views of the market, and different goals and objectives. More recently, companies now recognize that the wide range of promotional tools must be coordinated to communicate effectively and present a consistent image to its target audiences. We now turn to the topic of integrated marketing communications and discuss its evolution, renewed perspective, growth, and importance.

The Evolution of IMC

During the 1980s, many companies realized the need for a strategic integration of their promotional tools. These firms began moving toward the process of **integrated marketing communications (IMC)**, which involves coordinating the various promotional tools and other marketing activities that communicate with a firm's customers.[14] As marketers embraced the concept of integrated marketing communication, they began asking their ad agencies to coordinate the use of a variety of promotional tools rather than relying primarily on media advertising. Companies also began to look beyond traditional advertising agencies and use other types of promotional specialists to develop and implement various components of their promotional plans. Many agencies responded to the need for coordinating the promotional tools by acquiring PR, sales promotion, and direct marketing companies and touting themselves as IMC agencies that offer one-stop shopping for all of their clients' promotional needs.[15]

A task force from the American Association of Advertising Agencies (the "4As") developed one of the first definitions of integrated marketing communications that focuses on the process of using all forms of promotion to achieve maximum communications impact:

> a concept of marketing communications planning that recognizes the added value of a comprehensive plan that evaluates the strategic roles of a variety of communication disciplines—for example, general advertising, direct response, sales promotion, and public relations—and combines these disciplines to provide clarity, consistency, and maximum communications impact.[16]

Many companies adopted an IMC perspective during the 1990s. They saw it as a way to coordinate and manage their marketing communication programs to ensure that they give customers a consistent message about the company and/or its brands. For these companies, the IMC approach represented an improvement over the traditional method of treating the promotional tools as virtually separate activities. More recently, this view of IMC has been challenged on the basis that it focuses primarily on the tactical coordination of various communication tools with the goal of making them look and sound alike.[17] It has been criticized as an "inside-out marketing" approach that is a relatively simple matter of bundling promotional mix elements together so they have one look and speak with one voice.[18] As IMC continues to evolve, both academicians as well as practitioners see the need for a renewed perspective that views the discipline from a more strategic perspective. IMC Perspective 1–1 describes how Procter & Gamble has adapted recently.

A Renewed Perspective of IMC

A renewed understanding of IMC involves more than just coordinating the various elements of their marketing and communications programs into a "one look, one voice" approach. As IMC evolves, it is being recognized as a business process that helps companies identify the most appropriate and effective methods for communicating and building relationships with customers and other stakeholders. Don Schultz of Northwestern University has developed what many think is a more appropriate definition of IMC, as follows:

> Integrated marketing communication is a strategic business process used to plan, develop, execute and evaluate coordinated, measurable, persuasive brand communications programs over time with consumers, customers, prospects, employees, associates and other targeted relevant external and internal audiences. The goal is to generate both short-term financial returns and build long-term brand and shareholder value.[19]

This definition views IMC as an ongoing strategic business process rather than just tactical integration of various communication activities. It also recognizes that there are a number of relevant audiences that are an important part of the process. Externally these include customers, prospects, suppliers, investors, interest groups, and the general public. It also views internal audiences such as employees as an important part of the IMC process. Finally, Schultz notes that this definition reflects the increasing emphasis that is being placed on the demand for accountability and measurement of the *outcomes* of marketing communication programs as well as marketing in general.

Many companies are realizing that communicating effectively with customers and other stakeholders involves more than just the tactical use of the traditional marketing communication tools. These firms, along with many advertising agencies, are embracing IMC and incorporating it into their marketing and business practices. It is true, however, that not all companies have moved beyond the stage of simply bundling promotional mix elements together and made the organization changes and investment that are needed for true integration. Moreover, some academics and practitioners have questioned whether IMC is just another "management fashion"

IMC PERSPECTIVE 1–1

New Vision for a Consumer Products Giant

Procter & Gamble (P&G)—the historically successful and large consumer products manufacturer of brands like Tide, Cover Girl, Old Spice, and Swiffer—overhauled its marketing and organizational operations, which had enormous implications for how P&G makes its promotional decisions. The change originated when managers decided to focus on when the consumer chooses to buy and use the product as the central drive for all decisions. This approach had implications for internal structure, working with communication agencies, and strategic priorities.

Organizationally, P&G marketing personnel joined other functional specialists on 200 retail teams worldwide, compared with 20 teams just a few years ago. Marketers in Canada work on multi-functional teams to customize worldwide product launches for local success. This has resulted in P&G in Canada typically using the original TV creative, but augmenting the campaign with more targeted IMC tools. P&G also augmented its market research to include observational methodologies in home and store environments, and attempted to measure results in new ways to account for the new communication developments.

From an agency perspective, P&G partnered with diverse types of agencies and employed multiple parties to execute new brand initiatives. For example, it began to work with more specialized agencies for emerging tools like in-store brand presentation and interactive applications. Furthermore, P&G expected strategic communication planning from its agencies, which were immersed in the newfound customer-centric direction of their client.

Innovative communication practices for the brands mentioned above resulted from these internal and external developments. The Canadian campaign for Cover Girl Outlast Lipstick featured motion-sensitive ads in bars and restaurants in Toronto. Old Spice dance events, known as "Red zone after hours," occurred at Canadian bars and included an online contest, out-of-home media, and a televised competition. The Canadian launch for Tide Cold Water included facets not used in other countries because of our high proportion of consumers who already do cold-water laundry (and our really cold water in winter!). Consumers received inserts with their energy bills that expressed the financial savings clearly and in the right context. For the home cleaning products under the Swiffer banner, P&G introduced a functional display for Wal-Mart stores that allowed the different implements and supplies to be shown in a way that was more logical and convenient for consumers.

Communications also occurred to bring brands together. P&G's Canadian division published *Rouge* magazine, which explained the new products and bundled different ones together to educate consumers. For example, one issue concentrated on all the beauty products and how they could be used together. This idea emerged on TV, as P&G sponsored a program and embedded ads that told a continuous story of consumers beautifying themselves.

Source: Lisa d'Innocenzo, "Inside P&G," *Strategy*, June 2006.

Questions

1. How have the changes been beneficial for Procter & Gamble?
2. What are the potential risks or disadvantages of the new initiatives?

whose influence will be transitory.[20] Critics of IMC argue that it merely reinvents and renames existing ideas and concepts and that it questions its significance for marketing and advertising thought and practice.[21]

While the debate over the value and relevance of IMC is likely to continue, proponents of the concept far outnumber the critics. IMC is proving to be a permanent change that offers significant value to marketers in the rapidly changing communications environment they are facing in the new millennium. IMC has been described as one of the "new-generation" marketing approaches being used by companies to better focus their efforts in acquiring, retaining, and developing relationships with customers and other stakeholders.[22] Some scholars have stated that IMC is undoubtedly the major communications development of the last decade of the 20th century.[23] We will now discuss some of the reasons for the growth and importance of IMC.

Reasons for IMC Growth

The IMC approach to marketing communications planning and strategy is being adopted by both large and small companies and has become popular among firms marketing consumer products and services as well as business-to-business marketers. There are a number of reasons why marketers are adopting the IMC approach, notably, planning efficiency and effectiveness, consumer adoption of new technology and media, and innovative marketing practices.

Planning Efficiency and Effectiveness One reason for IMC growth is that marketers understand the value of strategically integrating the various communication functions rather than having them operate autonomously. By coordinating their marketing communications efforts, companies can avoid duplication, take advantage of synergy among various promotional tools, and develop more efficient and effective marketing communications programs. Advocates of IMC argue that it is one of the easiest ways for a company to maximize the return on its investment in marketing and promotion.[24]

Consumer Adoption of Technology and Media The move to integrated marketing communications also reflects an adaptation by marketers to consumer adoption of technology and media. For example, cable TV and digital satellite systems have vastly expanded the number of channels available to households. A quick scan of the offerings of any television service provider reveals that consumers can easily select programming from more than 100 channels. Every day more consumers are surfing the World Wide Web. Online services provide information and entertainment as well as the opportunity to shop for and order a vast array of products and services. Marketers are responding by developing websites where they can advertise their products and services interactively as well as transact sales, such as at WestJet's website, shown in Exhibit 1–11. New applications for advertising on the Internet are invented each year, allowing marketers greater opportunity to reach particular audiences.

Exhibit 1–11
Travellers can use WestJet's website to purchase tickets and reserve seats

Even as new technologies and formats create new ways for marketers to reach consumers, they are affecting the more traditional media. Television, radio, magazines, and newspapers are becoming more fragmented and reaching smaller and more selective audiences. Marketers are also facing the problem of consumers being less responsive to traditional advertising. They recognize that many consumers are turned off by advertising and tired of being bombarded with sales messages. These factors are prompting many marketers to look for alternative ways to communicate with their target audiences.

Innovative Marketing Practices The integrated marketing communications movement is also being driven by factors that change the relative emphasis of all promotional tools.[25]

- *A shifting of marketing dollars from media advertising to other forms of promotion, particularly consumer and trade-oriented sales promotions.* Many marketers feel that traditional media advertising has become too expensive and is not cost-effective.
- *A movement away from relying on advertising-focused approaches, which emphasize mass media such as network television and national magazines, to solve communication problems.* Many companies are turning to lower-cost, more targeted communication tools. For example, many new digital devices offer advertisers numerous opportunities to directly advertise or promote their products.
- *A shift in marketplace power from manufacturers to retailers.* Due to consolidation in the retail industry, large retailers are using their clout to demand larger promotional fees and allowances from manufacturers, a practice that often siphons money away from advertising. Moreover, checkout scanners give retailers information on the effectiveness of manufacturers' promotional programs, leading marketers to shift their focus to sales promotions.
- *The development of database marketing.* Many companies are building databases containing customer names; geographic, demographic, and psychographic profiles; purchase patterns; media preferences; credit ratings; and other characteristics. Marketers are using this information to target consumers through a variety of direct-marketing methods rather than relying on mass media.
- *The pervasiveness of the Internet, which is changing the very nature of how companies communicate and interact with consumers.* The Internet is an *interactive* medium that is becoming an integral part of communications strategy. Consumers rely on the Internet for information when making purchase decisions while advertisers distribute customized print and video messages.

Importance of IMC

A successful IMC program requires that a firm find the right combination of promotional tools and techniques, define their role and the extent to which they can or should be used, and coordinate their use. This perspective becomes important for organizations because of the many audiences it communicates with, the vast number of messages consumers receive from many brands, and the emergence of strong marketing relationships.

Audience Contacts The promotional mix elements are the major tools that marketers use to communicate with current and/or prospective customers as well as other relevant audiences. Many companies are taking an *audience contact* perspective in developing their IMC programs whereby they consider all of the potential ways of reaching their target audience and presenting the company or brand in a favourable manner. They recognize that there are a variety of ways customers may come into contact with a company or brand. These contacts can range from simply seeing or hearing an ad for a brand to actually having the opportunity to use or experience a brand at a company-sponsored event.

A key aspect of integrated marketing communications is that it encourages marketers to consider a variety of communication tools and how they can be used to deliver messages about their company or brands. Figure 1–5 shows the various ways by which consumers can come into contact with a company or brand. Marketers must determine how valuable each of these contact tools are for communicating with their target audience and how they can be combined to form an effective IMC program. This is generally done by starting with the target audience and determining which IMC tools will be most effective in reaching, informing, and persuading them and ultimately influencing their behaviour. It is the responsibility of those involved in the marketing communications process to determine how the various contact tools will be used to reach the target audience and help achieve the company's marketing objectives. IMC Perspective 1–2 shows how the Internet allows companies to reach particular target audiences.

Consumer's Point of View As a marketer, it is important to keep concepts distinct so that you can communicate with other people within your organization or other organizations when making decisions. For example, if you are planning a sales promotion, it is useful to refer to it as a sales promotion so that everyone involved can discuss its merits appropriately and allocate the sales promotion expenditure within the correct budget. Do we have the right sales promotion (i.e., coupon versus bonus pack)? Is the incentive strong enough to encourage the target audience to switch to our brand? Consumers, on the other hand, receive many exposures from many different brands, each using many different promotional tools. In fact, consumers receive so many exposures that they have the habit of often referring to any promotional tool as "advertising." Given this situation, the need for planning with an IMC perspective becomes imperative. All the elements of the promotional campaign have to be carefully linked in some manner so that the message is clear and does not misrepresent the brand.

FIGURE *1–5* IMC Audience Contact Tools

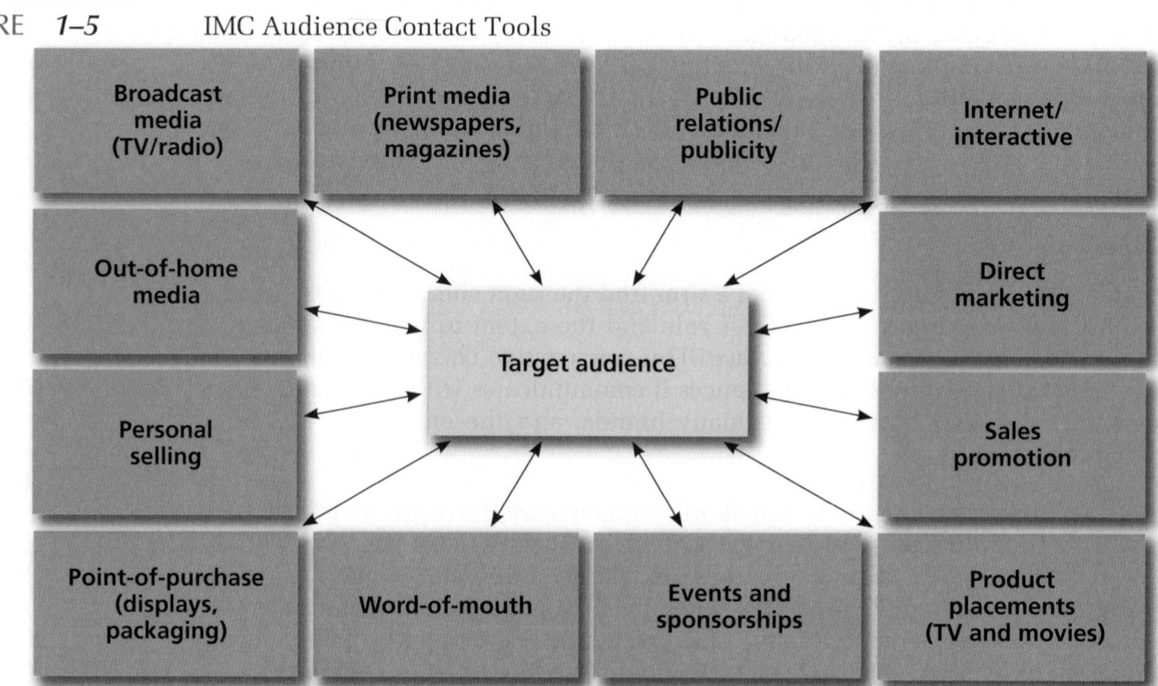

IMC PERSPECTIVE *1–2*

Innovative Marketing Communication with Technology

Marketing communication exploded recently with an interesting array of digital applications such as social networking sites, simulations, and video on demand that promotional managers integrated into their plans or investigated with small pilot projects.

By mid 2007, less than a year after its introduction to our country, 2.8 million Canadians had registered with the Facebook social network with a growth rate of 5 percent per week compared to 3 percent worldwide. Some brands initiated "sponsored groups," where consumers could join and receive brand messages and promotional offerings like contests and samples. For instance, Toyota created the F1 Canada group and offered desktop wallpapers and ringtones for its 3,000 members. Other communication applications included targeted banner ads based on consumer profile variables like demographics, psychographics, and media consumption preferences.

Telus experimented with a virtual-reality world that 120,000 of its 1.2 million customers experienced. Word of the new venture spread through blogs and newspaper articles. With essentially no monetary investment in the venture, the media exposure Telus received helped convey it as a technologically advanced company. But more importantly, Telus planned some promotions to customers based on the behaviours exemplified in the simulated game.

YouTube video appeared as an avenue for advertisers to disseminate their commercials prior to releasing them on television or in movie theatres. The highly successful "Dove evolution" ad, which revealed the transformation of a young woman to a model, fit nicely with the overall "Campaign for real beauty." Coke jumped into the action with its own animated execution, which replicated a character from the video game Grand Theft Auto who is kind and helpful while demonstrating "The Coke side of life."

Sources: Michelle Halpern, "In Your Face," *Marketing Magazine*, July 16, 2007; and Rob Gerlsbeck, "Socially Awkward," *Marketing Magazine*, November 20, 2006.

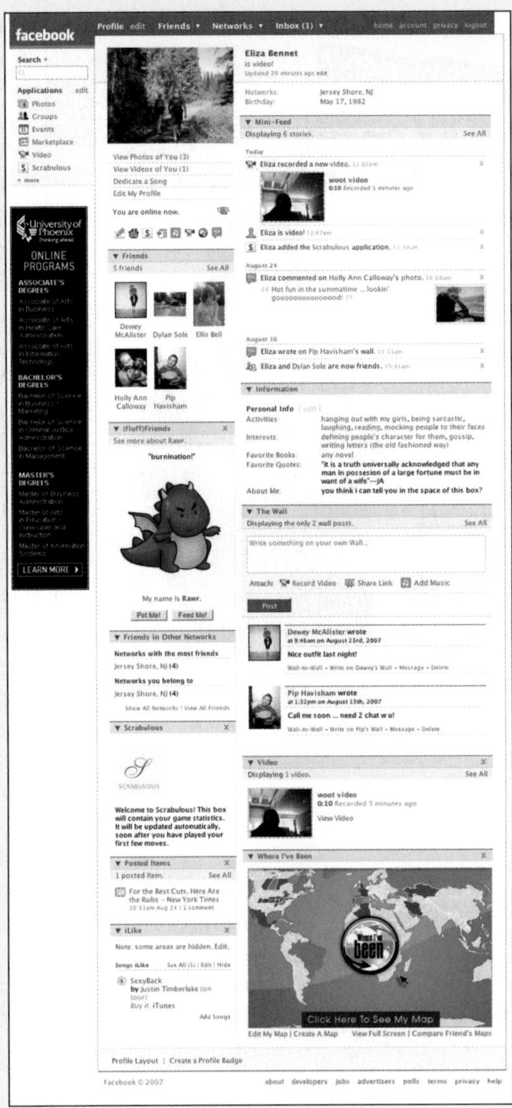

Question

1. Debate whether these technological innovations are effective media channels to reach consumers.

L'Oréal Canada built its Maybelline and L'Oréal Paris brands through innovative use of advertising, sales promotion, sponsorship, public relations, and Internet marketing. Faced with constraints of key marketing activities decided at the brand headquarters of Paris, New York, and Tokyo, L'Oréal Canada created a Canadian identity for its primary consumer brands. Maybelline sponsored the hit Quebec television reality show *Star Académie* and tweaked its famous slogan to fit the show's "star"

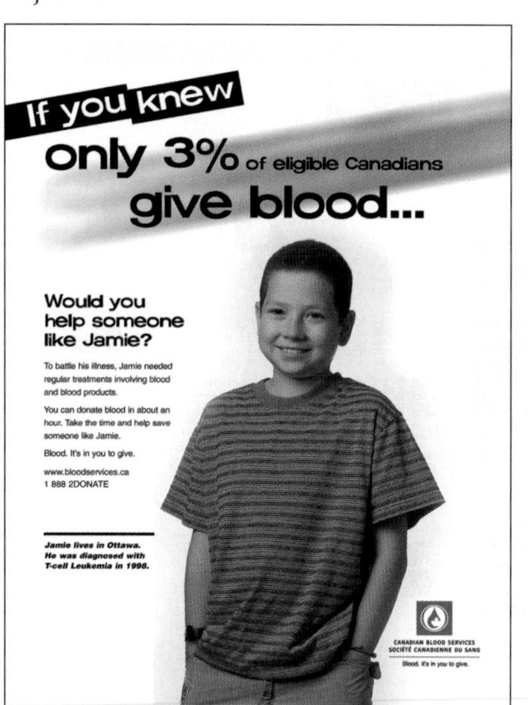

Exhibit 1–12 Many non-profit organizations use advertising to meet their marketing objectives

theme, allowed its make-up artists to interact with the public on the Internet, organized autograph session in shopping malls with contestants who had been eliminated, and continued its advertising message on other media like radio. L'Oréal Paris also sponsored the hit show *Canadian Idol*. In addition to regular commercials and a highlighted presence on the website for *Canadian Idol*, the show featured sponsorship announcements and on-air promotions that linked consumers to interactive, stylish fun on the L'Oréal Paris website. L'Oréal Canada received positive publicity for its interactive campaign in honour of International Women's Day that provided needed money for the Canadian Women's Foundation's Economic Development Fund. Promotional support for other fashion and arts events permitted L'Oréal Canada to keep its profile high. And to help facilitate these media, L'Oréal Canada worked with pharmacy retailers to deliver contest promotions and much-needed communication at the point of sale. Collectively, L'Oréal Canada's success indicates the importance of a well planned communications strategy that carefully considers the consumer's response to many tools.[26]

Relationship Marketing Today, most marketers are seeking more than just a one-time exchange or transaction with customers. The focus of market-driven companies—and many non-profit organizations (Exhibit 1–12)—is on developing and sustaining *relationships* with their customers. This has led to a new emphasis on **relationship marketing**, which involves creating, maintaining, and enhancing long-term relationships with individual customers as well as other stakeholders for mutual benefit.[27]

This relationship focus is generally more profitable since it is often more cost-effective to retain customers than to acquire new ones. Furthermore, these retained customers tend to buy more products or expand their purchases to other products that an organization offers. Marketers are giving more attention to the *lifetime value* of a customer because studies have shown that reducing customer defections by just 5 percent can increase future profit by as much as 30 to 90 percent.[28] Recently, the AMA adopted a revised and more strategic definition of **marketing**, which is as follows:

> Marketing is an organizational function and a set of processes for creating, communicating and delivering value to customers and for managing customer relationships in ways that benefit the organization and its stakeholders.[29]

Relationship marketing makes IMC planning imperative as well. Marketers must recognize which tools within the promotional mix are enhancing the relationship. And since their customers are involved so closely with the firm, the need for consistency becomes even more critical.

Integrated Marketing Communications Planning

In developing a promotional strategy, a company combines the promotional mix elements, balancing the strengths and limitations of each, to produce an effective promotional campaign. **Promotional management** involves coordinating the promotional mix elements to develop a controlled, integrated program of effective marketing communications. The marketer must consider which promotional tools to use and how to combine them to achieve its marketing and promotional objectives. Companies also face the task of distributing the total promotional budget across the promotional mix elements. What percentage of the budget should they allocate to advertising, sales promotion, public relations, direct marketing, and interactive marketing?

The marketing communications program is generally developed with a specific purpose in mind and is the end product of a detailed marketing and promotional planning process. As with any business function, planning plays a fundamental role in the development and implementation of an effective promotional program. The individuals involved in promotion design a **promotional plan** that provides the framework for developing, implementing, and controlling the organization's integrated marketing communications programs and activities. Promotional planners must decide on the role and function of the specific elements of the promotional mix, develop strategies for each element, and implement the plan. A model of the IMC planning process is shown in Figure 1–6 on page 24. The remainder of this chapter presents a brief overview of the steps involved.

Review the Marketing Plan

The first step in the IMC planning process is to review the marketing plan and objectives. Before developing a promotional plan, marketers must understand where the company (or the brand) has been, its current position in the market, where it intends to go, and how it plans to get there. Most of this information should be contained in the **marketing plan**, a written document that describes the overall marketing strategy and programs developed for an organization, a particular product line, or a brand. Marketing plans can take several forms but generally include five basic parts:

- A detailed situation analysis that consists of an internal marketing audit and review and an external analysis of the market, company, consumer, competition, and macro-environment.
- Specific marketing objectives that provide direction, a time frame for marketing activities, and a mechanism for measuring performance.
- A marketing strategy and program that include selection of target market(s) and decisions and plans for the four elements of the marketing mix.
- A program for implementing the marketing strategy, including determining specific tasks to be performed and responsibilities.
- A process for monitoring and evaluating performance and providing feedback so that proper control can be maintained and any necessary changes can be made in the overall marketing strategy or tactics.

For most firms, the promotional plan is an integral part of the marketing strategy. Thus, the promotional planners must know the roles advertising and other promotional mix elements will play in the overall marketing program. The promotional plan is developed similarly to the marketing plan and often uses its detailed information. Promotional planners focus on information in the marketing plan that is relevant to the promotional strategy.

Assess the Marketing Communications Situation

After the marketing plan is reviewed, the next step in developing a promotional plan is to conduct the situation analysis. In the IMC program, the situation analysis focuses on those factors that are relevant to development of a promotional strategy. Like the overall marketing situation analysis, the promotional program situation analysis includes both an internal and an external analysis.

FIGURE 1–6 An integrated marketing communications planning model

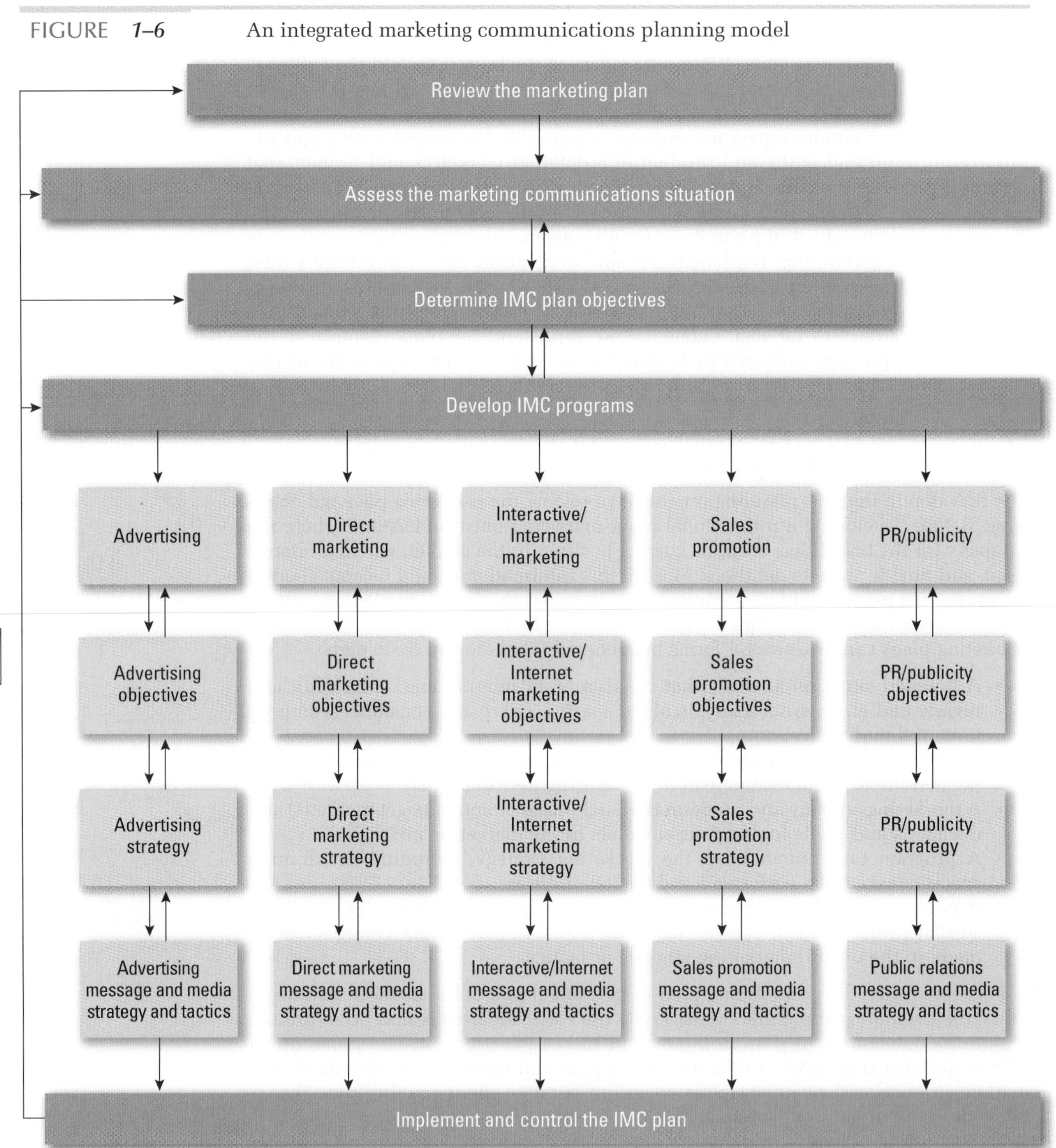

Internal Analysis The **internal analysis** assesses relevant areas of the product offering and the firm itself. The internal analysis assesses the relative strengths and limitations of the product; the product's unique selling points, attributes, or benefits; its packaging, price, and design; and so on. This information is important to the creative personnel who must develop the brand's advertising message.

Since the firm is planning a new promotional plan, it is imperative that a review of the firm's previous promotional programs is undertaken. Specifically, the objectives,

FIGURE 1–6 (concluded)

An integrated marketing communications planning model

Review the Marketing Plan
Focus on market company, consumer, competitive, and environmental information
Examine marketing objectives, strategy, and programs
Understand role of promotion within marketing plan

Assess the Marketing Communications Situation
Internal analysis
- Relative strengths and weaknesses of products/services
- Previous promotional programs
- Brand image
- Promotional organization and capabilities

External analysis
- Customer behaviour analysis
- Competitive analysis
- Environmental analysis

Determine IMC Plan Objectives
Establish IMC communication objectives
Establish IMC behaviour objectives

Develop IMC Programs
For advertising, sales promotion, public relations, direct marketing, and Internet marketing:
- Set specific communication and behaviour objectives for each IMC tool
- Determine budget requirements
- Develop relevant message strategy and tactics
- Select suitable media strategy and tactics

Investigate integration options across all five programs

Implement and Control the IMC Plan
Design all promotional materials internally or with agencies and buy media space/time
Measure promotional program results/effectiveness and make adjustments

budgets, strategies, and tactics of all promotional mix elements should be closely examined to understand the strengths and limitations. Furthermore, if the firm has utilized marketing research to track the results of previous programs, this information needs to be examined closely.

Another aspect of the internal analysis is assessing the strengths and limitations of the firm or the brand from an image perspective. Often the image the firm brings to the market will have a significant impact on the way it can advertise and promote itself as well as its products and services. Companies or brands that are new to the market or those for whom perceptions are negative may have to concentrate on their images, not just the benefits or attributes of the specific product or service. On the other hand, a firm with a strong image is already a step ahead when it comes to marketing its products. For example, Starbucks has an outstanding image that is a result of the quality of its coffee and other products as well as its reputation as a socially responsible company. The company is recognized as a good citizen in its dealings with communities, employees, suppliers, and the environment. Starbucks recognizes that being recognized as a socially responsible company is an important part of its tremendous growth and success. The company publishes a Corporate Social Responsibility Annual Report each year that describes its social, environmental, and economic impacts on the communities in which it does business (Exhibit 1–13 on page 26).

Reviewing the capabilities of the firm and its ability to develop and implement a successful promotional program, and the organization of the promotional

Exhibit 1–13 Starbucks has a strong image as a socially responsible company

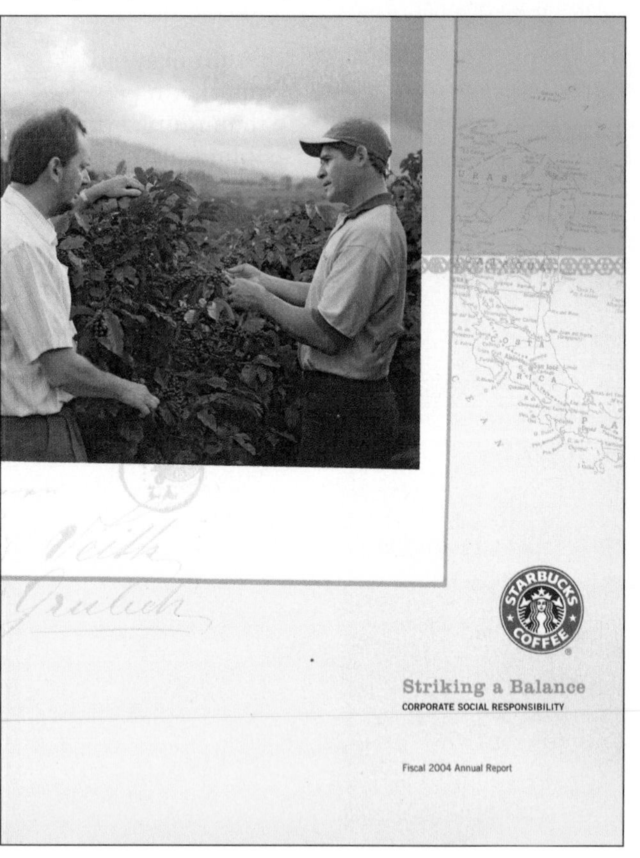

department, the analysis may indicate the firm is not fully capable of planning and implementing the promotional program. If this is the case, it would be wise to look for assistance from an advertising agency or some other promotional facilitator. If the organization is already using an ad agency, the focus will be on the quality of the agency's work and the results achieved by past and/or current campaigns.

Figure 1–7 is a checklist of some of the areas one might consider when performing analyses for promotional planning purposes. Addressing internal areas may require information the company does not have available internally and must gather as part of the external analysis.

External Analysis The **external analysis** focuses on factors such as characteristics of the firm's customers, market segments, competitors, and environment as shown in Figure 1–7. An important part of the external analysis is a detailed consideration of customers' characteristics and buying patterns, their decision processes, and factors influencing their purchase decisions. Attention must also be given to consumers' perceptions and attitudes, lifestyles, and criteria for making purchase decisions. Often, marketing research studies are needed to answer some of these questions. A key element of the external analysis is an assessment of the market. The attractiveness of various market segments must be evaluated and the segments to target identified.

The external phase of the promotional program situation analysis also includes an in-depth examination of both direct and indirect competitors. While competitors were analyzed in the overall marketing situation analysis, even more attention is devoted to promotional aspects at this phase. Focus is on the firm's primary competitors: their specific strengths and limitations; their segmentation, targeting, and positioning strategies; and the promotional strategies they employ. The size and allocation of their promotional budgets, their media strategies, and the messages they are sending to the marketplace should all be considered.

Determine IMC Plan Objectives

An important part of this stage of the promotional planning process is establishing communication goals and objectives. In this text, we stress the importance of distinguishing between communication and marketing objectives. **Marketing objectives** refer to what is to be accomplished by the overall marketing program. They are often stated in terms of sales, market share, or profitability.

Communication objectives refer to what the firm seeks to accomplish with its promotional program. They are often stated in terms of the nature of the message to be communicated or what specific communication effects are to be achieved. The promotional planner must think about the process consumers will go through in responding to marketing communications. Communication objectives may include creating awareness or knowledge about a product and its attributes or benefits; creating an image; or developing favourable attitudes, preferences, or purchase intentions. Communication objectives should be the guiding force for the overall marketing communications strategy and the objectives for each promotional mix area. Behaviour objectives in terms of trial purchase or repeat purchase may be defined along with the communication objectives.

FIGURE 1–7 Areas covered in the situation analysis

Internal Factors	External Factors
Assessment of firm's promotional organization and capabilities	**Customer behaviour analysis**
Organization of promotional department	Who buys our product or service?
Capability of firm to develop and execute promotional programs	Who makes the decision to buy the product?
Determination of role and function of ad agency and other promotional facilitators	Who influences the decision to buy the product?
Assessment of firm's previous promotional programs	How is the purchase decision made? Who assumes what role?
Promotional objectives	What does the customer buy? What needs must be satisfied?
Promotional budgets and allocations	Why do customers buy a particular brand?
Promotional mix strategies and programs	Where do they go or look to buy the product or service?
Results of promotional programs	When do they buy? Any seasonality factors?
Assessment of firm or brand image	What are customers' attitudes toward our product/service?
Assessment of relative strengths and weaknesses of product/service	What social factors might influence the purchase decision?
What are its key attributes and benefits?	Do the customers' lifestyles influence their purchase decisions?
Does it have any unique selling points?	Do demographic factors influence the purchase decision?
Are the package and label consistent with the brand image?	**Competitive analysis**
	Who are our direct and indirect competitors?
	What key benefits and positioning are used by our competitors?
	What is our position relative to the competition?
	How big are competitors' promotion budgets?
	What promotion strategies are competitors using?
	Environmental analysis
	Are there any current trends or developments that might affect the promotional program?

As these objectives are determined, some attention is given to the promotional budget. Two basic questions are asked at this point: What will the promotional program cost? How will these monies be allocated? Ideally, the amount a firm needs to spend on promotion should be determined by what must be done to accomplish its communication objectives. In reality, promotional budgets are often determined using a more simplistic approach, such as how much money is available or a percentage of a company's or brand's sales revenue. At this stage, the budget is often tentative. It may not be finalized until specific promotional mix strategies are developed.

Develop IMC Programs

Developing the IMC program is generally the most involved and detailed step of the promotional planning process. As discussed earlier, each promotional mix element has certain strengths and limitations. At this stage of the planning process, decisions have to be made regarding the role and importance of each element and their coordination with one another. As Figure 1–6 shows, each promotional mix element has its own set of objectives and a budget and strategy for meeting them. Decisions must be made and activities performed to implement the promotional programs and evaluate performance to make any necessary changes.

For example, the advertising program will have its own set of objectives, usually involving the communication of some message or appeal to a target audience. A budget will be determined, providing the advertising manager and the agency with some idea of how much money is available for developing the ad campaign and purchasing media to disseminate the ad message.

Two important aspects of the advertising program are development of the message and the media strategy. Message development, often referred to as *creative strategy*, involves determining the basic message the advertiser wishes to convey to the target audience. This process, along with the ads that result, is to many students the most fascinating aspect of promotion. *Media strategy* involves determining which communication channels will be used to deliver the advertising message to the target audience. Decisions must be made regarding which types of media will be used (e.g., newspapers, magazines, radio, TV, billboards) as well as specific media selections (e.g., a particular magazine or TV program). This task requires careful evaluation of the media options' strengths and limitations, costs, and ability to deliver the message effectively to the target audiences.

Once the message and media strategies have been determined, steps must be taken to implement them. Most large companies hire advertising agencies to plan and produce their messages and to evaluate and purchase the media that will carry their ads. However, most agencies work very closely with their clients as they develop the ads and select media, because it is the advertiser that ultimately approves (and pays for) the creative work and media plan.

A similar process takes place for the other elements of the IMC program as objectives are set, an overall strategy is developed, message and media strategies are determined, and steps are taken to implement them. While the marketer's advertising agencies may be used to perform some of the other IMC functions, they may also hire other communication specialists.

Alternatively, if a firm considers using multiple tools for its complete plan it must decide which ones best fit together to solve a particular marketing communication problem. For example, in its first major promotional campaign in many years, Melitta Coffee increased its budget substantially and selected three IMC tools (Figure 1–8).[30] In addition, an IMC plan might evolve from an initial plan from one tool used, especially advertising. For example, Visa's "Win what you buy" sales promotion built upon the same message of "disappearing debt" conveyed in the television and print ads.[31]

Implement and Control the IMC Plan

It is important to determine how well the promotional program is meeting communications objectives and helping the firm accomplish its overall marketing goals and objectives. The promotional planner wants to know not only how well the

FIGURE *1–8* Melitta Coffee campaign

Budget:	**$1.8 million (previous year $50,000)**
Target:	**Women 25–54**
Advertising Message:	**Everyday indulgence**
Advertising Media:	**Radio (Vancouver, Calgary, Toronto, Montreal)** **Television (Prime, Deja View, Mystery, Cool TV, W)** **Print (*Canadian Living, Coup de Pouce, Canadian Grocer*)** **March to May, and September to December**
Sales Promotion:	**Product placement on *Me, My House and I*** **Contest supported by *Spectacular Spas* television show and newspaper** **Gift Basket giveaway** **June to August**
Internet:	**MochaSofa/Mokasofa.com**

promotional program is doing but also why. For example, problems with the advertising program may lie in the nature of the message or in a media plan that does not reach the target market effectively. The manager must know the reasons for the results in order to take the right steps to correct the program.

This final stage of the process is designed to provide managers with continual feedback concerning the effectiveness of the promotional program, which in turn can be used as input into the planning process. As Figure 1–6 shows, information on the results achieved by the promotional program is used in subsequent promotional planning and strategy development.

IMC Planning: Organization of Text

The purpose of this book is to provide a thorough understanding of the field of advertising and other elements of a firm's promotional mix and show how they are combined to form an integrated marketing communications program. The previous section developed the perspective for IMC planning, and we continue with this idea of an IMC planning section to conclude each chapter throughout the text. Its purpose is to relate the specific chapter material to the overall direction of an IMC plan. The final section of this chapter establishes this approach by illustrating how the entire book is organized around the IMC planning perspective. The book is organized around five major parts to facilitate this goal.

Part I, "Understand Integrated Marketing Communications," is comprised of four chapters. This initial chapter introduces the basic tools of IMC and how they relate to marketing. The chapter also gives a brief description of IMC and the content of a promotional plan. We discuss how firms organize for IMC and make decisions regarding ad agencies and other firms that provide marketing and promotional services in Chapter 2. To plan, develop, and implement an effective IMC program, those involved must understand consumer behaviour and the communications process. We focus on consumer behaviour and the target audience decision, and summarize various communication response models in Chapters 3 and 4, respectively. Combined, these two chapters establish a conceptual foundation for developing the subsequent set of decisions of an IMC plan.

The heart of marketing communication lies in what we are trying to say. Part II, "Articulate the Message," concerns a number of decisions firms make to put together a persuasive message. Chapter 5 explains how to set communication objectives to achieve the desired communication effects. Perhaps the most exciting aspects of IMC are discussed in Chapters 6, 7, and 8, where we illustrate the brand positioning strategy, creative strategy, and creative tactics decisions that result in vibrant and exciting ads. Chapter 9 examines how to measure advertising effectiveness, which also sets the stage for understanding how to assess the effects of all IMC tools.

Part III, "Deliver the Message," explores the key media strategy and media tactics decisions in Chapter 10 and the six traditional media choices (i.e., television, radio, magazines, newspapers, out-of-home, and support) within Chapters 11, 12, and 13. Collectively, Parts II and III provide a foundation for the IMC program. As all other IMC tools share this message and media characteristic, the general ideas can be applied throughout the IMC plan.

Our interest turns to the other areas of the promotional mix—sales promotion, public relations, direct marketing, and Internet marketing—in Part IV, "Strengthen the Message." Each tool is explored in its own chapter and related to communication objectives as done in Part III. The book concludes with Part V, "Advertising and Society," which examines advertising regulation and the ethical, social, and economic effects on an organization's advertising and promotional program.

SUMMARY

Advertising and other forms of promotion are an integral part of the marketing process in most organizations. The basic task of marketing is to combine the four controllable elements, known as the marketing mix, into a comprehensive program that facilitates exchange with a group of customers. The elements of the marketing mix are the product, price, place (distribution), and promotion (market communication).

Promotion is accomplished through a promotional mix that includes advertising, sales promotion, public relations, direct marketing, Internet marketing, and personal selling. The inherent advantages and disadvantages of each of these promotional mix elements influence the roles they play in the overall marketing program. In developing the promotional program, the manager must decide which tools to use and how to combine them to achieve the organization's objectives. Many organizations assist promotional managers in developing or implementing their plans including advertising agencies, media organizations, and specialized communication services firms like direct-response agencies, sales promotion agencies, interactive agencies, and public relations firms.

Historically, companies used mass-media advertising extensively in their promotional plans. Eventually, companies linked their promotional elements to achieve a more efficient and effective communication program. Managers referred to this practice as integrated marketing communication (IMC). Today, IMC is viewed as a strategic and comprehensive planning perspective for all facets of an organization's marketing communication.

Reasons for the growth of IMC feature improved efficiency and effectiveness with better communication planning, increased consumer adoption of technology and media, and innovative marketing practices used by organizations such as shifting marketing dollars from advertising to sales promotion, relying on database marketing more extensively, using the Internet with greater emphasis, and viewing communication problems as requiring advertising less frequently.

The emergence of IMC has become even more important for organizations as they view their environment as comprising many different audiences, such as, for example, current customers or prospective customers. When planning for IMC, managers have to consider how each promotional tool will communicate the brand effectively depending on who is receiving the brand message. Moreover, an IMC perspective for promotional planning has become critical as audiences receive messages from competing brands across different IMC tools. Finally, the evolution of marketing where organizations attempt to build long-term relationships with their customers has altered the communication perspective of many promotional planners.

Promotional management involves coordinating the promotional mix elements to develop an integrated program of effective marketing communication. The model of the IMC planning process in Figure 1–6 contains a number of steps: a review of the marketing plan; promotional program situation analysis; analysis of the communications process; budget determination; development of an integrated marketing communications program; integration and implementation of marketing communications strategies; and monitoring, evaluation, and control of the promotional program.

KEY TERMS

advertising, *9*
advertising agency, *14*
brand equity, *6*
clients, *14*
collateral services, *15*
communication objectives, *26*
direct channels, *8*
direct marketing, *12*
direct-response advertising, *12*
exchange, *4*
external analysis, *26*
indirect channels, *8*
integrated marketing communications (IMC), *15*
interactive media, *13*
internal analysis, *24*
marketing *22*
marketing mix, *4*
marketing objectives, *26*
marketing plan, *23*
media organizations, *14*
personal selling, *14*
product symbolism, *5*
promotion, *8*
promotional management, *22*
promotional mix, *8*
promotional plan, *23*
publicity, *12*
public relations, *10*
relationship marketing, *22*
sales promotion, *9*
specialized marketing communication services, *15*

DISCUSSION QUESTIONS

1. Discuss how integrated marketing communication differs from traditional advertising and promotion. What are some of the reasons why more marketers are taking an IMC perspective to their advertising and promotion programs?

2. Many sales promotions often look like ads these days. Why might this be occurring?

3. Why have companies been using public relations to an increasing degree in their IMC plans during the past 15 years?

4. Discuss the role of direct marketing as an IMC tool, giving attention to the various forms of direct marketing.

5. Analyze the role of the Internet in a company's IMC program. Discuss how the Internet can be used to execute the various elements of the promotional mix.

6. Discuss the role IMC plays in the brand-building process. How are marketers changing the ways they go about building strong brands?

7. What are customer contact points? Select a company or brand and discuss the various contact points that marketers can use to reach consumers of this product.

8. Discuss the role IMC plays in relationship marketing. How might the customization of advertising and other forms of marketing communication be possible?

9. Why is it important for those who work in the field of advertising and promotion to understand and appreciate all various IMC tools, not just the area in which they specialize?

10. What parts of the IMC planning model are similar to and different from a marketing planning model?

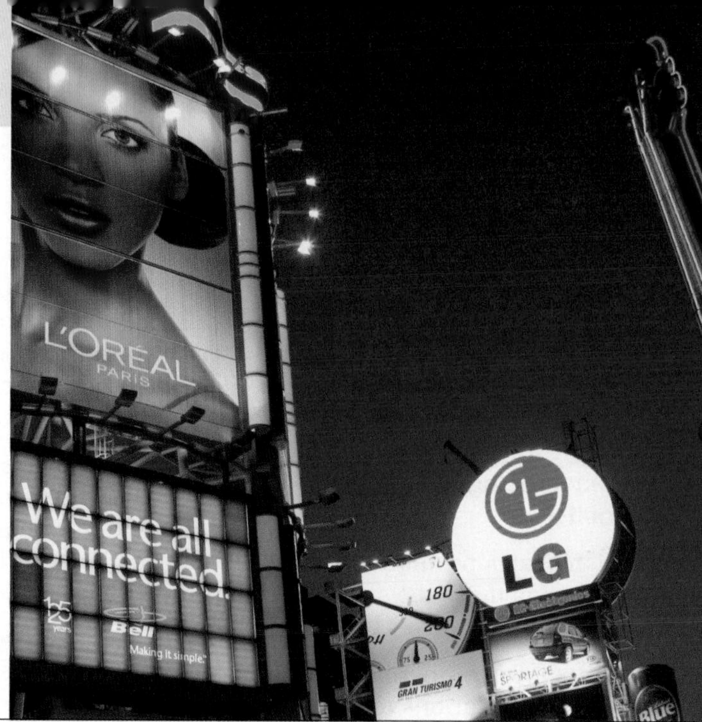

CHAPTER 2

ORGANIZING FOR INTEGRATED MARKETING COMMUNICATIONS

Chapter Objectives

- To understand how companies organize for advertising and other aspects of integrated marketing communications.
- To examine methods for selecting, compensating, and evaluating advertising agencies.
- To explain the role and functions of specialized marketing communications organizations.
- To examine various perspectives on the use of integrated services and responsibilities of advertisers versus agencies.

Happiness happens at TELUS.

Judges Hail a Creative Taxi

The Agency of the Year award bestowed by *Marketing Magazine* is based on producing superior creative, obtaining a significant number of new clients, and demonstrating vision. For 2005, Taxi sped past other fine agencies like Rethink, Publicis Canada, BBDO Canada, DDB Canada, and Cossette Communication Group and captured this distinction once again, just four years after being named Agency of the Year in 2001.

Taxi piled up an impressive list of achievements for 2005. It continued building on successful campaigns for its long-term clients that contributed to Taxi winning the $30-million WestJet and $50-million Canadian Tire accounts. The U.S. Clio Awards recognized Taxi as second best for its Global Agency of the Year award. Internationally, the prestigious Gunn Report selected Taxi as one of the most successful agencies in the world. And to cap it off, Taxi's successful creative work for Viagra and the Mini impressed worldwide judges, who awarded two gold lions at the International Advertising Festival in Cannes, France.

Clearnet PCS and Telus represent one of Taxi's greatest achievements. The creative theme of nature to represent the simplicity of using new wireless communication in its "The future is friendly" campaign has stood the test of time. Taxi not only clearly established Clearnet versus three other strong competitors in the late 1990s, but also skillfully transitioned the creative to the newly named Telus beginning in 2001. For example, by 2002 Telus Mobility gained substantially higher revenue per unit and obtained nearly half a million new subscribers. In subsequent years and in 2005, Taxi continued to build Telus Mobility as one of the leading wireless phone providers with innovative use of new characters from the natural world.

The launch of Viagra and the Mini promoted Taxi to the upper echelons of advertising in Canada and abroad. In both cases, the agency's television ads resulted in overwhelmingly positive results in terms of awareness and sales. The initial Viagra ad showed an elated consumer having a "Good morning" after an obvious good evening. The first Mini ad illustrated "David vs. Goliath" challenges to show the power and performance of the new car. In fact, head offices for both brands recognized the Canadian executions as being the best in the world. These initial creative themes continued for both brands into 2005, culminating in Taxi's impressive award.

Sources: Paul-Mark Rendon, "The New Establishment," *Marketing Magazine,* November 28, 2005; Taxi.ca.

Questions

1. Explain how Taxi achieved its award.
2. Which of its clients has the most creative campaigns?

Developing and implementing an integrated marketing communications program is usually a complex and detailed process involving the efforts of many persons from both the marketing firm and the advertising and other types of agencies. To manage this process, firms ensure that they are organized internally and have strong relationships with advertising agencies and other communication specialists.

This chapter discusses how companies organize internally for advertising and promotion. For many companies, advertising is planned and executed by an outside ad agency. Many large agencies offer a variety of other IMC capabilities, including public relations, sales promotion, and direct marketing. Thus, we will devote particular attention to the ad agency's role and the overall relationship between company and agency. We also examine the role of these specialized marketing communications organizations (such as direct-response, sales promotion, and interactive agencies and public relations firms) in the promotional process. The chapter concludes with a discussion of whether marketers are best served by using the integrated services of one large agency or the separate services of a variety of communications specialists.

Organizing for Advertising and Promotion in the Firm

The way a company organizes for marketing communications depends on several factors, including its size, the number of products it markets, the role of advertising and promotion in its marketing mix, the advertising and promotion budget, and its marketing organization structure. Many individuals throughout the organization may be involved in the promotions decision-making process. Marketing personnel have the most direct relationship with advertising and are often involved in many aspects of the decision process, such as providing input to the campaign plan, agency selection, and evaluation of proposed programs. Top management is usually interested in how the advertising program represents the firm, and this may also mean being involved in advertising decisions even when the decisions are not part of its day-to-day responsibilities.

While many people both inside and outside the organization have some input into the advertising and promotion process, direct responsibility for administering the program must be assumed by someone within the firm. Many companies have an advertising department headed by an advertising or communications manager operating under a marketing director. An alternative used by many large multiproduct firms is a decentralized marketing (brand management) system.

The Centralized System

In many organizations, marketing activities are divided along functional lines, with advertising placed alongside other marketing functions such as sales, marketing research, and product planning, as shown in Figure 2–1. The **advertising manager** is responsible for all promotions activities except sales. In the most common example of a **centralized system**, the advertising manager controls the entire promotions operation, including budgeting, coordinating the creation and production of ads, planning media schedules, and monitoring and administering the sales promotions programs for all the company's products or services. Basic functions the manager and staff perform include the following.

FIGURE 2–1 The advertising department under a centralized system

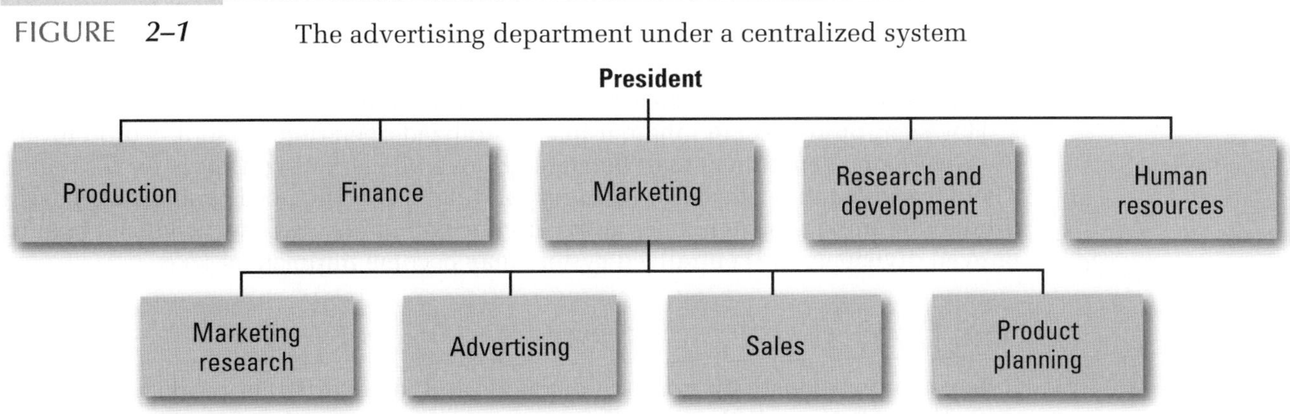

Planning and Budgeting The advertising department is responsible for developing advertising and promotions plans that will be approved by management and recommending a promotions program based on the overall marketing plan, objectives, and budget. Formal plans are submitted annually or when a program is being changed significantly, as when a new campaign is developed. While the advertising department develops the promotional budget, the final decision on allocating funds is usually made by top management.

Administration and Execution The manager must organize the advertising department and supervise and control its activities. The manager also supervises the execution of the plan by subordinates and/or the advertising agency. This requires working with such departments as production, media, art, copy, and sales promotion. If an outside agency is used, the advertising department is relieved of much of the executional responsibility; however, it must review and approve the agency's plans.

Coordination with Other Departments The manager must coordinate the advertising department's activities with those of other departments, particularly those involving other marketing functions. For example, the advertising department must communicate with marketing research and/or sales to determine which product features are important to customers and should be emphasized in the company's communications. Research may also provide profiles of product users and nonusers for the media department before it selects broadcast or print media. The advertising department may also be responsible for preparing material for the sales force, such as sales promotion tools, advertising materials, and point-of-purchase displays.

Coordination with Outside Agencies and Services Many companies have an advertising department but still use many outside services. For example, companies may develop their advertising programs in-house while employing media buying services to place their ads and/or use collateral services agencies to develop brochures, point-of-purchase materials, and so on. The department serves as liaison between the company and any outside service providers and also determines which ones to use. Once outside services are retained, the manager will work with other marketing managers to coordinate their efforts and evaluate their performances.

A centralized organizational system is often used when companies do not have many different divisions, product or service lines, or brands to advertise. Many companies prefer a centralized advertising department because developing and coordinating advertising programs from one central location facilitates communication regarding the promotions program, making it easier for top management to participate in decision making. A centralized system may also result in a more efficient operation because fewer people are involved in the program decisions, and as their experience in making such decisions increases, the process becomes easier.

However, problems are inherent in a centralized operation. First, it is difficult for the advertising department to understand the overall marketing strategy for the brand. The department may also be slow in responding to specific needs and problems of a product or brand. As companies grow and develop or acquire new products, brands, or even divisions, the centralized system may become impractical.

The Decentralized System

In large corporations with multiple divisions and many different products, it is very difficult to manage all the advertising, promotional, and other functions through a centralized department. These types of companies generally have a **decentralized system**, with separate manufacturing, research and development, sales, and marketing departments for various divisions, product lines, or businesses. Many companies that use a decentralized system, such as Procter & Gamble, Gillette Co., and Nestlé, assign each product or brand to a **brand manager** who is responsible for the total management of the brand, including planning, budgeting, sales, and profit performance. (The term *product manager* is also used to describe this position.) The brand manager, who may have one or more assistant brand managers, is also responsible for the planning, implementation, and control of the marketing program.[1]

Under this system, the responsibilities and functions associated with advertising and promotions are transferred to the brand manager, who works closely with the outside advertising agency and other marketing communications specialists as they develop the promotional program.[2] In a multiproduct firm, each brand may have its own ad agency and may compete against other brands within the company, not just against outside competitors. For example, Exhibit 2–1 shows ads for Cheer and Tide, which are both Procter & Gamble products that compete for a share of the laundry detergent market.

As shown in Figure 2–2, the advertising department is part of marketing services and provides support for the brand managers. The role of marketing services is to assist the brand managers in planning and coordinating the integrated marketing communications program. In some companies, the marketing services group may

Exhibit 2–1
Many of Procter & Gamble's brands compete against each other

FIGURE 2–2 A decentralized brand management system

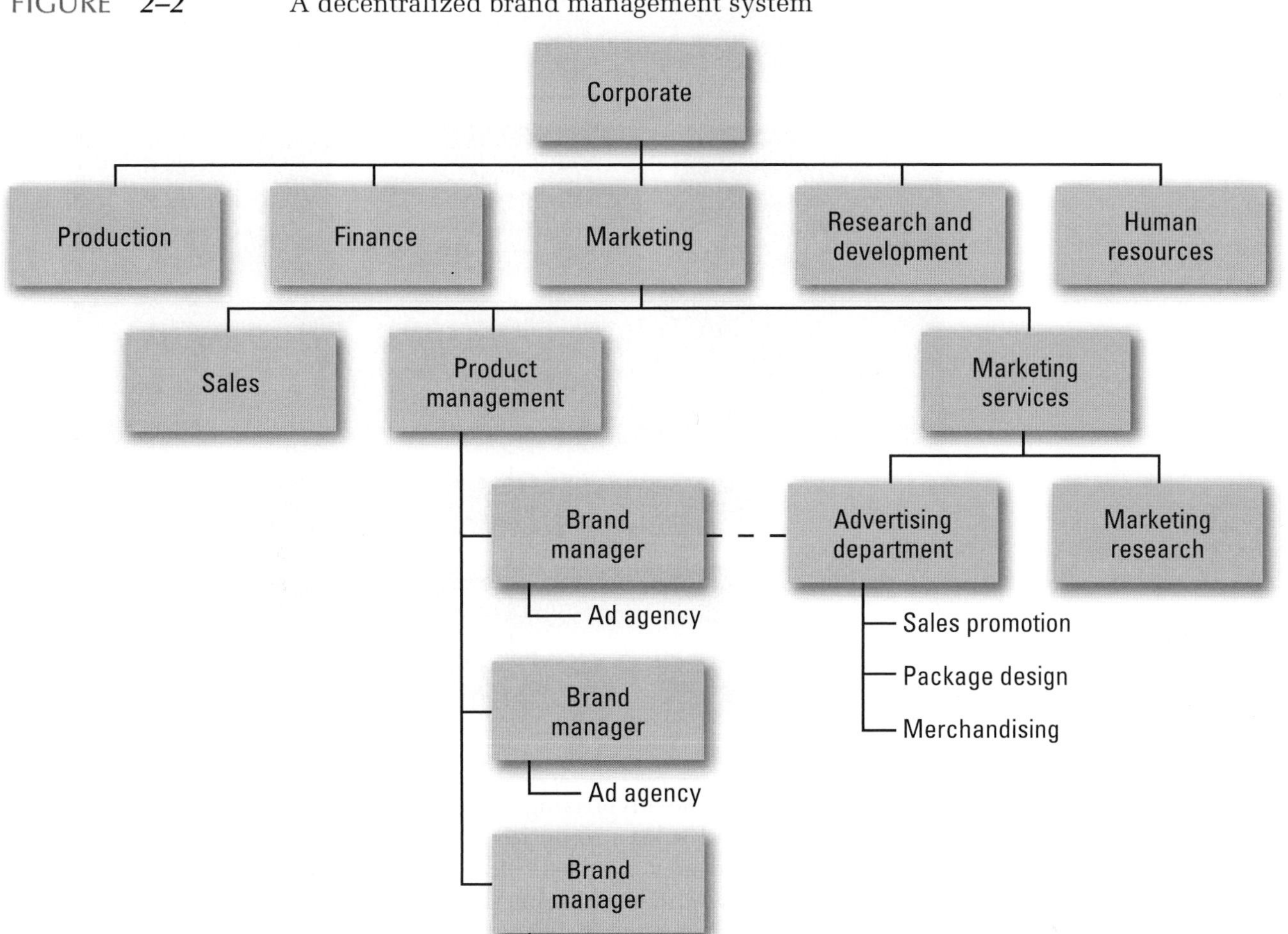

include sales promotion. The brand managers may work with sales promotion people to develop budgets, define strategies, and implement tactical executions for both trade and consumer promotions. Marketing services may also provide other types of support services, such as package design and merchandising.

Some companies may have an additional layer(s) of management above the brand managers to coordinate the efforts of all the brand managers handling a related group of products. An example is the organizational structure of Procter & Gamble, shown in Figure 2–3 on page 38. This system—generally referred to as a **category management system**—includes category managers as well as brand and advertising managers. The category manager oversees management of the entire product category and focuses on the strategic role of the various brands in order to build profits and market share.[3]

The advertising manager may review and evaluate the various parts of the program and advise and consult with the brand managers. This person may have the authority to override the brand manager's decisions on advertising. In some multiproduct firms that spend a lot on advertising, the advertising manager may coordinate the work of the various agencies to obtain media discounts for the firm's large volume of media purchases.

An advantage of the decentralized system is that each brand receives concentrated managerial attention, resulting in faster response to both problems and opportunities. The brand manager system is also more flexible and makes it easier to

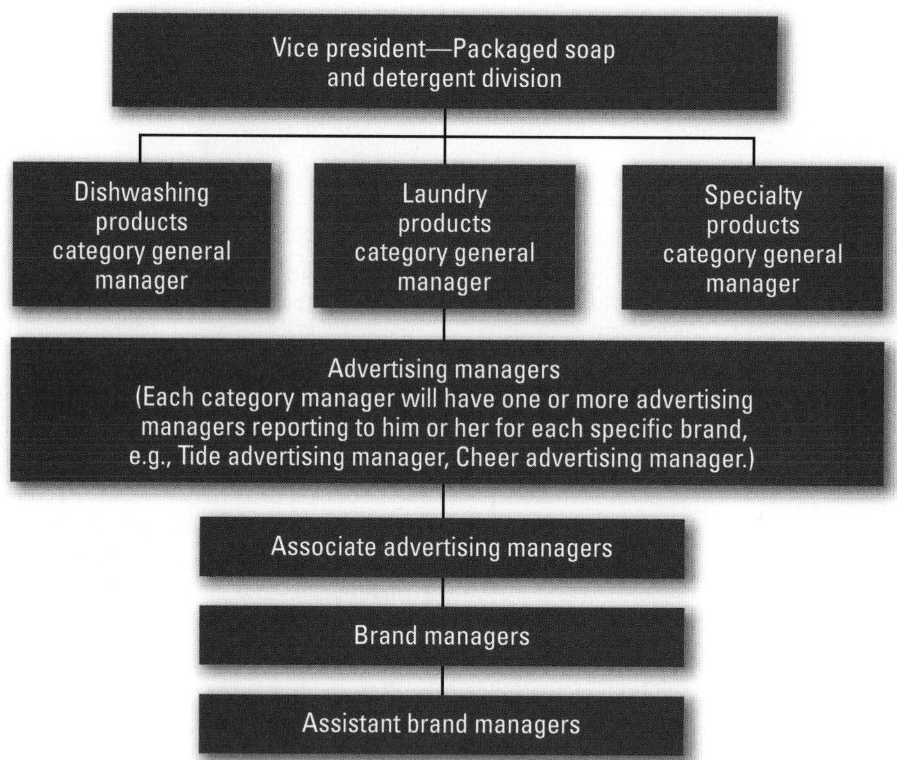

FIGURE 2–3

A Procter & Gamble division, using the category management system

adjust various aspects of the advertising and promotional program, such as creative platforms and media and sales promotion schedules.[4] The brand manager system is also more flexible and makes it easier to adjust the advertising and promotional program, such as creative themes and media and sales promotion schedules.[5]

There are some drawbacks to the decentralized approach. Brand managers often lack training and experience. The promotional strategy for a brand may be developed by a brand manager who does not really understand what advertising or sales promotion can and cannot do and how each should be used. Brand managers may focus too much on short-run planning and administrative tasks, neglecting the development of long-term programs.

Another problem is that individual brand managers often end up competing for management attention, marketing dollars, and other resources, which can lead to unproductive rivalries and potential misallocation of funds. The manager's persuasiveness may become a bigger factor in determining budgets than the long-run profit potential of the brands. These types of problems were key factors in Procter & Gamble's decision to switch to a category management system.

Finally, the brand management system has been criticized for failing to provide brand managers with authority over the functions needed to implement and control the plans they develop.[6] Some companies have dealt with this problem by expanding the roles and responsibilities of the advertising and sales promotion managers and their staff of specialists. The staff specialists counsel the individual brand managers, and advertising or sales promotion decision making involves the advertising and/or sales promotion manager, the brand manager, and the marketing director.

Advertising Agencies

The use of an advertising agency is unique for each advertiser. And as you might expect, there are many different types. In this section we provide a general overview that describes the situation. We review the advertising agency decision, describe the activities of a full-service agency, highlight the agency industry, and identify other types of agencies.

Advertising Agency Decision

Irrespective of whether an advertiser uses a centralized or decentralized organizational structure, there remains the choice of whether a firm will have its own in-house agency or whether it will employ an external advertising agency. We now briefly discuss the relative merits and concerns of both options.

In-House Agency Option Some companies, in an effort to reduce costs and maintain greater control over agency activities, have set up their own advertising agencies internally. An **in-house agency** is an advertising agency that is set up, owned, and operated by the advertiser. Some in-house agencies are little more than advertising departments, but in other companies they are given a separate identity and are responsible for the expenditure of large sums of advertising dollars. Many companies use in-house agencies exclusively; others combine in-house efforts with those of outside agencies. For example, Benetton handles most of its advertising in-house, but it does use an outside agency for some of its creative work (Exhibit 2–2).

A major reason for using an in-house agency is to reduce advertising and promotion costs. Companies with very large advertising budgets pay a substantial amount to outside agencies in the form of media commissions. With an internal structure, these commissions go to the in-house agency. An in-house agency can also provide related work such as sales presentations and sales force materials, package design, and public relations at a lower cost than outside agencies. A study by M. Louise Ripley found that creative and media services were the most likely functions to be performed outside, while merchandising and sales promotion were the most likely to be performed in-house.[7]

Saving money is not the only reason companies use in-house agencies. Time savings, bad experiences with outside agencies, and the increased knowledge and understanding of the market that come from working on advertising and promotion for the product or service day by day are also reasons. Companies can also maintain tighter control over the process and more easily coordinate promotions with the firm's overall marketing program. Some companies use an in-house agency simply because they believe it can do a better job than an outside agency could.[8]

Exhibit 2–2 Benetton's in-house agency works with outside agencies to develop ads

Opponents of in-house agencies say they can give the advertiser neither the experience and objectivity of an outside agency nor the range of services. They argue that outside agencies have more highly skilled specialists and attract the best creative talent and that using an external firm gives a company a more varied perspective on its advertising problems and greater flexibility. In-house personnel may become narrow or grow stale while working on the same product line, but outside agencies may have different people with a variety of backgrounds and ideas working on the account. Flexibility is greater because an outside agency can be dismissed if the company is not satisfied, whereas changes in an in-house agency could be slower and more disruptive.

Advertising Agency Option Many major companies use an advertising agency to assist them in developing, preparing, and executing their promotional programs. An ad agency is a service organization that specializes in planning and executing advertising programs for its clients. Probably the main reason outside agencies are used is that they provide the client with the services of highly skilled individuals who are specialists in their chosen fields. An advertising agency staff may include artists, writers, media analysts, researchers, and others with specific skills, knowledge, and experience who can help market the client's products or services. Many agencies specialize in a particular type of business and use their knowledge of the industry to assist their clients.

An outside agency can also provide an objective viewpoint of the market and its business that is not subject to internal company policies, biases, or other limitations. The agency can draw on the broad range of experience it has gained while working on a diverse set of marketing problems for various clients. For example, an ad agency that is handling a travel-related account may have individuals who have worked with airlines, cruise ship companies, travel agencies, hotels, and other travel-related industries. The agency may have experience in this area or may even have previously worked on the advertising account of one of the client's competitors. Thus, the agency can provide the client with insight into the industry (and, in some cases, the competition). IMC Perspective 2–1 shows a newfound source of inspiration for ads.

Advertising Agency Industry

The Canadian advertising agency industry is similar to others—there is a combination of domestic firms and international organizations, especially from the U.S. Many of the latter have extensive sales in Canada; however, recent legal changes pertaining to accounting practices do not permit the release of sales revenue for its subsidiaries. Consequently, it is impossible to fully describe the size and scope of the industry. According to Statistics Canada, the advertising agencies earned $2.2 billion during 2004.[9] Given the limited data, we still present the top five Canadian-based advertising agencies in Figure 2–4 for reference. Figure 2–5 on page 42 puts the context of the Canadian revenue into perspective compared to the large multinational firms.

The strong presence of international ad agencies in Canada reflects a global trend. The advertising industry underwent major changes as large agencies merged with or acquired other agencies and support organizations during the past 20 years. These **superagencies** were formed so that agencies could provide clients with integrated

FIGURE *2–4*

Domestic revenue of Canada's top 5 communications services companies

Ranking	Company	2005 Revenues ($C M)
1	Cossette Communication Group	143.4
2	MDC Partners	61.6
3	Maritz Canada	51.9
4	Carlson Marketing Group Canada	48.0
5	Nurun	33.2

Source: *Marketing Magazine*, June 19, 2006.

IMC PERSPECTIVE 2–1
Homemade Advertising

The latest fad in advertising is consumer-generated advertising. Advertisers and ad agencies ask consumers to enter contests to submit their best ideas to promote their brand. In some cases, the agency will produce the idea; in others, the consumer actually produces a finished 30-second spot. "It's a great way to build buzz, but a debatable way to build a brand," says Harvard Business School consumer marketing professor Stephen Greyser.

Although the idea appears attractive to advertisers, there are a lot of hurdles and risks. It takes time to sort through the ideas, find an ad in good taste, determine if it fits the brand strategy, assess whether it is affordable to produce, and finally sign the contracts. But what happens when a non-winning consumer claims that the commercial on the Super Bowl is his or her idea, while the winning consumer who produced a similar submission is the lucky one who got credit—and big bucks—for it?

This approach may make sense as a short-term promotional tactic. Smaller companies with limited budgets might consider this path, if the alternative is to not advertise at all. But if homemade ads are part of a sustained effort to turn over the reins of brand communication to consumers, then there is certainly cause for concern.

Lack of brand consistency is one reason why homemade advertising might not make any sense. Brand strength is developed by expressing and delivering the brand promise consistently across all touch points and over time. So why would a marketer want to run a bunch of ads created by different people with different messages using different creative approaches?

Moreover, these ads likely miss the opportunity to demonstrate brand leadership; that is, to express the unique and compelling brand point of view that transcends the product or service being sold. The ads everyone points to as having been the most successful are ones that represent brand leadership. It is likely that no consumer, no matter how talented or cool or brand fanatical, would ever have conceived Nike's original Just Do It campaign.

Consumers know what they know at the moment—they know why they like a product, but they don't know the vision of the brand. They don't know the company's dreams and aspirations for the brand, and so they lack the insight and foresight to realize an ad's full potential. Just as product development should involve the consumer, so should creative development. But innovative companies don't ask consumers to actually develop new products for them, and in the same way shouldn't ask consumers to develop ads for them, either.

Sources: Marc Brownstein, "About Consumer-Generated Ads: Have We Gone Mad?" *Advertising Age,* November 16, 2006; and Denise Lee Yohn, "Do Consumers Always Know Best?" *Brandchannel.com,* July 3, 2006.

Questions

1. Do you think that homemade consumer advertising is a fad?
2. Can you think of any situations where this type of advertising can have merit?

marketing communications services worldwide. Many of the mid-size agencies were acquired by or forged alliances with larger agencies because their clients wanted an agency with international communications capabilities and their alignment with larger organizations gave them access to a network of agencies around the world.[10] Recent merger and acquisition activity has seen major agencies acquiring companies specializing in areas such as interactive communications, direct marketing, and sales promotion so that they can offer their clients an ever-broader range of integrated marketing communication services.[11]

Full-Service Advertising Agencies

Since ad agencies can range in size from a one- or two-person operation to large organizations with over 1,000 employees, the services offered and functions performed will vary. In order to understand the variety of agencies, we focus on the largest and most complex. Many companies employ what is known as a **full-service agency**,

FIGURE 2–5

World's top ad organizations

World's Top 10 Agency Brands

RANK 2005	RANK 2004	AGENCY	WORLDWIDE REVENUE ($US M) 2005	2004	% CHANGE
1	1	Dentsu	2,165.9	2,205.5	−1.8
2	2	McCann Erickson Worldwide	1,461.1	1,455.5	0.4
3	3	JWT	1,313.5	1,324.9	−0.9
4	4	BBDO Worldwide	1,295.7	1,165.6	11.2
5	6	DDB Worldwide Communications	1,190.6	1,090.2	9.2
6	5	Publicis Worldwide	1,083.2	1,037.3	4.4
7	9	TBWA Worldwide	950.2	873.3	8.8
8	8	Leo Burnett Worldwide	807.3	823.7	−2.0
9	10	Ogilvy & Mather Worldwide	801.4	752.6	6.5
10	9	Hakuhudo	788.0	802.0	−1.7

Source: Based on "2006 issue Worlds top 10 agency brands" Advertising Age, May 1, 2006, pg 37.

which offers its clients a full range of marketing, communications, and promotions services, including planning, creating, and producing the advertising; performing research; and selecting media. A full-service agency may also offer nonadvertising services such as strategic market planning; sales promotions, direct marketing, and interactive capabilities; package design; and public relations and publicity.

The full-service agency is made up of departments that provide the activities needed to perform the various advertising functions and serve the client, as shown in Figure 2–6. We now summarize these main characteristics.

Account Services Account services, or account management, is the link between the ad agency and its clients. Depending on the size of the client and its advertising budget, one or more account executives serve as liaison. The **account executive** is responsible for understanding the advertiser's marketing and promotions needs and interpreting them to agency personnel. He or she coordinates agency efforts in planning, creating, and producing ads. The account executive also presents agency recommendations and obtains client approval.

As the focal point of agency–client relationships, the account executive must know a great deal about the client's business and be able to communicate this to specialists in the agency working on the account.[12] The ideal account executive has a strong marketing background as well as a thorough understanding of all phases of the advertising process.

Marketing Services Over the past two decades, use of marketing services has increased dramatically. One service gaining increased attention is research, as agencies realize that to communicate effectively with their clients' customers, they must have a good understanding of the target audience. As shown in Chapter 1, the advertising planning process begins with a thorough situation analysis, which is based on research and information about the target audience.

Most full-service agencies maintain a *research department* whose function is to gather, analyze, and interpret information that will be useful in developing advertising for their clients. This can be done through primary research—where a study is designed, executed, and interpreted by the research department—or through the use of secondary (previously published) sources of information. Sometimes the research department acquires studies conducted by independent syndicated research firms

FIGURE 2–6 Full-service agency organizational chart

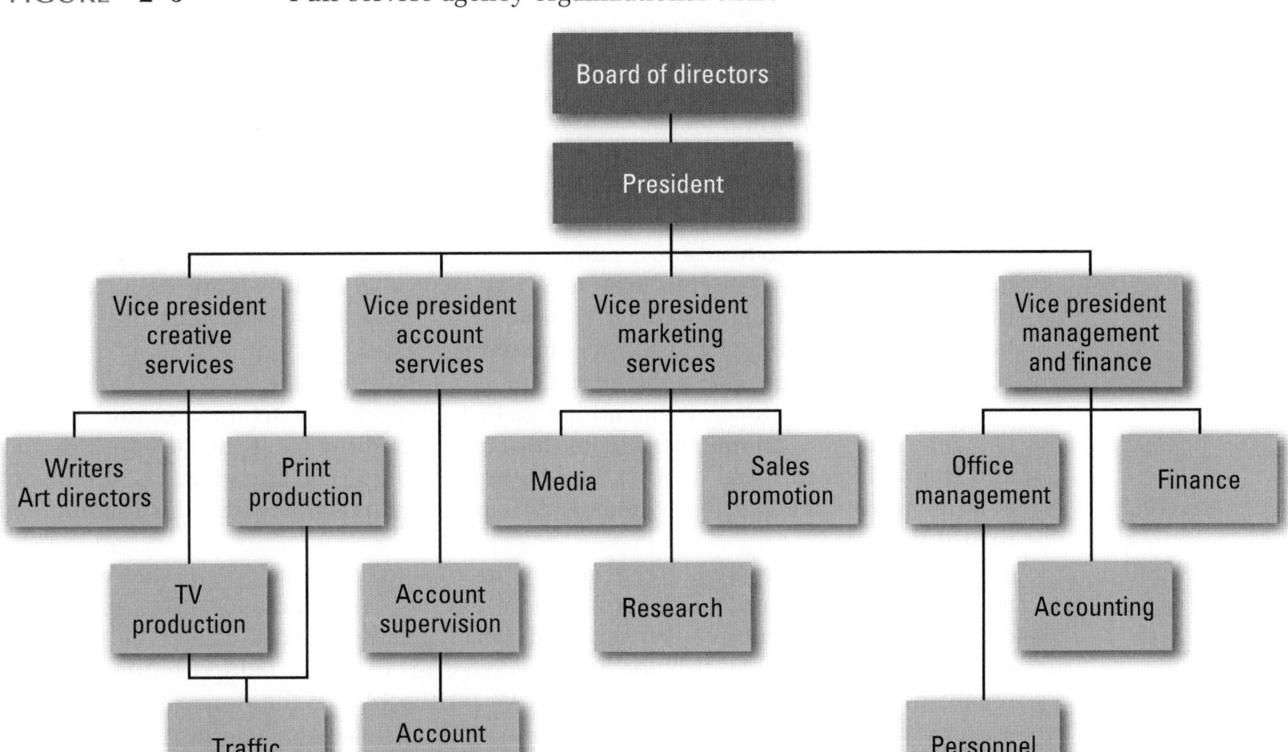

or consultants. The research staff then interprets these reports and passes on the information to other agency personnel working on that account.

The research department may also design and conduct research to pretest the effectiveness of advertising the agency is considering. For example, copy testing is often conducted to determine how messages developed by the creative specialists are likely to be interpreted by the receiving audience.

The *media department* of an agency analyzes, selects, and contracts for space or time in the media that will be used to deliver the client's advertising message. The media department is expected to develop a media plan that will reach the target audience and effectively communicate the message. Since most of the client's ad budget is spent on media time and/or space, this department must develop a plan that both communicates with the right audience and is cost-effective.

Media specialists must know what audiences the media reach, their rates, and how well they match the client's target audience. The media department reviews information on demographics, magazine and newspaper readership, radio listenership, and consumers' TV viewing patterns to develop an effective media plan. The media buyer implements the media plan by purchasing the actual time and space. The media department is becoming an increasingly important part of the agency business as many large advertisers consolidate their media buying with one or a few agencies to save money and improve media efficiency. An agency's strategic ability to negotiate prices and effectively use the vast array of media vehicles available is becoming as important as its ability to create ads.

The research and media departments perform most of the functions that full-service agencies need to plan and execute their clients' advertising programs. Some agencies offer additional marketing services to their clients to assist in other promotional areas. An agency may have a sales promotion department, or merchandising department, that specializes in developing contests, premiums, promotions, point-of-sale materials, and other sales materials. It may have direct-marketing specialists and package designers, as well as a PR/publicity department. Many agencies have developed interactive media departments to create websites for their clients. The growing popularity of integrated marketing communications has prompted many full-function agencies to develop capabilities and offer services in these other promotional areas.

Creative Services The creative services department is responsible for the creation and execution of advertisements. The individuals who conceive the ideas for the ads and write the headlines, subheads, and body copy (the words constituting the message) are known as **copywriters**. They may also be involved in determining the basic appeal or theme of the ad campaign and often prepare a rough initial visual layout of the print ad or television commercial.

While copywriters are responsible for what the message says, the *art department* is responsible for how the ad looks. For print ads, the art director and graphic designers prepare *layouts*, which are drawings that show what the ad will look like and from which the final artwork will be produced. For TV commercials, the layout is known as a *storyboard*, a sequence of frames or panels that depict the commercial in still form.

Members of the creative department work together to develop ads that will communicate the key points determined to be the basis of the creative strategy for the client's product or service. Writers and artists generally work under the direction of the agency's creative director, who oversees all the advertising produced by the organization. The director sets the creative philosophy of the department and may even become directly involved in creating ads for the agency's largest clients.

Once the copy, layout, illustrations, and mechanical specifications have been completed and approved, the ad is turned over to the *production department*. Most agencies do not actually produce finished ads; they hire printers, engravers, photographers, typographers, and other suppliers to complete the finished product. For broadcast production, the approved storyboard must be turned into a finished commercial. The production department may supervise the casting of people to appear in the ad and the setting for the scenes as well as choose an independent production studio. The department may hire an outside director to turn the creative concept into a commercial. Copywriters, art directors, account managers, people from research and planning, and representatives from the client side may all participate in production decisions, particularly when large sums of money are involved.

Creating an advertisement often involves many people and takes several months. In large agencies with many clients, coordinating the creative and production processes can be a major problem. A *traffic department* coordinates all phases of production to see that the ads are completed on time and that all deadlines for submitting the ads to the media are met. The traffic department may be located in the creative services area of the agency, or be part of media or account management, or be separate.

Management and Finance Like any other business, an advertising agency must be managed and perform basic operating and administrative functions such as accounting, finance, and human resources. It must also attempt to generate new business. Large agencies employ administrative, managerial, and clerical people to perform these functions. The bulk of an agency's income (approximately 64 percent) goes to salary and benefits for its employees. Thus, an agency must manage its personnel carefully and get maximum productivity from them.

Structure Full-function advertising agencies must develop an organizational structure that will meet their clients' needs and serve their own internal requirements. Most medium-size and large agencies are structured under either a departmental or a group system. Under the **departmental system**, each of the agency functions shown in Figure 2–6 is set up as a separate department and is called on as needed to perform its specialty and serve all of the agency's clients. Ad layout, writing, and production are done by the creative department, marketing services is responsible for any research or media selection and purchases, and the account services department handles client contact. Some agencies prefer the departmental system because it gives employees the opportunity to develop expertise in servicing a variety of accounts.

Many large agencies use the **group system**, in which individuals from each department work together in groups to service particular accounts. Each group is headed by an account executive or supervisor and has one or more media people, including media planners and buyers; a creative team, which includes copywriters, art directors, artists, and production personnel; and one or more account executives. The group may also include individuals from other departments such as marketing research, direct marketing, or sales promotion. The size and composition of the group varies depending on the client's billings and the importance of the account to the agency. For very important accounts, the group members may be assigned exclusively to one client. In some agencies, they may serve a number of smaller clients. Many agencies prefer the group system because employees become very knowledgeable about the client's business and there is continuity in servicing the account.

Other Types of Agencies and Services

Not every agency is a large full-service agency. Many smaller agencies expect their employees to handle a variety of jobs. For example, account executives may do their own research, work out their own media schedule, and coordinate the production of ads written and designed by the creative department. Many advertisers, including some large companies, are not interested in paying for the services of a full-service agency but are interested in some of the specific services agencies have to offer. Over the past few decades, several alternatives to full-service agencies have evolved, including creative boutiques and media buying services.

Creative Boutiques A **creative boutique** is an agency that provides only creative services. These specialized agencies have creative personnel but do not have media, research, or account planning capabilities. Creative boutiques have developed in response to some companies' desires to use only the creative services of an outside agency while managing the other functions internally. While most creative boutiques work directly for companies, full-service agencies often subcontract work to creative boutiques when they are very busy or want to avoid adding full-time employees to their payrolls. Many creative boutiques have been formed by members of the creative departments of full-service agencies who leave the firm and take with them clients who want to retain their creative talents. Exhibit 2–3 on page 46 highlights an example of Canada's most successful creative boutiques.

One area where Canadian agencies have worked with specialized creative firms is in the development of messages targeted to specific ethnic markets. It is very expensive and difficult for large agencies to be set up for each ethnic community that it may try to reach in a campaign, so they rely on specialists who have the expertise. With a tremendous growth of Chinese immigrants in Toronto and Vancouver, firms such as Ford have used tailored messages and ethnic media to influence the attitudes of this target audience that has very different beliefs than other consumers because of their heritage. Ford could not succeed in establishing a unique brand position with this target audience without the assistance of those more familiar. One trade-off that advertisers need in order to make this work is to put the media savings from lower-cost publications or TV programming into the production of appropriate creative messages.[13]

Exhibit 2–3
An example of Rethink's creative talent

Media Buying Services **Media buying services** are independent companies that specialize in the buying of media, particularly radio and television time. The task of purchasing advertising media has grown more complex as specialized media proliferate, so media buying services have found a niche by specializing in the analysis and purchase of advertising time and space. Agencies and clients usually develop their own media strategies and hire the buying service to execute them. Some media buying services do help advertisers plan their media strategies. Because media buying services purchase such large amounts of time and space, they receive large discounts and can save the small agency or client money on media purchases.

Media buying services have been experiencing strong growth in recent years as clients seek alternatives to full-service agency relationships. Many companies have been unbundling agency services and consolidating media buying to get more clout from their advertising budgets. As noted earlier, many of the major agencies have formed independent media services companies that handle the media planning and buying for their clients and also offer their services separately to companies interested in a more specialized or consolidated approach to media planning, research, and/or buying. The rise of the independent media-buying services, operating outside the structure of the traditional ad agency media department, and the divestment of these departments from the agency system are two of the most significant developments that have occurred in the advertising industry in recent years. Exhibit 2–4 shows how Initiative, which is one of the largest media specialist companies, promotes its services.

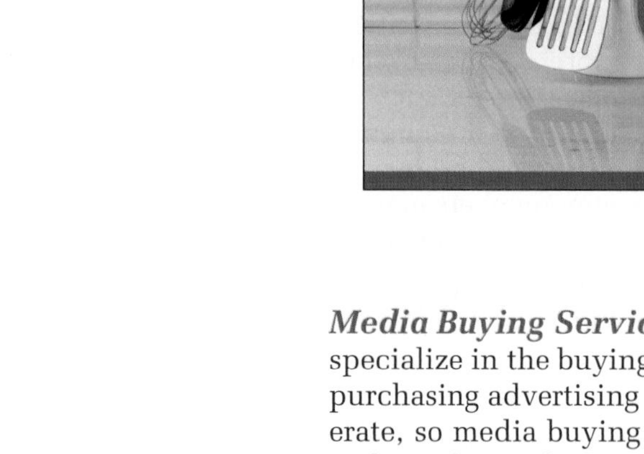

Exhibit 2–4 Initiative is one of the leading media specialist companies

Agency Compensation

Agencies use a variety of compensation methods depending on the type and amount of service they provide to their clients. We review a number of methods since there is no one method of compensation to which everyone subscribes. We also examine the related topic of performance evaluation and explore reasons why clients switch agencies.

COMMISSIONS FROM MEDIA

The traditional method of compensating agencies is through a **commission system**, where the agency receives a specified commission (usually 15 percent) from the media on any advertising time or space it purchases for its client. This system provides a simple method of determining payments, as shown in the following example.

Assume an agency prepares a full-page magazine ad and arranges to place the ad on the back cover of a magazine at a cost of $100,000. The agency places the order for the space and delivers the ad to the magazine. Once the ad is run, the magazine will bill the agency for $100,000, less the 15 percent ($15,000) commission. The media will also offer a 2 percent cash discount for early payment, which the agency may pass along to the client. The agency will bill the client $100,000 less the 2 percent cash discount on the net amount, or a total of $98,300, as shown in Figure 2–7. The $15,000 commission represents the agency's compensation for its services.

The commission system to compensate agencies has been quite controversial despite its prevalent use for decades. Critics argue that the commission system encourages agencies to recommend high-priced media to increase their commission level. Another concern regarding the commission system is that it ties agency compensation to media costs, allowing the agency to be disproportionately rewarded. Critics of the system have argued that it provides an incentive for agencies to recommend mass-media advertising when other forms of communication such as direct marketing or public relations might do a better job.[14]

Defenders of the commission system argue that it is easy to administer and it keeps the emphasis in agency competition on non-price factors such as the quality of the advertising developed. Proponents argue that agency services are proportional to the size of the commission, since more time and effort are devoted to the large accounts that generate high revenue for the agency. They also say the system is more flexible than it appears because agencies often perform other services for large clients at no extra charge, justifying such actions by the large commission they receive.

A recent study of agency compensation conducted by the Association of Canadian Advertisers (ACA) indicates that agency compensation based on the traditional 15 percent commission is becoming rare.[15] The survey found that the commission model was one of many approaches used and that no one model stood out as being the very best. In fact, a trend toward so many other models implies that the 15 percent commission is on a significant decline. Many advertisers have gone to a **negotiated commission** system to compensate their agencies. In this system, commissions average 8 to 10 percent, and are based on a sliding scale that becomes lower as clients' media expenditures increase. Agencies are also relying less on media commissions for their income as their clients expand their integrated marketing communications programs to include other forms of promotion and cut back on mass-media advertising. The percentage of agency income from media commissions is declining, and a greater percentage is coming through other methods such as fees and performance incentives.

Media Bills Agency		Agency Bills Advertiser	
Costs for magazine space	$100,000	Costs for magazine space	$100,000
Less 15% commission	–15,000	Less 2% cash discount	–1,700
Cost of media space	$ 85,000	Advertiser pays agency	$ 98,300
Less 2% cash discount	–1,700		
Agency pays media	$ 83,300	Agency income	$ 15,000

FIGURE 2–7
Example of commission system payment

Other Compensation Systems

Many agencies and their clients have developed a fee arrangement or cost-plus agreement for agency compensation in response to commission system concerns. Some are using incentive-based compensation, which is a combination of a commission and a fee system.

Fee Arrangement There are two basic types of fee arrangement systems. In the straight or **fixed-fee method**, the agency charges a basic monthly fee for all of its services and credits to the client any media commissions earned. Agency and client agree on the specific work to be done and the amount the agency will be paid for it. Sometimes agencies are compensated through a **fee-commission combination**, in which the media commissions received by the agency are credited against the fee. If the commissions are less than the agreed-on fee, the client must make up the difference. If the agency does much work for the client in noncommissionable media, the fee may be charged over and above the commissions received.

Both types of fee arrangements require that the agency carefully assess its costs of serving the client for the specified period, or for the project, plus its desired profit margin. To avoid any later disagreement, a fee arrangement should specify exactly what services the agency is expected to perform for the client. A recent interview of four agency executives suggests that the fee arrangement is becoming the more accepted method of compensation in Canada.[16]

Cost-Plus Agreement Under a **cost-plus system**, the client agrees to pay the agency a fee based on the costs of its work plus some agreed-on profit margin (often a percentage of total costs). This system requires that the agency keep detailed records of the costs it incurs in working on the client's account. Direct costs (personnel time and out-of-pocket expenses) plus an allocation for overhead and a markup for profits determine the amount the agency bills the client. An agency can add a markup of percentage charges to various services the agency purchases from outside providers (e.g., market research, artwork, printing, photography).

Fee agreements and cost-plus systems are commonly used in conjunction with a commission system. The fee-based system can be advantageous to both the client and the agency, depending on the size of the client, advertising budget, media used, and services required. Many clients prefer fee or cost-plus systems because they receive a detailed breakdown of where and how their advertising and promotion dollars are being spent. However, these arrangements can be difficult for the agency, as they require careful cost accounting and may be difficult to estimate when bidding for an advertiser's business. Agencies are also reluctant to let clients see their internal cost figures.

Incentive-Based Compensation Clients expect accountability from their agencies and link agency compensation to performance through some type of **incentive-based system**. The basic idea is that the agency's ultimate compensation level will depend on how well it meets predetermined performance goals. These goals often include objective measures such as sales or market share as well as more subjective measures such as evaluations of the quality of the agency's creative work. Companies using incentive-based systems determine agency compensation through media commissions, fees, bonuses, or some combination of these methods.

A recent study, Performance by Results (PBR), commissioned by the Institute of Communications and Advertising, highlights the importance of clearly identifying the objectives of the promotional plan and measuring the performance of the plan based on these objectives. One focus of the study is to investigate and define an advertising remuneration process where the basic advertising agency fee is adjusted by a reward based on the degree of achieving mutually agreed upon objectives between the client and the agency. Another focus of the study is to view the remuneration as a part of a system of linking performance, its measurement, and reward within the client–

agency relationship, something that has been characteristic of supply relationships in other industries. The benefits of the PBR system are:

- Greater efficiency and accountability
- Achievement of cost efficiencies
- Higher productivity
- Fewer barriers of self-interest
- Stronger mutual understanding
- Improved retention of creative talent
- Increased agency strategic input
- Improved client–agency communication

Performance measures are a key element of the PBR system and the study highlights three general groups that should comprise the evaluation: overall business performance, marketing communication effectiveness, and agency process evaluation. Business measures include sales, market share, profitability, and margins. Marketing communication effectiveness measures include brand awareness, brand image ratings, and likability of advertising. This group also includes four objectives that are more behavioural: intent to purchase, trial, repeat purchase, and brand loyalty. The final group concerns the various services the agency provides and its overall management process.

The PBR system recognizes that there is no standard formula in applying these measures. The relative importance of each measure needs to be investigated for each brand and its marketing situation. Furthermore, the measures should take into account the role of promotion in the marketing mix and how promotion contributes to business results for the brand and within the product category or industry. In addition, the PBR study provides the following suggestions. Objectives can be short term and long term. An appropriate number of objectives should be used to focus the organization. The objectives should be consistent with other performance measures used in the organization. Objectives should be periodically re-evaluated by the client and the agency. Although some of these recommendations may be intuitive, the Canadian PBR study is the most thorough, published examination of the PBR system in the world. Another remarkable achievement for our marketing communication industry![17]

Over the past five years, about one-third of all Canadian marketers compensate their agencies with some form of payment by results. However, this overall figure varies depending upon the size of the communications budget. A total of 58 percent of firms spending more than $100 million use incentives, compared to only 18 percent of firms spending less than $15 million. Moreover, about two-thirds of clients compensating their agencies in this manner report improved performance. Larger firms, like Univer, for example, employ this compensation method for all of their service agencies including sales promotion and public relations.[18]

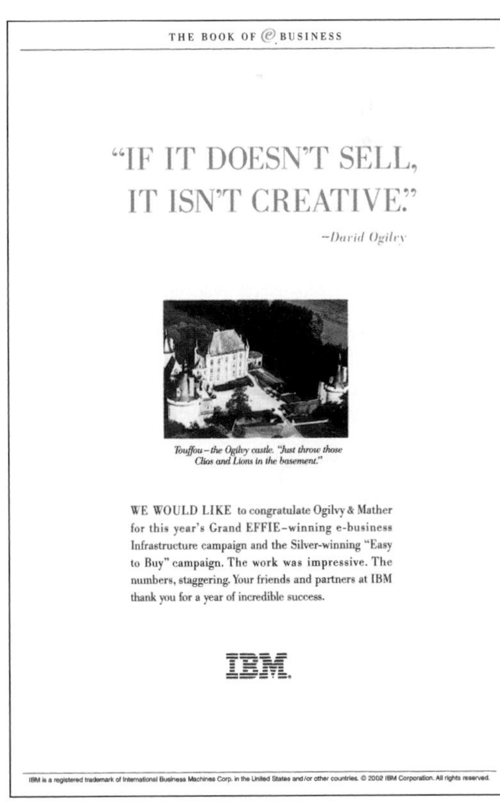

Exhibit 2–5 IBM congratulates its agency for developing an award-winning campaign

Evaluation of Agencies

Regular reviews of the agency's performance are necessary. The agency evaluation process usually involves two types of assessments, one financial and operational and the other more qualitative. The **financial audit** focuses on how the gency conducts its business. It is designed to verify costs and expenses, the number of personnel hours charged to an account, and payments to media and outside suppliers. The **qualitative audit** focuses on the agency's efforts in planning, developing, and implementing the client's advertising programs and considers the results achieved. Sometimes it may appear that an evaluation is not required when the advertiser publicly praises its agency (Exhibit 2–5).

The agency evaluation is often done on a subjective, informal basis, particularly in smaller companies where ad budgets are low or advertising is not seen as the most critical factor in the firm's marketing performance. Some companies have developed formal, systematic evaluation systems, particularly when budgets are large and the advertising function receives much emphasis. As advertising costs continue to rise, the top management of these companies wants to be sure money is being spent efficiently and effectively.

As part of its mandate as an industry resource, the Institute of Communications and Advertising provides a Guide to Best Practice that includes information to facilitate agency evaluation (the Guide and the PBR study are both available at www.ica-ad.com). The document provides guidelines on the client–agency relationship and includes many forms that can be used as a basis for evaluating an agency in all areas of performance such as account management, creative, planning and research, production, media planning and buying, budget and financial, agency management, direct marketing, interactive marketing, and public relations.

One example of a formal agency evaluation system is that used by Whirlpool, which markets a variety of consumer products. Whirlpool management meets once a year with the company's agencies to review their performance. Whirlpool managers complete an advertising agency performance evaluation, part of which is shown in Figure 2–8. These reports are compiled and reviewed with the agency at each annual meeting. Whirlpool's evaluation process covers six areas of performance. The company and the agency develop an action plan to correct areas of deficiency.

FIGURE 2–8
Whirlpool's ad agency performance evaluation

CREATIVE SERVICES

Always	Often	Occasionally	Seldom	Never	NA	Marks Scored
4	3	2	1	0		

1. Agency produces fresh ideas and original approaches
2. Agency accurately interprets facts, strategies and objectives into usable advertisements and plans
3. Creative group is knowledgeable about company's products, markets and strategies
4. Creative group is concerned with good advertising communications and develops campaigns and ads that exhibit this concern
5. Creative group produces on time
6. Creative group performs well under pressure
7. Creative group operates in a businesslike manner to control production costs and other creative charges
8. Agency presentations are well organized with sufficient examples of proposed executions
9. Creative group participates in major campaign presentations
10. Agency presents ideas and executions not requested but felt to be good opportunities
11. Agency willingly accepts ideas generated by other locations/agency offices vs. being over-protective of its own creative product
12. Other areas not mentioned
13. Agency demonstrates commitment to client's business
14. Agency creative proposals are relevant and properly fulfill creative brief

Value—(marks)

Rating:			
	Excellent	90–100%	Total marks scored
	Good	80–89%	
	Average	70–79%	Total possible marks
	Fair	60–69%	
	Poor	below 60%	Score

ACCOUNT REPRESENTATION & SERVICE

Always	Often	Occasionally	Seldom	Never	NA	Marks Scored
4	3	2	1	0		

1. Account representatives act with personal initiative
2. Account representatives anticipate needs in advance of direction by client (ie: are proactive)
3. Account group takes direction well
4. Agency is able to demonstrate results of programs implemented
5. Account representatives function strategically rather than as creative advisors only
6. Account representatives are knowledgeable about competitive programs and share this information along with their recommendations in a timely manner
7. Account representatives respond to client requests in a timely fashion
8. Account group operates in a business-like manner to control costs
9. Agency recommendations are founded on sound reasoning and supported factually, and appropriately fit within budget constraints
10. Agency is able to advise the client on trends and developments in technology
11. Account representatives demonstrate a high degree of professionalism in both written and oral communication
12. Agency presents ideas and executions not requested by felt to be good opportunities
13. Agency makes reasoned recommendations on allocation of budgets
14. Agency demonstrates commitment to client's business
15. There is a positive social relationship between client and agency

Value—(marks)

Rating:			
	Excellent	90–100%	Total marks scored
	Good	80–89%	
	Average	70–79%	Total possible marks
	Fair	60–69%	
	Poor	below 60%	Score

Reasons for Agencies Losing Clients

The evaluation process described above provides valuable feedback to both the agency and the client, such as indicating changes that need to be made by the agency and/or the client to improve performance and make the relationship more productive. Many agencies have had very long-lasting relationships with their clients (see Exhibit 2–6); however, long-term relationships are becoming less common.

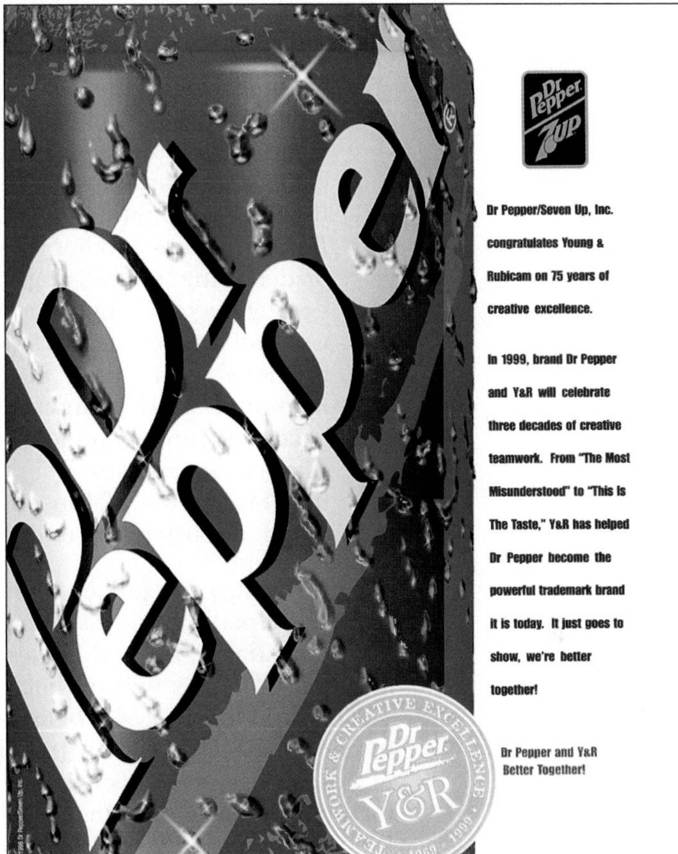

Dr Pepper
Dr Pepper 7UP
Dr Pepper/Seven Up, Inc. congratulates Young & Rubicam on 75 years of creative excellence.
In 1999, brand Dr Pepper and Y&R will celebrate three decades of creative teamwork. From "The Most Misunderstood" to "This Is The Taste," Y&R has helped Dr Pepper become the powerful trademark brand it is today. It just goes to show, we're better together!
Teamwork & Creative Excellence
Dr Pepper
Y&R
1969 · 1999
Dr Pepper and Y&R
Better Together!

Exhibit 2–6 Young & Rubicam has been the agency for Dr Pepper for more than three decades

Agency-of-record (AOR) is the term used to describe those situations where a client works with an exclusive agency for a number of years. It is the very foundation on which the advertising agency business exists—a service provider whose foremost interest is in building the client's brand. A recent trend is that some advertisers do not have a specific AOR, but work with different agencies at once, or in succession, depending upon their communication needs. In essence, agencies engage in project-like work for a client by developing a short campaign or performing creative work only. For example, a client can contract the creative work to an agency but rely on its own market research resources. Advertisers believe they are saving money, finding the best ideas for an assignment, and putting pressure on agencies to perform. Critics believe this allows marketing investments to gravitate away from advertising and limit brand development, minimizes consistency across multiple campaigns, or constrains creativity to position the brand effectively.[19]

While the debate continues, many Canadian campaigns such as Coors, Shoppers Drug Mart, Mr. Sub, Budget, Apple, and WestJet are the result of project work. In some cases, the brand had an AOR status but the client decided to use a smaller or different agency for a particular assignment. Advertisers cite the need to remain flexible and the desire to test out new agencies for future relationships. In fact, a considerable amount of the project work went to smaller independent agencies or creative boutiques, which suggests longer-term relationships could be in the future.[20]

There are a number of reasons why clients switch agencies. Some of the more common reasons agencies lose clients are as follows:

- *Poor performance or service.* The client becomes dissatisfied with the quality of the advertising and/or the service provided by the agency.
- *Poor communication.* The client and agency personnel fail to develop or maintain the level of communication necessary to sustain a favourable working relationship.
- *Unrealistic demands by the client.* The client places demands on the agency that exceed the amount of compensation received and reduce the account's profitability.
- *Personality conflicts.* People working on the account on the client and agency sides do not have enough rapport to work well together.
- *Personnel changes.* A change in personnel at either the agency or the advertiser can create problems. New managers may wish to use an agency with which they have established ties. Agency personnel often take accounts with them when they switch agencies or start their own.

- *Changes in size of the client or agency.* The client may outgrow the agency or decide it needs a larger agency to handle its business. If the agency gets too large, the client may represent too small a percentage of its business to command attention.
- *Conflicts of interest.* A conflict may develop when an agency merges with another agency or when a client is part of an acquisition or merger.
- *Changes in the client's corporate and/or marketing strategy.* A client may change its marketing strategy and think a new agency is needed to carry out the new program.
- *Declining sales.* When sales of the client's product or service are stagnant or declining, advertising may be seen as contributing to the problem. A new agency may be sought for a new creative approach.
- *Conflicting compensation philosophies.* Disagreement may develop over the level or method of compensation. As more companies move toward incentive-based compensation systems, disagreement over compensation is becoming more commonplace.
- *Changes in policies.* Policy changes may result when either party reevaluates the importance of the relationship, the agency acquires a new (and larger) client, or either side undergoes a merger or acquisition.

If the agency recognizes these warning signs, it can try to adapt its programs and policies to make sure the client is satisfied. Some of the situations discussed here are unavoidable, and others are beyond the agency's control. But to maintain the account, problems within the agency's control must be addressed.

The time may come when the agency decides it is no longer in its best interest to continue to work with the client. Personnel conflicts, changes in management philosophy, and/or insufficient financial incentives are just a few of the reasons for such a decision. Then the agency may terminate the account relationship. IMC Perspective 2–2 cites some alarming levels of dissatisfaction currently experienced by clients.

Specialized Services

Many companies assign the development and implementation of their promotional programs to an advertising agency. But several other types of organizations provide specialized services that complement the efforts of ad agencies. Direct-response agencies, sales promotion agencies, and public relations firms are important to marketers in developing and executing IMC programs. Let us examine the functions these organizations perform.

Sales Promotion Agencies

Developing and managing sales promotion programs such as contests, sweepstakes, refunds and rebates, premium and incentive offers, and sampling programs is a very complex task. Most companies use a **sales promotion agency** to develop and administer these programs. Some large ad agencies have created their own sales promotion department or acquired a sales promotion firm. However, most sales promotion agencies are independent companies that specialize in providing the services needed to plan, develop, and execute a variety of sales promotion programs.

Sales promotion agencies often work in conjunction with the client's advertising and/or direct-response agencies to coordinate their efforts with the advertising and direct-marketing programs. Services provided by large sales promotion agencies include promotional planning, creative, research, tie-in coordination, fulfillment, premium design and manufacturing, catalogue production, and contest/sweepstakes

IMC PERSPECTIVE 2–2

Client Discontent with Advertising Agencies

According to a survey by Forrester Research, ad agencies are failing miserably to deliver what clients want—never mind that most marketers can't measure what they're getting from their shops anyway. The rather bleak report employed the net promoter score, a popular test of loyalty that's based on a simple question: How likely are you to recommend a particular product or service? Agencies turned in a dismal aggregate score of 21 percent, meaning that very few clients would recommend their agency's services to others. Yet the report also found that a whopping 76 percent of marketers had no way to determine their return on investment from their lead agencies. Sixty-nine percent said ROI is too difficult to measure.

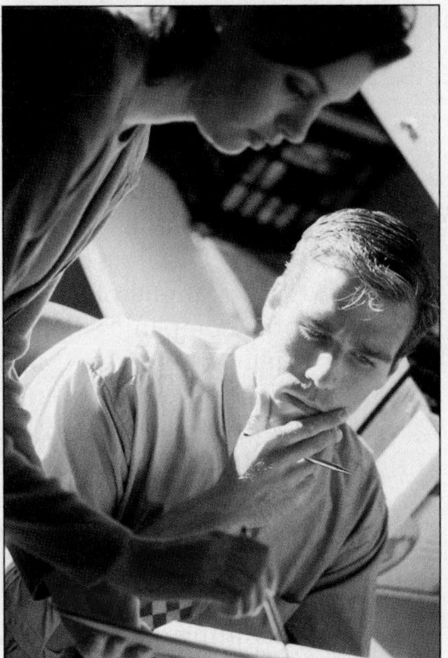

The survey of agencies put a fine point on one of the major challenges facing the advertising industry today: How can agencies remain central marketing partners in an age of increased specialization driven by an increasingly digital media environment?

"There's always an undercurrent of discontent with agencies," said Peter Kim, a senior analyst at Forrester. "What surprised me is that three-quarters do not measure agency ROI. They're dissatisfied, yet on what basis? It's not because the agency didn't help them drive sales or meet some other business outcome. It's a vague disenchantment or dis-appointment; it's a feeling that there isn't data to back up."

The bright side for the advertising industry is that, for all their shortcomings, agencies still exert a big influence on how marketing budgets are spent, responsible for nearly 60 percent of spending, and marketers continue to regard them as strong business partners. That figure could be at risk, however, especially if agencies aren't quick to solve the digital-talent shortage that's plaguing the business.

The relationship will also be helped along by a better focus on measurement. Arthur Anderson, a principal at Morgan Anderson Consulting, said marketers have generally been good at measuring business outcomes, such as sales, or marketing results, such as awareness, but are less so when it comes to evaluating work practices and nuts and bolts, such as sharing marketing plans.

Source: Matthew Creamer, "Survey: Marketers Can't Grade Agencies But Fail Them Anyway," *Advertising Age*, February 26, 2007.

Questions

1. Why do you think clients are so dissatisfied with their agencies?
2. How does the shortage of digital talent affect current satisfaction levels?

management. Many sales promotion agencies are also developing direct/database marketing and telemarketing to expand their integrated marketing services capabilities. Sales promotion agencies are generally compensated on a fee basis.

Public Relations Firms

Many large companies use both an advertising agency and a PR firm. The **public relations firm** develops and implements programs to manage the organization's publicity, image, and affairs with consumers and other relevant publics, including employees, suppliers, shareholders, government, labour groups, citizen action groups, and the general public. The PR firm analyzes the relationships between the client and these various publics, determines how the client's policies and actions relate to and affect these publics, develops PR strategies and programs, implements these programs using various public relations tools, and evaluates their effectiveness.

The activities of a public relations firm include planning the PR strategy and program, generating publicity, conducting lobbying and public affairs efforts, becoming involved in community activities and events, preparing news releases and other communications, conducting research, promoting and managing special events, and managing crises. As companies adopt an IMC approach to promotional planning, they are coordinating their PR activities with advertising and other promotional areas. Many companies are integrating public relations and publicity into the marketing communications mix to increase message credibility and save media costs.[21]

Direct-Response Agencies

One of the fastest-growing areas of IMC is direct marketing, where companies communicate with consumers through telemarketing, direct mail, television, the Internet, and other forms of direct-response advertising. As this industry has grown, numerous direct-response agencies have evolved that offer companies their specialized skills in both consumer and business markets. Many of the top direct-marketing agencies such as Rapp Collins Worldwide, Draft, Wunderman, and OgilvyOne are subsidiaries of large agency holding companies. However, there are also a number of independent direct-marketing agencies including those that serve large companies as well as smaller firms that handle the needs of local companies (Exhibit 2–7).

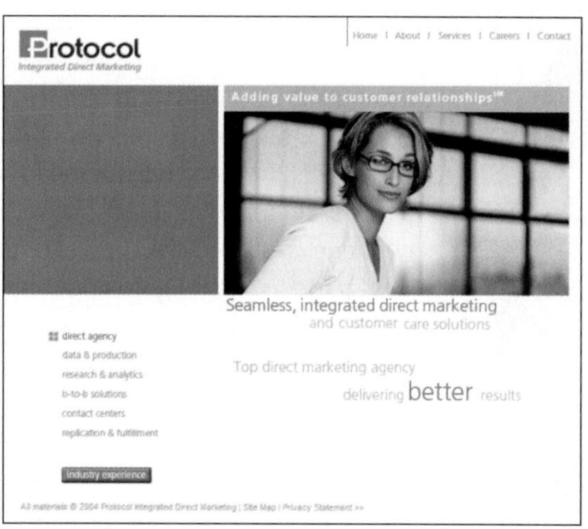

Exhibit 2–7 Protocol promotes its direct-marketing services

Direct-response agencies provide a variety of services, including database management, direct mail, research, media services, and creative and production capabilities. While direct mail is their primary weapon, many direct-response agencies are expanding their services to include such areas as infomercial production and database management. Database development and management is becoming one of the most important services provided by direct-response agencies. Many companies are using database marketing to pinpoint new customers and build relationships and loyalty among existing customers.[22]

A typical direct-response agency is divided into three main departments: account management, creative, and media. Some agencies also have a department whose function is to develop and manage databases for their clients. The account managers work with their clients to plan direct-marketing programs and determine their role in the overall integrated marketing communications process. The creative department consists of copywriters, artists, and producers. Creative is responsible for developing the direct-response message, while the media department is concerned with its placement.

Interactive Agencies

With the rapid growth of the Internet and other forms of interactive media, a new type of specialized marketing communications organization has evolved—the interactive agency. Many marketers are using **interactive agencies** that specialize in the development and strategic use of various interactive marketing tools such as websites for the Internet, banner ads, CD-ROMs, text messages, search engines, and kiosks. They recognize that the development of successful interactive marketing programs requires expertise in technology as well as areas such as creative website design, database marketing, digital media, and customer relationship management. Many traditional advertising agencies have established interactive capabilities, ranging from a few specialists within the agency to an entire interactive division.

While many agencies have or are developing interactive capabilities, a number of marketers are turning to more specialized interactive agencies to develop websites and interactive media. They feel these companies have more expertise in designing and developing websites as well as managing and supporting them. Interactive agencies range from smaller companies that specialize in website design and creation to full-service interactive agencies that provide all the elements needed for a successful Internet/interactive marketing program. These services include strategic consulting regarding the use of the Internet and online branding, technical knowledge, systems integration, and the development of electronic commerce capabilities.

IMC Planning: Agency Relationships

Currently, marketers can choose from a variety of organizations to assist them in planning, developing, and implementing an integrated marketing communications program. Companies must decide whether to use specialized organizations for each marketing communications function or consolidate them with a large advertising agency that offers all of these services. In this final section, we discuss the issue as to whether an advertiser would want to use an integrated services agency or not, assess the agency–client responsibilities for IMC, and summarize the current situation regarding the agency–client relationship in the context of an IMC environment.

Integrated IMC Services

It has been argued that the concept of integrated marketing is nothing new, particularly in smaller companies and communication agencies that have been coordinating a variety of promotional tools for years. And larger advertising agencies have been trying to gain more of their clients' promotional business for over 20 years. However, in the past, the various services were run as separate profit centres. Each was motivated to push its own expertise and pursue its own goals rather than develop truly integrated marketing programs. Moreover, the creative specialists in many agencies resisted becoming involved in sales promotion or direct marketing. They preferred to concentrate on developing magazine ads or television commercials rather than designing coupons or direct-mail pieces.

Proponents of the integrated marketing services agency (the one-stop shop) contend that past problems are being solved and the various individuals in the agencies and subsidiaries are learning to work together to deliver a consistent message to the client's customers. They argue that maintaining control of the entire promotional process achieves greater synergy among each of the communications program elements. They also note that it is more convenient for the client to coordinate all of its marketing efforts—media advertising, direct mail, special events, sales promotions, and public relations—through one agency. An agency with integrated marketing capabilities can create a single image for the product or service and address everyone, from wholesalers to consumers, with one voice.

But not everyone wants to turn the entire IMC program over to one agency. Opponents say the providers become involved in political wrangling over budgets, do not communicate with each other as well and as often as they should, and do not achieve synergy. They also claim that agencies' efforts to control all aspects of the promotional program are nothing more than an attempt to hold on to business that might otherwise be lost to independent providers. They note that synergy and economies of scale, while nice in theory, have been difficult to achieve and competition and conflict among agency subsidiaries has been a major problem.[23] Many companies use a variety of vendors for communication functions, choosing the specialist they believe is best suited for each promotional task, be it advertising, sales promotion, or public relations.

Compounding these concerns is the opinion that advertising agencies are neither sufficiently staffed to ensure complete integration, nor are they fully cognizant of multiple target audiences. Advertising agency personnel are trained in particular aspects of the process and are less inclined to consider many marketing variables in their decisions. Furthermore, they tend to consider only the end user or consumer rather than all the parties in the marketing process who are connected to the results of the communications plan. It is recommended that marketers ensure that the agencies consider the needs of all (e.g., customer service staff, sales representatives, distributors, and retailers) in their communication plans.[24]

Agency–Client Responsibility

Surveys of advertisers and agency executives have shown that both groups believe integrated marketing is important to their organizations' success and that it will be even more important in the future.[25] However, marketers and agency executives have very different opinions regarding who should be in charge of the integrated marketing communications process. Many advertisers prefer to set strategy for and coordinate their own IMC campaigns, but most agency executives see this as their domain.

While agency executives believe their shops are capable of handling the various elements an integrated campaign requires, many marketers, particularly larger firms, disagree. Marketing executives say the biggest obstacle to implementing IMC is the lack of people with the broad perspective and skills to make it work. Agencies are felt to lack expertise in database marketing, marketing research, and information technology. Internal turf battles, agency egos, and fear of budget reductions are also cited as major barriers to successful integrated marketing campaigns.[26]

Many ad agencies are adding more resources to offer their clients a full line of services. They are expanding their agencies' capabilities in interactive and multimedia advertising, database management, direct marketing, public relations, and sales promotion. However, many marketers still want to set the strategy for their IMC campaigns and seek specialized expertise, more quality and creativity, and greater control and cost efficiency by using multiple providers.

Most marketers do recognize that ad agencies will no longer stick primarily to advertising and will continue to expand their IMC capabilities. There is an opportunity for agencies to broaden their services beyond advertising—but they will have to develop true expertise in a variety of integrated marketing communications areas. They will also have to create organizational structures that make it possible for individuals with expertise in a variety of communications areas to work well together both internally and externally. One thing is certain: as companies continue to shift their promotional dollars away from media advertising to other IMC tools, agencies will continue to explore ways to keep these monies under their roofs.

Agency–Client Partnership

In a series of interviews, an executive from each of BMO Financial Group, Levi Strauss & Co., Nestlé Canada, and Moosehead Breweries offered his or her opinion on broad questions surrounding agency–client relations. What do marketers (i.e., clients) want from their agency partners? Are agencies meeting these needs? What can marketers do to forge stronger relations with agency partners?[27]

The needs of marketers are broad and varied, including more integrated plans using a range of communication tools, constant messages across many tools, greater understanding of the marketer's brand, overall good quality, more precise measurement of communication effects, insight into market positioning strategies, and of course, very creative ads.

Agencies appear to be performing very well in some areas, but there appears to be room for improvement. While there have been increased attempts at integration, there may be certain biases of individuals toward one tool versus another. Improved creative planning has emerged; however, concern regarding full accountability currently exists. Agencies offer greater services with larger multinationals, although this has not always been completely beneficial for clients. The creative planning process has become very efficient, but the process has not changed significantly to reflect evolution of IMC. Although measurement of communication effects is recognized as a priority, there remains a need to find innovative ways to know if communication dollars have been invested properly. Finally, clients prefer to have more strategic thinking along with the outstanding creative ads that agencies continue to deliver!

Marketers believe they can help agencies in the relationship by being better clients through good personnel, clear decision-making, sufficient budgets and lead times, and solid market research. In addition, clients should provide clear direction of their needs at the start of the creative process and involve the agency completely. This also includes sharing sensitive and confidential information so that the agency understands the client's business, marketing, and market positioning objectives. In the end, the agency and client must be viewed as one team, not two organizations.

Some of these and other findings emerged from a recent survey of agency and clients conducted in both Canada and the U.S. In partnership, *Marketing Magazine* and *Brandweek* administered over 10,000 addressed e-mail questionnaires. A highlight of this research is that it tried to obtain a balanced perspective on many advertising industry issues by having an independent research organization design the study and collect the data rather than industry associations.[28]

A survey of the marketers reported the following:

- 45 percent maintained a primary relationship with an ad agency, while many preferred working on a project basis or with multiple specialty agencies.
- Agencies from all disciplines were used; advertising (79 percent), public relations (59 percent), direct marketing (54 percent), sales promotion (54 percent), events (46 percent), and interactive marketing (46 percent).
- Clients valued creativity, strategic insights, and excellence in execution fairly equally.
- Agencies tended to have poor performance in multidisciplined thinking (31 percent), strategic depth (30 percent), creative breadth (26 percent), and resource availability (26 percent).
- Additional services deemed important were independent ROI audits and training of agency staff with respect to marketing versus advertising only.

A survey of the agencies revealed a few noteworthy facts:

- About half focused on multiple disciplines while the other half specialized on one.
- Agencies tended to have one or two dominant clients and only one-third had 15 or more clients.
- Business of the AOR and the project was split roughly equally.
- Approximately 60 percent of all relationships lasted three years or more.
- Agencies viewed client relationships, client loyalty, and strategic involvement as the most important factors compared to profits or performance-based rewards.

In reviewing the two perspectives of the agency–client relationship, some issues for future collaboration appear relevant. Some divergence on the type of partnership between agency and client is emerging. A different view regarding performance-based remuneration is a challenge for agreement. Long-term relationships appear to be more difficult to maintain. The degree to which claimed and actual integration across disciplines occur is at odds. The ability of agencies to deliver independent marketing ideas and focus on ROI may be a limitation that clients will desire with increased frequency.

SUMMARY

Companies use two basic systems to organize internally for advertising and promotion. Centralized systems offer the advantages of facilitated communications, lower personnel requirements, continuity in staff, and more top-management involvement. Disadvantages include a lower involvement with overall marketing goals, longer response times, and difficulties in handling multiple product lines.

Decentralized systems offer the advantages of concentrated managerial attention, more rapid responses to problems, and increased flexibility, though they may be limited by ineffective decision making, internal conflicts, misallocation of funds, and a lack of authority.

Firms have to decide if they will hire an external advertising agency or use an in-house service to create their ads and purchase media. In-house agencies, while offering the advantages of cost savings, control, and increased coordination, have the disadvantage of less experience, objectivity, and flexibility.

Many firms use advertising agencies to help develop and execute their programs. These agencies may take on a variety of forms, including full-service agencies, creative boutiques, and media buying services. The first offers the client a full range of services (including creative, account, marketing, and financial and management services); the other two specialize in creative services and media buying, respectively.

Agencies are compensated through commission systems, and fee- and cost-based systems. Recently, the emphasis on agency accountability has increased. Agencies are being evaluated on both financial and qualitative aspects, and some clients are using incentive-based compensation systems that tie agency compensation to performance measures such as sales and market share.

In addition to using ad agencies, marketers use the services of other marketing communication specialists, including direct marketing agencies, sales promotion agencies, public relations firms, and interactive agencies. A marketer must decide whether to use a different specialist for each promotional function or have all of its integrated marketing communications done by an advertising agency that offers all of these services under one roof.

Recent studies have found that most marketers believe it is their responsibility, not the ad agency's, to set strategy for and coordinate IMC campaigns. The lack of a broad perspective and specialized skills in nonadvertising areas is seen as the major barrier to agencies' increased involvement in integrated marketing communications.

KEY TERMS

account executive, *42*
advertising manager, *34*
brand manager, *36*
category management system, *37*
centralized system, *34*
commission system, *47*
copywriters, *44*
cost-plus system, *48*
creative boutique, *45*
decentralized system, *36*
departmental system, *44*
direct-response agencies, *54*
fee-commission combination, *48*
financial audit, *49*
fixed-fee method, *48*
full-service agency, *41*
group system, *45*
incentive-based system, *48*
in-house agency, *39*
interactive agencies, *54*
media buying services, *46*
negotiated commission, *47*
public relations firm, *53*
qualitative audit, *49*
sales promotion agency, *52*
superagencies, *40*

DISCUSSION QUESTIONS

1. What are some of the specific responsibilities and duties of an advertising manager under a centralized advertising department structure? Why is an advertising manager needed if a company uses an outside agency?

2. Discuss the pros and cons of using an in-house advertising agency. What are some of the reasons why companies might change from using an in-house agency and hire an outside agency?

3. Discuss the various functions a full-service advertising agency performs for its clients. Might any one of these functions be more important than another?

4. Discuss some of the reasons why traditional advertising agencies have been developing more IMC capabilities. What changes might these agencies have to make to improve their service?

5. Why might a company choose to use a creative boutique rather than a larger full-service agency?

6. Why are marketers likely to use a media buying service to handle their media planning and buying versus the media department of an agency?

7. Discuss the various methods by which advertising agencies are compensated. What factors will determine the type of compensation arrangement a company uses with an agency?

8. Why are many companies moving away from the traditional commission system and using incentive-based compensation for their advertising agencies? Why might an ad agency be reluctant to accept an incentive-based compensation system?

9. Discuss the various reasons why marketers often choose to switch advertising agencies. Find an example of a company that has recently changed advertising agencies and analyze the reasons given for the change.

10. Discuss the reasons why a company might want to have all its integrated marketing communication activities performed versus having these activities performed by several different agencies who specialize in various areas of IMC, like public relations, direct marketing, sales promotion, and Internet marketing.

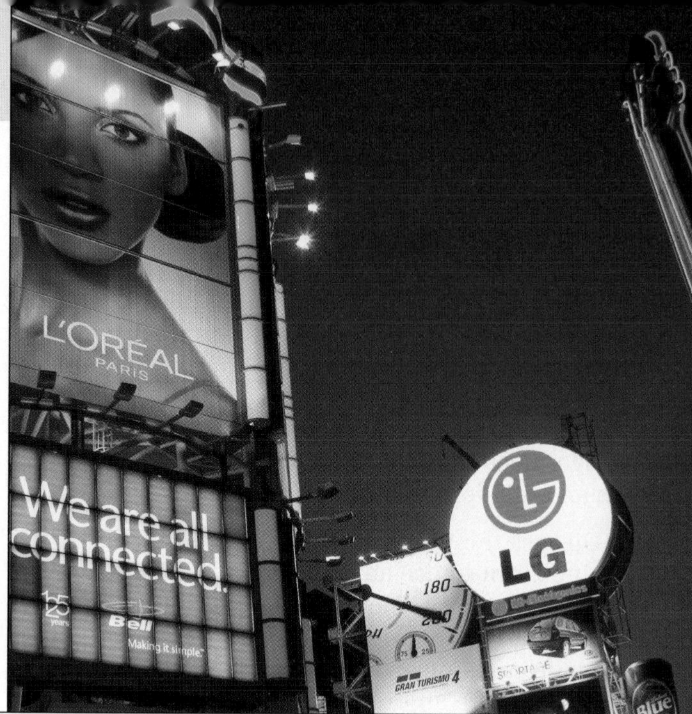

CHAPTER 3

CONSUMER BEHAVIOUR AND TARGET AUDIENCE DECISIONS

Chapter Objectives

- To understand the consumer decision-making process and how it varies for different types of purchases.
- To understand various internal psychological processes, their influence on consumer decision making, and implications for advertising and promotion.
- To understand the similarities and differences of target market and target audience.
- To understand the various options for making a target audience decision for marketing communication.

Marketers Seeking 50-Plus Consumers

Nintendo is famous for its video games. DaimlerChrysler features a wide selection of car brands. Tabi is known for its classic women's clothing. While seemingly unrelated, these brands have recently shared a similar strategy.

As these established companies expanded beyond their current customer base, each brand attempted new marketing communication programs containing a more emotional message aimed at the 50-plus demographic. The 50-plus crowd not only is a sizable market, but also is a very lucrative one; they control 55 percent of all discretionary spending in Canada due to their relatively high net worth. And while the brands all looked toward the fifty-plus market, additional segmentation based on an understanding of consumer behaviour revealed subtle differences in their approach.

For Nintendo, the saturated youth market proved to be a no-growth avenue. With industry sales hitting the billion-dollar level, penetration levelling off at 30 percent of Canadian homes, and research indicating that 75 percent of teens perceived lower interest in gaming, Nintendo looked to new users. However, convincing 50-plus consumers of the value of buying a device to play "brain-training" games like Sudoku on a hand-held device appeared to be a significant communication challenge because these consumers use iPods, cell phones, and PDAs.

DaimlerChrysler marketed its new vehicles—the Chrysler 300, Dodge Magnum, and Dodge Charger—to the older crowd as well, but diverged the communication plans according to different consumer behaviour considerations. For example, its Dodge ads conveyed the benefits of value and distinctive styling, while Chrysler expressed a luxurious styling. Moreover, despite both brands targeting the 50-plus market, alternate media appeared promising as Chrysler consumers leaned toward talk radio, theatre, and dramas, while Dodge consumers yearned for classic rock, movies, and sitcoms.

Tabi took the targeting in its own direction by breaking the older age demographic into several different "personality cohorts" reflecting many lifestyles. As this influenced product selection in the store, Tabi used this approach in its advertising and other promotional tools. Tabi sought to find new fashion models, and ran a contest in conjunction with *Canadian Living* with the intention of selecting three women who represented Tabi customers.

Sources: Lisa D'Innocenzo, "Boom Goes Your Brand," *Strategy Magazine*, May 2006, p. 33; Michelle Halpern, "Mind Games," *Marketing Magazine*, April 10, 2006; and Sylvain Desofosses, "Shifting Values," *Marketing*, September 11, 2006.

Questions

1. Why do marketers tend to overlook older consumers?
2. Explain some reasons why older consumers are good markets.

The companies described in the opening vignette reveal that the development of effective marketing communication programs begins with understanding why consumers behave as they do. This understanding helps marketers to know how to encourage new consumers to buy a product (e.g., Nintendo), what to emphasize in communications to specific audiences (e.g., DaimlerChrysler), and which types of IMC tools might be used (e.g., Tabi). These types of communication problems or opportunities, and others, can be addressed with a thorough understanding of consumer behaviour.

It is beyond the scope of this text to examine consumer behaviour in depth. However, promotional planners need a basic understanding of consumer decision making, factors that influence it, and how this knowledge can be used in developing promotional strategies and programs. This chapter addresses these topics and concludes with a summary of the options a promotional planner has for the initial decision, the target audience for an ad or promotional campaign.

Consumer Decision-Making Process

Consumer behaviour can be defined as the process and activities people engage in when searching for, selecting, purchasing, using, evaluating, and disposing of products and services so as to satisfy their needs and desires. The conceptual model in Figure 3–1 will be used as a framework for analyzing the consumer decision-making process. We will discuss what occurs at the various stages of this model and how advertising and promotion can be used to influence decision making. The five-stage decision process model of Figure 3–1 views the consumer as a problem solver and information processor who engages in mental processes to evaluate alternative brands and determine the degree to which they might satisfy needs or purchase motives. This model is a form of cognitive learning. Consumer learning has been defined as "the process by which individuals acquire the purchase and consumption knowledge and experience they apply to future related behaviour."[1] There are other perspectives regarding how consumers acquire the knowledge and experience they use in making purchase decisions. However, this model is the most widely accepted and managerially useful.

Need Recognition

Figure 3–1 shows that the first stage in the consumer decision-making process is **need recognition**, which occurs when the consumer perceives a need and becomes motivated to enter a decision-making process to resolve the felt need. Marketers are required to know the specific needs consumers are attempting to satisfy and how they translate into purchase criteria. This information allows markets to accurately portray the need in promotional messages or place messages in an appropriate location.

Need recognition is caused by a difference between the consumer's *ideal state* and *actual state*. A discrepancy exists between what the consumer wants the

FIGURE *3–1* A basic model of consumer decision making

A. Stages in the Consumer Decision-Making Process

Need recognition → Information search → Alternative evaluation → Purchase decision → Postpurchase evaluation

B. Relevant Internal Psychological Processes

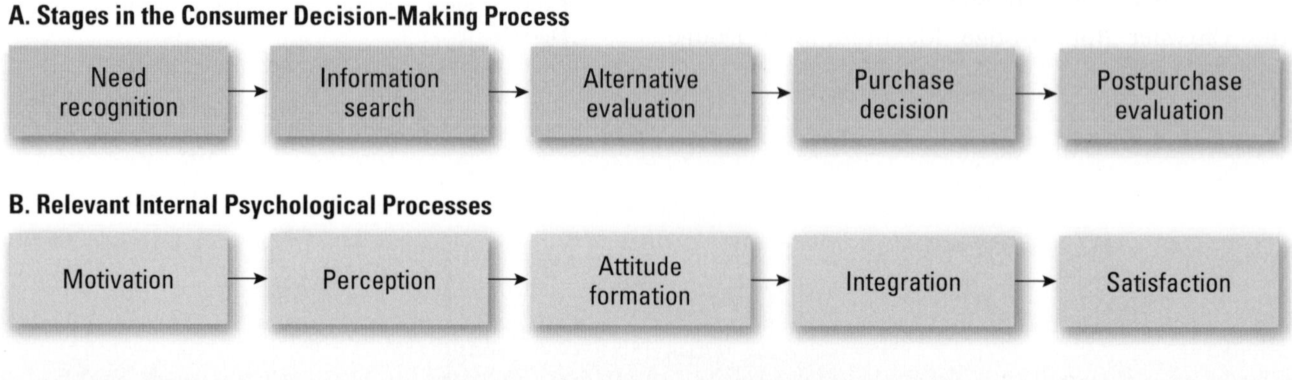

Motivation → Perception → Attitude formation → Integration → Satisfaction

situation to be like and what the situation is really like. A goal exists for the consumer, and this goal may be the attainment of a more positive situation from a neutral state. Or, the goal could be a shift from a negative situation, and the consumer wishes to be at a neutral state.

The causes of need recognition may be very simple or very complex and may result from changes in the consumer's current and/or desired state. These causes may be influenced by both internal and external factors.

Out of Stock Need recognition occurs when consumers use their existing supply of a product and must replenish their stock. The purchase decision is usually simple and routine and is often resolved by choosing a familiar brand or one to which the consumer feels loyal.

Dissatisfaction Need recognition is created by the consumer's dissatisfaction with the current state of affairs and/or the product or service being used. For example, a consumer may think her ski boots are no longer comfortable or stylish enough. Advertising may be used to help consumers recognize when they have a need to make a purchase. The Energizer ad shown in Exhibit 3–1 helps users realize that some batteries are superior.

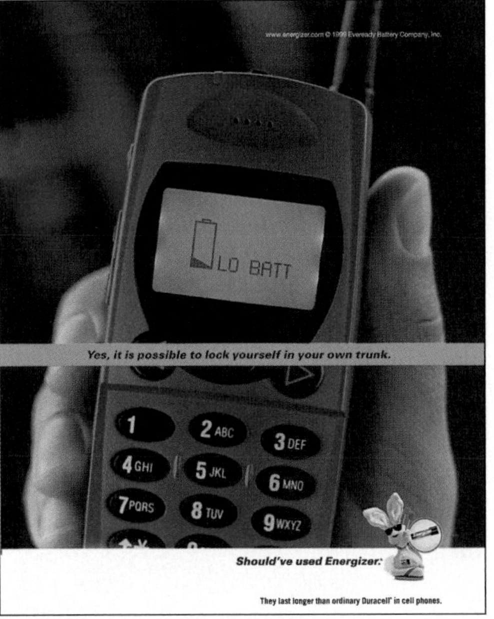

Exhibit 3–1 This Energizer ad shows how its batteries last longer

New Needs/Wants Changes in consumers' lives often result in new needs and wants. For example, changes in one's financial situation, employment status, or lifestyle may create new needs. As you will see, when you graduate from college or university and begin your professional career, your new job may necessitate a change in your wardrobe. (Good-bye blue jeans, hello business suits.)

Not all product purchases are based on needs. Some products or services sought by consumers are not essential but are nonetheless desired. A **want** has been defined as a felt need that is shaped by a person's knowledge, culture, and personality.[2] Many products sold to consumers satisfy their wants rather than their basic needs.

Related Products/Purchases Need recognition can also be stimulated by the purchase of a product. For example, the purchase of a new camera may lead to the recognition of a need for accessories, such as additional lenses or a carrying case. The purchase of a personal computer may prompt the need for software programs or upgrades.

Marketer-Induced Need Recognition Another source of need recognition is marketers' actions that encourage consumers not to be content with their current state or situation. Ads for personal hygiene products such as mouthwash, deodorant, and foot sprays may be designed to create insecurities that consumers can resolve through the use of these products. Marketers change fashions and clothing designs and create perceptions among consumers that their wardrobes are out of style. Marketers also take advantage of consumers' tendency toward *novelty-seeking behaviour*, which leads them to try different brands. Consumers often try new products or brands even when they are basically satisfied with their regular brand. Marketers encourage brand switching by using advertising and sales promotion techniques that encourage consumers to reconsider their current consumption habits. The BlackBerry ad in Exhibit 3–2 on page 64 demonstrates the need for communication when out of the office.

New Products Need recognition can also occur when innovative products are introduced. For example, the Rogers ad shown in Exhibit 3–3 on page 64 introduces a new camera phone that allows the user to do more than ever before. Marketers'

Exhibit 3–2 The importance of communication is featured in this BlackBerry ad

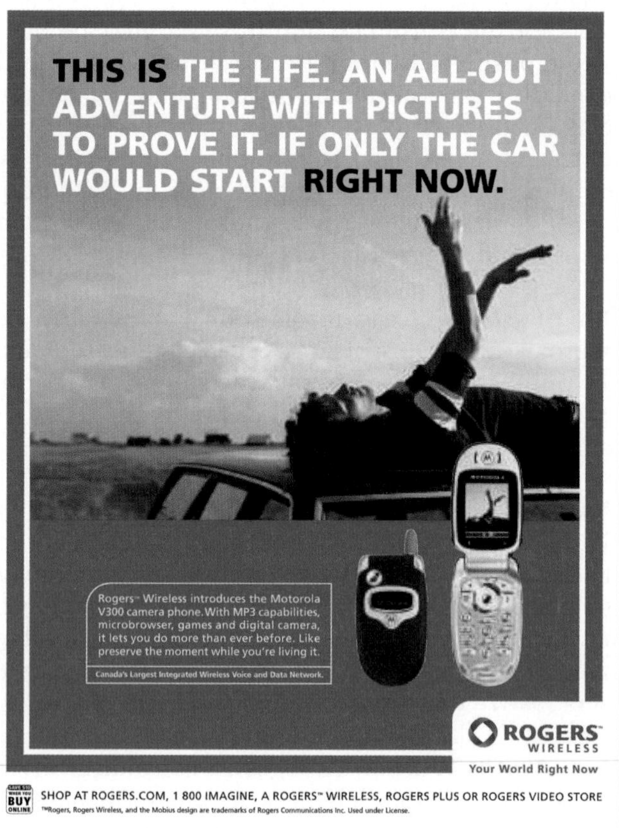

Exhibit 3–3 Rogers introduces a camera phone

attempts to create need recognition among consumers are not always successful. Consumers may not see a need for the product the marketer is selling. A main reason why many consumers were initially reluctant to purchase a personal computer was that they failed to see how it fulfilled their needs. One way PC manufacturers successfully activated need recognition was by stressing how a computer helps children improve their academic skills and do better in school.

Consumer Motivation

While need recognition is often a basic, simple process, the way a consumer perceives a purchase situation and becomes motivated to resolve it will influence the remainder of the decision process. For example, one consumer may perceive the need to purchase a new watch from a functional perspective and focus on reliable, low-priced alternatives. Another consumer may see the purchase of a watch as more of a fashion statement and focus on the design and image of various brands. To better understand the reasons underlying consumer purchases, marketers devote considerable attention to examining **motives**—that is, those factors that compel a consumer to take a particular action.

One of the most popular approaches to understanding consumer motivations is based on the classic theory of human motivation popularized many years ago by psychologist Abraham Maslow.[3] His **hierarchy of needs** theory postulates five basic levels of human needs, arranged in a hierarchy based on their importance. As shown in Figure 3–2, the five needs are (1) *physiological*—the basic level of primary needs for things required to sustain life, such as food, shelter, clothing, and sex; (2) *safety*—the need for security and safety from physical harm; (3) *social/love and belonging*—the desire to have satisfying relationships with others and feel a sense of love, affection, belonging, and acceptance; (4) *esteem*—the need to feel

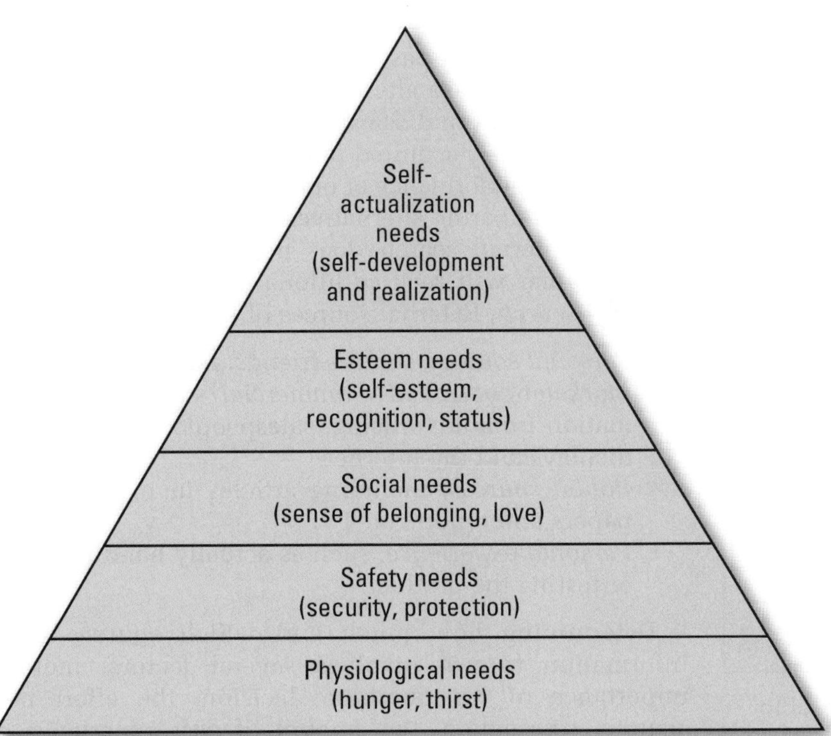

FIGURE 3–2

Maslow's hierarchy of needs

a sense of accomplishment and gain recognition, status, and respect from others; and (5) *self-actualization*—the need for self-fulfillment and a desire to realize one's own potential.

According to Maslow's theory, the lower-level physiological and safety needs must be satisfied before the higher-order needs become meaningful. Once these basic needs are satisfied, the individual moves on to attempting to satisfy higher-order needs such as self-esteem. In reality, it is unlikely that people move through the needs hierarchy in a stairstep manner. Lower-level needs are an ongoing source of motivation for consumer purchase behaviour. However, since basic physiological needs are met in most developed countries, marketers often sell products that fill basic physiological needs by appealing to consumers' higher-level needs. For example, in marketing its wipes, Huggies focuses on the love between parent and child (social needs) in addition to the gentleness of the product (Exhibit 3–4).

Exhibit 3–4 Huggies appeals to needs for love and belonging in this ad

While Maslow's needs hierarchy has flaws, it offers a framework for marketers to use in determining what needs they want their products and services to be shown satisfying. Advertising campaigns can then be designed to show how a brand can fulfill these needs. Marketers also recognize that different types of consumers have different need levels. For example, a young single person may be attempting to satisfy social or self-esteem needs in purchasing a car, while a family with children will focus more on safety needs. Chrysler used ads like the one in Exhibit 3–5 on page 66 to communicate that its cars meet the security needs of consumers with children.

Information Search

The second stage in the consumer decision-making process is *information search*. Once consumers perceive a need that can be satisfied by the purchase of a product, they begin to search for information needed to make a purchase decision. The initial

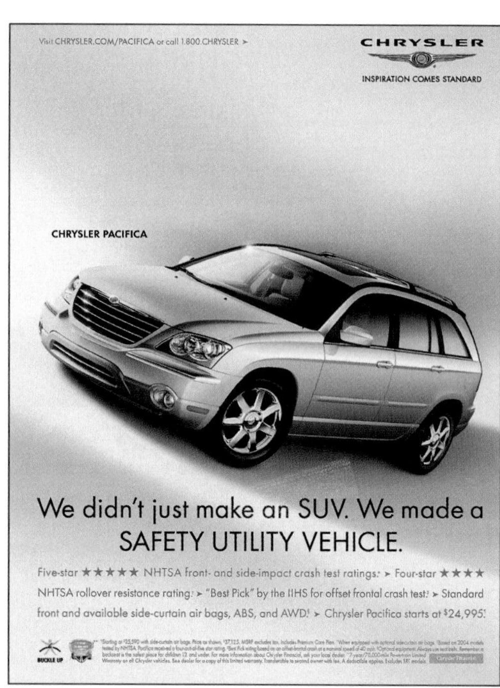

Visit CHRYSLER.COM/PACIFICA or call 1.800.CHRYSLER
CHRYSLER
INSPIRATION COMES STANDARD
CHRYSLER PACIFICA
We didn't just make an SUV. We made a SAFETY UTILITY VEHICLE.
Five-star ★★★★★ NHTSA front- and side-impact crash test ratings ➤ Four-star ★★★★ NHTSA rollover resistance rating ➤ "Best Pick" by the IIHS for offset frontal crash test ➤ Standard front and available side-curtain air bags, ABS, and AWD ➤ Chrysler Pacifica starts at $24,995
BUCKLE UP

Exhibit 3–5 Chrysler uses an appeal to security needs

search effort often consists of an attempt to scan information stored in memory to recall past experiences and/or knowledge regarding various purchase alternatives.[4] This information retrieval is referred to as **internal search**. For many routine, repetitive purchases, previously acquired information that is stored in memory (such as past performance or outcomes from using a brand) is sufficient for comparing alternatives and making a choice.

If the internal search does not yield enough information, the consumer will seek additional information by engaging in **external search**. External sources of information include:

- *Personal sources*, such as friends, relatives, or co-workers.
- *Marketer-controlled (commercial) sources*, such as information from advertising, salespeople, or point-of-purchase displays and the Internet.
- *Public sources*, including articles in magazines or newspapers and reports on TV.
- *Personal experience*, such as actually handling, examining, or testing the product.

Determining how much and which sources of external information to use involves several factors, including the importance of the purchase decision, the effort needed to acquire information, the amount of past experience relevant, the degree of perceived risk associated with the purchase, and the time available. For example, the selection of a movie to see on a Friday night might entail simply talking to a friend or checking the movie guide in the daily newspaper. A more complex purchase such as a new car might use a number of information sources—perhaps a review of *Road & Track, Motor Trend*, or *Consumer Reports*; discussion with family members and friends; and test-driving of cars. At this point in the purchase decision, the information-providing aspects of advertising are extremely important.

The Internet influences consumers' external search patterns significantly for many products. For the travel industry, 60 percent indicated in 2006 that the Internet is very or extremely important for making travel plans, compared to one-third in 2002. TNS Canadian Facts research also noted that website satisfaction reached 36 percent, compared with 27 percent previously. The type of information sought involved significant moves from simple things like researching the weather or the destination to more complex comparisons of travel costs and accommodations.[5]

Perception

Knowledge of how consumers acquire and use information from external sources is important to marketers in formulating communication strategies. Marketers are particularly interested in (1) how consumers sense external information, (2) how they attend to various sources of information, (3) how this information is interpreted and given meaning, and (4) how the information is retained. These four processes are all part of **perception**, the process by which an individual receives, attends to, interprets, and stores information to create a meaningful picture of the world.[6] Perception is an individual process; it depends on internal factors such as a person's beliefs, experiences, needs, moods, and expectations. The perceptual process is also influenced by the characteristics of a stimulus (such as its size, colour, and intensity) and the context in which it is seen or heard. Selectivity occurs throughout the four stages of the consumer's perceptual process. Perception may be viewed as a filtering process in which internal and external factors influence what is received and how it is processed and interpreted. The sheer number and complexity of the marketing stimuli a person is exposed to in any given day require that this filtering occur. **Selective perception** may occur within all four stages of the perceptual process, as shown in Figure 3–3.

FIGURE 3–3 The selective perception process

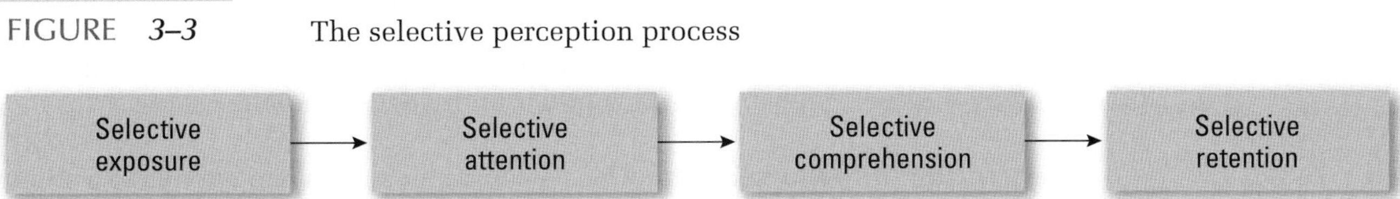

Sensation **Sensation** is the immediate, direct response of the senses (taste, smell, sight, touch, and hearing) to a stimulus such as an ad, package, brand name, or point-of-purchase display. Perception uses these senses to create a representation of the stimulus. Marketers recognize that it is important to understand consumers' physiological reactions to marketing stimuli. For example, the visual elements of an ad or package design must be designed so that consumers sense their existence. This is one reason why many TV ads start with a particular sound effect or visual movement.

Marketers sometimes try to increase the level of sensory input so that their advertising messages will get noticed. For example, marketers of colognes and perfumes often use strong visuals as well as scent strips to appeal to multiple senses and attract the attention of magazine readers. Some advertisers have even inserted microcomputer chips into their print ads to play a song or deliver a message. **Selective exposure** occurs as consumers choose whether or not to make themselves available to information. For example, a viewer of a television show may change channels or leave the room during commercial breaks.

Selecting Information Sensory inputs are important but are only one part of the perceptual process. Other determinants of whether marketing stimuli will be attended to and how they will be interpreted include internal psychological factors such as the consumer's personality, needs, motives, expectations, and experiences. These psychological inputs explain why people focus attention on some things and ignore others. Two people may perceive the same stimuli in very different ways because they select and attend to messages differently. An individual's perceptual processes usually focus on elements of the environment that are relevant to his or her needs and tune out irrelevant stimuli. Think about how much more attentive you are to advertising for personal computers, tires, or stereos when you are in the market for one of these products.

Selective attention occurs when the consumer chooses to focus attention on certain stimuli while excluding others. One study of selective attention estimates the typical consumer is exposed to nearly 1,500 ads per day yet perceives only 76 of these messages.[7] Other estimates range as high as 3,000 exposures per day. This means advertisers must make considerable effort to get their messages noticed. Advertisers often use the creative aspects of their ads to gain consumers' attention. For example, some advertisers set their ads off from others by showing their products against a vibrant colour background (Exhibit 3–6). Marketers also place ads in certain times or locations so that consumers will notice them more easily. For example, a

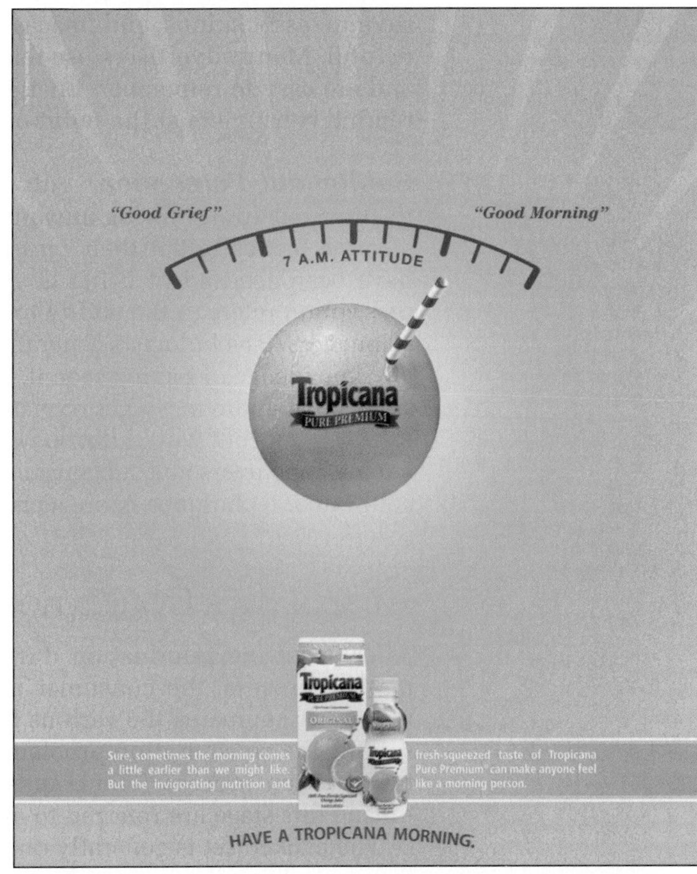

Exhibit 3–6 Tropicana uses colour to focus attention on orange juice

consumer may pay more attention to a commercial that is heard alone at home than to one heard in the presence of friends, at work, or anywhere distractions may be present. If advertisers can isolate a particular time when the listener is likely to be attentive, they will probably earn his or her undivided attention.

Interpreting the Information Once a consumer selects and attends to a stimulus, the perceptual process focuses on organizing, categorizing, and interpreting the incoming information. This stage of the perceptual process is very individualized and is influenced by internal psychological factors. The interpretation and meaning an individual assigns to an incoming stimulus also depend in part on the nature of the stimulus. For example, many ads are objective, and their message is clear and straightforward. Other ads are more ambiguous, and their meaning is strongly influenced by the consumer's individual interpretation.

Even if the consumer does notice the advertiser's message, there is no guarantee it will be interpreted in the intended manner. Consumers may engage in **selective comprehension**, interpreting information on the basis of their own attitudes, beliefs, motives, and experiences. They often interpret information in a manner that supports their own position. For example, an ad that disparages a consumer's favourite brand may be seen as biased or untruthful, and its claims may not be accepted.

Retaining the Information The final stage of the perceptual process involves the storage of the information in short-term or long-term memory. Consumers may make mental notes or focus on some aspect of an advertising message to ensure that they will not forget, thus permitting easy retrieval during the information search stage. **Selective retention** means consumers do not remember all the information they see, hear, or read even after attending to and comprehending it. Advertisers attempt to make sure information will be retained in the consumer's memory so that it will be available when it is time to make a purchase. **Mnemonics** such as symbols, rhymes, associations, and images that assist in the learning and memory process are helpful. Many advertisers use telephone numbers that spell out the company name and are easy to remember. Energizer put pictures of its pink bunny on packages to remind consumers at the point of purchase of its creative advertising.

Subliminal Perception Advertisers know consumers use selective perception to filter out irrelevant or unwanted advertising messages, so they employ various creative tactics to get their messages noticed. One controversial tactic advertisers have been accused of using is appealing to consumers' subconscious. **Subliminal perception** refers to the ability to perceive a stimulus that is below the level of consciousness. Psychologists generally agree it is possible to perceive something without any knowledge of having seen it. The possibility of using hidden persuaders such as subliminal audio messages or visual cues to influence consumers might be intriguing to advertisers but would not be welcomed by consumers. The idea of marketers influencing consumers at a subconscious level has strong ethical implications. The use of subliminal techniques is *not* a creative tactic we would recommend to advertisers.

ALTERNATIVE EVALUATION

After acquiring information during the information search stage of the decision-making process, the consumer moves to alternative evaluation. In this stage, the consumer compares the various brands he or she has identified as being capable of solving the consumption problem and satisfying the needs or motives that initiated the decision process. The brands identified as purchase options to be considered during this stage are referred to as the consumer's *evoked set*.

The evoked set is generally only a subset of all the brands of which the consumer is aware. The consumer reduces the number of brands to be reviewed during the alternative evaluation stage to a manageable level. The exact size of the evoked set varies from one consumer to another and depends on such factors as the importance of the purchase and the amount of time and energy the consumer wants to spend comparing alternatives.

The goal of most advertising and promotional strategies is to increase the likelihood that a brand will be included in the consumer's evoked set and considered during alternative evaluation. Marketers use advertising to create *top-of-mind awareness* among consumers so that their brands are part of the evoked set of their target audiences. Popular brands with large advertising budgets use *reminder advertising* to maintain high awareness levels and increase the likelihood they will be considered by consumers in the market for the product. Marketers of new brands or those with a low market share need to gain awareness among consumers and break into their evoked sets.

Once consumers have identified an evoked set and have a list of alternatives, they must evaluate the various brands. This involves comparing the choice alternatives on specific criteria important to the consumer. **Evaluative criteria** are the attributes of a product that are used to compare different alternatives. Evaluative criteria can be objective or subjective. For example, in buying an automobile, consumers use objective attributes such as price, warranty, and fuel economy as well as subjective attributes such as image or styling.

Many marketers view their products as *bundles of attributes*, but consumers also tend to think about products or services in terms of their *consequences* or bundles of benefits. J. Paul Peter and Jerry Olson define consequences as specific events or outcomes that consumers experience when they purchase and/or consume a product.[8] Functional benefits are concrete outcomes of product usage that are tangible and directly related to product performance. The taste of a soft drink or a potato chip, the acceleration of a car, and the clarity of a fax transmission are examples of functional consequences. Experiential benefits are related to how a product makes the consumer feel while consuming the product. These emotions can be feelings of happiness or joy, for example, as seen by some car ads illustrating consumers enjoying the drive in a particular brand. Psychological benefits can refer to the status a consumer encounters when associated with a brand.

Marketers should distinguish between product attributes and benefits because the importance and meaning consumers assign to an attribute are usually determined by its consequences for them. Moreover, advertisers must be sure consumers understand the link between a particular attribute and a benefit. For example, the Ping ad in Exhibit 3–7 focuses on the benefit of using the new Ping golf club. Product attributes and the benefits consumers think they will experience from a particular brand are very important, for they are often the basis on which consumers form attitudes and decide among various choice alternatives.

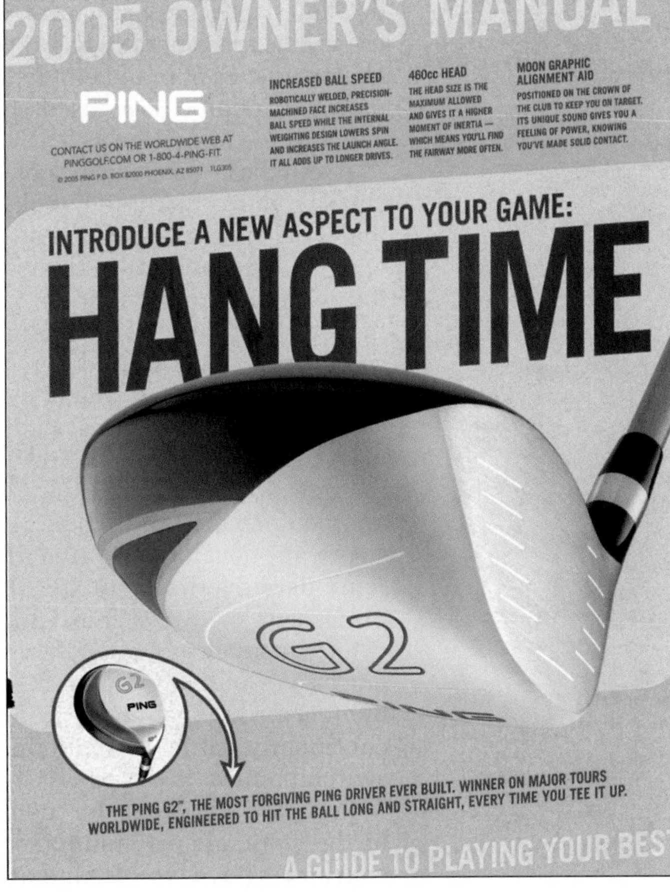

Exhibit 3–7 This ad emphasizes the positive benefits of using a Ping G2 driver

Attitudes

Attitudes are one of the most heavily studied concepts in consumer behaviour. According to Gordon Allport's classic definition, "attitudes are learned predispositions to respond to an object."[9] More recent perspectives view attitudes as a summary construct that represents an individual's overall feelings toward or evaluation of an object.[10] Consumers hold attitudes toward a variety of objects that are important to marketers, including individuals (celebrity endorsers such as Tiger Woods or Michael Jordan), brands (Cheerios), companies (Microsoft), product categories (beef, pork, tuna), retail stores (The Bay, Sears), or even advertisements (the Energizer bunny ads).

Attitudes are important to marketers because they theoretically summarize a consumer's evaluation of an object (or brand or company) and represent positive or negative feelings and behavioural tendencies. Marketers' keen interest in attitudes is based on the assumption that they are related to consumers' purchase behaviour. Considerable evidence supports the basic assumption of a relationship between attitudes and behaviour.[11] The attitude–behaviour link does not always hold; many other factors can affect behaviour.[12] But attitudes are very important to marketers. Advertising and promotion are used to create favourable attitudes toward new products/services or brands, reinforce existing favourable attitudes, and/or change negative attitudes.

Purchase Decision

At some point in the buying process, the consumer must stop searching for and evaluating information about alternative brands in the evoked set and make a *purchase decision.* As an outcome of the alternative evaluation stage, the consumer may develop a **purchase intention** or predisposition to buy a certain brand. Purchase intentions are generally based on a matching of purchase motives with attributes or characteristics of brands under consideration. Their formation involves many of the personal subprocesses discussed in this chapter, including motivation, perception, and attitude formation.

A purchase decision is not the same as an actual purchase. Once a consumer chooses which brand to buy, he or she must still implement the decision and make the actual purchase. Additional decisions may be needed, such as when to buy, where to buy, and how much money to spend. Often, there is a time delay between the formation of a purchase intention or decision and the actual purchase, particularly for highly involved and complex purchases such as automobiles, personal computers, and consumer durables.

For nondurable products, which include many low-involvement items such as consumer package goods, the time between the decision and the actual purchase may be short. Before leaving home, the consumer may make a shopping list that includes specific brand names because the consumer has developed **brand loyalty**—a preference for a particular brand that results in its repeated purchase. Marketers strive to develop and maintain brand loyalty among consumers. They use reminder advertising to keep their brand names in front of consumers, maintain prominent shelf positions and displays in stores, and run periodic promotions to deter consumers from switching brands. Maintaining consumers' brand loyalty is not easy. Competitors use many techniques to encourage consumers to try their brands, among them new product introductions and free samples. Marketers must continually battle to maintain their loyal consumers while replacing those who switch brands.

Purchase decisions for nondurable, convenience items sometimes take place in the store, almost simultaneous with the purchase. Marketers must ensure that consumers have top-of-mind awareness of their brands so that they are quickly recognized and considered. These types of decisions are influenced at the actual point of purchase. Packaging, shelf displays, point-of-purchase materials, and promotional tools such as on-package coupons or premium offers can influence decisions made through constructive processes at the time of purchase.

Integration Processes

A key part of the purchase decision stage is the way consumers combine information about the characteristics of brands. **Integration processes** are the way product knowledge, meanings, and beliefs are combined to evaluate two or more alternatives.[13] Analysis of the integration process focuses on the different types of *decision rules* or strategies consumers use to decide among purchase alternatives.

Consumers often make purchase selections by using formal integration strategies or decision rules that require examination and comparison of alternatives on specific attributes. This process involves a very deliberate evaluation of the alternatives, attribute by attribute. When consumers apply such formal decision rules, marketers need to know which attributes are being considered so as to provide the information the consumers require.

Sometimes consumers make their purchase decisions using more simplified decision rules known as **heuristics**. Peter and Olson note that heuristics are easy to use and are highly adaptive to specific environmental situations (such as a retail store).[14] For familiar products that are purchased frequently, consumers may use price-based heuristics (buy the least expensive brand) or promotion-based heuristics (choose the brand for which I can get a price reduction through a coupon, rebate, or special deal).

One type of heuristic is the **affect referral decision rule**,[15] in which consumers make a selection on the basis of an overall impression or summary evaluation of the various alternatives under consideration. This decision rule suggests that consumers have affective impressions of brands stored in memory that can be accessed at the time of purchase. How many times have you gone into a store and made purchases based on your overall impressions of the brands rather than going through detailed comparisons of the alternatives' specific attributes?

Marketers selling familiar and popular brands may appeal to an affect referral rule by stressing overall affective feelings or impressions about their products. Market leaders, whose products enjoy strong overall brand images, often use ads that promote the brand as the best overall (Exhibit 3–8).

Exhibit 3–8 Market leaders such as Labatt can appeal to consumer affect

Postpurchase Evaluation

The consumer decision process does not end with the purchase. After consumption, the consumer assesses the level of performance of the product or service. The postpurchase evaluation process is important because the feedback acquired from actual use of a product will influence the likelihood of future purchases. Positive performance means the brand is retained in the evoked set and increases the likelihood it will be purchased again. Unfavourable outcomes may lead the consumer to form negative attitudes toward the brand, lessening the likelihood it will be purchased again or even eliminating it from the consumer's evoked set.

Consumers engage in a number of activities during the postpurchase evaluation process. They may seek out reassurance and opinions from others to confirm the wisdom of their purchase decision, lower their attitudes or opinions of the unchosen alternative, deny or distort any information that does not support the choice they made, or look for information that does support their choice. An important source of supportive information is advertising; consumers tend to be more attentive to advertising for the brand they have chosen.[16] Thus, it may be important for companies to advertise to reinforce consumer decisions to purchase their brands.

Satisfaction

The most significant psychological concept during the postpurchase evaluation process is satisfaction. A leading expert in satisfaction research has recently defined

satisfaction as a judgment that consumers make with respect to the pleasurable level of consumption-related fulfillment.[17] The notion of fulfillment implies that a consumer's goal has been achieved (i.e., needs met), and that the fulfillment is "judged with reference to a standard." Thus, consumers make a comparison between the consumption outcome and some other referent.

Consumers can make many comparisons. One is to compare the level of product performance to the expectations of the product that consumers had prior to purchase. Satisfaction can occur when the consumer's expectations are either met or exceeded, whereas dissatisfaction results when performance is below expectations. Consumers can also compare the product performance to some absolute standard of quality to perceive satisfaction or dissatisfaction.

Another aspect of satisfaction is **cognitive dissonance**, a feeling of psychological tension or postpurchase doubt that a consumer experiences after making a difficult purchase choice. Dissonance is more likely to occur in important decisions where the consumer must choose among close alternatives (especially if the unchosen alternative has unique or desirable features that the selected alternative does not have).

Marketers must recognize the importance of the postpurchase evaluation stage. Dissatisfied consumers not only are unlikely to repurchase the marketer's product but also may spread negative word-of-mouth information that deters others from purchasing the product or service. The best guarantee of favourable postpurchase evaluations is to provide consumers with a quality product or service that always meets their expectations. Marketers must be sure their advertising and other forms of promotion do not create unreasonable expectations their products cannot meet.

Marketers have come to realize that postpurchase communication is also important. Some companies send follow-up letters and brochures to reassure buyers and reinforce the wisdom of their decision. Many companies have set up toll-free numbers for consumers to call if they need information or have a question or complaint regarding a product. Marketers also offer liberalized return and refund policies and extended warranties and guarantees to ensure customer satisfaction. Some have used customers' postpurchase dissatisfaction as an opportunity for gaining new business.

Variations in Consumer Decision Making

We have reviewed the consumer decision-making process with respect to individual purchases. However, variations in this process arise depending upon the type of purchase and whether the individual is making the decision with other people. We now discuss these two variations in the consumer decision-making process.

Types of Decision Making

The preceding pages describe a general model of consumer decision making. But consumers do not always engage in all five steps of the purchase decision process or proceed in the sequence presented. They may minimize or even skip one or more stages if they have previous experience in purchasing the product or service or if the decision is of low personal, social, or economic significance. To develop effective promotional strategies and programs, marketers need some understanding of the problem-solving processes their target consumers use to make purchase decisions.[18]

Many of the purchase decisions we make as consumers are based on a habit known as **routine problem solving** or routine response behaviour. For many low-priced, frequently purchased products, the decision process consists of little more than recognizing the need, engaging in a quick internal search, and making the purchase. The consumer spends little or no effort engaging in external search or alternative evaluation.

Marketers of products characterized by a routine response purchase process need to get and/or keep their brands in the consumer's evoked set and avoid anything that may result in their removal from consideration. Established brands that have strong market share position are likely to be in the evoked set of most consumers. Marketers of these brands want consumers to follow a routine choice process and continue to purchase their products. This means maintaining high levels of brand awareness through reminder advertising, periodic promotions, and prominent shelf positions in retail stores.

Marketers of new brands or those with a low market share face a different challenge. They must find ways to disrupt consumers' routine choice process and get them to consider different alternatives. High levels of advertising along with sales promotion efforts in the form of free samples, special price offers, high-value coupons, and the like may encourage consumers to reconsider their habit or routine choice.

A more complicated decision-making process may occur when consumers have limited experience in purchasing a particular product or service and little or no knowledge of the brands available and/or the criteria to use in making a purchase decision. They may have to learn what attributes or criteria should be used in making a purchase decision and how the various alternatives perform on these dimensions. For products or services characterized by **limited problem solving** or **extended problem solving** marketers should make information available that will help consumers decide. Advertising that provides consumers with detailed information about a brand and how it can satisfy their purchase motives and goals is important. Marketers may also want to give consumers information at the point of purchase, through either displays or brochures. Distribution channels should have knowledgeable salespeople available to explain the features and benefits of the company's product or service and why it is superior to competing products.

The Fidelity Investments ad in Exhibit 3–9 is a good example of how advertising can appeal to consumers who may be engaging in extended problem solving when considering retirement investing. Notice how the ad communicates with consumers who know little about how to purchase this product. The ad also makes more detailed information available by offering a toll-free number and a website.

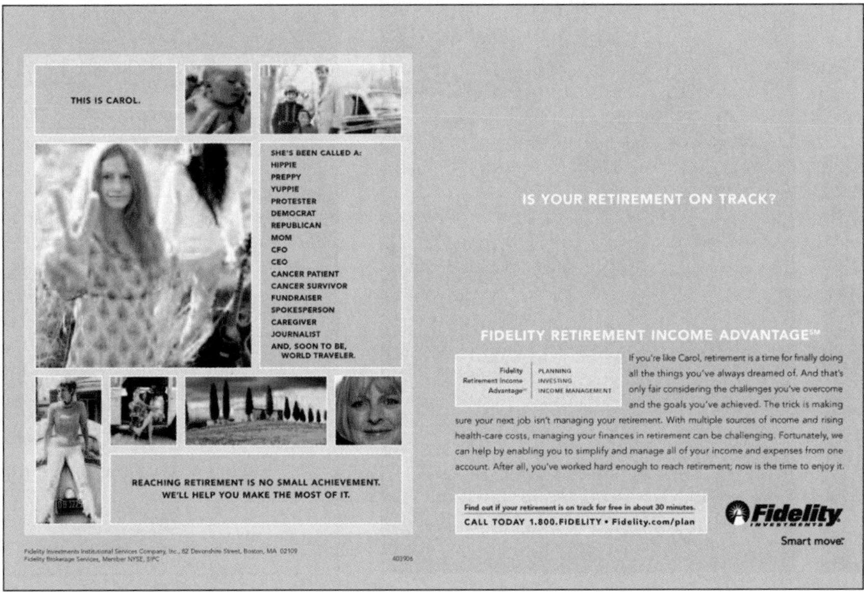

Exhibit 3–9 This ad for Fidelity Investments shows how marketers can appeal to consumers engaging in extended problem solving

Group Decision Making

Think about the last time you attended a party. As you dressed for the party, you probably asked yourself (or someone else) what others would be wearing. Your selection of attire may have been influenced by those likely to be present. This simple example reflects one form of impact that groups may exert on your behaviour.

A group has been defined as "two or more individuals who share a set of norms, values, or beliefs and have certain implicitly or explicitly defined relationships to one another such that their behavior is interdependent."[19] Groups are one of the primary factors influencing learning and socialization, and group situations constitute many of our purchase decisions.

A **reference group** is "a group whose presumed perspectives or values are being used by an individual as the basis for his or her judgments, opinions, and actions." Consumers use reference groups as a guide to specific behaviours, even when the groups are not present.[20] In the party example, your peers—although not present—provided a standard of dress that you referred to in your clothing selection. Likewise, your college classmates, family, and co-workers, or even a group to which you aspire, may serve as referents, and your consumption patterns will typically conform to the expectations of the groups that are most important to you. Global Perspective 3–1 highlights the influence of group norms.

Marketers use reference group influences in developing advertisements and promotional strategies. The ads in Exhibits 3–10 and 3–11 are examples of *aspirational* reference groups (to which we might like to belong) and *disassociative* groups (to which we do not wish to belong), respectively.

In some instances, the group may be involved more directly than just as a referent. Family members may serve as referents to each other, or they may actually be involved in the purchase decision process—acting as an individual buying unit. As shown in Figure 3–4 on page 76, family members may assume a variety of roles in the decision-making process.[21] As the example indicates, there can be group interaction at every stage of the consumer decision-making process since various members take on a role.

Exhibit 3–10 These ads are examples of aspirational reference groups

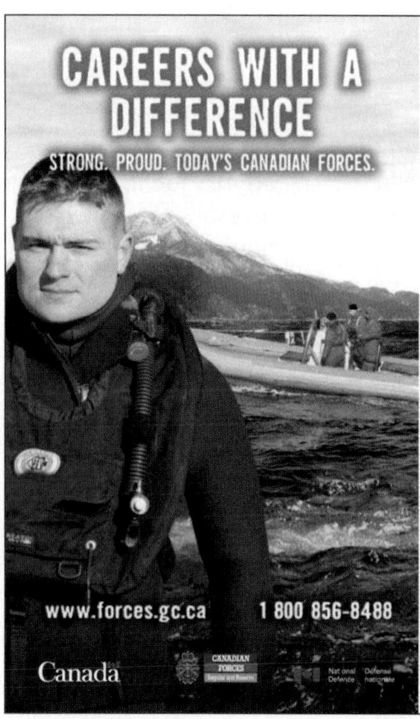

Exhibit 3–11 This ad represents a disassociative reference group

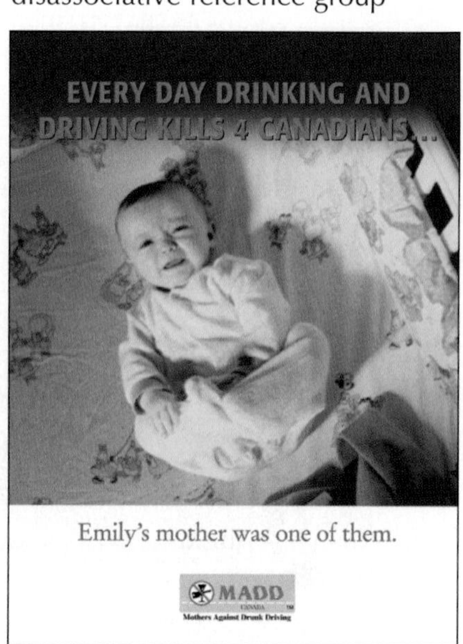

GLOBAL PERSPECTIVE 3–1

Axe Slices through the Deodorant Market

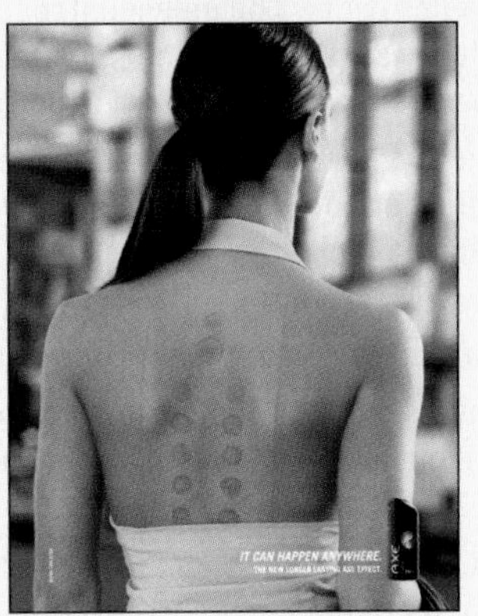

In the highly lucrative and competitive deodorant market, companies are always looking for the edge that will give them an advantage over competitors. Unilever may just have found it, and they call it *ethnography*. The European-based company hired a U.S.-based research organization specializing in cultural anthropology to observe young males between the ages of 18 and 22 and their friends in their everyday environs to learn more about their likes, dislikes, activities, and decision-making behaviours. The 28 young men—from Los Angeles and Pittsburgh—were videotaped, and then the tapes were analyzed to gain insights through the participants' own descriptions of their activities while being observed in everyday facets of their lives.

Once the tapes were finished, executives from Unilever, their advertising and public relations agencies, and their event specialist agency met to take a "deep dive" into the young men's psyches. More specifically, the executives wanted to understand the participant's mating life, that is, what he is about, why he does what he does, what excites him, and what he fears. Not surprisingly, much of the young men's lives focused on sex. Their interest was not just dating: They preferred to go to parties with other male friends and "hook up." Relationships were avoided whenever possible, as were the words *boyfriends* and *girlfriends*. They just wanted to have sex. The anthropologists even typed the males into groups based upon their characteristics into classifications such as "pimp daddy," "player," "sweetheart," and "shy guy."

So what does this have to do with marketing deodorant? A lot! Based upon these findings the basis for the integrated marketing campaign theme was developed—"Wear this deodorant and you'll pick up chicks!" Simply put, using AXE products (deodorant, body spray, shower gel, and more) will help you in your mating attempts. (In Ireland and Australia, the product is called Lynx, though the same theme is used.) The television commercials focus on spontaneous sexual encounters and the need to be ready at any time, while protected (and enhanced) by AXE. The AXE man is always ready. The commercials have won the Gold Lion—the top award given at the Cannes Film Festival for international advertising quality—two of the past four years, and 10 times overall. The advertising campaign theme is also maintained through other integrated strategies.

In Colombia, female AXE patrols visit bars and nightclubs, frisking guys and spraying them with body spray. The "AXE angels" (also female) pass out samples at various events including the MTV Video Awards. The viral marketing campaign launched a fake website including videos, fake recordings of phone calls, and pictures. Axe produced a one-hour TV program, *The AXE House Party: Hundreds of Girls, Rock Stars, and a Beach House*. Invitations to the party were passed out by street teams, through public relations activities, and via an ad campaign that directed consumers to the website for a chance to win an invitation. The promotion won a Promotional Marketing Association Reggie Award for excellence.

Print and online promotions were also used to promote the seduction skills used in an online digital fantasy game called Mojo Master. The game, which cost over a million dollars to produce, challenges young men armed with AXE deodorant body spray, shower gel, deodorant stick, and invisible solid to pick up girls. Each time one of the products is used it enhances the male's "mojo," and helps him enhance his "attraction meter." If one is good enough, he qualifies to use the AXE fragrance. What are the girls in the game like? "Absolutely stunning," says the director of the company that developed the game.

But can ethnography lead to successful product marketing? Consider the following: *The AXE House Party* generated attention from MTV, VH-1, *Rolling Stone,* and *Jimmy Kimmel Live*. In the four weeks following the promotion, brand awareness among 11–24-year-olds increased 22 percent, and market share jumped from 3 percent to 3.7 percent. In regard to the bottom line, the campaign's results are equally impressive: (1) First launched in 1983, the products are now marketed in more than 60 countries; (2) the AXE brand is number one in several European and Latin American markets as well as in Asia and the United States, where it has been marketed only since 2003; (3) sales are almost seven times those of the competitive Old Spice brand introduced at the same time; and (4) sales of the body spray in the United States in 2004 were over $60 million, making it the category leader. In this case, ethnography and IMC seem to have produced a winning combination.

Sources: Ian Herbert, "Spray It, Don't Say It," *U.S. News & World Report,* May 30, 2005, p. 58; Kris Oser, "AXE's Latest Sex Ad Is a Digital Game," www.Adage.com, May 20, 2005, pp. 1–3; Christine Bittar, "Bringing Down the House: AXE Shakes Its Groove Thang," *Brandweek,* March 22, 2004, p. R4; Jack Neff, "Analyzing AXE Man," *Advertising Age,* June 21, 2004, pp. 4–5.

Questions:

1. What is your opinion regarding the promotional activities used by Axe?
2. Did the research arrive at a reasonable conclusion about young men?

FIGURE 3–4

Roles in the family decision-making process

The initiator. The person responsible for initiating the purchase decision process; for example, the mother who determines she needs a new car.

The information provider. The individual responsible for gathering information to be used in making the decision; for example, the teenage car buff who knows where to find product information in specific magazines or collects it from dealers.

The influencer. The person who exerts influence as to what criteria will be used in the selection process. All members of the family may be involved. The mother may have her criteria, whereas others may each have their own input.

The decision maker(s). That person(s) who actually makes the decision. In our example, it may be the mother alone or in combination with another family member.

The purchasing agent. That individual who performs the physical act of making the purchase. In the case of a car, a husband and wife may decide to choose it together and sign the purchase agreement.

The consumer. The actual user of the product. In the case of a family car, all family members are consumers. For a private car, only the mother might be the consumer.

Each role has implications for marketers. First, the advertiser must determine who is responsible for the various roles in the decision-making process so that messages can be targeted at that person (or those people). These roles will also dictate media strategies, since the appropriate magazines, newspapers, or TV or radio stations must be used. Second, understanding the decision-making process and the use of information by individual family members is critical to the design of messages and choice of promotional program elements. In general, to create an effective promotional program, a marketer must have an overall understanding of how the decision process works and the role that each group member plays.

Target Audience Decision

We reviewed the consumer decision-making process since marketers need to thoroughly understand the behaviour they are trying to influence through their promotional plans. Marketers also try to understand consumers as much as possible since an IMC plan, IMC program (e.g., advertising campaign), or ad is directed to a particular target audience, which is usually a primary decision made prior to any other communication decision.

Recall that the information and decisions of a marketing plan are key inputs for all promotional plan decisions. Futhermore, the direction of the target audience decision is derived from the segmentation and target market decisions of the marketing plan. In this section, we review the target market process to understand the context of promotional planning. Next, we summarize approaches for market segmentation and identify how it is used for target market selection. Finally, we explore how these marketing decisions provide direction for target audience options.

Target Market Process

The process of developing and implementing the target market decision is summarized in Figure 3–5. This model consists of four major components: the organization's situation analysis, the target market process, the marketing program development (which includes the promotional mix), and the target market. As the model shows, the marketing process begins with the development of a marketing strategy and analysis in which

FIGURE 3–5 Marketing and promotions process model

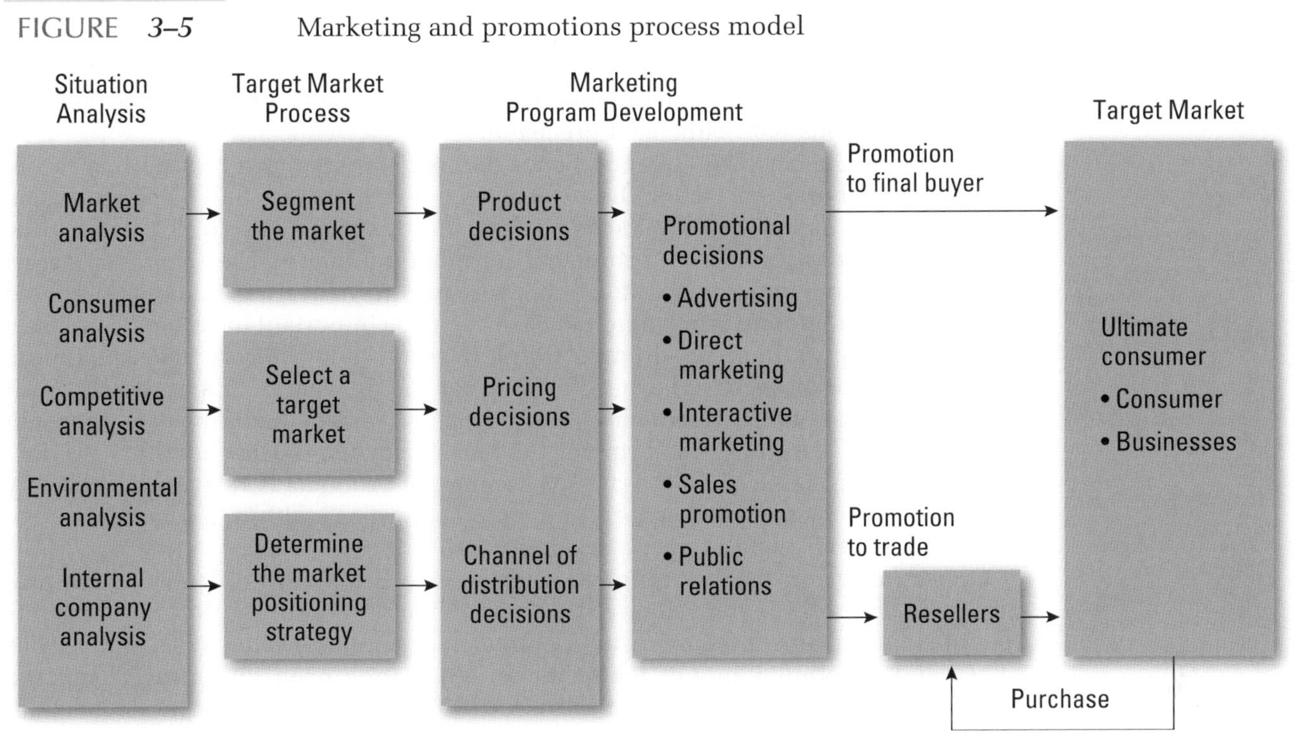

the company decides the product areas and particular markets where it wants to compete. The company must then coordinate the various elements of the marketing mix into a cohesive marketing program that will reach the target market effectively. Note that a firm's promotion program is directed not only to the final buyer but also to the channel or "trade" members that distribute its products to the ultimate consumer. These channel members must be convinced there is a demand for the company's products so they will carry them and will aggressively merchandise and promote them to consumers. Promotions play an important role in the marketing program for building and maintaining demand not only among final consumers but among the trade as well.

The target market is the focus of the firm's marketing effort, and specific sales, market share, and profitability objectives are set according to where the company wants to be and what it hopes to accomplish in this market. The method by which marketers do this (presented in Figure 3–6) is referred to as the **target market process** and involves three basic steps: segment the market, select a target market, and determine the market positioning strategy of one's product or service. The selection of the target market (or markets) in which the firm will compete is an important part of its marketing strategy and has direct implications for its advertising and promotional efforts. Specific communication objectives are derived and the promotional mix strategies are developed to achieve these objectives. Thus, different objectives may be established, different budgets may be used, and the promotional mix strategies may vary, depending on the market selected.

As we introduced this section, we used the terms target market and target audience. We concur with a recent perspective that suggests promotional planners should make a careful distinction between these concepts since an advertising plan or IMC plan is one part of the overall marketing plan.[22] The **target market** is the

FIGURE 3–6

The target market process

group of consumers toward which an overall marketing program is directed. The **target audience** is a group of consumers toward which the advertising campaign, for example, is directed. Conceptually, these targets are interdependent but their distinction allows promotional planners the ability to make more effective communication decisions with enhanced precision.

The difference between target audience and target market can be seen in a recent campaign for Imodium Quick Dissolve tablets, a diarrhea remedy. The campaign tried to reach Canadian vacationers to foreign countries who do not want to be inconvenienced with this unfortunate gastronomic ailment. The secondary target audience was frequent business travellers who may have overlooked being prepared for their discomfort and who could not afford to miss important meetings. Combined together, it appears that Imodium is trying to reach new category users. Imodium used humour to cleverly point out the need for the product with a message, "Visit the country, not just its restrooms," and visuals of various facilities used throughout the world. Naturally, the product has other consumers, and how this product is positioned in the marketplace versus competing products is relevant, but clearly Imodium has selected a certain part of the market to speak within this campaign that is a sub-set of the overall target market.[23]

Opportunities in the environment often lead to firms developing selective promotional programs beyond their normal target market. For example, tea represents the fourth most consumed drink after coffee, milk, and tap water. With many types of tea and different kinds of tea drinkers, tea brands need to approach specific audiences with their communication efforts. The health benefits perceived with tea have recently attracted many young Canadian consumers toward specialty teas. In particular, sales for green, red, and white teas rose substantially in 2006; however, herbal and black tea dropped slightly. Although the main tea consumer is women over 40, according to Twinings tea, the well-established brand developed its latest campaign toward newer consumers (i.e., younger) with a strong emphasis to teach the less experienced more about tea and the various types. Its communication consisted of door-hangers and samples to specific locations and in displays for select retailers, as seen in the next two examples.

Market Segmentation

To identify a target market, the marketer identifies the specific needs of groups of people (or segments), selects one or more of these segments as a target, and develops marketing programs directed to each. This approach has found increased applicability in marketing for a number of reasons, including changes in the market (consumers are becoming much more diverse in their needs, attitudes, and lifestyles); increased use of segmentation by competitors; and the fact that more managers are trained in segmentation and realize the advantages associated with this strategy. Perhaps the best explanation, however, comes back to the basic premise that you must understand as much as possible about consumers to design marketing programs that meet their needs most effectively. Furthermore, as marketers establish a common ground with consumers, the more effective they will be in addressing these requirements in their communications programs and informing and/or persuading potential consumers that the product or service offering will meet their needs.

Marketers competing in nearly all product categories are constantly searching for ways to segment their markets in an attempt to better satisfy customers' needs (Exhibit 3–12). The remainder of this section discusses ways to approach this task and make the final segmentation decision. As shown in Figure 3–7 on page 80, several methods are available for segmenting markets. Marketers may use one of the segmentation variables or a combination of approaches. Consider the market segmentation strategy that might be employed to market snow skis. The consumer's lifestyle—active, fun-loving, enjoys outdoor sports—is certainly important. But so are other factors, such as age, income, and marital status. Let us review the basis for segmentation and examine some promotional strategies employed in each.

Geographic Segmentation In the **geographic segmentation** approach, markets are divided into different geographic units. These units may include nations, provinces, states, counties, or even neighbourhoods. Consumers often have different buying habits depending on where they reside. To address this, advertisers might use different IMC tools or advertising messages.

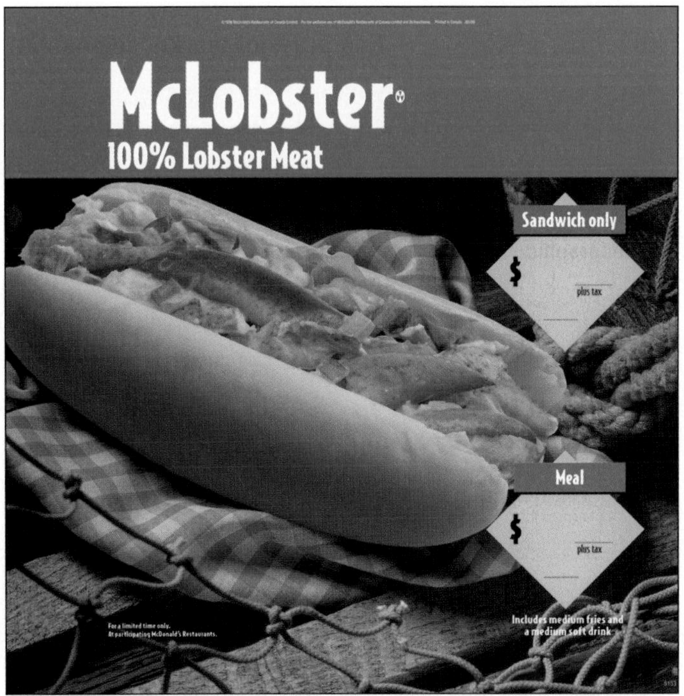

Exhibit 3–12 McDonald's offers a variety of products in different geographic markets

Demographic Segmentation Dividing the market on the basis of demographic variables such as gender, age, marital status, household size, and socioeconomic variables like income, education, and occupation is called **demographic segmentation**. For example, the Alberta Securities Commission targeted young adults aged 24–35 who had very little knowledge of investing and had a perceived need for financial advice as indicated by market research. Print and radio ads directed interested consumers to an education link on the Commission's website. A second phase of the advertising message featured links on Web portals that also highlighted a contest.[24]

While demographics is a common method of segmenting markets, it is important to recognize that other factors may be the underlying basis for homogeneity and/or consumer behaviour. The astute marketer will identify additional approaches for segmenting and will recognize the limitations of demographics.

Psychographic Segmentation Dividing the market on the basis of lifestyle, personality, culture, and social class is referred to as **psychographic segmentation**. Each of these variables can be the basis for segmentation.

Lifestyle Many consider lifestyle the most effective criterion for segmentation. The determination of lifestyles is usually based on an analysis of the activities, interests, and opinions (AIOs) of consumers. These lifestyles are then correlated with the consumers' product, brand, and/or media usage. For many products and/or services, lifestyles may be the best discriminator between use and nonuse, accounting for differences in food, clothing, and car selections, among numerous other consumer behaviours.[25] Notice how the ad for MEC in Exhibit 3–13 reflects the life of the target audience member.

Psychographic segmentation has been increasingly accepted with the advent of the values and lifestyles (VALS) program. Developed by the Stanford Research Institute (SRI), VALS has become a very popular method for applying lifestyle segmentation. VALS 2 divides Americans into eight lifestyle segments that exhibit distinctive attitudes, behaviours, and decision-making patterns.[26] SRI believes that when combined with an estimate of the resources the consumer can draw on (education, income, health, energy level, self-confidence, and degree of consumerism), the VALS 2 system is an excellent predictor of consumer behaviours. PRIZM, developed by Claritas, is another American lifestyle segmentation approach that has been adapted for the Canadian market through the research firm Environics. PRIZM$_{ce}$ associates the lifestyle questions asked on the survey with demographic data from the federal government's Census. The analysis provides 66 different lifestyle segments and

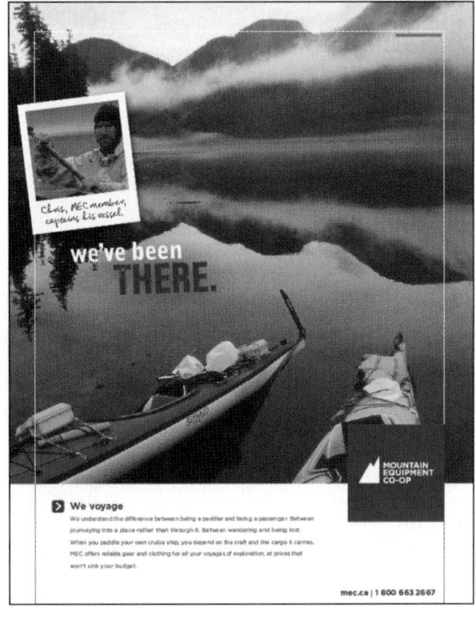

Exhibit 3–13 Mountain Equipment Co-op appeals to the active lifestyle

FIGURE 3–7 Examples of market segmentation variables

Main Dimension	Segmentation Variables	Typical Breakdowns
Customer Characteristics		
Geographic	Region	West, Central, East
	City size	Under 10,000; 10,000–24,999; 25,000–49,999; 50,000–99,999; 100,000–249,999; 250,000–499,999; 500,000–999,999; 1,000,000 or more
	Metropolitan area	Census Metropolitan Area (CMA); etc.
	Density	Urban; suburban; small town; rural
Demographic	Gender	Male; female
	Age	Under 6 yrs; 6–11 yrs; 12–17 yrs; 18–24 yrs; 25–34yrs; 35–44yrs; 45–54 yrs; 55–64 yrs; 65–74 yrs; 75 yrs plus
	Race	Asian; Black; Hispanic; Indian; White/Caucasian; etc.
	Life stage	Infant; preschool; child; youth; collegiate; adult; senior
	Birth era	Baby boomer (1949–1964); Generation X (1965–1976); baby boomlet/ Generation Y (1977–present)
	Household size	1; 2; 3–4; 5 or more
	Residence tenure	Own home; rent home
	Marital status	Never married; married; separated; divorced; widowed
Socioeconomic	Income	<$15,000; $15,000–$24,999; $25,000– $34,999; $35,000–$49,999; $50,000–$74,999; $75,000+
	Education	Some high school or less; high school graduate; some college or university; university/college graduate; etc
	Occupation	Managerial and professional specialty; technical, sales, and administrative support; service; farming, forestry, and fishing; etc.
Psychographic	Lifestlye	Activities, interests, options
	Values	Actualizers; fulfilleds; achievers; experiencers; believers; strivers; makers; strugglers
	Personality	Gregarious; compulsive; introverted; aggressive; ambitious; etc.
	Culture	Ethnic; social
	Social class	Low middle class; upper middle class; etc
Buying situations		
Outlet type	In-store	Department; specialty; outlet; convenience; supermarket; superstore/mass merchandiser; catalogue
	Direct	Mail order/catalogue; door-to-door; direct response; Internet
Benefits sought	Product feature	Situation specific; general
	Needs	Quality; service; price/value; financing; warranty; etc.
Usage	Usage rate	Light user; medium user; heavy user
	User status	Nonuser; ex-user; prospect; first-time user; regular user
Awareness and intentions	Product knowledge	Unaware; aware; informed; interested; intending to buy; purchaser; rejection
Behaviour	Involvement	Minimum effort; comparison; special effort

18 social groups based on whether the respondent is a pre-boomer, boomer, or post-boomer. $PRIZM_{ce}$ claims that the segmentation system is useful for communication decisions like target audience profiling and media planning, and many other marketing strategy decisions for virtually all industries.

Personality Borrowing from psychological theory, we are interested in consumers' personality traits—the relatively enduring characteristics of one's personality that lead people to respond in a reasonably consistent manner. Often, such characteristics like introvert versus extrovert are used to describe a group of consumers more precisely.

Culture The broadest and most abstract of the external factors that influence consumer behaviour is **culture**, or the complexity of learned meanings, values, norms, and customs shared by members of a society. Cultural norms and values offer direction and guidance to members of a society in all aspects of their lives, including their consumption behaviour.

Marketers must also be aware of changes that may be occurring in a particular culture since it could be the basis for effective segmentation. Marketing researchers monitor these changes and their impact on the ways companies market their products and services. IMC Perspective 3–2 on page 82 demonstrates how some Canadian firms target their communications to specific ethnic cultures.

While marketers recognize that culture exerts a demonstrable influence on consumers, they often find it difficult to respond to cultural differences in different markets. The subtleties of various cultures are often difficult to understand and appreciate, but marketers must understand the cultural context in which consumer purchase decisions are made and adapt their advertising and promotional programs accordingly.

For example, Bell Mobility rang in the Chinese New Year early in 2004 with an advertising and promotion campaign directed to Asian customers in Western Canada, the first of many specific communication efforts to appeal to a large group of potential customers. To resonate with the people of this culture more significantly, Bell Mobility introduced new creative messages to celebrate the Year of the Monkey. It also edited existing television ads to include scenes reflecting Asian lifestyles more accurately while also translating ads into Cantonese and Mandarin.[27]

Within a given culture are generally found smaller groups or segments whose beliefs, values, norms, and patterns of behaviour set them apart from the larger cultural mainstream. These **subcultures** may be based on age, geographic, religious, racial, and/or ethnic differences. A number of subcultures exist within Canada. These racial/ethnic subcultures are important to marketers because of their size, growth, purchasing power, and distinct purchasing patterns. Marketers develop specific marketing programs for various products and services for these target markets.

Other types of subcultures are also targeted through promotional communication. For example, many major brands including Honda Civic, RadioShack, Adidas Canada, and Athletes World target those within the hip-hop culture. The firms have included the hip-hop culture in their television ads and marketing events.[28]

Social Class Virtually all societies exhibit some form of stratification whereby individuals can be assigned to a specific social category on the basis of criteria important to members of that society. **Social class** refers to relatively homogeneous divisions in a society into which people sharing similar lifestyles, values, norms, interests, and behaviours can be grouped. While a number of methods for determining social class exist, class structures in Canada are usually based on occupational status, educational attainment, and income. For example, sociologists generally agree there are three broad levels of social classes in North America: the upper (14 percent), middle (70 percent), and lower (16 percent) classes.[29]

IMC PERSPECTIVE 3–2

Canada's Mosaic Population

Approximately 4 million Canadians are visible minorities in a country with about 31 million citizens. Some experts believe that significant retail growth will come from this sizable group of Canadians, especially considering that immigration accounted for more than half of the population growth between the two most recent census tabulations of 1996 and 2001. And as all good marketers know, segmenting the market using this valuable characteristic can be profitable if brands are looking to target a more specific audience.

The largest minority group in Canada is Chinese at 1.1 million. Research suggests that Chinese consumers are interested in luxury brands more than any other ethnic group and use luxury brands as a way of displaying their economic achievement, seek status through products significantly more than white Canadians, and purchase extensively on the Internet. Noting these ideas and the fact that 70 percent of all Chinese children study a musical instrument, the Toronto Symphony Orchestra (TSO) looked to this segment as a source of attracting new customers and tailored a communications offering of advertising, public relations, and promotional incentives in the Chinese language. After its initial success, the TSO continued with even more customized communication including Chinese brochures, designing part of its website in Chinese, advertising in Chinese media, offering a slogan that fits the Chinese culture more specifically, and even setting up a hot-line in both Cantonese and Mandarin. The TSO expanded these ideas to similar communication programs in other languages such as Italian, Russian, and Korean.

And the TSO is not the only firm targeting the Chinese community. A Rona store in Vancouver experienced similar success with customized communication to Chinese consumers that increased sales so much that the store received a hardware retailer of the year award. However, Rona's main office had yet to customize its national brand advertising for distinct ethnic markets as it preferred to keep a consistent message through translation of uniform advertising messages.

Combined with these examples, market research firms focus on Chinese consumers extensively, with one firm developing eight demographic/psychographic profiles ranging in size of about 12,000 to 93,000. Consumers in one of the largest groups, "Ethnic Cruisers-Chinese Technocrats," are university educated; have a household income of $95,000; work in management, sales, and service industries; have young families; and participate in sports, health clubs, social clubs, and investing.

On the other hand, Wal-Mart recently offered its commercials in Italian, Portuguese, Spanish, Cantonese, Mandarin, and Southeast Asian languages on various specialty ethnic channels. The ads show real customers speaking about their Wal-Mart experiences in their own language. This appears to go a step beyond Zellers' effort of dubbing its English ads into other languages.

While slightly smaller at 900,000, Canadians from India and other nearby South Asian countries present another sizable ethnic segment that has its own unique characteristics that marketers attempt to attract. For example, Telus adapted a television ad that included monkeys by changing the background music such that the meaning of the message more closely fit Indian culture and adding a combination of English and Hindi known as "Hinglish." In addition, Telus changed the animal theme in its ad for camera phones for the Indian market since the national campaign showed pigs, an unappealing animal in that culture.

Sources: Eve Lazarus, "Building Better Relationships," *Marketing Magazine*, May 19, 2003; Chris Daniels, "Shopping Mosaic," *Marketing Magazine*, May 17, 2004; Loretta Lam, "Music to Ethnic Ears," *Marketing Magazine*, May 19, 2003; Michelle Warren, "Telus, Fat Free Tailor Indian Ad Effort," *Marketing Magazine*, November 17, 2003; Judy Waytiuk, "Discounter Diversity," *Marketing Magazine*, May 19, 2003; Rebecca Harris, "Home Away From Home," *Marketing Magazine*, February 13, 2006.

Question

1. Explain why some of the promotional activities are effective.

Social class is an important concept to marketers, since consumers within each social stratum often have similar values, lifestyles, and buying behaviour. Thus, the various social class groups provide a natural basis for market segmentation. Consumers in the different social classes differ in the degree to which they use various products and services and in their leisure activities, shopping patterns, and media habits. Marketers respond to these differences through the positioning of their products and services, the media strategies they use to reach different social classes, and the types of advertising appeals they develop.

With smaller Canadian households (2.5 persons) and rising disposable household income, marketers of premium products find that the middle-class consumers behave as upper-class consumers for selective purchases. A sizable group of middle-class consumers who cannot afford premium or luxury goods for all their purchases are "trading up" for items such as clothing, home furnishings, or alcohol.[30] As a profile variable for target audience decisions, social class offers potential for expanding a brands market.

Benefit Segmentation In purchasing products, consumers are generally trying to satisfy specific needs and/or wants. They are looking for products that provide specific benefits to satisfy these needs. The grouping of consumers on the basis of attributes sought in a product is known as **benefit segmentation** and is widely used.

Consider the purchase of a wristwatch. While you might buy a watch for particular benefits such as accuracy, water resistance, or stylishness, others may seek a different set of benefits. Watches are commonly given as gifts for birthdays, Christmas, and graduation. Certainly some of the same benefits are considered in the purchase of a gift, but the benefits the purchaser derives are different from those the user will obtain. Ads that portray watches as good gifts stress different criteria to consider in the purchase decision. The next time you see an ad or commercial for a watch, think about the basic appeal and the benefits it offers.

Another example of benefit segmentation can be seen in the cough remedy market. Some consumers want a product with fever reliever (NeoCitran); others prefer one that helps them to sleep (NyQuil). Buckley's offers that their cough mixture "tastes awful ... and it works" (Exhibit 3–14).

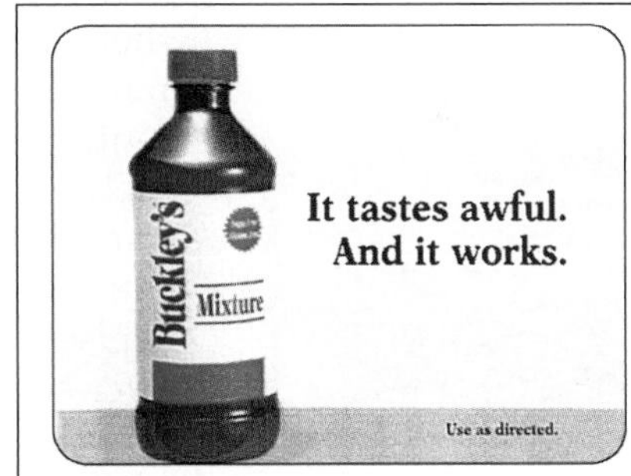
Buckley's
Mixture
It tastes awful.
And it works.
Use as directed.

Exhibit 3–14 Buckley's stresses the benefit of its superior cough remedy.

Behaviouristic Segmentation Dividing consumers into groups according to their usage, loyalties, or buying responses to a product is **behaviouristic segmentation**. For example, product or brand usage, degree of use (heavy versus light), and/or brand loyalty are combined with demographic and/or psychographic criteria to develop profiles of market segments. In the case of usage, the marketer assumes that nonpurchasers of a brand or product who have the same characteristics as purchasers hold greater potential for adoption than nonusers with different characteristics. A profile (demographic or psychographic) of the user is developed, which serves as the basis for promotional strategies designed to attract new users. For example, teenagers share certain similarities in their consumption behaviours. Those who do not currently own an iPod are more likely to be potential buyers than people in other age groups.

Another way of viewing behaviouristic segmentation is to examine the specific situation in which consumers plan to use the product or brand since it directly affects their perceptions, preferences, and purchasing behaviours.[31] Two types of **situations** may be relevant: the specific usage situation and the purchase situation.

Usage refers to the circumstance in which the product will be used. For example, purchases made for private consumption may be thought of differently from those that will be obvious to the public. Furthermore, purchases made for oneself versus for others as gifts offer another way to view consumer markets. The *purchase* situation more directly involves the environment operating at the time of the purchase. Time constraints, store environments, and other factors guide consumers' behaviour, which opens the door for inventive ways of segmenting the market.

Target Market Selection

As we have seen, a number of alternative segmentation approaches may be used. Each time a specific segment is identified, additional information is gathered to help the marketer understand this group. For example, once a specific segment is identified on the basis of benefits sought, the marketer will examine lifestyle characteristics and demographics to help characterize this group and to further its understanding of this market. Behaviouristic segmentation criteria will also be examined. In the purchase of ski boots, for example, specific benefits may be sought—flexibility or stiffness—depending on the type of skiing the buyer does. All this information will be combined to provide a complete profile of the skier.

Promotional planners will refer to the segmentation approach used in the marketing plan. The market segmentation may be based on demographics so the target market could be men ages 18–24 or women 25–44. And, it may be incumbent upon the promotional planner to perform additional research to develop a more complete profile. Alternatively, the market segmentation used in the marketing plan could employ one variable as a starting point and offer additional variables to further define the target market as seen in the ski boots example.

The promotional planner must consider whether the target segment is substantial enough to support individualized strategies. More specifically, they consider whether this group is accessible. Can it be reached with a communications program? For example, you will see in Chapter 10 that in some instances there are no media that can be used to reach some targeted groups. Or the promotions manager may identify a number of segments but be unable to develop the required programs to reach them. For example, the firm may have insufficient funds to develop the required advertising campaign. The more marketers segment the market, the more precise is their understanding of it. But the more the market becomes divided, the fewer consumers are in each segment. Thus, a key decision is: How far should one go in the segmentation process?

While we have given a couple of promotional implications indicating the degree to which marketers may segment the market, similar arguments hold true for the other marketing mix variables. However, another issue arises as to which segmentation variable is used first and which others are used as additional profile variables. The answer to this question is the art of marketing; the insight promotional planners see in the information to understand their target market and target audience options.

Target Audience Options

We now turn to the Rossiter and Percy (R&P) perspective of identifying and selecting the target audience for promotional communication.[32] R&P state that the primary and most logical factor for initially defining a target audience is the current behaviour of consumers. This factor is critical since it is the individual decision of each customer to purchase a brand that dictates a firm's total sales. Furthermore, this behaviour is a manifestation of a consumer's attitude toward the brand. Thus, in setting the direction for any IMC plan or component of an IMC plan (i.e., advertising), the manager must have a clear idea of the customer status of the target audience. Essentially, this decision hinges on a key question. Is the communication directed toward customer groups or non-customer groups?

Customer Groups A promotional planner has the opportunity to direct communications to **brand loyal customers** who regularly buy their firm's products. Recent marketing strategies (i.e., relationship marketing discussed in Chapter 1) and communication strategies regularly focus on a firm's current customers to ensure that customers maintain their current purchasing and consumption behaviour. As we noted in Chapter 1, it is generally very profitable to maintain a stable core of current customers. From a communication standpoint, it suggests that we do not have to advertise as often or we do not have to have as many sales promotions. However, we still see campaigns directed toward current loyal customers. For example, The Movie Network ran an eight-week television, radio, and outdoor campaign in early 2004 that was entirely devoted to its current subscribers base.[33]

To put this idea into another context we highlight the fact that one-third of all Canadians do not drink beer at all and that 74 percent of all Canadian beer drinkers claim they are loyal to their favourite beer.[34] This raises the question as to whether beer company ads should target their loyal customers and ensure future purchases by strengthening the loyalty with relevant messages, or target the remaining customers who claim they are not loyal to a specific beer.

Favourable brand switchers are a second customer group highlighted by R&P. These customers buy the promotional planner's brand but also buy other brands within a given relevant time period for the product category. For some product categories, consumers habitually purchase from a few favourites or those brands within their evoked set. These types of purchases may occur for many reasons. Consumers often face different purchase situations (e.g., own purchase versus gift). Sometimes certain moods influence brand choice. Whatever the motivation or external influencing factor, consumers adjust their purchases accordingly. While a promotional planner would dearly love to have all customers be truly loyal, favourable brand switchers are an important source of purchases and are loyal to a degree. For these reasons, marketers would like to communicate directly with these consumers so that their brand remains in the evoked set. Alternatively, continued communication may influence stronger loyalty in the future. Butter is always competing with margarine for increased loyalty (Exhibit 3–15).

Exhibit 3–15 Butter advertises to avoid switching to substitute products

Returning to our beer example, it turns out that Canadian beer drinkers may not be strongly aligned to one beer, as 30 to 40 percent will switch brands if a promotional offer coincides with an advertising message.[35] In reality, it appears many Canadian beer drinkers are loyal to their favourite beer to a degree, but they will also include it along with other brands, thereby categorizing themselves as favourable brand switchers.

Non-Customer Groups Communication directed to non-customers is the focus of much advertising and promotion. R&P identify three key groups: **new category users**, **other brand switchers**, and **other brand loyals**. These consumers are more difficult to attract as they do not currently purchase the promotional planner's brand.

New category users, as the name implies, are those customers that are not purchasing within a product category. For example, after graduating from college or university many young adults begin to enter numerous categories partly because they have the income but also because they are at a stage of their life when new or latent needs emerge. Advertisers attempt to court this target audience since many of these consumers are potentially ready to make a purchase. Later on in life consumers face different needs and move into a product category, as shown in Exhibit 3–16. Marketers believe that steady communication may entice these customers to their brand

Exhibit 3–16 Toyota suggests the need for a minivan in many of its recent prints ads

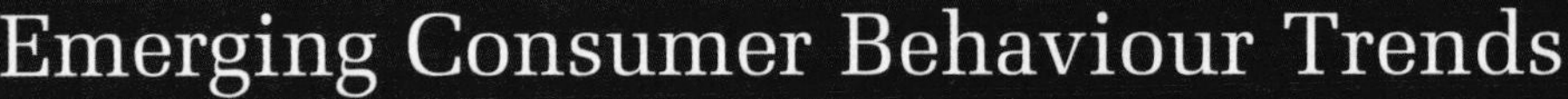

IMC PERSPECTIVE 3–3

Emerging Consumer Behaviour Trends

According to research by the Boston Consulting Group, consumers are justifying select luxuries, such as plasma televisions, but are looking for bargains on mundane products. This is the result of a rise of roughly $9,000 in real family income over the past ten years, thanks largely to an increased contribution from women. Holding the middle ground is an increasingly untenable business strategy, says Cliff Grevler of the Boston Consulting Group. For example, in the past five years the premium beer category has grown 6 percent, while the discount beer category has increased its share by 7 percent. Meanwhile, the middle—held primarily by core Molson and Labatt brands—has dropped 13 percent. No wonder Labatt was advertising its flagship brand, Blue, as "The good stuff, not the okay stuff" in the summer of 2007.

Another trend is that young people are not wearing watches as much as older people. Investment banker Piper Jaffray Co. found that the number of teens who do not wear a watch soared last year, to 59 percent up from 48 percent in 2004. "Teens just aren't interested in buying watches anymore," said Neely Tamminga, a Piper Jaffray analyst. She says that teens are getting the time from other gadgets, in particular cell phones. Tamminga goes on to say that cell phones are more fashionable, but also have technological advances over watches because they can do more things, such as change time zones automatically. Tamminga says that watch makers are caught in a generally downward cycle. They need to inject some verve back into the industry. She says that if teens have an extra $65 they want to spend it on retro shoes, not a watch.

Another 82 percent of teenagers polled by Piper Jaffray in the United States and Canada said they have no plans to buy a watch over the next six months, up from 76 percent at the same time last year. The number of teens who said they wore a watch daily declined to 13 percent last year, from 18 percent the year before. Makers of expensive watches, such as Rolex and Patek Phillippe, are suffering too, according to the marketing researcher NPD Group. They found that the number of people buying watches that sell over $1,000 declined 2 percent last year—even though they are still popular with older people, who see the watch as an accessory.

Sources: "Soft in the Middle," *Canadian Business*, July 17, 2006; Kevin Restivo, "Clock Ticking for Watch Sales," *Financial Post*, May 5, 2006.

Questions

1. With the growth of some luxury products, such as plasma televisions, do you feel that middle-of-the-road brands in some product categories are in trouble?
2. Can you think of a marketing strategy to encourage teens to wear watches?

when the time comes for these consumers to actually purchase. IMC Perspective 3–3 identifies an emerging group of new category users as a target audience for a watch brand.

Other brand switchers are like the switchers in the customer group in that they purchase a few different brands within a category. However from a promotional planner's perspective, they are fundamentally different, as they are not purchasing their brand. This is a challenging target audience, as the brand needs to break into consumers' evoked set and within the brands that these consumers are currently purchasing. This is a formidable task but still the focus of a considerable amount of advertising and promotion. (Exhibit 3–17 is an ad to attract drinkers of other brands of beer.)

For example, Coffee Crisp recently started advertising on television after a 10-year hiatus. As the brand manager noted, "Because Coffee Crisp hasn't been advertised for so many years, we haven't brought in a new generation of Coffee Crisp consumers." Naturally, many young consumers were eating other brands of chocolate bars, so Coffee Crisp faced the challenge of appealing to these other brand switchers with a taste alternative. Research showed that Coffee Crisp "owned" the coffee association in the chocolate bar market, and with a generation of young coffee drinkers that frequent cafés the brand had a good opportunity to improve sales with its new ads. In fact, the room for growth is impressive, as the famous bar that was once ranked number one or two in Canada had fallen to number five with a lack of advertising for so many years.[36]

R&P's final group for target audience selection concerns other brand loyals. As this implies, these consumers purchase only one other brand. For example, Porter Airlines attempts to draw from Air Canada's customers (Exhibit 3–19). It is difficult to say how much advertising and promotion expenditures are directed to these types of consumer across many industries. Logically, it would be very difficult to break the strongly held behaviour in which these consumers currently engage. Nevertheless, this is still a potential target to which a firm may wish to deliver some form of advertising and promotion. The ad in Exhibit 3–18 shows a strong message to encourage non-users to switch.

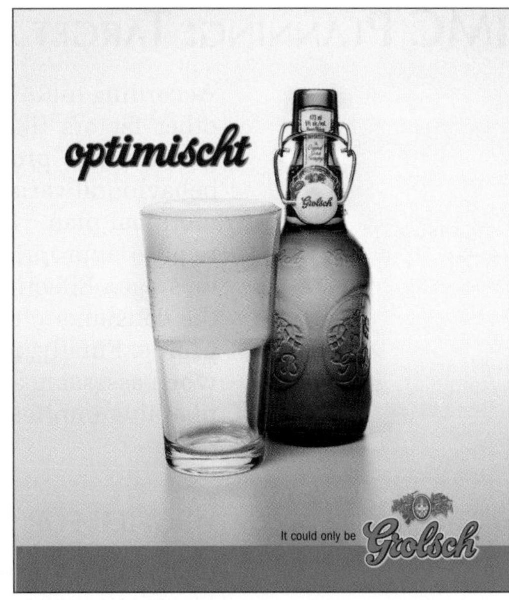

Exhibit 3–17 Grolsch plays on its name to attract new customers

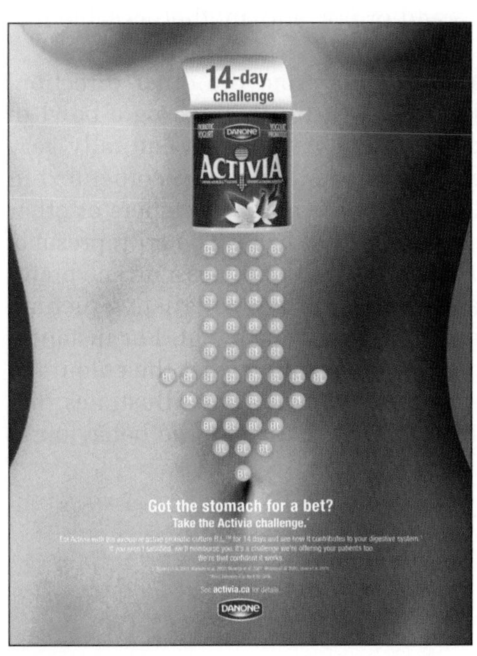

Exhibit 3–18 Danone challenges new users to try its brand of yogurt

Exhibit 3–19 Porter Airlines' "rules" campaign sways Air Canada customers

IMC Planning: Target Audience Profile

According to R&P, after prioritizing the target audience in terms of customer groups other factors like lifestyle or demographics are used to develop a complete target audience profile. A complete profile of the target audience beyond the initial behavioural variable is necessary for direction of the remaining decisions in the promotional plan. Creative decisions involving the main message to be communicated require appropriate content so that consumers will attend to and understand the message. Effective media decisions require the promotional planner to match the consumer characteristics of the specific media with a complete target audience profile. Finally, more information about the target audience allows greater precision when assessing and choosing IMC tools to deliver the message. We now explore the planning implications of these three ideas.

Profile for Messages

In later chapters we will identify different aspects of constructing the main message a promotional planner would want to develop for its advertising or sales promotion or any other IMC tool like the Internet or public relations. For the message to be completely understood, the content of the message must be consistent with the background or experiences of the intended audience. For example, if the ad uses language or references to a lifestyle that is unfamiliar to the target audience, there is less likelihood of it influencing in the direction intended. Thus, a complete profile of the target audience will be useful when finalizing the body copy in a print ad or the scenes in a television commercial.

Many companies target a younger demographic. We may read in the press or in marketing trade publications that a firm is targeting an 18–24-year-old demographic. While this may be true, often there is an inherent behavioural variable implied. Sometimes it is more like a new category user, since young adults start to consume new categories of products as they mature. Other times, it is more like favourable brand switchers in an attempt to make these consumers exhibit stronger loyalty. Thus, a communication message has to resonate with the target audience based on their current behaviour, whether they buy the brand or not, and another variable like demographics.

One clever ad by Tide detergent illustrates this point from the other direction. The ad shows a child sitting in a highchair who has just finished eating a bowl of spaghetti. The picture clearly shows the child's face and the child is naturally very messy. The headline reads, "The day I switched to Tide," and there is no other text in the ad. It appears that this message is targeted toward other brand switchers or other brand loyals who are at a particular stage of the family life cycle. The ad represents the significant decision they undertook to finally stop consuming a current brand and move on to a presumably better brand. Had the ad shown an alternative picture, the additional profile variable would have been considerably different. For instance, a young woman wearing athletic clothing who observes a stain or that the colours of her clothing are fading too quickly suggests an active lifestyle. This illustrates that any marketing segmentation variable can be used to further profile the behavioural variable.

Profile for Media

Later in this text, we will also identify the different media decisions. For example, the promotional planner could select television or radio to deliver its message, or the promotional planner might consider newspapers or magazines or a multitude of other media. Each medium offers many avenues that also must be considered. For instance, would the promotional planner place the television commercial on a TSN sports event during the day, or on a CTV drama in the evening? A detailed profile of the target audience allows the message to be more precisely delivered in a medium that has a higher proportion of the target audience.

Some contend that the advent of many different television channels leading to greater audience fragmentation has led to television being less efficient, since an advertiser is required to place a commercial on more than one station to reach a larger audience. In contrast, the detailed target audience profile for media helps a promotional planner move toward greater effectiveness. With the possibility of offering a more customized message to different audiences, promotional planners can have one type of commercial oriented toward younger non-customers on one channel and another message to older current customers on a different channel. Or, with the extensive number of new television channels in languages other than the two official languages, advertisers can provide more customized messages on the respective channels. For example, the OpenRoad brand of car dealerships selling Toyota, Lexus, Honda, Acura, Hyundai, and Audi vehicles has successfully used different combinations of media to effectively reach the Vancouver resident with a Chinese background.[37]

Profile for IMC Tools

Similarly, in a later part of the book, we investigate the decisions involved for other IMC tools like sales promotion, public relations, direct marketing, and the Internet. Each of these represents additional avenues for reaching target audiences, and each represents a tool with a greater opportunity for building the brand. Like media, there is also the possibility of more closely aligning the use of a tool with a promotional planner's target audience, provided sufficient profiling is done.

Western Union created cultural events for Toronto, Vancouver, and Winnipeg residents with Filipino heritage to encourage usage when sending money to their previous country. This idea arose after research indicated an interest in entertainment, in particular performers and celebrities from the former country. Ethnically based media advertising supported this effort to convince these consumers that the brand was not an overpriced, indifferent global company.[38]

From another angle, Canadian Tire—historically geared for men—continues to evolve with a greater emphasis toward women. Altering its product offerings and store design was just one step, as it offers a substantially different set of communications directed to women with a stylish-home kind of lifestyle. Its television advertising featured creative messages more fitting for women, placed on specialty channels. Canadian Tire featured print advertising in stylish publications like *Wish, Style at Home,* and *Canadian House & Home.* Store displays appeared more inspiring and less informational, also to fit with this newfound audience.[39]

SUMMARY

This chapter introduced you to the field of consumer behaviour and examined its relevance to promotional strategy. Consumer behaviour is best viewed as the process and activities that people engage in when searching for, selecting, purchasing, using, evaluating, and disposing of products and services to satisfy their needs and desires.

A five-stage model of the consumer decision-making process consists of need recognition, information search, alternative evaluation, purchase, and postpurchase evaluation. Internal psychological processes that influence the consumer decision-making process include motivation, perception, attitude formation and change, and integration processes. The decision process model views consumer behaviour primarily from a cognitive orientation.

This chapter also investigated how promotional planners make a target audience decision for any aspect of an IMC plan. To understand the context of this decision, the chapter examined the role of promotion in the overall marketing process, as shown in Figure 3–5. The process includes a situation analysis, target market process, and marketing program development all directed toward a prescribed target market.

One of the key aspects pertains to the target marketing process, which includes segmenting the market, selecting a target market, and determining the market positioning strategy, as this process gives direction to the target audience decision. Accordingly, we reviewed how marketing planners and promotional planners segment the market, and explained how each made the target market and target audience decision, respectively.

Finally, the chapter concluded by identifying a model to profile a target audience by considering the current purchase behaviour of the target audience with respect to the promotional planner's brand as the primary segmentation variable. Promotional messages can be directed to current customers, such as brand-loyal or favourable brand switchers. Alternatively, promotional messages could be targeted to non-customers, like new category users, other brand switchers, or other brand loyals. Other variables to more accurately define the audience in terms of lifestyle or psychographics became relevant after this initial direction became finalized. This descriptive profile becomes useful for all facets of the promotional plan (i.e., message, media, IMC tools).

KEY TERMS

affect referral decision rule, *71*
behaviouristic segmentation, *83*
benefit segmentation, *83*
brand loyal customers, *84*
brand loyalty, *70*
cognitive dissonance, *72*
consumer behaviour, *62*
culture, *81*
demographic segmentation, *79*
evaluative criteria, *69*
extended problem solving, *73*
external search, *66*
favourable brand switchers, *85*
geographic segmentation, *79*
heuristics, *71*
hierarchy of needs, *64*
integration processes, *70*
internal search, *66*
limited problem solving, *73*
mnemonics, *68*
motives, *64*
need recognition, *62*
new category users, *85*
other brand loyals, *85*
other brand switchers, *85*
perception, *66*
psychographic segmentation, *79*
purchase intention, *70*
reference group, *74*
routine problem solving, *72*
satisfaction, *72*
selective attention, *67*
selective comprehension, *68*
selective exposure, *67*
selective perception, *66*
selective retention, *68*
sensation, *67*
situations, *83*
social class, *81*
subcultures, *81*
subliminal perception, *68*
target audience, *78*
target market, *77*
target market process, *77*
want, *63*

DISCUSSION QUESTIONS

1. A number of factors may lead to need recognition among consumers. Discuss the various causes of need recognition, and give an example of each.

2. Explain how consumers might engage in each of the processes of selective perception described in the chapter. Provide examples.

3. Explain the concept of an *evoked set*. Why is this concept important to marketers? Give examples of an evoked set, and how marketers might attempt to influence consumers to gain consideration.

4. After buying a new car, a customer receives many pieces of direct mail such as a driving magazine or information on automobile care from the manufacturer. Explain why this is effective or ineffective communication.

5. In the text it was indicated that families may influence the consumer decision-making process. Describe how various family members may assume the different roles described in Figure 3–4. Also explain how these roles might change depending upon the product under consideration.

6. Some marketers contend that demographics is not really a basis for segmentation but is a descriptor of the segment. Discuss examples to support both positions.

7. A number of approaches to segmentation have been cited in the text. Provide examples of companies and/or brands that employ each in their promotional communications.

8. In what situations is the target audience and the target market the same? In what situations is the size of the target audience larger or smaller than the target market?

9. When defining a target audience for communications, why is it a good idea to use consumer behaviour with respect to your brand as the primary variable before using other variables such as demographics or lifestyle?

10. How is it possible for a brand to communicate to both customers and non-customers in an IMC plan?

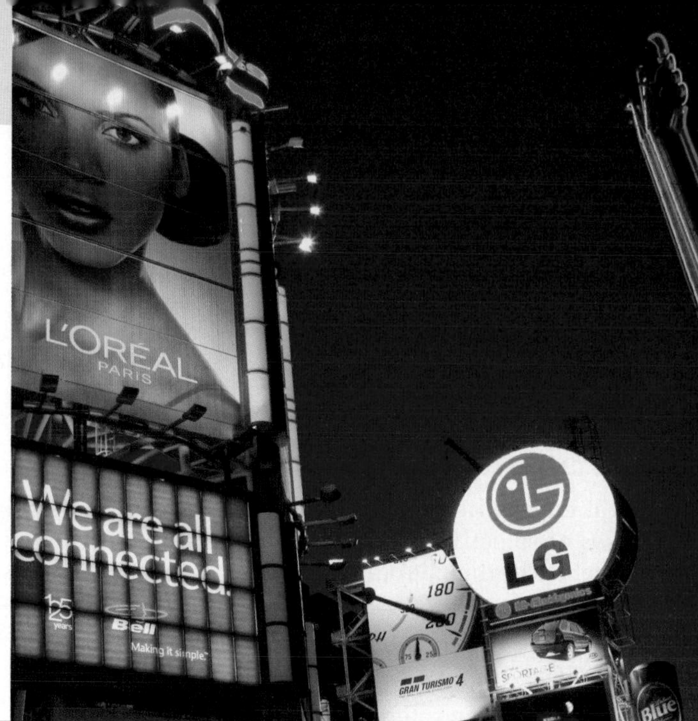

CHAPTER 4

COMMUNICATION RESPONSE MODELS

Chapter Objectives

- To understand the basic elements of the communication process and the role of communications in marketing.
- To summarize traditional communication response models.
- To analyze the response processes of receivers of marketing communications, including alternative response hierarchies and cognitive processing.
- To summarize an integrative communication response model from a theoretical and managerial perspective.

Mobile Channels of Communication

We've all seen ads on TV, heard ads on radio, smelled ads in magazines, and practically tasted and felt visually stunning street ads, but the newest media is a total experience in one's personal space. Text messaging from marketers to consumers' cell phones is the latest channel used to deliver brand content. In fact, researchers estimate that more than 500 text message campaigns occurred during the three years ending in 2006. Although many of the campaigns appeared to be one-time tests of the new channel, industry participants predict that, starting in 2007, advertisers will consider text messages as part of their overall IMC plan.

Leading-edge marketers found innovative uses of text messages in 2006. CBC sent news updates, advertising of television shows, and Olympic highlights to registered users. During the World Cup, Rogers delivered alerts, country flags and anthems, and video highlights providing an immediate update for keen soccer fans. Intrawest, owner of ski and other tourist resorts, offered discounts on its hotels with an amazing 52 percent response rate. Pfizer Canada launched "Reactine mobile pollen alerts" so consumers would know when and where the highest pollen locations were occurring. In the "Molson Canadian Rocks Revealed" event interested concertgoers discovered the name of a mystery band and texted their answer to win tickets. Likewise, potential Nissan buyers responded to digital signage to inquire about the new Versa small car.

The market potential of text messaging appears unlimited—Canadians sent 8.7 million text messages per day in 2006, up from 3.7 million in 2005. However, of the 50 percent of Canadians who own a cell phone, only about 25 percent of them actively use text messages, thus limiting the overall reach of the media channel compared to the near-universal use of television. On the bright side, the usage rate of text messages in Europe reaches 70 to 85 percent in the UK, Germany, and France, versus Canada's 25 percent.

Despite this opportunity, consumers are reluctant to receive advertising in a device that is viewed as more personal than other channels. One Yankee Group study of 2,000 cell phone users determined that only 12 to 22 percent desired to receive some form of advertising message on their cell phone, depending upon the content and type of message. Furthermore, in the past year 11 percent received an unwanted message, 15 percent received a message but deleted it, 3 percent received a relevant message, and 70 percent did not receive a message. Clearly advertisers have a challenge on their hands, but how to use the new channel is up for debate. Some view it as an ideal support to more traditional media to reach more specific target audiences. More innovative marketers believe text messages are the primary channel to reach unique target audiences.

Source: Sarah Dobson, "Mobile Matter," *Marketing Magazine*, October 9, 2006.

Question

1. Based on the statistics described, what is your opinion on the use of text messages for advertising?

The function of an integrated marketing communications program is to communicate. An organization's IMC strategy is implemented through the communication tools and messages it sends to current or prospective customers as well as other relevant publics. Organizations communicate in many ways, such as through advertisements, brand names, logos and graphic systems, websites, press releases, package designs, promotions, and visual images. Thus, those involved in the planning and implementation of an IMC program need to understand the communications process. Marketers must understand how consumers will perceive and interpret their messages and how these reactions will shape consumers' responses to the company and/or its product or service.

This chapter takes a historical perspective to illustrate how academics and practitioners have evolved in their thinking to understand how persuasion works in the context of marketing communication. We begin with a basic model of communication to illustrate the complexity of the communication process. Next, we examine the response process of consumers that is explained by traditional models, alternative hierarchies, and cognitive processing of communications. Finally, we summarize with a framework that illustrates an IMC planning perspective.

A Basic Model of Communication

Communication has been defined as the passing of information, the exchange of ideas, or the process of establishing a commonness or oneness of thought between a sender and a receiver.[1] These definitions suggest that for communication to occur, there must be some common thinking between two parties and information must be passed from one person to another (or from one group to another). This section elaborates on this idea by introducing a model of communication and discussing its elements.

Overview of Model

The communication process is often very complex. Success depends on such factors as the nature of the message, the audience's interpretation of it, and the environment in which it is received. The receiver's perception of the source and the medium used to transmit the message may also affect the ability to communicate, as do many other factors. Words, pictures, sounds, and colours may have different meanings to different audiences, and people's perceptions and interpretations of them vary. Marketers must understand the meanings that words and symbols take on and how they influence consumers' interpretation of products and messages. This can be particularly challenging to companies marketing their products in foreign countries, as discussed in Global Perspective 4–1.

Over the years, a basic model of the communication process has evolved, as shown in Figure 4–1 on page 96.[2] Two elements represent the major participants in the communication process, the sender and the receiver. Another two are the major communication tools: message and channel. Four others are the major communication functions and processes: encoding, decoding, response, and feedback. The last element, noise, refers to any extraneous factors in the system that can interfere with the process and work against effective communication.

Source/Encoding

The sender, or **source**, of a communication is the person or organization that has information to share with another person or group of people. The source may be an individual (say, a salesperson or hired spokesperson, such as a celebrity, who appears in a company's advertisements) or a nonpersonal entity (such as the brand

GLOBAL PERSPECTIVE 4–1

B.C. Hemlock Producers Branch Out

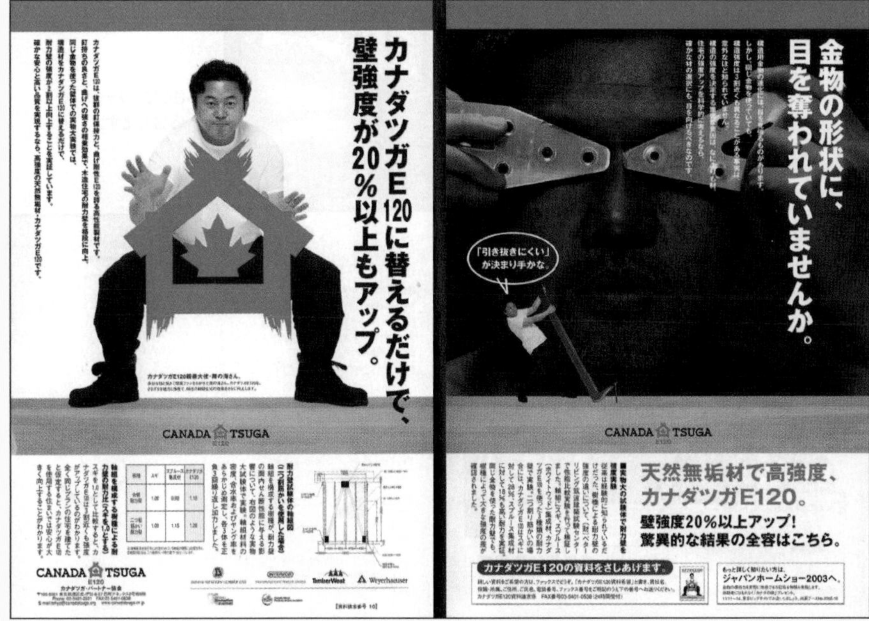

How can Canadian wood producers get their message of better quality hemlock understood by Japanese construction industry members? Enter Mai-no-umi, a 165 cm, 120 kg Japanese Sumo wrestler who has taken on and beaten much larger opponents and has achieved hero-like status as an underdog who performs. The Coastal Forest and Lumber Association (CFLA), an association designed to assist the marketers of many British Columbia wood producers, recently cast this unlikely spokesperson to demonstrate the strength of Canadian Tsuga, a new brand name for Hemlock grown in Canada and distributed in Japan.

B.C.'s share in Japan dropped from 38 percent in 1995 to 26 percent in 2002 due to competition from Europe and Russia. Since hemlock is one of B.C.'s most critical forest products and Japan is a critical foreign market beyond North America, it proved to be a communication challenge to change the negative perceptions of the strength of the wood. Research indicated that Japanese builders considered B.C. hemlock as weak and did not perceive any difference between it and American hemlock. In fact, Japanese referred to all hemlock as Bei Tsuga, Bei meaning American and Tsuga the Latin name for hemlock. With scientific research supporting that Canadian hemlock had the greatest bending stiffness and the greatest nail-holding grip compared to any other species, CFLA had to figure out a way to communicate this so that members of the Japanese construction industry would believe in the superior strength of the product.

Communication featured a new brand name, Canada Tsuga, and a red logo depicting a Japanese house with a red maple leaf placed between the two words of the brand name. Advertising in engineering and architectural journals reached the key decision makers, but the full effect and understanding of the message occurred with the Sumo spokesperson adopted in the past year. CFLA clearly linked the strength of a Sumo to the strength of the product. "We are saying, just as you have the strength of the Sumo and the technical attributes of his game, you have the strength of our Canada Tsuga and the technical attributes of our product."

As a result, Canada Tsuga became the preferred brand for post-and-beam construction in Japan with the Canadian market share climbing 2 percent in the past year. CFLA executives attributed most of this performance to the education and marketing campaigns implemented.

Source: Eve Lazarus, "Branching Out," *Marketing Magazine*, October 20, 2003.

Question

1. Explain why branding something like wood is a good idea.

or organization itself). Because the receiver's perceptions of the source influence how the communication is received, marketers must be careful to select a communicator the receiver believes is knowledgeable and trustworthy or with whom the receiver can identify or relate in some manner.

The communication process begins when the source selects words, symbols, pictures, and the like, to represent the message that will be delivered to the receiver(s). This process, known as **encoding**, involves putting thoughts, ideas, or information into a symbolic form. The sender's goal is to encode the message in

FIGURE 4–1 A model of the communication process

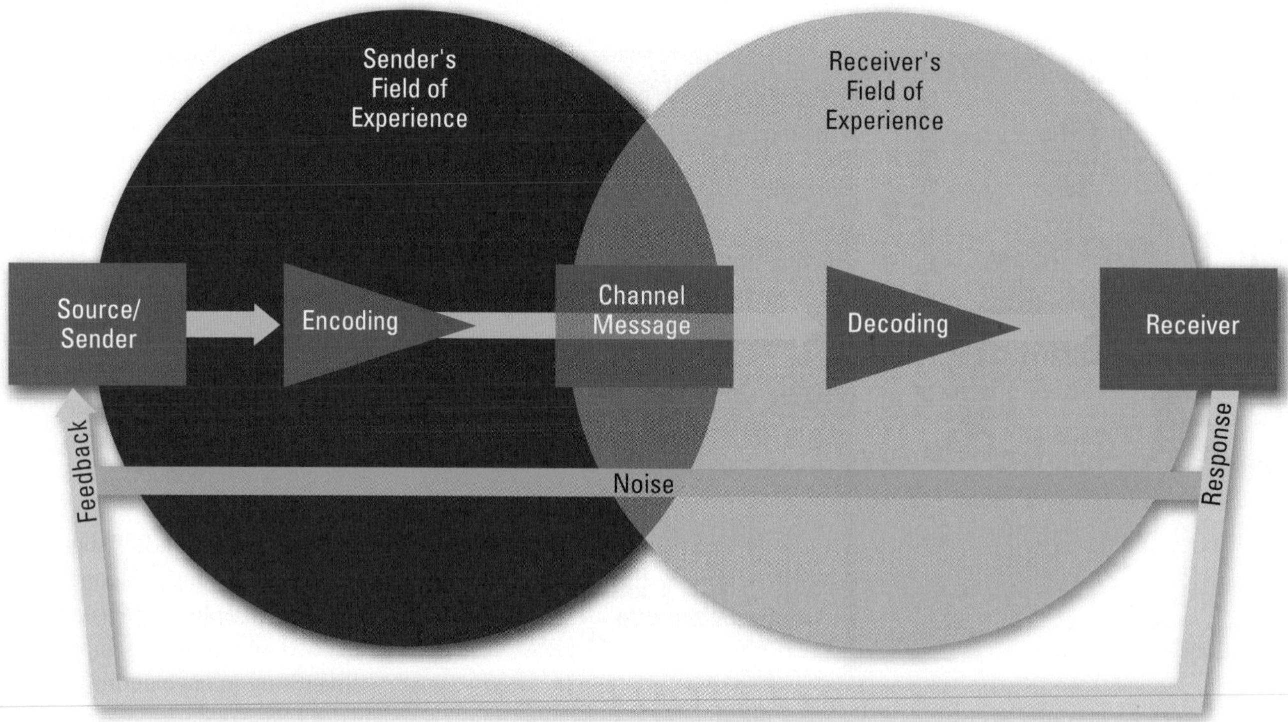

such a way that it will be understood by the receiver. This means using words, signs, or symbols that are familiar to the target audience. Many symbols have universal meaning, such as the familiar circle with a line through it to denote no parking, no smoking, and so forth. Many companies also have highly recognizable symbols—such as McDonald's golden arches, Nike's swoosh, or the Coca-Cola trademark—that are known to consumers around the world.

Message

The encoding process leads to development of a **message** that contains the information or meaning the source hopes to convey. The message may be verbal or nonverbal, oral or written, or symbolic. Messages must be put into a transmittable form that is appropriate for the channel of communication being used. In advertising, this may range from simply writing some words or copy that will be read as a radio message to producing an expensive television commercial. For many products, it is not the actual words of the message that determine its communication effectiveness but rather the impression or image the ad creates. Notice how the Coach ad shown in Exhibit 4–1 uses only a picture to deliver its message. However, the brand name and picture help communicate a feeling of eloquence and the classic design of its handbag.

To better understand the symbolic meaning that might be conveyed in a communication, advertising and marketing researchers have begun focusing attention on **semiotics**, which studies the nature of meaning and asks how our reality—words, gestures, myths, signs, symbols, products/services, theories—acquires meaning.[3] Semiotics is important in marketing communications since products and brands acquire meaning through the way they are advertised and consumers use products and brands to express their social identities.

Marketers may use individuals trained in semiotics and related fields such as cultural anthropology to better understand the conscious and subconscious meanings the nonverbal signs and symbols in their ads transmit to consumers. For example, Levi

Strauss & Co.'s agency hired a cultural anthropologist to help it better understand the image and meaning of clothing and fashion among young consumers. As part of the process, the agency research team recruited hip-looking young people in the streets of the East Village section of New York City, an area picked because they felt it is the best reflection of today's youth life. Those chosen were handed a piece of red cardboard and a white marker and asked to "write down something you believe in; something that's true about you or your world." The process provided the agency with insight into the teen market and was the impetus for an ad campaign featuring teenagers holding placards inscribed with their philosophical messages.[4] Exhibit 4–2 shows the thinking behind the elements of one of the ads used in the campaign as explained by Sean Dee, the director of the Levi's brand.

Some advertising and marketing people are skeptical about the value of semiotics. They question whether social scientists read too much into advertising messages and are overly intellectual in interpreting them. However, the meaning of an advertising message or other form of marketing communication lies not in the message but with the people who see and interpret it. Moreover, consumers behave on the basis of meanings they ascribe to marketplace stimuli. Thus, marketers must consider the meanings consumers attach to the various signs and symbols. Semiotics may be helpful in analyzing how various aspects of

Exhibit 4–1 The image projected by an ad often communicates more than words

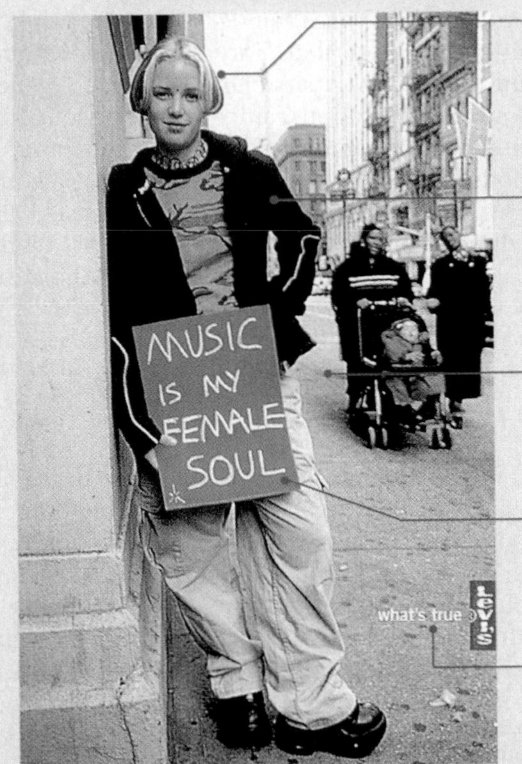

THE MODEL: A premed student at New York University
"We wanted people who are not defined by what they do but by what they are. We chose her because she looks like a Levi's type. She's young. She has her own point of view. She's sexy, but in an understated way. She's not trying too hard. She's definitely got something about her."

THE CLOTHES: Levi's cargo pants, her own T-shirt, zip-up sweatshirt, combat boots, and accessories
"It's important that she wore what she wanted. We're not trying to create a Levi's uniform; that wouldn't be very 'real.' We didn't use a professional stylist or a hairdresser; that wouldn't be real."

THE SETTING: Manhattan's East Village
"We picked New York City because it's the best reflection of today's youth life. We drove around the grittiest parts of the city. The people in the background [of this image] give it a street feel; it's obviously not staged in a studio."

THE STATEMENT: "Music is my female soul"
"It's hard for people to believe, but the [language] came totally from the kids; there was no prompting.... We liked the music theme [in this statement] because we do a lot to promote original music; we see music as being *the* voice of the young people."

THE TAG LINE: "What's true"
"The challenge with youth marketing these days is not to dictate to kids. This [line] is both a statement and a question. Is what we're saying true? Or is it a declaration? It works because it's provocative and ambiguous."

Exhibit 4–2 Semiotic analysis is used to describe the various elements of this Levi's ad

the marketing program—such as advertising messages, packaging, brand names, and even the nonverbal communications of salespeople (gestures, mode of dress)—are interpreted by receivers.[5]

Channel

The **channel** is the method by which the communication travels from the source or sender to the receiver. At the broadest level, channels of communication are of two types, personal and nonpersonal. *Personal channels* of communication are direct interpersonal (face-to-face) contact with target individuals or groups. Salespeople serve as personal channels of communication when they deliver their sales message to a buyer or potential customer. Social channels of communication such as friends, neighbours, associates, co-workers, or family members are also personal channels. They often represent *word-of-mouth communication*, a powerful source of information for consumers.[6]

Many companies are working to generate positive word-of-mouth discussion for their companies or brands. Knowing that the average consumer often listens to what others say about a brand, marketers will target specific groups of influential consumers such as trendsetters or loyal customers. A recent study conducted by David Godes and Diane Mayzlin on the effects of a word-of-mouth campaign for a chain store examined the characteristics of the most successful "agents" so that firms could better understand at whom they should target their buzz marketing efforts.[7] They found that agents who were not loyal customers of the store were more effective at generating sales through word of mouth than were loyal customers. The explanation offered for these somewhat counterintuitive findings is that loyal customers have already told their friends and acquaintances about a product and are already generating positive word of mouth. On the other hand, nonloyal customers may be more responsive to buzz marketing campaigns designed to encourage them to spread the word about a product. However, marketers still have to identify the best generators of buzz among both loyal and nonloyal customers—such as those who are considered opinion leaders by their peers and "social butterflies," who have a high propensity to meet new people and connect with friends.

Nonpersonal channels of communication are those that carry a message without interpersonal contact between sender and receiver. Nonpersonal channels are generally referred to as the **mass media** or mass communications, since the message is sent to many individuals at one time. For example, a TV commercial broadcast on a prime-time show may be seen by 1 million households in a given evening. Nonpersonal channels of communication consist of two major types, print and broadcast. Print media include newspapers, magazines, direct mail, and billboards; broadcast media include radio and television. The technical capabilities of the Internet allow innovative marketers to use it as a personal channel and a non-personal channel with both print and broadcast characteristics. IMC Perspective 4–2 highlights a new direction as well.

Receiver/Decoding

The **receiver** is the person(s) with whom the sender shares thoughts or information. Generally, receivers are the consumers in the target market or audience who read, hear, and/or see the marketer's message. The target audience may consist of individuals, groups, niche markets, market segments, or a general public or mass audience as discussed in the previous chapter.

Decoding is the process of transforming the sender's message back into thought. This process is heavily influenced by the receiver's frame of reference or **field of experience**, which refers to the experiences, perceptions, attitudes, and values he or she brings to the communication situation. For effective communication to occur, the message decoding process of the receiver must match the encoding of the sender. Simply put, this means the receiver understands and correctly interprets what the source is trying to communicate. As Figure 4–1 showed, the source and

IMC PERSPECTIVE 4–2

Channel Changes from Broadcast to Broadband

The wide acceptance of the Internet can be seen in its recent competition with TV for audience share. For Canada's broadcasters, the Internet began as a dumping ground of sorts—a place to show old and cancelled programs and video clips, and to advertise their main network offerings. That practice has all but disappeared in the quest for eyeballs and supplementary advertising. Canada's broadcasters now view their online sites as mini-networks—places to air original content, bonus material, and special events. CTV Television is perhaps farthest along toward the fully digital world; its seven-channel CTV Broadband Network currently offers a couple thousand hours of full-length programming, plus live streams from sources such as CTV Newsnet.

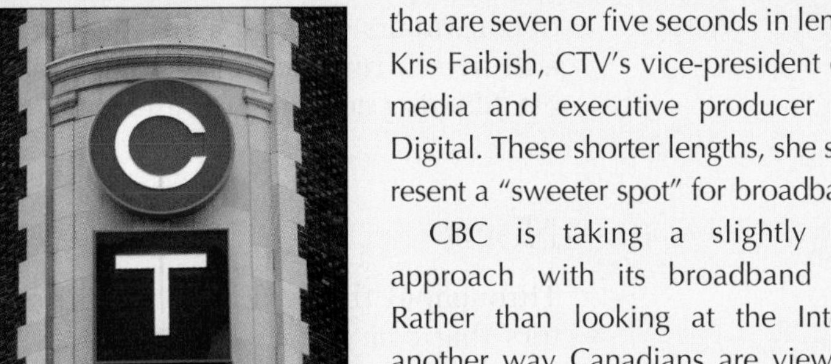

Although CTV is still figuring out what works online versus what works on the airwaves, the broadcaster believes many tenets of old-fashioned television apply to the digital world: good programming rules, and people want to be entertained. Big events such as the final game of the World Junior Hockey Championship in Sweden drew TV-type numbers for TSN.ca, with 118,000 unique viewers watching streaming video of the afternoon match.

CTV operates under the premise that broadband today caters to two very different audiences: a younger demographic, which views digital as its primary entertainment platform, and people who don't have access to TV during the day but have a broadband connection at work and might jump in to catch up on news and gossip or to view a cult show such as *Nip/Tuck*. The broadband model also affords advertisers the opportunity to experiment with different ad formats. CTV is encouraging agencies to urge clients to consider everything from 15-second commercials to spots that are seven or five seconds in length, says Kris Faibish, CTV's vice-president of digital media and executive producer of MTV Digital. These shorter lengths, she says, represent a "sweeter spot" for broadband ads.

CBC is taking a slightly different approach with its broadband offering. Rather than looking at the Internet as another way Canadians are viewing television, the public broadcaster considers it a way to air programming that can't be squeezed onto the main network. CBC's plans for the NHL hockey playoffs are a good example. Its new broadcast deal with the league actually comes into effect with the playoffs, spurring it to produce both pre- and post-game shows and consider providing streaming live-game telecasts free on CBCsports.ca.

Faibish compares the current state of broadband TV to the nascent days of the iPod. "We're in early adopter mode right now with kids who are naturally going to the net," she says. But as the technology, the encoding, and the resolution allow for simultaneous distribution on broadband and portable devices, these alternative channels will take off like the iPod. "People will consume entertainment when and where they want it. And when it hits the mass market that is when it really will get traction."

Source: Paul Brent, "From Broadcast to Broadband," *Marketing Magazine,* April 30, 2007.

Questions

1. Do you think a day will come when broadband replaces broadcast?
2. Why would someone watch a show on broadband that is available on both broadcast and broadband?

the receiver each have a frame of reference (the circle around each) that they bring to the communication situation. Effective communication is more likely when there is some *common ground* between the two parties. (This is represented by the overlapping of the two circles.) The more knowledge the sender has about the receivers, the better the sender can understand their needs, empathize with them, and communicate effectively. Advertisers spend millions of dollars every year to understand the frames of reference of the target audiences who receive their messages. They also spend much time and money pretesting messages to make sure consumers understand and decode them in the manner the advertiser intended.

While this notion of common ground between sender and receiver may sound basic, it often causes great difficulty in the advertising communications process. Marketing and advertising people often have very different fields of experience from the consumers who constitute the mass markets with whom they must communicate. Most advertising and marketing people are university-educated and work and/or reside in large urban areas such as Toronto or Montreal. Yet they are attempting to develop commercials that will effectively communicate with millions of consumers who have never attended university, work in blue-collar occupations, and live in rural areas or small towns. Another factor that can lead to problems in establishing common ground between senders and receivers is age.

Noise

Throughout the communication process, the message is subject to extraneous factors that can distort or interfere with its reception. This unplanned distortion or interference is known as **noise**. Errors or problems that occur in the encoding of the message, distortion in a radio or television signal, or distractions at the point of reception are examples of noise. Perhaps the foremost distraction is advertising clutter, whereby the receiver is confronted with many competing messages.

Noise may also occur because the fields of experience of the sender and receiver don't overlap. Lack of common ground may result in improper encoding of the message—using a sign, symbol, or words that are unfamiliar or have different meaning to the receiver. The more common ground there is between the sender and the receiver, the less likely it is this type of noise will occur.

Response/Feedback

The receiver's set of reactions after seeing, hearing, or reading the message is known as a **response**. Receivers' responses can range from nonobservable actions such as storing information in memory to immediate action such as dialing a toll-free number to order a product advertised on television. Marketers are very interested in **feedback**, that part of the receiver's response that is communicated back to the sender. Feedback, which may take a variety of forms, closes the loop in the communications flow and lets the sender monitor how the intended message is being decoded and received.

Because advertisers are not in direct contact with the customers, they must use other means to determine how their messages have been received. While the ultimate form of feedback occurs through sales, it is often hard to show a direct relationship between advertising and purchase behaviour. So marketers use other methods to obtain feedback, among them customer inquiries, store visits, coupon redemptions, visits to websites, and reply cards. Research-based feedback analyzes readership and recall of ads, message comprehension, attitude change, and other forms of response. With this information, the advertiser can determine reasons for success or failure in the communication process and make adjustments.

Successful communication is accomplished when the marketer selects an appropriate source, develops an effective message or appeal that is encoded properly, and then selects the channels or media that will best reach the target audience so that the message can be effectively decoded and delivered. Since these decisions must consider how the target audience will respond to the promotional message, the remainder of this chapter examines the process by which consumers respond to advertising and other forms of marketing communications.

The Response Process

Perhaps the most important aspect of developing effective communication programs involves understanding the *response process* the receiver may go through in moving toward a specific behaviour (like purchasing a product) and how the promotional efforts of the marketer influence consumer responses. To explain the response process we now review two types of response hierarchy models—traditional and alternative.

Traditional Response Hierarchy Models

A number of models have been developed to depict the stages a consumer may pass through in moving from a state of not being aware of a company, product, or brand to actual purchase behaviour. Figure 4–2 shows four of the best-known response hierarchy models. While these response models may appear similar, they were developed for different reasons.

The **AIDA model** was developed to represent the stages a salesperson must take a customer through in the personal selling process.[8] This model depicts the buyer as passing successively through attention, interest, desire, and action. The salesperson must first get the customer's attention and then arouse some interest in the company's product or service. Strong levels of interest should create desire to own or use the product. The action stage in the AIDA model involves getting the customer to make a purchase commitment and closing the sale. To the marketer, this is the most important stage in the selling process, but it can also be the most difficult. Companies train their sales reps in closing techniques to help them complete the selling process.

Perhaps the best known of these response hierarchies is the model developed by Robert Lavidge and Gary Steiner as a paradigm for setting and measuring advertising objectives.[9] Their **hierarchy of effects model** shows the process by which advertising works; it assumes a consumer passes through a series of steps in sequential order from initial awareness of a product or service to actual purchase. A basic premise of this model is that advertising effects occur over a period of time. Advertising communication may not lead to immediate behavioural response or purchase; rather, a series of effects must occur, with each step fulfilled before the consumer can move to

FIGURE 4–2 Models of the response process

Stages	Models: AIDA model	Hierarchy of effects model	Innovation adoption model	Information processing model
Cognitive stage	Attention	Awareness Knowledge	Awareness	Presentation Attention Comprehension
Affective stage	Interest Desire	Liking Preference Conviction	Interest Evaluation	Yielding Retention
Behavioural stage	Action	Purchase	Trial Adoption	Behaviour

the next stage in the hierarchy. As we will see in Chapter 5, the hierarchy of effects model has become the foundation for objective setting and measurement of advertising effects in many companies.

The **innovation adoption model** evolved from work on the diffusion of innovations.[10] This model represents the stages a consumer passes through in adopting a new product or service. Like the other models, it says potential adopters must be moved through a series of steps before taking some action (in this case, deciding to adopt a new product). The steps preceding adoption are awareness, interest, evaluation, and trial. The challenge facing companies introducing new products is to create awareness and interest among consumers and then get them to evaluate the product favourably. The best way to evaluate a new product is through actual use so that performance can be judged. Marketers often encourage trial by using demonstration or sampling programs or allowing consumers to use a product with minimal commitment (Exhibit 4–3). After trial, consumers either adopt the product or reject it.

The final hierarchy model shown in Figure 4–2 is the **information processing model** of advertising effects, developed by William McGuire.[11] This model assumes the receiver in a persuasive communication situation like advertising is an information processor or problem solver. McGuire suggests the series of steps a receiver goes through in being persuaded constitutes a response hierarchy. The stages of this model are similar to the hierarchy of effects sequence; attention and comprehension are similar to awareness and knowledge, and yielding is synonymous with liking. McGuire's model includes a stage not found in the other models: retention, or the receiver's ability to retain that portion of the comprehended information that he or she accepts as valid or relevant. This stage is important since most promotional campaigns are designed not to motivate consumers to take immediate action but rather to provide information they will use later when making a purchase decision.

Implications of the Traditional Hierarchy Models

The hierarchy models of communication response are useful to promotional planners from several perspectives. First, they delineate the series of steps potential purchasers must be taken through to move them from unawareness of a product or service to readiness to purchase it. Second, potential buyers may be at different stages in the hierarchy, so the advertiser will face different sets of communication problems. For example, a company introducing an innovative product like Zenith's high-definition television (HDTV) may need to devote considerable effort to making people aware of the product, how it works, and its benefits (Exhibit 4–4). Marketers of a mature brand that enjoys customer loyalty may need only supportive or reminder advertising to reinforce positive perceptions and maintain the awareness level for the brand.

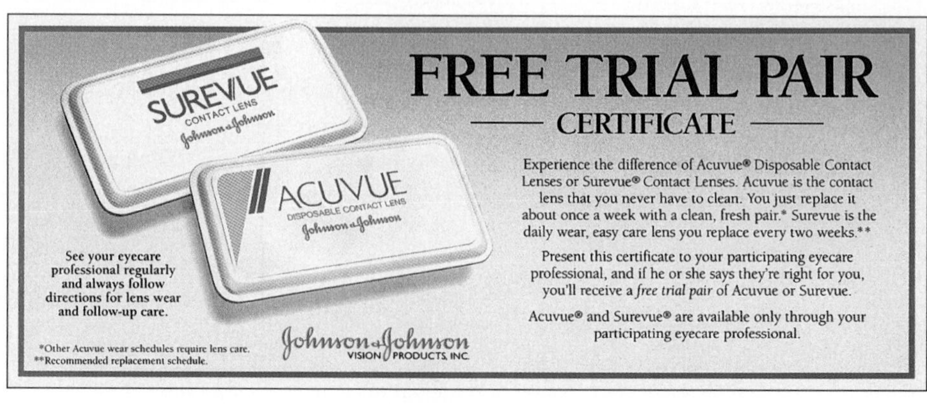

Exhibit 4–3
Sampling or demonstration programs encourage trial of new products such as disposable contact lenses

Exhibit 4–4 Advertising for innovative new products such as HDTV must make consumers aware of their features and benefits

Third, the hierarchy models can also be useful as intermediate measures of communication effectiveness that could guide future communication decisions. The marketer needs to know where audience members are on the response hierarchy. For example, research may reveal that one target segment has low awareness of the advertiser's brand, whereas another is aware of the brand and its various attributes but has a low level of liking or brand preference.

For the first segment of the market, the communication task involves increasing the awareness level for the brand. The number of ads may be increased, or a product sampling program may be used. For the second segment, where awareness is already high but liking and preference are low, the advertiser must determine the reason for the negative feelings and then attempt to address this problem in future advertising.

As shown in Figure 4–2, the four models presented all view the response process as consisting of movement through a sequence of three basic stages. The *cognitive stage* represents what the receiver knows or perceives about the particular product or brand. This stage includes awareness that the brand exists and knowledge, information, or comprehension about its attributes, characteristics, or benefits. The *affective stage* refers to the receiver's feelings or affect level (like or dislike) for the particular brand. This stage also includes stronger levels of affect such as desire, preference, or conviction. The *conative* or *behavioural stage* refers to the consumer's action toward the brand: trial, purchase, adoption, or rejection.

All four models assume a similar ordering of these three stages. Cognitive development precedes affective reactions, which precede behaviour. One might assume that consumers become aware of and knowledgeable about a brand, develop feelings toward it, form a desire or preference, and then make a purchase. While this logical progression is often accurate, the response sequence does not always operate this way. Over the past few decades, considerable research in marketing, social psychology, and communications has led to questioning of the traditional cognitive → affective → behavioural sequence of response. Several other configurations of the response hierarchy have been theorized.

Alternative Response Hierarchies

Michael Ray has developed a model of information processing that identifies three alternative orderings of the three stages based on perceived product differentiation and product involvement.[12] Figure 4–3 on page 104 identifies the alternative response hierarchies as the standard learning, dissonance/attribution, and low-involvement models.[13]

The Standard Learning Hierarchy In many purchase situations, the consumer will go through the response process in the sequence depicted by the traditional communication models. Ray terms this a **standard learning model**, which consists of a learn → feel → do sequence. Information and knowledge acquired or *learned*

FIGURE 4–3

Alternative response hierarchies

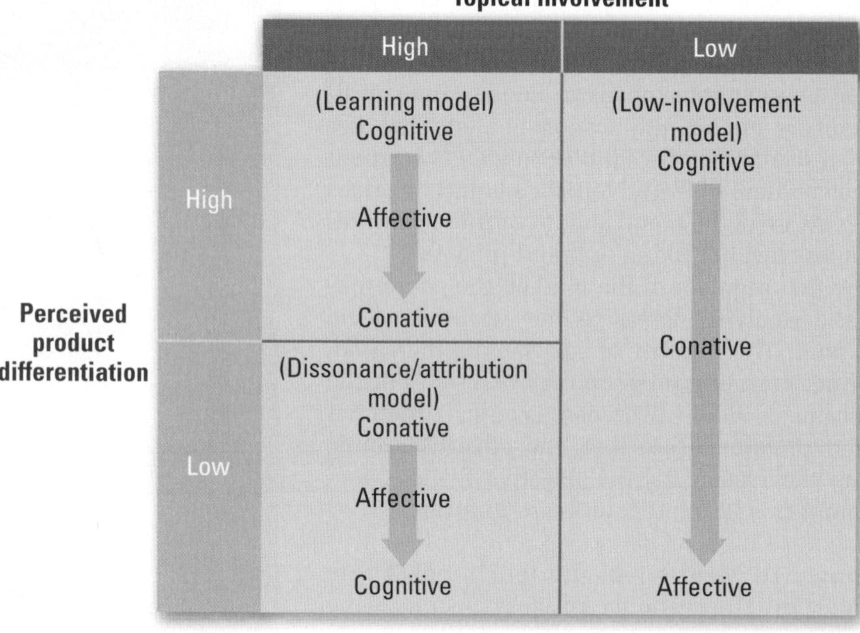

about the various brands are the basis for developing affect, or *feelings,* that guide what the consumer will do (e.g., actual trial or purchase). In this hierarchy, the consumer is viewed as an active participant in the communication process who gathers information through active learning.

Ray suggests the standard learning hierarchy is likely when the consumer is highly involved in the purchase process and there is much differentiation among competing brands. High-involvement purchase decisions such as those for industrial products and services and consumer durables like personal computers, printers, cameras, appliances, and cars are areas where a standard learning hierarchy response process is likely. Ads for products and services in these areas are usually very detailed and provide customers with information that can be used to evaluate brands and help them make a purchase decision (Exhibit 4–5).

Exhibit 4–5 Ads for high-involvement products provide consumers with information to help them evaluate brands

THINK LIKE YOU'VE NEVER THOUGHT.
FEEL LIKE YOU'VE NEVER FELT. DRIVE LIKE YOU'VE NEVER DRIVEN.

Introducing the all-new Subaru B9 Tribeca. A dynamic, progressive design that will change the way you think about SUVs. It's equipped with a powerful 250-hp, 6-cylinder Subaru boxer engine, Vehicle Dynamics Control and signature Symmetrical All-Wheel Drive standard. Providing stability, agility and control you just don't expect from an SUV. Feel the cockpit wrap around and connect you with a state-of-the-art available touch screen navigation system that intuitively guides you to places near or far. And while the available 9" widescreen DVD entertainment system can capture the attention of up to 7 passengers, the engaging drivability and real world versatility will capture yours. Simply put, you'll never think, feel, drive, the same way again. **subaru.com**

SUBARU B9 TRIBECA

Think. Feel. Drive.

SUBARU

The Dissonance/Attribution Hierarchy A second response hierarchy proposed by Ray involves situations where consumers first behave, then develop attitudes or feelings as a result of that behaviour, and then learn or process information that supports the behaviour. This **dissonance/attribution model**, or do → feel → learn, occurs in situations where consumers must choose between two alternatives that are similar in quality but are complex and may have hidden or unknown attributes. The consumer may purchase the product on the basis of a recommendation by some nonmedia source and then attempt to support the decision by developing a positive attitude toward the brand and perhaps even developing negative feelings toward the rejected alternative(s). This reduces any *postpurchase dissonance* or anxiety the consumer may experience resulting from doubt over the purchase (as discussed in Chapter 3). Dissonance reduction involves *selective learning*, whereby the consumer seeks information that supports the choice made and avoids information that would raise doubts about the decision.

According to this model, marketers need to recognize that in some situations, attitudes develop *after* purchase, as does learning from the mass media. Ray suggests that in these situations the main effect of the mass media is not the promotion of original choice behaviour and attitude change but rather the reduction of dissonance by reinforcing the wisdom of the purchase or providing supportive information. For example, the ad shown in Exhibit 4–6 reinforces consumers' decision to use a Visa credit card by reassuring them of the layers of security the company provides to its cardholders.

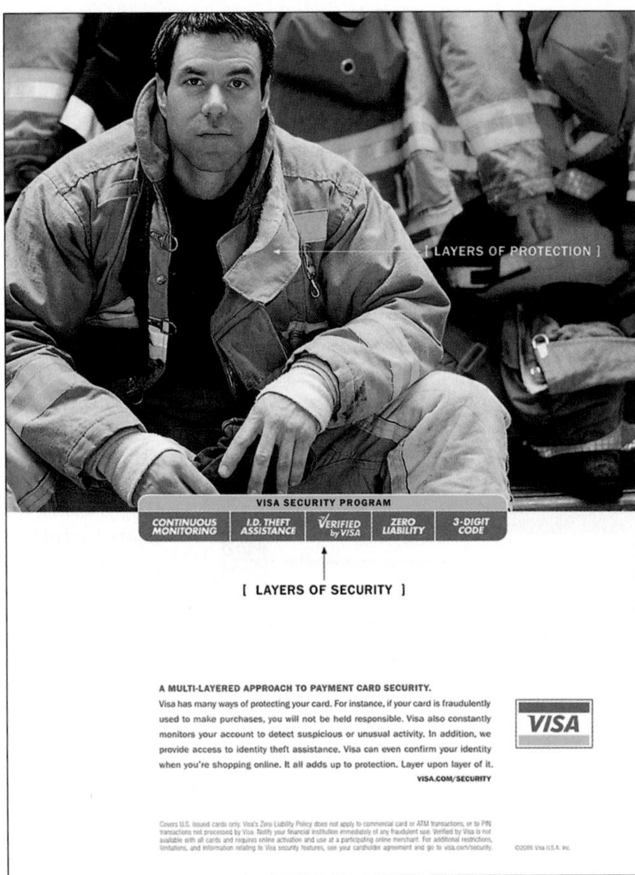

Exhibit 4–6 This ad reinforces the wisdom of the decision to use a Visa credit card

As with the standard learning model, this response hierarchy is likely to occur when the consumer is involved in the purchase situation; it is particularly relevant for postpurchase situations. For example, consumers are not worried about using their Visa credit card due to fraudulent use of the account numbers.

Some marketers resist this view of the response hierarchy because they can't accept the notion that the mass media have no effect on the consumer's initial purchase decision. But the model doesn't claim the mass media have no effect—just that their major impact occurs after the purchase has been made. Marketing communications planners must be aware of the need for advertising and promotion efforts, not just to encourage brand selection but also to reinforce choices and ensure that a purchase pattern will continue.

The Low-Involvement Hierarchy Perhaps the most intriguing of the three response hierarchies proposed by Ray is the **low-involvement hierarchy**, in which the receiver is viewed as passing from cognition to behaviour to attitude change. This learn → do → feel sequence is thought to characterize situations of low consumer involvement in the purchase process. Ray suggests this hierarchy tends to occur when involvement in the purchase decision is low, there are minimal differences among brand alternatives, and mass-media (especially broadcast) advertising is important.

The notion of a low-involvement hierarchy is based in large part on Herbert Krugman's theory explaining the effects of television advertising.[14] Krugman wanted to find out why TV advertising produced a strong effect on brand awareness and recall but little change in consumers' attitudes toward the product. He hypothesized that TV is basically a low-involvement medium and the viewer's perceptual defences are reduced or even absent during commercials. In a low-involvement situation, the consumer does not compare the message with previously acquired beliefs, needs, or past experiences. The commercial results in subtle changes in the consumer's knowledge structure, particularly with repeated exposure. This change in the consumer's knowledge does not result in attitude change but is related to learning something about the advertised brand, such as a brand name, ad theme, or slogan. According to Krugman, when the consumer enters a purchase situation, this information may be sufficient to

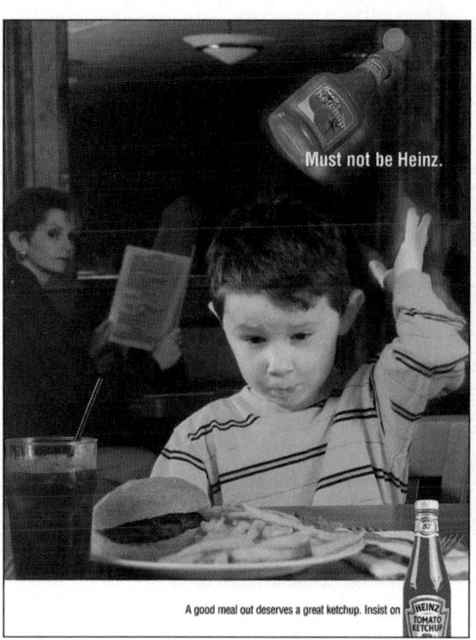

Must not be Heinz.
A good meal out deserves a great ketchup. Insist on
HEINZ TOMATO KETCHUP

Exhibit 4–7 Advertising promoting taste quality has helped Heinz dominate the ketchup market

trigger a purchase. The consumer will then form an attitude toward the purchased brand as a result of experience with it.

In the low-involvement hierarchy, the consumer engages in passive learning and random information catching rather than active information seeking. The advertiser must recognize that a passive, uninterested consumer may focus more on nonmessage elements such as music, characters, symbols, and slogans or jingles than actual message content. The advertiser might capitalize on this situation by developing a catchy jingle that is stored in the consumer's mind without any active cognitive processing and becomes salient when he or she enters the actual purchase situation.

Advertisers of low-involvement products also repeat simple product claims such as a key copy point or distinctive product benefit. A study by Scott Hawkins and Stephen Hoch found that under low-involvement conditions, repetition of simple product claims increased consumers' memory of and belief in those claims.[15] They concluded that advertisers of low-involvement products might find it more profitable to pursue a heavy repetition strategy than to reach larger audiences with lengthy, more detailed messages. For example, Heinz has dominated the ketchup market for over 20 years by repeatedly telling consumers that its brand is the thickest and richest. Heinz has used a variety of advertising campaigns over the years, but they all repeat the same basic theme and focus on the consistent quality of the brand (Exhibit 4–7).

Implications of the Alternative Response Models

Advertising and consumer researchers recognize that not all response sequences and behaviours are explained adequately by either the traditional or the alternative response hierarchies. Advertising is just one source of information consumers use in forming attitudes and/or making purchase decisions. Consumers are likely to integrate information from advertising, other sources, and direct experience in forming judgments about a brand. For example, in a recent study Robert Smith found that advertising can lessen the negative effects of an unfavourable trial experience on brand evaluations when the ad is processed before the trial. However, when a negative trial experience precedes exposure to an ad, cognitive evaluations of the ad are more negative.[16] More recent research has also shown that advertising can affect consumers' objective sensory interpretation of their experiences with a brand and what they remember about it.[17]

The response models offer an interesting perspective on the ways consumers respond to advertising and other forms of marketing communications. They also provide insight into promotional strategies marketers might pursue in different situations. A review of these alternative models of the response process shows that the traditional standard learning model does not always apply. The notion of a highly involved consumer who engages in active information processing and learning and acts on the basis of higher-order beliefs and a well-formed attitude may be inappropriate for some types of purchases. Sometimes consumers make a purchase decision on the basis of general awareness resulting from repetitive exposure to advertising, and attitude development occurs after the purchase, if at all. The role of advertising and other forms of promotion may be to induce trial, so consumers can develop brand preferences primarily on the basis of their direct experience with the product.

From a promotional planning perspective, it is important that marketers examine the communication situation for their product or service and determine which type of response process is most likely to occur. They should analyze involvement levels and product/service differentiation as well as consumers' use of various information

IMC PERSPECTIVE 4–3

Movie Theatres Seek New Features

Movie theatres are facing shrinking audiences due to the narrowing gap between a movie's premiere in theatres and its debut in video stores—from six months a few years ago, to about four months or less today. With the window getting smaller, people don't want to leave the house. For some viewers, especially adults, their kids who see the big blockbusters have essentially become focus groups that help the parents decide whether they should see a movie when it comes out on DVD. A quarter-century ago, Hollywood made most of its money from showing films in theatres. Now the largest revenues come from DVDs and pay TV.

Many people in the movie business believe that digital movies will bring audiences back to the theatre, since it offers a much better picture for the viewers—something consumers are becoming accustomed to in their homes. Print quality for film can vary drastically across frames and copies. The quality of projection may also vary; there are still theatres that run the projector lamp at less than proper brightness. Film has degradation problems, much like other media. The combination of a big screen and digital could be a key factor for movie fans. Finally, digital is significantly less expensive compared to current technology. The current method of shooting with film, copying, delivering to theatres, and projecting on the screen are very costly. It is estimated that digital would cut print and shipping costs about 80 percent.

Who, then, is against digital? Well, some studio chiefs worry that a movie on disc is much easier to duplicate; piracy is a huge drain on their income. But it's mainly theatre owners who are worried. When they hear the word digital, they reach for their digitals. Already feeling the hit from the 13 percent slump in movie-going over the past three years, they aren't eager to spend the more than $3 billion or so that it would cost to convert approximately 36,000 film projectors to digital. "Digital cinema is probably a lot further away than most people would think," says Kurt Hall, president and CEO of National CineMedia, the marketing arm of AMC, Cinemark, and Regal Entertainment Group. "There's still a lot of work to be done on the technology making it secure for the content owners."

On the positive side, Cineplex has been experimenting with new uses for theatres. Cineplex's success with high-definition, pay-per-view National Hockey League games, and the recently introduced direct-from-satellite performances of the New York Metropolitan Opera live from Lincoln Center, has convinced Cineplex to look into putting on more special events. Professional wrestling, World Cup soccer, speakers' series, and big-screen video-game competitions have already appeared at Cineplex theatres, along with pay-per-view concerts by David Bowie and Bon Jovi. Cineplex plans to talk to Broadway producers about getting some plays shown at its theatres.

Sources: Guy Dixon, "Cineplex Looks to Broadway after Opera Hit," *The Globe and Mail,* January 31, 2007; Richard Corliss, "Can This Man Save the Movies?" *Time,* March 20, 2006.

Questions

1. How can consumers be persuaded to visit movie theatres instead of watching the DVD version at home?
2. Can you think of programs other than the ones Cineplex has introduced that might be successful in movie theatres?

sources and their levels of experience with the product or service. Once the manager has determined which response sequence is most likely to operate, the integrated marketing communications program can be designed to influence the response process in favour of the company's product or service. IMC Perspective 4–3 conveys a very challenging communication task for changing consumer attitudes.

Cognitive Processing of Communications

The hierarchical response models were for many years the primary focus of approaches for studying the receiver's responses to marketing communications. Attention centred on identifying relationships between specific controllable variables (such as source and message factors) and outcome or response variables (such as attention, comprehension, attitudes, and purchase intentions). This approach has been criticized on a number of fronts, including its black-box nature, since it can't explain what is causing these reactions.[18] In response to these concerns, researchers began trying to understand the nature of cognitive reactions to persuasive messages. This section reviews two widely accepted approaches for understanding consumers' cognitive processing of advertising messages.

The Cognitive Response Approach

One of the most widely used methods for examining consumers' cognitive processing of advertising messages is assessment of their **cognitive responses**, the thoughts that occur to them while reading, viewing, and/or hearing a communication.[19] These thoughts are generally measured by having consumers write down or verbally report their reactions to a message. The assumption is that these thoughts reflect the recipient's cognitive processes or reactions and help shape ultimate acceptance or rejection of the message.

The cognitive response approach has been used in research by both academicians and advertising practitioners. Its focus has been to determine the types of responses evoked by an advertising message and how these responses relate to attitudes toward the ad, brand attitudes, and purchase intentions. Figure 4–4 depicts the three basic categories of cognitive responses researchers have identified—product/message, source-oriented, and ad execution thoughts—and how they may relate to attitudes and intentions.

Product/Message Thoughts The first category of thoughts comprises those directed at the product or service and/or the claims being made in the communication. Much attention has focused on two particular types of responses, counterarguments and support arguments.

Counterarguments are thoughts the recipient has that are opposed to the position taken in the message. For example, consider the ad for Ultra Tide shown in Exhibit 4–8. A consumer may express disbelief or disapproval of a claim made in an ad. ("I don't believe that any detergent could get that stain out!") Other consumers who see this ad may generate **support arguments**, or thoughts that affirm the claims made in the message. ("Ultra Tide looks like a really good product—I think I'll try it.")

FIGURE 4–4 A model of cognitive response

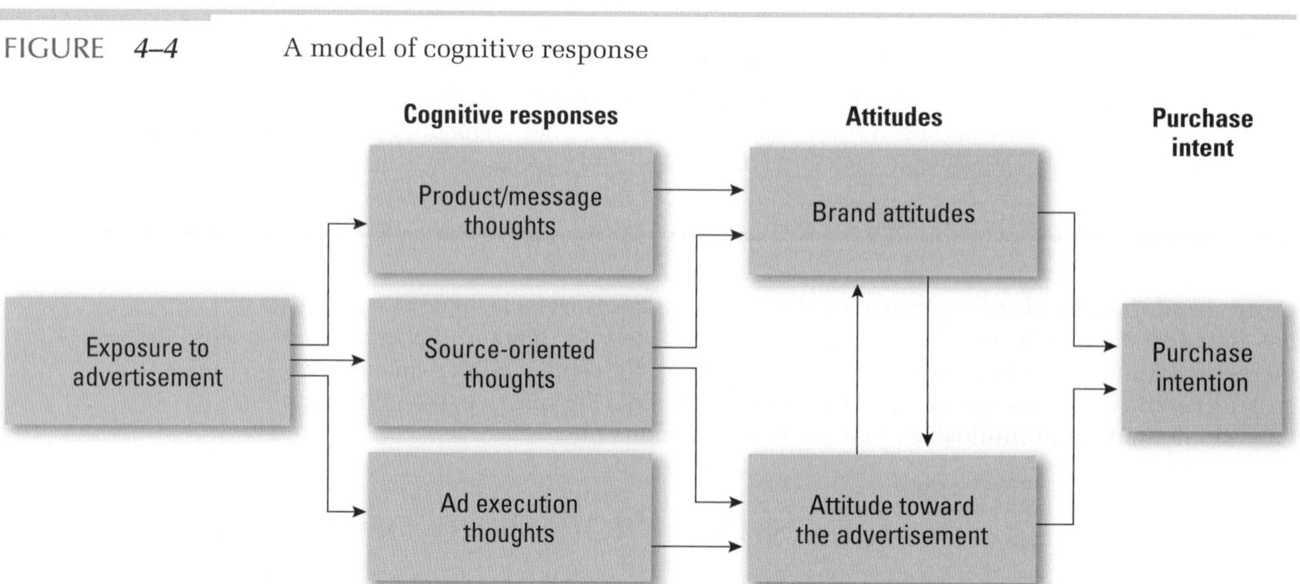

The likelihood of counterarguing is greater when the message makes claims that oppose the receiver's beliefs. For example, a consumer viewing a commercial that attacks a favourite brand is likely to engage in counterarguing. Counterarguments relate negatively to message acceptance; the more the receiver counterargues, the less likely he or she is to accept the position advocated in the message.[20] Support arguments, on the other hand, relate positively to message acceptance. Thus, the marketer should develop ads or other promotional messages that minimize counterarguing and encourage support arguments.

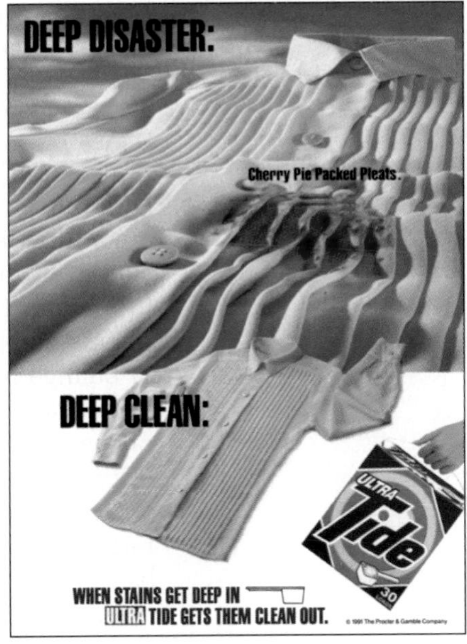

Exhibit 4–8 Consumers often generate support arguments in response to ads for quality products

Source-Oriented Thoughts A second category of cognitive responses is directed at the source of the communication. One of the most important types of responses in this category is **source derogations**, or negative thoughts about the spokesperson or organization making the claims. Such thoughts generally lead to a reduction in message acceptance. If consumers find a particular spokesperson annoying or untrustworthy, they are less likely to accept what this source has to say.

Of course, source-related thoughts are not always negative. Receivers who react favourably to the source generate favourable thoughts, or **source bolsters**. As you would expect, most advertisers attempt to hire spokespeople their target audience likes so as to carry this effect over to the message. Considerations involved in choosing an appropriate source or spokesperson will be discussed in Chapter 7. How might consumers react to the model in Exhibit 4–9?

Exhibit 4–9 The source in this ad could elicit both types of source thoughts

Ad Execution Thoughts The third category of cognitive responses shown in Figure 4–4 consists of the individual's thoughts about the ad itself. Many of the thoughts receivers have when reading or viewing an ad do not concern the product and/or message claims directly. Rather, they are affective reactions representing the consumer's feelings toward the ad. These thoughts may include reactions to ad execution factors such as the creativity of the ad, the quality of the visual effects, colours, and voice tones. **Ad execution-related thoughts** can be either favourable or unfavourable. They are important because of their effect on attitudes toward the advertisement as well as the brand.

In recent years, much attention has focused on consumers' affective reactions to ads, especially TV commercials.[21] **Attitude toward the ad** (A → ad) represents the receivers' feelings of favourability or unfavourability toward the ad. Advertisers are interested in consumers' reactions to the ad because they know that affective reactions are an important determinant of advertising effectiveness, since these reactions may be transferred to the brand itself or directly influence purchase intentions. One study found that people who enjoy a commercial are twice as likely as those who are neutral toward it to be convinced that the brand is the best.[22]

Consumers' feelings about the ad may be just as important as their attitudes toward the brand (if not more so) in determining an ad's effectiveness.[23] The importance of affective reactions and feelings generated by the ad depend on several factors, among them the nature of the ad and the type of processing engaged in by the receiver.[24] Many advertisers now use emotional ads designed to evoke feelings and affective reactions as the basis of their creative strategy. The success of this strategy depends in part on the consumers' involvement with the brand and their likelihood of attending to and processing the message. Global Perspective 4–4 shows how feelings were an important part of LG's international campaign.

The Elaboration Likelihood Model

Differences in the ways consumers process and respond to persuasive messages are addressed in the simplified **elaboration likelihood model (ELM)** of persuasion, shown in Figure 4–5.[25] The ELM was devised by Richard Petty and John Cacioppo to explain the process by which persuasive communications (such as ads) lead to persuasion by influencing *attitudes.* According to this model, the attitude formation or change process depends on the amount and nature of *elaboration*, or processing, of relevant information that occurs in response to a persuasive message. High elaboration means the receiver engages in careful consideration, thinking, and evaluation of the information or arguments contained in the message. Low elaboration occurs when the receiver does not engage in active information processing or thinking but rather makes inferences about the position being advocated in the message on the basis of simple positive or negative cues.

The ELM shows that elaboration likelihood is a function of two elements, motivation and ability to process the message. *Motivation* to process the message depends on such factors as involvement, personal relevance, and individuals' needs and arousal levels. *Ability* depends on the individual's knowledge, intellectual capacity, and opportunity to process the message.

Central Route Under the **central route to persuasion**, the receiver is viewed as a very active, involved participant in the communication process whose ability and motivation to attend, comprehend, and evaluate messages are high. When central processing of an advertising message occurs, the consumer pays close attention to message content and scrutinizes the message arguments. A high level of cognitive response activity or processing occurs, and the ad's ability to persuade the receiver

FIGURE 4–5

Simplified elaboration likelihood model of persuasion

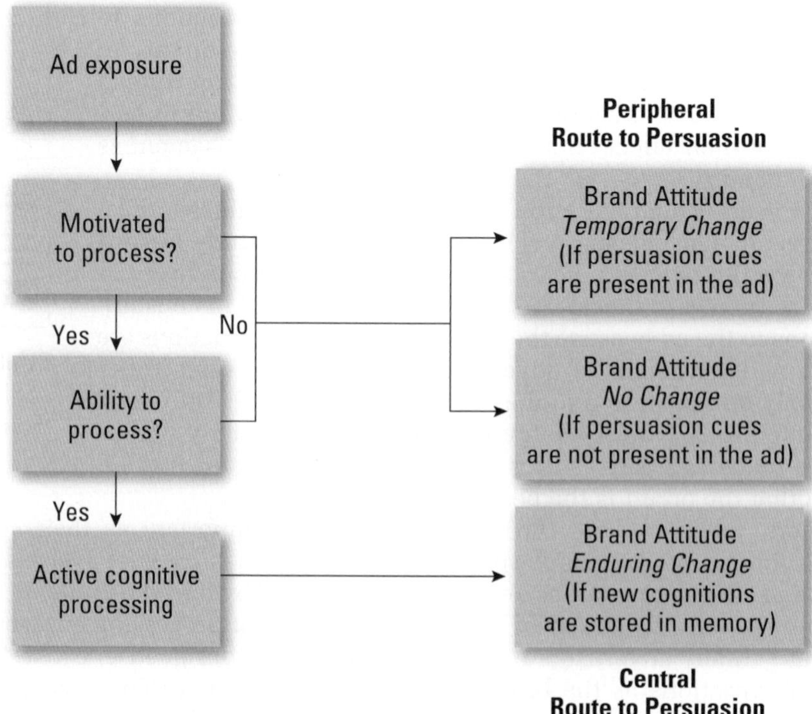

GLOBAL PERSPECTIVE 4–4

LG Connects with Consumers

MUSIC. VIDEO.
Easy As...Rockin' As...Smart as LG.
LG
Life's Good
www.LGUSA.com

For many years, the consumer electronics market was dominated by Japanese companies including Sony, Panasonic, Fujitsu, and Mitsubishi. However, these companies, as well as others such as Philips Electronics from the Netherlands and U.S.-based Motorola, find themselves up against two other formidable competitors from a country that is rapidly emerging as a major force in a variety of areas. That country is South Korea, the home of two of the fastest growing consumer electronic firms in the world—Samsung Electronics and LG Electronics. While Samsung is currently the better known of the two companies, LG is quickly gaining ground on its Korean counterpart and is taking steps to become a market leader.

The company began in 1958 as Goldstar and shortened its name to LG in 1995 to broaden its global appeal. LG is already the world's top manufacturer of household air conditioners, the number-three appliance manufacturer, and a global leader in such products as plasma display panels (PDP) and liquid crystal displays for TVs. Many consumers have probably already used an LG Electronics product, but the name on it was Dell, Apple, or IBM, as the company has made products for these other companies for many years. Now LG is aggressively pursuing market share under its own brand name as a manufacturer of stylish, cutting-edge, performance-driven products.

LG's promotional program connects with consumers on an emotional level beyond the functionality of its products. LG uses the same slogan that the company uses around the world, "Life's Good," which underscores the company's commitment to delivering products that enhance the human experience and help make life better. In 2004, LG initiated a major integrated marketing communications program designed to increase recognition of the company and to position the company as a digital convergence leader.

In mid-2005, LG launched an integrated marketing campaign designed to differentiate its phones from those of its competitors, to educate consumers in the various ways in which its phones fit into their lives, and to provide cross-promotional opportunities with LG wireless carriers and retail partners. The campaign is based on the theme "six degrees" and illustrates the many ways in which LG phones ensure that consumers are constantly in touch with their worlds. The creative marketing features images of trendy, fashionable young adults using LG phones in both traditional and innovative ways such as listening to music, text messaging, and accessing the Internet, all of which illustrate how LG mobile phones can fit into the lives of consumers, keeping them connected, entertained, and informed.

The "six degrees" integrated campaign also included a Concierge program that provided celebrity influencers with special fittings by experts with the latest LG products as well as customized point-of-sale displays accentuating the advertising theme. The online elements included a Web-based community for LG customers to share tips and reviews of LG products and to enter online promotions and contests as well as online games incorporating LG products and themes.

LG's chief executive, Kim Ssang Su, has noted that the company is no longer content with being a second-tier player and wants to be a global market leader. Success in cellular handsets is an important part of the company's strategy as LG managers believe that once consumers have an LG phone in their hands, they're more likely to consider the brand when they are purchasing a TV, refrigerator, or DVD player. While LG is likely to face stiff competition from competitors who defend their market share, it appears that its rivals now have another fast-moving Korean company to contend with. And one that understands the importance of connecting with consumers.

Sources: "LG Electronics MobileCom Launches Integrated Marketing and Advertising Campaign," press release, www.biz.yahoo.com, May 31, 2005; Moon Ihlwan, "Korea's LG May Be the Next Samsung," *BusinessWeek*, January 24, 2005, pp. 51–52; Beth Snyder Bulik, "LG's $100 Mil Charge Apes Samsung Tack," *Advertising Age*, June 21, 2004, pp. 1, 33.

Question

1. Why is the "six degrees" campaign a good idea?

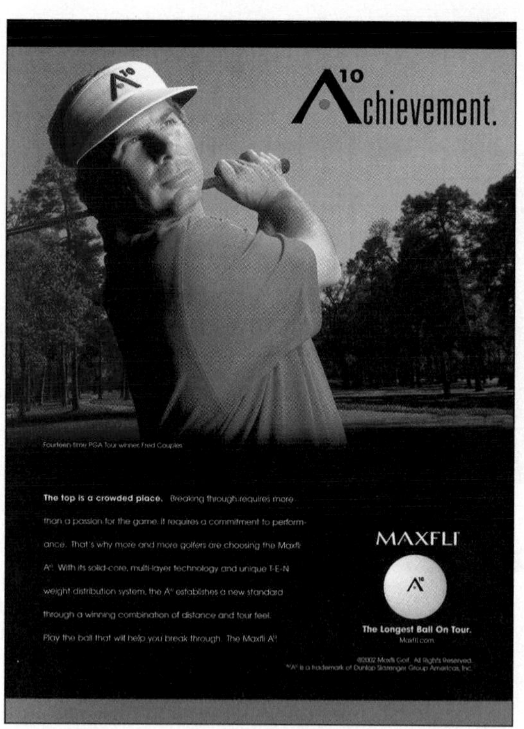

Exhibit 4–10 This ad contains peripheral cues, most notably a celebrity endorser

depends primarily on the receiver's evaluation of the quality of the arguments presented. Predominantly favourable cognitive responses (support arguments and source bolsters) lead to favourable changes in cognitive structure, which lead to positive attitude change, or persuasion.

Conversely, if the cognitive processing is predominantly unfavourable and results in counterarguments and/or source derogations, the changes in cognitive structure are unfavourable and *boomerang*, or result in negative attitude change. Attitude change that occurs through central processing is relatively enduring and should resist subsequent efforts to change it.

Peripheral Route Under the **peripheral route to persuasion**, the receiver is viewed as lacking the motivation or ability to process information and is not likely to engage in detailed cognitive processing. Rather than evaluating the information presented in the message, the receiver relies on peripheral cues that may be incidental to the main arguments. The receiver's reaction to the message depends on how he or she evaluates these peripheral cues.

The consumer may use several types of peripheral cues or cognitive shortcuts rather than carefully evaluating the message arguments presented in an advertisement.[26] Favourable attitudes may be formed if the endorser in the ad is viewed as an expert or is attractive and/or likable or if the consumer likes certain executional aspects of the ad such as the way it is made, the music, or the imagery. Notice how the ad in Exhibit 4–10 contains several positive peripheral cues, including a popular celebrity endorser (pro golfer Fred Couples) and excellent visual imagery. These cues might help consumers form a positive attitude toward the brand even if they do not process the message portion of the ad.

Peripheral cues can also lead to rejection of a message. For example, ads that advocate extreme positions, use endorsers who are not well liked or have credibility problems, or are not executed well (such as low-budget ads for local retailers) may be rejected without any consideration of their information or message arguments. As shown in Figure 4–5, the ELM views attitudes resulting from peripheral processing as temporary. So favourable attitudes must be maintained by continual exposure to the peripheral cues, such as through repetitive advertising.

Explanation for ELM One reason for explaining how the peripheral route to persuasion works lies in the idea of **classical conditioning**. Classical conditioning assumes that learning is an *associative process* with an already existing relationship between a stimulus and a response. This process is transferred to a **conditioned stimulus** that elicits a **conditioned response** resembling the original unconditioned reaction. Two factors are important for learning to occur through the associative process. The first is contiguity, which means the unconditioned stimulus and conditioned stimulus must be close in time and space. The other important principle is *repetition,* or the frequency of the association. The more often the unconditioned and conditioned stimuli occur together, the stronger the association between them will be.

Buyers can be conditioned to form favourable impressions and images of various brands through the associative process. Advertisers strive to associate their products and services with perceptions, images, and emotions known to evoke positive reactions from consumers. Many products are promoted through image advertising, in which the brand is shown with an unconditioned stimulus that elicits pleasant feelings. When the brand is presented simultaneously with this unconditioned stimulus, the brand itself becomes a conditioned stimulus that elicits the same favourable

Exhibit 4–11 Lancome associates itself with moisture

response. The ad for Lancome in Exhibit 4–11 shows an application of this strategy. Notice how this ad associates Lancome's moisture with the freshness of a rose.

Classical conditioning can also associate a product with a favourable emotional state. A study by Gerald Gorn used this approach to examine how background music in ads influences product choice.[27] He found that subjects were more likely to choose a product when it was presented against a background of music they liked rather than music they disliked. These results suggest the emotions generated by a commercial are important because they may become associated with the advertised product through classical conditioning. Kellaris and colleagues also showed that music that was congruent with the message enhanced both ad recall and recognition.[28] Advertisers often attempt to pair a neutral product stimulus with an event or situation that arouses positive feelings, such as humour.

Implications of the ELM The elaboration likelihood model has important implications for marketing communications, particularly with respect to involvement. For example, if the involvement level of consumers in the target audience is high, an ad or sales presentation should contain strong arguments that are difficult for the message recipient to refute or counterargue. If the involvement level of the target audience is low, peripheral cues may be more important than detailed message arguments.

An interesting test of the ELM showed that the effectiveness of a celebrity endorser in an ad depends on the receiver's involvement level.[29] When involvement was low, a celebrity endorser had a significant effect on attitudes. When the receiver's involvement was high, however, the use of a celebrity had no effect on brand attitudes; the quality of the arguments used in the ad was more important.

The explanation given for these findings was that a celebrity may serve as a peripheral cue in the low-involvement situation, allowing the receiver to develop favourable attitudes based on feelings toward the source rather than engaging in extensive processing of the message. A highly involved consumer, however, engages in more detailed central processing of the message content. The quality of the message claims becomes more important than the identity of the endorser.

The ELM suggests that the most effective type of message depends on the route to persuasion the consumer follows. Many marketers recognize that involvement levels are low for their product categories and consumers are not motivated to process advertising messages in any detail. That's why marketers of low-involvement products often rely on creative tactics that emphasize peripheral cues and use repetitive advertising to create and maintain favourable attitudes toward their brand.

IMC Planning: Response Model for Decision Making

In this final section we attempt to reconcile the models presented in this chapter by summarizing the theoretical debate and by presenting the most relevant response model for decision making. The first section concludes that traditional communication response models based on a hierarchy or adaptation of a hierarchy are somewhat limited in their ability to explain how advertising works. The subsequent section summarizes another part of the Rossiter and Percy perspective that is managerially oriented and will be used to set communication objectives and plan for creative messages in subsequent chapters.

Theoretical Debate

Vakratsas and Ambler recently reviewed more than 250 journal articles and books in an effort to better understand how advertising works and affects the consumer.[30] On the basis of their review of these studies, they concluded that although effects hierarchies have been actively employed for nearly 100 years, there is little support for the concept of a hierarchy of effects in the sense of temporal sequence. They note that in trying to understand the response process and the manner in which advertising works, there are three critical intermediate effects between advertising and purchase (Figure 4–6). These include *cognition*, the "thinking" dimension of a person's response; *affect*, the "feeling" dimension; and *experience*, which is a feedback dimension based on the outcomes of product purchasing and usage.

The authors conclude that individual responses to advertising are mediated or filtered by factors such as motivation and ability to process information, which can radically alter or change the individual's response to advertising. They suggest that the effects of advertising should be evaluated using these three dimensions, with some intermediate variables being more important than others depending on factors such as the product category, stage of the product life cycle, target audience, competition, and impact of other marketing-mix components.

Other researchers have been critical of the hierarchy models as well. For example, Hall argues that advertisers need to move away from explicit and implicit reliance

FIGURE 4–6

A framework for studying how advertising works

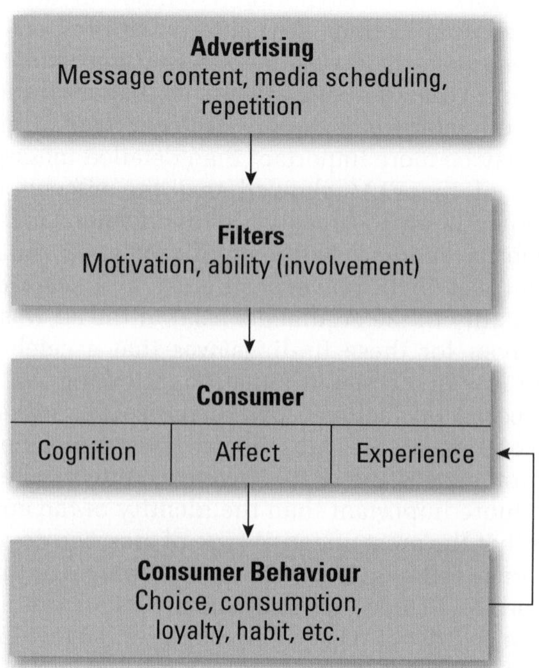

on hierarchical models of advertising effects and develop models that place affect and experience at the centre of the advertising process.[31] The implication of these criticisms is that marketers should focus on cognition, affect, and experience as critical variables that advertising may influence. However, they should not assume a particular sequence of responses but, rather, engage in research and analysis to better understand how advertising and other forms of promotion may affect these intermediate variables in various product/market situations.

William Weilbacher has noted that marketing communications programs include more than just advertising.[32] Consumers are continually immersed in brand-sponsored communications that include public relations, a broad range of sales promotion activities, websites, direct marketing, event sponsorships, movie and TV show product placements, and other forms of marketing communication. He argues that hierarchy models must move beyond just explaining the effects of advertising and consider how, and with what effects, consumers synthesize information from all the various integrated marketing communications activities for a brand.

While a number of issues and concerns regarding hierarchy of effects models have been noted, many believe that they are of value to advertising practice and research. For example, Thomas Barry contends that despite their limitations, hierarchical models do help predict behaviour. He notes that these models also provide insight into whether advertising strategies need to focus on impacting cognition, affect, and/or behaviour based on audience or segmentation experiences and that they provide valuable planning, training, and conceptual frameworks.[33]

Based on this theoretical debate regarding the exactness of how advertising works, we suggest a few conclusions that are relevant for managers in making advertising and promotion decisions. After all, academics will continue this investigation while managers still need to make decisions.

First, it appears that managers should consider and plan for both the cognitive and the affective responses of the receiver when the latter is processing advertising or any promotional message. Receivers typically have both cognitive and emotional reactions to the messages they see all around them every day.

Second, managers are undoubtedly concerned with the resulting effects of the advertising or promotional message for a time period after the receiver has received and processed the message. As suggested in many of the models, managers want to know if their messages are improving awareness or attitudes.

Finally, the primary characteristic that influences communication success appears to be the receiver's previous brand experience. This implies managers should be cognizant of to whom exactly they are directing their message. As discussed in Chapter 3, the manager needs a detailed profile of the target audience to have some understanding to gauge communication success. Thus, managers require a decision framework that addresses these points, which is the topic of the next section.

Managerial Approach

We introduced the Rossiter and Percy (R&P) perspective in Chapter 3 when identifying options for the target audience decision. This perspective suggests promotional planners initially consider the message as being directed to either customers purchasing their brand or non-customers who have not purchased their brand. This managerial view starts with the consumer and is based on the consumer's previous brand experience and degree of brand loyalty, two critical factors that influence how motivated or involved the audience would be when responding to promotional messages.

A continuation of the R&P perspective is a communication response model that takes a managerial view by identifying the responses in terms of the promotional manager's brand for any type of marketing communication decision. Figure 4–7 on page 116 shows the initial processing stage that highlights the immediate responses to any advertising message while receiving the ad exposure. This implies the

FIGURE 4–7

Planning for processing and communication effects

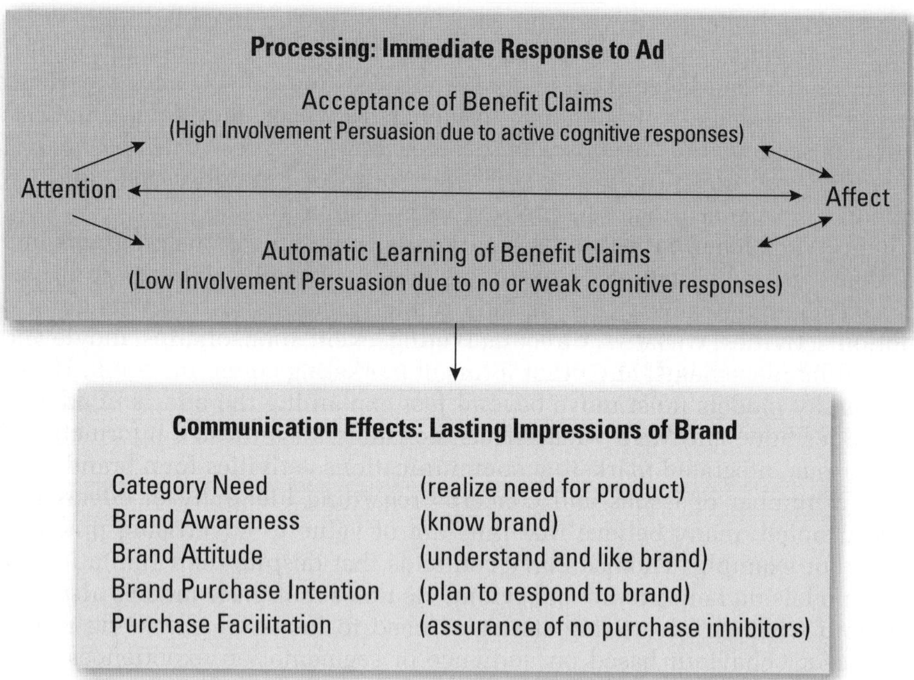

psychological experiences that occur in the target audience's mind while watching a television commercial, for example. Communication effects refer to the lasting brand impressions that remain with the target audience after the target audience processes the message. This implies the target audience's memory of the brand that results after watching the television commercial. We now explore the planning implication of this perspective.

Processing of Messages After attending to the ad, the target audience may have low or high involvement in terms of how much thought regarding the brand's benefit claims is generated while receiving the message. In addition, affect, or emotional responses, will influence and be generated as a result of these cognitive responses. This notion of processing is consistent with the previous models discussed.

From an IMC planning perspective, managers need to design brand messages with the understanding of the target audience. For instance, to attract new customers, the manager may consider brand messages that will support high-involvement processing. And, as we will see in the media chapters and the chapters relating to other communication tools, the manager may consider more involving avenues for delivering the message.

Alternatively, companies often have programs to both attract and retain customers. This could require promotional planners to strategically evaluate the balance of their messages. Should messages that attempt to generate high involvement be primary or secondary in the overall message strategy? Analytical questions such as this emerge by considering the processing stage as a key precursor to planning for the communication effects stage.

Communication Effects of Messages Figure 4–7 also distinguishes the brand communication effects that are established more permanently in the target audience's memory. Overall, R&P summarize five **communication effects** for the target audience.

- *Category need:* Target audience's perception of requiring a product to satisfy a need.
- *Brand awareness:* Target audience's ability to recognize and/or recall the brand within the category in sufficient detail to make a purchase.
- *Brand attitude:* Target audience's overall evaluation of the brand in relation to its ability to satisfy the reason they want it.
- *Brand purchase intention:* Target audience's self-instruction to respond (purchase; purchase-related action) to the brand.
- *Purchase facilitation:* Target audience's perception that a marketing factor could affect their purchase or use of the brand.

Three important planning implications are realized with the R&P model. First, there is an obvious and clear connection to the target audience's purchase of the promotional manager's particular brand. This is apparent with its reference to the brand in three communication effects. It is also seen in the connection to category need, which addresses the underlying reason why the target audience is motivated to buy the promotional manager's brand, and where the target audience understands the brand fits in the market in relation to other brands. Moreover, it is observed with the link to purchase facilitation, which highlights the importance of communicating information to make sure the promotional manager's brand is purchased by the target audience.

Second, the R&P model uses brand attitude as a central communication effect. Note that the other models viewed the entire process (i.e., cognition, affect, behaviour) as reflecting an attitude, and that some models argued consumers experienced various steps in various orders depending upon the purchase situation. The target audience's brand attitude evaluation includes both cognitive and affective components, acknowledging that each aspect is relevant for planning for all purchase situations.

Third, the R&P model can be applied for all aspects of an IMC program. It can guide individual television ads, as previously suggested, and it can be used for any ad in any media environment. For example, promotional planners can consider this model for print ads or video-type ads placed on the Internet. Moreover, the model can be used for planning any IMC tool. In another direction, the communication effects can be used to assess the target audience's reaction to an overall advertising campaign consisting of many different types of media. An entire and comprehensive IMC program can be planned using these target audience responses. And finally, planners can use the same effects whether planning for one or multiple target audiences.

The R&P model and some of the other communication response models will be revisited in the next chapter. Promotional planners use a communication response model to determine the communication objectives for advertising and other promotional tools. It is important to base marketing communication decisions on a model and translate them into specific objectives since promotional planners need clear guidance for the remaining marketing communication decisions.

SUMMARY

The function of all elements of the promotional mix is to communicate, so promotional planners must understand the communication process. This process can be very complex; successful marketing communications depend on a number of factors, including the nature of the message, the audience's interpretation of it, and the environment in which it is received. For effective communication to occur, the sender must encode a message in such a way that it will be decoded by the receiver in the intended manner. Feedback from the receiver helps the sender determine whether proper decoding has occurred or whether noise has interfered with the communication process.

Promotional planning begins with the receiver or target audience, as marketers must understand how the audience is likely to respond to various sources of communication or types of messages. Traditional response models provide an initial understanding of this process. Different orderings of the traditional response hierarchy include the standard learning, dissonance/attribution, and low-involvement models.

The cognitive response approach examines the thoughts evoked by a message and how they shape the receiver's ultimate acceptance or rejection of the communication. The elaboration likelihood model of attitude formation and change recognizes two forms of message processing, the central and peripheral routes to persuasion, which are a function of the receiver's motivation and ability to process a message.

Theoretical research concludes that there are three critical intermediate effects between advertising and purchase including cognition, affect, and experience. Those responsible for planning the IMC program should learn as much as possible about their target audience and how it may respond to advertising and other forms of marketing communications. A managerial view of the response process provides direction for understanding how promotional planners should determine their brands' communication strategies.

KEY TERMS

ad execution-related thoughts, *109*
AIDA model, *101*
attitude toward the ad, *109*
central route to persuasion, *110*
channel, *98*
classical conditioning, *112*
cognitive responses, *108*
communication, *94*
communication effects, *117*
conditioned response, *112*
conditioned stimulus, *112*
counterarguments, *108*
decoding, *98*
dissonance/attribution model, *104*
elaboration likelihood model (ELM), *110*
encoding, *95*
feedback, *100*
field of experience, *98*
hierarchy of effects model, *101*
information processing model, *102*
innovation adoption model, *102*
low-involvement hierarchy, *105*
mass media, *98*
message, *96*
noise, *100*
peripheral route to persuasion, *112*
receiver, *98*
response, *100*
semiotics, *96*
source, *94*
source bolsters, *109*
source derogations, *109*
standard learning model, *103*
support arguments, *108*

DISCUSSION QUESTIONS

1. Discuss the various elements of the communications process. Find an example of an advertising campaign being used by a company and analyze this campaign in terms of these elements of the communications model.

2. Discuss how semiotics can be of value to the field of integrated marketing communications. Select a marketing stimulus such as an advertisement, package, or other relevant marketing symbol and conduct a semiotic analysis of it such as the one shown in Exhibit 4–2.

3. Explain why the four response models of Figure 4–2 are limited in planning for an IMC campaign.

4. How do the response models in Chapter 4 relate to the consumer decision-making process described in Chapter 3?

5. What are the key differences between traditional response models and alternative response hierarchies?

6. Assume that you are the marketing communications manager for a brand of paper towels. Discuss how the low-involvement hierarchy could be of value in developing an advertising and promotion strategy for this brand.

7. Find an example of a print ad and evaluate it using the cognitive response model shown in Figure 4–4. Identify the specific types of cognitive responses that the ad might elicit from consumers and discuss why they might occur.

8. Explain what is meant by a central versus peripheral route to persuasion and the factors that would determine when each might be used by consumers in response to an advertisement.

9. Select an ad you think would be processed by a central route to persuasion and one where you think peripheral processing would occur. Show the ads to several people and ask them to write down the thoughts they have about each ad. Analyze their thoughts using the cognitive response categories discussed in the chapter.

10. Why do cognition and affect components for both processing and communication effects exist in the R&P model?

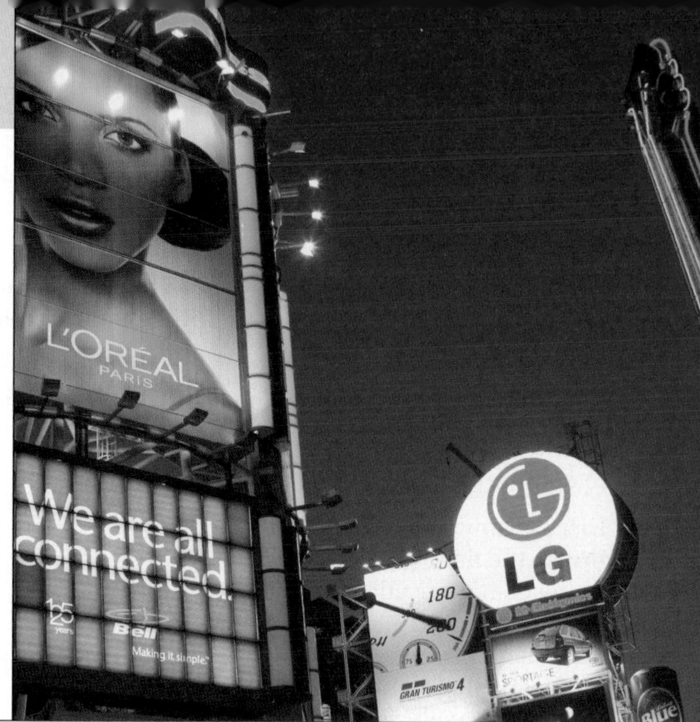

CHAPTER 5

OBJECTIVES FOR THE IMC PLAN

Chapter Objectives

- To recognize the value of setting specific objectives for advertising and promotion.
- To know the differences between marketing and communication objectives and the issues regarding the use of each.
- To know the historical approaches for setting communication objectives for advertising.
- To understand a comprehensive framework for setting communication and behavioural objectives for all aspects of the IMC plan.

Lenovo's Evolving Objectives

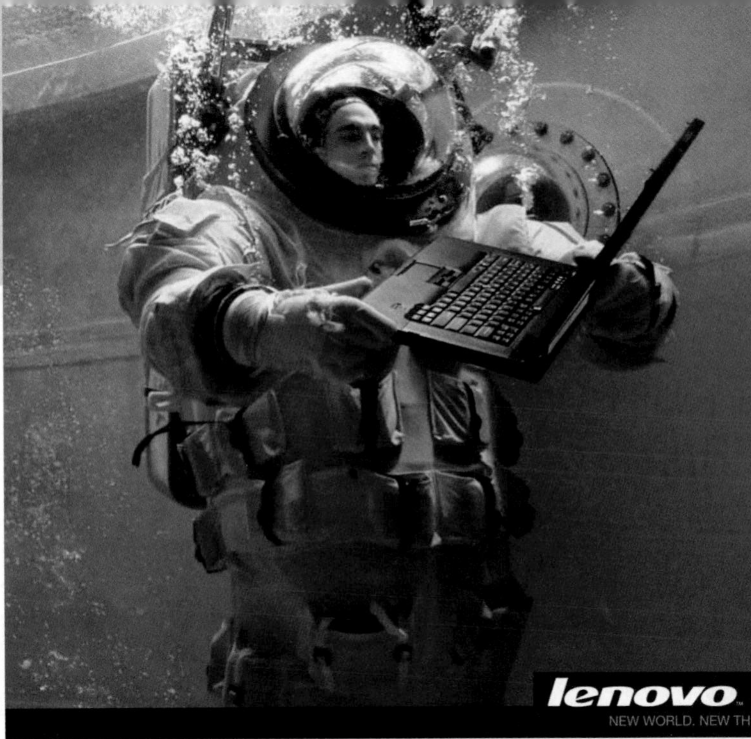

In 2005, Lenovo acquired the rights for IBM's Personal Computer Division, bringing along the successful ThinkPad. As one of the leading PC manufacturers in China with one-third of the consumer market, Lenovo faced the challenging task of building a new brand for itself in Canada while retaining the equity in the IBM ThinkPad name.

Lenovo observed enormous potential in the Canadian computer market. ThinkPad had 12 percent of the total notebook PC market, and 19 percent of the commercial segment. Although HP-Compaq held 55 percent of the retail desktop market, Lenovo noticed an opportunity to become a strong second to other small-share brands. Coupled with strong growth in all facets of the computer market, Lenovo looked forward to the new communication task.

Specifically, the managers went from communicating a brand with significant recognition and a reputation for technology and innovation to an unknown brand. With a formidable communication problem, Lenovo planned three phases, each with its own objectives.

In the first phase, Lenovo ensured continuity and trust with its current customers. It emphasized that it was the same organization that had designed, manufactured, and sold the original ThinkPad. Its communication featured the ThinkPad brand, ThinkCenter messaging system, and the ThinkPad logo. The second part of this initial phase independently built the Lenovo brand by linking it to innovation, service excellence, and high quality.

The second phase occurred in the fall of 2005. Lenovo's objective this time addressed linking ThinkPad with Lenovo as it introduced product innovations. Lenovo's message highlighted the commitment to ThinkPad innovation and quality with the new models. The company slowly introduced the Lenovo name with ThinkPad. By the end of the year, the Lenovo name became more prominent.

February 2006 marked the start of the third phase. During the Winter Olympics, Lenovo launched a new product line aimed at small business in need of affordable computing resources. Initially, Lenovo communicated to resellers to ensure this audience understood the positioning of the brand. In April, Lenovo started ads directed toward the consumer market. At this time, Lenovo continued to communicate its improvements in the ThinkPad line to signal its commitment to the newly acquired brand. Lenovo highlighted the common message of innovation, quality, and customer service for both product lines while simultaneously emphasizing the unique characteristics of both.

Sources: Chris Daniels, "Becoming Big Blue," *Marketing Magazine*, June 20, 2005; "Lenovo Makes Global Push for Its Computer Brand," *Marketing Magazine*, February 24, 2006; Janice Dawes, "The Rise of Lenovo," *Marketing Magazine*, September 11, 2006.

Questions

1. Identify the communication objectives Lenovo established.
2. Do you agree with these objectives and the three phases used to establish them?

Many companies have difficulty with the most critical step in the promotional planning process—setting realistic objectives that will guide the development of the IMC program. Complex marketing situations, conflicting perspectives regarding what advertising and other promotional mix elements are expected to accomplish, and uncertainty over resources make the setting of marketing communication objectives "a job of creating order out of chaos."[1] While the task of setting objectives can be complex and difficult, it must be done properly, because specific goals and objectives are the foundation on which all other promotional decisions are made. Budgeting for advertising and other promotional areas, as well as creative and media strategies and tactics, evolves from these objectives. They also provide a standard against which performance can be measured.

This chapter examines the nature and purpose of objectives and the role they play in guiding the development, implementation, and evaluation of an IMC program. First, we examine the distinction between marketing and communication objectives. Then we consider the approaches of setting communication objectives for communication based on the response models previously discussed in Chapter 4. We then present a comprehensive approach for setting communication and behavioural objectives for each element of the IMC plan and for the overall IMC plan that will be consistently referred to in Parts 2, 3, and 4 of the book.

Objective Setting

Setting specific objectives should be an integral part of the planning process. However, many companies either fail to use specific marketing communication objectives or set ones that are inadequate for guiding the development of the promotional plan or measuring its effectiveness. This section discusses the value of objectives and distinguishes between marketing and communication objectives.

Value of Objectives

Perhaps one reason why many companies fail to set specific objectives for their integrated marketing communications programs is that they don't recognize the value of doing so.Advertising and promotional objectives are needed for several reasons, including the functions they serve in communications, planning and decision-making, and measurement and evaluation.

Communications Specific objectives for the IMC program facilitate coordination of the various groups working on the campaign. Many people are involved in the planning and development of an integrated marketing communications program on the client side as well as in the various promotional agencies. The advertising and promotional program must be coordinated within the company, inside the ad agency, and between the two. Any other parties involved in the promotional campaign, such as public relations and/or sales promotion firms, research specialists, or media buying services, must also know what the company hopes to accomplish through its marketing communications program. Many problems can be avoided if all parties have written approved objectives to guide their actions and serve as a common base for discussing issues related to the promotional program. For example, the ad and Ford's involvement with the cause shown in Exhibit 5–1 was dependent upon all participants understanding Ford's objectives.

Planning and Decision Making Specific promotional objectives also guide development of the integrated marketing communications plan. All phases of a firm's promotional strategy should be based on the established objectives, including budgeting, creative, and media decisions as well as supportive programs such as direct marketing, public relations/publicity, sales promotion, and/or reseller support.

Meaningful objectives can also be a useful guide for decision making. Promotional planners are often faced with a number of strategic and tactical options in terms of choosing creative options, selecting media, and allocating the budget among various elements of the promotional mix. Choices should be made based on how well a particular strategy matches the firm's promotional objectives.

Measurement and Evaluation of Results An important reason for setting specific objectives is that they provide a benchmark against which the success or failure of the promotional campaign can be measured. Without specific objectives, it is extremely difficult to determine what the firm's advertising and promotion efforts accomplished. One characteristic of good objectives is that they are measurable; they specify a method and criteria for determining how well the promotional program is working. By setting specific and meaningful objectives, the promotional planner provides measures that can be used to evaluate the effectiveness of the marketing communications program. Most organizations are concerned about the return on their promotional investment, and comparing actual performance against measurable objectives is the best way to determine if the return justifies the expense.

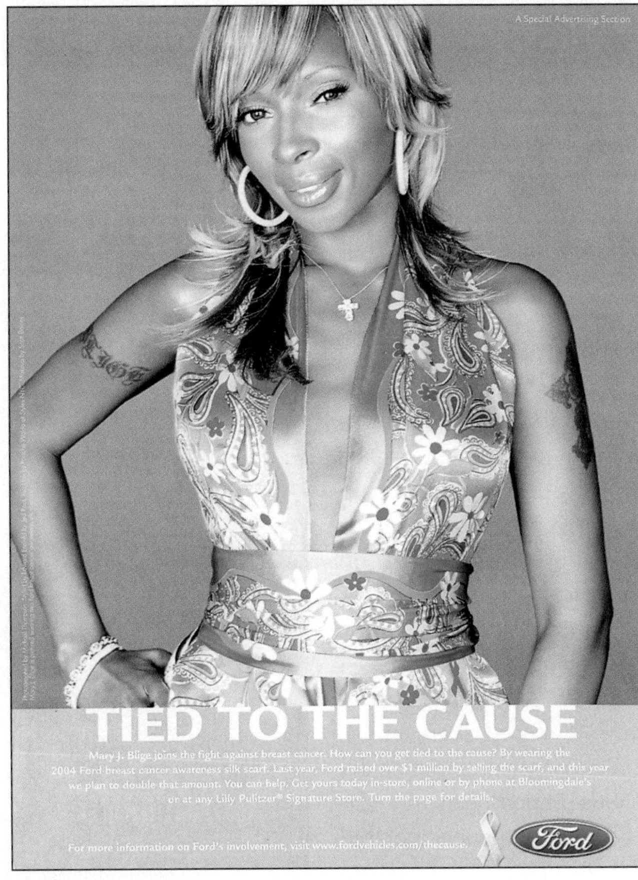

Exhibit 5–1 The objective of this ad is to demonstrate Ford's support for a cause

Marketing Objectives

Marketing objectives are generally stated in the firm's marketing plan and are statements of what is to be accomplished by the overall marketing program within a given time period. Marketing objectives are usually defined in terms of specific, measurable outcomes such as sales volume, market share, profits, or return on investment. Good marketing objectives are quantifiable; they delineate the target market and note the time frame for accomplishing the goal (often one year). For example, a copy-machine company may have as its marketing objective "to increase sales by 10 percent in the small-business segment of the market during the next 12 months." To be effective, objectives must also be realistic and attainable.

The choice of the type of marketing objective is likely a function of market conditions. A company with a very high market share may seek to increase its sales volume by stimulating growth in the product category. It might accomplish this by increasing consumption by current users or encouraging nonusers to buy the product. A firm in a fast-growing market may have market share as its marketing objective since this reflects that it is growing more quickly than its direct competitors. Alternatively, in mature markets with limited growth, firms tend to focus on profit as the key marketing objective. Finally, a firm that faces unique consumer preferences across various geographic markets (i.e., Ontario versus Quebec) may in fact have a separate marketing objective for each region.

IMC PERSPECTIVE 5–1

Molson Muscles in the U.S.

Does achieving communications objectives lead to an increase in sales? The answer to this question is maybe or maybe not, as sales are a function of a number of factors beyond just advertising and promotion. At the same time, there is more and more evidence of a strong relationship between the two. Take the case (not a case!) of Molson Canadian beer for example.

Although it is the number-one-selling domestic beer in Canada, Molson Canadian saw its market share in the United States drop during the 1990s. Import beers as a category had experienced rapid growth during this time, but Molson's sales dropped by about 50 percent due largely to lack of attention from Miller Brewing Company, which owned the rights to the product in the United States. In order to save the brand, and turn the declining sales trend around, Molson bought back the rights from Miller and embarked on a communications strategy to reposition Molson Canadian.

The new strategy began with an in-depth research study of the beer-drinking culture of the target market—males 21 to 27. The research team visited clubs, restaurants, bars, and virtually anywhere else these guys could buy a bottle of imported beer. They watched what the men drank, how they held the bottle, the difference between "Wednesday night beers" (with the guys) and "Friday night beers" (with the ladies), even where the beer was placed on the bar or table in front of them. Their conclusion? Guys go to bars to meet women, and beer, like clothing, is used as a signal to make them more attractive to the opposite sex. Beer labels, like designer labels, are a badge to show who they are. Unfortunately for Molson, the Molson Canadian brand had no badge. Essentially the label had no identity, evoked no meaning or relevance, and, worst of all, provided no assistance in making them more attractive to the opposite sex.

Once the marketing communications manager has reviewed the marketing plan, he or she should understand the marketing objectives of the marketing program, how it intends to get there, and the role advertising and promotion will play. Marketing goals defined in terms of sales, profit, or market share increases are usually not appropriate promotional objectives. They are objectives for the entire marketing program, and achieving them depends on the proper coordination and execution of all the marketing mix elements, including not just promotion but also product planning and production, pricing, and distribution. In contrast, many promotional planners approach promotion from a communications perspective and believe the objective of advertising and other promotional mix elements is usually to communicate information or a selling message about a product or service. IMC Perspective 5–1 illustrates the debate between sales and communication objectives.

Based on this information, the brand team at Molson established two goals: (1) make the label mean something; and (2) give it relevance to males by helping them build confidence and succeed in their quest to meet women. To do this, a second label, dubbed the Twin Label, was added to the bottles to serve as a signalling device to women by communicating something about the bottle holder. In all, 232 different labels were developed in categories including pickup lines, icebreakers, comebacks, and other statements reflecting strength and physical prowess. The Twin Labels effort was supported with an advertising campaign called "Friends," which ran print ads in *Cosmopolitan*, *Maxim*, *Stuff*, and *FHM*, the former to let women know that Molson men were caring and sensitive, the latter three (all men's magazines) to inform the target audience that they are programming women to have a favourable impression of the Molson drinker. The ads suggested that the men save the labels to use the next time they buy a woman a drink. Other "phony" materials—pictures of adoring grandparents, orphans admiring the man's largesse, and puppy and kitten pictures—were available on the Molson U.S. website. So, too, were business cards for luxury yachts, private-jet charters, and other items that could be used to impress women. Television commercials communicated the same message ending with the tagline "Let your Molson do the talking," with a mild disclaimer to male beer fans that Molson would not really help them get women.

The efforts earned Molson and their agency a Jay Chiat Planning Gold and Grand Prix award from the American Association of Advertising Agencies (AAAA). But, did it work? Molson tracked the opinions of the target audience to determine if its efforts had an impact on the brand image. Beer drinkers were asked to finish the following sentence, "Molson is for __________." After six months there was a 23 percent increase among those who said "Young people in their 20s," a 36 percent increase among those who said "Guys who are successful with the ladies," and a 17 percent increase among those who said "Guys who go out on the town a lot." The number of men who had never tried Molson but said they would consider trying it increased by 26 percent. "But what about sales?" you ask. Depending on whom you talk to, sales increased by somewhere between 32.5 percent and 48 percent as a result of the campaign.

However, not everyone is impressed. The Marin Institute, an industry watchdog, says the ads violated the industry trade group's (The Beer Institute's) voluntary advertising code, and were neither responsible nor in good taste. The watchdog group said the ads promoted lying and deception, and were offensive and cynical. Molson's response? A company spokesperson said the ads did not promote deception but promoted the brand in a humorous light, noting further that "No one really takes it seriously." Except for the sales.

Sources: Stan Sutter, "Scandal, Beer and Vaughn," *Marketing Magazine,* March 22–28, 2005, p. 3; Christopher Lawton, "In Molson Ads, Tips to Magazine Get Girls Turns Some Off," *The Wall Street Journal,* July 28, 2004, p. B1; "Gold and Grand Prix Nontraditional Advertising Communications," American Association of Advertising Agencies, 2004, pp. 99–105.

Questions

1. Is it a good idea for Molson to have a different approach for the U.S. market?
2. Do you agree that the campaign was offensive?

Sales Objectives Debate

In contrast to the conclusion of the previous section, some managers believe the only meaningful objective for their promotional program is sales. They take the position that the basic reason a firm spends money on advertising and promotion is to sell its product or service. Promotional spending represents an investment of a firm's scarce resources that requires an economic justification. Rational managers generally compare investment options on a common financial basis, such as return on investment (ROI). They believe that monies spent on advertising and other forms of promotion should produce measurable results, such as increasing sales volume by a certain percentage or dollar amount or increasing the brand's market share. These beliefs are partly a result of marketing and brand managers being under pressure to show sales results. They often take a short-term perspective in evaluating advertising and sales promotion programs and look for a quick fix for declining sales or loss of market share.

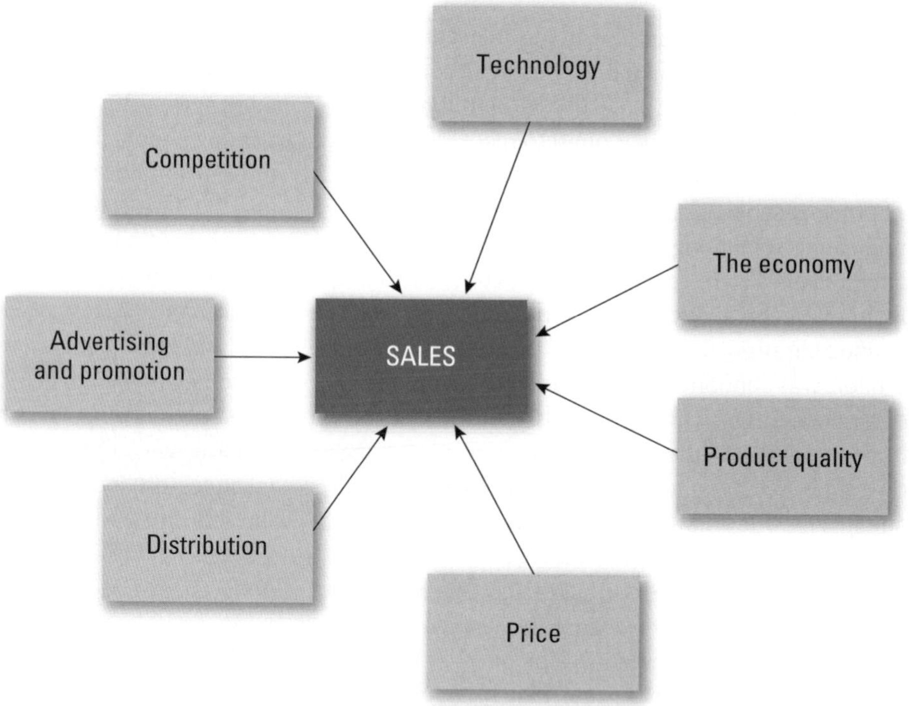

FIGURE 5–1

Factors influencing sales

One problem with sales objectives for promotion is that poor sales results can be due to any of the other marketing mix variables, including product design or quality, packaging, distribution, or pricing. Advertising can make consumers aware of and interested in the brand, but it can't make them buy it, particularly if it is not readily available or is priced higher than a competing brand. As shown in Figure 5–1, sales are a function of many factors, not just advertising and promotion.

Another problem with sales objectives is that the effects of advertising often occur over an extended period. Many experts recognize that advertising has a lagged or **carryover effect**; if monies spent on advertising do not necessarily have an immediate impact on sales.[2] Advertising may create awareness, interest, and/or favourable attitudes toward a brand, but these feelings will not result in an actual purchase until the consumer enters the market for the product, which may occur later. A review of econometric studies that examined the duration of cumulative advertising effects found that for mature, frequently purchased, low-priced products, advertising's effect on sales lasts up to nine months.[3] Models have been developed to account for the carryover effect of advertising and to help determine the long-term effect of advertising on sales.[4] The carryover effect adds to the difficulty of determining the precise relationship between advertising and sales.

A third problem with sales objectives is that they offer little guidance to those responsible for planning and developing the promotional program. The creative and media people working on the account need some direction as to the nature of the advertising message the company hopes to communicate, the intended audience, and the particular effect or response sought. Communication objectives are recommended because they provide operational guidelines for those involved in planning, developing, and executing the advertising and promotional program.

The counterargument to these three points is that sales objectives are appropriate when the above three factors are not relevant. If a marketer is certain that other marketing or environmental factors were not influencing sales, that the carryover effect was not occurring, or that the managers involved did not require guidance, then a sales objective could be plausible. In general, the likelihood of such conditions arising appears quite remote, which necessitates the use of communication objectives as the primary approach for promotional planning purposes. To illustrate this point we will discuss two examples: direct-response advertising and the marketing practices of packaged-goods firms.

Direct-response advertising is one type of advertising that typically evaluates its effectiveness on the basis of sales. Merchandise is advertised in material mailed to customers, in newspapers and magazines, or on television. The consumer purchases the merchandise by mail or by calling a toll-free number. The direct-response advertiser generally sets objectives and measures success in terms of the sales response generated by the ad. For example, objectives for and the evaluation of a direct-response ad on TV are based on the number of orders received each time a station broadcasts the commercial. Because advertising is really the only form of communication and promotion used in this situation and response is generally immediate, setting objectives in terms of sales appears appropriate.

However, this is an example where a carryover effect may be working. Consumers receive the ad many times during the campaign and decide not to purchase. During subsequent campaigns during the year, these consumers have the communication effect of the previous campaign combined with word-of-mouth communication and evaluation considerations. The cumulative impact of all communications can influence the consumer as he or she proceeds through the usual decision-making process. Establishing communication objectives is still a critical step in understanding the effectiveness of the ads, once again indicating that sales objectives alone are not sufficient.

We now turn to our second example. Many packaged-goods companies compete in mature markets with established channels of distribution, stable competitive prices and promotional budgets, and products of similar quality. They view advertising and sales promotion as the key determinants of a brand's sales or market share, so it may be possible to isolate the effects of these promotional mix variables.[5] Many companies have accumulated enough market knowledge with their advertising, sales promotion, and direct-marketing programs to have considerable insight into the sales levels that should result from their promotional efforts. Thus, they believe it is reasonable to set objectives and evaluate the success of their promotional efforts in terms of sales results.

Again, this appears to be a plausible explanation; however, we can surmise a few factors that make the setting of communication objectives an important step for predicting the sales results. Even mature categories have new customers entering the market, to which communication effects are important considerations for seeing if these customers are gravitating to one's own or a competing brand. Consumer perceptions of campaign-message changes and promotional-mix alterations may have a delayed effect on sales, and an understanding of consumer psychological reactions (i.e., attitude) may be more immediately forthcoming.

Communication Objectives

Communication objectives are statements of what the communications will accomplish. In general, objectives are based on one or more consumer response models discussed in Chapter 4. We can speak of communication objectives on three levels depending upon the decision at hand. There are communication objectives for the overall IMC plan. We can also speak of communication objectives for individual IMC tools (i.e., advertising). Often, as was shown in Chapter 1,

Every car company is concerned about the people inside its cars.
But what about the people outside?

To help reduce pedestrian injuries, the modified windshield-wiper system helps absorb energy in the event of an accident.
The energy-absorbing space under the front fenders is designed to minimize injury.
Honda redesigned the hood hinge so it bends with the force of an impact to help minimize pedestrian injuries.
The specially designed hood creates a space between the engine and the hood to lessen the severity of an impact.
As part of Honda's commitment to "Safety for Everyone," we are leading the industry in technology to help protect pedestrians in the event of an accident. Approximately 70,000 pedestrians a year are involved in traffic crashes. And about 5,000 of these end in fatalities. In our efforts to help reduce injuries, especially to the head, Honda created POLAR II, a unique pedestrian test dummy with sensors that help analyze the types of injuries that could be sustained in an accident. Our pioneering research has led to the development of a number of pedestrian-protection features, including injury-reducing designs that minimize direct contact with the most rigid part of the vehicle. More than 2 million U.S. Honda and Acura vehicles on the road today have this equipment. Honda is firmly committed to advancing our safety technologies, with our goal of "Safety for Everyone" leading the way.
POLAR II has instruments that measure the level of injury throughout the body, including the head, neck, chest, abdomen and legs.
Created by Honda engineers, POLAR II is the most advanced pedestrian test dummy, and simulates the kinematics of the human body.

HONDA
The Power of Dreams
safety.honda.com

Exhibit 5–2 Honda's communication objectives for this ad are very unique

these communication objectives are referred to as objectives for the particular tool (i.e., advertising objectives). When working in this field, marketers may use either of these terms depending upon their background or company practices. Finally, we can also use the concept of communication objectives for individual elements of a communication tool. When we design an individual print ad, we want to make sure it achieves the communication objectives we set for it. For example, Honda had very specific safety objectives for this ad that is quite unique (Exhibit 5–2).

Irrespective of whether we are speaking of communication objectives for the IMC plan, a particular tool, or a specific ad, **the communication objectives should be based on the particular communication tasks required to deliver the appropriate messages to the specific target audience at a relevant point within the target audience's purchase decision-making process and consumption experience.**

Managers must be able to translate general marketing goals into communication goals and specific promotional objectives. Some guidance in doing this may be available from the situation analysis of the marketing plan, which includes the following:

128

- The market segments the firm wants to target and the target audiences (customer status, demographics, psychographics, and purchase motives) that the firm wishes to communicate with.
- The product's main features, attributes, benefits, uses, and applications.
- The company's and competitors' brands (sales and market share in various segments, market positioning, competitive strategies, promotional expenditures, creative and media strategies, and tactics).

After reviewing all the information, the promotional planner should see how integrated marketing communications fit into the marketing program and what the firm hopes to achieve through advertising and other promotional elements. The importance of setting communication objectives of a promotional plan is featured in IMC Perspective 5–2. The Dove example also illustrates the different levels of communication objectives. Clearly the whole IMC campaign has certain esteem objectives. The advertising contributed to these IMC objectives, but also had more specific emotional effects. Finally, the sponsorship attempts to achieve its own behavioural change objective.

When setting specific communication objectives, promotional planners often are not sure what constitutes adequate levels of awareness, knowledge, liking, preference, or conviction. No formulas provide this information. The promotional manager will have to use his or her personal experience and that of the brand or product managers, as well as the marketing history of this and similar brands. Average scores on various communication measures for this and similar products should be considered, along with the levels achieved by competitors' products. We now turn to various approaches for setting communication objectives that provide guidelines for some of these concerns.

IMC PERSPECTIVE 5–2

Objectives for Dove's Campaign

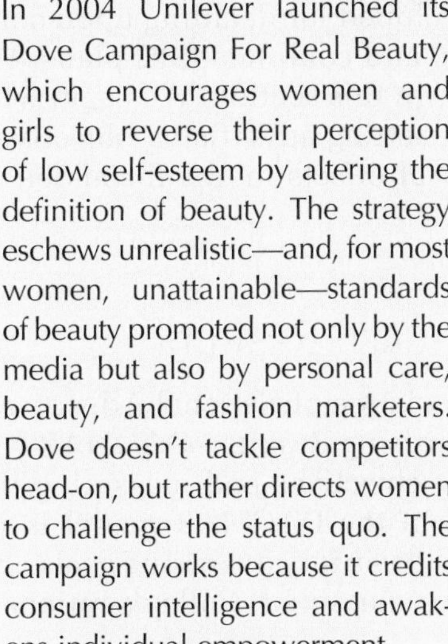

In 2004 Unilever launched its Dove Campaign For Real Beauty, which encourages women and girls to reverse their perception of low self-esteem by altering the definition of beauty. The strategy eschews unrealistic—and, for most women, unattainable—standards of beauty promoted not only by the media but also by personal care, beauty, and fashion marketers. Dove doesn't tackle competitors head-on, but rather directs women to challenge the status quo. The campaign works because it credits consumer intelligence and awakens individual empowerment.

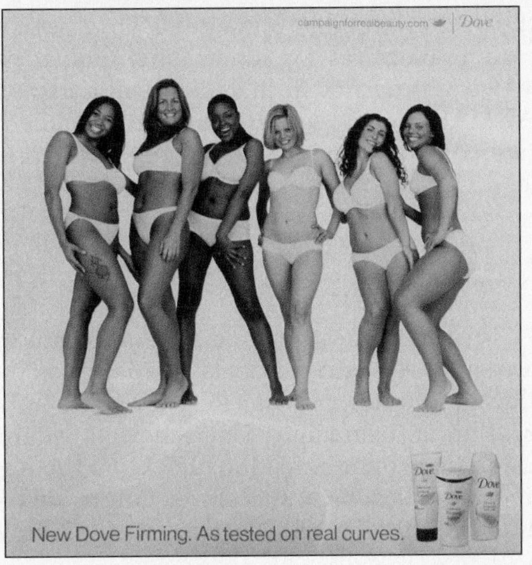

New Dove Firming. As tested on real curves.

It's a global strategy with regional executions. In 2005, the multifaceted campaign won Best of Show at the Canadian Media Innovation Awards for an effort that included LED billboards depicting a Reubenesque woman and a toll-free number to call to vote on whether she looked "fat" or "fab." Ogilvy & Mather's Toronto office created the latest work, which makes a direct play to our protective instincts through TV and cinema spots that reveal the inner emotions of young girls, including "Thinks she's ugly," "Wishes she were blonde," and "Thinks she's fat." The "Little Girls" spots—which keep it real by using actual girls rather than models—hit the U.S. airwaves to much acclaim in February during the Super Bowl broadcast, but actually broke in Canada and won a silver in the cinema single category at the 2006 Marketing Awards.

The current phase in the Campaign For Real Beauty attempts to raise girls' self-esteem by challenging harmful stereotypes and embracing healthy, authentic, and positive ways of being beautiful. It includes the Dove Self-Esteem Fund, which provides information and learning tools designed to help young people deal with their feelings about physical appearance, and funding to the National Eating Disorder Information Centre in English Canada and the ANFB, a similar organization, in Quebec. Dove also conducts Real Beauty Workshops for girls in communities across Canada.

The source of information that provided direction for the campaign's communication objectives is a study that Unilever released to the public in February 2006. The study, "Beyond Stereotypes: Rebuilding the Foundation of Beauty Beliefs," surveyed 3,300 girls and women age 15 to 64 in Canada, the U.S., Mexico, Brazil, the U.K., Italy, Germany, Japan, China, and Saudi Arabia. The study found that women's anxiety about their appearance is a global phenomenon. Two-thirds of women admitted to avoiding such basic activities as meeting friends, exercising, voicing an opinion, dating, and even seeking medical help because they feel badly about the way they look.

Age 13 is the time when Canadian girls first become concerned over physical appearance, facial appearance, and body weight and shape, according to the study. It's also the age at which Canadian girls start wearing makeup, manicuring their nails, or straightening their hair—and, for a minority, compulsive eating and throwing up or refusing to eat, and dieting. Ninety-three percent of Canadian women surveyed want to change some aspect of themselves, with body weight and shape at the top of the list followed by height. Forty-one percent of girls age 15 to 17 want to change their skin complexion, 34 percent want to change their hair, 22 percent want to change their skin colour, and 27 percent want to change their eye colour. Canadian girls' wishes for the future include becoming more athletic (32%), thinner (23%), more confident (22%), and taller (18%).

The study found that girlfriends and mothers, followed by the media, are the earliest and most powerful influencers of a young girl's feelings about her appearance, and that women have a strong desire to encourage young girls to have a realistic and healthy body image and to eat healthily rather than diet. While the study cautions that women are not "passive idiots who simply swallow the dictates of the style industry," it describes our contemporary relationship to beauty as "tragic" because "beauty is not felt to be a birthright but a ... desire that is hard to attain."

Most Canadian respondents (61%), wish that when they were younger they had seen girls and women in magazines that looked more like them. Mothers with daughters under 17 universally hope they have not passed on feelings of self-doubt or insecurity to their daughters; 41 percent want children to know that beautiful women come in different colours, shapes, and sizes.

Source: Angela Kryhul, "Dove's Beautiful Goal," *Marketing Magazine*, April 17–24, 2006.

Questions

1. What aspects of consumer attitudes is Dove attempting to influence with its campaign?
2. How does the research help guide the development of communication objectives?

From Communication Response Models to Communication Objectives

Over the years, a number of methods have been developed for deciding upon communication objectives for advertising, related tools, and complete IMC plans. We review two approaches from a historical perspective in this section. We begin with the DAGMAR model, which provided guidance for setting advertising objectives. Next, we consider Lavidge and Steiner's hierarchy of effects model discussed in Chapter 4.

Defining Advertising Goals for Measured Results

In 1961, Russell Colley prepared a report for the Association of National Advertisers titled Defining Advertising Goals for Measured Advertising Results—**DAGMAR.**[6] In it, Colley developed a model for setting advertising objectives and measuring the results of an ad campaign. The major contribution of the DAGMAR model is its conclusion that communication effects are the logical basis for advertising goals and objectives against which success or failure should be measured. Colley's rationale for communication-based objectives was as follows:

> Advertising's job, purely and simply, is to communicate to a defined audience information and a frame of mind that stimulates action. Advertising succeeds or fails depending on how well it communicates the desired information and attitudes to the right people at the right time and at the right cost.[7]

Under the DAGMAR approach, an advertising goal involves a communication task that is specific and measurable. A **communication task**, as opposed to a marketing task, can be performed by, and attributed to, advertising rather than to a combination of several marketing factors. Colley proposed that the communication task be based on a hierarchical model of the communication process with four stages:

- Awareness—making the consumer aware of the existence of the brand or company.
- Comprehension—developing an understanding of what the product is and what it will do for the consumer.
- Conviction—developing a mental disposition in the consumer to buy the product.
- Action—getting the consumer to purchase the product.

The DAGMAR approach to setting objectives has had considerable influence on the advertising planning process. Many promotional planners use this model as a basis for setting objectives and assessing the effectiveness of their promotional campaigns. DAGMAR also emphasized the value of using communications-based rather than sales-based objectives to measure advertising effectiveness and encouraged the measurement of stages in the response hierarchy to assess a campaign's impact. Colley's work has led to improvements in the advertising and promotional planning process by providing a better understanding of the goals and objectives toward which planners' efforts should be directed.

A second major contribution of DAGMAR to the advertising planning process was its definition of what constitutes a good objective. Colley argued that advertising objectives should specify a target audience, be stated in terms of concrete and measurable communication tasks, indicate a benchmark starting point and the degree of change sought, and specify a time period for accomplishing the objective(s).

Target Audience An important characteristic of good objectives is a well-defined target audience. The primary target audience for a company's product or service is described in the situation analysis. It may be based on descriptive variables such as geography, demographics, and psychographics (on which advertising media selection decisions are based) as well as on behavioural variables such as customer status (i.e, brand-loyal users), usage rate, or benefits sought. This step is critical since the communication effect has to be interpreted from the perspective of the intended receiver.

Concrete, Measurable Tasks The communication task specified in the objective should be a precise statement of what appeal or message the advertiser wants to communicate to the target audience. Advertisers generally use a copy platform to describe their basic message. The objective or copy platform statement should be specific and clear enough to guide the creative specialists who develop the advertising message. According to DAGMAR, the objective must also be measurable. There must be a way to determine whether the intended message has been communicated properly.

Benchmark and Degree of Change Sought To set objectives, one must know the target audience's present status concerning response hierarchy variables (e.g., awareness) and then determine the degree to which consumers must be changed by the advertising campaign. Determining the target audience's present position regarding the various response stages requires **benchmark measures**. Often a marketing research study must be conducted to determine prevailing levels of the response hierarchy. In the case of a new product or service, the starting conditions are generally at or near zero for all the variables, so no initial research is needed.

Establishing benchmark measures gives the promotional planner a basis for determining what communication tasks need to be accomplished and for specifying particular objectives. For example, a preliminary study for a brand may reveal that awareness is high but consumer perceptions and attitudes are negative. The objective for the advertising campaign must then be to change the target audience's perceptions of and attitudes toward the brand.

Quantitative benchmarks not only are valuable in establishing communications goals and objectives but also are essential for determining whether the campaign was successful. Objectives provide the standard against which the success or failure of a campaign is measured. An ad campaign that results in a 90-percent awareness level for a brand among its target audience cannot really be judged effective unless one knows what percentage of the consumers were aware of the brand before the campaign began. A 70-percent pre-campaign awareness level would lead to a different interpretation of the campaign's success than would a 30-percent level.

Specified Time Period A final consideration in setting advertising objectives is specifying the time period in which they must be accomplished. Appropriate time periods can range from a few days to a year or more. Most ad campaigns specify time periods from a few months to a year, depending on the situation facing the advertiser and the type of response being sought. For example, awareness levels for a brand can be created or increased fairly quickly through an intensive media schedule of widespread, repetitive advertising to the target audience. Repositioning of a product requires a change in consumers' perceptions and takes much more time.

Comprehensive Response Model Applications

The DAGMAR model was the impetus for the application of more involved or comprehensive response models for setting communication objectives. Over time, advertising theorists prefer the Lavidge and Steiner hierarchy of effects model, as it is more specific and provides a better way to establish and measure results.[8] Thus, this particular hierarchical model has been used as a basis for analyzing the

FIGURE 5–2

Effects of advertising on consumers: movement from awareness to action

Related behavioural dimensions	Movement toward purchase	Example of types of promotion or advertising relevant to various steps
Conative The realm of motives. Ads stimulate or direct desires.	Purchase	Point-of-purchase Retail store ads Deals "Last-chance" offers Price appeals Testimonials
	Conviction	
Affective The realm of emotions. Ads change attitudes and feelings.	Preference	Competitive ads Argumentative copy
	Liking	"Image" copy Status, glamour appeals
Cognitive The realm of thoughts. Ads provide information and facts.	Knowledge	Announcements Descriptive copy Classified ads Slogans Jingles Skywriting Teaser campaigns
	Awareness	

communication response processes of consumers and has been the foremost application for setting communication objectives.

Figure 5–2 shows the various steps in the Lavidge and Steiner hierarchy of effects model as the consumer moves from awareness to purchase, along with examples of types of promotion or advertising relevant to each step. Recall from Chapter 4 that consumers pass through three successive stages: cognitive, affective, and behavioural. As consumers proceed through the three stages, they move closer to making a purchase. Consumers are not expected to respond immediately; rather, advertisers realize they must provide relevant information and create favourable predispositions toward the brand before purchase behaviour will occur. For example, the ad for Philips in Exhibit 5–3 is designed to inform consumers of the company's focus on technology that makes sense and is simple. While there is no call for immediate action, the ad creates favourable impressions about the company by creating a distinct image. Consumers will consider this image when they enter the market for products in this category.

Setting communication objectives with a model like this is the same way that a pyramid is built, by first accomplishing lower-level objectives such as awareness and knowledge or comprehension.[9] Subsequent tasks involve moving consumers who are aware of or knowledgeable about the product or service to higher levels in the pyramid (Figure 5–3). The initial stages, at the base of the pyramid, are easier to accomplish than those toward the top, such as trial and repurchase or regular use. Thus, the percentage of prospective customers will decline as they move up the pyramid. Figure 5–4 on page 134 shows how a company introducing a new brand of shampoo targeted at 18- to 34-year-old females might set its IMC objectives using the communications effects pyramid.

The communication effects pyramid can also be used to determine promotional objectives for an established brand. The promotional planner must determine where the target audience lies with respect to the various blocks in the pyramid. If awareness levels for a brand and knowledge of its features and benefits are low, the communication objective should be to increase them. If these blocks of the pyramid are already in place, but liking or preference is low, the advertising goal may be to change the target markets' image of the brand and move consumers through to purchase.

Even though comprehensive response models have been used to set communication objectives for many years, research shows that its acceptance has been limited over time. A 1969 study showed that most advertising agencies did not state appropriate objectives for determining advertising success.[10] Another more recent study found that most advertisers in their sample did not set concrete advertising objectives, specify objective tasks, measure results in terms of stages of a hierarchy of effects, or match objectives to evaluation measures.[11] The authors concluded: "Advertising practitioners have only partially adopted the concepts and standards of objective setting and evaluation set forth 25 years ago."[12] Finally, another recent study measured the attitudes of chairs, presidents, and other senior managers of business-to-business advertising companies; more than half of the 427 respondents said they did not know whether their advertising was working and fewer than 10 percent thought it was working well.[13]

© 2005 Philips Electronics North America Corporation.
Things start uncomplicated. Why change them?
Life is complicated enough. Technology shouldn't add to the problem. So Philips is committed to making technology that makes sense. Technology that's as simple as the box it comes in. Technology that's easy to use. Technology designed around the way you live and work. In other words, technology that's pure simplicity.
Join us on our journey at www.philips.com/simplicity
PHILIPS
sense and simplicity

Exhibit 5–3 Philips creates an image for its products

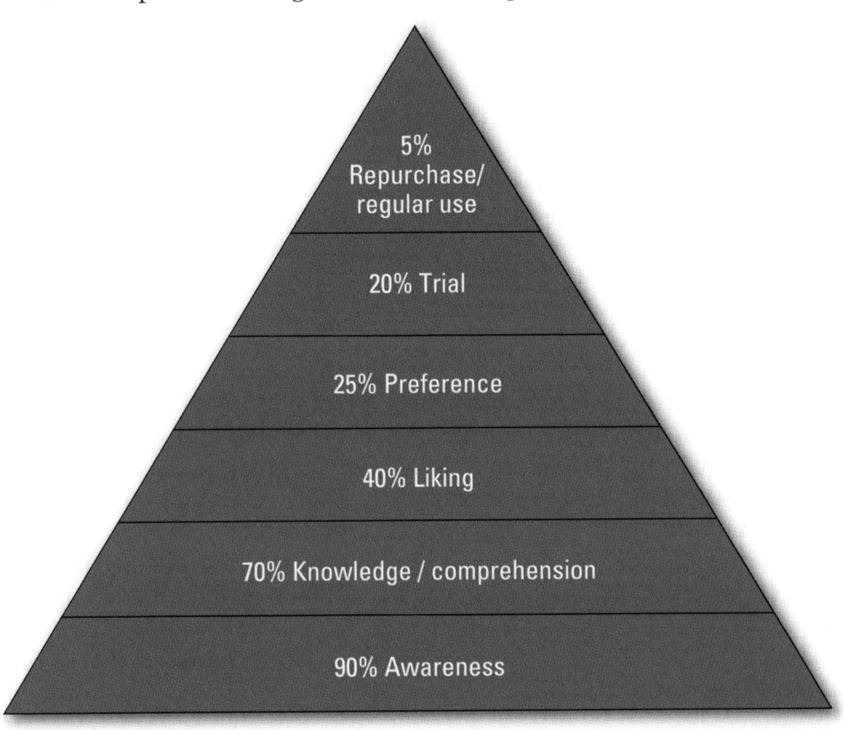

FIGURE 5–3
Communication effects pyramid

FIGURE 5–4

Setting objectives using the communications effects pyramid

Product: Backstage Shampoo

Time period: Six months

Objective 1: Create awareness among 90 percent of target audience. Use repetitive advertising in newspapers, magazines, TV and radio programs. Simple message.

Objective 2: Create interest in the brand among 70 percent of target audience. Communicate information about the features and benefits of the brand—i.e., that it contains no soap and improves the texture of the hair

Objective 3: Create positive feelings about the brand among 40 percent and preference among 25 percent of the target audience. Create favourable attitudes by conveying information, promotions, sampling, etc.

Objective 4: Obtain trial among 20 percent of the target audience. Use sampling and cents-off coupons along with advertising and promotions.

Objective 5: Develop and maintain regular use of Backstage Shampoo among 5 percent of the target audience. Use continued reinforcement advertising, fewer coupons and promotions

Setting IMC Objectives

We now turn our attention to the Rossiter and Percy (R&P) perspective of setting objectives. We first introduced the ideas of R&P in Chapter 3 when discussing the guidelines for target audience identification and selection, and in Chapter 4 when summarizing communication response models. An additional feature of their perspective is to provide guidelines for setting behavioural objectives that are based on their view of target audience identification and selection and for setting communication objectives that are based on their view of communication effects.

Compared to the previous approaches of setting communication objectives, the R&P perspective has three main characteristics. First, it is completely consistent with a critical part of the original DAGMAR model. The R&P perspective makes a direct connection between the target audience decision and the type of communication objectives required for each target audience. Secondly, it provides guidelines for communication objectives that are more managerially useful and do not completely rely on a set hierarchy of effects. Finally, it provides guidelines for behavioural or action objectives that are not specified completely in the previous approaches. This step is critical for linking communication objectives and marketing objectives (i.e., sales). This section will review the options promotional planners should consider when setting behavioural and communication objectives. We include the R&P perspective since it attempts to resolve the limitations of other communication models and approaches for objective setting. Furthermore, the R&P perspective provides guidelines for creative tactics, as will be seen in Chapter 8.

Options for Behavioural Objectives

A key part of R&P's approach is to have a clear behavioural objective for each target audience since summating the individual purchasing behaviour of many customers leads to a firm's overall sales. From another perspective, the link between marketing objectives (i.e., sales) and communication objectives (i.e., attitude toward the brands) is behavioural objectives. Advertising and promotion can focus on influencing a particular form of behaviour based on the nature of the advertising message or IMC tool used. We now discuss various types of behavioural objectives.

Trial A **brand trial purchase** is defined as a consumer's first purchase of a brand. For many everyday products, this purchase occurred many years ago; it is probably difficult to remember when one purchased their first soft drink or snack food. However, these firms continue to have a **brand trial objective** to some degree as consumers naturally enter the market when they attain a certain age or have income (i.e., allowance from parents). In fact, a brand trial objective is a behavioural objective for almost all firms, but it is not necessarily the primary behavioural objective for all campaigns or all communication tools.

Alternatively, it is quite unlikely that consumers continue to purchase the same brand of soft drink as the first trial purchase. In fact, many people consume more than one brand of soft drink. Many brand managers are faced with this dilemma. For whatever reason, it is possible that consumers have not purchased a brand for a period of time (i.e., perhaps a year). Thus, the manager's firms would like consumers to have a new trial experience of the brand. A **brand re-trial purchase** is defined as a consumer's first purchase of a brand after some time delay. The length of the delay to focus on when setting a **brand re-trial objective** is a decision the promotion manager makes. It depends upon the purchase frequency of the product, among other factors observed from the situation analysis.

A manager may plan for a brand trial or brand re-trial objective when consumers are purchasing another brand. A **brand-switching purchase** is defined as a consumer's purchase toward a brand from some other competing brand. A brand-switching purchase occurs whereby the consumer makes a re-trial purchase of a brand and leaves the new favourite. A brand-switching purchase also occurs when the consumer makes a trial purchase of a brand from a competing brand. Thus, brand trial or brand re-trial objectives are also known as **brand-switching objectives**.

Now let's put the trial purchase in another perspective: consider the purchase of a cell phone that many young adults currently own. The cell phone is a different kind of product and likely a somewhat involved purchase for many consumers. Despite this, cell phone companies and service providers had trial objectives as they attempted to attract consumers who did not own such technology. While this is obviously a brand trial purchase, it is also something broader. A **category trial purchase** is defined as a consumer's first purchase in a product category that the consumer has not purchased in previously. Marketers of new products, like the cellphone, have a dual challenge of attaining both **category trial objectives** and brand trial objectives.

Repeat Purchase In the age of relationship marketing and a focus on customer retention, this form of purchase behaviour is most critical. A **repeat purchase** is defined as a consumer's continued purchase of a brand within a specified time period. Again, the time factor is at the discretion of the marketer, and once again it is contingent upon purchase frequency of the product or other factors derived from the situation analysis.

Firms can have a **repeat-purchase objective** in many situations. As noted above, marketers desire to have a stable core of customers that remain loyal to the brand. Many firms communicate with these consumers to maintain their positive attitude toward the brand. For example, some argue that most of Coca-Cola's advertising and promotions are directed toward its repeat customers. In many product categories, a group of consumers habitually consume two or three brands continuously. For instance, of 15 purchases, over 10 consecutive purchases might be of the brand with the remaining five purchases spread across two other brands. This is another situation where a marketer may emphasize a repeat-purchase objective in its communications plan. While this type of consumer does not purchase the brand for every single occasion, the consumer is a consistent contributor to the firm's sales and a marketer would want to communicate appropriately to ensure future sales.

The repeat-purchase objective is pervasive for most organizations. Thus, we identify three alternatives to guide managers in setting their behavioural objectives for IMC: how often to purchase, how much to purchase, and when to purchase.

The first alternative concerns the rate, or how often to purchase the brand. This implies that a marketer may set an objective pertaining to consumers purchasing its brand every week instead of every two weeks. This example shows an option where a manager may want to increase the rate of purchase from a "half" product per week to "one" product per week. A second managerial option is to maintain the rate of purchase. While this is a more conservative objective, it is still a viable option in very competitive environments. Finally, a manager may want to decrease the rate of purchase. This option may be viable in unique situations of high demand or with products that have potentially negative consequences (i.e., alcohol).

The amount or how much to purchase each occasion is the second alternative. As this alternative implies, a marketer may set an objective where consumers purchase two products per occasion versus one per occasion. As above, this option is to increase the amount per occasion, but a marketer could still evaluate whether to maintain or decrease the amount per occasion.

The final alternative is the timing, or when to purchase. Certain products are seasonal, have a peak in their sales, or can be easily stored. Marketers may have a behavioural objective to influence when consumers will make the purchase. For example, Wendy's restaurant advertises on television in the evening and communicates the fact that its drive-through service stays open late, thus prompting consumers to purchase at a certain time of day. Consistent with the other two alternatives, we can conceive three options: maintain, accelerate, and delay.

An evolution in its message from "Perspective Is Everything" to "Don't Miss a Day" signals how the *Globe and Mail* newspaper specified its repeat-purchase objectives over time. Faced with competition from other newspapers, the "perspective" message conveyed one aspect of quality in an attempt to maintain its readership. Recognizing that some readers may not purchase or read its newspaper every day, the *Globe and Mail* focused its message on increasing the frequency of reading the newspaper in its more recent "day" message.[14]

Purchase-Related Behaviour Often, communication is designed to encourage a consumer to progress through the decision-making process more smoothly. Or, communication is deemed a necessary part of the process. For example, most people find it imperative to visit a car dealership prior to buying a car. So the focus of some parts of an IMC plan is to have consumers take action that will lead them one step closer to the final destination of a purchase. **Purchase-related behaviour** is an action consumers take that will lead to a higher probability of purchasing the brand. Many types of purchase-related action exist, but in general, most concern the consumer seeking some amount of information (e.g., visiting a website) about the brand or some kind of experience with the brand (e.g., demonstration, sample). Accordingly, marketers can have many purchase-related behaviour objectives to know whether enough of the target audience is involved with the brand during the decision-making process. For example, the firm can track the number of sales inquiries or requests for samples, or demonstrations to gauge how well it is performing for the objective.

Repeat Consumption Thus far we have considered repeat purchase as a behavioural objective. Related to this is repeat consumption as a behavioural objective. **Repeat consumption** is defined as the continued consumption of the brand once purchased. Marketers may have a **repeat-consumption objective** when communicating with their current customers who have previously purchased the brand and have the product at their home or work. Some communications have an objective of modifying how often to consume the brand, how much to consume each occasion, and when to consume.

Exhibit 5–4 Kit-Kat associated with a situational use to increase repeat purchases

To give an idea of a repeat-consumption objective in action, we will cite two common approaches. Often, food and drink products advertise certain television commercials that show consumption visuals that may prompt consumers to snack or have another beverage. The Kit-Kat ad in Exhibit 5–4 reinforces continued consumption when its customers "take a break." Another approach is to show consumers how to enjoy the product for other uses, or in new or alternative situations.

Milk faces a unique problem of 100-percent trial and 99-percent household penetration, yet its consumption continues to decline. The B.C. Dairy Foundation identified teens and young adults as an audience for a campaign to maintain consumption since research indicated that consumption levels dropped off during the ages of 16–23. Since many of these people still lived at home, the print and television messages "Don't take your body for granted" and "What would life be like without a body?" tried to ensure that this age group would not stop consuming milk prior to moving out on their own. Exciting outdoor events geared toward this audience attempted to make drinking milk as "cool" as any other beverage![15]

The type of purchase and consumption behaviour that firms may try to influence is quite varied. If a firm has multiple target audiences to reach, quite likely it will have to carefully specify the type of behaviour associated with each target audience so that it can develop the most appropriate message and select the most relevant IMC tool. To assist a manager in making these subsequent decisions, it is important to set clear communication objectives.

The Canadian Tourism Commission and Toyota presented an interesting example of a campaign designed to increase repeat consumption. This dual branded message encouraged Canadians to "drive the world's greatest country" in a series of newspaper, television, and radio ads followed by a second wave of Internet and dealer promotions. Since it was assumed that most Canadians had previously taken a road vacation to see various Canadian sites, this campaign attempted to capitalize on the growing trend of domestic travel.[16]

Options for Communication Objectives

Earlier in this chapter we saw how communication response hierarchy models can be used to formulate communication objectives. The R&P approach is similar since it translates their perspective of communication effects into clear options for managers to set communication objectives. In fact, it offers a number of options for each of the five communication objectives that can be applied to one target audience or multiple target audiences.

These options for communication objectives can be viewed as a universal framework for (i) a specific communication like one print ad or television commercial, (ii) a specific campaign like advertising or sponsorship, and (iii) a complete IMC program that includes all promotional tools. It should be noted that the characteristics of good objectives still retain the characteristics set forth earlier (i.e., specific benchmark with the degree of change sought within a specified time period). Furthermore, the framework is flexible enough to apply the various communication objectives to each stage of the buyer decision-making process. We now turn to summarizing the various options for each communication objective and show this application to the buyer decision process.

Category Need **Category need** pertains to whether the target audience feels the need to purchase within the actual product category. Before describing the three options available for managers, it is useful to understand what we mean by category. Cell phones are a clear product for which some people are consumers and some are not. A cell phone company may try to build demand by convincing new users of the benefits of owning a cell phone versus not owning one. This type of message is likely to be different than the type of message used to convince a current user to switch to another brand when the technology improves with new features. In this example, it is a question of whether the target audience feels their life would be more fulfilled with the product or without it. IMC Perspective 5–3 discusses the evolution of another new category.

Another example of category need occurs with transportation. If you were thinking about buying a "car" upon graduation, your choice may in fact be a truck or a sports utility vehicle. In a broad sense, all vehicles can be used for transportation, but consumers have particular needs that are satisfied more easily with some types or categories of vehicles versus others. A marketer for SUVs may try to communicate in a way so that a target audience will feel the need for an SUV more strongly than the need for a sporty sub-compact, which might be the initial category of product that young consumers would gravitate toward. In this example, it is a question of which distinct yet related category fulfills the target audience's need more completely.

A car purchase is certainly not restricted to one's first purchase and category need is a communication objective managers need to consider as an option when marketing to current car owners. For example, 64 percent of all Canadian minivan owners who bought a new vehicle purchased another minivan in 2000; however, this dropped to 48 percent in 2003. In contrast, corresponding numbers rose for large SUVs (e.g., 28 percent to 38 percent) and small cars (e.g., 49 percent to 63 percent). Research suggests consumers "wanted something different" as the most heavily cited reason for changing the type of vehicle.[17] It appears that astute marketers anticipate changing needs and adjust their advertising accordingly and introduce category need as an objective when it is appropriate even in existing markets.

We can describe category need in another perspective. Sticking with the transportation theme, public transit services illustrate their benefits by comparing themselves to the limitations of commuting with a car. Recent television ads in Montreal featured the message "Discover Public Transit" by demonstrating how one could not travel quickly on the highways. The irony of the ad existed in its use of "car-like" visuals—travelling freely at great speed—but then coming to a sudden stop due to traffic. Outdoor signs supported the message at precisely the time when drivers would be experiencing the problem and possibly considering an alternative.[18]

In either of these situations or others, a manager has three options with respect to the category need objective:

- *Category need is omitted.* If the need is quite apparent, then it does not need to be the focus of a particular message or campaign.
- *Category need is reminded.* One obvious example of this is reminder advertising (discussed in Chapter 8), where the brand is communicated and the need for the product is communicated clearly. Often, the reminder option of category need

IMC PERSPECTIVE 5–3

Maple Leaf Prime™ Naturally* Branded Chicken

Designating a brand name for a commodity like chicken appeared to be the final frontier in food marketing, but that's the recent strategy for Maple Leaf Poultry, a division of Maple Leaf Foods Inc. when it launched M.L. Prime™ Naturally* branded chicken, a 100% vegetable-grain with no animal by products fed poultry. With no initial competition for branded chicken, M.L. Prime™ Naturally* had the jump on competitors in the 1990s when it was initially marketed as M.L. Prime™ chicken, the first national brand of air chilled chicken. Over time, regional producers entered the market with a similar offering. These entrants included brands like Olymel's Flamingo in Quebec, Lilydale Chicken in Western Canada, and Granny's Poultry Co-op in Manitoba, with Loblaw's President's Choice distributed nationally in its many grocery store formats. In July 2001, in response to increased competition, M.L. Poultry, launched Maple Leaf Prime™ Naturally* chicken — a line of chicken that has been raised on 100% vegetable grain feed with no animal by products.

Two earlier creative ads helped to establish the importance of higher quality chicken and to set the stage for consumers to understand that a premium category of chicken existed (i.e., establish category need). One showed a recruiter interviewing a chicken who desired to be a Prime™ Naturally* chicken, while another ad showed chickens working out to strengthen their thighs so that they would be selected. The underlying message had been to communicate that Prime™ Naturally* is better, leaner, and healthier chicken by clearly making a connection between how the product is "produced" to the resulting benefits.

Some market research indicated that the campaign achieved success. During early stages of the advertising, 32 percent of all consumers studied could recall the Prime™ Naturally* chicken without any prompting other than to name a brand of chicken, according to the Chicken Farmers of Canada. It is also the number one branded chicken in Canada in terms of sales according to ACNielsen, an international firm specializing in marketing research.

M.L. Prime™ Naturally* chicken was part of an overall corporate strategy at Maple Leaf Foods to brand its traditional commodity like products. For example, with the success of Prime™ Naturally* chicken, Maple Leaf Pork introduced an all vegetable-grain fed fresh pork product branded as Maple Leaf Medallion™ Naturally**. Using chicken as a template, Maple Leaf Foods planned to establish a premium category for fresh pork and retain a number one position as well. Maple Leaf Foods as a whole continued with this higher quality direction across all corporate branding communications with an umbrella message of "We take care."

Source: Lesley Young, "Plucky Branding," *Marketing Magazine*, October 6, 2003.

Questions

1. How does branding chicken make it easier to develop a marketing communications program?
2. Is it possible to establish a premium category for chicken?

* Canada's leading brand of chicken
** Canada's leading brand of pork

is the focus of campaigns for lapsed users. For example, the ad for Dairyland Milk 2 Go products (Exhibit 5–5 on page 140) reminds consumers that it is a convenient drink when away from home, like soft drinks or sport drinks.

- *Category need is emphasized* (that is, "sold"). The above two examples (that is, cell phones and vehicles) show two situations where we actively attempt to persuade the target audience to feel the need for the product.

Exhibit 5–5 This ad for Dairyland Milk 2 Go products is part of a campaign designed to increase sales and market share

The Swiss Water Decaffeinated Coffee Company required category need as its communication objective as it faced the difficult task of explaining that its process for decaffeinating coffee used water instead of chemicals. Known as the Swiss Water Process, brand name coffees use this approach and highlight the fact on their packages much like the famous "Intel Inside" or the VQA designation on Canadian wines indicating an adherence to quality production. Swiss Water used the message "Decaf without the chemistry" to highlight the difference, yet not scare the target audience toward other products like decaffeinated tea.[19] Thus, a category need objective is usually imperative when competing technologies or substitute products emerge on the market thus creating two subcategories instead of one general category.

Brand Awareness **Brand awareness** is a universal communication objective. This means that every single point of communication should contribute to a target audience's understanding and knowledge of the brand name. This understanding and knowledge should go even further such that the target audience knows the category that the brand typically competes in when the consumer is in position to make a purchase or some other related action. This stronger interpretation of awareness is important for the brand to be considered in the decision-making process.

Essentially, there are two types of brand awareness:

- *Brand awareness through recognition.* If the target audience makes a choice at the point of purchase, then simple recognition of past brand messages can be sufficient for brand consideration or purchase.
- *Brand awareness through recall.* If the target audience feels the need for a product but needs to remember what brands to consider away from the point of purchase, then recall becomes the focus of the campaign.

Naturally, if both forms of brand awareness are relevant, then a manager may have both as awareness objectives.

Brand recall is often referred to as unaided brand awareness when measuring. After its launch in western Canada in 2001, Bell had achieved only 10 percent unaided brand recall. What this means is that when people are thinking about buying a cell phone service, only one in 10 will think of Bell. Obviously, this reduces Bell's chances of having many consumers enter Bell stores or call to enquire about its services.[20]

Bell Mobility's continued expansion westward included enhanced network and call centre investments along with more intense distribution of Bell World locations and other retail outlets. As expected, brand awareness remained an important communication objective in 2003 when it also launched its new "Making It Simple" campaign. With an eye to new customers in the 18–34 age range and an emphasis on quality and innovation, Bell Mobility improved its awareness to 27 percent.[21]

In defining brand awareness we must be careful in distinguishing it from advertising awareness, which concerns itself with whether consumers are aware of a brand's television or print ads. While there is some logical connection between the two, they are not identical. For example, one study pegged Ford's unaided brand awareness at 78 percent but its unaided advertising awareness at 57 percent. Four other major car firms, GM, Chrysler, Toyota, and Honda, also showed a consistent 20-percent difference between the two types of awareness.[22]

Brand Attitude **Brand attitude** is another universal communication objective. Like brand awareness, every aspect of a firm's IMC program or any particular element, such as a television commercial, should contribute to some aspect of the overall evaluation of the brand from the perspective of the target audience. A logical conclusion to this point is that there should be no such thing as an "awareness campaign," as the campaign should surely influence brand awareness and some aspect of brand attitude.

Since brand attitude is such an important communication objective, prior understanding of the existing brand attitude is a critical guide for each option:

- *Brand attitude is established.* A new target audience that has no awareness and therefore no prior attitude toward the brand generally requires extensive communication so that an attitude is created or established. The Sonicare ad in Exhibit 5–6 needs to establish a favourable brand attitude with its new features.
- *Brand attitude is maintained.* Often, advertising is performed so that existing attitude levels will remain constant in order to ensure future sales. Stopping communication is one reason for declining sales that have been seen in many examples over time. In contrast, many major advertisers (e.g., Coca-Cola) consistently follow this approach to maintain sales.
- *Brand attitude is increased.* Target audiences who are familiar with the brand and moderately favourable toward the brand can be influenced. For example, we can increase their brand attitude by getting the target audience to believe that the brand delivers better performance on a particular attribute or benefit.
- *Brand attitude is modified.* Similar to the previous option, if the target audience is moderately favourable, we still seek to improve their attitude. However, we modify the brand attitude if no increase is possible. In this option, marketers use a different point of reference in communicating the benefits. Typically, marketers focus on a new consumer motive for purchasing the brand that the target audience will be receptive toward.
- *Brand attitude is changed.* Negative attitudes are difficult to influence, but in some communication situations the marketer is faced with the challenge of changing the brand attitude for a target audience.

Brand Purchase Intention There are two fairly simple options for **brand purchase intention** here:

- *Brand purchase intention is assumed.* In situations (i.e., low involvement) where the strength of an intention to purchase is consistent (i.e., highly correlated) with brand attitude, a marketer is not required to include this objective.
- *Brand purchase intention is generated.* In contrast, managers need the target audience to have a plan to purchase a brand in situations of high involvement.

Exhibit 5–6 A strong basis for differentiation could establish a clear brand attitude

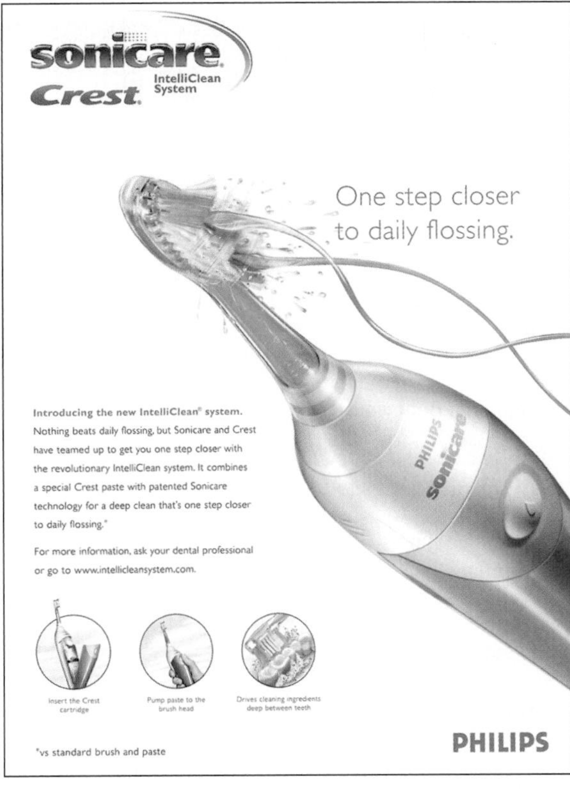

Brand Purchase Facilitation A proactive interpretation of marketing communication pervades **brand purchase facilitation** by these two options:

- *Purchase facilitation is included.* If the target audience believes that some aspect of the marketing mix is weak or problematic (i.e., availability at certain types of stores), then the marketer should take this into account when designing ads, and offer reassurance, explanation, or information.
- *Purchase facilitation is omitted.* Naturally, this is not a focus of the ad if there are no perceived problems.

IMC Planning: Objectives for Buyer Decision Stages

In Chapter 3, we presented a model of consumer decision making that showed the stages typically experienced when making a purchase. We outlined several steps: need recognition, information search, alternative evaluation, purchase decision, and post-purchase evaluation. One important role of marketing communications is to help the target audience move through these stages. Marketers require specific communication tools and messages that will resonate with each target audience as they proceed through these stages. We assess this decision-making process for each target audience and make a conclusion as to which communication objectives are most relevant for each stage. Figure 5–5 illustrates how this works.

The analysis occurs in the first six rows, where the marketer includes the target audience information and makes a conclusion on the key communication objectives that need to be attained so that the target audience will continue to the next stage. We have addressed some of these ideas already. The first question (Who?) looks at the key participants in the decision. We highlighted these roles in Chapter 3. The

FIGURE 5–5 Assessing the consumer decision-making process

Analysis & Conclusions	Need Recognition	Information Search	Alternative Evaluation	Purchase Decision	Post-purchase Evaluation
Who? (Roles)					
Where? (Location)					
When? (Time, Timing)					
How? (Shopping Behaviour)					
Why? (Key motivator)					
Communication Objectives					
Behavioural Objectives					
Message Options					
Communication Tool Options					

next three questions are descriptors of where, when, and how the shopping behaviour will occur. This is based on market research, managerial experience, flashes of inspiration, and assumptions. The key point is that we need to make clear the behaviour that we are trying to influence.

After summarizing these questions, we determine which communication objectives are necessary to ensure that the consumer continues through all stages. For example, what aspect of brand attitude needs to be addressed at the need-recognition stage versus the alternative-evaluation stage? Is recall an awareness objective at the need-recognition stage and recognition an awareness objective at the purchase-decision stage? We also need to determine the most relevant behavioural objective. For example, we may wish to encourage phone enquiries at the information search stage. Or perhaps we may desire Internet visits to compare brands at the alternative evaluation stage.

Once this assessment has been done, then the marketer can outline preliminary options concerning the types of messages and communication tools that would be most useful. Returning to the first question above, a marketer may decide to have a fun television commercial (e.g., communication tool option) that emphasizes the emotional attachment (e.g., brand attitude) to the product. It should be noted that when identifying some options, the marketer has not fully committed or recommended that this is exactly the plan, but rather that this is the template of analysis for making the final decision.

The Rogers@Home "Download Rigor Mortis" IMC campaign is an excellent example of these concepts. In the spring and fall of 2000, Rogers put together a campaign to attract new users for its high-speed cable Internet service. It featured the humorous result of consumers requiring medical attention after experiencing rigor mortis when they waited for Internet downloads to occur through regular phone lines. The campaign included TV, print, radio, billboards, Web, and direct mail, and resulted in 100,000 new subscribers. As one Rogers executive noted, "I don't think any one piece works entirely on its own. That's what is nice about integrated campaigns; each piece layered on helps build it."

We can now surmise how each IMC tool played a key role in achieving key communication objectives at each stage of the decision-making process. TV worked well at the need-recognition stage, as it generated initial awareness and allowed consumers to easily see the benefit of a new type of Internet service for them (i.e., category need) and understand that Rogers could deliver the key attribute of speed (i.e., brand attitude). Print and Web enhanced the belief that Rogers could deliver the complete service package, as they contained more information (i.e., brand attitude) that consumers would be seeking at the information-search stage. Radio and posters likely reminded consumers to seek additional information (i.e., purchase facilitation) by phoning the company or visiting the website, if the consumer had not done so previously when they were in the purchase-intention stage. Direct mail encouraged consumers to act (i.e., purchase decision).[23]

The rest of this book focuses on how to make IMC plan decisions that are based on the target audience, behaviour objectives, and communication objectives established at the start of the plan. Chapters 6–9 focus on the message, while Chapters 10–17 focus on the communication tools. As we noted at the start of this chapter, content of this framework becomes the key criteria for making all promotional decisions and the criteria by which the results are measured. While all firms may not be able to afford comprehensive studies to assess communication effects, they would benefit from the use of the framework because it provides disciplined thinking before investing in promotion.

SUMMARY

This chapter has examined the role of objectives in the planning and evaluation of the IMC. Specific objectives are needed to guide the development of the promotional program, as well as to provide a benchmark against which performance can be measured and evaluated. Objectives serve important functions as communications devices, as a guide to planning the IMC program and deciding on various alternatives, and for measurement and evaluation.

Objectives for IMC evolve from the organization's overall marketing plan and are based on the roles various promotional mix elements play in the marketing program. Many managers use sales or a related measure such as market share as the basis for setting objectives. However, many promotional planners believe the role of advertising and other promotional mix elements is to communicate because of the various problems associated with sales-based objectives. They use communications-based objectives like those in the response hierarchy as the basis for setting goals. The first approach for this was DAGMAR, which outlined four principles for setting communication objectives for advertising: well-defined target audience, concrete measurable tasks, benchmark with degree of change sought, and a specified time period.

Much of the emphasis in setting objectives has been on traditional advertising-based views of marketing communications. Many of the principles used in setting advertising objectives can be applied to other elements in the promotional mix.

We presented a comprehensive framework for setting behaviour objectives and communication objectives for all levels: IMC plans, individual IMC tools (i.e., advertising), and specific elements (i.e., print ad). The framework identified options for behaviour objectives to guide the formation of communication objectives. It also presented many options for setting communication objectives. The framework was then linked to the buyer decision-making model to see the connection between a consumer's behaviour and a particular brand's objectives.

KEY TERMS

DISCUSSION QUESTIONS

1. Discuss the value of setting objectives for the integrated marketing communications program. What important functions do objectives serve?

2. In meeting with your new boss, she informs you that the only goal of advertising and promotion is to generate sales. Present your argument as to why communications objectives must also be considered.

3. What are some of the problems associated with using sales objectives as the only measure of advertising performance? Can you think of any situation where it may be the best and only measure?

4. What are the strengths and weaknesses of using traditional hierarchy models for setting communication objectives?

5. Some claim that promotion is all about communication, so we should focus only on communication objectives and not worry about behavioural objectives. Convince them otherwise.

6. If a firm cannot afford large market research studies to quantitatively assess whether communication objectives have been achieved, why should the firm bother setting communication objectives?

7. How is the framework discussed in the last section similar to and different from setting communications objectives based on the traditional hierarchy models?

8. In what situations would brand awareness be the only communication objective for an advertising campaign?

9. A firm is running a campaign with advertising, sales promotion, and public relations. Why might it have different communication objectives for each IMC tool?

10. Find a print ad and explain what its communication objectives are. Look at the company's website and determine whether the communication objectives are similar or different.

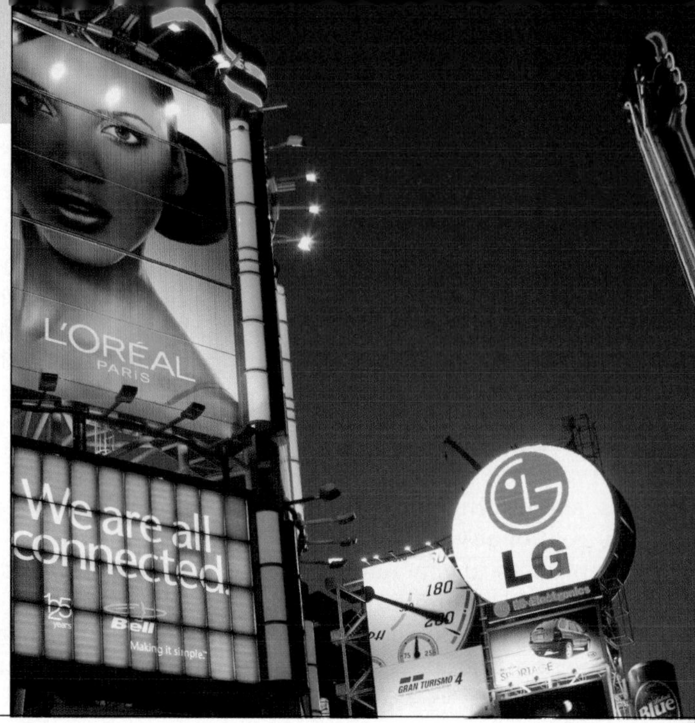

CHAPTER 6

BRAND POSITIONING STRATEGY DECISIONS

Chapter Objectives

- To review the concepts of market positioning strategy and market position.
- To apply the positioning concept in an advertising context by defining brand positioning strategy and brand position.
- To illustrate how to formulate the brand positioning strategy decisions.
- To summarize various brand repositioning strategy opportunities.

Never Quit with Toyota Tacoma

Toyota Tacoma's positioning needed an overhaul with its re-launch for 2005. The compact pickup truck enjoyed moderate success against the competition from Ford, Chrysler, and GM when initially launched in 1995; however, it eventually experienced a decline, with virtually no advertising support from 1998 onward as market share hovered around 6 percent during the intervening seven years.

During this time, Toyota Trucks (i.e., trucks and SUVs) positioned its vehicles as recreational, with messages like "I don't want to work all day," and "You belong outside," which allowed it to compete indirectly with the work-like emphasis of domestic brands (e.g., "Built Ford tough"). Moreover, the entire compact truck category declined as consumers gravitated to larger trucks. Toyota planned in the future to connect its brand directly with the redesigned and larger Tundra for 2007; a recreational approach for the Tacoma required a complete revision because its new positioning needed to start the new truck direction for Toyota.

The promotional planners initially considered three different positioning strategies along the idea of "tough." The first involved a "work-tough" positioning by showing the Tacoma at work on Canadian oil fields and farms. A second, "recreation-tough," would show the Tacoma engaged in off-road activities. Finally, "international-tough" intended to demonstrate the Tacoma's use throughout the world. The final choice won out as the planners used live footage of Toyota trucks involved in delivering aid during international disasters to create the launch television commercial. The concept carried over to newspaper and magazine ads along with dealer events during the initial phase and carried the tagline "Never Quit."

Results over the next year provided evidence of a strong positioning. Some key communication effects improved substantially during the first seven months. Brand awareness gained from 83 percent to 95 percent, advertising awareness rose from 5 percent to 19 percent, and purchase intention increased from 22 percent to 40 percent. Many consumer perception ratings rose significantly and reached levels superior to those of competitors. For example, more than 70 percent of the consumers surveyed rated the Tacoma as high quality, dependable, well-built, and trusted. Sales for the first seven months grew by 176 percent and for the first 13 months reached 88 percent, with market share moving to the 14-percent to 16-percent range. These remarkable results occurred with Chevrolet re-branding its S-10 to Colorado and brands like Dodge Dakota and Ford Ranger spending more money on advertising than the Tacoma.

Source: Based on case studies at www.cassies.ca.

Questions

1. Why has the stronger truck emphasis in its advertising been successful for the Tacoma?
2. Do you agree with the idea of associating to "tough" as an appropriate positioning?
3. What is the connection of the "Never Quit" tagline with the "international-tough" positioning?

As the opening vignette implies, advertising and all IMC tools occur within a marketing strategy. In fact, marketing strategy influences the role of all promotional decisions, which must be coordinated to support other marketing programs within the marketing mix. Thus, promotion has a significant contribution toward the overall positioning of the product to selected target markets, or what is known as a market positioning strategy. However, advertising and all promotional activities described in the vignette have their own unique communication objectives to persuade a very particular target audience. In this sense, we can understand how various promotional tools and the whole promotional program influences the positioning of a brand to a designated target audience, or what is known as a brand positioning strategy.

Our investigation in this chapter—to understand positioning for both marketing strategy and marketing communication—is consistent with the distinction between target market and target audience (Chapter 3) and the importance of linking the overall communication strategy and objectives with the overall marketing strategy and objectives (Chapter 5). First, we review market positioning strategy, define brand positioning strategy, and subsequently describe the brand positing strategy decision process. We then define and illustrate the four decisions for developing a comprehensive brand positioning strategy. Finally, we explore opportunities for changing the brand positioning strategy, known as repositioning.

POSITIONING

In this section, we distinguish between positioning within the marketing strategy and positioning within the communications strategy. We also highlight the difference between the decision a manager makes in terms of a positioning strategy and the resulting effects in terms of the position in which the target market or target audience perceives the firm or brand to be competing. We end the section with an overview of the decision-making process for a brand positioning strategy.

MARKET POSITIONING STRATEGY

Any organization that wants to exchange its products or services in the marketplace successfully should have a **strategic marketing plan** to guide the allocation of its resources. A strategic marketing plan usually evolves from an organization's overall corporate strategy and serves as a guide for specific marketing programs and policies.

In Chapter 1 we emphasized the importance of advertising professionals to use the marketing plan as an important information source when planning for marketing communication decisions. The marketing plan summarizes the situation analysis comprising an evaluation of the company, consumers, environment, market, competition, the market positioning strategy, and specific marketing programs. In particular, those creating ads should be familiar with their client's or organization's market positioning strategy since it gives direction for how a brand should be positioned in the promotional program.

Positioning has been defined as "the art and science of fitting the product or service to one or more segments of the broad market in such a way as to set it meaningfully apart from competition."[1] A **market positioning strategy** concerns the final decision of the market(s) in which firms wish to compete, combined with the specific elements of the marketing mix that are designed to fulfill the respective needs of the market(s). Typically, firms will write a market positioning strategy statement in their marketing plan to accurately communicate this decision. This statement will be the guiding principle and direction for each of the four areas of decision within the marketing program development phase: product, price, distribution, and marketing communications.

IMC PERSPECTIVE 6–1

Lacoste Alligator On the Loose Again

The Lacoste brand of clothes with the alligator logo is a good example of a brand that once had a quality image, then a discount image, and finally repositioned itself as a quality product. The "alligator shirt," as it was called, had its heyday in North America in the late 70s and early 80s. But during the 1980s shoppers moved on; the owner General Mills cut prices and quality, dumping the shirts at Wal-Mart and other discount retailers. In 1992, General Mills sold the U.S. rights to the logo (by then rebranded as Izod) back to the Lacoste family. The brand languished until 2002, when the company relaunched it in North America as a quality brand using better material. To create a quality brand image, the company removed the brand from discount stores and began selling it to upscale department stores. Lacoste also opened freestanding boutiques in affluent shopping districts. The price point of Lacoste's shirt moved to $69, versus $35 back in the discount days. Although the intensely private operation won't share dollar figures, it says U.S. sales have soared 1000 percent in the past five years, making it Lacoste's largest and most profitable market to date.

Resurrecting a brand is cheaper than starting a brand from scratch. "The cost to build a new brand from scratch in North America is $100 million," says John Torella, a senior partner with J.C. Williams Group, a Toronto-based retail consultancy. Torella says that revitalizing an existing brand, especially if there remains an awareness of the brand, doesn't cost nearly as much. That a label is able to be revitalized has to do with the little fact of "brand biology." Like ants or dolphins, logos have life cycles. They go through periods where they grow in popularity, then become mainstream, and eventually die. A brand has to stay upstream. "Once a brand goes mainstream, it dies," says Torella. "Lacoste expanded, and soon its little alligator logo was on everything from socks to sweatbands. Lacoste got to the point where it was omnipresent," says Torella. "That's the way you kill a brand."

Sources: Greg Lindsay, "The Alligator's New Look," *Business 2.0*, April 2006; "Lacoste's Alligator Sheds Its Skin," *Business Week*, February 27, 2006; Christopher Shulgan, "Brand Renew," *The Ottawa Citizen* October 4, 2003.

Questions

1. How did Lacoste change its market position from discount to premium?
2. Can you think of other brands that have attempted such a transformation?

For example, different market segments in the personal computer (PC) industry include the home, education, science, and business markets. These segments can be even further divided. The business market consists of both small companies and large corporations; the education market can range from elementary schools to colleges and universities. A company that is marketing its products in the PC industry must decide in which particular market segment or segments it wishes to compete. This decision depends on the amount and nature of competition the brand will face in a particular market.

Fashion and luxury brands extend their name beyond their initial product success as the popularity of high-end brands reaches to consumers who are not typically considered wealthy. The ad for Chanel reinforces its place as a stylish brand compared to other more common brands (Exhibit 6–1). IMC Perspective 6–1 shows how a famous brand has changed its market positioning strategy over time.

As the firm develops its market positioning strategy, it may consider many combinations of product attributes with varying price levels across different retail outlets. Alternatively, it could evaluate narrow product choices with very wide distribution and a mass advertising appeal. A firm will consider as many feasible options as possible so that it does not miss a market opportunity. At this stage, the firm uses its market research and experience

Exhibit 6–1 Chanel is just one of many companies competing in the luxury goods market

wisely to put together a "package of benefits" that will be acceptable to the target market selected.

Once the marketing programs are developed and implemented, organizations may find results at, above, or below expectations. For example, sales or market share objectives may or may not be obtained. The reactions of consumers may be very close to what the firm intended, or they could be quite different. We define this response to be the **market position** of a firm. This distinction signifies that it is not the current or past strategic plans of the marketing managers, but rather the intended or unintended consumer beliefs of the organization's efforts.

To expand on these ideas, we will use the Canadian airline industry as an example. As of 2001, Air Canada represented essentially the only full-service national airline. While it has had various ad campaigns over the years, it has always attempted to maintain this full-service position, especially when it faced competition from Canadian Airlines. WestJet, previously a small regional discount carrier, purchased larger, newer jets so that it could offer services for cross-country routes.[2] Advertising now had to maintain its discount market position throughout the country.

We illustrate this situation with a simple market position diagram, recognizing that alternative interpretations may be feasible (Figure 6–1). We graph two axes, full and limited service versus high and low price. WestJet and Air Canada are opposite ends of the service spectrum. It appears that both companies have followed some kind of target market process and are putting together the most appropriate marketing program to be successful. While these initial market positioning strategies appear as suitable attempts to successfully deliver needed airline services, time would tell whether consumers truly believed that each occupies the intended market space and has the correct market position in terms of consumers' perceptions.

Over the next few years WestJet experienced substantial success in the market; however, it realized that consumers in general perceived a discount or low-cost airline to offer a "no-frills" or "bring your own seatbelt" kind of flight experience. Alternatively, it appeared that WestJet offered greater service than perceived—in other words, WestJet needed to improve its market position by moving from the bottom left of Figure 6–1 to somewhere closer to the horizontal line or even above it. This problem was one of two things that prompted the successful "WestJetters Are Owners" campaign. From an overall marketing standpoint, the campaign represented a new market positioning strategy. And the results materialized as four key measures of airline stature improved an average of 8 percent in a few short months.

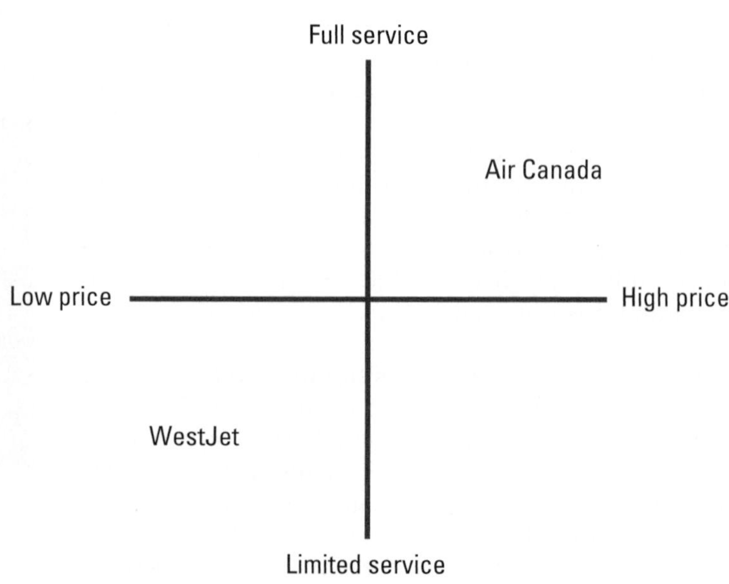

FIGURE *6–1*

Hypothetical illustration of market position of airlines

Brand Positioning Strategy

Since promotion is so visible, it is tempting to believe that it alone defines the market positioning strategy. While this may be true in some situations, in most cases, advertising and IMC campaigns typically focus on a particular message that helps consumers understand the product in comparison to other brands *within* a specific product market or category. Furthermore, most ads or other IMC tools speak to a very specific target audience. A bank can have a direct-mail piece to a current customer to obtain a mortgage renewal and focus the message on the ease of continuity and the good follow-up service. Or it may run a TV ad with a message of attractive interest rates and specialized options that may attract customers from competing banks. Since these are obviously different target audiences with different competitive reference points, we need to use the positioning concept appropriately in a communications context that is distinct from positioning in a marketing context. This notion of positioning in marketing communication is the topic to which we now turn.

Many advertising practitioners consider positioning the most important decision in establishing a brand in the marketplace. David Aaker and John Myers note that the term position has been used to indicate the brand's or product's image in the marketplace.[3] Jack Trout and Al Ries suggest that this brand image must contrast with competitors'. They say, "In today's marketplace, the competitors' image is just as important as your own. Sometimes more important."[4] Thus, a **brand positioning strategy**, as used in this text, relates to the intended image of the product or brand relative to a competing brand for a given competitive space as defined by certain product market or category characteristics. The brand positioning strategy is a key decision prior to determining the most effective selling message of the advertising or the IMC. The ad in Exhibit 6–2 targets consumers who drink bottled water and might enjoy carbonation.

Now consider consumer reactions to having seen television commercials or any other communication for any type of product or service. What do consumers think about the brand, having experienced the message? Do they have positive or negative feelings for the brand? What unique attributes or benefits come to mind when considering the brand? All of these questions pertain to the reactions consumers have to promotions, and constitute what we will refer to as the **brand position**. We need to distinguish between what the firm plans to do with its image versus what the actual image of the brand is, since both occur at different points in time and reside in different locations. The brand positioning strategy is a part of the overall advertising or IMC plan, while the brand position exists within the target audience.

Exhibit 6–2
Pepsi's Sparkling Aquafina targets a new audience

Let us return to our airline example. In the course of developing its discount market positioning strategy, WestJet has a number of options to communicate, of which we will highlight a couple. It could encourage those who never or rarely travel to consider flying since it is now so affordable. Or it may try to convince those who buy the cheapest economy-class tickets (i.e., red-eye flights back east) to buy a WestJet ticket and travel at a more civilized time of the day. In either case, there is a distinct brand positioning strategy decision made to reach each unique target audience. Accordingly, each target audience will have its own unique brand position based on its experiences with the ads and the service.

We continue this idea with a more competitive angle since Air Canada has entered the discount market with Tango. Both WestJet and Tango will compete to be the leader in the discount market, and WestJet may need some elements of its IMC plan to encourage WestJet customers not to switch to Tango or to switch Tango customers to WestJet. These are just a few examples of how WestJet could be using a brand positioning strategy to speak

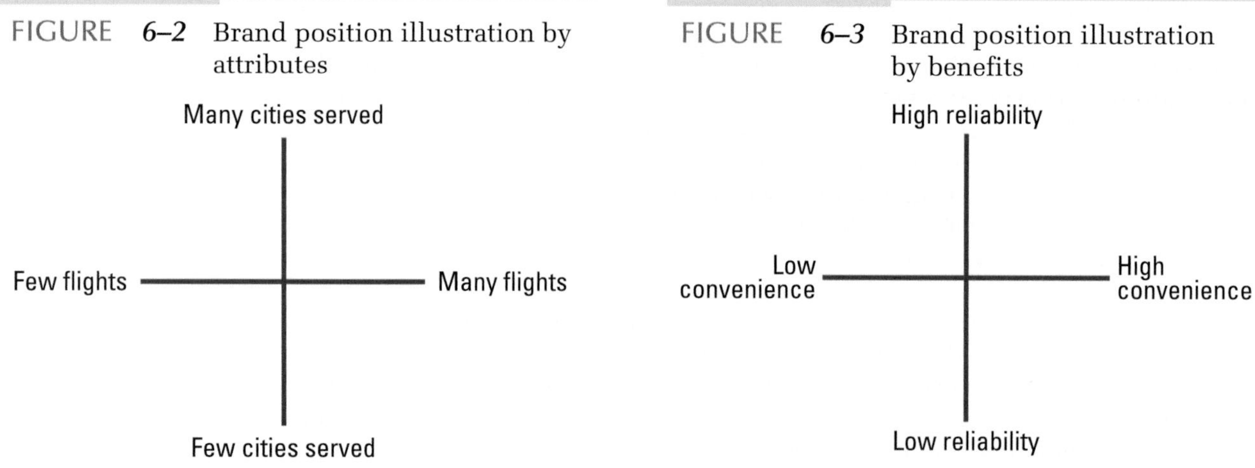

FIGURE 6–2 Brand position illustration by attributes

FIGURE 6–3 Brand position illustration by benefits

with unique target audiences who are a part of the overall target market and may be receptive to the overall market positioning strategy.

We now return to our brand position (i.e., consumer perceptions) diagram whereby WestJet and Tango are competing on certain **salient attributes**. Figure 6–2 shows two axes on which the companies *may* compete: frequency of flights and number of cities serviced. We hesitate to locate exactly where both of these firms are, since the discount market is starting to develop. We can also surmise that the airlines *may* be competing on certain **salient benefits** (Figure 6–3) of reliability (i.e., on-time departures, no mechanical delays) and convenience (i.e., check-in, ticket purchase).

The "WestJetters Are Owners" campaign addressed another concern. Focusing its message on superior customer service during the whole pre-flight, flight, post-flight experience allowed WestJet to attract dissatisfied Air Canada travellers who had possibly received poorer service. Preliminary research suggested that this target audience existed in sufficient numbers to ensure financial viability of the marketing communication investment. Follow-up research indicated that two measures of travel experience improved by 9 percent, and a third improved by 20 percent.

Two important implications arise from this example. The first concerns how the campaign contributed to both market position and the brand position for a specific target audience. The campaign allowed WestJet to establish an improved market position by indicating that it did not offer a discount experience. In this respect it inched closer to being a "full-fledged" airline in the eyes of most travellers. And, as established in the previous paragraph, the campaign also focused on a salient benefit that would be critical for motivating dissatisfied Air Canada passengers to switch. The second implication concerns how the salient consumer benefits for positioning evolve over time or differ across various target audiences. As WestJet became more established, the dynamics of how it could compete allowed it to compete on superior customer service.

Let us turn to another example to illustrate the importance of developing a distinct brand positioning strategy for a new target audience. Sleeman Brewery has maintained an authentic quality position as a microbrewer that makes craft beer (its market position). Much of Sleeman's recent success can be attributed to reaching a core of loyal drinkers in the 35+ age demographic who value its ingredients and brewing methods (brand position). Seeking to grow, Sleeman tried to attract a group of drinkers who were looking to switch as they matured (i.e., aged 25–35). So the issue focused on the appropriate brand positioning strategy to encourage these potential customers to believe that they would now value some of the attributes and benefits of this kind of beer, Sleeman beer in particular. Naturally, the brand positioning strategy that Sleeman used for its new target audience should not alienate the brand position of its loyal drinkers while at the same time maintaining its clear market position. This is quite the challenge and the ads seemed to work.

Sleeman decided to minimize the use of its long-time spokesperson John Sleeman for its English ads in 2001 while connecting consumption experiences with an attribute of the bottle. The clear glass shows the product clearly such that there is "nothing to hide." Picking up on this idea, the ads symbolically conveyed this with social situations where consumers had "nothing to hide." For example, we do not conceal our true thoughts and feelings when meeting someone. Sleeman continued the theme in 2002 and focused on the fact that the beer does not have a label. It played on the meaning of the word "label" and featured new music groups that had not been signed by a "record label." In both cases, these messages resonate more with a new younger audience.[5]

Brand Positioning Strategy Decision Process

We present a five-step process for making the brand positioning strategy, adapted from other sources.[6] Chapter 1 briefly outlined this process, but we investigate the actual steps in more detail here to fully understand the brand positioning strategy decisions.

Develop a Market Partition A useful approach for defining the market is to make it consistent with how consumers make a purchase decision. It is suggested that promotional planners view the market broadly as a general product category and subsequently divide the market into various sub-categories until consumers perceive brands as being relatively similar. The criteria for market partitioning include the type of product, end benefit, usage situation, and brand name. Figures 6–4 to 6–7 show a basic partition of the car market for each of these four approaches,

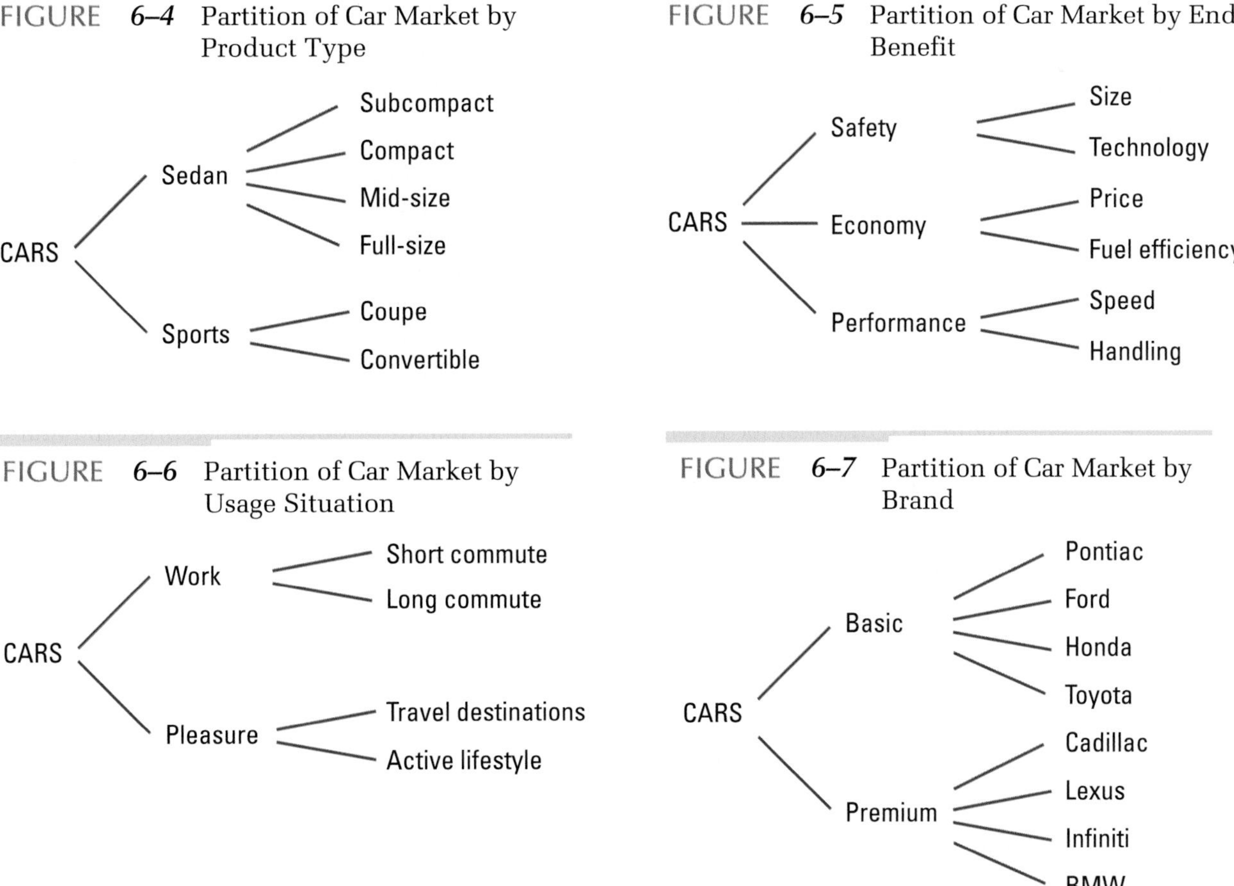

FIGURE *6–4* Partition of Car Market by Product Type

FIGURE *6–5* Partition of Car Market by End Benefit

FIGURE *6–6* Partition of Car Market by Usage Situation

FIGURE *6–7* Partition of Car Market by Brand

and these simple illustrations can be expanded or altered to the decision maker's requirements. This task is important for establishing the initial parameters for identifying the most important competitors to determine a unique positioning strategy that can be communicated.

Assess Competitors' Position Once we define the competitors through the market partition, we must determine how consumers perceive them by assessing their respective brand positions. To do so, we rely on new or existing consumer research. Oftentimes the research is a survey, indicating how consumers perceive the key brands on the more relevant and important attributes and benefits that consumers use when evaluating a brand. The data from these types of surveys are used to formulate the brand position maps shown previously in Figures 6–2 and 6–3.

Sometimes, preliminary consumer research may be necessary to ensure that promotional planners do not overlook key aspects some competitors may be communicating to establish a differential brand position. For example, cars compete on numerous attributes and benefits, and over time newer product characteristics may become important and need to be added to usual competitive profiles to accurately assess the brand positions.

Assess Brand Position Consumer research for the promotional planner's brand, either existing or new, is used to assess how consumers currently perceive the brand. This research would be compared with the previously determined brand positioning strategy (e.g., last year, or the prior 2–4 years). If current efforts are not working it may be time to consider an alternative strategy. Unless there is strong reason to believe a change in positioning is necessary, promotional planners are advised to maintain the current brand positioning strategy.

In situations where there is no established brand position, such as with a new product or where there has been no advertising for many years, promotional planners could assess characteristics that may be related to the corporate brand or complementary products in the organization's portfolio.

Determine Brand Positioning Strategy Going through the first three steps should provide direction for where to establish a brand position. The content of the decision is the focus of the remainder of this chapter. We will present a structure and summarize the parts for a well-developed brand positioning strategy. It is at this point in the process that the promotional planner will construct a detailed description by writing a brand positioning strategy statement.

The final decision is not always clear and well defined. The research used may provide direction, but not give a definitive picture. In that case, promotional planners will make subjective judgments based on experience. For example, promotional planners will consider whether there are sufficient resources to establish the brand position over time. Promotion generally requires substantial investment in media or other IMC tools for sufficient consumers in the target audience to receive and retain the message. In addition, they will assess the degree to which the brand positioning strategy will be strong enough in the face of competition.

Monitor Brand Positioning Strategy Once a brand position has been established, we want to monitor how well it is being maintained. Tracking studies measure the image of the brand over time. Changes in consumers' perceptions can be determined, with any slippage immediately noted and reacted to. At the same time, the impact of competitors can be assessed.

The brand positioning strategy decisions are an important requirement for setting the overall strategy for advertising. From this direction, the content of the advertising message, its creative strategy, and tactics can be formulated.

Thus, the next step is to ensure that the creativity and the content of the message persuades the target audience appropriately and is consistent with the brand positioning strategy. We illustrate this connection between strategy and the creativity and content of the message in the context of advertising since it is so pervasive and familiar. Many of the uniquely Canadian examples cited used advertising along with other tools and communicated a consistent brand positioning strategy. The decisions are consistent with other promotional communication tools. For example, prior to launching a public relations or publicity campaign, a marketer would specify the positioning of its brand to its intended target audience before deciding upon the exact content of its message and how he or she would creatively present it.

Brand Positioning Strategy Decisions

The essence of positioning the brand in the context of advertising is to clearly indicate where the brand is competing, with whom it is competing, how it is competing, and finally why consumers will purchase the brand. Each of these questions must be addressed through four decisions within the brand positioning strategy: market definition, differential advantage, target audience brand attitude, and consumer purchase motive.

Market Definition

A primary decision for positioning is how the promotional planners define the market and where they intend for the brand to compete with its benefit claims. The market partition illustrations showed that brands compete against other brands on end benefits, brand name, usage situation, and product category. One purpose of advertising is to contribute to developing a perceived advantage over competing brands within the competitive space. Thus, each of these offer tremendous opportunity to communicate benefit claims and establish a perceived differential advantage.

Positioning by End Benefit A common approach to positioning is setting the brand apart from competitors on the basis of the specific characteristics or benefits offered. Sometimes a product may be positioned on more than one product benefit. Marketers attempt to identify salient attributes (those that are important to consumers and are the basis for making a purchase decision).

For example, the focus of Harvey's advertising message, "Long Live the Grill," emphasizes an attribute regarding how they cook their hamburgers (Exhibit 6–3). Consequently, many consumers can easily interpret a benefit of good taste or better flavour compared with other fast food retailers.[7] Advertisers require good research and reasons for justifying this kind of positioning recommendation because moving toward a specific attribute like this precludes messages regarding other attributes and benefits.

Exhibit 6–3 Harvey's positions its hamburgers with a specific attribute

Selecting the right benefit is a very basic, but critical decision, and one that is often determined too quickly or without sufficient research. Recent research for Schick's Intuition razor for women, a one-step lather and shave design, revealed that women perceived "easy to use" as being much different than "convenient" despite these two usage benefits appearing very similar. This discovery created a substantially different positioning and gave the creative specialists different focus.

While we refer to benefits in this discussion, often marketers will make a direct link between a particular attribute and the derived benefit, or they may highlight the attribute and allow the target audience to interpret the benefit. Again, research for Schick's Quattro for women indicated indifference regarding the engineered four blades, but a distinct desire to know that the brand produced a truly long-lasting shave.[8]

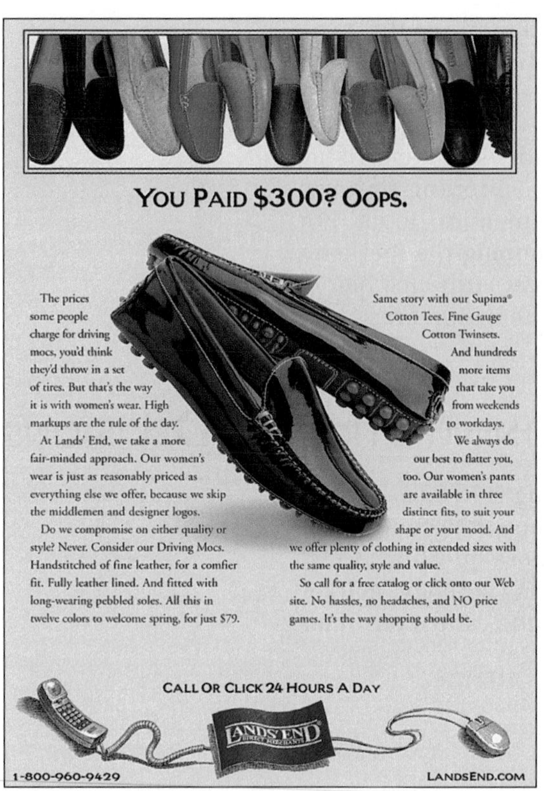

Exhibit 6–4 Lands' End positions its brand as having high quality for the right price

Exhibit 6–5 Arm & Hammer baking soda demonstrates numerous product uses

Positioning by Brand Name Marketers often use price/quality characteristics to position their brands. One way they do it is with ads that reflect the image of a high-quality brand where cost, while not irrelevant, is considered secondary to the quality benefits derived from using the brand. Premium brands positioned at the high end of the market use this approach to positioning.

Another way to use price/quality characteristics for positioning is to focus on the quality or value offered by the brand at a very competitive price. For example, the Lands' End ad shown in Exhibit 6–4 uses this strategy by suggesting that quality can be affordable. Remember that although price is an important consideration, the product quality must be comparable to, or even better than, competing brands for the positioning strategy to be effective.

Positioning by Usage Situation Another way to communicate a specific image or position for a brand is to associate it with a specific use. For example, Black & Decker introduced the SnakeLight as an innovative solution to the problem of trying to hold a flashlight while working. A TV commercial showed various uses for the product, while creative packaging and in-store displays were used to communicate the uses. While this strategy is often used to enter a market based on a particular use, it is also an effective way to expand the situational usage of a product. For example, Arm & Hammer baking soda has been promoted for multiple uses (Exhibit 6–5).

Positioning by Product Category Often the competition for a product comes from outside the product category. For example, airlines know that while they compete with other airlines, trains and buses are also viable alternatives. Via Rail has positioned itself as an alternative to airplanes, citing cost savings, enjoyment, and other advantages. Many margarines position themselves against butter. Rather than positioning against another brand, an alternative strategy is to position the brand against another product category.

Differential Advantage

Brand benefit claims embodied in the positioning and represented in the ads contribute to the differential advantage for a brand. While it is generally expected that a brand positioning strategy should take a differential positioning approach and have a product benefit focus, we highlight some situations where brands do not follow this pattern.

Differential vs. Central Positioning In the previous section, we mentioned the importance of advertising contributing to the perceived differential advantage for the brand. This is true for most brands; however, market circumstances allow brands to claim a central position within the product category. A central brand positioning strategy is possible when the brand can claim and deliver on the most salient benefits. This may be a function of the brand being the market share leader, achieving success during the growth stage of the product life cycle, or having unique brand characteristics that essentially define the category. A new brand of sub-compact car illustrates one successful central positioning strategy.

After a successful launch in Canada, Toyota changed its entry into the sub-compact car market from the Echo to the Yaris due to a change in international strategy. The problem appeared particularly vexing because the switch from Tercel to Echo had occurred just a few years previously. Moreover, the Echo sedan and hatchback established a 42-percent market share, so the change could have emerged as a significant risk for Toyota. The task seemed even more challenging when promotional planners acknowledged that the Yaris had improved styling, a higher price, and no advantageous standard features in a category that consumers perceived as an economic compromise with a rational purchase process. Finally, Toyota's research indicated a trend of its customers getting older, so a younger-oriented positioning also appeared necessary.

The solution emerged in the form of "Uncle Yaris," a fictional character to reflect the lifestyle associated with the brand and act as an adviser to young people without the stigma of the message arising from one's parents. The promotional planners decided to move away from the idea of a sub-compact car specifically and let its advertising act as a leader to attract consumers through its innovative creativity. It appears that the Yaris planners envisioned a market partition along the end benefit "fun to drive"—a more emotional criterion for purchase. Follow-up research indicated sales far superior to the Echo launch, a younger clientele, and a solid position as category leader with the consumer perception of being a fun car.

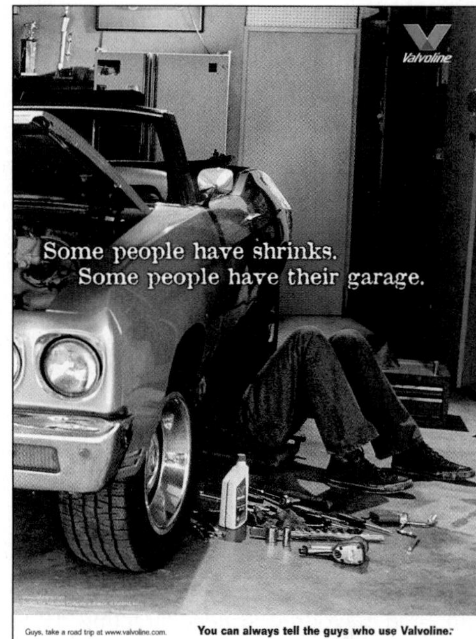

Exhibit 6–6 Valvoline positions by product user

Achieving central positioning in a category through advertising is not an easy task for most promotional planners. The Yaris example demonstrates that a market leader—or one of the market leaders—can attempt this position in mature product categories. It should be noted that the sub-compact market recently appeared in transition for a period as five-door hatchback vehicles and small cars in general made a comeback thanks to rising gasoline costs. In this sense, the market segment undertook renewed growth as consumers switched from other preferences and first-time buyers considered small cars more frequently.

In another market context, being the first brand in a product category is a good start, but research suggests it is not a guarantee; the second and third entries after the initial pioneer have established strong positions in some categories. As IMC Perspective 6–2 on page 158 illustrates, Clearly Canadian literally invented the alternative beverage category, yet was unable to establish itself with a central position—as evidenced by some of its recent strategies that are in the process of changing.

Brand Benefit versus User Positioning We have thus far implied that most positioning decisions involve unique and differential benefit claims that the brand can deliver. The market partition and competitive analysis gives promotional planners the opportunity to identify and determine the most important ones to claim in advertising. Again, while this is true for many product categories and brands, some situations allow for a user positioning. Often, a brand is positioned by association with a particular user or group of users. An example is the Valvoline ad shown in Exhibit 6–6. This campaign emphasizes identification or association with a specific group, in this case car enthusiasts. A user brand positioning strategy occurs in situations where the individual is motivated for social or individual reasons and the ads emphasize how good the consumer feels while using the brand (Exhibit 6–7).

Exhibit 6–7 Positioning that focuses on the product user

The Dodge SX 2.0 employed a user positioning in its advertising to re-brand its compact car from the previously named Chrysler Neon. The compact market is particularly competitive; it is the largest in sales and

IMC PERSPECTIVE 6–2

Clearly Canadian Rebounds

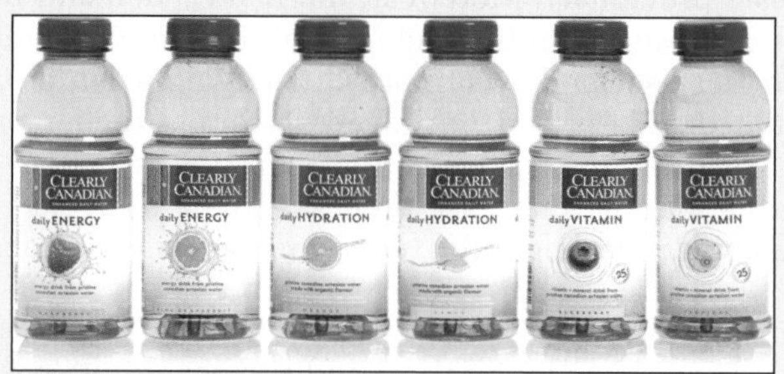

Since joining Clearly Canadian Beverage Corporation as president, Brent Lokash has been on a mission to put some fizz back into the troubled Vancouver-based drink company. He's signed home-grown sports heroes as pitchmen, branched into the fast-growing organic foods business, and has just cut a deal with a U.S. station to turn every move he and Clearly Canadian make into a reality TV series.

But getting the brand—which pretty much pioneered the alternative beverage category in the late 1980s with its flavoured waters and light blue bottles—back into shape won't be easy. The product category it helped create is now packed with a host of companies—including heavyweights like Pepsi and Coca-Cola—peddling everything from flavoured waters and iced teas to energy drinks. Clearly Canadian's sales have been on a steady slide for years, and earnings have also been non-existent.

Gone are novelty products such as Orbitz—a drink with edible coloured balls floating around inside. In its place Clearly Canadian is focusing on healthy drinks. It launched Enhanced Daily Waters, a line of energy, vitamin, and flavoured waters targeting 18-to 35-year-olds with names like dailyEnergy, dailyVitamin, and dailyHydration. "We've taken our original core drink, which is sparkling flavoured water, and brought it back to its traditional roots," he says.

Organic snack food is another part of Clearly Canadian's comeback. The company bought DMR Food Corporation, a company that sells organic snacks under the name Sweet Selections in Eastern Canada. Lokash also bought Ontario-based My Organic Baby. Lokash says he is emulating the Pepsi/Frito Lay model by connecting beverages and snack food. But while Pepsi links soft drinks and chips, Clearly Canadian is focusing on healthy foods, natural and organic snacks, organic baby food, and water.

Industry-watchers will be able to witness the results, thanks to the Clearly Canadian reality show airing in January 2008 on the U.S.-based MOJO high-definition cable network. Though televising your company's attempt at a comeback may sound bizarre, the idea, says Lokash, is to create an eight-episode *Venture*-like show, where Clearly Canadian is the star. According to a company press release, the show will give viewers full access to the "corporate drama, deal-making, and pressure that exists in the high stakes corporate world" as the film crew follows the company through promotional events, trade shows, distribution drives, and meetings with national retailers.

Lokash says that as well as showcasing the product to consumers, the show will help with distribution. "Distribution is the key to the beverage industry," he says. "We are not a company that can afford to spend big money on traditional media so this is a great thing."

Adding to the celebrity blitz, Lokash signed the NBA's Most Valuable Player, Steve Nash, to a three-year endorsement deal and recruited baseball player Justin Morneau, another B.C. native and American League MVP for the Minnesota Twins. "Sports figures are great for any beverage," he says. "For us we focus on Canadian because we are Clearly Canadian so it's a play on the word and a play on the personalities." Nash recently made an appearance in a video and contest for Clearly Canadian.

Source: Eve Lazarus, "Clearly a Comeback?" *Marketing Magazine*, April 16, 2007.

Question

1. How will the new IMC tools help re-establish the brand position for Clearly Canadian?

number of brands, and is an entry-level point for young buyers purchasing their first vehicle. Neon's sales had declined for seven consecutive years and languished at 3 percent of the small car market, yet still represented one-quarter of DaimlerChrysler's sales. This, combined with an older consumer compared to its major competitors, meant the renamed Dodge SX 2.0 needed a more youthful appeal. However, with no model makeover to speak of other than the brand name, and no obvious differential benefit to emphasize, the message needed to focus on the user. Enter the "Born to Be Alive" music, intended to connect with exuberant young adults who desired a car that could express their "be bold and powerful" outlook on life that consumer research supported. Moreover, this positioning contributed to the belief that young buyers looked for an expressive car that would be accepted by their peers.

Success came quickly for the newly branded Dodge SX 2.0. Market share moved to almost 5 percent in just six months—and a main competitor, Sunfire, saw its share decline by nearly 1 percent while receiving a substantial model improvement. Awareness and purchase intentions strengthened compared to Neon's old levels. These gains all occurred with the product changing virtually not at all, a slightly higher price, and no discount financing promotions.

Target Audience Brand Attitude

Previously in this chapter we identified the concepts of salient attributes or salient benefits. This notion is based on the idea that consumers may hold a number of different beliefs about brands in any product or service category. However, not all of these beliefs are activated in forming an attitude. Beliefs concerning specific attributes or benefits that are activated and form the basis of an attitude are referred to as **salient beliefs**. Marketers should identify and understand these salient beliefs. They must also recognize that the saliency of beliefs varies among different target audiences, over time, and across different consumption situations. To understand which attributes and benefits to emphasize in advertising, marketers often use a specific model that can be used to develop persuasive brand positioning strategies.

Brand Attitude Model Consumer researchers and marketing practitioners have been using multiattribute attitude models to study consumer attitudes for two decades.[9] A **multiattribute attitude model** views an attitude object, such as a product or brand, as possessing a number of attributes that provide the basis on which consumers form their attitudes. According to this model, consumers have beliefs about specific brand attributes and attach different levels of importance to these attributes. Using this approach, an attitude toward a particular brand can be represented as

$$A_B = \sum_{i=1}^{n} B_i \times E_i$$

where A_B = attitude toward a brand
B_i = beliefs about the brand's performance on attribute i
E_i = importance attached to attribute i
n = number of attributes considered

For example, a consumer may have beliefs (B_i) about various brands of toothpaste on certain attributes. One brand may be perceived as having fluoride and thus preventing cavities, tasting good, and helping control tartar buildup. Another brand may not be perceived as having these attributes, but consumers may believe it performs well on other attributes such as freshening breath and whitening teeth.

To predict attitudes, one must know how much importance consumers attach to each of these attributes (E_i). For example, parents purchasing toothpaste for their children may prefer a brand that performs well on cavity prevention, a preference that leads to a more favourable attitude toward the first brand. Teenagers and young adults may prefer a brand that freshens their breath and makes their teeth white and thus prefer the second brand.

Brand Attitude Persuasion Multiattribute models help marketers understand and diagnose the underlying basis of consumers' attitudes. By understanding the beliefs that underlie consumers' evaluations of a brand and the importance of various attributes or benefits, the marketer is better able to develop communication strategies for establishing, maintaining, increasing, modifying, or changing brand attitudes. The multiattribute model provides insight into several ways marketers can influence and persuade consumer attitudes.

Influence Attribute Belief The first strategy is commonly used by advertisers. They identify an attribute or benefit that is important and remind consumers how well their brand performs in either case. In situations where consumers do not perceive the marketer's brand as possessing an important attribute or the belief strength is low, advertising strategies may be targeted at changing the belief rating. Even when belief strength is high, advertising may be used to increase the rating of a brand on an important attribute. The Harvey's campaign for grill-cooked hamburgers illustrates this approach. Other quick-service food retailers focused on fast drive-through or convenient locations, along with enhanced menus with healthier foods. Harvey's appeared disadvantaged in comparison and faced declining sales and a reduced number of franchises. The grill attribute positioning conjured both functional benefits (e.g., fresh, natural, healthy) and emotional benefits (e.g., outdoor BBQ, male bonding). The positioning succeeded with unaided awareness moving from 13 percent to 22 percent, key brand attitude measures improving, purchase intention rising from 21 percent to 38 percent, and negative sales growth of 3 percent reversed to positive growth of 2 percent.

Influence Attribute Importance Marketers often attempt to influence consumer attitudes by changing the relative importance of a particular attribute. This second strategy involves getting consumers to attach more importance to the attribute in forming their attitude toward the brand. Marketers using this strategy want to increase the importance of an attribute their particular brand has. The print ads for Jergens Ultra Care moisturizer highlight the importance to a woman of regularly applying lotion all over her body. The positioning was intended to demonstrate that moisturizing was as important as all the other beauty activities that women engage in every day. The main message suggested that women "Take care of what you wear every day" with a visual showing the lotion on a woman's body, and obviously associated a woman's skin with her wardrobe. The positioning was initiated in Quebec as the brand underachieved significantly compared to other parts of Canada. Research indicated that women from Quebec did not separate beauty and skin care from health. This insight suggested that new users could be attracted to the brand if the ads conveyed the sensuality of moisturized skin. A 50 percent increase in sales in Quebec allowed the brand's positioning to be extended in English rather than continuing with the planned U.S. ads.

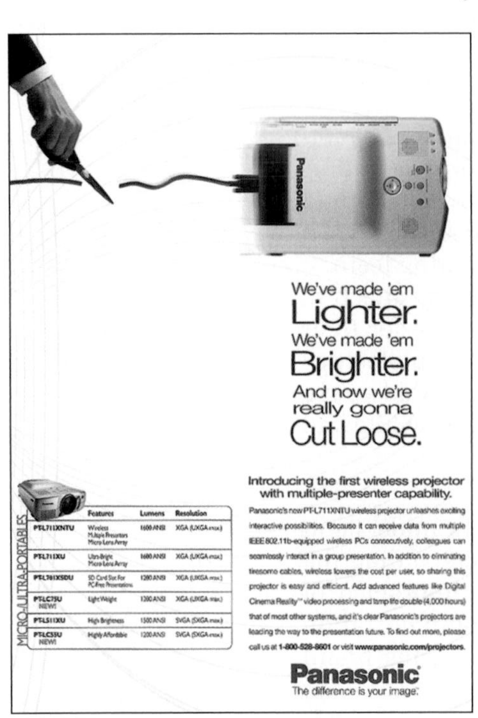

Exhibit 6–8 Panasonic adds a new attribute for customers to consider

Add New Attribute Belief The third strategy for influencing consumer attitudes is to add or emphasize a new attribute that consumers can use in evaluating a brand. Marketers often do this by improving their products or focusing on additional benefits or consequences associated with using the brand. Exhibit 6–8 shows how Panasonic is introducing wireless technology in an attempt to influence consumers' attitudes. Wonder Plus, a line extension of the famous Wonder bread, needed to communicate that it had the same great taste as the original, but that it had the nutrition of whole wheat bread. The new brand attempted to influence lapsed users of Wonder Bread due to the perception that white bread was no longer healthy. Yet at the same time, managers knew that the message had to reinforce the attitude of loyal customers. Adding the health benefit worked with clever imagery of twins eating both types of bread and believing that they both taste the same, yet one is now whole wheat. The positioning of this advertising produced significant gains for all communication effects and sales.

Influence Attribute Belief of Competitor Brand A final strategy marketers use is to change consumer beliefs about the attributes of competing brands or product categories. This strategy has become much more common with the increase in comparative advertising, where marketers compare their brands to competitors' on specific product attributes. An example of this is the comparative ad shown in Exhibit 6–9.

Exhibit 6–9 Influencing beliefs of competitor brand

Consumer Purchase Motive

Since positioning involves presenting the brand's benefit claims to a target audience, the portrayal of the benefits influences how consumers will respond to the brand's delivery and whether the target audience perceives them as important. The portrayal of benefits is reflected by the purchase motivation associated with the brand. Thus, the purchase motivation of the target audience is another important decision for the brand positioning strategy.

Importance of Purchase Motives As we suggested with the Harvey's attribute positioning, given the content of the ad, the underlying reason for enjoying a grilled hamburger appears to be the taste sensation. However, another perspective is that it could reflect healthier eating (i.e., compared to fried hamburgers) since there is less fat retained in the meat and consequently less fat consumed and a consumer can feel better about oneself and their dietary choices. This connection between the cooking attribute and healthier eating could have been communicated with some subtle changes in the ads of the current campaign. Thus, the attribute positioning still requires the right kind of motivation or reason for purchase demonstrated in the ad to be completely successful.

Keep in mind that the reasons for the Harvey's hamburger purchase are quite distinct: the sensory enjoyment of the hamburger versus the individual accomplishment of eating properly. We highlight these two ideas since they are two of eight basic consumer purchase motives that are more managerially useful to guide the brand positioning strategy decision within Rossiter and Percy's framework we have discussed previously. Figure 6–8 summarizes these motives into two types consistent with psychological theory.

Informational motives are negatively based since the consumer perceives their current consumption situation as some kind of deficit in which the purchase of the product would minimize the shortfall and bring the consumer a neutral or normal state. Exhibit 6–10 suggests an informational motive for non-users. **Transformational motives** imply consumers perceive their consumption situation as requiring some improvement from a neutral state. Negative and positive oriented motives are consistent with psychological theories of motivation and are similar to Maslow's theory—however, there is no implied hierarchy. Exhibit 6–11 on page 162 conveys a transformational motive for runners.

Exhibit 6–10 Ad implies incomplete satisfaction of competing brands

Informational Motives Problem removal motives reflect consumption situations where consumers perceive a problem, for example dandruff, and seek a product that resolves the problem, like anti-dandruff shampoo. Many such products in this

Informational Motives	Transformational Motives
Problem removal	Sensory gratification
Problem avoidance	Intellectual stimulation or mastery
Incomplete satisfaction	Social approval
Mixed approach-avoidance	
Normal depletion	

FIGURE 6–8

Eight basic consumer purchase motives

Exhibit 6–11 Ad captures the personal dedication of training

category have emphasized this motive in their ads while attempting to highlight its unique attribute or benefit positioning. However, more recent ads for Head and Shoulders in Canada have mentioned the problem while emphasizing how beautiful one's hair feels with their anti-dandruff shampoo, thus reflecting a different primary motive beyond the initial problem removal. Herein lies the reason for connecting the purchase motive shown in the ad to the brand positioning strategy—it identifies the particular way to communicate effectively with a target audience that the brand has profiled in great detail.

Problem avoidance motives occur when consumers anticipate a problem if they do not take some pre-emptive action through the purchase of a product. Listerine successfully illustrated a problem avoidance motive in its ad messages by colourfully showing how mouthwash superheroes fight germs that cause bad breath. While a positioning by use may be operational, the underlying reason for purchase more precisely defines the overall strategy.

Incomplete satisfaction motives are based on the consumer perceptions that they are not fully satisfied with their current brand choice and are seeking a better product. The Canada food retailer New York Fries, with 180 outlets in Canada, Australia, and the Middle East, emphasized fresh-cut potatoes and cooked to order in a new "Authentically New York" ad message.[10] A positioning on quality, directed toward teens and young adults who purchase high volumes of quick-service food, resonates with those who are not completely satisfied with french fries from multiple competing outlets. From another perspective, we can see ads that indicate an incomplete satisfaction motive yet have a positioning by competitor focus. For example, Bell Mobility ran ads inviting Fido users to switch their cell phone provider.[11]

Mixed approach-avoidance motives are active for consumers in purchase situations where they enjoy some elements of a product but dislike other parts and are seeking alternative solutions. WestJet proclaimed itself a low-fare leader in its initial advertising messages. As it developed its service, it also evolved the message to show that it flew more destinations with fun and friendly service.[12] It appears WestJet employed a price/quality brand positioning strategy and its ability to find a competitive niche against Air Canada suggests a mixed approach-avoidance motive, where some consumers liked Air Canada but were seeking a more affordable alternative that had reasonably comparable service levels.

Consumers requiring a product because they have none in stock occurs regularly, and so a normal depletion as a reason for purchase is almost an everyday situation;

however, it is not a viable option for a primary brand positioning strategy. A message focusing on a reminder purchase when a consumer does not have the product is featured in seasonal purchases. For example, gardening products in the spring and back to school supplies in the fall are two obvious ad messages we commonly see. In essence, a normal depletion motive is not a long-term strategy, however, it is useful for short-term situations and reaching particular target audiences at a particular point in time to maximize total sales during a year.

Transformational Motives As the term implies, sensory gratification motives are predicated on the product providing a positive experience via one of the five senses. Clearly, this is a valuable approach for indicating purchase in motive for many types of products, but it is important to focus on the right aspect with the right reference point. Encouragement to attend horse racing in Alberta for similar reasons as going to the movies, for the entertainment value, demonstrated a brand repositioning strategy or perhaps positioning by product class to non-users and indicated a sensory gratification motive. Small ads designed like movie ads and placed in the entertainment section of newspapers (versus the sports section to reach current users) provided an entertainment alternative and increased awareness and attendance.[13]

Intellectual stimulation or mastery is an individual motive linked to some element of self-improvement through the purchase of a particular product. Working with its Canadian agency, US Organic Orange Growers sought to develop the Canadian market with the same message "Grown in the U.S.A." that worked well south of the border. Research indicated that Canadians knew that most oranges originated from the U.S., in addition to a few other countries, however, they perceived this attribute with less importance compared to the fact that organic oranges contained 30 percent more vitamin C.[14] Appealing with a health attribute brand positioning strategy, we surmise that improved diet indicates an intellectual stimulation motive as consumers demonstrated their concern for well-being and heightened involvement in their nourishment needs.

Personal recognition is suggested with the social approval motive whereby consumers are motivated to purchase certain product or brands because consumers aspire to be accepted in certain social groups. An anti-smoking message by the Nova Scotia Office of Health Promotion illustrates a social approval motive within the context of positioning toward the product user. The characters from the Canadian cult film *Fubar* provided great tongue-in-cheek reasons to smoke by emphasizing the benefits of body odour and emphysema. The campaign thus positioned non-smoking to non-users of tobacco as something socially desirable.[15]

Competing Positioning Motives Oftentimes, various brands within a product category will compete on a similar motive yet emphasize unique attributes and benefits with a memorable creative campaign. However, we also see instances where the positioning of competing brands will imply different motives. For example, recent ads for Subway focused on health benefits and dietary concerns, implying an intellectual stimulation motive, while Mr. Sub and Quiznos ads addressed the "quality ingredients" and "toasted buns" respectively, implying a sensory gratification motive.[16] Subway competed beyond the sub sandwich market (i.e., fast-food hamburgers and chicken) and communicated a different and more unique motive from both direct and indirect competitors. The art of positioning and its connection to the creative ad message is challenging, and subtle changes must be done with careful consideration to be successful.

Brand Repositioning Strategy

The brand positioning strategy may have to be changed due to many factors found in situation analysis. For example, marketing objectives such as sales or share may be below forecast, or advertising claims from competitors may threaten the current strategy. Developing a new brand positioning strategy is referred to as repositioning.

This is often difficult to achieve because of established attitudes to the brand. The options for altering the brand positioning strategy typically focus on the same four topics previously defined: market definition, differential advantage, target audience, and a salient motive.

Market Definition

McCain's Crescendo Rising Crust Pizza experienced weak results after battling with Kraft's Delissio for five years. Despite McCain introducing the first product and establishing the frozen pizza category, Kraft outsold McCain by a four to one margin in the $400-million market due to heavier retail and advertising expenditures. The initial message from both brands positioned the products against pizza ordered from a restaurant (i.e., pizzeria) and delivered or picked up from the location. For example, McCain claimed, "Who can tell it from takeout?" while Kraft exclaimed, "It's not delivery, it's Delissio!" Clearly, both brands defined the market in terms of a store purchase for home preparation versus a restaurant takeout/delivery purchase, thus exhibiting a product category positioning.

McCain repositioned Crescendo on the key benefit of a "rising crust," distancing it from the established product category positioning that Kraft owned. The rising crust claim implied quality, freshness, and taste. The repositioning also featured a change in target audience to teens who recommended or influenced the pizza purchase to their parents, who did the shopping and paid for the groceries. The "Tan Lines" campaign, with the tagline "Nothing rises like Crescendo," carried out this positioning as oblivious teens got slight tan lines on their faces while they watched the crust rise as it baked.

Media included television and billboards, while teens with makeup tan lines offered coupons and buttons at street promotional events. Impressive results emerged as sales rose 34 percent, market share increased 8 percent, and some research reported increased awareness. Finally, the campaign garnered publicity as it was spoofed on *Air Farce* and *This Hour Has 22 Minutes,* satirized by Aislin in a *Montreal Gazette* cartoon, and featured in a newspaper article that jokingly questioned scientists as to whether one could get tan lines through an oven door.

Differential Advantage

As discussed earlier, determining the differential advantage concerned a differential versus central positioning, and product benefits versus user positioning. RBC's "First for You" campaign launched in 2004 appears to have repositioned the brand on both accounts. RBC looked to have an overall campaign for each of its three businesses—personal banking, corporate, and institutional—with the goal of increasing the number of products purchased by its current customers from its current 2.46.

Previous messages focused on benefits of RBC's products and services with an emphasis on differentiation. Instead, the new campaign emphasized the innovativeness of the organization over time through such things like sports sponsorship, personal services, and credit card rewards with the intention to convey RBC as the market leader in the banking industry. In other words, the brand moved from a differentiated positioning strategy to a central positioning strategy. Depicting a customer representing the letter "I" in the word "first" and emphasizing their satisfaction in selecting RBC contributed to a shift from a product benefit positioning strategy to a user positioning strategy.

The launch featured multiple media, and over the course of the first two years RBC ran 19 TV ads, 140 print ads, and 30 posters. The campaign also included events, direct, Internet, and corporate communication. Total spending amounted to

$26 million annually, about the same as previous years. Results for RBC imply the new positioning is headed in the right direction. Some awareness, attitudinal, and brand equity measures suggest RBC is in the top 20 percent for all financial ads. Products per customer rose, suggesting a strong ROI for the advertising investment.

New Target Audience

As we saw in Chapter 3, organizations target advertising messages to both customers such as brand loyals and favourable brand switchers, and non-customers such as new category users, other brand switchers, and other brand loyals. We now illustrate various repositioning strategies for each of these target audiences.

Brand-Loyal Customers Gatorade experienced a decline in the sports drink market for the first time in 20 years during 2004. Faced with competition within its category from Powerade, and pressure from emerging product categories such as energy drinks and new formats for water (enhanced, flavoured), Gatorade saw its share slip from 73 percent to 68 percent. Although the efficacy of Gatorade for hydration is scientifically established, regulations do not allow this benefit claim to be communicated in broadcast media. Finally, despite an established brand position as "the" sport drink for all male athletes who play their best at all times and desire maximum performance, Gatorade required a new approach to maintain its past success.

Consumer insight suggested that Canadian sports people enjoyed playing and watching many sports despite being overwhelmingly passionate about hockey. This differed significantly from American male athletes and indicated an opportunity to associate a unique consumption experience for the new flavour, X-Factor. A key execution in this reformulated strategy showed the many sports in which Gatorade might be consumed in a montage of scenes moving from the letter A to the letter X, ending with a product shot of the new entrant. For example, for the letter B, the visual showed an overhead picture of a hockey net, which outlines the letter (for example, Exhibit 6–12).

Exhibit 6–12
Gatorade has a history of creative commercials to position its brand

The positioning established important effectiveness measures as "level of enjoyment" and "relevance" hit levels well beyond average—as did purchase intention. Sales and share improved while Powerade's sales declined, giving some indication that Gatorade had regained some of its loyal customers with a new image.

Favourable Brand Switcher Customers For the 2005 model year, Toyota had its hands full in the compact car category as the well-established Corolla attempted to defend its share against a new model from Honda Civic and more recent models from Mazda, Pontiac, and Chevrolet, along with newer Korean brands offering very good value. In 2004, the Civic led the category with 46,000 units sold; Corolla and Mazda were close behind.

Research indicated that among various key benefits 56 percent of consumers believed the Corolla to be reliable and dependable, compared to the 34 percent of consumers believing compact cars could deliver reliability or dependability. This fit well with the psychographic profile of Corolla buyers, who tended to balance form and function when buying almost anything, and to whom minimizing risk when buying something like a car appeared very important. So while the positioning on reliability to compact consumers in the market during 2005 may have seemed kind of boring, the resulting message of "One thing you can count on" hit the mark just right. By May 2006 Corolla edged ahead of the Honda Civic, even while spending less than half as much money on communication.

New Category Users With 3 percent of the juice drink market, Five Alive faced the task of growing beyond its predominant sales to mothers aged 25–54 purchasing mostly for their children. The new target audience identified young adults 25–34, of which one-third were regular users despite awareness at 72 percent. In particular, the brand focused on a psychographic group labelled "experiencers," who desired to try new experiences in all facets of life (e.g., social and leisure activities) just prior to moving on to "family life" in a few years. In addition, the five fruit juices provided a unique drink for this lifestyle that appeared healthier than pop or iced tea and easier to consume than 100-percent juice. Although Five Alive could not claim "Five Alive makes you feel alive" due to legal regulations, it could claim that "Five Alive captures the spirit of feeling alive." Thus, the ads communicated the positioning of the five fruit flavours as a unique characteristic of the brand.

Over five years, Five Alive employed many TV and out-of-home ads to produce impressive results. Brand and advertising awareness and attitudinal measures increased substantially. For instance, ad awareness improved from 44 percent to 82 percent despite actually lowering the amount of money spent on advertising over time. Purchase intentions rose from 30 percent to 38 percent and trial rates improved from 70 percent to 75 percent. By the end of five years sales had nearly doubled to $40 million while the category shrank by 4 percent, allowing Five Alive to move market share from 2.5 percent to 5.2 percent.

Other Brand Loyals Scotiabank tackled the problem of attracting non-customers after spending considerable time building loyalty among its own customers. Many consumers of other banks believed that switching banks would not be worth the effort, with an attitude that "all banks are the same." Since the four other major banks attained about 30 percent household penetration each, Scotiabank envisioned an opportunity to move beyond its level of 19 percent. Research indicated a prevailing theme of some consumers needing banking services to help manage their money more effectively on a month-to-month basis. Many experienced frustration while working hard and making sufficient income, yet feeling like they did not have sufficient resources.

Scotiabank's positioning on enhanced financial service, encapsulated by the phrase "You're richer than you think," allowed the brand to connect with consumers dissatisfied with their experiences at other banks. The ads to support this positioning clearly showed how Scotiabank would help consumers find money they did not know they had by managing their loans and financing more effectively. IMC tools employed to support this innovative brand positioning strategy included TV and magazine ads, branch point-of-sale, direct mail, Internet, permission-based e-mail, and financial seminars.

The new positioning appeared promising for Scotiabank after 18 months; brand awareness increased from 36 percent to 56 percent, and unaided TV advertising awareness moved from 6 percent to 22 percent while aided grew from 15 percent to 39 percent. Scotiabank noted stronger brand associations, and purchase intentions grew to 33 percent from 24 percent. Finally, business results improved—$40 million profit with a 38 percent increase in new customers per month.

Other Brand Switchers With share dwindling to below 5 percent because of lagging product innovation and weak advertising expenditure, Juicy Fruit managers determined that the brand required a radical change in the positioning strategy with respect to its target audience. Its historical target of reasonably loyal adults aged 18–34 who comprised half the brand's sales would be teens who accounted for only 6 percent of sales. Moreover, teens represented the heaviest users and exhibited fickle preferences across brands due to their impulse purchase habits, whereby 84 percent purchased chewing gum weekly.

Preliminary qualitative research produced the concept of "sweet." The meaning to teens implied both "cool" and "don't to take things too seriously." To establish this positioning, it meant Juicy Fruit had to literally destroy the old positioning to show "cool" things to teens with the iconic smashing guitar scenes in the TV ads. Sweet described the brand's classic fruit flavour, so the double meaning appeared as another catchy way to reinvent Juicy Fruit's old image. Sweet also allowed Juicy Fruit to have an overall positioning for all its product formats (i.e., sugar free, blue, red).

Overall market share more than doubled to almost 11 percent by the end of 2004 and returned the brand to profitability. Awareness undoubtedly improved, but critical brand image statistics supported the idea that Juicy Fruit had established a new brand position with teens. A tracking study suggested stronger attitudes toward Juicy Fruit compared to Dentyne Ice and Trident for characteristics like "fun," "cool," and "brand I can relate to." Teen consumption shifted from the initial 6 percent of sales to 19 percent.

Purchase Motivation

A brand repositioning strategy through consumer purchase motivation implies a shift from one type of motive to another. The most significant shift would be moving from an informational motive to a transformational motive or vice versa. We present two examples to show successful repositioning through a new consumer purchase motivation.

Problem–Solution Moores Clothing for Men found great success by altering the purchase motive conveyed in its ads. Originally named Moores: The Suit People, an entry-level retailer, initial advertising promised the line, "Well Made. Well Priced. Well Dressed." Although quality perceptions grew, because of the "high-end" look of some of its ads consumers became confused as to whether the brand represented a discount clothing store or a fashion store. The new positioning clearly showed men with various wardrobe problems like *suit too tight* or *suit out of style,* and offered Moores as a solution (see Exhibit 6–13 on page 168). This positioning connected with a group of men who wore business clothes for work yet preferred not to wear such

Moores
Two business men walking down the street wearing the same suit.
The business man on the right bought his suit from Moores.
The street light turns red and the man on the right stops while the one on the left continues.
The business man on the left gets hit by a cyclist and falls to the ground.
Moores
Well Made.
Well Priced.
Well Dressed.

Exhibit 6–13 Moore's repositioning introduced a purchase motive not seen for clothes

clothes and would rather spend their disposable income on other life purchases. For this target audience, shopping was a necessary activity rather than entertaining or adventurous. Moores certainly carved out a niche with this positioning, as sales growth reversed from 4.5 percent to 6.5 percent.

Intellectual Stimulation Listerine's established position as a mouthwash that "kills germs that cause bad breath" had run its course as consumers became more active in their oral health instead of relying completely on their dentist. From a competitive standpoint, consumers believed the brand to be "old," "serious," and "authoritarian," and Listerine fell behind the market leader Scope and private-label brands as consumers did not perceive much difference. As part of the increased awareness and behaviour change for oral health, consumers became more concerned about the health of their gums. Listerine's clinical research proved that it could be effective against gingivitis, but the connection for this gum disease and mouthwash appeared to be very distant in the eyes of consumers. Listerine targeted "therapy seekers," those consumers who actively managed their health including their oral health. They appeared receptive to an empowering message oriented to their personal decision to be a healthier person.

The creative to support this positioning emerged as "Listerine: The action hero for your gums." Over the course of six years, the new positioning allowed Listerine to grow remarkably. In the first three years, Listerine improved its key brand image ratings—such as helps fight gingivitis, promotes healthy mouth, and kills germs—from an average of about 50 percent to 80 percent. Purchase intention and usage rates improved by about 10 percent each as well. Awareness of the ads showed strong numbers, and many consumers could link the ads to the brand. These numbers remained very strong for the remaining three years and showed continued modest gains. Finally, Listerine moved its market share from 39 percent to 52 percent while Scope's declined from 28 percent to 20 percent.

IMC Planning: Brand Positioning Extensions

From an IMC planning perspective, we can extend or adapt the concepts encompassing the brand positioning strategy decisions in three directions: multiple target audiences, buyer decision stages, and corporate brands. The idea is to work with the general model for the positioning decisions and modify it for different parts of the IMC plan.

Multiple Target Audiences

Throughout this chapter we have examined the brand positioning strategy for a single target audience of end users. Many organizations target multiple audiences for their marketing communications based on many reasons. For example, in

Chapter 3 we outlined different customer and non-customer groups; brands in fact do have the opportunity to invest in communications devoted to each group. This raises the question as to whether the brand should develop exactly the same positioning strategy for each target audience, or whether some variation should exist. And if variation is necessary, what aspects of the brand positioning strategy need to be customized? A number of the examples in Chapter 3 implied this issue; however, after describing positioning strategy, we need to return to the opportunity for promotional planners to fully consider their options.

Although promotional planners could consider customizing all four brand positioning strategy decisions, the first two, market definition and differential advantage, would likely remain relatively constant across customer and non-customer groups. The specific messages to influence brand attitude and the purchase motive communicated offer greater opportunity for getting the right message at the right time. One IMC tool to execute this customized brand positioning strategy is the Internet. For example, advertisers might consider consumers who visit websites to gather information while searching for a vehicle as more likely to be brand switchers, and will include messages that position the brand against its strongest competitor on specific benefits and portray those benefits along the lines of the target audience having some dissatisfaction with their current brand. While this is just one example, promotional planners can look at all advertising options and all IMC tools for opportunities to deliver a more specific message to a particular target audience that reinforces a particular brand positioning strategy.

Another interpretation for multiple target audiences involves group decision making, another topic introduced in Chapter 3. For example, in traditional family situations an advertiser may attempt one brand positioning strategy for mothers/ fathers and a relatively different one for children. McDonald's has historically employed this approach with communication directed to children featuring Ronald McDonald and other characters, while parents received messages of the special time they could enjoy with their family. Keeping the husband and wife scenario, automobile brands can use print ads to emphasize certain car features that appeal to men in magazines where men represent a higher proportion of the audience, and similarly for women.

Buyer Decision Stages

In the IMC Planning section of Chapter 5 we noted that marketers should consider various message and communication tool options for each stage of the consumer decision-making process. Various message options can be discerned from the brand positioning strategy decisions outlined in this chapter. First, promotional planners can decide which part of the brand positioning strategy would be most relevant or effective at each stage. Market definition and differential advantage may be more appropriate at the pre-purchase stage or need-recognition stage. For example, the marketing for the Mini in Canada used television advertising to signal that it competed against two markets: regular compact cars like Honda Civic, and other smaller sports cars like the BMW 3 Series. It also emphasized its advantage of being small in size, but not too small.

In contrast, Internet microsites (mini.ca/experiment, mini.ca/choice, mini.ca/ family, mini.ca/date) offered positioning on specific benefits with a transformational motive for consumers actively searching for information about the new brand. In fact, the Internet microsites facilitated customer relationships by inviting prospects to register. Mini reported an average response rate of 20 percent for each of the four sites. The brand positioning strategies along buyer decision stages also illustrated the second option. Specifically, promotional planners can use different IMC tools to communicate certain elements of the brand positioning strategy. Finally, promotional planners can use various media to convey specific attributes that are not in other media. For example, Mini used billboards to communicate its British heritage and speed, and magazines to illustrate its safety.

Corporate Brands

Thus far we have defined brand positioning strategy and illustrated examples where the brand is at the product level. For instance, our initial brand positioning strategy example involved WestJet and how its communications intended to establish an enhanced brand position among dissatisfied Air Canada customers. Corporate brands are also part of integrated marketing communications and are the focus of the public relations topics in Chapter 15. In this context, corporate brands often have varied target audiences, for example investors or members of a particular community.

Given the broader scope of the corporate brand, the initial positioning decision for market definition would concern brand name in most cases. Establishing a differential advantage from a corporate brand entails both differential and central positioning. For example, corporate brand-building activities for Honda suggest that it attempted to establish a central positioning concerning environmental responsibility. This would coincide with its marketing activities of introducing the first hybrid vehicle. Again, the organization-wide communication would imply that most corporate brand positioning would focus on brand benefit positioning over user positioning; however, recent "green marketing" efforts by companies suggest potential for the latter with an appropriate message that signifies altruistic feelings upon the target audience.

All marketing communication decisions are or should be designed to influence target audience attitudes, so corporate brand attitude persuasion is entirely relevant. For example, organizations often involve themselves in various sponsorship activities to signal that they are socially responsible, a key attribute to communicate to the general public or to future employees or other stakeholders. Finally, most corporate brand communication is intended along the lines of transformational motives; the clearest examples are television commercials with triumphant music and everlasting positive images.

SUMMARY

The strategic marketing plan describes all marketing decisions including promotion and the supporting analysis and justification. It typically includes the market positioning strategy, which summarizes the markets the organization is competing in (i.e., target market) and how the marketing mix fulfills the needs of this market. The resulting consumer perception as to where the consumer believes the organization to be competing is known as the market position. Oftentimes, market research illuminates where consumers perceive an organization with respect to its competitors, which can be graphed on a market position diagram or perceptual map. Promotional planners rely on this document for all decisions including the overall IMC direction, creative strategy, and creative tactics for advertising or any other IMC tool such as sales promotion, public relations, direct, or Internet.

For many communication problems or opportunities, promotional messages are directed to target audiences. These audiences are a subset of the target market or an entirely different group depending upon the communications situation. As discussed in Chapter 3, promotional planners require a detailed profile of the target audience with most appropriate segmentation variables, including whether the target is a customer or non-customer. Advertising or any other promotional message is guided by the brand positioning strategy that specifies how it is intended to influence its target audience with a given product category or product market. The resulting promotions result in a brand position in terms of the target audience's perceptions.

The process for developing a brand positioning strategy in the context of marketing communications is similar to developing a positioning strategy for the overall marketing. However, it differs by evaluating or integrating very micro-level aspects of consumer behaviour in its planning by closely considering the nature of the purchase decision. The direction of the decisions is much different, with the goal of finding the most appropriate message, media, or IMC tool versus determining optimal product design features.

The brand positioning strategy comprises four decisions: market definition, differential advantage, target audience brand attitude, and consumer purchase motive. The market definition decision allows the promotional planner to consider whether to define the market in which the brand is competing by benefits, brand name, usage situation, or product category. Differential advantage decisions include whether the brand takes a differential or central positioning and whether the brand focuses its positioning on its benefit claims or the user. Target audience attitude decisions consider how the message is expected to persuade existing beliefs to the desired beliefs about the brand. Finally, promotional planners decide what type of purchase motive should be associated with the brand.

In some communication situations—such as new competitors, changing consumer tastes, or poor brand performance—promotion planners need to reposition their brand. The repositioning can follow the same decisions as described above, where the promotional planner can consider an alternative market definition, communicate a new differential advantage, emphasize different benefit claims, or focus on another motivational option.

KEY TERMS

brand position, *151*
brand positioning strategy, *151*
informational motive, *161*
market position, *150*
market positioning strategy, *148*
multiattribute attitude model, *159*
positioning, *148*
salient attributes, *152*
salient beliefs, *159*
salient benefits, *152*
strategic marketing plan, *148*
transformational motive, *161*

DISCUSSION QUESTIONS

1. Establishing brand image is often difficult for new companies. Explain what these companies must do to establish a strong brand image.

2. Describe how the market positioning strategy adopted for a brand would need to be supported by all other elements of the marketing mix.

3. What is meant by brand positioning strategy? How is it similar to or different from a market positioning strategy?

4. Why is it useful to distinguish between brand positioning strategy and brand position?

5. Develop a market position for chocolate bars.

6. How do major chocolate bar brands define their market?

7. Explain why a central positioning is feasible. Do any brands currently use this approach in their communications?

8. Why is the brand model important for brand positioning strategy?

9. What problem would a brand encounter if it communicated with an incorrect motive?

10. What factors would lead a marketer to the use of a repositioning strategy?

CHAPTER 7

CREATIVE STRATEGY DECISIONS

Chapter Objectives

- To explore the creative strategy planning process.
- To identify three key decisions that comprise a creative strategy: creative theme, message appeal, and message source.
- To explore various approaches used for determining the creative theme that forms the basis of an advertising campaign.
- To summarize the different types of message appeals that advertisers use to persuade their target audience.
- To highlight the source or communicator options a marketer has for a promotional message.

Bell's Talking Beavers

If this offer were any bigger, I'd need a bigger head.

An offer worth getting excited about – sign up for Sympatico™ High Speed Internet service from Bell and receive:

- Consistently fast service that's never shared
- Automatically updated and fully supported security services
- Quick and easy installation
- 24/7 technical support

3 months free

Limited time offer

1 866 439-7875 Visit a Bell store bell.ca/sympatico

Frank and Gordon's first spots—in "The Waiting Room," and then "The Audition," and finally "The Gig"—launched the friendly beavers as industrious, reliable, and Canadian, just like Bell. With this exclusive television placement and the beavers' cross-country debut during the NFL playoffs in 2006, the telecommunications giant instantaneously created something it had never done previously. For the first time, Bell established a national creative strategy across its entire line of products and services for both English and French audiences.

Most Canadians became familiar with the humorous duo as Bell's "spokespersons" a few weeks later, when Bell advertised the brand as a sponsor of the Turin Olympics. In follow-up research, half of all Canadians could accurately identify an Olympic sponsor, and a quarter could say the same for Bell—easily double retention for McDonald's, in second place.

On the surface, the computer-generated rodents appeared similar to the dogs of Fido or the multiple insects, reptiles, and animals of Telus; however, the personification of *Castor Canadensis,* Latin for beaver, put the witty pair in an entirely different light. Right away the classic comedy routine allowed Bell to explain its features and benefits in a humorous manner, as one beaver always seemed to be showing the other how a product or service worked. Research a year later identified an 80–20 split on like–dislike for Frank and Gordon.

Post-Olympics ads focused on Sympatico, Express-Vu, various types of phones, and PVRs, and in all instances Frank and Gordon demonstrated a particular characteristic of the product through their dialogue or antics. For example, during the NHL playoffs, Frank watched the games on his phone and showed Gordon how badly their team was losing. Of course, the gag centred on Gordon shaving off his playoff beard. And the pair turned into singers for an Internet song entitled "There's Nothing More Canadian," which proclaimed their love of hockey. In addition, a text-and-win contest let fans win season tickets in Montreal, Ottawa, or Edmonton.

In total Bell spent approximately $50 million on mass media, including 20 original television executions and many print, direct, and outdoor vehicles. Subsequent tracking research suggested incredible advertising recall as virtually everyone who saw the ads could connect the Bell name to the animated rodents. Sales and store traffic increased during ad rotation. Bell reacquired about 100,000 customers since the campaign began. And the budget got more efficient with lower production costs in using the same creative across all communication tools, which allowed Bell to buy more media placements.

Sources: David Brown, "The Year of Frank and Gordon," *Marketing Magazine,* November 20, 2006; Sarah Dobson, "Bell's Frank and Gordon Back for the NHL Playoffs," *Marketing Magazine,* April 25, 2006; Paul-Mark Rendon, "The Frank and Gordon Show," *Marketing Magazine,* February 6, 2006; Dave Scholze and Jean-Marc Leger, "Year of the Beavers," *Marketing Magazine,* April 10, 2006; Paul-Mark Rendon, "Working Overtime," *Marketing Magazine,* March 12, 2007.

Questions

1. Why are these characters so memorable for Bell?
2. For how long will Bell be able to use Frank and Gordon as "spokespersons" for the brand?

One of the most important components of an integrated marketing communications program is the advertising message. From the marketer's perspective, the advertising message is a way to tell consumers how the product can solve a problem or help satisfy desires or achieve goals. Advertising can also be used to create images or associations and establish a brand position as well as transform the experience of buying and/or using a product. Many of you may not be directly involved in the design and creation of ads. However, because advertising messages are often so crucial to the success of the firm's promotional effort, everyone involved in the promotional process should understand the strategic decisions that underlie the development of advertising campaigns and messages, as well as the creative options available to the advertiser.

One need only watch an evening of commercials or peruse a few magazines to realize there are myriad ways to convey an advertising message. Underlying all of these messages is a **creative strategy** that determines what the advertising message will communicate and **creative tactics** for how the message will be executed. In this chapter, we focus on three creative strategy decisions. First, we describe approaches to determine the big idea that will be used as the central theme of the advertising campaign and translated into attention-getting, distinctive, and memorable messages. Second, we review the many appeals that advertisers use to develop messages designed to persuade consumers. Third, we focus on the key source characteristics that advertisers typically use to gain attention and alter consumers' attitudes. Prior to these decisions, we explore the process of planning for creative strategy. We also conclude with our IMC planning perspective.

Advertising Creativity

Upon determining the direction for the communications program, the advertising agency, or the department in the organization responsible for developing ads, focuses on finding an appropriate creative approach to communicate a message that reinforces the brand positioning strategy. Good advertising creativity can often be central to determining the success of a product as it clearly contributes to a strong brand position with its intended target audience. The essence of advertising is its creativity and we now provide a working definition and indicate its importance.

Definition of Advertising Creativity

For many students, as well as many advertising and marketing practitioners, the most interesting aspect of advertising is the creative side. We have all at one time or another been intrigued by an ad and admired the creative insight that went into it. A great ad is a joy to behold and often an epic to create, as the cost of producing a TV commercial can exceed $1 million. Many companies see this as money well spent. They realize that the manner in which the advertising message is developed and executed is often critical to the success of the promotional program, which in turn can influence the effectiveness of the entire marketing program (Exhibit 7–1).

Creativity is probably one of the most commonly used terms in advertising. Ads are often called creative. The people who develop ads and commercials are known as creative specialists. These specialists work for ad agencies that develop ad campaigns or for marketers that handle their own advertising without the help of an agency. Perhaps so much attention is focused on the concept of creativity because many people view the specific challenge given to those who develop an advertising message as being creative. It is their job to turn all of the information regarding product features and benefits, marketing plans, consumer research, and communication objectives into a creative concept that will bring the advertising message to life. This begs the question: What is meant by *creativity* in advertising?

Exhibit 7–1 Excellent advertising helps create an image for BMW automobiles

Advertising creativity is the ability to generate fresh, unique, and appropriate ideas that can be used as effective solutions to communications problems. To be *appropriate* and *effective*, a creative idea must be relevant to the target audience. Relevance, as an important characteristic of creativity, has to instantly capture the target audience's attention and generate critical brand associations through specific cognitive and emotional responses. The relevance is even more critical when an advertiser takes into account the selective attention of the target audience. Moreover, the creativity has to crystallize the brand so that it is understood by the target audience, which is also experiencing selective comprehension when faced with many competing promotional messages. Extending this further, the relevance of the creativity to the target audience is critical to establishing an important link to the brand, its benefits, and why the target audience would purchase it. In other words, relevance clearly supports the brand positioning strategy.

Advertising creativity is not the exclusive domain of creative specialists, as creative thinking occurs from everyone involved in the promotional planning process. Agency people, such as account executives, media planners, researchers, and attorneys, as well as those on the client side, such as marketing and brand managers, must all seek creative solutions to problems encountered in planning, developing, and executing an advertising campaign.

For example, the creative strategy for Absolut vodka plays off the distinctive shape of its bottle and depicts it with visual puns and witty headlines that play off the Absolut name. The agency and client carried the advertising campaign further by tailoring the print ads for the magazines or regions where they appear. Absolut's media schedule includes over 100 magazines, among them various consumer and business publications. The creative and media departments work together selecting magazines and deciding on the ads that will appeal to the readers of each publication. The creative department is often asked to create media-specific ads to run in a particular publication.

Importance of Advertising Creativity

Perspectives on what constitutes creativity in advertising differ. At one extreme are people who argue that advertising is creative only if it sells the product. An advertising message's or campaign's impact on sales counts more than whether it is innovative. At the other end of the continuum are those who judge the creativity of an ad in terms of its artistic or aesthetic value and originality. They contend creative ads can break through the competitive clutter, grab the consumer's attention, and have a positive communication effect. Both perspectives indicate the importance of advertising creativity as it either presents a good public exposure or contributes to a brand positioning strategy and ultimately sales.

Perspectives on advertising creativity often depend on one's role. A study by Elizabeth Hirschman examined the perceptions of various individuals involved in the creation and production of TV commercials, including management types (brand managers and account executives) and creatives (art director, copywriter, commercial director, and producer).[1] She found that product managers and account executives view ads as promotional tools whose primary purpose is to communicate favourable impressions to the marketplace. They believe a commercial should be evaluated in terms of whether it fulfills the client's marketing and communicative objectives. The perspective of those on the creative side was much more self-serving, as Hirschman noted:

> In direct contrast to this client orientation, the art director, copywriter, and commercial director viewed the advertisement as a communication vehicle for promoting their own aesthetic viewpoints and personal career objectives. Both the copywriter and art director made this point explicitly, noting that a desirable commercial from their standpoint was one which communicated their unique creative talents and thereby permitted them to obtain "better" jobs at an increased salary.[2]

What constitutes creativity in advertising is probably somewhere between the two extremes. To break through the clutter and make an impression on the target audience, an ad often must be unique and entertaining. Research has shown that a major determinant of whether a commercial will be successful in changing brand preferences is its "likability," or the viewer's overall reaction.[3] TV commercials and print ads that are well designed and executed and generate emotional responses can create positive feelings that are transferred to the product or service being advertised. Many creative specialists believe this type of advertising can come about only if they are given considerable latitude in developing advertising messages. But ads that are creative only for the sake of being creative often fail to communicate a relevant or meaningful message that will lead consumers to purchase the product or service. Everyone involved in planning and developing an advertising campaign must understand the importance of balancing the "it's not creative unless it sells" perspective with the novelty/uniqueness perspective.

Another perspective on the issue of creativity is that some Canadian creative people believe that advertising should play an important role in society and be financially accountable. Advertising can have subtle flair and finesse reflecting current social trends and enhance the collective intelligence of society while still cleverly indicating a motive for purchase to ensure a positive investment from a business standpoint.[4] Whether all marketers and agencies agree with this perspective, it still highlights the inherent tension between creativity and financial results.

Planning Creative Strategy

Creative specialists must take all the research, creative briefs, strategy statements, communications objectives, and other input and transform them into an advertising message. Their job is to write copy, design layouts and illustrations, or produce commercials that effectively communicate the central theme on which the campaign is based. Rather than simply stating the features or benefits of a product or service, they must put the advertising message into a form that will engage the audience's interest and make the ads memorable.[5] In this section, we describe the creative challenge, illustrate the creative process, and summarize the end result—the copy platform—when planning for creative promotional communication.

Creative Challenge

The job of the creative team is challenging because every marketing situation is different and each campaign or advertisement may require a different creative approach. Numerous guidelines have been developed for creating effective advertising.[6] Many creative people follow proven formulas when creating ads because they are safe. Clients can feel uncomfortable with advertising that is too different. Bill Tragos, former chair of TBWA, the advertising agency noted for its excellent creative work for Absolut vodka, Evian, and many other clients, says, "Very few clients realize that the reason that their work is so bad is that they are the ones who commandeered it and directed it to be that way. I think that at least 50 percent of an agency's successful work resides in the client."[7]

Many creative people say it is important for clients to take some risks if they want breakthrough advertising that gets noticed. One agency that has been successful in getting its clients to take risks is Wieden & Kennedy, best known for its excellent creative work for companies such as Nike and Microsoft (see Exhibit 7–2). The agency's founders believe a key element in its success has been a steadfast belief in taking risks when most agencies and their clients have been retrenching and becoming more conservative.[8] The agency can develop great advertising partly because clients like Nike are willing to take risks and agree with the agency's priority system, which places the creative work first and the client–agency relationship second. The agency has even terminated relationships with large clients when they interfered too much with the creative process. Several major advertisers including Procter & Gamble and Coca-Cola have added Wieden & Kennedy to their agency roster in efforts to increase the creativity of their advertising.[9] IMC Perspective 7–1 on page 180 describes a message that took a creative risk by the award-winning agency Taxi.

Exhibit 7–2 Wieden & Kennedy's belief in taking risks has led to creative advertising for clients such as Nike

Not all agree that advertising has to be risky to be effective, however. Many marketing managers are more comfortable with advertising that simply communicates product or service features and benefits and gives the consumer a reason to buy. They see their ad campaigns as multimillion-dollar investments whose goal is to sell the product rather than finance the whims of their agency's creative staff. They argue that some creative people have lost sight of advertising's bottom line: Does it sell?

Creative Process

Some advertising people say creativity in advertising is best viewed as a process and creative success is most likely when some organized approach is followed. This does not mean there is an infallible blueprint to follow to create effective advertising; as we saw earlier, many advertising people reject attempts to standardize creativity or develop rules. However, most do follow a process when developing an ad.

One of the most popular approaches to creativity in advertising was developed by James Webb Young, a former creative vice president at the J. Walter Thompson agency. Young said, "The production of ideas is just as definite a process as the production of Fords; the production of ideas, too, runs an assembly line; in this production the mind follows an operative technique which can be learned and controlled; and that its effective use is just as much a matter of practice in the technique as in the effective use of any tool."[10] Working from a sociological view, Young's process of creativity follows a four-stage approach:

- *Preparation.* Read background information regarding the problem.
- *Incubation.* Get away and let ideas develop.
- *Illumination.* See the light or solution.
- *Verification.* Refine the idea and see if it is an appropriate solution.

Models of the creative process such as Young's are valuable to those working in the creative area of advertising, since they offer an organized way to approach an advertising problem. These models do not say much about how this information

IMC PERSPECTIVE 7–1

Pfizer's Creative Ads

Pfizer's ad campaigns and its consumer product launches have put it in the forefront of marketing. Pfizer's ambitious and innovative marketing programs resulted in it being recognized as Marketer of the Year by *Marketing Magazine* for 2002.

Viagra, of course, was the main attraction as the creative strategy broke new ground with its direct-to-consumer (DTC) ad that showed a smiling middle-aged man who jumps a newspaper vending machine, joins in a kids' basketball game, and frolics down the street while the song "Good Morning" plays. The ad, launched in the spring and fall of 2002, closed with the brand name Viagra and a message to talk to your doctor. The song was translated into French to make the ad truly national. The ad communicated that it was not a performance-enhancing drug, but rather something that allowed a man to feel good about himself.

The communication results were simply astounding. Not only did the ad score unprecedented awareness levels, 80 percent agreed or strongly agreed that Viagra projected a positive image and 25 percent of those who had erectile dysfunction (ED) claimed the ad persuaded them to talk to their doctor or partner about the problem or about Viagra. This was especially successful since the ad did not and could not give an explicit description of what Viagra could do medically because of the laws governing Canadian DTC ads. Advertisers could only communicate the brand name or what the product could do, not both.

This Viagra ad built on a 2001 ad that showed the difficulty of men speaking about the topic. In the ad "Doctor's Office" we saw a reluctant man not approach the subject with his doctor. The purpose of this ad was to minimize the stigma attached with such a concern. And somehow this uncomfortable looking character resonated with men as 80 percent of the target audience could recall seeing the ad, nearly double the norm. Even doctors claimed the ad was completely realistic at illustrating the problem they experienced. Later in 2001, another ad, featuring famous hockey player Guy Lafleur, continued with this idea of ED being a frequent problem.

In between the two "Good Morning" campaigns during 2002, Pzifer ran a more informational message called "Straight Goods" that described many facts about ED, again with the idea that men should talk to their doctor. For 2003, Viagra released the "We are the champions" ad showing men celebrating their reclaimed potency.

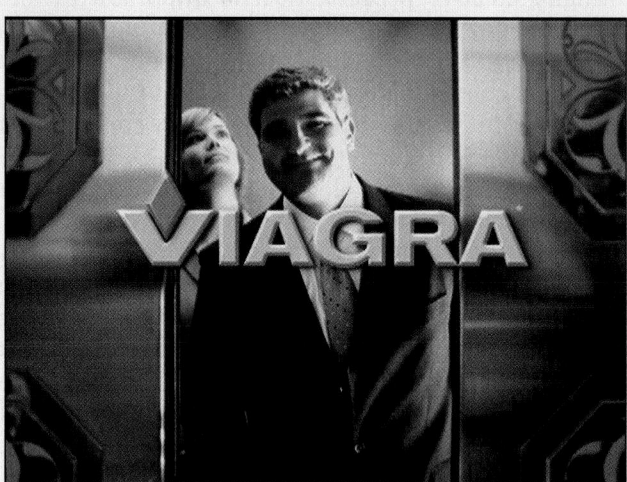

In 2004, Viagra launched its third branded ad with men of many nationalities singing the song "My Way" while in the shower. Research suggested that Viagra's ads have a recognizable creative strategy as viewers could identify the ad as a Viagra ad before the presentation of the brand name.

In 2005, Viagra ran four ads where the dialogue was "bleeped," allowing the viewer to consider what kind of "adult" conversations took place. This campaign won a Gold Lion at Cannes. Viagra continued the hockey angle with a "Viagra Legends of Hockey" event that included Guy Lafleur and other former NHL stars. By the start of 2006, Pfizer retained two-thirds of the market in the face of competition from Cialis and Levitra. Success of the Canadian campaign can also be viewed in two other ways. Initial research demonstrated that American-produced ads would not resonate north of the border, thus allowing the campaign to start. And Pfizer subsidiaries from around the world picked up the campaign—which is being shown in Europe, Latin America, and the United States.

Sources: Annette Bourdeau, "Sexual Healing: Viagra's Vericona Piacek," *Marketing Magazine,* February 2006. Lesley Young, "Viagra's Wake-up Call," *Marketing Magazine,* April 1, 2002; Danny Kucharsky, "Pfizer Finds Its Ad Groove," *Marketing Magazine,* February 10, 2003; Editorial, "Marketing Ménage á Trois," *Marketing Magazine,* April 5, 2004; Lesley Young, "Pfizer's Men Sing for Their Viagra," *Marketing Magazine,* March 8, 2004.

Question

1. In what ways are all the Viagra ads connected so that consumers understand the creative theme?

will be synthesized and used by the creative specialist because this part of the process is unique to the individual. Despite this limitation, the models offer a useful way of describing the creative process.

The creative specialist first learns as much as possible about the product, the target audience, the competition, and any other relevant **research**. Much of this information would come from the marketing plan and advertising plan, which would give the creative specialist an idea as to the direction of the brand positioning strategy. The creative specialist can acquire background information in numerous ways. Some informal fact-finding techniques have been noted by Sandra Moriarty:

- Read anything related to the product or market.
- Talk to people (e.g., marketing personnel, designers, engineers, consumers).
- Visit stores and malls.
- Use the product or service and become familiar with it.
- Work in and learn about the business.[11]

Humpty Dumpty saw the importance of research for making advertising and promotion decisions. A brand of potato chips that had seen little change in its communications for some time undertook a comprehensive review of its identity with a market research firm and its advertising agency. The results indicated that while the brand was outdated, old-fashioned, and tired, the teenage target audience would still be receptive to the brand. A key challenge was to find the right creative message that would modify the target's attitude. TV ads led this IMC campaign and the initial two spots communicated taste and flavour attributes while "re-inventing" the Humpty Dumpty character as strong and confident. It appears that consumers were connecting with the brand with shelf space and sales starting to grow.[12]

Creative people use both general and product-specific preplanning input. **General preplanning input** can include books, periodicals, trade publications, scholarly journals, pictures, and clipping services, which gather and organize magazine and newspaper articles on the product, the market, and the competition, including the latter's ads. Another useful general preplanning input concerns market trends and developments. Information is available from a variety of sources, including local, provincial, and federal governments, secondary research suppliers, and industry trade associations, as well as advertising and media organizations that publish research reports and newsletters. Those involved in developing creative strategy can also gather relevant and timely information by reading Canadian publications like *Marketing* or *Strategy,* and American publications like *Adweek, Advertising Age,* and *Brand Week.*

In addition to getting general background research, creative people receive **product/service-specific preplanning input**. This information generally comes in the form of specific studies conducted on the product or service, the target audience, or a combination of the two. Quantitative consumer research includes attitude studies, market structure, and positioning studies such as perceptual mapping and psychographic or lifestyle profiles. Some agencies conduct psychographic studies annually and construct detailed psychographic or lifestyle profiles of product or service users. DDB Needham conducts a large-scale psychographic study each year using a sample of 4,000 U.S. adults. The agency's Life Style Study provides its creative teams with a better understanding of the target audience for whom they are developing ads.

Qualitative research is used to gain insight into the underlying causes of consumer behaviour. Methods employed include in-depth interviews, projective techniques, association tests, and focus groups in which consumers are encouraged to bring out associations related to products and brands (see Figure 7–1 on page 182). This research is often referred to as motivation research. In general, motivation research is considered important in assessing how and why consumers buy. Focus groups and in-depth interviews are valuable methods for gaining insights into consumers' feelings, and projective techniques are often the only way to get around stereotypical or socially desirable responses.

FIGURE 7–1

Some of the marketing research methods employed to probe the mind of the consumer

In-depth interviews
Face-to-face situations in which an interviewer asks a consumer to talk freely in an unstructured interview using specific questions designed to obtain insights into his or her motives, ideas, or opinions.

Projective techniques
Efforts designed to gain insights into consumers' values, motives, attitudes, or needs that are difficult to express or identify by having them project these internal states upon some external object.

Association tests
A technique in which an individual is asked to respond with the first thing that comes to mind when he or she is presented with a stimulus; the stimulus may be a word, picture, ad, and so on.

Focus groups
A small number of people with similar backgrounds and/or interests who are brought together to discuss a particular product, idea, or issue.

Focus groups are a prevalent research tool at this stage of the creative process. Focus groups are a research method whereby consumers (usually 10 to 12 people) from the target audience are led through a discussion regarding a particular topic. Focus groups give insight as to why and how consumers use a product, what is important to them in choosing a particular brand, what they like and don't like about various products, and any special needs they might have that aren't being satisfied. A focus group session might also include a discussion of types of ad appeals to use or evaluate the advertising of various companies. Focus group interviews bring the creative people and others involved in creative strategy development into contact with the customers. Listening to a focus group gives copywriters, art directors, and other creative specialists a better sense of who the target audience is, what the audience is like, and who the creatives need to write, design, or direct to in creating an advertising message.

Since motivation research studies typically use so few participants, there is also concern that they really discover the idiosyncracies of only a few individuals and their findings are not generalizable to the whole population. Still, it is difficult to ignore motivation research in furthering our understanding of consumer behaviour. Its insights can often be used as a basis for advertising messages aimed at buyers' deeply rooted feelings, hopes, aspirations, and fears.

Toward the end of the creative process, members of the target audience may be asked to evaluate rough creative layouts and to indicate what meaning they get from the ad, what they think of its execution, or how they react to a slogan or theme. The creative team can gain insight into how a TV commercial might communicate its message by having members of the target audience evaluate the ad in storyboard form. A **storyboard** is a series of drawings used to present the visual plan or layout of a proposed commercial. It contains a series of sketches of key frames or scenes along with the copy or audio portion for each scene (Exhibit 7–3).

Evaluating a commercial in storyboard form can be difficult because storyboards are too abstract for many consumers to understand. To make the creative layout more realistic and easier to evaluate, the agency may produce an **animatic**, a videotape of the storyboard along with an audio soundtrack. Storyboards and animatics

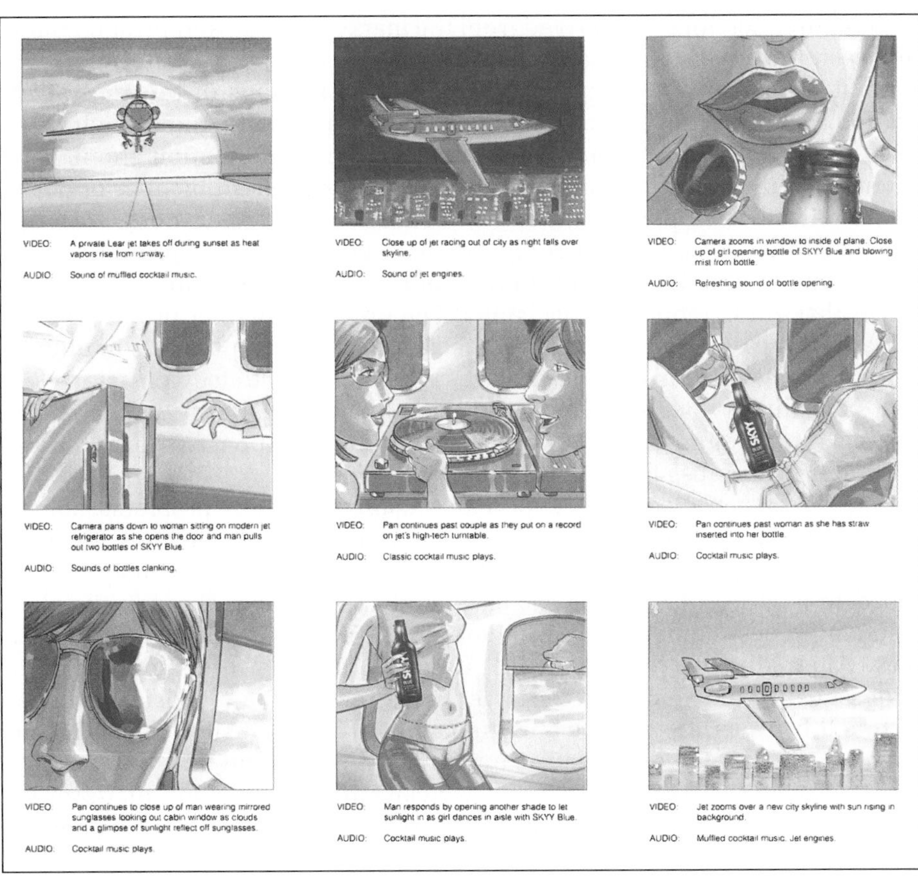

Exhibit 7–3 Marketers can gain insight into consumers' reactions to a commercial by showing them a storyboard

are useful for research purposes as well as for presenting the creative idea to other agency personnel or to the client for discussion and approval. At this stage of the process, the creative team is attempting to find the best creative strategy before moving ahead with the actual production of the ad. The process may conclude with more formal, extensive pretesting of the ad before a final decision is made. Pretesting and related procedures are examined in detail in Chapter 9.

Copy Platform

The end result of the creative process is the written document referred to as copy platform. It specifies the basic elements of the creative strategy and other relevant information. The **copy platform** may have other names depending upon the firm. Essentially, it is a plan that summarizes the entire creative approach that is agreed upon by the creative team and the marketing managers. Figure 7–2 shows a sample copy-platform outline. Just as there are different names for the copy platform, there are variations in the outline and format used and in the level of detail included.

FIGURE 7–2

Copy-platform outline

1. Basic problem or opportunity the advertising must address
2. Target audience(s) and behaviour objective(s)
3. Communication objectives
4. Brand positioning strategy statement
5. Creative strategy (creative theme, message appeal, source characteristic)
6. Supporting information and requirements

The first three sections are derived from the marketing plan and prior communication between the creative specialists and brand managers. The planning framework of this text, shown in Chapter 1, also supports all sections of this copy platform illustration. Chapter 1 reviewed the marketing mix and highlighted the importance of the marketing plan for promotional planning. This information should provide sufficient background on the nature of the communication problem or opportunity. Chapter 3 described important aspects of consumer behaviour along with options for target audience selection and guidelines for a target audience profile. Combined, Chapters 4 and 5 explained the usefulness of response models and communication objectives that guide remaining decisions. The previous chapter indicated different brand positioning options that creative specialists might propose as communication solutions. The rest of this chapter describes the creative strategy decisions that the creative specialists typically recommend. Finally, copy platforms may also include supporting information and requirements that should appear in any message to ensure uniformity across the ads used in a campaign.

At times, creative specialists experience communication problems among the participants of the creative process. Part of the problem is attributed to creative personnel not actually writing a copy platform. The creative process may be initially described in a series of notes or sketches, and as it evolves through the stages of the creative process some of the original participants may not be aware of all the changes. Alternatively, the lack of full description leads to misunderstanding of how the sequence of events, for example, would occur in a television commercial. And while it is important to have a written copy platform, it should be brief enough so that all participants could read it quickly and easily and still demonstrate the creativity of the advertising. In the end we can say that the copy platform should (1) be objective, (2) have proper vocabulary, spelling, and grammar, (3) demonstrate logical thinking, (4) be both creative and brief, (5) have specific recommendations, and (6) be viewed as a firm agreement.[13]

Creative Theme

Most ads are part of a series of messages that make up an IMC or **advertising campaign**, which is a set of interrelated and coordinated marketing communication activities that centre on a single theme or idea that appears in different media across a specified time period. Determining the unifying theme around which the campaign will be built is a critical part of the creative process, as it sets the tone for the individual ads and other forms of marketing communications that will be used. A **campaign theme** should be a strong idea, as it is the central message that will be communicated in all the advertising and other promotional activities.

The **creative theme** is a critical part of a marketing communication program since it must reflect the market positioning strategy and directly communicate the brand positioning strategy to its intended target audience. In this section, we cover three related decisions that comprise the creative theme. First, we discuss various ways to determine the creative theme. Next, we explore the issue of consistency of the creative theme across many parts of the promotional program. We conclude by exploring the importance of unique Canadian creative advertising and its success.

Origin of Creative Theme

Some advertising experts argue that for an ad campaign to be effective it must contain a big idea that attracts the consumer's attention, gets a response, and sets the advertiser's product or service apart from the competition's. Well-known adman John O'Toole describes the *big idea* as "that flash of insight that synthesizes the purpose of the strategy, joins the product benefit with consumer desire in a fresh, involving way, brings the subject to life, and makes the reader or audience stop, look, and listen."[14] Of course, the real challenge to the creative team is coming up with the big idea to use in the ad. Many products and services offer virtually nothing unique, and it can be difficult to find something interesting to say about them.

While really great ideas in advertising are difficult to come by, there are many big ideas that became the basis of very creative, successful advertising campaigns. A classic example is the "Pepsi generation" theme and subsequent variations like "the taste of a new generation" and "GenerationNext." More recent big ideas that have resulted in effective advertising campaigns include the "Intel inside" campaign for Intel microprocessors that go in personal computers; Nike's "Just do it"; and the "It keeps going and going" theme for Energizer batteries, featuring the pink bunny. It is difficult to pinpoint the inspiration for a big idea or to teach advertising people how to find one. However, several approaches can guide the creative team's search for a creative theme. Some of the best-known approaches follow:

- Using a unique selling proposition.
- Creating a brand image.
- Finding the inherent drama.
- Positioning.

Unique Selling Proposition The concept of the **unique selling proposition (USP)** was developed by Rosser Reeves, former chair of the Ted Bates agency, and is described in his influential book *Reality in Advertising.* Reeves noted three characteristics of unique selling propositions:

- Each advertisement must make a proposition to the consumer. Not just words, not just product puffery, not just show-window advertising. Each advertisement must say to each reader: "Buy this product and you will get this benefit."
- The proposition must be one that the competition either cannot or does not offer. It must be unique either in the brand or in the claim.
- The proposition must be strong enough to move the mass millions, that is, pull over new customers to your brand.[15]

Reeves said the attribute claim or benefit that forms the basis of the USP should dominate the ad and be emphasized through repetitive advertising. An example of advertising based on a USP is the campaign for Trident gum (Exhibit 7–4). The brand's unique attributes make it the only chewing gum with the seal of approval from the Canadian Dental Association.

For Reeves's approach to work, there must be a truly unique product or service attribute, benefit, or inherent advantage that can be used in the claim. The approach may require considerable research on the product and consumers, not only to determine the USP but also to document the claim.

Exhibit 7–4 This ad uses a unique selling proposition

Trident
Because it actually prevents cavities. maybe our gum should have looked like this.
You know how important a toothbrush is in preventing cavities, well you're about to find out how chewing gum can help as well. Trident' gum, that is. You see, Trident has Dentec' which is proven to prevent cavities. Helping to reduce them not by a little, but quite significantly. By up to 62%* in fact. That's 62% fewer cavities than you would get with a normal oral hygiene program alone. So treat your kids to a good chew, anytime. **Trident. A smile in every chew.**
*Based on a two year study when used in conjunction with a proper oral hygiene program

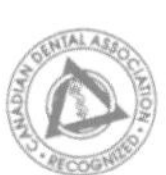

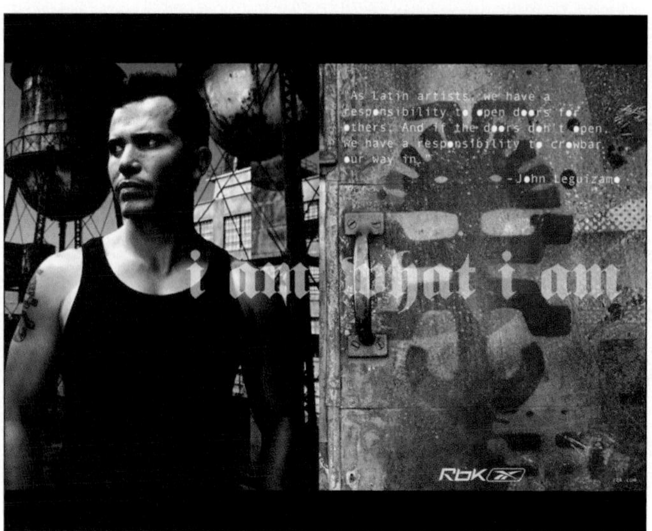

Exhibit 7–5 Reebok's "I am what I am" campaign creates an image of the brand as about being yourself

Creating a Brand Image In many product and service categories, competing brands are so similar that it is very difficult to communicate a unique attribute or benefit. Many of the packaged-goods products that account for most of the advertising dollars spent are difficult to differentiate on a functional or performance basis. The creative theme used to communicate these products is based on the development of a strong, memorable identity for the brand through **image advertising**.

David Ogilvy popularized the idea of brand image in his famous book *Confessions of an Advertising Man*. Ogilvy said that with image advertising, "every advertisement should be thought of as a contribution to the complex symbol which is the brand image." He argued that the image or personality of the brand is particularly important when brands are similar.

Image advertising has become increasingly popular and is used as the creative theme for a variety of products and services, including soft drinks, liquor, cigarettes, cars, airlines, financial services, perfume/colognes, and clothing. Many people consume certain brands of these products because of image. The key to successful image advertising is developing an image that will appeal to product users. For example, in 2005 Reebok initiated a $50-million global ad campaign using the "I am what I am" theme, which uses image advertising to promote the athletic shoe company as the brand for young consumers.[16] The campaign is designed to create an image for Reebok as a brand that is about being yourself rather than trying to become something you are not. The ads feature a variety of celebrity personalities including tennis star Andy Roddick, NHL star Sidney Crosby, and film star Lucy Liu. The image-oriented ads feature a portrait of the celebrity next to a visual symbol of an aspect of the star's private life and a quote about his or her life (see Exhibit 7–5).

Finding the Inherent Drama Another approach to determining the creative theme is finding the **inherent drama** or characteristic of the product that makes the consumer purchase it. The inherent drama approach expresses the advertising philosophy of Leo Burnett, founder of the Leo Burnett agency in Chicago. Burnett said inherent drama "is often hard to find but it is always there, and once found it is the most interesting and believable of all advertising appeals."[17] He believed advertising should be based on a foundation of consumer benefits with an emphasis on the dramatic element in expressing those benefits.

Burnett advocated a down-home type of advertising that presents the message in a warm and realistic way. Some of the more famous ads developed by his agency using the inherent drama approach are for McDonald's, Maytag appliances, Kellogg's cereals, and Hallmark cards. Notice how the Hallmark commercial shown in Exhibit 7–6 uses this approach to deliver a poignant message.

Positioning Since advertising helps establish or maintain the brand position, it can also be the source of the creative theme. Positioning is often the basis of a firm's creative strategy when it has multiple brands competing in the same market. For example, Procter & Gamble markets many brands of laundry detergent—and positions each one differently. Positioning is done for companies as well as for brands. For example, the ad shown in Exhibit 7–7 is part of "the other IBM" campaign that is designed to position the company as a provider of business consulting and more than just a technology provider. The integrated campaign, which includes print ads, television and online ads, sponsorships, and a micro website, is designed to reveal a side of IBM that has been largely unknown to many potential business consulting and services clients.[18]

LEO BURNETT COMPANY, INC. — HALLMARK CARDS, INC.

AS FILMED AND RECORDED (4/96) "Report Card" 2:00 HMHF6359

1. (MUSIC: UNDER THROUGHOUT)

2. MAXX: Hi, Mom, I'm home!
MOM: Hi. Is your coat on the floor?
MAXX: No...

3. MAXX: Can I go over to Lee's house?
MOM: Do you have any homework?
MAXX: Yeah.
MOM: After you finish it you can go.

4. MAXX: Cool.
MOM: Did you turn in your milk money?
MAXX: Yeah.

5. Hey--who moved my lunar module?

6. MOM: Maxx, what's this?
MAXX: Did Amy move my lunar module?
MOM: Maxx?

7. MAXX: It's something from Mrs. Bennett.
MOM: What'd she give you a card for?
MAXX: Cause I was nice to somebody.

8. MOM: Who were you nice to?
MAXX: Scott.
MOM: Who's Scott?

9. MAXX: The boy who comes to school just once in a while cause he's sick.
MOM: Was he at the school play?
MAXX: Nope. can we get an armadillo?

10. MOM: How were you nice to him?

11. MAXX: Well, Mrs. Bennett always has me sit next to him. Scott can't go out for recess and stuff so I stay in and play Yahtzee with him.

12. MOM: I didn't know you were doing that.
MAXX: I like him. It's no big deal. Could I see your card?

13. MAXX: Sure. MOM: (READING): "You didn't have to do what you did. And that's what made it so special." Maxx? Do you know what this means?

14. MAXX: Kinda.
MOM: It means you should be very proud of yourself. I know I am.

15. MAXX: Mom?
MOM: Yeah?
MAXX: You're squooshing me.

Exhibit 7–6 This Hallmark commercial uses an inherent drama approach

Exhibit 7–7 This ad is part of a campaign that positions IBM as a provider of business consulting and services

Trout and Ries originally described positioning as the image consumers had of the brand in relation to competing brands in the product or service category, but the concept has been expanded beyond direct competitive positioning.[19] As discussed in Chapter 6, products can be positioned on the basis of end benefit, brand name, usage situation, or product category. Any of these can spark a creative theme that becomes the basis of the creative strategy and results in the brand's occupying a particular place in the minds of the target audience. Since brand positioning can be done on the basis of a distinctive attribute, the positioning and unique selling proposition approaches can overlap.

Molson Export returned to its well-established position as an authentic beer in Quebec as the origin for a clever theme. Research indicated that consumers young and old alike still perceived Export as having a strong 100-year history and associated it with classic beer-drinking moments, even though the brand had inconsistent advertising and weak marketing support in recent years. The slogan captured the essence of the repositioning: "Molson Ex. Today's beer since 1903." The first few executions of the creative strategy showed the progression and similarity of Export consumption since its inception. For example, the first spot, "Evolution," says it all as a number of scenes depicted people bringing cases of Export to various parties over the course of time. Using the computer morphing techniques, the images also showed how the labels of the brand had changed.[20]

Creative Consistency

Consistency in promotional creativity is generally regarded as a key success factor so that the target audience retains the brand position. We explore examples of consistency in the creative theme across time, creative execution, advertising media, promotional tools, and products. The essential point is that when the target audience is exposed to a series of messages across different contexts, the creative theme should not change such that there is a clear reinforcement of the brand positioning strategy. Deviation of the theme allows the possibility that the target audience will process the message alternatively and arrive at a different interpretation of the brand.

Consistency Across Time Advertising or communication plans are generally done on an annual basis, thus the creative theme is often short-term in nature. However, the creative themes are usually developed with the intention of being used for a longer time period. While some marketers change their campaign themes often, a successful creative theme may last for years.

A consistent creative theme across time builds on the established awareness of the brand's current customers by encouraging continued processing of future advertising messages. Moreover, the familiarity of the creative theme is recognizable to a brand's non-customers when they may be entering the product category or considering switching their purchases.

Pepsi-Cola's campaign in Quebec has starred comedian Claude Meunier for more than 16 years. The campaign is a unique creative strategy for Pepsi from a worldwide perspective, and it is the longest running campaign and celebrity endorsement in the history of the brand. In fact, the relationship is so established that Meunier writes many of the spots and creates the characters he portrays.[21]

Despite this consistent creative theme, Pepsi introduced Patrick, Etienne, Paco, Sebastien, and Ivon (first letters spell PEPSI) in a TV ad as five guys who really, really like Pepsi to continue with its advertising theme of humour, entertainment, and youthful energy. However, this deviation was not the end of Meunier as Pepsi planned on his continued participation.[22]

The Dairy Farmers of Canada took creative consistency of their "spokesperson" to a new level during the past three Olympic Games. For the 1998 Olympics in Nagano, Japan, the cows were in the barn watching the Games. For the 2000 Sydney Summer

Games, they were seen on their way to the Olympics. They finally made it by attending events in Salt Lake City during 2002. In fact, they surprised a pair of figure skaters with a bale of hay as a reward at the end of one spot.[23] During the 2004 Summer Games, the cows became little blue animated cows that participated in the actual events.

A consistent creative theme is not the only criteria of success. In the late 90s, Nissan asked its agency to change the popular "Enjoy the ride" campaign that was widely praised for its amusing, creative executions but was not helping increase sales.[24] Nissan dealers complained that the ads did not focus enough attention on the product, and in some cases comparisons with the competition were used. However, in late 2002 Nissan launched a new advertising campaign using "Shift" as the umbrella tagline.[25] The new campaign used a combination of emotional and product-focused ads designed to strengthen Nissan's brand image while showing its revitalized product line (Exhibit 7–8).

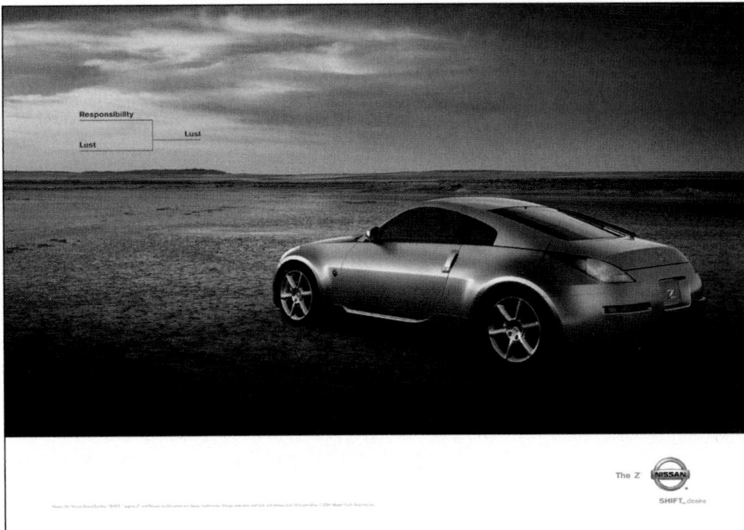

Exhibit 7–8 In Nissan's new ads, the cars are once again the stars

Consistency Across Executions As we noted above, an advertising campaign features a series of creative executions over time and it is important that marketers ensure that all ads feature a similar "look and feel." Exactly what this entails is a matter of interpretation, but most advertisers and consumers would say they recognize it when they see it. For example, many would say that the creative theme for Absolut vodka is consistent in all of their print ads even though we see the distinctive bottle in many different types of scenes or situations that fit with the specific target audience of the many magazines the ads are placed in.

Kraft Canada has used the same creative theme of an angel consuming Philadelphia cream cheese in the clouds of heaven throughout all of its television executions. This creative approach for communicating the brand's benefits has served it well as a distinctive presentation that is recognizable and consistent with positioning the brand as a tasty and healthy food product.[26]

Consistency Across Media Often a successful creative theme is one that is amenable to more than one media. For instance, the essence of creativity in a print ad is still captured in a follow-up radio ad. Or, the big idea found in a TV commercial transfers to an outdoor billboard. In both cases, the creativity of the initial media is seen in a supportive media—one less central to the primary media, yet still important to continue exposing a similar idea to the target audience. Interestingly, this idea is difficult to convey with visual creative themes moving to radio. For quite some time, listeners heard a "friendly thought" from Telus that differed significantly from the nature theme portrayed in all visual media.

Consistency Across Promotional Tools Using the advertising creative theme across the various promotional tools is an issue to be resolved. The argument for the same "look and feel" is pervasive. For example, Telus Mobility keeps its nature theme in all of its communications—from TV ads to promotional displays to its website and finally all of its public relations and publicity. Action such as this supports the notion that the creative theme for the integrated marketing communication must support the broad market positioning and all brand positioning strategies for its many target audiences.

Consistency Across Products The same kind of use of a consistent theme across all IMC tools is evident in RBC Financial Group's "First" campaign. However, this theme pervades all tools for all of its products and services. And so the campaign's consistent theme works on multiple levels. It is positioning the overall firm as an innovative and forward-looking organization. Yet, the campaign adapts well to a variety of purchase and consumption situations for credit or investment products that can be also adjusted depending on whether the target audience is a loyal customer or a potential one that RBC Financial Group is attempting to switch.

Canadian Creative Themes

We now present ideas regarding creative themes used in Canadian advertising and promotional communication. We begin with a perspective that supports the importance for unique ways of speaking to Canadian consumers. Since many brands are part of a North American or international marketing strategy, there is a tendency to standardize the message. As further evidence of the importance for Canadian creativity in communication, we highlight recent success stories.

Importance of Canadian Creative Themes The need for unique creative advertising can be found in divergence of values between Canadians and Americans. Decades of consumer research by Environics researcher Michael Adams suggests that while the citizens of North America share similar aspects of society, the underlying values are quite distinct.[27] For example, in 1992, 17 percent of Canadians and 34 percent of Americans agreed that "a widely advertised product is probably a good product"; however, in 2000, the percentage for Canadians had remained unchanged while the percentage for Americans had risen to 44 percent.[28] Statistics such as these have led to a profound conclusion.

> Canadians operate by a fundamentally different set of social values than Americans do, and marketers need to be sensitive to these differences. Americans are much more outer-directed, risk-taking, and yet are more concerned with maintaining social order and tradition. In contrast, Canadians are more inner-directed, more security-seeking, and yet are more socially liberal and tolerant of individual diversity. Americans celebrate those who have lived the American Dream—working hard, taking chances and striking it rich—so visual markers of success such as expensive cars, homes and vacations become important indicators of one's status on the social hierarchy. Canadians, on the other hand, believe in greater interdependence, achieving equitable balances, and the "fair" distribution of the wealth of the nation—the Canadian Dream is a strong social safety net. As a result, Canadians are more suspicious of wealth, are less trusting of business and are more skeptical of advertising.[29]

These unique Canadian values influence the motivation for consumption—Canadians buy products for what they can do for us versus what they say about us. Canadians favour experiences over possessions and are less inclined toward conspicuous consumption. For example, Canadians are more likely to believe that a car is basic transportation versus a statement of personal style or image. Therefore, certain types of advertising messages are more palatable for Canadians since the underlying reasons for purchase are more accurately reflected in the dialogue of a commercial or the body copy of a print ad produced by Canadian advertisers.

In fact, one author believes that Canada is truly in an advertising renaissance where agencies are consistently producing world-calibre creative campaigns.[30] Furthermore, the distinctiveness of Canadians derived from this data may be strong evidence for allowing Canadian managers more latitude in developing unique creative messages.[31]

Putting together a creative for Canada can be met with some obstacles. Canadian managers who market U.S. brands in Canada often feel the pressure to run the same campaign in Canada that is being run in the U.S. While this obviously saves on production costs of new ads, it can be more than offset with lower sales due to messages not resonating with Canadian culture. Sometimes firms need to perform specific market research to demonstrate that a unique creative is warranted for the Canadian market. For example, Lever Pond's of Canada felt the U.S. creative for Degree deodorant featuring CEOs and race car drivers would not be acceptable to Canadian consumers. Research was done, a discussion ensued with U.S. managers, and finally a humorous campaign that looked at stressful situations where the dryness benefit of the product could be understood. Ironically, the ads in the U.S. barely registered with consumers in follow-up research while the Canadian campaign tested above average.[32]

Successful Canadian Creative Themes Historically and recently, insightful and innovative Canadian creative themes demonstrate effective advertising and promotional communication. We take this time to identify the Canadian organizations that recognize creative themes that have been truly outstanding. Specifically, we summarize the CASSIES, the Marketing Awards, the Bessies, and the Extra Awards. We also highlight Canada's performance at the prestigious Cannes competition held in France.

CASSIES Awarded by The Institute of Communication and Advertising (ICA), The Association of Quebec Advertising Agencies, and Publicité Club de Montréal, this recognition is perhaps the most significant in Canada as it identifies Canadian advertising success stories. Initiated in Canada in 1993, the award is based on a similar idea started during the 1980s in the United Kingdom. Originally awarded every second year from 1993 until 2001, the CASSIES are now an annual event.

The CASSIES award recognizes advertising and promotional campaigns that document a direct cause and effect relationship between the campaign and communication and business results. Entrants have to submit the details of their campaign in the form of a business case that summarizes the performance of the brand prior to the campaign and indicates the degree to which the performance has improved. The website, cassies.ca, provides the complete entry requirements, identifies the winners, and contains the actual case history submitted.

The Grand Prix is the single most prestigious award presented each year. It has been won by seven firms since inception: Pepsi in Quebec during 1993, Listerine in Quebec during 1995, Chrysler Minivan for 1997, Sunlight Laundry Detergent in 1999, Molson Canadian for 2001, Diet Pepsi in 2002, Familiprix in 2003, and the Quebec Federation of Milk Producers in 2006.

Marketing Awards Sponsored by *Marketing Magazine*, these annual awards identify the top Canadian creative communication launched each year in a number of categories. For example, there is an overall winner for best multimedia campaign, a winner for best single ad and campaign across all major media (with television having more awards by various product categories), and awards for non-traditional media, point-of-purchase, and public service announcements.

Bessies These awards are given by the Television Bureau of Canada (TVB), an organization whose members comprise television stations, networks, and specialty services. The TVB promotes the use of television as an effective medium and has an important role as an information resource for its members. The Bessies recognize the best in English TV advertising each year and have been doing so since the early 1960s, shortly after the invention of television (an equivalent award for French TV advertising is awarded at La Fête de la Pub).

Extra Awards The Canadian Newspaper Association is similar to the TVB but for daily newspapers. Its Extra Awards recognize outstanding creative advertising in this media by giving ads a gold, silver, bronze, or merit award in nine product categories and types of ads (i.e., local ad, local campaign, national campaign, small-space ad).

Cannes On a global level, the Cannes International Advertising Film Festival is widely considered the most prestigious advertising award competition. The Cannes competition receives entries from agencies around the world hoping to win Lions (the name of the award) in each of the major categories: television; print and poster; online (cyber) advertising; media buying and planning; and direct. Canada has done fabulously at Cannes competitions over the past decade, winning an average of about seven Lions per year.

In the past, some questioned the overall effectiveness of Canadian creativity due to the nature of our culture to not take risks and the fact that many of the brands advertised are part of American or other global brands. However, others contend the increased presence of Canadians in attendance and on the juries of all five categories bodes well for future Canuck creative advertising and our recognition on the international stage. In fact, some argue that countries that have emerged recently with stronger advertising is a result of their advertisers taking the competition more seriously by sending a large contingent of committed creative specialists who learn considerably from international counterparts.[33]

Message Appeals

The **message appeal** refers to the approach used to influence consumers' attitude toward the product, service, or cause. A message appeal can also be viewed as "something that moves people, speaks to their wants or needs, and excites their interest."[34] The **creative execution** style is the way a particular appeal is turned into an advertising message presented to the consumer. According to William Weilbacher:

> The appeal can be said to form the underlying content of the advertisement, and the execution the way in which that content is presented. Advertising appeals and executions are usually independent of each other; that is, a particular appeal can be executed in a variety of ways and a particular means of execution can be applied to a variety of advertising appeals. Advertising appeals tend to adapt themselves to all media, whereas some kinds of executional devices are more adaptable to some media than others.[35]

As this implies, the message appeal is a creative strategy decision whereas the execution style is more of a creative tactic decision. (We will discuss the tactics in more detail in the next chapter.) One of the advertiser's most important creative strategy decisions involves the choice of an appropriate appeal. Hundreds of different appeals can be used as the basis for advertising messages. We concentrate on five broad appeals: rational appeals, emotional appeals, fear appeals, humour appeals, and combined rational and emotional appeals. In this section, we focus on ways to use these appeals as part of a creative strategy and consider how they can be combined in developing the advertising message.

Rational Appeals

Rational appeals focus on the consumer's practical, functional, or utilitarian need for the product or service and emphasize features of a product or service and/or the benefits or reasons for owning or using a particular brand. The content of these messages emphasizes facts, learning, and the logic of persuasion.[36] Rational-based appeals tend to be informative, and advertisers using them generally attempt to convince consumers that their product or service has a particular attribute(s) or provides a specific benefit that satisfies their needs. Their objective is to persuade the target audience to buy the brand because it is the best available or does a better job of meeting consumers' needs. For example, the Nordica ad shown in Exhibit 7–9 uses a rational appeal to explain the features and benefits of its Beast Synergy System ski collection.

Weilbacher identified several types of advertising appeals that fall under the category of rational approaches, among them feature, comparative, favourable price, news, and product/service popularity appeals. We also include reminder appeals in this list.

Ads that use a *feature appeal* focus on the dominant traits of the product or service. These ads tend to be highly informative and present the customer with a number of important product attributes or features that will lead to favourable attitudes and can be used as the basis for a rational purchase decision. Technical and high-involvement products often use message appeal. Exhibit 7–10 shows an ad for MacGregor golf clubs that focuses on the features and benefits of the club's technology.

A *comparative appeal* is the practice of either directly or indirectly naming competitors in an ad and comparing one or more specific attributes.[37] A comparative appeal can also be made for different product formats, as shown in Exhibit 7–11 on page 194. Some studies show that recall is higher for comparative than noncomparative messages, but comparative ads are generally not more effective for other response variables, such as brand attitudes or purchase intentions.[38] Advertisers must also consider how comparative messages affect credibility. Users of the brand being attacked in a comparative message may be especially skeptical about the advertiser's claims.

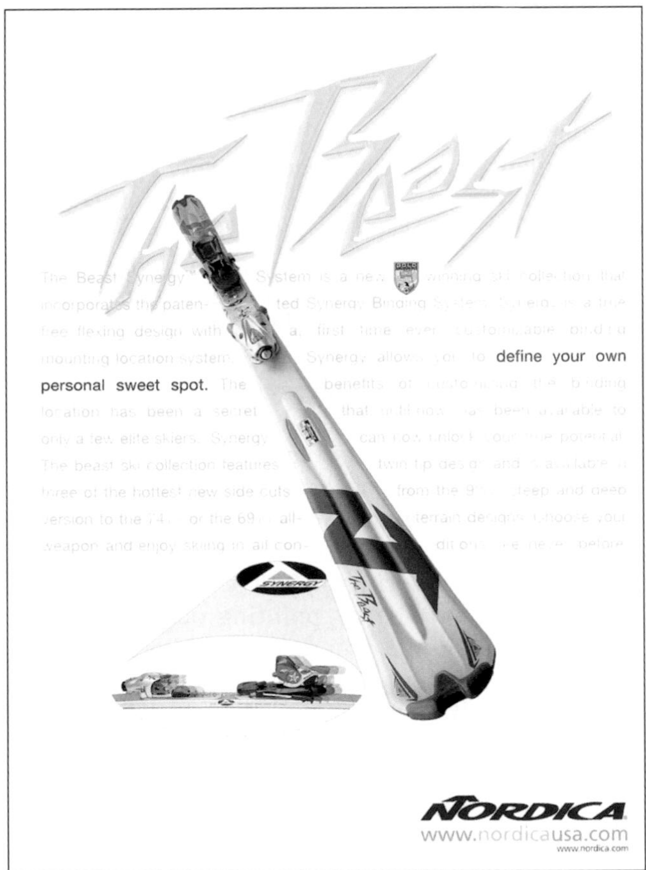

Exhibit 7–9 Nordica uses a rational appeal to advertise the features of its skis and bindings

Exhibit 7–10 MacGregor Golf uses a feature appeal to promote its clubs

Exhibit 7–11 A comparative appeal across product formats

OUR "AAA" STEAK HOUSE BURGERS HAVE NEVER BEEN FROZEN. NOT EVER.

At Casey's we take the time and care to make it fresh. Everyday.

FRESH. EVERYDAY.

OUR FRIES ARE HOT AND CRISPY BECAUSE OUR POTATOES ARE NEVER FROZEN. NOT EVER.

At Casey's we take the time and care to make it fresh. Everyday.

FRESH. EVERYDAY.

Comparative appeals may be particularly useful for new brands, since they allow a new market entrant to position itself directly against the more established brands and to promote its distinctive advantages. Direct comparisons can help position a new brand in the evoked, or choice, set of brands the customer may be considering.

Comparative appeals are often used for brands with a small market share. They compare themselves to an established market leader in hopes of creating an association and tapping into the leader's market. Market leaders, on the other hand, often hesitate to use comparison ads, as most believe they have little to gain by featuring competitors' products in their ads.

A *favourable price appeal* makes the price offer the dominant point of the message. Price appeal advertising is used most often by retailers to announce sales, special offers, or low everyday prices. Price appeal ads are often used by national advertisers during recessionary times. Many fast-food chains have made price an important part of their marketing strategy through promotional deals and "value menus" or lower overall prices, and their advertising strategy is designed to communicate this. Many other types of advertisers use price appeals as well.

Exhibit 7–12 Boeing uses a news appeal to promote its 777-200LR Worldliner

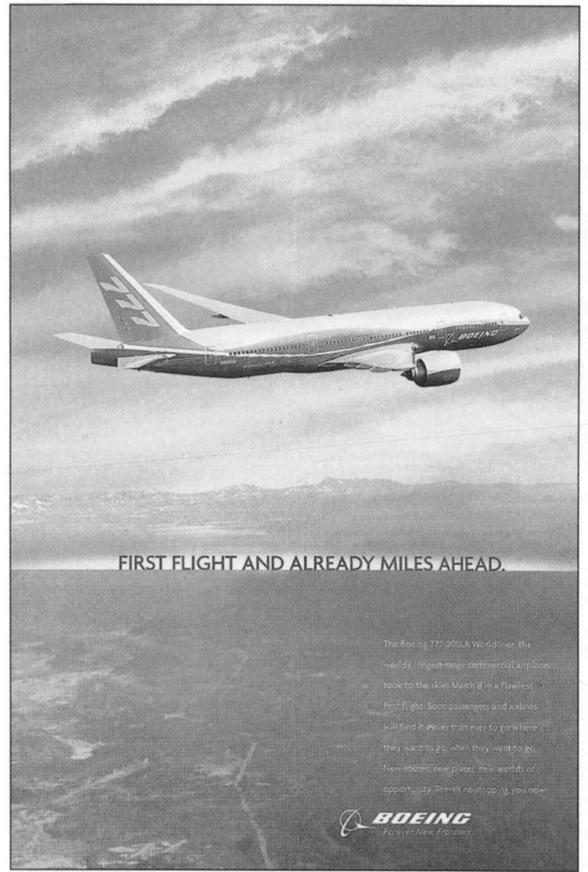

News appeals are those in which some type of news or announcement about the product, service, or company dominates the ad. This type of appeal can be used for a new product or service or to inform consumers of significant modifications or improvements. This appeal works best when a company has important news it wants to communicate to its target market. Exhibit 7–12 shows an ad using a news appeal that was run by Boeing to announce the first flight of the company's new Boeing 777-200LR Worldliner, which is the world's longest-range commercial airplane. The ad was run a few days after the inaugural flight to create interest and excitement in the new plane, which can connect any two cities in the world with nonstop service.

Product/service popularity appeals stress the popularity of a product or service by pointing out the number of consumers who use the brand, the number who have switched to it, the number of experts who recommend it, or its leadership position in the market. The main point of this advertising appeal is that the wide use of the brand proves its quality or value and other customers should consider using it. The ad for Neutrogena's Healthy Skin Anti-Wrinkle cream shown in Exhibit 7–13 uses a product popularity appeal by noting that it is the brand most recommended by dermatologists as well as the sales leader in the category.

A *reminder appeal* has the objective of building brand awareness and/or keeping the brand name in front of consumers. Well-known brands and market leaders often use a reminder appeal, which is often referred to as reminder advertising. Products and services that have a seasonal pattern to their consumption also use reminder advertising, particularly around the appropriate period. For example, marketers of candy products often increase their media budgets and run reminder advertising around Halloween, Valentine's Day, Christmas, and Easter.

Exhibit 7–13 This Neutrogena ad uses a product popularity appeal

Emotional Appeals

Emotional appeals relate to the customer's social and/or psychological needs for purchasing a product or service. Many of consumers' motives for their purchase decisions are emotional, and their feelings about a brand can be more important than knowledge of its features or attributes. Advertisers for many products and services view rational-based appeals as dull. Many advertisers believe appeals to consumers' emotions work better at selling brands that do not differ markedly from competing brands, since rational differentiation of them is difficult.[39]

The choice between rational or emotional appeal is a challenge and careful consideration must take place to ensure the advertising resonates with the target audience and evokes relevant processing responses connected to the purchase decision or consumption experience. For example, Gaz Métro, the largest natural gas provider in Quebec, repositioned itself to expand sales in the residential market after well establishing itself in the industrial, institutional, and commercial sectors. Faced with strong electric power competition from Hydo Quebec, Gaz Métro needed to educate and reassure consumers that natural gas was a secure alternative to electricity when consumers were renovating or upgrading their household energy requirements. While some might have expected Gaz Métro to use a rational argument, it instead used an emotional appeal that showed how comfortable one's home would feel with the seductive blue flame of natural gas in a stunning visually oriented television commercial.[40]

Many feelings or needs can serve as the basis for advertising appeals designed to influence consumers on an emotional level, as shown in Figure 7–3. These appeals are based on the psychological states or feelings directed to the self (such as pleasure or excitement), as well as those with a more social orientation (such as status or recognition).

FIGURE 7–3

Bases for emotional appeals

Personal States or Feelings		Social-Based Feelings
Safety	Arousal/stimulation	Recognition
Security	Sorrow/grief	Status
Fear	Pride	Respect
Love	Achievement/accomplishment	Involvement
Affection	Self-esteem	Embarrassment
Happiness	Actualization	Affiliation/belonging
Joy	Pleasure	Rejection
Nostalgia	Ambition	Acceptance
Sentiment	Comfort	Approval
Excitement		

Advertisers can use emotional appeals in many ways in their creative strategy. Kamp and Macinnis note that commercials often rely on the concept of *emotional integration*, whereby they portray the characters in the ad as experiencing an emotional benefit or outcome from using a product or service.[41] Ads using humour, sex, and other appeals that are very entertaining, arousing, upbeat, and/or exciting can affect the emotions of consumers and put them in a favourable frame of mind.

Marketers use emotional appeals in hopes that the positive feeling they evoke will transfer to the brand and/or company. Research shows that positive mood states and feelings created by advertising can have a favourable effect on consumers' evaluations of a brand.[42] Studies also show that emotional advertising is better remembered than nonemotional messages.[43]

Mercedes-Benz Canada successfully used an emotional appeal in its first Canadian-made television commercial in 2003. Preliminary research indicated that many potential buyers had a very positive attitude toward Mercedes-Benz but delayed purchasing for various reasons. Brand associations of Mercedes-Benz being "older money and prestige," and "distancing and intimidating," along with consumers feeling they had not "arrived yet" led to a sizable target audience of young consumers who have never bought previously. Enter the positioning message, "Mercedes-Benz. You're Ready" along with "The Story of Raymond," which traces the life of one who delays buying ice-cream as a boy and throughout much of his adult life. At the conclusion, we see a few shots of the car and realize the creative is a metaphor for desiring a Mercedes-Benz yet postponing the purchase. Subsequent research revealed outstanding levels for emotions, entertainment value, and consumer understanding of the key message. In fact, Mercedes-Benz received e-mail and telephone responses from consumers saying the ad spurred them to purchase.[44]

Fear Appeals

Fear is an emotional response to a threat that expresses, or at least implies, some sort of danger. Ads sometimes use **fear appeals** to evoke this emotional response and arouse individuals to take steps to remove the threat. Some, like anti-smoking ads, stress physical danger that can occur if behaviours are not altered. Others—like those for deodorant, mouthwash, or dandruff shampoos—threaten disapproval or social rejection. IMC Perspective 7–2 shows a fear appeal for cars.

Before deciding to use a fear appeal–based message strategy, the advertiser should consider how fear operates, what level to use, and how different target audiences may respond. One theory suggests that the relationship between the level of fear in a message and acceptance or persuasion is curvilinear, as shown in Figure 7–4.[45] This means that message acceptance increases as the amount of fear used rises—to a point. Beyond that point, acceptance decreases as the level of fear rises.

FIGURE *7–4*

Relationship between fear levels and message acceptance

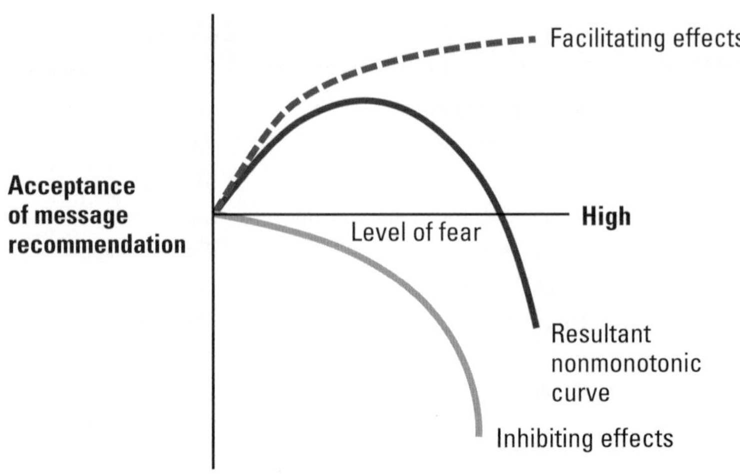

IMC PERSPECTIVE 7–2

Safety Happens with VW

An ad for the Volkswagen Jetta shows people driving in their Jetta—and then suddenly the calm is broken by another vehicle that appears out of nowhere and crashes into them. Heads mash into airbags and passengers are stunned and confused. What makes this ad different from previous car ads is that real actors are used instead of crash-test dummies. At the end of the ad, a slogan reads "Safe Happens," along with a reference to its government rating for side-impact safety, the most-desired new technology according to the company. In another version for the Volkswagen Passat a similar scenario occurs, with reference made to the ratings for front-end safety.

VW admits that reaction varies to the ad, but the ads are getting people to think about the brand and safety. Dealers say the ad is working because there is more traffic coming through the door. VW officials have defended the raw honesty of their ads, saying they show what the Jetta does to protect passengers in real-world situations. The ads are also designed to resonate with consumers between the ages of 18 and 34, the target age of a Jetta buyer in North America. Consumers at this age range are also most likely to watch graphic horror movies such as the *Saw* trilogy, so a little car crash without any blood and gore really is nothing much to them.

J. D. Power & Associates, in a recent survey, showed that safety is the number-one priority of new-car buyers, and other automobile manufacturers are strong competitors. VW is fighting to position itself as a safe brand in an automotive world increasingly populated by safe brands. First among them, of course, is Volvo, the Swedish division of Ford. "Safety is a Volvo differentiator," stated Paul Gustavsson, director of product planning and strategy at Volvo. To retain its safety halo, Volvo plans to heavily promote both the active and passive safety features of its latest model, the 2007 Volvo S80. Not every manufacturer is opting for the scare approach. Lexus has used TV commercials to show off various safety features in North America, but the overall approach remains cautious. That is, there are no images of crashes to be found in the commercials.

Sources: Jeremy Cato, "Fear Is a Powerful Motivator," *The Globe and Mail,* October 19, 2006; Theresa Howard, "Volkswagen Hits the Mark with Jarring Jetta Ads," *USA Today,* May 1, 2006.

Question

1. Do you feel that the realistic VW ads using a fear appeal is appropriate to demonstrate safety?

This relationship between fear and persuasion can be explained by the fact that fear appeals have both facilitating and inhibiting effects.[46] A low level of fear can have facilitating effects; it attracts attention and interest in the message and may motivate the receiver to act to resolve the threat. Thus, increasing the level of fear in a message from low to moderate can result in increased persuasion. High levels of fear, however, can produce inhibiting effects; the receiver may emotionally block the message by tuning it out, perceiving it selectively, or denying its arguments outright. Figure 7–4 illustrates how these two countereffects operate to produce the curvilinear relationship between fear and persuasion.

A recent study by Anand-Keller and Block provides support for this perspective on how fear operates.[47] Their study indicated that a communication using a low level of fear may be ineffective because it results in insufficient motivation to elaborate on the harmful consequences of engaging in the destructive behaviour (smoking). However, an appeal arousing high levels of fear was ineffective because it resulted in too much elaboration on the harmful consequences. This led to defensive tendencies such as message avoidance and interfered with processing of recommended solutions to the problem.

Another approach to the curvilinear explanation of fear is the protection motivation model.[48] According to this theory, four cognitive appraisal processes mediate the individual's response to the threat: appraising (1) the information available regarding the severity of the perceived threat, (2) the perceived probability that the threat will occur, (3) the perceived ability of a coping behaviour to remove the threat, and (4) the individual's perceived ability to carry out the coping behaviour.

This model suggests that both the cognitive appraisal of the information in a fear appeal message and the emotional response mediate persuasion. An audience is more likely to continue processing threat-related information, thereby increasing the likelihood that a coping behaviour will occur. The protection motivation model suggests that ads using fear appeals should give the target audience information about the severity of the threat, the probability of its occurrence, the effectiveness of a coping response, and the ease with which the response can be implemented.[49]

It is also important to consider how the target audience may respond. Fear appeals are more effective when the message recipient is self-confident and prefers to cope with dangers rather than avoid them.[50] They are also more effective among nonusers of a product than among users. Thus, a fear appeal may be better at keeping non-smokers from starting than persuading smokers to stop.

In reviewing research on fear appeals, Herbert Rotfeld has argued that some of the studies may be confusing different types of threats and the level of potential harm portrayed in the message with fear, which is an emotional response.[51] He concludes that the relationship between the emotional responses of fear or arousal and persuasion is not curvilinear but rather is monotonic and positive, meaning that higher levels of fear do result in greater persuasion. However, Rotfeld notes that not all fear messages are equally effective, because different people fear different things. Thus they will respond differently to the same threat, so the strongest threats are not always the most persuasive. This suggests that marketers using fear appeals must consider the emotional responses generated by the message and how they will affect reactions to the message.

Humour Appeals

Humorous ads are often the best known and best remembered of all advertising messages. Humour is usually presented through radio and TV commercials as these media lend themselves to the execution of humorous messages. However, humour is occasionally used in print ads as well.

Advertisers use **humour appeals** for many reasons. Humorous messages attract and hold consumers' attention. They enhance effectiveness by putting consumers in a positive mood, increasing their liking of the ad itself and their feeling toward the product or service. And humour can distract the receiver from counterarguing against the message.[52] Critics argue that funny ads draw people to the humorous situation but distract them from the brand and its attributes. Also, effective humour can be difficult to produce and some attempts are too subtle for mass audiences.

Clearly, there are valid reasons both for and against the use of humour in advertising. Not every product or service lends itself to a humorous approach. A number of studies have found that the effectiveness of humour depends on several factors, including the type of product and audience characteristics.[53] For example, humour has been more prevalent and more effective with low-involvement, feeling products than high-involvement, thinking products.[54] An interesting study surveyed the research and creative directors of the top 150 advertising agencies.[55] They were asked to name which communications objectives are facilitated through the appropriate situational use of humour in terms of media, product, and audience factors. The general conclusions of this study are shown in Figure 7–5.

Combined Rational and Emotional Appeals

In many advertising situations, the decision facing the creative specialist is not whether to choose an emotional or a rational appeal but rather determining how to combine the two approaches. As noted copywriters David Ogilvy and Joel Raphaelson have stated:

- Humour does aid awareness and attention, which are the objectives best achieved by its use.
- Humour may harm recall and comprehension in general.
- Humour may aid name and simple copy registration.
- Humour may harm complex copy registration.
- Humour may aid retention.
- Humour does not aid persuasion in general.
- Humour may aid persuasion to switch brands.
- Humour creates a positive mood that enhances persuasion.
- Humour does not aid source credibility.
- Humour is generally not very effective in bringing about action/sales.
- Creatives are more positive on the use of humour to fulfill all the above objectives than research directors are.
- Radio and TV are the best media in which to use humour; direct mail and newspapers are least suited.
- Consumer nondurables and business services are best suited to humour; corporate advertising and industrial products are least suited.
- Humour should be related to the product.
- Humour should not be used with sensitive goods or services.
- Audiences that are younger, better educated, upscale, male, and professional are best suited to humour; older, less educated, and downscale groups are least suited to humour appeals.

FIGURE 7–5
Conclusions of the humour study

Few purchases of any kind are made for entirely rational reasons. Even a purely functional product such as laundry detergent may offer what is now called an emotional benefit—say, the satisfaction of seeing one's children in bright clean clothes. In some product categories the rational element is small. These include soft drinks, beer, cosmetics, certain personal care products, and most old-fashioned products. And who hasn't experienced the surge of joy that accompanies the purchase of a new car?[56]

Consumer purchase decisions are often made on the basis of both emotional and rational motives, and attention must be given to both elements in developing effective advertising. Sometimes appeals are difficult to interpret and they may be considered a combined rational and emotional appeal, as shown in the Altoids ad (Exhibit 7–14).

Advertising researchers and agencies have given considerable thought to the relationship between rational and emotional motives in consumer decision making and how advertising influences both. McCann-Erickson Worldwide, in conjunction with advertising professor Michael Ray, developed a proprietary research technique known as *emotional bonding.* This technique evaluates how consumers feel about brands and the nature of any emotional rapport they have with a brand compared to the ideal emotional state they associate with the product category.[57]

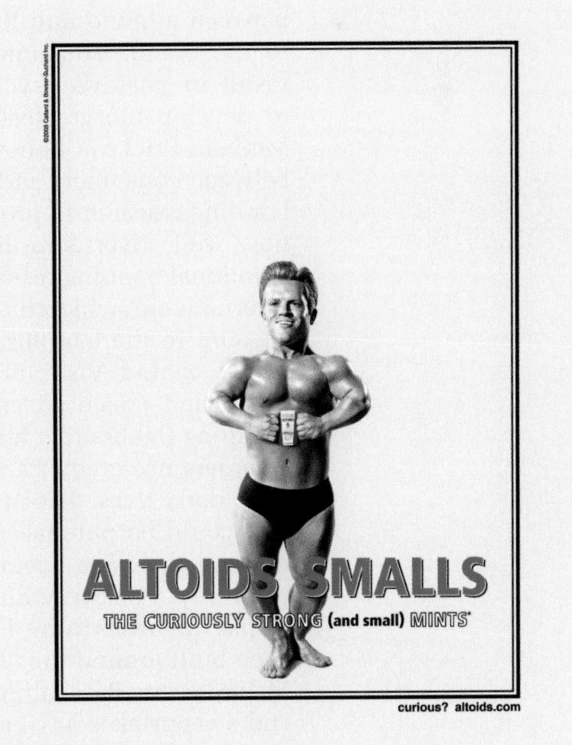

Exhibit 7–14 Altoids uses humour and facts in its reminder ads

FIGURE 7–6

Levels of relationships with brands

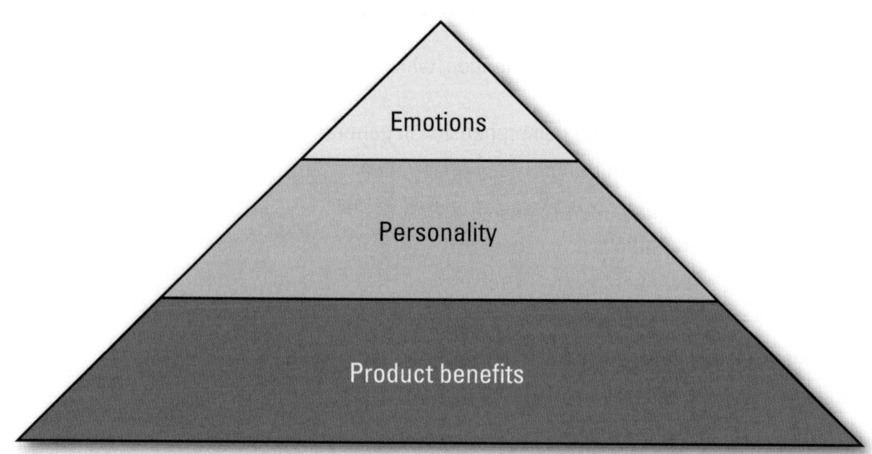

The basic concept of emotional bonding is that consumers develop three levels of relationships with brands, as shown in Figure 7–6. The most basic relationship indicates how consumers *think* about brands in respect to product benefits. This occurs, for the most part, through a rational learning process and can be measured by how well advertising communicates product information. Consumers at this stage are not very brand loyal, and brand switching is common.

At the next stage, the consumer assigns a *personality* to a brand. For example, a brand may be thought of as self-assured, aggressive, and adventurous, as opposed to compliant and timid. The consumer's judgment of the brand has moved beyond its attributes or delivery of product/service benefits. In most instances, consumers judge the personality of a brand on the basis of an assessment of overt or covert cues found in its advertising.

McCann-Erickson researchers believe the strongest relationship that develops between a brand and the consumer is based on feelings or emotional attachments to the brand. Consumers develop *emotional bonds* with certain brands, which result in positive psychological movement toward them. The marketer's goal is to develop the greatest emotional linkage between its brand and the consumer. McCann-Erickson believes advertising can develop and enrich emotional bonding between consumers and brands. McCann and its subsidiary agencies use emotional bonding research to provide strategic input into the creative process and determine how well advertising is communicating with consumers. McCann-Erickson used emotional bonding research as the basis for the "Priceless" campaign for MasterCard International, which has been extremely successful. When the agency took over the account in the late 90s, MasterCard had become the third card in the consumer's wallet behind Visa and American Express. The challenge was to reposition the brand and create an emotional bond between consumers and MasterCard while retaining the brand's functional appeal. The idea behind the campaign is that good spenders use credit cards to acquire things that are important to them and enrich their daily lives. The creative execution involves showing a shopping list of items that could be purchased for a certain dollar amount and one key item that could not and thus was deemed "Priceless." The tagline "There are some things money can't buy. For everything else there's MasterCard," positions the card as the way to pay for everything that matters. An entire integrated marketing campaign has been built around the "Priceless" campaign theme that includes sponsorships with Major League Baseball, the National Hockey League, and the PGA golf tour. Contests and sweepstakes have also been part of the campaign. The campaign now runs in 80 countries and has won numerous creative awards. Exhibit 7–15 shows one of the print ads from the campaign.

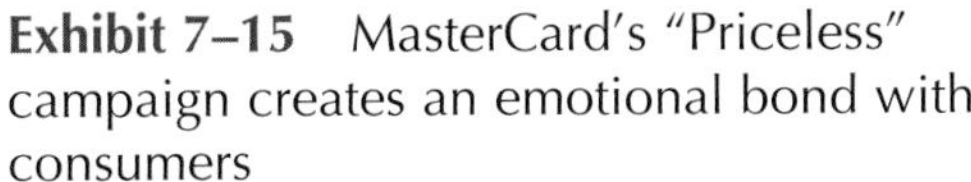
Exhibit 7–15 MasterCard's "Priceless" campaign creates an emotional bond with consumers

Exhibit 7–16 Porsche used teaser ads to create interest in the new Cayenne SUV

A unique example of combining rational and emotional appeals is the use of **teaser advertising**. Advertisers introducing a new product often use teaser advertising, which is designed to build curiosity, interest, and/or excitement about a product or brand by talking about it but not actually showing it. Teasers, or *mystery ads* as they are sometimes called, are also used by marketers to draw attention to upcoming advertising campaigns and generate interest and publicity for them. For example, Porsche used teaser ads to generate interest and excitement in the Cayenne SUV (Exhibit 7–16).

Nike also used teaser ads to start its campaign for its successful "RunTO 10K" running event in Toronto in 2003. Looking to generate awareness of the race, establish a stronger link between Nike products and running, and encourage average or non-runners to participate (register online or in-store, and actually run), the creative featured "Running Guy," who represented all novice runners determined to complete the challenge despite not being in the best of shape. Messages at various out-of-home locations and in newspapers such as "10 km to a collapsed lung" and "10 km to the fetal position" preceded "Running Guy," thus provoking curiosity and introducing his persona. The campaign garnered significant media publicity, especially with "Running Guy" participating in the morning show of a radio station consistent with the target audience. In total, 7,500 runners finished the challenge, which easily surpassed the per capita participation rate of other major international cities.[58]

Source Characteristics

The third creative strategy decision is the source of the message appeal. We use the term **source** to mean the person involved in communicating a marketing message, either directly or indirectly. A *direct source* is a spokesperson who delivers a message and/or demonstrates a product or service—like tennis star Andre Agassi, who endorses Head tennis rackets in Exhibit 7–17 on page 202. An *indirect source,* say, a model, doesn't actually deliver a message but draws attention to and/or

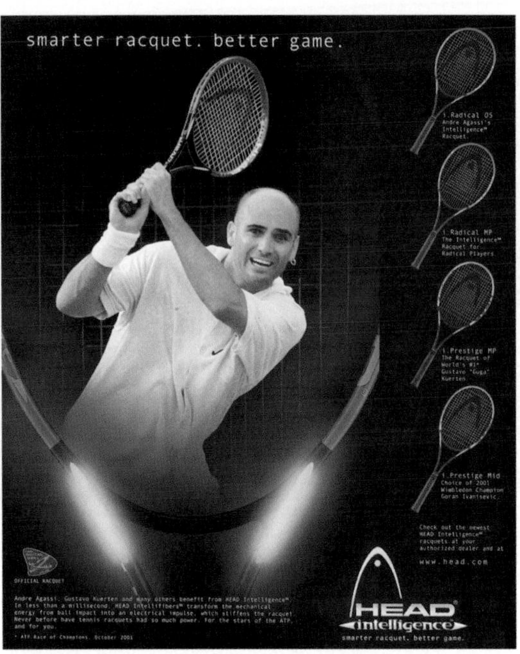

Exhibit 7–17 Tennis star Andre Agassi serves as spokesperson for Head

enhances the appearance of the ad. Some ads use neither a direct nor an indirect source; the source is the organization with the message to communicate. Since most research focuses on individuals as a message source, our examination of source factors follows this approach.

Companies are very careful when selecting individuals to deliver their selling messages. Many firms spend huge sums of money for a specific person to endorse their product or company. They recognize that the characteristics of the source affects the sales and advertising message. Marketers try to select individuals whose traits will maximize message influence. The source may be knowledgeable, popular, and/or physically attractive; typify the target audience; or have the power to reward or punish the receiver in some manner. Herbert Kelman developed three basic categories of source attributes: credibility, attractiveness, and power.[59] Each influences the recipient's attitude or behaviour through a different process (see Figure 7–7). This section looks at the first two characteristics in the context of advertising. Source power is omitted, as compliance is not really possible in most promotional communication.

Source Credibility

Credibility is the extent to which the recipient sees the source as having relevant knowledge, skill, or experience and trusts the source to give unbiased, objective information. There are two important dimensions to credibility, expertise and trustworthiness.

A communicator seen as knowledgeable—someone with expertise—is more persuasive than one with less expertise. But the source also has to be trustworthy—honest, ethical, and believable. The influence of a knowledgeable source will be lessened if audience members think he or she is biased or has underlying personal motives for advocating a position (such as being paid to endorse a product).

One of the most reliable effects found in communications research is that expert and/or trustworthy sources are more persuasive than sources who are less expert or trustworthy.[60] Information from a credible source influences beliefs, opinions, attitudes, and/or behaviour through a process known as **internalization**, which occurs when the receiver adopts the opinion of the credible communicator since he or she believes information from this source is accurate. Once the receiver internalizes an opinion or attitude, it becomes integrated into his or her belief system and may be maintained even after the source of the message is forgotten.

A highly credible communicator is particularly important when message recipients have a negative position toward the product, service, company, or issue being promoted, because the credible source is likely to inhibit counterarguments. As

FIGURE *7–7*

Source attributes and receiver processing modes

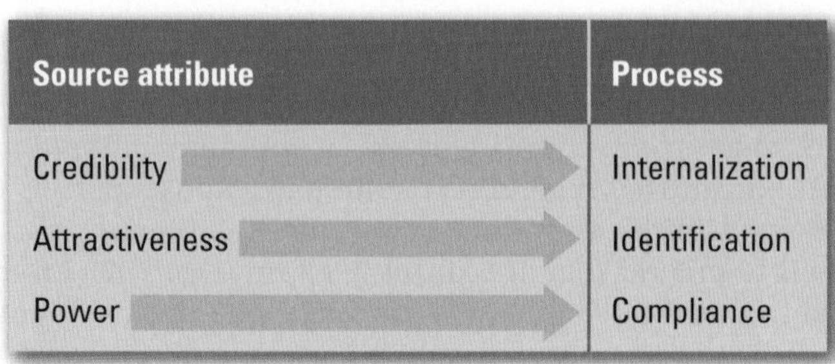

discussed in Chapter 4, reduced counterarguing should result in greater message acceptance and persuasion.

Applying Expertise Because attitudes and opinions developed through an internalization process become part of the individual's belief system, marketers want to use communicators with high credibility. Spokespeople are often chosen because of their knowledge, experience, and expertise in a particular product or service area. Endorsements from individuals or groups recognized as experts, such as doctors or dentists, are also common in advertising (Exhibit 7–18). The importance of using expert sources was shown in a study by Roobina Ohanian, who found that the perceived expertise of celebrity endorsers was more important in explaining purchase intentions than their attractiveness or trustworthiness. She suggests that celebrity spokespeople are most effective when they are knowledgeable, experienced, and qualified to talk about the product they are endorsing.[61]

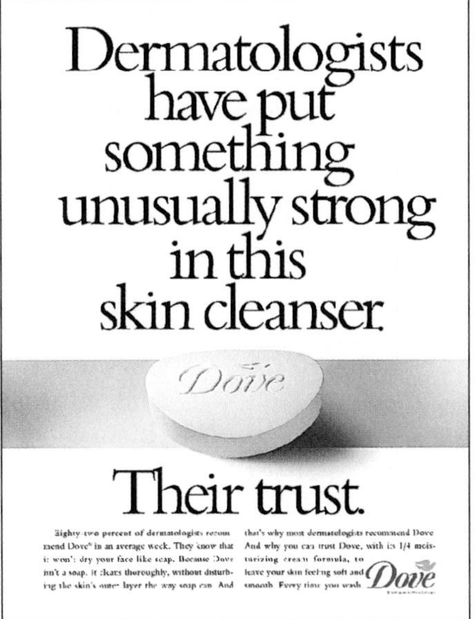

Exhibit 7–18 Dove promotes the fact that it is recommended by experts in skin care

Applying Trustworthiness While expertise is important, the target audience must also find the source believable. Finding celebrities or other figures with a trustworthy image is often difficult. Many trustworthy public figures hesitate to endorse products because of the potential impact on their reputation and image. Advertisers use various techniques to increase the perception that their sources are trustworthy. Hidden cameras are used to show that the consumer is not a paid spokesperson and is making an objective evaluation of the product. Disguised brands are compared. (Of course, the sponsor's brand always performs better than the consumer's regular brand, and he or she is always surprised.) Most consumers are skeptical of these techniques, so they may have limited value in enhancing perceptions of credibility.

Using Corporate Leaders as Spokespeople Another way of enhancing source credibility is to use the company president or chief executive officer as a spokesperson in the firm's advertising. Many companies believe the use of their president or CEO is the ultimate expression of the company's commitment to quality and customer service. Some research suggests the use of a company president or CEO can improve attitudes and increase the likelihood that consumers will inquire about the company's product or service.[62] It is becoming common for local retailers to use the owner or president in their ads. Companies are likely to continue using their top executives in their advertising, particularly when they have celebrity value that helps enhance the firms' image. However, there can be problems with this strategy. CEO spokespeople who become very popular may get more attention than their company's product/service or advertising message. And if a firm's image becomes too closely tied to a popular leader, there can be problems if that person leaves the company. Perhaps the most prolific corporate leader in recent years is Frank D'Angelo, who promotes his beer and energy drink brands.

Limitations of Credible Sources Several studies have shown that a high-credibility source is not always an asset, nor is a low-credibility source always a liability. High- and low-credibility sources are equally effective when they are arguing for a position opposing their own best interest.[63] A very credible source is more effective when message recipients are not in favour of the position advocated in the message.[64] However, a very credible source is less important when the audience has a neutral position, and such a source may even be less effective than a moderately credible source when the receiver's initial attitude is favourable.[65]

Another reason why a low-credibility source may be as effective as a high-credibility source is the **sleeper effect**, whereby the persuasiveness of a message increases with the passage of time. The immediate impact of a persuasive message may be inhibited because of its association with a low-credibility source. But with time, the association of the message with the source diminishes and the receiver's attention focuses more on favourable information in the message, resulting in more support arguing. However, many studies have failed to demonstrate the presence of a sleeper effect.[66] Many advertisers hesitate to count on the sleeper effect, since exposure to a credible source is a more reliable strategy.[67]

Source Attractiveness

A source characteristic frequently used by advertisers is **attractiveness**, which encompasses similarity, familiarity, and likability.[68] *Similarity* is a supposed resemblance between the source and the receiver of the message. *Familiarity* refers to knowledge of the source through exposure. *Likability* is an affection for the source as a result of physical appearance, behaviour, or other personal traits. Even when the sources are not famous, consumers often admire their physical appearance, talent, and/or personality.

Source attractiveness leads to persuasion through a process of **identification**, whereby the receiver is motivated to seek some type of relationship with the source and thus adopts similar beliefs, attitudes, preferences, or behaviour. Maintaining this position depends on the source's continued support for the position as well as the receiver's continued identification with the source. If the source changes position, the receiver may also change. Unlike internalization, identification does not usually integrate information from an attractive source into the receiver's belief system. The receiver may maintain the attitudinal position or behaviour only as long as it is supported by the source or the source remains attractive.

One requirement for a national campaign with an identifiable and likeable spokesperson who actually speaks in the ads is the fact that the person has to be fluent in both official languages. Danone did this with actress Sophie Lorain, who convincingly played a strong central character in all of their commercials. She demonstrated that Danone was for women who wanted yogurt as a healthy part of their busy everyday lives. Lorain had previously been the spokesperson in the Quebec ads for two years when Danone tested her in an English ad. The results were encouraging and the rest is history. While the language was a necessary requirement for success, Danone executives believed that Lorain's character (i.e., likability, similarity) communicated the benefits of the brand effectively, which was the primary concern.[69]

Applying Similarity Marketers recognize that people are more likely to be influenced by a message coming from someone with whom they feel a sense of similarity.[70] If the communicator and receiver have similar needs, goals, interests, and lifestyles, the position advocated by the source is better understood and received. Similarity can be used to create a situation where the consumer feels empathy for the person shown in the commercial. In a slice-of-life commercial, the advertiser usually starts by presenting a predicament with the hope of getting the consumer to think, "I can see myself in that situation." This can help establish a bond of similarity between the communicator and the receiver, increasing the source's level of persuasiveness. Many companies feel that the best way to connect with consumers is by using regular-looking, everyday people with whom the average person can easily identify.

Applying Familiarity Familiarity through exposure from some other context can provide a strong source. In fact the connection can be quite surprising and very effective in some circumstances, especially for the British Columbia Automobile Association (BCAA). Three television commercials advertised its new Premier Membership with three former B.C. premiers, Dave Barrett, Bill Vander Zalm, and

Glen Clark, each who faced varying political fortunes while leading Canada's westernmost province. Seeking to stay ahead of new competitive entrants in the road-side assistance market, BCAA sought to retain its market leadership position through higher sales growth while maintaining its reputation for strong products and excellent customer service. The answer of a risky creative that captured former premiers in humorous, self-deprecating situations that poked fun at themselves seemed the best bet to break through clutter and clearly identify the brand name Premier. Each "actor" agreed to waive the fee in lieu of a donation to his favourite charity. Initial sales in the spring topped 2,000 and BCAA looked to up that to 10,000 by the end of 2004.[71]

Applying Likability: Using Celebrities Advertisers recognize the value of using spokespeople who are admired: TV and movie stars, athletes, musicians, and other popular public figures (Exhibit 7–19). Why do companies spend huge sums to have celebrities appear in their ads and endorse their products? They think celebrities have stopping power. That is, they draw attention to advertising messages in a very cluttered media environment. Marketers think a popular celebrity will favourably influence consumers' feelings, attitudes, and purchase behaviour. And they believe celebrities can enhance the target audience's perceptions of the product in terms of image and/or performance. For example, a well-known athlete like Sidney Crosby may convince potential buyers that the product will enhance their own performance (Exhibit 7–20 on page 206).

Exhibit 7–19 Maria Sharapova has endorsement contracts with a number of companies including Nike, Canon, Motorola, and Tag Heuer

A number of factors must be considered when a company decides to use a celebrity spokesperson, including the dangers of overshadowing the product and being overexposed, and the target audience's receptivity.

Overshadowing the Product How will the celebrity affect the target audience's processing of the advertising message? Consumers may focus their attention on the celebrity and fail to notice the brand. Advertisers should select a celebrity spokesperson who will attract attention and enhance the sales message, yet not overshadow the brand. For example, Chrysler Corp. chose singer Celine Dion to appear in ads for various brands including the Pacifica sport wagon, Crossfire sports coupe, and Town & Country minivan and also signed on as the sponsor of her Las Vegas show "A New Day." She starred in a number of lavish TV commercials that were part of Chrysler's "Drive & Love" campaign, which was developed to give Chrysler a more upscale image and help achieve a premium positioning for the brand. However, the campaign was not successful as it was believed that her celebrity persona overshadowed the products and did more to sell her than the cars.[72]

Overexposure Consumers are often skeptical of endorsements because they know the celebrities are being paid.[73] This problem is particularly pronounced when a celebrity endorses too many products or companies and becomes overexposed. Advertisers can protect themselves against overexposure with an exclusivity clause limiting the number of products a celebrity can endorse. However, such clauses are usually expensive, and most celebrities agree not to endorse similar products anyway. Many celebrities try to earn as much endorsement money as possible, yet they must be careful not to damage their credibility by endorsing too many products. For example, Wayne Gretzky received some criticism for being a spokesperson for too many brands shortly after he retired from the NHL.

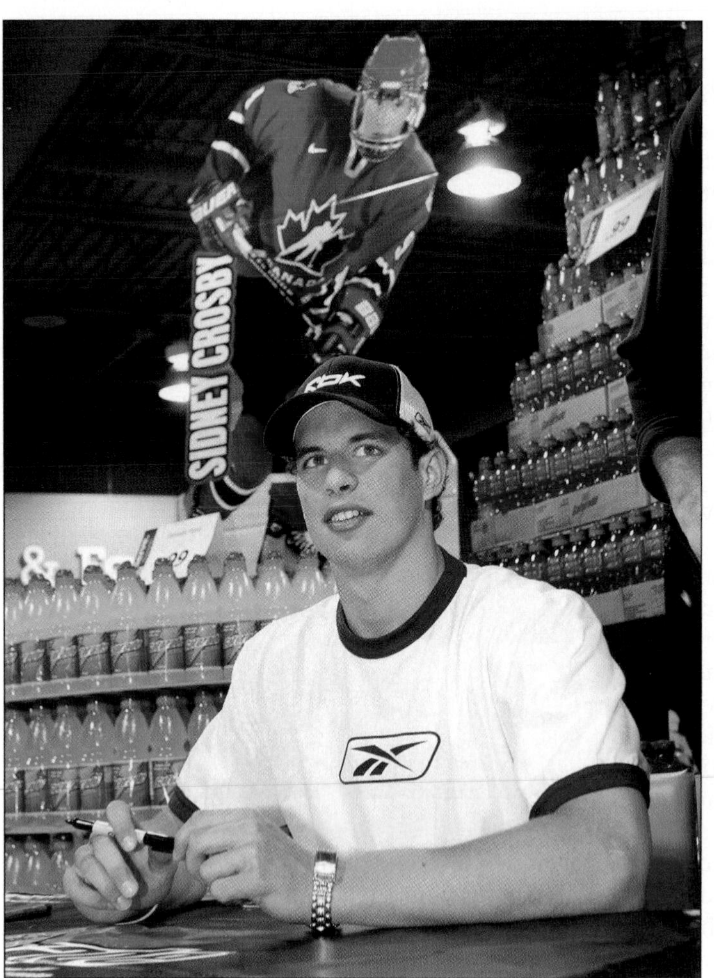

Exhibit 7–20 Sidney Crosby is featured at this Gatorade promotional event

Target Audience's Receptivity One of the most important considerations in choosing a celebrity endorser is how well the individual matches with and is received by the advertiser's target audience. Consumers who are particularly knowledgeable about a product or service or have strongly established attitudes may be less influenced by a celebrity than those with little knowledge or neutral attitudes. One study found that college-age students were more likely to have a positive attitude toward a product endorsed by a celebrity than were older consumers.[74] The teenage market has generally been very receptive to celebrity endorsers, as evidenced by the frequent use of entertainers and athletes in ads targeted to this group for products such as apparel, cosmetics, and beverages. However, many marketers are finding that teenage consumers are more skeptical and cynical toward the use of celebrity endorsers and respond better to ads using humour, irony, and unvarnished truth. Some marketers targeting teenagers have responded to this by no longer using celebrities in their campaigns or by poking fun at their use.

Understanding the Meaning of Celebrity Endorsers Advertisers must try to match the product or company's image, the characteristics of the target audience, and the personality of the celebrity.[75] The image that celebrities project to consumers can be just as important as their ability to attract attention. An interesting perspective on celebrity endorsement was developed by Grant McCracken.[76] He argues that credibility and attractiveness don't sufficiently explain how and why celebrity endorsements work and offers a model based on meaning transfer (Figure 7–8).

FIGURE *7–8* Meaning movement and the endorsement process

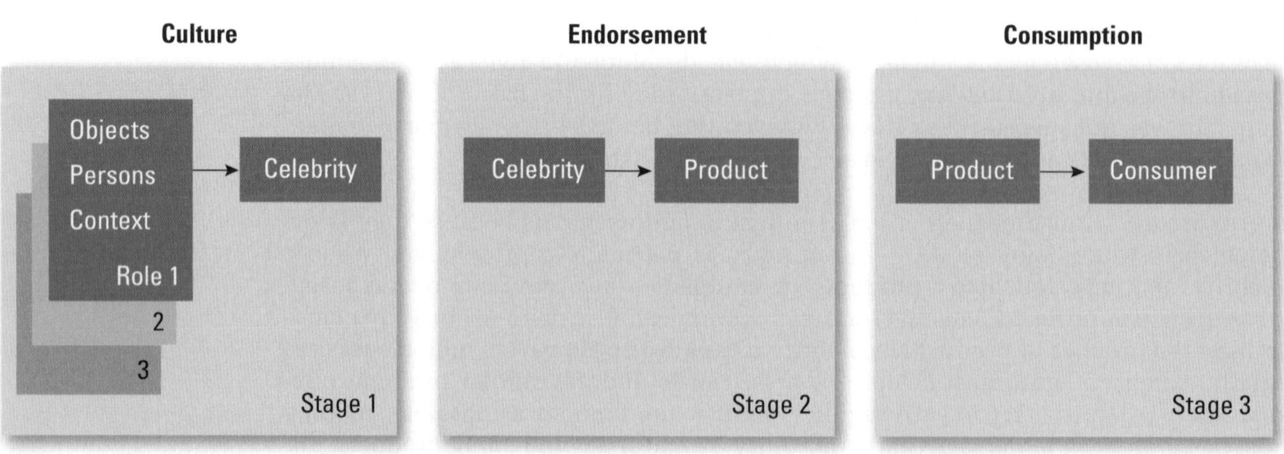

According to this model, a celebrity's effectiveness as an endorser depends on the culturally acquired meanings he or she brings to the endorsement process. Each celebrity contains many meanings, including status, class, gender, and age as well as personality and lifestyle. In explaining stage 1 of the meaning transfer process, McCracken notes:

> Celebrities draw these powerful meanings from the roles they assume in their television, movie, military, athletic, and other careers. Each new dramatic role brings the celebrity into contact with a range of objects, persons, and contexts. Out of these objects, persons, and contexts are transferred meanings that then reside in the celebrity.[77]

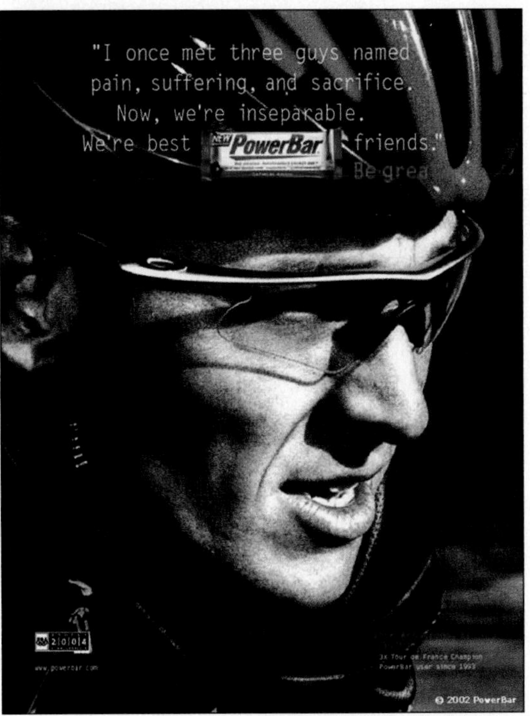

Exhibit 7–21 Cyclist Lance Armstrong helps position PowerBar as a product that provides energy to athletes

For example, cyclist Lance Armstrong has developed a very favourable image as a fierce competitor and an All-American superhero by winning the gruelling Tour de France cycling race four times after overcoming a life-threatening form of testicular cancer. McCracken suggests celebrity endorsers bring their meanings and image into the ad and transfer them to the product they are endorsing (stage 2 of the model in Figure 7–8). For example, PowerBar, the leading brand of energy performance bars, takes advantage of Armstrong's image as a competitor and champion with great determination in ads such as the one shown in Exhibit 7–21. He is also an effective endorser for the product since he competes in a very gruelling and demanding sport where the benefits of sustained energy are very important.

In the final stage of McCracken's model, the meanings the celebrity has given to the product are transferred to the consumer. By using Armstrong in its ads, PowerBar hopes to enhance its image as a product that can provide extra energy to athletes and enhance their performance. McCracken notes that this final stage is complicated and difficult to achieve. The way consumers take possession of the meaning the celebrity has transferred to a product is probably the least understood part of the process.

The meaning transfer model has some important implications for companies using celebrity endorsers. Marketers must first decide on the image or symbolic meanings important to the target audience for the particular product, service, or company. They must then determine which celebrity best represents the meaning or image to be projected. An advertising campaign must be designed that captures that meaning in the product and moves it to the consumer. Marketing and advertising personnel often rely on intuition in choosing celebrity endorsers for their companies or products, but some companies conduct research studies to determine consumers' perceptions of celebrities' meaning.

Marketers may also pretest ads to determine whether they transfer the proper meaning to the product. When celebrity endorsers are used, the marketer should track the campaign's effectiveness. Does the celebrity continue to be effective in communicating the proper meaning to the target audience? Celebrities who are no longer in the limelight may lose their ability to transfer any significant meanings to the product.

As we have seen, marketers must consider many factors when choosing a celebrity to serve as an advertising spokesperson for the company or a particular brand. Studies have shown that advertising and marketing managers take these various factors into account when choosing a celebrity endorser.[78] Among the most important factors are the celebrity's match with the target audience and the product/service or brand, the overall image of the celebrity, the cost of acquiring the celebrity, trustworthiness, the risk of controversy, and the celebrity's familiarity and likability among the target audience. Global Perspective 7–3 on page 208 shows how some entertainment celebrities are as selective as the marketing experts when choosing where to endorse brands.

GLOBAL PERSPECTIVE 7–3

Celebrities Turn to Japan

While many celebrities make huge sums of money endorsing products and serving as advertising spokespeople, some big stars won't appear in ads in the United States as they don't want fans to think they've sold out. There has also long been a feeling among actors and actresses that appearing in commercials might devalue their image among the powerful Hollywood producers and directors. However, this has been changing in recent years as even some of the biggest names in entertainment have decided to cash in on their celebrity and appear in commercials. For example, Nicole Kidman was paid $8 million to appear in commercials for the Chanel No. 5 fragrance line for one year while Catherine Zeta-Jones is getting $20 million for four years to appear for the wireless service provider T-Mobile. And Brad Pitt was paid an estimated $1 million for one airing of a Heineken commercial during the 2005 Super Bowl that showed him dodging paparazzi on his way to pick up a six-pack of the Dutch beer.

While some of the A-list celebrities still resist the temptation to cash in on their fame in the United States, they are only too happy to appear in ads in foreign countries. And nowhere are ads starring American celebrities more prevalent than in Japan. Even the rich and famous have trouble saying no to Japanese advertisers who will pay them between $1 million and $3 million for a few hours' work to make 10-second spots that their Western fans across the Pacific will never see. In Japan, celebrities make more money for less work and because the commercials will never air in the United States, they think they can make the money without looking like they are selling their artistic souls.

Megastars such as Charlize Theron, Brad Pitt, Sean Connery, and Harrison Ford are paid millions for appearing in Japanese commercials. Theron has appeared in an ad for Honda and for Lux bath products, while Ford received several million dollars for appearing sweaty and bare-chested in Kirin beer commercials and print ads. Pitt has appeared in ads for canned coffee and blue jeans, former Beatle Ringo Starr has promoted an apple drink, and David Bowie has advertised Vittel water. Sometimes celebrities are forced to change their images or personalities to suit the advertising style of Japanese companies and the tastes of audiences in Japan. Japanese commercials have a totally different feel than those in the United States and Europe and have often been described as "tacky" or "cheesy" by Western standards. For example, one ad showed actor Dennis Hopper sitting in a tub with a rubber ducky to promote a brand of shampoo and body wash while, in another, Sean Connery was shown carrying a ham into a room to a James Bond tune. Many of the commercials show myriad images of the celebrities during the short spots, putting even the best music video editors to shame.

There are several reasons why Japanese companies are willing to shell out huge sums of money for these stars. Many Japanese are fascinated by American culture and its celebrities, and endorsement of a brand by a star gives it a certain international cachet. Also, Japanese advertising emphasizes style and mood rather than substance; consumers expect to be entertained rather than bored by product information or testimonials. Because most Japanese commercials last only 10 seconds, advertisers think that an instantly recognizable Western celebrity who can capture viewers' attention is well worth the money. Some movie studios also encourage celebrities to do commercials in Japan because it boosts their visibility and helps the marketing of their films in Japan and other Asian markets.

While many celebrities are cashing in on endorsement deals in Japan, they still try to protect their image at home. For example, the stars commonly have nondisclosure clauses in their contracts, specifying that the ads cannot be shown—or sometimes even discussed (oops!)—outside of Japan. However, with the growth of the Internet, such blatant moneymaking is no longer a secret. A small Canadian Web company, Zero One Design, is dedicated to showing U.S. celebrities pitching products in Japan at gaijinagogo.com and a Vancouver-based English teacher runs the spots on his Japander.com website. Recently, several celebrities, including Arnold Schwarzenegger, Meg Ryan, and Leonardo DiCaprio, threatened legal action against the sites for showing their commercials, arguing that they infringed on the stars' intellectual property rights.

Sources: Sasha Haines-Stiles, "And Hello, A-Listers!," *Forbes*, July 4, 2005, p. 60; Hugh Davies, "Pitt's Five Million Reasons to Do a Beer Advert," news.telegraph.co.uk, May 2, 2005; Debra Lau, "Movie Stars Moonlight in Japan," Forbes.com, March 14, 2001.

Questions

1. Are some celebrities overreacting on the potential damage to their image with product endorsements?
2. Why are Japanese brands willing to pay so much for these endorsers?

Applying Likability: Decorative Models Advertisers often draw attention to their ads by featuring a physically attractive person who serves as a passive or decorative model rather than as an active communicator. Research suggests that physically attractive communicators generally have a positive impact and generate more favourable evaluations of both ads and products than less attractive models.[79] The gender appropriateness of the model for the product being advertised and his or her relevance to the product are also important considerations.[80] Products such as cosmetics or fashionable clothing are likely to benefit from the use of an attractive model, since physical appearance is very relevant in marketing these items.

Some models draw attention to the ad but not to the product or message. Studies show that an attractive model facilitates recognition of the ad but does not enhance copy readership or message recall. Thus, advertisers must ensure that the consumer's attention will go beyond the model to the product and advertising message.[81] Marketers must also consider whether the use of highly attractive models might negatively impact advertising effectiveness. Some recent studies have shown that some women experience negative feelings when comparing themselves with beautiful models used in ads and the images of physical perfection they represent.[82]

Exhibit 7–22 Dove's "Campaign for Real Beauty" uses everyday women rather than supermodels in its ads

Some companies have developed marketing campaigns that undermine the traditional approach to beauty care advertising by telling women, as well as young girls, that they're beautiful just the way they are. For example, Unilever's Dove brand has long eschewed the use of supermodels in its ads and used everyday women and girls who resemble its typical consumers. The company recently developed an interesting global integrated marketing campaign designed to appeal to everyday women.[83] The "Campaign for Real Beauty" includes magazine ads, extensive public relations, and a website (www.campaignforrealbeauty.ca) where women can discuss beauty-related issues (Exhibit 7–22). Dove has taken a social advocacy approach in the campaign, which it proclaims "aims to change the status quo and offer in its place a broader, healthier, more democratic view of beauty."[84]

IMC Planning: Message and Source Combinations

As noted at the outset of this chapter, the creative strategy comprises decisions regarding the creative theme, message appeal, and source characteristic. In the creative theme section, we noted that promotional planners determine the degree to which there is creative consistency across time, executions, media, promotional tools, and products. In this IMC planning section, we present a table that allows promotional planners to consider various combinations of message and source decisions.

MDG computers, the largest Canadian-owned PC manufacturer and retailer, recently ran newspaper ads that included Steve Nash, the two-time NBA MVP. At the same time, it ran newspaper ads without Steve Nash, the two-time NBA MVP. So, here we have an IMC program that selectively included its key spokesperson for the brand. Moreover, the website for MDG computers selectively placed the image of Steve Nash on its community page with more of an emotional appeal. The website featured Steve Nash on the pages describing the Apton performance computer with a rational appeal, but not on the pages for other types of computers. In fact, the Vision household computer included images of families. This example begins to illustrate how promotion can be put together to influence target audience attitudes; the MDG brand combined various messages and sources to effectively resonate with its various target audiences.

Figure 7–9 presents a table summarizing the possible combinations of all message and source decisions. Essentially any ad or IMC tool has one of these 15 combinations. Promotional planners can consider using certain combinations for certain parts of the IMC plan. For example, a brand may select a more credible source with a rational appeal for its print communication and possibly consider a familiar source with an emotional appeal for its television commercials. As noted in the creative consistency section, Telus has used a different message appeal and source on television and radio. Television ads feature likable critters with emotional appeals, while radio ads feature a trustworthy source with rational appeals.

	Rational Appeal	Emotional Appeal	Combined Appeal
Credible			
Trustworthy			
Similar			
Familiar			
Likable			

FIGURE 7–9

Possible combinations for message and source decisions

While a number of combinations exist—and we have shown two examples where brands have adapted the source and message across IMC tools or media—promotional planners can certainly decide to keep the same source and message appeal for all their tools and media.

SUMMARY

The creative development and execution of the advertising message are a crucial part of a firm's integrated marketing communications program. The creative specialist or team is responsible for developing an effective way to communicate the marketer's message to the customer and reinforce the brand positioning strategy. Marketers often turn to ad agencies to develop, prepare, and implement their creative strategy since these agencies are specialists in the creative function of advertising.

The challenge facing the writers, artists, and others who develop ads is to be creative and come up with fresh, unique, and appropriate ideas that can be used as solutions to communications problems. Creativity in advertising is a process of several stages, including preparation, incubation, illumination, and verification. Various sources of information are available to help the creative specialists determine the best creative strategy.

Creative strategy is guided by marketing goals and objectives and is based on a number of factors, including the basic problem the advertising must address, the target audience, behavioural and communication objectives the message seeks to accomplish, and key benefits the advertiser wants to communicate as reflected in the brand positioning strategy. These factors and the creative strategy decisions are generally stated in a copy platform, which is a work plan used to guide development of the ad campaign.

The creative strategy often contains three key decisions. An important part of creative strategy is determining the creative theme of the campaign. There are several approaches to doing this, including using a unique selling proposition, creating a brand image, looking for inherent drama in the brand, and positioning. In general, the creative theme guides much of the advertising campaign or IMC program. Consistency and originality and its ability to effectively communicate are three key strengths of a good creative.

A message appeal, the second decision of the creative strategy, is the central message used in the ad to elicit cognitive and emotional processing responses and communication effects from the target audience. Appeals can be broken into two broad categories, rational and emotional. Rational appeals focus on consumers' practical, functional, or utilitarian need for the product or service; emotional appeals relate to social and/or psychological reasons for purchasing a product or service. Numerous types of appeals are available to advertisers within each category.

Selection of the appropriate source or communicator to deliver a message is the third creative strategy decision. Three important attributes are source credibility, attractiveness, and power. Marketers enhance message effectiveness by hiring communicators who are experts in a particular area and/or have a trustworthy image. The use of celebrities to deliver advertising messages has become very popular; advertisers hope they will catch the receivers' attention and influence their attitudes or behaviour through an identification process. The chapter discusses the meaning a celebrity brings to the endorsement process and the importance of matching the image of the celebrity with that of the company or brand.

KEY TERMS

advertising campaign, ***184***
advertising creativity, ***177***
animatic, ***182***
attractiveness, ***204***
campaign theme, ***184***
creative execution, ***192***
creative strategy, ***176***
creative tactics, ***176***
creative theme, ***184***
credibility, ***202***
copy platform, ***183***
emotional appeal, ***195***
fear appeal, ***196***
focus groups, ***182***
general preplanning input, ***181***
humour appeal, ***198***
identification, ***204***
image advertising, ***186***
inherent drama, ***186***
internalization, ***202***
message appeal, ***192***
product/service-specific preplanning input, ***181***
rational appeal, ***192***
research, ***181***
sleeper effect, ***203***
source, ***201***
storyboard, ***182***
teaser advertising, ***201***
unique selling proposition (USP), ***185***

DISCUSSION QUESTIONS

1. Television commercials can use unusual creativity that has very little to do with the product being advertised. Explain why creative specialists would recommend such ads and why the brand managers would approve the production and placement.

2. Assume you have been assigned to work on the advertising campaign for a new brand of bottled water. Describe the types of general and product-specific preplanning input you might evaluate.

3. What is your opinion of advertising awards, such as the Cannes Lions, that are based solely on creativity? If you were a marketer looking for an agency, would you take these creative awards into consideration in your agency evaluation process? Why or why not?

4. Find an example of a print ad that you think is very creative and an ad you feel is dull and boring. Evaluate each ad from a creative perspective. What makes one ad creative and the other bland?

5. Find an example of an ad or campaign that you think reflects one of the approaches used to develop a creative theme such as unique selling proposition, brand image, inherent drama, or positioning. Discuss how the creative theme is used in this ad or campaign.

6. Discuss the pros and cons of using a comparative advertising appeal for the following products: beer, cellphones, furniture, airlines.

7. Assume that you have been asked to consult for a government agency that wants to use a fear appeal to encourage college and university students not to drink and drive. Explain how fear appeals might affect persuasion and what factors should be considered in developing the ads.

8. It has been observed that Canadian advertisers use fewer celebrity endorsers compared to American advertisers. Do you agree with this? If it is true, what is the explanation?

9. Find a celebrity who is currently appearing in ads for a particular company or brand and analyze and use McCracken's meaning transfer model (shown in Figure 7–8) to analyze the use of the celebrity as a spokesperson.

CHAPTER 8

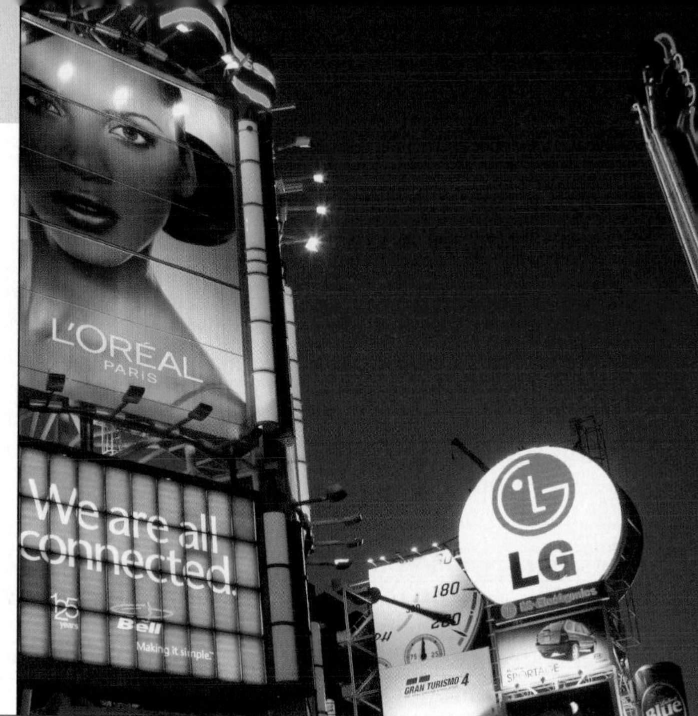

CREATIVE TACTICS DECISIONS

Chapter Objectives

- To identify three key decisions for creative tactics: execution style, message structure, and design elements.
- To analyze the creative execution styles that advertisers can use and the situations where they are most appropriate.
- To examine different types of message structures that can be used to develop a promotional message.
- To analyze design elements involved in the creation of print advertising and TV commercials.
- To understand a planning model for making creative tactics decisions.
- To consider how clients evaluate the creative work of their agencies and discuss guidelines for the evaluation and approval process.

Clever Tactics or IMC Imperatives?

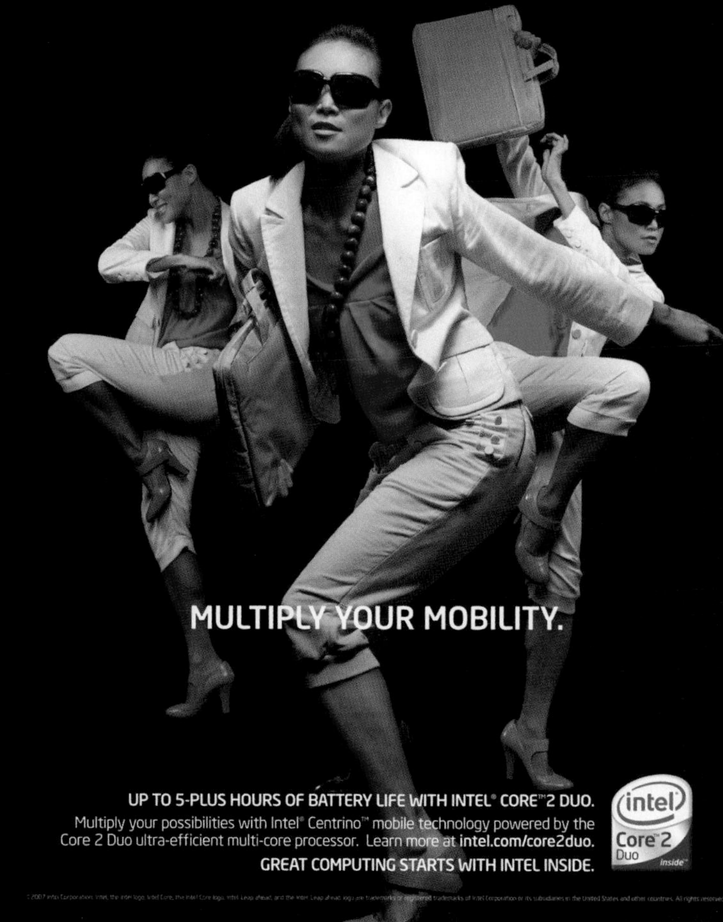

MULTIPLY YOUR MOBILITY.
UP TO 5-PLUS HOURS OF BATTERY LIFE WITH INTEL® CORE™2 DUO.
Multiply your possibilities with Intel® Centrino™ mobile technology powered by the Core 2 Duo ultra-efficient multi-core processor. Learn more at intel.com/core2duo.
GREAT COMPUTING STARTS WITH INTEL INSIDE.
intel
Core 2
Duo
inside

The great debate on the role of taglines and audio logos in promotional messages continues. Some contend that the tagline is not worth the time and money invested; it is "the period at the end of the sentence," with the ad being the sentence. Moreover, a good tagline is the result of a good advertising message. Others suggest that the tagline is less prevalent these days but still very relevant. For example, one executive believes a good tagline, "communicates a brand position or brand benefit." With such divergence of opinion, which direction should firms go in this age of multiple media and IMC tools?

Audio logos tell a similar tale, but it appears more tilted in favour of the positive. Intel's famous three-second soundtrack, introduced in 1995, helped it become one of the top ten most recognized brands. Heard across all forms of media with audio sound, the familiar notes allowed listeners to instantly recognize the brand and experience positive emotional feelings.

Firms that offer many types of goods and services view the audio logo as one way of connecting brand messages across multiple media and IMC tools, much like a visual logo. For example, the Rogers audio logo can be heard for many of its services like wireless and cable. Continuity and consistency in the promotional message across IMC tools—like television, radio, wireless, interactive displays, Internet, and podcasts—makes simple reminders all the more critical.

This was the thinking, too, with taglines; however, the recent decline in their use appears puzzling, as some brands like Gap and Apple do not consistently use them in all ads. Part of the problem is the volume of ads consumers are exposed to each day. So many competing messages make it hard for target audiences to recall a verbal phrase. Moreover, some firms try to encapsulate everything about the brand and company so that the tagline becomes overly general or too abstract, making it much less memorable.

Despite these recent constraints, some believe that taglines are worth attempting if they can create a movement or culture, the way Nike did with its "Just Do It" or DeBeer's did with its "A diamond is forever." And here lies another concern: most memorable taglines lasted for quite some time, as marketers had to repeat the phrase many times before it became synonymous with the brand.

And this might explain the growth of audio logos over taglines. Research suggests that about 75 percent of all broadcast ads (TV and radio) use music, and that people process and remember music much more easily than words. In this age of delivering multiple messages across many media, a familiar sound just might be the glue that holds it all together.

Sources: Michelle Warren, "Flight of the Stinger," *Marketing Magazine,* May 1, 2006; Michelle Warren, "The Trouble with Tag Lines," *Marketing Magazine,* March 6, 2006.

Question

1. Will assessing consumer reaction to advertising using market research over the Internet improve the quality of information in the future?

In the previous chapter, we identified and described the three creative strategy decisions. This chapter focuses on the three main creative tactics decisions. It examines various execution styles that can be used to develop the ad, the important message structure choices available, and the elements involved in the design and production of effective advertising messages. We also present a framework for guiding the creative tactics decisions. We conclude by presenting some guidelines marketers can use to evaluate the creative recommendations they need to approve to effectively communicate their brand positioning strategy.

Creative Execution Style

Once the specific message appeal has been determined, the creative specialist or team decides the creative tactics. One critical creative tactic is the **creative execution style**, which is the way a message appeal is presented. While it is obviously important for an ad to have a meaningful message appeal to communicate to the consumer, the manner in which the ad is executed is also important.

Message appeals can be presented or executed in numerous ways:

- Straight sell/factual message
- Scientific/technical evidence
- Demonstration
- Comparison
- Testimonial
- Slice of life
- Animation
- Personality symbol
- Imagery
- Dramatization
- Humour
- Combinations

We now examine these formats and considerations involved in their use. Many of these techniques can be combined to present the message appeal.

Straight Sell/Factual Message

One of the most basic types of creative executions is the straight sell or factual message. This type of ad relies on a straightforward presentation of information concerning the product or service. This execution is often used with rational appeals, where the focus of the message is the product and its specific attributes and/or benefits.

Straight-sell executions are commonly used in print ads. A picture of the product or service occupies part of the ad, and the factual copy takes up the rest of the space. They are also used in TV advertising, with an announcer generally delivering the sales message while the product/service is shown on the screen. Ads for high-involvement consumer products as well as industrial and other business-to-business products generally use this format. The ad for the Hitachi line form series plasma TV shown in Exhibit 8–1 is part of a campaign that uses a straight-sell execution style.

Exhibit 8–1 Hitachi uses a straight-sell execution style in this ad

Scientific/Technical Evidence

In a variation of the straight sell, scientific or technical evidence is presented in the ad. Advertisers often cite technical information, results of scientific or laboratory studies or endorsements by scientific bodies or agencies to support their advertising claims. The ad for Eagle One's NanoWax shown in Exhibit 8–2 positions the brand as the most technologically advanced car wax available and uses scientific evidence to support this claim.

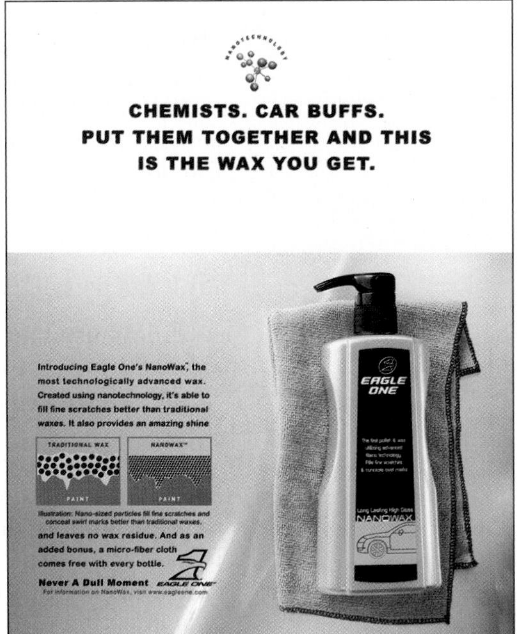

Exhibit 8–2 This ad uses scientific evidence to promote Eagle One NanoWax

Demonstration

Demonstration is designed to illustrate the key advantages of the product by showing it in actual use or in some staged situation. Demonstration executions can be very effective in convincing consumers of a product's utility or quality and of the benefits of owning or using the brand. TV is particularly well suited for demonstration executions, since the benefits or advantages of the product can be shown right on the screen. Although perhaps a little less dramatic than TV, demonstration ads can also work in print. The Mentadent toothpaste ad shown in Exhibit 8–3 uses this style to demonstrate how the brand's Liquid Calcium technology replenishes the surface enamel to whiten teeth. Dove soap provides an example of demonstration presentation tactic across IMC tools. The magazine ads, TV ad, direct mail, and in-store demonstrations encouraged consumers to use litmus paper to test the alkalinity of various soaps. The key attribute of mildness of Dove was naturally communicated, albeit in a subtle manner, and the brand name was not highlighted in an obvious manner in the print and TV ads.[1]

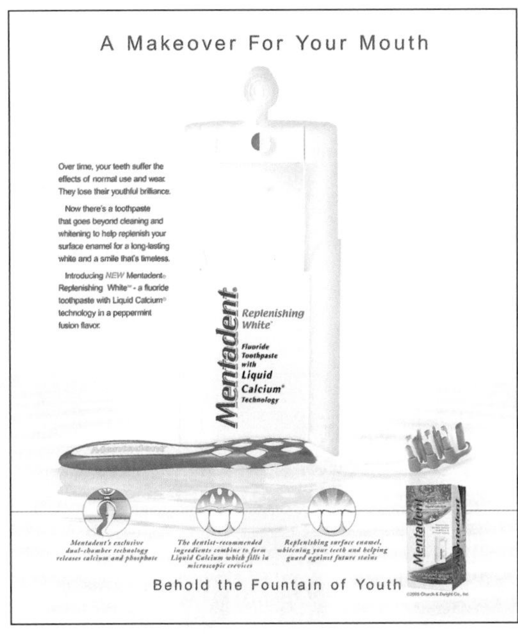

Exhibit 8–3 This ad uses demonstration execution to explain the benefits of Mentadent

Comparison

Brand comparisons can also be the basis for the advertising execution. The comparison execution approach is increasingly popular among advertisers, since it offers a direct way of communicating a brand's particular advantage over its competitors or positioning a new or lesser-known brand with industry leaders. Comparison executions are often used to execute comparative appeals, as discussed in the previous chapter.

Testimonial

Many advertisers prefer to have their messages presented by way of a testimonial, where a person praises the product or service on the basis of his or her personal experience with it. Testimonial executions can have ordinary satisfied customers discuss their own experiences with the brand and the benefits of using it. This approach can be very effective when the person delivering the testimonial is someone with whom the target audience can identify or who has an interesting story to tell. The testimonial must be based on actual use of the product or service to avoid legal problems, and the spokesperson must be credible. Testimonials can be particularly effective when they come from a recognizable or popular source.

Toyota dealers in western Canada used actual customers to communicate their product's quality and dependability. Among the four initially produced, a country veterinarian drove his 13-year-old Toyota 4Runner with 742,000 km in one spot and a travelling salesperson complained that the odometer of his Corolla only had six digits in another spot. All ads were based on actual customer experiences and although the campaign was a risky departure, the initial results appeared promising for a regional launch prior to the spring buying season in 2003.[2]

Endorsements can also be from professional associations. Recall that the unique selling proposition for Trident was supported with an endorsement from the Canadian Dental Association as shown in Exhibit 7–4 in the previous chapter.

Slice of Life

A widely used advertising format, particularly for packaged-goods products, is the slice-of-life execution. This type of ad portrays a situation that consumers might face in their daily lives. The ad then shows how the advertiser's product can resolve the problem.

Slice-of-life executions are often criticized for being unrealistic and irritating to watch because they are often used to remind consumers of problems of a personal nature, such as dandruff, bad breath, body odour, and laundry or cleaning problems. Often these ads come across as contrived, silly, phony, or even offensive to consumers. However, many advertisers still prefer this style because they believe it is effective at presenting a situation to which most consumers can relate and at registering the product feature or benefit.

Execution is critical in using the technique effectively, as these ads are designed to be dramatizations of a supposedly real-life situation that consumers might encounter. Getting viewers to identify with the situation and/or characters depicted in the ad can be very challenging. Since the success of slice-of-life ads often depends on how well the actors come across and execute their roles, professional actors are often used to achieve credibility and to ensure that the commercial is of high quality. Smaller companies and local advertisers often do not have ad budgets large enough to hire the talent or to pay for the production quality needed to effectively create slice-of-life spots. Thus, this execution technique is more likely to be used by companies with ad budgets that are large enough to fund the use of professional talent and production of quality commercials.

Many marketers like to use the slice-of-life genre as they believe it can be an effective way of addressing a problem or issue and offering a solution. For example, Listerine used a slice-of-life commercial effectively to introduce a new Natural Citrus flavour of the popular mouthwash.[3] The spot was designed to address the problem that some consumers have with the intense taste of the original flavour of the product. The spot opens with a mother returning home from the store with two surprises: danish and Listerine. However, when her husband and two kids see the mouthwash they run and hide. The mother then tells them it is Natural Citrus Listerine, which tastes less intense. The humorous spot ends with the father coming out of a kitchen cupboard and pots and pans dangling as one of the boys climbs down from the top of the kitchen island and the voiceover says, "You can handle it. Germs can't" (see Exhibit 8–4).

Exhibit 8–4 Listerine uses a slice-of-life execution to introduce a new flavour

Animation

An advertising execution approach that has become popular in recent years is animation. With this technique, animated scenes are drawn by artists or created on the computer, and cartoons, puppets, or other types of fictional characters may be used. Cartoon animation is especially popular for commercials targeted at children for products like toys and cereal.

IMC PERSPECTIVE 8–1

Ronald McDonald Gets a Lifestyle Change

One of the most popular personality symbols is Ronald McDonald. In recent ads he appears snowboarding and skateboarding and dressed in a sporty version of his trademark yellow suit. The popular icon for the fast-food giant seems to be having an identity crisis. McDonald's executives are branding the icon as "an ambassador for a balanced active lifestyle."

The makeover of the burger giant's 42-year-old personality symbol is part of the second phase of McDonald's latest marketing blitz promoting healthy lifestyles. Customers can now substitute bottled water and apple slices for soft drinks and fries, or skip the bun and get a lettuce-wrapped burger. McDonald's also has hired as consultants Oprah Winfrey's personal trainer Bob Greene and best-selling author and nutritionist Dr. Dean Ornish to design fitness programs and promote good eating habits. McDonald's strategy seems to be working.

Three versions of a TV spot called "Active Ronald, You and I" are playing on Teletoon and YTV in Canada. They depict Ronald changing from his clown suit into a track suit and kicking soccer balls, riding snowboards, and running and jumping his way around town. The two-minute, 30-second and 15-second ads encourage kids to get up off the couch and get moving. Noticeably absent are the usual burgers, fries, and golden arches. A new tagline—"It's what I eat and what I do ... I'm lovin' it"—accompanies the spots.

"Some of the TV ads are done in a different kind of format than what consumers are accustomed to seeing from McDonald's," says Ron Christianson, manager of corporate communications for McDonald's Canada. "The spots don't mention product and essentially showcase Ronald encouraging kids to be active all day by playing sports, skipping, running, and jumping."

McDonald's ranked eighth in *Business Week's* Top 100 brands for 2006. A new healthy-living marketing campaign, and the premium-priced sandwiches and salads that come with it, have led to a fourth year of sales gains.

Sources: "The 100 Top Brands," *Business Week Online* at http://bwnt.businessweek.com/brand/2006; Gail Powell, "Salad, Fries and Exercise," *Marketing*, June 27, 2005; Gina Piccalo, "McDonald's Markets a Healthy Makeover," *The Toronto Star*, July 22, 2005.

Question

1. How will consumers react to the new image of Ronald McDonald?

Animation is a key element of a long-standing television commercial for Bits & Bites, a snack food directed to adults. The ad featured a man standing behind a fence as a friendly neighbour with his dog. First conceived in the 1970s, the light-hearted commercial continued to run into the 1980s and 1990s due to its significant appeal to consumers as indicated by market research. Faced with increased competition from a variety of snack foods, Kraft refreshed the graphics by brightening the colour of the scenes and adding more detail to the drawings. And for the first time ever, Kraft developed new versions of the ad by having three different "blooper out-takes" (i.e., line flubs, staging collapses, and character mishaps).[4]

PERSONALITY SYMBOL

Another type of advertising execution involves developing a central character or personality symbol that can deliver the advertising message and with which the product or service can be identified. This character can be a person, like the Maytag repairman, who sits anxiously by the phone but is never needed because the company's appliances are so reliable. IMC Perspective 8–1 shows how McDonald's is changing the image of its famous personality.

Canadian brands have been at the forefront in developing and nurturing a personality. Kool-Aid's "Face" icon and three-dimensional Kool-Aid pitcher provide an instantly recognizable character. In fact, established in Canada, the personality has been used in campaigns in the U.S. and Mexico. The American headquarters for Clorox invented The Man From Glad personality about 40 years ago, although he has not been seen in ads south of the border for 20 years while continuously appearing in Canadian ads. Captain High Liner has been extolling the virtues of his brand of frozen fish products for over 25 years in Canada. A&W has used two types of personalities over the years, a person dressed as a bear and many family members to represent the different names of their burger products. Over time however, some personalities are changed or possibly retired. The St-Hubert chicken has been updated many times over the last 50 years, but executives are uncertain of its future since research indicates that it does not quite fit its new restaurant format and decor.[5]

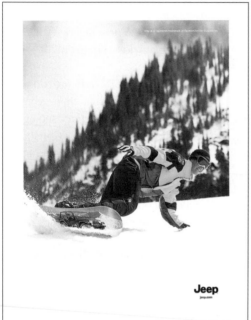

Exhibit 8–5 This ad associates the Jeep Wrangler with images of the outdoors and adventure

Imagery

Some ads contain little or no information about the brand or company and are almost totally visual. These advertisements use imagery executions whereby the ad consists primarily of visual elements such as pictures, illustrations, and/or symbols rather than information. An imagery execution is used when the goal is to encourage consumers to associate the brand with the symbols, characters, and/or situation shown in the ad. Imagery ads are often the basis for emotional appeals that are used to advertise products or services where differentiation based on physical characteristics is difficult, such as soft drinks, liquor, designer clothing, and cosmetics. However, image is important for all types of products and services as marketers want the target audience to hold a favourable set of psychosocial associations for their company or brand.

An imagery execution may be based on *usage imagery* by showing how a brand is used or performs and the situation in which it is used. For example, advertising for trucks and SUVs often shows the vehicles navigating tough terrain or in challenging situations such as towing a heavy load. Notice how the clever Jeep ad shown in Exhibit 8–5 uses only the image of the vehicle on the bottom of a snowboard to associate the vehicle with the outdoors and adventuresome activities. This type of execution can also be based on *user imagery* where the focus is on the type of person who uses the brand. Ads for cosmetics often use very attractive models in the hope of getting consumers to associate the model's physical attractiveness with the brand (see Exhibit 8–6). Most Nike ads have very little copy and rely primarily on images of athletes achieving success by using the company's products. Image executions rely heavily on visual elements such as photography, colour, tonality, and design to communicate the desired image to the consumer. Marketers who rely on image executions have to be sure that the usage or user imagery with which they associate their brand evokes the right feelings and reactions from the target audience.

Exhibit 8–6 This bebe ad uses an attractive model to create a favourable image for the brand

Dramatization

Another execution technique particularly well suited to television is dramatization, where the focus is on telling a short story with the product as the star. Dramatization is akin to slice-of-life execution, but it uses more excitement and suspense in telling the story. The purpose of using drama is to draw the viewer into the action it portrays. Advocates of drama note that when it is successful, the audience becomes lost in the story and experiences the concerns and feelings of the characters.[6]

Although we typically see dramatization used in television or radio ads, because they have audio capabilities, it is possible to use this execution style in print. Good Year Tires conveyed the drama of driving in bad winter snow conditions with an effective newspaper ad that showed a car skidding through the weather page! Designed to look like the worst type of January weather, the fall campaign reminded consumers the importance of purchasing new snow tires before it was too late.[7]

The real challenge facing the creative team is how to encompass all these elements in a 30-second commercial. A good example of the dramatization execution technique is the ad for Zerex antifreeze in Exhibit 8–7, which shows a woman's sense of relief when her car starts at the airport on a cold winter night. The ad concludes with a strong identification slogan, "The temperature never drops below Zerex," which connects the brand name to its product benefit.

Humour

Like comparisons, humour was discussed in Chapter 7 as a type of message appeal, but this technique can also be used as a way of presenting other message appeals. Humorous executions are particularly well suited to television or radio, although some print ads attempt to use this style.

The Golf Pride ad in Exhibit 8–8 uses a humour execution style for a mostly rational message appeal. The snowman represents a score of 8 on a hole that golfers want to avoid. The visual likely attracts the audience's attention, and the copy explains how Golf Pride can improve their performance with new grips.

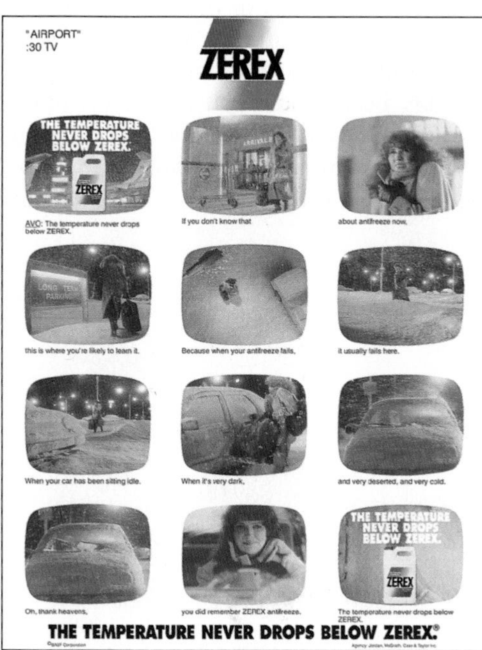

Exhibit 8–7 This Zerex ad uses a dramatization execution

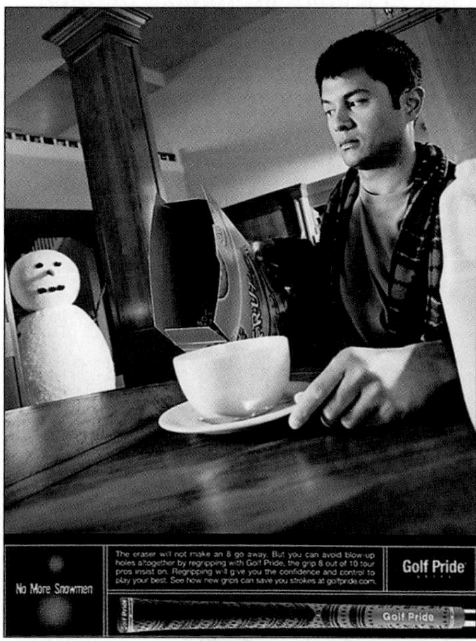

Exhibit 8–8 This Golf Pride ad uses a humour executional style to communicate an important product benefit

Message Structure

Marketing communications usually consist of a number of message points that the communicator wants to convey. It is important to communicate these points to overcome any opposing viewpoints audience members may hold. Extensive research has been conducted on how the structure of a persuasive message can influence its effectiveness, including order of presentation, conclusion drawing, message sidedness, and verbal versus visual message characteristics. This section summarizes the second creative tactic decision, message structure.

Order of Presentation

A basic consideration in the design of a persuasive message is the arguments' order of presentation. Should the most important message points be placed at the beginning of the message, in the middle, or at the end? Research on learning and memory generally indicates that items presented first and last are remembered better than those presented in the middle (see Figure 8–1).[8] This suggests that a communicator's strongest arguments should be presented early or late in the message but never in the middle.

Presenting the strongest arguments at the beginning of the message assumes a **primacy effect** is operating, whereby information presented first is most effective. Putting the strong points at the end assumes a **recency effect**, whereby the last arguments presented are most persuasive.

Whether to place the strongest selling points at the beginning or the end of the message depends on several factors. If the target audience is opposed to the communicator's position, presenting strong points first can reduce the level of counterarguing. Putting weak arguments first might lead to such a high level of counterarguing that strong arguments that followed would not be believed. Strong arguments work best at the beginning of the message if the audience is not interested in the topic, so they can arouse interest in the message. When the target audience is predisposed toward the communicator's position or is highly interested in the issue or product, strong arguments can be saved for the end of the message. This may result in a more favourable opinion as well as better retention of the information.

The order of presentation can be critical when a long, detailed message with many arguments is being presented. For short communications, such as a 15- or 30-second TV or radio commercial, the order may be less critical. However, many product and service messages are received by consumers with low involvement and minimal interest. Thus, an advertiser may want to present the brand name and key selling points early in the message and repeat them at the end to enhance recall and retention.

FIGURE 8–1

Ad message recall as a function of order of presentation

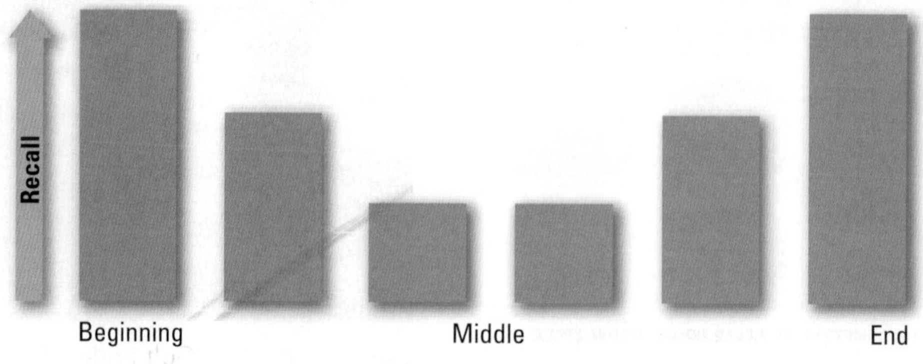

Conclusion Drawing

Marketing communicators must decide whether their messages should explicitly draw a firm conclusion or allow receivers to draw their own conclusions. Research suggests that, in general, messages with explicit conclusions are more easily understood and effective in influencing attitudes. However, other studies have shown that the effectiveness of conclusion drawing may depend on the target audience, the type of issue or topic, and the nature of the situation.[9]

More highly educated people prefer to draw their own conclusions and may be annoyed at an attempt to explain the obvious or to draw an inference for them. But stating the conclusion may be necessary for a less educated audience, who may not draw any conclusion or may make an incorrect inference from the message. Marketers must also consider the audience's level of involvement in the topic. For highly personal or ego-involving issues, message recipients may want to make up their own minds and resent any attempts by the communicator to draw a conclusion. One study found that open-ended ads (without explicit conclusions) were more effective than closed-ended arguments that did include a specific conclusion—but only for involved audiences.[10]

Whether to draw a conclusion for the audience also depends on the complexity of the topic. Even a highly educated audience may need assistance if its knowledge level in a particular area is low. Does the marketer want the message to trigger immediate action or a more long-term effect? If immediate action is an objective, the message should draw a definite conclusion. When immediate impact is not the objective and repeated exposure will give the audience members opportunities to draw their own conclusions, an open-ended message may be used. Drawing a conclusion in a message may make sure the target audience gets the point the marketer intended. But many advertisers believe that letting customers draw their own conclusions reinforces the points being made in the message. The ad for Silk Soymilk in Exhibit 8–9 is a very good example of an open-ended message. The question in the headline encourages consumers to be open to the idea of drinking soymilk.

Message Sidedness

Another message structure decision facing the marketer involves message sidedness. A **one-sided message** mentions only positive attributes or benefits. A **two-sided message** presents both good and bad points. One-sided messages are most effective when the target audience already holds a favourable opinion about the topic. They also work better with a less educated audience.[11]

Two-sided messages are more effective when the target audience holds an opposing opinion or is highly educated. Two-sided messages may enhance the credibility of the source.[12] A better-educated audience usually knows there are opposing arguments, so a communicator who presents both sides of an issue is likely to be seen as less biased and more objective.

Most advertisers use one-sided messages. They are concerned about the negative effects of acknowledging a weakness in their brand or don't want to say anything positive about their competitors. There are exceptions, however. Sometimes advertisers compare brands on several attributes and do not show their product as being the best on every one.

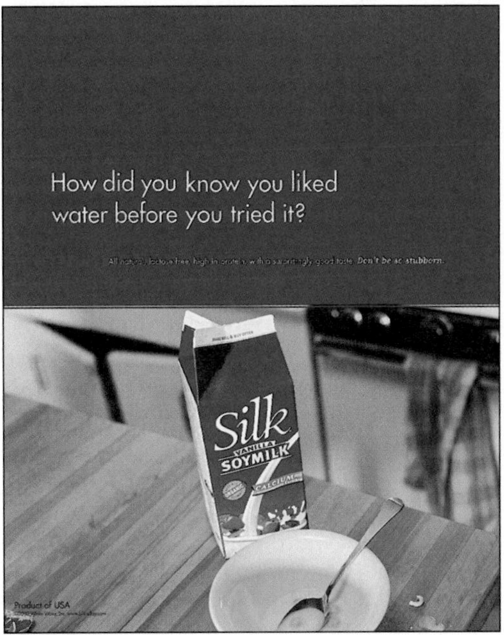

Exhibit 8–9 This ad makes effective use of an open-ended approach

In some situations, marketers may focus on a negative attribute as a way of enhancing overall perceptions of the product. For example, W. K. Buckley Limited has become one of the

No one said it would be easy.
Buckley's
Mixture
COUGHS & CONGESTION
It tastes awful. And it works.

Exhibit 8–10 Buckley's Cough Syrup uses a two-sided message to promote the product's effectiveness

leading brands of cough syrup by using a blunt two-sided slogan: "Buckley's Mixture. It tastes awful. And it works." Ads for the brand poke fun at the cough syrup's terrible taste but also suggest that the taste is a reason why the product is effective (Exhibit 8–10). They have used this slogan for many years and have built the brand from 2 percent to now 16 percent market share. It helps that this slogan is a bit of truth in advertising that consumers certainly appreciate.[13]

A special type of two-sided message is known as a **refutation**. The communicator presents both sides of an issue and then refutes the opposing viewpoint. Since this tends to "inoculate" the target audience against a competitor's counterclaims, they are more effective than one-sided messages in making consumers resistant to an opposing message.[14] Refutational messages may be useful when marketers wish to build attitudes that resist change and must defend against attacks or criticism of their products or the company. Market leaders, who are often the target of comparative messages, may find that acknowledging competitors' claims and then refuting them can help build resistant attitudes and customer loyalty.

Verbal versus Visual Messages

Thus far our discussion has focused on the information, or verbal, portion of the message. However, the nonverbal, visual elements of an ad are also very important. Many ads provide minimal amounts of information and rely on visual elements to communicate. Pictures are commonly used in advertising to convey information or reinforce copy or message claims.

Both the verbal and visual portions of an ad influence the way the advertising message is processed.[15] Consumers may develop images or impressions based on visual elements such as an illustration in an ad or the scenes in a TV commercial. In some cases, the visual portion of an ad may reduce its persuasiveness, since the processing stimulated by the picture may be less controlled and consequently less favourable than that stimulated by words.[16]

Pictures affect the way consumers process accompanying copy. A recent study showed that when verbal information was low in imagery value, the use of pictures providing examples increased both immediate and delayed recall of product attributes.[17] However, when the verbal information was already high in imagery value, the addition of pictures did not increase recall. Advertisers often design ads where the visual image supports the verbal appeal to create a compelling impression in the consumer's mind.

Sometimes advertisers use a different approach; they design ads in which the visual portion is incongruent with or contradicts the verbal information presented. The logic behind this strategy is that the use of an unexpected picture or visual image will grab consumers' attention and get them to engage in more effortful or elaborative processing.[18] A number of studies have shown that the use of a visual that is inconsistent with the verbal content leads to more recall and greater processing of the information presented.[19]

Design Elements for IMC Tools

Once the creative strategy and initial two tactics decisions have been determined, attention turns to creating the actual advertisement. The design and production of advertising messages involve a number of activities, among them writing copy, developing illustrations and other visual elements of the ad, and bringing all of the pieces together to create an effective message. In this section, we examine the verbal and visual elements of an ad and discuss tactical considerations in creating print ads and TV commercials. Most of the points here can be applied to other media and IMC tools.

Design for Print Messages

The basic components of a print ad are the headline, the body copy, the visual or illustrations, and the layout (the way they all fit together). The headline and body copy portions of the ad are the responsibility of the copywriters; artists, often working under the direction of an art director, are responsible for the visual presentation. Art directors also work with the copywriters to develop a layout, or arrangement of the various components of the ad: headlines, subheads, body copy, illustrations, captions, logos, and the like. We briefly examine the three components of a print ad and how they are coordinated.

Headlines The **headline** is the words in the leading position of the ad—the words that will be read first or are positioned to draw the most attention.[20] Headlines are usually set in larger, darker type and are often set apart from the body copy or text portion of the ad to give them prominence. Most advertising people consider the headline the most important part of a print ad.

The most important function of a headline is attracting readers' attention and interesting them in the rest of the message. While the visual portion of an ad is obviously important, the headline often shoulders most of the responsibility of attracting readers' attention. Research has shown the headline is generally the first thing people look at in a print ad, followed by the illustration. Only 20 percent of readers go beyond the headline and read the body copy.[21] So in addition to attracting attention, the headline must give the reader good reason to read the copy portion of the ad, which contains more detailed and persuasive information about the product or service. To do this, the headline must put forth the main theme, appeal, or proposition of the ad in a few words. Some print ads contain little if any body copy, so the headline must work with the illustration to communicate the entire advertising message.

Headlines also perform a segmentation function by engaging the attention and interest of consumers who are most likely to buy a particular product or service. Advertisers begin the segmentation process by choosing to advertise in certain types of publications (e.g., a travel, general interest, or fashion magazine). An effective headline goes even further in selecting good prospects for the product by addressing their specific needs, wants, or interests.

Types of Headlines There are numerous headline possibilities. The type used depends on several factors, including the creative strategy, the particular advertising situation (e.g., product type, media vehicle(s) being used, timeliness), and its relationship to other components of the ad, such as the illustration or body copy. Headlines can be categorized as direct and indirect. **Direct headlines** are straightforward and informative in terms of the message they are presenting and the target audience they are directed toward. Common types of direct headlines include those offering a specific benefit, making a promise, or announcing a reason why the reader should be interested in the product or service.

Indirect headlines are not straightforward about identifying the product or service or getting to the point. But they are often more effective at attracting readers' attention and interest because they provoke curiosity and lure readers into the body copy to learn an answer or get an explanation. Techniques for writing indirect headlines include using questions, provocations, how-to statements, and challenges.

Exhibit 8–11 This ad uses a question-style headline and strong visual image that motivate consumers to read the copy

Indirect headlines rely on their ability to generate curiosity or intrigue so as to motivate readers to become involved with the ad and read the body copy to find out the point of the message. This can be risky if the headline is not provocative enough to get the readers' interest. Advertisers deal with this problem by using a visual appeal that helps attract attention and offers another reason for reading more of the message. For example, the ad for the Lexus GS sports sedan shown in Exhibit 8–11 uses a question as the headline that invites consumers to read the copy to learn more about the features of the car and decide how to categorize it. The visual portion of the ad supports the positioning theme by showing the GS 430 being driven on a windy road.

While many ads have only one headline, it is also common to see print ads containing the main head and one or more secondary heads, or **subheads**. Subheads are usually smaller than the main headline but larger than the body copy. They may appear above or below the main headline or within the body copy. The Cambridge SoundWorks ad shown in Exhibit 8–12 uses subheads within the body copy.

Subheads are often used to enhance the readability of the message by breaking up large amounts of body copy and highlighting key sales points. Their content reinforces the headline and advertising slogan or theme.

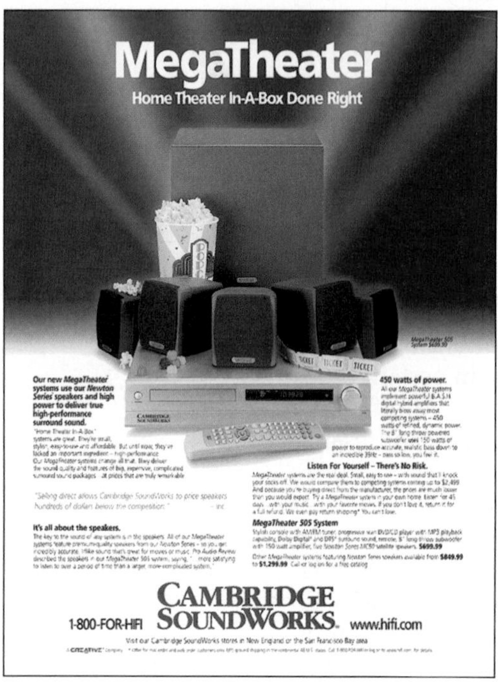

Exhibit 8–12 This ad uses subheads to make the copy easier to read

Body Copy The main text portion of a print ad is referred to as the **body copy** (or sometimes just *copy*). While the body copy is usually the heart of the advertising message, getting the target audience to read it is often difficult. The copywriter faces a dilemma: The body copy must be long enough to communicate the advertiser's message yet short enough to hold readers' interest.

Body copy content often flows from the points made in the headline or various subheads, but the specific content depends on the type of advertising appeal and/or execution style being used. For example, straight-sell copy that presents relevant information, product features and benefits, or competitive advantages is often used with the various types of rational appeals discussed earlier in the chapter. Emotional appeals often use narrative copy that tells a story or provides an interesting account of a problem or situation involving the product.

Advertising body copy can be written to go along with various types of creative appeals and executions—comparisons, price appeals, demonstrations, humour, dramatizations, and the like. Copywriters choose a copy style that is appropriate for the type of appeal being used and effective for executing the creative strategy and communicating the advertiser's message to the target audience.

An interesting example of the use of a long copy occurred with Rogers (AT&T) Wireless. Borrowing from the idea that a picture is worth a thousand words, the poster ads extolled upon the attributes and benefits of picture messaging with a small photo of the product and exactly one thousand words! To garner attention and full processing of the copy, the ads involved the reader in personally relevant conversations that the target audience would be familiar with such as a woman talking to her man-friend about which shoes to wear to her high-school reunion, and a man talking to his buddy about his golfing triumphs. The entertaining dialogue provided a quick and enjoyable read, giving the feeling that one was actually experiencing the conversation.[22]

Visual Elements The third major component of a print ad is the visual element. The illustration is often a dominant part of a print ad and plays an important role in determining its effectiveness. The visual portion of an ad must attract attention, communicate an idea or image, and work in a synergistic fashion with the headline and body copy to produce an effective message. In some print ads, the visual portion of the ad is essentially the message and thus must convey a strong and meaningful image. For example, the award-winning ad for Sims Snowboards shown in Exhibit 8–13 uses a powerful visual image. In a scene reminiscent of the protestor blocking military vehicles in Beijing's Tiananmen Square during the 1989 student uprising, a snowboarder stands in the path of snow-grooming machines (which pack the snow, to the distress of snowboarders). The single line of copy, "In a courageous act of solidarity, a lone snowboarder stands up for freedom," reinforces the message presented by the visual image.

Exhibit 8–13 This ad for Sims Snowboards uses a strong visual image and a layout that resembles a newspaper page

Many decisions have to be made regarding the visual portion of the ad: what identification marks should be included (brand name, company or trade name, trademarks, logos); whether to use photos or hand-drawn or painted illustrations; what colours to use (or even perhaps black and white or just a splash of colour); and what the focus of the visual should be.

Layout While each individual component of a print ad is important, the key factor is how these elements are blended into a finished advertisement. A **layout** is the physical arrangement of the various parts of the ad, including the headline, subheads, body copy, illustrations, and any identifying marks. The layout shows where each part of the ad will be placed and gives guidelines to the people working on the ad. For example, the layout helps the copywriter determine how much space he or she has to work with and how much copy should be written. The layout can also guide the art director in determining the size and type of photos. In the ad for Sims Snowboards shown in Exhibit 8–13, the layout is designed to make the ad look like it was reprinted from a newspaper page. Notice how this theme is carried through in the copy, which reads like a newspaper photo caption and ends with "Story on 2C." Layouts are often done in rough form to visualize what the ad will look like before moving on to the more costly stages of print production.

Design for Television Messages

As consumers, we see so many TV commercials that it's easy to take for granted the time, effort, and money that go into making them. Creating and producing commercials that break through the clutter on TV and communicate effectively is a detailed, expensive process. On a cost-per-minute basis, commercials are the most expensive productions seen on television.

TV is a unique and powerful advertising medium because it contains the elements of sight, sound, and motion, which can be combined to create a variety of advertising appeals and executions. However, for regular TV commercials, the viewer does not control the rate at which the message is presented, so there is no opportunity to review points of interest or reread things that are not communicated clearly. As with any form of advertising, one of the first goals in creating TV commercials is to get the viewers' attention and then maintain it. This can be particularly challenging because of the clutter and because people often view TV commercials while doing other things.

As you know, TV commercials have video and audio components that must work together to create the right impact and communicate the advertiser's message.

Video The video elements of a commercial are what the consumer sees on the TV screen. The visual portion generally dominates the commercial, so it must attract viewers' attention and communicate an idea, message, and/or image. A number of visual elements may have to be coordinated to produce a successful ad. Decisions have to be made regarding the product, the presenter, action sequences, demonstrations, and the like, as well as the setting(s), the talent or characters who will appear in the commercial, and such other factors as lighting, graphics, colour, and identifying symbols. Many TV commercials cost a small fortune in production costs to get the product and actors looking just right.

In attempting to attract new users who were of a younger demographic, Becel margarine used a new filming technique called Dogme that is very inexpensive but highly interesting—and, as it turns out, highly effective. The filming is predicated on 35-mm film, no lighting, no sets, all shooting on location, natural sounds, and natural actors (no wardrobe or make-up). Becel was placed in several places to remind customers of the alternative, which was both a healthier way to live and a key reinforcement of Becel's positioning. For example, Becel was placed between elevator doors so that consumers would use the stairs. Executives at the head office in Amsterdam took notice of the technique and message to new younger consumers and considered running the ads internationally.[23]

Audio The audio portion of a commercial includes voices, music, and sound effects. Voices are used in different ways in commercials. They may be heard through the direct presentation of a spokesperson or as a conversation among various people appearing in the commercial. A common method for presenting the audio portion of a commercial is through a **voiceover**, where the message is delivered or action on the screen is narrated or described by an announcer who is not visible. A trend among major advertisers is to have celebrities with distinctive voices do the voiceovers for their commercials.[24]

Music is also an important part of many TV commercials and can play a variety of roles.[25] In many commercials, the music provides a pleasant background or helps create the appropriate mood. Advertisers often use **needledrop**, which Linda Scott describes as follows:

> Needledrop is an occupational term common to advertising agencies and the music industry. It refers to music that is prefabricated, multipurpose, and highly conventional. It is, in that sense, the musical equivalent of stock photos, clip art, or canned copy. Needledrop is an inexpensive substitute for original music; paid for on a one-time basis, it is dropped into a commercial or film when a particular normative effect is desired.[26]

In some commercials, music is much more central to the advertising message. It can be used to get attention, break through the advertising clutter, communicate a key selling point, help establish an image or position, or add feeling.[27] For example, music can work through a classical conditioning process to create positive emotions that become associated with the advertised product or service. Music can also create a positive mood that makes the consumer more receptive toward the advertising message.[28]

Because music can play such an important role in the creative strategy, many companies have used popular songs in their commercials that reflect the selling message so uniquely. For example, Mitsubishi has made music a key element of its commercials, which usually show a group of young, fun adults in the car bopping to the beat or singing to the tunes of songs such as "Start the Commotion" or "One Week" by the Barenaked Ladies. Bud Light spoofed love songs of the 1970s for its Bud Light Institute campaign. One infamous title is "I Love You Dearly Because You Let Me Go Out With My Friends On A Weekly Basis." Unexpectedly, people requested the songs, and the company responded by selling a complete CD entitled "Ulterior Emotions." Consumers can download the music featured in recent commercials from Coca-Cola and Bell Canada's websites. The widespread diffusion of technology has clearly created opportunities for marketers to enhance awareness.[29]

Sometimes, marketers creatively use music that previously existed. PEI tourism organizations asked Stompin' Tom Connors to re-record his song "Dial an Island" in a television ad that encouraged Canadians to call the toll-free phone number for information. With visuals of old home movies, the lyrics to the song along with a bouncing ball made music an integral part of the message to suggest PEI as a holiday option for the summer of 2004.[30] The Dairy Farmers of Canada used Beethoven's "Ode to Joy" in their ads that reminded us to "Drink milk, love life."[31]

Often music is composed specifically for a commercial. Musicians and composers participate early on in the process of developing the ad; alternatively, the creative specialists produce the ad look for very specific types of music to support the visuals. For example, the original musical score for the Canadian launch of the Mini was written after filming the ad. The visuals and the musical request led to a very unique sound that contributed to the brand positioning strategy in such a way that people thought it was previously recorded. In fact some in the industry believe that custom-written music is the best since it almost always works.[32]

Another important musical element in both TV and radio commercials is **jingles**, catchy songs about a product or service that usually carry the advertising theme and a simple message. For example, "Black's is photography" and "You always have time for Tim Hortons" are two retail jingles that have stood the test of time. In some commercials, jingles are used more as a form of product identification and appear at the end of the message. Jingles are often composed by companies that specialize in writing commercial music for advertising. These jingle houses work with the creative team to determine the role music will play in the commercial and the message that needs to be communicated.

Production of TV Commercials Advertisers recognize that they need to do more than talk about, demonstrate, or compare their products or services. Their commercials have to break through the clutter and grab viewers' attention; they must often appeal to emotional, as well as rational, buying motives. Television is essentially an entertainment medium, and many advertisers recognize that their commercials are most successful when they entertain as well as inform. Many of the most popular advertising campaigns are characterized by commercials with strong entertainment value. On the other hand, sometimes what the producers of television commercials think is appropriate is different than what the public believes, as evidenced in Ethical Perspective 8–2 on page 230.

The elements of a TV commercial are brought together in a **script**, a written version of a commercial that provides a detailed description of its video and audio content. The script shows the audio components of the commercial—the copy to be spoken by voices, the music, and sound effects. The video portion of the script provides the visual plan of the commercial—camera actions and angles, scenes, transitions, and other important descriptions. The script also shows how the video corresponds to the audio portion of the commercial.

Once the basic script has been conceived, the writer and art director get together to produce a storyboard, a series of drawings used to present the visual plan or layout of a proposed commercial. The storyboard contains still drawings of the video scenes and descriptions of the audio that accompanies each scene. Like layouts

ETHICAL PERSPECTIVE 8–2

Style Goes Wrong

The Dairy Farmers of Canada's "Stop Cooking with Cheese" campaign is the kind of advertising that easily grates on the nerves of the ad creative community, but gets embraced by a less discriminating general public. The crotchety old lady who delivers the "Can't get your kids to leave home? Stop cooking with cheese" punch line in each spot depicting parents going to extremes to get their grown-up children to move out was quickly absorbed into the pop culture lexicon. But even early on there was sporadic criticism of the campaign for its implicit "anti-family" subtext.

Then came the execution "Protection." In it two parents lament to a teenage boy that his girlfriend is "not good enough for him" and is "cheap," with the reveal that they are talking about their own daughter. The old lady then pops up on the couch to sign off with, "Can't stop your daughter's boyfriend coming over? Stop cooking with cheese."

The cheese quickly hit the fan. A wave of complaints from the general public—and from members of the Dairy Farmers of Canada—cast the ad as too "mean spirited" and "anti-family," Nathalie Nol, DFC director of marketing, told *The Globe and Mail.* A committee of dairy farmers made the decision to pull the campaign and call an account review to develop a new approach to cheese marketing, Nol said. "Our organization is a farmer-based organization. We have to consider what they have to say."

As a result of the concerns and the demise of the campaign, the account was put into review. Cossette Communication-Marketing, the original agency-of-record that produced the ads and received the approval of the execution style from its client, attempted to regain the business from the $16.8-million cheese and butter advertising account.

Source: Stan Sutter, "When Values Collide," *Marketing Magazine,* January 15, 2007.

Question

1. Why do seemingly annoying execution styles such as the one described above continue to be produced and shown on TV?

for print ads, storyboards provide those involved in the production and approval of the commercial with a good approximation of what the final commercial will look like. In some cases an aniamatic (a videotape of the storyboard along with the soundtrack) may be produced if a more finished form of the commercial is needed for client presentations or pretesting.

Once the storyboard or aniamatic of the commercial is approved, it is ready to move to the production phase, which involves three stages:

- *Preproduction*—all the work and activities that occur before the actual shooting/recording of the commercial.
- *Production*—the period during which the commercial is filmed or videotaped and recorded.
- *Postproduction*—activities and work that occur after the commercial has been filmed and recorded.

The activities of each phase are shown in Figure 8–2. Before the final production process begins, the client must usually review and approve the creative strategy and tactics that will be used for the advertising message.

FRAMEWORKS FOR CREATIVE TACTICS

In this section, we present two planning models that guide the decision for selecting the most appropriate creative tactics. Each model builds on a perspective of the consumer response processes that we described in Chapter 4. We discuss the models from a historical perspective to explain how the more recent model is an improvement over the initial model.

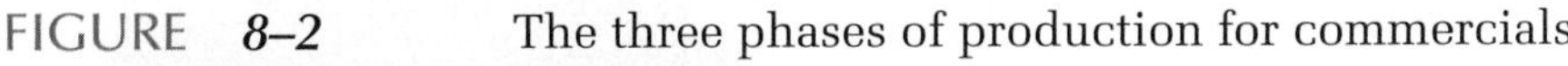

FIGURE 8–2 The three phases of production for commercials

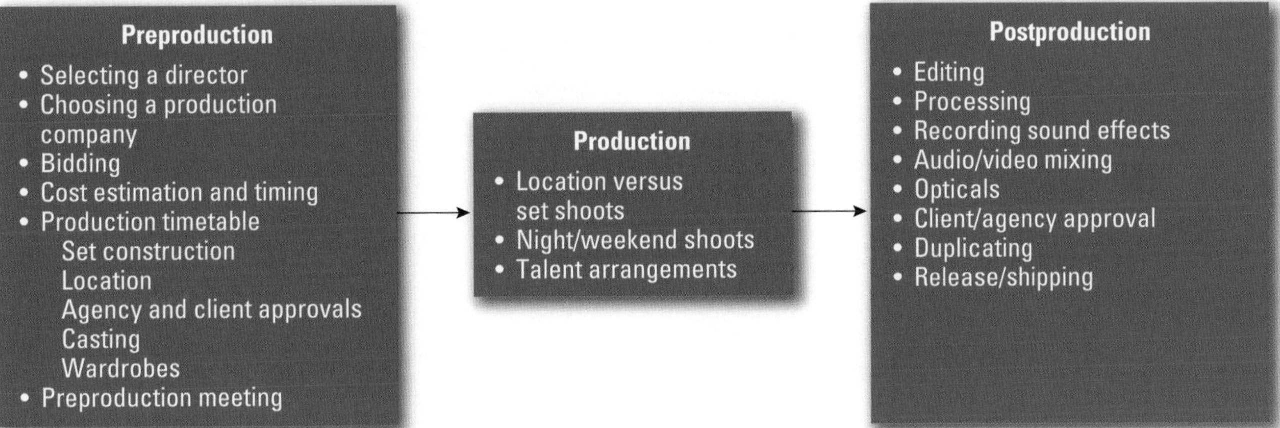

The FCB Planning Model

An interesting approach to analyzing the communication situation comes from the work of Richard Vaughn of the Foote, Cone & Belding advertising agency. Vaughn and his associates developed an advertising planning model by building on traditional response theories such as the hierarchy of effects model and its variants and research on high and low involvement.[33] They added the dimension of thinking versus feeling processing at each involvement level by bringing in theories regarding brain specialization. The right/left brain theory suggests the left side of the brain is more capable of rational, cognitive thinking, while the right side is more visual and emotional and engages more in the affective (feeling) functions. Their model, which became known as the FCB grid, delineates four primary advertising planning quadrants—informative, affective, habit formation, and satisfaction—along with the most appropriate variant of the alternative response hierarchies (Figure 8–3 on page 232).

Vaughn suggests that the *informative strategy* is for highly involving products where rational thinking and economic considerations prevail and the standard learning hierarchy is the appropriate response model. The *affective strategy* is for highly involving/feeling purchases. For these types of products, advertising should stress psychological and emotional motives such as building self-esteem or enhancing one's ego or self-image. The *habit formation strategy* is for low-involvement/thinking products with such routinized behaviour patterns that learning occurs most often after a trial purchase. The response process for these products is consistent with a behaviouristic learning-by-doing model known as operant conditioning. The *self-satisfaction strategy* is for low-involvement/feeling products where appeals to sensory pleasures and social motives are important. Vaughn acknowledges that some minimal level of awareness (passive learning) may precede purchase of both types of low-involvement products, but deeper, active learning is not necessary.

The FCB grid provides a useful way for those involved in the advertising planning process, such as creative specialists, to analyze consumer–product relationships and develop appropriate promotional strategies. Consumer research can be used to determine how consumers perceive products or brands on the involvement and thinking/feeling dimensions.[34] This information can then be used to develop effective creative options such as using rational versus emotional appeals, increasing involvement levels, or even getting consumers to evaluate a think-type product on the basis of feelings. Although the FCB model did not explicitly give

FIGURE 8–3

The Foote, Cone & Belding (FCB) grid

	Thinking	Feeling
High involvement	**1. Informative (thinker)** Car–house–furnishings. model: Learn–feel–do **Possible implications** Media: Long copy format Reflective vehicles Creative: Specific information Demonstration	**2. Affective (feeling)** Jewellery–cosmetics–fashion apparel. model: Feel–learn–do **Possible implications** Media: Large space Image specials Creative: Executional Impact
Low involvement	**3. Habit formation (doer)** Food–household items model: Do–learn–feel **Possible implications** Media: Small space ads 10-second I.D.s Radio; POS Creative: Reminder	**4. Self-satisfaction (reactor)** Liquor–candy model: Do–feel–learn **Possible implications** Media: Billboards Newspapers POS Creative: Attention

detailed suggestions for all quadrants, Vaughn concluded that the four responses guide the content of how messages could be executed by suggesting possible implications.

The R&P Planning Model

We highlighted the R&P perspective in Chapter 5 when discussing objectives for the IMC plan. Another part of their framework concerns recommendations for creative tactics so that the appropriate communication effects will occur with the target audience while they are processing the message. On the surface, their planning model appears similar to the FCB planning model as both represent consumer attitudes and explain how marketers use creative tactics to influence attitudes. However, we will discuss four improvements as we explain the R&P model.

Brand Awareness Tactics The first consideration is that the R&P model argues that brand awareness is a necessary precursor to brand attitude. According to R&P, both brand awareness and brand attitude are universal communication objectives for all circumstances (i.e., one ad, ad campaign, IMC plan). In this view, all communications should strive to achieve awareness to make brand attitude operational. R&P have three suggestions for awareness:

- Match the brand stimuli and the type of response behaviour of the target audience so that understanding of the brand in a category is unambiguous.
- Use a unique brand execution style to connect the brand to the category.
- Maximize brand contact time in the exposure to reinforce name and category connection.

In order for awareness to be fully established, the target audience needs to understand the context (brand, behaviour, category) as this is a clue as to how or why the brand exists. If the context is not clear, then the target audience has trouble remembering when it comes time to purchase. A unique execution style helps cut through the clutter. The connection to the category and sufficient exposure is required to make sure that the message is retained. For example, TV ads can sometimes show the package or brand name for too short a time for target audiences to fully grasp where the brand competes in the market.

We also noted that R&P suggest that awareness can be achieved via recognition and/or recall. R&P have two suggestions for recognition that require less media frequency as consumers need only to be familiar with the brand stimuli at the point of purchase:

- The brand package and name should have sufficient exposure in terms of time or size depending on the media.
- Category need should be mentioned or identified.

Since recall is a more difficult mental task, R&P have six suggestions for this aspect of awareness. Recall also requires high levels of frequency since the brand has to be remembered prior to being at the point of purchase:

- The brand and the category need should be connected in the primary benefit claim.
- The primary benefit claim should be short to be easily understood.
- Within an exposure, the primary benefit claim should be repeated often.
- The message should have or imply a clear personal reference.
- A bizarre or unusual execution style can be used if it is consistent with the brand attitude objective.
- A jingle or similar "memory" tactics should be included.

We have many more specific recommendations for recall since it is a much more difficult mental task for consumers. Advertisers have to help their target audience know their brand prior to purchasing. Thus, careful attention has to be put on all three creative tactics decisions to ensure the target audience can retrieve the brand name from long-term memory when the need to purchase a product category arises.

Brand Attitude Grid Tactics The R&P view of consumer attitudes is also framed as a matrix, with the dimensions of involvement and motivation. For each of these dimensions, R&P argue that their view is a more accurate representation of attitude for planning purposes than the FCB model, and the use of these two concepts represents the second and third improvements.

Low-involvement decision Informational motivation	Low-involvement decision Transformational motivation
High-involvement decision Informational motivation	High-involvement decision Transformational motivation

The involvement dimension is similar to the FCB model, from low involvement to high involvement. However, R&P argue that theirs is specific to the brand as the target audience makes a purchase decision. Further, the high- and low-involvement levels are also consistent with the central and peripheral routes to persuasion. More precisely, R&P interpret involvement as the degree of risk perceived by the target audience (i.e., new category user or loyal customer) in choosing a particular brand for the next purchase occasion. One extension of this idea, not fully developed by R&P, is that the concept can extend to purchase-related behaviour that we discussed in Chapter 5. For example, how much risk does a person buying a car for the first time take in deciding to visit a particular dealer for a test drive?

The motivation dimension is a continuum from negative motive, or informational-based attitude, to positive motive, or transformational-based attitude. The historic interpretation of an informational-based attitude implies that it is based on careful reasoning that results from the cognitive responses that the target audience has while experiencing advertising messages. This purely cognitive orientation is also the foundation of the "think" dimension of the FCB model. However, R&P argue that this is too limiting as attitude is based on both cognition and affect. Accordingly, they suggest that creative tactics for this side of the matrix should account for the benefit claims (i.e., cognition) and the emotional portrayal of the motive (i.e., affect). Thus, in order for it to be an informational-based attitude, the emphasis of the benefit claim is stronger than the emotional portrayal of the negative motive.

The notion of transformational-based attitude is partly based on a recent idea. A transformational ad is defined as "one which associates the experience of using (consuming) the advertised brand with a unique set of psychological characteristics which would not typically be associated with the brand experience to the same degree without exposure to the advertisement."[35]

Transformational advertising can help differentiate a product or service by making the consumption experience more enjoyable by suggesting the type of experiences consumers might have when they consume the product or service. This type of advertising is often used by companies in the travel industry to help consumers envision the experience or feeling they might have when they take a trip such as a cruise or visit a particular destination.

Image advertising, which is designed to give a company or brand a unique association or personality, is often transformational in nature. It is designed to create a certain feeling or mood that is activated when a consumer uses a particular product or service. For example, the Lambesis agency has created a unique image for Skyy vodka by creating ads that associate the brand with cinematic-based cocktail moments (see Exhibit 8–14). IMC Perspective 8–3 discusses how the agency is using a different transformational advertising approach based on image attributes of sophistication and style to introduce Skyy90, a new line extension to compete in the ultra-premium segment of the vodka market against brands such as Grey Goose and Ketel One.

Exhibit 8–14 Advertising for Skyy vodka uses a cinematic theme to create an image for the brand

Just like the informational-based attitude is not purely cognitive, the transformational-based attitude is not purely based on emotion but includes some cognitive elements. Intuitively, this makes a lot of sense as some ads with a very strong fear appeal often leave us thinking. Overall, the emphasis of the emotional portrayal is stronger than the benefit claim for transformational-based attitude. Providing information in transformational ads is at the heart of two recent Saturn car ads. From a transformational perspective, both ads showed emotional elements of the purchase-and-consumption experience of owning a Saturn by demonstrating situations where the salesperson goes above and beyond "normal" service-level expectations to deliver a new Saturn. In both cases, however, key attribute information was conveyed. In one, online purchasing and its simplicity were communicated, while in the other, Saturn's 30-day/2,500-kilometre guarantee was explained.[36]

IMC PERSPECTIVE *8–3*

Skyy Goes After the Ultra-Premium Market

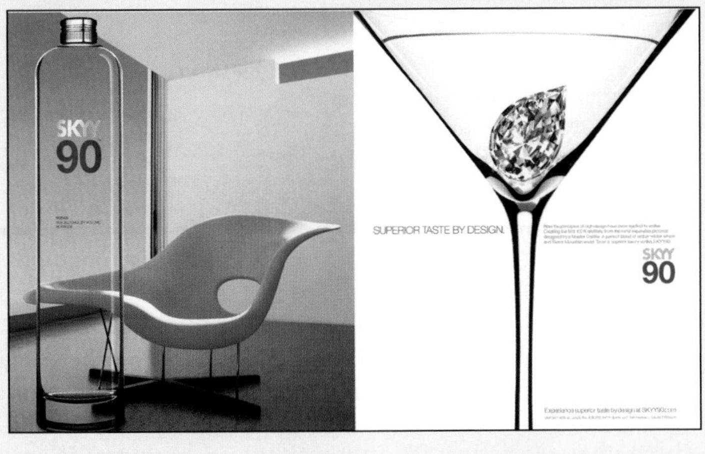

The last decade has been a great time for marketers of vodka as the product category has experienced strong growth and one wave of chic new brands has been followed by another. Consumption of vodka has increased steadily since 1998, and the vodka category is double the size of the next distilled spirits segment, rum. Ironically, a bland-tasting product that was best known for helping Russians make it through a cold, bleak winter has become a status symbol for many trendy twenty- and thirtysomethings. Marketers have tried to capitalize on the growing popularity of vodka and the growth of the "cocktail culture" that has brought more young adults to the spirits market by creating a distinct image for their brands and getting consumers to think of them as cutting-edge, edgy, and hip.

While myriad new vodka brands have been introduced over the past decade, one of the most successful has been Skyy, which has overtaken Stolichnaya as the number-two super-premium vodka in the United States. Skyy trails only Absolut, a brand which achieved iconic status through ads that focused on the distinctive shape of the bottle with visual puns and witty headlines. Skyy Spirits was founded in 1992 by Maurice Kanbar, who developed it as a premium brand for older connoisseurs, like himself, desirous of the perfect martini. Kanbar developed a four-stage distillation process that extracts many of the congers, which are natural impurities that remain in alcohol after distillation and may contribute to headaches. He created what he believed to be the purest of vodkas.

Much of Skyy's initial growth was driven by word of mouth. The company successfully placed its eye-catching blue bottle into swanky Hollywood parties and nightclubs known for attracting a hip crowd. Skyy quickly generated a buzz on the nightclub circuit, where word spread that its quadruple-distilled formula reduced the likelihood of hangovers. The company spent much of its limited marketing budget on sponsoring independent film festivals and producing artsy short films that were shown at these events. Skyy also uses the Internet to feature these films as a way of expanding its presence on the Web and shows them as part of the festivals and movie premieres that it sponsors.

Image advertising became an important part of Skyy's brand-building efforts. The Lambesis agency took over the account in 1998 and created the "Skyy Cinema" campaign to target 21- to 34-year-old urban, metro consumers. The ads do not contain any copy but rather rely on stylish, seductive visuals that set up various noir-inspired story lines but leave the actual scenarios up to the mind of the viewer. All of the ads establish Skyy's distinctive cobalt blue bottle as the "star" and showcase the brand as a catalyst for a great cocktail moment. The campaign has helped Skyy vodka sales increase from 3,000 cases in 1993 to nearly 2 million cases in 2004.

While sales of Skyy continue to increase, the new growth occurs in the ultra-premium category where brands such as Grey Goose, Ketel One, Belvedere, and Level (which is made by Absolut) dominate. To compete in this market, Skyy has introduced a brand extension called Skyy90, which is being positioned as the world's first modern luxury vodka with taste by design. The advertising and other communications for the brand focus on the art of modern luxury and how the same principles of design used in modern art, architecture, and technology have guided Skyy's master distiller in the creation of Skyy90. The objective is to create an image for Skyy90 as the brand for those who desire the taste of modern luxury by associating it with sophistication and style.

All photography, illustrations, and copy for Skyy90 reflect a higher aesthetic and integrate modern luxury icons and environments. The Skyy90 bottle was designed to echo simple and pure design principles and serve as an expression of modern luxury. Lambesis has also created a mini website (SKYY90.com) for Skyy90 that has an ultra-modern tone, feel, and style and provides information on the ingredients, facilities, innovative processes, and technology that are involved in distilling the brand.

Skyy Sprits recognizes that it will face stiff competition in the ultra-premium category where brands such as Grey

Goose and Ketel One spend more than $18 million and $10 million per year, respectively, on advertising. Grey Goose, the market leader in the segment, advertises the brand as the world's best-tasting vodka and saw its sales increase by 27 percent in 2004.

Sources: Christopher Lawton, "Stolichnaya Marketer Takes Shot at Dated Ads for Grey Goose," *The Wall Street Journal,* April, 15, 2005, p. B5; James B. Arndorfer, "Spirits Makers Raise the Bar on Lux Brands," *Advertising Age,* November 1, 2004, pp. 4, 62; Kenneth Hein, "Strategy: Skyy Sets the Stage in Sultry Cinematic Scenes," *Adweek,* June 17, 2002; Theresa Howard, "Marketers of the Next Generation: Teresa Zepeda," *Brandweek,* November 8, 1999, pp. 38–21.

Question

1. How do the ads for each vodka elicit different emotional responses for consumers?

The fourth improvement of the R&P model is that its guidelines for creative tactics balance elements in the ad for both cognitive and emotional responses that contribute to both aspects of brand attitude. On the emotional side, we are concerned with how the motive is portrayed or conveyed in the ad. To consider this, we have three characteristics: its authenticity, or how real it appears to the target audience; whether the target audience likes the ad; and finally, the target audience's reaction to the execution style. On the informational side, we are concerned with the brand's message with respect to the benefit claims. We also have three characteristics to consider: the number, the intensity, and the repetition of the claims.

While the guidelines for all six characteristics may be a function of all three creative tactics decisions, we can make a stronger connection for some. The authenticity and whether the target audience likes the ad are typically associated with the design elements of the ad. Quite obviously, there is a direct connection between the execution style of the framework and that particular creative tactic decision discussed in this chapter. The benefit claims are mostly a function of the message structure since the latter concerns the details of explaining the product's benefits. It is also a function of the relative balance between a verbal and visual message. We now turn our attention to creative tactics recommendations for the four brand attitude cells.

Low Involvement—Informational Creative Tactics Ads designed to influence target audiences' attitude based on low involvement—informational persuasion should have a very obvious benefit claim with an unusual execution style. Since the intention is to persuade the target audience so that they automatically learn the connection between the brand, its category, and the benefit, consumer acceptance or rejection of the message is not a factor. Further, the emotion demonstrated in the ad and whether the target audience likes the ad are not necessary as the message is intended to make a creative link among the brand, category, and benefit.

Low Involvement—Informational

Emotional portrayal of motive	
Authenticity	Not necessary.
Like ad	Not necessary.
Execution style	Unusual, problem-solution format.
Benefit claim of brand message	
Number of benefits	One or two, or one clear group.
Intensity of benefit claim	State extremely.
Repetition of benefit claim	Few required for reminder.

Low Involvement—Transformational Creative Tactics Three emotional portrayal guidelines are critical for this type of attitude. These points are consistent with transformational ads described above. For example, the representation of the consumption of the brand in the drama or story of the ad must "ring true" with the target audience such that it is perceived as a very enjoyable ad. In a low-involvement situation, some benefit claims are still included but may be indirectly communicated through the story or emotion surrounding the story. Actual acceptance of the benefit claim is not a requirement; however, rejection of the overall message can lead to a reduction in the attitude of the target audience.

Low Involvement—Transformational

Emotional portrayal of motive	
Authenticity	Key element and is the single benefit.
Like ad	Necessary.
Execution style	Unique to the brand.
Benefit claim of brand message	
Number of benefits	One or two, or one clear group.
Intensity of benefit claim	Imply extremely by association.
Repetition of benefit claim	Many exposures to build-up before trial purchase and reinforce attitude after trial.

High Involvement—Informational Creative Tactics This side of the model illustrates the importance of information as high involvement implies the requirement of considerable and accurate benefit claims. Many benefits can be claimed here but they must be organized and presented in a manner that respects the current attitude of the target audience. Since this is an informational-based attitude, the emotional portrayal is important but not the primary consideration. Furthermore, the high-involvement characteristic means that the target audience has to accept the benefit claims. Rejection of the benefit claims may not result in any negative change in attitude if the copy respected the prior attitude of the target audience.

High Involvement—Informational

Emotional portrayal of motive	
Authenticity	Key element early in product life cycle and declines as product reaches later stages.
Like ad	Not necessary.
Execution style	Unusual.
Benefit claim of brand message	
Number of benefits	Overall claim to summarize multiple (no more than seven) benefits.
Intensity of benefit claim	Initial attitude is key reference point. Very accurate claim; cannot over-claim or under-claim. Comparative or refutation messages are strong options.
Repetition of benefit claim	Many claims within an exposure.

High Involvement—Transformational Creative Tactics Persuasion through this type of attitude formation requires strong emphasis of the emotion. A positive attitude toward the ad leads to a positive brand attitude. Likewise, the target audience must truly relate to the execution style and feel like the ad supports their lifestyle. The end result is that if the target audience rejects the message because the emotion is not accurate, then the persuasion will not work and may even cause significant attitude reduction. The remaining guidelines illustrate that considerable information is required similar to what is seen for the high involvement—informational attitude. Once again this implies that acceptance of the benefit claims is critical for the attitude to take hold with the target audience.

High Involvement—Transformational

Emotional portrayal of motive	
Authenticity	Paramount; must reflect lifestyle of target audience.
Like ad	Necessary.
Execution style	Unique; target audience must identify with product, people, or consumption situation shown.
Benefit claim of brand message	
Number of benefits	Acceptable number to provide key information.
Intensity of benefit claim	Very accurate claim; may over-claim but do not under-claim.
Repetition of benefit claim	Many are required to support informational message.

IMC Planning: Guidelines for Creative Evaluation

While the creative specialists have much responsibility for determining the message appeal and execution style to be used in a campaign, the marketer must evaluate and approve the creative approach before any ads are produced. A number of people may be involved in evaluating the creative recommendation, including the advertising or communications manager, product or brand managers, marketing director or vice president, representatives from the legal department, and sometimes even the president or chief executive officer (CEO) of the company or the board of directors.

In situations where an advertising agency is used, top management is involved in selecting an ad agency and must approve the theme and creative strategy for the campaign. Evaluation and approval of the individual ads proposed by the agency often rest with the advertising and product managers who are primarily responsible for the brand. The account executive and a member of the creative team present the creative concept to the client's advertising and product and/or marketing managers for their approval before beginning production. A careful evaluation should be made before the ad actually enters production, since this stage requires considerable time and money as suppliers are hired to perform the various functions required to produce the actual ad.

The evaluation of the print layout or commercial storyboard can be difficult, since the advertising or brand manager is generally not a creative expert and must be careful not to reject viable creative approaches or accept ideas that will result in inferior advertising. Advertisers use numerous criteria to evaluate the recommended creative approach. In some instances, the advertiser may want to have the rough layout or storyboard pretested to get quantitative information to assist in the evaluation. However, the evaluation can be more subjective; the advertising or brand manager relies on qualitative considerations. Basic criteria for evaluating the creative approach focus on a number of questions requiring managerial judgment:

- *Is the creative approach consistent with the brand's marketing and advertising objectives?* One of the most important factors the advertiser must consider is whether the creative strategy and tactics recommended by the agency are consistent with the marketing strategy for the brand and the role advertising and promotion have been assigned in the overall marketing program. This means the creative approach must be compatible with the image of the brand and the way it is positioned in the marketplace.

- *Is the creative approach consistent with the communication objectives?* The creative strategy and tactics must meet the established communication objectives. Creative specialists can lose sight of what the advertising message is supposed to be and come up with an approach that fails to execute the advertising strategy. Individuals responsible for approving the ad should ask the creative specialists to explain how the creative strategy and tactics achieve the creative and communications objectives.
- *Is the creative approach appropriate for the target audience?* Generally, much time has been spent defining, locating, and attempting to understand the target audience for the advertiser's product or service. Careful consideration should be given to whether the creative strategy and tactics recommended will appeal to, be understood by, and communicate effectively with the target audience. This involves studying all elements of the ad and how the audience will respond to them. Advertisers do not want to approve advertising that they believe will receive a negative reaction from the target audience.
- *Does the creative approach communicate a clear and convincing message to the customer?* Most ads are supposed to communicate a message that will help sell the brand. Many ads fail to communicate a clear and convincing message that motivates consumers to use a brand. While creativity is important in advertising, it is also important that the advertising communicate information attributes, features and benefits, and/or images that give consumers a reason to buy the brand.
- *Does the creative approach keep from overwhelming the message?* A common criticism of advertising, and TV commercials in particular, is that so much emphasis is placed on creative approach that the advertiser's message gets overshadowed. Many creative, entertaining commercials have failed to register the brand name and/or selling points effectively.

With the increasing amount of clutter in most advertising media, it may be necessary to use a novel creative approach to gain the viewer's or reader's attention. However, the creative approach cannot overwhelm the message. Advertisers must walk a fine line: Make sure the sales message is not lost, but be careful not to stifle the efforts of the creative specialists and force them into producing dull, boring advertising.

- *Is the creative approach appropriate for the media environment in which it is likely to be seen?* Each media vehicle has its own specific climate that results from the nature of its editorial content, the type of reader or viewer it attracts, and the nature of the ads it contains. Consideration should be given to how well the ad fits into the media environment in which it will be shown.
- *Is the ad truthful and tasteful?* Marketers also have to consider whether an ad is truthful, as well as whether it might offend consumers. The ultimate responsibility for determining whether an ad deceives or offends the target audience lies with the client. It is the job of the advertising or brand manager to evaluate the approach suggested by the creative specialists against company standards. The firm's legal department may be asked to review the ad to determine whether the creative appeal, message content, or execution could cause any problems for the company. It is much better to catch any potential legal problems before the ad is shown to the public.

The advertising manager, brand manager, or other personnel on the client side can use these basic guidelines in reviewing, evaluating, and approving the ideas offered by the creative specialists. There may be other factors specific to the firm's advertising and marketing situation. Also, there may be situations where it is acceptable to deviate from the standards the firm usually uses in judging creative output. As we shall see in the next chapter, the client may want to move beyond these subjective criteria and use more sophisticated pretesting methods to determine the effectiveness of a particular approach suggested by the creative specialists.

SUMMARY

In this chapter, we examined how the advertising message is implemented and executed. Once the creative strategy that will guide the ad campaign has been determined, attention turns to the specific creative tactics that will enhance the cognitive and emotional processing of the message. This chapter summarizes three decisions that are critical when developing creative tactics: execution style, message structure, and design elements.

The creative execution style is the way the advertising appeal is presented in the message. A number of common execution techniques were examined in the chapter, along with considerations for their use. The most appropriate style is a matter of balancing uniqueness in the market versus effective communication to achieve the stated objectives.

The design of the advertising message is a critical part of the communication process and is the second creative tactic discussed. There are various options regarding the message structure, including order of presentation of message arguments, conclusion drawing, message sidedness, refutation, and verbal versus visual traits.

Attention was also given to tactical issues involved in creating print and TV advertising. The components of a print ad include headlines, body copy, illustrations, and layout. We also examined the video and audio components of TV commercials and various considerations involved in the planning and production of commercials. Together, these showed some of the important design decisions that have to be made to complete the creative approach.

We presented a framework for creative specialists and marketers to help them make the appropriate decisions for the creative tactics. The framework uses the target audience's attitude as the key factor when deciding upon the correct execution style, message structure, and design.

Creative specialists are responsible for determining the creative strategy and tactics from the marketer's input. However, the client must review, evaluate, and approve the creative approach before any ads are produced or run. A number of criteria can be used by advertising, product or brand managers, and others involved in the promotional process to evaluate the advertising messages before approving final production.

KEY TERMS

body copy, *226*
creative execution style, *216*
direct headlines, *225*
headline, *225*
high-involvement decision, *233*
indirect headlines, *225*
informational motivation, *233*
jingles, *229*
layout, *227*
low-involvement decision, *233*
needledrop, *228*
one-sided message, *223*
primacy effect, *222*
recency effect, *222*
refutation, *224*
script, *229*
subheads, *226*
transformational motivation, *233*
two-sided message, *223*
voiceover, *228*

DISCUSSION QUESTIONS

1. Discuss the difference between a message appeal and a creative execution style. Why is it important to make this distinction?

2. Explain how the dramatization advertising execution technique could be used for the following products: beer, cellphones, furniture, airlines.

3. Discuss the use of the slice-of-life execution style. For what types of products might this approach work best?

4. Explain how a humour execution style differs from a humour message appeal.

5. What is transformational advertising? Why is it an important option for advertisers?

6. What is meant by one-sided versus two-sided message? Discuss some the reasons marketers may or may not want to use a two-sided message.

7. Discuss the role of headlines and subheads in print advertisements. Would you say that headlines are more important for processing (i.e., gaining attention) or establishing a communication effect (i.e., awareness).

8. Discuss the role of music in advertising. Why might companies such as Microsoft, Cadillac, and Nike pay large sums of money for the rights to use popular songs in their commercials?

9. What are the similarities and differences of creative tactics across the four cells of the R&P planning model?

10. Explain how the guidelines for creative evaluation can be applied to ads seen on the Internet.

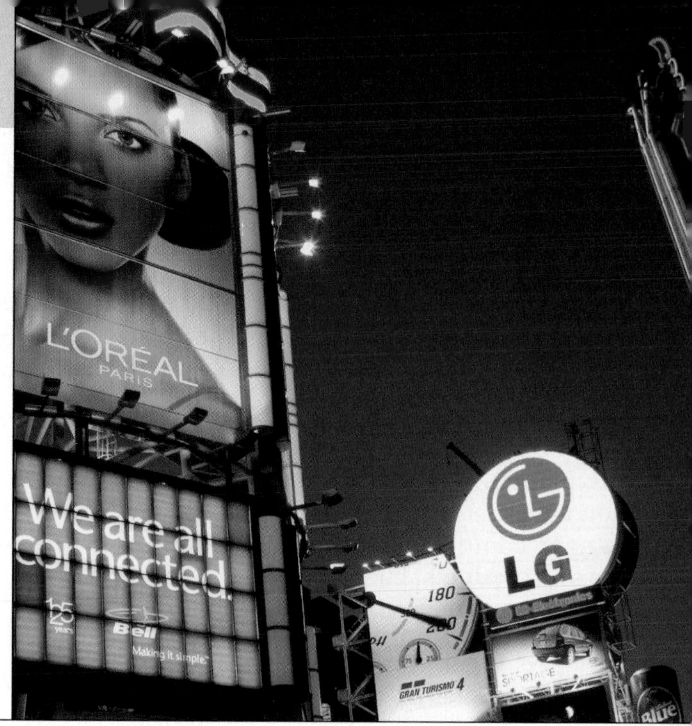

CHAPTER 9

MEASURING THE EFFECTIVENESS OF THE PROMOTIONAL MESSAGE

Chapter Objectives

- To understand reasons for measuring promotional program effectiveness.
- To know the various measures used in assessing promotional program effectiveness.
- To evaluate alternative methods for measuring promotional program effectiveness.
- To understand the requirements of proper effectiveness research.

Emotionally Involved Researchers Measure Ad Effectiveness

Imagine sitting in an office wondering how consumers would react to new ads shown as storyboards developed by an advertising agency. Or perhaps consider whether the completed print ads should be placed in magazines for the next campaign. For that matter, if managers are wondering about *any* message to be delivered across any or multiple media, how or what evaluation should be implemented to ensure success? Although many standard or traditional approaches for promotional effectiveness exist, new methods continue to emerge.

One promising development is a method allowing researchers to get a better read on consumer emotions. Many approaches toward effectiveness tend to measure consumer knowledge in terms of brand recall or recognition, advertising recall or recognition, and rational thoughts connected to the brand. Typically, consumers have difficulty expressing their emotional attachment to a brand as they often convey their brand usage in relation to product attributes or benefits.

This dilemma led Ipsos-ASI to innovate with a measurement tool designed to gauge consumers' emotional reactions to an ad by asking three questions: How do you feel toward the ad? What feeling is the advertiser trying to get across? What emotions do you associate with being a brand user? Consumers selected their emotional response from a group of facial pictures drawn by artists that exhibited many emotions.

Their research also identified 11 personality traits that could be used to assess brands. Some of these traits include social, outgoing, extroverted; emotional, touching, sensitive; reserved, quiet, introverted; and spontaneous, creative, impulsive. Finally, building on existing motivation research, their investigation examined 11 different motivators for purchasing a brand, such as self-sufficient, independent, autonomous; experience personal success or achievement; and pleasurable sensuous feeling. Overall, these measures have allowed Ipsos-ASI to distinguish between categories like cars or beer, and brands such as Ford and Audi or Budweiser and Heineken.

New advances for measuring audience involvement with marketing communication messages gained ground as well. In fact, the notion of measuring involvement recently expanded to all marketing communication points beyond television. Working together, many agency and research firms explore varying approaches to understand the degree of consumer reaction to marketing messages. For example, MediaCom's new measurement tool attempts to measure the depth of involvement with the message. The Media Company's new research method looks to understand the amount of involvement of people who are actually exposed to an advertising message on television. Finally, Carat Canada's research indicated that mothers with children were less involved when receiving messages with their children versus without their children.

Sources: Paul Brent, "The New Tools of Engagement," *Marketing Magazine,* August 14, 2006; Pattie Summerfield, "Getting to Engagement," *Strategy Magazine,* June 2006; Rebecca Harris, "Measuring Emotions," *Marketing Magazine,* September 25, 2006; John Hallward, "The Creators of Motivation: Advancement in the Exploration of Emotions," *Ipsos-ASI,* June 2004.

Questions

1. Why are advertisers so concerned with measuring emotions and involvement?
2. Should promotional planners measure these two variables for other IMC tools, such as sales promotions or direct response?

Measuring the effectiveness of the promotional program is a critical element in the promotional planning process. Research allows the marketing manager to assess the performance of specific program elements and provide input into the next period's situation analysis. We are concerned with research that is conducted in an evaluative role—that is, to measure the effectiveness of advertising and promotion and/or to assess various strategies before implementing them. This is not to be confused with research discussed earlier in the text to help develop the promotional program, although the two can (and should) be used together.

In this chapter, we explore the measuring effectiveness debate. Next we examine key research decisions for evaluative research. Finally, we summarize research methods and conclude with our IMC planning perspective. Our primary focus concerns measuring the effects of advertising because much more time and effort have been expended developing evaluation measures in advertising than in the other promotional areas. Furthermore, since most other promotional tools have an advertisement-like message, most of these research techniques can be applied. In fact, advertising research approaches are often adapted to other tools. We will highlight methods of measuring effectiveness for these tools in their respective chapters later in the text.

The Measuring Effectiveness Debate

In business, employees are generally given objectives to accomplish, and their job evaluations are based on their ability to achieve these objectives. Advertising and promotion should not be an exception. It is important to determine how well the communications program is working and to measure this performance against some standards or the objectives established in the promotional plan. Although this may appear logical, some consider this to be debatable.

Reasons for Measuring Effectiveness

Assessing the effectiveness of ads both before they are implemented and after the final versions have been completed and fielded offers a number of advantages:

Avoiding Costly Mistakes Total advertising topped $10 billion in 2004. This is a lot of money to be throwing around without some understanding of how well it is being spent. If the program is not achieving its objectives, the marketing manager needs to know so he or she can stop spending (wasting) money on it.

Just as important as the out-of-pocket costs is the opportunity loss due to poor communications. If the advertising and promotions program is not accomplishing its objectives, not only is the money spent lost but so too is the potential gain that could result from an effective program. Thus, measuring the effects of advertising does not just save money. It also helps the firm maximize its investment. For example, one mass merchant discovered that promoting Tide detergent generated more cross-selling opportunities than did promotions of nonpremium brands (Exhibit 9–1). At the same time, promotions of motor oil had no cross-selling impact.[1]

Evaluating Alternative Strategies Typically a firm has a number of strategies under consideration. For example, there may be some question as to which medium should be used or whether one message is more effective than another. Or the decision may be between two promotional program elements. For example, should research be spent on sponsorships or on advertising? One retailer found that advertising do-it-yourself products on the radio was effective in rural areas but not in urban locales.[2] Research may be designed to help the manager determine which strategy is most likely to be effective. Companies often test alternate versions of their advertising in different cities to determine which ad communicates most effectively.

Exhibit 9–1 Tide has been shown to be an effective promotional draw

Increasing Advertising Efficiency You may have heard the expression "can't see the forest for the trees." Sometimes advertisers get so close to the project they lose sight of what they are seeking, and because they know what they are trying to say, they expect their audience will also understand. They may use technical jargon that not everyone is familiar with. Or the creative department may get too creative or too sophisticated and lose the meaning that needs to be communicated. How many times have you seen an ad and asked yourself what it was trying to say, or how often have you seen an ad that you really like, but you can't remember the brand name? Conducting research helps companies develop more efficient and effective communications. An increasing number of clients are demanding accountability for their promotional programs and putting more pressure on the agencies to produce.

Reasons for Not Measuring Effectiveness

Companies give a number of reasons for not measuring the effectiveness of advertising and promotions strategies.

Cost Perhaps the most commonly cited reason for not testing (particularly among smaller firms) is the expense. Good research can be expensive, in terms of both time and money. Many managers decide that time is critical and they must implement the program while the opportunity is available. Many believe the monies spent on research could be better spent on improved production of the ad, additional media buys, and the like.

While the first argument may have some merit, the second does not. Imagine what would happen if a poor campaign were developed or the incentive program did not motivate the target audience. Not only would you be spending money without the desired effects, but the effort could do more harm than good. Spending more money to buy media does not remedy a poor message or substitute for an improper promotional mix. For example, one firm watched its test-market sales for a new brand of beer fall short of expectations. The solution, it decided, was to buy all the TV time available that matched its target audience. After two months, sales had not improved, and the product was abandoned in the test market. Analysis showed the problem was not in the media but rather in the message, which communicated no reason to buy. Research would have identified the problem, and millions of dollars and a brand might have been saved. The moral: spending research monies to gain increased exposure to the wrong message is not a sound management decision.

Research Problems A second reason cited for not measuring effectiveness is that it is difficult to isolate the effects of promotional elements. Each variable in the marketing mix affects the success of a product or service. Because it is rarely possible to measure the contribution of each marketing element directly, some managers become frustrated and decide not to test at all. They say, "If I can't determine the specific effects, why spend the money?"

This argument also suffers from weak logic. While we agree that it is not always possible to determine the dollar amount of sales contributed by promotions, research can provide useful results. Communications effectiveness can be measured and may carry over to sales.

Disagreement On What to Test The objectives sought in the promotional program may differ by industry, by stage of the product life cycle, or even for different people within the firm. The sales manager may want to see the impact of promotions on sales, top management may wish to know the impact on corporate image, and those involved in the creative process may wish to assess recall and/or recognition of the ad. Lack of agreement on what to test often results in no testing.

Again, there is little rationale for this position. With the proper design, many or even all of the above might be measured. Since every promotional element is designed to accomplish its own objectives, research can be used to measure its effectiveness in doing so.

Objections of Creative Specialists It has been argued by many (and denied by others) that the creative department does not want its work to be tested and many agencies are reluctant to submit their work for testing. This is sometimes true. Ad agencies' creative departments argue that tests are not true measures of the creativity and effectiveness of ads; applying measures stifles their creativity; and the more creative the ad, the more likely it is to be successful. They want permission to be creative without the limiting guidelines marketing may impose.

At the same time, the marketing manager is ultimately responsible for the success of the product or brand. Given the substantial sums being allocated to advertising and promotion, it is the manager's right, and responsibility, to know how well a specific program—or a specific ad—will perform in the market.

Decisions for Measuring Effectiveness

We now identify some broad issues for measuring the communication effects of advertising. This section considers what elements to evaluate, as well as when and where such evaluations should occur. The issue of how to measure is covered in the next section.

What to Test

The focus of the testing is mostly on the creative strategy and creative tactics decisions that the advertiser makes while putting a campaign together. In the beer example discussed earlier, the message never provided a reason for consumers to try the new product. In other instances, the message may not be strong enough to pull readers into the ad by attracting their attention, or it may not be clear enough to help them evaluate the product. Sometimes the message is memorable but doesn't achieve the other goals set by management. One study showed that 7 of the 25 products that scored highest on interest and memorability in Video Storyboard Tests' ad test had flat or declining sales.[3] As these few examples show, many of the creative strategy and creative tactics decisions regarding the message can be tested.

Creative Strategy Decisions The primary creative strategy decision—the creative theme—can be tested. When a company decides to change its theme or is planning to launch an unusual attention-getting approach, it may want to see the reactions of the target audience prior to investing in the media placement. Similarly, different message appeals can be tested (i.e., rational versus emotional), or different versions of one appeal can be tested. Finally, another important question is whether the spokesperson being used is effective and how the target audience will respond to him or her. A product spokesperson may be an excellent source initially but, owing to a variety of reasons, may lose impact over time in terms of attractiveness or likeability. Thus, all major creative strategy decisions can be tested.

Creative Tactics Decisions Different execution styles displayed on storyboards can be presented to members of the target audience in focus groups for their reaction. The message structure can be looked at such as reading the body-copy in an interview or some other method. Specific design elements, such as the music in a television ad or the headline of a print ad, can also be the focus of research. Overall, advertisers use a variety of research methods to test essentially any creative tactic that they are unsure about or that requires confirmation.

Other Promotional Tools Many of the other tools we will discuss in this book have an associated creative or message. Many sales promotions have a visual as well as some advertising-like message that reinforces the brand position in the target audience's mind. Similarly, firms use many creative tactics to gain the attention of media personnel so that their story will get picked up by the media in order to get publicity exposure. Thus, while we have examined the creative in the context of advertising in the book, as we noted previously, all the decisions are relevant in the other promotional tools, and as expected, the same research is possible if the advertiser believes it necessary. We review a few specifics in each of the subsequent chapters to measure the effectiveness of other promotional tools.

When to Test

Virtually all test measures can be classified according to when they are conducted. **Pretests** are measures taken before the campaign is implemented; **posttests** occur after the ad or commercial has been in the field. A variety of pretests and posttests are available to the marketer, each with its own methodology designed to measure some aspect of the advertising program. Figure 9–1 classifies these testing methods.

Pretesting Pretests may occur at a number of points, from as early on as idea generation to rough execution to testing the final version before implementing it. More than one type of pretest may be used. For example, concept testing (which is discussed later in this chapter) may take place at the earliest development of the ad

FIGURE 9–1

Classification of testing methods

Pretests	Lab	Field
Concept	Concept tests	
Rough/copy/commercial	Rough tests Consumer juries	Comprehension and reaction tests
Finished print ads	Portfolio Readability	Dummy advertising vehicles
Finished TV ads	Theatre Physiological	On-air
Posttests		
Finished print ads in magazines		Inquiry tests Recognition tests Recall tests Tracking studies
Finished TV ads on-air		Recall tests Comprehensive measures Test marketing Single-source Tracking studies

or commercial, when little more than an idea, basic concept, or positioning statement is under consideration. In other instances, layouts of the ad campaign that include headlines, some body copy, and rough illustrations are used. For TV commercials, storyboards and animatics may be tested.

The methodologies employed to conduct pretests vary. In focus groups, participants freely discuss the meanings they get from the ads, consider the relative advantages of alternatives, and even suggest improvements or additional themes. In addition to or instead of the focus groups, consumers are asked to evaluate the ad on a series of rating scales. (Different agencies use different measures.) In-home interviews, mall intercept, or laboratory methods may be used to gather the data.

The advantage of pretesting at this stage is that feedback is relatively inexpensive. Any problems with the concept or the way it is to be delivered are identified before large amounts of money are spent in development. Sometimes more than one version of the ad is evaluated to determine which is most likely to be effective.

A study of 4,637 on-air commercials designed to build normative intelligence conducted by McCollum Spielman Worldwide (MSW) found that only 19 percent were considered outstanding or really good. Nearly twice as many (34 percent) were failures. On the other hand, of those spots that were pretested before the final form was aired, the share of good to outstanding rose to 37 percent, while the failure rate fell to 9 percent.[4] This is certainly a testimonial to the value of pretesting.

The disadvantage is that mock-ups, storyboards, or animatics may not communicate nearly as effectively as the final product. The mood-enhancing and/or emotional aspects of the message are very difficult to communicate in this format. Another disadvantage is time delays. Many marketers believe being first in the market offers them a distinct advantage over competitors, so they forgo research to save time and ensure this position.

Posttesting Posttesting is also common among both advertisers and ad agencies (with the exception of testing commercials for wearout). Posttesting is designed to (1) determine if the campaign is accomplishing the objectives sought and (2) serve as input into the next period's situation analysis. An excellent example of using research to guide future advertising strategies is reflected in an experiment conducted by Lowes, a home improvement retailer in the U.S. In a study designed to test 36 different versions of covers for its catalogues (which are sent to between 30 and 40 million homes per year), the company determined that by putting more products on the covers, using real pictures rather than cartoons, and reducing the size of the catalogue, the catalogues were more effective. Other tests varying the number of TV spots, newspaper ads, and sports sponsorships led to increases in advertising spending and affirmation of the company's sponsorship of NASCAR auto racing.[5] A variety of posttest measures are available, most of which involve survey research methods.

Where to Test

In addition to when to test, decisions must be made as to *where.* These tests may take place in either laboratory or field settings.

Laboratory Tests In **laboratory tests**, people are brought to a particular location where they are shown ads and/or commercials. The testers either ask questions about them or measure participants' responses by other methods—for example, pupil dilation, eye tracking, or galvanic skin response.

The major advantage of the lab setting is the *control* it affords the researcher. Changes in copy, illustration, formats, colours, and the like can be manipulated inexpensively and the differential impact of each assessed. This makes it much easier for the researcher to isolate the contribution of each factor.

The major disadvantage is the lack of *realism.* Perhaps the greatest effect of this lack of realism is a **testing bias**. When people are brought into a lab (even if it has been designed to look like a living room), they may scrutinize the ads much more closely than they would at home. A second problem with this lack of realism is that it cannot duplicate the natural viewing situation, complete with the distractions or comforts of home. Looking at ads in a lab setting may not be the same as viewing at home; however some testing techniques have made progress in correcting this deficiency. Overall, however, the control offered by this method probably outweighs the disadvantages, which accounts for the frequent use of lab methods.

Field Tests **Field tests** are tests of the ad or commercial under natural viewing situations, complete with the realism of noise, distractions, and the comforts of home. Field tests take into account the effects of repetition, program content, and even the presence of competitive messages.

The major disadvantage of field tests is the lack of control. It may be impossible to isolate causes of viewers' evaluations. If atypical events occur during the test, they may bias the results. Competitors may attempt to sabotage the research. And field tests usually take more time and money to conduct, so the results are not available to be acted on quickly. Thus, realism is gained at the expense of other important factors. It is up to the researcher to determine which trade-offs to make.

Methods of Measuring Effectiveness

Testing may occur at various points throughout the development of an ad or a campaign: (1) concept generation research, (2) rough, prefinished art, copy, and/or commercial testing, (3) finished art or commercial pretesting, and (4) market testing of ads or commercials (posttesting). In this section, we describe various methods used for each of these four stages.

Concept Generation and Testing

Figure 9–2 describes the process involved in advertising **concept testing**, which is conducted very early in the campaign development process in order to explore the targeted consumer's response to a potential ad or campaign or have the consumer evaluate advertising alternatives. Positioning statements, copy, headlines, and/or illustrations may all be under scrutiny. The material to be evaluated may be just a headline or a rough sketch of the ad. The colours used, typeface, package designs, and even point-of-purchase materials may be evaluated.

One of the more commonly used methods for concept testing is focus groups, which usually consist of 8 to 10 people in the target audience for the product. Companies have tested everything from product concepts to advertising concepts using focus groups. For most companies, the focus group is the first step in the research process. The number of focus groups used varies depending on group consensus, strength of response, and/or the degree to which participants like or dislike the concepts. In general, about 10 are usually needed to test a concept sufficiently.

While focus groups continue to be a favourite of marketers, they are often overused. The methodology is attractive in that results are easily obtained, directly

FIGURE 9–2
Concept testing

Objective:	Explores consumers' responses to various ad concepts as expressed in words, pictures, or symbols.
Method:	Alternative concepts are exposed to consumers who match the characteristics of the target audience. Reactions and evaluations of each are sought through a variety of methods, including focus groups, direct questioning, and survey completion. Sample sizes vary depending on the number of concepts to be presented and the consensus of responses.
Output:	Qualitative and/or quantitative data evaluating and comparing alternative concepts.

FIGURE 9–3

Weaknesses associated with focus group research

- The results are not quantifiable.
- Sample sizes are too small to generalize to larger populations.
- Group influences may bias participants' responses.
- One or two members of the group may steer the conversation or dominate the discussion.
- Consumers become instant "experts."
- Members may not represent the target market. (Are focus group participants a certain type of person?)
- Results may be taken to be more representative and/or definitive than they really are.

FIGURE 9–4

Rough testing terminology

A rough commercial is an unfinished execution that may fall into three broad categories:

Animatic Rough
Succession of drawings/cartoons
Rendered artwork
Still frames
Simulated movement: Panning/zooming of frame/rapid sequence

Photomatic Rough
Succession of photographs
Real people/scenery
Still frames
Simulated movements: Panning/zooming of frame/rapid sequence

Live-Action Rough
Live motion
Stand-in/nonunion talent
Nonunion crew
Limited props/minimal opticals
Location settings

A Finished Commercial Uses
Live motion/animation
Highly paid union talent
Full union crew
Exotic props/studio sets/special effects

observable, and immediate. A variety of issues can be examined, and consumers are free to go into depth in areas they consider important. Also, focus groups don't require quantitative analysis. Unfortunately, many managers are uncertain about research methods that require statistics, and focus groups, being qualitative in nature, don't demand much skill in interpretation. Weaknesses with focus groups are shown in Figure 9–3. Clearly, there are appropriate and inappropriate circumstances for employing this methodology.

Another way to gather consumers' opinions of concepts is mall intercepts, where consumers in shopping malls are approached and asked to evaluate rough ads and/or copy. Rather than participating in a group discussion, individuals assess the ads via questionnaires, rating scales, and/or rankings. New technologies allow for concept testing over the Internet, where advertisers can show concepts simultaneously to consumers throughout Canada, garnering feedback and analyzing the results almost instantaneously. IMC Perspective 9–1 highlights recent trends in communication research done through the Internet.

Rough Art, Copy, and Commercial Testing

Because of the high cost associated with the production of an ad or commercial (many network commercials cost hundreds of thousands of dollars to produce), advertisers are increasingly spending more monies testing a rendering of the final ad at early stages. Slides of the artwork posted on a screen or animatic and photomatic **rough tests** may be used at this stage. (See Figure 9–4 for an explanation of terminology.) Because such tests can be conducted for about $3,000 to $5,000, research at this stage is becoming ever more popular.

IMC PERSPECTIVE 9–1

Advertising Research Adopts the Internet

The Internet is reinventing market research by making it cheaper, more engaging, and more creative. Consider the experience of a large U.S. retailer client who pretested a major television campaign before taking it to air. Using its own nationwide panel of about 30,000 customers, this retailer carefully selected a sub-sample of 1,000 and conducted an online poll that involved respondents viewing several versions of the TV campaign and completing a short questionnaire. The study was completed in 48 hours and cost $3,000—about the same as a conventional focus group with 12 participants. Ten years ago the only viable method for gauging the views of a large group of respondents to stimuli such as an ad campaign was through shopping mall interviews or by mailing them test videos. Using either method, a study on the scale undertaken by the U.S. retail client would have taken weeks to complete and cost $50,000 to $100,000.

Technology is rapidly changing roles and relationships for the three principal players in market research: marketers, researchers, and respondents. On the client side, corporate research departments—which were sometimes ignored during the 80s and 90s—are on the ascendancy. That's because the new speed, cost, and quality equation allows for more timely and relevant research than was ever possible before. Marketer-side researchers can respond within hours to C-suite requests for information on everything from new concepts to competitive threats, thus making research part of the fast-moving decision cycle of most large companies.

The second role transformation associated with the current technological revolution involves companies and researchers on the "supply" side of the research industry. Here the story is about the re-emergence of small and mid-size consultancies—because, in the new era, size is becoming increasingly irrelevant. Previously, smaller research companies lacked the resources and infrastructure necessary to undertake large, complex research missions. But now the same dynamic that is liberating marketers is providing highly creative researchers with a changing environment for their practices. With market research, as with so many other areas touched by the Internet, small is once again beautiful.

The third, and in many respects most important, role change occurring today involves respondents: the men and women who participate in market research surveys, focus groups, and market simulations. Historically, the market research industry grew on the fertile ground of citizen and consumer civility. Millions of people have answered the questions and responded to the pokes and prods of researchers because answering the questions of strangers on the other end of the phone line was considered a polite and socially acceptable thing to do. Across North America and increasingly around the world, respondent engagement has become a huge threat to the market research industry as non-cooperation rates often exceed 80 percent. In many respects the Internet can be a convivial tool for collecting opinions as respondents can choose the time and place for completing a survey. And because the high cost of call centre distribution has been eliminated, it's economically feasible to provide a small incentive to encourage participation.

Another significant change the Internet promises for respondents concerns the ability of this technology to make the survey experience itself much more pleasant. Most online surveys are little more than telephone scripts that have been placed on a screen. But that's starting to change as 3D animation, simulated shopping experiences, and online shopping games find traction. It's all about visuals and engagement—a phenomenon that will only accelerate as more households move to high-speed Internet connections.

Source: Angus Reid, "Market Research Liberated," *Marketing Magazine*, September 25, 2006.

Question

1. Will assessing consumer reaction to advertising using market research over the Internet improve the quality of information in the future?

FIGURE 9–5
Consumer juries

Objective:	Potential viewers (consumers) are asked to evaluate ads and give their reactions to and evaluation of them. When two or more ads are tested, viewers are usually asked to rate or rank order the ads according to their preferences.
Method:	Respondents are asked to view ads and rate them according to either (1) the order of merit method or (2) the paired comparison method. In the former, the respondent is asked to view the ads, then rank them from one to *n* according to their perceived merit. In the latter, ads are compared only two at a time. Each ad is compared to every other ad in the group, and the winner is listed. The best ad is that which wins the most times. Consumer juries typically employ 50 to 100 participants.
Output:	An overall reaction to each ad under construction as well as a rank ordering of the ads based on the viewers' perceptions.

FIGURE 9–6
Questions asked in a consumer jury test

1. Which of these ads would you most likely read if you saw it in a magazine?
2. Which of these headlines would interest you the most in reading the ad further?
3. Which ad convinces you most of the quality or superiority of the product?
4. Which layout do you think would be most effective in causing you to buy?
5. Which ad did you like best?
6. Which ad did you find most interesting?

But cost is only one factor. The test is of little value if it does not provide relevant, accurate information. Rough tests must indicate how the finished commercial would perform. Some studies have demonstrated that these testing methods are reliable and the results typically correlate well with the finished ad.[6] Most of the tests conducted at the rough stage involve lab settings. Popular tests include comprehension and reaction tests and consumer juries.

Comprehension and Reaction Tests One key concern for the advertiser is whether the ad or commercial conveys the meaning intended. The second concern is the reaction the ad generates. Obviously, the advertiser does not want an ad that evokes a negative reaction or offends someone. **Comprehension and reaction tests** are designed to assess these responses. Tests of comprehension and reaction employ no one standard procedure. Personal interviews, group interviews, and focus groups have all been used for this purpose, and sample sizes vary according to the needs of the client; they typically range from 50 to 200 respondents.

Consumer Juries This method uses consumers representative of the target audiences to evaluate the probable success of an ad. **Consumer juries** may be asked to rate a selection of layouts or copy versions presented in pasteups on separate sheets. The objectives sought and methods employed in consumer juries are shown in Figure 9–5.[7] Sample questions asked of jurists are shown in Figure 9–6.

While the jury method offers the advantages of control and cost effectiveness, serious flaws in the methodology limit its usefulness:

- *The consumer may become a self-appointed expert.* One of the benefits sought from the jury method is the objectivity and involvement in the product or service that the targeted consumer can bring to the evaluation process. Sometimes, however, knowing they are being asked to critique ads, participants try to become more expert in their evaluations, paying more attention and being more critical than usual. The result may be a less than objective evaluation or an evaluation on elements other than those intended.
- *The number of ads that can be evaluated is limited.* Whether order of merit or paired comparison methods are used, the ranking procedure becomes tedious

as the number of alternatives increases. Consider the ranking of 10 ads. While the top two and the bottom two may very well reveal differences, those ranked in the middle may not yield much useful information. In the paired comparison method, 15 evaluations are required for six alternatives. As the number of ads increases, the task becomes even more unmanageable.

- *A halo effect is possible.* Sometimes participants rate an ad as good on all characteristics because they like a few and overlook specific as weaknesses. This tendency, called the **halo effect**, distorts the ratings and defeats the ability to control for specific components. (Of course, the reverse may also occur—rating an ad as bad overall due to only a few bad attributes.)
- *Preferences for specific types of advertising may overshadow objectivity.* Ads that involve emotions or pictures may receive higher ratings or rankings than those employing copy, facts, and/or rational criteria. Even though the latter are often more effective in the marketplace, they may be judged less favourably by jurists who prefer emotional appeals.

Some of the problems noted here can be remedied by the use of ratings scales instead of rankings. But ratings are not always valid either. Thus, while consumer juries have been used for years, questions of bias have led researchers to doubt their validity. As a result, a variety of other methods (discussed later in this chapter) are more commonly employed.

Pretesting of Finished Ads

Pretesting finished ads is one of the more commonly employed studies among marketing researchers and their agencies. At this stage, a finished advertisement or commercial is used; since it has not been presented to the market, changes can still be made.

Many researchers believe testing the ad in final form provides better information. Several test procedures are available for print and broadcast ads, including both laboratory and field methodologies.

Print methods include portfolio tests, analyses of readability, and dummy advertising vehicles. Broadcast tests include theatre tests and on-air tests. Both print and broadcast may use physiological measures.

Pretesting Finished Print Messages A number of methods for pretesting finished print ads are available. One is described in Figure 9–7. The most common of these methods are portfolio tests, readability tests, and dummy advertising vehicles.

Portfolio Tests **Portfolio tests** are a laboratory methodology designed to expose a group of respondents to a portfolio consisting of both control and test ads. Respondents are then asked what information they recall from the ads. The assumption is that the ads that yield the *highest recall* are the most effective.

Objective:	Tests recall and readers' impressions of print ads.
Method:	Mall intercepts in two or more cities are used to screen respondents and have them take home "test magazines" for reading. Participants are phoned the next day to determine opinions of the ads, recall of ad contents, and other questions of interest to the sponsor. Approximately 225 people constitute the sample.
Output:	Scores reported include related recall of copy and visual elements, sales messages, and other nonspecific elements. Both quantitative (table) scores and verbatim responses are reported.

FIGURE 9–7 Diagnostic Research Inc.'s print test

While portfolio tests offer the opportunity to compare alternative ads directly, a number of weaknesses limit their applicability:

- Factors other than advertising creativity and/or presentation may affect recall. Interest in the product or product category, the fact that respondents know they are participating in a test, or interviewer instructions (among others) may account for more differences than the ad itself.
- Recall may not be the best test. Some researchers argue that for certain types of products (those of low involvement) ability to recognize the ad when shown may be a better measure than recall.

One way to determine the validity of the portfolio method is to correlate its results with readership scores once the ad is placed in the field. Whether such validity tests are being conducted or not is not readily known, although the portfolio method remains popular in the industry.

Readability Tests The communications efficiency of the copy in a print ad can be tested without reader interviews. This test uses the **Flesch formula**, named after its developer, Rudolph Flesch, to assess readability of the copy by determining the average number of syllables per 100 words. Human interest appeal of the material, length of sentences, and familiarity with certain words are also considered and correlated with the educational background of target audiences. Test results are compared to previously established norms for various target audiences. The test suggests that copy is best comprehended when sentences are short, words are concrete and familiar, and personal references are drawn.

This method eliminates many of the interviewee biases associated with other tests and avoids gross errors in understanding. The norms offer an attractive standard for comparison.

Disadvantages are also inherent, however. The copy may become too mechanical, and direct input from the receiver is not available. Without this input, contributing elements like creativity cannot be addressed. To be effective, this test should be used only in conjunction with other pretesting methods.

Dummy Advertising Vehicles In an improvement on the portfolio test, ads are placed in "dummy" magazines developed by an agency or research firm. The magazines contain regular editorial features of interest to the reader, as well as the test ads, and are distributed to a *random sample* of homes in predetermined geographic areas. Readers are told the magazine publisher is interested in evaluations of editorial content and asked to read the magazines as they normally would. Then they are interviewed on their reactions to both editorial content and ads. Recall, readership, and interest-generating capabilities of the ad are assessed.

The advantage of this method is that it provides a more natural setting than the portfolio test. Readership occurs in the participant's own home, the test more closely approximates a natural reading situation, and the reader may go back to the magazine, as people typically do.

But the dummy magazine shares the other disadvantages associated with portfolio tests. The testing effect is not eliminated, and product interest may still bias the results. Thus, while this test offers some advantages over the portfolio method, it is not a guaranteed measure of the advertising's impact.

While all the previously described measures are available, the most popular form of pretesting of print ads now involves a series of measures that account for the shortcomings cited above. The tests can be used for rough and/or finished ads and are most commonly conducted in the respondents' homes enabling the researcher to collect multiple measures from many samples. One example is shown in Figure 9–8.

Pretesting Finished Broadcast Ads A variety of methods for pretesting broadcast ads are available. The most popular are theatre tests, on-air tests, and physiological measures.

Objective:	To assist advertisers in copy testing of print advertisements to determine (1) main idea communication, (2) likes and dislikes, (3) believability, (4) ad attribute ratings, (5) overall likability, and (6) brand attribute ratings.
Method:	Tests are conducted in current issues of newsstand magazines. The recall measure consists of 150 responses. Diagnostic measures range from 105 to 150 responses. Highly targeted audiences are available through a version known as the Targeted Print Test.
Output:	Standard scores and specific diagnostics.

FIGURE 9–8
Ipsos-ASI's Next*Print

Theatre Tests In the past, one of the most popular laboratory methods for pretesting finished commercials was **theatre testing**. In tests, participants are invited by telephone, mall intercepts, and/or tickets in the mail to view pilots of proposed TV programs. In some instances, the show is actually being tested, but more commonly a standard program is used so that audience responses can be compared with normative responses established by previous viewers. Sample sizes range from 250 to 600 participants.

On entering the theatre, viewers are told a drawing will be held for gifts and asked to complete a product preference questionnaire asking which products they would prefer if they win. This form also requests demographic data. Participants may be seated in specific locations in the theatre to allow observation by age, sex, and so on. They view the program and commercials, and a form asking for evaluations is distributed. Participants are then asked to complete a second form for a drawing so that changes in product preference can be noted. In addition to product/brand preference, the form may request other information:

- Interest in and reaction to the commercial.
- Overall reaction to the commercial as measured by an adjective checklist.
- Recall of various aspects of the commercial.
- Interest in the brand under consideration.
- Continuous (frame-by-frame) reactions throughout the commercial.

The methods of theatre testing operations vary, though all measure brand preference changes. For example, many of the services now use videotaped programs with the commercials embedded for viewing in one's office rather than in a theatre. Others establish viewing rooms in malls and/or hotel conference rooms. Some do not take all the measures listed here; others ask the consumers to turn dials or push buttons on a keypad to provide the continual responses. An example of one methodology is shown in Figure 9–9.

Those opposed to theatre tests cite a number of disadvantages. First, they say the environment is too artificial. The lab setting is bad enough, but asking respondents to turn dials or, as one service does, wiring people for physiological responses takes them too far from a natural viewing situation. Second, the contrived measure of brand preference change seems too phony to believe. Critics contend that participants will see through it and make changes just because they think they are

Advertising Control for Television (ACT), a lab procedure of The MSW Group, uses about 400 respondents representing four cities. It measures initial brand preference by asking participants which brands they most recently purchased. Respondents are then divided into groups of 25 to view a 30-minute program with seven commercials inserted in the middle. Four are test commercials; the other three are control commercials with established viewing norms. After viewing the program, respondents are given a recall test of the commercials. After the recall test, a second 30-minute program is shown, with each test commercial shown again. The second measure of brand preference is taken at this time, with persuasion measured by the percentage of viewers who switched preferences from their most recently purchased brand to one shown in the test commercials.

FIGURE 9–9
The AD*VANTAGE/ACT theatre methodology

supposed to. Finally, the group effect of having others present and overtly exhibiting their reactions may influence viewers who did not have any reactions themselves.

Proponents argue that theatre tests offer distinct advantages. In addition to control, the established norms (averages of commercials' performances) indicate how one's commercial will fare against others in the same product class that were already tested. Further, advocates say the brand preference measure is supported by actual sales results.

Despite the limitations of theatre testing, most major consumer product companies have used it to evaluate their commercials. This method may have shortcomings, but it allows them to identify strong or weak commercials and to compare them to other ads.

On-Air Tests Some of the firms conducting theatre tests also insert the commercials into actual TV programs in certain test markets. Typically, the commercials are in finished form, although the testing of ads earlier in the developmental process is becoming more common. This is referred to as an **on-air test** and often includes single-source ad research (discussed later in this chapter).

On-air testing techniques offer all the advantages of field methodologies, as well as all the disadvantages. Further, there are negative aspects to the specific measures taken through the on-air systems. One concern is associated with **day-after recall scores**, the primary measure used in these tests. Lyman Ostlund notes that measurement errors may result from the natural environment—the position of the ad in the series of commercials shown, the adjacent program content, and/or the number of commercials shown.[8] While the testing services believe their methods overcome many of these criticisms, each still uses recall as one of the primary measures of effectiveness. Since recall tests best reflect the degree of attention and interest in an ad, claims that the tests predict the ad's impact on sales may be going too far. (In 28 studies reviewed by Jack Haskins, only two demonstrated that factual recall could be related to sales.)[9] Joel Dubow's research indicates that recall is a necessary but not sufficient measure, while research by Jones and Blair was even more demonstrative, noting that "it is unwise to look to recall for an accurate assessment of a commercial's sales effect."[10]

On the plus side, most of the testing services have offered evidence of both validity and reliability for on-air pretesting of commercials. Some firms claim their pretest and posttest results yield the same recall scores 9 out of 10 times—a strong indication of reliability and a good predictor of the effect the ad is likely to have when shown to the population as a whole.

In summary, on-air pretesting of finished or rough commercials offers some distinct advantages over lab methods and some indications of the ad's likely success. Whether the measures used are as strong an indication as the providers say still remains in question.

Physiological Measures A less common method of pretesting finished commercials involves a laboratory setting in which physiological responses are measured. These measures indicate the receiver's *involuntary* response to the ad, theoretically eliminating biases associated with the voluntary measures reviewed to this point. (Involuntary responses are those over which the individual has no control, such as heartbeat and reflexes.) Physiological measures used to test both print and broadcast ads include pupil dilation, galvanic skin response, eye tracking, and brain waves:

Pupil dilation. Research in **pupillometrics** is designed to measure dilation and constriction of the pupils of the eyes in response to stimuli. Dilation is associated with action; constriction involves the body's conservation of energy.

Advertisers have used pupillometrics to evaluate product and package design as well as to test ads. Pupil dilation suggests a stronger interest in (or preference for) an ad or implies arousal or attention-getting capabilities. Other attempts to determine the affective (liking or disliking) responses created by ads have met with less success.

Because of high costs and some methodological problems, the use of pupillometrics has waned over the past decade. But it can be useful in evaluating certain aspects of advertising.

Galvanic skin response. Also known as **electrodermal response**, GSR measures the skin's resistance or conductance to a small amount of current passed between two electrodes. Response to a stimulus activates sweat glands, which in turn increases the conductance of the electrical current. Thus, GSR/EDR activity might reflect a reaction to advertising. In their review of the research in this area, Paul Watson and Robert Gatchel concluded that GSR/EDR (1) is sensitive to affective stimuli, (2) may present a picture of attention, (3) may be useful to measure long-term advertising recall, and (4) is useful in measuring ad effectiveness.[11] In interviews with practitioners and reviews of case studies, Priscilla LaBarbera and Joel Tucciarone also concluded that GSR is an effective measure and is useful for measuring affect, or liking, for ads.[12] While a number of companies have offered skin response measures, this research methodology is not commonly used now, and LaBarbera and Tucciarone believe that it is underused, given its potential.

Eye tracking. A methodology that is more commonly employed is **eye tracking** (Figure 9–10), in which viewers are asked to view an ad while a sensor aims a beam of infrared light at the eye. The beam follows the movement of the eye and shows the exact spot on which the viewer is focusing. The continuous reading of responses demonstrates which elements of the ad are attracting attention, how long the viewer is focusing on them, and the sequence in which they are being viewed.

Eye tracking can identify strengths and weaknesses in an ad. For example, attractive models or background action may distract the viewer's attention away from the brand or product being advertised. The advertiser can remedy this distraction before fielding the ad. In other instances, colours or illustrations may attract attention and create viewer interest in the ad.

Brain waves. **Electroencephalographic (EEG) measures** can be taken from the skull to determine electrical frequencies in the brain. These electrical impulses are used in two areas of research, alpha waves and hemispheric lateralization.

- **Alpha activity** refers to the degree of brain activation. People are in an alpha state when they are inactive, resting, or sleeping. The theory is that a person in an alpha state is less likely to be processing information (recall correlates negatively with alpha levels) and that attention and processing require moving from this state. By measuring a subject's alpha level while viewing a commercial, researchers can assess the degree to which attention and processing are likely to occur.
- **Hemispheric lateralization** distinguishes between alpha activity in the left and right sides of the brain. It has been hypothesized that the right side of the brain processes visual stimuli and the left processes verbal stimuli. The right hemisphere is thought to respond more to emotional stimuli, while the left responds to logic. The right determines recognition, while the left is responsible for recall.[13] If these hypotheses are correct, advertisers could design ads to increase learning and memory by creating stimuli to appeal to each hemisphere. However, some researchers believe the brain does not function laterally and an ad cannot be designed to appeal to one side or the other.

While EEG research has engaged the attention of academic researchers, it has been much less successful in attracting the interest of practitioners, although this may be changing, as shown in IMC Perspective 9–2 on page 258.

FIGURE *9–10*

Eye movement research

Objective:	Tracks viewers' eye movements to determine what viewers read or view in print ads and where their attention is focused in TV commercials or billboards.
Method:	Fibre optics, digital data processing, and advanced electronics are used to follow eye movements of viewers and/or readers as they process an ad.
Output:	Relationship among what readers see, recall, and comprehend. Scan paths on print ads, billboards, commercials, and print materials. (Can also be used to evaluate package designs.)

IMC PERSPECTIVE 9–2

Measuring Brain Waves for Ad Success

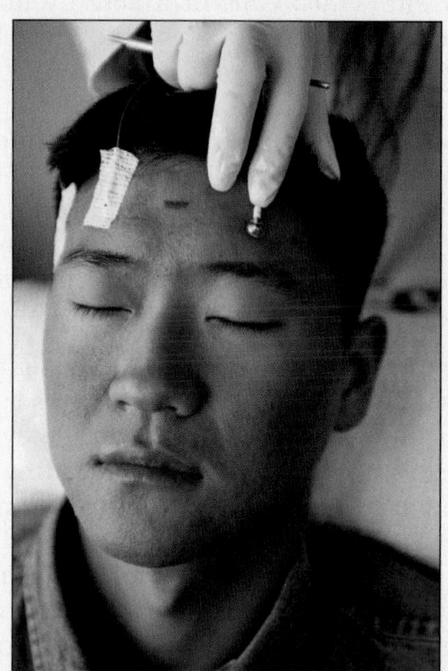

Thirty-four users of bathroom cleansers visited a U.S. research lab to watch "Prison Visitor," the much-awarded TV spot by Zig for Unilever's Vim brand. The ad shows a young girl visiting her distraught mother, who appears to be behind a prison glass but is revealed to be scrubbing a grimy shower. Researchers wanted a "clean read" on the ad, so they tested consumers in the U.S.—where the ad never aired and where the product isn't available. Participants reacted strongly to the "hands on glass" sequence, particularly during the dramatic "I love you, Mama!" "I love you too, baby!" exchange. However, the scenes showing the product demonstration and brand message evoked a much weaker response.

How did researchers measure viewers' response to such emotionally charged advertising? Each participant in the study was asked how they felt about the ad—while six electrodes were attached to their head. This was U.K.-based research firm Millward Brown's first foray into measuring brain activity to discover how consumers respond to brands and advertising. Working with Brainwave Science, a Seattle-based neuroscience company, Millward Brown used the electroencephalography (EEG) technique and then compared the results to its verbal survey-based technique, called Link.

"The idea was really to see, can we find out something new, can we find out something meaningful (from the brainwave test)," says Graham Page, global director of innovation at Millward Brown in London, England. The two sets of results tied up closely: Elements of the ad that evoked negative emotions as measured by the Link test corresponded strongly with the scenes that generated the strongest brainwave response. Page describes the measurement as "every market researcher's dream": an objective view of consumers' thoughts without the influence of interviewer questions and biases. While he's enthusiastic about the new approach, he's not ready to replace tried-and-true research techniques with electrodes. "There are still big barriers to it," he says.

But such research has its drawbacks. First, it's expensive. And second, it's a "small numbers" problem. For example, Ipsos Reid can ask 1,000 Canadians what they think of Prime Minister Stephen Harper, but "you're not going to put 1,000 people through a scanner." At this early stage, advertising agencies aren't convinced the technology will change the way they craft their messages, either. "I would have a difficult time justifying going to a client and saying, 'What I want to do is an MRI and I think this will help make better ads for you,'" says Michael Szego, senior planner at Ogilvy & Mather in Toronto. "At this point, I couldn't do that with a straight face." Furthermore, Szego says, there are very few client enquiries. But, he adds, "The biggest brands with the biggest budgets tend to arrive at new ideas and approaches first." This stems from the fact if global brands can improve by one or two percent, "it's a huge impact," explains Szego. "But at the Canadian marketers level, the benefits just aren't clear at this stage." Szego adds there are many disciplines in science used by marketers that aren't MRI-based, such as semiotics, anthropology, and neurolinguistic programming.

Millward Brown's Page believes researchers still require a survey to make sense of the findings. For example, while the "Prison Visitor" spot elicited strong negative emotional response—often crucial in an ad to generate humour—overall, the consumers who participated in Millward Brown's study didn't respond that favourably to the spot. Says Page, "They realized it was a joke but they actually found it quite distasteful." Those latter findings came from the verbal survey, which also revealed the ad had a well-below-average enjoyment rating, evoking such verbal responses as "you end up feeling emotionally used."

"We actually got quite a different response to this ad (in the U.S.) perhaps than what you get in Canada or what we would have gotten in the U.K., just because of the humour," says Page. Still, he believes the testing will become part of the marketer's tool kit but "it won't be the first tool out of the bag in most instances." Other experts agree. "We're not going to get rid of focus groups, telephone surveys and mall intercepts," says Moore. "It's going to be a supplement to them." That said, "I think it will grow and become more important and fairly widely adopted in five to ten years."

Source: Rebecca Harris, "Brain Waves," *Marketing Magazine*, June 5, 2006.

Question

1. Express your feelings on whether you would volunteer as a respondent to this kind of research.

Market Testing of Ads

The fact that the ad and/or campaign has been implemented does not mean there is no longer a need for testing. The pretests were conducted on smaller samples and may in some instances have questionable merit, so the marketer must find out how the ad is doing in the field. In this section, we discuss methods for posttesting an ad. Some of the tests are similar to the pretests discussed in the previous section and are provided by the same companies.

Posttests of Print Ads A variety of print posttests are available, including inquiry tests, recognition tests, and recall tests.

Inquiry Tests Used in both consumer and business-to-business market testing, **inquiry tests** are designed to measure advertising effectiveness on the basis of inquiries generated from ads appearing in various print media, often referred to as "bingo cards." The inquiry may take the form of the number of coupons returned, phone calls generated, or direct inquiries through reader cards. Figure 9–11 shows that the reader response card is still the most commonly employed response to trade ads. For example, if you called in a response to an ad in a local medium recently, perhaps you were asked how you found out about the company or product or where you saw the ad. This is a very simple measure of the ad's or medium's effectiveness.

More complex methods of measuring effectiveness through inquiries may involve (1) running the ad in successive issues of the same medium, (2) running **split-run tests**, in which variations of the ad appear in different copies of the same newspaper or magazine, and/or (3) running the same ad in different media. Each of these methods yields information on different aspects of the strategy. The first measures the cumulative effects of the campaign; the second examines specific elements

FIGURE 9–11

Ad response methods

Despite the rise in popularity of electronic response mechanisms, the traditional reader service, or "bingo card," remains the most common way to respond to trade publication advertising.

Ad Response Methods Used Frequently or Very Frequently*	
Indirect Methods	
Return reader service cards	41%
Save ads for reference	35
Discuss advertised products with others	30
Pass ads on to others for possible action	26
Direct Methods	
Send back reply cards/coupons	31%
Contact vendors' websites	28
Telephone manufacturers	23
Telephone local distributors/reps	22
Go to magazine websites	21
Stop at vendors' trade show exhibits	20
Discuss products with sales reps	20
Send faxes to vendors	17
Contact distributors' websites	15
Send e-mail messages	10
Mail notes to vendors	6

*The 2,705 respondents could name more than one method.

of the ad or variations on it. The final method measures the effectiveness of the medium rather than the ad itself.

While inquiry tests may yield useful information, weaknesses in this methodology limit its effectiveness. For example, inquiries may not be a true measure of the attention-getting or information-providing aspects of the ad. The reader may be attracted to an ad, read it, and even store the information but not be motivated to inquire at that particular time. Time constraints, lack of a need for the product or service at the time the ad is run, and other factors may limit the number of inquiries. But receiving a small number of inquiries doesn't mean the ad was not effective; attention, attitude change, awareness, and recall of copy points may all have been achieved. At the other extreme, a person with a particular need for the product may respond to any ad for it, regardless of specific qualities of the ad.

Major advantages of inquiry tests are that they are inexpensive to implement and they provide some feedback with respect to the general effectiveness of the ad or medium used. But they are usually not very effective for comparing different versions or specific creative aspects of an ad.

Recognition Tests Perhaps the most common posttest of print ads is the **recognition method**, most closely associated with Roper ASW. The *Starch Ad Readership Report* lets the advertiser assess the impact of an ad in a single issue of a magazine, over time, and/or across different magazines (see Figure 9–12). Starch measures over 75,000 ads in more than 1,000 issues representing more than 100 consumer, farm, and business magazines and newspapers per year and provides a number of measures of the ad's effectiveness. An example of a Starch report is shown in Exhibit 9–2.

Exhibit 9–2 The Starch method of testing is widely employed

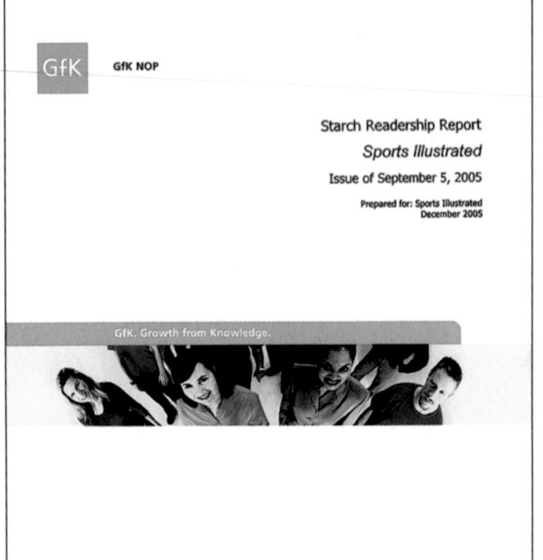

Starch also offers the *Starch Impression Study* and the *Starch Ballot Readership Study*. The impression study provides consumers' qualitative impressions of ads (for example, company image and important features); the readership study measures readership in business magazines.

Starch claims that (1) the pulling power of various aspects of the ad can be assessed through the control offered, (2) the effectiveness of competitors' ads can be compared through the norms provided, (3) alternative ad executions can be tested, and (4) readership scores are a useful indication of consumers' involvement in the ad or campaign. (The theory is that a reader must read and become involved in the ad before the ad can communicate. To the degree that this readership can be shown, it is a direct indication of effectiveness.)

FIGURE *9–12*

The *Starch Ad Readership Report*

Objective:	Determining recognition of print ads and comparing them to other ads of the same variety or in the same magazine.
Method:	Samples are drawn from 20 to 30 urban areas reflecting the geographic circulation of the magazine. Personal interviewers screen readers for qualifications and determine exposure and readership. Samples include a minimum of 200 males and females, as well as specific audiences where required. Participants are asked to go through the magazines, looking at the ads, and provide specific responses.
Output:	*Starch Ad Readership Reports* generate three recognition scores: • Noted score—the percentage of readers who remember seeing the ad. • Seen-associated score—the percentage of readers who recall seeing or reading any part of the ad identifying the product or brand. • Read-most score—the percentage of readers who report reading at least half of the copy portion of the ad.

Of these claims, perhaps the most valid is the ability to judge specific aspects of the ad. Many researchers have criticized other aspects of the Starch recognition method (as well as other recognition measures) on the basis of problems of false claiming, interviewer sensitivities, and unreliable scores:

False claiming. Research shows that in recognition tests, respondents may claim to have seen an ad when they did not. False claims may be a result of having seen similar ads elsewhere, expecting that such an ad would appear in the medium, or wanting to please the questioner. Interest in the product category also increases reporting of ad readership. Whether this false claiming is deliberate or not, it leads to an overreporting of effectiveness. On the flip side, factors such as interview fatigue may lead to an underreporting bias—that is, respondents not reporting an ad they did see.

Interviewer sensitivities. Any time research involves interviewers, there is a potential for bias. Respondents may want to impress the interviewer or fear looking unknowledgeable if they continually claim not to recognize an ad. There may also be variances associated with interviewer instructions, recordings, and so on, regardless of the amount of training and sophistication involved.

Reliability of recognition scores. Starch admits that the reliability and validity of its readership scores increase with the number of insertions tested, which essentially means that to test just one ad on a single exposure may not produce valid or reliable results.

In sum, despite critics, the Starch readership studies continue to dominate the posttesting of print ads. The value provided by norms and the fact that multiple exposures can improve reliability and validity may underlie the decisions to employ this methodology.

Recall Tests There are several tests to measure recall of print ads. Perhaps the best known of these are the Ipsos-ASI Next*Print test and the Gallup & Robinson Magazine Impact Research Service (MIRS) (described in Figure 9–13). These **recall tests** are similar to those discussed in the section on pretesting broadcast ads in that they attempt to measure recall of specific ads.

In addition to having the same interviewer problems as recognition tests, recall tests have other disadvantages. The reader's degree of involvement with the product and/or the distinctiveness of the appeals and visuals may lead to higher-than-accurate recall scores, although in general the method may lead to lower levels of recall than actually exist (an error the advertiser would be happy with). Critics contend the test is not strong enough to reflect recall accurately, so many ads may score as less effective than they really are, and advertisers may abandon or modify them needlessly.

On the plus side, it is thought that recall tests can assess the ad's impact on memory. Proponents of recall tests say the major concern is not the results themselves but how they are interpreted. In one very interesting study of the effects of

FIGURE 9–13

Gallup & Robinson Magazine Impact Research Service

Objective: Tracking recall of advertising (and client's ads) appearing in magazines to assess performance and effectiveness.

Method: Test magazines are placed in participants' homes and respondents are asked to read the magazine that day. A telephone interview is conducted the second day to assess recall of ads, recall of copy points, and consumers' impressions of the ads. Sample size is 150 people.

Output: Three measurement scores are provided:

- Proven name registration—the percentage of respondents who can accurately recall the ad.
- Idea communication—the number of sales points the respondents can recall.
- Favourable buying attitude—the extent of favourable purchase reaction to the brand or corporation.

brand name suggestiveness on recall, Kevin Keller, Susan Heckler, and Michael Houston found that suggestive brand names (those that convey relevant attribute or benefit information about the product) facilitate the initial recall of the brand's benefits but inhibit recall of subsequently advertised claims. These results would seem to indicate that a suggestive brand name could facilitate initial positioning of the brand but make it more difficult to introduce new attributes at a later time. The authors suggest that these results might be useful in explaining why Jack in the Box has had trouble developing a more adult image and why Old Spice and Oldsmobile have had difficulty with younger audiences.[14]

A very extensive longitudinal study was conducted by the Netherlands Institute of Public Opinion (NIPO) to assess the relationship between recall and recognition. The results indicated that the average correlation between recall and recognition in both newspapers and magazines was very high (r = .96 and .95, respectively). The study concluded that recall actually stems from recognition, in that 99 percent of 3,632 cases of recall also had recorded recognition. In addition, likable and interesting ads doubled the recall scores and increased the recall share of recognition. Creative advertising was much more effective for creating perceptions and recall than was the size of the ad.[15]

Posttests of Broadcast Commercials A variety of methods exist for posttesting broadcast commercials. The most common provide a combination of day-after recall tests, persuasion measures, and diagnostics. Test marketing and tracking studies, including single-source methods, are also employed.

Day-After Recall Tests The most popular method of posttesting employed in the broadcasting industry for decades was the *Burke Day-After Recall test.* While a number of companies offered day-after recall methodologies, the "Burke test" for all intents and purposes became the generic name attached to these tests. While popular, day-after recall tests also had problems, including limited samples, high costs, and security issues (ads shown in test markets could be seen by competitors). In addition, the following disadvantages with recall tests were also suggested:

- DAR tests may favour unemotional appeals because respondents are asked to verbalize the message. Thinking messages may be easier to recall than emotional communications, so recall scores for emotional ads may be lower.[16] A number of other studies have also indicated that emotional ads may be processed differently from thinking ones; some ad agencies, for example Leo Burnett and BBDO Worldwide, have gone so far as to develop their own methods of determining emotional response to ads.[17]
- Program content may influence recall. The programs in which the ad appears may lead to different recall scores for the same brand. The net result is a potential inaccuracy in the recall score and in the norms used to establish comparisons.[18]
- A prerecruited sample may pay increased attention to the program and the ads contained therein because the respondents know they will be tested the next day. This effect would lead to a higher level of recall than really exists.

The major advantage of day-after recall tests is that they are field tests. The natural setting is supposed to provide a more realistic response profile. These tests are also popular because they provide norms that give advertisers a standard for comparing how well their ads are performing. In addition to recall, a number of different measures of the commercial's effectiveness are now offered, including persuasive measures and diagnostics. (The Burke test itself no longer exists.)

Comprehensive Measures As noted earlier in our discussion of pretesting broadcast commercials, a measure of a commercial's persuasive effectiveness is gathered by asking consumers to choose a brand that they would want to win in a drawing and then—after exposure to the ad—asking the question again. In theatre settings, this is accomplished by announcing a series of prize drawings, with viewers

FIGURE *9–14*

Ipsos-ASI's Next*TV

Objective:	To assist advertisers in copy testing of their commercials through multiple measures to determine (1) the potential of the commercial for impacting sales, (2) how the ad contributes to brand equity, (3) how well it is in line with existing advertising strategies and objectives, and (4) how to optimize effectiveness.
Method:	Consumers are recruited to evaluate a TV program, with ads embedded into the program as they would be on local prime-time television. Consumers view the program on a videotape in their homes to simulate actual field conditions. (The option to use local cable television programs with commercial inserts is also provided.)
Output:	Related recall (day-after recall) scores; persuasion scores, including brand preference shifts, purchase intent and frequency, brand equity differentiation, and relevance and communication; and reaction diagnostics to determine what viewers take away from the ad and how creative elements contribute to or distract from advertising effectiveness.

indicating which of the brands they would choose if they won. In field settings, it is accomplished by taking a brand preference measure when the video is delivered and then again the next day. Some of the services offer additional persuasion measures, including purchase-intent and frequency-of-purchase criteria.

Copy testing firms also provide diagnostic measures. These measures are designed to garner viewers' evaluations of the ads, as well as how clearly the creative idea is understood and how well the proposition is communicated. Rational and emotional reactions to the ads are also examined. While each of the measures just described provides specific input into the effectiveness of a commercial, many advertisers are interested in more than just one specific input. Thus, some companies provide comprehensive approaches in which each of the three measures just described (i.e., recall, persuasion, diagnostics) can be obtained through one testing program. Figure 9–14 describes one such comprehensive program, Ipsos-ASI's Next*TV test (Exhibit 9–3).

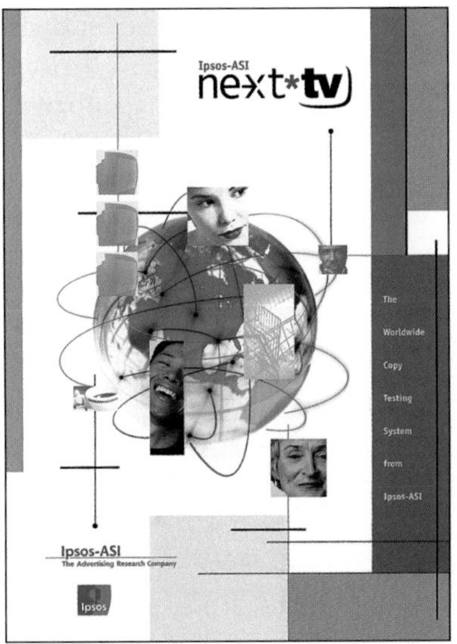

Exhibit 9–3 Ipsos-ASI offers a comprehensive testing measure

Test Marketing Many companies conduct tests designed to measure their advertising effects in specific test markets before releasing them nationally. The markets chosen are representative of the target market. For example, a company may test its ads in London, Ontario, Peterborough, Ontario, or Winnipeg, Manitoba, if the demographic and socioeconomic profiles of these cities match the product's market. A variety of factors may be tested, including reactions to the ads (for example, alternative copy points), the effects of various budget sizes, or special offers. The ads run in finished form in the media where they might normally appear, and effectiveness is measured after the ads run.

The advantage of test marketing of ads is realism. Regular viewing environments are used and the testing effects are minimized. A high degree of control can be attained if the test is designed successfully. For example, an extensive test market study was designed and conducted by Seagram and Time, Inc., over three years to measure the effects of advertising frequency on consumers' buying habits. This study demonstrated just how much could be learned from research conducted in a field setting but with some experimental controls. It also showed that proper research can provide strong insights into the impact of ad campaigns. (Many advertising researchers consider this study one of the most conclusive ever conducted in the attempt to demonstrate the effects of advertising on sales.)

The Seagram study also reveals some of the disadvantages associated with test market measures, not the least of which are cost and time. Few firms have the luxury to spend three years and hundreds of thousands of dollars on such a test. In addition, there is always the fear that competitors may discover and intervene in the research process. Test marketing can provide substantial insight into the effectiveness of advertising if care is taken to minimize the negative aspects of such tests.

Single-Source Tracking Studies Since the 1980s, the focus of many research efforts has been on single-source tracking methods. **Single-source tracking methods** track the behaviours of consumers from the television set to the supermarket checkout counter. Participants in a designated area who have cable TV and agree to participate in the studies are given a card (similar to a credit card) that identifies their household and gives the research company their demographics. The households are split into matched groups; one group receives an ad while the other does not, or alternate ads are sent to each. Their purchases are recorded from the bar codes of the products bought. Commercial exposures are then correlated with purchase behaviours.

Earlier we mentioned the use of single-source ad research in pretesting commercials. One study demonstrated that the single-source method can also be used effectively to posttest ads, allowing for a variety of dependent measures and tracking the effects of increased ad budgets and different versions of ad copy—and even ad effects on sales.[19]

A 10-year study conducted by Information Resources' BehaviorScan service demonstrated long-term effects of advertising on sales. The study examined copy, media schedules, ad budgets, and the impact of trade promotions on sales in 10 markets throughout the United States and concluded that advertising can produce sales growth as long as two years after a campaign ends.[20] (The study also concluded that results of copy recall and persuasion tests were unlikely to predict sales reliably.) A number of single-source methods have been used, among them BehaviorScan (Information Resources) and MarketSource. The ACNielsen company's Scantrack is another commonly employed single-source tracking system.

Many advertisers believe these single-source measures will change the way research is conducted due to the advantages of control and the ability to measure directly the ads' effects on sales. A number of major corporations and ad agencies are now employing this method, including Campbell Soup, Colgate-Palmolive, Nestlé, General Foods, P&G, Pepsi-Cola, Leo Burnett, and J. Walter Thompson. After using scanner data to review the advertising/sales relationship for 78 brands, John Jones concluded that single-source data are beginning to fulfill their promise now that more measurements are available.[21]

While single-source testing is a valuable tool, it still has some problems. One researcher says, "Scanner data focus on short-term sales effects, and as a result capture only 10 to 30 percent of what advertising does."[22] Others complain that the data are too complicated to deal with, as an overabundance of information is available. Still another disadvantage is the high cost of collecting single-source data. While the complexity of single-source data resulted in a slow adoption rate, this method of tracking advertising effectiveness became widely adopted in the 1990s.

Exhibit 9–4 Tracking studies provide useful measures

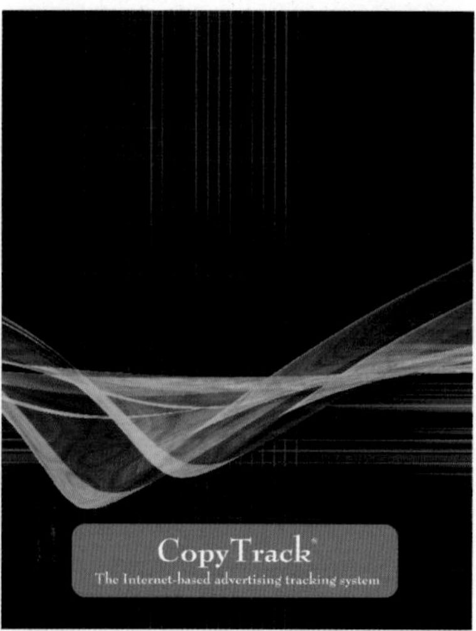

Tracking Print/Broadcast Ads One of the more useful and adaptable forms of posttesting involves tracking the effects of the ad campaign by taking measurements at regular intervals. **Tracking studies** have been used to measure the effects of advertising on awareness, recall, interest, and attitudes toward the ad and/or brand as well as purchase intentions. (Ad tracking may be applied to both print and broadcast ads but is much more common with the latter.) Personal interviews, phone surveys, mall intercepts, and even mail surveys have been used. Sample sizes typically range from 250 to 500 cases per period (usually quarterly or semiannually). Tracking studies yield perhaps the most valuable information available to the marketing manager for assessing current programs and planning for the future. (See Exhibit 9–4.)

The major advantage of tracking studies is that they can be tailored to each specific campaign and/or situation. A standard set of questions can track effects of the campaign over time. The effects of various media can also be determined, although with much less effectiveness. Tracking studies have also been used to measure the differential impact of different budget sizes, the effects of flighting, brand or corporate image, and recall of

1. Properly defined objectives
2. Alignment with sales objectives
3. Properly designed measures (e.g., adequate sample size, maximum control over interviewing process, adequate time between tracking periods)
4. Consistency through replication of the sampling plan
5. Random samples
6. Continuous interviewing (that is, not seasonal)
7. Evaluate measures related to behaviour (attitudes meet this criterion; recall of ads does not)
8. Critical evaluative questions asked early to eliminate bias
9. Measurement of competitors' performance
10. Skepticism about questions that ask where the advertising was seen or heard (TV always wins)
11. Building of news value into the study
12. "Moving averages" used to spot long-term trends and avoid seasonality
13. Data reported in terms of relationships rather than as isolated facts
14. Integration of key marketplace events with tracking results (e.g., advertising expenditures of self and competitors, promotional activities associated with price changes in ad campaigns, introductions of new brands, government announcements, changes in economic conditions)

FIGURE *9–15*

Factors the make or break tracking studies

specific copy points. Finally, when designed properly, as shown in Figure 9–15, tracking studies offer a high degree of reliability and validity.[23]

Some of the problems of recall and recognition measures are inherent in tracking studies, since many other factors may affect both brand and advertising recall. Despite these limitations, however, tracking studies are a very effective way to assess the effects of advertising campaigns.

In summary, you can see that each of the testing methods considered in this chapter has its strengths and its limitations. You may wonder: Can we actually test advertising effectiveness? What can be done to ensure a valid, reliable test? The next section of this chapter suggests some answers.

IMC Planning: Program for Measuring Effectiveness

Our discussion of what should be tested, when, and where was general and designed to establish a basic understanding of the overall process of evaluative research. Many research methods discussed in the last section showed the complexities of good research. In this section, we offer some prescriptions for managers planning for evaluative research. In a significant industry move, 21 of the largest U.S. ad agencies endorsed a set of principles aimed at "improving the research used in preparing and testing ads, providing a better creative product for clients, and controlling the cost of TV commercials."[24] This set of nine principles, called **PACT (Positioning Advertising Copy Testing)**, defines *copy testing* as research "which is undertaken when a decision is to be made about whether advertising should run in the marketplace. Whether this stage utilizes a single test or a combination of tests, its purpose is to aid in the judgment of specific advertising executions."[25] The nine principles of good copy testing are shown in Figure 9–16 on page 266.

Criteria for Effective Research

When testing methods are compared to the criteria established by PACT, it is clear that some of the principles important to good copy testing can be accomplished readily, whereas others require substantially more effort. For example, principle 6

FIGURE 9–16

Positioning Advertising Copy Testing (PACT)

1. Provide measurements that are relevant to the objectives of the advertising.
2. Require agreement about how the results will be used in advance of each specific test.
3. Provide multiple measurements (because single measurements are not adequate to assess ad performance).
4. Be based on a model of human response to communications—the reception of a stimulus, the comprehension of the stimulus, and the response to the stimulus.
5. Allow for consideration of whether the advertising stimulus should be exposed more than once.
6. Require that the more finished a piece of copy is, the more soundly it can be evaluated and require, as a minimum, that alternative executions be tested in the same degree of finish.
7. Provide controls to avoid the biasing effects of the exposure context.
8. Take into account basic considerations of sample definition.
9. Demonstrate reliability and validity.

(providing equivalent test ads) should require a minimum of effort. The researcher can easily control the state of completion of the test communications. Also fairly easy are principles 1 and 2 (providing measurements relative to the objectives sought and determining a priori how the results will be used).

Slightly more difficult are principles 3, 5, and 8, although again these factors are largely in the control of the researcher. Principle 3 (providing multiple measurements) may require little more than budgeting to make sure more than one test is conducted. At the most, it may require considering two similar measures to ensure reliability. Likewise, principle 5 (exposing the test ad more than once) can be accomplished with a proper research design. Finally, principle 8 (sample definition) requires little more than sound research methodology; any test should use the target audience to assess an ad's effectiveness. You would not use a sample of nondrinkers to evaluate new liquor commercials.

The most difficult factors to control—and the principles that may best differentiate between good and bad testing procedures—are PACT requirements 4, 7, and 9. Fortunately, however, addressing each of these contributes to the attainment of the others.

The best starting point is principle 4, which states the research should be guided by a model of human response to communications that encompasses reception, comprehension, and behavioural response. It is the best starting point, in our opinion, because it is the principle least addressed by practising researchers. If you recall, Chapter 4 proposed a number of models that could fulfill this principle's requirements. Yet even though these models have existed for quite some time, few if any common research methods attempt to integrate them into their methodologies. Most current methods do little more than provide recall scores, despite the fact many researchers have shown that recall is a poor measure of effectiveness. Models that do claim to measure such factors as attitude change or brand preference change are often fraught with problems that severely limit their reliability. An effective measure must include some relationship to the communications process.

It might seem at first glance that principle 7 (providing a nonbiasing exposure) would be easy to accomplish. But lab measures, while offering control, are artificial and vulnerable to testing effects. And field measures, while more realistic, often lose control. The Seagram and Time study may have the best of both worlds, but it is too large a task for most firms to undertake. Some of the improvements associated with the single-source systems help to solve this problem. In addition, properly designed ad tracking studies provide truer measures of the impact of the communication. As technology develops and more attention is paid to this principle, we expect to see improvements in methodologies soon.

Last but not least is principle 9, the concern for reliability and validity. Most of the measures discussed are lacking in at least one of these criteria, yet these are two of the most critical distinctions between good and bad research. If a study is properly designed, and by that we mean it addresses principles 1 through 8, it should be both reliable and valid.

As you can see, advertisers and their clients are concerned about developing *appropriate* testing methods. Adherence to these principles may not make for perfect testing, but it goes a long way toward improving the state of the art and providing guidelines for effectiveness research.

Guidelines for Effective Testing

Simply put, good tests of advertising effectiveness must address the nine principles established by PACT. One of the easiest ways to accomplish this is by following the decision sequence model in formulating promotional plans.

- *Use a consumer response model.* Early in this text we reviewed hierarchy of effects models and cognitive response models, which provide an understanding of the effects of communications and lend themselves to achieving communications goals. We also presented Rossiter and Percy's model for stating communication objectives which could also be a basis for measurement.
- *Establish communications objectives.* It is nearly impossible to show the direct impact of advertising on sales. The marketing objectives established for the promotional program are not good measures of communication effectiveness. On the other hand, attainment of communications objectives can be measured and leads to the accomplishment of marketing objectives.
- *Use both pretests and posttests.* From a cost standpoint—both actual cost outlays and opportunity costs—pretesting makes sense. It may mean the difference between success or failure of the campaign or the product. But it should work in conjunction with posttests, which avoid the limitations of pretests, use much larger samples, and take place in more natural settings. Posttesting may be required to determine the true effectiveness of the ad or campaign.
- *Use multiple measures.* Many attempts to measure the effectiveness of advertising focus on one major dependent variable—perhaps sales, recall, or recognition. As noted earlier in this chapter, advertising may have a variety of effects on the consumer, some of which can be measured through traditional methods, others that require updated thinking (recall the discussion on physiological responses). For a true assessment of advertising effectiveness, a number of measures may be required.
- *Understand and implement proper research.* It is critical to understand research methodology. What constitutes a good design? Is it valid and reliable? Does it measure what we need it to? There is no shortcut to this criterion, and there is no way to avoid it if you truly want to measure the effects of advertising.

A major study sponsored by the Advertising Research Foundation (ARF), involving interviews with 12,000 to 15,000 people, addressed some of these issues.[26] While we do not have the space to analyze this study here, note that the research was designed to evaluate measures of copy tests, compare copy testing procedures, and examine some of the PACT principles. Information on this study has been published in a number of academic and trade journals and by the ARF.

SUMMARY

This chapter introduced issues and decisions concerning the measurement of advertising and promotion effectiveness. All marketing managers want to know how well their promotional programs are working. This information is critical for planning the next period, since program adjustments and/or maintenance are based on evaluation of current strategies.

While the need for understanding how programs are working appears critical, this chapter summarized the debate regarding whether measurement is in fact needed. We conclude that research measuring the effectiveness of advertising is important to the promotional program and should be an integral part of the planning process.

We summarized many types of decisions for advertising research. Managers must consider what parts of the promotional message need to be tested. Moreover, this test could occur prior to or after the campaign, which represents another key decision. Whether a lab or field test is required also should be determined.

The chapter described many research methods that cover the stages of developing a promotional program. Many of the tests originated with one firm and were later adapted by other firms. Many companies have developed their own testing systems in conjunction with their advertising or communication agency.

Concept tests, focus groups, and mall intercepts are used to test initial ideas for creative strategies and promotional messages. Comprehension and reaction tests along with consumer juries appeared useful to testing rough or preliminary examples of print ads and television storyboards.

Finished ads are also tested prior to launching the campaign. Investment in these tests reassures managers so that costly media buys can be avoided. We reviewed porfolio tests, readability tests, and dummy advertising vehicles for evaluating completed print ads. Finished broadcast ads can be examined with theatre tests, on-air tests, and physiological measures.

Evaluations after the ads have been launched, known as posttests, offer greater confirmation of the promotion effectiveness. Print ad posttests include inquiry tests, recognition tests, and recall tests. Broadcast posttests include day-after recall tests, comprehensive measures, test marketing, single-source tracking studies, and tracking studies.

Single-source research data such as BehaviorScan, Scantrack, and Market Source were discussed for measuring the effects of advertising. These single-source systems offer strong potential for improving the effectiveness of ad measures in the future, since commercial exposures and reactions may be correlated to actual purchase behaviours.

Finally, we reviewed the criteria (defined by PACT) for sound research and suggested some ways to accomplish effective studies. It is important to recognize that different measures of effectiveness may lead to different results. Depending on the criteria used, one measure may show that an ad or promotion is effective while another states that it is not. This is why clearly defined objectives, evaluations occurring both before and after the campaigns are implemented, and the use of multiple measures are critical to determining the true effects of an IMC program.

KEY TERMS

alpha activity, *257*
comprehension and reaction tests, *252*
concept testing, *249*
consumer juries, *252*
day-after recall scores, *256*
electrodermal response, *257*
electroencephalographic (EEG) measures, *257*
eye tracking, *257*
field tests, *249*
Flesch formula, *254*
halo effect, *253*
hemispheric lateralization, *257*
inquiry tests, *259*
laboratory tests, *248*
on-air test, *256*
PACT (Positioning Advertising Copy Testing), *265*
portfolio tests, *253*
posttests, *247*
pretests, *247*
pupillometrics, *256*
recall tests, *261*
recognition method, *260*
rough tests, *250*
single-source tracking methods, *264*
split-run tests, *259*
testing bias, *248*
theatre testing, *255*
tracking studies, *264*

DISCUSSION QUESTIONS

1. Discuss some of the reasons why some companies decide not to measure the effectiveness of their promotional programs. Explain why this may or may not be a good strategy.

2. Discuss the differences between pretesting and posttesting. Give examples of each.

3. What is the difference between a lab test and a field test? When should each be employed?

4. Give examples of the various types of rough testing methodologies. Describe why a company might wish to test at this phase of the process. When might they wish to test only completed ads?

5. The bottom line for advertisers is to evoke some behaviour—for example, sales. Explain why it may be difficult to use sales to measure advertising effectiveness.

6. Why might a firm use theatre testing, on-air tests, and physiological measures to pretest its finished broadcast ads?

7. What limitations exist if one uses inquiry tests, recall tests, and recognition tests when performing market testing of ads?

8. Why are the PACT criteria important for testing effectiveness?

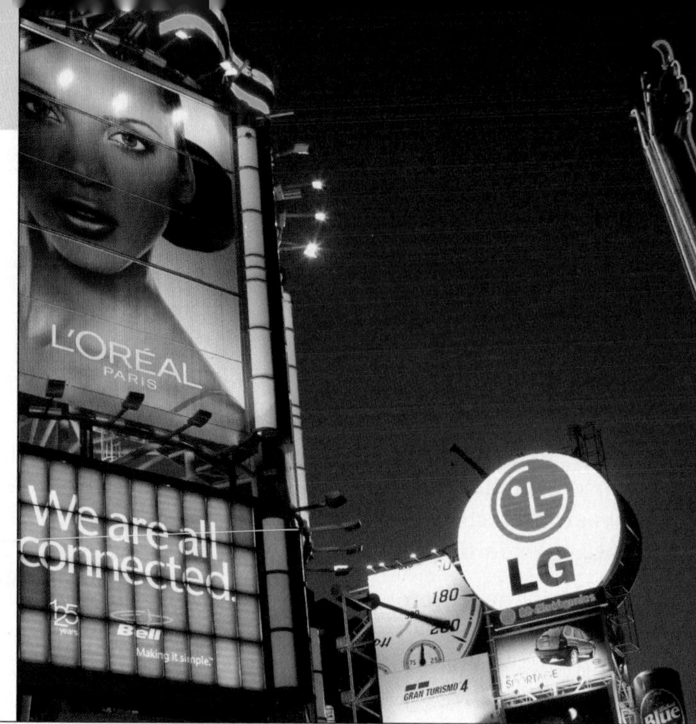

CHAPTER 10

MEDIA PLANNING AND BUDGETING FOR IMC

Chapter Objectives

- To understand the key terminology used in media planning.
- To know how a media plan is developed.
- To know the process of deciding and implementing media strategies and tactics.
- To understand the theoretical and managerial approaches for media budget setting.

Media Planners Adapt to a New Reality

Media planners are finding their task much more challenging as the media environment continues to change on many fronts. New technology—and consumer adaptation to technology—is evolving. Media firms are changing how they organize and offer their services. Communication strategists are looking for new avenues to deliver their messages. And, established media planning truisms are being criticized.

Media consumption by consumers is moving in new directions thanks to new technology. For example, the Internet represents 16 percent of all time spent with media for Canadians age 12 and older, not far behind television at 22 percent and radio at 19 percent. Broadband Internet access and DVD player adoption reached 50 percent faster than PCs, CDs, and VCRs. Television networks CTV and Global expanded online to offer broadband programs, allowing advertisers to reach consumers in a new commercial environment. Almost half of Canadian households access digital TV, leading to strong growth for video-on-demand. And with all this adoption, consumers age 29 and younger demonstrate a discernable trend toward less TV and radio, at 31 percent versus 49 percent for those 30 and older.

As consumers diverge in their media consumption, media firms are converging. Steady concentration of media ownership means that the media firms can offer deals for advertisers to place messages across many avenues, to reach as many consumers as possible. For example, with its recent purchase of CHUM, Bell Globemedia can put together TV, radio, print, and Internet packages for innovative advertisers. In addition, Transcontinental, owner of many newspapers, magazines, and direct-marketing services, expanded to online content to offer wider coverage for advertisers.

Observing these trends, marketing executives now consider media to be almost any channel in which a promotional message is delivered, even it appears to be a unique IMC tool. Managers are experimenting with a variety of new initiatives that are Internet-based, yet appear to be planned at the same time and in contrast to traditional media. Moreover, managers are looking for as many message contact points as possible, such as public relations and brand partnerships in sponsorship arrangements. In fact, the role of the media agency is now viewed to be as strategically important as that of the agency of record by two-thirds of marketing executives recently surveyed.

As the idea of media evolves to include traditional media and various IMC tools, the notion of some basic ideas like how many consumers to reach through these channels becomes murkier. And, with managers feeling the pressure to demonstrate strong return on investment for their budget, the trend is to spend on those media—like in-store events and direct marketing—that produce more measurable results.

Sources: Natalia Williams, "State of the National," *Strategy Magazine,* March 2006; Michael Szego, "Moving Beyond Reach," *Marketing Magazine,* May 22, 2006; Chris Powell, "Whetting the Media Appetite," *Marketing Magazine,* September 25, 2006; and Chris Powell, "Consumption on Demand," *Marketing Magazine,* December 4, 2006.

Question

1. Explain how these trends make the selection of what media to use so difficult for media planners.

As the opening vignette suggests, a marketer has many media opportunities available that require in-depth knowledge of all the alternatives. Media planners must now consider new options as well as recognize the changes that are occurring in traditional sources. Planning when, where, and how the message will be delivered is a complex and involved process resulting in a media plan. The purpose of the media plan is to identify and justify the decisions that will deliver the message to the target audience cost efficiently and will communicate the product, brand, and/or service message effectively.

This chapter illustrates the media planning process, discusses the development of decisions for media strategy and tactics, and presents issues and decisions related to setting an IMC budget. Later chapters will explore the relative strengths and limitations of the various media and examine each in more detail.

Media Planning

Media planning is the series of decisions involved in delivering the promotional message to the prospective purchasers and/or users of the product or brand. Media planning is a process whereby the decisions may be altered or abandoned as the plan develops. One primary decision is the type of media selected. Options include mass media such as television, newspapers, radio, and magazines, as well as out-of-the-home media such as outdoor advertising, transit advertising, and electronic billboards (Figure 10–1). A variety of other media such as direct marketing, digital media, promotional products advertising, and in-store point-of-purchase options must also be considered. Each medium has its own particular strengths and limitations that must be considered in light of the communication problem or opportunity with which the marketer is faced. This makes the media selection and all other media decisions very difficult. For example, the media planning process becomes even more complicated when the manager has to choose among alternatives within the same medium. In this section, we review the media plan content and highlight key media planning challenges.

Media Plan

The media plan determines the best way to get the advertiser's message to the market. In a basic sense, the goal of the media plan is to find that combination of media that enables the marketer to communicate the message in the most effective manner to the largest number of potential customers at the lowest cost. Most media plans have a prescribed budget that the media planner must respect. Often, media planners face the challenge of developing a plan with limited financial resources.

A number of decisions must be made throughout the media planning process. The promotional planning model in Chapter 1 discussed the process of identifying target audiences, establishing objectives, and formulating strategies for attaining them. The development of the media plan and strategies follows a similar path, except that the focus is to determine the best way to deliver the message. Thus, the media plan is generally comprised of a short section containing **media objectives**, an explanation of the **media strategy** decisions, and fine-tuning details that are known as media execution or **media tactics**. The activities involved in developing the media plan and the purposes of each are presented in Figure 10–2 on page 274. Although this simplified template illustrates broadcast and print media, the general process is similar for all media and IMC tools.

Media Objectives Just as the situation analysis leads to establishment of marketing and communications objectives, it should also lead to specific media objectives. The media objectives are not ends in themselves. Rather, they are derived from and are designed to lead to the attainment of communication and behavioural objectives,

FIGURE *10–1* Canadian market data: Net advertising revenues

COMPONENTS OF NET ADVERTISING REVENUE BY MEDIUM (IN MILLIONS OF DOLLARS)

Medium		2000	%	2001	%	2002	%	2003	%	2004	%	2005	%
Television	Total	2,450	26%	2,553	26%	2,593	26%	2,826	27%	2,963	26%	3,013	26%
	National Spot	1,200	13%	1,209	12%	1,210	12%	1,312	12%	1,308	12%	1,300	11%
	Local Spot	428	4%	418	4%	386	4%	389	4%	384	3%	385	3%
	Network	425	4%	469	5%	480	5%	503	5%	546	5%	541	5%
	Specialty	381	4%	438	5%	509	5%	607	6%	708	6%	768	7%
	Infomercial	17	0%	20	0%	18	0%	17	0%	18	0%	19	0%
Radio	Total	1,001	11%	1,049	11%	1,080	11%	1,171	11%	1,209	11%	1,299	11%
Daily Newspapers (ex. classified)	Total	1,731	18%	1,678	17%	1,684	17%	1,697	16%	1,752	16%	1,784	15%
Consumer Magazines	Total	514	5%	541	6%	558	6%	610	6%	647	6%	665	6%
Outdoor & Transit	Total	263	3%	281	3%	273	3%	284	3%	303	3%	344	3%
Internet	Total	110	1%	97	1%	176	2%	237	2%	364	3%	519	4%
Other	Total	3,449	36%	3,487	36%	3,547	36%	3,781	36%	3,981	35%	4,109	35%
	Catalogue/ Direct Mail	1,255	13%	1,264	13%	1,295	13%	1,399	13%	1,499	13%	1,547	13%
	Phone Directories	1,029	11%	1,046	11%	1,060	11%	1,121	11%	1,168	10%	1,206	10%
	Other Print (religious, school, farm, trade publication, community newspaper, weekend supp)	1,165	12%	1,177	12%	1,192	12%	1,261	12%	1,314	12%	1,356	12%
Total (All Media)		9,519	100%	9,685	100%	9,911	100%	10,607	100%	11,218	100%	11,738	100%

Sources: TVB

Television: *CRTC;* **Daily Newspaper:** *CNA for Total, estimates for breakdown;* **Radio:** *CRTC;* **General Magazine:** *Magazines Canada;* **Outdoor:** *NMR;* **Direct Mail:** *Canada Post/TVB estimate;* **Internet:** IAB; **Phone Directories:** *TeleDirect;* **Other:** *includes estimates for Community Newspaper, Trade & Other Print*

Note: Some figures may differ from previous charts due to updating.

Figures in GREEN represent Industry estimates. Broadcast revenue is based on the broadcast calendar ie. in each year indicated, the figures represent the revenue from Sept.01 of the previous year to Aug.31 of the indicated year. All other figures are based on revenue for the indicated calendar year.

Source: Reproduced from *Media Digest* 06/07, p.12

and contribute to achieving marketing objectives. Media objectives are the goals for the media program and should be limited to those that can be accomplished through media strategies. We now present examples of media objectives that relate to three communication and two behavioural objectives.

FIGURE 10–2 Activities involved in developing the media plan

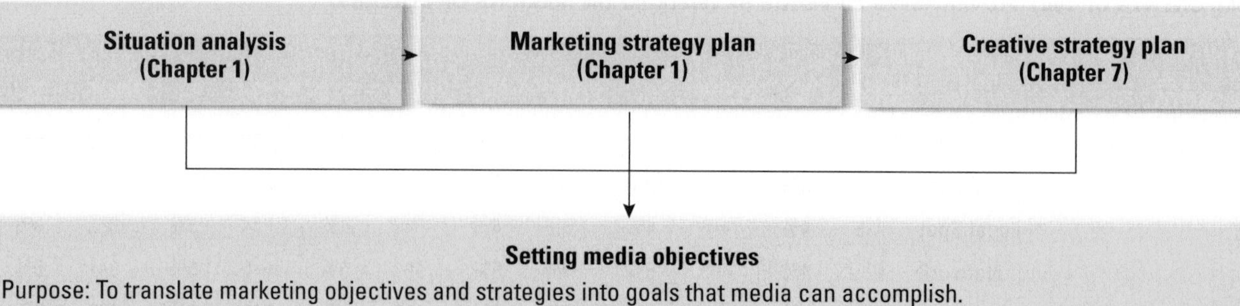

Setting media objectives

Purpose: To translate marketing objectives and strategies into goals that media can accomplish.

Determining media strategy

Purpose: To translate media goals into a strategic direction that will guide the planner's selection and use of media.

Selecting broad media classes

Purpose: To determine which broad class of media best fulfills the criteria. Involves intermedia comparison of broad media classes such as newspapers, magazines, radio, television, outdoor, transit, etc.

Selecting media within classes

Purpose: To compare and select the best media within broad classes, again using predetermined criteria.

1. If magazines were recommended, then what types?
   a. General interest
   b. Special topic
2. If television was recommended, then
   a. Broadcast or cable television?
   b. Network or spot television?
   c. If network, which program(s)?
   d. If spot, which markets?

Media vehicle broadcast

1. What specific shows?
2. Desired reach and frequency levels?
3. On which days and months are commercials to appear?
4. Placement of spots in programs or between programs?

Media vehicle print

1. What specific publications?
2. Desired reach or frequency levels?
3. Number of ads to appear and on which days and months?
4. Placements of ads: Any preferred position within media?
5. Special treatment: Gatefolds, bleeds, colour, etc.

Category Need

- Select media to sufficiently demonstrate how the target audience requires the product category.
- Provide sufficient number of exposures to ensure 80 percent of target audience understands the need for the product category.

Brand Awareness

- Select media to provide coverage of 80 percent of the target audience over a six-month period.
- Provide sufficient number of exposures to ensure 60-percent target audience brand recognition.
- Concentrate advertising during the target audience's peak purchasing time.

Brand Attitude

- Select media to ensure that 40 percent of the target audience have favourable beliefs regarding the brand's benefits and have positive emotions associated with the brand.
- Schedule creative executions over six months to heighten emotions associated with the brand and minimize message fatigue.

Brand Trial

- Select media to allow immediate purchase of brand.
- Schedule sufficient number of opportunities for target audience brand engagement.

Brand Repeat Purchase

- Select media to remind target audience of brand purchase.
- Provide sufficient advertising throughout the year to minimize target audience switching.

The content and exact number of media objectives is at the promotional planner's discretion. These examples merely illustrate the degree to which the link between objectives is not an easy step. The media objectives give direction for the media strategy and tactics decisions. Upon implementation, marketers need to know whether or not they were successful. Measures of effectiveness must consider two factors: (1) How well did these strategies achieve the media objectives? (2) How well did this media plan contribute to attaining the overall marketing and communications objectives? If the strategies were successful, they should be used in future plans. If not, their flaws should be analyzed.

Media Strategy As Figure 10–2 indicates, the primary media strategy decision concerns the use of media, moving from a broad perspective to a more specific one. The **medium** is the general category of available delivery systems, which includes broadcast media (like TV and radio), print media (like newspapers and magazines), direct marketing, out-of-home advertising, and other support media. After or during this evaluation, the media planner will consider the relative strengths and limitations of broad **media class** options. IMC Perspective 10–1 on page 276 shows how the advertising industry recognizes good media selection.

IMC PERSPECTIVE 10–1

Media Innovation Awards I

Media Innovation Awards selected by a committee designated by *Marketing Magazine* recognized the important contribution of media in marketing communication. For 2006, the evaluation committee examined 260 entries and granted 82 medal winners—10 gold, 14 silver, 19 bronze, and 39 certificates. The criteria for the awards are the following:

- The strategic media insight: What was the big idea that significantly improved the targeting precision of the delivery of the advertising message? Was there a bold new understanding of the message from the recipients' interaction with the selected medium or media?
- Tactical media creativity: What was the big idea that made the receptivity of the advertising message significantly greater? How did the tactics enhance the creative message carried and/or how did the tactics capitalize on a given medium's intrinsic attributes?
- Executional skill: What kind of "degree of difficulty" was involved in the implementation in terms of size and scope, budgetary limitations, and regulatory or media convention hurdles overcome?
- Results: Would results data substantiate exceptional achievement? What tangible evidence was there of the specific effect of the media contribution?

Best of show and stunt/PR gold went to the Assaulted Women's Helpline. Faced with the problem of getting the phone number out to women who may not have the opportunity to record it due to the presence of the one causing the assault, the crisis service used a very unique approach to discreetly deliver the message. A container that looked like a lipstick tube carried the phone number on a small piece of paper. The delivery device allowed women complete privacy and symbolically suggested they not "cover up" the experience. Distributed to women's shelters, service organizations, and emergency rooms for one year, the 9,500 tubes resulted in a 10 percent increase in call volume.

Rogers' "Shine" campaign received gold for mixed media. Rogers wanted to visually connect its target audience of consumers looking to switch cell phone providers with a clear message that illustrated the new features of its cool phones. Perhaps the most creative aspect of the campaign featured the billboard's electronically charged paper, which flashed and illuminated the "Shine" message sequentially. Carefully chosen billboard locations ensured that the message could be seen by drivers on dark winter nights. In cinemas, restaurants, bars, and malls, the target audience received audio and three-dimensional "Shine" messages. Conventional broadcast media executions acted as support to the more creative out-of-home approaches. Measured success of the campaign showed an increase in sales of 35 percent—with 216,000 new customers, awareness 60 percent higher than normal, and brand linkage greater than 75 percent.

Source: Media Innovation Awards, *Marketing Magazine,* November 9, 2006.

Question

1. Do the two winners appear to meet the criteria for winning?

In making the media strategy decisions, a media planner will consider the strategic implications of three concepts. **Reach** is a measure of the number of different audience members exposed at least once to a media vehicle in a given period of time. **Coverage** refers to the potential audience that might receive the message through a vehicle. Coverage relates to potential audience; reach refers to the actual audience delivered. (The importance of this distinction will become clearer later in this chapter.) Finally, **frequency** refers to the number of times the receiver is exposed to the media vehicle in a specified period.

Media Tactics After the general strategic direction of the media plan has been established, the media planner looks to more specific media decisions like the media vehicle. The **media vehicle** is the specific carrier within a media class.

For example, *Maclean's* is a print vehicle; *Hockey Night in Canada* is a television vehicle. As described in later chapters, each vehicle has its own characteristics as well as its own relative strengths and limitations. Specific decisions must be made as to the value of each in delivering the message.

While making the media vehicle decision, the media planner evaluates the options carefully to maximize coverage, reach, and frequency, and minimize costs. For example, according to Figure 10–2, once print has been established the media planner has to decide which specific magazine(s) to select. In addition, certain placement factors need to be carefully evaluated. The tactical decisions include relative cost estimates that may lead to refinements in the allocation of the media dollars. Finally, the complete plan is summarized in a blocking chart. The chart may indicate gaps in media coverage or some other concern that would lead the media planner to perform additional evaluation prior to completing the media plan.

Flexibility While most media plans are written annually, advertisers find it necessary to alter their objectives and strategies due to the marketing environment. An effective media plan requires a degree of flexibility. If the plan has not built in some flexibility, opportunities may be lost and/or the company may not be able to address new threats. Flexibility may be needed to address the following:

- *Market opportunities.* Sometimes a market opportunity arises that the advertiser wishes to take advantage of. For example, a special television show may prompt an advertiser to shift its expenditures from another medium.
- *Market threats.* External factors may pose a threat to the firm, and a change in media strategy is dictated. For example, a competitor may alter its media strategy to gain an edge. Failure to respond to this challenge could create problems for the firm.
- *Availability of media.* Sometimes a desired medium (or vehicle) is not available to the marketer. Perhaps the medium does not reach a particular target audience or has no time or space available. There are still some geographic areas that certain media do not reach. Alternative vehicles or media must then be considered.
- *Changes in media vehicles.* A change in a particular media vehicle may require a change in the media strategy. A drop in ratings or a change in editorial format may lead the advertiser to use different programs or print alternatives.

Media Planning Challenges

Since media planning is a series of decisions, a number of problems contribute to the difficulty of establishing the plan and reduce its effectiveness. These problems include insufficient information, inconsistent terminologies, and difficulty measuring effectiveness.

Insufficient Information While a great deal of information about markets and the media exists, media planners often require more than is available. Some data are just not measured, either because they cannot be or because measuring them would be too expensive. For example, continuous measures of radio listenership exist, but only periodic listenership studies are reported due to sample size and cost constraints.

The timing of measurements is also a problem; some audience measures are taken only at specific times of the year. (For example, **sweeps periods** in February, May, July, and November are used for measuring TV audiences and setting advertising rates.) This information is then generalized to succeeding months, so future planning decisions must be made on past data that may not reflect current behaviours. Think about planning for TV advertising for the fall season. There are no data on the audiences of new shows, and audience information taken on existing programs during the summer may not indicate how these programs will do in the fall because summer viewership is generally much lower. While the advertisers can review these programs before they air, they do not have actual audience figures.

The lack of information is even more of a problem for small advertisers, who may not be able to afford to purchase the information they require. As a result, their decisions are based on limited or out-of-date data that was provided by the media themselves, or no data at all.

Compared to media planners in the United States, Canadian media planners face additional pressures of insufficient information. The size of the American population permits extensive economies of scale, so it is not unexpected that larger U.S.-based media-buying organizations would have valuable resources. Combined with similar media consumption (e.g., popular television shows) between American and English-Canadians, there is a movement to coordinate media purchasing across North America. The end result may be improved efficiency and effectiveness of the media purchase with the sharing of information.[1]

Inconsistent Terminologies Problems arise because the cost bases used by different media often vary and the standards of measurement used to establish these costs are not always consistent. For example, print media may present cost efficiency data in terms of the cost to reach a thousand people (cost per thousand, or CPM), while broadcast and outdoor media use the cost per ratings point (CPRP). Audience information that is used as a basis for these costs has also been collected by different methods. Finally, terms that actually mean something different (such as *reach* and *coverage*) may be used synonymously, adding to the confusion.

Difficulty Measuring Effectiveness Because it is so hard to measure the effectiveness of advertising and promotions in general, it is also difficult to determine the relative effectiveness of various media or media vehicles. While progress is being made in this regard (particularly in the area of direct-response advertising), the media planner must usually guess at the impact of these alternatives.

While these problems complicate the media planning process, they do not render it an entirely subjective exercise. Media planners try to ensure that all media decisions are quantitatively determined, but sometimes managers rely on their experience and judgment when faced with these concerns. The next section of this chapter explores in more detail how media strategies are developed and ways to increase their effectiveness.

Media Strategy Decisions

Having determined what is to be accomplished, media planners consider how to achieve the media objectives. They develop and implement media strategies that consist of five main topics for decision:

- media mix
- target audience coverage
- geographic coverage
- scheduling
- reach vs frequency

The Media Mix

A wide variety of media are available to advertisers. While it is possible that only one might be employed, it is much more likely that a number of alternatives will be used. The objectives sought, the characteristics of the product or service, the size of the budget, and individual preferences are just some of the factors that determine what combination of media will be used.

FIGURE *10–3* Ad techniques—What's acceptable for Canadians?

	Acceptable		
	2004	2005	2006
Print advertising in newspapers	78%	82%	94%
Print advertising in magazines			91%
Posters on buses or subways	70%	75%	88%
Radio advertising	72%	77%	85%
Television advertising	68%	72%	82%
Digital video signs in public			69%
Billboards along roads	56%	61%	68%
Product placement in television shows	53%	52%	64%
Ads in washrooms	47%	46%	57%
Roadside billboards with a video display			47%
Banner advertising on the Internet	31%	33%	46%
Ads placed on personal property	29%	30%	35%
Ads on cell phone displays	20%	20%	28%
Pop up windows with advertising on the Internet	12%	12%	14%

Source: Dave Scholz, "Bring On the Ads," *Marketing Magazine*, December 4, 2006.

As an example, consider a promotional situation in which a product requires a visual demonstration to be communicated effectively. In this case, TV may be the most effective medium. If the promotional strategy calls for coupons to stimulate trial, print media may be necessary. For in-depth information, the Internet may be best.

While an evaluation of each media occurs within the perspective of the communication situation a media planner faces, each media has certain degrees of acceptability with Canadians, as shown in Figure 10–3. The results of this major study conducted by *Marketing Magazine* and Leger Marketing find that 86 percent of all Canadians believe there is more advertising compared to ten years ago, yet 64 percent believe it to be an acceptable level.

The context of the medium in which the ad is placed may also affect viewers' perceptions. A specific creative strategy may require certain media. Because TV provides both sight and sound, it may be more effective in generating emotions than other media; magazines may create different perceptions from newspapers. It is possible to increase the success of a product significantly through a strong creative campaign. In some situations, the media strategy to be pursued may be the driving force behind the creative strategy, as the media and creative departments work closely together to achieve the greatest impact with the audience of the specific media.

By employing a media mix, advertisers can add more versatility to their media strategies, since each medium contributes its own distinct advantages. By combining media, marketers can increase coverage, reach, and frequency levels while improving the likelihood of achieving overall communications and marketing goals. Chapters 11, 12, and 13 summarize the characteristics of each medium that make it better or worse for attaining specific communication objectives. We have organized these as media and media-usage characteristics.

Media Characteristics	**Media-Usage Characteristics**
• target audience selectivity	• control for selective exposure
• target audience coverage	• attention
• geographic coverage	• creativity for cognitive responses
• scheduling flexibility	• creativity for emotional responses
• reach	• amount of processing time
• frequency	• involvement
• cost efficiency	• clutter
• absolute cost for placement and production	• media image

Figure 10–4 provides a summary of the strengths and limitations of the media reviewed in the next three chapters. We continue with these characteristics for direct marketing and Internet marketing in their respective chapters. With so many competing variables, it becomes clear why media planners spend considerable efforts getting the media mix decision right. Finally, keep in mind that these are general characteristics that give guidance to the media mix decision. Citing these to make a media mix decision is not sufficient. Each strength and limitation needs to be related to the communication situation a specific brand faces and how the media characteristics will help the brand reach its relevant objectives.

FIGURE *10–4*

Strengths and limitations of media characteristics

	Strengths	Limitations
Television	Target audience coverage	Selective exposure
	Geographic coverage	Target audience selectivity
	Creativity for emotional responses	Absolute cost
	Creativity for cognitive responses	Amount of processing time
	Reach	Involvement
	Frequency	Clutter
	Scheduling flexibility	Media image
	Cost efficiency	
	Attention	
	Media image	
Radio	Cost efficiency	Amount of processing time
	Absolute cost	Selective exposure
	Target audience selectivity	Attention
	Geographic coverage	Clutter
	Scheduling flexibility	Creativity for emotional responses without visual
	Creativity for cognitive responses	Involvement
	Reach	Target audience coverage
	Frequency	
	Media image	
Magazines	Target audience selectivity	Target audience coverage
	Geographic coverage	Reach
	Selective exposure	Frequency
	Attention	Scheduling flexibility
	Involvement	Cost efficiency
	Amount of processing time	Absolute cost
	Creativity for cognitive responses	Clutter
	Creativity for emotional responses	
	Media image	

	Strengths	Limitations
Newspapers	Scheduling flexibility Reach Frequency Geographic coverage Cost efficiency Absolute cost Target audience coverage Media image Involvement Processing time Creativity for cognitive responses	Target audience selectivity Clutter Selective exposure Attention Creativity for emotional responses
Outdoor	Frequency Attention Geographic coverage Reach Cost efficiency Selective exposure Creativity for emotional responses Scheduling flexibility	Amount of processing time Media image Target audience selectivity Target audience coverage Absolute cost Clutter Low involvement Creativity for cognitive responses
Transit	Geographic coverage Reach Frequency Amount of processing time Selective exposure Scheduling flexibility Cost efficiency Absolute cost	Target audience coverage Target audience selectivity Creativity for cognitive responses Creativity for emotional responses Involvement Media image Clutter Attention

FIGURE 10–4

(Continued)

Target Audience Coverage

The media planner determines which target audiences should receive the most media emphasis. Developing media strategies involves matching the most appropriate media to this audience by asking, "Through which media and media vehicles can I best get my message to prospective buyers?" The issue here is to get coverage of the audience, as shown in Figure 10–5 on page 282. The optimal goal is full audience coverage, shown in the second pie chart. But this is a very optimistic scenario. More realistically, conditions shown in the third and fourth charts are most likely to occur. In the third chart, the coverage of the media does not allow for coverage of the entire audience, leaving some potential customers without exposure to the message. In the fourth chart, the marketer is faced with a problem of overexposure (also called **waste coverage**), in which the media coverage exceeds the targeted audience. If media coverage reaches people who are not sought as buyers and are not potential users, then it is wasted. This term is used for coverage that reaches people who are not potential buyers and/or users. Consumers may not be part of the intended target audience but may still be considered as potential—for example, those who buy the product as a gift for someone else.

FIGURE 10–5

Marketing coverage possibilities

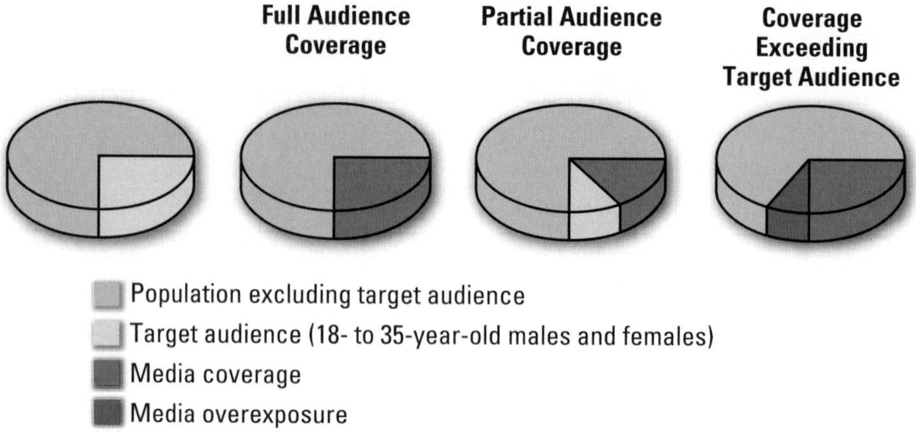

The goal of the media planner is to extend media coverage to as many of the members of the target audience as possible while minimizing the amount of waste coverage. The situation usually involves trade-offs. Sometimes one has to live with less coverage than desired; other times, the most effective media expose people not sought. In this instance, waste coverage is justified because the media employed are likely to be the most effective means of delivery available and the cost of the waste coverage is exceeded by the value gained from their use.

A variety of factors can assist media planners in making the target audience coverage decision. Some will require primary research, whereas others will be available from published (secondary) sources. This research can show the number of consumers for a particular product category across many demographic variables. We review audience information in Chapters 11, 12, and 13 as each medium has its own method.

When examining this data, media planners are often more concerned with the percentage figures and index numbers than with the raw numbers. This is largely due to the fact that the numbers provided may not be specific enough for their needs, or they question the numbers provided because of the methods by which they were collected. Another key reason is that index numbers and percentages provide a comparative view of the market.

Overall, the **index number** is considered a good indicator of the potential of the market. This number is derived from the formula

$$\text{Index} = \frac{\text{Percentage of users in a demographic segment}}{\text{Percentage of population in the same segment}} \times 100$$

An index number over 100 means use of the product is proportionately greater in that segment than in one that is average (100) or less than 100. Depending on their overall strategy, marketers may wish to use this information to determine which groups are now using the product and target them or to identify a group that is currently using the product less and attempt to develop that segment. While the index is helpful, it should not be used alone. Percentages and product usage figures are also needed to get an accurate picture of the market. Just because the index for a particular segment of the population is very high, that doesn't always mean it is the only attractive segment to target. The high index may be a result of a low denominator (a very small proportion of the population in this segment).

Understanding coverage in a multimedia environment is proving difficult for media planners. Recent research suggests that younger consumers frequently engage in the consumption of more than one medium at a time. It suggests that up to 34 percent of young people aged 12–17 use the Internet while watching television.[2] This is a significant trend since coverage historically implied a reasonably close association with exposure and processing of the advertising message. Clearly, the communication is limited even further if other media are competing for the young people's attention.

Geographic Coverage

The question of where to promote relates to geographic considerations. The question is, where will the ad dollars be more wisely spent? Should we allocate additional promotional monies to those markets where the brand is already the leader to maintain market share, or does more potential exist in those markets where the firm is not doing as well and there is more room to grow? Perhaps the best answer is that the firm should spend advertising and promotion dollars where they will be the most effective—that is, in those markets where they will achieve the desired objectives. Two useful calculations that marketers examine to make this decision are the Brand Development Index and the Category Development Index.

The **Brand Development Index (BDI)** helps marketers factor the rate of product usage by geographic area into the decision process.

$$\text{BDI} = \frac{\text{Percentage of brand to total Canadian sales in the market}}{\text{Percentage of total Canadian population in the market}} \times 100$$

The BDI compares the percentage of the brand's total sales in a given market area with the percentage of the total population in the market to determine the sales potential for that brand in that market area. An example of this calculation is shown in Figure 10–6. The higher the index number, the more market potential exists. In this case, the index number indicates this market has high potential for brand development.

The **Category Development Index (CDI)** is computed in the same manner as the BDI, except it uses information regarding the product category (as opposed to the brand) in the numerator:

$$\text{CDI} = \frac{\text{Percentage of product category total sales in market}}{\text{Percentage of total Canadian population in market}} \times 100$$

The CDI provides information on the potential for development of the total product category rather than specific brands. When this information is combined with the BDI, a much more insightful promotional strategy may be developed. One might first look at how well the product category does in a specific market area. In Alberta, for example, the category potential is low (see Figure 10–7). The marketer

FIGURE 10–6

Calculating BDI

$$\begin{aligned}\text{BDI} &= \frac{\text{Percentage of product category sales in Alberta}}{\text{Percentage of total Canadian population in Alberta}} \times 100 \\ &= \frac{50\%}{38\%} \times 100 \\ &= 132\end{aligned}$$

FIGURE 10–7

Using CDI and BDI to determine market potential

$$\begin{aligned}\text{CDI} &= \frac{\text{Percentage of product category sales in Alberta}}{\text{Percentage of total Canadian population in Alberta}} \times 100 \\ &= \frac{8\%}{10\%} \times 100 \\ &= 80\end{aligned}$$

$$\begin{aligned}\text{BDI} &= \frac{\text{Percentage of total brand sales in Alberta}}{\text{Percentage of total Canadian population in Alberta}} \times 100 \\ &= \frac{15\%}{10\%} \times 100 \\ &= 150\end{aligned}$$

FIGURE 10–8

Using BDI and CDI indexes

	High BDI	Low BDI
High CDI	High market share Good market potential	Low market share Good market potential
Low CDI	High market share Monitor for sales decline	Low market share Poor market potential

High BDI and high CDI	This market usually represents good sales potential for both the product category and the brand.
High BDI and low CDI	The category is not selling well, but the brand is; probably a good market to advertise in but should be monitored for declining sales.
Low BDI and high CDI	Both the product category and the brand are doing poorly; not likely to be a good place for advertising.
Low BDI and low CDI	The product category shows high potential but the brand is not doing well; the reasons should be determined.

analyzes the BDI to find how the brand is doing relative to other brands in this area. This information can then be used in determining how well a particular product category and a particular brand are performing and figuring what media weight (or quantity of advertising) would be required to gain additional market share, as shown in Figure 10–8.

In addition to the BDI and CDI considerations, some geographic decisions are based on the availability of the product. For example, Primus launched the first national Web telephone service in North America using voice over Internet protocol (VOIP) technology. The Talk Broadband offering promises long-distance savings of 15 percent and attempts to pre-empt cable companies in the long-distance phone market and sway current telephone users. While national in scope for the long term, the radio, print, and transit ads are shown in Toronto, Montreal, Vancouver, Halifax, Calgary, Ottawa, and Edmonton, cities where the product is initially sold.[3]

Scheduling

Obviously, companies would like to keep their advertising in front of consumers at all times as a constant reminder of the product and/or brand name. In reality, this is not possible or necessary for a variety of reasons. The primary objective of scheduling is to time promotional efforts to coincide with the highest potential buying times. For some products these times are not easy to identify; for others they are very obvious. Three scheduling methods available to the media planner—continuity, flighting, and pulsing—are shown in Figure 10–9.

Continuity refers to a continuous pattern of advertising, which may mean every day, every week, or every month. The key is that a regular (continuous) pattern is developed without gaps or nonadvertising periods. Such strategies might be used

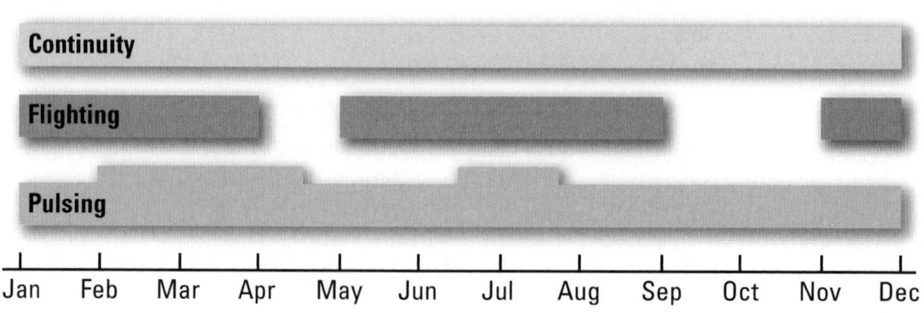

FIGURE 10–9

Three methods of promotional scheduling

for advertising for food products, laundry detergents, or other products consumed on an ongoing basis without regard for seasonality.

A second method, **flighting**, employs a less regular schedule, with intermittent periods of advertising and nonadvertising. At some time periods there are heavier promotional expenditures, and at others there may be no advertising. Many banks, for example, spend no money on advertising in the summer but maintain advertising throughout the rest of the year. Snow skis are advertised heavily between October and April; less in May, August, and September; and not at all in June and July.

Pulsing is actually a combination of the first two methods. In a pulsing strategy, continuity is maintained, but at certain times promotional efforts are stepped up. In the automobile industry, advertising continues throughout the year but may increase in April (income-tax refund time), September (when new models are brought out), and the end of the model year.

There are certain advantages and disadvantages to each scheduling method, as shown in Figure 10–10. One comprehensive study indicates that continuity is more effective than flighting. On the basis of the idea that it is important to get exposure to the message as close as possible to when the consumer is going to make the purchase, the study concludes that advertisers should continue weekly schedules as long as possible.[4] The key here may be the "as long as possible" qualification. Given a significant budget, continuity may be more of an option than it is for those with more limited budgets.

An interesting twist on scheduling is with Campbell's soup, where ads are run when the temperature drops below –5 degrees. A 10-second ad appearing on The Weather Network demonstrates the falling temperature of a thermometer turning into a Campbell's soup can. The voice-over concludes with, "When it's cold outside ... warm up with Campbell's," while the visual shows a bowl of soup and the Campbell's slogan "M'm! M'm! Good!" The campaign also features a Web banner in ads in daily e-mails sent by The Weather Network and in newspaper ads adjacent to the weather information in some Toronto newspapers.[5]

FIGURE *10–10*

Characteristics of scheduling methods

	Continuity
Advantages	Serves as a constant reminder to the consumer
	Covers the entire buying cycle
	Allows for media priorities (quantity discounts, preferred locations, etc.)
Disadvantages	Higher costs
	Potential for overexposure
	Limited media allocation possible

	Flighting
Advantages	Cost efficiency of advertising only during purchase cycles
	May allow for inclusion of more than one medium or vehicle with limited budgets
Disadvantages	Weighting may offer more exposure and advantage over competitors
	Increased likelihood of wearout
	Lack of awareness, interest, retention or promotional message during nonscheduled times
	Vulnerability to competitive efforts during nonscheduled periods

	Pulsing
Advantages	All of the same as the previous two methods
Disadvantages	Not required for seasonal products (or other cyclical products)

Reach versus Frequency

Since advertisers have a variety of objectives and face budget constraints, they usually must trade off reach and frequency. They must decide whether to have the message be seen or heard by more people (reach) or by fewer people more often (frequency).

How Much Reach Is Necessary? A universal communication objective is awareness of the product and/or brand. The more consumers are aware, the more they are likely to consider the brand throughout the decision-making process. Achieving awareness requires reach—that is, exposing potential buyers to the message. New brands or products need a very high level of reach, since the objective is to make all potential buyers aware. High reach is also desired at later purchase-decision stages. For example, a promotional strategy might use a free sample to encourage brand trial. An objective of the marketer is to reach a larger number of people with the sample, in an attempt to make them learn of the product, use it, and develop a favourable attitude toward it that may lead to an initial brand purchase.

It is possible to be exposed to more than one media vehicle with an ad. If one ad is placed on one TV show one time, the number of people exposed is the reach. If the ad is placed on two shows, the total number exposed once is **unduplicated reach**. Some people will see the ad twice. The reach of the two shows, as depicted in Figure 10–11, includes a number of people who were reached by both shows (C). This overlap is referred to as **duplicated reach**. Both unduplicated and duplicated reach figures are important. Unduplicated reach indicates potential new exposures, while duplicated reach provides an estimate of frequency. Most media buys include both forms of reach.

The problem arises because there is no known way of determining how much reach is required to achieve levels of awareness, attitude change, or buying intentions, nor can we be sure an ad placed in a vehicle will actually reach the intended audience. If advertising time on a popular news program is purchased, will everyone who is tuned to the program see the ad? No. Many viewers will leave the room, be distracted during the commercial, and so on, as shown in Figure 10–12. These data provide a good example of the difference between reach and coverage. This

FIGURE *10–11*

Representation of reach and frequency

A. Reach of One TV Program

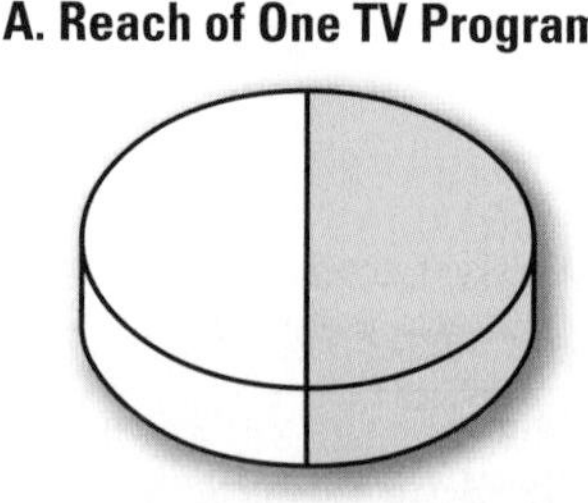

Total market audience reached

B. Reach of Two Programs

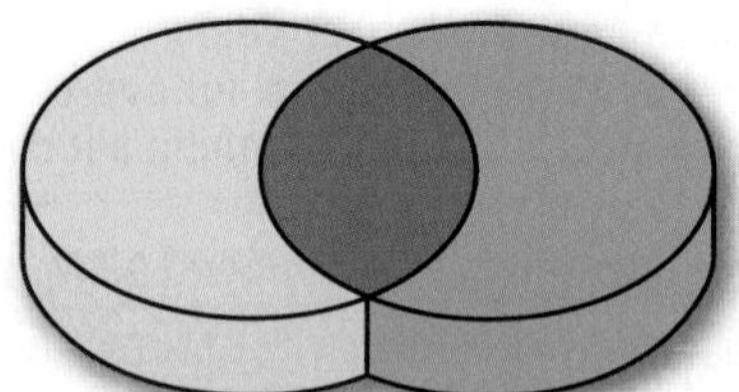

Total market audience reached

C. Duplicate Reach

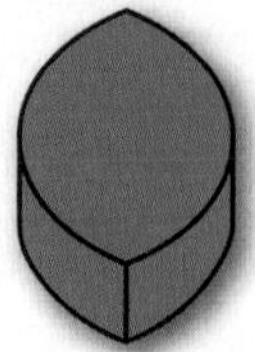

Total market reached with both shows

D. Unduplicated Reach

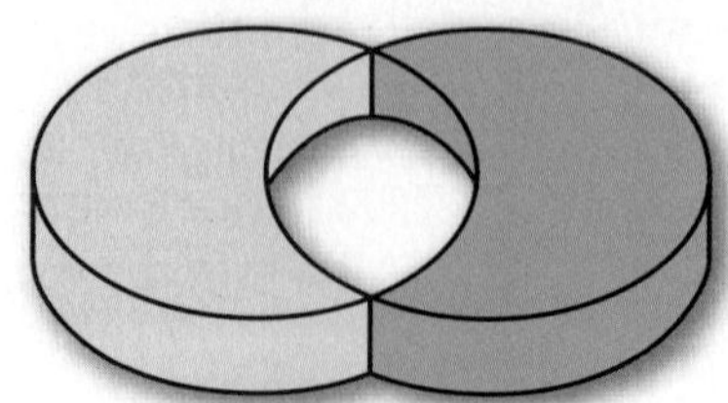

Total reach less duplicated reach

FIGURE 10–12 Who's still there to watch the ads?

How many viewers actually watch a commercial? R.D. Percy & Co. reports that its advanced people meters, equipped with heat sensors that detect viewers present, indicate that spots retain, on average, 82 percent of the average-minute ratings for the quarter hour. During early morning news programs, "commercial efficiency" (as Percy calls it), is lower because so many people are bustling about, out of the room (green), but the rate rises at night.

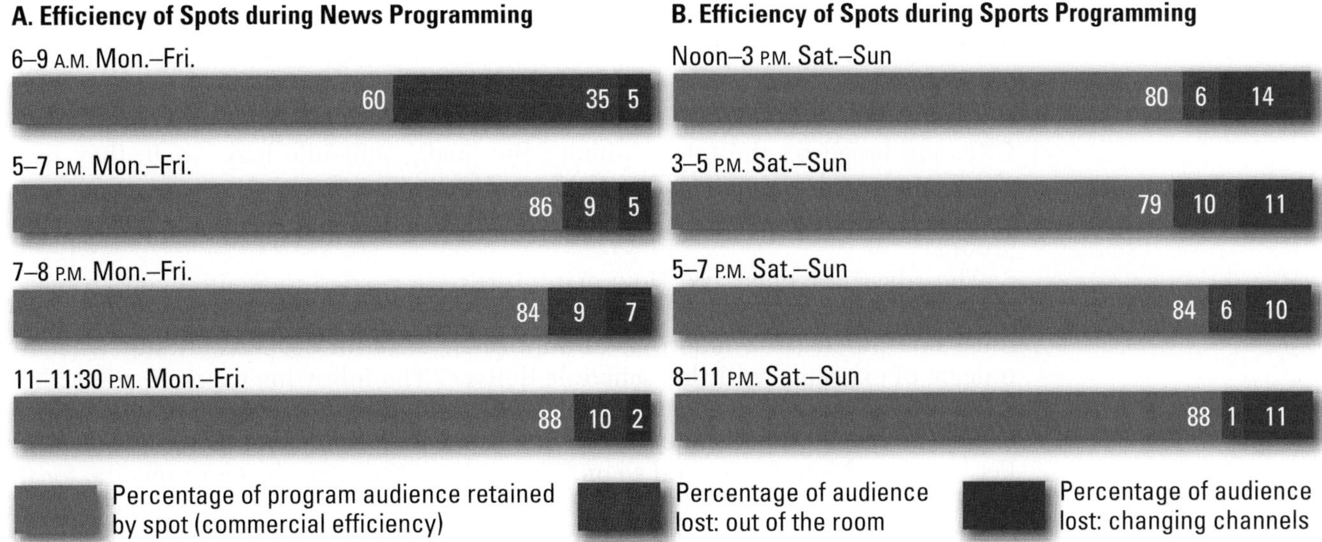

leads to the next question: What frequency of exposure is necessary for the ad to be seen and to have a communication effect?

What Frequency Level Is Needed? With respect to media planning, *frequency* carries a particular meaning. Here frequency is the number of times one is exposed to the media vehicle, not necessarily to the ad itself. While one study has estimated the actual audience for a commercial may be as much as 30 percent lower than that for the program, not all researchers agree.[6] Figure 10–12 demonstrates that, depending on the program, this number may range from 12 percent to 40 percent.

Most advertisers do agree that a 1:1 exposure ratio does not exist. So while the ad may be placed in a certain vehicle, the fact that a consumer has been exposed to that vehicle does not ensure that it has been seen. As a result, the frequency level expressed in the media plan overstates the actual level of exposure to the ad. This overstatement has led some media buyers to refer to the reach of the media vehicle as "opportunities to see" an ad rather than actual exposure to it.

Because the advertiser has no sure way of knowing whether exposure to a vehicle results in exposure to the ad, the media and advertisers have adopted a compromise: One exposure to the vehicle constitutes reach, given that this exposure must occur for the viewer even to have an opportunity to see the ad. Thus, the exposure figure is used to calculate reach and frequency levels. But this compromise does not help determine the frequency required to make an impact. The creativity of the ad, the involvement of the receiver, noise, and many other intervening factors confound any attempts to make a precise determination.

Given the complexity and uncertainty for reach and frequency, it is not too surprising to see that these decisions are not always made on hard data. Says Joseph

Ostrow, executive vice president/director of communications services with Young and Rubicam, "Establishing frequency goals for an advertising campaign is a mix of art and science but with a definite bias toward art."[7] Let us first examine the process involved in setting reach and frequency levels and then discuss the logic of each.

Using Gross Ratings Points The media buyer typically uses a numerical indicator to know how many potential audience members may be exposed to a series of commercials. A summary measure that combines the program rating and the average number of times the home is reached during this period (frequency of exposure) is a commonly used reference point known as **gross ratings points (GRP)**:

$$\text{GRP} = \text{Reach} \times \text{Frequency}$$

GRPs are based on the total audience the media schedule may reach; they use a duplicated reach estimate. GRPs can be calculated for the total population aged 2+, Adults 18+, Adults 18–34, Adults 18–49, or several other measured demographic groups.

The advertiser must ask: How many GRPs are needed to attain a certain reach? How do these GRPs translate into effective reach? For example, how many GRPs must one purchase to attain an unduplicated reach of 50 percent, and what frequency of exposure will this schedule deliver? The following example shows how this process works. A purchase of 100 GRPs could mean 100 percent of the market is exposed once or 50 percent of the market is exposed twice or 25 percent of the market is exposed four times, and so on. This information must be more specific for the marketer to use it effectively. To know how many GRPs are necessary, the manager needs to know how many members of the intended audience the schedule actually reaches. The chart in Figure 10–13 helps make this determination.

In Figure 10–13, a purchase of 100 GRPs on one network would yield an estimated reach of 32 percent of the total households in the target audience. This figure would climb to 37.2 percent if two networks were used and 44.5 percent with three. Working backward through the formula for GRPs, the estimate of frequency of exposure—3.125, 2.688, and 2.247, respectively—demonstrates the trade-off between reach and frequency. This naturally leads to the question of how much frequency is required.

Figure 10–14 summarizes the effects that can be expected at different levels of exposure, on the basis of research in this area. A number of factors may be operating, and direct relationships may be difficult to establish.[8] In addition to the results shown in Figure 10–14, Joseph Ostrow has shown that while the number of repetitions increases awareness rapidly, it has much less impact on attitudinal and behavioural responses.[9] IMC Perspective 10–2 highlights the significance of the seventh point in Figure 10–14 as media needs to be linked with creative.

FIGURE *10–13*

Estimates of reach for network GRPs

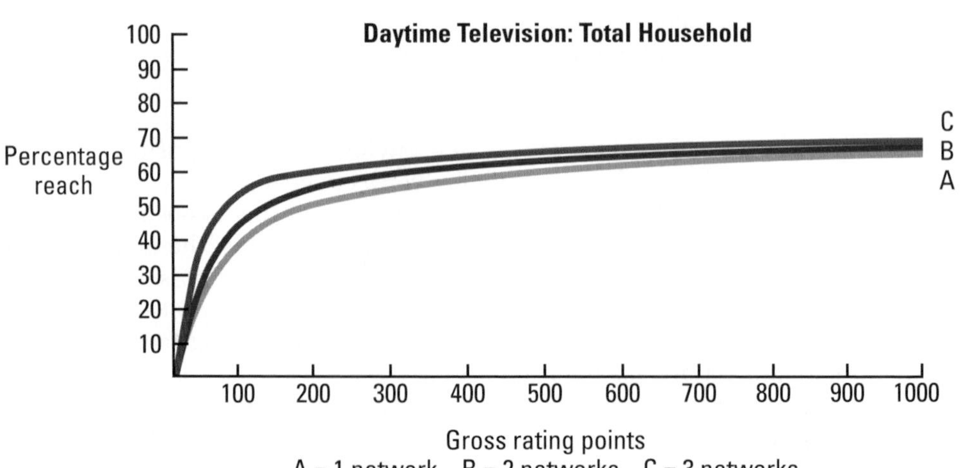

IMC PERSPECTIVE 10–2

Creative and Media Integration

"Things like creative and strategy, media people don't always get," says Esmé Röttschäfer, the creative director of media at Saatchi & Saatchi in Toronto. "But things like reach, frequency, and market coverage, creatives don't always get, either."

It's the big reason why, just over a year ago, Röttschäfer was installed in the role of overseeing Saatchi's in-house media team while simultaneously liaising with its creative unit. Part of her job, she says, is to lead the agency's exploration of new consumer touchpoints, figuring out how traditional media plans can be augmented. For the agency's work on Toyota's Yaris launch last year, it employed more than 40 touchpoints including branded pizza boxes, branded music compilations, and bathroom graffiti.

Indicative of a growing belief that to thrive in an increasingly fragmented media landscape creative agencies and their counterparts at media shops must forge a stronger bond, Rottschafer's position—or one akin to it—has been created at other agencies as well.

Last month, Toronto's Y&R hired Catharine Dunlop to become its first-ever creative channel director, a role that is rooted in the agency's creative department but that will see her liaising with sister agency Mediaedge:cia. "It's recognition of the changing media landscape and so much consumer choice," she says of her new job. "I'm just another resource and a new perspective at the table."

Steve Meraska, senior vice-president and director of connections planning at Toronto's Leo Burnett (and a 19-year veteran of the agency, who spent most of that time at sister shop Starcom MediaVest Group), says he made the move to his current role last year as a response to the shift. He says brands today differentiate themselves not only in what they say, but also by the medium in which they choose to say it. The emergence of a hybrid creative/media role, he says, points to how complicated a brand's life has become. "I think it says a lot about where the industry is going."

Where it's already been, says Röttschäfer, is a place where media plans were often drawn months before creative or strategy were produced, resulting in incongruent campaigns. Unfortunately, the situation persists. "I can't count how many times I see things on the street that make me go, 'What happened there?' That creative shouldn't be on that billboard. What were they thinking? There was a disconnect."

To that point, Meraska says a role like his isn't about sidelining media directors but rather ensuring that things stay on strategy and figuring out new intersections where it makes sense for media and creative to meet. "We can all go paint the side of a building, or paint a plane and fly it around and do whatever we want," he says. "But if it has nothing to do with the brand, then to me it's just more clutter."

Source: Paul-Mark Rendon, "It's the Medium Stupid!" *Marketing Magazine,* October 23, 2006.

Question

1. Explain how these new roles will lead to better IMC plans and results.

1. One exposure of an ad to a target group within a purchase cycle has little or no effect in most circumstances.
2. Since one exposure is usually ineffective, the central goal of productive media planning should be to enhance frequency rather than reach.
3. The evidence suggests strongly that an exposure frequency of two within a purchase cycle is an effective level.
4. Beyond three exposures within a brand purchase cycle or over a period of four or even eight weeks, increasing frequency continues to build advertising effectiveness at a decreasing rate but with no evidence of decline.
5. Although there are general principles with respect to frequency of exposure and its relationship to advertising effectiveness, differential effects by brand are equally important.
6. Nothing we have seen suggests that frequency response principles or generalizations vary by medium.
7. The data strongly suggest that wearout is not a function of too much frequency; it is more of a creative or copy problem.

FIGURE *10–14*

The effects of reach and frequency

Determining Effective Reach and Frequency Since marketers have budget constraints, they must decide whether to increase reach at the expense of frequency or increase the frequency of exposure but to a smaller audience. A number of factors influence this decision. For example, a new product or brand introduction will attempt to maximize reach, particularly unduplicated reach, to create awareness in as many people as possible as quickly as possible. At the same time, for a high-involvement product or one whose benefits are not obvious, a certain level of frequency is needed to achieve effective reach.

Effective reach represents the percentage of a vehicle's audience reached at each effective frequency increment. This concept is based on the assumption that one exposure to an ad may not be enough to convey the desired message. As we saw earlier, no one knows the exact number of exposures necessary for an ad to make an impact, although advertisers have settled on three as the minimum. Effective reach (exposure) is shown in the shaded area in Figure 10–15 in the range of 3 to 10 exposures. Fewer than 3 exposures is considered insufficient reach, while more than 10 is considered overexposure and thus ineffective reach. This exposure level is no guarantee of effective communication; different messages may require more or fewer exposures. For example, Jack Myers, president of Myers Reports, argues that the three-exposure theory was valid in the 1970s when consumers were exposed to approximately 1,000 ads per day. Now that they are exposed to 3,000 to 5,000 per day, three exposures may not be enough. Adding in the fragmentation of television, the proliferation of magazines, and the advent of a variety of alternative media leads Myers to believe that 12 exposures may be the minimum level of frequency required. Also, Jim Surmanek, vice president of International Communications Group, contends that the complexity of the message, message length, and recency of exposure also impact this figure.[10]

Since they do not know how many times the viewer will actually be exposed, advertisers typically purchase GRPs that lead to more than three exposures to increase the likelihood of effective reach and frequency.

Determining effective reach is further complicated by the fact that when calculating GRPs, advertisers use a figure that they call **average frequency**, or the average number of times the target audience reached by a media schedule is exposed to the vehicle over a specified period. The problem with this figure is revealed in the following scenario:

Consider a media buy in which:

50 percent of audience is reached 1 time.
30 percent of audience is reached 5 times.
20 percent of audience is reached 10 times.
Average frequency = 4

FIGURE *10–15* Graph of effective reach

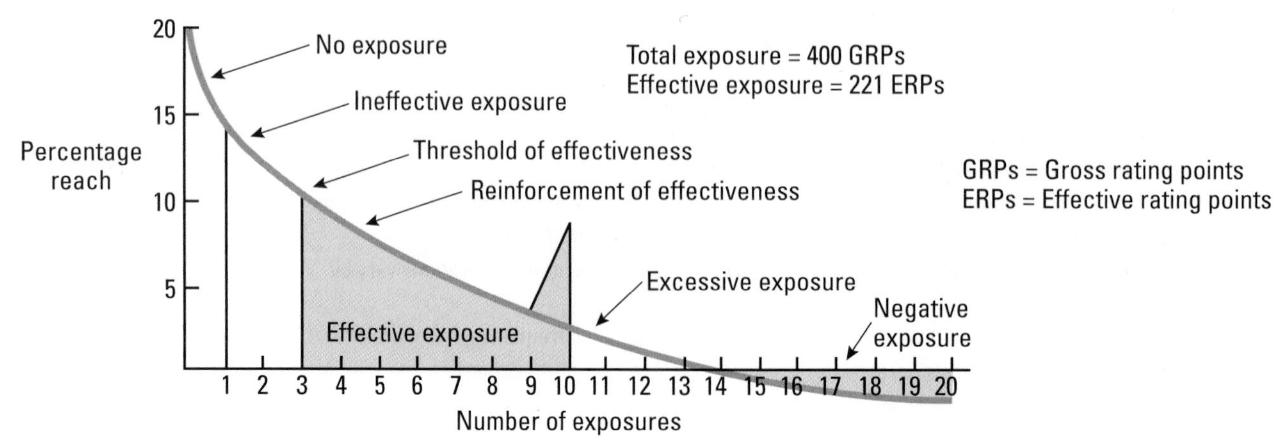

In this media buy, the average frequency is 4, which is slightly more than the number established as effective. Yet a full 50 percent of the audience receives only one exposure. Thus, the average frequency number can be misleading, and using it to calculate GRPs might result in underexposing the audience.

Although GRPs have their problems, they can provide useful information to the marketer. A certain level of GRPs is necessary to achieve awareness, and increases in GRPs are likely to lead to more exposures and/or more repetitions—both of which are necessary to have an effect on higher-order objectives. Perhaps the best advice for purchasing GRPs is offered by Ostrow, who recommends the following strategies:[11]

- Instead of using average frequency, the marketer should decide what minimum frequency goal is needed to reach the advertising objectives effectively and then maximize reach at that frequency level.
- To determine effective frequency, one must consider marketing factors, message factors, and media factors. (See Figure 10–16.)

FIGURE ***10–16***

Factors important in determining frequency levels

Marketing Factors

- *Brand history.* New brands generally require higher frequency levels.
- *Brand share.* The higher the brand share, the lower the frequency level required.
- *Brand loyalty.* The higher the loyalty, the lower the frequency level required.
- *Purchase cycles.* Shorter purchasing cycles require higher frequency levels to maintain top-of-mind awareness.
- *Usage cycle.* Products consumed frequently usually require a higher level of frequency.
- *Share of voice.* Higher frequency levels are required with many competitors.
- *Target audience.* The ability of the target group to learn and to retain messages has a direct effect on frequency.

Message or Creative Factors

- *Message complexity.* The simpler the message, the less frequency required.
- *Message uniqueness.* The more unique the message, the lower the frequency level required.
- *New versus continuing campaigns.* New campaigns require higher levels of frequency.
- *Image versus product sell.* Image ads require higher levels of frequency than specific product sell ads.
- *Message variation.* A single message requires less frequency; a variety of messages requires more.
- *Wearout.* Higher frequency may lead to wearout.
- *Advertising units.* Larger units of advertising require less frequency than smaller ones.

Media Factors

- *Clutter.* The more advertising that appears in the media used, the more frequency is needed to break through the clutter.
- *Editorial environment.* The more consistent the ad is with the editorial environment, the less frequency is needed.
- *Attentiveness.* Media vehicles with higher attention levels require less frequency.
- *Scheduling.* Continuous scheduling requires less frequency than does flighting or pulsing.
- *Number of media used.* The fewer media used, the lower the level of frequency required.
- *Repeat exposures.* Media that allow for more repeat exposures require less frequency.

In summary, the reach-versus-frequency decision, while critical, is very difficult to make. A number of factors must be considered, and concrete rules do not always apply. The decision is often more of an art than a science.

Media Tactics Decisions

Once the initial media strategy has been determined, the marketer addresses three media tactics decisions: media vehicle, relative cost estimates, and blocking chart.

Media Vehicle

Once the medium or media has been determined, the media planner must consider the most suitable media vehicle. Certain media vehicles enhance the creativity of a message because they create a mood that carries over to the communication. For example, think about the moods created by the following magazines: *Gourmet, Skiing, Travel,* and *House Beautiful.* Each of these special-interest vehicles puts the reader in a particular mood. The promotion of fine wines, ski boots, luggage, and home products is enhanced by this mood. What different images might be created for a product advertised in the following media?

The *National Post* versus the *Toronto Star*
Architectural Digest versus *Reader's Digest*
A highly rated prime-time TV show versus an old rerun

The message may require a specific medium and a certain media vehicle to achieve its objectives. Likewise, certain media and vehicles have images that may carry over to the perceptions of messages placed within them. The explanation of these considerations is the **vehicle option source effect**, "the differential impact that the advertising exposure will have on the same audience member if the exposure occurs in one media option rather than another."[12] People perceive ads differently depending on their context.[13]

Once the media vehicle consideration is resolved, the media planner considers some other fine-tuning. The location within a particular medium (front page versus back page) and size of ad or length of commercial also merit examination. For example, research has demonstrated that readers pay more attention to larger ads.[14]

Relative Cost Estimates

One of the more important decisions in the development of media strategy is cost estimating. The value of any strategy can be determined by how well it delivers the message to the audience with the lowest cost and the least waste. We have already explored a number of factors, such as reach, frequency, and availability, that affect this decision. The marketer tries to arrive at the optimal delivery by balancing cost with each of these. As the following discussion shows, understanding cost figures may not be as easy as it seems and knowledge of them can improve a media plan as it reaches the tactical stage.

Advertising and promotional costs can be categorized in two ways. The **absolute cost** of the medium or vehicle is the actual total cost required to place the message. For example, a full-page four-colour ad in *Chatelaine* magazine costs about $42,000. **Relative cost** refers to the relationship between the price paid for advertising time or space and the size of the audience delivered; it is used to compare media vehicles. Relative costs are important because the manager must try to optimize audience delivery within budget constraints. Since a number of alternatives are available for delivering the message, the advertiser must evaluate the relative costs associated with these choices. The way media costs are provided and problems in comparing these costs across media often make such evaluations difficult.

	Canadian Living	*Chatelaine*
Per-page cost	$35,500	$46,505
Circulation	519,045	586,136
Calculation of CPM	$\frac{\$35,500 \times 1,000}{519,045}$	$\frac{\$46,505 \times 1,000}{586,136}$
CPM	$68.39	$79.34

FIGURE *10–17*

Cost per thousand computations: *Canadian Living* versus *Chatelaine*

To evaluate alternatives, advertisers must compare the relative costs of media as well as vehicles within these media. Unfortunately, the broadcast, print, and out-of-home media do not always provide the same cost breakdowns, nor necessarily do vehicles within the print media. Following are the cost bases used:

1. **Cost per thousand (CPM).** For years the magazine industry has provided cost breakdowns on the basis of cost per thousand people reached. The formula for this computation is

$$\text{CPM} = \frac{\text{Cost of ad space (absolute cost)}}{\text{Circulation}} \times 1{,}000$$

Figure 10–17 provides an example of this computation for two vehicles in the same medium—*Canadian Living* and *Chatelaine*—and shows that (all other things being equal) *Canadian Living* is a more cost-efficient buy. (We will come back to "all other things being equal" in a moment.)

Like magazines, newspapers now use the cost-per-thousand formula to determine relative costs. As shown in Figure 10–18, the *National Post* costs significantly more to advertise in than does *The Globe and Mail* (again, all other things being equal).

2. **Cost per ratings point (CPRP).** The broadcast media provide a different comparative cost figure, referred to as cost per ratings point or *cost per point (CPP),* based on the following formula:

$$\text{CPRP} = \frac{\text{Cost of commercial time}}{\text{Program rating}}$$

An example of this calculation for a spot ad in a local TV market is shown in Figure 10–19 on page 294. It indicates that *Survivor* would be more cost-effective than *CSI.*

293

	Globe and Mail	*National Post*
Cost per page	$64,800	$53,070
Circulation	335,013	240,030
Calculation	$\text{CPM} = \frac{\text{Page cost} \times 1,000}{\text{Circulation}}$	
	$= \frac{\$64,800 \times 1,000}{335,013}$	$\frac{\$53,070 \times 1,000}{240,030}$
	= $193.43	$221.10

FIGURE *10–18*

Comparative costs in newspaper advertising

FIGURE 10–19

Comparison of cost per ratings point: *CSI* versus *Survivor* in a local TV market

	CSI	*Survivor*
Cost per spot ad	$9,000	$8,000
Rating	20	19
Reach (households)	195,140	185,383
Calculation	$9,000/20	$8,000/19
CPRP (CPP)	$450	$421

As you can see, it is difficult to make comparisons across various media. What is the broadcast equivalent of cost per thousand? In an attempt to standardize relative costing procedures, the broadcast and newspaper media have begun to provide costs per thousand, using the following formulas:

$$\text{Television}: \frac{\text{Cost of 1 unit of time} \times 1{,}000}{\text{Program rating}} \qquad \text{Newspapers}: \frac{\text{Cost of ad space} \times 1{,}000}{\text{Circulation}}$$

While the comparison of media on a cost-per-thousand basis is important, intermedia comparisons can be misleading. The ability of TV to provide both sight and sound, the longevity of magazines, and other characteristics of each medium make direct comparisons difficult. The media planner should use the cost-per-thousand numbers but must also consider the specific characteristics of each medium and each media vehicle in the decision.

The cost per thousand may overestimate or underestimate the actual cost efficiency. Consider a situation where some waste coverage is inevitable because the circulation exceeds the target audience. If the people reached by this message are not potential buyers of the product, then having to pay to reach them results in too low a cost per thousand, as shown in scenario A of Figure 10–20. We must use the potential reach to the target audience—the destination sought—rather than the overall circulation figure. A medium with a much higher cost per thousand may be a wiser buy if it is reaching more potential receivers. (Most media buyers rely on **target CPM (TCPM)**, which calculates CPMs based on the target audience, not the overall audience.)

CPM may also underestimate cost efficiency. Magazine advertising space sellers have argued for years that because more than one person may read an issue, the actual reach is underestimated. They want to use the number of **readers per copy** as the true circulation. This would include a **pass-along rate**, estimating the number of people who read the magazine without buying it. Scenario B in Figure 10–20 shows how this underestimates cost efficiency. Consider a family in which a father, mother, and two teenagers read each issue of *Maclean's*. While the circulation figure includes only one magazine, in reality there are four potential exposures in these households, increasing the total reach.

While the number of readers per copy makes intuitive sense, it has the potential to be extremely inaccurate. The actual number of times the magazine changes hands is difficult to determine. While research is conducted, pass-along estimates are very subjective and using them to estimate reach is speculative. These figures are regularly provided by the media, but managers are selective about using them. At the same time, the art of media buying enters, for many magazines' managers have a good idea how much greater the reach is than their circulation figures provided.

In addition to the potential for over- or underestimation of cost efficiencies, CPMs are limited in that they make only quantitative estimates of the value of media. While they may be good for comparing very similar vehicles, they are less valuable in making intermedia comparisons. We have already noted some differences among media that preclude direct comparisons.

FIGURE 10–20

Cost per thousand estimates

Scenario A: Overestimation of Efficiency

Target audience	18–49
Magazine circulation	400,000
Circulation to target audience	65% (260,000)
Cost per page	$15,600

$$\text{CPM} = \frac{\$15,600 \times 1,000}{400,000} = \$39$$

$$\text{CPM (actual target audience)} = \frac{\$15,600 \times 1,000}{260,000} = \$60$$

Scenario B: Underestimation of Efficiency

Target audience	All age groups, male and female
Magazine circulation	400,000
Cost per page	$15,600
Pass-along rate	3

$$\text{CPM (based on readers per copy)} = \frac{\text{Page cost} \times 1,000}{260,000 + 3(260,000)} = \frac{\$15,600 \times 1,000}{1,040,000}$$

$$= \$15.00$$

*Assuming pass-along was valid.

Blocking Chart

The media planning process typically concludes with a blocking chart. The **blocking chart** summarizes many of the media strategy and media tactics decisions made thus far, and includes extensive implementation details that guide the media buyers as they attempt to achieve the media objectives. An example for the Toyota Sienna is shown in Figure 10–21.

A blocking chart is typically formatted according to some type of calendar. While it is often done on a weekly basis, a firm with limited communications may organize it monthly. On the other hand, a firm with extensive communications may produce a blocking chart on a daily basis for all or critical parts of its annual media plan. For example, if a firm launches a new product, daily communications during the first few weeks can be critical and specific media exposure is planned in minute detail.

A synopsis of the media choice decisions with respect to television, print, and out-of-home media may also be contained in the blocking chart. In this age of IMC,

FIGURE 10–21 The Toyota Sienna blocking chart shows all media and IMC tools

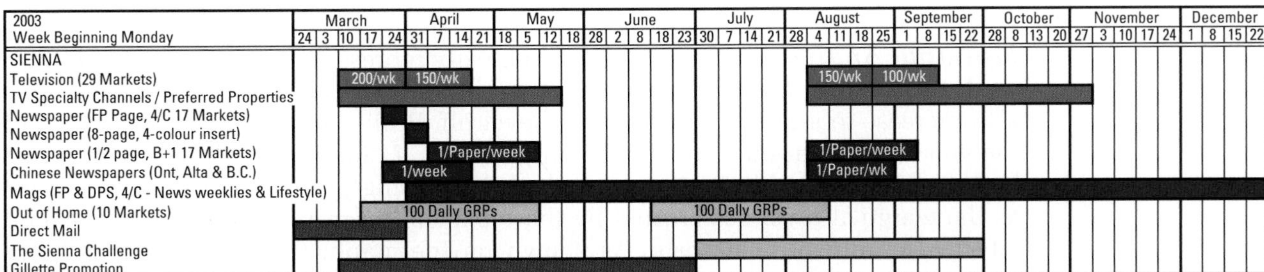

Source: www.cassies.ca

the blocking chart can also contain elements of other communication tools such as marketing events, public relations, or direct response tools. In all likelihood, the blocking chart will break these media choices down by different vehicles and different geographic markets.

Another key detail of the blocking chart is showing the relative weight of media expenditures. For example, it could illustrate the number of GRPs per week for each city. Related to this is a clear indication of the reach and frequency of each media decision.

Because the blocking chart concludes the media planning process, the media expenditures have to be included either in summary form or accompanying the blocking chart. This information allows managers to assess the quality of the media plan and to determine if any adjustments need to be made during the planning time frame.

While we have briefly highlighted the nature of a blocking chart, it may in fact be more than one chart. If a firm is using multiple media across many months and geographic markets, it may have one summary chart and other supporting charts that break the information down into more readable and action-oriented subsections. Remember that a blocking chart is also a communication tool that has to be organized and presented so that all participants are familiar with all decisions.

Budget Setting

We noted earlier in this chapter that the media plan has to contribute its part in achieving communication objectives such as brand awareness and brand attitude. While establishing media and communication objectives is an important part of the planning process, the degree to which these objectives can be obtained is a function of the media budget or how much the firm wishes to invest in advertising. No organization has an unlimited budget, so objectives must be set with the budget in mind and the budget has to be realistic to achieve any media and communication objectives.

We include budget issues in this chapter because of this inherent trade-off between objectives and financial resources. We do not discuss budget issues for other IMC tools extensively in this book for two reasons. First, the remaining IMC tools are often dependent on media expenditures. For example, aspects of public relations campaigns use media. Advertisers use media advertising to direct visitors to their websites. Second, as we noted earlier in this book, the planning process for all marketing communications follows or is consistent with established planning processes of advertising. Thus, the budgeting concepts here directly transfer to other IMC tools.

The remainder of this section provides insight into some underlying theory with respect to budget setting, discusses how companies budget for promotional efforts, and demonstrates the inherent strengths and weaknesses associated with these theoretical and managerial approaches.

Theoretical Approaches in Budget Setting

Most of the approaches used to establish advertising budgets are based on marginal analysis or sales response models.

Marginal Analysis Figure 10–22 graphically represents the concept of **marginal analysis**. As advertising/promotional expenditures increase, sales and gross margins also increase to a point, but then they level off. Profits are shown to be a result of the gross margin minus advertising expenditures. Using this theory to establish its budget, a firm would continue to spend advertising/promotional dollars as long as the marginal revenues created by these expenditures exceeded the incremental advertising/promotional costs. As shown on the graph, the optimal expenditure

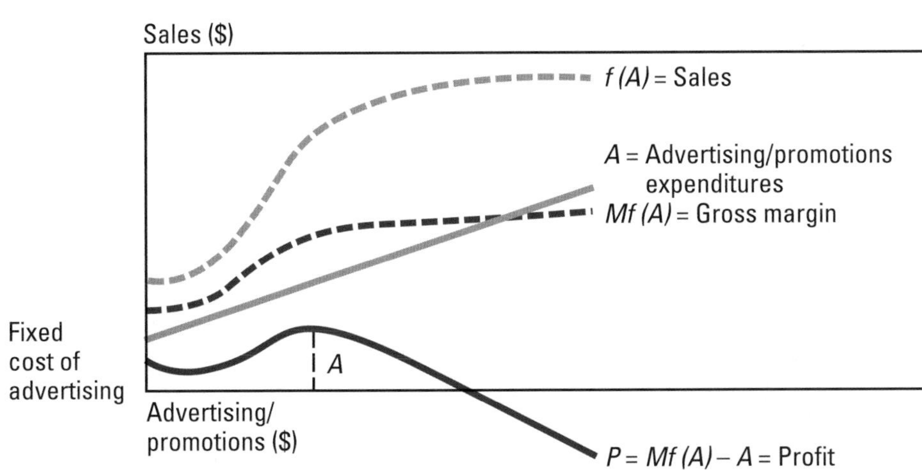

FIGURE 10–22
Marginal analysis

level is the point where marginal costs equal the marginal revenues they generate (point A). If the sum of the advertising/promotional expenditures exceeded the revenues they generated, one would conclude the appropriations were too high and scale down the budget. If revenues were higher, a higher budget might be in order.

While marginal analysis seems logical intuitively, certain weaknesses limit its usefulness. These weaknesses include the assumptions that (1) sales are a direct result of advertising and promotional expenditures and this effect can be measured and (2) advertising and promotion are solely responsible for sales. Let us examine each of these assumptions in more detail.

1. *Assumption that sales are a direct measure of advertising and promotions efforts.* Previously, we discussed the fact that the advertiser needs to set communications objectives that contribute to accomplishing overall marketing objectives but at the same time are separate. One reason for this strategy is that it is often difficult, if not impossible, to demonstrate the effects of advertising and promotions on sales. In studies using sales as a direct measure, it has been almost impossible to establish the contribution of advertising and promotion.[15] Thus, to try to show that the size of the budget will directly affect sales of the product is misleading. A more logical approach would be to examine the impact of specific budgets for each communication tool on the attainment of specific communications objectives for each tool.
2. *Assumption that sales are determined solely by advertising and promotion.* This assumption ignores the remaining elements of the marketing mix—price, product, and distribution—which do contribute to a company's success. Environmental factors may also affect the promotional program, leading the marketing manager to assume the advertising was or was not effective when some other factor may have helped or hindered the accomplishment of the desired objectives.

Sales Response Models The sales curve in Figure 10–22 shows sales levelling off even though advertising and promotions efforts continue to increase. The relationship between advertising and sales has been the topic of much research and discussion designed to determine the shape of the response curve.

Almost all advertisers subscribe to one of two models of the advertising/sales response function: the concave-downward function or the S-shaped response curve.

- *The concave-downward function.* After reviewing more than 100 studies of the effects of advertising on sales, researchers concluded that the effects of advertising budgets follow the microeconomic law of diminishing returns.[16] That is, as the amount of advertising increases, its incremental value decreases.

FIGURE 10–23 Advertising sales/response functions

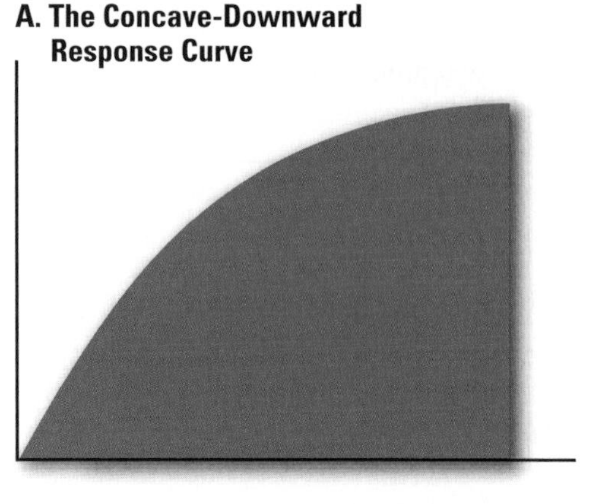

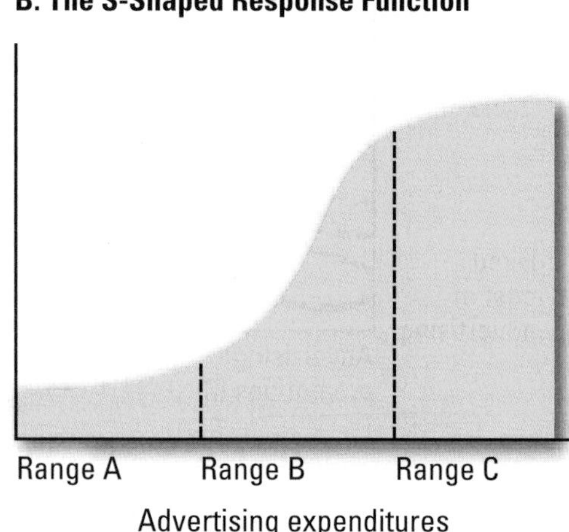

The logic is that those with the greatest potential to buy will likely act on the first (or earliest) exposures, while those less likely to buy are not likely to change as a result of the advertising. For those who may be potential buyers, each additional ad will supply little or no new information that will affect their decision. Thus, according to the **concave-downward function model**, the effects of advertising quickly begin to diminish, as shown in Figure 10–23A. Budgeting under this model suggests that fewer advertising dollars may be needed to create the optimal influence on sales.

- *The S-shaped response curve.* Many advertising managers assume the **S-shaped response curve** (Figure 10–23B), which projects an S-shaped response function to the budget outlay (again measured in sales). Initial outlays of the advertising budget have little impact (as indicated by the essentially flat sales curve in range A). After a certain budget level has been reached (the beginning of range B), advertising and promotional efforts begin to have an effect, as additional increments of expenditures result in increased sales. This incremental gain continues only to a point, however, because at the beginning of range C additional expenditures begin to return little or nothing in the way of sales. This model suggests a small advertising budget is likely to have no impact beyond the sales that may have been generated through other means (for example, word of mouth). At the other extreme, more does not necessarily mean better: Additional dollars spent beyond range B have no additional impact on sales and for the most part can be considered wasted. As with marginal analysis, one would attempt to operate at that point on the curve in area B where the maximum return for the money is attained.

Even though marginal analysis and the sales response curves may not apply directly, they give managers insight into a theoretical basis of how the budgeting process should work. Some empirical evidence indicates the models may have validity. One study, based on industry experience, has provided support for the S-shaped response curve; the results indicate that a minimum amount of advertising dollars must be spent before there is a noticeable effect on sales.[17]

A weakness in attempting to use sales as a direct measure of response to advertising is that various situational factors may have an effect. In one comprehensive study, 20 variables were shown to affect the advertising/sales ratio. Figure 10–24 lists these factors and their relationships.[18] For a product characterized by emotional buying motives, hidden product qualities, and/or a strong basis for differentiation, advertising would have a noticeable impact on sales. Products characterized as large

FIGURE 10–24 Factors influencing advertising budgets

Factor	Relationship of Advertising/Sales	Factor	Relationship of Advertising/Sales
Product Factors		**Customer Factors**	
Basis for differentiation	+	Industrial products users	—
Hidden product qualities	+	Concentration of users	+
Emotional buying motives	+	**Strategy Factors**	
Durability	—	Regional markets	—
Large dollar purchase	—	Early stage of brand life cycle	+
Purchase frequency	Curvilinear	High margins in channels	—
Market Factors		Long channels of distribution	+
Stage of product life cycle		High prices	+
Introductory	+	High quality	+
Growth	+	**Cost Factors**	
Maturity	—	High profit margins	+
Decline	—		
Inelastic demand	+		
Market share	—		
Competition			
Active	+		
Concentrated	+		
Pioneer in market	—		

Note: + relationship means the factor leads to a positive effect of advertising on sales; — relationship indicates little or no effect of advertising on sales.

dollar purchases and those in the maturity or decline stages of the product would be less likely to benefit. The study showed that other factors involving the market, customer, costs, and strategies employed have different effects.

The results of this study are interesting but limited, since they relate primarily to the percentage of sales dollars allocated to advertising and the factors influencing these ratios. As we will see later in this chapter, the percentage-of-sales method of budgeting has inherent weaknesses in that the advertising and sales effects may be reversed. So we cannot be sure whether the situation actually led to the advertising/sales relationship or vice versa. Thus, while these factors should be considered in the budget appropriation decision, they should not be the sole determinants of where and when to increase or decrease expenditures.

Managerial Approaches in Budget Setting

The theoretical approaches to establishing the promotional budget are seldom employed. Instead, a number of methods developed through practice and experience are implemented. This section reviews some of the more traditional methods of setting budgets and the relative advantages and disadvantages of each. It is important to review many approaches since firms may employ more than one method. Budgeting methods also vary according to the size and sophistication of the firm. For example, small firms rely on some of the simpler approaches.

Types of Budgeting Approaches

One approach discussed in this section may be referred to as **top-down budgeting** because an amount is established (usually at an executive level) and then the monies are passed down to the various departments (as shown in Figure 10–25). These budgets are essentially predetermined and have no true theoretical basis. Top-down methods include the affordable method, arbitrary allocation, percentage of sales, competitive parity, and return on investment (ROI).

The major flaw associated with the top-down methods is that these judgmental approaches lead to predetermined budget appropriations often not linked to objectives and the strategies designed to accomplish them. A more effective budgeting strategy would be to consider the firm's communications objectives and budget what is deemed necessary to attain these goals. As noted earlier, the promotional planning model shows the budget decision as an interactive process, with the communications objectives on one hand and the promotional mix alternatives on the other. The idea is to budget so these promotional mix strategies can be implemented to achieve the stated objectives. This is known as bottom-up budgeting; we review two approaches, the objective and test method and payout planning.

The Affordable Method In the **affordable method**, the firm determines the amount to be spent in various areas such as production and operations. Then it allocates what's left to advertising and promotion, considering this to be the amount it can afford. The task to be performed by the advertising/promotions function is not considered, and the likelihood of under- or overspending is high, as no guidelines for measuring the effects of various budgets are established.

This approach is common among small firms where cash flow concerns are prominent. Unfortunately, it is also used in large firms, particularly those that are not marketing-driven and do not understand the role of advertising and promotion. For example, some high-tech firms focus on new product development and engineering and assume that the product, if good enough, will sell itself. In these companies, little money may be left for performing the advertising and promotions tasks.

The logic for this approach stems from "We can't be hurt with this method" thinking. That is, if we know what we can afford and we do not exceed it, we will not get into financial problems. While this may be true in a strictly accounting

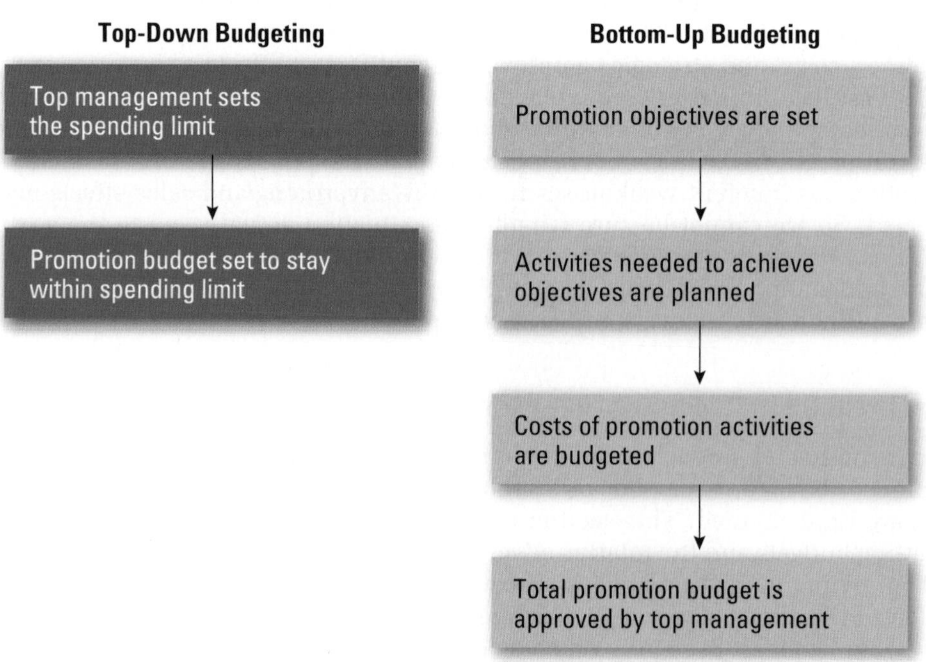
Top-Down Budgeting
Top management sets the spending limit
Promotion budget set to stay within spending limit
Bottom-Up Budgeting
Promotion objectives are set
Activities needed to achieve objectives are planned
Costs of promotion activities are budgeted
Total promotion budget is approved by top management

FIGURE *10–25*

Top-down versus bottom-up approaches to budget setting

sense, it does not reflect sound managerial decision making from a marketing perspective. Often this method does not allocate enough money to get the product off the ground and into the market. In terms of the S-shaped sales response model, the firm is operating in range A. Or the firm may be spending more than necessary, operating in range C. When the market gets tough and sales and/or profits begin to fall, this method is likely to lead to budget cuts at a time when the budget should be increased.

Arbitrary Allocation Perhaps an even weaker method than the affordable method for establishing a budget is **arbitrary allocation**, in which virtually no theoretical basis is considered and the budgetary amount is often set by fiat. That is, the budget is determined by management solely on the basis of what is felt to be necessary. In a discussion of how managers set advertising budgets, Melvin Salveson reported that these decisions may reflect "as much upon the managers' psychological profile as they do economic criteria."[19] While Salveson was referring to larger corporations, the approach is no less common in small firms and nonprofit organizations.

The arbitrary allocation approach has no obvious advantages. No systematic thinking has occurred, no objectives have been budgeted for, and the concept and purpose of advertising and promotion have been largely ignored. Other than the fact that the manager believes some monies must be spent on advertising and promotion and then picks a number, there is no good explanation why this approach continues to be used. Yet budgets continue to be set this way, and our purpose in discussing this method is to point out only that it is used—not recommended.

Percentage of Sales Perhaps the most commonly used method for budget setting (particularly in large firms) is the **percentage-of-sales method**, in which the advertising and promotions budget is based on sales of the product. Management determines the amount by either (1) taking a percentage of the sales dollars or (2) assigning a fixed amount of the unit product cost to promotion and multiplying this amount by the number of units sold. These two methods are shown in Figure 10–26.

Proponents of the percentage-of-sales method cite a number of advantages. It is financially safe and keeps ad spending within reasonable limits, as it bases spending on the past year's sales or what the firm expects to sell in the upcoming year. Thus, there will be sufficient monies to cover this budget, with increases in sales leading to budget increases and sales decreases resulting in advertising decreases. The percentage-of-sales method is simple, straightforward, and easy to implement. Regardless of which basis—past or future sales—is employed, the calculations used to arrive at a budget are not difficult. Finally, this budgeting approach is generally

Method 1: Straight Percentage of Sales		
2000	Total dollar sales	$1,000,000
	Straight % of sales at 10%	$100,000
2001	Advertising budget	$100,000
Method 2: Percentage of Unit Cost		
2000	Cost per bottle to manufacturer	$4.00
	Unit cost allocated to advertising	$1.00
2001	Forecast sales, 100,000 units	
2001	Advertising budget (100,000 × $1)	$100,000

FIGURE *10–26*

Alternative methods for computing percentage of sales for Eve Cologne

stable. While the budget may vary with increases and decreases in sales, as long as these changes are not drastic the manager will have a reasonable idea of the parameters of the budget.

At the same time, the percentage-of-sales method has some serious disadvantages, including the basic premise on which the budget is established: sales. Letting the level of sales determine the amount of advertising and promotions dollars to be spent reverses the cause-and-effect relationship between advertising and sales. It treats advertising as an expense associated with making a sale rather than an investment.

Another problem with this approach was actually cited as an advantage earlier: stability. Proponents say that if all firms use a similar percentage, that will bring stability to the marketplace. But what happens if someone varies from this standard percentage? The problem is that this method does not allow for changes in strategy either internally or from competitors. An aggressive firm may wish to allocate more monies to the advertising and promotions budget, a strategy that is not possible with a percentage-of-sales method unless the manager is willing to deviate from industry standards.

The percentage-of-sales method of budgeting may result in severe misappropriation of funds. If advertising and promotion have a role to perform in marketing a product, then allocating more monies to advertising will, as shown in the S-shaped curve, generate incremental sales (to a point). If products with low sales have smaller promotion budgets, this will hinder sales progress. At the other extreme, very successful products may have excess budgets, some of which may be better appropriated elsewhere.

The percentage-of-sales method is also difficult to employ for new product introductions. If no sales histories are available, there is no basis for establishing the budget. Projections of future sales may be difficult, particularly if the product is highly innovative and/or has fluctuating sales patterns.

Finally, if the budget is contingent on sales, decreases in sales will lead to decreases in budgets when they most need to be increased. Continuing to cut the advertising and promotion budgets may just add impetus to the downward sales trend (Figure 10–27). On the other hand, some of the more successful companies have allocated additional funds during hard times or downturns in the cycle of sales. Companies that maintain or increase their ad expenditures during recessions achieve increased visibility and higher growth in both sales and market share (compared to those that reduce advertising outlays). For example, Sunkist can attribute at least some of its success in maintaining its strong image to the fact that it has maintained consistent levels of advertising expenditures over 80 years, despite recessions.[20]

FIGURE *10–27*

Investments pay off in later years

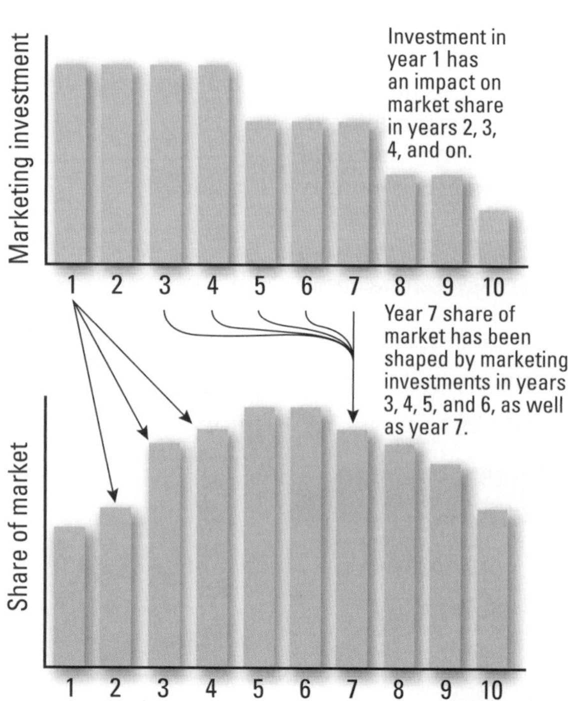
Marketing investment
Investment in year 1 has an impact on market share in years 2, 3, 4, and on.
1 2 3 4 5 6 7 8 9 10
Year 7 share of market has been shaped by marketing investments in years 3, 4, 5, and 6, as well as year 7.
Share of market
1 2 3 4 5 6 7 8 9 10

A variation on the percentage-of-sales method uses a percentage of projected future sales as a base. This method also uses either a straight percentage of projected sales or a unit cost projection. One advantage of using future sales as a base is that the budget is not based on last year's sales. As the market changes, management must factor the effect of these changes on sales into next year's forecast rather than relying on past data. The resulting budget is more likely to reflect current conditions and be more appropriate. While this appears to be a remedy for some of the problems discussed here, the reality is that problems with forecasting, cyclical growth, and uncontrollable factors limit its effectiveness.

Competitive Parity In many industries or product categories, we observe firms with similar advertising expenditures resulting from a competitive analysis. Competitors' advertising expenditures are available from market research firms, trade associations, and other advertising industry periodicals. Larger corporations often subscribe to services that track media and other communication expenditures. For example, videotape services provide competitors with information, and Nielsen's new technology (discussed in Chapter 11) allows full reporting of all commercials. Smaller companies often use a **clipping service**, which clips competitors' ads from local print media, allowing the company to work backward to determine the cumulative costs of the ads placed.

In the **competitive parity method**, managers establish budget amounts by matching the competition's percentage-of-sales expenditures. The argument is that setting budgets in this fashion takes advantage of the collective wisdom of the industry. It also takes the competition into consideration, which leads to stability in the marketplace by minimizing marketing warfare. If companies know that competitors are unlikely to match their increases in promotional spending, they are less likely to take an aggressive posture to attempt to gain market share. This minimizes unusual or unrealistic ad expenditures.

The competitive parity method has a number of disadvantages, however. For one, it ignores the fact that advertising and promotions are designed to accomplish specific objectives by addressing certain problems and opportunities. Second, it assumes that because firms have similar expenditures, their programs will be equally effective. This assumption ignores the contributions of creative executions and/or media allocations, as well as the success or failure of various promotions. Further, it ignores possible advantages of the firm itself; some companies simply make better products than others. A study by Yoo and Mandhachitara indicates that a competitive parity strategy must consider the fact that a competitor's advertising can actually benefit one's own firm, and that one competitor's gain is not always the other's loss. As shown in Figure 10–28 there are four different situations to determine how the competitive budgets may impact sales—only one of which involved the zero-sum scenario.[21]

FIGURE *10–28* Competitors' advertising outlays do not always hurt

Competitor's Advertising Affects Your Sales...	Your Advertising Affects Competitor's Sales... Negatively	Your Advertising Affects Competitor's Sales... Positively
Positively	**Advertiser's Advantage** • Your brand is stronger than the competing brand. • Rely on advertising rather than other promotional tools. • Attack with your advantage.	**Symbiotic Competition** • The brands are strong complements to each other. • The market is growing. • Maintain modest advertising.
Negatively	**Zero-Sum Competition** • The brands are strong substitutes for each other. • The market is not growing. • Increase advertising to defend your position.	**Competitor's Advantage** • The competing brand is stronger than your brand. • Find a niche position. • Improve product quality. • Use different promotional tools rather than advertising. • Decrease advertising.

Also, there is no guarantee that competitors will continue to pursue their existing strategies. Since competitive parity figures are determined by examination of competitors' previous years' promotional expenditures (short of corporate espionage), changes in market emphasis and/or spending may not be recognized until the competition has already established an advantage. Further, there is no guarantee that a competitor will not increase or decrease its own expenditures, regardless of what other companies do. Finally, competitive parity may not avoid promotional wars.

In summary, few firms employ the competitive parity method as a sole means of establishing the promotional budget. This method is typically used in conjunction with the percentage-of-sales or other methods. It is never wise to ignore the competition; managers must always be aware of what competitors are doing. But they should not just emulate them in setting goals and developing strategies.

Return on Investment (ROI) In the percentage-of-sales method, sales dictate the level of advertising appropriations. But advertising causes sales. In the marginal analysis and S-shaped curve approaches, incremental investments in advertising and promotions lead to increases in sales. The key word here is *investment.* In the **ROI budgeting method**, advertising and promotions are considered investments, like plant and equipment. Thus, the budgetary appropriation (investment) leads to certain returns. Like other aspects of the firm's efforts, advertising and promotion are expected to earn a certain return.

While the ROI method looks good on paper, the reality is that it is rarely possible to assess the returns provided by the promotional effort—at least as long as sales continue to be the basis for evaluation. Thus, while managers are certain to ask how much return they are getting for such expenditures, the question remains unanswered, and ROI remains a virtually unused method of budgeting.

Objective and Task Method It is important that objective setting and budgeting go hand in hand rather than sequentially. It is difficult to establish a budget without specific objectives in mind, and setting objectives without regard to how much money is available makes no sense. For example, a company may wish to create awareness among X percent of its target market. A minimal budget amount will be required to accomplish this goal, and the firm must be willing to spend this amount.

The **objective and task method** of budget setting consists of three steps: (1) defining the communications objectives to be accomplished, (2) determining the specific strategies and tasks needed to attain them, and (3) estimating the costs associated with performance of these strategies and tasks. The total budget is based on the accumulation of these costs.

Implementing the objective and task approach is somewhat more involved. The manager must monitor this process throughout and change strategies depending on how well objectives are attained. As shown in Figure 10–29, this process involves several steps:

1. *Isolate objectives.* When the promotional planning model is presented, a company will have two sets of objectives to accomplish—the marketing objectives for the product and the communications objectives. After the former are established, the task involves determining what specific communications objectives will be designed to accomplish these goals. Communications objectives must be specific, attainable, and measurable, as well as time limited.
2. *Determine tasks required.* A number of elements are involved in the strategic plan designed to attain the objectives established. (These strategies constitute the remaining chapters in this text.) These tasks may include advertising in various media, sales promotions, and/or other elements of the promotional mix, each with its own role to perform.
3. *Estimate required expenditures.* Buildup analysis requires determining the estimated costs associated with the tasks developed in the previous step. For example, it involves costs for developing awareness through advertising, trial through sampling, and so forth.

4. *Monitor.* As we saw in Chapter 9 on measuring effectiveness, there are ways to determine how well one is attaining established objectives. Performance should be monitored and evaluated in light of the budget appropriated.
5. *Reevaluate objectives.* Once specific objectives have been attained, monies may be better spent on new goals. Thus, if one has achieved the level of consumer awareness sought, the budget should be altered to stress a higher-order objective such as evaluation or trial.

The major advantage of the objective and task method is that the budget is driven by the objectives to be attained. The managers closest to the marketing effort will have specific strategies and input into the budget-setting process.

The major disadvantage of this method is the difficulty of determining which tasks will be required and the costs associated with each. For example, specifically what tasks are needed to attain awareness among 50 percent of the target audience? How much will it cost to perform these tasks? While these decisions are easier to determine for certain objectives—for example, estimating the costs of sampling required to stimulate trial in a defined market area—it is not always possible to know exactly what is required and/or how much it will cost to complete the job. This process is easier if there is past experience to use as a guide, with either the existing product or a similar one in the same product category.

However, the process is especially difficult for new product introductions. As a result, budget setting using this method is not as easy to perform or as stable as some of the methods discussed earlier. Given this disadvantage, many marketing managers have stayed with those top-down approaches for setting the total expenditure amount. The objective and task method offers advantages over methods discussed earlier but is more difficult to implement when there is no track record for the product. The following section addresses the problem of budgeting for new product introductions.

Payout Planning The first months of a new product's introduction typically require heavier-than-normal advertising and promotion appropriations to stimulate higher levels of awareness and subsequent trial. After studying more than 40 years of Nielsen figures, James O. Peckham estimated that the average share of advertising to sales ratio necessary to launch a new product successfully is approximately 1.5:2.0.[22] This means that a new entry should be spending at approximately twice the desired market share, as shown in the two examples in Figure 10–30 on page 306. For example, in the food industry, brand 101 gained a 12.6 percent market share by spending 34 percent of the total advertising dollars in this category. Likewise, brand 401 in the toiletry industry had a 30 percent share of advertising dollars to gain 19.5 percent of sales.

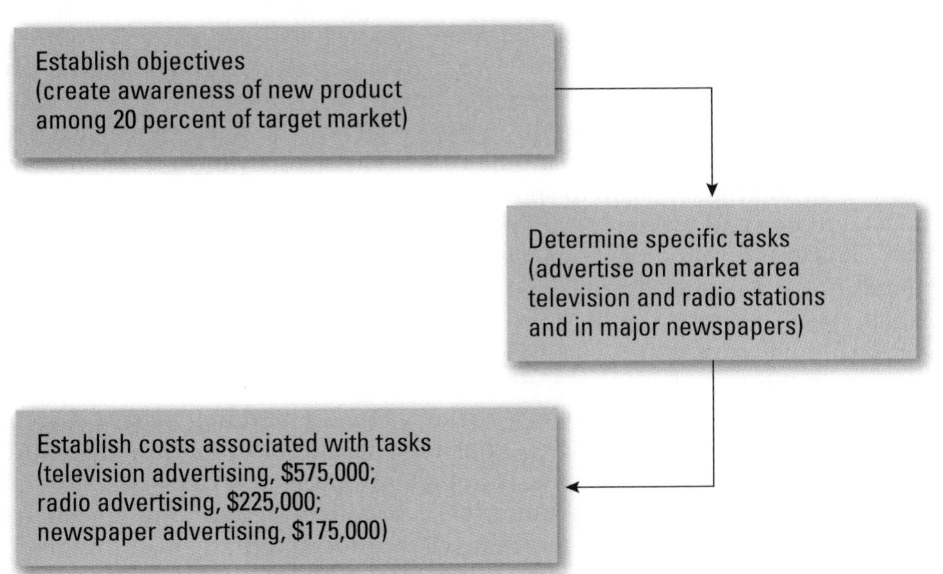

FIGURE 10–29
The objective and task method

FIGURE *10–30*

Share of advertising/sales relationship (two-year summary)

A. New Brands of Food Products

Brand	Average share of advertising	Attained share of sales	Ratio of share of advertising to share of sales
101	34%	12.6%	2.7
102	16	10.0	1.6
103	8	7.6	1.1
104	4	2.6	1.5
105	3	2.1	1.4

B. New Brands of Toiletry Products

Brand	Average share of advertising	Attained share of sales	Ratio of share of advertising to share of sales
401	30%	19.5%	1.5
402	25	16.5	1.5
403	20	16.2	1.2
404	12	9.4	1.3
405	16	8.7	1.8
406	19	7.3	2.6
407	14	7.2	1.9
408	10	6.0	1.7
409	7	6.0	1.2
410	6	5.9	1.0
411	10	5.9	1.7
412	6	5.2	1.2

To determine how much to spend, marketers often develop a **payout plan** that determines the investment value of the advertising and promotion appropriation. The basic idea is to project the revenues the product will generate, as well as the costs it will incur, over two to three years. Based on an expected rate of return, the payout plan will assist in determining how much advertising and promotions expenditure will be necessary when the return might be expected. A three-year payout plan is shown in Figure 10–31. The product would lose money in year 1, almost break even in year 2, and finally begin to show substantial profits by the end of year 3.

The advertising and promotion figures are highest in year 1 and decline in years 2 and 3. This appropriation is consistent with Peckham's findings and reflects the additional outlays needed to make as rapid an impact as possible. For example, that shelf space is limited, and store owners are not likely to wait around for a product to become successful. The budget also reflects the firm's guidelines for new product expenditures, since companies generally have established deadlines by which the product must begin to show a profit. Finally, building market share may be more difficult than maintaining it—thus the substantial dropoff in expenditures in later years. While the payout plan is not always perfect, it does guide the manager in establishing the budget. When used in conjunction with the objective and task method, it provides a much more logical approach to budget setting than the top-down approaches previously discussed.

	Year 1	Year 2	Year 3
Product sales	15.0	35.50	60.75
Profit contribution (@ $0.50/case)	7.5	17.75	30.38
Advertising/promotions	15.0	10.50	8.50
Profit (loss)	(7.5)	7.25	21.88
Cumulative profit (loss)	(7.5)	(0.25)	21.63

FIGURE *10–31*

Example of three-year payout plan ($ millions)

Summary of Budgeting Methods

Why have we discussed some budgeting methods if they are not recommended for use or have severe disadvantages that limit their effectiveness? It is important knowledge to understand the various methods used in order to recognize their limitations, especially since these flawed methods are commonly employed by marketers throughout the United States, Europe, and Canada, as demonstrated in the results of a number of research studies shown in Figure 10–32. Tradition and top management's desire for control are probably the major reasons why top-down methods continue to be popular. These data highlight some trends over time. The use of percentage-of-sales methods and competitive parity remains high. Unfortunately, the affordable method appears to be on the increase; however, the use of the objective and task method also continues to increase.

FIGURE *10–32* Comparison of methods for budgeting

Study	San Augustine and Foley (1975)	Patti and Blasko (1981)	Lancaster and Stern (1983)	Blasko and Patti (1984)	Hung and West (1991)
Population	Large Consumer/ Industrial Advertisers	Large Consumer/ Services Advertisers	Large Consumer Advertisers	Large Industrial Advertisers	Large & Medium Advertisers in U.K., U.S., & Canada
Sample	50/50	54	60	64	100
Methods					
Quantitative models	2/4	51	20	3	NA
Objective and task	6/10	63	80	74	61
Percent anticipated sales	50/28	53	53	16	32
Unit anticipated sales	8/10	22	28	NA	9
Percent past year's sales	14/16	20	20	23	10
Unit past year's sales	6/4	NA	15	2	NA
Affordable	30/26	20	13	33	41
Arbitrary	12/34	4	NA	13	NA
Competitive parity	NA	24	33	21	25
Previous budget	NA	NA	3	NA	NA
Share of voice	NA	NA	5	NA	NA
Others	26/10	NA	12	NA	NA

Note: Figures exceed 100% due to multiple responses. NA = No answer.

In a more recent study of how managers make decisions regarding advertising and promotion budgeting decisions, George Low and Jakki Mohr interviewed 21 managers in eight consumer-product firms. Their research focused on the decision processes and procedures used to set spending levels on the factors that influence the allocation of advertising and promotion dollars.

On the basis of their results, the authors concluded that the budget-setting process is still a perplexing issue to many managers and that institutional pressures led to a greater proportion of dollars being spent on sales promotions than managers would have preferred. In addition, the authors concluded that to successfully develop and implement the budget, managers must (1) employ a comprehensive strategy to guide the process, avoiding the piecemeal approach often employed, (2) develop a strategic planning framework that employs an integrated marketing communications philosophy, (3) build in contingency plans, (4) focus on long-term objectives, and (5) consistently evaluate the effectiveness of programs.[23]

IMC Planning: Budget Allocation

Once the overall budget has been determined, the next step is to allocate it. The allocation decision involves determining the relative expenditures across IMC tools and markets while accounting for market-share goals, client/agency policies, and organizational characteristics.

IMC Tools

The promotional budget is allocated to broadcast, print, and out-of-home media as suggested in the media plan, and among other IMC tools such as sales promotion, public relations, Internet, and direct marketing. As noted in Chapter 1, firms are increasingly evaluating and employing all IMC tools to achieve their communication and behavioural objectives. The degree to which a firm engages in more tools to achieve its objectives influences the relative emphasis. Figure 10–33 summarizes examples of traditional media plans and others with evolving IMC tools.[24]

FIGURE *10–33* Summary of examples of target and media choices

Brand	Target	Media
Toronto Star $500,000	Potential classified ad purchasers, ages 40–59, married, suburbs	Magazine, newspaper, radio, TV in elevators; high-traffic display, GO transit buses and shelters
Sprite $170,000	New consumers, urban youth, males, ages 16–18	Virtual community Habbo Hotel, transit shelter; donated basketball backboard and net to community centres; court chalk art; Sprite's animated spokesperson, Miles Thirst, hosts own MusiquePlus VJ show
Thermasilk $200,000	New consumers (repositioning); girls, ages 15–20	Virtual community Habbo Hotel, banner ads, microsite, contest, TV advertising
Home Depot	Women ages 30–49, professional, house proud	Domestic Divas via *Chatelaine* Internet site, contests, *Chatelaine* magazine, e-newsletter
BMW 525i	Men who like to drive; high income, urban; manager travelling in three major cities	*Air Canada* magazine and in-flight television; radio; outdoor (billboard, garages, elevator, gas pump); banner ads

These examples are reflected in macro statistics cited earlier. As shown in Figure 10–1, total Canadian expenditures for media advertising, Internet, and catalogue/direct mail total about $12 billion. Some of these IMC tools continue their strength over time. For example, television advertising consistently commands approximately one-quarter of all media expenditures at about $3 billion. However, the ratio among different types of television advertising has evolved, with less emphasis on spot advertising and greater emphasis for specialty channel advertising.

Representing print media, newspaper, consumer magazines, and specialty print typically constitute one-third of all media expenditures at approximately $4 billion. In contrast, Internet has grown from no expenditures in 1996 to more than $500 million ten years later and accounts for 4 percent of all media expenditures. This amount equals the decline in catalogue/direct mail and phone directory advertising, which has declined from 27 percent to 23 percent.

In comparison, other promotional tools constitute extensive expenditures. Public relations activities like sponsorship approach $1 billion, while promotional products approximate $2 billion in Canada. And while an accurate accounting for all sales promotion expenditures is difficult to achieve, estimating sales promotion expenditures at 2 percent of all Canadian retail sales culminates in a total of $7 billion.

As these macro statistics indicate, firms have a variety of tools and approaches for delivering messages to their target audiences, and careful consideration of the allocation across the tools each year is a central task for IMC planning.

Market Share Goals

While the budget should be allocated according the specific promotional tools needed to accomplish the objectives, the size of the market affects the amount of money invested in promotion. In smaller markets, it is often easier and less expensive to reach the target audience. Too much of an expenditure in these markets will lead to saturation and a lack of effective spending. In larger markets, the target audience may be more dispersed and thus more expensive to reach.

For a variety of reasons, some markets hold more potential than others. When particular markets hold higher potential, the marketing manager may decide to allocate additional monies to them. Keep in mind that just because a market does not have high sales does not mean it should be ignored. The key is potential—and a market with low sales but high potential may be a candidate for additional appropriations.

Two studies in the *Harvard Business Review* discussed advertising spending with the goal of maintaining and increasing market share.[25] John Jones compared the brand's share of market with its share of advertising voice (the total value of the main media exposure in the product category). Jones classified the brands as "profit taking brands, or underspenders" and "investment brands, those whose share of voice is clearly above their share of market." His study indicated that for those brands with small market shares, profit takers are in the minority; however, as the brands increase their market share, nearly three out of five have a proportionately smaller share of voice.

Jones noted that three factors can be cited to explain this change. First, new brands generally receive higher-than-average advertising support. Second, older, more mature brands are often "milked"—that is, when they reach the maturity stage, advertising support is reduced. Third, there's an advertising economy of scale whereby advertising works harder for well-established brands, so a lower expenditure is required. Jones concluded that for larger brands, it may be possible to reduce advertising expenditures and still maintain market share. Smaller brands, on the other hand, have to continue to maintain a large share of voice.

FIGURE 10–34

The share of voice (SOV) effect and ad spending: priorities in individual markets

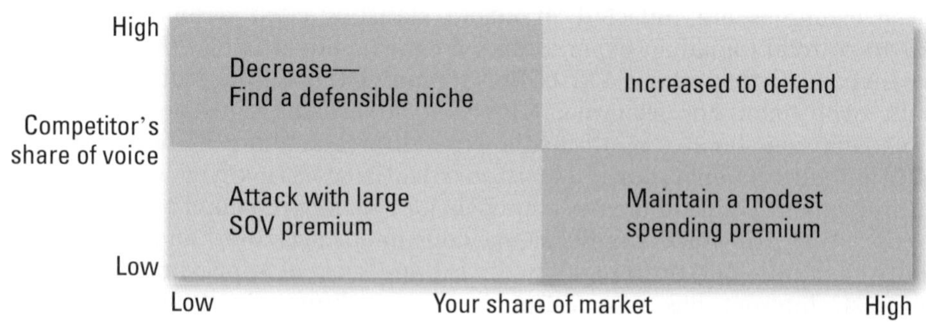

James Schroer addressed the advertising budget in a situation where the marketer wishes to increase market share. His analysis suggests that marketers should focus on markets where competition is weak and/or underspending instead of advertising nationally. Figure 10–34 shows Schroer's suggestions for spending priorities in various markets.

One factor influencing these suggestions is **economies of scale** in advertising. It is argued that larger advertisers can maintain advertising shares that are smaller than their market shares because they get better advertising rates, have declining average costs of production, and accrue the advantages of advertising several products jointly. In addition, they are likely to enjoy more favourable time and space positions, cooperation of intermediaries, and favourable publicity.

Some studies have presented evidence that firms and/or brands maintaining a large share of the market have an advantage over smaller competitors and thus can spend less money on advertising and realize a better return.[26] Reviewing the studies in support of this position and then conducting research over a variety of small package products, Kent Lancaster found that this situation did not hold true and that in fact larger brand share products might actually be at a disadvantage.[27] His results indicated that leading brands spend an average of 2.5 percentage points more than their brand share on advertising. The results of this and other studies suggest there really are no economies of scale to be accrued from the size of the firm or the market share of the brand.[28]

Client/Agency Policies

Another factor that may influence budget allocation is the individual policy of the company or the advertising agency. The agency may discourage the allocation of monies to sales promotion, preferring to spend them on the advertising area.

The agency may take the position that these monies are harder to track in terms of effectiveness and may be used improperly if not under its control. (In many cases commissions are not made on this area, and this fact may contribute to the agency's reluctance.)[29]

The orientation of the agency or the firm may also directly influence where monies are spent. Many ad agencies are managed by officers who have ascended through the creative ranks and are inclined to emphasize the creative budget. Others may have preferences for specific media. For example, some agencies position themselves as experts in cable TV programming and often spend more client money in this medium. Others tend to spend more monies on the Internet. Both the agency and the client may favour certain aspects of the promotional program, perhaps on the basis of past successes, that will substantially influence where dollars are spent.

Organizational Characteristics

In a review of the literature on how allocation decisions are made between advertising and sales promotion, George Low and Jakki Mohr concluded that organizational factors play an important role in determining how communications dollars are spent.[30] The authors note that the following factors influence the allocation decision. These factors vary from one organization to another, and each influences the relative amounts assigned to advertising and promotion:

- The organization's structure—centralized versus decentralized, formalization, and complexity.
- Power and politics in the organizational hierarchy.
- The use of expert opinions (e.g., consultants).
- Characteristics of the decision maker (preferences and experience).
- Approval and negotiation channels.
- Pressure on senior managers to arrive at the optimal budget.

One example of how these factors might influence allocations relates to the level of interaction between marketing and other functional departments, such as accounting and operations. The authors note that the relative importance of advertising versus sales promotion might vary from department to department. Accountants, being dollars-and-cents minded, would argue for the sales impact of promotions, while operations would argue against sales promotions because the sudden surges in demand that might result would throw off production schedules. The marketing department might be influenced by the thinking of either of these groups in making its decision.

SUMMARY

The media strategy must be designed to supplement and support the overall marketing and communications objectives. The objectives of this plan are designed to deliver the message the program has developed.

The basic task involved in the development of media strategy is to determine the best matching of media to the target audience, given the constraints of the budget. The media planner attempts to balance reach and frequency and to deliver the message to the intended audience with a minimum of waste coverage. Media strategy development has been called more of an art than a science because while many quantitative data are available, the planner also relies on creativity and nonquantifiable factors.

This chapter discussed many media strategy decisions, including developing a proper media mix, determining target audience coverage, geographic coverage, scheduling, and balancing reach and frequency. A summary chart of strengths and limitations of various media was provided.

The list provides a starting point for planners who select the right combination of media based on the communication problem or opportunity.

The chapter also looked at key tactics decisions that fine-tune the media strategy. The media vehicle plays a key part in the media plan as the media planner makes a careful match between the viewers, listeners, and readers of the media and the profile of the target audience. Relative cost estimates guide the media planner's final decisions for vehicle selection by finding the most cost-efficient placement. Fine-tuning scheduling details are finalized with the realization of a blocking chart that summarizes all media decisions and costs across relevant time periods and geographic locations.

This chapter summarized theoretical and managerial approaches for budget setting. Theoretical methods feature economic models (i.e., marginal analysis, sales response) that attempt to demonstrate the effects of advertising on sales, often without accounting for the effects of other marketing mix variables. Top-down managerial approaches include affordable, arbitrary allocation, percentage of sales, competitive parity, and return on investment. The methods are often viewed as lacking in any theoretical basis while ignoring the role of advertising and promotion in the marketing mix.

Bottom-up managerial approaches include the objective and task method and payout planning. In particular, the former connects the cost of advertising and promotion to the communication and behavioural objectives expected for the communication program as opposed to broader marketing objectives expected for the marketing program. While the objective and task method offers an improvement over the top-down approaches, firms continue to use a combination of approaches to make the budget decision.

KEY TERMS

absolute cost, *292*
affordable method, *300*
arbitrary allocation, *301*
average frequency, *290*
blocking chart, *295*
Brand Development Index (BDI), *283*
Category Development Index (CDI), *283*
clipping service, *303*
competitive parity method, *303*
concave-downward function model, *298*
continuity, *284*
cost per ratings point (CPRP), *293*
cost per thousand (CPM), *293*
coverage, *276*
duplicated reach, *286*
economies of scale, *310*
effective reach, *290*
flighting, *285*
frequency, *276*
gross ratings points (GRP), *288*
index number, *282*
marginal analysis, *296*
media class, *275*
media objectives, *272*
media planning, *272*
media strategy, *272*
media tactics, *272*
media vehicle, *276*
medium, *275*
objective and task method, *304*
pass-along rate, *294*
payout plan, *306*
percentage-of-sales method, *301*
pulsing, *285*
reach, *276*
readers per copy, *294*
relative cost, *292*
ROI budgeting method, *304*
S-shaped response curve, *298*
sweeps periods, *277*
target CPM (TCPM), *294*
top-down budgeting, *300*
unduplicated reach, *286*
vehicle option source effect, *292*
waste coverage, *281*

DISCUSSION QUESTIONS

1. Describe what is meant by waste coverage. The decision must often be made between waste coverage and undercoverage. Give examples when the marketer might have to choose between the two, and when it may be acceptable to live with waste coverage.

2. Media planning involves a trade-off between reach and frequency. Explain what this means. Under what circumstances would a planner emphasize reach? Frequency?

3. What is meant by readers per copy? How is this different from CPM? Explain the advantages and disadvantages associated with the use of both.

4. One long-time advertising agency executive noted that buying media is both an art and a science, with a leaning toward art. Explain what this means and provide examples.

5. Discuss some of the factors that are important in determining frequency levels. Give examples of each factor.

6. Describe the three methods of promotional scheduling. Give examples of products that might use each method.

7. Discuss some of the reasons managers continue to set budgets using "top-down" budgeting methods.

8. Explain the difference between investing in advertising and spending. Cite examples of companies that have successfully invested.

9. Figure 10–28 shows that advertising spending and effects may differ in different competitive environments. Explain each of the four scenarios presented and give examples of brands in each of the cells.

10. Explain the difference between the two sales response models. Provide examples of types of products that might follow each of these response curves.

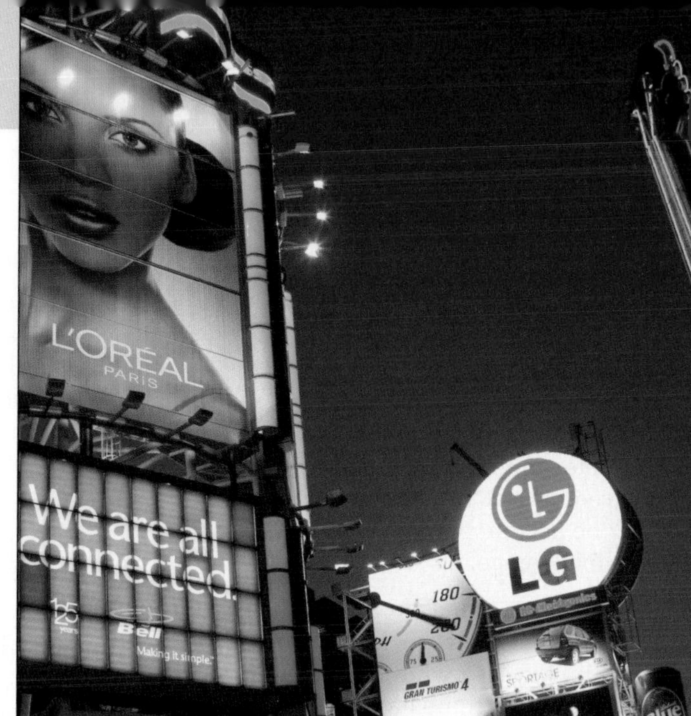

CHAPTER 11

BROADCAST MEDIA

Chapter Objectives

- To examine the structure of the television and radio industries and the role of each medium in the advertising program.
- To consider the strengths and limitations of TV and radio as advertising media.
- To explain how advertising time is purchased for television and radio media, how audiences are measured, and how rates are determined.

The Evolution of Television

Television still commands the lion's share of advertising revenue in Canada, at $3.1 billion in 2006. With projected worldwide revenue of $186 billion for 2009 compared to a projected $32 billion for Internet advertising, it is clear that TV commercials will not disappear overnight as some predicted a few years ago. Television media will continue to play a major role in many promotional planners' budgets, but naturally will evolve along with the media landscape.

CTV launched broadband Internet channels supported by advertising. Viewers watched TV shows normally seen on conventional channels, giving new meaning to sponsored entertainment, information, sports, comedy, and drama shows. Moreover, digital Internet technology allows viewers to see their favourite programs on the smaller screens of cell phones and BlackBerrys. In this sense, the television medium has found new audiences who watch very little television, or reached audiences that may be watching less traditional TV, or allowed advertisers to deliver their commercials more frequently or ensure more successful exposure and involvement with their messages. Whatever the case, viewers can see CTV's *Canadian Idol* or *Corner Gas* online and watch business reports on mobile phones.

Surprisingly, television viewership is still strong; individuals watch an average of 21 hours per week, despite the growth of the Internet the past seven years. In fact, the most significant drop in TV viewership occurred between 1995 and 2000 as it lowered from 24 hours per week. What has changed recently is the possible shift in media habits for teens and young adults, something the macro statistics do not reveal. One recent study pegs adults ages 18 to 34 viewing 12 hours of TV and using the Internet 15 hours, while another found 14 percent of people ages 14 to 29 had watched a TV show online in the past week. However, these surveys relied on consumer memory through self-reported behaviour. Actual behaviour as measured by television viewing technology shows that those under 25 continue to watch about 15 hours per week, unchanged since the advent of the Internet.

Television brands are building their new online channels with the idea that advertising can support a value-added service for new-media consumers and avoid the illegal use of content that the music industry dealt with previously. Future success hinges on advertisers knowing the size of their audience, and new portable audience measuring technology will eventually allow advertisers a degree of knowledge in their planning that they currently do not possess. Innovative advertisers are jumping at the opportunity despite the limited measures—like Ford, which launched the Edge on conventional TV, broadband TV, and mobile programming on Bell Mobility. As this recent example shows, brands will continue to use conventional TV advertising and employ emerging television media for greater exposure.

Sources: William D. Ratcliffe, "Teens and the Tube," *Marketing Magazine,* January 16, 2006; Pia Musngi, "An Audience of One," *Strategy Magazine,* March 2006; Chris Daniels, "Television Redefined," *Marketing Magazine,* November 2006; Terry Poulton, "The Future of Viewership," *Strategy Magazine,* July 2006; and Chris Powell, "Global Forecast," *Marketing Magazine,* April 3, 2006.

Question

1. As an advertiser, why might you avoid online TV advertising? Why might you consider both conventional and new forms of TV ads?

TV has virtually saturated households throughout Canada and most other countries and has become a mainstay in the lives of most people. The average Canadian household watches almost six hours of TV a day, and the average person (age 2+) watches about 3.5 hours of TV per day.[1] The large numbers of people who watch television are important to the TV networks and stations because they can sell time on these programs to marketers who want to reach that audience with their advertising messages. Moreover, the qualities that make TV a great medium for news and entertainment also encourage creative ads that can have a strong impact on customers.

Radio is also an integral part of our lives. For many people, radio is a constant companion in their cars, at home, even at work for information and entertainment. The average Canadian listens to the radio about three hours each day.[2] Like TV viewers, radio listeners are an important audience for marketers. In this chapter, we examine TV and radio media, including the general characteristics of each as well as their specific strengths and limitations. We examine how advertisers use TV and radio as part of their advertising and media strategies, how they buy TV and radio time, and how audiences are measured and evaluated for each medium.

Television

It has often been said that television is the ideal advertising medium. Its ability to combine visual images, sound, motion, and colour presents the advertiser with the opportunity to develop the most creative and imaginative appeals of any medium. However, TV does have certain characteristics that limit or even prevent its use by many advertisers.

Strengths of Television

TV has numerous strengths compared to other media, including creativity, target audience coverage, cost efficiency, attention, scheduling flexibility, geographic coverage, reach, frequency, and media image.

Creativity for Cognitive and Emotional Responses Perhaps the greatest advantage of TV is the opportunity it provides for presenting the advertising message. The interaction of sight, sound, and motion offers tremendous creative flexibility and makes possible dramatic, lifelike representations of products and services. TV commercials can be used to convey a mood or image for a brand as well as to develop emotional or entertaining appeals that help make a dull product appear interesting. The overall impact of TV's characteristics provides unlimited options for generating optimal cognitive and emotional responses to highly imaginative ads.

Television is also an excellent medium for demonstrating a product or service. For example, print ads are effective for showing a car and communicating information regarding its features, but only a TV commercial can put you in the driver's seat and give you the sense of actually driving, as shown by the Porsche commercial in Exhibit 11–1.

Target Audience Coverage Television advertising makes it possible to reach large audiences. Nearly everyone, regardless of age, sex, income, or educational level, watches at least some TV. During prime time (7:00 p.m. to 11:00 p.m.), an average of 40 percent of adults will tune in (see Figure 11–1). Most people do so on a regular basis, since 99 percent of all Canadian households own a TV, and 65 percent have more than one. Marketers selling products and services that appeal to broad target audiences find that TV lets them reach mass markets.

Exhibit 11–1 This TV commercial helps viewers feel the sensation of driving a sports car

Cost Efficiency Compared to many other media, the cost to reach individuals by television is reasonably affordable. For example, one estimate is that the average cost per thousand (CPM) to reach English-speaking women 18 to 49 is about $18.[3] Because of its ability to reach large audiences in a cost-efficient manner, TV is a popular medium among companies selling mass-consumption products. Companies with widespread distribution and availability of their products and services use TV to reach the mass market and deliver their advertising messages at a very low cost per thousand. Television has become indispensable to large consumer packaged-goods companies, carmakers, and major retailers.

Attention Television is basically intrusive in that commercials impose themselves on viewers as they watch their favourite programs. Unless we make a special effort to avoid commercials, most of us are exposed to thousands of them each year. This seemingly continuous exposure implies that viewers devote some attention (i.e., selective attention) to many advertising messages. As discussed in Chapter 4, the low-involvement nature of consumer learning and response processes may mean TV ads have an effect on consumers simply through heavy repetition and exposure to catchy slogans and jingles.

FIGURE *11–1* Percentage distribution of weekly per-capita hours by daypart: total Canada

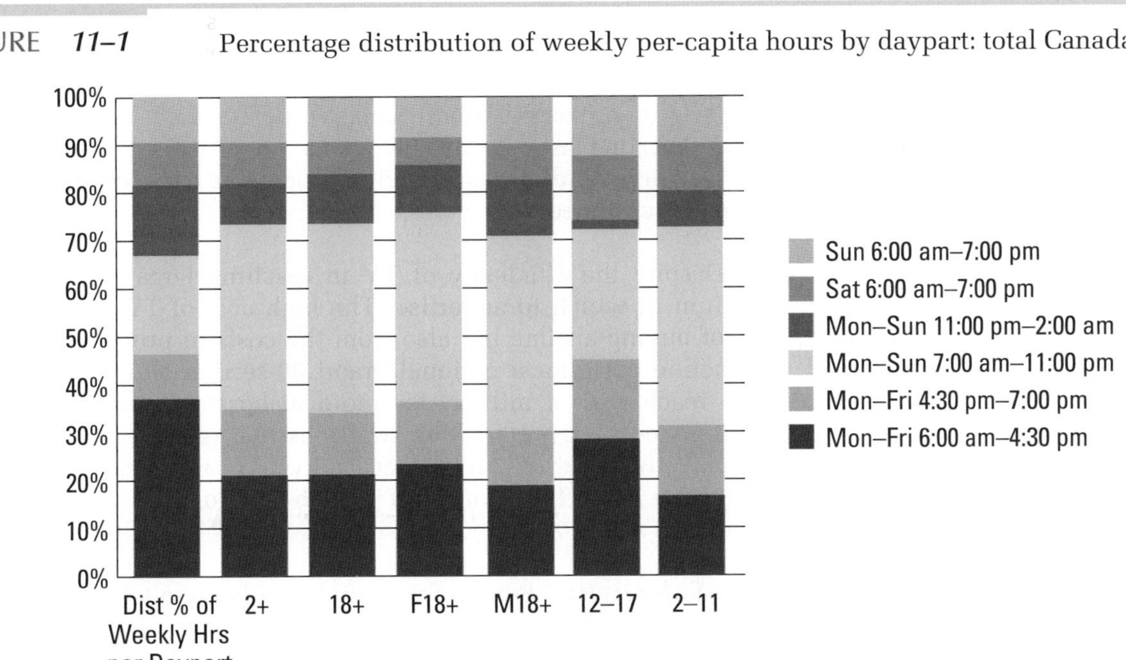

Scheduling Flexibility Television has often been criticized for being a nonselective medium, since it is difficult to reach a precisely defined target audience through the use of TV advertising. But some selectivity is possible due to variations in the composition of audiences as a result of broadcast time and program content. For example, Saturday morning TV caters to children; Saturday and Sunday afternoon programs are geared to the sports-oriented male; and weekday daytime shows appeal heavily to homemakers. With the growth of specialty channels, advertisers refine their coverage further by appealing to groups with specific interests such as sports, news, history, the arts, or music.

Geographic Coverage Advertisers can also adjust their media strategies to take advantage of different geographic markets through spot ads in specific market areas. Ads can be scheduled to run repeatedly in more favourable markets. Alternatively, advertisers can obtain national coverage or regional coverage depending upon their marketing objectives.

Reach Television viewing is a closely monitored activity such that the size of the audience for a television program is known fairly quickly. Placement of TV ads on certain combinations of shows allows an advertiser to reach as many in its target audience as it feels necessary. Availability of airtime and amount of budget are the main constraints on allowing an advertiser to reach as large an audience as possible.

Frequency Scheduling television permits frequency in concentrated blocks throughout a program, evening, week, month, or season. Heightened frequency may be necessary for a new product launch or an effort to obtain switching, while lower levels of frequency may be feasible for advertisers desiring more continuous exposure.

Media Image Given the prominence television has with its mass-market characteristic, TV advertising often carries a high degree of acceptability. Television is usually viewed favourably due to the higher costs of placement and production that demonstrates a level of acceptance or establishment for those who advertise with this medium. In fact, Figure 10–4 in the previous chapter shows that the degree of acceptability of advertising on television is at a remarkable 72-percent acceptance level.

Limitations of Television

Although television is unsurpassed from a creative perspective, the medium has several limitations that preclude its use by many advertisers. These problems include absolute cost, target audience selectivity, processing time, clutter, selective exposure, involvement, and media image.

Absolute Cost Despite the efficiency of TV in reaching large audiences, it is an expensive medium in which to advertise. The high cost of TV stems not only from the expense of buying airtime but also from the costs of producing a quality commercial. Production costs for a national brand 30-second spot average nearly $300,000 and can reach over a million for more elaborate commercials.[4] More advertisers are using media-driven creative strategies that require production of a variety of commercials, which drive up their costs. Even local ads can be expensive to produce and often are not of high quality. The high costs of producing and airing commercials often price small- and medium-size advertisers out of the market.

Target Audience Selectivity Some selectivity is available in television through scheduling, but advertisers who are seeking a very specific, often small, target audience find the coverage of TV often extends beyond their market. Geographic selectivity can be a problem for local advertisers such as retailers, since a station bases its rates on the total market area it reaches. For example, stations in Ottawa reach viewers in western Quebec and eastern Ontario. The small company whose market is limited to the immediate Ottawa area may find TV an inefficient media buy, since the stations cover a larger geographic area than the merchant's trade area.

Audience selectivity is improving as advertisers target certain groups of consumers through the type of program or day and/or time when they choose to advertise. However, TV still does not offer as much audience selectivity as radio, magazines, newspapers, or direct mail for reaching precise segments of the market.

Processing Time TV commercials usually last only 30 or 15 seconds and leave nothing tangible for the viewer to examine or consider. Commercials have become shorter as the demand for a limited amount of broadcast time has intensified and advertisers try to get more impressions from their media budgets. Commercials lasting 15 seconds have grown from 21 percent in 1991 to 27 percent in 2006, while 30-second commercials moved from 67 percent to 61 percent.

An important factor in the decline in commercial length has been the rising media costs over the past two decades. Many advertisers see shorter commercials as the only way to keep their media costs in line. A 15-second spot typically sells for about two-thirds the price of a 30-second spot. By using 15-second commercials, advertisers think they can run additional spots to reinforce the message or reach a larger audience. Some advertisers believe shorter commercials can deliver a message just as effectively as longer spots for much less money.

Clutter The problems of short messages are compounded by the fact that the advertiser's message is only one of many spots and other nonprogramming material seen during a commercial break, so it may have trouble being noticed. One of advertisers' greatest concerns with TV advertising is the potential decline in effectiveness because of such *clutter*.

Imagine counting the number of commercials, promotions for the news or upcoming programs, or public service announcements that appear during a station break and the concern for clutter becomes obvious. In the USA, one study sponsored by the advertising industry found a record level of clutter during prime-time television broadcasts on the major networks. The study analyzed one week of broadcasts during May and November of 1999 and found that the four major networks averaged 16 minutes and 43 seconds of nonprogramming content.[5] With all of these messages competing for target audiences' attention, it is easy to understand why the viewer comes away confused or even annoyed and unable to remember or properly identify the product or service advertised.

One cause of clutter is the use of shorter commercials and **split-30s**, 30-second spots in which the advertiser promotes two different products with separate messages. The Canadian Radio-television and Telecommunications Commission (CRTC), which regulates television, permits only 12 minutes of commercials per hour. However, when simulcast Canadian commercials are run, there is extra time since U.S. TV stations often show more than 12 minutes of commercials. To fill this time, Canadian stations run ads for other shows, public service announcements, or news/entertainment vignettes. Thus, Canadian viewers experience a different kind of clutter than their American counterparts.

Selective Exposure When advertisers buy time on a TV program, they are not purchasing guaranteed exposure but rather the opportunity to communicate a message to large numbers of consumers. But there is increasing evidence that the size of the viewing audience shrinks by a third during a commercial break for a variety of reasons.[6] Thus, viewers engage in selective exposure to television commercials resulting from zapping and zipping.

Zapping refers to changing channels to avoid commercials. An observational study found as much as a third of program audiences may be lost to electronic zapping when commercials appear.[7] The Nielsen study found that most commercial zapping occurs at the beginning and, to a lesser extent, the end of a program. Zapping at these points is likely to occur because commercial breaks are so long and predictable. Zapping has also been fuelled by the emergence of 24-hour continuous-format programming on cable channels. Viewers can switch over for a few news headlines, sports scores, or a music video and then switch back to the program. Research shows that young adults zap more than older adults, and men are more likely to zap than women.[8]

How to inhibit zapping? The networks use certain tactics to hold viewers' attention, such as previews of the next week's show or short closing scenes at the end of a program. Some programs start with action sequences before the opening credits and commercials. Some advertisers believe that producing different executions of a campaign theme is one way to maintain viewers' attention. Others think the ultimate way to zap-proof commercials is to produce creative advertising messages that will attract and hold viewers' attention.

A study on zapping among viewers of the five major commercial channels in the Netherlands was conducted by Lex van Meurs.[9] He found that during commercial breaks, 29 percent of the audience stopped watching television or switched away to another channel. This loss of viewers was partially compensated for by an average increase of 7 percent of new viewers who zapped in from another channel. The study also found that people stop viewing TV during a commercial break because they have a reason to stop watching television altogether or they want to find out what is being shown on other channels. The number of people zapping in and out during breaks was not caused by the type of products being advertised or by specific characteristics of the commercials.

In a representative sample of Canadians on what they do to limit their exposure to television, radio, and online advertising it shows a number of alternatives. Figure 11–2 illustrates the frequencies of those efforts that most pertain to television.

FIGURE *11–2*

How Canadians avoid television advertising

	Age					
	Total (n=1285)	15–19 (n=120)*	20–29 (n=204)*	30–39 (n=246)*	40–49 (n=270)*	50+ (n=445)*
Change TV channels	61	83	79	66	64	43
Use mute button	18	7	7	14	14	29
Leave room/walk away	14	8	9	13	17	18
Do something else	12	7	7	11	13	15
Turn it off	7	10	8	6	6	7
Fast forward through ads	6	1	4	5	8	9
Get food/drink	6	3	2	5	7	10
Do household task	4	2	3	3	4	5
Ignore it	4	2	4	2	3	6
Read something	3	1	1	1	2	7
Watch TV channels that don't have ads	2	–	3	2	2	2
Turn down volume	2	1	–	2	2	3
Other/don't know	4	4	4	5	3	3

*n = the number of respondents.
Note: Total does not equal 100 percent because more than one response was accepted.
Source: The Strategic Counsel, Toronto.

Canadians engage in considerable zapping—at 61 percent or about double the amount of zapping cited in previous studies. Actual amount of zapping versus perceived amount of zapping may account for this difference. This would suggest that people's attitude toward an ad and their actual behaviour toward it are dramatically at odds. Alternatively, the different statistics may indicate a trend to increased zapping or more technological usage on the part of Canadians to avoid ads.[10]

Zipping occurs when customers fast-forward through commercials as they play back a previously recorded program. A study of VCR use found that most viewers fully or partially zipped commercials when watching a prerecorded program.[11] Primarily provided by Bell ExpressVu and Rogers, PVR technology entered Canada in 2001, about five years after the launch of the TiVo and Relay brands in the United States. By 2006, household penetration reached 6 percent in Canada and 25 percent in the U.S. In Canada, about two-thirds of all PVR owners claimed increased TV viewing enjoyment. A study by Forrester Research in the U.S. suggests that users watch 60 percent of their viewing from recorded programming and skip about 90 percent of the ads. However, another study released by *Mediaweek* found that most consumers could recognize the brands advertised as they zip through the commercials.[12]

Involvement The cumulative effect of the varied television characteristics generally implies that it is a low-involvement medium. While its invasiveness can expose the message to us readily and perhaps hold our attention with significant creative strategies and tactics, the relative short processing time and clutter make for less effective media for an advertiser to significantly persuade a target audience. This is a very topical issue for advertisers, as shown in IMC Perspective 11–1 on page 322.

Media Image To many critics of advertising, TV commercials personify everything that is wrong with the industry. Critics often single out TV commercials because of their pervasiveness and the intrusive nature of the medium. Consumers are seen as defenceless against the barrage of TV ads, since they cannot control the transmission of the message and what appears on their screens. Viewers dislike TV advertising when they believe it is offensive, uninformative, or shown too frequently or when they do not like its content.[13] Studies have shown that of the various forms of advertising, distrust is generally the highest for TV commercials.[14] Also, concern has been raised about the effects of TV advertising on specific groups, such as children or the elderly.[15]

Buying Television Advertising Time

A number of options are available to advertisers that choose to use TV as part of their media mix. They can purchase ads on shows that are shown across the national or regional network versus a local spot announcement in a few cities. They can sponsor an entire program. They can purchase time in a variety of program formats that appeal to various types and sizes of audiences. With the growth of new television services, advertisers decide the degree to which they want to advertise on specialty channels. We explore these four decisions in this section.

The purchase of TV advertising time is a highly specialized phase of the advertising business, particularly for large companies spending huge sums of money. Large advertisers that do a lot of TV advertising generally use agency media specialists or specialized media buying services to arrange the media schedule and purchase TV time. Consequently, we conclude this section with a discussion on measuring TV audiences since it is a critical input for TV decisions.

IMC PERSPECTIVE 11–1

Are Consumers Engaged by TV Commercials?

Ratings agencies measure how many people watched a certain program and, with minute-to-minute ratings, can even provide an estimate of how many people watched a certain TV commercial. What the likes of Nielsen Media Research and BBM can't do, however, is measure whether viewers paid any attention to a particular spot. For many years, agencies have been attempting to measure engagement, first with print, then radio, then television, and, most recently, with the Internet. It's hardly an overstatement to say engagement, which the Advertising Research Foundation defines as "a measurable level of involvement resulting from a marketing communication," is highly sought by media buyers.

Genesis Media, a Canadian media firm, says that levels of engagement on specific channels vary depending on the types of products and advertisers and the demographics the advertisers are targeting. One surprising fact that has come through its research is that high-rated programming on conventional stations tends to generate a proportionately lower consumer response than less heralded shows. "Perhaps they are too engaged in the programs," says Claassen, chief executive of Genesis Media, adding there is no definitive answer for the phenomenon.

One solution, harkening back to the dawn of television, when major packaged-goods manufacturers sponsored entire programs, was tried recently by Procter & Gamble Co. Billed as a "showmercial," the series of commercials ran as a mini-program during commercial breaks during an airing of CanWest Global's broadcast of *The Gilmore Girls*, documenting the makeover of a mother and daughter using P&G health and beauty products. "It wasn't an actual commercial sell, it was a makeover using the products," says Doug Checkeris, president and CEO of the Media Company. "You are trying to build relevance, trying to build interest, trying to engage the consumer with the message rather than simply bombarding them with another simple outgoing message." He said the media buyer has not yet measured the impact of the program on P&G's business. Regardless of individual cases, it will be some years, if ever, before media buyers can come up with a hard-and-fast measure of engagement.

While media buyers continue to grapple with consumer engagement, there are signs advertisers are becoming more demanding—Toyota Motor Co. has announced a deal with U.S. broadcaster NBC that guarantees a specific level of viewer engagement from a major network. Based on the theory that there is a strong correlation between recall of program details and viewers' retention of the accompanying advertising, NBC says it will measure viewer attentiveness with the use of an audience panel surveyed by a third-party firm. "Beyond audience size, we want the networks to focus on attention-grabbing, highly engrossing shows that keep audiences tuned in," says Kim McCullough, Toyota's corporate manager, marketing communications.

Source: Paul Brent, "The New Tools of Engagement," *Marketing Magazine*, August 14–21, 2006.

Question

1. Why is involvement an important measurement for advertisers to expect from broadcasters?

TYPES OF TELEVISION ADVERTISING

A basic decision for all advertisers is allocating their TV media budget to network versus local or spot announcements. Most national advertisers use network schedules to provide national coverage and supplement this with regional or local spot purchases to reach markets where additional coverage is desired.

Network Advertising A common way advertisers disseminate their messages is by purchasing airtime from a **television network**. A network assembles a series of affiliated local TV stations, or **affiliates**, to which it supplies programming and services. These affiliates, most of which are independently owned, contractually agree to preempt time during specified hours for programming provided by the networks and to carry the national advertising within the program. The networks share the advertising revenue they receive during these time periods with the affiliates.

Station	FALL 2001	2002	2003	2004	2005
Conventional Station					
CBC	4.4	4.5	4.7	4.2	4.6
CBC Affiliates	0.9	0.7	0.7	0.7	0.7
CBC TOTAL	**5.4**	**5.3**	**5.6**	**5.1**	**5.5**
CTV	11.3	12.2	11.9	13.1	13.4
Independent English	7.6	8	9.4	8.8	8.3
Global	7.7	7.9	7.5	7.2	7.4
Radio Canada	4.1	3.4	2.7	3.8	3.4
Radio Canada Affiliates	0.9	0.8	0.6	0.8	0.7
RADIO CANADA TOTAL	**5.1**	**4.2**	**3.3**	**4.6**	**4.2**
TVA	8.7	8.7	8.2	8.1	7.9
Télé-Québec	0.6	0.7	0.7	0.7	0.7
Quatre Saisons	3.4	3.5	4.1	3.1	2.9
Total Cdn. Convent	**49.8**	**50.4**	**50.7**	**50.7**	**50.6**
US Conventional TV					
US: ABC Affiliates	2.4	2.1	1.9	1.7	1.7
NBC Affiliates	2.3	2.0	2.1	2.0	2.0
CBS Affiliates	2.1	2.1	2.2	2.1	2.1
FOX Affiliates	2.5	2.0	2.0	1.7	1.5
PBS	1.4	1.1	1.1	1.0	0.9
Independent/UPN/WB	1.5	1.6	1.4	1.2	2.4
Total U.S. Convent	**12.2**	**10.9**	**10.7**	**9.7**	**9.3**
Cable	0.3	0.4	0.3	0.3	0.3
International	0.1	0.1	0.1	0.1	0.2
Provincial	1.2	1.4	1.2	1.4	1.5
VCR	4.2	4.5	4.5	4.9	4.7
PVR	–	–	–	0.1	0.3
CDN. Specialty/Pay	21.4	22.8	23.8	23.7	25.8
U.S. Specialty/Pay	9.2	8	7.2	7.1	4.7
Others	1.4	1.4	1.6	1.9	1.2
Total Hours (Millions)	**642.9**	**659.4**	**667.4**	**666.5**	**678.7**

Source: BBM Fall 2005 Sweep Surveys (Mon–Sun 6A-2A)

FIGURE *11–3*

Share of hours tuned by station group, TVBasics 2006–2007

The affiliates are also free to sell commercial time in non-network periods and during station breaks in the pre-empted periods to both national and local advertisers. Figure 11–3 summarizes the Canadian and U.S. networks and independent stations, along with the amount of consumption for each.

Canada's television industry features three national networks. The Canadian Broadcasting Corporation (CBC) is a Crown corporation of the federal government of Canada. Its full network includes 34 stations, including 19 private affiliates that reach 99 percent of English-language homes. Radio-Canada is the CBC cousin for the French-language network consisting of 13 stations (7 in Quebec, 6 outside of Quebec). The Canadian Television Network (CTV) operates as a national English-language service and owns 22 stations in most Canadian provinces.

Canada has a number of regional networks. The CBC also consists of five regional networks; Atlantic, Central (Ontario and English Montreal), Pacific (B.C.), Western, and North (NWT). CTV has three regional networks: Ontario, Atlantic, and Saskatchewan. Global Television Network sends its signal from Toronto to 14 transmitters to reach 97 percent of the Ontario population. Global Atlantic operates in a similar manner to reach the majority of people in New Brunswick, PEI, and Nova Scotia. NewNet is an amalgamation of five Ontario stations reaching over 4 million people. Citytv, based in Toronto, reaches an audience of 4 million households from Windsor to Ottawa. CHTV operates similarly out of Toronto/Hamilton and covers 90 percent of Ontario through its seven transmitters. There are three regional networks in Quebec. TVA has 10 stations and reaches 99 percent of the province. Television Quatre Saisons has nine stations and reaches 94 percent of the province. Finally, sports programming has reached the regional network status as Sportsnet operates in four regions: Pacific, West, Ontario, and East.

The networks have affiliates throughout the nation for almost complete national coverage. When an advertiser purchases airtime from one of the national networks, the commercial is transmitted across the nation through the affiliate station network. Network advertising truly represents a mass medium, as the advertiser can broadcast its message simultaneously throughout the country.

A major advantage of network advertising is the simplification of the purchase process. The advertiser has to deal with only one party or media representative to air a commercial nationwide. The networks also offer the most popular programs and generally control prime-time programming. Advertisers interested in reaching huge nationwide audiences generally buy network time during the prime viewing hours of 8 to 11 p.m. eastern time.

Availability of time can also be a problem as more advertisers turn to network advertising to reach mass markets. Traditionally, most prime-time commercial spots, particularly on the popular shows, are sold during the buying period in May/June/July that occurs before the TV season begins. Advertisers hoping to use prime-time network advertising must plan their media schedules and often purchase TV time as much as a year in advance. Demands from large clients who are heavy TV advertisers force the biggest agencies to participate in the up-front market. However, TV time is also purchased during the **scatter market** that runs through the TV season. Some key incentives for buying up front, such as cancellation options and lower prices, are becoming more available in the quarterly scatter market. Network TV can also be purchased on a regional basis, so an advertiser's message can be aired in certain sections of the country with one media purchase.

The marketing and selling of advertising time by the network producers of television shows to buyers of advertising can be less challenging with an established brand like the television series *Canadian Idol*. However, the challenge can be enormous for new television shows with a low profile. The producers of the hit show *Corner Gas* marketed to television viewers directly to build the audience, thus making the show very attractive to advertisers. CTV used publicity, on-air ads, website promotions, and a cross-country tour of Brent Butt (a comedian and star of the show) to appeal to a core group who would like a show that was described as original, familiar, and fun. At its peak, *Corner Gas* is in the top 15 shows watched in Canada with an audience of 1.5 million, topping many American situation comedies.[16]

Similarly, Alliance Atlantis Broadcasting takes a packaged-goods marketing approach in its planning and organizing to develop the market for its imported specialty channels like HGTV, National Geographic Channel, and BBC Canada or domestic specialty channels like Showcase and History Television. In addition, it uses innovative creative tactics to ensure large audiences for its advertisers. For example, during the *Six Feet Under* launch, it used an unusual mobile display to a record-breaking 735,000 viewers, establishing it as the most watched specialty-channel program.[17]

Spot Advertising **Spot advertising** refers to commercials shown on local TV stations, with time negotiated and purchased directly from the individual stations or their national station representatives. **Station reps** act as sales agents for a number of local stations in dealing with national advertisers.

Spot advertising offers the national advertiser flexibility in adjusting to local market conditions. The advertiser can concentrate commercials in areas where market potential is greatest or where additional support is needed. This appeals to advertisers with uneven distribution or limited advertising budgets, as well as those interested in test marketing or introducing a product in limited market areas. National advertisers sometimes use spot television advertising through local retailers or dealers as part of their cooperative advertising programs and to provide local dealer support. This attractive option is most prevalent in Canada with about 60 percent of all TV ads.

Sponsorship Advertising Under a **sponsorship** arrangement, an advertiser assumes responsibility for the production and usually the content of the program as well as the advertising that appears within it. In the early days of TV, most programs were produced and sponsored by corporations and were identified by their name. Today most shows are produced by either the networks or independent production companies that sell them to a network, however, sponsorship is a good option in some situations.

A company might choose to sponsor a program for several reasons. Sponsorship allows the firm to capitalize on the prestige of a high-quality program, enhancing the image of the company and its products. Another reason is that the sponsor has control over the number, placement, and content of its commercials. Commercials can be of any length as long as the total amount of commercial time does not exceed network or station regulations. Advertisers introducing a new product line often sponsor a program and run commercials that are several minutes long to introduce and explain the product. While these factors make sponsorship attractive to some companies, the high costs of sole sponsorship limit this option to large firms.

Scotiabank provides an excellent example of innovative sponsorship. Historically, Scotiabank was successful with its sponsorship of CTV's "Business Report," shown during its *Canada AM* morning show. Looking for a consistent message across many of CTV's banners, Scotiabank hit on the solution of using the Report on Business Television's financial news show *Dollars & Sense*, as shown in Figure 11–4.[18]

FIGURE *11–4*

The *Dollars & Sense* breakout

Participants: Report on Business Television, CTV Newsnet, Canada *AM, CTV News,* CTV.ca, ROBTV.com and other Bell Globemedia relevant websites.

Run: For 10 weeks starting Oct. 6, 2003 and for 20 weeks starting Jan. 5, 2004.

Production: 150 original two-minute *Dollars & Sense* segments airing on Report on Business Television; 30 original 30-second *Dollars & Sense* interstitial vignettes airing on CTV Newsnet and *Canada AM.*

Online: Digitized content so interstitials and long-version *Dollars & Sense* segments are available online supporting the advertising.

Component breakdown:

Report on Business Television runs two-minute editorial segments titled *Dollars & Sense*; airing four times per day, with unique content, Monday to Friday. Editorial segments are sponsored by Scotiabank and packaged with a 10-second opening and closing billboard and a 30-second adjacent Scotiabank commercial. Scotiabank-branded stock ticker appears on screen during the editorial content.

CTV Newsnet runs 30-second *Dollars & Sense* interstitial vignettes (similar content to longer version but more compact and focused in-content delivery), airing two times per day, Monday to Friday; 30-second commercial adjacency following interstitial; 10-second customized closed captioning campaign promoting "*Dollars & Sense* brought to you by Scotiabank," Monday to Saturday.

Canada AM runs 30-second *Dollars & Sense* interstitial in fixed position on Wednesdays and Fridays with 30-second commercial adjacency.

CTV News runs 10-second customized closed-captioning campaign promoting "*Dollars & Sense* brought to you by Scotiabank," Monday to Friday.

FIGURE 11–5

Common television dayparts

Morning	7:00 a.m.–9:00 a.m., Monday through Friday
Daytime	9:00 a.m.–4:30 p.m., Monday through Friday
Early fringe	4:30 p.m.–7:30 p.m., Monday through Friday
Prime-time access	7:30 p.m.–8:00 p.m., Sunday through Saturday
Prime time	8:00 p.m.–11:00 p.m., Monday through Saturday, and 7:00 p.m.–11:00 p.m., Sunday
Late news	11:00–11:30 p.m., Monday through Friday
Late fringe	11:30–1:00 a.m., Monday through Friday

FIGURE 11–6 Television hours by daypart

PERCENT DISTRIBUTION OF WEEKLY PER CAPITA HOURS BY DAYPART: TOTAL CANADA						
Dayparts	All 2+	Adults 18+	Women 18+	Men 18+	Teens 12–17	Children 2–11
M–F 6a–4:30p	21.5	20.8	23.7	17.6	17.5	30.9
M–F 4:30p–7p	12.9	12.5	13.2	11.8	14.5	15.9
M–Su 7p–11p	39.8	40.9	39.7	42.3	41.4	27.1
M–Su 11p–2a	10.0	10.9	9.5	12.3	8.4	2.5
Sa 6a–7p	7.4	6.8	6.4	7.2	9.2	12.0
Su 6a–7p	8.4	8.1	7.5	8.8	9.1	11.5

Note: From BBM Fall 2001 & 2005
Source: *Media Digest* 06–07, p. 21

Time Periods and Programs

Another decision in buying TV time is selecting the right period and program for the advertiser's commercial messages. The cost of TV advertising time varies depending on the time of day and the particular program, since audience size varies as a function of these two factors. TV time periods are divided into **dayparts**, which are specific segments of a broadcast day.

The time segments that make up the programming day vary from station to station. However, a typical classification of dayparts for a weekday is shown in Figure 11–5. The various daypart segments attract different audiences in both size and nature, so advertising rates vary accordingly. Figure 11–6 shows how the viewership distribution varies across different dayparts. Prime time draws about 40 percent of per capita television consumption. Since firms that advertise during prime time must pay premium rates, this daypart is dominated by the large national advertisers.

The various dayparts are important to advertisers since they attract different demographic groups. For example, daytime TV generally attracts women; early morning attracts women and children. The late-fringe (late-night) daypart period has become popular among advertisers trying to reach young adults. Audience size and demographic composition also vary depending on the type of program.

Specialty Television Advertising

Canada has an extensive variety of specialty networks and digital specialty networks that advertisers run commercials on to reach specific target audiences. These specialty networks require either cable or satellite technology on the part of consumers to access this entertainment. We will briefly review these two technologies and then discuss the advertising on these specialty channels.

Cable and Satellite Technology Perhaps the most significant development in the broadcast media has been the expansion of **cable television**. Cable, or CATV (community antenna television), which delivers TV signals through fibre or coaxial wire rather than the airways, was developed to provide reception to remote areas that couldn't receive broadcast signals. Canadians readily accepted cable in the 1970s since it was the easiest or only method of receiving the feed of American channels. Today, cable penetration stands at about 66 percent, down from 76 percent in 1995.

Direct broadcast satellite (DBS) services emerged in the 1990s. TV and radio programs are sent digitally from a satellite to homes equipped with a small dish. DBS companies have been aggressively marketing their service, superior picture quality, and greater channel choice as subscribers receive as many as 200 channels that include news, music, and sports in crisp, digital video and CD-quality sound. However, the pendulum can swing back the other way as more cable operators offer digital cable that allows them to match the number of channels received on satellites. Total satellite and digital cable penetration reached 41 percent in 2005.

Cable and satellite subscribers pay a monthly fee and receive many channels, including the local Canadian and American network affiliates and independent stations, various specialty networks, American superstations, and local cable system channels. Both operators also offer programming that is not supported by commercial sponsorship and is available only to households willing to pay a fee beyond the monthly subscription charge (e.g., The Movie Channel). Cable and satellite broadens the program options available to the viewer as well as the advertiser by offering specialty channels, including all-news, pop music, country music, sports, weather, educational, and cultural channels as well as children's programming. One feature offered by these television service providers is time shifting, where viewers can watch a program from another time zone. As discussed in IMC Perspective 11–2 on page 328, this has led to some unexpected challenges.

Specialty Networks The proliferation of channels in both technologies has influenced the nature of television as an advertising medium. Expanded viewing options have led to considerable audience fragmentation. Much of the audience growth of specialty networks has come at the expense of national and regional networks. Specialty networks now have about 28 percent of the viewing audience. Many specialty networks have become very popular among consumers, leading advertisers to re-evaluate their media plans and the prices they are willing to pay for network and spot commercials on network affiliate stations. Advertising on specialty networks reached $768 million in 2005, up from $438 million in 2001. In comparison, all other television ad revenue increased from $2.553 billion in 2001 to $3.013 billion.

This change in advertising revenue indicates that advertisers are using specialty networks to reach specific target audiences. Advertisers are also interested in specialty networks because of their low cost and flexibility. Advertising rates on cable programs are much lower than those for the shows on the major networks. This makes TV a much more viable media option for smaller advertisers with limited budgets and those interested in targeting their commercials to a well-defined target audience. Also, specialty network advertisers generally do not have to make the large up-front commitments the networks require, which may be as much as a year in advance.

In addition to costing less, specialty networks give advertisers much greater flexibility in the type of commercials that can be used. While most network commercials are 30- or 15-second spots, commercials on specialty networks can be longer (i.e., **infomercials** ranging from 3 to 30 minutes in length). Direct-response advertisers often use these longer ads to describe their products or services and encourage consumers

IMC PERSPECTIVE 11–2

Time-Shifting Problems Emerge

Time shifting allows viewers to watch network feeds from other time zones. If viewers in Toronto miss their favourite show at 8 p.m., for example, they can watch the Vancouver feed three hours later. The problem is that those viewers are also seeing ads intended for Vancouver residents.

So, while a national company may run a price promotion intended only for Western Canada, someone in the East may see the ad while watching a time-shifted signal and become annoyed when the promotion doesn't seem to exist. "We are just understanding how it impacts our business," says Andeen Pitt, vice-president of media and business development for Wasserman & Partners in Vancouver. "You have to start thinking about the kind of message you deliver in a world where you can't pinpoint the when and where someone will see your message."

For local advertisers, time shifting also cuts into a buy's reach. One week last fall, Global's hit reality show *Survivor* garnered a 16.6 rating among adults ages 18 to 49 in Edmonton—yet only a 9.8 from the Global Edmonton station. The rest of the ratings came from viewers tuning in to Global feeds from, among other places, Nova Scotia and Ontario. "The advertiser is not reaching the audience they could be," says Sharon Dixon, manager, MEC MediaLab Canada.

While programs may attract droves of viewers, say broadcast executives, it is not always reflected in the ratings. The broadcasters say they've lost revenue as a result. Kathy Gardner, senior VP, integrated media research at CanWest MediaWorks, says her company lost $16 million in the 2005–06 broadcast year because of time shifting.

Even though Canada is the only country that allows time shifting, broadcasters recognize this is how cable and satellite companies have, in part, sold digital TV services. CanWest has proposed to the CRTC that satellite and cable providers adopt "simultaneous substitution"—a solution modelled on how Canadian networks simulcast American programs. The upshot is that no matter where a program is broadcast from, it would include local commercials.

Source: Chris Daniels, "Shift Disturbers," *Marketing Magazine*, April 30, 2007.

Questions

1. Why should advertisers be concerned with reaching viewers beyond the local market?
2. Do you agree with the proposed "simultaneous substitution" solution?

to call in their orders during the commercial. The use of infomercials by direct-response advertisers is discussed in Chapter 16. Finally, specialty network advertising can be purchased on a national or a regional basis. Many large marketers advertise on specialty networks to reach large numbers of viewers across the country with a single media buy. Regional advertising on specialty networks is available but limited.

While specialty networks have become increasingly popular among national, regional, and local advertisers, they still have limitations. One concern is that specialty networks are overshadowed by the networks. The average person will watch more hours per week of a CBC or CTV affiliate than a single specialty network, although this is changing. Figure 11–7 shows a summary of the more highly viewed specialty channels. The average Canadian watches TSN an average of 1.9 hours per week, while the average person in Ottawa watches the CBC affiliate 2.5 hours per week. Although specialty networks' share of the TV viewing audience has increased significantly, the viewers are spread out among the large number of channels available. Collectively, the specialty channels contribute to greater audience fragmentation as the number of viewers who watch any one cable channel is generally quite low. Figure 11–8 on page 330 shows a breakout of television viewership across all formats.

FIGURE 11–7

Average hours watched per week for selected specialty channels

COMMERCIAL SPECIALTY NETWORKS

Weekly Hours Tuned & Weekly Reach by Network* All Persons 2+ Mo–Su 8a–12m Total Canada

	Fall 2004			Fall 2005		
SPECIALTY	Hours (000)	Reach (000)	Avg Hrs	Hours (000)	Reach (000)	Avg Hrs
Bravo	5,376	5,927	0.9	4,816	5,190	0.9
Canal D	3,584	2,530	1.4	3,808	2,424	1.6
Canal Evasion	560	896	0.6	672	924	0.7
Canal Nouvelles, TVA	2,128	1,856	1.1	2,464	1,917	1.3
Canal Vie	4,032	2,209	1.8	3,920	2,091	1.9
Canal Z	2,128	1,239	1.7	2,576	1,329	1.9
CBC Newsworld	6,048	5,686	1.1	4,704	5,464	0.9
CLT	560	1,158	0.5	n/a	n/a	n/a
Country Music Television	4,368	4,587	1.0	3,920	4,397	0.9
CP24	1,904	2,192	0.9	1,904	2,484	0.8
CTV NewsNet	2,688	3,013	0.9	3,696	3,681	1.0
Discovery	9,296	7,447	1.2	9,632	7,561	1.3
Food Network Canada	3,136	2,841	1.1	3,136	3,154	1.0
HGTV Canada	5,488	4,434	1.2	4,928	4,857	1.0
Historia	1,568	1,103	1.4	1,344	1,116	1.2
History Television	7,392	4,986	1.5	6,496	5,145	1.3
Life Network	2,688	5,152	0.5	2,576	4,652	0.6
MétéoMédia	784	1,762	0.4	1,120	1,929	0.6
Much More Music	2,464	4,284	0.6	2,464	4,225	0.6
MuchMusic	4,256	5,796	0.7	3,920	5,564	0.7
Musimax	784	1,499	0.5	560	1,325	0.4
Musique Plus	1,232	1,963	0.6	1,292	1,820	0.7
Outdoor Life	1,456	2,987	0.5	1,568	3,143	0.5
Prime TV	6,272	4,930	1.3	5,264	5,136	1.0
RDS -La Reseau des Sports	3,024	2,126	1.4	7,056	2,814	2.5
RDI -Le Reseau de L'information	4,256	2,437	1.7	4,480	2,291	2.0
Report on Business Television	1,120	679	1.6	1,008	740	1.4
Score Television Network	1,792	2,652	0.7	3,024	3,616	0.8
Series +	4,704	1,324	3.6	4,928	1,287	3.8
Showcase	6,720	6,482	1.0	6,944	6,913	1.0
Space	8,176	4,838	1.7	7,176	4,797	1.7
SportsNet	11,088	5,888	1.9	15,008	7,254	2.1
Star TV	1,232	2,175	0.6	1,344	1,999	0.7
Teletoon English	9,184	5,516	1.7	10,528	5,856	1.8
Teletoon French	4,480	1,827	2.5	4,816	1,878	2.6
The Comedy Network	4,928	5,641	0.9	5,040	5,857	0.9
The Family Channel	9,856	5,917	1.7	n/a	n/a	n/a
The Movie Network	7,952	2,214	3.6	7,168	2,385	3.0
The Weather Network	4,877	2,912	0.6	2,576	4,882	0.5
Treehouse	10,192	3,059	3.3	n/a	n/a	n/a
TSN	9,744	7,525	1.3	17,136	8,594	1.9
TV5	1,232	1,674	0.7	1,344	1,741	0.8
Vision TV	2,240	2,731	0.8	2,352	2,557	0.9
VRAK TV	3,920	1,983	2.0	n/a	n/a	n/a
W Network	6,160	5,574	1.1	6,832	5,791	1.2
YTV	11,760	6,317	1.9	12,320	7,097	1.7
TOTAL DIGITAL NETWORKS	17,136	5,117	3.3	18,928	5,854	3.2

*Numbers represent an average of eight weeks: Sep 27–Oct 3, '04 to Nov 15–Nov 21, '04; Fall 2005 Weeks 5–12 (8-week average)

Stations that do not appear on this list, or where n/a appears, are not Nielsen subscribers.

Source: Nielsen Media Research, People Meter Data

FIGURE 11–8

Viewing habits of Canadians 2+ by station groups

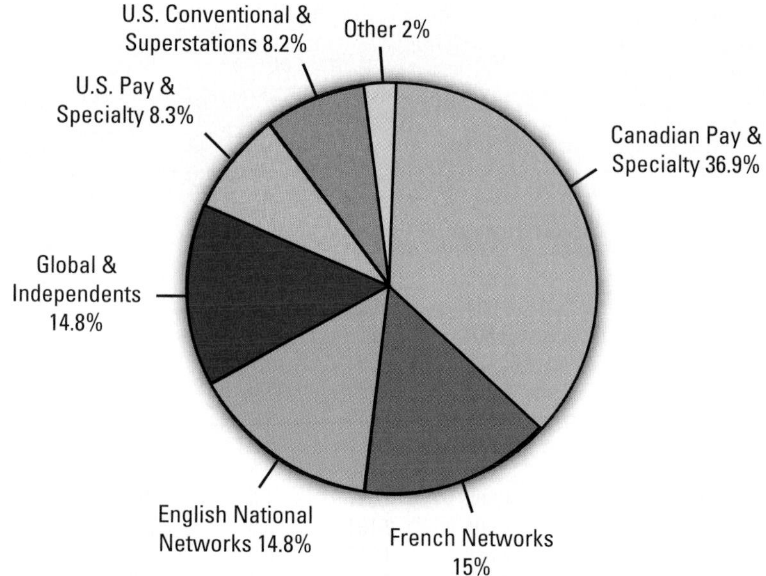

The emergence of dozens of digital specialty channels a few years ago raises the question as to how well they are performing in attracting audiences in sufficient numbers for advertisers to consider them as a viable television vehicle. While their share of 1 or 2 percent of the television market may be considered disappointing, another perspective suggests that a more realistic benchmark should be used. Since access to a specific digital specialty channel requires a subscription similar to that of magazines, a more important comparison is to look at the leaders for each media. In fact, about three-quarters of the digital specialty channels have more than half a million subscribers, something only three subscription magazines can claim.[19]

Recent research suggests that over the past few years, 45 percent of all viewers watch more programs on specialty channels with 41 percent indicating their perception that these channels have more interesting/entertaining programming versus conventional channels. Furthermore, 37 percent devote more than half of their viewing time to specialty channels and a similar number will consider a specialty channel first when they do not have a planned program to watch. With cost per rating point being about 50 percent lower and a greater ability to target an audience, it is not surprising to see that advertising revenues for specialty channels is growing significantly faster compared to conventional channels.[20]

Measuring the TV Audience

One of the most important considerations in TV advertising is the size and composition of the viewing audience. Audience measurement is critical to advertisers as well as to the networks and stations. Advertisers want to know the size and characteristics of the audience they are reaching when they purchase time on a particular program. And since the rates they pay are a function of audience size, advertisers want to be sure audience measurements are accurate.

Audience size and composition are also important to the network or station, since they determine the amount it can charge for commercial time. Shows are frequently cancelled because they fail to attract enough viewers to make their commercial time attractive to potential advertisers. Determining audience size is not an exact science and has been the subject of considerable controversy through the years. In this section, we examine how audiences are measured and how advertisers use this information in planning their media schedules.

Audience Measurement Resources The size and composition of television audiences are important to media planners as they weigh the value of buying commercial time on a program. In Canada, television audiences are measured and communicated by the Bureau of Broadcast Measurement of Canada (BBM Canada) and Nielsen Media Research (NMR). In 2006, BBM and NMR formed a joint venture to reduce the duplication of audience measurement. A third organization, the Television Bureau of Canada, offers additional information related to television audiences.

BBM Canada BBM Canada is a not-for-profit broadcast research company based on cooperation among the Canadian Association of Broadcasters, the Association of Canadian Advertisers, and Canadian advertising agencies. BBM Canada produces audience measurement data for its TV and radio members. This member relationship gives BBM Canada a reputation as the industry's rating service.

BBM Canada uses the diary research method for collecting television audience information in 33 smaller local markets during the fall and spring, and 9 larger local markets during the fall, spring, and summer. A booklet for each television owned in the household is sent to a representative sample of households. BBM gathers viewership information from this sample and then projects this information to the total viewing area.

The diary method works as follows. Each person aged two years or older records his or her viewing for one week in the booklet. The recordings are based on 15-minute increments from 6:00 A.M. until 2:00 A.M. Viewers write down station call letters, channel numbers, programs, and who is watching. The booklet also contains a number of basic demographic questions to be completed by each individual. All participants receive a small incentive to encourage their responses. BBM receives completed diaries from about 40 percent of those that are mailed, although the rates vary by region and other factors. These and other aspects of the research process are done according to standard market research practices to ensure valid and reliable information; however, one drawback is that some diaries are not filled out correctly.

To help its customers understand the data, BBM Canada provides an extensive array of products. Market reports are a summary of the audience sizes across all markets by time block, program listings, and time period. Their reach book summarizes the demographic information across each province, data area, and station. BBM Canada also offers guidelines on population estimates and booklets that assist its members in understanding the geographic boundaries studied and the research methodology. BBM Canada's television data book breaks down the viewing habits across different markets with user-friendly graphs and charts. The EM Stats Card provides detailed information for each extended market in terms of cable, satellite, PVR, and VCR penetration in addition to other similar macro-level data. Finally, two different documents tabulate the audiences for the different television shows. As a complement, BBM Canada also offers four different software packages that allow its members to analyze the data in a variety of ways.

Nielsen Media Research Nielsen Media Research (NMR) is a Canadian subsidiary of an American firm with the same name. NMR gathers viewership information from a panel of TV homes that is a representative sample. It then projects this information to the total viewing area. The resulting data is presented as the Nielsen Television Index (NTI). In Canada, the only technique used to gather audience measurement information is the electronic meter. Nielsen had previously used both the diary and electronic meter in Canada, like the practice done in the United States. Currently NMR's technology measures audiences for the national market and for the Vancouver, Calgary, and Toronto/Hamilton markets. NMR has recently launched a similar service to measure the audiences for the new digital channels offered on both cable and satellite.

NMR provides audience viewing information by household across a number of variables including income, language, cable status, pay TV, children residing, household size, age of head of household, number of TVs, rent or own home, kind of dwelling, ownership of VCRs and other durables, principal shopper, and restaurant and movie usage. The data is also presented by age, gender, education, and occupation. NMR also provides various data management tools and services to help its clients understand the data.

BBM–NMR Historically, BBM measured local market audiences with the diary method and NMR measured national audiences with its meter technology. Over time, NMR moved to a few local cities and BBM followed by introducing meter technology for national and some local markets. As part of this development, BBM introduced portable meter technology to measure French-speaking audiences in Quebec. For a period of a few years, duplication of audience measurement in Canada existed between the two organizations, something no other country could claim. In response to industry requests, BBM–NMR formed a joint venture in 2006 to end the redundancy.

The agreement means that BBM–NMR will use the meter technology for national, Toronto, Ontario, Calgary, and Vancouver markets, and will be the only organization releasing the data to BBM and NMR, which in turn will release the data to their members or subscribers and third-party clients. The agreement allows BBM to continue with its portable meter technology in Quebec. BBM will also have access to all of NMR's measurement technology, which is used worldwide. Most advertising industry members applaud the change; however, the Association of Canadian Advertisers expressed concerns regarding less competition with a single supplier of information.[21]

Television Bureau of Canada (TVB) The TVB is an industry association for television networks, television stations, and sales firms that sell television advertising time. It offers resources to those in the television industry to demonstrate the value and importance of television as a media versus competing media (i.e., magazines). It publishes basic facts garnered from various sources and conducts primary research through independent market research firms.

Most of the information is from BBM Canada or NMR. Based on this research, television consistently outperforms the other media on a number of variables. Television reaches 85 percent of the country on a daily basis, with the average Canadian watching about 3.5 hours per day. Furthermore, television is perceived as being the most authoritative (43 percent) and most influential (71 percent) compared to radio, the Internet, daily newspapers, and magazines.

Audience Measures We now review some of the concepts associated with television audience measurement that are the basis for the reports published by these three organizations.

Television Households The number of households in the market that own a TV is sometimes referred to as the *universe estimate* (UE). Since more than 98 percent of Canadian households own a TV set, **television households** generally correspond to the number of households in a given market.

Program Rating Probably the best known of all audience measurement figures is the **program rating**, the percentage of TV households in an area that are tuned to a specific program during a specific time period. The program rating is calculated by dividing the number of households tuned to a particular show by the total number of households in the area. For example, if 1.2 million households (HH) watched a show, the national rating would be 10.9, calculated as follows:

$$\text{Rating} = \frac{\text{HH tuned to show}}{\text{Total HH}} = \frac{1,200,000}{11,000,000} = 10.9$$

A **ratings point** represents 1 percent of all the television households in a particular area tuned to a specific program. On a national level, 1 ratings point represents 110,000 households. Thus, a top-rated program with an average rating of 19 reaches 2.1 million households each week (19 × 110,000).

The program rating is the key number to the stations, since the amount of money they can charge for commercial time is based on it. Ratings points are very important to the networks as well as to individual stations. A 1 percent change in a program's ratings over the course of a viewing season can gain or lose millions of dollars in advertising revenue. Advertisers also follow ratings closely, since they are the key measure for audience size and commercial rates.

Households Using Television The percentage of homes in a given area where TV is being watched during a specific time period is called **households using television (HUT)**. This figure, sometimes referred to as sets in use, is always expressed as a percentage. For example, if 5.5 million Canadian TV households have their sets turned on at 10 p.m. on a Thursday night, the HUT figure is 50 percent (5.5 million out of 11 million). Television usage varies widely depending on the time of day and season of the year.

Share of Audience Another important audience measurement figure is the **share of audience**, which is the percentage of households using TV in a specified time period that are tuned to a specific program. This figure considers variations in the number of sets in use and the total size of the potential audience, since it is based only on those households that have their sets turned on. Audience share is calculated by dividing the number of households (HH) tuned to a show by the number of households using television (HUT). Thus, if 5.5 million Canadian households had their sets turned on during the 10 p.m. time slot, the share of audience would be 20, calculated as follows:

$$\text{Share} = \frac{\text{HH tuned to show}}{\text{Households using TV}} = \frac{1.1}{5.5} = 20$$

Audience share is always higher than the program rating unless all the households have their sets turned on (in which case they would be equal). Share figures are important since they reveal how well a program does with the available viewing audience. For example, late at night the size of the viewing audience drops substantially, so the best way to assess the popularity of a late-night program is to examine the share of the available audience it attracts relative to competing programs.

Ratings services also provide an audience statistic known as **total audience**, the total number of homes viewing any five-minute part of a telecast. This number can be broken down to provide audience composition figures that are based on the distribution of the audience into demographic categories.

Audience Measurement Technology

Nielsen Television Index The source of national and network TV audience information is the Nielsen Television Index (NTI), which provides daily and weekly estimates of TV viewing and national sponsored network and major cable program audiences. Historically, Nielsen provided this information using a two-pronged system consisting of a national sample of metered households along with a separate sample of diary households. In the metered households, an electronic measurement device known as the **audimeter** (audience meter) was hooked up to the TV set to continuously measure the channels to which the set was tuned. Network viewing for the country (the famous Nielsen ratings) was based on the results provided by audimeters placed in a national sample of homes carefully selected to represent the population of households. The metered households were supported by a separate panel of households that recorded viewing information in diaries. Since the audimeter could measure only the channel to which the set was tuned, the diary panel was used to gather demographic data on the viewing audience.

For many years, the television and advertising industries expressed concern over the audimeter/diary system. The information from diaries was not available to the network and advertising analysts for several weeks, and studies indicated the method was overstating the size of some key demographic audiences. Cooperation rates among diary keepers declined, and often the person who kept a household's diary did not note what other family members watched when he or she wasn't home. The complex new video environment and explosion in viewing options also made it difficult for diary keepers to maintain accurate viewing records. As a result of these problems, in 1987 Nielsen made the people meter the sole basis of its national rating system and eliminated the use of the diary panel.

Exhibit 11–2 Nielsen Media Research uses the People Meter to measure national TV audiences

The People Meter The **People Meter** is an electronic measuring device that incorporates the technology of the audimeter in a system that records not only what is being watched but also by whom in a representative sample of homes. The actual device is a small box with eight buttons—six for the family and two for visitors—that can be placed on the top of the TV set (Exhibit 11–2). A remote control unit permits electronic entries from anywhere in the room. Each member of the sample household is assigned a button that indicates his or her presence as a viewer. The People Meter collects what station is being tuned and, through interaction with the meter, who is sitting down and watching the programs.

The viewership information the People Meter collects from the household is stored in the Home Unit, which in turn reports television use over a telephone line to a central computer. Data collected include when the set is turned on, which channel is viewed, when the channel is changed, and when the set is off, in addition to who is viewing. The demographic characteristics of the viewers are also in the system, and viewership can be matched to these traits. The operation centre processes all this information each night for release to the TV and advertising industries.

The People Meter is an improvement over the diary method, but it still requires cooperation on an ongoing basis from people in the metered homes. Viewers in the panel of households, including young children, must punch a preassigned number on the remote control device each time they start or stop watching.

The TV measurement system received newfound criticism due to ad-avoidance technologies like personal video recorders (PVRs). Viewership is reported for "live" and "live plus seven days," which means that it counts a playback within a week of recording. Recently, the networks wanted to adopt live-plus-seven as an industry standard. Advertisers wanted the live standard—because, they contended, many commercials have a limited shelf life, like spots that promote a movie opening on a certain weekend or a sale that lasts just 24 hours. A likely compromise of "live plus three" appears forthcoming in future negotiations.[22]

Radio

Television has often been referred to as the ideal advertising medium, because of its characteristics and national programming. In contrast, radio has evolved into a primarily local advertising medium characterized by highly specialized programming appealing to very narrow segments of the population. The importance of radio is best demonstrated by the numbers. There are 1,141 radio stations in Canada, including 195 AM and 407 FM stations. Radio reaches 93 percent of all Canadians over the age of 12 each week and has grown into a ubiquitous background to

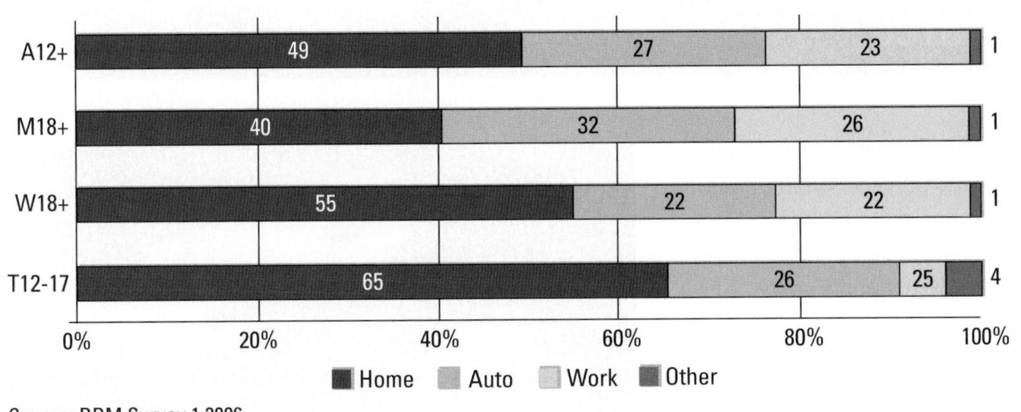

FIGURE 11–9

Percentage of listening by location

Source: BBM Survey 1 2006, National, Mo–Su, 5a-1a, p.32.

many activities, among them reading, driving, running, working, and socializing (Figure 11–9). The average Canadian listens to radio three hours per day or 21 hours per week.

The pervasiveness of this medium has not gone unnoticed by advertisers; radio advertising revenue grew from $1.05 billion in 2001 to $1.3 billion in 2005. Radio has survived and flourished as an advertising medium because it offers advertisers certain strengths for communicating messages to their potential customers. However, radio has inherent limitations that affect its role in the advertiser's media strategy. IMC Perspective 11–3 on page 336 highlights radio's recent attractiveness.

Strengths of Radio

Radio has many strengths compared to other media, including cost efficiency and absolute cost, reach and frequency, target audience selectivity, geographic coverage, scheduling flexibility, creativity for cognitive responses, and image.

Cost Efficiency and Absolute Cost One of the main strengths of radio as an advertising medium is its low cost. Radio commercials are very inexpensive to produce. They require only a script of the commercial to be read by the radio announcer or a copy of a prerecorded message that can be broadcast by the station. The cost for radio time is also low. The low relative costs of radio make it one of the most efficient of all advertising media, and the low absolute cost means the budget needed for an effective radio campaign is often lower than that for other media.

Reach and Frequency The low cost of radio means advertisers can build more reach and frequency into their media schedule within a certain budget. They can use different stations to broaden the reach of their messages and multiple spots to ensure adequate frequency. Radio commercials can be produced more quickly than TV spots, and the companies can afford to run them more often.[23] Many national advertisers also recognize the cost efficiency of radio and use it as part of their media strategy. Figures 11–10 and 11–11 on page 337 indicate the degree of reach.

Target Audience Selectivity Another major advantage of radio is the high degree of audience selectivity available through the various program formats and geographic coverage of the numerous stations. Radio lets companies focus their advertising on specialized audiences such as certain demographic and lifestyle groups. Most areas have radio stations with formats such as adult contemporary, easy listening, classical music, country, news/talk shows, jazz, and all news, to name a few. For example, among 18- to 24-year olds, the most popular radio format is top 40, while those between the ages of 45 and 54 prefer news/talk. Elusive consumers like teenagers, students, and working adults can be reached more easily through radio than most other media.

IMC PERSPECTIVE 11–3

Radio's Resurgence

Experts predicted the collapse of radio when other media like TV emerged; in the face of MP3 players, satellite radio, Internet radio, and podcasting, it again seems like radio is doomed. However, radio's advertising revenue continues to grow rapidly due to creative uses by national brands, new digital technology, expanded radio programming available on the Internet, and widespread consumer usage.

Brand development through radio appeared as a strong possibility and Goodyear Canada made this traditional media work. Building on the successful image from its TV ads, the radio ads used the highly recognizable spokesperson Tom Sharp with his distinctive and recognizable voice. The campaign focused on safety by informing consumers that various safety vehicles (e.g., ambulance, police car, or school bus) used Goodyear tires.

Technologically, radio is going digital like television. Compared to traditional analogue-based AM and FM stations, DAB offers CD-quality sound and a screen display that can communicate song credits, traffic, and emergency information, and possibly marketing messages. A consortium of major radio broadcasters (e.g., Chum, Rogers) launched a radio campaign describing these benefits of DAB with a suggestion to visit its website digitalradio.ca for more information. Many stations already offer DAB; however, consumers need to purchase a relatively inexpensive receiver.

Radio stations' Internet sites have been a key competitive tool to continue building the unique and local relationships stations have with their listeners. On these sites, loyal listeners can sign up to be "members," offer feedback, learn more about the on-air personalities, obtain artist and concert information, and participate in promotions. For some ardent radio listeners, the radio station's site has become a key portal for local entertainment and information. A Radio Marketing Bureau study reported that one-third of all Canadians 18 and older have visited a radio station's Internet site. For example, Standard Radio instituted a new division to develop Internet sites for its 52 stations and received 2.6 million unique visitors in one month. On average, each visitor accessed the site about 20 minutes a day for almost five days per week.

While the Internet offers a more value-added radio experience, radio's original benefit of "live" information with a local flavour continues to attract listeners at all times of the day in a variety of settings and situations. Extensive penetration of radios, and the fact that so much listening occurs in cars, allows radio to have substantial availability of advertising exposure—something most brand managers appreciate. Finally, radio is like a friend or companion that is always by one's side, allowing listeners to feel connected to their community.

Overall, radio's numbers speak for themselves. Its daily share of media time (i.e., three hours) is equal to television at 37 percent with daily newspapers trailing in third with 10 percent. Radio advertising revenues reached a total of $1.3 billion, easily surpassing all other media beyond television and daily newspapers. In fact, advertisers are tracking positive results and buy radio for 52 weeks a year. Moreover, with such an extensive investment, these kinds of advertisers look for ways to integrate radio with their other media.

Sources: Scott Gardiner, "Radio Days," *Marketing Magazine*, May 22, 2006; David Brown, "Radio.com," *Marketing Magazine*, May 22, 2006; and Andrea Zoe Aster, "Radio's New Wavelength," *Marketing Magazine*, February 2, 2004.

Question

1. Visit the Internet site of a popular radio station and assess how well it enhances the listener's enjoyment of the brand.

Radio can reach consumers other media can't. Light television viewers spend considerably more time with radio than with TV and are generally an upscale market in terms of income and education level. Light readers of magazines and newspapers also spend more time listening to radio. As mass marketing gives way to market segmentation and regional marketing, radio will continue to grow in importance.

FIGURE 11–10
Percentage weekly reach & hours tuned by major demographic

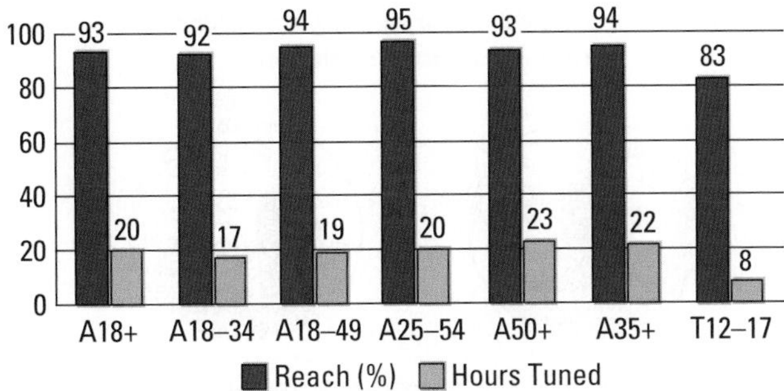

Source: BBM Survey 1 2006, National, Mo–Su, 5a-1a

Geographic Coverage Radio is essentially a local media. In this respect, since all listeners can tune in, it offers excellent coverage within its geographic scope. Radio stations become an integral part of many communities, and the deejays and program hosts may become popular figures. Advertisers often use radio stations and personalities to enhance their involvement with a local market and to gain influence with local retailers. Radio also works very effectively in conjunction with place-based/point-of-purchase promotions. Retailers often use on-site radio broadcasts combined with special sales or promotions to attract consumers to their stores and get them to make a purchase. Live radio broadcasts are also used in conjunction with event marketing.

FIGURE 11–11
Percentage weekly reach by major demographic, by location

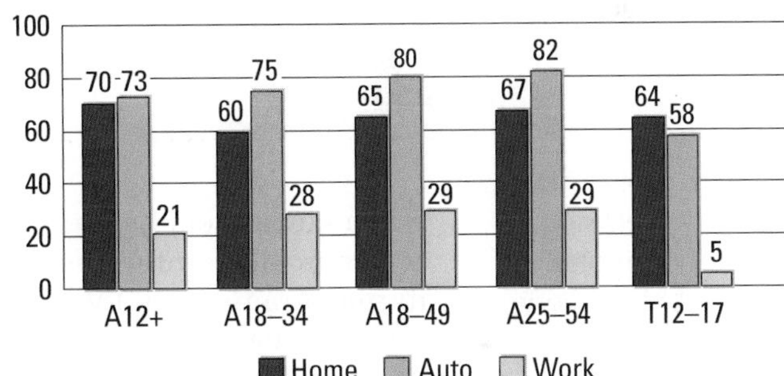

Source: BBM Survey 1 2006, Mo–Su, 5a-1a

Scheduling Flexibility Radio is probably the most flexible of all the advertising media because it has a very short closing period, which means advertisers can change their message almost up to the time it goes on the air. Radio commercials can usually be produced and scheduled on very short notice. Radio advertisers can easily adjust their messages to local market conditions and marketing situations.

Creativity for Cognitive Responses The verbal nature of radio ads makes them ideal for long copy to select target audiences who may appreciate greater detailed information for some products. Alternatively, radio ads can also provide more concise brand information in a timely manner. Moreover, both of these factors are highly relevant for those listening in their car, which is a significant percentage of radio listenership. In either case, the informative nature of radio advertising makes it an opportunistic media to connect with a target audience on a more rational level.

Media Image Radio advertising in general has a good media image. Consumers rely on radio for news, weather, and traffic information, not to mention the obvious program content. Thus, radio is well appreciated and this spills over to the ads as 77 percent of Canadians feel that radio advertising is acceptable.

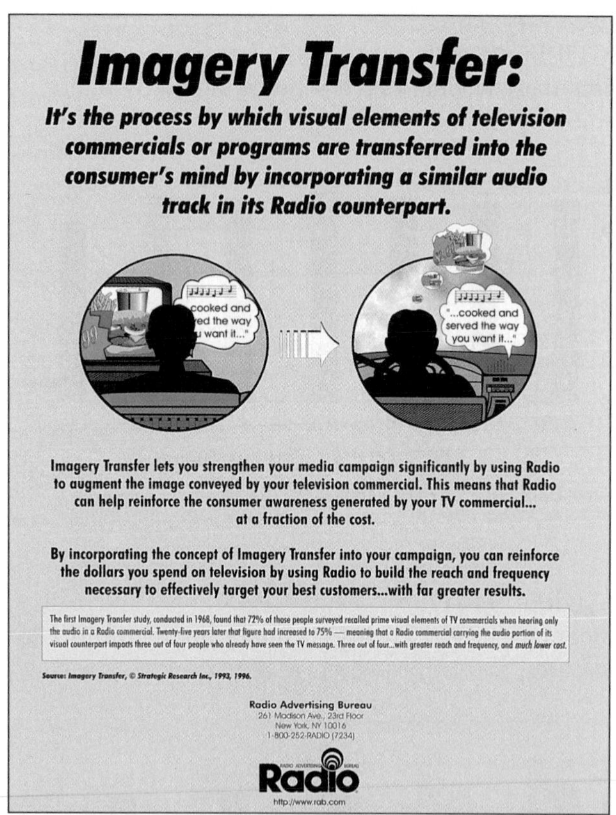

Exhibit 11–3 The Radio Advertising Bureau promotes the concept of imagery transfer

LIMITATIONS OF RADIO

Several factors limit the effectiveness of radio as an advertising medium, among them creativity for emotional responses, amount of processing time, target audience coverage, listener attention, selective exposure, clutter, and involvement. The media planner must consider them in determining the role the medium will play in the advertising program.

Creativity for Emotional Responses A major drawback of radio as an advertising medium is the absence of a visual image. The radio advertiser cannot show the product, demonstrate it, or use any type of visual appeal or information. While the creative options of radio are limited, many advertisers take advantage of the absence of a visual element to let consumers create their own picture of what is happening in a radio message. Some ads encourage listeners to use their imagination when processing a commercial message.

Radio may also reinforce television messages through a technique called **image transfer**, where the images of a TV commercial are implanted into a radio spot.[24] First the marketer establishes the video image of a TV commercial. Then it uses a similar, or even the same, audio portion (spoken words and/or jingle) as the basis for the radio counterpart. The idea is that when consumers hear the radio message, they will make the connection to the TV commercial, reinforcing its video images. Image transfer offers advertisers a way to make radio and TV ads work together. This promotional piece put out by the Radio Advertising Bureau of the U.S. shows how the image transfer process works (Exhibit 11–3).

Amount of Processing Time A radio commercial is, like a TV ad, a short-lived and fleeting message that is externally paced and does not allow the receiver to control the rate at which it is processed.

Target Audience Coverage Another problem with radio is the high level of audience fragmentation due to the large number of stations. The percentage of the market tuned to any particular station is usually very small. The top-rated radio station in many major metropolitan areas with a number of AM and FM stations may attract less than 10 percent of the total listening audience. Advertisers that want a broad reach in their radio advertising media schedule have to buy time on a number of stations to cover even a local market. With recent media mergers in Canada, syndicated radio stations now provide advertisers with greater coverage, thus minimizing this limitation to a lesser degree. Figures 11–12 and 11–13 highlight the major players for English and French listeners.

Listener Attention Another problem that plagues radio is that it is difficult to retain listener attention to commercials. Radio programming, particularly music, is often the background to some other activity and may not receive the listener's full attention. Thus they may miss all or some of the commercials.

Selective Exposure One environment where radio has a more captive audience is in cars. But getting listeners to expose themselves to commercials can still be difficult. Most people preprogram their car radio and change stations during commercial breaks. A study by Avery Abernethy found large differences between exposure to radio programs versus advertising for listeners in cars. They were exposed to only half of the advertising broadcast and changed stations frequently to avoid commercials.[25] Another factor that is detracting from radio listening in motor vehicles is the rapid growth of cellular phones. A recent study found that half of commuters surveyed who own a cellphone reported listening to less radio than they did a year earlier.[26]

FIGURE 11–12
Share of radio hours tuned by major station—English 18+

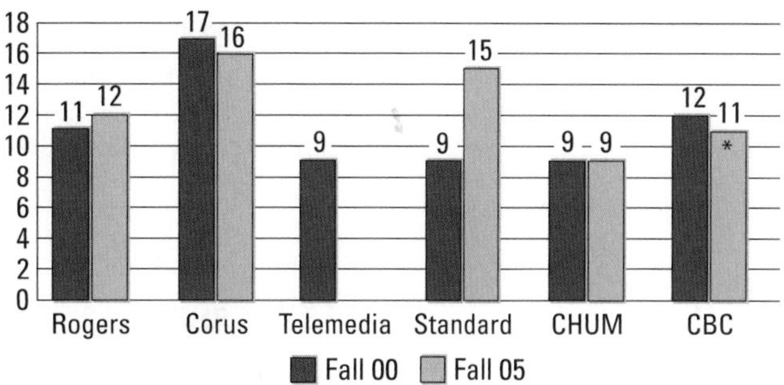

*Fall 04 data. Fall 05 data not representative because of disruption of regular programming.

Source: BBM, Mo–Su, 5a-1a; as reported in CMDC Ownership and Market Share Report

Clutter Clutter is just as much a problem with radio as with other advertising media. Radio stations can play as many minutes of advertising as they like. Most radio stations carry an average of nearly 10 minutes of commercials every hour. During the popular morning and evening rush hours, the amount of commercial time may exceed 12 minutes. Advertisers must create commercials that break through the clutter or use heavy repetition to make sure their messages reach consumers. In a study of radio listeners conducted by Edison Research, perceptions of increased ad clutter were cited by participants as a reason for spending less time listening to radio.[27]

Involvement Similar to television, radio is generally considered a low-involvement media since it is faced with the same characteristics of short processing time and clutter. In fact, it may be seen as being less involving since it has the additional limitation of no visual.

FIGURE 11–13
Share of radio hours tuned by major station—French 18+

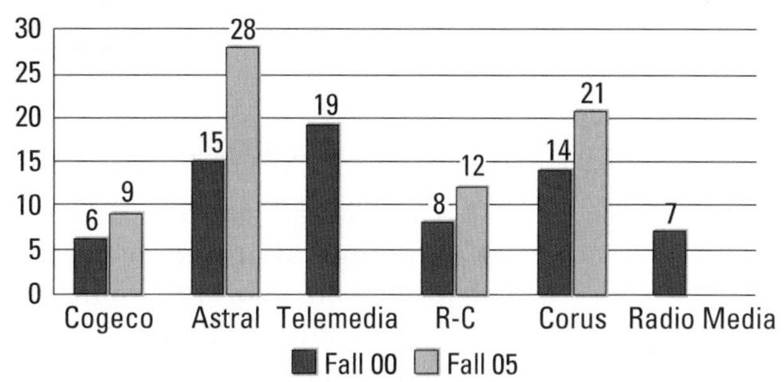

Source: BBM, Mo–Su, 5a-1a; as reported in CMDC Ownership and Market Share Report

Buying Radio Time

The purchase of radio time is similar to that of television, as advertisers can make either network, or spot buys. Since these options were reviewed in the section on buying TV time, they are discussed here only briefly.

Network Radio Advertising time on radio can be purchased on a network basis. This is a relatively new option for advertisers who can now run ads on the CHUM radio network, The Team Sports Radio Network, and a few others. Using networks minimizes the amount of negotiation and administrative work needed to get national or regional coverage, and the costs are lower than those for individual stations. However, the number of affiliated stations on the network roster and the types of audiences they reach may vary, so the use of network radio reduces advertisers' flexibility in selecting stations.

Spot Radio National advertisers can also use spot radio to purchase airtime on individual stations in various markets. The purchase of spot radio provides greater flexibility in selecting markets, individual stations, and airtime and adjusting the message for local market conditions. By far the heaviest users of radio are local advertisers; the majority of radio advertising time is purchased from individual stations by local companies. Auto dealers, retailers, restaurants, and financial institutions are among the heaviest users of local radio advertising.

FIGURE 11–14

Audience composition by daypart (%)

Time Block		Women 18+	Men 18+	Teens	Total
Breakfast	Mo–Fr 6–10a	48	48	4	100
Midday	Mo–Fr 10a–4p	51	48	1	100
Drive	Mo–Fr 4–7p	46	49	5	100
Evening	Mo–Fr 7p–12a	44	42	9	100

Source: BBM Survey 1 2006, National, AQH Audience

Time Classifications

As with television, the broadcast day for radio is divided into various time periods or dayparts, as shown in Figure 11–14. The size of the radio listening audience varies widely across the dayparts, and advertising rates follow accordingly. The largest radio audiences (and thus the highest rates) occur during the early morning and late afternoon drive times. Radio rates also vary according to the number of spots or type of audience plan purchased, the supply and demand of time available in the local market, and the ratings of the individual station. Rate information is available directly from the stations and is summarized in CARD. Some stations issue grid rate cards. But many stations do not adhere strictly to rate cards. Their rates are negotiable and depend on factors such as availability, time period, and number of spots purchased.

Measuring the Radio Audience

As noted earlier, BBM Canada also provides information on radio listenership using a diary method similar to television. Surveys are done up to three times per year in over 130 radio markets. BBM Canada publishes many reports associated with these surveys. Market reports summarize each radio station's audience by occupation, language, and other important characteristics. Other similar reports with greater aggregation across regions are also published. As for television, BBM Canada provides its members with many supporting documents to understand how to use radio as a communication tool. It also offers many software applications so that advertisers can purchase radio media effectively and efficiently. The three basic elements in the BBM Canada reports are:

- Person estimates—the estimated number of people listening.
- Rating—the percentage of listeners in the survey area population.
- Share—the percentage of the total estimated listening audience.

These three estimates are further defined by using quarter-hour and cume figures. The **average quarter-hour (AQH) figure** expresses the average number of people estimated to have listened to a station for a minimum of five minutes during any quarter-hour in a time period. This figure helps to determine the audience and cost of a spot schedule within a particular time period.

Cume stands for cumulative audience, the estimated total number of different people who listened to a station for at least five minutes in a quarter-hour period within a reported daypart. Cume estimates the reach potential of a radio station.

The **average quarter-hour rating (AQH RTG)** expresses the estimated number of listeners as a percentage of the survey area population. The **average quarter-hour share (AQH SHR)** is the percentage of the total listening audience tuned to each station. It shows the share of listeners each station captures out of the total listening audience in the survey area.

Audience research data on radio are often limited, particularly compared with TV, magazines, or newspapers. The BBM audience research measurement mostly focuses on demographics and a handful of lifestyle factors. Most users of radio are local companies that cannot support research on radio listenership in their markets. Thus, media planners do not have as much audience information available to guide them in their purchase of radio time as they do with other media.

The Radio Marketing Bureau (RMB) is an organization that plays a similar role for radio as the Television Bureau of Canada, discussed earlier in this chapter. It acts as a resource for radio stations and those involved with selling airtime for radios. Its mission is to educate advertisers on the effective use of the radio medium and to assist advertisers in meeting their communication objectives. The Radio Marketing Bureau offers professional services to advertisers if needed. It also offers a training and certificate program for those working in the radio industry. Finally, this organization does some research to help support radio as a viable communication medium.

IMC Planning: Strategic Use of Broadcast Media

We continue with our IMC planning sections by relating the use of TV and radio with respect to achieving communication and behavioural objectives in general and in terms of the different stages of the consumer decision-making process for the target audience. This builds on our discussions in earlier chapters and highlights the importance of planning creative and media together.

Television

The creative opportunities and many types of television allow it to play a variety of roles in the decision-making process for the target audience. We link the different types of ads with communication objectives and decision-making processes because the integration of television with other media or tools is predicated upon which types of TV ads will be run. For example, the suggestion to combine TV with Internet advertising, an event sponsorship, or perhaps out-of-home media is contingent on how the two media are planned to influence the target audience. As promotional planners decide upon TV as part of their IMC plan, it is critical to consider its communication objectives in relation to the objectives the other tools will contribute.

Promotional managers can plan for ads to influence their target audience at the pre-purchase and need recognition stages. These kinds of ads could focus on one key benefit or consumption experience, and identify the brand sufficiently to contribute to awareness. For example, some car ads fit this role quite nicely, like the commercials positioning the Toyota Corolla as a reliable vehicle. The plan included other media to encourage further progress through the decision-making process. In this case, the Corolla utilized newspaper advertising for additional explanation and support of the reliability (e.g., information search), and transit station posters as a reminder for a test drive (e.g., purchase decision). For Corolla, the media selection, including television, planned a particular role for each selection to encourage all aspects of the decision-making process, each with particular attitudinal communication objectives.

Alternatively, marketers could provide a television message with information to influence their target audience while evaluating alternative brands. The WestJet ads communicated the enhanced service level compared to its previous discount offering to encourage Air Canada consumers to switch; this message would be critical at the alternative evaluation stage. The many executions showed the variety of customer experiences enhanced by the commitment level of the staff to serve its customers in an exemplary manner.

Finally, planners often schedule ads that have more immediate purchase intention or purchase facilitation objectives for the target to take action. An additional type of car ad communicates a promotional event or encourages a dealer visit for a test drive. Virtually all car brands resort to TV ads like this, yet the intensity of the "call to action" and the frequency varies considerably. When these ads are run, car brands typically are not running other types of TV ads but might have instructions to consult the newspaper for additional information. Another example in the social marketing realm is The United Way of Toronto's TV ads that showed a "helping hand" in two different scenarios with a verbal message requesting donations and the Internet address shown visually.

Radio

While all media are inherently in competition for advertising revenue spent by media planners, radio finds itself with a very significant niche of flexibility that allows it to be in the plans for national brands like Bell and local advertisers like the pizzeria just around the corner. Moreover, the characteristics of the medium allow planners to integrate radio with virtually any other media or IMC tool.

Whether we are considering a national advertiser like Bell or a local business, oftentimes the purchase decision stage is the one where maximum influence occurs. For example, many radio messages have a time frame for encouraging purchase through participation with a price promotion. Retailers use radio extensively for various sales, for instance. Alternatively, other radio messages might remind the target audience of entertainment and leisure activities occurring in the city or province within a time frame requiring more immediate action. In these situations, the key communication objectives attained are brand purchase intention or brand purchase facilitation. As we can see from these points, the scheduling flexibility of radio permits attainment of particular communication objectives or messaging consumers exactly when they are planning to make a purchase decision.

The lower costs associated with radio can contribute to building brand equity or an identifiable positioning through the affordability of repetition. A recent example of this is the prevalent use of radio by Sleep Country Canada, with owner Christine McGee as the spokesperson. The radio ads give the central positioning as a leading mattress retailer much added frequency beyond its television commercials, thus indicating a natural way to build brands by integrating a consistent message across two broadcast media.

Radio's flexibility and cost implications allow it to support other IMC tools. It can suggest that the target audience visit a brand's Internet site or look for a direct mail piece sent to their home—again, both are action-oriented with a time frame—or with some kind of intention on the part of the receiver of the message. As noted above with price promotions, many other sales promotions can be communicated through radio, particularly those affiliated with sponsorships. Radio can be a key integrating media to generate awareness of the other IMC tools for further communication in the target audience's decision making.

SUMMARY

Television and radio media are the most pervasive media in most consumers' daily lives and offer advertisers the opportunity to reach vast audiences. Both media are time rather than space oriented and organized similarly in that they use a system of affiliated stations belonging to a network, as well as individual stations, to broadcast their programs and commercial messages. Advertising on radio or TV can be done on national or regional network programs or purchased in spots from local stations.

TV has grown faster than any other advertising medium in history and has become the leading medium for national advertisers. No other medium offers its creative capabilities; the combination of sight, sound, and movement give the advertiser a vast number of options for presenting a commercial message with high impact. Television also offers advertisers mass coverage at a low relative cost. Variations in programming and audience composition, along with the growth of cable, are helping TV offer more audience selectivity to advertisers. While television is often viewed as the ultimate advertising medium, it has several limitations, including the high absolute cost of producing and airing commercials, low target audience selectivity, short processing time, extensive clutter, high selective exposure, and distrustful image.

Information regarding the size and composition of national and local TV audiences is provided by BBM Canada and Nielsen Media Research. The amount of money networks or stations can charge for commercial time on their programs is based on its audience measurement figures. This information is also important to media planners, as it is used to determine the combination of shows needed to attain specific levels of reach and frequency with the advertiser's target audience.

The role of radio as an entertainment and advertising medium has changed with the rapid growth of television. Radio has evolved into a primarily local advertising medium that offers highly specialized programming appealing to narrow segments of the market. Radio offers advertisers cost efficiency and absolute cost, reach and frequency, target audience selectivity, geographic coveage, scheduling flexibility, creativity for cognitive responses, and media image.

The major drawback of radio is its weak creativity owing to the absence of a visual image. The short and fleeting nature of the radio commercial, the highly fragmented nature of the radio audience, low involvement, and clutter are also problems.

As with TV, the rate structure for radio advertising time varies with the size of the audience delivered. The primary sources of listener information are BBM and RMB.

KEY TERMS

DISCUSSION QUESTIONS

1. Discuss the strengths of television as an advertising medium and the importance of these factors to major national advertisers and to smaller local companies.

2. Television is often described as a mass medium that offers little selectivity to advertisers. Do you agree with this statement? What are some of the ways selectivity can be achieved through TV advertising?

3. Choose a particular television daypart other than prime time and analyze the products and services advertised during this period. Why do you think these companies have chosen to advertise during this daypart?

4. Explain what is meant by zapping and zipping and how they affect television viewing behaviour. Discuss some of the ways that advertisers can deal with these problems.

5. Discuss the strengths and limitations of advertising on specialty channels. Discuss how both large national advertisers and small local companies might use cable TV effectively in their media plans.

6. Discuss the methods used to measure network and local TV viewing audiences. Do you think the measurement methods used for each are producing reliable and valid estimates of the viewing audiences? How might they be improved?

7. Discuss how personal video recorders will influence consumers' television viewing and how advertisers will likely respond to the changes.

8. What are the strengths and limitations of advertising on radio? What types of advertisers are most likely to use radio?

9. What is meant by image transfer in radio advertising? Find an example of a radio campaign that is using this concept and evaluate it.

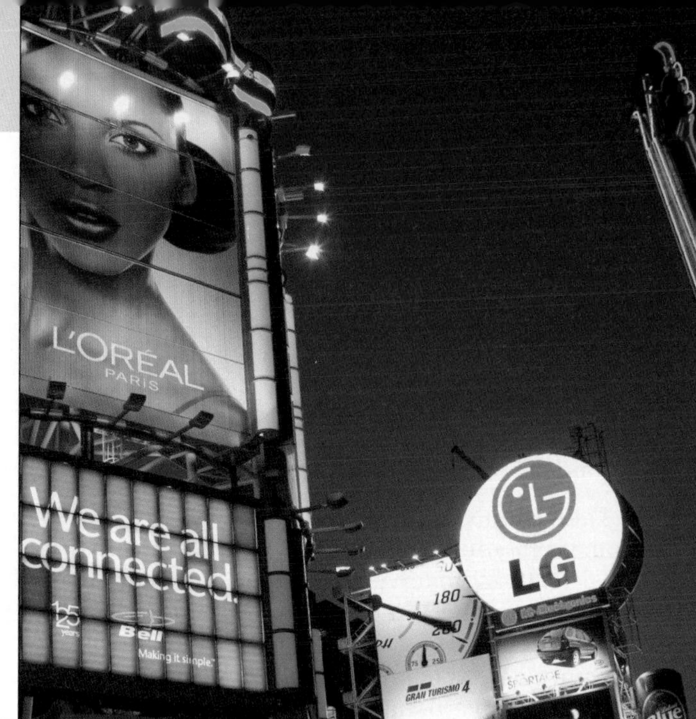

CHAPTER 12

PRINT MEDIA

Chapter Objectives

- To examine the structure of the magazine and newspaper industries and the role of each medium in the advertising program.
- To analyze the strengths and limitations of magazines and newspapers as advertising media.
- To examine the various types of magazines and newspapers and the value of each as an advertising medium.
- To discuss how advertising space is purchased in magazines and newspapers, how readership is measured, and how rates are determined.

Custom Publications Find a Niche

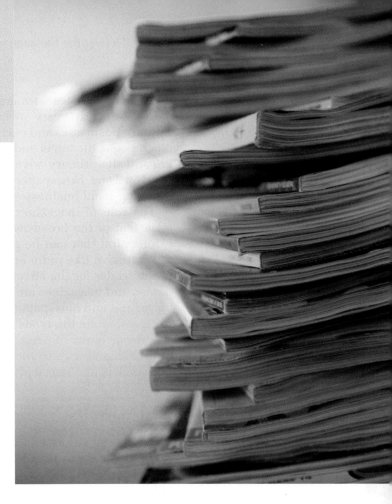

Segmenting the market and tailoring an offering is the hallmark of marketing and brand advertising; HBC has followed suit with its novel approach for magazines directed to its current customers, titled *Belle* and *Living Spree.* Introduced in 2004, *Belle* targeted upscale females ages 35 to 55 with household income greater than $100,000—representing HBC's best customers in 325,000 Canadian homes. Past purchasing behaviour through credit cards and rewards cards identified this attractive segment as being interested in fashion, beauty, and home décor. *Belle* offers editorial content to fit the target's lifestyle while showing selective products and brands sold at The Bay and Home Outfitters. Its aspirational tone allows Belle readers to dream and fulfill their lifestyle with a magazine tailored to their liking.

HBC appeared to have found a winning package with *Belle.* A previous magazine missed the mark of selectivity and relationship building with a mass appeal and distribution to 1.5 million households. However, *Living Spree,* launched in 2003, is targeted to moderate-income households with children. Its editorial content focuses on practical solutions for the family and is distributed to 500,000 households three times per year. Thus, rather than one general custom publication, HBC offers two more targeted titles to different types of current customers.

The allure of a custom publication allows brands to track the effectiveness of the vehicle specifically through shopping behaviour. In light of recent media fragmentation, PVRs, and privacy legislation, advertisers find these publications useful as a way of communicating directly yet with the flair and editorial content of a traditional magazine. In fact, a key mandate is authentic editorial content, since consumers are sensitive to too strong a hard-sell if the lines between editorial and content become blurred. Finally, the magazines are generally cost-efficient and cost-effective, giving marketers the best of both worlds financially. For example, one custom publication issue approximately equals 12 minutes of television advertising, compared to the average of 20 minutes readers spend perusing a magazine.

RBC is another brand that investigated custom publications with *life, etc.*, directed to customers of its Visa loyalty cards. While testing the concept, RBC examined spending and redemption habits of consumers who did and did not receive the publication to assess its communication effectiveness. Similar kinds of "experiments" or tests are possible in future using the strong database developed through these publications. For example, *Belle* planned to offer more customized promotional offers depending on the purchasing habits consumers developed.

Sources: Lynn Chambers, "Ringing Her Belle," *Marketing Magazine,* March 6, 2006; and Lisa D'Innocenzo, "Next Wave Customer Pubs: The New Black," *Strategy Magazine,* November 2004.

Question

1. Given that HBC and RBC are using custom publications, why do they continue to advertise in regular magazines?

Thousands of magazines are published in Canada and throughout the world. They appeal to nearly every specific consumer interest and lifestyle, as well as to thousands of businesses and occupations. By becoming a highly specialized medium that reaches specific target audiences, the magazine industry has prospered. Newspapers are still the primary advertising medium in terms of both ad revenue and number of advertisers. Newspapers are particularly important as a local advertising medium for many retail businesses and are often used by large national advertisers as well.

The role of magazines and newspapers in the advertiser's media plan differs from that of the broadcast media because they allow the presentation of detailed information that can be processed at the reader's own pace. The print media are not intrusive like radio and TV, and they generally require some effort on the part of the reader for the advertising message to have an impact. For this reason, newspapers and magazines are often referred to as *high-involvement media.*[1] While both magazines and newspapers are print media, their strengths and limitations are quite different, as are the types of advertising each attracts. This chapter focuses on these two major forms of print media. It examines the specific strengths and limitations of each, along with factors that are important in determining when and how to use newspapers and magazines in the media plan.

Evaluation of Magazines

Magazines serve the educational, informational, and entertainment needs of a wide range of readers in both the consumer and business markets. Magazines are the most specialized of all advertising media. While some magazines are general mass-appeal publications, most are targeted to a very specific audience. There is a magazine designed to appeal to nearly every type of consumer in terms of demographics, lifestyle, activities, interests, or fascination. Numerous magazines are targeted toward specific businesses and industries as well as toward individuals engaged in various professions. The wide variety makes magazines an appealing medium to many advertisers.

Classifications of Magazines

To gain some perspective on the various types of magazines available and the advertisers that use them, consider the way magazines are generally classified. Canadian Advertising Rates and Data (CARD), the primary reference source on periodicals for media planners, divides magazines into three broad categories based on the audience to which they are directed: consumer, farm, and business publications. Each category is then further classified according to the magazine's editorial content and audience appeal. We also examine the opportunity of foreign publications.

Consumer Magazines Consumer magazines are bought by the general public for information and/or entertainment. CARD divides 830 domestic consumer magazines into 46 classifications, among them general interest, sports, travel and tourism, and women's. Another way of classifying consumer magazines is by distribution: They can be sold through subscription, store distribution, or controlled distribution (free) to selected individuals. Figures 12–1 and 12–2 show the top Canadian magazines in terms of circulation. Magazines can also be classified by frequency; weekly, monthly, and bimonthly are the most common.

Consumer magazine advertising reached $665 million in 2005, up from $541 million in 2001. Annual circulation hit 751 million copies in 2005. Consumer magazines are best suited to marketers interested in reaching general consumers of products and services as well as to companies trying to reach a specific target audience. Gardening, homes, and women's magazines have grown significantly the past decade. IMC Perspective 12–1 on page 350 traces the decline of one magazine format. Figure 12–3 on page 350 shows the most prevalent advertising product categories.

FIGURE 12–1 Top English-language magazines by circulation and readership*

English Publications	Magazine Class	Average Total Circulation	1P 4CB Rate ($)	Total Canada Readers Per Copy 12+ (000s)	English Canada Average Readers Per Issue 18+ (000S)			
					Total	Male	Female	% Reach 18+
CAA Magazine	General Interest	753,237	28,887	1.3	1863	852	1011	9
Canadian Living	Women's	519,045	35,500	8.2	4105	991	3114	21
Chatelaine	Women's	586,136	46.505	6.4	4022	728	3294	20
Famous Magazine	Entertainment	511,045	25,000	3.2	1077	564	513	5
Food & Drink	Food & Beverage	522,213	18,056	4.2	2018	762	1255	10
Homemakers Magazine	Women's	512,201	23,230	4.9	1856	333	1523	9
Maxim	Men's	2,503,218	28,350					
Movie Entertainment	Entertainment	854,512	20,080					
Québec Vacation Guide	Travel	1,629,283	9,950					
Reader's Digest	General Interest	921,588	37,305	7.2	6411	2779	3632	32
Starweek	TV & Radio	641,900	16,935	2	1215	588	628	6
Stuff Magazine	Men's	1,310,900	14,535					
Touring (Eng)	General Interest	615,696	12,700	1.9	243	139	105	1
Tribute Magazine	Entertainment	500,019	19,900	3.4	1273	676	597	6
TV Times Magazines	TV & Radio	1,696,179	48,391	1.5	1936	876	1060	10
Westworld	General Interest	646,999	27,700	1.3	1356	676	680	7

Note: Consumer Magazines: Circulation, Page Rates & Readership: English Canada (Audited Circ. of 30,000+)

Source: *Media Digest*, p. 56.

FIGURE 12–2 Top French-language magazines by circulation and readership*

French Publications	Magazine Class	Average Total Circulation	1P 4CB Rate ($)	Total Canada Readers Per Copy 12+ (000s)	French Canada Average Readers Per Issue 18+ (000S)			
					Total	Male	Female	% Reach 18+
Bébé Progresse	Babies & Moms	459,848	17,500					
Châtelaine	Women's	200,115	15,800	6.2	1089	374	715	20
Coup de Pouce	Women's	221,289	12,510	6.2	1238	342	896	23
L'actualité	News	185,157	17,500	6.0	979	464	515	18
Place des Arts Magazine	Entertainment	200,000	7,350					
Primeurs	TV & Radio	409,434	7,875	1.9	668	378	290	13
Qu'est-ce qui mijore**	Food & Beverage	551,000	14,000	1.9	982	260	721	18
Sélection du Reader's Digest	General Interest	242,970	12,105	5.2	1154	490	663	22
Senass!	Women's	200,000	6,750					
Style de Vie	Women's	206,667	8,750	0.9	135	41	94	3
Télé Horaire - Le journal de Montreal	TV & Radio	272,360	5,271					
Touring (French)	General Interest	615,696	12,700	1.9	843	434	409	16
TV 7 Jours/TV Hebdo	TV & Radio	248,000	9,575	4.1	816	314	503	15
Virage	Marure Marker	224,023	4,730					
Voilà!	TV & Radio	581,391	16,215	1.2	528	211	317	10
Voir	City & Regional	199,000	14,323	2.8	483	223	260	9

Note: Rates and circulation as of April 2005 CARD. PMB 2006 2 year Readership study with the exception of those magazines noted with
*** PMB 2006 1 year Readership Study PUBLISHER SWORN CIRCULATION NUMBER*
*Consumer Magazines: Circulation, Page Rates & Readership: English Canada (Audited Circ. of 30,000+)

Source: *Media Digest*

IMC PERSPECTIVE 12–1

The Decline of Men's Magazines

After four years, 29 issues, and one rumination on The Hulk's sexual orientation, *Toro Magazine*—Canada's would-be rival to the likes of *Esquire* and *GQ*—suspended publication in February 2007. In the accompanying death notice, *Toro* publisher Dinah Quattrin cited a "limited advertising pool" in the men's category as the reason for its demise. It could be argued that things are tough in every sector, but *Toro's* closure brings the number of general interest men's magazines in Canada to six—three fewer than are devoted to horses and horse racing. Clearly, readers and advertisers aren't saying nay to every magazine category.

But if Toro's remaining competitors have any misgivings about the viability of men's magazines, they aren't saying. The day after its demise, in fact, auto title *Driven* tooted its own horn by issuing a release stating "Men's magazines need the right formula to succeed in Canada," and that *Toro's* demise was "further validation" of its own editorial concept—which features a mix of fashion, technology, travel, lifestyle, and cars. *Toro,* it charged, "failed to assess exactly what men are interested in." An odd assertion, since all the things mentioned in the release were prominent ingredients in *Toro's* editorial mix, along with other typical male pursuits like sports, drink, food, and, yes, sex. Why then, did *Toro* fail while *Driven,* according to publisher Michel Crpault, is flourishing?

Some rival publishers and media buyers believe *Toro's* editorial product—characterized as everything from "a bit T&A," to "juvenile" and "derivative" of U.S. publications like *Details*—either frightened off or failed to attract the prestige advertisers it coveted. Much of the blame, however, seems to focus on *Toro's* controlled-circulation model, which saw the magazine distributed for free in *The Globe and Mail.* In addition to making *Toro* entirely reliant on ad dollars for its survival, some believe there was no natural fit between the two products.

It was in September 2003 that *Marketing* ran a feature entitled "The Rise of Men's Mags" outlining the increased activity in a category previously dormant in Canadian publishing. At the time, one media buyer predicted that the sector would heat up before levelling out. Four years later, it hasn't levelled out so much as it has flatlined. Nearly all of the titles cited in that piece (*Rev, Razor, Menz, Toro*) have closed, with only Ottawa's appropriately titled *UMM (Urban Male Magazine)* still standing.

According to the April edition of *Canadian Advertising Rates & Data* (CARD), the men's magazine category in Canada now consists of *Chill Magazine* (a freebie available at The Beer Store), *Driven, Maxim, Ontario Out of Doors, UMM,* the French-language title *Summum,* and the regional title *Winnipeg Men Magazine.* So perhaps there really

FIGURE 12–3

Top 10 magazine ad categories

Advertiser Category	2006 Rank*
Toiletries and toilet goods	1
Food and food products	2
Business and consumer services	3
Retail stores	4
Automotive	5
Drugs and remedies	6
Travel, hotels and resorts	7
Entertainment and amusement	8
Computer and business equipment	9
Home entertainment	10

*Advertising dollars

Source: LNA 2006

While large national advertisers tend to dominate consumer magazine advertising in terms of expenditures, consumer magazines are also important to smaller companies selling products that appeal to specialized markets. Special-interest magazines assemble consumers with similar lifestyles or interests and offer marketers an efficient way to reach these people with little wasted coverage or circulation. For example, a manufacturer of ski equipment such as Nordica, Rossignol, or Salomon

isn't a demand for Canadian men's titles outside of the male-friendly news and business categories. Brian Segal, president and CEO of Rogers Publishing, says the company is in the "dual-audience" magazine business, electing to cover off the men's category with male-oriented titles like *Canadian Business, Maclean's,* and *Profit.* "Why tip the apple cart when you can start adding fashion pages to *Maclean's*?" reasons Shelagh Tarleton, VP, publisher with Kontent Publishing's *FQ* and *Sir* titles.

Segal says Rogers did explore the men's category "very thoroughly" four or five years ago, but couldn't see a viable ad market or even a place for a Canadian title that wouldn't merely ape the U.S. and U.K. imports that crowd Canadian newsstands. "We looked at a variety of ways of growing our business, but concluded that the women's market was the place to go in Canada," adds Segal, whose company instead added several female-oriented titles, including *Loulou, Chocolat, and Hello!,* to its portfolio.

According to 2005 figures from the Audit Bureau of Circulations, the U.S. edition of *Maxim* has a paid circulation of 148,636 in Canada, followed by *Men's Health* with 105,241. Other U.S. men's titles with paid Canadian circulation include *GQ* (23,116), *Esquire* (11,099), *Men's Journal* (10,486), and *Details* (7,093). Interestingly, some take that to mean there's a viable market for a quality Canadian men's magazine. "Do I think there's room in this country to talk to men? Absolutely," says Kontent's Tarleton. "Advertisers are hungry for it, and frankly I think guys are too."

Sir caters to a psychographic of what Tarleton describes as "young-minded if not youngish" urban males. Like *Toro* was, it is distributed inside *The Globe and Mail.* The magazine, which is presented to advertisers as a package with *FQ,* has developed into a "really solid property" since its 2005 debut, says Tarleton. She expects it to break even this year as it broadens its advertiser base. *Sir's* 86-page spring/summer issue features 39 pages of advertising from the likes of BMW, Cadillac, and Mini (a full-page ad costs $17,000). "We're getting a ton of automotive and a much broader mix of fashion than we've had in the past," says Tarleton.

Even *UMM,* a publication that will never be confused with *Toro* or *Sir,* is booming. Its current issue features a raft of advertisers like Calvin Klein, Honda, Ford, P&G (both its Gillette and Old Spice brands), Kenneth Cole, and Dial Canada. "I think with UMM, they've figured out where the niche is and they're milking it, and good for them," says Ivey. "They've said there's room for a magazine that's all about the pictures and not too much about the editorial."

Source: Chris Powell, "Maximed Out," *Marketing Magazine,* May 14, 2007.

Question

1. What reasons explain why so many men's magazines did not survive the past few years?

might find *Ski Canada* magazine the best vehicle for advertising to serious skiers. Not only are these specialty magazines of value to firms interested in reaching a specific market segment, but their editorial content often creates a very favourable advertising environment for relevant products and services (see Exhibit 12–1).

Farm Publications The second major CARD category consists of all the magazines directed to farmers and their families. About 80 publications are tailored to nearly every possible type of farming or agricultural interest (e.g., *Ontario Milk Producer, Ontario Produce Farmer*). A number of farm publications are directed at farmers in specific provinces or regions, such as Alberta Beef (see Exhibit 12–2 on page 352). Farm publications are not classified with business publications because historically farms were not perceived as businesses.

Business Publications Business publications are those magazines or trade journals published for specific businesses, industries, or occupations. CARD breaks down magazines and trade journals into 90 categories. The major categories include

- Magazines directed at specific professional groups, such as *Canadian Lawyer* for lawyers and *Canadian Architect* for architects.

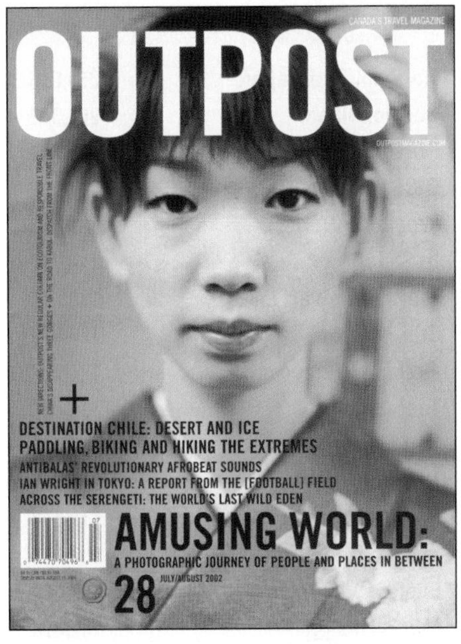

Exhibit 12–1 Outpost magazine is an excellent vehicle for reaching adventure travel tourists

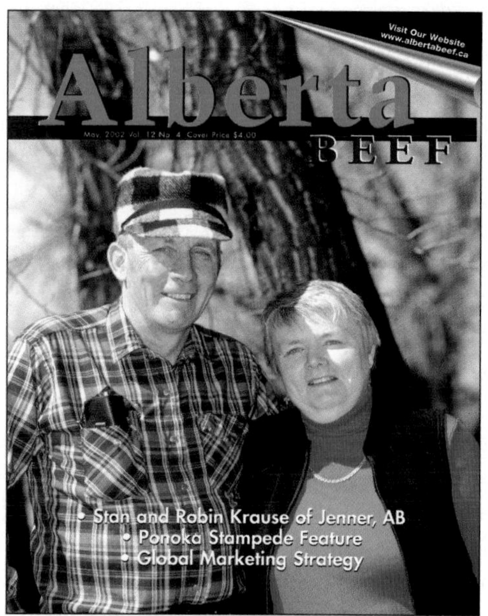

Exhibit 12–2 Alberta Beef is read by many cattle ranchers

- Industrial magazines directed at businesspeople in various manufacturing and production industries—for example, *Process Equipment and Control News and Heavy Construction.*
- Trade magazines targeted to wholesalers, dealers, distributors, and retailers, among them *Canadian Grocer.*
- General business magazines aimed at executives in all areas of business, such as *Canadian Business.*

The numerous business publications reach specific types of professional people with particular interests and give them important information relevant to their industry, occupation, and/or careers. Business publications are important to advertisers because they provide an efficient way of reaching the specific types of individuals who constitute their target market. Much marketing occurs at the trade and business-to-business level, where one company sells its products or services directly to another.

Foreign Publications

Canadian magazines face significant competition from foreign publications, particularly American consumer magazines that account for about 90 percent of newsstand sales. These U.S. print vehicles are another means for Canadian advertisers to reach Canadian consumers. Current legislation allows for foreign publications to accept up to 18 percent of their advertising space from Canadian advertisers for magazines sold in Canada. In addition, foreign publications can accept greater amounts of advertising if the majority of editorial content is Canadian.[2]

Figure 12–4 shows that only 16 U.S. publications had circulations greater than 100,000 in 2005; the opportunity for Canadian advertisers is to a degree limited in comparison to circulation figures for Canadian titles shown in Figures 12–1 and 12–2. As Figure 12–5 shows, the spillover of American magazines has declined substantially over the past decade, while the growth of Canadian magazine pages has risen sharply during the same time period as shown in Figure 12–6. Research done by the Canadian Magazine Publishers indicates that Canadians prefer domestic magazines but have difficulty identifying them in the face of foreign competition. An extensive communications campaign over the past six years to brand Canadian magazines appears to have contributed to a steady increase in the number of pages and Canadian titles.[3]

FIGURE *12–4*

U.S. magazines with a circulation of 100,000+ in Canada

Magazine Name	Total Paid CDN Circ.
National Geographic	378,816
Cosmopolitan	262,342
Prevention	194,930
O Oprah	167,189
Woman's World	161,143
In Style	140,229
Martha Stewart Living	130,137
Star	126,670
First For Women	121,036
Teen People	119,859
Vanity Fair	117,517
National Enquirer	114,681
Maxim	112,578
In Touch Weekly	107,133
Endless Vacation	105,002
Men's Health	102,870

Source: ABC, December 2005

Strengths of Magazines

Magazines have a number of characteristics that make them attractive as an advertising medium. Strengths of magazines include their target audience selectivity, geographic coverage, creativity, reader involvement and amount of processing time, media image, and selective exposure and attention.

Target Audience Selectivity One of the main advantages of using magazines as an advertising medium is their **selectivity**, or ability to reach a specific target audience. Magazines are the most selective of all media except direct mail. Most magazines are published for readers with very specific interests. The thousands of magazines published in Canada reach all types of consumers and businesses and allow advertisers to target their advertising to segments of the population who buy their products. For example, *PhotoLife* is targeted toward camera buffs, *Exclaim!* reaches those with an avid interest in music, and *What!* claims to be "the voice and choice of Canadian youth." Many new magazines are introduced each year targeting new interests and trends.

One of the most recent and interesting titles to come about is *Vice.* This Canadian success story has an international circulation of 350,000 and has versions in the U.S., the U.K., and Japan, with plans for versions in Scandinavia, Germany, Holland, and France. Designed for the hip, urban, young consumer, *Vice* has steadily built an "edgy" reputation—making some advertisers critical of the magazine's content and wary of advertising in it. In contrast, Canada now has *Nuvo* magazine, a refined publication (non-paid circulation) catering to the very affluent who appreciate a refined lifestyle of luxury.[4] IMC Perspective 12–2 on page 354 describes a new magazine format for greater-sell activity.

In addition to providing selectivity based on interests, magazines can provide advertisers with high demographic selectivity. *Demographic selectivity,* or the ability to reach specific demographic groups, is available in two ways. First, most magazines are, as a result of editorial content, aimed at fairly well-defined demographic segments. *Canadian Living* and *Chatelaine* are read predominantly by women; *The Hockey News* is read mostly by men. Older consumers can be reached through publications like *FiftyPlus.*

FIGURE 12–5 U.S. spill trends

	Ttl Spill Circ ('000)	Avg Circ/Title	Index
2005	7,509	13,243	50
2004	7,899	14,055	53
2002	8,160	15,396	59
2000	8,518	15,716	60
1998	9,155	16,203	62
1989	9,969	21,031	80
1983	10,705	26,303	100

*Measured Titles (ABC)

Source: ABC, December 2005

FIGURE 12–6

Canada continues to outpace the U.S. in magazine page growth

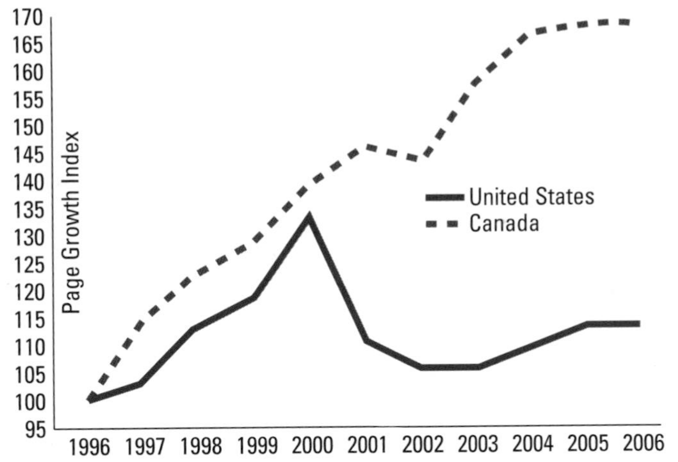

Source: PIB: Leading National Advertisers, 1996–2006

Selectivity through demographics is an approach used to reach different target audiences that participate in group purchase decisions. Sun-Rype's Fruit to Go used magazines to deliver specific appeals to mothers and their children in a recent campaign. Ads in *Canadian Living, Canadian House & Home,* and *Today's Parent* communicated the health benefits of the 100-percent fruit bars. Ads in YTV's *Whoa!, Kidsworld, Pop!* and *News for Kids* delivered fun consumption and lifestyle benefits. Overall response has been positive according to a Sun-Rype executive, who claims that both mothers and children have positive views of the brand and that sales have increased dramatically.[5]

Selectivity can be applied effectively by tailoring the message by language. As you might expect, Canada has magazines written in both English and French. In fact the latter has seen tremendous change recently with the relaunching of several titles prompting significant readership and ad revenue growth.[6]

Two technological developments allow advertisers to deliver personalized messages to tightly targeted audiences: selective binding and ink-jet imaging. **Selective binding** is a computerized production process that allows the creation of hundreds

IMC PERSPECTIVE 12–2

Shopping Magazines for Women

Canadian publishers joined an international trend of shopping magazines in 2004 with the launch of three titles, *Shopping Clin d'Oeil, Fashion Shops,* and *Loulou.* Shopping magazines are fashion and beauty publications designed to show women the selection available and the prices for a variety of products. In contrast, typical fashion/beauty lifestyle magazines continue to offer editorial content on celebrities, fashion trends, and the like.

Lucky, the most acclaimed international shopping magazine, racked up a circulation of 900,000 in just three years, turned a profit recently, and received the award for Magazine of the Year from *Advertising Age.* With a simple formula of a fashion magazine stripped of its thin models and editorial content, *Lucky* provided interested shoppers with detailed product information, prices, and store locations. In fact, it added stickers to allow consumers to mark items as "yes" or "maybe." Follow-up research supported the venture by showing that 80 percent of the readers bought something after seeing an ad for it in *Lucky.*

Shopping Clin d'Oeil, based on the women's magazine *Clin d'Oeil,* offered the first Canadian shopping magazine in March of 2004. It planned three initial issues of 144 pages each to be distributed to existing readers representing 25- to 35-year-old women. Similarly, the anticipated *Fashion Shops,* an off-shoot of *Fashion,* is viewed by its publishers as the 11th and 12th issues. Despite its brand extension status, *Fashion Shops* would contain planning tools and shopping lists to help facilitate consumer purchases. *Loulou,* targeted to urban professional women ages 18–34 known as "label queens" who love to shop, found success after its launch of three issues in 2004, eight issues for 2005, and 10 issues for 2006. Published in English and French, its circulation reached about 195,000.

Naturally, this new publishing format attracted advertisers who jumped at the opportunity to build their brand one step closer to the purchase action or the actual purchase decision. Some advertising executives believed shopping magazines could replace some of their traditional advertising placements that have less reach or greater per reader costs. Another predicted that by the end of 2005, shopping magazines would be a normal placement on the part of advertisers even though audience characteristics and sizes would not be ascertained until 2007 by the Print Measurement Bureau. However, advertisers look to existing PMB research that indicates over 40 percent of the 7.5 million Canadian women aged 18–49 really enjoy shopping for clothes and try to stay informed of style and fashion trends.

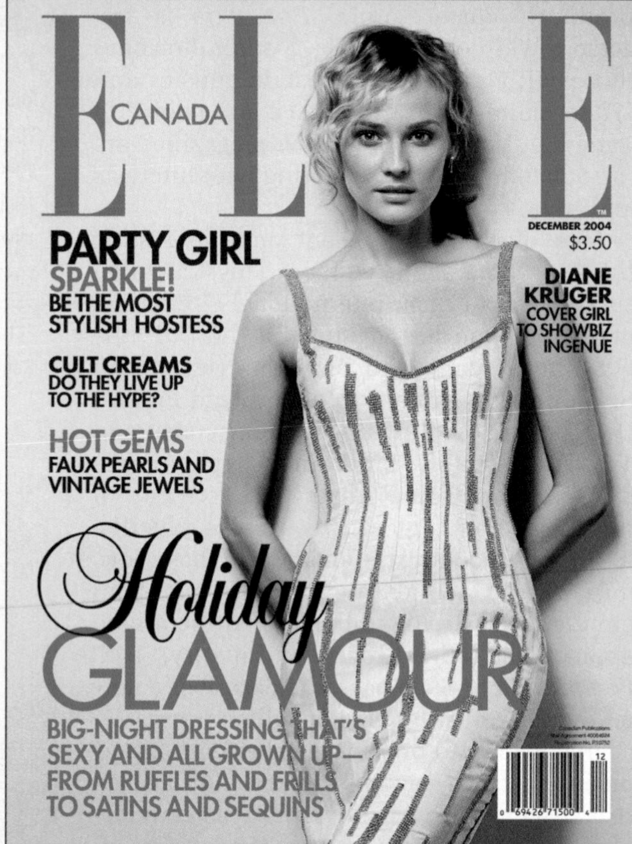

Sources: David Chilton, "Reaching the Label Queens," *Marketing Magazine,* April 17, 2006; Orville Manangan, "Pick and Choose," *Marketing Magazine,* April 19, 2004; Chris Powell, "Mags Target Shopping Fashionistas," *Marketing Magazine,* November 24, 2003; Andrea Zoe, "Aster Shopping Basics," *Marketing Magazine,* April 19, 2004.

Question

1. Why would women enjoy reading a shopping magazine devoted to fashion that did not contain any articles for reading pleasure?

of copies of a magazine in one continuous sequence. Selective binding enables magazines to target and address specific groups within a magazine's circulation base. They can then send different editorial or advertising messages to various groups of subscribers within the same issue of a publication. **Ink-jet imaging** reproduces a message by projecting ink onto paper rather than using mechanical plates. This process makes it possible to personalize an advertisings message. These innovations permit advertisers to target their messages more finely and let magazines compete more effectively with direct mail and other direct-marketing vehicles. Exhibit 12–3 shows how *Newsweek* promotes the capabilities of ink-jet imaging for targeting advertising messages.

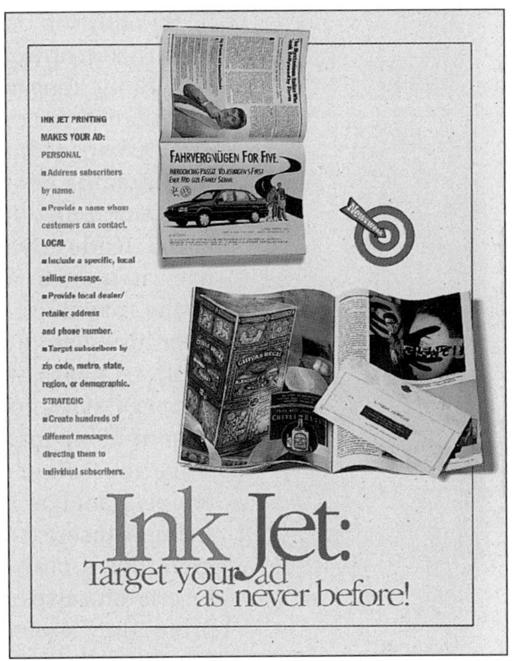

Exhibit 12–3 Newsweek promotes the value of ink-jet imaging

Geographic Coverage One way to achieve specific geographic coverage is by using a magazine that is targeted toward a particular area. One of the more successful media developments of recent years has been the growth of city magazines in some Canadian cities. *Toronto Life, Vancouver Magazine,* and *Montréal Scope,* to name a few, provide residents of these areas with articles concerning lifestyle, events, and the like, in these cities and their surrounding metropolitan areas (Exhibit 12–4).

Another way to achieve selective geographic coverage in magazines is through purchasing ad space in specific geographic editions of national or regional magazines. A number of publications (e.g., *Maclean's, Chatelaine*) divide their circulation into groupings based on regions or major metropolitan areas and offer advertisers the option of concentrating their ads in these editions.

CARD lists the consumer magazines offering geographic editions. Regional advertisers can purchase space in editions that reach only areas where they have distribution, yet still enjoy the prestige of advertising in a major national magazine. National advertisers can use the geographic editions to focus their advertising on areas with the greatest potential or those needing more promotional support. They can also use regional editions to test-market products or alternative promotional campaigns in various regions of the country.

Ads in regional editions can also list the names of retailers or distributors in various markets, thus encouraging greater local support from the trade. The trend toward regional marketing is increasing the importance of having regional media available to marketers. The availability of regional and demographic editions can also reduce the cost per thousand for reaching desired audiences.

Exhibit 12–4 City magazines such as Toronto Life offer advertisers high geographic selectivity

Creativity for Cognitive and Emotional Responses One of the most valued attributes of magazine advertising is the reproduction quality of the ads. Magazines are generally printed on high-quality paper stock and use printing processes that provide excellent reproduction in black and white or colour. Since magazines are a visual medium where illustrations are often a dominant part of an ad, this is a very important property. The reproduction quality of most magazines is far superior to that offered by the other major print medium of newspapers, particularly when colour is needed. The use of colour has become a virtual necessity in most product categories.

In addition to their excellent reproduction capabilities, magazines also offer advertisers options in terms of the type, size, and placement of the advertising material. Some magazines offer (often at extra charge) a variety of special opportunities to enhance the creative appeal of the ad such as gatefolds, bleed pages, inserts, and creative space buys.

Gatefolds enable an advertiser to make a striking presentation by using a third page that folds out and gives the ad an extra-large spread. Gatefolds are often found at the inside cover of large consumer magazines or on some inside pages. Advertisers use gatefolds to make a very strong impression, especially on special occasions such as the introduction of a new product or brand. For example, automobile advertisers often use gatefolds to introduce new versions of their cars each model year.

Bleed pages are those where the advertisement extends all the way to the end of the page, with no margin of white space around the ad. Bleeds give the ad an impression of being larger and make a more dramatic impact.

Various other **inserts** are used in many magazines. These include return cards, recipe booklets, coupons, and even product samples. Cosmetics companies use scented inserts to introduce new fragrances, and some companies use them to promote deodorants, laundry detergents, or other products whose scent is important. Inserts are also used in conjunction with direct-response ads and as part of sales promotion strategies. Current technologies are being refined and made more cost effective, and newer options include anaglyphic images (three-dimensional materials that are viewed with coloured glasses); lenticular (colour) images printed on finely corrugated plastic that seem to move when tilted; and pressure- or heat-sensitive inks that change colour on contact.

Creative space buys are another option of magazines. Some magazines let advertisers purchase space units in certain combinations to increase the impact of their media budget. For example, WD-40, an all-purpose lubrication product, uses half- or quarter-page ads on consecutive pages of several magazines, mentioning a different use for the product on each page, as shown in Exhibit 12–5. This strategy gives the company greater impact for its media dollars and is helpful in promoting the product's variety of uses.

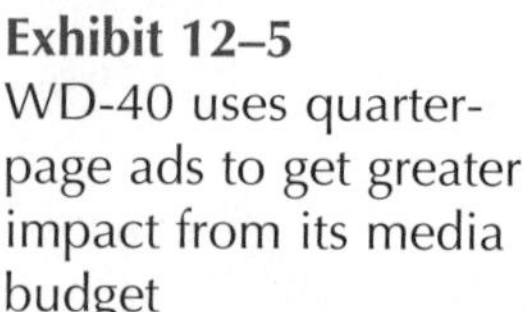

Exhibit 12–5
WD-40 uses quarter-page ads to get greater impact from its media budget

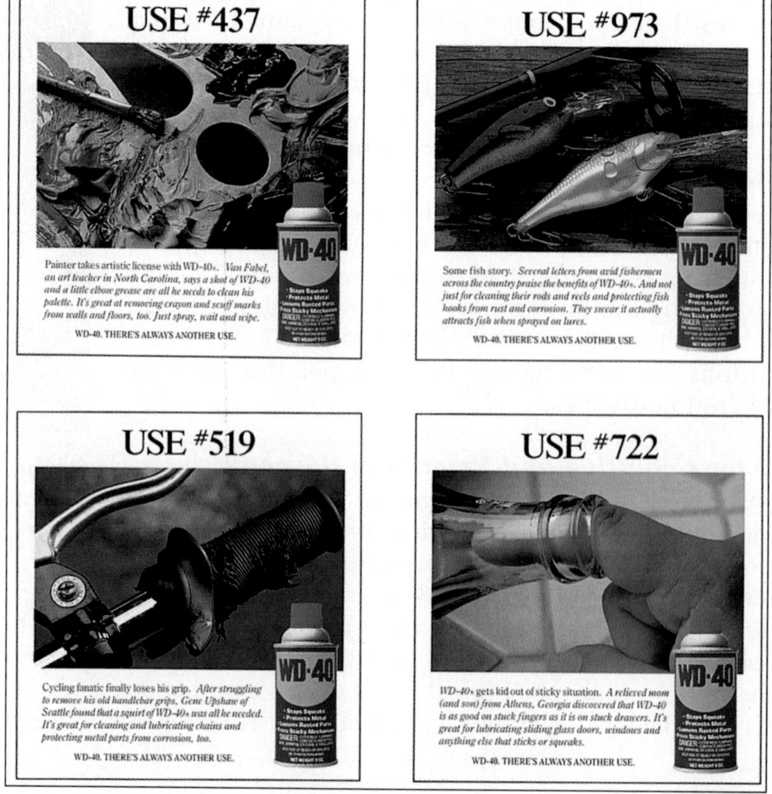

Reader Involvement and Amount of Processing Time A distinctive strength offered by magazines is their long life span. TV and radio are characterized by fleeting messages that have a very short life span; newspapers are generally discarded soon after being read. Magazines, however, are generally read over several days and are often kept for reference. They are retained in the home longer than any other medium and are generally referred to on several occasions. A study of magazine audiences found that readers devote nearly an hour over a period of two or three days to reading an average magazine.[7] Studies have also found that nearly 75 percent of consumers retain magazines for future reference.[8] One benefit of the longer life of magazines is that reading occurs at a less hurried pace and there is more opportunity to examine ads in considerable detail. This means ads can use longer and more detailed copy, which can be very important for high-involvement and complex products or services. The permanence of magazines also means readers can be exposed to ads on multiple occasions and can pass magazines along to other readers.

Media Image Another positive feature of magazine advertising is the prestige the product or service may gain from advertising in publications with a favourable image. Companies whose products rely heavily on perceived quality, reputation, and/or image often buy space in prestigious publications with high-quality editorial content whose consumers have a high level of interest in the advertising pages. For example, *Flare* covers young women's fashions in a very favourable environment, and a clothing manufacturer may advertise its products in these magazines to enhance the prestige of its lines. *Canadian Geographic* provides an impressive editorial environment that includes high-quality photography. The magazine's upscale readers are likely to have a favourable image of the publication that may transfer to the products advertised on its pages.

While most media planners recognize that the environment created by a publication is important, it can be difficult to determine the image a magazine provides. Subjective estimates based on media planners' experience are often used to assess a magazine's prestige, as are objective measures such as reader opinion surveys. Magazines are a preferred choice for some products, as described in IMC Perspective 12–3 on page 358.

Selective Exposure and Attention With the exception of newspapers, consumers are more receptive to advertising in magazines than in any other medium. Magazines are generally purchased because the information they contain interests the reader, and ads provide additional information that may be of value in making a purchase decision.

In addition to their relevance, magazine ads are likely to be received favourably by consumers because, unlike broadcast ads, they are nonintrusive and can easily be ignored. Studies show that the majority of magazine readers welcome ads; only a small percentage have negative attitudes toward magazine advertising.[9] Some magazines, such as bridal or fashion publications, are purchased as much for their advertising as for their editorial content. Some studies have shown that magazine readers are more likely to attend to and recall ads than are TV viewers.

Limitations of Magazines

Although the strengths offered by magazines are considerable, they have certain drawbacks too. These include the costs of advertising, their limited reach and frequency, the long lead time required in placing an ad, weak target audience coverage, and the problem of clutter.

Absolute Cost and Cost Efficiency The cost of advertising in magazines varies according to the size of the audience they reach and their selectivity. Advertising in

IMC PERSPECTIVE 12–3

Timeless and Everlasting Quality of Magazines

While the Internet and mobile communications are taking an increasingly prominent role in marketing plans, Rolex remains steadfast in its support of traditional media. According to Nielsen Media Research, $1.5 million of the $1.7 million the 102-year-old company spent on measured media advertising in 2006 went toward either magazines or daily newspapers. The luxury watch company's in-house media department builds its plans around a list of publications that include *Elle, Canadian Geographic, Report On Business, FQ, Time Canada, Sir,* and various city magazines, newspapers like *The Globe and Mail,* and a smattering of TV.

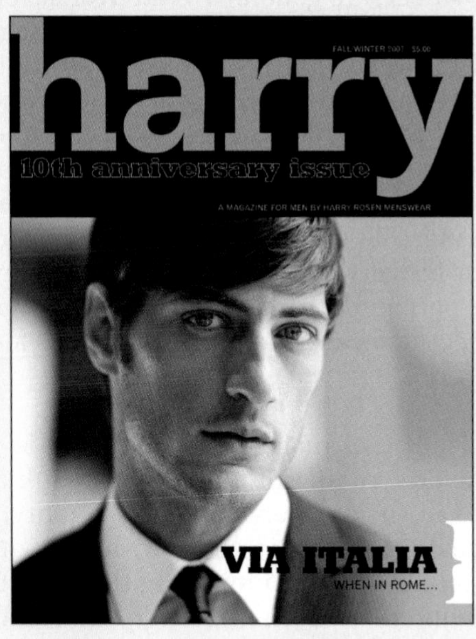

"Alternatives have come along over the years," explains Royce, "but so far we haven't seen anything that truly is going to replace the approach we currently take. I firmly believe you get the best results from the print medium." Rolex's luxurious print ads boast a who's who of celebrities from the arts and sports worlds, including the world's top-ranked tennis player, Roger Federer, cellist Yo-Yo Ma, and opera star Placido Domingo. "The consumer needs to see the product. This is one of the big advantages of the glossy magazine look, because you can really show it exactly as it is. The consumer can see it in a very clear, concise way."

"Magazines are going to give you a much more beautiful image of a luxury product, like a Louis Vuitton handbag, than a transitory image on the web," agrees Karin Macpherson, managing partner of Toronto media management firm The Media Company. "The stuff just looks great, and it hangs around for a while. Vogue magazine hangs around for months and months—it doesn't just disappear."

Larry Rosen, chair and CEO of upscale men's fashion retailer Harry Rosen, says his company likes magazines so much it operates its own custom book, *Harry*. Marking its 10th anniversary this year, the twice-yearly publication—which is distributed to the chain's top 100,000 customers and has a newsstand presence of about 10,000—averages 50 pages of paid advertising from the likes of Mercedes, Lexus, Armani, and Hugo Boss (a page sells for $16,500). "It's a smashing success," says Rosen. "To the point where we can't take all

large mass-circulation magazines like *Maclean's* can be very expensive. For example, a full-page, four-colour ad in *Maclean's* magazine's national edition (circulation 383,000) cost $34,000 in 2006. Popular positions such as the back cover cost even more.

Like any medium, magazines must be considered not only from an absolute cost perspective but also in terms of relative costs. Most magazines emphasize their effectiveness in reaching specific target audiences at a low cost per thousand. Media planners generally focus on the relative costs of a publication in reaching their target audience. However, they may recommend a magazine with a high cost per thousand because of its ability to reach a small, specialized market segment. Of course, advertisers with limited budgets will be interested in the absolute costs of space in a magazine and the costs of producing quality ads for these publications.

Reach and Frequency Magazines are generally not as effective as other media in offering reach and frequency. While adults in Canada read one or more consumer magazines each month, the percentage of adults reading any individual publication tends to be much smaller, so magazines have a thin penetration of households. For example, *Maclean's* has a high circulation, but it represents only 3 percent of the 12.8 million households in Canada.

Thus, advertisers seeking broad reach must make media buys in a number of magazines, which means more negotiations and transactions. For a broad reach strategy, magazines are used in conjunction with other media. Since most magazines are

the advertisers." *Harry* is also selective about the type of ads it accepts. "I will only take advertisers whose brands are consistent with Harry Rosen," he says. "I've turned down all sorts of ads. I think what makes it a valuable vehicle is the consistency of the kind of advertiser that's in there. The reader knows that it speaks to a certain element."

The look and feel of print isn't the only reason luxury marketers are attracted to the medium. Canadian households with an annual income surpassing $100,000 read more magazines and newspapers and spend less time with radio and TV than do lower-income households, according to Print Measurement Bureau (PMB) data. Such data indicate that reaching luxury consumers is a fairly straightforward proposition. However, PMB data also reveals that households with income above $150,000 spend an average of 8.5 hours per week on the Internet (excluding e-mail) and households between $100,000 and $150,000 spend 7.2 hours. That compares with 5.9 hours per week for households earning $50,000 to $100,000 and 4.2 hours for households with income below $50,000.

The increasing democratization of luxury means that marketers face what Macpherson says is a "big debate" about straddling the line between traditional media and the "universe of interaction" that is digital media. "They have to be so careful, because the [luxury] brand is the hero," she says. "It's a fine line between still providing that mystique and that notion of exclusivity and still making it democratic and for the masses."

The Media Company handles media buying for several luxury brands, including BMW and LVMH Moët Hennessy Louis Vuitton S.A., a French holding company that is the world's largest luxury goods conglomerate with brands such as Louis Vuitton, Tag Heuer, Givenchy, and Christian Dior. In the early '90s, Macpherson says, luxury goods marketers were largely focused on baby boomers. Now, the focus is shifting toward their offspring, the Gen-Xers, who grew up surrounded by material goods and are now reaching their maximum earning potential.

With an average customer age of about 38—and roughly a quarter of its clientele under 30—Harry Rosen continues to use print advertising while at the same time dabbling in everything from banner ads on the national dailies' websites to paid search. "Every time a 65-year-old drops out of the workforce, and buys less clothing, we have to add a 22-year-old who's going to be starting his life cycle buying quality clothing," says Rosen. "You're always finding new vehicles and new ways of keeping younger people coming in."

Source: Chris Powell, "Rich Media," *Marketing Magazine,* June 25, 2007.

Question

1. Would magazines be an optimal medium to reach both customers and non-customers for luxury brands?

monthly or at best weekly publications, the opportunity for building frequency through the use of the same publication is limited. Using multiple ads in the same issue of a publication is an inefficient way to build frequency. Most advertisers try to achieve frequency by adding other magazines with similar audiences to the media schedule.

Scheduling Flexibility Another drawback of magazines is the long lead time needed to place an ad thus reducing scheduling flexibility. Most major publications have a 30- to 90-day lead time, which means space must be purchased and the ad must be prepared well in advance of the actual publication date. No changes in the art or copy of the ad can be made after the closing date. This long lead time means magazine ads cannot be as timely as other media, such as radio or newspapers, in responding to current events or changing market conditions.

Target Audience Coverage The flipside of the strength of target audience selectivity is the limitation of magazines in providing extensive target audience coverage. Even though a magazine may draw an audience with a particular interest, for example, hockey with *The Hockey News*, the number of people reading the publication versus the number of people who actually play hockey is substantially disproportionate.

Clutter While the problem of advertising clutter is generally discussed in reference to the broadcast media, magazines also have this drawback. Clutter is not as serious an issue for the print media as for radio or TV, since consumers tend to be more receptive and tolerant of print advertising. They can also control their exposure to a magazine ad simply by turning the page. The clutter problem for magazines is something of a paradox: The more successful a magazine becomes, the more advertising pages it attracts, and this leads to greater clutter. In fact, magazines generally gauge their success in terms of the number of advertising pages they sell.

Magazine publishers do attempt to control the clutter problem by maintaining a reasonable balance of editorial pages to advertising. However, many magazines contain ads on more than half of their pages. This clutter makes it difficult for an advertiser to gain readers' attention and draw them into the ad. Thus, many print ads use strong visual images, catchy headlines, or some of the creative techniques discussed earlier to grab the interest of magazine readers. Some advertisers create their own custom magazines to sidestep the advertising clutter problem as well as to have control over editorial content. A number of companies have also been publishing their own magazines to build relationships with their customers.

Fashion retailer Holt Renfrew custom-published its own shopping magazine, *Holt's,* to reach a sophisticated clientele who shop all around the world. This contributed to Holt Renfrew's established connections with the high-profile publication *Lucky,* where the fashion retailer consistently linked its brand with the world-renowned fashion and beauty brands through product placement and cooperative media opportunities. In the future, Holt Renfrew looks to establish more permanent advertising placements in Canada's newest fashion magazines *Loulou, Fashion Shops,* and *Shopping Clin d'Oeil* and achieve an optimal balance between custom-published and regular magazines.[10]

Buying Magazine Advertising Space

The strengths and limitations of magazines are part of the decision to use this media. Another key factor is a complete understanding of the readers of magazines to assess whether there is a fit between them and the target audience of the promotion plan. In this section, we review a few issues related to this part of the decision: circulation and readership, audience measurement, and magazine advertising rates.

Magazine Circulation and Readership

Two of the most important considerations in deciding whether to use a magazine in the advertising media plan are the size and characteristics of the audience it reaches. Media buyers evaluate magazines on the basis of their ability to deliver the advertiser's message to as many people as possible in the target audience. To do this, they must consider the circulation of the publication as well as its total readership and match these figures against the audience they are attempting to reach.

Circulation Circulation figures represent the number of individuals who receive a publication through either subscription or store purchase, or through controlled distribution (free). Given that circulation figures are the basis for a magazine's advertising rates and one of the primary considerations in selecting a publication for placement, the credibility of circulation figures is important. Most major publications are audited by the Audit Bureau of Circulations (ABC), which was organized in 1914 and is sponsored by advertisers, agencies, and publishers. The Canadian division of this U.S.-based organization is known as the Canadian Circulations Audit Board. ABC collects and evaluates information regarding the subscriptions and sales of magazines and newspapers to verify their circulation figures. Only publications with 70 percent or more paid circulation (which means the purchaser paid at least half the magazine's established base price) are eligible for verification audits by ABC. Certain business publications are audited by the Business Publications Audit (BPA) of Circulation. Many of these are published on a **controlled-circulation basis**, meaning copies are sent (usually free) to individuals who the publisher believes can influence the company's purchases.

ABC provides media planners with reliable figures regarding the size and distribution of a magazine's circulation, which helps them evaluate its worth as a media vehicle. The ABC statement also provides detailed circulation information that gives a media planner an indication of the quality of the target audience. For example, it shows how the subscription was sold, the percentage of circulation sold at less than full value, the percentage of circulation sold with some kind of incentive, and the percentage of subscriptions given away. Many advertisers believe that subscribers who pay for a magazine are more likely to read it than are those who get it at a discount or for free. Media buyers are generally skeptical about publications whose circulation figures are not audited and will not advertise in unaudited publications. Circulation data, along with the auditing source, are available from CARD or from the publication itself.

Readership Advertisers are often interested in the number of people a publication reaches as a result of secondary, or pass-along, readership. **Pass-along readership** can occur when the primary subscriber or purchaser gives a magazine to another person or when the publication is read in doctors' waiting rooms or beauty salons, on airplanes, and so forth.

Advertisers generally attach greater value to the primary in-home reader than the pass-along reader or out-of-home reader, as the former generally spends more time with the publication, picks it up more often, and receives greater satisfaction from it. Thus, this reader is more likely to be attentive and responsive to ads. However, the value of pass-along readers should not be discounted. They can greatly expand a magazine's readership.

The **total audience, or readership**, of a magazine is calculated by multiplying the readers per copy (the total number of primary and pass-along readers) by the circulation of an average issue. For example, *Flare* has a circulation of 160,000 and 11 readers per copy for a total audience of 1.5 million. However, rate structures are generally based on the more verifiable primary circulation figures, and many media planners devalue pass-along readers by as much as 50 percent. Total readership estimates are reported by the Print Measurement Bureau (PMB), to which we now turn our attention.

Magazine Audience Measurement—PMB

Print Measurement Bureau (PMB) is a non-profit Canadian industry association of nearly 500 members drawn from advertisers, print magazine publishers, and advertising agencies. Its primary mandate is to collect readership information for print magazines, which allows all three constituents to make more effective advertising decisions. Its foremost research is known simply as the **PMB study**.

The first national PMB study was conducted in 1973 and originally concerned print magazines only. It has grown since then and is now Canada's primary syndicated source for print and non-print media exposure, as well as responses to survey questions. The current study has resulted in a two-year database of 30,000 respondents, over 2,500 products, and over 3,500 brands.

The research method is an in-home interview conducted throughout the year. Respondents are screened by asking whether they have read any of the listed publications within the past 12 months; they are subsequently qualified if they have read the publications recently enough, depending upon the frequency of publication (e.g., weekly, monthly). A number of reading-related questions are asked, including frequency of reading, number of reading occasions, time spent reading, source of copy, where read, and interest.

Respondents are then asked many demographic, lifestyle, media consumption, product usage, retail shopping, and psychographic questions. The demographic questions are quite exhaustive and total over 20 in number. The lifestyle questions include life events, leisure activities, education, sporting activities, and attendance of sporting events. Media consumption questions are very extensive and include TV viewing, radio listening, community and daily newspaper reading, transit usage, distance travelled, shopping mall trips, and Yellow Pages usage. Product usage data is recorded for 17 broad product categories (e.g., personal care, groceries, financial, business, and so on). Questions pertaining to shopping at approximately 30 different retail environments are also asked. And finally, many questions are asked to determine psychographic clusters for nine broad product categories and one general societal category.

The data available for analysis is a virtual gold mine of information for media planners. They can relate many of the variables together to accurately reach a specific target audience in terms of their behaviour (i.e., the primary target variable), demographics, lifestyle, and psychographics. The database works with specialized software to allow media planners to make their effective decisions efficiently.

One final useful feature of the PMB study is "return to sample." Individual firms can confidentially re-contact respondents to ask them proprietary questions with respect to specific brand attitudes, purchase intentions, or purchase influences. An advertiser would then have the broad data tied in with some specific measures of their own brand.

Magazine Advertising Rates

Magazine rates are primarily a function of circulation: the greater the circulation, the higher cost of the ad. Other variables include the size of the ad, its position in the publication, the particular editions (geographic, demographic) chosen, any special mechanical or production requirements, the number and frequency of insertions, and whether the circulation is controlled (free) or paid.

Advertising space is generally sold on the basis of space units such as full page, half page, and quarter page, although some publications quote rates on the basis of column inches. The larger the ad, the greater the cost. However, many advertisers use full-page ads since they result in more attention and readership. Studies have found that full-page ads generated 36 percent more readership than half-page ads.[11]

Ads can be produced or run using black and white, black and white plus one colour, or four colours. The more colour used in the ad, the greater the expense because of the increased printing costs. On average, a four-colour ad costs 30 percent more than a black-and-white ad. Advertisers generally prefer colour ads because they have greater visual impact and are superior for attracting and holding attention.[12] Starch INRA Hooper, Inc., analyzed the effect of various factors on the readership of magazine ads. The "noted" scores (the percentage of readers who remember seeing the ad in a publication they read) are 45 percent higher for a four-colour full-page ad than for a black-and-white ad. A four-colour spread (two facing pages) outperforms a black-and-white spread by 53 percent.[13] Ads requiring special mechanical production such as bleed pages or inserts may also cost extra.

Rates for magazine ad space can also vary according to the number of times an ad runs and the amount of money spent during a specific period. The more often an advertiser contracts to run an ad, the lower are the space charges. Volume discounts are based on the total space purchased within a contract year, measured in dollars or number of insertions.

Evaluation of Newspapers

Newspapers, the second major form of print media, are the largest of all advertising media in terms of total dollar volume. In 2005 more than $1.8 billion was spent on daily newspaper advertising, or about 15 percent of the total advertising expenditures in Canada. Community newspapers accounted for almost $800 million, or 9 percent. Newspapers are an especially important advertising medium to local advertisers, particularly retailers. However, newspapers are also valuable to national advertisers. Many of the advertising dollars spent by local retailers are actually provided by national advertisers through cooperative advertising programs (discussed in Chapter 14). Newspapers vary in terms of their characteristics and their role as an advertising medium.

Types of Newspapers

The traditional role of newspapers has been to deliver prompt, detailed coverage of news as well as to supply other information and features that appeal to readers. The vast majority of newspapers are daily publications serving a local community. However, weekly, national, and special-audience newspapers have special characteristics that can be valuable to advertisers.

Daily Newspapers Daily newspapers, which are published each weekday, are found in cities and larger towns across the country. Many areas have more than one daily paper. Daily newspapers are read by about 50 percent of adults each weekday and nearly 80 percent each week. They provide detailed coverage of news, events, and issues concerning the local area as well as business, sports, and other relevant information and entertainment. In 2005, there were 134 daily newspapers in Canada; of these, 120 were English-language papers and 14 were French-language papers.

Community Newspapers Most community newspapers publish weekly and originate in small towns or suburbs where the volume of news and advertising cannot support a daily newspaper. These papers focus primarily on news, sports, and events relevant to the local area and usually ignore national and world news, sports, and financial and business news. Community newspapers appeal primarily to local advertisers because of their geographic focus and lower absolute cost. Most national advertisers avoid community newspapers because of their duplicate circulation with daily papers in the large metropolitan areas.

While smaller daily and community newspapers have historically been a fragmented market and difficult for national or regional advertisers to use as an effective newspaper vehicle, their emerging force in Ontario promises to create an interesting opportunity. Recently, Osprey Media Group purchased many daily newspapers in small towns and cities (e.g., Kingston, Sarnia, Sudbury, etc.) with a total circulation of 622,000. When combined with weekly newspapers, the new media giant can reach nearly 1 million people in 45 markets. In total, Osprey owns 22 dailies and 24 weeklies. In comparison, two other similar companies own 60-plus newspapers, thus indicating the beginning of some concentration in the media option. The implication for advertisers is significant. In addition to providing advertisers with the ability to reach many local markets easily, these newspapers allow advertisers to reach a very attractive market since disposable income tends to be higher in those towns and cities with lower property/mortgage costs.[14]

National Newspapers Newspapers in Canada with national circulation include the *National Post* and *The Globe and Mail.* Both are daily publications and have editorial content with a national appeal. The *National Post* has a weekday circulation of about 240,000 and a Saturday circulation of almost 260,000. *The Globe and Mail* has a weekday circulation of about 335,000 and a Saturday circulation of approximately 335,000. National newspapers appeal primarily to large national advertisers and to regional advertisers that use specific geographic editions of these publications.

Internet Newspapers Major Canadian daily newspapers, the two national newspapers, and some community newspapers offer an Internet version of their publications. Regular newspapers charge for subscription or individual papers at a newsstand and rely on advertising revenue to support the distribution of editorial content. Internet versions are similar in this respect; the publishing firms have experimented with different combinations of fees and banner ads. Recently, CanWest allowed newspaper subscribers free access to the complete digital version of the newspaper. Online readership has grown from 10 percent in 2001 to almost 20 percent, but it is substantially lower than the 80 percent for the original version. Consumers are currently in the process of evolving their newspaper consumption habits, but the implications for advertisers remain unclear. For example, portals like Sympatico offer news and features similar to online newpapers, so the competition for an audience may be different in a new media environment.[15]

Special-Audience Newspapers A variety of papers offer specialized editorial content and are published for particular groups, including labour unions, professional organizations, industries, and hobbyists. Many people working in advertising and marketing read *Marketing Magazine*. Specialized newspapers are also published in areas with large foreign-language-speaking ethnic groups, among them Chinese. Newspapers targeted at various religious and educational groups compose another large class of special-interest papers. A recent trend has been the establishment of local business newspapers. In western Canada, *Business Edge* reaches 47,000 readers in Alberta and 30,000 in B.C. It receives advertising from regional and small firms, and also from large firms like Telus and Rogers Wireless.[16]

Newspaper Supplements Although not a category of newspapers per se, some papers include magazine-type supplements. For example, *The Globe and Mail* publishes a glossy *Report On Business* magazine at the end of each month.

Types of Newspaper Advertising

The ads appearing in newspapers can also be divided into different categories. The major types of newspaper advertising are display and classified. Other special types of ads and preprinted inserts also appear in newspapers.

Display Advertising **Display advertising** is found throughout the newspaper and generally uses illustrations, headlines, white space, and other visual devices in addition to the copy text. Display ads account for approximately 70 percent of the advertising revenue of the average newspaper. The two types of display advertising in newspapers are local and national (general).

Local advertising refers to ads placed by local organizations, businesses, and individuals who want to communicate with consumers in the market area served by the newspaper. Supermarkets and department stores are among the leading local display advertisers, along with numerous other retailers and service operations such as banks and travel agents. Local advertising is sometimes referred to as retail advertising because retailers account for 85 percent of local display ads.

National or general advertising refers to newspaper display advertising done by marketers of branded products or services that are sold on a national or regional level. These ads are designed to create and maintain demand for a company's product or service and to complement the efforts of local retailers that stock and promote the advertiser's products. Major retail chains, automakers, and airlines are heavy users of newspaper advertising.

Classified Advertising **Classified advertising** also provides newspapers with a substantial amount of revenue. These ads are arranged under subheads according to the product, service, or offering being advertised. Employment, real estate, and automotive are the three major categories of classified advertising. While most classified ads are just text set in small type, some newspapers also accept classified display advertising. These ads are run in the classified section of the paper but use illustrations, larger type sizes, white space, borders, and even colour to stand out.

Special Ads and Inserts Special advertisements in newspapers include a variety of government and financial reports and notices and public notices of changes in business and personal relationships. Other types of advertising in newspapers include political or special-interest ads promoting a particular candidate, issue, or cause. **Preprinted inserts** are another type of advertising distributed through newspapers. These ads do not appear in the paper itself; they are printed by the advertiser and then taken to the newspaper to be inserted before delivery. Many retailers use inserts such as circulars, catalogues, or brochures in specific circulation zones to reach shoppers in their particular trade areas.

Strengths of Newspapers

Newspapers have a number of characteristics that make them popular among both local and national advertisers. These include their reach and frequency, scheduling flexibility, geographic coverage, reader involvement and amount of processing time, media image, creativity for cognitive responses, absolute cost and cost efficiency, and target audience coverage.

Reach and Frequency One of the primary strengths of newspapers is the high degree of market coverage, or penetration, they offer an advertiser. In most areas, 60 percent or more of households read a daily newspaper, and the reach figure may exceed 70 percent among households with higher incomes and education levels. Most areas are served by one or two daily newspapers.

The extensive penetration of newspapers makes them a truly mass medium and provides advertisers with an excellent opportunity for reaching all segments of the population with their message. Also, since many newspapers are published and read daily, the advertiser can build a high level of frequency into the media schedule.

Scheduling Flexibility Another strength of newspapers is the flexibility they offer advertisers in terms of requirements for producing and running the ads. Newspaper ads can be written, laid out, and prepared in a matter of hours. For most dailies, the closing time by which the ad must be received is usually only 48 hours before publication (although closing dates for special ads, such as those using colour, and supplements are longer). The short production time and closing dates make newspapers an excellent medium for responding to current events or presenting timely information to consumers. For example, the Archdiocese of Montreal ran an ad a few days after the terrorist attacks of September 11, 2001 that showed the repeated text of the Lord's Prayer in the shape of the twin towers. The meanings of this message are numerous for many people; however, the most significant point is that the message would not have been as effective if it had been placed in a magazine a month later.[17]

Geographic Coverage Newspapers generally offer advertisers targeted geographic or territorial coverage. Advertisers can vary their coverage by choosing a paper—or combination of papers—that reaches the areas with the greatest sales potential. National advertisers take advantage of the geographic coverage of newspapers to concentrate their advertising in specific areas they can't reach with other media or to take advantage of strong sales potential in a particular area. For example, more expensive automobile manufacturers advertise in Toronto newspapers that reach the greater Toronto area and beyond with their wide distribution.

A number of companies use newspapers in their regional marketing strategies. Newspaper advertising lets them feature products on a market-by-market basis, respond and adapt campaigns to local market conditions, and tie in to more retailer promotions, fostering more support from the trade.

Local advertisers like retailers are interested in geographic coverage within a specific market or trade area. Their media goal is to concentrate their advertising on the areas where most of their customers are. Many newspapers now offer advertisers various geographic areas or zones for this purpose.

Reader Involvement and Amount of Processing Time Another important feature of newspapers is consumers' level of acceptance and involvement with papers and the ads they contain. The typical newspaper reader spends considerable time each day reading. Most consumers rely heavily on newspapers not only for news, information, and entertainment but also for assistance with consumption decisions.

Many consumers actually purchase a newspaper *because* of the advertising it contains. Consumers use retail ads to determine product prices and availability and to see who is having a sale. One aspect of newspapers that is helpful to advertisers is readers' knowledge about particular sections of the paper. Most of us know that ads for automotive products and sporting goods are generally found in the sports section, while ads for financial services are found in the business section. The weekly food section in many newspapers is popular for recipe and menu ideas as well as for the grocery store ads and coupons offered by many stores and companies.

Media Image The value of newspaper advertising as a source of information has been shown in several studies. One study found that consumers look forward to ads in newspapers more than in other media. In another study, 80 percent of consumers said newspaper ads were most helpful to them in doing their weekly shopping. Newspaper advertising has also been rated the most believable form of advertising in numerous studies.

Creativity for Cognitive Responses Newspapers offer the opportunity for extremely long copy, perhaps a thousand words extolling the attributes and benefits of a product. The option of considerable explanation of a product could be quite important for marketers looking to persuade consumers who are at the information search stage of the decision-making process. Furthermore, newspapers offer numerous creative options as ads can be run in various sizes, shapes, and formats to persuade the reader. Magazine innovations described earlier are adapted to newspapers as well. *Metro* agreed to print all 540,000 copies of an entire edition on special green paper for Dove's Cool Moisture product line. The special media buy included a front-page ad, a double-page spread inside, and a product sample attached to the front.[18]

Absolute Cost and Cost Efficiency Newspapers assist small companies through free copywriting and art services. Small advertisers without an agency or advertising department often rely on the newspaper to help them write and produce their ads. Production costs of ads are reasonable since many are comprised of simple copy with a standard image or photo-stock visual. The creative flexibility of newspapers in terms of size and format of the ad makes it difficult to exactly conclude the cost implications of this media. Small and local businesses can run a small ad with a reasonable CPM (cost per thousand) compared to magazines.

Target Audience Coverage Coverage of a specific target audience is argued to be a limitation for newspapers in comparison to its print cousin, magazines. However, placement of ads in certain sections of the newspaper that occur every day (e.g., sports, business, entertainment) or once a week (e.g., food, cars, finances) can be advantageous for some marketers.

LIMITATIONS OF NEWSPAPERS

While newspapers have many strengths, like all media they also have limitations that media planners must consider. The limitations of newspapers include their creativity for emotional responses, selective exposure and attention, target audience selectivity, and clutter.

Creativity for Emotional Responses One of the greatest limitations of newspapers as an advertising medium is their poor reproduction quality. The coarse paper stock used for newspapers and the absence of extensive colour limits the quality of most newspaper ads. Newspapers have improved their reproduction quality in recent years, and colour reproduction has become more available. Also, advertisers desiring high-quality colour in newspaper ads can turn to such alternatives as freestanding inserts or supplements. However, these are more costly and may not be desirable to many advertisers. As a general rule, if the visual appearance of the product is important, the advertiser will not rely on newspaper ads. Ads for food products and fashions generally use magazines to capitalize on their superior reproduction quality and colour.

Selective Exposure and Attention Unlike magazines, which may be retained around the house for several weeks, a daily newspaper is generally kept less than a day. So an ad is unlikely to have any impact beyond the day of publication, and repeat exposure is very unlikely. Compounding this problem are the short amount of time many consumers spend with the newspaper and the possibility they may not even open certain sections of the paper. Media planners can offset these problems somewhat by using high frequency in the newspaper schedule and advertising in a section where consumers who are in the market for a particular product or service are likely to look.

Target Audience Selectivity While newspapers can offer advertisers geographic selectivity, they are not a selective medium in terms of demographics or lifestyle characteristics. Most newspapers reach broad and very diverse groups of consumers, which makes it difficult for marketers to focus on narrowly defined market segments. For example, manufacturers of fishing rods and reels will find newspapers very inefficient because of the wasted circulation that results from reaching all the newspaper readers who don't fish. Thus, they are more likely to use special-interest magazines. Any newspaper ads for their products will be done through cooperative plans whereby retailers share the costs or spread them over a number of sporting goods featured in the ad.

Clutter Newspapers, like most other advertising media, suffer from clutter. Because a substantial amount of the average daily newspaper in Canada is devoted to advertising, the advertiser's message must compete with numerous other ads for consumers' attention and interest. Moreover, the creative options in newspapers are limited by the fact that most ads are black and white. Thus, it can be difficult for a newspaper advertiser to break through the clutter without using costly measures such as large space buys or colour. Some advertisers use creative techniques like island ads—ads surrounded by editorial material. Island ads are found in the middle of the stock market quotes on the financial pages of many newspapers.

Buying Newspaper Advertising Space

The strengths and limitations of newspapers are part of the decision to use this medium. Another key factor is a complete understanding of the readers of newspapers to assess whether there is a fit between them and the target audience of the promotion plan. In this section, we review a few issues related to this part of the decision: circulation and readership, audience measurement, and newspaper advertising rates.

Newspaper Circulation and Readership

As with any medium, the media planner must understand the nature and size of the audience reached by a newspaper in considering its value in the media plan. Since newspapers as a class of media do an excellent job of penetrating their market, the typical daily newspaper gives advertisers the opportunity to reach most of the households in a market. But, while local advertisers aim to cover a particular market or trade area, national advertisers want to reach broad regions or even the entire country. They must purchase space in a number of papers to achieve the desired level of coverage. IMC Perspective 12–4 looks at Toronto's competitive newspaper market.

Circulation The basic source of information concerning the audience size of newspapers comes from circulation figures available through CARD, discussed earlier in this chapter. The Audit Bureau of Circulation (ABC) verifies circulation figures for many newspapers, as illustrated in the magazine media section. Advertisers using a number of papers in their media plan generally find CARD to be the most convenient source. The Canadian Community Newspapers Association (CCNA) verifies the circulation if an advertiser decides to use this vehicle.

The CCNA is a network of seven regional newspaper associations: Atlantic Community Newspapers Association, the Quebec Community Newspapers Association, the Ontario Community Newspapers Association, the Manitoba Community News-papers Association, the Saskatchewan Weekly Newspapers Association, the Alberta Weekly Newspapers Association, and the British Columbia & Yukon Community Newspapers Association. Membership of an individual community newspaper in a regional association includes membership in the national association. CCNA currently represents more than 700 English-language community newspapers with a total first-edition circulation of more than 9 million copies per week.

The CCNA gives an individual community newspaper a national voice in working with the public, business, and government, and its mission is to ensure a strong community newspaper industry. For advertisers, the CCNA plays a strong role in coordinating the placement of ads throughout the network. Its services include a one-order–one-bill system, ROP ads and pre-printed inserts, digital transmission of ads, Geographic Information System (GIS), and national or regional classified advertising. Presently, CCNA does not have audience information like NADbank; however, in June 2002, CCNA announced the implementation of a readership study. Despite this limitation, the CCNA claims community newspapers offer key benefits: precise coverage of specific markets with no wasted circulation, strong household penetration, state-of-the-art newspaper reproduction, and audited circulation figures.

CCNA has a self-administered audit program for all its members. The program includes a manual with detailed instructions and necessary forms. The member newspaper collects its own circulation data according to the VC rules and regulations. These data are reported to the CCNA and the CCNA Circulation Auditor or a Public (Chartered) Accountant audits the data thoroughly and a circulation report is published.

IMC PERSPECTIVE 12–4

Newspaper Wars in Toronto

Imagine a city with six daily newspapers, each with its own identity and target market, something few cities in the world can claim. *Metro Toronto* and *24 hours* joined the established papers *Globe and Mail, National Post, Toronto Star,* and *Toronto Sun* a few years ago and have given the latter a run for its money. Metro boasted a cumulative five-day readership of 824,000, while *24 hours* posted 728,000 readers with the *Toronto Sun* trailing at 453,000. Similar results emerged in Vancouver and Montreal; however, some believe that in those two cities the market for newspaper expanded rather than switching readers.

Metro Toronto, printed on semi-gloss paper and distributed in key locations along TTC and GO transit routes, looked every bit the supermarket tabloid with its content featuring wire-copy "human interest" stories. However, with a publishing record targeting females aged 18–34 and major advertisers like Rogers, Fido, and Expedia.ca, this formidable competitor appeared ready to battle the new up-start *24 hours.* With a track record of delivering strong readership and many advertising options (e.g., cover wraps and unusually shaped ads), *Metro Toronto* confidently raised its rates by 20 percent signalling a premium quality compared to *24 hours.*

Alternatively, *24 hours* targeted the outlying regions of Toronto and looked to find a content niche that would appeal to a broader target market of females aged 25–49. To entice advertisers, *24 hours* discounted its rates substantially to offer a $20 CPM, considerably less than other

newspapers. And some media buyers began experimenting with short test runs to see if the new publication delivered results more efficiently than *Metro Toronto.* Finally, internal research for *24 hours* revealed that 27 percent of its readers indicated that they had not read any daily newspaper prior to its initial publication.

Sources: Chris Powell, "Attack of the Freebies," *Marketing Magazine,* April 17, 2006; Chris Powell, "Second Time Around," *Marketing Magazine,* February 9, 2004; Chris Powell, "The Spin on NADbank," *Marketing Magazine,* April 19, 2004.

Question

1. How does the availability of so many newspapers help or hinder advertisers?

Newspaper circulation figures are generally broken down into three categories: the city zone, the retail trading zone, and all other areas. The **city zone** is a market area composed of the city where the paper is published and contiguous areas similar in character to the city. The **retail trading zone** is the market outside the city zone whose residents regularly trade with merchants within the city zone. The "all other" category covers all circulation not included in the city or retail trade zone.

Sometimes circulation figures are provided only for the primary market, which is the city and retail trade zones combined, and the other area. Both local and national advertisers consider the circulation patterns across the various categories in evaluating and selecting newspapers.

Readership Circulation figures provide the media planner with the basic data for assessing the value of newspapers and their ability to cover various market areas. However, the media planner also wants to match the characteristics of a newspaper's readers with those of the advertiser's target audience. Data on newspaper audience size and characteristics are available from NADbank. Figures 12–7 and 12–8 on page 370 give you an overview of the Canadian newspaper reader.

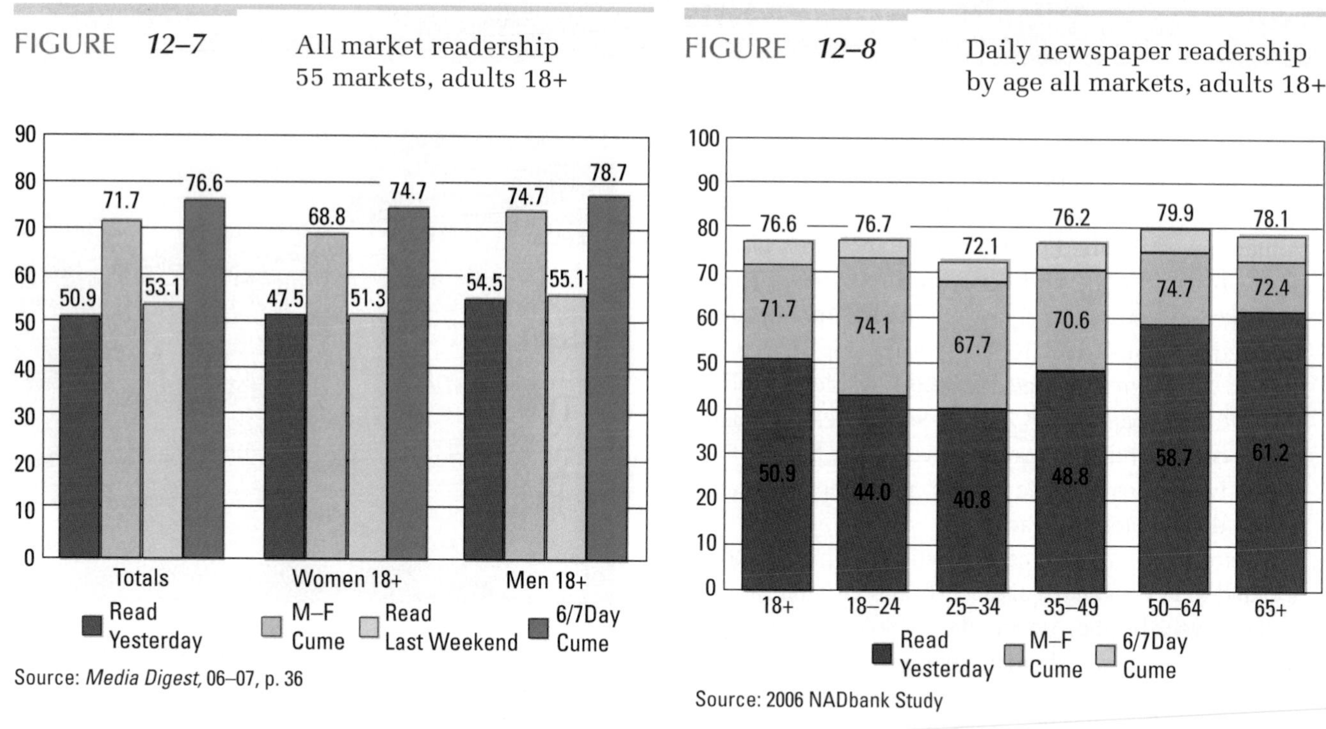

FIGURE 12–7 All market readership 55 markets, adults 18+

Source: *Media Digest*, 06–07, p. 36

FIGURE 12–8 Daily newspaper readership by age all markets, adults 18+

Source: 2006 NADbank Study

Daily Newspaper Audience Measurement

NADbank Newspaper Audience Databank Inc. (NADbank) is an organization comprised of newspaper, advertising agency, and advertiser members. Its primary mandate is to publish audience research information of Canadian daily newspapers. The purpose of this research is to provide its members with valid readership information to facilitate the buying and selling of newspaper advertising space.

NADbank uses a phone interview of respondents that takes approximately 15 minutes. The interview asks questions pertaining to readership of local and non-local newspapers, time spent reading, frequency of reading, method of receipt of newspapers into the home or outside the home, readership of TV magazine publications, radio listening, TV viewing and magazine readership, Internet readership of online newspapers, demographics, and media reliance. Product usage data is collected by a self-completion questionnaire that is sent to respondents after the telephone interview. These questions focus on 29 product categories and 20 retail shopping categories.

The study is conducted in 55 Canadian urban markets covering 81 Canadian daily newspapers. Nineteen markets annually are measured for both the readership and product data, while 36 markets are measured for readership data every three years. The measurement period for NADbank 2006 is comprised of two waves. The Winter/Spring wave covers the period from January to June. The Fall wave measures the period from September to December.

The readership study indicated that adults read the newspaper an average of 48 minutes per weekday and an average of 88 minutes on the weekend. The reach of newspaper is quite pervasive even though there are many media choices and reading is more time-consuming and involving than other media. For example, 57 percent of adults 18 and older across all markets read a newspaper yesterday, 64 percent read a newspaper last weekend, and 83 percent have read a newspaper in the past week.

As we have seen in the audience measurement for other media, the NADbank data is available to use with specialized software that is available through two authorized suppliers (IMS and Harris/Telmar). It provides consultation services to assist its members who use the information. Proprietary questions may also be added to the survey if an advertiser or marketer wants to link brand-specific data with the media and product usage data.

ComBase ComBase administers the audience measurement for CCNA. ComBase is also the name of the study. ComBase is an organization with a similar composition and mandate as NADbank. The independent board features newspapers, advertisers, and advertising agencies. Its mandate is to publish audience research information of the 700 community newspapers throughout Canada to allow them to sell their advertising space more effectively. In addition, ComBase accounts for listenership of 900 radio stations. The first bi-annual study surveyed 24,000 English-speaking Canadians in over 400 markets in 2003.

The "Recent Reading" methodology used by ComBase is as thorough as the Nadbank and PMB studies. In fact, an independent organization, the Canadian Advertising Research Foundation (CARF), appraised and endorsed the methodology. Of note, the survey determines all the publications read with an intensive investigation over a three-month time period. The survey also features excellent sample sizes and response rates and conducts the survey appropriately over time to ensure authenticity.

ComBase conducts 10-minute telephone interview in English of adults selected at random. The interviewer asks questions pertaining to readership of community newspapers, local and non-resident; readership of daily newspapers, including nationals; readership of other print press including shoppers, agricultural press, alternative publications; number of papers read; frequency of reading; newspaper preferred if more than one read; rating of newspapers read; radio listening, TV viewing; and demographic information about the respondent and household.

Results of the data can be compiled along a number of dimensions: Census Metropolitan Area (CMA) with population of 100,000 or more in an urbanized core; Census Agglomeration (CA) with population of 10,000 or more in an urbanized core; suburbs; newspaper distribution areas; Census Subdivisions (CSD) like towns and villages; economic regions with areas of common economic interests as defined by Statistics Canada; and provinces. Data can be accessed and used with existing media software, a similar situation we saw with NADbank. The following results demonstrate the significance of community newspapers:

- 70 percent read last weekday's issue of their community newspaper
- 48 percent read yesterday's weekday daily
- 25 percent of readers are exclusive
- 40 percent of Canadians are light TV viewers
- 26 percent of Canadians did not listen to radio yesterday.

Newspaper Advertising Rates

Advertisers are faced with a number of options and pricing structures when purchasing newspaper space. The cost of advertising space depends on the circulation, and whether the circulation is controlled (free) or paid. It also depends on factors such as premium charges for colour in a special section, as well as discounts available. National rates can be about 15 percent higher than local rates, to account for agency commission. Figures 12–9 and 12–10 on page 372 provide a summary of newspaper advertising rates.

FIGURE *12–9* 2005 daily newspaper circulation and cost by region

	Atlantic	Quebec	Ontario	Prairies	BC & Yukon	Total
Number of Markets	13	6	38	15	26	98
Number of Dailies	14	14	52	20	34	134
Circulation	331,575	1,347,863	3,130,757	942,444	600,447	6,353,086
B/W Line Rate ($)	24	45	181	46	52	348
Full Page B/W ($)	65,721	96,632	435,203	122,206	110,656	830,418
Full Page Colour ($)	80,028	124,320	494,257	145,261	132,160	976,026

Note: Rates used are open line rates.

Source: *April 2006 CARDonline*

FIGURE *12–10* 2005 daily newspaper circulations and costs by population groups

	IMM+	500M–1MM	100M–500M	50M–100M	Under 50M	Total
Number of Markets	6	3	26	19	44	98
Number of Dailies	23	6	35	22	48	134
Circulation	3,631,385	598,965	1,234,540	368,568	519,628	6,353,086
B/W Line Rate ($)	165	22	85	26	48	346
Full Page B/W ($)	360,263	58,409	228,565	66,103	117,078	830,418
Full Page Colour ($)	418,926	69,120	268,355	77,583	142,042	976,026

Note: Rates used are open line rates.

Source: *April 2006 CARDonline*

Newspaper space is sold by the **agate line** and **column width**. A line (or agate line) is a unit measuring one column wide and 1⁄14-inch deep. One problem with this unit is that newspapers use columns of varying width, from 6 columns per page to 10 columns per page, which affects the size, shape, and costs of an ad. (Note that these columns are not the actual columns viewed while reading the newspaper.) This results in a complicated production and buying process for national advertisers that purchase space in a number of newspapers.

Advertisers need to know the number of lines and number of columns on a newspaper page in order to calculate the cost of an ad. For example, the following calculation is for the weekday cost of a full-page ad in the national edition of the *National Post.* The paper has 301 lines and 10 columns per page, and the open cost per line is $17.69.

10 columns × 301 lines × $17.69/line per column = $53,247

This calculation could be done differently with the same result when the entire length of the paper is known (301 lines/14 agate lines per column inch).

10 columns × 21.5 inches × 14 agate lines per column inch × $17.69 = $52,247

This principle can be used to calculate the cost of ads of various sizes. For example, for an ad that is 5 columns wide and 6 inches deep, the calculation would then be the following:

5 columns × 6 inches × 14 agate lines per column inch
× $17.69 per column inch = $7,430

Newspaper rates for local advertisers continue to be based on the column inch, which is 1 inch deep by 1 column wide. Advertising rates for local advertisers are quoted per column inch, and media planners calculate total space costs by multiplying the ad's number of column inches by the cost per inch.

Most newspapers have an **open-rate structure**, which means various discounts are available. These discounts are generally based on frequency or bulk purchases of space and depend on the number of column inches purchased in a year. The above calculations used the most expensive cost based on a one-time ad. The maximum discount puts the cost per line at $11.82, about one-third less expensive. A full-page ad would drop from $53,247 to $35,578, a savings of $17,669.

Newspaper space rates also vary with an advertiser's special requests, such as preferred position or colour. The basic rates quoted by a newspaper are **run of paper (ROP)**, which means the paper can place the ad on any page or in any position it desires. While most newspapers try to place an ad in a requested position, the advertiser can ensure a specific section and/or position on a page by paying a higher **preferred position rate**. Colour advertising is also available in many newspapers on an ROP basis or through preprinted inserts or supplements.

Recently, advertising rates have come under fire from media buyers with an equally contentious response from the media vendors. Historically, media buyers paid what newspapers set as their price without much criticism. However, newspaper rates have been questioned from larger advertising agencies and media buying organizations that have emerged with amalgamations in the industry. While media buyers usually investigate and evaluate the audience size and price for television advertising rates, this behaviour was not generally expected with newspapers. In particular, the *National Post* and *The Globe and Mail* reacted strongly to those buyers who have put increased pressure on lower rates as they represent very large advertisers who purchase millions of agate lines per year. To contribute to the discussion, *The Globe and Mail* worked with an independent data analysis firm that tracked the sales impact of newspaper ad placement.[19]

IMC Planning: Strategic Use of Print Media

In the previous chapter, we ended with a discussion of the use of broadcast media to achieve strategic IMC objectives. In this IMC planning section, we investigate the use of magazines and newspapers to achieve communication and behavioural objectives at different stages of the target audience's decision-making process.

Magazines

The selectivity and creativity options for magazines allow promotional planners a multitude of opportunities for establishing and maintaining very unique brand positions across all potential target audiences. For example, if research indicates a high proportion of non-users in certain lifestyle publications, the promotional planner can develop print ads with extensive copy to build category need as well as sufficient brand coverage for awareness while communicating the most appropriate brand benefit message for persuasion. Alternatively, research in other publications might indicate strong brand development and a high degree of current customers, thus allowing the promotional planner the opportunity to use messages that maintain the strong brand equity. This might suggest a more emotional message with enticing visuals for low-involvement processing.

While the decision to offer more customized messages to each audience is met with some amount of risk, it is mitigated by the consistency in the creative theme and creative tactics such as the design elements (e.g., layout). This possible scenario for promotional planners suggests that ads directed toward non-users could be developed to influence the pre-purchase and need recognition stages, whereas the ads for the customer could attempt to influence the purchase decision stage, as the brand would be encouraging a repeat purchase objective.

Extending this argument geographically is another strategic opportunity for promotional planners. For example, if the brand has a low brand development index in one part of the country, more persuasive switching messages directed to consumers at the purchase decision stage might be considered through regional or city editions. Alternatively, other regional editions could be examined if the brand has a high brand development index and the promotional planner concentrates on brand maintenance messages that focus, for example, on post-purchase satisfaction.

As the use of these key strengths of magazines implies, promotional planners can use magazines to attain virtually any of the communication objectives with any type of target audience and create the unique brand positions desired. Granted, certain costs are associated with this strategic use of magazines; the promotional planner can schedule the placements over time so as not to break the budget.

These strengths of magazines allow print to work with other media and IMC tools. Visuals can be the same as those from TV commercials to enhance message frequency. Headlines could be consistently used across out-of-home media and print ads. Sales promotions can be added to the message, like coupons or Internet site links to register for samples. Brand-building charity sponsorship or events can be communicated if they especially resonate with the readership audience. In short, magazines offer a degree of potential integration in the IMC plan.

Newspapers

The strategic use of this media is similar to radio in that national and local advertisers design messages with related objectives. National advertisers employ newspapers for brand-building messages they wish to disseminate across the country or in select regions. These ads take a few general forms. One kind of ad builds awareness and benefit beliefs at the pre-purchase and need recognition stages due to the broad reach of newspapers. With the majority of Canadian households reading newspapers on a regular basis, brands naturally reach their target audience and those who may not be in the market for such products. Other types of ads contribute at the information search stage for the target audience. The involved nature of the messages that can be creatively communicated in a more rational manner to fit the editorial context permits promotional planners to persuade their audience via high-involvement, informational brand attitude. One limitation with the opportunity is that the number of consumers actually in the market at this stage is fewer, thus making the purchase less cost-efficient. Finally, national advertisers utilize newspapers for executing information regarding sales promotions. For example, automobile manufacturers and large retailers are some of the largest advertisers who communicate their price and other promotions in newspapers to influence consumers at the purchase decision stage.

As noted in the cost implications discussion, newspapers offer local advertisers and small businesses (e.g., retailers, services) a tremendous opportunity for reaching an entire city for a reasonable cost. These advertisers can design ads to meet any communication objectives. A perusal of the local newspaper will identify ads that are clearly trying to build awareness and communicate certain brand benefits. However, the daily/weekly time frame of newspapers reveals that many ads have stronger purchase intention objectives.

Like magazines, newspapers offer good potential for integrating with other media and IMC tools. Oftentimes, television and radio commercials suggest that consumers "see newspaper for details." In this case, the initial ads are influencing the target audience at the need recognition stage and the newspaper is influencing the information search stage. Many public relations activities like sponsorship of charity events in the local community are conveyed in newspapers since they act as a planning resource for things to do in one's city.

SUMMARY

Magazines and newspapers, the two major forms of print media, play an important role in the media plans and strategy of many advertisers. Magazines are a very selective medium and are very valuable for reaching specific types of customers and market segments. The three broad categories of magazines are consumer, farm, and business publications. Each of these categories can be further classified according to the publication's editorial content and audience appeal.

In addition to their selectivity, the strengths of magazines include their target audience selectivity, geographic coverage, creativity, reader involvement and amount of processing time, media image, and selective exposure and attention levels. Limitations of magazines include their high cost, limited reach and frequency, long lead time, weak target audience coverage, and the advertising clutter in most publications.

Advertising space rates in magazines vary according to a number of factors, among them the size of the ad, position in the publication, particular editions purchased, use of colour, and number and frequency of insertions. Rates for magazines are compared on the basis of the cost per thousand, although other factors such as the editorial content of the publication and its ability to reach specific target audiences must also be considered.

Newspapers represent the largest advertising medium in terms of total volume, receiving about a fourth of all advertising dollars. Newspapers are a very important medium to local advertisers, especially retailers. Newspapers are a broad-based medium that reaches a large percentage of households in a particular area. Newspapers' other advantages include scheduling flexibility, geographic coverage, reader involvement and amount of processing time, media image, creativity for cognitive responses, and absolute cost and cost efficiency. Drawbacks of newspapers include their creativity for emotional responses, selective exposure and attention, target audience selectivity, and clutter.

Trends toward market segmentation and regional marketing are prompting many advertisers to make more use of newspapers and magazines. However, both magazines and newspapers face increasing competition from such other media as direct marketing and the Internet, and both are working to improve the quality of their circulation bases.

KEY TERMS

agate line, *372*
bleed pages, *356*
city zone, *369*
classified advertising, *365*
column width, *372*
controlled-circulation basis, *361*
creative space buys, *356*
display advertising, *364*
gatefolds, *356*
ink-jet imaging, *355*
inserts, *356*
open-rate structure, *373*
pass-along readership, *361*
PMB study, *361*
preferred position rate, *373*
preprinted inserts, *365*
retail trading zone, *369*
run of paper (ROP), *373*
selective binding, *353*
selectivity, *352*
total audience/readership, *361*

DISCUSSION QUESTIONS

1. Discuss the strengths and limitations of magazines as an advertising medium. How do magazines differ from television and radio as advertising media?

2. Describe what is meant by selectivity with regard to the purchase of advertising media and discuss some of the ways magazines provide selectivity to advertisers.

3. Explain why advertisers of products such as cosmetics or women's clothing would choose to advertise in magazines such as *Flare, Elle Canada,* or *Chatelaine.*

4. Discuss how circulation figures are used in evaluating magazines and newspapers as part of a media plan and setting advertising rates.

5. If you were purchasing magazine ad space for a manufacturer of snowboarding equipment, what factors would you consider? Would your selection of magazines be limited to snowboarding publications? Why or why not?

6. The number of magazines has increased substantially in the past five years. What could have caused this recent trend?

7. Discuss the strengths and limitations of newspapers as an advertising medium. How might the decision to use newspapers in a media plan differ for national versus local advertisers?

8. What factors could explain the lower readership of newspapers compared to a few years ago?

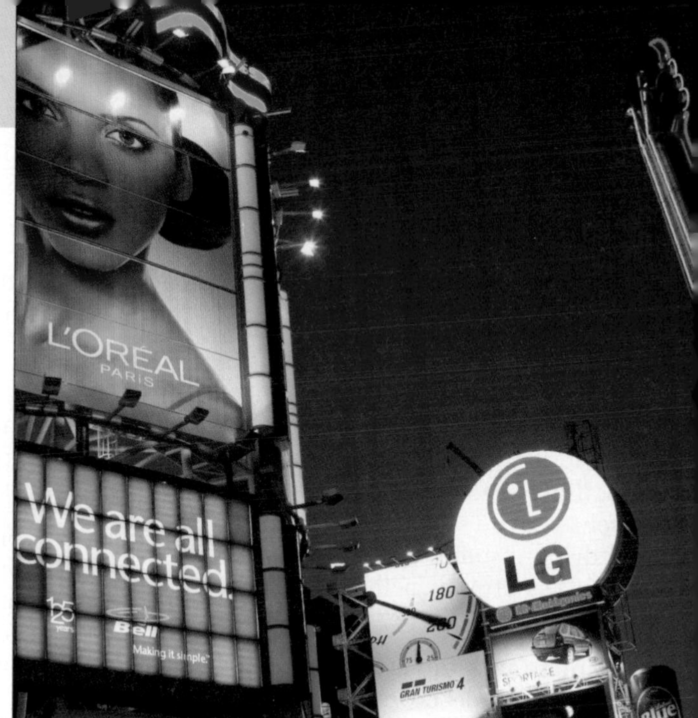

CHAPTER 13

OUT-OF-HOME AND SUPPORT MEDIA

Chapter Objectives

- To describe out-of-home and support media available to the marketer in developing an IMC program.
- To develop an understanding of the strengths and limitations of out-of-home and support media.
- To know how audiences for out-of-home and support media are measured.

Outdoor Ads Turn Heads

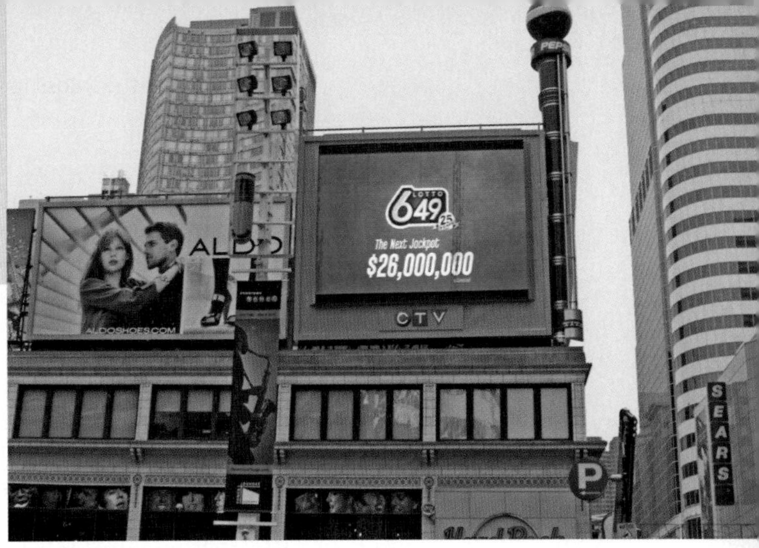

Although outdoor ads do not attract significant levels of advertising revenue compared to broadcast and print media, they nevertheless get a lot of consumer attention as brands continue to innovate creatively and with new technology. On the creative front, Nike placed two huge billboards on a barge that sailed around Vancouver. The pictures depicted Vancouver Canuck star Markus Naslund in a tug-of-war battle with a tugboat to advertise Nike's new training products—which included the resistance bands demonstrated in the unreal battle. Entitled "Barge Resistance," the ad was one of many outdoor initiatives to encourage young athletes to visit Nike's hockey training Internet site. Other grand visuals included "training poses" of Naslund and Calgary Flame Jarome Iginla in a few major cities. Smaller versions found their way into local hockey arenas—and eventually to children's homes! And while Nike planned to generate the aforementioned consumer action, it also hoped to help the brand at the store level, where it faced significant competition for retail shelf space.

Full-motion video billboards emerged a few years ago, but advertisers now understand how to use the newer technology more creatively. For example, to launch a can version of its famous draught beer Guinness used this option extensively in downtown Toronto in March to coincide with St. Patrick's Day celebrations. A Nokia display showed real people walking along the street, invited them to test a new camera, and instantly e-mailed the photos to an Internet site. Tim Hortons alters its messages based on the time of day, offering different products. Radio station Q107 showed the song playing on-air at that very moment.

Consumer response to full-motion video billboards is positive. One study found very positive results for questions pertaining to awareness, seen in the past week, favourable impression, enliven the surroundings, and better than regular billboards. Growth in video billboards is expected as it hit a critical mass of reaching 13 million people in Toronto, Hamilton, Winnipeg, Calgary, and Edmonton, with about 700,000 travelling by the Yonge–Dundas square display in Toronto each week. However, some cities—like Vancouver—are reluctant to approve these ads or have less viable locations for installation.

The future of outdoor ads is going digital, as text messaging and other applications are allowing consumers to "interact" with new forms of displays. For instance, The Jean Machine used digital boards in food courts with full-motion, full-colour ads that invited consumers to enter a shopping spree contest by entering a text message. The campaign attracted 2,000 entries in ten malls in the Toronto area. Nokia ventured into this realm as well by encouraging people in Montreal to change the lights on a Christmas tree that demonstrated the innovation and technology associated with the brand. Radio messaging allows consumers to receive communication from billboards to their cell phones providing additional product information, Internet site links, or a coupon. Nintendo is looking at this idea to allow gamers to download applications from billboards. Three-dimensional holographic images provide new and fascinating visuals or short commercials.

Sources: Paul Brent, "Blowing Up the Brand," *Marketing Magazine,* May 15, 2006; Patti Summerfield, "The Great Outdoor," *Strategy Magazine,* April 2006; and Michelle Warren, "Looking Way Up," *Marketing Magazine,* July 2006.

Question

1. From the perspective of the receiver of the message, are full-motion video billboards more similar to regular billboards or to television commercials?

Every time we step out of the house, we encounter media directing an advertising message to us. Often we see ads while travelling. Most places we go have some form of advertising. And when we shop, we continue to see more ads! **Out-of-home media** is quite pervasive, and it delivers the advertising messages that we encounter while moving throughout our town or city, accomplishing our day-to-day activities. Some are new to the marketplace, and others have been around a while. In this chapter, we review three broad categories of out-of-home media: outdoor, transit, and place-based (Figure 13–1). We discuss the relative strengths and limitations, cost information, and audience measurement of each. We use the term out-of-home media because it is a general term that encompasses all media that go beyond the traditional media—broadcast or print—that are located in public spaces.

We also encounter ads from non-traditional media. **Support media** are used to reach those people in the target audience that the primary media may not have reached or to reinforce the message contained in primary media. We conclude this chapter by summarizing two broad categories of support media: promotional products and product placement.

FIGURE *13–1*

Out-of-home media

Outdoor	Transit	Place-Based
Horizontal/vertical poster	Exterior bus posters	Bar, restaurant, hotel
Backlit poster	Interior overhead door card	Cinema
Superboard	Station poster	Mall
Electronic	Transit shelter	Parking lot
Street level	Super-bus, bus mural	Arena, stadium
Wall banner, mural	Subway online	Golf, ski, fitness centre
Mobile mural/poster	Airport display	Washroom, floor
Aerial, bench, receptacle	In-flight	Elevator, escalator

Outdoor Media

Outdoor media is pervasive, and it appears that we are surrounded. However, the amount spent on this medium is approximately $200 million, which is about 10 percent of TV or newspaper advertising revenue. Despite this, outdoor media have just about doubled recently, compared to the 25- to 35-percent growth for TV and newspaper media. The role of outdoor media in contributing to sales may be a key factor. In a study reported by BBDO advertising, 35 percent of consumers surveyed said they had called a phone number they saw on an out-of-home ad.[1] A study reported by Mukesh Bhargava and Naveen Donthu showed that outdoor advertising can have a significant effect on sales, particularly when combined with a promotion.[2] IMC Perspective 13–1 highlights findings from other research. We now turn our attention to the many outdoor media options available for an advertiser.

Outdoor Media Options

Posters describe the typical billboard, which can be horizontal (e.g., 3m by 6m) or vertical (e.g., 4m by 5m). These displays are front lit for visibility at night and are located in high vehicle-traffic areas. They may be purchased on an individual basis or for a certain level of GRPs in cities such as Toronto or in smaller markets such as Timmins, Ontario. As the name implies, **backlit posters** are posters of generally the same size that have a light behind them so that they are more clearly illuminated. These units are located at major intersections or high traffic-volume areas in or near major cities in Canada.

IMC PERSPECTIVE 13–1

Commuter Habits Help Out-of-Home Ads

The Out-of-Home Marketing Association of Canada's new "A Day in the Life" study determined that out-of-home advertising boasts considerable ability to reach and influence Canada's car commuters. The study, based on telephone interviews with 2,500 Canadians age 12+ in major markets, found that the typical urban Canadian drives nearly 130 kilometres a week, with commuting to and from work accounting for half this distance. On a typical weekday, urban Canadians spend an average of 0.7 hours commuting to and from work.

The study revealed that 73 percent of urban workers use a vehicle to get to work, with the incidence of travelling by vehicle increasing significantly among suburbanites. For example, while 53 percent of metro Toronto residents travel to work by vehicle, that figure increases to 89 percent among suburban residents. The same is true in both Montreal (where 45 percent of metro residents and 75 percent of suburban residents use a vehicle to get to work) and Vancouver (where 64 percent of metro residents and 85 percent of suburban residents use a vehicle to get to work).

On a typical weekday, urban Canadians spend as much time exposed to out-of-home media (3.8 hours) as to television. On weekend days, the amount of time they are exposed to out-of-home advertising jumps to 4.7 hours, putting it ahead of TV (3.1 hours), the Internet (2.5 hours), and radio (1.2 hours).

The study also found that urban Canadians are prone to shopping on the way home from work, with 44 percent listing it as a time when they shop (82 percent of workers say they shop on the weekends or days when they're not at work). In addition, 45 percent of people ages 12 to 17 said they are more likely to spontaneously shop on the way to and from work, followed by 41 percent of adults ages 18 to 24 and 39 percent of adults ages 25 to 34. About one-third of people age 35 and older shop on their way to and from work.

Out-of-home advertising also wields considerable influence on purchase decisions. The study found that in the past three months, 30 percent of people visited a specific website after seeing it promoted on out-of-home advertising, 25 percent learned about a store/product/sale that motivated them to visit a specific store, and 17 percent were prompted to purchase or seek information about a new product. Those numbers increased to 45 percent, 41 percent, and 32 percent, respectively, when taking the past year into account.

Source: Chris Powell, "Reaching Daytrippers," *Marketing Magazine*, October 23, 2006.

Question

1. How can advertisers take advantage of the results of this study?

Taking a cue from retail merchandising used by The Gap, Scotiabank recently added posters to its exterior windows and placed interior posters throughout each of its branches. The overall strategy called for significant visuals that emphasized the current customer service strategy and meshed with other communication materials. A guiding constraint included the task of making the posters fit with the decor of each bank location, much like Scotiabank managers had observed at The Gap. Each poster featured a horizontal split with a simple 10-word message on one side and a strong visual on the other. External window posters and those near personal banking offices communicated the Scotiabank brand of "human," while posters near customer service representatives and automatic banking machines communicated specific products. A dual messaging approach permitted specific brand experiences for unique target audiences. Scotiabank planned to expand the customized message for each brand depending upon customer mix for each local market.[3]

Larger billboards, known as **bulletins**, **superboards**, or **spectaculars**, are larger displays (two to three times larger) that have a variety of sizes depending upon the

FIGURE 13–2 Outdoor rates by daily GRP delivery

Type of Poster and Markets	25 GRPs Daily # of panels	25 GRPs Daily 4-week rate Cost range (000s)	50 GRPs Daily # of Panels	50 GRPs Daily 4-week rate Cost range (000s)	75 GRPs Daily # of Panels	75 GRPs Daily 4-week rate Cost range (000s)
Horizontal Posters						
Top 3 Markets	91–159	$210–316	214–308	$363–446	321–474	$533–704
Top 10 Markets	154–284	$298–456	340–557	$576–718	475–881	$721–1237
Vertical Posters						
Top 3 Markets	106–143	$170–219	248–253	$367–379	357–364	$530–540
Top 10 Markets	144–188	$244–293	317–328	$483–495	457–470	$686–696
Street Level/TSAs						
Top 3 Markets	152–185	$122–136	309–479	$229–267	465–567	$334–399
Top 10 Markets	238–300	$167–201	480–707	$344–389	719–906	$497–576
Mall						
Top 3 Markets	77	$38	151	$88	228	$125
Top 10 Markets	132	$70	255	$146	384	$206
Backlit (Weekly GRPs)						
Top 3 Markets	16	$30	29–31	$55–79	43–47	$83–118
Top 10 Markets	25	$45	44–48	$81–114	63–69	$116–163

*Source: *CARD, April 2006/Vendor Rate Cards*

media company. These displays are sold on a per location basis due to their size and the low number of options available in major Canadian markets. Smaller backlit displays, known as **street-level posters** and measuring about 2m by 1m, are available across the country.

Exhibit 13–1 Outdoor media goes beyond two dimensions

The aforementioned outdoor options are typically purchased for four weeks and provide anywhere from 25 GRPs to 150 GRPs per day, depending upon the number of displays or showings chosen within a local market. Recall from Chapter 10 that one GRP represents 1 percent of the market seeing the ad once. Thus, buying 50 GRPs implies that the marketer is reaching 50 percent of the market every day. (Figure 13–2 shows some outdoor rates broken down by three GRP levels.)

Most outdoor operators can present examples of past outdoor campaigns producing awareness and other communication effects. The examples can be for a product category or for individual campaigns. The operators can also provide maps to illustrate the posters' locations and other relevant data (e.g., demographics).

A number of innovative outdoor tools have emerged in Canada. Some firms are setting up large video-display units that have full animation and colour. For example, Dundas Square, near the Eaton Centre in downtown Toronto, features a 12-metre-wide by 9-metre-high full-colour video screen in addition to eight display faces and Canada's largest neon sign, at 18 metres in diameter. Many of Canada's largest advertisers secure space in this very prominent location, which receives extensive pedestrian and vehicular traffic (see Exhibit 13–1).[4] Electronic message signs offer short ads (e.g., 10 seconds) on

2-or 3-minute rotation. As expected, both of these displays are located in high-traffic locations in a few large urban markets, with various sizes and packages available depending on the media firm. Murals and wall banners are sold in a few major markets in Canada (e.g., Toronto, Vancouver) with varying sizes. A number of firms offer **mobile signage** by placing displays on trucks or vehicles (see Exhibit 13–2). These are sold by the number of vehicles and the number of months.

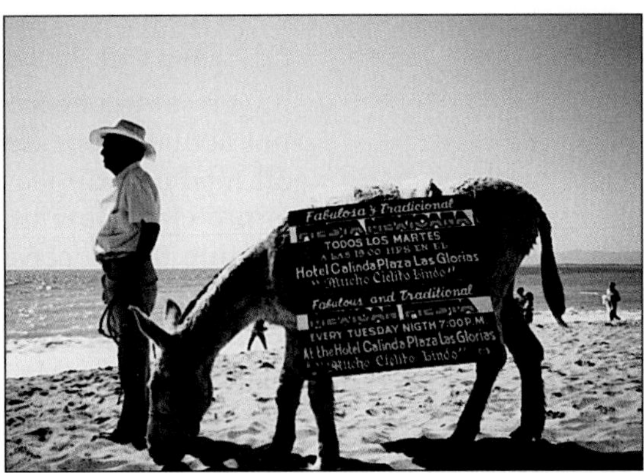

Exhibit 13–2 An interesting and unusual example of a mobile billboard

Finally, we find outdoor media in some unusual outdoor locations. Signage is placed on benches, bicycle racks, garbage receptacles, and in the air through aerial advertising on airplanes or hot-air balloons. It seems that no matter where we turn outside, there will be some form of advertising message directed toward us.

Despite the pervasiveness of outdoor advertising, there is some concern. In a Maritz AmeriPoll asking consumers about their opinions of billboards, 62 percent of the respondents said that they thought billboards should not be banned, while 52 percent said that they should be strictly regulated. When asked if billboards were entertaining, 80 percent of those surveyed said no; when asked if billboards could be beautiful, only 27 percent said yes.[5] Media buyers have not completely adopted outdoor media, partially because of image problems and the limited message that can be communicated.

Historically, advertisers considered outdoor ads as a support media to broadcast or print. However, current usage indicates it can be used successfully as a primary media as seen by Clover Leaf's recent strategic emphasis. Hoping to expand the overall tuna category to both men and women with their flavoured varieties (e.g., sun-dried tomato and basil), the only nationally distributed tuna producer showed interesting and innovative ways of thinking about tuna (e.g., salad or wrap) with its more exotic taste sensations. Outdoor (e.g., posters, transit shelters, street columns) became the focal point to communicate the images and messages that easily transferred to other out-of-home media (e.g., in-store, health club posters) and sales promotions (e.g., coupons, samples).[6]

Audience Measurement for Outdoor Media

Audience measurement to determine the amount of reach and frequency is done by the Canadian Outdoor Measurement Bureau (COMB), an independent organization comprised of members from advertisers, advertising agencies, and media firms known as outdoor operators. COMB maintains a national database of all products for outdoor operators in order to calculate daily or weekly audience averages for each media in all markets. COMB acts as an auditor to ensure an authentic media purchase and produces specific reports as documentation. COMB conducts 6,000 randomly selected field audits per year, calculates performance statistics for all operators, and disseminates these findings to all members.

COMB's methodology to determine the reach and frequency is comprehensive. COMB obtains traffic circulation numbers from municipalities. This data is then analyzed with respect to three key questions:

- What is the average number of people in the vehicle?
- What is the vehicle's origin within the CMA?
- Is the sign illuminated? If so, for how long?

This analysis is known as the total number of circulations. These circulations are applied to each poster along a certain part of the road that is known as a link. The numbers are adjusted to account for time-of-day variations throughout the week to arrive at an adjusted circulation, which is then divided by the target population so that the reach is expressed as 1 percent of the population.

This involved measurement process has resulted in a system that COMB claims as being the most accurate and reliable method in the world. In contrast, some media buyers are concerned that the measurement tracks opportunity for exposure and not actual exposure to the ads. While this discrepancy is an inherent problem with all media, it appears to be particularly strong with outdoor media. Furthermore, it is not clear how many people are in each vehicle that may be exposed to the ads. Despite this success and constructive criticism, COMB strives to find the best system possible to ensure a larger piece of the advertising industry beyond its usual 4-percent share compared to broadcast or print.

Recently, COMB tested the use of a global positioning system (GPS) to track driving behaviour more accurately in selected Canadian cities. The device was installed in cars to track driving patterns and to track which outdoor ads drivers had driven past. Pre- and posttest interviews obtained demographic and other information that was linked to other data sources to estimate reach and frequency. Preliminary results indicated that people were exposed to many ads but with less frequency to each ad, thus suggesting the usefulness of maximizing reach over frequency with outdoor ads.

The future of measurement in Canada may be found in the United Kingdom where an innovative technology that tracks a driver's eye movement while behind the wheel can assess which ads are actually seen. Taking into the account the size of the ad and the distance from the road, this new method is demonstrating more accurate numbers and some believe it has led to a growth of advertising revenue that now stands at 8 percent.[7] IMC Perspective 13–2 highlights the new technology.

Strengths of Outdoor Media

Reach With proper placement, a broad base of exposure is possible in a given market, with both day and night presence. A 100 GRP **showing** (the percentage of duplicated audience exposed to an outdoor poster daily) could yield exposure to an equivalent of 100 percent of the marketplace daily! This level of coverage is likely to yield high levels of reach.

Frequency Because purchase cycles for outdoor media are typically for 4-week periods, consumers are usually exposed a number of times, resulting in high levels of frequency.

Geographic Coverage Outdoor media can be placed along highways, near stores, or on mobile billboards, almost anywhere that the law permits. Local, regional, or even national markets may be covered.

Creativity for Emotional Responses As shown in Exhibits 13–1 and 13–2, outdoor ads can be very creative. Large print, colours, and other elements attract attention and tend to generate short emotional responses that connect the target audience to the brand.

Cost Efficiency Outdoor ads usually have a very competitive CPM when compared to other media. The average CPM of outdoor ads is less than that of radio, TV, magazines, and newspapers.

Scheduling Flexibility Modern technologies have reduced production times for outdoor advertising to allow for rapid turnaround time. Placement can be done on a monthly basis assuming availability exists.

IMC PERSPECTIVE 13–2

Outdoor Advertising Tested

Eye tracking—a technology that's at least 20 years old—is enjoying renewed interest. In essence, a test subject is shown a visual stimulus and his or her eye movements are tracked using a recording medium. These stimuli could be anything, but out-of-home advertising is probably the commercial field where most of the research is currently being conducted.

Rosanne Caron, president of the Toronto-based Out-of-Home Marketing Association of Canada (OMAC), says the out-of-home industry is pushing hard on eye-tracking research, citing Britain and Australia as two countries where it is becoming more prominent. Caron also points to developments here, including the Outdoor Advertising Consumer Exposure Study (OACES), which she bills as the first study of its kind.

Mary Falbo, vice-president of business development for Oakville, Ont.-based Pattison Outdoor Advertising, which commissioned OACES along with Astral Media Outdoor and CBS Outdoor, says curiosity was the impetus for the research. "We were very curious about how consumers interacted with outdoor products," says Falbo. The study was carried out by Toronto-based VisionTrack in the Ottawa and Montreal markets in September 2005. The study used 27 randomly selected drivers and passengers in each city, who were asked to drive a pre-determined route that passed by a variety of outdoor advertising products, including trio boards, standard posters, superboards, and bus shelters, while also providing exposure to a variety of different driving conditions (in town, city, congestion, etc.).

The route was driven at different times of day (morning peak, morning non-peak, afternoon non-peak, afternoon peak, and night) and respondents' eye movements were tracked using a headband eye camera (their entire visual interaction was also recorded onto videotape). There were two significant differences among the Canadian and European and U.S. studies, says Falbo: in Europe the research was conducted under simulated conditions, while in the U.S. the drivers of test cars weren't tested, only their passengers.

Michele Erskine, director of marketing for CBS Outdoor in Toronto, says eye tracking research is "pretty concrete. You can tell that somebody's eye paused and actually saw the ad, because there's a measure of when the eye is fixated," she explains. "I think in a lot of ways it takes us to a level that some of the other media (haven't reached). We are finding out what percentage of ads was actually looked at as (a test car) drove by."

During OACES, an outdoor ad was considered "seen" if a driver or passenger fixated on it for at least 200 milliseconds. The study found that 55 percent of the ads selected for analysis were seen by the 27 drivers and passengers tested. Passengers, unsurprisingly, were more likely to see them (some 73 percent, versus 52 percent of drivers who saw them). It was also found that women were slightly more likely to see outdoor advertising, registering 57 percent against 53 percent. Those people who looked at advertising looked at an ad an average of 2.04 times on a single drive-by. Out-of-home ads with three rotating faces were looked at more often, 2.46 times, compared with 1.9 times for a standard poster. In total, 535 outdoor exposures were eye-tracked during the study.

The test drive in Montreal took about 90 minutes and most of the advertising seen was in French (in Ottawa, most of the out-of-home advertising seen was in English). However, analysis showed that language made no difference to the study's findings. Neither drivers nor passengers knew the study was related to advertising. In fact, says Erskine with a laugh, most of them thought it was something to do with the transport ministry.

VisionTrack president Gerry Grundland—clients include Cadbury Adams Canada, Procter & Gamble, Unilever, and Warner Lambert—is emphatic about the rigour behind eye tracking. Grundland is understandably bullish about eye tracking, but he's also cautious: "It brings a whole new degree of understanding the consumer," says Grundland. "But it does not negate what marketers already know. It's a powerful piece of information, but only one part of the marketing mix."

Source: David Chilton, "Eying Outdoors," *Marketing Magazine*, October 26, 2006.

Question

1. Explain why the data from this kind of research would be highly valued by advertisers.

Selective Exposure On the one hand, outdoor ads are difficult for consumers to avoid since they are so pervasive. Moreover, a consumer has little control like television or radio to change the channel or station. On the other hand, consumers can deliberately ignore outdoor ads; however, the high profile of the ads makes this a difficult task at times.

Attention The sheer size, strategic placement, and the creative elements of colour make outdoor advertising an attractive medium to draw the attention of the target audience.

Limitations of Outdoor Media

Target Audience Coverage With the broad base reach of outdoor advertising, it is difficult to ensure that the specific target audience coverage is sufficient. While it is possible to reach an audience with select location placement, in many cases the purchase of outdoor ads results in a high degree of waste coverage. It is not likely that everyone driving past a billboard is part of the target audience.

Amount of Processing Time Because of the speed with which most people pass by outdoor ads, exposure time is short, so messages are limited to a few words and/or an illustration.

Creativity for Cognitive Responses Lengthy appeals are not physically possible in many instances, and if they were, they have less likelihood of complete comprehension. Thus, it is expected that outdoor ads suffer from their inability to fully persuade consumers with an involved message.

Absolute Cost A basic level of 25 GRPs per day over four weeks in 10 or even three major cities can be quite prohibitive for many advertisers. For smaller businesses selecting a few strategic locations in a local market could overcome this limitation.

Media Image Outdoor advertising has suffered some image problems as well as some disregard among consumers. This may be in part due to fatigue of the high frequency of exposures that may lead to wearout—people are likely to get tired of seeing the same ad every day.

Target Audience Selectivity Reaching a specific target audience is challenging due to the broad exposure of outdoor media in general. However, strategic use can overcome this limitation, for example by using reminder ads for a type of product near the retail outlets.

Clutter By its very nature, outdoor ads have competing messages. At any streetscape or location where outdoor ads are featured, it is very likely that other messages will be also vying for consumer attention.

Low Involvement The overall effect of the short repeated message is that outdoor ads tend to be considered a low-involvement media.

Transit Media

Another form of out-of-home advertising is **transit advertising**. While similar to outdoor in the sense that it uses billboards and electronic messages, transit is targeted at the millions of people who are exposed to commercial transportation facilities, including buses, subways, light-rail trains, and airplanes. The first three we cover in the form of local transit options, and then we consider the airplane option.

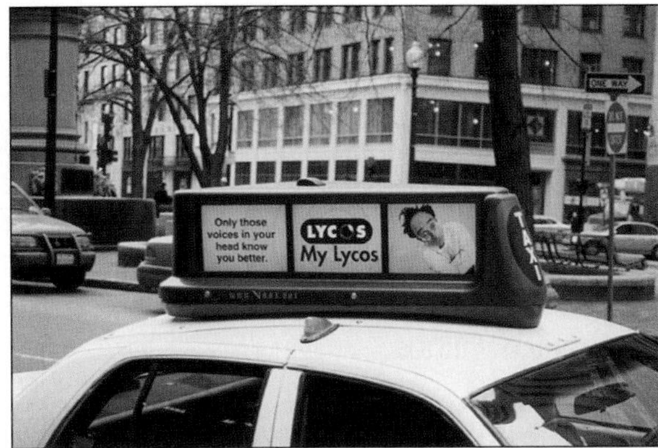

Exhibit 13–3 Electronic outside posters often appear on taxicabs

Commuter Transit Options

Some of the most common commuter ads viewed are the **interior transit cards** placed above the seating area that advertise restaurants, TV or radio stations, or myriad other products and services. Ads are positioned in backlit units above windows and along both sides of the bus, streetcar, subway, or light-rail transit cars. **Interior door cards** are available in major markets where there is subway-like transit. These cards are placed on both sides of the doors and are about 50 percent larger than the aforementioned cards. **Exterior posters** may appear on the sides, backs, and/or roofs of buses, taxis, trains, and subway and street cars (see Exhibit 13–3).

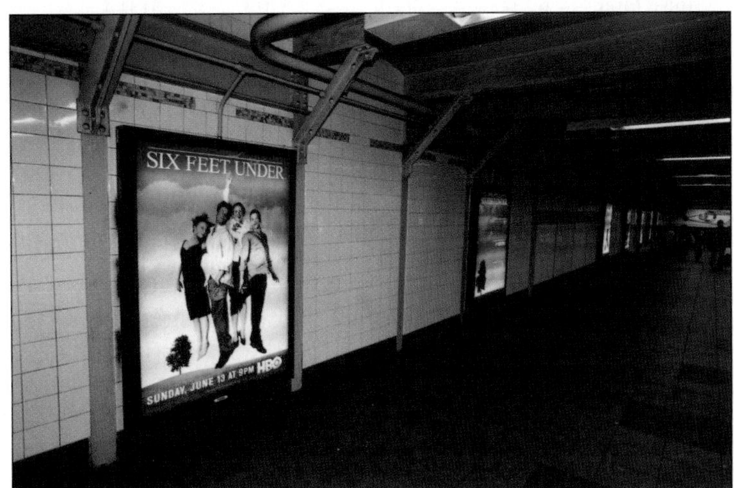

Exhibit 13–4 Station posters can be used to attract attention

Discovery Channel has always used out-of-home media to establish itself as a legitimate television alternative and to advertise its specific series, specials, or theme weeks. For example, during Shark Week in 2002, they turned transit shelters into giant shark tanks. Following this, a summer transit shelter campaign in downtown Toronto attempted to establish an audience for *Nefertiti Resurrected* and to increase awareness and viewership of Discovery Channel in general. The ads featured an air of glamour and mystery to attract new viewers. In addition, Nefertiti models passed by the transit ads during a two-week period and allowed people to ask questions and take photographs. Discovery Channel believes these transit ads and street-level events played an important supporting role with the on-air ads in setting a record audience, 10 percent higher than previously achieved.[8]

Station posters are of varying sizes and forms that attempt to attract the attention of those waiting for a subway-like ride. The most common size is 1m by 2m. As Exhibit 13–4 shows, station posters can be very attractive and attention-getting. Similar-sized posters are found at bus or street car **transit shelters** and often provide the advertiser with expanded coverage where other outdoor boards may be restricted.

Transit media are sold in select markets on a four-week basis with a certain desired level of GRPs. The range of GRPs is quite varied, going from a low of 5 GRPs to a high of 100 GRPs. Other purchases of transit media are based on the number of showings. For example, if an operator has the rights to 400 buses or subway cars, then an advertiser could typically buy displays in varying numbers (i.e., 25 percent, 50 percent, 75 percent, 100 percent) over a four-week time period. (Figure 13–3 on page 388 shows some transit rates broken down by a number of GRP levels.)

Recent innovations in transit media include the super-bus, where an advertiser "owns the bus" and places a vinyl ad on the entire surface of the bus. This is often done for a longer-term contract of a half- or full year because of the application on the bus. On a less grand scale in a few select markets, smaller bus murals can be

FIGURE *13–3* Transit advertising rates for selected buys (all costs in $000s)

		Exterior 70s				Exterior Kings			
		25 Daily GRPs		50 Daily GRPs		25 Daily GRPs		50 Daily GRPs	
Markets*	Fleet	Cost/4wks.	#Units	Cost/4wks.	#Units	Cost/4wks.	#Units	Cost/4wks.	#Units
Top 3 total	6,137	$103.3	340	$202.1	690	$118.8	283	$231.2	566
Top 10 total	9,337	$153.9	555	$299.7	1,120	$177.7	464	$344.9	928
Top 25 total	10,906	$201.4	707	$394.2	1,429	$232.4	602	$452.1	1,204

		Interior Singles				Interior Doubles			
		½ Showing		Full Showing		½ Showing		Full Showing	
Markets*	Fleet	Cost/4wks.	#Units	Cost/4wks.	#Units	Cost/4wks.	#Units	Cost/4wks.	#Units
Top 3 total	6,137	$71.1	3,079	$134.4	6,312	$139.0	3,079	$261.1	6,312
Top 10 total	9,337	$100.7	5,036	$182.1	9,292	$191.9	5,036	$345.4	9,292
Top 25 total	10,906	$114.6	5,721	$208.9	10,697	$218.5	5,721	$396.3	10,697

**Top 3, 10 & 25: Based upon Top 25 markets by population. Check other available suppliers in CARD.*
Source: April 2006, CARD, p. 71.

applied to the side or tail for a shorter period of time. Recently, the Toronto and Montreal subway systems have featured station domination, where a single advertiser can be the sole sponsor of all points of communication within that station. **Subway online** is located in the 10 busiest subway stations in Toronto. It features digital news centres with video capabilities that deliver news, sports, and weather highlights with 20-second ads.

Strengths of Transit Media

Amount of Processing Time Long length of exposure to an ad is a major strength of indoor forms. The audience is essentially a captive one, with nowhere else to go and nothing much to do. As a result, riders are likely to read the ads—more than once.

Reach Transit advertising benefits from the absolute number of people exposed. Millions of people ride mass transit every week, providing a substantial number of potential viewers that can be reached.

Frequency Because our daily routines are standard, those who ride buses, subways, and the like are exposed to the ads repeatedly. If you rode the same subway to work and back every day, in one month you would have the opportunity to see the ad 20 to 40 times. The locations of station and shelter signs also afford high frequency of exposure.

Geographic Coverage For local advertisers in particular, transit advertising provides an opportunity to reach a very select segment of the population. A purchase of a location in a certain neighbourhood will lead to exposure to people of specific ethnic backgrounds, demographic characteristics, and so on.

Absolute Cost and Cost Efficiency Transit advertising tends to be one of the least expensive media in terms of both absolute and relative costs. An ad on the side of a bus can be purchased for a very reasonable CPM.

Selective Exposure Similar to outdoor advertising, transit ads are quite pervasive for those using the service and consumers have little control over the use of the media.

Scheduling Flexibility The capacity available for transit ads makes it fairly good for placement. Ads can be produced quickly and inserted internally or externally.

Limitations of Transit Media

Media Image To many advertisers, transit advertising does not carry the image they would like to represent for their products or services. Some advertisers may think having their name on the side of a bus or in a bus does not reflect well on the firm.

Target Audience Selectivity While a strength of transit advertising is the ability to provide exposure to a large number of people, this audience may have certain lifestyles and/or behavioural characteristics that are not true of the target audience as a whole. For example, in rural or suburban areas, mass transit is limited or nonexistent, so the medium is not very effective for reaching these people.

Target Audience Coverage While geographic selectivity may be an advantage, not everyone who rides a transportation vehicle or is exposed to transit advertising is a potential customer. For products that do not have specific geographic segments, this form of advertising incurs a good deal of waste coverage. Another problem is that the same bus may not run the same route every day. To save wear and tear on the vehicles, some transit companies alternate city routes (with much stop and go) with longer suburban routes. Thus, a bus may go downtown one day and reach the desired target group but spend the next day in the suburbs, where there may be little market potential.

Creativity for Emotional and Cognitive Responses It may be very difficult to place colourful and attractive ads on cards, thus limiting their emotional content. And while much copy can be provided on inside cards, the short copy on the outside of a bus provides less rational persuasion.

Clutter Inside ads suffer from clutter of competing ads and outside ads feel the pressure of other street-level ads. Furthermore, the environment is cluttered in another sense as sitting or standing on a crowded subway may not be conducive to reading advertising, let alone experiencing the mood the advertiser would like to create.

Attention The smaller size and location of interior transit ads make it difficult to use the creative elements to attract attention. The movement of transit vehicles makes it difficult to perceive the message.

Involvement Like outdoor advertising, with shorter copy and seemingly fleeting messages of short copy, transit ads are generally considered to be low-involvement media.

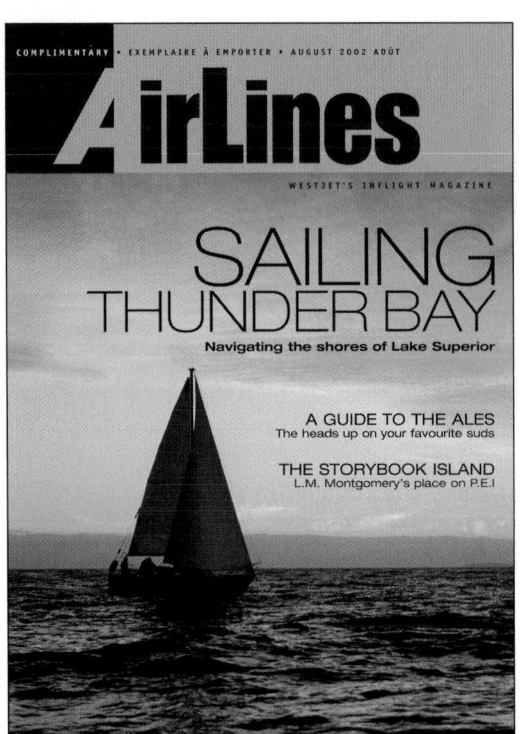

Exhibit 13–5
In-flight magazines are available on most carriers

Airline Transit Options

Related to transit media while travelling *within* cities and towns is media while travelling *between* cities and towns. As the number of flying passengers increases so too does the attractiveness of four **in-flight advertising** options and many airport terminal options. In-flight magazines are free magazines published by the airlines and are offered on almost every plane in the air (see Exhibit 13–5). In-flight videos have been common on international flights for some time and are now being used on domestic flights. Commercials were not originally included in these videos. Now, Air Canada sells different packages depending on the type of show (e.g., news, movie). Some of these commercial messages are as long as three minutes. In-flight radio is a pleasant way to pass the time while flying, and it offers another opportunity for advertisers to deliver an audio message beyond standard radio. Ads can be placed on various collateral material such as boarding passes, ticket jackets, and meal trays. Finally, similar to transit and outdoor, **airport displays** are available ranging from smaller backlit posters in the terminal to superboards near the terminal and various other types of displays depending upon the media company and airport terminal. Since we have covered broadcast, print, and poster ads thus far in the text, the strengths and limitations of these media in an airline context are readily transferred. The following points are a few unique strengths and limitations of using media in this particular context that are consistent with the same terminology used previously.

Strengths of In-Flight Advertising

Target Audience Selectivity In-flight allows the advertiser to reach specific demographic groups, as well as travellers to a specific destination. Both business and tourist travellers tend to be upscale, an attractive audience to companies targeting these groups. Many of these passengers hold top management positions in their firms.

Selective Exposure The audience in an airplane cannot leave the room. Particularly on long flights, many passengers are willing (and even happy) to have in-flight magazines to read, news to listen to, and even commercials to watch.

Absolute Cost The cost of in-flight commercials is lower than that of business print media. For example, $10,000 can get considerable exposure on Air Canada flights.

Limitations of In-Flight Advertising

Media Image Many consumers are not pleased with the idea of ads in general and believe they are already too intrusive. In-flight commercials are just one more place, they think, where advertisers are intruding.

Scheduling Flexibility Many airlines limit the amount of time they allow for in-flight commercials. Japan Air Lines, for example, allows a mere 220 seconds per flight.

Attention Many passengers may decide to tune out the ads, not purchase the headsets required to get the audio, or simply ignore the commercials.

Place-Based Media

As noted earlier in this chapter, the variety of out-of-home media continues to increase, and discussing or even mentioning all of it is beyond the scope of this text. The idea of bringing the advertising medium to consumers wherever they may be underlies the strategy behind place-based media. However, the following are provided to illustrate a few of the many options.

Place-Based Media Options

An original example of place-based media is signage and displays in malls. The popular mall poster is often backlit like the transit shelter or transit-station poster and is located throughout a shopping mall. The key feature of the mall poster is that it is in the shopping environment and therefore one step closer to the actual purchase. These posters are sold in most markets across the country similarly to outdoor posters with individual spot buys and varying levels of GRPs. Firms also sell various sizes of mall banners for branding purposes.

A number of place-based media are outdoor media brought into a particular environment. Backlit posters, superboards, electronic message signs, and video displays are used in many other locations such as convention centres, movie theatres, hotels, sports stadiums or arenas, or wherever there is a sufficient number of people. The method of selling the time or space is similar to what was described above.

Continuing this idea of bringing a message to a target audience based on where they are illustrates two emerging place-based media outlets. Firms attempt to reach younger consumers on the campuses of many universities and colleges with various sizes of indoor posters that are standard and non-standard. Furthermore, with closed-circuit television, firms attempt to reach travellers or patients in designated hotel rooms or hospital or doctor waiting rooms, respectively. And to reach virtually anyone and everyone, it is possible to place small print ads inside elevators or washrooms and on floors or escalator handrails.

Strengths of Place-Based Media

Target Audience Selectivity The main purpose of place-based media is to reach a specific target audience or to reach the target audience while closer to the purchase decision.

Absolute Cost and Cost Efficiency The absolute cost and CPM are generally reasonable compared to other media options.

Creativity for Cognitive and Emotional Responses Because the target and place are intertwined, the message may generate more in-depth cognitive responses or stronger emotional responses.

Selective Exposure and Attention Since many of these media options have or nearly have captive audiences, the opportunity for consumers to avoid the ads or direct their attention elsewhere is minimal compared to other media.

Involvement With the above strengths of many place-based media options, the collective conclusion suggests that the target audience may be more involved with the advertising message than some other similar media in different contexts.

Limitations of Place-Based Media

Media Image Often, place-based media are exposed to consumers when they do not expect a selling message to occur, which may cause some amount of resentment.

Clutter The clutter that consumers feel while watching television or reading a magazine may also be experienced.

Reach and Frequency Place-based media plays more of a supporting role to other media since it is very difficult to ensure high levels of either reach or frequency. Some exceptions to these can be considered, but in general media planners will look for other media to maximize these two factors.

Target Audience and Geographic Coverage The logistical availability of these types of media makes full coverage difficult or quite challenging to implement or nearly impossible to get complete geographic coverage.

Amount of Processing Time For the most part, place-based media suffer from very short messages to target audiences that are more likely preoccupied with some other task.

Scheduling Flexibility While not a complete or comprehensive limitation, the logistics of changing place-based media makes the scheduling, which is done on a monthly basis, put certain restrictions on an advertiser for a timely message.

Place-Based Media at the Movies

We now turn our attention to a specific form of place-based media: movie theatres. It is estimated that about $25 to $30 million in advertising is spent in theatres on commercials, slides, posters, and sales promotions, with about $15 million of that for the commercials. And with the commercials lasting 60 to 90 seconds, advertisers have a unique opportunity to communicate for a longer period of time than with a TV ad, which typically runs 30 seconds. In fact, 95 percent of the theatre ads are also shown on television, albeit in a shortened format. A wide variety of products have been advertised using the medium including cars, government, telcos, food, video games, and health and beauty products, representing main brand names such as Toyota, Nissan, Telus, Bell Mobility, Health Canada, Department of National Defence, and Pepsi-Cola.

As a medium grows so does its sophistication, and theatre media is no exception; it now reports audience measurement information. One study estimated that total recall (aided plus unaided) reached 74 percent compared to 37 percent for radio and 32 percent for television. Yet while there appears to be good communication effect, and the cost is reasonable, the overall revenue is still only 1 percent of the TV advertising revenue per year. Part of the problem is that the reach is still limited—only 3.6 million per month for Cineplex Odeon, for example.[9]

Strengths of Movie Theatres as a Medium

Control for Selective Exposure The viewers constitute a captive audience who cannot avoid the ad messages unless they are in another part of the theatre.

Cost The cost of advertising in a theatre varies from one setting to the next. However, it is low in terms of both absolute and relative costs per exposure.

Clutter Lack of clutter is another advantage offered by advertising in movie theatres. Most theatres limit the number of ads.

Target Audience Selectivity The movie titles and ratings enable advertisers to place their commercials to reach specific target audiences. Furthermore, moviegoers are generally above average in income and education.

Target Audience Coverage Coverage is positive for most advertisers as all cities and larger towns have theatres and the chains can accommodate the placement in various locations.

Geographic Coverage Certain cities or towns can be featured in a campaign depending upon the needs of an advertiser.

Creativity for Processing Responses Movie ads tend to be repeats of those in other media to launch a brand-new campaign. In either case, advertisers expect similar response to what is found, for example, on television. However, the special mood created in the movie theatre compared to at-home consumption makes the experience richer and advertisers use theatre ads as an emotional spike that can transfer to the product more readily, especially if the theatre is located next to a mall or store where the product may be sold.

Attention and Involvement The larger screen and the fact that consumers are facing the screen with little opportunity to avoid the ads deliver strong attention and involvement.

Limitations of Movie Theatres as a Medium

Media Image Perhaps the major disadvantage is that many people do not wish to see advertising in this medium. A number of studies suggest that these ads may create a high degree of annoyance.[10] This dissatisfaction may carry over to the product itself, to the movies, or to the theatres. Mike Stimler, president of the specialty video label Water Bearer Films, says, "People boo in movie theatres when they see product advertising."[11] Anne-Marie Marcus, vice president of sales for Screenvision, contends that the furor has died down.[12]

In a study by Michael Belch and Don Sciglimpaglia, many moviegoers stated that they not only would not buy the product advertised, but also would consider boycotting it. So advertisers should be cautious in their use of this medium. If they want to use movies, they may want to consider an alternative—placing products in the movies.

Cost While the cost of advertising in local theatres has been cited as a strength because of the low rates charged, ads exposed nationally can be expensive, with a corresponding high CPM compared to other media.

Reach and Frequency As suggested in the introduction for this section, while the number of people attending movies is substantial, the ability to reach large numbers of consumers with repeated messages is limited. In this sense, some advertisers would view this exposure as support to other media used.

Scheduling Flexibility Placement for ads generally requires eight weeks, and category exclusivity in certain distribution outlets further limits the availability and scheduling ease with this media option.

Amount of Processing Time Similar to television ads, we see short fleeting messages; however, considerable research suggests that the environment of the theatre and the large screen contributes to strong recall.

Promotional Products

The Promotional Products Association International (PPAI), a trade association, defines **promotional products marketing** as "the advertising or promotional medium or method that uses promotional products, such as ad specialties, premiums, business gifts, awards, prizes, or commemoratives." Promotional product marketing is a recent name for what used to be called specialty advertising. Specialty advertising has now been provided with a new definition:

> A medium of advertising, sales promotion, and motivational communication employing imprinted, useful, or decorative products called advertising specialties, a subset of promotional products. Unlike premiums, with which they are sometimes confused (called advertising specialties), these articles are always distributed free—recipients don't have to earn the specialty by making a purchase or contribution.[13]

Specialty advertising is often considered both an advertising and a sales promotion medium. In our discussion, we treat it as an advertising medium in the IMC program, as it often communicates or represents the brand and its positioning.

The promotional product industry in Canada is substantial, and the Canadian trade association (www.promocan.com) is known as the Promotional Products Association of Canada (PPAC). One of its main tasks is to compile research information for its members, which we highlight briefly. Distributor revenue topped $2.1 billion in 2001, up from $1.1 billion in 1998 and $800 million in 1993. Although this Canadian data is somewhat dated, we can put this amount into context. The 2001 figure is four times greater than all Internet advertising in 2005. Furthermore, inflation grew 16 percent during that nine-year period, and distributor revenue climbed 160 percent. Figure 13–4 shows the percentage of sales by product category. Wearables/apparel accounted for the bulk at 37 percent, while the next highest,

FIGURE *13–4*

Distributor product category breakdown

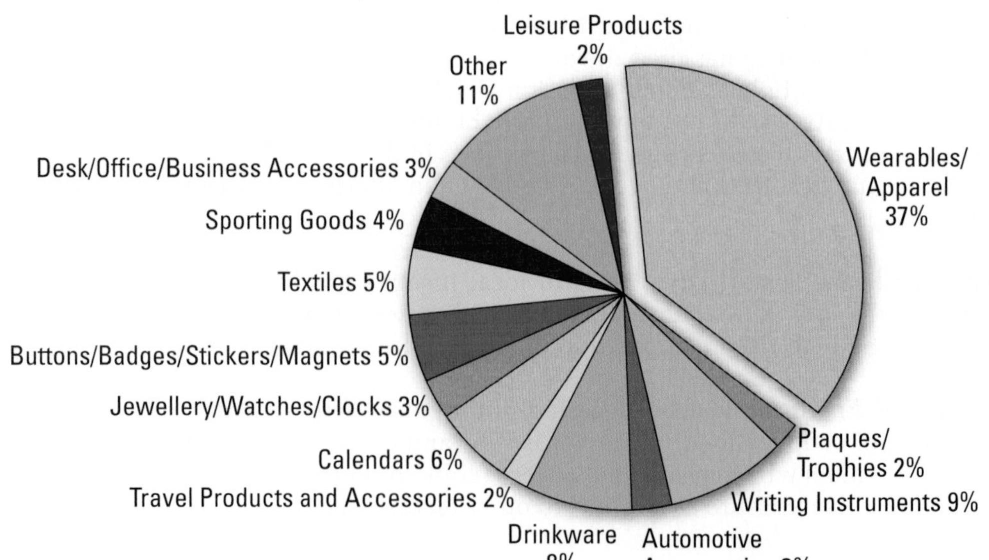

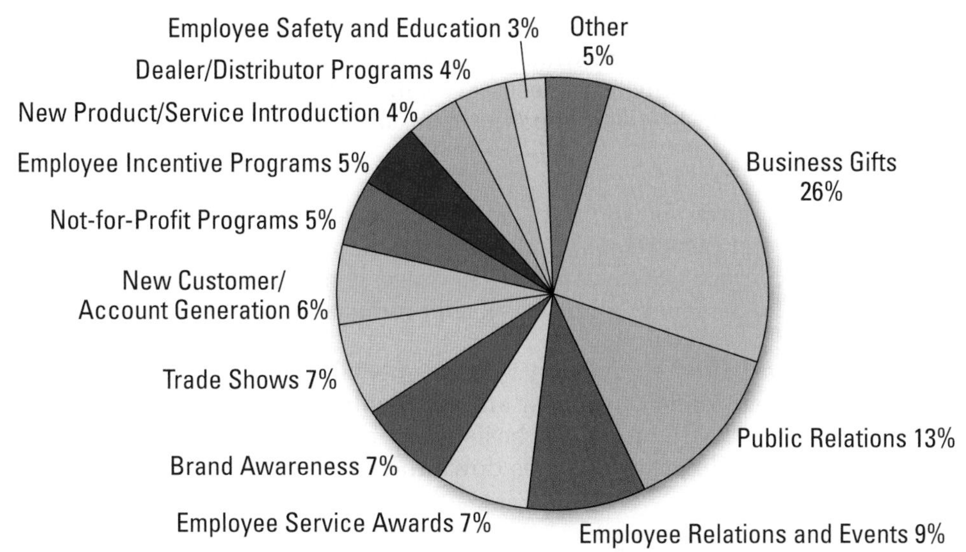

FIGURE 13–5

Distributor sales by program type

writing instruments, clipped in at 9 percent. Figure 13–5 shows the percentage of sales by program type. Business gifts, public relations, and employee relations and events account for nearly half of all revenue.[14]

Some trends are supporting the growth of promotional products. Thanks to the Internet, it is now logistically easier to distribute the products than in the past. Since clothing is the largest product category, its growth stemmed from a steady change toward more casual dressing at work and from many name brands such as Nike getting into the market. Other big brands like Apple make their product lines available, thus spurring on the overall demand for promotional products. Promotional products organizations have become more sophisticated in their selling as they try to build a brand with promotional planners. For example, both parties carefully consider whether the promotional product needs to be directly tied to the type of product, and the degree to which the promotional product needs to last a long time or for a shorter time period.[15]

As suggested above, thousands of advertising specialty items exist—ballpoint pens, coffee mugs, key rings, calendars, T-shirts, and matchbooks. Unconventional specialties such as plant holders, wall plaques, and gloves with the advertiser's name printed on them are also used to promote a company or its product; so are glassware, trophies, awards, and vinyl products. Specialty items are used for many promotional purposes. It can generate or improve awareness when introducing new products or reinforcing the name of an existing company or products. The variety of promotional products makes it a virtual certainty that a manager will be able to strengthen attitudes with an item that represents the brand appropriately. Oftentimes promotional products are used to thank customers for patronage and encourage repeat purchasing. Promotional products support other IMC tools like sales promotion or public relations, so they contribute substantially to the overall promotional mix. In summary, many companies use promotional products as a way to fully communicate with their customers, suppliers, employees, and the general public.

Strengths of Promotional Products

Target Audience Selectivity and Coverage Because specialty advertising items are generally distributed directly to target customers, the medium offers a high degree of selectivity. The communication is distributed to the desired recipient, reducing waste coverage.

Creativity for Cognitive Responses As the variety of specialty items in Figure 13–4 demonstrates, this medium offers a high degree of flexibility. A message as simple as a logo or as long as is necessary can be distributed through a number of means. Both small and large companies can employ this medium, limited only by their own creativity.

Frequency Most forms of specialty advertising are designed for retention. Key chains, calendars, and pens remain with the potential customer for a long time, providing repeat exposures to the advertising message at no additional cost. One set of statistics suggests 50 percent of all promotional products are kept for a year or longer.

Absolute Cost and Cost Efficiency Some specialty items are rather expensive (for example, leather goods), but most are affordable to almost any size organization. While they are costly on a CPM basis when compared with other media, the high number of repeat exposures drives down the relative cost per exposure of this advertising medium.

Creativity for Emotional Responses Promotional products are perhaps the only medium that generates goodwill in the receiver. Because people like to receive gifts and many of the products are functional (key chains, calendars, etc.), consumers are grateful to receive them. In a recent study of users of promotional products, goodwill was cited as the number 1 reason for use.

Attention, Involvement, Amount of Processing Time These would all be considered strengths of promotional products assuming the recipient appreciates the actual item, whether it is clothing or some kind of office product. Certainly the selection of the item in question will heavily influence consumer reaction.

Limitations of Promotional Products

Media Image While most forms of specialty advertising are received as friendly reminders of the store or company name, the firm must be careful choosing the specialty item. The company image may be cheapened by a chintzy or poorly designed advertising form.

Clutter With so many organizations now using this advertising medium, the marketplace may become saturated. While one can always use another ballpoint pen or book of matches, the value to the receiver declines if replacement is too easy, and the likelihood that you will retain the item or even notice the message is reduced. The more unusual the specialty, the more value it is likely to have to the receiver.

Scheduling Flexibility The lead time required to put together a promotional products message is significantly longer than that for most other media.

Reach An advertiser hoping to expand the market through wider reach would likely find promotional products a weaker choice. As a support media, it thrives on assisting existing media that have reach as their strength.

Geographic Coverage While promotional products can be distributed essentially anywhere, the cost implications would severely curtail this as a feasible feature for most advertisers.

Selective Exposure Recipients of promotional products are in complete control as to whether they choose to display or show the item. It is entirely possible that a tremendous investment could receive very minimal exposure to the intended target audience.

Promotional Products Research

Owing to the nature of the industry, specialty advertising has no established ongoing audience measurement system. Research has been conducted in an attempt to determine the impact of this medium, however, including the following reports.

A study by Schreiber and Associates indicated 39 percent of people receiving advertising specialties could recall the name of the company as long as six months later, and a study conducted by AC Nielsen found that 31 percent of respondents were still using at least one specialty item they had received a year or more earlier.[16]

A study by Gould/Pace University found the inclusion of a specialty item in a direct-mail piece generated a greater response rate and 321 percent greater dollar purchases per sale than mail pieces without such items.[17] Studies at Baylor University showed that including an ad specialty item in a thank-you letter can improve customers' attitudes toward a company's sales reps by as much as 34 percent and toward the company itself by as much as 52 percent.[18] Finally, Richard Manville Research reported the average household had almost four calendars; if they had not been given such items free, two-thirds of the respondents said they would purchase one, an indication of the desirability of this particular specialty item.[19]

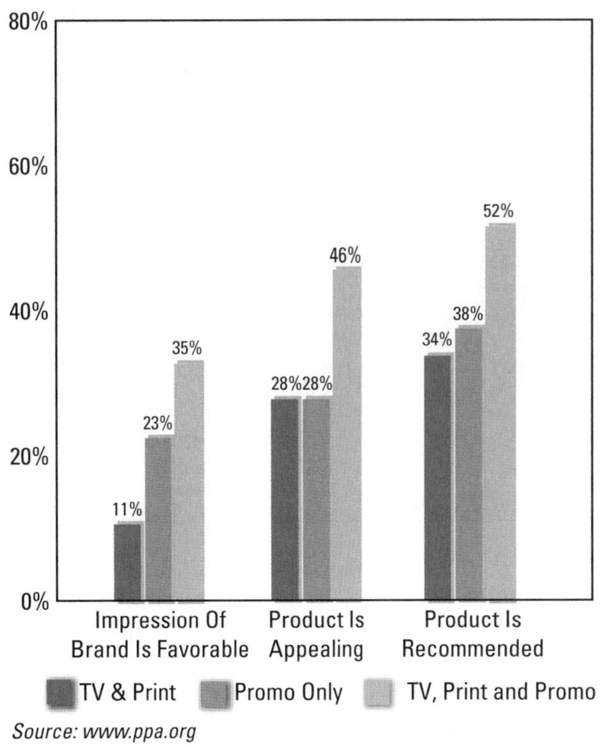

FIGURE 13–6
Respondents' evaluation of brand or product

More recent research conducted by PPAI (www.ppai.org) shows the pronounced communication effect of promotional products when combined with media. The results of one experiment shown in Figure 13–6 illustrate the stronger impressions that occur when a promotional product is combined with TV and print ads for a local pizzeria. Another survey of more than 550 business travellers at a U.S. airport found that 71 percent had received a promotional product within the past 12 months; 34 percent actually had the item with them at the time of the survey; and 76 percent recalled the brand name. A field experiment at a trade show indicated that visits to a firm's booth increased significantly when a modest promotional product (i.e., magnet) and a promise to receive a more valuable item (i.e., T-shirt) were mailed to registrants prior to the show compared with a simple invitation.

Product Placement

An increasingly common way to promote a brand is **product placement** where the actual product or an ad for it is part of a movie, TV show, or video game. Like specialty advertising, product placement is sometimes considered a promotion rather than an advertising form. This distinction is not a critical one, and we have decided to treat product placement as a form of advertising. We review a few key product placement decisions and their corresponding strengths and limitations.

Product Placement Decisions

With up to $4 billion in North American revenue and up to 50 percent of all movies and television shows using product placement, advertising through this promotional medium is certainly big business. For example, we have recently seen the Apple

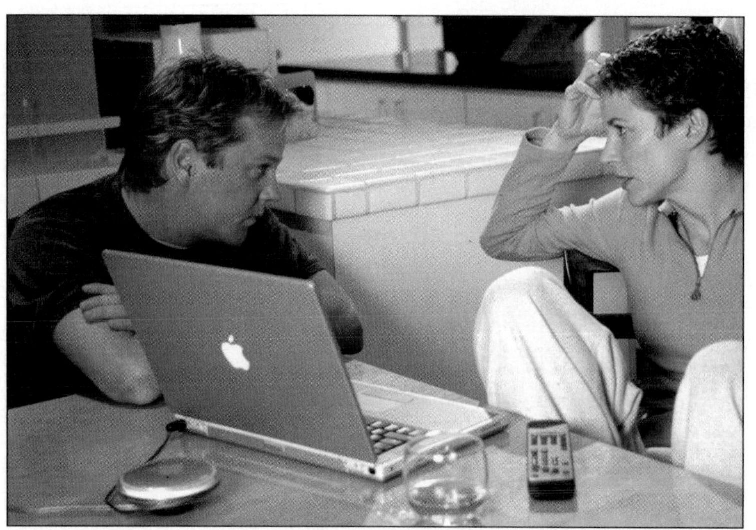

Exhibit 13–6 Apple Computers makes frequent use of product placements

computer in many entertainment vehicles (see Exhibit 13–6). In the gaming world, North American advertising revenue is expected to reach close to $1 billion by 2008. Assuming a marketer selected the right movie or TV vehicle for exposure, product placement contributes to higher awareness by its sheer volume of exposure. More successful product placement contributes to its brand position and requires a number of decisions.[20] Similarly for video games, research supports about 30 percent unaided brand recall; 70 percent believe that ads in games make the experience feel realistic.[21]

A primary issue to resolve concerns the source as represented by the plot, scenes, or characters of the movie or TV show. The creative use of the product profoundly impacts the experience ranging from a central role in the scene to a mere showing of the product to having a central character use or talk about the product.[22] Recent examples of product placement occurring in Canada or as a result of movie or television production being filmed in Canada are quite numerous.[23]

Related to the above two issues is the amount of time the product is featured and how many different vehicles a marketer wants to be exposed in. While a marketer and its agent obviously try to negotiate the most favourable situation on all these issues, they are also dependent upon the director's final artistic decision.[24] For example, product placement moved to animated shows with the placement of the Reach 400 Max toothbrush on the TV sitcom *Bob and Margaret* in the form of a five-to-10-second virtual placement that was blended into the show's program about a dentist. Reach managers felt the placement balanced the requirements of not too blatant, but noticed. Placement support included a tune-in spot for the show that featured the toothbrush along with the Reach commercial in the promotion schedule, and closed captioning sponsorship of the show. The Reach toothbrush's placement offered more control than usual since the program already existed with an established time slot, and the virtual placement material (i.e., logo, product visual) provided by Reach fit appropriately into established scenes.[25] Ethical Perspective 13–3 discusses a newer form of product placement.

Finally, as a support medium, product placement needs to work with other marketing communication tools to achieve its maximum contribution. Much of the product placement in Quebec reality television shows is linked with sponsorship arrangements. For example, GM Canada sponsors *Le Grand blond avec un show surnois*—a late-night talk show, and *Testostérone*—a men's show, in addition to having product placement as an important element. Similarly, *Ma Maison Rona* is a sponsored reality television show based on renovating someone else's home that naturally included trips to Rona for material.[26] Rona goes one step further as this product placement occurs during its mass media campaign.[27]

As promising as product placement appears, research indicates that its greatest strength lies in maintaining existing loyalty of current customers who see the product they consume actually consumed in a realistic situation by a character they can relate to or identify with. Furthermore, consumers indicate that real products are expected and preferred compared to some kind of generic unrecognizable brand.[28]

ETHICAL PERSPECTIVE 13–3

Virtual Ads: Now You See Them—Now You Don't

During the last couple of seasons of *Will & Grace*, it seemed that Eric McCormack, the show's Toronto-born star, was ordering from his favourite Canadian pizza joint. Truth is, the Pizza Pizza box and company logo, which also appeared on a salad container and the spine of a phone book, were totally virtually integrated into the show. This form of camera trickery is the latest way networks are battling commercial-skipping technologies like personal video recorders.

In a primitive form, virtual advertising has been used for several years by Global TV to hawk Canadian brands—such as a virtual Primus blimp, and a virtual billboard ad for Canadian Tire during an NFL broadcast. Now, technological advances have led to bolder applications and Global continues to lead the pack. For a couple of years now, Global has digitally inserted consumer products into several U.S. programs.

Much of the high-tech wizardry that goes into Global's virtual ads is done by PVI, a New Jersey–based media company. Editors spend hours blending a two-dimensional image of a product into a show, shot by shot. "Scenes with little variation in lighting and a steady camera work best," says Nezik Tahri, an art director with Global. "When there are harsh camera movements the graphic may not move well with the shot. The product can't shift a millimetre. It has to be seamless."

Virtual products are often added to the background or foreground of a scene, be it a box of Splenda on a kitchen shelf, or a package of Tylenol on a coffee table in *Will & Grace*. But transition shots—usually outdoor city images—provide a blank canvas on which to plaster ads. "They're usually only three seconds," says Tahri, "but they have an impact because there are no competing elements."

An overt example of the practice showed up in the closing scene of *The Apprentice*. During Global's Ontario simulcast, the New York cab that whisks away The Donald's castoff each week displayed an ad for Orillia, Ont.–based Casino Rama (it replaced the original Yahoo!Jobs ad). Virtual ads can be cheaper than traditional advertising and standard product placement. The Casino Rama/*Apprentice* deal reportedly cost less than $10,000 an episode. "We would not advertise on an actual New York cab, but I like the idea of how it looks to the average Torontonian viewing *The Apprentice* and seeing the backlit ad on a New York cab," said Jeff Craik, director of marketing services for Casino Rama. A 30-second spot on the same broadcast is $36,000. While virtual ads are an inconsequential sliver of Canada's $3-billion TV advertising market, they are on the minds of executives at every major network in large part because they provide an unregulated revenue source. The CRTC monitors virtual ads, but has no plans to force networks to include them in the 12 minutes of ad time permitted during each 60-minute slot.

Sources: John Intini, "*Will & Grace* Loved Their *Maclean's*," *Maclean's*, June 26, 2006; Keith McArthur, "No, Those Casino Rama Ads Aren't Running in NYC," *The Globe and Mail*, March 15, 2006.

Question

1. Do you believe it's ethical for advertisers to place a virtual ad embedded in a U.S. television program directed toward Canadian viewers?

Strengths of Product Placement

Reach A large number of people see movies each year. The average film is estimated to have a life span of three and one-half years, and most of these moviegoers are very attentive audience members. When this is combined with the increasing home video rental market and network and specialty channels, the potential exposure for a product placed in a movie is enormous.

Frequency Depending on how the product is used in the movie (or program), there may be ample opportunity for repeated exposures (many, for those who like to watch a program or movie more than once).

Creativity for Emotional Responses We previously discussed the advantage of source identification that occurs with a creative message. When consumers see their favourite movie star wearing Oakleys, drinking Gatorade, or driving a Mercedes, this association may lead to a favourable product image. Most of those involved in product placement believe that association with the proper source is critical for success.

Cost Efficiency While the cost of placing a product may range from free samples to $1 million, these are extremes. The CPM for this form of advertising can be very low, owing to the high volume of exposures it generates.

Geographic Coverage The potential for geographic coverage is substantial as a top movie or television show could have national or international coverage. We emphasize the importance of this qualifying aspect, as entertainment viewers can be fickle.

Selective Exposure It is very difficult for a theatre audience member to physically avoid the product placement through some form of zipping or zapping!

Clutter With category exclusivity rights within a vehicle and the fact that any show or movie has only a few product placements, the potential for clutter is very low. However, the plot, scenes, and dialogue act as a form of clutter that can be overcome with creative use of product placement.

Involvement A product placement done properly has direct relevance for the character or situation and is almost a transformational experience for the audience member who is paying full attention to the entertainment.

Limitations of Product Placement

Absolute Cost While the CPM may be very low for product placement in movies, the absolute cost of placing the product may be very high, pricing some advertisers out of the market.

Amount of Processing Time and Attention While the way some products are exposed to the audience has an impact, there is no guarantee viewers will notice the product. Some product placements are more conspicuous than others. When the product is not featured prominently, the advertiser runs the risk of not being seen (although, of course, the same risk is present in all forms of media advertising). Furthermore, some product placements last only for a few seconds.

Creativity for Cognitive Responses The appeal that can be made in this media form is limited. There is no potential for discussing product benefits or providing detailed information. Rather, appeals are limited to source association, use, and enjoyment. The endorsement of the product is indirect, and the flexibility for product demonstration is subject to its use in the film.

Scheduling Flexibility In many movies, the advertiser has no say over when and how often the product will be shown. Fabergé developed an entire Christmas campaign around its Brut cologne and its movie placement, only to find the movie was delayed until February.

Exhibit 13–7 Ads often appear in the strangest places

Media Image Many TV viewers and moviegoers are incensed at the idea of placing ads in programs or movies. These viewers want to maintain the barrier between program content and commercials. If the placement is too intrusive, they may develop negative attitudes toward the brand.

Target Audience Selectivity By its very nature of being cast in a movie, the potential for exposure beyond a brand's target audience is enormous. Although a certain amount of selectivity is viable through the type of movie or show, there is likely considerable wasted coverage.

Target Audience Coverage Movie attendance is historically strong, however, in many cases it will be difficult to reach a substantial portion of one's audience with a single movie. Similarly, even a hit television show may reach only a portion of a brand's target audience.

Audience Measurement for Product Placement

To date, no audience measurement is available except from the providers. Potential advertisers often have to make decisions based on their own creative insights (see Exhibit 13–7) or rely on the credibility of the source. However, at least two studies have demonstrated the potential effectiveness of product placements. Research provided by Pola Gupta and Kenneth Lord showed that prominently displayed placements led to strong recall.[29] A study by Pola Gupta and Stephen Gould indicated that viewers are accepting of promotional products and in general evaluate them positively, though some products (alcohol, guns, cigarettes) are perceived as less acceptable.[30]

IMC Planning: Strategic Use of Out-of-Home and Support Media

Previously, the strategic use of out-of-home and support media might have been considered an oxymoron, as both types appeared in promotional planners' budgets after money had been allocated to other more "valuable" media. An IMC perspective toward media selection provides a new look at how these types of opportunities can achieve communication and behavioural objectives, primarily at the pre-purchase and purchase decision stages.

Out-of-Home Media

For the most part, outdoor, transit, and place-based media tend to have two primary objectives. The first is awareness, as these media share common strengths of cost efficiency with extensive reach and frequency levels in the geographic areas in which the media are located or placed. The ability to use clever images and headlines or very short-copy messages permits these messages to have some emotional relevance to help ensure brand recognition or recall. Moreover, these two design elements can be consistent with creative messages from other media to ensure additional message frequency with the intention to build awareness more strongly.

In general, these media are limited in their ability to build category need or influence brand attitudes beyond maintaining the current attitude of the target audience. Many brands will use these media as an inexpensive, yet cost-effective way of communicating simple brand preference messages directed toward current customers or messages to reinforce the general market position of the brand to all potential consumers. Given the limited nature of these media to influence attitudes extensively with short messages, they typically are good for building communication effects at the pre- and post-purchase stages.

Most place-based media typically offer the opportunity for promotional planners to achieve a second objective: brand purchase intention. Since the messages for place-based media are context-dependent in terms of location or time, they can provide the right situational motive to spur on a store visit or more immediate sale. Some particular place-based media, like movie theatres, are vehicles for additional exposure of the more traditional broadcast and print media ads and thus permit strong brand positioning strategy opportunities. As noted in the chapter, movie theatres can show longer and more specialized ads that brands may be reluctant to show in a broadcast environment.

Given the broad reach and public nature of these media, oftentimes they are more general and have a less clear behavioural objective. However, given that many messages are reinforcing existing attitudes, it appears a substantial number of these ads attempt to influence repeat purchasing.

From an integration perspective, out-of-home of transit media provide additional frequency of a creative message that has been placed in broadcast or print media. Typically, we do not see advertisers using these media for executing sales promotions except in some poster locations. This medium is also used to some extent for public relations activities, and we infrequently observe any connection to direct marketing or Internet applications.

Support Media

The size and growth of support media such as promotional products and product placement is almost hidden given the degree to which it fits into our everyday life or our normal TV, movie, and video game consumption habits. In this regard, they are similar to out-of-home media that are a part of our everyday experiences. However, for these two support media, the exposure is both more widespread and more narrow. Promotional products are more widespread as we are selectively observing them virtually everywhere depending on the product. Given that a high percentage is wearable, we witness brand names on shirts, hats, and so on almost constantly. Product placement is clearly narrower, as it is limited within the time frame and scope of the vehicle it is delivered in. These characteristics suggest that both are excellent for building awareness, much like out-of-home media, and could be especially useful for all stages of the target audience's decision-making process.

Promotional products and product placement offer brand-building capabilities much like some specialized place-based media such as movie theatres. The vehicle in which the brand is associated provides an additional source effect that puts significant context around the brand experience. For example, observing a particular brand in a movie approximates an endorsement from both the character and the actor. This is consistent with viewing a television commercial with the same actor, but even more so as the emotion and involvement with the movie compounds the positive effect. Given this more profound viewing experience, it is no wonder advertisers are willing to pay substantial parts of their budget to have the brand featured in a few seconds of a popular movie.

The independence of these kinds of media suggests more limited opportunity for integration. However, some opportunities are pursued. Public relations activities are often used to connect the brand and its product placement in a movie or television show. For example, for some blockbuster placements, like showing a new car model in a movie, news media will report the appearance in both traditional versions and on the Internet. Recently, news media have reported upon the placement of brands in various video games. Naturally, the Internet offers a wide variety of information content, and a brand can highlight its placement on its own site.

SUMMARY

This chapter introduced the vast number of out-of-home and support media available to marketers. Out-of-home media include outdoor, transit, and place-based. Support media include promotional products and product placement. While these constitute many examples and options for a marketer, it seems the choices are quite endless at times.

Collectively, these media offer a variety of strengths. Cost, ability to reach the target audience, and flexibility are just a few of those cited in this chapter. In addition, many of the media discussed here have effectively demonstrated the power of their specific medium to get results.

But each of these media has limitations. Perhaps the major weakness with most is the lack of audience measurement and verification. The advertiser is forced to make decisions without hard data or based on information provided by the media. As the number and variety of media continue to grow, it is likely the major weaknesses will be overcome.

KEY TERMS

airport displays, *390*
backlit posters, *380*
bulletins, *381*
exterior posters, *387*
in-flight advertising, *390*
interior door cards, *387*
interior transit cards, *387*
mobile signage, *383*
out-of-home media, *380*
posters, *380*
product placement, *397*
promotional products marketing, *394*
showing, *384*
spectaculars, *381*
station posters, *387*
street-level posters, *382*
subway online, *388*
superboards, *381*
support media, *380*
transit advertising, *386*
transit shelters, *387*

DISCUSSION QUESTIONS

1. What are promotional products? List some of the advantages and disadvantages of this medium. Provide examples where the use of this medium would be appropriate.

2. Discuss some of the merits of in-flight advertising. What types of products might most effectively use this medium?

3. Explain how out-of-home and support media might be used as part of an IMC program. Take any three of the media discussed in the chapter and explain how they might be used in an IMC program for automobiles, cellular telephones, and Internet services.

4. A prevalent strategy among advertisers is to get themselves into television shows and movies. Discuss the possible advantages and disadvantages that might result from such exposures.

5. Explain how outdoor ads can be creative and foster emotional responses. Why would brands use outdoor ad for this purpose?

6. Discuss advantages and disadvantages associated with advertising in movie theatres. For what types of products and/or services might these media be most effective?

7. What are place-based media? Explain what type of advertisers would most benefit from their use.

8. Many forms of transit advertising exist. What products might be successfully advertised in each type?

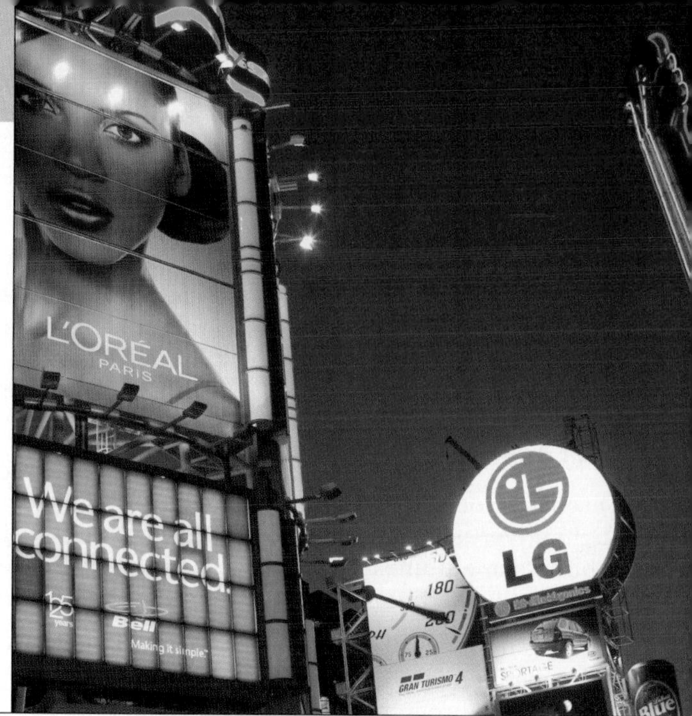

CHAPTER 14

SALES PROMOTION

Chapter Objectives

- To understand the role of sales promotion in a company's integrated marketing communications program and to examine why it is increasingly important.
- To examine the objectives, strategy, and tactical components of a sales promotion plan.
- To examine the consumer and trade sales promotion strategy options and the factors to consider in using them.
- To understand key IMC issues related to sales-promotion decisions.

Event Marketing Gets Personal

A novel way to launch your brand into a market is to hand out free concert tickets. When Best Buy opened in Montreal, 13,000 lucky people watched the Black Eyed Peas courtesy of the new electronics retailer. A similar idea worked in Toronto, where Our Lady Peace played to celebrate the opening of new stores. Best Buy executives looked at concerts as a way of distinguishing the brand from its main competitors. The bands are young, fun, and entertaining, something Best Buy hoped consumers would believe about the new entry. The Montreal launch included many other IMC tools including shopping spree giveaways, charity donations, visits from the Best Buy mascot, and local celebrity autograph sessions—along with television commercials highlighting the store's no-commission policy, a key differentiator versus Future Shop.

The bandwagon for music events has gathered speed as many other brands look to music events to connect with consumers and involve them with sales promotions like samples, coupons, demonstrations, and contests. In fact, both consumers and managers prefer the relaxed music environment to build the brand relationship. Some other notable examples include General Motors, Panasonic, and Garnier.

General Motors used a "Kar Karaoke" event at a concert where consumers jumped in a car and sang a song. The musical interlude attracted 1,000 potential customers per event, with some participants spending up to 20 minutes in the car. These events essentially brought the dealership visit to the consumer in a fun environment that was substantially more enjoyable and less stressful.

Panasonic promoted its Lumix camera at concerts by inviting patrons to have their picture taken on a red carpet, just like rock stars. Participants proudly carried their newly printed photographs around their necks immediately after the shoot. The photo-op allowed consumers to interact with the product for a minute or so, and for many minutes after with a keepsake. Panasonic reached 250 individuals per evening, attracting a long lineup each time.

Garnier located promotional events at music concerts that fit its products and target audiences. For example, the brand featured styling products at shows by hip bands to appeal to younger listeners, while shampoo products appeared at venues for older women. These specific, targeted activities worked along with online communication and contests, samples, in-store displays, and television.

Sources: Libby Biason, "Music to Their Ears," *Marketing Magazine,* September 18, 2006; and Danny Kucharsky, "Sound Strategy," *Marketing Magazine,* January 9, 2006.

Question

1. Why are concerts good venues to develop marketing events for these brands?

As discussed in the opening vignette, marketers realize that advertising alone is not always enough to move their products off store shelves and into the hands of consumers. Companies also use sales promotion methods targeted at both consumers and the wholesalers and retailers that distribute their products to stimulate demand. Most companies' integrated marketing communications programs include consumer and trade promotions that are coordinated with advertising, direct marketing, and publicity/public relations campaigns as well as salesforce efforts.

This chapter focuses on the role of sales promotion in a firm's IMC program. We examine how marketers use both consumer and trade promotions to influence the purchase behaviour of consumers, and wholesalers and retailers respectively. We explore the objectives of sales promotion programs and the types of sales promotion tools that can be used at both the consumer and trade level. We also consider how sales promotion can be integrated with other elements of the promotional mix, and look at problems that can arise when marketers become overly dependent on consumer and trade promotions.

Sales Promotion Planning

Of all the IMC tools available to a promotional planner, sales promotion potentially allows brands to achieve multiple objectives or provides the opportunity to enhance an IMC plan due to the nature of its characteristics and the many types that are available. We review these two topics in this section and highlight some of the reasons why sales promotion has grown so tremendously, thus indicating some of the relative strengths of sales promotion.

Characteristics of Sales Promotion

Sales promotion has been defined as "a direct inducement that offers an extra value or incentive for the product to the sales force, distributors, or the ultimate consumer with the primary objective of creating an immediate sale."[1] This definition indicates two distinguishing features of sales promotion.

First, sales promotion involves some type of inducement that provides an *extra incentive* to buy. This incentive is usually the key element in a promotional program: it may be a coupon or price reduction, the opportunity to enter a contest or sweepstakes, a money-back refund or rebate, or an extra amount of a product. The incentive may also be a free sample of the product, given in hopes of generating a future purchase, or a premium that serves as a reminder of the brand and reinforces its image. Most sales promotion offers attempt to add some value to the product or service. While advertising appeals to the mind and emotions to give the consumer a reason to buy, sales promotion appeals more to the pocketbook and provides an incentive for purchasing a brand.

Sales promotion can also provide an inducement to marketing intermediaries such as wholesalers and retailers. A trade allowance or discount gives retailers a financial incentive to stock and promote a manufacturer's products. A trade contest directed toward wholesalers or retail personnel gives them extra incentive to perform certain tasks or meet sales goals.

A second point is that sales promotion is essentially an *acceleration tool,* designed to speed up the selling process and maximize sales volume.[2] By providing an extra incentive, sales promotion techniques can motivate consumers to purchase a larger quantity of a brand or shorten the purchase cycle of the trade or consumers by encouraging them to take more immediate action.

Companies also use limited-time offers such as price-off deals to retailers or a coupon with an expiration date to accelerate the purchase process.[3] Sales promotion attempts to maximize sales volume by motivating customers who have not responded to advertising. The ideal sales promotion program generates sales that would not be

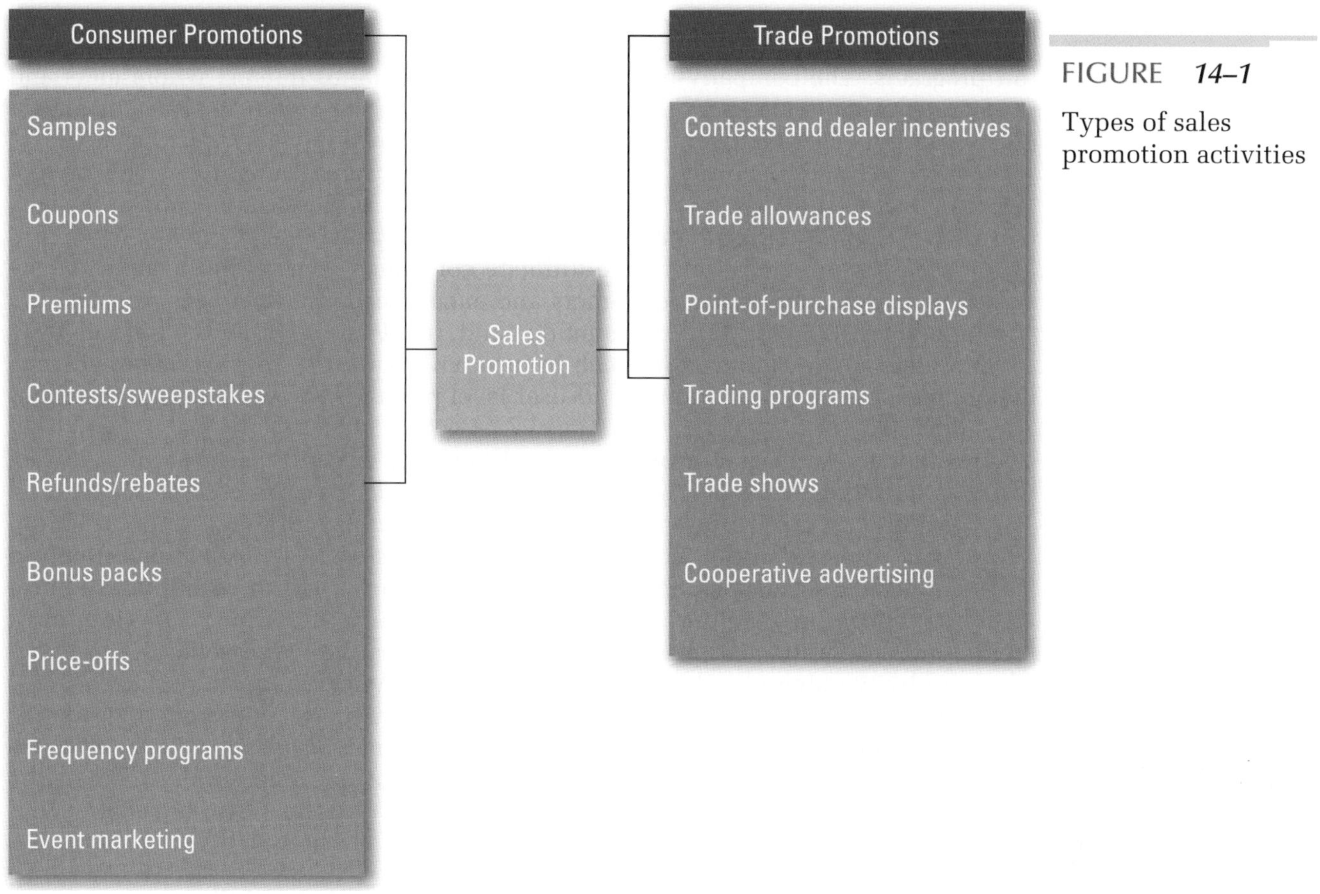

FIGURE *14–1*

Types of sales promotion activities

achieved by other means. However, as we shall see later, many sales promotion offers end up being used by current users of a brand rather than attracting new users.

Types of Sales Promotion

Sales promotion activities can be *targeted to different audiences* in the marketing channel. As shown in Figure 14–1, sales promotion can be directed to consumers and trade members. Activities involved in **consumer sales promotion** include sampling, couponing, premiums, contests and sweepstakes, refunds and rebates, bonus packs, price-offs, and event marketing. These promotions are directed at consumers, the end purchasers of goods and services, and are designed to induce them to purchase the marketer's brand. Consumer promotions are also used by retailers to encourage consumers to shop in their particular stores. **Trade sales promotion** includes dealer contests and incentives, trade allowances, point-of-purchase displays, sales training programs, trade shows, cooperative advertising, and other programs designed to motivate distributors and retailers to carry and merchandise a product.

Many marketing programs include both trade and consumer promotions, since motivating both groups maximizes the effectiveness of the promotional program. Programs designed to persuade the trade to stock, merchandise, and promote a manufacturer's products are part of a **promotional push strategy**. The goal of this strategy is to push the product through the channels of distribution by aggressively selling and promoting the item to the resellers, or trade. A push strategy tries to convince resellers they can make a profit on a manufacturer's product and to encourage them to order the merchandise and push it through to their customers. Promotion to the trade includes all the elements of the promotional mix. Company sales representatives call on resellers to explain the product, discuss the firm's plans for building demand among ultimate consumers, and describe special programs being offered to the trade, such as introductory discounts, promotional allowances, and cooperative ad programs. The company may use **trade advertising** to interest wholesalers and retailers and motivate them to purchase its products for resale to their customers. Trade advertising usually appears in publications that serve the particular industry.

Sometimes manufacturers face resistance from channel members who do not want to take on an additional product line or brand. In these cases, companies may turn to a **promotional pull strategy**, spending money on advertising and sales promotion efforts directed toward the ultimate consumer. The goal of a pull strategy is to create demand among consumers and encourage them to request the product from the retailer. Seeing the consumer demand, retailers will order the product from wholesalers (if they are used), which in turn will request it from the manufacturer. Thus, stimulating demand at the end-user level pulls the product through the channels of distribution.

Whether to emphasize a push or a pull strategy depends on a number of factors, including the company's relations with the trade, its promotional budget, and demand for the firm's products. Companies that have favourable channel relationships may prefer to use a push strategy and work closely with channel members to encourage them to stock and promote their products. A firm with a limited promotional budget may not have the funds for advertising and sales promotion that a pull strategy requires and may find it more cost effective to build distribution and demand by working closely with resellers. When the demand outlook for a product is favourable because it has unique benefits, is superior to competing brands, or is very popular among consumers, a pull strategy may be appropriate. Companies often use a combination of push and pull strategies, with the emphasis changing as the product moves through its life cycle. IMC Perspective 14–1 shows how consumer and trade promotions support one another.

Growth of Sales Promotion

While sales promotion has been part of the marketing process for a long time, its role and importance in a company's integrated marketing communications programs has evolved. For many years advertising was the major component in the promotional mix of most consumer-products companies. In the 1980s, the proportion of the marketing budget allocated to sales promotion rose sharply, while the amount spent on media advertising declined. The increase in spending on sales promotion at the expense of media advertising continued throughout the decade of the 90s and into the new millennium. Currently, estimates are that marketers spend between 60 and 75 percent of their promotional budgets on sales promotion, with the remainder being allocated to media advertising.[4]

Many factors have led to the shift in marketing dollars to sales promotion. Among them are the strategic importance of sales promotion, reaching a specific target audience, increased promotional sensitivity, declining brand loyalty, brand proliferation, short-term focus, increased accountability, growing power of retailers, and competition.

Strategic Importance of Sales Promotion A major reason for the increase in spending on sales promotion is that the promotion industry has matured. Increased sophistication and a more strategic importance have elevated the discipline and its role in the IMC program of many companies.[5] In the past, sales promotion specialists would be brought in after key strategic branding decisions were made. Promotional agencies were viewed primarily as tacticians whose role was to develop a promotional program that could create a short-term increase in sales. However, many companies include promotional specialists as part of their strategic brand-building team, a move that puts sales promotion on par with media advertising. Promotional agencies have expanded their integrated marketing capabilities as

IMC PERSPECTIVE 14–1

Kraft and Crayola Draw Up a Winning Promotion

Kraft, Crayola, YTV, and grocery retailers illustrate the importance of partnership for the success of joint consumer and trade promotional programs. Consumers found a unique PIN/prize code stamped on a game piece in the shape of a school bus in specially marked Kraft or Christie product packages. Consumers then could go online to play a game and claim a prize. Kraft then sent a prize that featured a new Crayola product. The promotion ran for 6 months with ads featured on TV, in *What's Cooking* and *Not for Adults* magazines, with in-store displays, and on Kraft Canada's website. Redemptions exceeded initial expectations as Kraft and Crayola gave away more than 500,000 Crayola products.

With multiple partners, it was imperative that each participant perceive strategic value. Kraft saw Crayola as a perfect partner for a back-to-school promotion right when consumers were buying such products. Crayola received excellent imagery exposure in grocery stores where it considered its presence weak historically. Grocery stores enjoyed the combination of two significant brands with a very creative point-of-sale display—a giant school bus. YTV increased its media consumption through its television spots and online execution. And received a free premium from Crayola, or in Crayola's eyes a cost-efficient and communication-effective method of distributing a sample.

The Kraft and Crayola promotion signals a growing trend of brands taking a more strategic orientation toward sales promotion that builds the brand with a positive brand experience, which reinforces the brand positioning strategy.

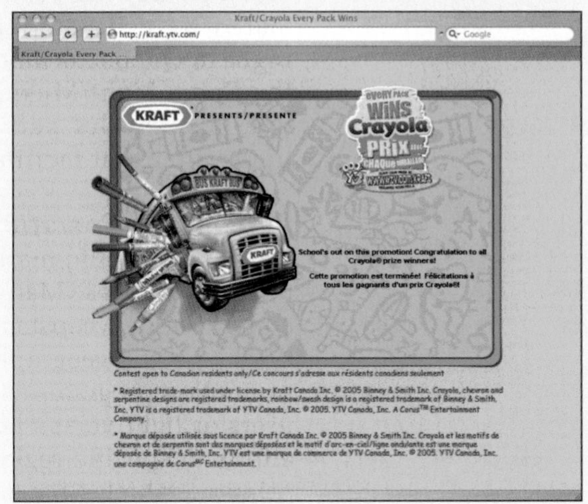

Advertisers are looking toward going beyond the "one-off" promotion that tried to move volumes of product and did not lend itself to build the brand successfully (i.e., brand position). In fact, once the significant promotional campaign is established, many believe it is important to continue in subsequent years or to maintain the consistent theme with promotions occurring throughout the year.

Sources: Matthew Diamond, "Leveraging the Big Idea," *Marketing Magazine,* October 6, 2003; Fawzia Sheikh, "Casting Off the One-Off," *Marketing Magazine,* May 10, 2004.

Question

1. Why are each of the partners motivated to participate in this promotion?

well as their expertise in programs designed to enhance brand equity. As noted in Chapter 1, *brand equity* is an intangible asset of added value or goodwill that results from consumers' favourable image, impressions of differentiation, and/or strength of attachment to a brand.

Marketing experts generally agree that advertising plays an important role in building and maintaining a brand's image and position, which are core components of its equity. Many are concerned that if the trend toward spending more on sales promotion at the expense of media advertising continues, brands may lose the equity that advertising helped create and be forced to compete primarily on the basis of price. Many of these concerns are justified, but not all sales promotion activities detract from the value of a brand, as this next example illustrates.

Coors Canada has used sales promotion to build its brand equity in the face of stiff sales promotion competition from other brands. Just a few years ago, Coors was offering only one sales promotion per year, its famous "Talking Can & Cap" campaign. Now Coors Canada spends 25 percent of its marketing budget on sales promotions, and 25 percent of its $4.8-million media budget is allocated to support the sales promotions. In 2001, it offered four in-case promotions in Western Canada, one in Quebec, and at least one in Ontario. Says one Coors Canada executive, "We are trying to make our in-case promotions build equity as much as they can for what they are, (but) we also have promotions that we're primarily trying to drive image with." Coors Canada's "Tracker" campaign for Coors Light in Quebec is an example of this. When a consumer opens a "tracker" bottle, the Coors Light/Musique Plus Tracker team greets the lucky winner with a trip to a Los Angeles party. The opened bottle triggers a Global Positioning System transmitter that facilitates the search![6]

Reaching a Specific Target Audience Most companies focus their marketing efforts on specific market segments and are always looking for ways to reach their target audiences. Many marketers are finding that sales promotion tools such as contests and sweepstakes, events, coupons, and samplings are very effective ways to reach specific geographic, demographic, psychographic, and ethnic markets. Sales promotion programs can also be targeted to specific user-status groups such as non-users or light versus heavy users. Many companies are tailoring their promotional efforts to specific regional markets. Sales promotion tools have become one of the primary vehicles for doing this, through programs tied into local flavour, themes, or events. For example, in an effort to increase traffic during lunch and dinner, a major western Canadian franchisee of 25 Denny's Restaurants used advertising (e.g., radio, newspaper), sales promotion (e.g., featured menu prices, guarantee), and public relations (e.g., sponsorship of junior hockey) to increase sales by 15 percent during 2001.[7]

Increased Promotional Sensitivity Marketers are making greater use of sales promotion in their marketing programs because consumers respond favourably to the incentives it provides. A major research project completed by Promotion Decisions, Inc., in 1999 tracked the purchase behaviour of over 33,000 consumers and their response to both consumer and trade promotions. The results showed that 42 percent of the total unit volume of the 12 packaged-good products analyzed was purchased with some type of incentive while 58 percent was purchased at full price. Coupons were particularly popular among consumers, as 24 percent of the sales volume involved the use of a coupon.[8]

An obvious reason for consumers' increased sensitivity to sales promotion offers is that they save money. Another reason is that many purchase decisions are made at the point of purchase by consumers who are increasingly time-sensitive and facing too many choices. Some studies have found that up to 70 percent of purchase decisions are made in the store, where people are very likely to respond to promotional deals.[9] Buying a brand that is on special or being displayed can simplify the decision-making process and solve the problem of overchoice.

Declining Brand Loyalty Another major reason for the increase in sales promotion is that consumers have become less brand loyal to one brand. Some consumers are always willing to buy their preferred brand at full price without any type of promotional offer. However, many consumers are loyal coupon users and/or are conditioned to look for deals when they shop. They may switch back and forth among a set of brands they view as essentially equal. These brands are all perceived as being satisfactory and interchangeable, and favourable brand switchers (discussed in Chapter 3) purchase whatever brand is on special or for which they have a coupon.

Brand Proliferation A major aspect of many firms' marketing strategies has been the development of new products. Consumer-product companies are launching more new products each year. The market has become saturated with new brands, which often lack any significant advantages that can be used as the basis of an advertising campaign. Thus, companies increasingly depend on sales promotion to encourage consumers to try these brands. Marketers are relying more on samples, coupons, rebates, premiums, and other innovative promotional tools to achieve trial usage of their new brands and encourage repeat purchase (Exhibit 14–1).

Promotions are also important in getting retailers to allocate some of their precious shelf space to new brands. The competition for shelf space for new products in stores is enormous. Supermarkets carry an average of 30,000 products (compared with 13,067 in 1982). Retailers favour new brands with strong sales promotion support that will bring in more customers and boost their sales and profits. Many retailers require special discounts or allowances from manufacturers just to handle a new product. These slotting fees or allowances, which are discussed later in the chapter, can make it expensive for a manufacturer to introduce a new product.

Exhibit 14–1
A premium offer is used to provide extra incentive to purchase Kellogg's Corn Flakes

Short-Term Focus Many businesspeople believe the increase in sales promotion is motivated by marketing plans and reward systems geared to short-term performance and the immediate generation of sales volume. Some think the packaged-goods brand management system has contributed to marketers' increased dependence on sales promotion. Brand managers use sales promotions routinely, not only to introduce new products or defend against the competition but also to meet quarterly or yearly sales and market share goals. The salesforce, too, may have short-term quotas or goals to meet and may also receive requests from retailers and wholesalers for promotions. Thus, reps may pressure marketing or brand managers to use promotions to help them move the products into the retailers' stores.

Many managers view consumer and trade promotions as the most dependable way to generate short-term sales, particularly when they are price related. The reliance on sales promotion is particularly high in mature and slow-growth markets, where it is difficult to stimulate consumer demand through advertising. This has led to concern that managers have become too dependent on the quick sales fix that can result from a promotion and that the brand franchise may be eroded by too many deals.

Increased Accountability In addition to pressuring their marketing or brand managers and salesforce to produce short-term results, many companies are demanding to know what they are getting for their promotional expenditures. Sales promotion is more economically accountable than advertising. In companies struggling to meet their sales and financial goals, top management is demanding measurable, accountable ways to relate promotional expenditures to sales and profitability.

Managers who are being held accountable to produce results often use price discounts or coupons, since they produce a quick and easily measured jump in sales. It takes longer for an ad campaign to show some impact and the effects are more difficult to measure. Marketers are also feeling pressure from the trade as powerful retailers demand sales performance from their brands. Real-time data available from computerized checkout scanners make it possible for retailers to monitor promotions and track the results they generate on a daily basis.

Growing Power of Retailers One reason for the increase in sales promotion is the power shift in the marketplace from manufacturers to retailers. Historically, consumer products manufacturers created consumer demand for their brands by using heavy advertising and some consumer promotions and exerted pressure on retailers to carry the products. Retailers did very little research and sales analysis; they relied on manufacturers for information regarding the sales performance of individual brands. With the advent of optical checkout scanners and sophisticated in-store computer systems, retailers gained access to data concerning how quickly products turn over, which sales promotions are working, and which products make money.[10]

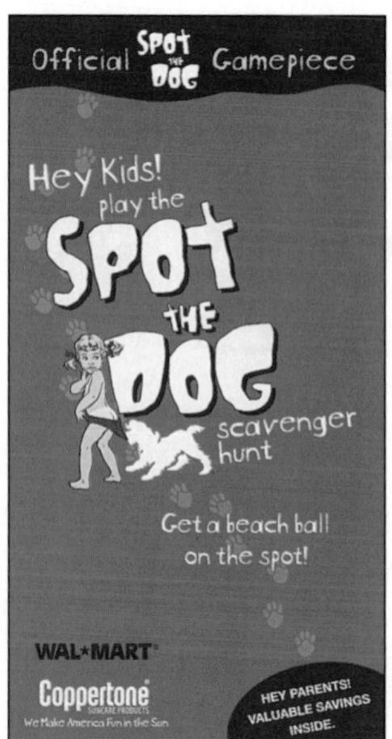

Exhibit 14–2 Coppertone developed an account-specific promotion for Wal-Mart

Retailers use this information to analyze sales of manufacturers' products and then demand discounts and other promotional support from manufacturers of lagging brands. Companies that fail to comply with retailers' demands for more trade support often have their shelf space reduced or even their product dropped.

Competition Another factor that led to the increase in sales promotion is manufacturers' reliance on trade and consumer promotions to gain or maintain competitive advantage. The markets for many products are mature and stagnant, and it is increasingly difficult to boost sales through advertising. Exciting, breakthrough creative ideas are difficult to come by, and consumers' attention to mass media advertising continues to decline. Rather than allocating large amounts of money to run dull ads, many marketers have turned to sales promotion.

Many companies are tailoring their trade promotions to key retail accounts and developing strategic alliances with retailers that include both trade and consumer promotional programs. A major development in recent years is **account-specific marketing** (also referred to as *comarketing*), whereby a manufacturer collaborates with an individual retailer to create a customized promotion that accomplishes mutual objectives (see Exhibit 14–2).

Retailers may use a promotional deal with one company as leverage to seek an equal or better deal with its competitors. Consumer and trade promotions are easily matched by competitors, and many marketers find themselves in a promotional trap where they must continue using promotions or be at a competitive disadvantage.

Sales Promotion Plan

In this section, we examine the various parts of a sales promotion plan. First, we consider some objectives marketers have for sales promotion programs. Next, we illustrate why the various sales promotion decisions are strategic options. Finally, we discuss the key tactics that are critical for all sales promotions. We focus on the consumer market to illustrate these ideas. Application to the trade market is readily done once the concept is understood.

Objectives of Consumer Sales Promotion

Sales promotion activities are designed to achieve the specific objectives. As with any promotional mix element, marketers must plan consumer promotions by conducting a situation analysis and determining sales promotion's specific role in the integrated marketing communications program. They must decide what the promotion is designed to accomplish and to whom it should be targeted. Setting clearly defined objectives and measurable goals for their sales promotion programs is consistent with the planning process explained in previous chapters.

While the basic goal of most consumer sales promotion programs is to induce purchase of a brand, the marketer may have a number of different objectives for both new and established brands. We use the ideas developed in Chapter 5 to highlight how sales promotions can help achieve behavioural and communication objectives. In particular, the latter considers the long-term cumulative effect on the brand's image and position.

Trial Purchase One of the most important uses of sales promotion techniques is to encourage consumers to try a new product or service. While thousands of new products are introduced to the market every year, as many as 90 percent of them fail within the first year. Many of these failures are due to the fact that the new product or brand lacks the promotional support needed to encourage initial trial by enough consumers. Many new brands are merely new versions of an existing product without unique benefits, so advertising alone cannot induce trial. Sales promotion tools have become an important part of new brand introduction strategies; the level of initial trial can be increased through techniques such as sampling, couponing, and refund offers.

A trial purchase objective is also relevant for an established brand that uses a sales promotion to attract nonusers of the product category. Attracting nonusers of the product category can be very difficult, as consumers may not see a need for the product. Sales promotions can appeal to nonusers by providing them with an extra incentive to try the product, but a more common strategy for increasing sales of an established brand is to attract consumers who use a competing brand. This can be done by giving them an incentive to switch, such as a coupon, premium offer, bonus pack, or price deal. Marketers can also get users of a competitor to try their brand through sampling or other types of promotional programs.

Repeat Purchase The success of a new brand depends not only on getting initial trial but also on inducing a reasonable percentage of people who try the brand to repurchase it and establish ongoing purchase patterns. Promotional incentives such as coupons or refund offers are often included with a sample to encourage repeat purchase after trial. For example, when Lever Brothers introduced its Lever 2000 brand of bar soap, it distributed millions of free samples along with a 75-cent coupon. The samples allowed consumers to try the new soap, while the coupon provided an incentive to purchase it.

A company can use sales promotion techniques in several ways to retain its current customer base through continued repeat purchases. One way is to load them with the product, taking them out of the market for a certain time. Special price promotions, coupons, or bonus packs can encourage consumers to stock up on the brand. This not only keeps them using the company's brand but also reduces the likelihood they will switch brands in response to a competitor's promotion.

Increasing Consumption Many marketing managers are responsible for established brands competing in mature markets, against established competitors, where consumer purchase patterns are often well set. Awareness of an established brand is generally high as a result of cumulative advertising effects, and many consumers have probably tried the brand. These factors can create a challenging situation for the brand manager. Sales promotion can generate some new interest in an established brand to help increase sales or defend market share against competitors.

Marketers attempt to increase sales for an established brand in several ways, and sales promotion can play an important role in each. One way to increase product consumption is by identifying new uses for the brand. Sales promotion tools like recipe books or calendars that show various ways of using the product often can accomplish this. One of the best examples of a brand that has found new uses is Arm & Hammer baking soda. Exhibit 14–3 shows a clever freestanding insert (FSI) coupon that promotes the brand's new fridge–freezer pack, which absorbs more odours in refrigerators and freezers.

Exhibit 14–3 Arm & Hammer used this FSI to promote a specific use for the product

Build Brand Equity A final objective for consumer promotions is to enhance or support the integrated marketing communications effort for a brand or company. Although maintaining or building brand equity and image has traditionally been viewed as being accomplished by media advertising, it has also become an important objective for sales promotions. Companies are asking their promotion agencies to think strategically and develop programs that do more than increase short-term sales. They want promotions that require consumer involvement with their brands. Sales promotion techniques such as contests or sweepstakes and premium offers are often used to draw attention to an ad, increase involvement with the message and product/service, and help build relationships with consumers.

Marketers often turn to sales promotion in the fall to reach students of all ages who are going back to school. For example, DaimlerChrysler displayed its new PT Cruiser and Neon RT to university students at nine campuses across Canada during frosh week in September 2001 as part of its "Coolest car on campus" campaign. A contest allowed students to paint a PT Cruiser with water-based paint, with the winning university receiving the car for a campus drive-safe program. In addition, students dressed up in costumes in front of the car, and photos were sent to their parents as part of the "I'll be graduating before you know it" campaign.[11]

Consumer Sales Promotion Strategy Decisions

Strategic decisions for sales promotions fall into three broad categories: sales promotion strategy options, application across product lines, and application across geographic markets.

Sales Promotion Strategy Options Our view of sales promotions is that the options identified in Figure 14–1 are important strategic choices for a marketer. Essentially, the key strategic decision for a marketer concerns the most appropriate sales promotion option(s) that will best achieve the behavioural objective(s) for the target audience(s). Two characteristics of sales promotions help guide the strategic direction of the sales promotion plan: the degree to which the sales promotion is "franchise building" and whether the incentive of the sales promotion is immediate or delayed.

Franchise-Building Characteristic Sales promotion activities that communicate distinctive brand attributes and contribute to the development and reinforcement of brand identity are **consumer franchise-building (CFB) promotions.**[12] Consumer sales promotion efforts cannot make consumers loyal to a brand that is of little value or does not provide them with a specific benefit. But they can make consumers aware of a brand and, by communicating its specific features and benefits, contribute to the development of a favourable brand attitude. Consumer franchise-building promotions are designed to build long-term brand preference and help the company achieve the ultimate goal of full-price purchases that do not depend on a promotional offer.

For years, franchise or image building was viewed as the exclusive realm of advertising, and sales promotion was used only to generate short-term sales increases. But now marketers are recognizing the image-building potential of sales promotion and realizing its CFB value. A survey of senior marketing executives found that 88 percent believe consumer promotions can help build a brand's equity, and 58 percent think trade promotions can contribute.[13]

Nonfranchise-Building Characteristic **Nonfranchise-building (non-FB) promotions** are designed to accelerate the purchase decision process and generate an immediate increase in sales. These activities do not communicate information about a brand's unique features or the benefits of using it, so they do not contribute to the building of brand equity and image. Price-off deals, bonus packs, and rebates or refunds are examples of non-FB sales promotion techniques. Trade promotions receive the most criticism for being nonfranchise building—for good reason. First, many of the promotional discounts and allowances given to the trade are never passed on to consumers. Most trade promotions that are forwarded through the channels reach consumers in the form of lower prices or special deals and lead them to buy on the basis of price rather than brand equity.

Many specialists in the promotional area stress the need for marketers to use sales promotion tools to build a franchise and create long-term continuity in their promotional programs. Whereas non-FB promotions merely borrow customers from other

FIGURE *14–2* Consumer sales promotion tools for various objectives

Consumer Reward Incentive	Trial purchase	Repeat purchase/ customer loading	Support IMC program/ build brand equity
	Communication and Behavioural Objectives		
Immediate	• Sampling • Instant coupons • In-store coupons • In-store rebates	• Price-off deals • Bonus packs • In- and on-package free premiums • Loyalty programs	• Events • In- and on-package free premiums
Delayed	• Media- and mail-delivered coupons • Mail-in refunds and rebates • Free mail-in premiums • Scanner- and Internet-delivered coupons	• In- and on-package coupons • Mail-in refunds and rebates • Loyalty programs	• Self-liquidating premiums • Free mail-in premiums • Contests and sweepstakes • Loyalty programs

brands, well-planned CFB activities can convert consumers to loyal customers. Short-term non-FB promotions have their place in a firm's promotional mix, particularly when competitive developments call for them. But their limitations must be recognized when a long-term marketing strategy for a brand is developed.

Incentive Characteristic Sales promotions provide consumers with an extra incentive or reward for engaging in a certain form of behaviour, such as purchasing a brand. For some sales promotion tools the incentive that the consumer receives is immediate, while for others the reward is delayed and not realized immediately. Using their situation analysis, marketers decide the relative balance between immediate or delayed incentives. The decision is based on the target audience(s) and the intended behavioural objective(s). The chart in Figure 14–2 outlines which sales promotion tools can be used to accomplish various behavioural objectives and identifies whether the extra incentive or reward is immediate or delayed.[14]

It should be noted that in Figure 14–2 some of the sales promotion techniques are listed more than once because they can be used to accomplish more than one objective with both immediate and delayed incentives. For example, loyalty programs can be used to retain customers by providing both immediate and delayed rewards. Shoppers who belong to loyalty programs sponsored by supermarkets, and who receive discounts every time they make a purchase, are receiving immediate rewards that are designed to retain them as customers. Some loyalty promotions, such as frequency programs used by airlines, car rental companies, and hotels, offer delayed rewards by requiring that users accumulate points to reach a certain level or status before the points can be redeemed. Loyalty programs can also be used by marketers to help build brand equity. For example, when an airline or car rental company sends its frequent users upgrade certificates, the practice helps build relationships with these customers and thus contributes to brand equity.

One explanation for how sales promotion incentives work lies in the theory of **operant conditioning**. The individual acts on some aspect of the environment that reinforces behaviour. In a promotion context, if a consumer buys a product with a sales promotion and experiences a positive outcome, the likelihood that the consumer will use this product again increases. If the outcome is not favourable, the likelihood of buying the product again decreases. Note that sales promotions have both immediate and delayed reinforcements that must fit with the particular target audience and the accompanying objectives desired.

Two aspects of reinforcement that are particularly relevant to sales promotion strategies are schedules of reinforcement and shaping. Different **schedules of reinforcement** result in varying patterns of learning and behaviour. Learning occurs most rapidly under a *continuous reinforcement schedule,* in which every response is rewarded—but the behaviour is likely to cease when the reinforcement stops. Learning occurs more slowly but lasts longer when a *partial or intermittent reinforcement schedule* is used and only some of the individual's responses are rewarded.

Promotional programs have partial reinforcement schedules. A firm may offer consumers an incentive to use the company's product. The firm does not want to offer the incentive every time (continuous reinforcement), because consumers might become dependent on it and stop buying the brand when the incentive is withdrawn. A study that examined the effect of reinforcement on bus ridership found that discount coupons given as rewards for riding the bus were as effective when given on a partial schedule as when given on a continuous schedule.[15] The cost of giving the discount coupons under the partial schedule, however, was considerably less.

Reinforcement schedules can also be used to influence consumer behaviour through a process known as **shaping**, the reinforcement of successive acts that lead to a desired behaviour pattern or response.[16] In a promotional context, shaping procedures are used as part of the introductory program for new products. Figure 14–3 provides an example of how samples and discount coupons can be used to introduce a new product and take a consumer from trial to repeat purchase. Marketers must be careful in their use of shaping procedures: If they drop the incentives too soon, the consumer may not establish the desired behaviour; but if they overuse them, the consumer's purchase may become contingent on the incentive rather than the product or service.

FIGURE *14–3*

Application of shaping procedures for sales promotion

Behaviour Change	Type of Sales Promotion
Induce product trial	Free samples distributed; large discount coupon
Induce purchase with little financial obligation	Discount coupon prompts purchase with little cost; coupon good for small discount on next purchase enclosed
Induce purchase with moderate financial obligation	Small discount coupon prompts purchase with moderate cost
Induce purchase with full financial obligation	Purchase occurs without coupon assistance

Application across Product Lines Another part of the strategic sales promotion decision is the degree to which each sales promotion tool is applied to the range of sizes, varieties, models, or products. Overall, there are three important product decisions for sales promotions. The first concerns whether the sales promotion should be run on the entire line or on individual items. If the latter option is selected (i.e., selective application), the second decision concerns which specific items. The marketer could run a promotion on either the more or less popular items. Similarly, the marketer could focus on higher or lower price points. Sometimes, a sales promotion is offered on a unique product format or size instead of the regular product. For example, Kellogg's bundled three brands of cereal with plastic in one sales promotion in which each size was not the standard size typically distributed. Thus, the third strategic issue concerns whether the sales promotion is run on the "regular" stock or some other special version.

Application across Geographic Markets Sales promotions can be run nationally or in select markets. Local or regional market conditions, with respect to consumer demand and competitive intensity, tend to dictate the degree of tailoring sales promotions for each geographic market. Intuitively, it appears that many marketers would be faced with situations where offering unique sales promotions for each geographic market would achieve optimal communication and behavioural effects; however, there are three factors that marketers need to consider. First, a regional focus requires additional managerial commitment in planning and implementation. Second, achieving objectives more specifically may result in greater expense, thus necessitating a cost–benefit analysis. Finally, national accounts may not be too receptive, with different types of sales promotions in one province versus another.

Consumer Sales Promotion Tactics Decisions

A coupon can be received with a value anywhere from 50¢ to $2.00 for many consumer products, early in the year or later in the year, often or not so often, or from any number of outlets (e.g., direct mail, magazine). As this implies, for each sales promotion option, the marketer faces a number of key tactical decisions: value of the incentive, timing, and distribution. We briefly describe each of these in order to put together a comprehensive sales promotion plan.

Value of Incentive Whether the marketer is offering some sort of price discount or a consumer franchise-building sales promotion such as a premium, eventually the marketer has to decide the value of the sales promotion. For example, should the coupon be the equivalent of a 10- or a 20-percent discount? This decision is contingent upon the threshold at which consumers will respond to a sales promotion and the number of potential consumer responses; each will contribute to the total cost of the sales promotion. Similarly, if a beer company is offering a premium, a strategic decision has to be made as to the relative value of the premium: for example, a T-shirt worth $10 to $15 or perhaps a "cozy" worth a couple of dollars.

A non-economic interpretation of value is also possible. Hostess Frito-Lay (HFL) has used various in-pack collectables (e.g., stickers) of well-known entertainment or pop-culture icons (e.g., *The Simpsons, Star Wars*) that attract young impulse-purchase consumers. The focus of these sales promotions transfers well to point-of-sale displays to attract consumers' attention and to meet retailers' need for innovative merchandising to move product off the shelves. In 2001, HFL used Marvel comic-book characters on packaging and convenience-store point-of-sale displays, and offered limited-edition comic books as part of a trivia challenge in association with Teletoon.[17]

Timing The time element of the sales promotion is important in a few directions that are mutually dependent. A marketer has to decide during which months, weeks, or days the sales promotion will be offered. Seasonal or some other consumption pattern discovered through market research or the situation analysis may guide this choice. Secondly, sales promotions can be offered for one day, one week, a few weeks, or even a few months. Target audience and behavioural objectives typically guide this duration decision. Finally, the frequency of the sales promotion is a final timing consideration. If coupons have been decided, the marketer needs to decide whether one will be offered every six months or perhaps two every six months.

Distribution For most sales promotions, there is a logistical consideration as to how the promotion will get to the consumer or how the consumer will get to the sales promotion. There are many choices for sales promotions, such as coupons (e.g., direct mail, in-ad), while for others, such as premiums, the choices may be limited. We discuss some of the distribution options for each sales promotion in the next section, where we describe each sales promotion and its strengths and limitations.

Consumer Sales Promotion Strategy Options

A number of consumer sales promotions that managers may select from to develop a strategic sales promotion plan were identified in Figure 14–1. Each of these options can assist the promotional planner in achieving the objectives just discussed. We now review each of these options by describing their characteristics, distribution methods, and strengths and limitations.

Sampling

Sampling involves a variety of procedures whereby consumers are given some quantity of a product for no charge to induce trial. Sampling is generally considered the most effective way to generate trial, although it is also the most expensive. As a sales promotion technique, sampling is often used to introduce a new product or brand to the market; however, sampling is used for established products as well. Some companies do not use sampling for established products, reasoning that samples may not induce satisfied users of a competing brand to switch and may just go to the firm's current customers, who would buy the product anyway. This may not be true when significant changes (new and improved) are made in a brand.

Manufacturers of packaged-goods products such as food, health care items, cosmetics, and toiletries are heavy users of sampling since their products meet the three criteria for an effective sampling program:

- The products are of relatively low unit value, so samples do not cost too much.
- The products are divisible, which means they can be broken into small sample sizes that are adequate for demonstrating the brand's features and benefits to the user.
- The purchase cycle is relatively short, so the consumer will consider an immediate purchase or will not forget about the brand before the next purchase occasion.

Strengths of Sampling Samples are an excellent way to induce a prospective buyer to try a product or service. A major study conducted by the Promotion Marketing Association in 2002 found that the vast majority of consumers receiving a sample either use it right away or save it to use sometime later.[18] Sampling generates much higher trial rates than advertising or other sales promotion techniques.

Getting people to try a product leads to a second benefit of sampling: consumers experience the brand directly, gaining a greater appreciation for its benefits. This can be particularly important when a product's features and benefits are difficult to describe through advertising. Many foods, beverages, and cosmetics have subtle features that are most appreciated when experienced directly. Nearly 70 percent of the respondents in the PMA survey indicated that they have purchased a product they did not normally use after trying a free sample. The study also found that samples are even more likely to lead to purchase when they are accompanied with a coupon.

Limitations of Sampling While samples are an effective way to induce trial, the brand must have some unique or superior benefits for a sampling program to be worthwhile. Otherwise, the sampled consumers revert back to other brands and do not become repeat purchasers. The costs of a sampling program can be recovered only if it gets a number of consumers to become regular users of the brand at full retail price.

Another possible limitation to sampling is that the benefits of some products are difficult to gauge immediately, and the learning period required to appreciate the brand may require supplying the consumer with larger amounts of the brand than are affordable. An example would be an expensive skin cream that is promoted as preventing or reducing wrinkles but has to be used for an extended period before any effects are seen.

Sampling Methods One basic decision the promotional manager must make is how the sample will be distributed. The sampling method chosen is important not only in terms of costs but also because it influences the type of consumer who receives the sample. The best sampling method gets the product to the best prospects for trial and subsequent repurchase. We now review the distribution options available.

Door-to-door sampling, in which the product is delivered directly to the prospect's residence, is used when it is important to control where the sample is delivered. This distribution method is very expensive because of labour costs, but it can be cost-effective if the marketer has information that helps define the target audience and/or if the prospects are located in a well-defined geographic area.

Sampling through media, in which some companies have samples delivered directly to consumers' homes by including them with newspapers or magazines. There are a number of newspapers that can now distribute a sample into a subscriber segment as small as 250 households with little increase in costs to marketers.[19]

Sampling through the mail is common for small, lightweight, nonperishable products. A major advantage of this method is that the marketer has control over where and when the product will be distributed and can target the sample to specific market areas. Many marketers are using information from geodemographic target marketing programs such as Claritas's Prizm or Microvision to better target their sample mailings. The main drawbacks to mail sampling are postal restrictions and increasing postal rates.

In-store sampling is increasingly popular, especially for food products. The marketer hires temporary demonstrators who set up a table or booth, prepare small samples of the product, and pass them out to shoppers. The in-store sampling approach can be very effective for food products, since consumers get to taste the item and the demonstrator can give them more information about the product while it is being sampled. Demonstrators may also give consumers a cents-off coupon for the sampled item to encourage immediate trial purchase. While this sampling method can be very effective, it can also be expensive and requires a great deal of planning, as well as the cooperation of retailers.

Exhibit 14–4
Armor All uses on-package samples for related products

On-package sampling, where a sample of a product is attached to another item, is another common sampling method (see Exhibit 14–4). This procedure can be very cost-effective, particularly for multiproduct firms that attach a sample of a new product to an existing brand's package. A drawback is that since the sample is distributed only to consumers who purchase the item to which it is attached, the sample will not reach nonusers of the carrier brand. Marketers can expand this sampling method by attaching the sample to multiple carrier brands and including samples with products not made by their company.

Event sampling has become one of the fastest-growing and most popular ways of distributing samples. Many marketers are using sampling programs that are part of integrated marketing programs that feature events, media tie-ins, and other activities that provide consumers with a total sense of a brand rather than just a few tastes of a food or beverage or a trial size of a packaged-goods product. Event sampling can take place in stores as well as at a variety of other venues such as concerts, sporting events, and other places.

Direct sampling is when, with the advancement of technology, marketers can deliver samples directly. Some companies send samples to consumers who call toll-free numbers to request them or mail in sample request forms. As discussed in Chapter 16, these sampling methods are becoming popular because they can help marketers build a database for direct marketing.

Location sampling allows many companies to use specialized sample distribution services that help the company identify consumers who are nonusers of a product or users of a competing brand and develop appropriate procedures for distributing a sample to them. Many university and college students receive sample packs at the beginning of the semester that contain trial sizes of such products as mouthwash, toothpaste, headache remedies, and deodorant.

The Internet is yet another way companies are making it possible for consumers to sample their products, and it is adding a whole new level of targeting to the mix by giving consumers the opportunity to choose the samples they want. Schick Canada created a three-page mini-site to let consumers order a free sample of its new unisex razor, Xtreme III. The home page (www.schick.ca) showed uncluttered images of the product and a couple indicating its unisex feature. The second page described a couple of features, while the third page permitted consumers to request the sample. A link on www.canadianfreestuff.com directed users to the site in addition to a viral e-mail. In the first three months, Schick Canada had received about 9,000 requests for samples.

Promotional planners are certainly not limited to one method. In fact, **multiple methods** may be quite useful, as shown in the following example. With the decline of wet cat food in a can category, Effem looked to samples to launch its Whiskas Flavour Lock pouch and its Temptations treat cat food in two new product formats—wet cat food in a convenient pouch and tasty treats as a cat snack. Using a database, Effem delivered samples to a total of 250,000 households in less than four months. Print ads, online ads, and retail point-of-sale supported the direct contact. Consumers also responded with an online request and received one of three samples through the mail. Consumers requested about 20 percent of the samples online, making this Canadian site the second most visited international site owned by Effem's parent, Mars Corporation. Whiskas' market share in the wet pouch category increased by 1.5 percent and volume by weight rose 20 percent, with Whiskas the only brand growing in the declining wet cat food category. Temptations increased its share by 7 percent and maintained its lead in the treat category.[20]

Coupons

The oldest, most widely used, and most effective sales promotion is the cents-off coupon. Research indicates that, on average, Canadians used about eight coupons per household, and that 83 percent of Canadians used coupons in 2005. In fact, 28 percent of all Canadians had used coupons in the past week during 2005.[21] And half of all Canadian households claim that coupons influence their brand purchase decision.

Figure 14–4 summarizes recent statistics indicating the scope of coupons in Canada. The number of coupons distributed by consumer packaged-goods marketers reached 3.5 billion in 2005, up substantially from the 2.3 billion in 2002. The number of coupons redeemed approximated 100 million over the past few years. The value of an average redeemed coupon hit 1.29 in 2005 and saved Canadians about $129 million.

Strengths of Coupons Coupons have a number of strengths that make them popular sales promotion tools for both new and established products. First, coupons make it possible to offer a price reduction only to those consumers who are price-sensitive. Such consumers generally purchase because of coupons, while those who

FIGURE 14–4

Coupon redemption rates

	2001	2002	2003	2004	2005
Quantity distributed	2.67 billion	2.32 billion	2.60 billion	2.94 billion	3.50 billion
Quantity redeemed	122 million	110 million	97 million	99 million	100 million
Average face value coupons *distributed*	$1.25	$1.25	$1.23	$1.55	$1.84
Average face value coupons *redeemed*	$1.05	$1.07	$1.08	$1.19	$1.29
Average valid period	234 days	219 days	214 days	206 days	183 days
Consumer savings	$128 million	$118 million	$105 million	$118 million	$129 million

are not as concerned about price buy the brand at full value. Coupons also make it possible to reduce the retail price of a product without relying on retailers for cooperation, which can often be a problem. Coupons are generally regarded as second only to sampling as a promotional technique for generating trial. Since a coupon lowers the price of a product, it reduces the consumer's perceived risk associated with trial of a new brand. Coupons can encourage repurchase after initial trial. Many new products include a cents-off coupon inside the package to encourage repeat purchase. Coupons can also be useful promotional devices for established products. They can encourage nonusers to try a brand, encourage repeat purchase among current users, and get users to try a new, improved version of a brand. Coupons may also help coax users of a product to trade up to more expensive brands.

Limitations of Coupons There are a number of problems with coupons. First, it can be difficult to estimate how many consumers will use a coupon and when. Response to a coupon is rarely immediate; it typically takes anywhere from two to six months to redeem one. A study of coupon redemption patterns by Inman and McAlister found that many coupons are redeemed just before the expiration date rather than in the period following the initial coupon drop.[22] Many marketers are attempting to expedite redemption by shortening the time period before expiration. The average length of time from issue date to expiration date for coupons in 2005 was 183 days. However, coupons remain less effective than sampling for inducing initial product trial in a short period.

A problem associated with using coupons to attract new users to an established brand is that it is difficult to prevent the coupons from being used by consumers who already use the brand. For example, General Foods decided to reduce its use of coupons for Maxwell House coffee when research revealed the coupons were being redeemed primarily by current users. Rather than attracting new users, coupons can end up reducing the company's profit margins among consumers who would probably purchase the product anyway.

Other problems with coupons include low redemption rates and high costs. Couponing program expenses include the face value of the coupon redeemed plus costs for production, distribution, and handling of the coupons. Figure 14–5 on page 424 shows the calculations used to determine the costs of a couponing program using an FSI (freestanding insert) in the newspaper and a coupon with an average face value of 75 cents. The marketer should track costs closely to ensure the promotion is economically feasible.

FIGURE 14–5

Calculating couponing costs

Cost per Coupon Redeemed: An Illustration

1.	Distribution cost 5,000,000 circulation × $15/M	$75,000
2.	Redemptions at 2%	100,000
3.	Redemption cost 100,000 redemptions × $.75 face value	$75,000
4.	Retailer handling cost and processor fees 100,000 redemptions × $10	$10,000
5.	Total program cost Items 1 + 3 + 4	$160,000
6.	Cost per coupon redeemed Cost divided by redemption	$1.60
7.	Actual product sold on redemption (misredemption estimated at 20%) 100,000 × 80%	80,000
8.	Cost per product moved Program cost divided by amount of product sold	$2.00

Recent research on coupon face value indicates that testing for the most appropriate level is important for determining the most efficient (i.e., cost per coupon redeemed) coupon program. Since a coupon program combines redemption, printing, distribution, and handling costs, the face value and corresponding redemption rate can influence the overall efficiency of the program. The research tested a number of direct mail and FSI offers from various firms selling major grocery brands with different face values and consistent communication elements across all offers. The results indicate that moving from $.50 to $1.00 off nearly doubles the redemption rate (e.g., 2 percent to 4 percent) while moving from $1.00 to $1.50 off improves the redemption rate at a slower rate (e.g., 4 percent to 5 percent). Overall, this curvilinear relationship between face value and redemption rate made the $1.00 offer 20 percent and 12 percent more cost efficient versus the $.50 and $1.50 offers, respectively. Conclusions from the research suggest the choice of face value should not make the program go over budget, the face value and redemption rate connection will vary by brand, lower face values may not be the most cost-efficient program, higher face values are good for brand trial, and lower face values good for brand retrial.[23]

Another problem with coupon promotions is misredemption, or the cashing of a coupon without purchase of the brand. Coupon misredemption or fraud occurs in a number of ways, including:

- Redemption of coupons by consumers for a product or size not specified on the coupon.
- Redemption of coupons by salesclerks in exchange for cash.
- Gathering and redemption of coupons by store managers or owners without the accompanying sale of the product.
- Gathering or printing of coupons by criminals who sell them to unethical merchants, who in turn redeem them.

Many manufacturers hold firm in their policy to not pay retailers for questionable amounts or suspicious types of coupon submissions. However, some companies are less aggressive, and this affects their profit margins. Marketers must allow a certain percentage for misredemption when estimating the costs of a couponing program. Ways to identify and control coupon misredemption, such as improved coding, are being developed, but it remains a problem.

Media Type	2003		2004		2005	
	D	R	D	R	D	R
Free Standing Inserts (FSI)	65%	13%	62%	11%	57%	13%
In-store	11%	45%	10%	44%	10%	37%
Instantly Redeemable (On Pack)	2%	11%	2%	8%	3%	8%
In/On Package	7%	10%	5%	14%	8%	22%
Direct to Home	5%	7%	7%	9%	6%	6%
Magazine	6%	4%	6%	3%	9%	3%
Charity (Cash for Kids)	1%	6%	2%	7%	1%	7%
Other	3%	4%	6%	4%	6%	4%

D = Distributed R = Redeemed

FIGURE *14–6*

Coupon distribution and redemption across all media

Coupon Distribution Coupons can be disseminated to consumers in a number of ways, including newspaper freestanding inserts, direct mail, newspapers (either in individual ads or as a group of coupons in a cooperative format), magazines, packages, and the Internet. Figure 14–6 summarizes the percentage distributed across all avenues and the percentage of coupons redeemed for each media type.

Distribution through newspaper *freestanding inserts* (FSIs) is by far the most popular method for delivering coupons to consumers, accounting for 57 percent of all coupons distributed in 2005. There are a number of reasons why FSIs are the most popular way of delivering coupons, including their high-quality four-colour graphics, competitive distribution costs, national same-day circulation, market selectivity, and the fact that they can be competition-free due to category exclusivity (by FSI company). Because of their consumer popularity and predictable distribution, coupons distributed in FSIs are also a strong selling point with the retail trade. On the other hand, FSIs suffer from a low redemption rate of 1 or 2 percent, and their widespread distribution may lead to a clutter problem.

Direct mail accounts for about 6 percent of all coupons distributed and account for 6 percent of all redemptions. Most are sent by local retailers or through co-op mailings where a packet of coupons for many different products is sent to a household. Direct-mail couponing has several advantages. First, the mailing can be sent to a broad audience or targeted to specific geographic or demographic segments. Firms that mail their own coupons can be quite selective about recipients. Another important advantage of direct-mail couponing is the redemption rate of nearly 6 percent, much higher than for FSIs.[24] Direct-mail couponing can also be combined with a sample, which makes it a very effective way to gain the attention of consumers. The major disadvantage of direct-mail coupon delivery is the expense relative to other distribution methods. The cost per thousand for distributing coupons through co-op mailings ranges from $10 to $15, and more targeted promotions can cost $20 to $25 or even more. Also, the higher redemption rate of mail-delivered coupons may result from the fact that many recipients are already users of the brand who take advantage of the coupons sent directly to them.

The use of *newspapers* and *magazines* as couponing vehicles offer a print media alternative. Distribution in magazines reached 9 percent in 2005 and corresponding numbers for newspaper were unavailable. The advantages of newspapers as a couponing vehicle include market selectivity, shorter lead times with timing to the day, cooperative advertising opportunities that can lead to cost efficiencies, and promotional tie-ins with retailers. Other advantages of newspaper-delivered coupons are the broad exposure and consumer receptivity. Many consumers actively search the newspaper for coupons, especially on Saturdays or "food day" (when grocery stores

Exhibit 14–5
Kellogg's uses an on-package coupon to encourage repurchase

advertise their specials). This enhances the likelihood of the consumer at least noticing the coupon. Distribution of coupons through magazines can take advantage of the selectivity of the publication to reach specific target audiences, along with enhanced production capabilities and extended copy life in the home. One feature of these print options is that the distribution cost is not a factor if the advertiser was planning to run a print ad in the first place. However, clearly there is a significant limitation with a 1 percent redemption rate.

Placing coupons either *inside* or on the *outside* of the package is a distribution method that accounted for about 8 percent of the coupons distributed in 2005 and accounted for 22 percent of all coupon redemptions. The in/on package coupon has virtually no distribution costs and a much higher redemption rate than other couponing methods, nearing 6 percent. An in/on pack coupon that is redeemable for the next purchase of the same brand is known as a **bounce-back coupon**. This type of coupon gives consumers an inducement to repurchase the brand.

Bounce-back coupons are often used with product samples to encourage the consumer to purchase the product after sampling. They may be included in or on the package during the early phases of a brand's life cycle to encourage repeat purchase, or they may be a defensive manoeuvre for a mature brand that is facing competitive pressure and wants to retain its current users. The main limitation of bounce-back coupons is that they go only to purchasers of the brand and thus do not attract non-users. A bounce-back coupon placed on the package for Kellogg's Eggo brand waffles is shown in Exhibit 14–5.

Another type of in/on pack coupon is the **cross-ruff coupon**, which is redeemable on the purchase of a different product, usually one made by the same company but occasionally through a tie-in with another manufacturer. Cross-ruff coupons have a redemption rate of about 5 percent and can be effective in encouraging consumers to try other products or brands. Companies with wide product lines, such as cereal manufacturers, often use these coupons.

Yet another type of package coupon is the **instant coupon**, which is attached to the outside of the package so that the consumer can rip it off and redeem it immediately at the time of purchase. Instant coupons have redemption levels of around 36 percent and give consumers an immediate point-of-purchase incentive. They can be selectively placed in terms of promotion timing and market region. Some companies prefer instant coupons to price-off deals because the latter require more cooperation from retailers and can be more expensive, since every package must be reduced in price. These coupons represent 3 percent and 8 percent of all coupons distributed and redeemed.

Another distribution method that has experienced strong growth is **in-store couponing**, which includes all co-op couponing programs distributed in a retail store environment. This medium now accounts for around 10 percent of total coupon distribution. Coupons are distributed to consumers in stores in several ways, including tear-off pads, handouts in the store (sometimes as part of a sampling demonstration), on-shelf dispensers, and electronic dispensers, with an 8-percent redemption rate. These in-store coupons have several advantages: They can reach consumers when they are ready to make a purchase, increase brand awareness on the shelf, generate impulse buying, and encourage product trial. They also provide category exclusivity. In-store couponing removes the need for consumers to clip coupons from FSIs or print ads and then remember to bring them to the store. The success of these coupons is seen by the fact that they are the most redeemed coupon, at 37 percent.

While many marketers are using the *Internet* for online promotions, online coupons account for a small percentage of all coupons distributed. One of the major problems that has kept marketers away from "e-couponing" is the risk of fraud, as it is too easy for consumers or unscrupulous retailers to mass-duplicate online coupons by printing out several, or by photocopying the black-and-white prints. There are ways to deal with this problem, such as coding coupons and verifying them in-store when they are redeemed. However, this is time-consuming and not very popular with retailers. Two alternatives are now on the scene in Canada. Two websites, coupons.com and save.ca, allow consumers to print or receive coupons in the mail, respectively. Currently, the fraud problem is not a significant concern in Canada.[25] The famous blue Valpak, distributed to households through the mail system, is now available online (Exhibit 14–6).

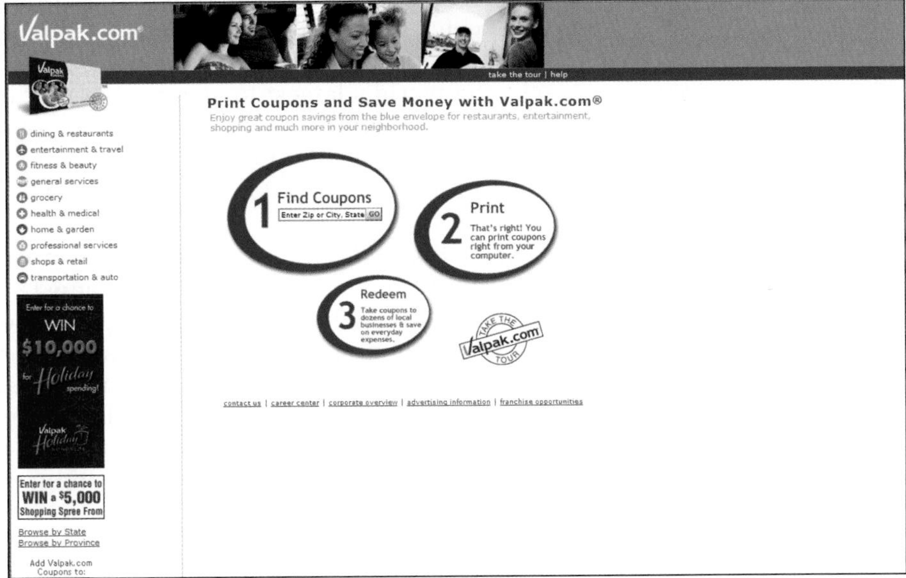

Exhibit 14–6
Valpak's coupons are now available online

PREMIUMS

Premiums are a sales promotion device used by many marketers. A **premium** is an offer of an item of merchandise or service either free or at a low price that is an extra incentive for purchasers. Many marketers are eliminating toys and gimmicks in favour of value-added premiums that reflect the quality of the product and are consistent with its image and positioning in the market. The two basic types of offers are the free premium and the self-liquidating premium.

Free Premiums Free premiums are usually small gifts or merchandise included in the product package or sent to consumers who mail in a request along with a proof of purchase. In/on-package free premiums include toys, balls, trading cards, or other items included in cereal packages, as well as samples of one product included with another. Surveys have shown that in/on-package premiums are consumers' favourite type of promotion.[26]

Package-carried premiums have high impulse value and can provide an extra incentive to buy the product. However, several problems are associated with their use. First, there is the cost factor, which results from the premium itself as well as from extra packaging that may be needed. Finding desirable premiums at reasonable costs can be difficult, particularly for adult markets, and using a poor premium may do more harm than good.

Exhibit 14–7
McDonald's Happy Meals use toys to help attract children

Since most free mail-in premium offers require the consumer to send in more than one proof of purchase, they encourage repeat purchase and reward brand loyalty. But a major drawback of mail-in premiums is that they do not offer immediate reinforcement or reward to the purchaser, so they may not provide enough incentive to purchase the brand. Few consumers take advantage of mail-in premium offers; the average redemption rate is only 2 to 4 percent.[27]

Free premiums have become very popular in the restaurant industry, particularly among fast-food chains such as McDonald's, which offers a premium in its kids' meals to attract children.[28] McDonald's has become the world's largest toymaker on a unit basis, commissioning about 750 million toys per year for its Happy Meals (Exhibit 14–7). Many of the premium offers used by the fast-food giants have cross-promotional tie-ins with popular movies and can be very effective at generating incremental sales.

Labatt's had a winner with the Labatt Blue NHL Crazy Coldie Program during the 2002 Stanley Cup Playoffs. Each case of Double Blue (i.e., 12 Blue and 12 Blue Light) had a coldie (i.e., holder to keep beer cold) in the shape of the jersey of one of the 30 teams. While the in-pack premium is relatively inexpensive, it resonated with the 19–34 male market that pushed sales to a 300-percent market share growth during the promotional program. Success can be partly attributed to the promotion's ads where three humorous spots showed consumers trying to wear the "coldie jersey" despite its obvious small size and a host of other promotional support activities such as a contest and special events.[29]

Perhaps the most successful in-package premium in Canada in 2001 was a General Mills giveaway of six CD-ROM computer games such as Monopoly Junior and Clue. Modelled after a similar premium offer in the U.S., the Canadian division worked with only one games supplier, Hasbro, versus a couple of partners used south of the border. Hasbro was selected because both it and General Mills represent quality and heritage. The premium was so popular that store employees witnessed consumers searching through cases to find the game they wanted, as well as some consumers who left the store with only the CD-ROM, after purchasing the cereal. For competitive reasons, executives at General Mills were not willing to reveal any results but did admit that the consumer reaction was beyond belief given the empty shelves.[30]

Self-Liquidating Premiums **Self-liquidating premiums** require the consumer to pay some or all of the cost of the premium plus handling and mailing costs. The marketer usually purchases items used as self-liquidating premiums in large quantities and offers them to consumers at lower-than-retail prices. The goal is not to make a profit on the premium item but rather just to cover costs and offer a value to the consumer.

In addition to cost savings, self-liquidating premiums offer several advantages to marketers. Offering values to consumers through the premium products can create interest in the brand and goodwill that enhances the brand's image. These premiums can also encourage trade support and gain in-store displays for the brand and the premium offer. Self-liquidating premiums are often tied directly to the advertising campaign, so they extend the advertising message and contribute to consumer franchise building for a brand.

General Mills Canada was at it again with a successful self-liquidating premium during Christmas of 2001. Customers received a beanbag version of the Pillsbury Doughboy for $2.99 with the purchase of two refrigerated-dough products. This marked the first time the brand icon had ever been directly merchandised! Pillsbury had the perfect opportunity because the Doughboy is the second-most recognized icon in North America, after Coca-Cola's Polar Bears. Even more impressive was the retailer participation and consumer acceptance. All retailers in Canada ran with the deal, and more than 200,000 Doughboys found a new home. And just to make sure that consumers liked the idea even more, the Doughboy came in three models: one holding a candy cane, another, a stocking, and the third, gifts.[31]

Self-liquidating premium offers have the same basic limitation as mail-in premiums: a very low redemption rate. Low redemption rates can leave the marketer with a large supply of items with a logo or some other brand identification that makes them hard to dispose of. Thus, it is important to test consumers' reaction to a premium incentive and determine whether they perceive the offer as a value. Another option is to use premiums with no brand identification, but that detracts from their consumer franchise-building value.

Contests and Sweepstakes

Contests and sweepstakes are an increasingly popular consumer sales promotion. These promotions seem to have an appeal and glamour that tools like cents-off coupons lack. Contests and sweepstakes are exciting because, as one expert has noted, many consumers have a "pot of gold at the end of the rainbow mentality" and think they can win the big prizes being offered.[32] Marketers are attracted to contests and sweepstakes as a way of generating attention and interest among a large number of consumers.

A **contest** is a promotion where consumers compete for prizes or money on the basis of skills or ability. The company determines winners by judging the entries or ascertaining which entry comes closest to some predetermined criteria. Contests usually provide a purchase incentive by requiring a proof of purchase to enter or an entry form that is available from a dealer or advertisement. Some contests require consumers to read an ad or package or visit a store display to gather information needed to enter. Marketers must be careful not to make their contests too difficult to enter, as doing so might discourage participation among key prospects in the target audience. IMC Perspective 14–2 on page 430 describes a contest where participation represented a key feature of the promotion.

A **sweepstakes** is a promotion where winners are determined purely by chance; it cannot require a proof of purchase as a condition for entry. Entrants need only submit their names for the prize drawing. While there is often an official entry form, handwritten entries must also be permitted. One form of sweepstakes is a **game**, which also has a chance element or odds of winning. Scratch-off cards with instant winners are a popular promotional tool. Some games occur over a longer period and require more involvement by consumers. Promotions where consumers must collect game pieces are popular among retailers and fast-food chains as a way to build store traffic and repeat purchases. For example, McDonald's has used promotions based on the game *Monopoly* several times in recent years.

Exhibit 14–8 Advertisements are often used to deliver messages about promotions such as sweepstakes

Because they are easier to enter, sweepstakes attract more entries than do contests. They are also easier and less expensive to administer, since every entry does not have to be checked or judged. Choosing the winning entry in a sweepstakes requires only the random selection of a winner from the pool of entries or generation of a number to match those held by sweepstakes entrants. Experts note that the costs of mounting a sweepstakes are also very predictable. Companies can buy insurance to indemnify them and protect against the expense of awarding a big prize. In general, sweepstakes present marketers with a fixed cost, which is a major advantage when budgeting for a promotion. Exhibit 14–8 shows an ad for a sweepstakes where the prize and brand are closely aligned to build brand equity, another key feature of these promotions.

IMC PERSPECTIVE 14–2

Bring Home the Cup

It's one of the most beloved pieces of sports hardware in the world. Measuring 88 centimetres tall and weighing 15 kilograms, the Stanley Cup is a Canadian icon. "There's a magic around the Stanley Cup—it's a celebrity, really," says Doug Brooks, managing director of corporate marketing in Canada for the NHL. "There's a respect and a reverence there. There's no other trophy in sports that has that mystique." The more than 700 Canadian hockey fans who participated in "Bring Home the Cup" would likely agree. The recent promo for the first time featured hockey's Holy Grail as part of a prize package.

Cashing in on the lofty status the Cup holds with Canadians, the NHL, CBC's *Hockey Night in Canada,* and corporate partners Pepsi, Lay's, and Gatorade launched the program in late March 2007, inviting fans to submit a video or photo showing their ritual for watching NHL playoff hockey and what the Cup means to them. The winner received a $25,000 grand prize package comprising a hockey shrine built in their home designed by *Hockey Night in Canada,* a Samsung HDTV home theatre system, *HNIC* leather chairs and memorabilia, an Xbox 360 game system, and a supply of Pepsi, Lay's, and Gatorade products.

This ultimate playoff party was captured for broadcast during a playoff game on *HNIC,* punctuated by six-time Stanley Cup champion Mark Messier delivering the Holy Grail itself as the guest of honour. The campaign was supported by *HNIC* broadcasts, a dedicated website, retail point-of-purchase creative, and special-edition Pepsi, Lay's, and Gatorade packaging.

"This was more than just a promotion," says Tony Chapman, president and CEO of Capital C, Toronto, the agency behind "Bring Home the Cup." "This struck a powerful emotional chord in so many different ways. It really focused on the ritual which is *Hockey Night in Canada,* and how people watch hockey, with their favourite chair, snacks, the TV." The video entries illustrate the partners' enthusiasm. The time, effort, and money Canadian hockey fans put into taping an homage to their favourite team, tributes to family matriarchs—even making their own primitive version of the Cup—illustrates their connection with NHL hockey.

One of the promotion's challenges was choosing a winner. The public selected 10 finalists, and then a panel of judges from the various partners narrowed it down to the final three. The public then viewed the finalists and voted for the ultimate winner, which was announced during game 2 of the Stanley Cup final featuring the Anaheim Ducks and Ottawa Senators.

The winning entry "True Hockey Spirit" showed the Villamere family of Madawaska, Ontario, and their remote fishing cabin with no running water or electricity where they watch *Hockey Night in Canada* via satellite TV powered by a generator. Unlike the second-place entry, from a Calgary Flames fan in Calgary, and the third-place finisher, a Toronto Maple Leafs fan in Halifax, the Villamere entry was non-partisan and showed how "true hockey spirit prevails."

Underscoring how popular the entries became, the winning submission was viewed online more than 16,000 times, the second-place entry more than 15,000, and the third-place finisher—the long-suffering Leafs fan—a fitting 6,000 views. During the promotion, the website attracted more than 100,000 visitors, 70 percent of them unique, and produced more than 700,000 page views. Finally, "Bring Home the Cup" increased consumer sales for all three companies, although exact data remained confidential.

Source: Wayne Karl, "The Cup Runneth Over," *Marketing Magazine,* August 27, 2007.

Question

1. What characteristics of this promotion made it so attractive for consumers to participate?

Strengths of Contests and Sweepstakes A recent study suggests that sales can be enhanced by trial and repeat purchases through a sweepstakes advertised via in-store ad-pads. A 12-week experiment of 20 mass-merchandiser outlets—10 test and 10 control stores—revealed that a major household product increased its sales by 70 percent in the test stores during the four-week test period compared to the previous four-week period that featured no advertising or promotion. Furthermore, during the posttest four-week period that had no ad-pad, sales hit a 30-percent increase.[33] Clearly, non-customers either recalled the sales promotion and ad message, or new or existing customers returned for a repeat purchase. In either case, the improved communication and behavioural effects of the promotion make it useful for both manufacturers and retailers.

Contests and sweepstakes can involve consumers with a brand by making the promotion product relevant or by connecting the prizes to the lifestyle, needs, or interests of the target audience. Procter & Gamble teamed up with MuchMusic for two contests to promote its Cover Girl brand of makeup. In January 2001, seven lucky winners received a live, on-air makeover with celebrity hair and makeup artists. Another contest, "Prom Night 2001," featured one winner and nine friends receiving a makeover and a limousine ride to their prom, among other prizes.[34]

Contests can be designed to be consistent with the brand positioning strategy used in advertising. Axe deodorant body spray used an unusual skill or ability in its recent contest in Quebec. It sent camera teams to popular clubs and asked men to recite their best "pick-up" lines. Winners received dinner and a shopping spree and their victorious efforts were shown on Musique Plus. While this is certainly provocative, it is quite fitting with the sexual allurement communicated in Axe's recent television commercials.[35]

Limitations of Contests and Sweepstakes While the use of contests and sweepstakes continues to increase, there are some limitations associated with these types of promotions. Many sweepstakes and/or contest promotions do little to contribute to consumer franchise building for a product or service and may even detract from it. The sweepstakes or contest often becomes the dominant focus rather than the brand, and little is accomplished other than giving away substantial amounts of money and/or prizes. Many promotional experts question the effectiveness of contests and sweepstakes. Some companies have cut back or even stopped using them because of concern over their effectiveness and fears that consumers might become dependent on them.[36]

Despite this challenge it is possible to overcome this limitation. O.K. Tire connected to the local community where its dealers are located with a positive consumer-franchise building contest to launch its re-branding strategy. O.K. Tire offered 40 prizes totalling $50,000 to local community groups that were identified on ballots entered at one of the 230 dealerships. Results included current customers filling out many ballots while visiting a dealership for service, new customers acting upon the television and radio ads to try O.K. Tire, increased word-of-mouth communication in many locales, and enhanced personal communication with an emphasis on the dealer as a trusted neighbourhood business.[37]

Numerous legal considerations affect the design and administration of contests and sweepstakes.[38] But companies must still be careful in designing a contest or sweepstakes and awarding prizes. Most firms use consultants that specialize in the design and administration of contests and sweepstakes to avoid any legal problems, but they may still run into problems with promotions.

A final problem with contests and sweepstakes is participation by professionals or hobbyists who submit many entries but have no intention of purchasing the product or service. Because it is illegal to require a purchase as a qualification for a sweepstakes entry, consumers can enter as many times as they wish. Professional players sometimes enter one sweepstakes several times, depending on the nature of the prizes and the number of entries the promotion attracts. Newsletters are even available that inform them of all the contests and sweepstakes being held, the entry dates, estimated probabilities of winning for various numbers of entries, how to enter, and solutions to any puzzles or other information that might be needed. The presence of these professional entrants not only defeats the purpose of the promotion but may also discourage entries from consumers who think their chances of winning are limited.

Refunds and Rebates

Refunds (also known as rebates) are offers by the manufacturer to return a portion of the product purchase price, usually after the consumer supplies some proof of purchase. Consumers are generally very responsive to rebate offers, particularly as the size of the savings increases. Rebates are used by makers of all types of products, ranging from packaged goods to major appliances, cars, and computer software.

Packaged-goods marketers often use refund offers to induce trial of a new product or encourage users of another brand to switch. Consumers may perceive the savings offered through a cash refund as an immediate value that lowers the cost of the item, even though those savings are realized only if the consumer redeems the refund or rebate offer. Redemption rates for refund offers typically range from 1 to 3 percent for print and point-of-purchase offers and 5 percent for in/on package offers.

Refund offers can also encourage repeat purchase. Many offers require consumers to send in multiple proofs of purchase. The size of the refund offer may even increase as the number of purchases gets larger. Some packaged-goods companies are switching away from cash refund offers to coupons or cash/coupon combinations. Using coupons in the refund offer enhances the likelihood of repeat purchase of the brand.

Strengths and Limitations of Refunds and Rebates Rebates can help create new users and encourage brand switching or repeat purchase behaviour, or they can be a way to offer a temporary price reduction. The rebate may be perceived as an immediate savings even though many consumers do not follow through on the offer. This perception can influence purchase even if the consumer fails to realize the savings, so the marketer can reduce price for much less than if it used a direct price-off deal.

Some limitations are associated with refunds and rebates. Many consumers are not motivated by a refund offer because of the delay and the effort required to obtain the savings. They do not want to be bothered saving cash register receipts and proofs of purchase, filling out forms, and mailing in the offer.[39] A study of consumer perceptions found a negative relationship between the use of rebates and the perceived difficulties associated with the redemption process.[40] The study also found that consumers perceive manufacturers as offering rebates to sell products that are not faring well. Nonusers of rebates were particularly likely to perceive the redemption process as too complicated and to suspect manufacturers' motives. This implies that companies using rebates must simplify the redemption process and use other promotional elements such as advertising to retain consumer confidence in the brand.

When small refunds are being offered, marketers may find other promotional incentives such as coupons or bonus packs more effective. They must be careful not to overuse rebate offers and confuse consumers about the real price and value of a product or service. Also, consumers can become dependent on rebates and delay their purchases or purchase only brands for which a rebate is available. Many retailers have become disenchanted with rebates and the burden and expense of administering them.[41]

Exhibit 14–9 Bonus packs provide more value for consumers

Bonus Packs

Bonus packs offer the consumer an extra amount of a product at the regular price by providing larger containers or extra units (Exhibit 14–9). Bonus packs result in a lower cost per unit for the consumer and provide extra value as well as more product for the money. There are several advantages to bonus pack promotions. First, they give marketers a direct way to provide extra value without having to get involved with complicated coupons or refund offers. The additional value of a bonus pack is generally obvious to the consumer and can have a strong impact on the purchase decision at the time of purchase.

Bonus packs can also be an effective defensive manoeuvre against a competitor's promotion or introduction of a new brand. By loading current users with large amounts of its product, a marketer can often remove these consumers from the market and make them less susceptible to a competitor's promotional efforts. Bonus packs may result in larger purchase orders and favourable display space in the store if relationships with retailers are good. They do, however, usually require additional shelf space without providing any extra profit margins for the retailer, so the marketer can encounter problems with bonus packs if trade relationships are not good. Another problem is that bonus packs may appeal primarily to current users who probably would have purchased the brand anyway or to promotion-sensitive consumers who may not become loyal to the brand.

Price-Off Deals

Another consumer sales promotion tool is the direct **price-off deal**, which reduces the price of the brand. Price-off reductions are typically offered right on the package through specially marked price packs, as shown in Exhibit 14–10. Typically, price-offs range from 10 to 25 percent off the regular price, with the reduction coming out of the manufacturer's profit margin, not the retailer's. Keeping the retailer's margin during a price-off promotion maintains its support and cooperation.

Exhibit 14–10 Examples of price-off packages

Marketers use price-off promotions for several reasons. First, since price-offs are controlled by the manufacturer, it can make sure the promotional discount reaches the consumer rather than being kept by the trade. Like bonus packs, price-off deals usually present a readily apparent value to shoppers, especially when they have a reference price point for the brand and thus recognize the value of the discount.[42] So price-offs can be a strong influence at the point of purchase when price comparisons are being made. Price-off promotions can also encourage consumers to purchase larger quantities, preempting competitors' promotions and leading to greater trade support.

Price-off promotions may not be favourably received by retailers, since they can create pricing and inventory problems. Most retailers will not accept packages with a specific price shown, so the familiar X amount off the regular price must be used. Also, like bonus packs, price-off deals appeal primarily to regular users instead of attracting nonusers. Finally, the federal government has regulations regarding the conditions that price-off labels must meet and the frequency and timing of their use.

Frequency Programs

One of the fastest growing areas of sales promotion is the use of **frequency programs** (also referred to as *continuity* or *loyalty programs*). Frequency programs have become commonplace in a number of product and service categories, particularly travel and hospitality, as well as among retailers. Virtually every airline, car rental company, and hotel chain has some type of frequency program. Loyalty programs are also used by a variety of retailers, including grocery stores, department stores, home centres, bookstores, and even local bagel shops.

There are a number of reasons why frequency programs have become so popular. Marketers view these programs as a way of encouraging consumers to use their products or services on a continual basis and as a way of developing strong customer loyalty. Many companies are also realizing the importance of customer retention and understand that the key to retaining and growing market share is building relationships with loyal customers. Frequency programs also provide marketers with the opportunity to develop databases containing valuable information on their customers that can be used to better understand their needs, interests, and characteristics as well

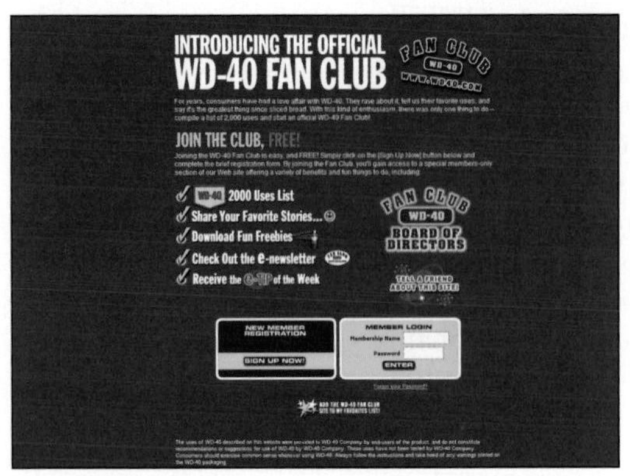

Exhibit 14–11 The WD-40 Fan Club is a popular customer loyalty program

as to identify and track a company's most valuable customers. These databases can also be used to target specific programs and offers to customers to increase the amount they purchase and/or to build stronger relationships with them.

For example, the WD-40 Fan Club is a loyalty program for the brand that provides members with product information, usage tips, newsletters, downloads of games, and other benefits (Exhibit 14–11). The fan club has nearly 70,000 members who educate each other about creative ways to use the solvent and serve as advocates for the brand.[43]

As frequency programs become more common, marketers will be challenged to find ways to use them as a means of differentiating their product, service, business, or retail store. It has been argued that many of the loyalty programs developed by marketers are really short-term promotions that overreward regular users and do little to develop long-term loyalty.[44] A recent study by a loyalty marketing firm found that 66 percent of consumers say that discounts are the main reason they participate in loyalty programs. This study also found that many consumers drop out of loyalty programs because of the length of time it takes to accumulate reward points.[45] Marketers must find ways to make their loyalty programs more than just discount or frequent-buyer programs. This will require the careful management of databases to identify and track valuable customers and their purchase history and the strategic use of targeted loyalty promotions.

Event Marketing

Event marketing has become very popular in recent years. It is important to make a distinction between *event marketing* and *event sponsorships,* as the two terms are often used interchangeably yet they refer to different activities. **Event marketing** is a type of promotion where a company or brand is linked to an event or where a themed activity is developed for the purpose of creating experiences for consumers and promoting a product or service. Event marketing allows marketers to develop integrated marketing programs including promotional tools that create experiences for consumers in an effort to associate their brands with certain lifestyles and activities. Marketers use events to distribute samples as well as information about their products and services or to actually let consumers experience the product. IMC Perspective 14–3 identifies how luxury brands are now using events.

An **event sponsorship** is an integrated marketing communications activity where a company develops actual sponsorship relations with a particular event (e.g., concert, art exhibition, cultural activity, social change, sports) and provides financial support in return for the right to display a brand name, logo, or advertising message and be identified as a supporter of the event. Part of the confusion between these two promotions arises from the fact that event marketing often takes place as part of a company's event sponsorship. We describe examples of the former concept here and address the latter in the next chapter as it more relates to public relations activities.

Two recent events to distribute samples in situations that reinforced their brand positioning strategy achieved great success. Aveeno, a marketer of skin care and moisturizer products, launched its 2004 Snowfest tour with product sampling, a contest, and an "Après Ski" party at 16 ski hills across Canada. Activities such as these

IMC PERSPECTIVE *14–3*

Luxury Products Try Event Marketing

While luxury goods marketers say they aren't abandoning traditional media, they are augmenting it with everything from online to events to "experiential" marketing. BMW Group Canada partnered with Fairmont Hotels & Resorts and luxury travel company Horizon & Co. for a summer promotion called "Cruising the Rockies." It's a high-end vacation package in which consumers pay around $4,000 and drive a BMW Z4 Roadster on a six-day tour through the Rocky Mountains, stopping at exclusive Fairmont resorts in Banff, Lake Louise, and Jasper along the way. It's being promoted through Fairmont Hotels' custom title, *Fairmont Magazine*.

The automaker's events differ depending on the campaign objective. It's supporting its "open-air" line of vehicles—including the Z4 and its 5 Series Cabriolet models—with online sponsorship of the America's Cup yacht race on TSN Broadband, while its xDrive all-wheel drive system is promoted through a series of comparison-drive events taking place in four Canadian cities. These invitation-only events enable participants to test drive BMWs equipped with the xDrive system, as well as competitors' cars, at a closed-track weekend event.

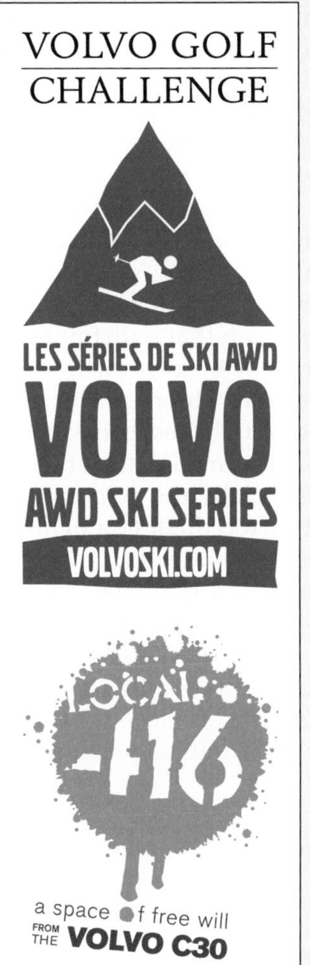

BMW competitor Volvo Cars of Canada, meanwhile, doubled its spending on event marketing in the past year, says president and CEO Steve Blyth. The bulk of those dollars are spent on established events like the Volvo Golf Challenge and Volvo Ski Series, but also includes new events like Local 416. The latter takes place in Toronto and involves artists creating work inspired by the automaker's new C30—a three-door coupe aimed at urban professionals ages 25–35 with no children (a marked contrast to Volvo's line of family-friendly vehicles). Each week for four weeks, the work of one artist, a DJ, and a fashion designer will be featured at a downtown art gallery. The event is being called a "physical extension" of Volvo's global positioning of the car as "a product of free will."

The car company's presence at Local 416 is subtle, says Blyth. "We want to be associated with it, we want to be seen as the hosts, but we don't want to be seen to compromise the arts and the artists." Volvo is launching four new vehicles, which has allowed the company to expand its marketing budget beyond mainstream media. And while daily newspaper and TV advertising is still part of the mix, Blyth echoes by-now familiar sentiments about its efficacy. "Traditional mainstream media is getting more and more cluttered and it's more difficult to get your message through and get any traction," he says. "That's why we've moved to a number of non-traditional media mixes."

Volvo also partnered with Cineplex Entertainment on an online contest built around the third instalment of the *Pirates of the Caribbean* franchise. The car company offered a grand prize of its XC90 SUV, which was promoted through in-theatre ads, along with full-page ads in *Famous* magazine and on websites (and attracted more than 27,000 entrants). Volvo also partnered with the youth-oriented online community iCoke on a promotion offering a C30 as a grand prize. The intention, says Blyth, is to create recognition of the Volvo brand among younger consumers. "There'll come a day when everybody needs to buy a car, I expect, and we'd like them to think Volvo," he says.

Source: Chris Powell, "Rich Media," *Marketing Magazine,* June 25, 2007.

Question

1. What are the strengths of the marketing events of these two brands of luxury automobiles?

can enhance the post-event advertising or can benefit from pre-event advertising. For instance, Aveeno used print and online ads to round out its IMC campaign.[46] An event run by Coffee-Mate was almost an anti-event with a "tease, taste and reveal" approach. It distributed 800,000 free cups of coffee with Coffee-Mate liquid at high-traffic locations (e.g., offices, commuter hubs, arenas) in six Canadian cities. To overcome the Coffee-Mate equals powder association, it did not disclose the brand until after the consumer had tasted the product.[47]

Subaru wanted to get consumers, sales consultants, and media representatives to be familiar with its new brands, Impreza WRX and Outback H6, so it developed the "2001 Subaru National Ride & Drive," its first event-marketing program. Members of each target audience in six Canadian cities (Quebec City, Montreal, Toronto, Calgary, Edmonton, and Vancouver) could test-drive the vehicles and talk to key Subaru employees.

Subaru enlisted more than 5,000 candidates through auto-show response cards and its website. From that enlistment, 3,000 qualified individuals received a direct-mail invitation to the event, of which 77 percent responded positively versus a 50- to 60-percent objective. The event included a classroom-style seminar, a vehicle and course walk-around, the test drive, and a demonstration by professional drivers with participants in the car. Subaru obtained enthusiastic written and verbal feedback on the event, especially the demonstration, and gave a thank-you card to all participants, which directed them to a dedicated website that had photos of the event.

The information received continued in the selling process. All information was passed on to the respective dealerships along with highlights of the event (e.g., statistics, photos). The program resulted in a 3 percent participant-to-sales conversion rate in the first six weeks; given the nature of car purchases, additional sales may be forthcoming to improve this ratio. Other statistics show the value of event marketing as post-event purchasing desires increased over the pre-event numbers, and 61 percent of all participants claimed that they would visit a Subaru dealership.[48]

Trade Sales Promotion

Objectives of Trade Sales Promotion

Like consumer promotions, sales promotion programs targeted to the trade should be based on well-defined objectives and measurable goals and a consideration of what the marketer wants to accomplish. Typical objectives for promotions targeted to marketing intermediaries such as wholesalers and retailers include obtaining distribution for new products, maintaining trade support for established brands, building retail inventories, and encouraging retailers to display established brands.

Obtain Distribution for New Products Trade promotions are often used to encourage retailers to give shelf space to new products. Essentially, this translates into a trial purchase objective like we saw with consumer promotions. Manufacturers recognize that only a limited amount of shelf space is available in supermarkets, drugstores, and other major retail outlets. Thus, they provide retailers with financial incentives to stock new products. For example, Lever Brothers used heavy sampling and high-value coupons in the successful introduction of Lever 2000 bar soap. However, in addition to these consumer promotions, the company used discounts to the trade to encourage retailers to stock and promote the new brand.

While trade discounts or other special price deals are used to encourage retailers and wholesalers to stock a new brand, marketers may use other types of promotions to get them to push the brand. Merchandising allowances can get retailers to display a new product in high-traffic areas of stores, while incentive programs or contests can encourage wholesale or retail store personnel to push a new brand.

Maintain Trade Support for Established Brands Trade promotions are often designed to maintain distribution and trade support for established brands. Clearly, this objective is akin to a repeat purchase objective that we saw with consumer sales promotion. Brands that are in the mature phase of their product life cycle are vulnerable to losing wholesale and/or retail distribution, particularly if they are not differentiated or face competition from new products. Trade deals induce wholesalers and retailers to continue to carry weaker products because the discounts increase their profit margins. Brands with a smaller market share often rely heavily on trade promotions, since they lack the funds required to differentiate themselves from competitors through media advertising. Even if a brand has a strong market position, trade promotions may be used as part of an overall marketing strategy.

Build Retail Inventories Manufacturers often use trade promotions to build the inventory levels of retailers or other channel members, another form of repeat purchasing. There are several reasons why manufacturers want to load retailers with their products. First, wholesalers and retailers are more likely to push a product when they have high inventory levels rather than storing it in their warehouses or back rooms. Building channel members' inventories also ensures they will not run out of stock and thus miss sales opportunities.

Some manufacturers of seasonal products offer large promotional discounts so that retailers will stock up on their products before the peak selling season begins. This enables the manufacturer to smooth out seasonal fluctuations in its production schedule and passes on some of the inventory carrying costs to retailers or wholesalers. When retailers stock up on a product before the peak selling season, they often run special promotions and offer discounts to consumers to reduce excess inventories.

Encourage Retailers to Display Established Brands Another objective of trade-oriented promotions is to encourage retailers to display and promote an established brand. This could be analogous to increased consumption as seen with consumer sales promotion objectives since the retailer demonstrates increased commitment. Marketers recognize that many purchase decisions are made in the store and promotional displays are an excellent way of generating sales. An important goal is to obtain retail store displays of a product away from its regular shelf location. A typical supermarket has approximately 50 display areas at the ends of aisles, near checkout counters, and elsewhere. Marketers want to have their products displayed in these areas to increase the probability shoppers will come into contact with them. Even a single display can increase a brand's sales significantly during a promotion.

Manufacturers often use multifaceted promotional programs to encourage retailers to promote their products at the retail level. For example, a manufacturer will combine its advertising and consumer sales promotions and offer them at the same time as the trade promotion.

Trade Sales Promotion Strategy Options

Manufacturers use a variety of trade promotion tools as inducements for wholesalers and retailers. Next we examine some of the most often used types of trade promotions and some factors marketers must consider in using them. These promotions include contests and incentives, events, trade allowances, point-of-purchase displays, sales training programs, trade shows, and cooperative advertising.

Contests and Incentives Manufacturers may develop contests or special incentive programs to stimulate greater selling effort and support from reseller management or sales personnel. Contests or incentive programs can be directed toward managers who work for a wholesaler or distributor as well as toward store or department managers at the retail level. Manufacturers often sponsor contests for resellers and use prizes such as trips or valuable merchandise as rewards for meeting sales quotas or other goals.

FIGURE *14–7*

Three forms of promotion targeted to reseller salespeople

- **Product or Program Sales**
  Awards are tied to the selling of a product, for example:
  Selling a specified number of cases
  Selling a specified number of units
  Selling a specified number of promotional programs
- **New Account Placements**
  Awards are tied to:
  The number of new accounts opened
  The number of new accounts ordering a minimum number of cases or units
  Promotional programs placed in new accounts
- **Merchandising Efforts**
  Awards are tied to:
  Establishing promotional programs (such as theme programs)
  Placing display racks, counter displays, and the like

Contests or special incentives are often targeted at the sales personnel of the wholesalers, distributors/dealers, or retailers. These salespeople are an important link in the distribution chain because they are likely to be very familiar with the market, more frequently in touch with the customer (whether it be another reseller or the ultimate consumer), and more numerous than the manufacturer's own sales organization. Manufacturers often devise incentives or contests for these sales personnel. These programs may involve cash payments made directly to the retailer's or wholesaler's sales staff to encourage them to promote and sell a manufacturer's product. These payments are known as **push money** (pm) or *spiffs.* For example, an appliance manufacturer may pay a $25 spiff to retail sales personnel for selling a certain model or size. In sales contests, salespeople can win trips or valuable merchandise for meeting certain goals established by the manufacturer. As shown in Figure 14–7, these incentives may be tied to product sales, new account placements, or merchandising efforts.

While contests and incentive programs can generate reseller support, they can also be a source of conflict between retail sales personnel and management. Some retailers want to maintain control over the selling activities of their sales staff. They don't want their salespeople devoting an undue amount of effort to trying to win a contest or receive incentives offered by the manufacturer. Nor do they want their people becoming too aggressive in pushing products that serve their own interests instead of the product or model that is best for the customer.

Events Often event marketing or event sponsorship programs directed to consumers are also linked to the trade as a way to foster good relationships among channel members and to enhance merchandising activities. For example, a tour of famous figure skaters—Kurt Browning, Elvis Stojko, Brian Orser, Isabelle Brasseur, Lloyd Eisler, Jose Chouinard, and Shae-Lynn Bourne—performed in many small Canadian cities with sponsorship from Procter & Gamble's Nice'n Easy brand of hair colouring for women. Usually, people in many of these towns did not have the opportunity to see such shows and P&G felt a need to more directly connect with markets that had strong consumer acceptance for this product. As part of the sponsorship, P&G ran various promotions with its retail distributors and customized the programs to meet their respective needs in addition to the usual contests and incentives. Zellers, Loblaws, and Shoppers Drug Mart hosted in-store autograph sessions. Wal-Mart organized tickets for the Children's Miracle Network and skating seminars for local clubs.[49]

Trade Allowances Probably the most common trade promotion is some form of **trade allowance**, a discount or deal offered to retailers or wholesalers to encourage them to promote, display, or stock the manufacturer's products. Types of allowances offered to retailers include buying allowances, promotional or display allowances, and slotting allowances.

Buying Allowances A buying allowance is a deal or discount offered to resellers in the form of a price reduction on merchandise ordered during a fixed period. These discounts are often in the form of an **off-invoice allowance**, which means a certain per-case amount or percentage is deducted from the invoice. A buying allowance can also take the form of *free goods*; the reseller gets extra cases with the purchase of specific amounts (for example, 1 free case with every 10 cases purchased).

Buying allowances are used for several reasons. They are easy to implement and are well accepted, and sometimes expected, by the trade. They are also an effective way to encourage resellers to buy the manufacturer's product, since they will want to take advantage of the discounts being offered during the allowance period. Manufacturers offer trade discounts expecting wholesalers and retailers to pass the price reduction through to consumers, resulting in greater sales. However, as discussed shortly, this is often not the case.

Promotional (Display) Allowances Manufacturers often give retailers allowances or discounts for performing certain promotional or merchandising activities in support of their brands. These merchandising allowances can be given for providing special displays away from the product's regular shelf position, running in-store promotional programs, or including the product in an ad. The manufacturer generally has guidelines or a contract specifying the activity to be performed to qualify for the promotional allowance. The allowance is usually a fixed amount per case or a percentage deduction from the list price for merchandise ordered during the promotional period.

Slotting Allowances Retailers often demand a special allowance for agreeing to accept a new product. *Slotting allowances,* also called *stocking allowances, introductory allowances,* or *street money*, are fees retailers charge for providing a slot or position to accommodate the new product. Retailers justify these fees by pointing out the costs associated with taking on so many new products each year, such as redesigning store shelves, entering the product into their computers, finding warehouse space, and briefing store employees on the new product.[50] They also note they are assuming some risk, since so many new product introductions fail.

Slotting fees can range from a few hundred dollars per store to $50,000 or more for an entire retail chain. Manufacturers that want to get their products on the shelves nationally can face several million dollars in slotting fees. Many marketers believe slotting allowances are not appropriate and say some 70 percent of these fees go directly to retailers' bottom lines. Retailers can continue charging slotting fees because of their power and the limited availability of shelf space in supermarkets relative to the large numbers of products introduced each year. Large manufacturers with popular brands are less likely to pay slotting fees than smaller companies that lack leverage in negotiating with retailers.

A recent study by Paul Bloom, Gregory Gundlach, and Joseph Cannon examined the views of manufacturers, wholesalers, and grocery retailers regarding the use of slotting fees. Their findings suggest that slotting fees shift the risk of new product introductions from retailers to manufacturers and help apportion the supply and demand of new products. They also found that slotting fees lead to higher retail prices, are applied in a discriminatory fashion, and place small marketers at a disadvantage.[51]

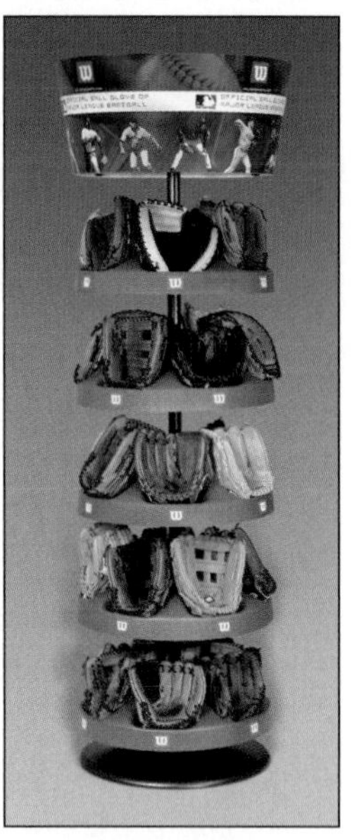

Exhibit 14–12
This award-winning point-of-purchase display plays an important role in the merchandising of Wilson

Problems with Trade Allowances Marketers give retailers these trade allowances so that the savings will be passed through to consumers in the form of lower prices, but companies such as Procter & Gamble claim that only 30 percent of trade promotion discounts actually reach consumers because 35 percent is lost in inefficiencies and another 35 percent is pocketed by retailers and wholesalers. Moreover, many marketers believe that the trade is taking advantage of their promotional deals and misusing promotional funds.

For example, retailers and wholesalers engage in a practice known as **forward buying**, where they stock up on a product at the lower deal or off-invoice price and resell it to consumers after the marketer's promotional period ends. Another common practice is **diverting**, where a retailer or wholesaler takes advantage of the promotional deal and then sells some of the product purchased at the low price to a store outside its area or to an intermediary who resells it to other stores.

In addition to not passing discounts on to consumers, forward buying and diverting create other problems for manufacturers. They lead to huge swings in demand that cause production scheduling problems and leave manufacturers and retailers always building toward or drawing down from a promotional surge. Marketers also worry that the system leads to frequent price specials, so consumers learn to make purchases on the basis of what's on sale rather than developing any loyalty to their brands.

The problems created by forward buying and diverting led Procter & Gamble, one of the country's most powerful consumer products marketers, to adopt **everyday low pricing (EDLP)**, which lowers the list price of over 60 percent of its product line by 10 to 25 percent while cutting promotional allowances to the trade. The price cuts leave the overall cost of the product to retailers about the same as it would have been with the various trade allowance discounts. Although some retailers reacted negatively to this strategy, P&G claimed success and continued with the plan internationally.[52]

Point-of-Purchase Displays Point-of-purchase displays are an important promotional tool because they can help advertisers obtain more effective in-store merchandising of products. In one sense, a display acts as a "medium" since it is an important method of transmitting an advertising-like message when consumers are making a purchase decision. In fact, the Point of Purchase Advertising Institute (POPAI) estimates that approximately two-thirds of consumers' purchase decisions are made in the store; some impulse categories demonstrate an 80-percent rate.[53] We put medium in quotes because often many types of displays do not appear to be typical media; in fact, however, a display shares similar characteristics with place-based media (discussed in Chapter 13). A display is also viewed as a sales promotion since many of the messages include a sales promotion and most require the participation of retailers that necessitates a payment that is often recorded as a trade promotion expense in the budget. Figure 14–8 identifies many types of point-of-purchase displays; Exhibit 14–12 shows a point-of-purchase display for Wilson baseball gloves.

It's easy to see why advertisers use point-of-purchase displays extensively. The main purpose is to reach the target audience while they are making the brand choice, so naturally a message or promotion attempting to influence a decider appears imperative. Indeed, key or deterministic benefits can be communicated just prior

FIGURE *14–8*

Types of point-of-purchase displays

On-premise sign	Pre-assembled display	Display card	TV display
Window display	Display shipper	Shelf sign	LED board
Modular display rack	Wall display	Stand-up rack	End-of-aisle display

to purchase as these benefits may become salient only during the final choice decision. Recent innovations in point-of-purchase options—such as video screens at cash registers—attempt to bring the emotion of television commercials to the store environment so that consumers feel the same way just prior to purchasing the product. Since consumers are in the process of shopping, point-of-sale media have a tremendous opportunity for attracting the attention of the target audience. In general, consumers are seeking additional information or sensory experience as they consider the product selection. Coverage objectives also can be achieved by distributing point-of-purchase displays across the country through retail chains. For example, a brand could have displays in virtually all grocery stores at the same time with placement agreed among personnel at a few head offices. A key strength of point-of-sale display is that it is communicating to virtually all people who are considering purchasing in a particular category except those going direct through the Internet or catalogues. It may be difficult to suggest that point-of-purchase displays are universally involving. However, it appears reasonable to suggest that if the target audience has not avoided a certain part of the store and also paid attention to a display, then the potential is strong that the relevant messages will resonate such that a sufficient amount of consideration will be given. And finally, the absolute cost and CPM are generally reasonable compared to other media options.

Despite these strengths, point-of-purchase displays have limitations. One source of discontent for a consumer is that shopping experience may be hindered by many promotional messages. Consumers have complete control over where they want to look in a store, how much time they prefer to stay in one area, and whether they want to look at any form of in-store communication. If an advertiser desires to be there, so does the competition. The clutter consumers feel while watching television or reading a magazine may be felt in the purchase environment. Processing of point-of-sale media requires a consumer's presence in the retail environment. So, except for circumstances where a consumer is entering an establishment repeatedly, the likelihood of an advertiser achieving sufficient frequency through this medium is quite limited. Finally, a marketer is reliant on the retailer, who may not install or set up the display correctly and also requires payment.

Sales Training Programs Another form of manufacturer-sponsored promotional assistance is sales training programs for reseller personnel. Many products sold at the retail level require knowledgeable salespeople who can provide consumers with information about the features, benefits, and advantages of various brands and models (e.g., cosmetics, appliances, computers). Manufacturers provide sales training assistance to retail salespeople through training sessions so that retail personnel can increase their knowledge of a product or a product line. These training sessions present information and ideas on how to sell the manufacturer's product and may also include motivational components.

Manufacturers also provide sales training assistance to retail employees through their own salesforce. Sales reps educate retail personnel about their product line and provide selling tips and other relevant information. The reps can provide ongoing sales training as they come into contact with retail sales staff on a regular basis and can update them on changes in the product line. Sales reps often provide resellers sales manuals, product brochures, reference manuals, and other material. Many companies provide videos for retail sales personnel that include product information, product-use demonstrations, and ideas on how to sell their product. These selling aids can often be used to provide information to customers as well.

Trade Shows Another important promotional activity targeted to resellers is the **trade show**, a forum where manufacturers can display their products to current as well as prospective buyers. According to the Trade Show Bureau, nearly 100 million people attend the 5,000 trade shows each year in the United States and Canada, and the number of exhibiting companies exceeds 1.3 million. In many industries, trade shows are a

Exhibit 14–13 The "Intel Inside" cooperative advertising program has been extremely successful

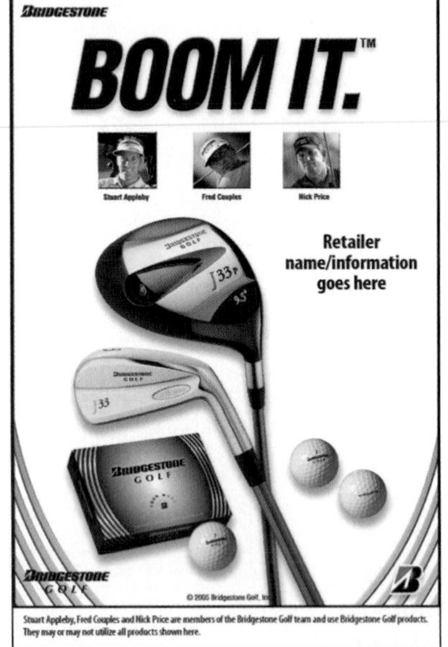

Exhibit 14–14 This Bridgestone Golf ad is an example of vertical cooperative advertising

major opportunity to display one's product lines and interact with customers. They are often attended by important management personnel from large retail chains as well as by distributors and other reseller representatives.

A number of promotional functions can be performed at trade shows, including demonstrating products, identifying new prospects, gathering customer and competitive information, and even writing orders for a product. Trade shows are particularly valuable for introducing new products, because resellers are often looking for new merchandise to stock. Shows can also be a source of valuable leads to follow up on through sales calls or direct marketing. The social aspect of trade shows is also important. Many companies use them to entertain key customers and to develop and maintain relationships with the trade. A recent academic study demonstrated that trade shows generate product awareness and interest and can have a measurable economic return.[54]

Cooperative Advertising The final form of trade-oriented promotion we examine is **cooperative advertising**, where the cost of advertising is shared by more than one party. There are three types of cooperative advertising. Although the first two are not trade-oriented promotion, we should recognize their objectives and purpose.

Horizontal cooperative advertising is advertising sponsored in common by a group of retailers or other organizations providing products or services to the market. For example, automobile dealers who are located near one another often allocate some of their ad budgets to a cooperative advertising fund. Ads are run promoting the location of the dealerships and encouraging car buyers to take advantage of their close proximity when shopping for a new automobile.

Ingredient-sponsored cooperative advertising is supported by raw materials manufacturers; its objective is to help establish end products that include the company's materials and/or ingredients. Companies that often use this type of advertising include DuPont, which promotes the use of its materials such as Teflon, Thinsulate, and Kevlar in a variety of consumer and industrial products, and NutraSweet, whose artificial sweetener is an ingredient in many food products and beverages. Perhaps the best-known, and most successful, example of this type of cooperative advertising is the "Intel Inside" program, sponsored by Intel Corporation (Exhibit 14–13).

The most common form of cooperative advertising is **vertical cooperative advertising**, in which a manufacturer pays for a portion of the advertising a retailer runs to promote the manufacturer's product and its availability in the retailer's place of business. Manufacturers generally share the cost of advertising run by the retailer on a percentage basis (usually 50/50) up to a certain limit.

The amount of cooperative advertising the manufacturer pays for is usually based on a percentage of dollar purchases. If a retailer purchases $100,000 of product from a manufacturer, it may receive 3 percent, or $3,000, in cooperative advertising money. Large retail chains often combine their co-op budgets across all of their stores, which gives them a larger sum to work with and more media options.

Cooperative advertising can take on several forms. Retailers may advertise a manufacturer's product in, say, a newspaper ad featuring a number of different products, and the individual manufacturers reimburse the retailer for their portion of the ad. Or the ad may be prepared by the manufacturer and placed in the local media by the retailer. Exhibit 14–14 shows a cooperative ad format that retailers can use by simply inserting their store name and location.

Once a cooperative ad is run, the retailer requests reimbursement from the manufacturer for its percentage of the media costs. Manufacturers usually have specific requirements the ad must meet to qualify for co-op reimbursement, such as size, use of trademarks, content, and format. Verification that the ad was run is also required, in the form of a tearsheet (print) or an affidavit from the radio or TV station (broadcast) and an invoice.

As with other types of trade promotions, manufacturers have been increasing their cooperative advertising expenditures in recent years. Some companies have been moving money out of national advertising into cooperative advertising because they believe they can have greater impact with ad campaigns in local markets. There is also a trend toward more cooperative advertising programs initiated by retailers, which approach manufacturers with catalogues, promotional events they are planning, or advertising programs they have developed in conjunction with local media and ask them to pay a percentage of the cost. Manufacturers often go along with these requests, particularly when the retailer is large and powerful.[55]

IMC Planning: Strategic Use of Sales Promotion

Rather than separate activities competing for a firm's promotional budget, advertising and sales promotion should be viewed as complementary tools. When properly planned and executed to work together, advertising and sales promotion can have a more complete and persuasive communication effect that is much greater than that of either promotional mix element alone. Proper coordination of advertising and sales promotion is essential for the firm to take advantage of the opportunities offered by each tool and get the most out of its promotional budget. Successful integration of advertising and sales promotion requires decisions concerning not only the allocation of the budget to each area but also the coordination of the ad and sales promotion themes, the timing of the various promotional activities, the brand equity implications of sales promotion, and the measuring of sales promotion effectiveness.

Budget Allocation

While many companies are spending more money on sales promotion than on media advertising, it is difficult to say just what percentage of a firm's overall promotional budget should be allocated to advertising versus consumer and trade promotions. This allocation depends on a number of factors, including the specific promotional objectives of the campaign, the market and competitive situation, and the brand's stage in its life cycle.

Consider, for example, how allocation of the promotional budget may vary according to a brand's stage in the product life cycle. In the introductory stage, a large amount of the budget may be allocated to sales promotion techniques such as sampling and couponing to induce trial. In the growth stage, however, promotional dollars may be used primarily for advertising to stress brand differences and keep the brand name in consumers' minds.

When a brand moves to the maturity stage, advertising is primarily a reminder to keep consumers aware of the brand. Consumer sales promotions such as coupons, price-offs, premiums, and bonus packs may be needed periodically to maintain consumer loyalty, attract new users, and protect against competition. Trade promotions are needed to maintain shelf space and accommodate retailers' demands for better margins as well as encourage them to promote the brand. A study on the synergistic effects of advertising and promotion examined a brand in the mature phase of its life cycle and found that 80 percent of its sales at this stage were due to sales promotions. When a brand enters the decline stage of the product life cycle, most of the promotional support will probably be removed and expenditures on sales promotion are unlikely.

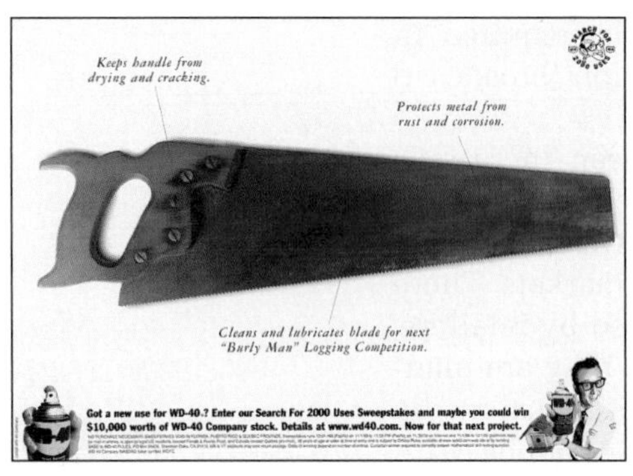

Exhibit 14–15 This WD-40 ad promotes the 2000 Uses Sweepstakes and is consistent with the positioning theme used for the brand

Creative Themes

To integrate the advertising and sales promotion programs successfully, the theme of consumer promotions should be tied in with the advertising and positioning theme wherever possible. Sales promotion tools should attempt to communicate a brand's unique attributes or benefits and to reinforce the sales message or campaign theme. In this way, the sales promotion effort contributes to the consumer franchise-building effort for the brand.

At the same time, media advertising should be used to draw attention to a sales promotion program such as a contest, sweepstakes, or event or to a special promotion offer such as a price reduction or rebate program. An example of a successful consumer brand-building promotion is the Search for 2000 Uses Sweepstakes promotion for WD-40, shown in Exhibit 14–15. The WD-40 Company positions its brand as the leading multipurpose problem solver that cleans, protects, penetrates, lubricates, and displaces moisture like no other product on earth. The marketing strategy for WD-40 is to continually promote the product's myriad uses. The Search for 2000 Uses Sweepstakes, which was launched to coincide with the new millennium, asked consumers to suggest their use for WD-40 in order to be entered for a chance to win various prizes, such as WD-40 can radios, T-shirts, baseball caps, and a grand prize of $10,000 in company stock. The sweepstakes reinforced WD-40's image as a multipurpose problem solver and also encouraged consumers to visit the company's website to enter their use.

Media Support

Media support for a sales promotion program is critical and should be coordinated with the media program for the ad campaign. Media advertising is often needed to deliver such sales promotion materials as coupons, sweepstakes, contest entry forms, premium offers, and even samples. It is also needed to inform consumers of a promotional offer as well as to create awareness, interest, and favourable attitudes toward the brand.

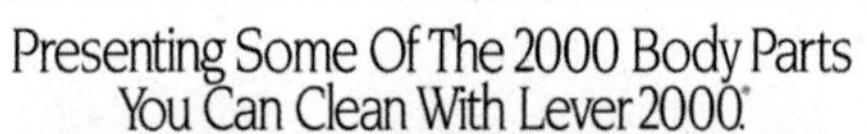

Exhibit 14–16 Creative advertising was coordinated with sales promotion in the successful introduction of Lever 2000 soap

By using advertising in conjunction with a sales promotion program, marketers can make consumers aware of the brand and its benefits and increase their responsiveness to the promotion. Consumers are more likely to redeem a coupon or respond to a price-off deal for a brand they are familiar with than one they know nothing about. Moreover, product trial created through sales promotion techniques such as sampling or high-value couponing is more likely to result in long-term use of the brand when accompanied by advertising.[56]

Using a promotion without prior or concurrent advertising can limit its effectiveness and risk damaging the brand's image. If consumers perceive the brand as being promotion dependent or of lesser quality, they are not likely to develop favourable attitudes and long-term loyalty. Conversely, the effectiveness of an ad can be enhanced by a coupon, a premium offer, or an opportunity to enter a sweepstakes or contest.

An example of the effective coordination of advertising and sales promotion is the introduction of Lever 2000 bar soap. The campaign used high-value coupons, sent samples, and offered discounts to retailers as part of its initial marketing blitz. These sales promotion efforts were accompanied by heavy advertising in print and TV with the tagline "Presenting some of the 2000 body parts you can clean with Lever 2000" (Exhibit 14–16).

Traditional	New and Improved
1. Primarily used to develop short-term tactics or concepts.	1. Used to develop long- and short-term promotional strategies as well as tactics.
2. Hired/compensated on a project-by-project basis.	2. Contracted on annual retainer, following formal agency reviews.
3. Many promotion agencies used a mix—each one hired for best task and/or specialty.	3. One or two exclusive promotion agencies for each division or brand group.
4. One or two contact people from agency.	4. Full team or core group on the account.
5. Promotion agency never equal to ad agency—doesn't work up front in annual planning process.	5. Promotion agency works on equal basis with ad agency—sits at planning table up front.
6. Not directly accountable for results.	6. Very much accountable—goes through a rigorous evaluation process.

FIGURE *14–9*

The shifting role of the promotion agency

Sales promotion was important in inducing trial for Lever 2000 and continued after introduction in the form of couponing. But it was the strong positioning created through effective advertising that converted consumers to regular users. Repeat sales of the brand were at about 40 percent even after heavy discounting ended. Just six months after its introduction, Lever 2000 became the number-two deodorant soap in dollar volume, with an estimated 8.4 percent of the bar-soap market.[57]

To coordinate their advertising and sales promotion programs more effectively, many companies are getting their sales promotion agencies more involved in the advertising and promotional planning process. Rather than hiring agencies to develop individual, nonfranchise-building types of promotions with short-term goals and tactics, many firms are having their sales promotion and advertising agencies work together to develop integrated promotional strategies and programs. Figure 14–9 shows how the role of sales promotion agencies is changing.

Brand Equity

The increasing use of sales promotion in marketing programs is a fundamental change in strategic decisions about how companies market their products and services. The value of this increased emphasis on sales promotion has been questioned by several writers, particularly with regard to the lack of adequate planning and management of sales promotion programs.[58] These concerns lead some to believe that sales promotion can be overused by too much frequency, too valuable an economic offering, or offering too many promotions.

Overuse of sales promotion can be detrimental to a brand in several ways. A brand that is constantly promoted may lose perceived value. Consumers often end up purchasing a brand because it is on sale, they get a premium, or they have a coupon, rather than basing their decision on a favourable attitude they have developed. When the extra promotional incentive is not available, they switch to another brand. A recent study by Priya Raghubir and Kim Corfman examined whether price promotions affect pretrial evaluations of a brand.[59] They found that offering a price promotion is more likely to lower a brand's evaluation when the brand has not been promoted previously compared to when it has been frequently promoted; that price promotions are used as a source of information about a brand to a greater extent when the evaluator is not an expert but does have some product or industry knowledge; and that promotions are more likely to result in negative evaluations when they are uncommon in the industry. The findings from this study suggest that marketers must be careful in the use of price promotions as they may inhibit trial of a brand in certain situations.

Alan Sawyer and Peter Dickson have used the concept of *attribution theory* to examine how sales promotion may affect consumer attitude formation.[60] According to this theory, people acquire attitudes by observing their own behaviour and considering why they acted in a certain manner. Consumers who consistently purchase a brand because of a coupon or price-off deal may attribute their behaviour to the external promotional incentive rather than to a favourable attitude toward the brand. By contrast, when no external incentive is available, consumers are more likely to attribute their purchase behaviour to favourable underlying feelings about the brand.

Another potential problem with consumer-oriented promotions is that a **sales promotion trap** or spiral can result when several competitors use promotions extensively.[61] Often a firm begins using sales promotions to differentiate its product or service from the competition. If the promotion is successful and leads to a differential advantage (or even appears to do so), competitors may quickly copy it. When all the competitors are using sales promotions, this not only lowers profit margins for each firm but also makes it difficult for any one firm to hop off the promotional bandwagon.[62] This dilemma is shown in Figure 14–10. A number of industries have fallen into this promotional trap. In the cosmetics industry, gift-with-purchase and purchase-with-purchase promotional offers were developed as a tactic for getting buyers to sample new products. But they have become a common, and costly, way of doing business.[63]

Marketers must consider both the short-term impact of a promotion and its long-term effect on the brand. The ease with which competitors can develop a retaliatory promotion and the likelihood of their doing so should also be considered. Marketers must be careful not to damage the brand franchise with sales promotions or to get the firm involved in a promotional war that erodes the brand's profit margins and threatens its long-term existence. Marketers are often tempted to resort to sales promotions to deal with declining sales and other problems when they should examine such other aspects of the marketing program as channel relations, price, packaging, product quality, or advertising.

FIGURE *14–10*

The sales promotion trap

All Other Firms	Our Firm: Cut back promotions	Our Firm: Maintain promotions
Cut back promotions	Higher profits for all	Market share goes to our firm
Maintain promotions	Market share goes to all other firms	Market share stays constant; profits stay low

Measuring Sales Promotion Effectiveness

Elizabeth Gardener and Minakshi Trivedi offer a communications framework to allow managers to evaluate sales promotion strategies over a given set of specific criteria. Borrowing from advertising applications, and using four communications goals—attention, comprehension (understanding), persuasion, and purchase—the researchers show the impact of four promotional tools and everyday low pricing (EDLP) on each goal (Figure 14–11). In addition, the impact of everyday low pricing, Procter & Gamble's strategy for discontinuing the use of sales promotions, is also discussed in the article.[64]

The implication of this study is that sales promotions can be evaluated with a framework similar to the one we summarized in Chapter 4. Much of the advertising research methods and measures discussed in Chapter 8 can be used in the context of sales promotions. For example, pre- or post-surveys can be used to assess brand awareness or brand attitude (i.e., attribute or benefit beliefs) associated with the sales promotion. Furthermore, assessment of attention, cognitive, and emotional responses of the promotional offer can also be measured with the appropriate method. From a behavioural standpoint, measurement of switching and loyalty is assessed with scanner data. Other aspects of behaviour can be measured by counting the number of inquiries, coupon redemptions, and contest entries.

FIGURE *14–11* Conceptual framework analysis

		Communication Factors			
		Attention/ Impression	Communication/ Understanding	Persuasion	Purchase
Sales Promotions	FSI coupons	33	333	33	33
	On-shelf coupons	333	333	333	333
	On-pack promotions	3	3	33	3
	Bonus packs	333	33	33	33
	EDLP	3	33	33	3

Promotional tendency to fulfill factor: 333 = Strong; 33 = Moderate; 3 = Weak

SUMMARY

Over the past decade, marketers have been allocating more of their promotional dollars to sales promotion to influence consumers' purchase behaviour. Some reasons for this shift include the strategic importance of sales promotions, reaching a specific target audience, increased promotional sensitivity, declining brand loyalty, brand proliferation, short-term focus and increased accountability of promotional managers, and growing power of retailers and the competition.

Sales promotions can be characterized as either franchise building or nonfranchise building. The former contribute to the long-term development and reinforcement of brand identity and image; the latter are designed to accelerate the purchase process and generate immediate increases in sales.

Sales promotion techniques can be classified as either trade or consumer oriented. A number of consumer sales promotion techniques were examined in this chapter, including sampling, couponing, premiums, contests and sweepstakes, refunds and rebates, bonus packs, price-off deals, frequency programs, and event marketing. The characteristics of these promotional tools were examined, along with their strengths and limitations. Various trade promotions were also examined, including trade contests and incentives, trade allowances, point-of-purchase displays, sales training programs, trade shows, and cooperative advertising.

Advertising and sales promotion should not be viewed as separate activities but rather as complementary tools. When planned and executed properly, advertising and sales promotion can produce a synergistic effect that is greater than the response generated from either promotional mix element alone. To accomplish this, marketers must coordinate budgets, advertising and promotional themes, media scheduling and timing, and target audiences.

Sales promotion abuse can result when marketers become too dependent on the use of sales promotion techniques and sacrifice long-term brand position and image for short-term sales increases. Many industries experience sales promotion traps when a number of competitors use promotions extensively and it becomes difficult for any single firm to cut back on promotion without risking a loss in sales. Overuse of sales promotion tools can lower profit margins and threaten the image and even the viability of a brand.

KEY TERMS

account-specific marketing, *414*
bonus packs, *432*
bounce-back coupon, *426*
consumer franchise-building (CFB) promotions, *416*
consumer sales promotion, *409*
contest, *429*
cooperative advertising, *442*
cross-ruff coupon, *426*
diverting, *440*
event marketing, *434*
event sponsorship, *434*
everyday low pricing (EDLP), *440*
forward buying, *440*
frequency programs, *433*
game, *429*
horizontal cooperative advertising, *442*
ingredient-sponsored cooperative advertising, *442*
instant coupon, *426*
in-store couponing, *426*
multiple methods *422*
nonfranchise-building (non-FB) promotions, *416*
off-invoice allowance, *439*
operant conditioning, *417*
premium, *427*
price-off deal, *433*
promotional pull strategy, *410*
promotional push strategy, *409*
push money, *438*
refund, *432*
sales promotion, *408*
sales promotion trap, *446*
sampling, *420*
schedules of reinforcement, *418*
self-liquidating premiums, *428*
shaping, *418*
sweepstakes, *429*
trade advertising, *410*
trade allowance, *439*
trade sales promotion, *409*
trade show, *441*
vertical cooperative advertising, *442*

DISCUSSION QUESTIONS

1. What are the differences between consumer and trade sales promotion? Discuss the role of each in a marketer's IMC program.

2. Discuss how sales promotion can be used as an acceleration tool to speed up the sales process and maximize sales volume.

3. Discuss the factors that have led to companies shifting more of their marketing budgets to sales promotion. Discuss the pros and cons of this reallocation of marketers' advertising and promotion budgets.

4. What are the differences between consumer franchise-building and nonfranchise-building promotions? Find an example of a promotional offer you believe contributes to the equity of a brand and explain why.

5. Discuss how sales promotion progress can be integrated with a company's online strategy and how the Internet can be used as part of a company's sales promotion efforts.

6. What is meant by a sales promotion trap? Find an example of an industry where a promotional war is currently taking place. What are the options for a marketer involved in such a situation?

7. Canadian Tire and Pillsbury used an aspect of their brand for a sales promotion for the first time ever. Does this damage the brand at all in light of some concerns about sales promotion raised in this chapter? What other brand has a long-standing icon that could be used for a sales promotion?

8. Explain why it is important for sales promotion to contribute to brand equity. In what circumstances will brand equity enhancement not be a priority?

9. The number of coupons directed to consumers grew significantly in recent years. Discuss why this occurred based on issues of distribution, redemption, profitability, type of coupon, and expiration date.

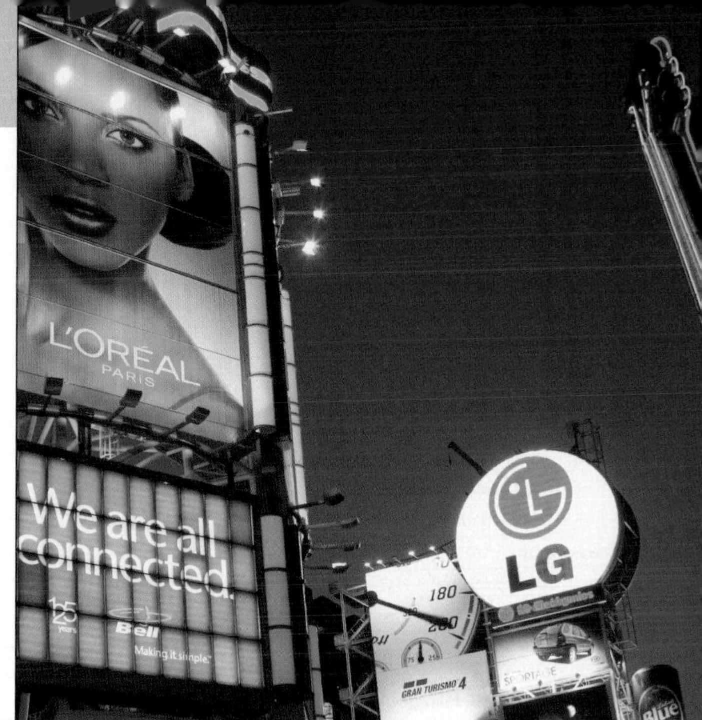

CHAPTER 15

PUBLIC RELATIONS

Chapter Objectives

- To recognize the role of public relations in the promotional mix.
- To know how to compile a public relations plan.
- To understand how public relations is generated through media publicity.
- To understand public relations and its strengths and limitations.
- To understand how public relations is managed through corporate advertising.

The Corporate Social Responsibility Debate

ETHOS | JWT

Are corporate social responsibility (CSR) programs beneficial for organizations? Should a company communicate to the public or its customers that it engages in ethical sourcing or fair-trade practices? Is it a factor when consumers make purchase decisions? A Canadian Business for Social Responsibility and Ipsos Reid study found that 75 percent of the surveyed Canadian companies had initiated CSR programs; however, the vast majority of consumers could not recall specific company practices despite 68 percent claiming they pay attention to such activities. It seems the disparity between what consumers believe or claim and what they actually do is quite significant. Other questions in the study asked respondents the criteria they used when forming opinions; factors like "quality" and "products meeting needs" occurred about 60 percent of the time compared to characteristics like "positively contributes to society" and "socially involved in sponsorship," which averaged less than 10 percent.

Social responsibility of the most enjoyed brands is possibly not the most significant topic on consumers' minds when actually deciding in the store or wherever purchases occur. Part of the problem is that while consumers might claim something like ethical business practices is very important, it is quite another thing for consumers to take specific purchase action. Another complication is that the indication of CSR being important to consumers is often overstated in the research as survey respondents often provide a "socially desirable" answer to the questions posed. After all, nobody wants to claim the environment is not important. Finally, some CSR programs are more corporate and too far removed from the consumer's purchase decision to have much consideration while evaluating competing alternative brands. Given these results, the question arises as to why organizations would develop CSR programs if there are not significant business results. One belief is that it enhances consumer goodwill and takes corporate reputations in a new direction. Alternatively, CSR may not be a deterministic factor for purchasing, but mismanagement could be a factor for *not* purchasing the brand.

In contrast, others believe consumers seek brands that make a difference in the world, as demonstrated by the actions of major agencies and brands. For example, JWT cites CSR research that demonstrates an increasing correlation between how well a company is behaving, what it stands for, how it engages with its stakeholders, and how well the business does. Its specialized division, Ethos, builds with its clients social strategies that achieve their corporate objectives by taking authentic stands on complex social issues and developing meaningful ways for organizations to engage with their stakeholders. Ethos works with both private and not-for-profit organizations; a few of their Canadian-based clients include Tim Hortons, TDBFG, HSBC, Magna, the Canadian Cancer Society, and the Heart and Stroke Foundation. Ethos is committed to achieving material outcomes for its clients; its recent Cassie award wins in both 2006 and 2007 for Sick Kids demonstrate how social strategies do achieve real business results.

L'Oréal's Professional Products division, which sells to salons, is an example of a major brand with a new initiative. Its program educates hair stylists about HIV/AIDS, who in turn communicate to their clients. In total, L'Oréal hopes to reach 500 million women through its 115 training centres in 50 countries, 400,000 salons, and 2 million stylists. The success of this program lies in the connection of the brand, type of product, target audience and delivery; all link together and are not so far removed from the social objective of managing the virus.

Sources: Natalia Williams, "Good Business," *Strategy Magazine,* August 2006; Angela Kryhul, "The Consumer Connection," *Marketing Magazine,* June 5, 2006.

Question

1. Are CSR programs a key part of brand communication or a fairly minor aspect?

Public relations, publicity, and corporate advertising all have promotional program elements that may be of great benefit to marketers. They are integral parts of the overall promotional effort that must be managed and coordinated with the other elements of the promotional mix. However, these three tools do not always have the specific objectives of product and service promotion, and often involve other methods of reaching their target audiences. Typically, these activities are designed more to change attitudes toward an organization or issue than to promote specific products or affect behaviours directly. However, some aspects of these tools assist the marketing of products periodically for firms with a new view of the role of these tools. This chapter explores the domain of public relations, its related topic of publicity generated by news media, corporate advertising, the strengths and limitations of each, and the process by which they are planned and implemented.

Public Relations

What is public relations? How does it differ from other elements of marketing discussed thus far? Perhaps a good starting point is to define what the term *public relations* has traditionally meant, to introduce its new role, and to compare it to publicity.

The Traditional Definition of PR

A variety of books define **public relations**, but perhaps the most comprehensive definition is that offered by the *Public Relations News* (the weekly newsletter of the industry):

> the management function which evaluates public attitudes, identifies the policies and procedures of an organization with the public interest, and executes a program of action (and communication) to earn public understanding and acceptance.[1]

Public relations is indeed a management function. The term *management* should be used in its broadest sense; it is not limited to business managements but extends to other types of organizations, including nonprofit institutions. In this definition, public relations requires a series of stages, including:

- The determination and evaluation of public attitudes.
- The identification of policies and procedures of an organization with a public interest.
- The development and execution of a communications program designed to bring about public understanding and acceptance.

This definition reveals that public relations involves much more than activities designed to sell a product or service. The PR program may involve some of the promotional program elements previously discussed but use them in a different way. For example, press releases may be mailed to announce new products or changes in the organization, special events may be organized to create goodwill in the community, and advertising may be used to state the firm's position on an issue.

The New Role of PR

An increasing number of marketing-oriented companies have established new responsibilities for public relations. PR takes on a broader (and more marketing-oriented) perspective, designed to promote the organization as well as its products and/or services.

The way that companies and organizations use public relations might best be viewed as a continuum. On one end of the continuum is the use of PR from a traditional perspective. In this perspective public relations is viewed as a nonmarketing function whose primary responsibility is to maintain mutually beneficial relationships between the organization and its publics. In this case, customers or potential customers are only part of numerous publics—employees, investors, neighbours, special-interest groups, and so on. Marketing and public relations are separate departments; if external agencies are being used, they are separate agencies.

At the other end of the continuum, public relations is considered primarily a marketing communications function. All noncustomer relationships are perceived as necessary only in a marketing context.[2] In these organizations, public relations reports to marketing. Thus, for many companies the PR function is moving more and more toward a "new role," which is much closer to a marketing function than a traditional one. The new role of public relations envisions both strong marketing and strong PR departments. Rather than each department operating independently, the two work closely together, blending their talents to provide the best overall image of the firm and its product or service offerings. Toyota Canada took this one step further by recently merging its advertising and public relations departments.[3]

Writing in *Advertising Age*, William N. Curry notes that organizations must use caution in establishing this relationship because PR and marketing are not the same thing, and when one becomes dominant, the balance required to operate at maximum efficiency is lost.[4] He says losing sight of the objectives and functions of public relations in an attempt to achieve marketing goals may be detrimental in the long run. Others take an even stronger view that if public relations and marketing distinctions continue to blur, the independence of the PR function will be lost and it will become much less effective.[5] In fact, as noted by Cutlip, Center, and Broom, marketing and public relations are complementary functions, "with each making unique but complementary contributions to building and maintaining the many relationships essential for organizational survival and growth. To ignore one is to risk failure in the other."[6] This position is consistent with our perception that public relations is an important part of the IMC process, contributing in its own way but also in a way consistent with marketing goals.

Exhibit 15–1
Firestone responds to negative publicity

Making It Right.
You have our word on that.

When you buy tires, you're not just buying rubber and steel... you want the confidence that your tires will get you to your destination—safely. Your safety is our primary concern. We want you to have confidence in the way Firestone tires are made and the way they perform. We'll do whatever it takes, however long it takes, to gain your trust.
We call this our "Making It Right" plan. With your satisfaction as our goal, Firestone is expanding warranties and making important enhancements in manufacturing and quality control. In the role of watchdogs, a new team of top technical and quality control managers has been assembled to continuously analyze tire and safety data. They'll act to uncover issues before they become problems. We believe in our tires. We want to prove to you that you can believe in them as well. We'll make it right. It's that simple.

PUBLICITY

Publicity refers to the generation of news about a person, product, service, or organization that appears in broadcast or print media, and now on the Internet. In some instances, it appears that publicity and public relations occur at the same time or in close proximity of one another. For example, a string of SUV accidents led to major problems for 102-year-old Bridgestone/Firestone. In response to the problem, Firestone replaced nearly 900,000 tires and implemented a communications program to counter the negative publicity, a program including television commercials, personal visits to dealers, and print advertising such as that shown in Exhibit 15–1. As a result of the campaign, Firestone lost none of its 10,000 independent tire dealers and two years later was on the road to recovery. In this case, consumers were exposed to both publicity and public relations at varying stages of the identification and solution to the problem.

In other instances, it seems that publicity is the end result or effect of the public relations effort. Because marketers like to have as much control as possible over the time and place where information is released, they often provide the news media with pre-packaged material. One way to do this is with the **video news release (VNR)**, a publicity piece produced by publicists so that

IMC PERSPECTIVE 15–1

Is All Publicity Good Publicity?

A hot and bothered cop, suicide attempts, a homoerotic kiss. This isn't a late-night detective drama, but a fresh crop of TV ads that have landed advertisers including Kia, General Motors, and Snickers in hot water with advocacy groups. Marketers say they're trying to "cut through the clutter," but are they just being provocative to get publicity?

"I don't think any advertiser deliberately tries to attract negative attention," says Karen Howe, vice-president, creative director at Due North Communications in Toronto. "They spend a lot of money and time putting their spots on air so the last thing you want to do is have to pull one off the air or re-edit it."

Still, that's what some marketers are doing. GM is removing a reference to suicide in a new ad after complaints from suicide prevention groups. The spot, which first aired during the Super Bowl, features a robot that gets fired from the GM assembly line for dropping a screw. After a series of menial jobs, the robot throws itself off a bridge. The spot ends with the robot waking up from a bad dream, while a voiceover tells viewers that GM's 160,000 km warranty has got everyone at GM obsessed about quality.

Snickers pulled an ad after its Super Bowl debut, following complaints from a gay rights group in the U.S. It showed two mechanics accidentally kissing while sharing a Snickers bar—then ripping out their chest hair to do something "manly." The Human Rights Campaign called the ad homophobic. Those complaints were widely publicized, but not all agency folks believe the adage "any publicity is good publicity." "No advertiser wants to be in the paper for something negative," says Bryan Tenenhouse, VP and creative director at Draft FCB in Toronto. But will it actually hurt the brand? Tenenhouse doubts it. "If you feel like Snickers, you're going to eat Snickers."

Rob Wilson, a professor of marketing at Ryerson University, says in the case of GM and Snickers, advocacy groups are "definitely being overly sensitive. I think these were tongue-in-cheek ads. They didn't go out of their way to insult, slander or demean anything."

So why pull an ad based on complaints from a small minority? In Canada, if complaints are made to Advertising Standards Canada, most advertisers will amend or pull the ads. That was the case with Kia Canada, which recently withdrew an ad showing a female police officer kissing a man she had pulled over in the driver's seat of his Spectra5. Quebec police unions complained the ad shows cops in a negative light. Kia initially moved the ad to a later time slot, then pulled it after Advertising Standards received several complaints. "We don't set out to upset anyone," says Duncan Bruce, executive creative director at Publicis, which created the ad. Kia is "a challenger brand, they don't spend as much as the competition, and their ads have to cut through the clutter, get noticed and seem fresh and unconventional." In Kia's case it may have worked. In January the automaker's ads were the fourth most noticed by Canadians according to Leger Marketing—right behind Bell's beavers, Familiprix's "Ah-Ha Moments," and Capital One's "Hand in Your Pocket" ads.

Source: Rebecca Harris, "Ads Gone Wild," *Marketing Magazine*, March 12, 2007.

Question

1. Is negative publicity from these ads damaging for the brands?

stations can air it as a news story. The videos almost never mention that they are produced by the subject organization, and most news stations don't mention it either.

There are at least three complications for understanding public relations and publicity. First is the fact that publicity typically lasts for a short period of time. The communication effect of an article in the newspaper about a new product may last for a few weeks. Alternatively, public relations is a concerted program with many exposures extending over a period of time that has a lasting communication effect. A second complication is that public relations is designed to provide positive information about a firm and is usually controlled by the firm or its agent. Publicity, on the other hand, is not always positive and is not always under the control of, or paid for by, the organization. One factor that distinguishes publicity from the other IMC program elements is its sheer power as a form of communication, which gives rise to the final complication. Some of the more powerful incidents of publicity are unplanned by the corporation, and the focus is on the successful and unsuccessful reactions of the organization to positive or negative events. IMC Perspective 15–1 identifies negative publicity some advertisers recently received and their public relations activities afterward.

Perhaps the most famous example of publicity and public relations occurring at the same time is Tylenol. Many years ago, seven people in the Chicago area died after taking Extra Strength Tylenol capsules that had been laced with cyanide (after the product reached the store). Within one week of the poisonings, Tylenol's market share fell from 35 to only 6.5 percent after extensive media coverage of the tampering. Strong public relations efforts combined with an already strong product and corporate image helped the product rebound. The Johnson & Johnson marketing efforts designed to aid recovery are a model in proficiency and have been studied by students of marketing (in both the classroom and the boardroom) for many years. A brand or firm with a lesser image would never have been able to come back. Tylenol regained almost 100 percent of its original brand share in just a few months.

Public Relations Plan

Public relations is an ongoing process requiring formalized policies and procedures for dealing with problems and opportunities. A public relations plan is required, as in the case for an advertising plan or a sales promotion plan. Moreover, the public relations plan needs to be integrated into the overall marketing communications program. A public relations plan can be structured like the other IMC tools we have discussed thus far. It starts with a situation analysis and includes decisions with respect to target audiences, behavioural objectives, communication objectives, strategy, and tactics. Once the plan is written, marketers should ask themselves some of the questions in Figure 15–1 to determine whether their public relations plan is complete. Given the broad nature of public relations, there are many options for each part of the plan that we now discuss.

Situation Analysis

Some elements of the situation analysis from the marketing plan or IMC plan are reviewed. An additional key piece of information is a current assessment of people's attitudes toward the firm, its product or service, or specific issues beyond those directed at a product or service. Why are firms so concerned with the public's attitudes?

One reason is that these attitudes may affect sales of the firm's products. A number of companies have experienced sales declines as a result of consumer boycotts. Procter & Gamble, Coors, and Nike are just a few companies that responded to organized pressures. Second, no one wants to be perceived as a bad citizen. Corporations exist in communities, and their employees may both work and live there. Negative attitudes carry over to employee morale and may result in a less-than-optimal working environment internally and in the community.

1. Does the plan reflect a thorough understanding of the company's business situation?
2. Has the PR program made good use of research and background sources?
3. Does the plan include full analysis of recent editorial coverage?
4. Do the PR people fully understand the product's strengths and weaknesses?
5. Does the PR program describe several cogent, relevant conclusions from the research?
6. Are the program objectives specific and measurable?
7. Does the program clearly describe what the PR activity will be and how it will benefit the company?
8. Does the program describe how its results will be measured?
9. Do the research, objectives, activities, and evaluations tie together?
10. Has the PR department communicated with marketing throughout the development of the program?

FIGURE 15–1

Ten questions for evaluating public relations plans

Due to their concerns about public perceptions, many privately held corporations, publicly held companies, utilities, and the media survey public attitudes. The reasons for conducting this research are many:

- *It provides input into the planning process.* Once the firm has determined public attitudes, these become the starting point in the development of programs designed to maintain favourable positions or change unfavourable ones.
- *It serves as an early warning system.* Once a problem exists, it may require substantial time and money to correct. By conducting research, the firm may be able to identify potential problems and handle them effectively before they become serious issues.
- *It secures support internally.* If research shows that a problem or potential problem exists, it will be much easier for the public relations arm to gain the support it needs to address this problem.
- *It increases the effectiveness of the communication.* The better it understands a problem, the better the firm can design communications to deal with it.[7]

Determine Relevant Target Audiences

The targets of public relations efforts may vary, with different objectives for each. Some may be directly involved in selling the product; others may affect the firm in a different way (e.g., they may be aimed at stockholders or legislators). These audiences may be internal or external to the firm.

Internal audiences may include the employees of the firm, stockholders and investors, members of the local community, suppliers, and current customers. Why are community members and customers of the firm considered internal rather than external? According to John Marston, it's because these groups are already connected with the organization in some way and the firm normally communicates with them in the ordinary routine of work.[8]

External audiences are those people who are not closely connected with the organization (e.g., the public at large). It may be necessary to communicate with both groups on an ongoing basis for a variety of reasons.

Employees of the Firm Maintaining morale and showcasing the results of employees' efforts are often prime objectives of the public relations program. Organizational newsletters, notices on bulletin boards, paycheque envelope stuffers, direct mail, and annual reports are some of the methods used to communicate with these groups. Personal methods of communicating may be as formal as an established grievance committee or as informal as an office Christmas party. Other social events, such as corporate sports teams or picnics, are also used to create goodwill.

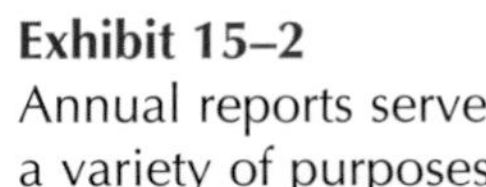

Exhibit 15–2
Annual reports serve a variety of purposes

Stockholders and Investors An annual report like the one in Exhibit 15–2 provides stockholders and investors with financial information regarding the firm. While this is one purpose, annual reports are also a communications channel for informing this audience about why the firm is or is not doing well, future plans, and other information that goes beyond numbers.

For example, McDonald's has successfully used annual reports to fend off potential PR problems. One year the report described McDonald's recycling efforts to alleviate consumers' concerns about waste; another report included a 12-page spread on food and nutrition. Other companies use similar strategies, employing shareholders' meetings, video presentations, and other forms of direct mail. General Motors' annual public interest report is sent to shareholders and community members to detail the company's high standards of corporate responsibility. Companies have used these approaches to generate additional investments, to bring more of their stocks "back home" (i.e., become more locally controlled and managed), and to produce funding to solve specific problems, as well as to promote goodwill.

Community Members People who live and work in the community where a firm is located or doing business are often the target of public relations efforts. Such efforts may involve ads informing the community of activities that the organization is engaged in—for example, reducing air pollution, or cleaning up water supplies. Demonstrating to people that the organization is a good citizen with their welfare in mind may also be a reason for communicating to these groups. Exhibit 15–3 features an ad to draw community members' attention to an energy company's concern for the environment.

Suppliers and Customers An organization wishes to maintain *goodwill* with its suppliers as well as its consuming public. If consumers think a company is not socially conscious, they may take their loyalties elsewhere. Suppliers may be inclined to do the same. Indirect indications of the success of PR efforts may include more customer loyalty, less antagonism, or greater cooperation between the firm and its suppliers or consumers. Historically, most people viewed public relations as a communications strategy to maintain customers. Cisco, Novell, and Sony recently used public relations effectively to attract new Canadian customers in their distribution channels. Each firm experienced substantial sales increases with specific tools to reach particular audiences that had not perceived the benefits offered.[9] Exhibit 15–4 shows how one firm reaches out to its customers and offers professional seminars.

The Media Perhaps one of the most critical external publics is the media, which determine what you will read in your newspapers or see on TV, and how this news will be presented. Because of the media's power, they should be informed of the firm's actions. Companies issue press releases and communicate through conferences, interviews, and special events. The media are generally receptive to such information so long as it is handled professionally; reporters are always interested in good stories.

Educators A number of organizations provide educators with information regarding their activities. The Canadian Marketing Association and the Promotional Products Association of Canada, among others, keep educators informed in an attempt to generate goodwill as well as exposure for their causes. These groups and major corporations provide information regarding innovations, state-of-the-art research, and other items of interest.

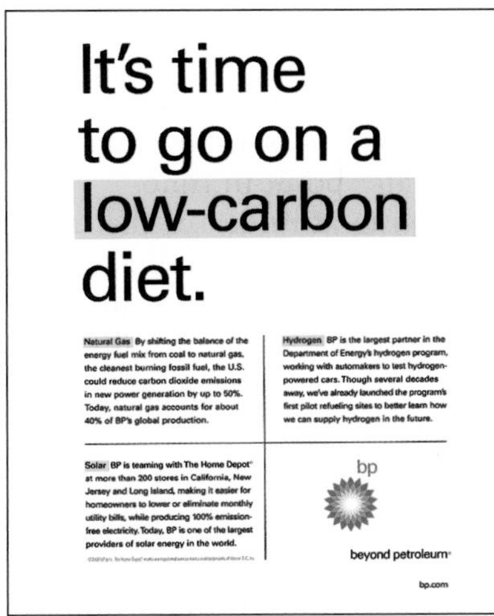

Exhibit 15–3 BP demonstrates concern for the public

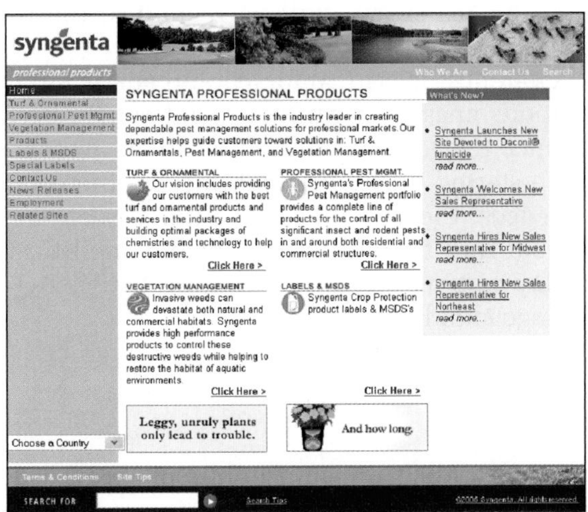

Exhibit 15–4 Syngenta provides information to customers

Civic and Business Organizations The local nonprofit civic organizations also serve as gatekeepers of information. Companies' financial contributions to these groups, speeches at organization functions, and sponsorships are all designed to create goodwill. Corporate executives' service on the boards of nonprofit organizations also generates positive public relations.

Governments Public relations often attempts to influence government bodies directly at both local and national levels. Successful lobbying may mean immediate success for a product, while regulations detrimental to the firm may cost it millions.

Financial Groups In addition to current shareholders, potential shareholders and investors may be relevant target markets. Financial advisers, lending institutions, and others must be kept abreast of new developments as well as financial information, since they offer the potential for new sources of funding. Press releases and corporate reports play an important role in providing information to these publics.

Behavioural Objectives

The framework for behavioural objectives discussed in Chapter 5 is readily applicable for public relations. Recall that behavioural objectives are trial purchase, repeat purchase, purchase-related action, or consumption. No matter what target audiences are selected in the prior step, an astute marketer will know that it is important to understand the type of behaviour desired as a result of the communication. The idea of a "purchase" seems incongruous for some public relations situations, so the marketer may have to view this as the target audience "buying into the idea" or some other specific behaviour in order to carefully define the objectives.

Communication Objectives

Similarly, the communication objectives of Chapter 5 can be used for public relations. Communication objectives include category need, brand awareness, brand attitude, purchase intention, and purchase facilitation. Each of these can be the focus of the public relations plan, although slight modifications are needed. For example, the "brand" may in fact be the corporation itself or a new product that is talked about in a press release. In addition, the notion of a "category" has to be adjusted. Some target audiences want to be affiliated with "good corporate citizens" that are responsible to the community, the environment, or some other issue. Often, then, the "category" will be related to the particular topic or focus of the public relations message.

Awareness is critical for a brand and is important for the organization. Many organizations engage in various social causes because the exposure of their name will enhance the general public's recall and recognition at a later point in time.

We started off by highlighting the importance of existing attitudes of the target audiences. Clearly, then, the public relations plan should have a specific section that outlines the attitude change or modification desired. It should also illustrate the key motives addressed and what attributes or benefits of the firm or product the message should focus on.

Strategy

The strategy decisions for public relations are twofold, as we saw with advertising: message and media. The primary message decisions concern the degree to which the message will have a marketing or corporation focus, and the creative associated with the message. We will briefly describe some issues related to this decision in this section. Like advertising, there are a number of options to disseminate the message, news media, advertising media, and events. We will discuss these in more detail in the next major section.

Focus of the Message Thomas L. Harris has referred to public relations activities designed to support marketing objectives as **marketing public relations (MPR)** functions.[10] Marketing objectives that may be aided by public relations activities include raising awareness, informing and educating, gaining understanding, building trust, giving consumers a reason to buy, and generating consumer acceptance. These points are consistent with the behavioural and communication objective of our framework. Marketing public relations can be used effectively in the following ways:

- Building marketplace excitement before media advertising breaks.
- Creating news about a new advertising or promotional campaign.
- Introducing a product with little or no advertising.
- Influencing the influentials—that is, providing information to opinion leaders.
- Defending products at risk with a message of reassurance.
- Constructively promoting a product.

Ikea Canada's innovative activities successfully increase media exposure and exemplify marketing public relations. In fact, a key source of many zany ideas originated from its consumer surveys—shopping at Ikea was seen as a bit stressful for some couples so it hosted relationship seminars on Valentine's Day. Ikea's Relax event noticed the fact that many Canadians found relaxing to be naughtier than sex. This prompted Ikea to issue instructions for making a restful home along with an "Ikea Adrenaline Index" on their website featuring humorous questions to assess people's stress levels. Store openings and catalogue launches both receive ambitious events to ensure that the media covers the story. Ikea sees the value of these activities and invests heavily with a 50-percent budget increase as well as each event receiving a $500,000 allotment.

The historical role of public relations is one of communicating a favourable image of the corporation as a whole. The domain of this image, or reputation management, concerns every facet of how the organization interacts with its many social, economic, political, and charitable constituents, in addition to the general public locally, nationally, and internationally.

Given the two broad directions of the actual message, marketing versus corporate, an organization has to decide the relative degree of the messages' impact over the course of a year or even longer, as public relations tends to have a lasting communication effect. Too much of a focus in either direction and the organization loses the opportunity to communicate fully.

Creative of the Message We will discuss the many tools for public relations shortly; however, in deciding what message to communicate, the marketer is faced with the decision as to whether the creative strategy of advertising or other IMC tools should be adopted for public relations. On the one hand, there is the argument that all communications should have a common look and feel to them. To counter this, one could argue that unique target audiences with a specific message should have an appropriate creative associated with it.

Delivery of the Message In the course of defining public relations and publicity, and explaining the content of a public relations plan, we have generally described two mechanisms for the delivery of the message. Various news media outlets are available and the media have the choice of publishing or not publishing the materials that organizations submit for their consideration. Alternatively, organizations can turn to other options where they control the dissemination of the message through different types of corporate advertising opportunities in which the organization is responsible for the costs, much like regular product advertising we have covered thus far. These two topics are quite involved, have their respective strengths and limitations, and will be discussed in their respective sections subsequently.

Tactics

The choice of news media or corporate advertising dictates the types of tactics employed. When using news media, a marketer would need to know how to make a media presentation, whom to contact, how to issue a press release, and what to know about each medium addressed, including TV, radio, newspapers, magazines, and direct-response advertising. In addition, decisions regarding alternative media such as news conferences, seminars, events, and personal letters, as well as insights on how to deal with government and other legislative bodies have to be made. Because this information is too extensive to include as a single chapter in this text, we suggest you peruse one of the many books available on this subject for additional insights. For corporate advertising, many tactical considerations have been addressed in Chapter 8. We briefly touch on a few more shortly.

Public Relations Effectiveness

As with the other promotional program elements, it is important to evaluate the effectiveness of the public relations efforts. In addition to determining the contribution of this program element to attaining communications objectives, the evaluation tells management:

- How to assess what has been achieved through public relations activities;
- How to measure public relations achievements quantitatively;
- How to judge the quality of public relations achievements and activities.

As shown in Figure 15–2, a number of exposure measures may be used to assess the effects of PR programs through news media. Raymond Simon suggests additional managerial approaches and research methods for accomplishing this evaluation process, including the following:[11]

- *Management by objectives.* Executives and their managers act together to identify communication objectives to be attained and the responsibilities of the managers. These objectives are then used as a standard to measure accomplishments.
- *Matching objectives and results.* Specific communications objectives should be related to actions, activities, or media coverage.
- *Personal observation and reaction.* Personal observation and evaluation by one's superiors should occur at all levels of the organization.
- *Public opinion and surveys.* Research in the form of public opinion surveys may be used to gather data to evaluate program goal attainment.
- *Internal and external audits.* Internal audits involve evaluations by superiors or peers within the firm to determine the performance of the employee (or his or her programs). External audits are conducted by consultants or other parties outside the organization.

FIGURE *15–2*

Criteria for measuring the effectiveness of PR

A system for measuring the effectiveness of the public relations program has been developed by Lotus HAL. The criteria used in the evaluation process follow:

- Total number of impressions over time
- Total number of impressions on the target audience
- Total number of impressions on specific target audiences
- Percentage of positive articles over time
- Percentage of negative articles over time
- Ratio of positive to negative articles
- Percentage of positive/negative articles by subject
- Percentage of positive/negative articles by publication or reporter
- Percentage of positive/negative articles by target audience

Others suggest comprehensive approaches like we have seen with advertising. Walter Lindenmann says three levels of measures are involved: (1) the basic, which measures the actual PR activities undertaken; (2) the intermediate, which measures audience reception and understanding of the message; and (3) the advanced, which measures the perceptual and behavioural changes that result.[12] We remind you that this approach is entirely consistent with the exposure, processing, communications effects model described in Chapter 4. An application of these concepts is conveyed in Figure 15–3, which is a model developed by Ketchum

FIGURE *15–3* The Ketchum Effectiveness Yardstick (KEY); a strategic approach to the measurement of public relations results

At Ketchum, we believe strongly that it is possible to measure public relations effectiveness. We also believe strongly that measuring public relations results can be done in a timely and cost-efficient manner.

Our strategic approach to public relations measurement involves a two-step process:

1. Setting in advance very specific and clearly defined public relations goals and objectives, and,
2. Pinpointing those levels of measurement that are crucial to the organization in determining to what extent those specific public relations goals and objectives have been met.

In the model, there are three levels for measuring PR effectiveness:

- Level #1—the Basic level for measuring public relations OUTPUTS. This measures the amount of exposure an organization receives in the media, the total number of placements, the total number of impressions, and/or the likelihood of having reached specific target audience groups. Research tools often used when conducting Level #1 measurement include content analysis or publicity tracking studies, secondary analysis, segmentation analysis, and basic public opinion polls.
- Level #2—the Intermediate level for measuring public relations OUTGROWTHS. Outgrowths measure whether or not target audience groups actually received the messages directed at them, paid attention to them, understood the messages, and retained those messages in any shape or form. Research tools often used when conducting Level #2 measurement include focus groups; in-depth interviews; telephone, mail, face-to-face, or mall intercept surveys; testing techniques; and recall studies.
- Level #3—the Advanced level for measuring public relations OUTCOMES. This measures opinion, attitude, and/or behaviour change to determine if there has been a shift in views and/or how people act when it comes to an organization, its products, or its services. Research tools often used when conducting Level #3 measurement include before-and-after studies, experimental and quasi-experimental research, ethnographic studies, communications audits, and multivariate analyses of data.
- The different levels of measuring public relations impact can be plotted on a yardstick in a hierarchial fashion. Here is a graphic displaying the KETCHUM EFFECTIVENESS YARDSTICK (KEY), which summarizes from left to right these levels of public relations measurement:

Level #1	Level #2	Level #3
Basic—Measuring	Intermediate—Measuring	Advanced—Measuring
OUTPUTS	OUTGROWTHS	OUTCOMES
Media placements	Receptivity	Opinion change
Impressions	Awareness	Attitude change
Targeted	Comprehension	Behaviour change
Audiences	Retention	

More detailed information about Ketchum's strategic approach to measuring public relations effectiveness may be obtained by contacting Graham Hueber, Vice President and Director of Research at Ketchum.

461

Public Relations for tracking the effects of public relations. Some organizations may use a combination of measures, depending on their specific needs. For example, Hewlett-Packard uses impression counts, awareness and preference studies, in-house assessments, press clippings counts, and tracking studies.[13]

Media Publicity

In this section, we discuss how organizations can acheive public relations communication objectives through publicity generated through the media. We refer to this as media publicity; that is, publicity that the firm attempts to control by influencing the media to report an organization's story to the public. In this section we review different ways to reach the media and consider the strengths and limitations of this option.

Media Options

A number of media options are available for communicating with various target audiences, including press releases, press conferences, exclusives, interviews, and community involvement.

Press Releases One of the most important publics is the press. To be used by the press, information must be factual, true, and of interest to the medium as well as to its audience. The source of the **press release** can do certain things to improve the likelihood that the "news" will be disseminated, such as ensuring that it reaches the right target audience, making it interesting, and making it easy to pass along.

The information in a press release won't be used unless it is of interest to the readers of the medium it is sent to. For example, financial institutions may issue press releases to business trade media and to the editor of the business section of a general-interest newspaper. Information on the release of a new rock album is of more interest to radio disc jockeys than to TV newscasters; sports news also has its interested audiences.

Press Conferences We are all familiar with **press conferences** held by political figures. While used less often by organizations and corporations, this form of delivery can be very effective as scenes of corporate spokespeople will be viewed on television. The topic must be of major interest to a specific group before it is likely to gain coverage. Companies often call press conferences when they have significant news to announce, such as the introduction of a new product or advertising campaign. On a local level, community events, local developments, and the like may receive coverage. Sports teams use this tool to attract fan attention and interest when a new star is signed.

A medium-sized Canadian company, Atelier America, used media relations to announce its innovative method of reproducing oil on canvas masterpieces. All major U.S. media organizations covered the press conference in New York City. The story circulated through all major U.S. cities and Europe and peaked with coverage on ABC's *World News Tonight* with Peter Jennings. Almost immediately, telephone orders emerged that could be tracked accurately with the media coverage. Previously weak Internet orders reversed overwhelmingly.[14]

Exclusives Although most public relations efforts seek a variety of channels for distribution, an alternative strategy is to offer one particular medium exclusive rights to the story if that medium reaches a substantial number of people in the target audience. Offering an **exclusive** may enhance the likelihood of acceptance and sometimes the media actually use these exclusives to promote themselves.

Interviews Interviews occur on a variety of news or information shows. Usually someone will raise specific questions, and a spokesperson provided by the firm will answer them. Ted Rogers often gives interviews pertaining to the many technological divisions that exist in the Rogers communications conglomerate.

Community Involvement Many corporations enhance their public images through involvement in the local community that often is covered by the media. This involvement may take many forms, including membership in local organizations and contributions to or participation in community events. For example, Rogers' employees work throughout many neighbourhoods on Halloween evening to promote community safety. It also includes organizations participating in emergencies.

Strengths of Media Publicity

Credibility Public relations communication through media publicity is not perceived in the same light as advertising. Consumers understand that most advertising is directly paid for by the sponsoring organization. Obviously some exceptions occur, such as public service announcements heard on the radio, for example. The fact that the media are not being compensated for providing the information may lead receivers to consider the news more truthful and credible. For example, an article in newspapers or magazines discussing the virtues of ibuprofen may be perceived as much more credible than an ad for a particular brand of ibuprofen. And while some firms present the media with news releases or press kits and incur some cost, consumers generally perceive the media source to be reasonably trustworthy with its reporting expertise.

Endorsement Information from media publicity may be perceived as an endorsement by the media vehicle in which it appeared. Automotive awards presented in magazines such as *Motor Trend* have long been known to carry clout with potential car buyers. Now marketers have found that even lesser media mean a lot as well. General Motors' Pontiac division played up an award given to Pontiac as "the best domestic sedan" by *MotorWeek* in a 30-minute program carried by about 300 public broadcasting stations. Likewise, Chrysler trumpeted the awards given to its Jeep Cherokee by *4-Wheel & Off Road* magazine.[15] It has become a common practice for car companies to promote their achievements. A number of auto manufacturers have also taken advantage in their ads of high customer satisfaction ratings reported by J. D. Powers & Associates, an independent research firm specializing in automotive research. Exhibit 15–5 shows that it extends to other industries.

Exhibit 15–5 Edward Jones promotes its J.D. Power Award

Cost In both absolute and relative terms, the cost of media publicity is very low, especially when the possible effects are considered. While a firm can employ public relations agencies and spend millions of dollars, for smaller companies this form of communication may be the most affordable alternative available. Many public relations programs require little more than the time and expenses associated with putting the program together and getting it distributed, yet they still accomplish their objectives.

Avoidance of Clutter Because they are typically perceived as news items, media publicity messages are not subject to the clutter of ads. A story regarding a new product introduction or breakthrough is treated as a news item and is likely to receive attention.

Lead Generation Information about technological innovations, medical breakthroughs, and the like results almost immediately in a multitude of inquiries. These inquiries may give the firm some quality sales leads.

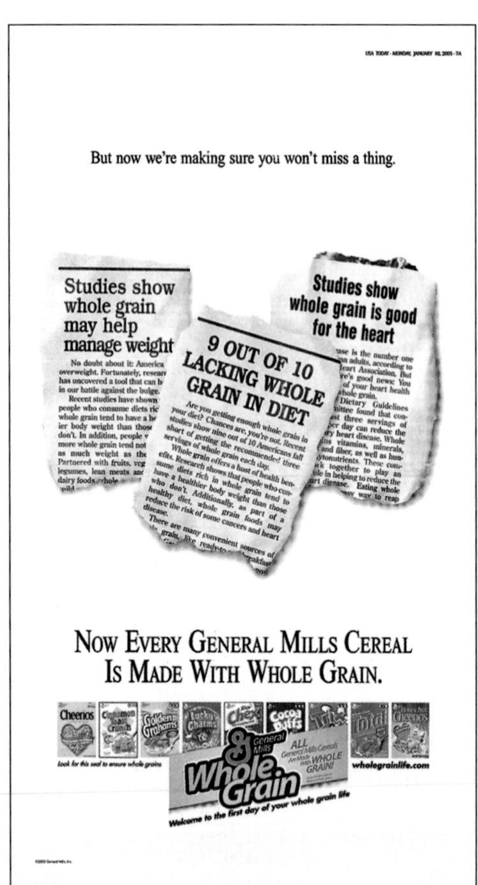

Exhibit 15–6 General Mills capitalizes on positive publicity

Reach Specific Audiences Because some products appeal only to small market segments, it is not feasible to engage in advertising and/or promotions to reach them. If the firm does not have the financial capabilities to engage in promotional expenditures, the best way to communicate to these groups is through media publicity.

Image Building Effective public relations helps to develop a positive image for the organization. The examples discussed thus far have indicated strong image building capabilities with proactive public relations. News about a product may in itself serve as the subject of an ad. Exhibit 15–6 demonstrates how General Mills used favourable publicity from a variety of sources to promote the importance of whole grains in a healthy diet and promote the use of whole grains in its cereal.

Frequency Potential Still another reason for publicity's power is the frequency of exposure it generates. For example, a successful public relations activity could generate exposure in multiple media (i.e., broadcast, print, Internet).

Limitations Media Publicity

Weaker Brand or Corporate Identification Effect Perhaps the major disadvantage of media publicity is the potential for not completing the communications process. While these messages can break through the clutter of commercials, the receiver may not make the connection to the source. Many firms' PR efforts are never associated with their sponsors in the public mind.

Inconsistent Message Media publicity may also misfire through mismanagement and a lack of coordination with the marketing department. When marketing and PR departments operate independently, there is a danger of inconsistent communications or redundancies in efforts.

Timing Timing of media publicity is not always completely under the control of the marketer. Unless the press thinks the information has very high news value, the timing of the press release is entirely up to the media—if it gets released at all. Thus, the information may be released earlier than desired or too late to make an impact.

Accuracy The information contained in a press release sometimes gets lost in translation—that is, it is not always reported the way the provider wishes it to be. As a result, inaccurate information, omissions, or other errors may result.

Corporate Advertising

The term **corporate advertising** tends to be used as a catchall for any type of advertising run for the direct benefit of the corporation rather than its products or services. For purposes of this text we use it to describe any type of advertising designed to promote the organization itself rather than its products or services. Corporate advertising is targeted at both internal and external audiences and involves the promotion of the organization as well as its ideas. Marketers seek attainment of corporate advertising's objectives by implementing image advertising, cause-related advertising, and sponsorship. More recently, the latter two have moved to the product level in communications strategy so the distinction has blurred. We cover these three topics in this section, but first we look at the reason for corporate advertising, namely the management of corporate reputation.

Corporate Reputation

Earlier in this text we suggested that the communications framework described for advertising can be applied to other communication tools, and previously in this chapter we highlighted that it can be used for various public relations tools. This thought is echoed with a summary of the planning process used by executives of a leading public relations firm, Fleishman-Hillard Canada, in its efforts to assist clients with reputation management:[16]

- Gain a detailed, forward-looking understanding of corporate business objectives, competitive positioning, and the desired corporate reputation or corporate brand. This is best accomplished through interviews with senior corporate and business unit executives.
- Define the key audience, derive audience-specific behavioural and attitudinal objectives, and audience-specific corporate positioning attributes.
- Assess current perceptions of the company held by each key stakeholder group or audience on each of the key reputational attributes.
- Implement reputation-management programs throughout the corporation.
- Establish an ongoing plan to measure and monitor corporate reputation, and use reputation measurement to refine communications programs.

We highlight the issue of corporate reputation, a term that is used in public relations to convey the idea of corporate image, since a key outcome of corporate advertising is to influence overall perceptions of the organization. Clearly, the notion of corporate reputation is attitudinal, thus indicating that the general framework suggested in this text can be applied to all IMC tools. Furthermore, all methods described in Chapter 9 (e.g., focus groups, interviews, surveys) are readily applied for measuring corporate advertising effectiveness. Various news organizations publish polls that ask Canadians their opinion about corporations. Figure 15–4 on page 466 summarizes the findings from a survey of 1500 who rated the quality of products offered by the companies.[17]

Shell Canada is an example of one company that takes its reputation seriously, as shown by its communications program that emphasized its sustainable development policies. After it launched the initial ads in the winter of 2002, Shell Canada's internal "favourability index" improved by several percentage points. A more recent campaign initiated in the fall of 2003 continued the theme of Shell Canada employees talking about their jobs in relation to the environment. In addition, print ads accentuated the importance of balancing profit and principles and portrayed Shell Canada as a company of ethical employees.[18]

Image Advertising

One form of corporate advertising is devoted to promoting the organization's overall image. **Image advertising** may accomplish a number of objectives, including creating goodwill both internally and externally, creating a position for the company, specifying a firm's perspective on an issue, and generating resources, both human and financial.

FIGURE *15–4*

Corporate reputation rankings

2007 Rank	Company	Score	Good Opinion	Bad Opinion	2006 Rank
1	Time Hortons	84	89.8%	5.9%	2
2	Canadian Tire	84	90.4%	6.7%	1
3	Sony	82	85.6%	3.2%	3
4	Staples	80	83.7%	3.7%	11
5	Panasonic	79	81.9%	2.5%	7
6	Sears	79	86.8%	8.0%	4
7	Subway	77	83.9%	6.5%	8
8	HBC: The Bay/Zellers	77	84.3%	7.6%	18
9	Toyota	76	78.6%	2.2%	17
10	Kraft	76	83.0%	6.9%	5
11	General Electric (GE)	76	81.1%	5.2%	20
12	The Home Depot	75	81.1%	5.8%	10
13	Honda	74	76.5%	2.4%	16
14	Nestle	74	80.8%	7.1%	6
15	Maple Leaf Foods	72	78.6%	6.2%	12
16	CBC	72	80.9%	8.8%	19
17	Home Hardware	71	74.4%	3.3%	14
18	Purolator	71	76.5%	5.4%	26
19	Canada Post	71	83.0%	12.1%	13
20	McCain	71	77.3%	6.6%	9

Source: www.marketingmag.ca

Exhibit 15–7 Tyco uses image advertising to avoid confusion

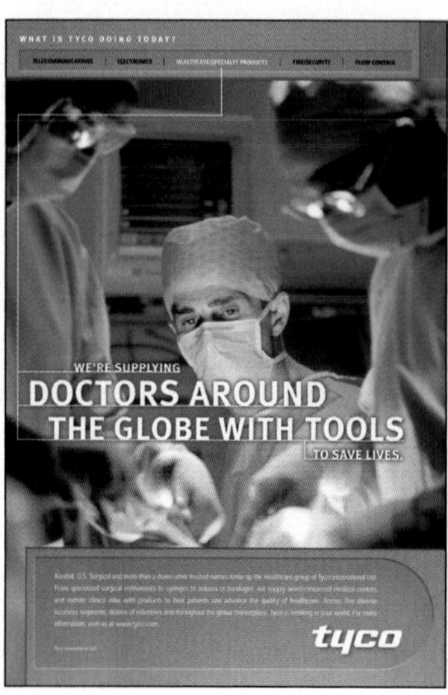

Positioning As shown in Exhibit 15–7, ads are often designed to create an image of the firm in the public mind. The exhibit shows how Tyco is attempting to create an image of itself as a market leader and health care expert, not a toy company.

This type of advertising also occurs when a company changes its name. In 2001, Andersen Consulting became Accenture, while Mutual Life Insurance became Clarica. Accenture was part of a worldwide make-over of 178 offices costing $263 million with 50 separate marketing teams. The Canadian team used public relations, direct mail to clients, and consumer print and TV ads created by an American agency. Clarica is the Latin root word for "clear" and that became the focus of all advertising messages, both print and television, as consumers truly wanted clear financial choices. Naturally, Clarica created a clear image of the "new" company through its corporate advertising efforts.[19]

Television Sponsorship A firm often runs corporate image advertising on TV programs or specials. For example, the Hallmark or IBM specials and documentaries on network TV are designed to promote the corporation as a good citizen. By associating itself with high-quality or educational programming, the firm hopes for a carryover effect that benefits its own image.

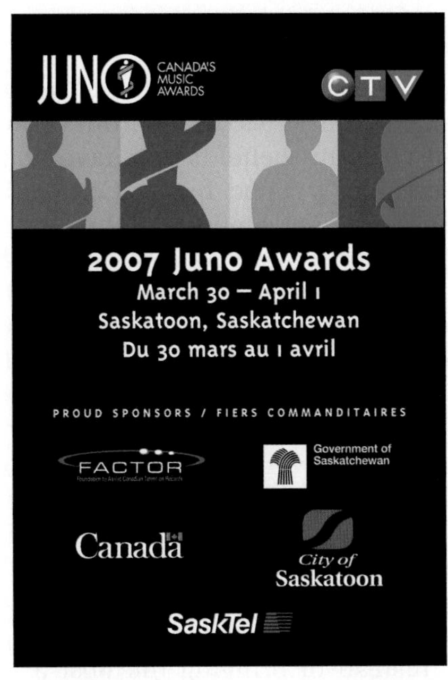

Exhibit 15–8 Some Juno Awards sponsors

Exhibit 15–9 Corporate image advertising designed to attract employees

According to John Bennett, senior VP for international marketing communications, the sponsorships are designed to fulfill specific business objectives while providing support for the recipients.[20] Exhibit 15–8 shows a few organizations that decided a Juno Awards sponsorship would be good for them.

Recruitment The promotional piece presented in Exhibit 15–9 is a good example of corporate image advertising designed to attract new employees. If you are a graduating senior considering a career in the new Internet economy, this ad, promoting a corporate image for the company, will interest you.

The employment section of most major metropolitan newspapers is an excellent place to see this form of corporate image advertising at work. Notice the ads in these papers and consider the images the firms are presenting.

Financial Support Some corporate advertising is designed to generate investments in the corporation. By creating a more favourable image, the firm makes itself attractive to potential stock purchasers and investors. More investments mean more working capital, more monies for research and development, and so on. In this instance, corporate image advertising is almost attempting to make a sale; the product is the firm.

Advocacy Firms often take positions on certain social, business, or environmental issues that influence its image and the public's perception. Such **advocacy advertising** is concerned with propagating ideas and elucidating controversial social issues of public importance in a manner that supports the interests of the sponsor.[21]

While still portraying an image for the company or organization, advocacy advertising does so indirectly, by adopting a position on a particular issue rather than promoting the organization itself. The ads may be sponsored by a firm or by a trade association and are designed to tell readers how the firm operates or management's position on a particular issue.

The reason for the advertising can be due to the firm's negative publicity, the firm's inability to place an important message through public relations channels, or the firm just wants to get certain ideas accepted or have society understand its concerns.

Exhibit 15–10
Whirlpool supports the effort for affordable housing

Cause-Related Advertising

An increasingly popular method of image building is **cause-related marketing**, in which companies link with charities or nonprofit organizations as contributing sponsors. The company benefits from favourable publicity, while the charity receives much-needed funds. Companies also take the opportunity to advertise their involvement (Exhibit 15–10). Spending on cause-related marketing has increased considerably in the past decade. Proponents of cause marketing say that association with a cause may differentiate one brand or store from another, increase consumer acceptance of price increases, generate favourable publicity, and even win over skeptical officials who may have an impact on the company.[22]

Cause marketing relationships can take a variety of forms. Making outright donations to a nonprofit cause, having companies volunteer for the cause, donating materials or supplies, running public service announcements, or even providing event refreshments are some of the ways companies get involved. KitchenAid found a unique way to get involved with the Canadian Breast Cancer Foundation. Its consumers hosted at-home parties and their guests donated money instead of bringing the host a gift (e.g., bottle of wine, flowers). Hosts could browse "cookforthecure.ca" for recipes, etc. and submit the funds that were raised. Success for this program is attributed to thorough competitive and consumer analysis that indicated it would resonate with its customers.[23]

Becel has supported the Heart and Stroke Foundation for 20 years with a variety of activities. About one-quarter of its media budget is spent on different initiatives each year, with 5 percent supporting the Becel Heart and Stroke Ride for Heart in three Canadian cities. In fact, the event recently raised $2.1 million and the recipient gratefully acknowledges the fundraising would not be as successful without the media presence paid for by the healthy margarine company.[24]

While companies receive public relations benefits from their association with causes, with 80 percent of consumers saying they have a more positive impression of companies that support a cause, they sometimes receive financial rewards as well.[25] An Ipsos Reid poll illustrated the current benefits that Canadians regard as socially responsible activities:

- 76 percent of Canadians think Canadian companies are doing a good job in terms of doing business in a socially responsible way (14 percent say companies are doing a "very good" job, while 62 percent say companies are doing a "somewhat good" job).
- 23 percent give Canadian companies poor marks (16 percent say companies are doing a "somewhat poor" job and 6 percent say they are doing a "very poor" job).
- 55 percent say they have consciously decided to buy a product or service from one company over another because they felt the company was a good corporate citizen, while 52 percent have consciously refused to buy a product or a service from a company not conducting business in a socially responsible way.
- While Canadians want to see companies operate in a socially responsible manner, they do question the motives of companies that undertake socially responsible activities (68 percent think companies are motivated by their bottom line, while 29 percent say companies care about being socially responsible).
- However, Canadians like good news (68 percent say that a corporate social responsibility news story about a company being singled out for a very positive action is more likely to grab their attention than a story about a company being highlighted for a very negative action).
- Women are more likely than men to want to read about a company's positive action (71 percent versus 64 percent).[26]

At the same time, not all cause marketing is a guarantee of success. Cause marketing requires more than just associating with a social issue, and it takes time and effort. Companies can get into trouble by misleading consumers about their relationships. It is also possible to waste money by hooking up with a cause that offers little connection or relation to their brand. Firms need to avoid picking the wrong cause—finding that their customers and potential customers either have little interest in or don't like the cause. Finally, the results of cause-marketing efforts can sometimes be hard to quantify.

SPONSORSHIP

Corporate sponsorships of charities and causes has become a popular form of public relations. While some companies sponsor specific events and/or causes with primarily traditional public relations objectives in mind, a separate and more marketing-oriented use of sponsorships is also on the increase. Such **event sponsorships** take on a variety of forms, as shown in Figure 15–5. In fact, some event sponsorships are now done for product-level brands compared to corporate brands.

In response to the growth of sponsorship, industry members recently established the Sponsorship Marketing Council of Canada to demonstrate sponsorship as a valuable communication tool by establishing practices and measurement tools to validate the investment.[27] Other activities include establishing an awards program recognizing the best sponsorship in four categories: arts and entertainment, sports, causes, and special interest. The Tackle Hunger program by Purolator and the CFL recently won the cause category even though it had a strong link to football, as the national courier would donate the quarterback's weight in food to the local food bank where events occurred each week.[28]

Sports receives the majority of event sponsorship monies. Among the most popular sporting events for sponsorship are auto racing, golf and tennis tournaments, and running events. Professional sports leagues and teams as well as Olympic teams are key recipients. Traditionally, beer and car companies have been among the largest sports event sponsors. Now a number of other companies have become involved in event sponsorships, including beverage companies, airlines, telecommunications and financial services companies, and high-tech firms.

As expected, there are a number of specific decisions associated with event sponsorship including the types of sponsorship, target audience fit, target audience exposure, and brand positioning. We explore these important sponsorship decisions in the context of sports sponsorship for illustrative purposes since it is the dominant expenditure and is projected to hit over $13 billion in North America in 2006. Each of these ideas can be readily adapted to other events (i.e., entertainment, festivals, or arts). Sport sponsorship can be successful with clear objectives,

FIGURE *15–5*

Annual sponsorship spending in North America by property ($ millions)

	1998	2002	2006
Sports	$4,556	$6,430	$8,935
Entertainment tours/attractions	680	865	1,377
Festivals, fairs, events	612	834	609
Causes	544	828	1,303
Arts	408	610	743
Associations/membership organizations			404
Total	$6,800	$9,567	$13,371

Source: Adapted from *Promo*, June 1, 2002; Promo Xtra Jan 24, 2007.

a good positioning strategy, adequate budget, appropriate sporting vehicle, and key tactical implementation, similar characteristics that we have seen in other types of promotional plans.[29]

Types of Sponsorship Sport sponsorship involves endorsement deals or sponsoring a team, league, event, athlete, or organization, along with stadium naming or broadcast rights. The goal is to associate a brand with its target audience's entertainment consumption or lifestyle, thus enriching the overall brand experience. One thought on the topic suggested three levels of sponsorship.[30] Proprietary has little or no external sanctioning or partnerships. Nike's RunTO featured a running event throughout the entire city of Toronto. Affiliated advertising utilizes the assets of a sponsorship or association. For example, the Esso Legends of Hockey brings together the Hockey Hall of Fame, NHL, NHLPA, and NHL Alumni. Programming lives within a larger event or sponsorship, for example Powerade's "Thirst for Soccer" that visits youth soccer tournaments across Canada. IMC Perspective 15–2 highlights issues regarding the privileges of certain investment levels, another key sponsorship decision.

Working with an athletic sponsorship is similar to sponsorship with a team, but we see a few unique issues. Foremost is ensuring a fit between the athlete and the company or brand. Exposure arrangements regarding an athlete's identity (e.g., name, image, and likeness), amount and type of service, and corporate logo placement need to be established. The strategic communication use of an athlete in advertising, public relations, or sales promotion and conditions such as investment protection (e.g., ethics clause) rounds out the arrangement.[31]

Brand Positioning Many companies are attracted to event sponsorships because effective IMC programs can be built around them and promotional tie-ins can be made to local, regional, national, and even international markets. Companies are finding event sponsorships an excellent platform from which to build equity and gain affinity with target audiences as well as a good public relations tool for the corporation in general.

While the overall market position of the brand may be well established throughout the marketing plan, sport sponsorship permits a brand positioning strategy to a unique and well-defined target audience that the brand has specific communication and behavioural objectives. For example, a sports sponsorship could enable a brand to establish awareness and new brand associations as it reaches new customers to develop trial purchases.

However, brands should be prepared to spend accordingly to achieve their objectives, as the initial sponsorship investment requires additional advertising or sales promotion expenditures. As the foundation is critical, brands should ensure that the rights and benefits of the sports sponsorship allow the brand to achieve its objectives and positioning. For example, sponsorship in hockey can have limits without the clearance from various stakeholders (e.g., NHL, NHLPA, and Hockey Canada). Finally, picking the right sponsorship that has the right profile at the right time and a partner that is receptive to making the deal work is paramount for successful implementation.

Target Audience Fit Most companies focus their marketing efforts on specific market segments and are always looking for ways to reach these target audiences. Many marketers are finding that event sponsorships are very effective ways to reach specific target audiences based on geographic, demographic, psychographic, and ethnic characteristics. For example, golf tournaments are a popular event for sponsorship by marketers of luxury automobiles and other upscale products and services. The golf audience is affluent and highly educated, and marketers believe that golfers care passionately about the game, leading them to form emotional attachments to brands they associate with the sport. Alternatively, brands will look to many similar venues to reach a consistent target audience that fits. For example,

IMC PERSPECTIVE 15–2

Getting the Most Out of Sponsorships

Let's say you want to align your brand with a major sports or charitable event, but you can't afford the title sponsor fees. As one of several lower-tier sponsors, are your fellow marketers friends or foes? Actually, they're both, according to Kim Smither, managing director of Octagon Canada in Toronto. Non-title sponsors are friends because they help promote and support an event, yet they're "enemies" because every marketer at an event is competing for the attention of the same attendees. The trick is ensuring your brand isn't lost among the sea of logos, or doesn't get overshadowed by the dominating presence of the title and presenting sponsors.

What a lower-tier sponsor can do is outsmart its "enemies" with a powerful activation campaign. By taking this approach, some second- and third-tier sponsors try to eclipse the brand awareness of even the event's title sponsor. The more "friendly" approach, meanwhile, is to partner or piggyback on the promotional efforts of the title sponsor and, in the process, reap the benefits of the extra exposure for a brand.

Levi's, for instance, embraces the powerful activation approach. In fact, Dave Soyka, consumer marketing manager for Levi's, believes this is the ideal way for a brand to sponsor an event: invest a modest amount of money, yet generate awareness levels as high as the title sponsor. That is exactly what happened last July when Levi Strauss & Co. was a secondary sponsor of Crankworx, a mountain bike festival in Whistler, B.C.

Levi's approach was to stage mock photo shoots during the nine-day festival. Levi's staff, acting as "model scouts," approached festival attendees in the brand's 17-to-24 target, to pose for mock ads. The posters were put up on-site, and event attendees were encouraged to vote for their favourite "model" via text messages or ballots (two winners later appeared in a real Levi's ad published in *Exclaim!* magazine). Levi's did the same thing at the two-day Virgin Festival in Toronto during September with a "Best Impressions" competition. Music festival goers voted for their favourite Levi's "model," and the winner appeared in the November issue of *Exclaim!*

Sometimes it can be impossible for brands with modest sponsorship investments to execute those creative promos due to restrictions to ensure all sponsors get their money's worth. Events like the Calgary Stampede and the Rogers Cup tennis tournament place companies in strict sponsorship categories based on their investment level. "This limits the kind of things a partner can get involved with," says Catherine McCleary, sponsorship manager of the Calgary Stampede. "If you are investing a certain amount of dollars, everyone in the same category receives similar exposure and value." For this reason McCleary says the Stampede has banned sampling programs—which was one way sponsors were able to gain maximum exposure with little investment. Instead, the Stampede sells a "Stampede Pack," stuffed with goodies from all of the event's sponsors. "This way it is contained, and people who attend the event can choose to get the samples."

At the Rogers Cup sampling is also restricted, to the entrance/exit of the event. Even then sampling, like all promotional programs, must be approved by Tennis Canada. "We are very conscious in terms of the equity model. We won't give a promotion to a bronze sponsor that would eclipse a gold level one," says Greg Wood, vice-president of corporate partnerships for Toronto-based Tennis Canada. "If an advertiser decides to do a big promotional event for the week, they would automatically be told they would have to invest more money; that would automatically raise their level of sponsorship."

Rather than compete, some advertisers have opted to cross-pollinate their brands with the title sponsor. McCain Foods and chocolate confectioner Ganong Bros. partnered in their sponsorships with the Canadian Breast Cancer Foundation's Run for the Cure. CIBC has been the title sponsor of the run for the past decade. Recognizing the financial institution is such a powerful title sponsor, McCain and Ganong—two of six other national sponsors—have created partnerships with CIBC. McCain donated juice boxes with pink straws toward a CIBC event called the Pink Pancake Breakfast leading up to the run. And Ganong supplied 50,000 bags of pink jelly beans to CIBC, which in turn sold them at its branches.

Source: Chris Daniels, "Take It Down a Notch," *Marketing Magazine,* December 4, 2006.

Question

1. Describe the reasons why each sponsorship is a good idea for the brand.

BMO Financial supports Figure Skating Canada, Equestrian at Spruce Meadows in Calgary, and the Canadian Opera Company.[32] The Telus World Ski and Snowboard Festival allows the national telecommunications firm to reach its youth market with its sponsorship investment.[33]

Clairol Canada signed a one-year, six-figure deal with the Canadian Football League to help launch their new hair colouring products for men. As one executive points out, "We're using the CFL and the Grey Cup to create excitement around hair colour and to make it more appealing to men, who may look at hair colour as something completely feminine. Also, Herbal Essences is targeted at men 15 to 25, and that's very much the target audience of the CFL and the Grey Cup." The deal includes national consumer promotion with in-store and media support. Other communications include on-field signage and in-stadium commercial messages during all playoff games, including the Grey Cup.[34]

Target Audience Exposure Many marketers are attracted to event sponsorship because it gets their company and/or product names in front of consumers. By choosing the right events for sponsorship, companies can get visibility among their target market. Canadian amateur athletes and semi-pro sports organizations have been working with marketers to develop sponsorships that benefit both parties. Alpine Canada Alpin (ACA), the governing body for Canadian alpine ski racing, generated $1.9 million in sponsorship deals representing 25 percent of its annual budget compared to 16 percent from the public sector for the 2000–01 season. It signed deals with Wrigley Canada, General Motors, and Fido cellphones. The key success factor in landing these deals is the fact that World Cup ski races had TV audiences of over 30 million.[35]

Measuring Sponsorship Effectiveness As we have seen with other communication tools, sponsorship planning follows a general framework of performing a situation analysis with relevant consumer and competitive research, establishing objectives (i.e., marketing, communication, behavioural), developing strategy and tactics, and outlining the criteria and measures of effectiveness to assess if objectives have been met. A major issue that faces the event sponsorship industry is incomplete research. As marketers become interested in targeted audiences, they will want more evidence that event sponsorship is effective and a good return on their investment.

Despite this concern, the growth in sponsorship investments has led to a corresponding emergence of measuring the effectiveness of sponsorships. Essentially, measures of sponsorship effectiveness can be categorized as exposure-based methods or tracking measures:[36]

- *Exposure methods.* Exposure methods can be classified as those that monitor the quantity and nature of the media coverage obtained for the sponsored event and those that estimate direct and indirect audiences. While commonly employed by corporations, scholars have heavily criticized these measures. Pham argues that media coverage is not the objective of sponsorships and should not be considered as a measure of effectiveness. He argues that the measures provide no indication of perceptions, attitude change, or behavioural change and should therefore not be considered as measures of effectiveness.[37]
- *Tracking measures.* These measures are designed to evaluate the awareness, familiarity, and preferences engendered by sponsorship based on surveys. A number of empirical studies have measured recall of sponsors' ads, awareness of and attitudes toward the sponsors and their products, and image effect including brand and corporate images. Moreover, the tracking measures could be done for current customers, potential customers, and the general public before, during, and after the event to get a complete picture of the sponsorship.[38]

1. Narrowly define objectives with specifics.
2. Establish solid strategies against which programming will be benchmarked and measure your programming and effectiveness against the benchmark.
3. Set measurable and realistic goals; make sure everything you do supports them.
4. Enhance, rather than just change, other marketing variables.
5. Programming should be crafted to reflect the particulars of your company's constituencies and target audiences.
6. Define the scope of your involvement. Will it involve multiple areas within the company? Who internally and externally comprises the team?
7. Think "long term." It takes time to build brand equity. Also, think of leveraging your sponsorship through programming for as long as possible, before and after the event.
8. Build evaluation and a related budget into your overall sponsoring program. Include items such as pre- and post-event attitude surveys, media analysis, and sales results.

FIGURE *15–6*

Eight steps to measuring event sponsorship

While each of these measures has its advantages and disadvantages, we suggest using several in assessing the impact of sponsorships. In fact, the selection of appropriate measures is so critical that some recommend they may have to be customized for each sponsorship activity.[39] One innovative and comprehensive measurement system is SponsorScope, developed by Fusion Alliance Marketing, a division of Cossette Communication Group. Their tool examined items like the media used, media and sponsor visibility, and usage of sales promotion tools along with items like the number of event sponsors, the event's reputation, category exclusivity, leveraging potential for employees, and the event's communication plan.[40] In addition to those mentioned here, the eight-step process suggested in Figure 15–6 could be used to guide these evaluations.

Strengths of Corporate Advertising

Positioning Firms, like products, need to establish an image or position in the marketplace. Corporate advertising activities are one way to accomplish this objective. A well-positioned product is much more likely to achieve success than is one with a vague or no image. The same holds true of the firm. Companies with strong positive corporate images have an advantage over competitors that may be enhanced when they promote any aspect of their organization or products.

Control of Message Exposure As the PR efforts of firms have increased, the attention paid to these events by the media has lessened (not because they are of any less value, but because there are more events to cover). The net result is that when a company engages in a public relations effort, there is no guarantee it will receive press coverage and publicity. Corporate advertising gets the message out, and though consumers may not perceive it as positively as information from an objective source, the fact remains that it can communicate what has been done.

Reach a Select Target Audience Corporate advertising should not be targeted to the general public. It is often targeted to investors and managers of other firms rather than to the general public. It doesn't matter if the general public does not appreciate this form of communication, as long as the target audience does. In this respect, this form of advertising may be accomplishing its objectives.

Limitations of Corporate Advertising

Questionable Effectiveness There is no strong evidence to support the belief that corporate advertising works. A study by Bozell & Jacobs Advertising of 16,000 ads concluded that corporate advertising contributed to only 4 percent of the variability in the company's stock price, compared with a 55-percent effect attributable to financial factors.[41] A second study also casts doubts on earlier studies that concluded corporate advertising worked.[42] A Gallup and Robinson study reported in *Advertising Age* found consumers were 35 percent less interested in corporate ads than in product-oriented advertising.[43] This may be because consumers do not understand the reasons behind such ads.

Questionable Ethics Some critics contend that since larger firms have more money, they can control public opinion unfairly. Nevertheless, many consumers still see such advertising as unfair and immediately take a negative view of the sponsor. Some critics believe the only time firms engage in corporate advertising is when they are in trouble—either in a financial sense or in the public eye—and are advertising to attempt to remedy the problem or divert attention from the real problem.

Poor Communication Strategy Given that the ads do not directly appeal to anyone, are not understood, and do not promote anything specific, critics say the monies could be better spent in other areas. Again, much of this argument has its foundation in the fact that corporate image ads are often intangible. They typically do not ask directly for a purchase; they do not ask for investors. Rather, they present a position or try to create an image. Because they are not specific, many critics believe their purpose is lost on the audience and these ads are not a wise investment of the firm's resources. In some cases, corporate advertising is a reflection of the top management who are involved in the message development and do not provide consistent direction to the task.

IMC Planning: Strategic Use of PR

As discussed in this chapter, public relations activities often communicate infrequently to a broader population and attempt to persuade the target audience on more global or abstract attributes of the company and its brand. With this in mind, public relations generally does not influence the decision-making process because the activities are not sequenced to match the purchase and consumption behaviour of consumers, as they are in advertising or sales promotion. For that matter, it is unlikely that a single public relations activity would coincide exactly with decision making for any other stakeholder that might be a target audience for the organization.

For example, the CIBC is the title sponsor for Run for the Cure, an annual event to raise funds for the Canadian Breast Cancer Foundation. The late-September event features considerable lead-up media exposure funded by CIBC and other sponsors; however, this timing does not necessarily fit for all customers and non-customers of CIBC since financial products and services are purchased year-round. Presumably, CIBC expects this sponsorship activity to have a broad, long-term benefit associated with the corporate brand that consumers and all other internal and external stakeholders would retain during the year and until the event returns.

Advertising and PR often reinforce one another. The launch of a new advertising campaign is helped with additional exposure through news media in the form of announcements in the newspaper, clips shown on television, or information and complete ads posted on the Internet. Sometimes, brands take advantage of favourable publicity and make note of this in their advertising or make it a central theme in a particular message. Alternatively, if the corporation involved itself with sponsorship of arts, a cause, or sports, the advertising can make reference of this for regular brand messages beyond advertising messages dedicated to communicating information about the sponsorship. For these reasons, it is no wonder we have seen extensive proliferation of various public relations expenditures in recent years.

PR and sales promotion often work hand-in-hand, and Tabi International provides a good example of this. Each season Tabi, like most fashion retailers or clothes designers, provides press releases to fashion, lifestyle, and marketing/business media with the intention of obtaining exposure through news articles in magazines, newspapers, or the Internet. To spark the presentation, the upscale retailer established the Tabi Face of 40+ contest as the central theme to launch its autumn fashions. The contest encouraged women over 40 to enter and be selected to model in a photo shoot published in the 40th anniversary edition of *Homemakers* magazine, along with *Canadian Living* magazine.[44]

Internet sites for corporations are a primary vehicle for communicating basic facts, especially the corporation's social and community interests, and for disseminating some common public relations tools. For example, firms regularly put copies of their press releases on their sites and also include video clips of various corporate activities like speeches or annual shareholder meetings. The ability of virtually anyone to obtain basic company information through the Internet makes it a desirable tool for firms to project their best image with timely content to ensure strong reputation management. However, the darker side of the Internet appears in the form of unwarranted negative publicity for many brands. It does not take much effort for the average person to try to sabotage organizations that have appropriate corporate missions, sell legitimate products, and follow the laws of the land.

SUMMARY

This chapter examined the role of the promotional elements of public relations. Public relations is typically done through publicity generated through news media and corporate advertising. We noted that these areas are all significant to the marketing and communications effort and are usually considered differently from the other promotional elements. The reasons for this special treatment stem from the facts that (1) they are typically not designed to promote a specific product or service and (2) in many instances it is harder for the consumer to make the connection between the communication and its intent.

Public relations was shown to be useful in its traditional responsibilities as well as in a more marketing-oriented role. In many firms, PR is a separate department operating independently of marketing; in others, it is considered a support system. Many large firms have an external public relations agency, just as they have an outside ad agency.

In the case of publicity, another factor enters the equation: lack of control over the communication the public will receive. In corporate advertising, the organization remains the source and retains much more control. Publicity often takes more of a reactive than a proactive approach, yet it may be more instrumental (or detrimental) to the success of a product or organization than all other forms of promotion combined.

While not all publicity can be managed, the marketer must nevertheless recognize its potential impact. Press releases and the management of information are just two of the factors under the company's control. Proper reaction and a strategy to deal with uncontrollable events are also responsibilities.

Corporate advertising was described as controversial, largely because the source of the message is top management, so the rules for other advertising and promoting forms are often not applied. This element of communication definitely has its place in the promotional mix. But to be effective, it must be used with each of the other elements, with specific communications objectives in mind.

Finally, in this chapter we tried to illustrate that the public relations plan is put together much like the advertising or sales promotion plans.

KEY TERMS

advocacy advertising, *467*
cause-related marketing, *468*
corporate advertising, *464*
event sponsorships, *469*
exclusive, *462*
external audiences, *456*
image advertising, *465*
internal audiences, *456*
marketing public relations (MRP), *459*
press conference, *462*
press release, *462*
public relations, *452*
publicity, *453*
video news release (VNR), *453*

DISCUSSION QUESTIONS

1. Some marketers and PR people believe public relations should replace advertising as the primary tool for introducing new products. Explain why this would or would not be a good plan.

2. Explain why traditional public relations practitioners might be unhappy with the organization's use of MPRs. Take a position as to whether this criticism is justified.

3. List and describe the advantages and disadvantages of the use of public relations in an IMC program. Provide an example of an appropriate use of public relations in this mix.

4. What is a video news release (VNR)? Provide an example of a situation in which a company might employ the use of a VNR. Discuss some of the ethical implications (if any) in using this tool.

5. Many companies are now taking the position that their charitable contributions should lead to something in return—for example, sales or increased visibility. Discuss the pros and cons of this position.

6. Many companies are now trying to generate as much free publicity as they can. Cite some examples of this, and discuss the advantages and disadvantages associated with this strategy.

7. Describe some criteria used by firms to measure public relations effectiveness.

CHAPTER 16

DIRECT MARKETING

Chapter Objectives

- To recognize the purpose of direct marketing as a communications tool.
- To appreciate the strategies and tactics involved in direct marketing.
- To demonstrate the use of direct-response media.
- To determine the scope and effectiveness of direct marketing.

Direct Mail Delivers for Knorr

For consumers, frozen dinners often evoke thoughts of convenience along with speed and ease of preparation—with the trade-off being a less tasty meal. Knorr looked to dispel that belief with its new line of frozen entrée dinners featuring delectable dishes like Grilled Chicken Alfredo and Ricotta Cheese Ravioli. However, the promotional message needed to convey the gourmet-like menu and premium ingredients along with altering consumer perceptions of the product category.

Enter the IMC campaign that featured the tagline "Frozen doesn't have to be a bad word." In the television commercial, a sound effect "bleeped out" the word "frozen" during the voice-over, so viewers heard, "They're unlike any [*beep*] dinner you've ever tried." Equating a swear word with traditional frozen dinners allowed Knorr to distance itself from its competitors. The slick production featured "great music, great voice, great cinematography, and great art direction," which suggested the premium product image.

Direct mail played a key role in the IMC program, which also featured print ads with the word "frozen" blacked out as though censored and an in-store program of signs, samples, and coupons. Knorr delivered direct mail pieces, also containing a coupon, to households according to demographic and purchase behaviour potential along ten different characteristics. Those most likely to respond included past Knorr consumers interested in the frozen food category who had sufficient disposable income to afford a premium product. The various combinations of the ten characteristics provided many opportunities to reach various target audiences ranging from very low to extremely high levels of audience attractiveness.

To read the direct mail message consumers placed the piece in the freezer, where the cold temperature activated the specialized ink and revealed the word "frozen"—keeping the consistent theme throughout all IMC tools. The results indicated a 10 percent response rate, substantially higher than the projected 3 percent. One of the more attractive target audiences attained a response rate of 50 percent. The need to hold back some of the mailing due to store stock-outs revealed a final indicator of success of the direct mail initiative.

Sources: Darren Warner, "Creative Eye," *Marketing Magazine,* May 8, 2006; Sarah Dobson, "Knorr Says 'Frozen' Doesn't Have to be a Bad Word," *Marketing Magazine,* April 11, 2006; 2007 Canadian Marketing Association Awards Magazine, November 16, 2007, www.the-cma-org.com; strategymag.com.

Questions

1. What is your reaction to the way Knorr used the word "frozen" in this campaign?
2. How valuable is the direct mail piece within the overall IMC campaign?

In this chapter, we discuss direct marketing and its role as a communications tool. Direct marketing includes programs such as direct mail, catalogues, telemarketing, and infomercials. In essence, it is communication in each of the media we have discussed thus far, but with a more immediate behavioural objective. Direct marketing is one of the fastest-growing forms of promotion in terms of dollar expenditures, and for many marketers it is rapidly becoming the medium of choice for reaching consumers. We begin with an overview of direct marketing and then examine direct-marketing programs. The chapter concludes with a discussion of the strengths and limitations of this marketing tool.

Direct Marketing

While most companies continue to rely primarily on the other promotional mix elements to move their products and services through intermediaries, an increasing number are going directly to the consumer. These companies believe that the traditional promotional mix tools, such as advertising and sales promotion, are effective in creating brand image, conveying information, and/or creating awareness. However, going direct with these same tools can generate an immediate behavioural response that makes direct marketing a valuable tool in the integrated communications program.

Defining Direct Marketing

As noted in Chapter 1, **direct marketing** is a system of marketing by which organizations communicate directly with target customers to generate a response or transaction. This response may take the form of an inquiry, a purchase, or even a vote. In his *Dictionary of Marketing Terms,* Peter Bennett defines direct marketing as:

> The total of activities by which the seller, in effecting the exchange of goods and services with the buyer, directs efforts to a target audience using one or more media (direct selling, direct mail, telemarketing, direct-action advertising, catalogue selling, cable TV selling, etc.) for the purpose of soliciting a response by phone, mail, or personal visit from a prospect or customer.[1]

Direct marketing is an aspect of total marketing—that is, it involves marketing research, segmentation, evaluation, and the like, just as our planning model in Chapter 1 did. Direct marketing uses a set of **direct-response media**, including direct mail, telemarketing, interactive TV, print, the Internet, and other media. These media are the tools by which direct marketers implement the communications process. Firms that use this marketing method range from major retailers to publishing companies to computer retailers to financial services. Business-to-business and industrial marketers have also significantly increased their direct-marketing efforts.

Growth of Direct Marketing

Direct marketing has been around since the invention of the printing press in the 15th century. However, the major impetus behind the growth of direct marketing may have been the development and expansion of the postal service, which made catalogues available to both urban and rural dwellers so that consumers could access goods that were otherwise unavailable during the late 1800s and early 1900s.

More recently, catalogues revolutionized North American buying habits; consumers could now shop without ever leaving their homes.

But catalogues alone do not account for the rapid growth of direct marketing. A number of factors in our society have led to the increased attractiveness of this medium for both buyer and seller:

- *Consumer credit cards.* A significant number of credit cards—bank, oil company, retail, and so on—are in circulation in Canada. This makes it feasible for consumers to purchase both low- and high-ticket items through direct-response channels and assures sellers that they will be paid. Of course, not all of this will be through direct marketing, but a high percentage of direct purchases do use this method of payment, and companies such as American Express, MasterCard, and Visa are among the heaviest direct advertisers.
- *Direct-marketing syndicates.* Companies specializing in list development, statement inserts, catalogues, and sweepstakes have opened many new opportunities to marketers. The number of these companies continues to expand, creating even more new users.
- *Structure of North American society.* One of the major factors contributing to the success of direct marketing is that so many of us are now "money-rich and time-poor."[2] The rapid increase in dual-income families and the reduced time available for shopping have increased the attractiveness of direct purchases.
- *Technological advances.* The rapid technological advancement of the electronic media and of computers has made it easier for consumers to shop and for marketers to be successful in reaching target markets. The majority of the 11 million households in Canada receive home shopping programs.
- *Miscellaneous factors.* A number of other factors have contributed to the increased effectiveness of direct marketing, including changing values, more sophisticated marketing techniques, and the industry's improved image. These factors will also ensure the success of direct marketing in the future.

Direct-Marketing Plan

To successfully implement direct-marketing programs, companies must make a number of decisions. As in other marketing programs, they must determine (1) what the program's objectives will be; (2) who to target by using a database; (3) what direct-response media strategy will be employed; and (4) how to measure direct-marketing effectiveness.

Direct-Marketing Objectives

The direct marketer seeks a direct response. The objectives of the program are normally consumer behaviours—for example, test-drives, votes, contributions, and/or purchases. A typical objective is defined through a set response, perhaps a 2 to 3 percent response rate.

Not all direct marketing seeks a behavioural response, however. Many organizations use direct marketing to build an image, maintain customer satisfaction, and inform and/or educate customers that may lead to future actions. Exhibit 16–1 shows how the province of Saskatchewan uses direct mail to encourage travel.

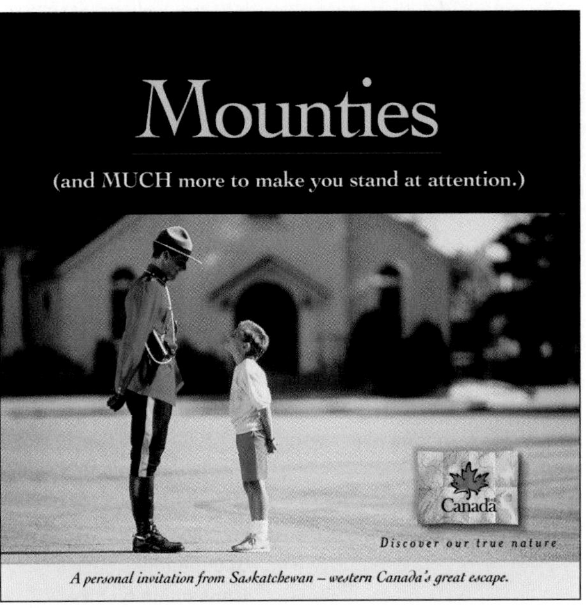

Exhibit 16–1 Saskatchewan encourages visits through direct mail

Developing a Database

As we have discussed throughout this text, market segmentation and targeting are critical components of any promotional program. Direct-marketing programs employ these principles even more than others, since the success of a direct-marketing program is in large part tied to the ability to reach a very significant target audience. To segment and target their audiences, direct marketers use a **database**, a listing of customers and/or potential customers. This database is a tool for **database marketing**—the use of specific information about individual customers and/or prospects to implement more effective and efficient marketing communications.[3]

Figure 16–1 demonstrates how database marketing works. The database marketing effort must be an integral part of the overall IMC program. At the very least, this list contains names, addresses, and postal codes; more sophisticated databases include information on demographics and psychographics, purchase transactions and payments, personal facts, neighbourhood data, and even credit histories (see Figure 16–2). The new privacy legislation introduced in 2004 places greater limitations on what marketers can do with information stored in their databases. We refer you to www.privcom.gc.ca for a complete guide.

FIGURE *16–1*

How database marketing works

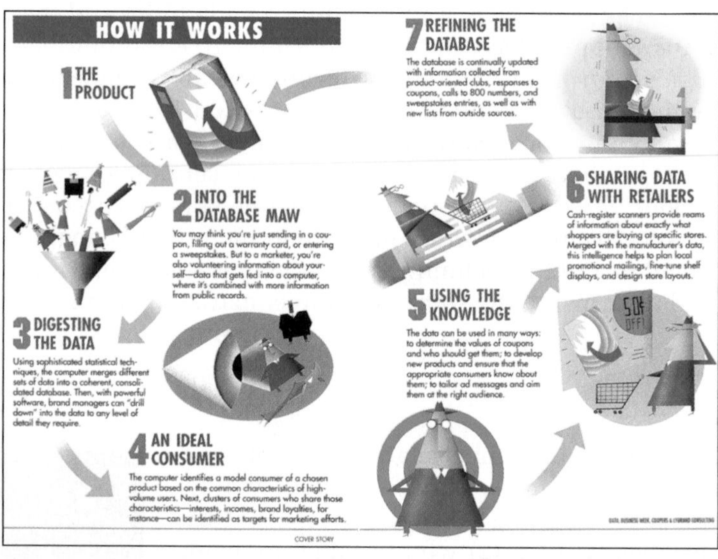

FIGURE *16–2*

Contents for a comprehensive database

Consumer Database	Business-to-Business Database
Name	Name of company/contact/decision maker(s)
Address/postal code	Title of contact
Telephone number	Telephone number
Length of residence	Source of order/inquiry or referral
Age	Credit history
Gender	Industrial classification
Marital status	Size of business
Family data (number of children, etc.)	Revenues
Education	Number of employees
Income	Time in business
Occupation	Headquarters location
Transaction history	Multiple locations
Promotion history	Purchase history
Inquiring history	Promotion history
Unique identifier	Inquiry history
	Unique identifier

This database serves as the foundation from which the direct-marketing programs evolve. Databases are used to perform the following functions:[4]

Exhibit 16–2 Blockbuster uses mailers to cross promote

- *Improving the selection of market segments.* Some consumers are more likely to be potential purchasers, users, voters, and so on than are others. By analyzing the characteristics of the database, a marketer can target a greater potential audience. For example, catalogue companies have become very specialized. Companies such as Lands' End, Sears, and The Gap have culled their lists and become much more efficient, targeting only those who are most likely to purchase their products.
- *Stimulate repeat purchases.* Once a purchase has been made, the customer's name and other information are entered into the database. These people are proven direct-marketing users who offer high potential for repurchase. Magazines, for example, routinely send out renewal letters and/or call subscribers before the expiration date. Companies from carpet cleaners to lawn care services to car dealers build a base of customers and contact them when they are "due" to repurchase.
- *Cross-sell.* Customers who demonstrate a specific interest also constitute strong potential for other products of the same nature. For example, the National Geographic Society has successfully sold globes, maps, videos, travel magazines, and an assortment of other products to subscribers who obviously have an interest in geography and/or travel. Likewise, Victoria's Secret has expanded its clothing lines primarily through sales to existing customers, and Kraft–General Foods has successfully cross-sold products in its varied food line. Notice how many cross-selling offers are contained in the Blockbuster piece in Exhibit 16–2.
- *Customer relationship management.* Customer relationship management (CRM) requires that the marketer develop and maintain a significant amount of information about its clients. The aim of CRM is to establish and maintain a relationship with one's customers through affinities, personalized communications, and product/service offerings. For CRM to work effectively, a database is required. While CRM relies on technology specifically designed for managing customer relationships, there are overlapping characteristics of CRM and database marketing. Suffice it to say at this point that many of the techniques employed in database marketing are necessary to develop an effective CRM program. Exhibit 16–3 shows how Hertz communicates its continuity program, a key part of CRM.

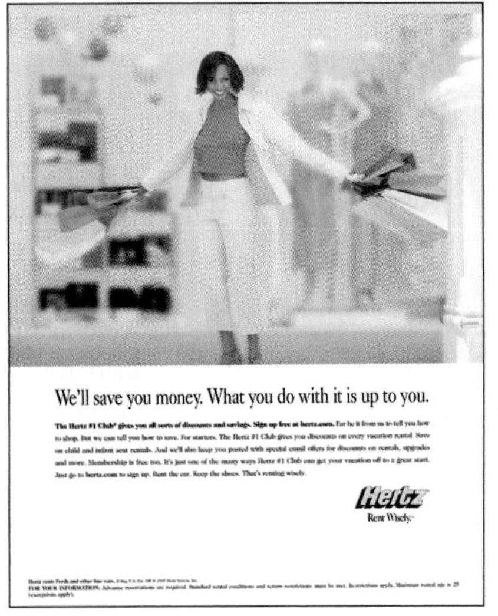

Exhibit 16–3 Hertz seeks permission to use receivers' names

Numerous other companies have established comprehensive databases on existing and potential customers both in North America and internationally. Database marketing has become so ubiquitous that many people are concerned about invasion of privacy. Direct marketers are concerned as well. The Canadian Marketing Association (CMA) and the Canadian Advertising Foundation (CAF) have asked members to adhere to ethical rules of conduct in their marketing efforts. They point out that if the industry does not police itself, the government will.

Sources of Database Information There are many sources of information for direct-marketing databases:

- *Statistics Canada.* Census data provide information on almost every household in Canada. Data include household size, demographics, income, and other information.

- *Canada Post.* Postal codes provide information on both household and business locations.
- *List services.* Many providers of lists are available. The accuracy and timeliness of the lists vary.
- *Info Canada.* Provincial Business Directory provides information regarding business lists. Published by province, Direct Mail List Rates and Data contains thousands of list selections.
- *Marketing research houses.* Large research houses conduct annual studies of customers who buy at home via mail or telephone. They compile information on total orders placed, types of products purchased, demographics, and purchase satisfaction, among others.
- *Loyalty programs.* Continuity programs designed to enhance loyalty are a new source of consumers with precise purchase patterns.
- *Others.* The Canadian Marketing Association, Dunn and Bradstreet, Fortune 500, *The Book of Lists,* and other published periodicals of this nature all contain listed information that can be used for these purposes.

Consumer-goods manufacturers, banks, credit bureaus, retailers, charitable organizations, and other business operations also sell lists and other selected information. Companies can build their own databases through completed warranty cards, surveys, and so on.

Determining the Effectiveness of the Database While many companies maintain a database, many do not use them effectively. Collecting names and information is not enough; the list must be kept current, purged of old and/or inactive customers, and updated frequently. The more information about customers that can be contained in the database, the more effective it will be. An **RFM scoring method** is often used for this purpose. RFM stands for the recency, frequency, and monetary transactions between the company and the customer. More specifically, data need to be entered each time there is a transaction so that the company can track how recently purchases have been made, how often they are made, and what amounts of money are being spent. In addition, tracking which products and/or services are used increases the ability for databases to conduct the activities previously mentioned in this section. By analyzing the database on a regular basis, the company or organization can identify trends and buying patterns that will help it establish a better relationship with its customers by more effectively meeting their needs.

Direct-Response Media

As with all other communications programs discussed in this text, marketers must decide the message to be conveyed, the size of the budget, and so on. Perhaps the major difference between direct-marketing programs and other promotional mix programs regards the use of media. Direct-response media include direct mail, telemarketing, broadcasting, the Internet, and print. Each medium is used to perform specific functions, although they generally follow a one- or two-step approach.

In the **one-step approach**, the medium is used directly to obtain an order. For example, TV commercials for products such as wrench sets, workout equipment, or magazine subscriptions urge viewers to phone a toll-free number to place an order immediately. Usually these ads accept credit cards or cash on delivery and give an address. Their goal is to generate an immediate sale when the ad is shown.

The **two-step approach** may involve the use of more than one medium. The first effort is designed to screen, or qualify, potential buyers. The second effort generates the response. For example, many companies use telemarketing to screen on the basis of interest, then follow up to interested parties with more information designed to achieve an order or use personal selling to close the sale.

A variation of the two-step approach emerged with the advent of the Internet. Many companies run direct-response television commercials to encourage website visits. For example, in its effort to move from a soup company to a food company, the Campbell Company of Canada ran nine ads with a celebrity chef demonstrating different cooking methods that directed consumers to a website, www.power2cook.ca, and followed up with extensive direct-mail pieces to 2 million Canadians.[5] IMC Perspective 16–1 on page 486 shows an innovative application of this method.

Exhibit 16–4 Porsche targets direct mail to upscale audiences

Direct Mail Direct mail is often called junk mail—the unsolicited mail received. Statistics show that 64 percent of Canadians read addressed direct mail right away when it arrives. Another 23 percent of Canadians keep it to review later at a time more convenient to them.[6] The low cost and extensive support provided by direct mail agencies and Canada Post allows small businesses to reach audiences. Large advertisers like financial institutions that have extensive databases of customers effectively use direct mail for cross-selling new products.

Many advertisers shied away from direct mail in the past, fearful of the image it might create or harbouring the belief that direct mail was useful only for low-cost products. But this is no longer the case. For example, Porsche Cars North America, Inc., uses direct mail to target high-income, upscale consumers who are most likely to purchase its expensive sports cars (Exhibit 16–4). In one example, Porsche developed a direct-mail piece that was sent to a precisely defined target market: physicians in specialties with the highest income levels. This list was screened to match the demographics of Porsche buyers and narrowed further to specific geographic areas. The direct-mail piece was an x-ray of a Porsche 911 Carrera 4 written in the language of the medical audience. This creative campaign generated one of the highest response rates of any mailing by Porsche.[7] The materials shown in Exhibit 16–5 are just some of the ones sent by Mercedes to market its SUV.

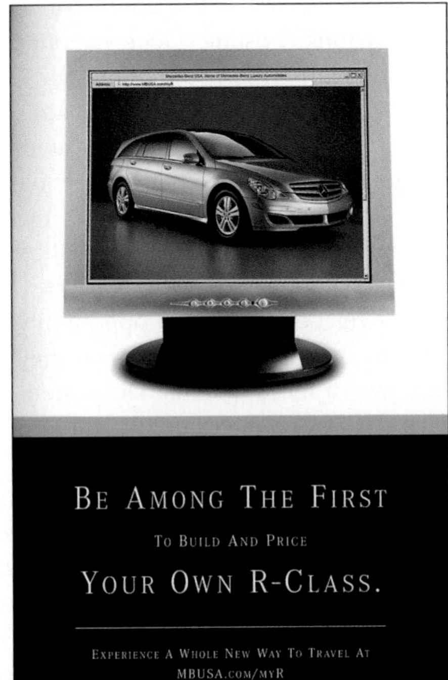

Exhibit 16–5 Mercedes used direct mail to introduce its new R-Class

Keys to the success of direct mail are the **mailing list**, which constitutes the database from which names are generated, and the ability to segment markets. Lists have become more current and more selective, eliminating waste coverage. Segmentation on the basis of geography (usually through postal codes), demographics, and lifestyles has led to increased effectiveness. The most commonly used lists are of individuals who have already purchased direct-mail products.

The importance of the list has led to a business of its own. It has been estimated that there are over 38 billion names on lists in North America, and many companies have found it profitable to sell the names of purchasers of their products and/or services to list firms. There are also a growing number of list-management companies springing up on the Internet. Canadian mailing lists by association or type of vocation are common. Canadian companies such as www.interactdirect.com, based in London, Ontario, are more common now.

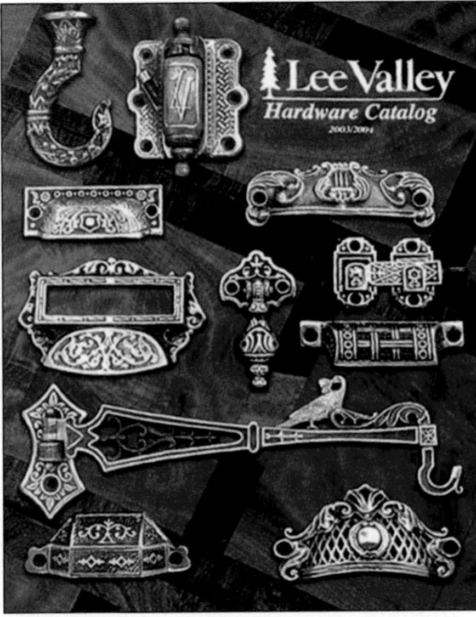

Exhibit 16–6 Lee Valley uses catalogues to communicate and sell directly

Catalogues Some companies rely solely on catalogue sales. For example, Yves Rocher is a firm that markets botanical beauty care products for women. It expanded into Canada with its small catalogues and sells directly to consumers. Lee Valley Tools of Ottawa began as a mail order catalogue company 30 years ago, but has branched out to retail stores across the country and online sales (Exhibit 16–6).

IMC PERSPECTIVE 16–1

Dove and Shoppers Drug Mart® Double Loyalty Club

With just over 10 million members, Shoppers Drug Mart isn't the only one happy about the success of its Shoppers Optimum loyalty program. Marketers often see sales of their brands spike when they invest in a Shoppers Optimum promotion since participating consumers receive bonus points toward in-store discounts. Now, Unilever—one of the drugstore chain's largest vendors—has upped the ante, running a loyalty initiative specifically for Dove that exists within the Shoppers Optimum program. Called Dove Optimum Rewards, membership gives consumers the opportunity to earn double the points when they buy two or more different Dove products. "We've created a club within a club," says Gabriel Verkade, retail activation manager of national accounts at Toronto-based Unilever.

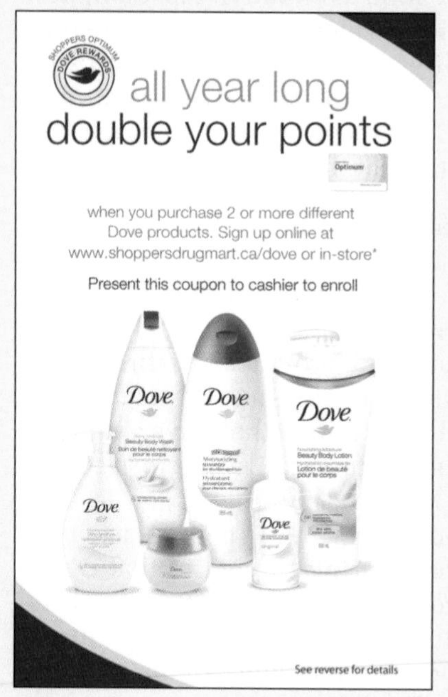

Dove Optimum Rewards is the first vendor program of its kind for Shoppers Drug Mart. As the loyalty segment matures, experts suggest this is just the start of what they're calling "loyalty program guardians," where marketers ranging from retailers to hotels create new and innovative partnerships with vendors. Before Shoppers Drug Mart partnered with Dove, rival packaged goods companies had approached the retailer about creating a vendor subprogram within Shoppers Optimum. Ultimately, Shoppers Drug Mart chose Dove because the brand ties nicely into the retailer's identity, focusing on health, beauty, and convenience, and had many SKUs to drive sales.

The four-week introductory campaign for Dove Optimum Rewards included a permission-based e-mail to one million Shoppers Optimum members, as well as to the permission-based e-mail lists of *Chatelaine* and mochasofa.ca; a national two-page flyer delivered to 4.4 million homes; an ad in *Glow* magazine; and signage, posters, and header cards in more that 974 Shoppers Drug Mart and Quebec-based Pharmaprix[MD] stores. The advertising included a coupon which, when scanned at the checkout, signed up Shoppers Optimum members to the Dove program. Shoppers Optimum members can also register online at www.shoppersdrugmart.ca/dove. Once registered, Shoppers Optimum card holders are automatically tagged as Dove Optimum Rewards members—in other words, no need for customers to carry yet another loyalty card.

Unilever aims to do more than just encourage trial among customers who typically only purchase a single Dove product. Unilever ultimately wants to develop a relationship with these customers through the new Dove Optimum database. Verkade says strict privacy regulations mean Shoppers Drug Mart doesn't give vendors access to its Shoppers Optimum database—which includes everything from the typical amount of a member's shopping basket to their demographic profile. But, the Shoppers Drug Mart/Unilever partnership does give Unilever access to information about the Dove Optimum Rewards members and the ability to work with Shoppers to better target them.

For Dove, the challenge is keeping the Dove Optimum Rewards program top of mind so that consumers realize that it is, in fact, a club within a club. "Once they are enrolled, our challenge is reminding them that they have joined an additional program and of the value they are receiving from it," says Verkade. That might mean a combination of direct mail, flyers, and e-mail or promotions on existing or new products, but also more value-added, enriched content, such as a booklet about beauty tips or information on managing sensitive skin.

Source: Chris Daniels, "The Layered Look," *Marketing*, March 26, 2007.

Questions

1. Explain how Dove's relationship to the Shoppers Optimum program works.
2. What concerns would you have about this joint promotion?

Companies also use catalogues in conjunction with their more traditional sales and promotional strategies. For example, companies such as Canadian Tire and Sears sell directly through catalogues but also use them to inform consumers of product offerings available in the stores.

In fact, Ikea prints 6 million catalogues per year and its executives view the catalogue as the company's "main marketing tool" since it naturally encourages consumers to visit the retail outlets or the Internet site. But, more importantly, it is a strong brand-building tool to demonstrate how Ikea's products improve the homes of millions of consumers.[8]

Home Depot started out as the headquarters for contractors and handy home renovators, but in Canada it started a decorating catalogue "The Home Depot DreamBook" to inspire women looking to improve their homes. Thus, catalogues can be used as a direct-marketing tool to attract a new target audience while not alienating the original loyal customer.[9]

In addition to the traditional hard copies, catalogues are now available on the Internet for both consumer and business-to-business customers. In some instances in the consumer market, the catalogue merchandise is available in retail stores as well. In others, the catalogue and retail divisions are treated as separate entities. For example, purchases made through the Eddie Bauer catalogue can be exchanged or returned to the retail stores. At The Gap, the catalogue is used to supplement the inventory in stock, and phone orders for different sizes and so on can be made from the store and shipped for free.

Broadcast Media Two broadcast media are available to direct marketers: television and radio. While radio was used quite extensively in the 1950s, its use and effectiveness have dwindled substantially in recent years. Thus, the majority of direct-marketing broadcast advertising now occurs on TV. Direct-response TV encompasses direct-response TV spots, infomercials, and home shopping shows (teleshopping).

TV Spots Referred to in the direct-marketing industry as *short-term programs*, these spots include direct-response commercials for products such as magazines and household goods. In **direct-response advertising**, the product or service is offered and a sales response is solicited, through either the one- or two-step approach. Toll-free phone numbers are included so that the receiver can immediately call to order.

Infomercials The lower cost of commercials on cable and satellite channels has led advertisers to a new form of advertising. An **infomercial** is a long commercial that ranges from 3 to 60 minutes. Many infomercials are produced by the advertisers and are designed to be viewed as regular TV shows. Consumers dial a 1-800 or 1-900 number to place an order. IMC Perspective 16–2 on page 488 highlights a unique adaptation of infomercials. This form of show is popular with small firms and infomercials have been adopted by many big, mainstream marketers. Apple Computer, Microsoft, Sony, Volvo, and Philips Electronics are just some of the many others now employing this method of communication (Exhibit 16–7).

As to their effectiveness, studies indicate that infomercials get watched and sell products. One study profiling infomercial viewers and buyers demonstrated that this advertising medium is indeed effective with a broad demographic base, not significantly different from the infomercial non-shopper in age, education, income, or gender. There are also a number of differences between infomercial shoppers and non-shoppers.[10]

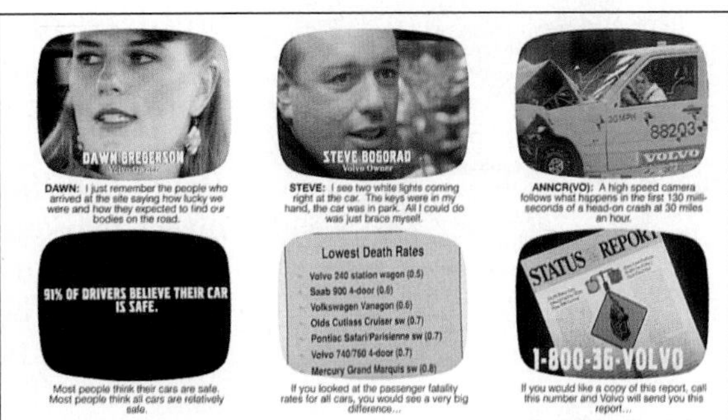

Exhibit 16–7 Volvo uses an infomercial to attract buyers

IMC PERSPECTIVE 16–2

Direct-Response Television Fundraising

Place of Miracles: Inside the Hospital for Sick Children aired November 2002 and ushered in the era of direct-response television to raise funds for the eminent facility located in downtown Toronto. As the drama continued throughout the one-hour show, viewers naturally felt they were watching an episode of a television show and not a plea for more money as they witnessed the heart-felt story of young Olivia and her quest for a new heart. And more importantly, viewers observed and identified with the parents of Olivia who related their experiences and explained their gratitude for the health-care service Olivia received. At the end of the film, Olivia received her transplanted heart and the requests for donations and a phone number were shown on the screen.

Pledges from direct-response television average about 45 percent of all callers, but *Place of Miracles* struck it rich with 61 percent. And direct-response television was part of the many direct-marketing tools that the foundation responsible for fundraising implements each year. With an annual goal of $54 million for 2003, the foundation also planned to use telemarketing, direct mail, door-to-door solicitation, radio, and a telethon. But the direct-response television played a key role because of its extensive reach and its ability to target those aged 35–50 who have children, a group the foundation did not reach with direct mail, which often reached those over age 55. Overall, the initial foray into this new direct-marketing alternative raised $850,000, double the expected target.

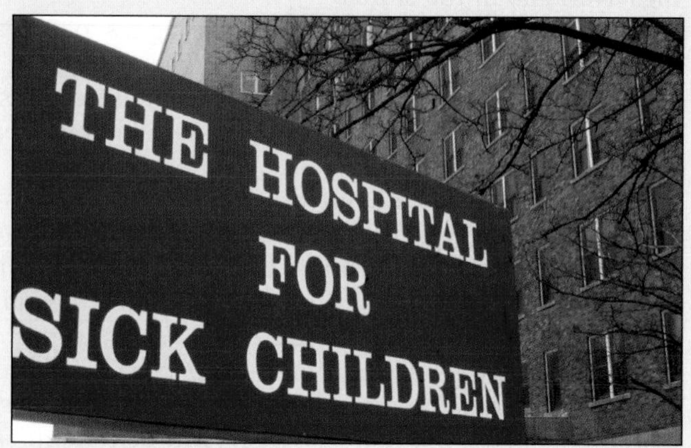

In choosing direct-response television, the hospital also recognized its value in building the overall brand, something unheard of previously. However, health-care facilities and other non-profit institutions face competition from all organizations and causes that seek funds from the general public. In fact, one advertising agency executive suggested that the fundraising in the not-for-profit world faced stronger competition than for the for-profit firms.

Source: Michelle Warren, "Sick Kids' Direct Drama," *Marketing Magazine*, February 10, 2003.

Question

1. Why was this infomercial so successful compared to other forms of direct-response media?

Exhibit 16–8 A direct-response print ad

Teleshopping The development of toll-free telephone numbers, combined with the widespread use of credit cards, has led to a dramatic increase in the number of people who shop via their TV sets. Jewellery, kitchenware, fitness products, electronics, and a variety of items are now promoted (and sold) this way. The Shopping Channel (TSC) is Canada's broadcast retailer available on all delivery formats (cable, satellite) across the country. And, of course, the lines of communication get blurred even more as TSC is available in catalogue form and on the Internet.

Print Media Magazines and newspapers are difficult media to use for direct marketing. Because these ads have to compete with the clutter of other ads and because the space is relatively expensive, response rates and profits may be lower than in other media. These ads are typically found in specific interest areas such as financial newspapers or sports, or hobby magazines. Exhibit 16–8 shows a direct ad that appeared in a magazine. Direct-to-consumer magazines hit Canada when the Hudson's Bay Company launched Canada's first publication, *Lifestyle*, to the 500,000 members within its HBC Rewards database. HBC planned to measure the consumer response to specific promotions, and advertisers within the magazine could also join in so that they too could track their results.[11]

FIGURE *16–3* The use of 800, 900, and 976 numbers in marketing

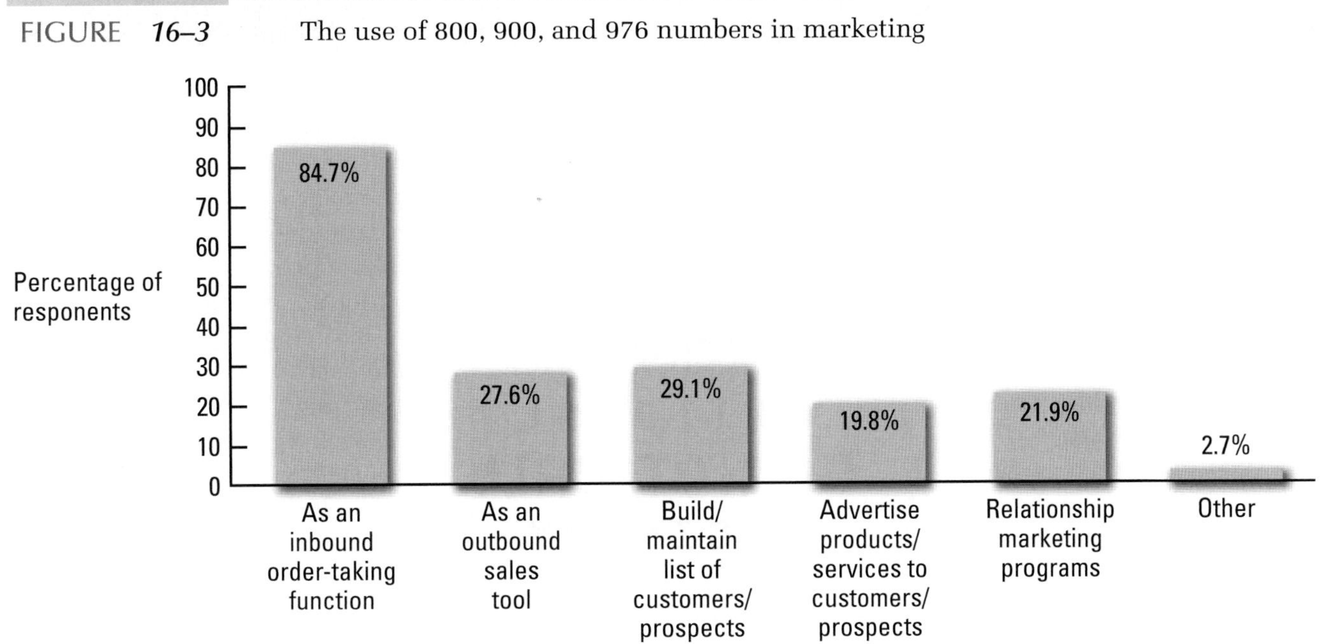

Note: *Direct* forecast survey was conducted by Jacobson Consulting Applications. The firms mailed a four-page questionnaire to direct-marketing executives, on an *n*th name basis from *Direct*'s circulation list. There were 565 responses.

Telemarketing Communication resulting in sales via the telephone is known as **telemarketing**. There are two types of telemarketing. Outbound telemarketing refers to calls made by a company or its sponsor to a potential buyer or client, soliciting the sale of products, services, donations, votes, or any other "value" issue. Inbound telemarketing occurs when a company has advertised its 1-800 number or its website address, for example, asking the customer to call the number, visit the store, or log on to the website. Both profit and charitable organizations have employed this medium effectively in both one- and two-step approaches.

As telemarketing continues to expand in scope, a new dimension referred to as **audiotex** or **telemedia** has evolved. Tom Eisenhart defines telemedia as the "use of telephone and voice information services (900, 800, and 976 numbers) to market, advertise, promote, entertain, and inform."[12] Many telemedia programs are interactive. Figure 16–3 shows more specifically how 800/900 numbers are used as marketing tools.[13]

Problems associated with telemarketing include its potential for fraud and deception and its potential for annoyance. However, data on call centres in Canada show that most call centres are well managed. The majority communicate clearly if the interaction is recorded, follow the laws governing telemarketing, and work with their employees to ensure appropriate interactions.[14] Those in the telemarketing and telemedia industry have responded to public criticisms. As more and more large companies use telemedia, its tarnished image will likely brighten up. IMC Perspective 16–3 on page 490 summarizes legislation limiting the use of telemarketing in the future.

Direct-Marketing Effectiveness

For direct-marketing programs that do not have an objective of generating an immediate behavioural response, traditional measures of advertising effectiveness can be applied. In those situations requiring a direct response, measuring the effectiveness should include some specific behavioural measure in addition to the communication measures. Using the cost per order (CPO), advertisers can evaluate the relative effectiveness of an ad in only a few minutes based on the number of calls generated.

IMC PERSPECTIVE 16–3

Telemarketers Losing Potential Customers

Canada's national Do-Not-Call (DNC) registry, slated for launch by the CRTC in the fall of 2007, is a major advance in the protection of privacy rights—and its value extends beyond reducing unwanted telemarketing calls. Canada's DNC legislation, like its American counterpart, has sharp teeth. Telemarketers will be required to regularly check the registry—most likely every 90 days—and "scrub" their calling lists. If they violate the legislation and call a registered household, the fine is expected to be $1,500 for individuals and $15,000 for companies.

The not-so-good news is that Do-Not-Call also entails short-term risk for marketing and public opinion research firms. The hard truth is that most people believe the registry will enable them to eliminate all unsolicited calls. Consumers are generally unaware that survey research firms—along with registered charities, political parties, and companies with a current business relationship with the consumer—are exempt. Many Canadians mistakenly think that once they register their phones are going to go silent. If this perception is not corrected, the result will be confusion, disappointment, and in some cases hostility.

Do-Not-Call will have a profound effect on Canadian marketers. The Marketing Research and Intelligence Association (MRIA) study conducted in fall 2006 revealed that 39 percent of Canadian adults were aware the registry is on the horizon, despite minimal media coverage. Such high awareness so early suggests the popularity of Canada's no-call list will match the U.S. experience. If this occurs, more than 9 million Canadian households could sign up within three years of the registry's launch. In the U.S., the number of registered households that are off-limits to unwanted telemarketers is now well over 90 million.

The period leading up to the registry's launch offers a unique opportunity to educate Canadians about the benefits of participating in survey research and to increase response rates. Strong, smart communication efforts—from both government and survey researchers—are needed during the registry's rollout in Canada to minimize confusion, manage expectations, and ensure unfettered access to survey respondents.

Source: Nik Nanos, "Calling Consumers," *Marketing Magazine*, March 26, 2007.

Question

1. Is continuing to allow certain people and organizations to call households a positive thing for consumers?

By running the same ad on different stations, a direct marketer can determine the relative effectiveness of the medium itself. For example, if the advertiser targets a $5 return per order and a broadcast commercial (production and print) costs $2,500, the ad is considered effective if it generates 500 orders. Similar measures have been developed for print and direct-mail ads.

Tracking the behavioural effects is exactly what Sprint Canada emphasized during the launch of its "Red Is Smarter" campaign. Each creative execution contained a unique toll-free number in a controlled region so that it could gauge the impact of different persuasive messages when the call centre received the inbound consumer response. Sprint Canada used the same idea for different promotional offers.[15]

Evaluation of Direct Marketing

Many of the strengths and limitations of direct marketing have already been presented. As we have done with other media, we now summarize these factors in a concluding section.

Strengths of Direct Marketing

Selective Reach Direct marketing lets the advertiser reach a large number of people and reduces or eliminates waste coverage. Intensive coverage may be obtained through broadcast advertising or through the mail. While not everyone drives on highways where there are billboards or pays attention to TV commercials, virtually everyone receives mail. A good list allows for minimal waste, as only those consumers with the highest potential are targeted. For example, a political candidate can direct a message at a very select group of people (those living in a certain postal code, or members of McGill University Alumni, or the Royal Vancouver Yacht Club, say); in the same vein, a music club can target recent purchasers of MP3 players, or a medical software supplier can target all M.D.s in the medical association directories.

Segmentation Capabilities Marketers can purchase lists of recent product purchasers, car buyers, bank card holders, and so on. These lists may allow segmentation on the basis of geographic area, occupation, demographics, and job title, to mention a few. Combining this information with the geocoding capabilities of PRIZM or VALS (discussed in Chapter 3), marketers can develop effective segmentation strategies.

Frequency Depending on the medium used, it may be possible to build frequency levels. The program vehicles used for direct-response TV advertising are usually the most inexpensive available, so the marketer can afford to purchase repeat times. Frequency may not be so easily accomplished through the mail, since consumers may be annoyed to receive the same mail repeatedly.

Flexibility Direct marketing can take on a variety of creative forms. For example, the Discovery Network sent 17-inch TV sets to media buyers through the mail. The only message accompanying the TV sets was one on the cord that said "Plug me in" and another on a videotape that read "Play me." Upon doing so, the recipient was greeted with a 7-minute promotional video. Direct-mail pieces also allow for detailed copy that provides a great deal of information. The targeted mailing of CDs or DVDs containing product information has increased dramatically, as companies have found this a very effective way to provide potential buyers with product information.

Timing While many media require long-range planning and have long closing dates, direct-response advertising can be much more timely. Direct mail, for example, can be put together very quickly and distributed to the target population. TV programs typically used for direct-response advertising are older, less sought programs that are likely to appear on the station's list of available spots. Another common strategy is to purchase available time at the last possible moment to get the best price.

Personalization No other advertising medium can personalize the message as well as direct media. Parents with children at different age levels can be approached, with their child's name included in the appeal. Car owners are mailed letters congratulating them on their new purchase and offering accessories. Computer purchasers are sent software solicitations. Graduating college and university students receive very personalized information that recognizes their specific needs and offers solutions (such as credit cards).

Costs While the CPM for direct mail may be very high on an absolute and a relative basis, its ability to specifically target the audience and eliminate waste coverage reduces the actual CPM. The ads used on TV are often among the lowest-priced available, and a video can be delivered for less than $1 (including postage). A second factor contributing to the cost effectiveness of direct-response advertising is the cost per customer purchasing. Because of the low cost of media, each sale generated is very inexpensive.

Measures of Effectiveness No other medium can measure the effectiveness of its advertising efforts as well as direct response. Feedback is often immediate and always accurate.

Limitations of Direct Marketing

Image Factors Many people believe unsolicited mail promotes junk products, and others dislike being solicited. Likewise, direct-response ads on TV are often low-budget ads for lower-priced products, which contributes to the image that something less than the best products are marketed in this way. Some of this image is being overcome by the home shopping channels, which promote some very expensive products. Telemarketing is found to be irritating to many consumers.

Accuracy One of the advantages cited for direct mail and telemarketing was targeting potential customers specifically. But the effectiveness of these methods depends on the accuracy of the lists used. People move, change occupations, and so on, and if the lists are not kept current, selectivity will decrease. Computerization has greatly improved the currency of lists and reduced the incidence of bad names; however, the ability to generate lists is becoming a problem.[16]

Content Support In our discussion of media strategy objectives in Chapter 9, we said that the ability of magazines to create mood contributes to the overall effectiveness of the ads they carry. In direct-response advertising, mood creation is limited to the surrounding program and/or editorial content.

IMC Planning: Strategic Use of Direct Marketing

Direct marketing is now an important component in the integrated marketing programs of many organizations. In some cases it is used as a tool for an immediate response and in other cases it plays a key role in building the brand by moving through the target audience's decision-making process. In addition, direct-marketing activities support and are supported by other elements of the promotional mix.

Decision-Making Process

As described in this chapter, direct marketing tools are typically employed to persuade immediate consumer action. At this point, it is critical that the promotional manager plan for a specific action in order to select the most appropriate direct-response media. In Chapter 5 we reviewed different types of behavioural objectives for promotional communication, which we will use to develop some IMC planning prescriptions. Trial and repeat purchasing objectives suggest that much of direct marketing involves influence at the purchase decision stage.

Trial objectives require a broader-based direct-response media, much like what is seen in advertising media decisions. Typically, wide-ranging direct-mail pieces targeted by census track and income dispersions allow firms to reach as many potential consumers as possible. In this situation, the database used relies on more public sources and a manager may use unaddressed drop-offs. Alternatively, for more targeted messages, brands may rely upon the list services and provide addressed mailings. Alternatively, with a database of existing customers, cross-selling of other products is now a trial purchase for the promotional planner's brand in a new product category. This trial purchase may be relatively new and be viewed as a purchase within the product category, thus requiring a direct-response medium providing considerable information.

We mentioned that existing customer databases are used for repeat purchases. Repeat purchasing objectives involve the timing, amount, and rate of consumer purchases. These different options suggest other criteria for evaluating the different direct-media options. For example, repeat purchasing objectives for specific timing might suggest telemarketing if the managers have current databases and permission to call upon its current customers. A favourite direct-response medium for many firms is bill inserts delivered monthly to enhance frequency and thus improve the amount and rate of purchase. Thus, the opportunity of promotional planners to match the specific objectives with the right direct-response medium requires full consideration.

Purchase-related behaviour objectives frequently involve influencing consumers at earlier stages in their decision-making. For example, direct-mail pieces may be delivered to encourage need recognition and prompt the target audience to make a sales enquiry at the retail location or over the telephone, or to visit the Internet site for further understanding of the brand during the information search stage. Alternatively, telephone calls can be made as follow up after the sales enquiry to ensure that the brand is seriously considered at the alternative evaluation stage.

Direct Marketing and IMC Tools

Obviously, direct marketing is in itself a form of advertising. Whether through mail, print, or TV, the direct-response offer is an ad. It usually contains a contact number, a form that requests mailing information, or a link to an Internet site. Sometimes the ad supports the direct-selling effort. For example, Victoria's Secret runs image ads to support its store and catalogue sales. Direct-response ads or infomercials are also referred to in retail outlet displays.

Public relations activities often employ direct-response techniques. Private companies may use telemarketing activities to solicit funds for charities or cosponsor charities that use these and other direct-response techniques to solicit funds. Likewise, corporations and/or organizations engaging in public relations activities may include contact numbers or Internet addresses in their ads or promotional materials.

Telemarketing and direct selling are two methods of personal selling. Non-profit organizations such as charities often use telemarketing to solicit funds. For-profit companies are also using telemarketing with much greater frequency to screen and qualify prospects (which reduces selling costs) and to generate leads. Direct-mail pieces are often used to invite prospective customers to visit auto showrooms to test-drive new cars; the salesperson then assumes responsibility for the selling effort.

Direct mail is often used to notify consumers of sales promotions like sales events or contests. Ski shops regularly mail announcements of special end-of-season sales. Whistler Ski Resort and Intrawest constantly mail out promotions to their customer database announcing promotional and seasonal vacation packages, room rates, and lift ticket specials. The Bay, Sears, and other retail outlets call their existing customers to notify them of special sales promotions. Each of these is an example of a company using direct-marketing tools to inform customers of sales promotions. In turn, the sales promotion event may support the direct-marketing effort (Exhibit 16–9). Databases are often built from the names and addresses acquired from a promotion, and direct mail and/or telemarketing calls follow.

Adding a promotional product to a direct mailer has proved to increase response rates. One company included a promotional product in half of its 10,000 mailers and not in the other half. The former generated 65 percent more orders. 3M used a promotional product as an incentive for people responding to a direct-mail offer. The incentive generated a 23 percent response rate versus only 9 percent for the regular mailer.

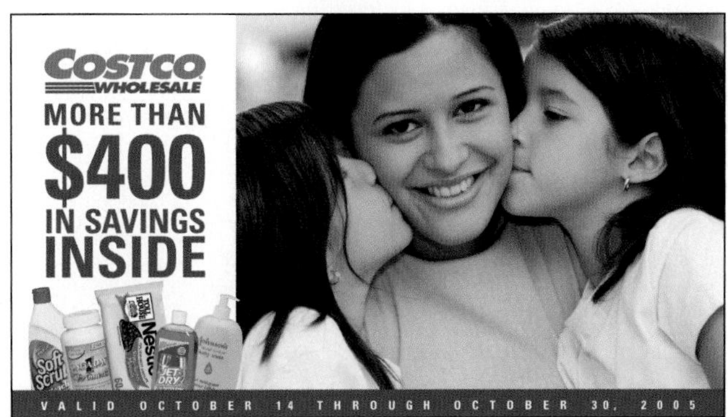

Exhibit 16–9 Costco sends promotional offers through the mail

SUMMARY

This chapter introduced the rapidly growing field of direct marketing, which involves a variety of methods and media beyond direct mail and telemarketing. The versatility of direct marketing offers many different types of companies and organizations a powerful promotional and selling tool.

Direct marketing continues to outpace other advertising and promotional areas in growth; many of the Fortune 500 companies now use sophisticated direct-marketing strategies. Database marketing has become a critical component of many marketing programs.

Advantages of direct marketing include its selective reach, segmentation, frequency, flexibility, and timing. Personalized and custom messages, low costs, and the ability to measure program effectiveness are also advantages of direct-marketing programs.

At the same time, a number of disadvantages are associated with the use of direct marketing. Image problems, the proliferating sale and use of databases (some of them based on inaccurate lists), lack of content support, and the intrusive nature of the medium make some marketers hesitant to use direct-marketing tools. However, self-policing of the industry and involvement by large, sophisticated companies have led to significant improvements. As a result, the use of direct marketing will continue to increase.

KEY TERMS

audiotex, *489*
database, *482*
database marketing, *482*
direct marketing, *480*
direct-response advertising, *487*
direct-response media, *480*
infomercial, *487*
mailing list, *485*
one-step approach, *484*
RFM scoring method, *484*
telemarketing, *489*
telemedia, *489*
two-step approach, *484*

DISCUSSION QUESTIONS

1. Explain how companies use database marketing. Name some of the companies that may have information in their database. Explain how this information is used to reach its target audience.

2. What is the difference between the one- and two-step approaches to direct marketing? Give examples of companies that pursue both methods.

3. As the Internet continues to grow in popularity, some marketers predict that the print catalogue will cease to exist, replaced by Internet catalogues. Others disagree. Explain some of the reasons why this situation may or may not occur.

4. Describe the various forms of direct-response advertising. Discuss some of the reasons for the success of direct-response advertising.

5. Many marketers thought that the Internet would hurt the direct-mail catalogue industry. In fact, this has not been the case. Explain some of the similar characteristics of catalogue shopping and shopping on the Internet. Then explain why you think the mail catalogue business has not been hurt.

6. Explain why companies like KitchenAid, Soloflex, and others have been successful in adopting direct-marketing techniques. Describe the conditions that contribute to the successful implementation of direct-marketing programs.

7. Identify some of the factors that have contributed to the growth of direct marketing. Do you see these factors being as relevant today? Discuss why or why not, and the impact they will have on direct marketing in the future.

8. One of the disadvantages associated with direct-marketing media is the high cost per exposure. Some marketers feel that this cost is not really as much of a disadvantage as is claimed. Argue for or against this position.

9. Give an example of how companies might use direct marketing as part of an IMC program. Provide examples of both consumer and business marketers.

10. Direct marketing has been beset by a number of problems that have tarnished its image. Discuss some of these and what might be done to improve direct marketing's image.

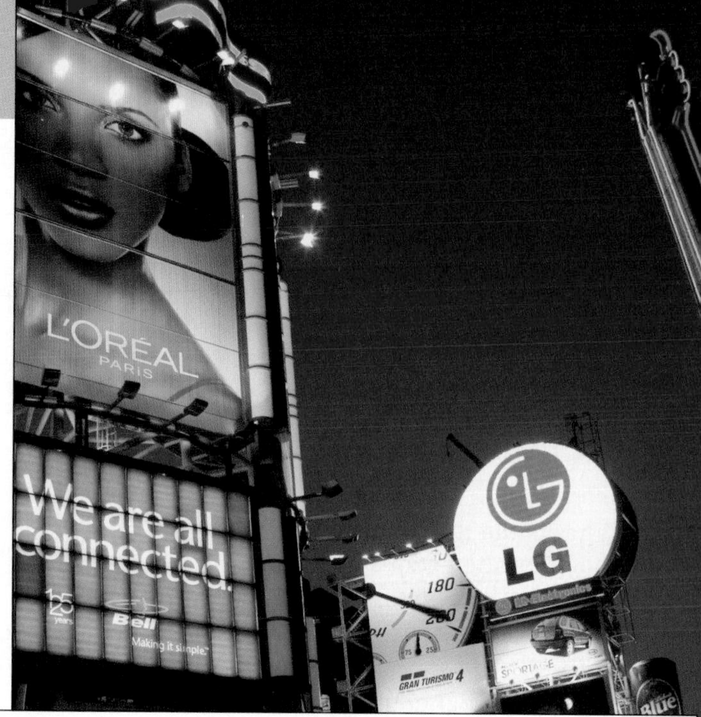

CHAPTER 17

INTERNET MEDIA

Chapter Objectives

- To explore the different ways the Internet is used to communicate.
- To review the strengths and limitations of Internet media.
- To understand the role of Internet media in an IMC program.
- To evaluate the effectiveness of communications through the Internet.

Advertising Goes Digital

The 2006 Digital Marketing Awards by *Marketing Magazine* certainly signals the arrival of Internet media as an important opportunity for advertisers to reach their audiences. Moreover, the variety of avenues advertisers use suggests that the development of a campaign for Internet media requires careful strategic and tactical planning as seen in other IMC tools.

Diesel of Montreal won Best of Show with its Internet site designed for the MGM Grand Hotel located in Las Vegas. The rich media images illuminated the experience of actually being in the hotel, with music and delightful scenes of an attractive young couple enjoying the hotel's attractions and amenities. The user-friendly design allowed consumers to move from scene to scene with ease or fast-forward or rewind video scenes. With the reservation section always in view, the site provided the opportunity to garner as many bookings as possible.

The TV show *Canada's Worst Handyman* won for best online/offline integrated campaign. The Internet site invited guests to see "Handy Ted," who incorrectly performed renovations like welding beside a live gas line in a game-like experience that the users controlled. Other media paid for by the Discovery Channel included TV, billboards, and transit shelters, making the show the top Canadian series in the spring of 2006. Air Canada received recognition for best online integrated campaign to promote its prepaid one-way flight credits. A micro-site featured passengers portrayed as "revolutionaries" who desire change in air travel. Banner ads with similar imagery directed interested consumers toward the site.

Subway sandwich wrappers contained a unique number for consumers to text in order to win prizes. This wireless application of Internet media advertising allowed non-winners to continue to interact, with trivia questions and ballot entries for additional contests. Results showed that 80 percent of consumers who participated carried on to the second stage of the promotion.

Finally, a microsite for Trojan condoms took best Internet site for consumer packaged goods. The image of an apartment building allowed voyeurs to vicariously witness the sexual antics of silhouetted couples in a variety of catchy scenes reminiscent of the different performance characteristics of its vast product line. Each scene concluded with the doorman voice-over remarking with sexual innuendo. A product description followed each vignette, allowing consumers to observe how the particular feature (e.g., extended pleasure) fit with the scene.

Source: Rob Gerlsbeck, "Maximum Digital," *Marketing Magazine*, November 6, 2006.

Question

1. Why were these Internet examples worthy of receiving recognition with an award?

The Internet has moved from a medium with almost no presence in the marketing environment to one that has a significant role in most firms' communication programs. The lead-in to this chapter illustrates that some companies effectively integrate the Internet into their marketing communications programs by viewing it as a medium to reach its target audience. In this chapter we will discuss Internet media from a communication perspective. Internet media is a valuable component of the integrated marketing communications program and, like other components, is most effective when used in conjunction with other program elements.

We begin this chapter by briefly exploring how promotional planners can view the Internet as a communication medium. Next, we investigate the many ways the Internet can be used within a promotional program. We conclude by summarizing the methods for measuring Internet communication effectiveness and presenting the key strengths and limitations of Internet media.

Internet Communication

The **Internet** is a worldwide means of exchanging information and communicating through a series of interconnected computers. It was started as a U.S. Defense Department project, but it is now accessible to anyone with a computer and a connection. The most popular component of the Internet is the **World Wide Web (WWW)**.

While the Internet and WWW are ways for marketers and consumers to conduct transactions for goods and services, our focus for this chapter is to consider the Internet as a medium for communication and facilitating all aspects of the promotional program. Like other media, the Internet has consumers—both current customers and potential customers—and marketers seeking or connecting with these consumers through advertising and other tools. And, like other media, advertisers would like to know as much as possible about Internet users as one means of knowing whether investments are worthwhile. In this section, we briefly review some basic facts about Canadian Internet users and explore the basic communication function of Internet media.

Internet Users

A profile of Canadian Internet users is summarized in Figure 17–1. Approximately two-thirds of all Canadians use the Internet at any location, with this usage rate equal between men and women. Internet usage declines with age; most young Canadians ages 18–34 use the Internet, while only a quarter of those over 65 use the Internet. Individuals from larger households are also more likely to use the Internet.

Internet use is greatly influenced by socio-economic status. Individuals with higher incomes and higher levels of education are much more likely to own a computer and use the Internet. For example, about 58 percent of individuals with incomes under $27,000 in 2005 had used the Internet from any location, compared to 83 percent of individuals with incomes of $46,000 or more. Thirty-one percent of adults 18 and over with less than a high school diploma used the Internet, whereas 89 percent of those with a university degree did so.[1]

Figure 17–2 on page 500 summarizes the types of usage, ranging from online purchases to searches of various types of information to entertainment activities, for individuals who have Internet access. Clearly, the variety of information and entertainment activities Canadians engage in on the Internet allows advertisers many opportunities for reaching specific customer groups, lifestyles, or virtually any marketing segmentation variable. Figure 17–3 on page 500 indicates that the amount of time Canadians use the Internet per week grew from 7.5 hours in 2000 to 9.9 hours in 2002, and hit 12.8 hours by 2006. In fact, 30 percent use the Internet two hours or more per day, rivalling the average of 3.5 hours per day for television.

FIGURE 17–1

Characteristics of individuals using the Internet

	2005 Location of Internet Access	
	Any Location[1]	Home
	% of all individual aged 18 years and over[2]	
All Internet users	**67.9**	**60.9**
Household type		
Single family households with unmarried children under age 18	80.9	74.1
Single family households without unmarried children under age 18	62.5	56.9
One-person households	48.7	38.2
Multi-family households	78.8	67.5
Sex		
Males	68.0	61.5
Females	67.8	60.3
Age		
18 to 34 years	88.9	77.3
35 to 54 years	75.0	68.3
55 to 64 years	53.8	49.3
65 years and over	23.8	22.5
Level of education		
Less than high school	31.2	26.5
High school or college	72.0	63.9
University degree	89.4	83.4
Personal income quartile[3]		
Lowest quartile	58.7	52.3
Second quartile	56.9	50.2
Third quartile	71.3	63.4
Highest quartile	83.2	77.7

1. Internet access from **any location** includes use from home, school, work, public library or other location, and counts an individual only once, regardless of use from multiple locations.
2. Percentage of all individuals, aged 18 years and over, who responded that they had used the Internet in the previous 12 months for personal non-business use from any location.
3. The survey respondents are divided into four equal groups based on their annual personal income, each group representing 25% of the income spectrum from highest to lowest. The lowest quartile is $13,000 or less, the second quartile is from $13,001 to $26,999, the third quartile is from $27,000 to $45,999 and the highest quartile is $46,000 and higher.

Source: Statistics Canada, CANSIM, tables 358-0123, 358-0124, 358-0125 and 358-0126. Last modified: 2006-08-15.

Website Communication

The role of the **website** is to act as the place where information is made available by the website owner to Internet users. To attract visitors to the site and have them return to it requires a combination of creativity, effective marketing, continual updating of the site, and the use of other media to direct consumers.

When major corporations first began to conduct business on the Internet, they put up websites primarily for information purposes. Companies had sites that were really not much more than online catalogues designed for information purposes only. The role of the website quickly changed, however; sites have become much more creative, and with technological advances it is possible to create fancier graphics, audio, and animation online. IMC Perspective 17–1 on page 501 describes a new use for websites.

FIGURE *17–2*

Internet use by individuals, by type of activity, 2005

	All Canadians[1]	Internet Users at Home[2]
	% of individuals	
Internet activity at home		
E-mail	55.6	91.3
Participating in chat groups or using a messenger	23.1	37.9
Searching for information on Canadian governments	31.7	52.0
Communicating with Canadian governments	13.8	22.6
Searching for medical or health related information	35.3	57.9
Education, training or school work	26.1	42.9
Travel information or making travel arrangements	38.5	63.1
Paying bills	33.5	55.0
Electronic banking	35.2	57.8
Researching investments	16.0	26.2
Playing games	23.5	38.7
Obtaining or saving music	22.3	36.6
Obtaining or saving software	19.4	31.8
Viewing the news or sports	37.6	61.7
Obtaining weather reports or road conditions	40.5	66.6
Listening to the radio over the Internet	15.9	26.1
Downloading or watching television	5.2	8.5
Downloading or watching a movie	5.0	8.3
Researching community events	25.8	42.3
General browsing (surfing)	51.2	84.0
Other Internet activity	6.7	10.9

1. Percentage of all individuals, aged 18 years and over.
2. Percentage of all individuals, aged 18 years and over, who responded that they had used the Internet in the previous twelve months for personal non-business use from home.

Source: Statistics Canada, CANSIM, table 358-0130.

FIGURE *17–3*

Time spent online per week by Canadian adults with Internet access (n = 797)

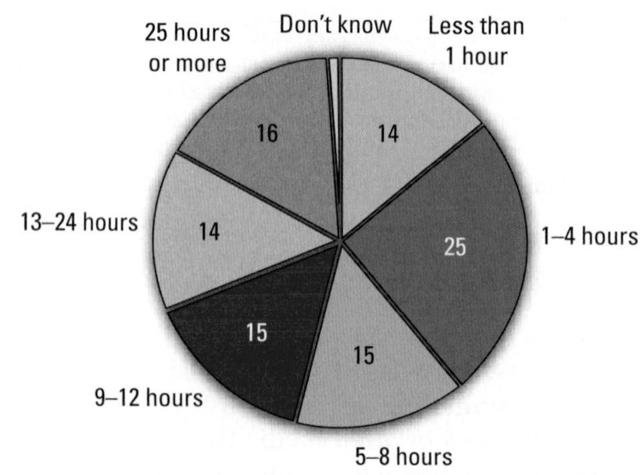

	02–2000 (n=1.066)	02–2001 (n=724)	02–2002 (n=704)	02–2003 (n=729)	02–2004 (n=789)	02–2005 (n=753)	02–2006 (n=797)
Mean Number of Hours	7.5	11.5	9.9	11.6	11.8	11.5	12.8

Source: Interactive Reid Report, Ipsos-Reid

IMC PERSPECTIVE 17–1

Procter & Gamble Encourages Moms to Spread the Word

Marketers have long understood that one of the most powerful forms of marketing is one that comes as an advocacy message from a trusted friend. Many companies have used the advocacy message as a way to connect with consumers in a meaningful way. In February 2006, Procter & Gamble, one of the world's largest consumer products companies, took the "trusted friend" advocacy message online by creating Vocalpoint (www.vocalpoint.com), a word-of-mouth advocacy program that targets moms who by nature love to talk to others and share information.

Vocalpoint is an online community, whose mission is to help companies do a better job developing products and services that moms care about and want to talk about. Vocalpoint offers moms access to information, products, and samples as well as the ability to influence products and programs and help shape marketing programs. The Vocalpoint moms are able to share their opinions and feedback on new ideas and products, and spread the word to friends if they think the idea or product is worth talking about. In essence, Vocalpoint moms are creating their own word-of-mouth marketing campaigns.

To date, P&G has recruited over half a million moms who have visited the Web site Vocalpoint.com and have signed up to participate in the online community. Membership in the community and the sharing of opinions is entirely voluntary, although on occasion Vocalpoint moms are asked to participate in research and are compensated in the same way as a focus group or any other paid consumer research program.

"Vocalpoint is a word-of-mouth advocacy program that focuses on the thoughts and opinions of 'moms'," said P&G spokeswoman Robyn Schroeder. "At P&G, we know that moms express terrific ideas and want to communicate with companies in a way that will allow their point of view to be heard. Vocalpoint provides them with that vehicle, as well as gives them a first-hand look at products or services to share with their social networks."

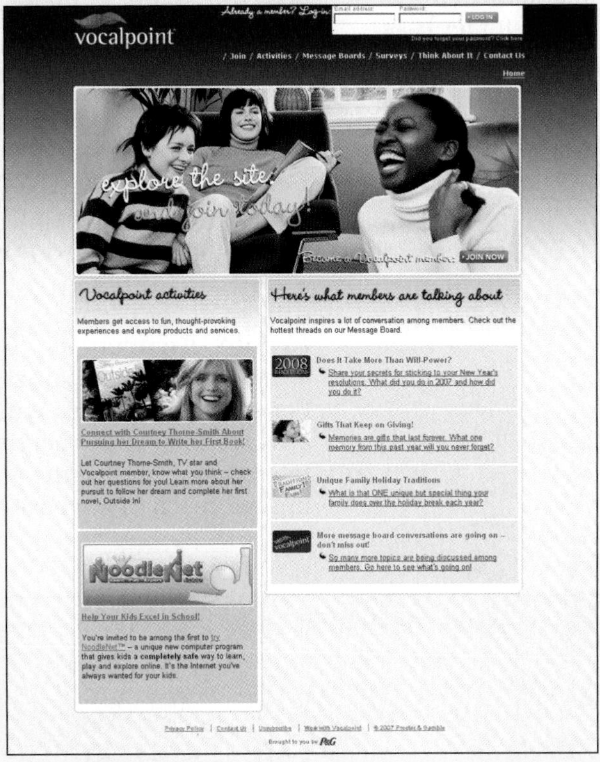

P&G won't say how big its budget is to create this network, or how many people it employs recruiting, training, and dealing with this giant army of moms but Vocalpoint has become an important program at P&G. In fact, not only does P&G use Vocalpoint for its own brands, it also offers the word-of-mouth and research services to other corporations.

Sources: Mathew Ingram, "Catering to Web-savvy Moms," *The Globe and Mail*, Jan 18, 2007; Stuart Elliott, "Online, P&G Gets a Little Crazy," *The New York Times*, December 14, 2006; Diane Francis, "P&G's Army of 'Moms'," *National Post*, July 7, 2006.

Question

1. Explain why the Vocalpoint program would be beneficial for P&G?

Thus, the website is a communications medium, allowing companies to create awareness, provide information, and influence attitudes, as well as pursue other communications objectives. As Figure 17–4 on page 502 indicates, the communication aspect is fairly strong. Let's first look at some of the communication objectives these companies want to achieve.

Website Communication Objectives

From a purely communication standpoint, websites typically attempt to achieve three broad communication objectives: create awareness, disseminate information, and build a brand image.

FIGURE *17–4*

Focus of online marketing efforts—by customer base

% Focusing on...	TOTAL	Customer Base: Business to Consumer	Customer Base: Business to Business	Customer Base: Both
Brand/Image building	52	46	65	60
Customer acquisition	43	54	39	47
Direct response	32	34	19	43
Promotion	42	49	39	51
Sales	38	39	40	47

BASE: Those doing online marketing (n=279)
Source: Canadian Marketing Association 2005 Fact Book.

Create Awareness Communicating on a website can be useful in creating awareness of an organization as well as its specific product and service offerings. For small companies with limited budgets, this is an opportunity to create awareness well beyond what might be achieved through traditional media. However, the Internet may not be the optimal medium for awareness in many situations due to its limited reach of a website without other communication to direct consumers.

Disseminate Information One of the primary objectives for using a website is to provide in-depth information about a company's products and services. In business-to-business markets, having a website has become a necessity, as more and more buyers expect that a company will have a site providing them with detailed information about its offerings. In the public sector, all levels of government use the Internet to provide citizens with a wide range of information on its services and policies. For example, we have cited Internet usage statistics in this chapter from research conducted by Statistics Canada. For many consumer companies, their websites serve as a means of communicating more information about their products and services. Exhibit 17–1 shows how Snapple creates a fun experience for consumers to learn about its brand.

Exhibit 17–1
Snapple offers a number of reasons to visit its website

Build a Brand Image Many websites are designed to reflect the image a company wants to portray. For example, the consumer sites at molsoncanadian.ca; and labattblue.ca are excellent examples of image building. Interestingly, one of the difficulties traditional marketers have experienced is that of creating a brand image on the Internet. While some companies have been successful, others have not fared as well and realize that branding and image-creating strategies must be specifically adapted to this medium. According to David Aaker, the Internet—as part of an integrated marketing communications program—can be a useful tool for branding.[2] Let's discuss a few of the many reasons why companies attempting to create branding through the Internet may not be achieving their goals.

Branding Is Challenging While creating a strong brand is not easy in any communications effort, some marketers feel that it may be even more difficult to do on the Internet. As noted by Karen Benezra, editor of *Brandweek* magazine, managers lack a clear understanding of the role the Web should assume in the branding process. New or less well known brands may have to assume different strategies than those used by more established brands such as Volvo, BMW, or The Gap. Another reason is that many marketers mistakenly believe that simply creating awareness will lead to a strong brand. Finally, notes Benezra, it takes a long time to establish a brand relationship with a customer, and the Internet hasn't been around long enough to prove its branding capabilities.[3]

Branding vs Direct Response Noting the similarities between the Internet and other direct-response media like catalogues or interactive TV, some marketers feel that the Internet is best suited to be a direct-response medium. They contend that direct marketing requires a very targeted effort, searching for high-probability buyers. Branding, on the other hand, is much less targeted and reaches out to numerous audiences. According to Erwin Ephron of *Advertising Age*, the Internet is somewhere in between, and trying to achieve both objectives at the same time has led to unsuccessful branding efforts.[4]

High Costs Successful branding does not take place overnight. Unfortunately, many marketers aren't willing—or feel that they can't afford—to wait. Such marketers may view the Internet as a "quick fix" that will allow them to instantly establish their brands. When they discover that the Internet is not able to provide instant identity, they may quickly return to their focus on ROI or the bottom line. Cutting advertising and brand identity efforts on the Internet will immediately reflect cost savings and a return to business as normal.[5]

The above are just a few of many reasons that can be offered as to why branding on the Internet has been less successful than many hoped. We believe that the Internet—as part of an integrated marketing communications program—can be used for branding purposes, as well as for other objectives.

This belief is reiterated in a recent article from an MSN Canada executive who believes the quality of the recent creative work on the Internet has vastly surpassed creative efforts from previous years. Combined with an average 30 hours per month on the Internet and advertising expenditures growing at a 40-percent annual rate, astute promotional planners will very soon master brand building on the Internet.[6]

Website Strategy

Making a site work and having one work successfully are not the same thing, however, and whether a site is effective is determined by what it is that management hopes to achieve through the site. As already noted, some sites are offered for informational purposes only (this tends to be more common in the business-to-business market than in the consumer market), while others approach the market much more aggressively. For example, Kimberly-Clark Corporation, the manufacturer of Huggies brand of diapers, Pull-Ups training pants, and Little Swimmers swim pants, has been extremely successful in its Internet marketing efforts. The Huggies homepage (Exhibit 17–2) goes well beyond providing information. The site has additional objectives, such as developing a long-term relationship with parents, establishing a brand image for the products, and supporting sales. The Huggies Baby Network provides expectant mothers with encouragement and ideas as to how to maintain a happy and healthy pregnancy. By clicking on this part of the site, the expectant mother is provided with informative articles, experts' opinions, weekly newsletters, and the opportunity to personalize the site to her personal needs. The site also provides information

Exhibit 17–2
Huggies homepage

to be used once the baby has been born. Tips on how to create a nursery, games to play with the baby, and more information from experts are just part of this section of the site. The site is designed to develop one-on-one relationships by offering very useful informaton, as well as product samples and more to anyone who sends in his or her name, address, and e-mail address. Thousands of people have responded to the offer, providing Kimberly-Clark with an enormous database the company can use for future marketing efforts. Also included are links to editorial partners and other content providers, as well as special offers, sweepstakes, and additional information about Huggies products. Finally, to support sales, the site directs customers to the nearest retail store that sells Huggies brands.

As the Huggies example demonstrates, a website can be an effective tool for the marketer. Depending on the nature of one's business and one's marketing objectives for the Internet, a website can range from a very simple source of information about the company and its products to a powerful tool for developing a brand image, sampling, and even generating sales.

Internet Media Options

The remarkable power of the Internet is the opportunity for promotional planners to view it as a multiple IMC tool. A primary decision for managers is to strategically use the features of the Internet to achieve communication and behavioural objectives. Various brands treat it as a media channel for advertising; a sales promotion through games and online experiences; a form of sophisticated public relations; and finally a direct-response communication mechanism. This perspective is different than using the Internet with advertising or using the Internet with sales promotion, which we examine toward the end of the chapter. We now investigate each of these options, but begin with the idea of how promotional planners target specific audiences with Internet media.

Methods of Reaching Target Audiences

Communicating to specific target audiences with Internet media is done with various methods resulting from the nature of the technology and consumer adaptation to the media within their everyday lives. The Advertising Research Foundation suggests reaching target audiences through behaviour, context, geography, site loyalty, and time of day. We now briefly define each of these approaches to illustrate that using the Internet as communication media shares some characteristics with the other media.[7]

Behavioural Targeting Another Internet advertising concept that has only recently gained acceptance is **behavioural targeting**. Behavioural targeting is based on advertisers' targeting consumers according to their website-surfing behaviours. By compiling clickstream data and Internet protocol (IP) information, segments of potential buyers can be identified and ads directed specifically to them. For example, by tracking an individual's visits to a number of automobile websites, an ad for cars or a dealership could be served to that individual. A frequent visitor to employment classifieds might be a promising target for an employment service firm, and so on.

Contextual Targeting Advertisers who target their ads based on the content of the Internet page are using **contextual targeting**. Whereas behavioural targeting tracks surfing behaviours, contextual ads are determined by the content on the web page. For example, an advertiser may place an airline ad on a travel site, or a golf club ad on a golf site, or even in or near a story about golf on another site. In September 2005, Yahoo! announced that it would provide a service to automatically place advertisers' messages near relevant content sites, including blogs—a service also offered by Google, though Google has had difficulty implementing the service.[8]

Geographic Targeting Increasingly, advertisers are adjusting their Internet communication messages depending upon where the user is located. This information can be determined with the user's voluntary declaration of residence (e.g., country, city, etc.) and to some degree with technological features. For example, different versions of travel websites (e.g., Travel Alberta) can emerge depending upon where the information seeker is living. Research suggests stronger consumer response with more tailored messages based on geography.

Site-Loyalty Targeting Websites fit into a variety of categories, much like television specialty channels, and recent research indicates that consumers have an affinity or are very loyal to particular sites for their information or entertainment needs. More loyal users tend to spend more time at a favourite site and have much more positive attitudes toward the site's relevance, content, and features. More importantly, users have more positive attitudes of the advertising for the sites they are more loyal toward and exhibit stronger awareness for advertised brands.

Time of Day Targeting Consumer variation in media usage akin to television and radio is found with Internet media. Television viewers are not consistently the same across the whole day, from early morning viewers to those watching daytime television versus the prime-time audience. Similarly, radio's audience size and composition varies considerably, especially during driving to and from work. Internet media are following a similar pattern, with groups of working people accessing Internet media during the day for business purposes, primarily in the morning. It declines during the afternoon and dinner time and then peaks once again during the evening for leisure purposes. Recent Canadian data suggest that the biggest growth in Internet media use is daytime access of news and information sites, at 21 percent versus overall Internet media use growth of 13 percent.[9]

ADVERTISING

Like broadcast or print, the Internet is an advertising medium. Companies and organizations working to promote their products and services must consider this medium as they would television, magazines, outdoor, and so on. The Interactive Advertising Bureau (IAB) of Canada estimated that online advertising reached $1 billion in 2006 (Figure 17–5). However, this is still lower than the almost $3 billion spent on television. The types of online advertising used by companies are shown in Figures 17–6 and 17–7 on page 506. We now discuss these various options.

Banners The most common form of advertising on the Internet is **banner ads**. Banner ads may take on a variety of forms, as shown in Exhibit 17–3 on page 506, as well as a number of names such as *side panels, skyscrapers,* or *verticals.* Initially banner ads constituted the vast majority of advertising on the Net, but studies indicating their questionable effectiveness have led to a decline in usage. Reports on click-through rates vary, but most studies indicate a less than 1 percent response rate.[10] At the same time, at least one study employing eye tracking methodology supports the likelihood of low click-through rates, but provides strong evidence that banner ads may be very effective in creating

FIGURE *17–5*

Canadian online advertising revenue trends, 2002–2007

Year	Revenue	% Increase
2006	$1,010 Million	80%
2005	$562 Million	54%
2004	$364 Million	54%
2003	$237 Million	37%
2002	$176 Million	

Source: Interactive Advertising Bureau of Canada

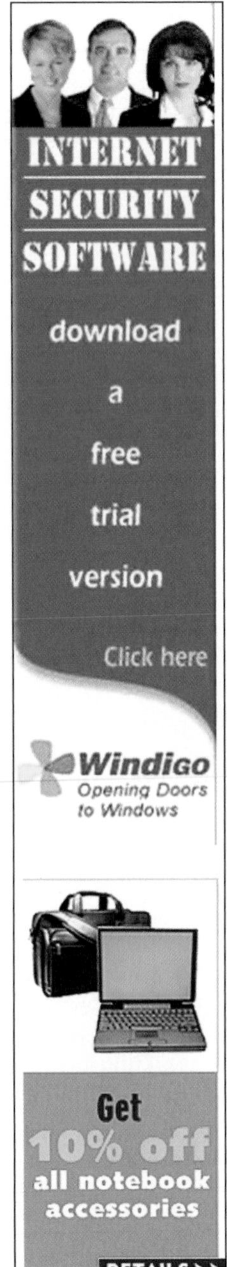

Exhibit 17–3
Banner ad formats

FIGURE 17–6 Types of online advertising used—by company revenue

% using...	TOTAL	Customer Base B2C	B2B	Both
E-mail marketing	75	78	77	84
Banner or tower ads on a third party website	52	62	58	56
Banner or tower ads on your company's website	42	58	44	43
Search engine optimization	41	45	52	44
Affiliate program	25	25	23	36
Pop-ups on your company's website	15	15	6	20
Pop-ups on a third party website	9	15	6	10
Other	8	10	4	13

BASE: Those doing online marketing
Source: Canadian Marketing Association 2005 Fact Book.

FIGURE 17–7 Canadian online advertising revenue, by advertising vehicle, as % of 2006 total revenue

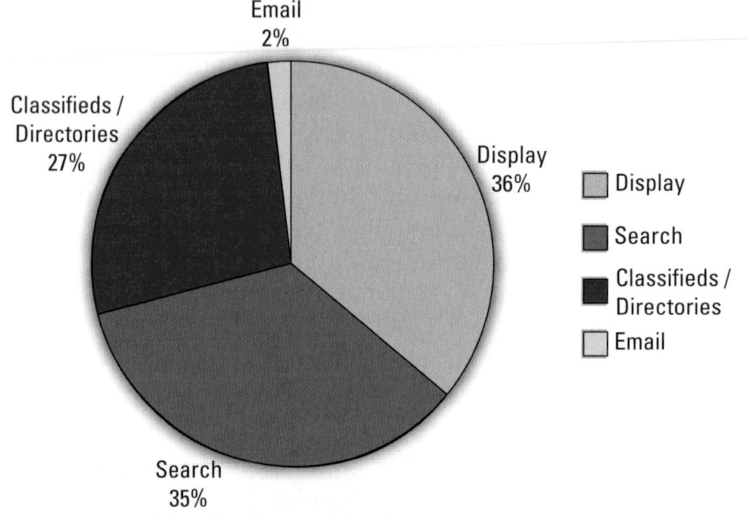

Source: Interactive Advertising Bureau of Canada

recall and brand building. The study also revealed a strong dislike for flashing banner ads, indicating that viewers almost immediately dismiss them.[11] In addition, a Ponemon Institute study conducted in 2004 showed that 66 percent of respondents said they would find relevant banner ads less annoying while 52 percent indicated they would even be likely to respond to a relevant banner ad.[12]

Sponsorship Another common form of advertising is **sponsorship**, of which there are two types. Regular sponsorship occurs when a company pays to sponsor a section of a site. A more involved agreement is the **content sponsorship**, in which the sponsor not only provides dollars in return for name association but also participates in providing the content itself. In some cases, the site is responsible for providing content and having it approved by the sponsor; in other instances, the sponsor may contribute all or part of the content.

For example, a Nature Valley/Sympatico microsite emerged when users selected certain subject sections from the Sympatico portal. The repackaged look of the website provided links to various outdoor activities like hiking, golfing, and skiing. These links informed users about these recreational activities, provided recommendations on how to enjoy their experiences, and gave suggestions on what to eat (i.e., Nature Valley Chewy Trail Mix). The microsite featured an advergame that was tied to receiving a free sample delivered to the user's home. Executives believed in promotions targeted to adults aged 25–49 who enjoyed an active lifestyle but were not health-obsessed. Post-promotion results appeared impressive. The Nature Valley brand received an 18-percent increase in message association scores, a 35-percent increase in unaided brand awareness, and 20,000 unique visitors played the advergame.[13]

Pop-Ups/Pop-Unders Often while browsing, a window or a creature of some sort appears on the screen with a message. These advertisements are known as **pop-ups**, and appear when users access certain sites. Pop-ups are usually larger than banner ads but smaller than a full screen. **Pop-unders** are ads that appear underneath the Web page and become visible only when the user leaves the site.

While some companies believe that pop-ups and pop-unders are effective forms of advertising, others disagree. Consumer complaints have led Google and others to no longer accept these advertising forms. A study conducted by TNS revealed that 93 percent of respondents found pop-up ads annoying or very annoying.[14] The frequency and effectiveness of pop-ups and pop-unders have been greatly reduced given the opportunity for Intenet users to purchase pop-up screeners, which will screen out the ads before they appear on the screen. Some marketers believe that pop-ups and pop-unders are in the decline stage of their life cycle.

Interstitials **Interstitials** are ads that emerge on the screen while a site's content downloads. Although some advertisers believe that interstitials are irritating and more of a nuisance than a benefit, a study conducted by Grey Advertising found that only 15 percent of those surveyed felt that the ads were irritating (versus 9 percent for banner ads) and that 47 percent liked the ads (versus 38 percent for banners). Perhaps more importantly, while ad recall of banner ads was approximately 51 percent, recall of interstitials was much higher, at 76 percent.

Push Technologies **Push technologies**, or **webcasting** technologies, allow companies to "push" a message to consumers rather than waiting for them to find it. Push technologies dispatch Internet pages and news updates and may have sound and video geared to specific audiences and even individuals. For example, a manager whose job responsibilities involve corporate finance might log on to his or her computer and find that new stories are automatically there on the economy, stock updates, or a summary of a speech. Companies provide screen savers that automatically "hook" the viewer to their sites for sports, news, weather reports, and/or other information that the viewer has specified. Users can use **personalization**—that is, they can personalize their sites to request the kinds of specific information they are most interested in viewing. For example, sports fans can have updates sent to them through sites providing sports information. The service is paid for by advertisers who flash their messages on the screen.

Links While considered by some as not a type of advertising, **links** serve many of the same purposes as are served by the types discussed above. A visitor to one site may click on a link that provides additional information and/or related materials at another site. Thus someone on TSN.ca may link to Nike.com and find information on sports-related products.

Paid Search By far the fastest growing form of advertising on the Internet is that of **paid search**, or search engine advertising in which advertisers pay only when a consumer clicks on their ad or link from a search engine page. In an effort to more specifically target customers that may be interested in their offerings, advertisers buy ads on search engine sites such as Google, Yahoo!, or MSN so that when the visitor to the site keys in a specific search word or phrase, an advertisement targeted

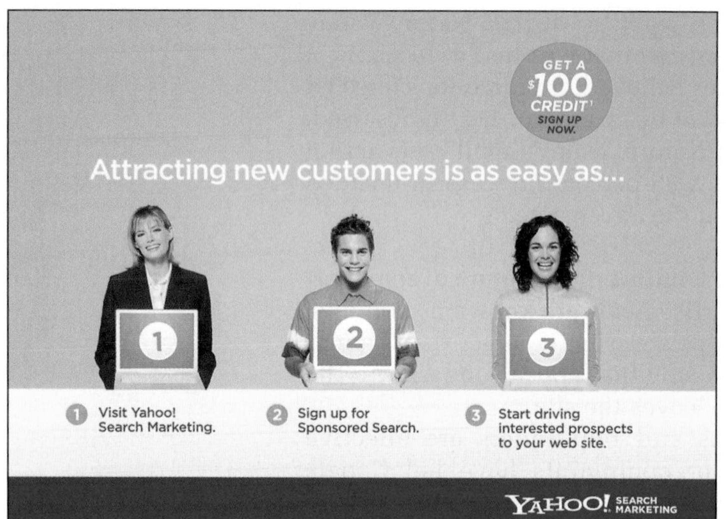

Exhibit 17–4
Yahoo! promotes its paid search program

to that category appears. Advertisers bid for the placement; those who pay the most get the best locations (Exhibit 17–4). For example, typing in the word *automobile* could lead to a Ford ad (or commercial).

Rich Media The increased penetration of broadband into households has increased the attention given to streaming video. **Rich media**, as defined by Wikipedia, are "a broad range of interactive digital media that exhibit dynamic motion, taking advantage of enhanced sensory features such as video, audio and animation."[15] Others state that rich media include all content that is created in Flash.[16] The successful adoption of music videos, sports clips, news, and more has led advertisers to create a variety of forms of streaming video advertising content. Types of rich media include the following.

Online Commercials The equivalent of traditional television commercials, online commercials are appearing on the Net. Some companies have created their own Web commercials, while others run the same spots they show on TV. A number of companies have been successful in blending the two media, showing the commercial on TV and then directing interested viewers to the Web if they wish to see it again or to view longer versions.

Radio-Canada, responsible for CBC programming in French, undertook an experiment with several industry personnel and placed its TV ads on the broadcaster's Internet site for a period of one month. TV spots directed viewers to this option. With an eye to see if consumers would be interested in the concept and to determine the most appropriate measurement and compensation system, the trial appeared successful. About 41,000 unique visitors watched an average of four commercials each, and 90 percent of the feedback e-mails contained positive comments. The future of this idea as a permanent option appears possible as those involved continued to investigate issues of viability, costs to marketers, fees to rights-holders, time, and bandwidth.[17]

Video on Demand Video clips of various entertainment activities (which include ads or are sponsored) are also available through the Internet. CTV's Broadband Network ushered in a new route for advertisers to reach their audiences via Internet media. Viewers watch free shows along with embedded commercials, similar to the existing television model. Initial programming had five or six minutes of commercials per 22-minute show, running before, after, and during the show. As an alternative, CHUM offered its shows on specific Internet sites for each program, such as MuchMusic, rather than a central "network" location.[18] The future of advertising through streamed television shows is a new, promising opportunity for promotional planners, even though the innovation is in the early stages of development for the sender and the receiver. Internet Protocol Television, IPTV, gained ground in 2006 and 2007, and service providers expected about one million Canadian subscribers by the end of 2008.[19]

Evolving Internet Media As the Internet evolves, more and more ways to deliver advertising messages appear. Unfortunately, we do not have the space to discuss all of these in this text; however, three of these media warrant attention here: podcasting, RSS, and blogs.

Podcasting **Podcasting** is a medium that uses the Internet to distribute radiolike files for downloading into iPods and other MP3 players. As the market for iPods and MP3 players grows, the attractiveness of this medium does as well.[20] Radio stations and television programs now podcast. The Podcast.net directory listed more than 4,000 different podcasters in 2005.[21] Traditional advertisers have adopted the medium, while others have found it useful as well. For example, Durex, a condom manufacturer, has purchased product placements in podcasts—in part to reach young listeners with risque marketing messages.[22]

RSS **Really Simple Syndication (RSS)** is a specification that uses XML to organize and format web-based content in a standard way. Content owners create an RSS feed, which usually consists of titles and brief descriptions of about 10 articles elsewhere on the site. The difference between web content and an RSS feed is that the latter can send out notifications whenever new material is available.[23] Because the alerts can be customized to the viewers' preferences, advertisers have found it useful for disseminating information to those who may be most interested.

Blogs A **blog** (or weblog) is a web-based publication consisting primarily of periodic articles, normally presented in reverse chronological order. As noted, blogs may reflect the writings of an individual, a community, a political organization, or a corporation, and they offer advertisers a new way to reach their target audiences. While some marketers are excited about the potential of blogs to reach large audiences at a small cost, others are more skeptical, noting numerous potential problems with their use. Given the fact that blogs have been around for only a short period of time, questions regarding the advantages and disadvantages of their use by marketers remain unanswered at this time.

Sales Promotion

Consumers experiencing Internet media through a variety of applications like websites, social utilities, blogs, podcasts, and video-on-demand allow promotional planners to offer innovative sales promotions, largely to encourage repeat purchasing or repeat consumption. Innovative advertisers create specialized groups on Facebook, a leading social utility application, to communicate and interact with loyal customers. In these environments, the members receive various treats. For example *Spiderman* movie fans who joined the Facebook group obtained electronic icons of the webbed hero for their computer. Loyal customers are rewarded with other related electronic items provided to them through social utilities and websites—such as ring-tones, wallpaper for one's computer, and emoticons, skins, winks, and pictures for instant message services. Related to this are virtual environments where consumers immerse themselves in alternative realities, as shown in IMC Perspective 17–2 on page 510.

In this sense, these services have become digital "gifts" or "premiums," as described in the sales promotion chapter. Although the non-virtual world usually considered tangible goods to be the premium, the digital age spawned the concept of intangible gifts that become highly valued. Another example occurs where various types of point systems allow repeat customers to generate even further rewards; a virtual continuity program for avid Internet media users who are brand loyal. Also, many brands offer advergames, skill-challenging endeavours that keep customers amused while offering brand messages during play. Thus, Internet media allow previously intangible sales promotions to create value through intangible benefits for continued usage.

Finally, one of the most significant rewards for loyal customers has been the delivery of enhanced content in terms of information or entertainment. Loyal customers are rewarded with exclusive video for their participation. To give thanks, advertisers provide enhanced levels of information where this is deemed valuable. In this sense, the content is not the product witnessed as it is perceived as a bonus, something fitting the original definition of a sale promotion.

IMC PERSPECTIVE 17–2

Sprite Visits Habbo Hotel

Adults have landmarks like The Plaza Hotel in New York, variations of The Ritz in many cities, and for majestic elegance there's always the Fairmont Banff Springs in Canada's own Banff National Park. But for teenagers around the world, the hotel of choice—an online icon of cool—is Habbo Hotel, a virtual space that simulates a hotel setting and that has, in only a couple of years, built a community of devoted visitors from around the world.

Habbo Hotel was developed by Finland-based Web developer Sulake as a Web destination that looks like a hotel and offers online visitors the opportunity to interact with one another as though they were guests in a hotel. It has developed a cult-like following, mostly among teens. Habbo Hotel websites based in the U.K., the U.S., and other countries around the world were the first to gain popularity. A Canadian site was launched in 2004 with partner CHUM City Interactive. Almost overnight, the Canadian Habbo Hotel had a population the size of a major Canadian city, with 300,000 youths visiting each month.

So when the Sprite brand team was looking for ideas on how to bring their hip, animated spokesperson, Miles Thirst, to life, Habbo Hotel immediately came to mind. From a pure reach perspective, considerably more teens can be reached in environments such as MSN Messenger or Hotmail. However, the real opportunity within Habbo Hotel was the prospect of going beyond display-based advertising. Instead of being merely associated with the environment, Sprite wanted to become an integral part of it.

With this in mind, Cossette Media, on behalf of Sprite, set out to negotiate the ideal presence from both a consumer and an advertiser perspective. They started with the largest club within Habbo Hotel and renovated and renamed it "Club Thirst." The changes were more than esthetic. They came up with ways that visitors could meet Miles Thirst. They created a penthouse and set it up as a place where Habbo visitors could get together with Miles twice a week over a six-month campaign.

In the Habbo Hotel virtual community, visitors can buy Habbo credits that can be used within the hotel experience, such as to purchase items to furnish their rooms. The credits are worth 10 cents each and are purchased via credit cards or SMS. Sprite turned Club Thirst into a popular celebrity destination within the hotel by giving Habbo patrons two Habbo credits every time they paid a visit to Miles Thirst. Another simulated experience at the Habbo Hotel is ordering virtual drinks from the bar. Normally, visitors are served a generic Habbo cola. In this campaign, visitors quenched their thirst with Sprite—a welcome addition that added an exciting new "real-life" dimension to the overall Habbo experience.

The results of the campaign were incredible. Brand likability, purchase intent, and consumption for Sprite improved dramatically. One control group study that compared teens who had not visited Habbo Hotel to those who had showed a 90-percent increase in Sprite product consumption among Habbo visitors. At the end of the campaign, Thirst received more than 9,000 "handwritten" comments from kids everywhere. Many of the e-mails included highly personalized daydreams and experiences. The Habbos just wanted to make sure that Miles Thirst appreciated how much the presence of Sprite and its spokesperson Thirst had brought to their community. And, more importantly, they were looking forward to seeing them again in the future.

Source: Nick Barbuto, "Virtual Thirst," *Marketing Magazine*, January 16, 2006.

Question

1. In what ways is this Sprite initiative viewed as a sales promotion?

Public Relations

The Internet is a useful medium for conducting public relations activities. Many sites devote a portion of their content to public relations activities, including the provision of information about the company, its philanthropic activities, and annual reports. Companies have used the Web to establish media, government, investor, and community relationships; deal with crises; and even perform corporate image, advocacy, and cause-related advertising. Companies have used their websites to address issues as well as to provide information about products and services, archive press releases, link to other articles and sites, and provide lists of activities and events. Other Internet tools, including e-mails and e-mail newsletters, have also been used effectively.

Shel Holtz, in his book *Public Relations on the Internet,* notes that the Internet offers a number of opportunities to public relations practitioners, including: (1) the development of media relations websites, (2) the ability to provide customized information dissemination, and (3) the development of positive e-mail relationships. Shel Holtz notes that while there are many similarities between public relations activities conducted in traditional media and those conducted on the Internet, three main elements account for the differences between the two:

- The Internet offers a more limited opportunity to gain attention due to short exposure times.
- The Internet offers the opportunity to build internal links that provide the media with instant access to additional sources of information on the issue.
- The Internet offers the ability to provide much more substantial information. Print and broadcast materials are confined by time and space limitations, while the Internet can literally provide volumes of information at a fingertip—or click of a mouse.[24]

An excellent example of the use of public relations on the Internet is provided by Chrysler (Exhibit 17–5). The site provides up-to-date news stories and other forms of content, photo images, and cross-references to other sites or media as well as press kits and a calendar of upcoming events. It also provides information about Chrysler automobiles and the corporation itself and allows for customer feedback and registration for updates. In addition, DaimlerChrysler's homepage contains many of the articles written about the corporation, including awards won and philanthropic efforts achieved such as its concern for the environment and its $1.1 million support for Hurricane Katrina victims.

Exhibit 17–5 Chrysler uses its website for public relations purposes

At the same time, many philanthropic and nonprofit organizations have found the Internet to be a useful way to generate funds. Several companies have developed sites to perform the functions that are required in traditional fundraising programs. For example, Ben & Jerry's uses its website to promote its products and image as well as showcasing the causes it supports and champions such as global warming, peace, and social and environmental issues (see Exhibit 17–6). Charitable organizations have also formed sites to handle public relations activities, provide information regarding the causes the charity supports, collect contributions, and so on. In an example of integrating the Internet with public relations and television, companies have found the Internet to be extremely useful for providing information in times of a crisis, and for gathering feedback about their products and services and about themselves.

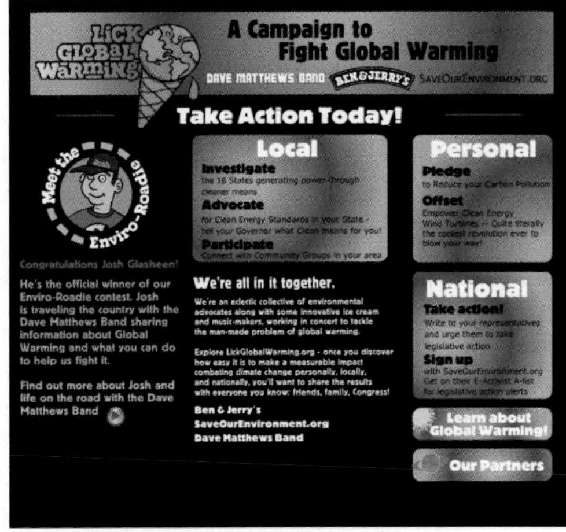

Exhibit 17–6 Ben & Jerry's supports global causes through its website

Direct Marketing

Our discussion of direct marketing and the Internet will approach the topic from the perspective of e-mail and short-message services.

IMC PERSPECTIVE 17–3

E-mail Messages Go Around

According to a study by Sharpe Partners, viral marketing with a touch of humour is spread the fastest, with 88 percent of respondents to the study saying they send along jokes or cartoons. The second most popular category was news, with a 56 percent pass-along rate, and health care and health information at 32 percent. Business and personal finance and sports and hobbies were found to be least popular, at 24 percent for each category.

"Humour is completely subjective, but we usually know most of the time, or believe we know, that when we think something is funny [we know others who] would find that humour funny," says Sharpe Partners CEO Kathy Sharpe.

Overall, the Sharpe study found that 89 percent of U.S. adult Internet users share content with others via e-mail. It also reported that 63 percent share content at least once a week, and a whopping 75 percent forward content to as many as six others. Those with no college education were only slightly more likely to pass along e-mails (64 percent) than those who are college educated (61 percent), while marital status, the presence of children, and household income were not factors.

As for the impression branded content makes on Internet users, three-quarters said it has no impact on whether they forward a message. Almost a fifth (19 percent) said branded content would have a positive impact on their passing along a viral marketing message. Only 7 percent said branded content creates a negative effect. The person most likely to share content, the study found, was a woman in her late 30s or early 40s in the U.S. Southwest or Midwest. The figures and geography are American (there's a dearth of Canadian numbers), but the study nevertheless points to the potential of viral marketing.

But Heather Clark, associate director of creative strategy at Henderson Bas in Toronto, who has worked on viral campaigns for ING Direct and Levi's, warns there is just as much potential for dismal failure. Clark says the chance of a commercial message being passed along using e-mail is extremely low. "Viral [marketing] doesn't often perform," she says, though there are steps marketers can take to give their viral campaigns a better shot at success.

Apart from humour, one tactic that will help is incentives, says Clark. She notes a big trend in viral marketing today is giving consumers a little something to persuade them to pass along a marketer's message, such as an extra entry in a sweepstakes contest. A third factor is recognizing the consumer is in charge with an optional "send to a friend" feature in any viral e-mail and a chance for recipients to personalize the message before they forward it.

Virgin Mobile used humour and consumer involvement (viewers could choose different plot lines) for its "Billy the Finger" campaign. James Powell, senior manager, brand and communications, says Virgin Mobile worked with Helios Design and Lowe Roche, both in Toronto, to come up with Billy the Finger to promote new rate plans.

"We just made the creative funny," says Powell. "We made it engaging—embedding things like the phone number (for Billy the Finger) in there, embedding risqué scenes that people will find hilarious. It is taking a risk because we were hoping that people would find it engaging, would find it funny enough to say, 'Hey, check out this website that I've found.'" In the first two weeks after the campaign launched, billythefinger.com was getting 50,000 unique visitors a day. Even now, six months later, it's pulling in 150 unique visitors every day, Powell says.

Source: David Chilton, "Spreading the Message," *Marketing Magazine*, March 6, 2006.

Question

1. How can advertisers ensure that their e-mail ads get passed along to others?

E-Mail Direct mail on the Internet is essentially an electronic version of regular mail. Like regular mail it is highly targeted, relies heavily on lists, and attempts to reach consumers with specific needs through targeted messages. Consumers can opt to have specific types of e-mail sent to them and other types not sent. For example, media firms and web portals will e-mail information about specific promotions, articles that will appear, books on sale, and other items that may be purchased. IMC Perspective 17–3 summarizes statistics of e-mail pass along.

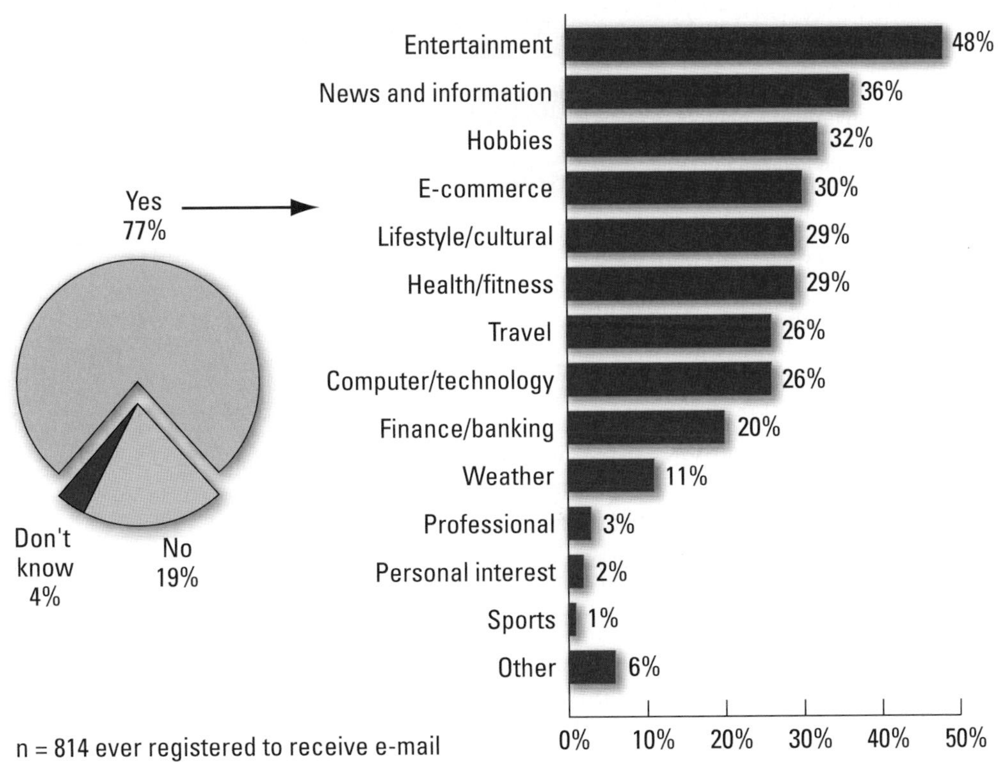

FIGURE *17–8*

Registering to receive e-mail/types of sites registered

Alternatively, companies can use e-mail for different purposes. For example, Bell Sympatico uses e-mail for customer stages. It sends e-mail to new consumers who sign up with Sympatico as their Internet service provider in order to obtain personal information and make the new user comfortable with the Internet. Later, when the data analysis of usage behaviour indicates a high probability of a customer leaving, Bell Sympatico sends out a customized e-mail to encourage the customer to stay. The results have been impressive as the firm has noted a substantial drop in its percentage of customers leaving, also known in the industry as churn. Finally, subsequent data analysis identifies customers who may be using services that do not fully meet their needs, and Bell Sympatico sends out an e-mail communicating a more appropriate service level. In some cases it has sent direct mail, but it received a substantially lower response rate.[25]

Sometimes, users may also receive less targeted, unwanted e-mails. The electronic equivalent of junk mail, these messages are referred to as **spam**. However, legitimate and enlightened marketers accept the practice of permission-based marketing where consumers register to willingly receive e-mail communications from organizations. Figure 17–8 summarizes the different types of advertising and promotion messages that Canadian consumers are most interested in receiving via e-mail and Figure 17–9 on page 514 indicates Canadian consumers' typical behavioural responses after receiving an e-mail.

Short-Message Service Canadian cellphone carriers agreed to connect their networks so that text messages could be sent to any cellphone hand-set, regardless of the carrier used. For example, instead of only being able to send messages from one Telus user to another, Telus customers could send messages to a friend who used Rogers, Bell Mobility, or Fido.[26]

This technological evolution paved the way for marketers to develop innovative two-way communication. Rather than send text messages one-way like e-mail,

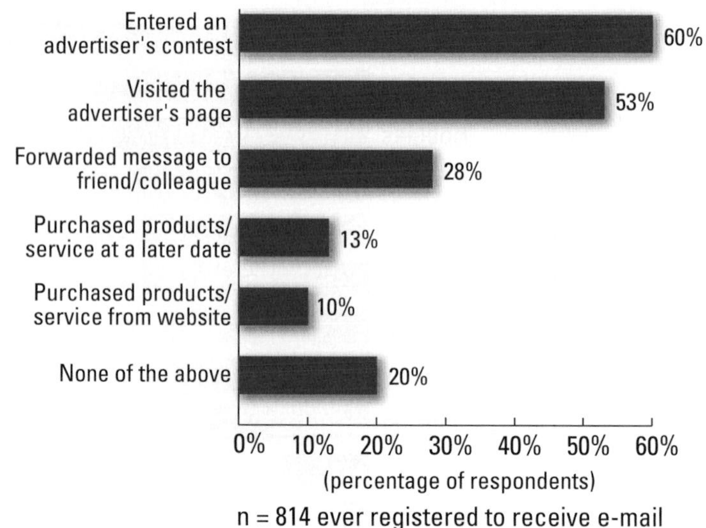

Source: Ipsos-Reid, 2004 E-mail Marketing Study

FIGURE *17–9*

Activities resulting from permission-based commercial e-mail

marketers conceived of the idea of creating short-code as part of a short-message service (SMS) so that consumers could immediately respond to relevant ads through their cell phone. For example, if "24BLUE" is seen on a billboard, the consumer could type this in and receive whatever promotional offer or information Labatt wanted to send as part of its overall promotional program. Overall, the SMS becomes a permission-based pull communication as only those interested in the promotional messages respond accordingly. Moreover, the marketer can reach any cell phone user with the technology standardization.[27]

Current research suggests that Canadians lag in text message usage, at 25 percent compared to 36 percent in the U.S. and 70 to 85 percent in various European countries. Although the domestic growth is impressive, moving from 3.7 million messages per day in 2005 to 8.7 million messages per day in 2006, only 12 percent are willing to receive relevant text messages from marketers. Despite the usefulness of SMS for marketing purposes remaining elusive, many brands planned and executed new communication and promotional offers. One expert estimated that main brands launched about 500 programs during the three years from 2005 to 2007.[28]

For example, Warner Music and 7-Eleven promoted to listeners of a local Winnipeg radio station to text in the message "Secret Events"; those who did received location directions just prior to the event commencing to ensure exclusivity for a free CD or free Slurpee. The success of this kind of communication is boosted by the fact that virtually all text messages are actually read by the cell phone customer.[29] Intrawest's promotional codes at point of sale generated a 50-percent redemption for a 25-percent discount on hotel rental. Reactine provided information on pollen levels at locations and times when allergy sufferers needed information. Molson Canadian Rocks Revealed allowed consumers to text the name of a mystery band based on clues provided. In turn, winners received virtual tickets scanned at the venue for admission. Various digital signage locations with unique words allowed Nissan to track which Versa messages received the most frequent contest entries.[30] Companies also found innovative ways to interact with their customers, going beyond promotional offers to attract switchers. For example, pharmaceutical company Janssen-Ortho, manufacturer of a contraceptive patch for women, sends weekly reminders to change the patch to women who have requested the alert.[31]

Multimedia Messaging Services The technological development of new cell phones permits the user to receive video content known as multimedia messaging services (MMS). For some it appears much like watching television, but with a few differences. The type of programming is currently limited to sports, entertainment, or news. Some experts believe that eventually the content on cell phones will be different than what is found on traditional TV, since the media consumption is more impulsive when users have free time while away from home.[32] For example, CHUM offered snippets of its show *Fashion Television* but added additional clips for cell phone users, which had greater potential for e-mailing to friends. Also, P&G sponsored a MuchMusic VJ search video sent to cell phones containing the advertiser's brand. Even with these content initiatives, some believe ads need to evolve to fit the small screen and the more personal link to the technology consumers have compared with television.[33]

Whatever programming implications arise, the development of this Internet media option is contingent upon the degree of advertising and the potential audience size. The method of advertising remains elusive as planners envision three payment options, as seen in TV: paid content where the user would pay a fee for each video received (i.e., a pay per view movie or hockey game); free content supported by advertising (i.e., a regular show or hockey game); or subscription content based on a monthly fee (i.e., a movie channel or centre-ice hockey package).[34] The size of the audience is relatively small. Preliminary estimates suggest there are 17 million cell phone users; 5 percent have video capability, of which only 10 percent actually watch video on their cell phone. Expected exponential growth suggests that video cell phones could reach 90 percent of all users by the end of 2008 or 2009, and with 20 percent downloading video the audience could grow from about 100,000 to almost 4 million.[35]

Measuring Internet Effectiveness

Measuring the effectiveness of the Internet is done by variety of methods, most of which can be done electronically. Audience information (demographics, psychographics, and so on) and exposure were the initial measures of effectiveness; however, fully measuring communication effects is an emerging trend.

Audience Measures

When the Internet industry first developed its own audience size measures, concerns with the research methods led to a slower adoption rate by traditional media buyers. In an attempt to respond to criticism of the audience metrics used, as well as to standardize the measures used to gauge effectiveness, the Interactive Advertising Bureau (IAB)—the largest and most influential trade group—formed a task force consisting of global corporations involved in advertising and research. The final reports of the task force are available from iab.net and contain both American and international guidelines (see also iabcanada.com).

The basic problem facing Internet media concerns a standardized method for determining the size of the audience. The report identified the technical procedures for accurately reporting whether an ad impression has occurred. This answers the fundamental expectation of advertisers as to whether the receiver of the message actually experienced an opportunity to see the ad (i.e., degree of exposure to the message). Another aspect concerns the accepted procedures for auditing the data, much like we see in traditional print media. Another key part of the report included guidelines for presenting data in terms of time of day, week, and month, much like we see in broadcast media. Finally, industry representatives agreed upon substantial guidelines for disclosure of research methodology, again consistent with all major media described in previous chapters. In future, advertisers can look forward to more authentic data to assess the viability of committing increased resources for

Clicks
Post-click conversions
Cost per conversion
Unique reach of delivered ads
Average frequency
Frequency to conversion ratios
Advertising exposure time
Ad interaction rate
View-through rate
Share of voice
Web page eye tracking
Offline sales lift
Cross-media econometric models

Source: 2005 DoubleClick, Inc.

FIGURE *17–10*

Measures of Internet effectiveness

Internet communication. With these standards in place, advertisers can view data such as those found in Figure 17–10 with greater confidence.

Processing and Communication Effects Measures

The movement for comprehensive communication effects measurement reveals that the Internet has its own set of criteria for measuring effectiveness and it is also borrowing from traditional measures. Many companies that provide research information in traditional media are now extending their reach into the Internet world. Academics are also beginning to publish articles related to measuring effectiveness on the Internet. Studies on consumers' attitudes toward a site, response variations in e-mail surveys, and similarities between bricks-and-mortar retailing and e-commerce are just a few of the many articles being published in academic journals to advance the measurement of the Internet.[36] We now summarize a few emerging communication effects measures.

Cross-Media Optimization Studies One of the more extensive attempts to measure the effectiveness of integrating interactive and traditional media are cross-media optimization studies. As noted by the IAB, the objective of these studies is the following:

> [To] help marketers and their agencies answer the question "What is the optimal mix of advertising vehicles across different media, in terms of frequency, reach and budget allocation for a given campaign to achieve its marketing goals?" . . . The [cross-media] studies simultaneously measure online and offline advertising in the same campaign to determine the optimal weight and mix of each medium.[37]

What makes these studies important is that they provide insight into (1) the relative contributions of each medium in the mix, (2) the combined contribution of multiple media, (3) optimal media budget allocations, and (4) actional media mix strategies. Colgate-Palmolive, ING Investment Management, and Universal Studios have participated in the most recent round of studies, while McDonald's, Kimberly-Clark's Kleenex, and Unilever's Dove participated in earlier ones. Figure 17–11 details the results of the most recent findings.

Online Measuring Firms are developing methods similar to those found in other media (i.e., PMB study) to measure demographics, psychographics, location of Web access, media usage, and buying habits. Clients can determine who saw their ads, determine reach, and ascertain whether the right target audience was reached. Advertisers can test the impact of their messages, receiving a report detailing impressions and clicks by time of day and day of the week.

Recall and Retention A number of companies use traditional measures of recall and retention to test their Internet ads. The same measures have been used to pretest online commercials as well.

Surveys Survey research, conducted both online and through traditional methods, is employed to determine everything from site usage to attitudes toward a site.

Tracking Some companies now provide information on specific communication measures like brand awareness, message association, brand attitude, and purchase intention.

FIGURE *17–11* Results of cross-media studies

Company and Product	Objective	Methodology	Results
Ford F-150 pick up truck	To increase sales	Use English/Spanish TV, outdoor, print, direct mail, radio, Internet, experimental design, behavioral tracking	49% exposure to online ads; 6% sales increase directly attributable to online; website visitors twice as likely to buy as nonvisitors
ING Investment Management funds	Brand familiarity; purchase consideration	Use TV, magazines, online, survey design, continuous tracking	Use of three media together more effective than any one or two alone
Universal Studios movies	Release of ET: *The Extra Terrestrial* on DVD; to generate purchase interest among 25–49 market	Survey design, continuous tracking	Use of TV and rich media more effective than banner ad or TV alone
Unilever Dove Nutrium soap products	To increase awareness, image, purchase intent	Use TV, print, interactive, ratings information, media cost	Combining interactive led to increase in awareness, branding, purchase, purchase intent

Sources of Measurement Data

The number of sources available that provide information about the Internet is enormous. Below we provide a partial list just to give you some indication of the types of information available. Most of the companies listed are the largest and/or most cited sources, and the list is by no means intended to be exhaustive:

- *Arbitron.* Arbitron provides demographic, media usage, and lifestyle data on users of the Internet as well as other interactive media.
- *MRI* and *SMRB.* Both of these companies now provide information regarding viewership profiles for the Internet and other interactive media. Nielsen offers similar data.
- *Audit Bureau of Circulations.* This print agency is developing a product called WebFacts to certify Web counts.
- *Internet Advertising Bureau (IAB).* A trade organization of the Internet, IAB provides information on statistics, usage, and strategies regarding the Internet.
- *eMarketer.* This company publishes comparative data from various research sources and explains the different methods used to arrive at the projections. It also publishes its own projections.
- *Nielson Net Ratings.* Nielson provides audience information and analysis based on click-by-click Internet behaviour through a meter installed on users' computers at home and work.
- *Jupiter MediaMetrics.* This large merged firm provides statistics and website information, including data on users, projections, trends, and so on.

Evaluation of Internet Media

As we have done for other media thus far in the text, we summarize the strengths and limitations of the Internet as media for delivering a message.

Strengths of Internet Media

Target Audience Selectivity A major strength of the Internet is the ability to target very specific groups of individuals with a minimum of waste coverage. For those in the business-to-business market, the Internet resembles a combination trade magazine and trade show, as only those most interested in the products and/or services that a site has to offer will visit the site (others have little or no reason to do so). In the consumer market, through personalization and other targeting techniques, sites are becoming more tailored to meet one's needs and wants. As a result of precise targeting, messages can be designed to appeal to the specific needs and wants of the target audience. The interactive capabilities of the Net make it possible to carry on one-to-one marketing with increased success in both the business and the consumer markets.

Involvement and Processing Time Because the Internet is interactive, it provides strong potential for increasing customer involvement and satisfaction and almost immediate feedback for buyers and sellers. A main objective of most websites is to provide significant brand content to allow consumers to enjoy a rich experience.

Control for Selective Exposure Perhaps the greatest strength of the Internet is its availability as an information source. Internet users can find a plethora of information about almost any topic of their choosing merely by conducting a search through one of the search engines. Once they have visited a particular site, users can garner a wealth of information regarding product specifications, costs, purchase information, and so on. Links will direct them to even more information if it is desired. Moreover, this control is very quick compared to all other media.

Creativity Creatively designed sites can enhance a company's image, lead to repeat visits, and positively position the company or organization. Technological advances have made the Internet as enjoyable to use as both broadcast and print media for both cognitive and emotional responses.

Costs For many smaller companies with limited budgets, the Internet enables them to gain exposure to potential customers that heretofore would have been impossible. For a fraction of the investment that would be required using traditional media, companies can gain national and even international exposure in a timely manner.

Limitations of Internet Media

Target Audience Coverage In the past, one of the greatest limitations of the Internet had been the lack of reliability of the research numbers generated. A quick review of forecasts, audience profiles, and other statistics offered by research providers will demonstrate a great deal of variance—leading to a serious lack of validity and reliability. The recent actions by IAB will reduce these concerns. And while the future looks promising, advertisers should continue to proceed with caution when using these data.

Clutter As the number of ads proliferates, the likelihood of one ad's being noticed drops accordingly. The result is that some ads may not get noticed, and some consumers may become irritated by the clutter. Some studies already show that banner ads may be losing effectiveness for this very reason.

Reach While the Internet numbers are growing in leaps and bounds, its reach is still far behind that of television. As a result, as discussed earlier, Internet companies have turned to traditional media to achieve reach and awareness goals.

Media Image A poor media image is due to annoying characteristics, deception, and privacy. Numerous studies have reported on the irritating aspects of some Internet tactics like e-mail spam, and pop-ups and pop-unders that deter visitors from repeat visits. Attempts by advertisers to target children with subtle advertising messages have proven to be a significant concern. In addition, data collection without consumers' knowledge and permission, hacking, and credit card theft are a number of problems confronting the Internet. Like direct marketing, Internet markets must be careful to respect users' privacy. Again IAB issued guidelines to improve this concern.

IMC Planning: Strategic Use of Internet Media

The print, video, and audio characteristics of Internet media, along with various types of applications (e.g., websites, banner ads, streaming video, sponsorship, promotions, social utilities, etc.), positions this media as capable of communicating with customers and non-customers to achieve all communication and behavioural objectives, and to influence consumers at every stage of their decision-making process. The challenge for promotional planners is to select the correct application that fits the target audience and allows for the achievement of the most relevant objective, along with the most appropriate message that supports the brand positioning strategy. This is not an easy task, as multiple combinations of opportunities for consideration exist.

Internet media often work with other IMC tools. Promotional planners using print, broadcast, or out-of-home media would need to investigate the degree to which the advertising campaign in these media would be directly transferred to Internet advertising. There are many examples of this and it is commonly done. Alternatively, the Internet advertising could take a substantially different direction as some microsites, for example, have allowed brands to take a more experiential or informational track and have a substantially different role and message compared to what is more publicly available, as seen in the award-winning Trojan condom website.

Internet advertising supports sales promotion activities designed to encourage trial and repeat purchases with banner ads or sponsored search links that direct consumers to contests or price promotional offers. Internet advertising is used successfully for public relations activities as links to corporate websites are found on relevant websites (e.g., financial information sites) and other mechanisms are available to direct consumers to corporate information to influence appropriate stakeholders. Finally, Internet advertising assists in direct-response marketing as it facilitates communication to the websites for conducting transactions.

Internet media as a sales promotion is a new opportunity for marketers, with some brands having success. This can work very well with media advertising and sales promotions, as seen in some of the decorative options delivered to computer users. These fun activities are consistent with both the brand image and consumer experience, with sales promotions offering additional exposure and increasing meaningful brand experiences. For example, note the value of branded emoticons or icons or murals (e.g., Spiderman, cited earlier) to continually remind consumers of past communication in other forms.

Internet media as public relations supports considerable media advertising for many consumer packaged-goods and food products. Broadcast and print ads for such products create images and persuade consumers with an appropriate brand positioning strategy. However, some consumers desire more information on usage or would like to know the exact ingredients in more detail. The Internet site for Becel margarine offers a wonderful array of information for consumers desiring a more involving message about the brand and acts as a tremendous public relations resource by presenting a comprehensive and honest assessment of the brand.

Internet as a direct-response medium works very well for Belairdirect. Many of the insurance company's print and radio ads suggest that consumers visit its Internet site to compare quotes from Belairdirect and up to five competitors. In this sense, the Internet media function beyond mere communication like a regular informational website, especially considering that for a few years the focus of all the ads has been to encourage a direct response via the Internet medium.

The general idea suggested here is that the power of the Internet allows promotional planners to adapt their utilization of Internet media as multiple IMC tools that can work with what we might call media advertising—and perhaps with each of the other tools with the right campaign and inventiveness.

SUMMARY

This chapter introduced the topic of Internet media. It explained some of the objectives for this medium and how it can be used in an IMC program as an important communication tool.

The discussion of the Internet focused on understanding the objectives sought when using the Internet, and Internet communications strategies. In addition, the role of the Internet in an IMC program was discussed, with an explanation of how all the IMC program elements can be used with the Internet.

We viewed the Internet as a communication medium to reach audiences much like other media. While there are no doubt broader marketing and business applications, our initial focus is to examine Internet media as a way to deliver a message and interact with current and potential customers. As such, we examined Internet media with the same criteria as other media. With this in mind, Internet media currently offer numerous strengths. Advertisers can direct tailored messages to very selective target audiences. And with technological advances, the creative messages can be richly experienced both cognitively and emotionally for considerable amounts of time as the users themselves decide what they would like to receive and not receive. Finally, this incredible messaging ability is possible at a reasonably low absolute and relative cost.

There are some limitations despite Internet media appearing to be the best possible. It is unclear to marketers the degree to which the target audience can be covered and reached. Internet media can be viewed as tremendous clutter as users move among various websites. And, finally, severe problems regarding advertising delivery, illegal activities, and privacy concerns remain significant drawbacks.

The Internet has been the most rapidly adopted medium of our time. It holds great potential for both business-to-business and consumer marketers. However, contrary to popular belief, the Internet is not a stand-alone medium. Its role in an integrated marketing communications program strengthens the overall program as well as the effectiveness of the Internet itself.

KEY TERMS

DISCUSSION QUESTIONS

1. While some believe that the Internet poses a threat to traditional media, others disagree, arguing that it is just another medium to marketers. Explain some of the arguments on both sides. What is your conclusion?

2. The Internet is growing at an extremely rapid pace. At the same time, there are indications that this growth will slow. Discuss some factors that may lead to decreased growth of the use of this medium.

3. Discuss the objectives marketers may be seeking in their use of the Internet. Which is the Internet best suited for?

4. Explain the different forms that advertisers might use to advertise on the Internet. Discuss some of the advantages and disadvantages associated with each.

5. One of the most difficult objectives to achieve on the Internet is creating a strong brand. Discuss the factors that make brand-building both difficult and possible.

6. Discuss some of the ways that marketers attempt to measure the effectiveness of their programs on the Internet. How do these measures relate to more traditional measures? Describe the advantages and disadvantages of traditional versus Internet measures.

7. Discuss some of the advantages of using the Internet. For which types of companies is the Internet best suited? Why?

8. Many marketers feel that the Internet offers much more potential to business-to-business marketers than it does to consumer marketers. Detail some of the reasons why they feel this way and draw a conclusion as to the merits of this argument.

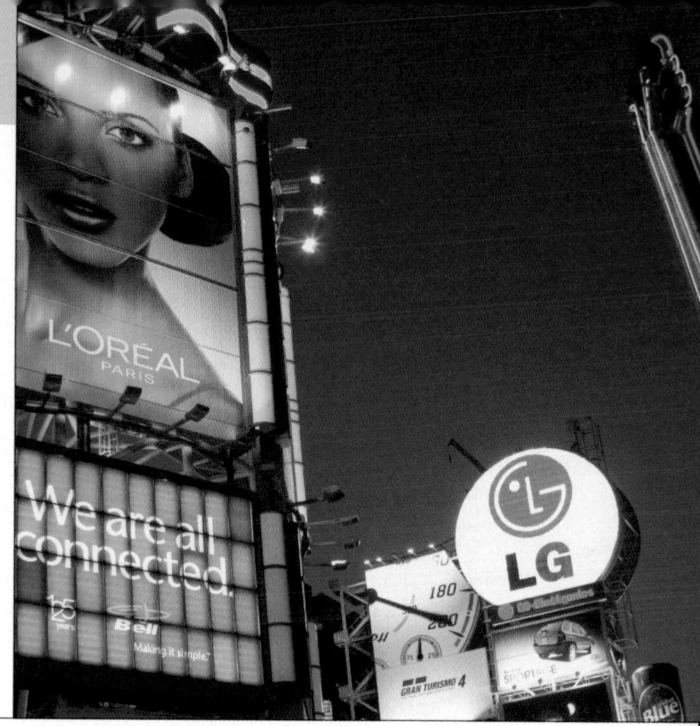

CHAPTER 18

REGULATORY, ETHICAL, SOCIAL, AND ECONOMIC ISSUES FOR IMC

Chapter Objectives

- To be familiar with the advertising regulation system in Canada.
- To evaluate the ethical perspectives of advertising.
- To understand the social effects of advertising.
- To examine the economic role of advertising and its effects on consumer choice, competition, and product costs and prices.

Dove Challenges the Stereotypical Norms of Beauty

share your views
in the news
campaignforrealbeauty | Dove
Real women have real curves
Firming the thighs of a size 2 supermodel is no challenge. Real Women have real bodies with real curves. And Dove wants to celebrate those curves.
Join these six real women who were asked to be in our ad campaign for NEW Dove® Firming. Get to know more about them and their experiences with the campaign. Help by telling more women to stand tall and celebrate their curves....
Meet the women, read their stories and see their beautiful curves.
Roll over each woman to see more.
View our pledge book
17,566 women stood firm for their curves by signing our virtual pledge book. Every name supported a $17,566 donation to uniquely ME! - a program to help boost girls' self-esteem.
> View our pledge book
Go behind the scenes
Get an inside look at the campaign. Watch exclusive footage and more.
> Watch the video
Share your thoughts
Meet the woman? Tell us what you think. What's your definition of beauty? What's your favorite curve?
> Share your thoughts

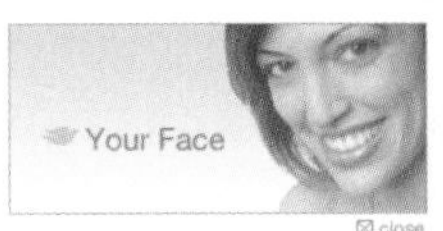

Your Face
close

WHAT DO YOU THINK?
oversized? outstanding?
> Vote now
Real Beauty Photo Exhibit
Explore images of beauty by world-renowned women photographers.
> Take a look
DOVE SELF-ESTEEM FUND
We're helping girls all over the world to overcome everyday beauty pressures.
> Learn more
> invite a friend
privacy policy
terms of use
contact us
dove.com

Most women firmly believe that the media and advertising set an unrealistic standard of beauty that they cannot achieve. More than two-thirds of the women in a recent worldwide study expressed this viewpoint. Only 13 percent of the women indicated that they are very satisfied with their body weight and shape, only 2 percent of the women around the world considered themselves beautiful, and more than half of the women said their bodies disgust them. Inspired by these findings, Unilever's Dove, the global beauty brand, recently launched an integrated marketing campaign that is intended to challenge the stereotypical view of beauty, celebrate diversity, and make women feel beautiful every day. The Dove Campaign for Real Beauty is a global effort that is intended to serve as a starting point for societal change and act as a catalyst for widening the definition and discussion of beauty.

Unilever launched the Dove Campaign for Real Beauty in September 2004 with a much-talked-about ad campaign featuring real women whose appearances are outside the stereotypical norms of beauty. The ads asked viewers to judge the women's looks (Oversized? Outstanding? or Wrinkled? Wonderful?) and invited them to cast their votes and join in a discussion of beauty issues on a special website (campaignforreal-beauty.ca). As part of the launch for the campaign, Dove invited women to rediscover the beauty in their own hair. Television ads were run challenging society's narrow vision that "one size fits all" hair is for everyone. A diverse group of women celebrated the individuality of their own beautiful hair as they shed the stereotypical long, blonde-haired image.

In June 2005, Dove kicked off the second phase of the Campaign for Real Beauty with advertising featuring six "real women" with real bodies and real curves. These "real women" are not professional models, vary in shape and size and come from all walks of life. The images of the real women show the women posing proudly and confidently in their underwear. The photos were not altered or retouched as is often done when shooting images of models. The new phase of the campaign addressed the issue of body image and encouraged women to "Stand Firm to Celebrate Their Curves." The second phase of the campaign supported the new line of Dove firming products with messages encouraging women to challenge beauty stereotypes. One of the ads shows an image of one woman along with two simple lines of copy: "New Dove Firming. As tested on real curves." The copy for another ad reads, "Let's face it, firming the thighs of a size 2 supermodel is no challenge."

Unilever developed an extensive IMC program for the Campaign for Real Beauty. The campaign reached women through national and local television and magazine advertising as well as interactive billboards, transit station signage, and bus ads. The website allowed women to engage in ongoing dialogue about beauty by posting to discussion boards, to hear other women's perspectives on beauty, and to download research studies about beauty. The campaign also featured customized retail promotions and partnerships, local events to foster discussion about real beauty, and cause-related marketing with the Dove Self-Esteem Fund.

Some critics remarked on a contradiction in the message of the "real beauty" campaign that implied consumers need to use the marketer's products to be beautiful. However, many feel that these ads send a message that many parents have tried to teach their daughters for years: Be happy with who you are.

Sources: Rich Thomaselli, "Beauty's New, ER, Face," *Advertising Age,* August 15, 2005, pp. 1, 21; Theresa Howard, "Ad Campaigns Tell Women to Celebrate Who They Are," *USA TODAY,* July 8, 2005, p. 5B; "Real Women Bare Their Real Curves," press release, Edelman/Unilever, June 23, 2005.

Question

1. What is your personal reaction to the campaign?

> If I were to name the deadliest subversive force within capitalism, the single greatest source of its waning morality—I would without hesitation name advertising. How else should one identify a force that debases language, drains thought, and undoes dignity?[1]

The primary focus of this text has been on the role of advertising and other promotional variables as marketing activities used to convey information to, and influence the behaviour of, consumers. We have been concerned with examining the advertising and promotion function in the context of a business and marketing environment and from a perspective that assumes these activities are appropriate. However, as you can see in this quote from economist Robert Heilbroner, not everyone shares this viewpoint. Advertising and promotion are the most visible of all business activities and are prone to scrutiny by those who are concerned about the methods marketers use to sell their products and services. Various parties—including scholars, economists, politicians, sociologists, government agencies, social critics, special-interest groups, and consumers—have attacked advertising for a variety of reasons, including its excessiveness, the way it influences society, the methods it uses, its exploitation of consumers, and its effect on our economic system.

Advertising is a very powerful force, and this text would not be complete without a look at the criticisms regarding its ethical, social, and economic effects as well as some defences against these charges. Before we entertain this debate, we will review the regulations affecting advertising in Canada. The various perspectives presented reflect judgments of people with different backgrounds, values, and interests. Some students may see nothing wrong with the ads for cigarettes or beer or sexually suggestive ads. Other students, however, may oppose these actions on moral and ethical grounds. While we attempt to present the arguments on both sides of these controversial issues, individuals will have to draw their own conclusions as to who is right or wrong.

Advertising Regulation in Canada

Regulation of advertising in Canada occurs through both government regulation and self-regulation. In this section, we review both of these topics. With respect to government regulation, we focus on four prevalent domains. The Canadian Radio-television and Telecommunications Commission (CRTC) is responsible for laws and regulations concerning broadcasting and telecommunications, so its role in advertising is relevant. The *Competition Act* regulates misleading or deceptive ads. Health Canada has placed stringent laws for tobacco promotion. Finally, the Quebec government has strong regulations with respect to advertising to children. In the other direction, the Advertising Standards Council (ASC) acts as the self-regulation body for the advertising industry. Responsibility for many of the federal laws regarding the content of advertising messages for specific product categories has been transferred to ASC by the request of the federal government.

Canadian Radio-television and Telecommunications Commission (CRTC)

The mandate of the CRTC is to ensure that the *Broadcasting Act of 1991* and the *Telecommunications Act of 1993* are upheld throughout Canada. The broad objective of both acts is to make certain that all Canadians can receive broadcasting and telecommunications services. In attaining its mandate, the CRTC is required to delicately balance the needs of citizens, industries, and various interest groups with respect to programming and costs. For purposes of advertising, we will concentrate on the broadcasting side.

The CRTC regulates over 5,900 media organizations (i.e., television, cable distribution, AM and FM radio, pay and specialty television, direct-to-home satellite systems, multipoint distribution systems, subscription television and pay audio). The CRTC is responsible for granting the licences for these media and ensuring that they comply with the *Broadcasting Act.* Within the context of the *Broadcasting Act,* the CRTC focuses on a number of relevant issues (i.e., content, competition, technology). There are three areas for broadcasting ads where the CRTC is involved significantly:

- *Signal substitution.* In an effort to keep advertising revenue in Canada, the CRTC allows television broadcasters to substitute Canadian-sponsored ads on programming originating from the U.S. when shows are delivered at the same time on both Canadian and American networks. While this appears acceptable to most Canadians most of the time, football viewers often feel left out when some U.S. ads are not part of the domestic feed for the Super Bowl.
- *Advertising limits.* The CRTC ensures that TV stations and specialty services carry 12 minutes of advertising during the broadcast day, which lasts 18 hours beginning at 6:00 a.m. However, public service announcements or "ads" for Canadian TV shows are not counted in this total.
- *Infomercials.* An infomercial is a program lasting more than 12 minutes that combines the promotion of a product in an engaging entertainment-like style. The CRTC approves all infomercials for any television station, network, or specialty service.

There are three areas where the CRTC is not involved significantly.

- *False or misleading ads.* The CRTC does not address complaints of these types of ads and refers complaints to the Competition Bureau of the Federal Government. The CRTC has left this for the ASC as well.
- *Alcohol and drugs.* There are regulations for advertising these products, but the CRTC has disbanded the screening process of the ads. This is now the responsibility of the ASC, and we will summarize this later in this section.
- *Internet.* For the time being, the CRTC has not provided any regulations on the content of the Internet, although the federal government provides extensive guideline booklets.

As a regulator, the CRTC recently evaluated two highly topical applications that would have changed the advertising industry substantially in Canada. The Canadian Cable Television Association requested that cable operators be allowed to carry a digital feed of U.S. specialty services (e.g., HBO, ESPN). The Canadian Association of Broadcasters countered with a defence that such services were not necessary since the programming was available on existing channels.[2] A marketing firm with the support of the Canadian Association of Advertisers wanted to insert Canadian ads during the feed of U.S. specialty services (e.g., TBS, A&E). Once again, the Canadian Association of Broadcasters argued against this change suggesting that sufficient advertising capacity existed in Canada, and that increased capacity would reduce advertising revenue.[3] In both cases, the CRTC denied the application.

Competition Act

The federal *Competition Act* prevents false or misleading advertising. Significantly revised in 1999, most of the act contains civil provisions to ensure compliance with the act rather than to seek punishment. In this situation, the goal is not so much to prove deliberate intent, but rather to remedy the situation with the most appropriate solution such as cease and desist orders. Some criminal provisions still exist for the most serious offences where false advertising occurred knowingly. Enforcement of the act falls under the jurisdiction of the Competition Bureau of Industry Canada. Some examples of what is not permissible are shown in Figure 18–1[4] on page 526.

FIGURE *18–1* Advertising and marketing law in Canada

Guideline	Advertising Claim	Misleading Content
Cannot make false claims	Buy this vacuum and get a year's supply of vacuum bags absolutely free	There is a $12 administration fee for the vacuum bags
Even if claim is true, do not give false impression	Drive away in a corvette for just $39,000	The visual display is a version with a sport package and costs $50,000
Avoid double meanings	Number one in the category	Best in sale, but not in quality
Disclaimers should not contradict headlines or body copy	Don't pay a cent until 2008	Fine-print says except for taxes and $750 freight

Source: Adapted from *Advertising and Marketing Law In Canada,* Brenda Pritchard and Susan Vogt, LexisNexis, Butterworths, 2006.

Regulation of Tobacco Advertising

Tobacco products are severely restricted by Health Canada regulations on their use of traditional advertising media. One avenue that tobacco companies turned to fairly quickly when the restrictions were enacted many years ago was to sponsor various arts, cultural, and sporting events; however, this option was discontinued in 2003. Print ads communicating these sponsorships were the only permitted advertising, so the new restriction appears to present even greater limits. Presently, tobacco firms also face significant packaging requirements such as presenting graphic images of the consequences of tobacco use, disallowing any reference to "light," and including a full list of ingredients. With such limited options to attract new users or retain existing consumers, the tobacco companies have been very creative with interesting media choices recently.

Underground marketing has emerged where communication of the brands occurs through exclusive distribution in select bars, pubs, and nightclubs. Through mechanisms such as these, the tobacco companies can get customers to register so that direct marketing techniques can take place, such as contest offers. And 1-800 numbers on tobacco packaging get customers to engage with the tobacco firms directly using creative angles. Point-of-sale communication has also been a competitive tactic that the companies aggressively pursue. Some companies have begun to use the Internet, but thus far mostly as a means of communicating sponsorship deals. Currently all of these IMC tools are legal, and we will find out whether the future looks bright for tobacco manufacturers, as they continue to innovate, or cloudy if the government steps in even further.[5]

Regulations on Advertising to Children

Although no federal laws specifically regulate advertising to children, the Broadcast Code for advertising to children acts as an important guide to ensure that children are not easily manipulated with exaggerated claims. In contrast, the province of Quebec provides strict regulations. According to the *Consumer Protection Act of Quebec,* it is illegal to direct commercial advertising messages to persons younger than 13 years of age. Provisions are in place to determine whether or not an ad is directed to children. Specifically, the provisions concern the product, the way the ad is presented, and the time and place the ad is shown. One exception to the law is a regularly published magazine that is for sale. These magazines, however, have 16 guidelines with respect to their advertising claims; the types of products; the portrayal of people's behaviour, motivation, or attitude reflected in the ad; and the source of the message (i.e., person or character).

To apply the law, the Quebec government provides summary guidelines for advertisers to follow, and it also provides screening services for advertisers if they are uncertain whether it contravenes the law. The purpose of the guidelines is to ensure that advertisers fully understand and correctly interpret the law. The guidelines pertain to precisely describing the types of advertising appeals that are not permitted, clearly defining what is meant by a children's TV program, and exactly stating the percentage of children in the audience that constitutes a children's TV program. The guidelines include the degree to which messages can be directed toward children depending upon whether the product is exclusively for children (i.e., candy), partially for children (i.e., cereal), or not for children. There are also specific guidelines for public service announcements directed to children, even though there is no commercial message.

Advertising Standards Council (ASC)

The ASC is a not-for-profit, self-regulatory industry body with a mandate to create and maintain community confidence in advertising. The ASC represents advertisers, media organizations, and advertising industry suppliers and has more than 200 corporate members. Its Standards Division administers the industry's self-regulatory codes (i.e., *Canadian Code of Advertising Standards, Gender Portrayal Guidelines*), handles complaints about advertising, and administers any disputes that arise between advertisers. Its Advertising Clearance Division previews advertisements in five industry categories, as well as ads directed toward children, ensuring that advertisers will follow applicable legislation, regulatory codes, and industry standards.

Canadian Code of Advertising Standards The Code, as it is known, describes what is not acceptable advertising. According to the ASC, "Advertising is defined as any message (the content of which is controlled directly or indirectly by the advertiser) expressed in any language and communicated in any medium to Canadians with the intent to influence their choice, opinion or behaviour." The Code pertains to the content of ads only. It does not limit the promotion of legal products or the demonstration of products for their intended purpose. The intention of the Code is to provide standards so that responsible and effective advertising results without minimizing the right of firms to advertise. It does not supersede any other laws or regulations.

The Code is used as the criteria to assess whether a complaint is legitimate or not, and the ASC is very clear in how it uses the Code to resolve complaints. "The context and content of the advertisement and the audience actually, or likely to be, or intended to be, reached by the advertisement, and the medium/media used to deliver the advertisement, are relevant factors in assessing its conformity with the Code."

The Code is supported by all member organizations as it sets the standard for advertising with respect to honesty, truth, accuracy, fairness, and propriety. Members are expected to follow the Code both in letter and in spirit and are expected to substantiate any advertised claims when requested. The Code contains 14 clauses.

1. Accuracy and Clarity
2. Disguised Advertising Techniques
3. Price Claims
4. Bait and Switch
5. Guarantees
6. Comparative Advertising
7. Testimonials
8. Professional or Scientific Claims
9. Imitation
10. Safety
11. Superstitions and Fears
12. Advertising to Children
13. Advertising to Minors
14. Unacceptable Depictions and Portrayals

In 2003, ASC updated clauses 6, 10, and 14 as part of its ongoing mandate to ensure that the Code reflects current practices and fairness. While on the surface the changes were just a few words for each clause, the meaning permitted a more reasonable and flexible interpretation. As part of the change, ASC began posting "interpretive guidelines" so that members could understand the code more thoroughly.[6]

Gender Portrayal Guidelines The Guidelines, based on a previous CRTC task force, attempts to ensure that women and men are portrayed appropriately and equally in advertising. The ASC presents the Guidelines as the direction of areas or topics from which complaints or issues have arisen over the past 30 years. Overall, there are six clauses pertaining to authority, decision making, sexuality, violence, diversity, and language.

When interpreting the Guidelines, ASC has four suggestions that advertisers should consider. The overall impression of the ad should not violate the spirit of gender equality. There are clauses specifically addressed toward women, as men are at less risk of being negatively portrayed. History and art should not be used as an excuse for violating a clause. Finally, certain products and how they are advertised are amenable to more appropriate media.

Complaint Process The Standards Division handles complaints in three streams. **Consumer complaints** are those from ordinary citizens who believe that an ad is unacceptable. The ASC receives these complaints directly as well as through government departments and agencies of all levels, the Better Business Bureau, the CRTC, and the Canadian Broadcast Standards Council. **Special interest group complaints** are those from a demonstrated organization that expresses a unified viewpoint. This is a new stream first recognized in the spring of 2002. Complaints from other advertisers are known as **trade disputes**. While there is a distinct complaint process for consumers and special interest groups, the general procedures for each have a degree of similarity that we will touch upon. A summary of all consumer complaints is published in an annual report.

The initial complaint is authenticated to make sure that it is, in fact, a consumer or special interest group complaint and not a trade dispute. From there, the complaint is evaluated to determine whether it legitimately violates a Code provision. This initial assessment occurs at the national (i.e., Toronto) or regional (i.e., Alberta, Atlantic, British Columbia) Consumer Response Councils for English ads, and le Conseil des normes in Montreal for French ads. If the complaint is valid, the advertiser is contacted and has an opportunity to respond to the complaint before the Council makes a formal ruling. On the other hand, the advertiser can take an appropriate action to remedy the complaint as part of the response. In these cases, the advertiser would not be identified in the ASC complaints report. An advertiser who responds and does not remedy the situation can be identified in the report if the Council upholds the complaint.

Complaints Report The ASC has published a more comprehensive annual report since 1997. This format includes the identification of advertisers and the details of all complaints. Previously the annual report provided global statistics. Figure 18–2 shows a capsule summary of the past few years. The ratio of the number of complaints to the number of ads indicates that the number of complaints per ad is less than two. This underscores the fact that the number of complaints is not a factor, but rather the content of the complaint is justification for investigating an ad. The percentage of complaints upheld has seen some modest movement, as expressed by the number of complaints received, pursued, and evaluated by council. In general, about half of all complaints originate from television. This has not deviated significantly over the years and is expected given its pervasiveness; television represents 25 percent of all media expenditures. Newspapers, out-of-home, radio, and Internet equally represent a third of all complaints. We now briefly review ads that received the most complaints in each of the past few years.

	2006	2005	2004
Number of Complaints (ads)			
Received	1,040 (723)	1,271 (804)	1,540 (860)
Pursued	696 (448)	874 (518)	1,116 (560)
Evaluated by Council	115 (57)	91 (73)	125 (87)
Upheld by Council	95 (40)	58 (52)	81 (55)
Upheld Complaints (ads)			
Received	9% (6%)	5% (6%)	5% (6%)
Pursued	14% (9%)	7% (10%)	7% (10%)
Evaluated by Council	83% (70%)	64% (71%)	65% (63%)

FIGURE 18–2

Summary of complaints from the Advertising Standards Council's annual Complaints Report

One of the most controversial rulings occurred in 2001. A Ford Motor Company TV ad showed a young female shoving a male store clerk into the hatchback of her car and driving away with him. This ad received nine complaints, and the Council upheld the complaint, citing Clause 14 as the ad depicted an abduction, which is an unlawful activity. Ford appealed the decision; however, the Appeal Panel confirmed the original decision. Ford's post-appeal statement makes this example an interesting debate:

> Ford of Canada did not intend to offend any segment of the population in this particular advertisement; rather the aim of the ad was to show the attributes of the Focus. The identical advertisement shown in Quebec (both in English and in French) was determined not to contravene the *Code* by the Consumer Response Council and Appeal Panel in Quebec. Particulars of this complaint were provided to the press by a consumer complainant even though this process is intended to be confidential. Subsequent to the Appeal Decision, Margaret Wente, in a lengthy *Globe and Mail* article dated January 31, 2002, gave strong positive support for the ad. However, in light of the decision of the ASC Appeal Panel, Ford of Canada will withdraw the current English advertisement.[7]

In 2002, nudity was an issue in a K-Rock 97.3 out-of-home ad. Billboard ads showed three apparently nude men with nutshells placed strategically across their anatomy. The campaign received 115 complaints and seven petitions totalling 455 signatures. Although Council recognized the display was consistent with the unusual personalities of the hosts, it nevertheless deemed that nudity was gratuitously exploited.

During 2003, another radio station, The Wolf 104.9, featured a mostly nude woman in a billboard ad that received 36 complaints. The image, taken from behind, focused on her buttocks and showed her hand resting on a guitar with a caption reading "Now turn us on." After the initial complaints, the word "censored" was used to cover the woman. In both cases, Council deemed the ads offensive and demeaning to women.

In early 2004, a television ad for an alcohol beverage depicted two women engaging in a passionate kiss. The 113 complaints indicated that the scene was inappropriate for family viewing programming. Council upheld this complaint stating, "the commercial displayed obvious indifference to conduct or attitudes that offended standard of public decency prevailing among a significant segment of the population." Council concluded that the ad in question did not contravene the code providing it was shown later than 9:30 in the evening.

In 2005, 13 complaints about a television commercial depicting abduction contravened Clause 14(b) of the Code. The ad showed the people using a communication device as they held another person captive without their consent.

Although the advertisers intended for the scene to be exaggerated and humorous, council ruled that it appeared too realistic.

A Kia Canada television commercial caused controversy during 2007 and received 77 complaints from individuals and those in the law-enforcement profession. The advertised vehicle contained two adults "making out," after which the woman returned to a police car wearing an officer's uniform. Council upheld the complaint citing Clause 14(c) and concluded that the ad demeaned female officers in particular and all law-enforcement officials in general. Kia responded to the complaint with the following statement:

> As a responsible advertiser, Kia Canada Inc. [Kia] is aware of Advertising Standards Canada [ASC] guidelines, of which its media service agencies are members, and strives to adhere to the spirit of which they have been written. While not in agreement with the Council's final decision, Kia respects it and the process by which it was achieved. Kia believes it has responded to the subject of the complaints by making revisions to the commercial in question, and in adherence to the ASC's Advertising Standards Code.[8]

However, Kia's concern became more public when it ran an edited version of the ad that did not show the woman leaving the car. Instead, words on the screen announced a more suitable ending for the commercial. The final scene featured a goat eating in a meadow while light-hearted music played. We leave the interpretation of this revised ending for interested students to debate!

Clearance Process The ASC provides clearance services for ads for many product categories and ads directed toward children for all jurisdictions except Quebec.

- *Alcohol.* The ASC adheres to the CRTC *Code for Broadcast Advertising of Alcoholic Beverages.* The CRTC disbanded the clearance services in 1997. This code gives 17 precise guidelines on what is not permitted in alcohol ads. Some of the guidelines pertain to not attracting under-age drinkers, non-drinkers, or problem drinkers. Many other guidelines focus on the message with respect to the type of consumption motivation, consumption situation, source, and appeal. The ASC will review all TV and radio ads across the country as well as print and out-of-home ads in British Columbia.
- *Cosmetics.* Health Canada transferred the clearance for cosmetic products ads to the ASC in 1992, although clearance is not an absolute requirement. The ASC follows the *Guidelines for Cosmetic Advertising and Labelling Claims.* The most recent version is a joint publication of the ASC, Health Canada, and the Canadian Cosmetic, Toiletry and Fragrance Association, and was published in 2000. The guidelines list acceptable and unacceptable claims for two types of hair care products, nail products, and five types of skin care products. Another set of guidelines list unacceptable and acceptable claims for toothpaste, deodorant, mouthwash, perfumes/fragrances/colognes, suncare products, vitamins, and aromatherapy products. Finally, the same is done for different benefit claims such as anti-wrinkle, healthy, ingredients, nourishment, relaxation, respiration, revitalization, therapy/treatment and lifting.
- *Non-prescription drugs.* Health Canada also transferred the clearance of non-therapeutic aspects of non-prescription drug ads directed toward consumers to the ASC in 1992. The ASC ensures that broadcast and print copy comply with Health Canada's *Consumer Drug Advertising Guidelines* and *The Food and Drugs Act and Regulations.* Health Canada has also given to the ASC the responsibility for resolving any complaints of advertising for this category. To facilitate this change, Health Canada has published a document

that describes its role, the ASC's role, and the claims that can be made in ads directed to consumers. Most of the guidelines in this document focus on the need for advertisers to provide factual information of the product's attributes and benefits and that the claims are scientifically valid.

- *Ads directed to children.* The ASC uses the *Broadcast Code for Advertising to Children (Children's Code),* published by the Canadian Association of Broadcasters in cooperation with the ASC, to assess whether ads directed toward children are appropriate. The code takes into account the unique characteristics of children to ensure adequate safety and has nine guidelines concerning factual presentation, product prohibitions, avoiding undue pressure, scheduling, source or endorser of the message, price, comparison claims, safety, and social values. The code also gives seven instructions on clearance procedures, such as when clearance is required or not, when ads can be directed to children, and during which programs ads can be directed to children.
- *Food.* The ASC evaluates broadcast ads with respect to *The Food and Drugs Act and Regulations* and the *Guide to Food Labelling and Advertising.* Its policy guidelines make a distinction between food claims that are exempt from clearance and those that require clearance in four categories: general advertising, occasion-greeting advertising (i.e., Christmas), promotional advertising, and sponsorship advertising. In addition, the ASC guidelines for the use of comparative advertising in food commercials outline six principles of appropriate executions of this presentation style. Finally, the ASC guidelines on claims based on research and survey data have requirements pertaining to all aspects of the research design (i.e., sample, data collection).

In conclusion, the Advertising Standards Council self-regulates advertising in Canada based on Canadian laws. However, as the name indicates, it is responsible only for advertising. Other brand messages arising from more innovative communication tools are not covered by these guidelines. For example, product reviews found on Internet sites or brand evaluations on blogs are not considered advertising, even though the actual effect may be quite similar in terms of awareness or influencing consumer opinion. Ethical Perspective 18–1 on page 532 highlights the growth of word-of-mouth communication that is also currently ungoverned, yet is approaching industry standards.

Ethical Effects of Advertising

While many laws and regulations determine what advertisers can and cannot do, not every issue is covered by a rule. Marketers must often make decisions regarding appropriate and responsible actions on the basis of ethical considerations rather than on what is legal or within industry guidelines. **Ethics** are moral principles and values that govern the actions and decisions of an individual or group.[9]

Ethical issues must be considered in integrated marketing communications decisions. And advertising and promotion are areas where a lapse in ethical standards or judgment can result in actions that are highly visible and often very damaging to a company. For example, many organizations and individuals have been critical of advertisers such as Calvin Klein for promoting sexual permissiveness and objectifying women in their ads (Exhibit 18–1). The company was heavily criticized and even boycotted over the controversial "kiddie porn" ads it ran a few years ago featuring intimate snapshots of teenagers in provocative states of undress.[10]

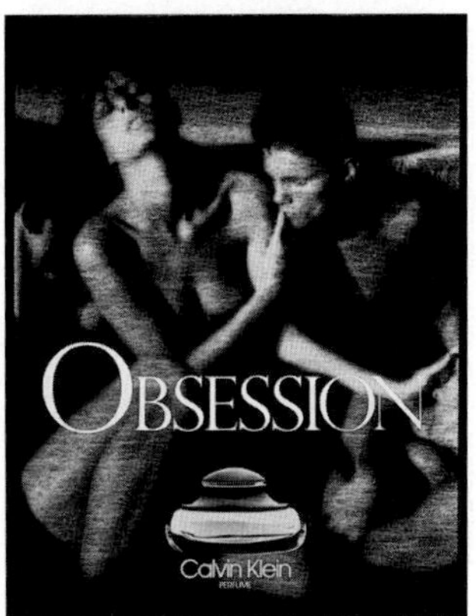

Exhibit 18–1 Ads by Calvin Klein have been the target of criticism by women's groups and others

ETHICAL PERSPECTIVE 18–1

Buzz Marketing

An IMC promotion tool that marketers are taking more seriously is word-of-mouth or buzz marketing. Buzzing is based on the premise of getting the "in" crowd to use your product, leading to a spike in sales due to their recommending the brand to their families and friends. While word-of-mouth campaigns can be seen as perhaps the oldest form of marketing, they have experienced a marked resurgence in the past five years as companies look for ways to impress their message upon a consumer base that is increasingly distracted and fragmented by new media and TV options.

Consumer products companies have also taken notice of Malcolm Gladwell's best-selling book *The Tipping Point,* which looked at how different types of key "influencers" within social networks could function to bring an idea or product to mass awareness. Today, many word-of-mouth campaigns are conducted for free through the Internet, and can involve contests and software giveaways. Word-of-mouth campaigns also hinge on events such as parties, concerts, and street theatre.

Agencies such as Toronto-based Matchstick and Agent Wildfire are in the business of "seeding" products. These companies are increasingly using armies of regular people to create a wave of buzz about items that might not typically get a lot of attention. BzzAgent, a controversial company based in Boston, is one of the leading exponents of word-of-mouth marketing. The company operates a network of volunteer "agents" who receive free samples of products. They then talk to their friends about them and give the participating companies feedback. In return for their work, they receive rewards through a points program.

Growth of word-of-mouth marketing has spawned the Word-of-Mouth Marketing Association (WOMMA), a trade and industry organization dedicated to development of this IMC tool. Its mandate includes protecting consumers and the industry with strong ethical guidelines, promoting word of mouth as an effective marketing tool, and setting standards to encourage its use. A key part of the first mandate is the dissemination of WOMMA's code of ethics, which features honesty of the marketing relationship, honesty of the recommender's opinion, and honesty of the identity of the brand endorsed. An element of the second directive includes extensive investigation of proper measurement of word-of-mouth success.

Sources: Emily Mathieu, "This Mayo Is Delicious," *National Post,* September 15, 2006; "Building Buzz: Marketing," *The Economist,* April 7, 2007; Hollie Shaw, "Grassroots and Growing," *National Post,* May 20, 2006; www.womma.org.

Question

1. If an agent or volunteer from this type of agency did not tell you of his/her affiliation with the agency or the brand, would you be upset?

Much of the controversy over advertising stems from the ways many companies use it as a selling tool and from its impact on society's tastes, values, and lifestyles (Exhibit 18–2). Specific techniques used by advertisers are criticized as deceptive or untruthful, offensive or in bad taste, and exploitative of certain groups, such as children. We discuss each of these criticisms, along with advertisers' responses.

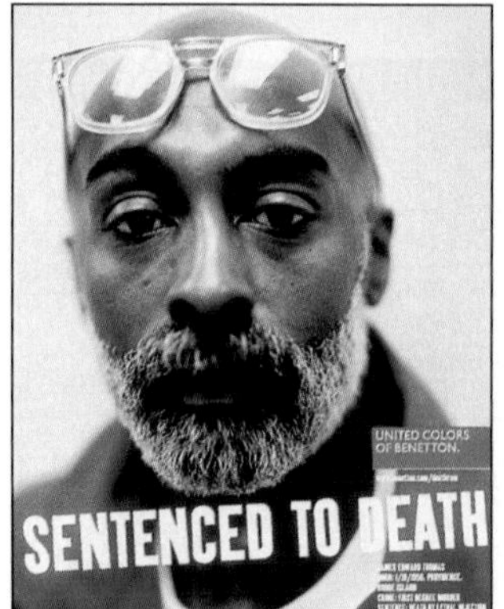

Exhibit 18–2 Benetton's "Death Row" ads created a major controversy

Advertising as Untruthful or Deceptive

One of the major complaints against advertising is that many ads are misleading or untruthful and deceive consumers. A number of studies have shown a general mistrust of advertising among consumers.[11] A study by Banwari Mittal found that consumers felt that less than one-quarter of TV commercials are honest and believable.[12] Sharon Shavitt, Pamela Lowery, and James Haefner recently conducted a major national survey of over 1,000 adult consumers to determine the general public's current attitudes toward and confidence in advertising. They found that consumers generally do not trust advertising, although they tend to feel more confidence in advertising claims when focused on their actual purchase decisions.[13]

Advertisers should have a reasonable basis for making a claim about product performance and may be required to provide evidence to support their claims. However, deception can occur more subtly as a result of how consumers perceive the ad and its impact on their beliefs.[14] The difficulty of determining just what constitutes deception, along with the fact that advertisers have the right to use puffery and make subjective claims about their products, tends to complicate the issue. **Puffery** has been legally defined as "advertising or other sales presentations which praise the item to be sold with subjective opinions, superlatives, or exaggerations, vaguely and generally, stating no specific facts."[15] But a concern of many critics is the extent to which advertisers are *deliberately* untruthful or misleading.

Sometimes advertisers have made overtly false or misleading claims or failed to award prizes promoted in a contest or sweepstakes. However, these cases usually involve smaller companies and a tiny portion of the hundreds of billions of dollars spent on advertising and promotion each year. Most advertisers do not design their messages with the intention to mislead or deceive consumers or run sweepstakes with no intention of awarding prizes. Not only are such practices unethical, but the culprits would damage their reputation and risk prosecution by regulatory groups or government agencies. National advertisers in particular invest large sums of money to develop loyalty to, and enhance the image of, their brands. These companies are not likely to risk hard-won consumer trust and confidence by intentionally deceiving consumers.

The problem of untruthful or fraudulent advertising and promotion exists more at the local level and in specific areas such as mail order, telemarketing, and other forms of direct marketing. Yet there have been many cases where large companies were accused of misleading consumers with their ads or promotions. Some companies test the limits of industry and government rules and regulations to make claims that will give their brands an advantage in highly competitive markets.

Periodically, we find unusual advertising that some may claim as deceptive. Labatt Breweries of Canada advertised in newspapers and communicated information about Carlsberg beer. However, upon reading the ad, it was not entirely clear that Labatt was the sponsor of the ad, especially when it no longer sells the beer! Labatt had sold Danish Carlsberg beer under licence for 15 years and lost the contract to Moosehead and yet, somehow, Labatt felt compelled to explain that Carlsberg was not exactly the same as it was before because it had a new brewer. It seems part of the motivation for such an ad arose from ads that Molson ran a few years before noting that even though Labatt gave the impression that its Kokanee beer was made with glacial mountain water from B.C., it was in fact brewed in London, Ontario, using the city's water supply.[16]

While many critics of advertising would probably agree that most advertisers are not out to deceive consumers deliberately, they are still concerned that consumers may not be receiving enough information to make an informed choice. They say advertisers usually present only information that is favourable to their position and do not always tell consumers the whole truth about a product or service.

Many believe advertising should be primarily informative in nature and should not be permitted to use puffery or embellished messages. Others argue that advertisers have the right to present the most favourable case for their products and services and should not be restricted to just objective, verifiable information.[17] They note that consumers can protect themselves from being persuaded against their will and that the various industry and government regulations suffice to keep advertisers from misleading consumers. Figure 18–3 on page 534 shows the advertising principles of the Association of Canadian Advertisers, which advertisers may use as a guideline in preparing and evaluating their ads.

FIGURE 18–3

Advertising principles of the Association of Canadian Advertisers

1. *Advertisers must behave responsibly.* ACA believes:
   - Industry self-regulation is in the best interests of all Canadians. Self-regulatory policy exists to ensure that Canadians' fundamental rights and social values are not only acknowledged, but also protected.
   - Advertisers already demonstrate their responsibility by endorsing the Canadian Code of Advertising Standards—the principal instrument of self-regulation for the advertising industry in Canada.
   - The Code of Advertising Standards is only one of many industry codes and guidelines. For example, there are guidelines for gender portrayal, advertising to children, and food labelling, to name just a few.
2. *Advertisers have a right to freedom of speech.* Specifically:
   - The ACA does not believe it is reasonable for a government to allow companies to manufacture and sell legal products, and collect taxes, and then restrict them from telling anyone about it.
   - The ACA remains vigilant in ensuring advertisers' commercial freedom of speech.
   - Advertising, including advertising of products we may not like, is an aspect of free speech, and that free speech is one of society's highest values.
3. *Advertisers make an important contribution to the Canadian economy and culture.* Specifically:
   - Advertising is important to the economic and cultural life of Canadians.
   - In all its forms, advertising is estimated to represent an annual $10-billion investment in the Canadian economy.
   - Advertising revenues fuel the Canadian broadcasting system. Advertisers pay for the production and delivery into Canadian homes of programs that entertain, inform, and educate. It also funds newspapers, magazines, and even movies and Internet sites.
   - Commercials reflect our life. They are a powerful tool and means of passing along our values, traditions, and lifestyles to new citizens and the next generation.
   - Locally produced commercials contribute to our sense of identity and promote national unity.
4. *Advertisers support a vibrant, competitive economy.* The ACA believes:
   - An increased reliance on market forces does not mean that a strong and enriched local and Canadian identity cannot be maintained.
   - Our ability to protect culture by limiting access to communications vehicles is becoming increasingly difficult. A prime example is the Internet.
   - In the rapidly changing world of communications, market conditions, not protectionism, should prevail.

Source: The Association of Canadian Advertisers, www.aca-online.com.

Advertising as Offensive or in Bad Taste

Another common criticism of advertising, particularly by consumers, is that ads are offensive, tasteless, irritating, boring, obnoxious, and so on. In the recent study by Shavitt and her colleagues, about half of the respondents reported feeling offended by advertising at least sometimes. A number of other studies have found that consumers feel most advertising insults their intelligence and that many ads are in poor taste.[18] Consumers can be offended or irritated by advertising in a number of ways, such as the type of product, fear appeals, sexual appeals, and shock appeals.

Product Type Some object when a product or service like contraceptives or personal hygiene products is advertised at all. Only in the last few years have media begun accepting ads for condoms, as the AIDS crisis forced them to reconsider their restrictions (Exhibit 18–3). A study of prime-time TV commercials found a strong product class effect with respect to the types of ads consumers perceived as distasteful or irritating. The most irritating commercials were for feminine hygiene products; ads for women's undergarments and hemorrhoid products followed.[19] Another study found that consumers are more likely to dislike ads for products they do not use and for brands they would not buy.[20] Ads for personal products have become more common on television and in print, and the public is more accepting of them.[21] However, advertisers must still be careful of how these products are presented and the language and terminology used. There are still many rules, regulations, and taboos advertisers must deal with to have their TV commercials approved by the networks.[22]

Exhibit 18–3 Many TV stations now accept ads for condoms

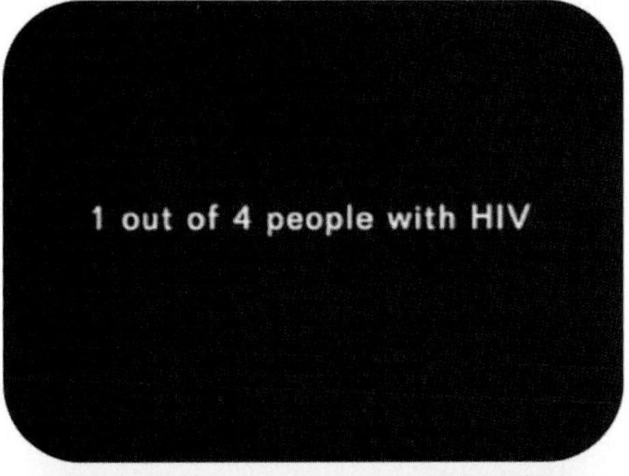

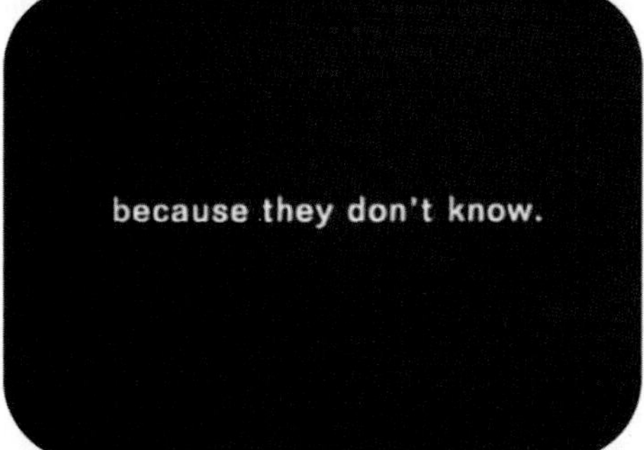

1 out of 4 people with HIV

don't tell their partners

because they don't know.

Use a condom every time.

Fear Appeals Another way advertising can offend consumers is by the type of appeal or the manner of presentation. For example, many people object to appeals that exploit consumer anxieties. Fear appeal ads, especially for products such as deodorants, mouthwash, and dandruff shampoos, are criticized for attempting to create anxiety and using a fear of social rejection to sell these products. Some ads for home computers were also criticized for attempting to make parents think that if their young children couldn't use a computer, they would fail in school.

Sexual Appeals The advertising appeals that have received the most criticism for being in poor taste are those using sexual appeals and/or nudity. These techniques are often used to gain consumers' attention and may not even be appropriate to the product being advertised. Even if the sexual appeal relates to the product, people may be offended by it. Many people object to both nudity in advertising and sexually suggestive ads.

Advertising critics are particularly concerned about the use of sexual appeals to glorify the image of liquor and beer or to suggest they can enhance one's own attractiveness. Some women's groups criticized the Airwalk ad shown in Exhibit 18–4 on page 536, arguing that it showed a submissive and sexually available woman. A critic argued that the ad contains a number of symbolic cues that are sexually suggestive and combine to reinforce an image of the woman's sexual submission to the man.[23] Thus, another common criticism of sexual appeals is that they can demean women (or men) by depicting them as sex objects.

Recently, Skyy Spirits has used provocative, sexually oriented ads to promote its popular namesake vodka brand. Some of its ads, which use stylized images placing the brand's distinctive blue bottle in suggestive situations, have been criticized by some groups (Exhibit 18–5 on page 536). However, a company spokesperson has responded to the criticisms by noting, "Style is a maker of interpretation and like with all art we appreciate all points of view."[24]

Attitudes toward the use of sex in advertising is a polarizing issue as opinions regarding its use vary depending upon the individual's values and religious orientation, as well as across various demographic groups including age, education, and gender. A recent study found major differences between men and women in their attitudes toward sex in advertising.[25] As shown in Figure 18–4 on page 536, while almost half of men said they liked sexual ads, only 8 percent of women felt the same way. Most men (63 percent) indicated that sexual ads have high stopping power and get their attention, but fewer women thought the same (28 percent). Also, most women (58 percent) said there is too much sex in advertising versus only 29 percent of the men. Women were also much more likely than men to say that sexual ads promote a deterioration of moral and social values and that they are demeaning of the models used in them.

FIGURE *18–4*

Attitudes toward Sex in Advertising: Men versus Women

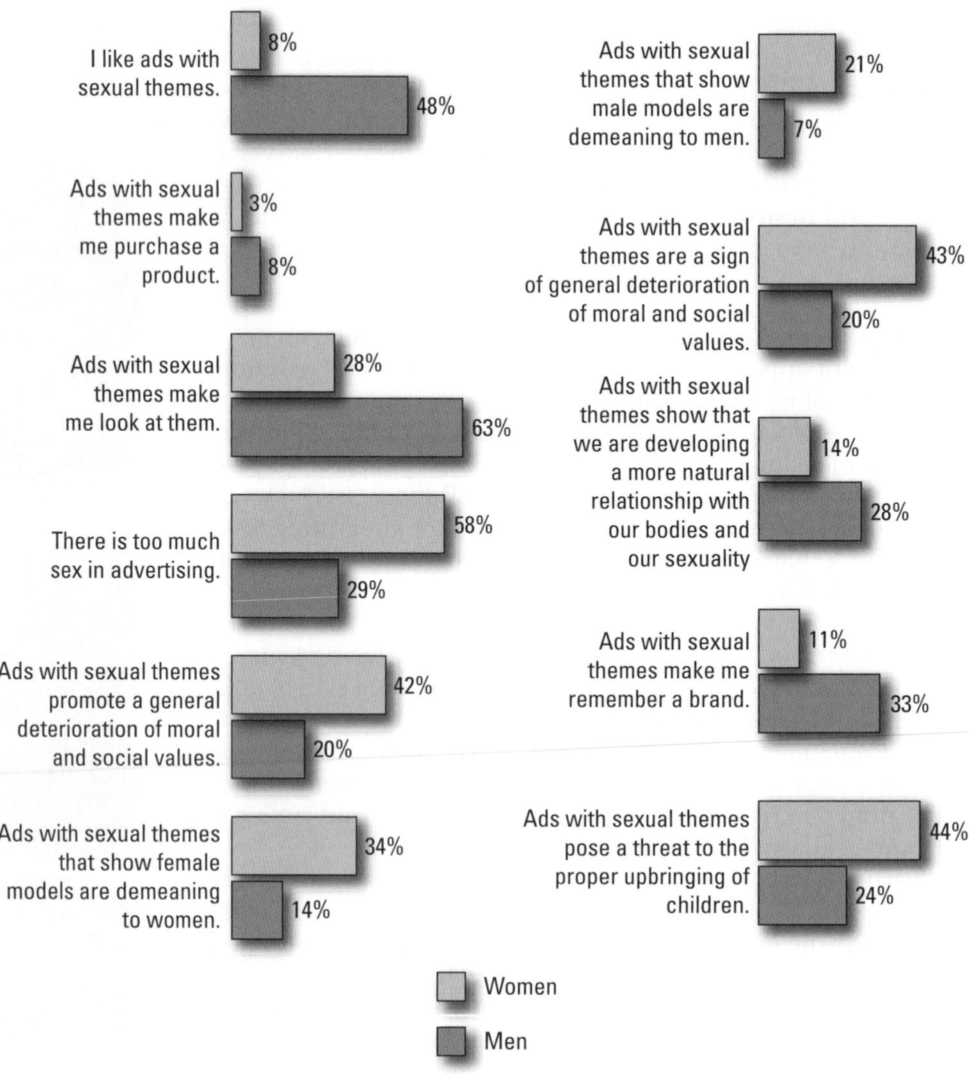
I like ads with sexual themes.
8%
48%
Ads with sexual themes make me purchase a product.
3%
8%
Ads with sexual themes make me look at them.
28%
63%
There is too much sex in advertising.
58%
29%
Ads with sexual themes promote a general deterioration of moral and social values.
42%
20%
Ads with sexual themes that show female models are demeaning to women.
34%
14%
Ads with sexual themes that show male models are demeaning to men.
21%
7%
Ads with sexual themes are a sign of general deterioration of moral and social values.
43%
20%
Ads with sexual themes show that we are developing a more natural relationship with our bodies and our sexuality
14%
28%
Ads with sexual themes make me remember a brand.
11%
33%
Ads with sexual themes pose a threat to the proper upbringing of children.
44%
24%
Women
Men

AIRWALK

Exhibit 18–4 This Airwalk ad was criticized for being suggestive and symbolizing sexual submission

Exhibit 18–5 Ads are often criticized for being sexually suggestive

Shock Appeals With the increasing clutter in the advertising environment, advertisers continue to use sexual appeals that may offend some people but catch the attention of consumers and may even generate publicity for their companies. In recent years there has been an increase in what is often referred to as a shock appeal, in which marketers use nudity, sexual suggestiveness, or other startling images to get consumers' attention. A shock appeal is not new, as Calvin Klein and Benetton have used this approach in their ads for many years. What is new is the pervasiveness of shock appeals in other domains, as we have seen in some of the ASC rulings summarized earlier. Many advertising experts argue that what underlies the increased use of shock appeals is the pressure on marketers and their agencies to do whatever it takes to get their ads noticed. However, critics argue that the more advertisers use the appeal, the more shocking the ads have to be to get attention. How far advertisers can go with this appeal will probably depend on the public's reaction. When advertisers have gone too far, they are likely to pressure the advertisers to change their ads and the media to stop accepting them. While marketers and ad agencies often acknowledge that their ads push the limits with regard to taste, they also complain about a double standard that exists for advertising versus editorial television program content. They argue that even the most suggestive commercials are bland compared with the content of many television programs.

Advertising and Children

One of the most controversial topics advertisers must deal with is the issue of advertising to children. TV is a vehicle through which advertisers can reach children easily. Children between the ages of 2 and 11 watch an average of 15.5 hours of TV a week. Studies show that television is an important source of information for children about products.[26] Concern has also been expressed about marketers' use of other promotional vehicles and techniques such as radio ads, point-of-purchase displays, premiums in packages, and the use of commercial characters as the basis for TV shows.

Critics argue that children, particularly young ones, are especially vulnerable to advertising because they lack the experience and knowledge to understand and evaluate critically the purpose of persuasive advertising appeals. Research has shown that preschool children cannot differentiate between commercials and programs, do not perceive the selling intent of commercials, and cannot distinguish between reality and fantasy.[27] Research has also shown that children need more than a skeptical attitude toward advertising; they must understand how advertising works in order to use their cognitive defences against it effectively.[28] Because of children's limited ability to interpret the selling intent of a message or identify a commercial, critics charge that advertising to them is inherently unfair and deceptive and should be banned or severely restricted.

At the other extreme are those who argue that advertising is a part of life and children must learn to deal with it in the **consumer socialization process** of acquiring the skills needed to function in the marketplace.[29] They say existing restrictions are adequate for controlling children's advertising. A recent study by Tamara Mangleburg and Terry Bristol provided support for the socialization argument. They found that adolescents developed skeptical attitudes toward advertising that were learned through interactions with socialization agents such as parents, peers, and television. They also found that marketplace knowledge plays an important role in adolescents' skepticism toward advertising. Greater knowledge of the marketplace appears to give teens a basis by which to evaluate ads and makes them more likely to recognize the persuasion techniques used by advertisers.[30]

The *Children's Code* discussed earlier recognizes the above debate explicitly, in the background section, to find a balance between these two points of view. A study comparing the attitudes of business executives and consumers regarding children's advertising found that marketers of products targeted to children believe advertising to them provides useful information on new products and does not disrupt the parent–child relationship. However, the general public did not have such a favourable opinion. Older consumers and those from households with children had particularly negative attitudes toward children's advertising.[31]

It is important to many companies to communicate directly with children. However, only by being sensitive to the naiveté of children as consumers will they be able to do so freely and avoid potential conflict with those who believe children should be protected from advertising.

Finally, while we have been concerned with ads directed toward children, advertisers need to be careful not to unwillingly produce ads directed toward adults that make an impression upon children. For example, ASC published a bulletin, consistent with CRTC regulations, stating that marketers of alcoholic beverages could not use a spokesperson that is perceived as a role model for children. This arose from Molson's use of Don Cherry for its "Bubba" beer ads.[32]

Social Effects of Advertising

Concern is often expressed over the impact of advertising on society, particularly on values and lifestyles. While a number of factors influence the cultural values, lifestyles, and behaviour of a society, the overwhelming amount of advertising and its prevalence in the mass media lead many critics to argue that advertising plays a major role in influencing and transmitting social values. While there is general agreement that advertising is an important social influence agent, opinions as to the value of its contribution are often negative. Advertising is criticized for encouraging materialism, manipulating consumers to buy things they do not really need, perpetuating stereotypes, and controlling the media.

Advertising Encourages Materialism

Many critics claim advertising has an adverse effect on consumer values by encouraging **materialism**, a preoccupation with material things rather than intellectual or spiritual concerns. Many critics believe that advertising:

- Seeks to create needs rather than merely showing how a product or service fulfills them.
- Surrounds consumers with images of the good life and suggests the acquisition of material possessions leads to contentment and happiness and adds to the joy of living.
- Suggests material possessions are symbols of status, success, and accomplishment and/or will lead to greater social acceptance, popularity, sex appeal, and so on.

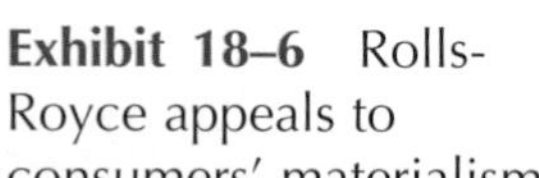

Exhibit 18–6 Rolls-Royce appeals to consumers' materialism

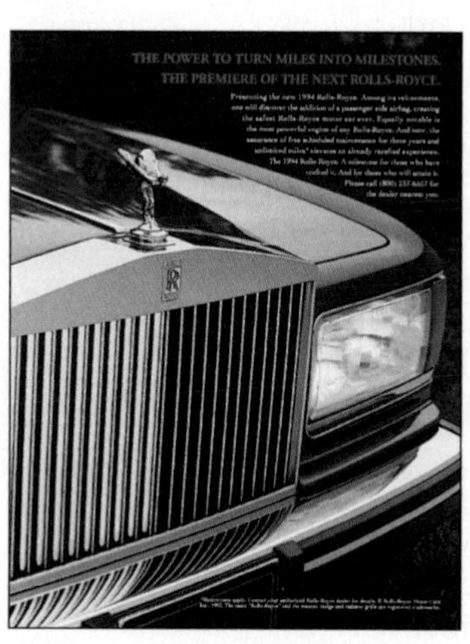

The ad shown in Exhibit 18–6 for Rolls-Royce automobiles is an example of how advertising can promote materialistic values.

This criticism of advertising assumes that materialism is undesirable and is sought at the expense of other goals. But many believe materialism is an acceptable part of the **Protestant ethic**, which stresses hard work and individual effort and initiative and views the accumulation of material possessions as evidence of success. Others argue that the acquisition of material possessions has positive economic impact by encouraging consumers to keep consuming after their basic needs are met. Many believe economic growth is essential and materialism is both a necessity and an inevitable part of this progress.

Economist John Kenneth Galbraith, often a vocal critic of advertising, describes the role advertising plays in industrialized economies by encouraging consumption:

> Advertising and its related arts thus help develop the kind of man the goals of the industrial system require—one that reliably spends his income and works reliably because he is always in need of more. In the absence of the massive and artful persuasion that accompanies the management of demand, increasing abundance might well have reduced the interest of people in acquiring more goods. Being not pressed by the need for these things, they would have spent less reliably to get more. The consequence—a lower and less reliable propensity to consume—would have been awkward for the industrial system.[33]

It has also been argued that an emphasis on material possessions does not rule out interest in intellectual, spiritual, or cultural values. Defenders of advertising say consumers can be more interested in higher-order goals when basic needs have been met. Raymond Bauer and Stephen Greyser point out that consumers may purchase material things in the pursuit of nonmaterial goals.[34] For example, a person may buy an expensive stereo system to enjoy music rather than simply to impress someone or acquire a material possession.

Even if we assume materialism is undesirable, there is still the question of whether advertising is responsible for creating and encouraging it. While many critics argue that advertising is a major contributing force to materialistic values, others say advertising merely reflects the values of society rather than shaping them.[35] They argue that consumers' values are defined by the society in which they live and are the results of extensive, long-term socialization or acculturation.

The argument that advertising is responsible for creating a materialistic and hedonistic society is addressed by Stephen Fox in his book *The Mirror Makers: A History of American Advertising and Its Creators.* Fox concludes advertising has become a prime scapegoat for our times and merely reflects society. Regarding the effect of advertising on cultural values, he says:

Exhibit 18–7 The advertising industry argues that advertising reflects society

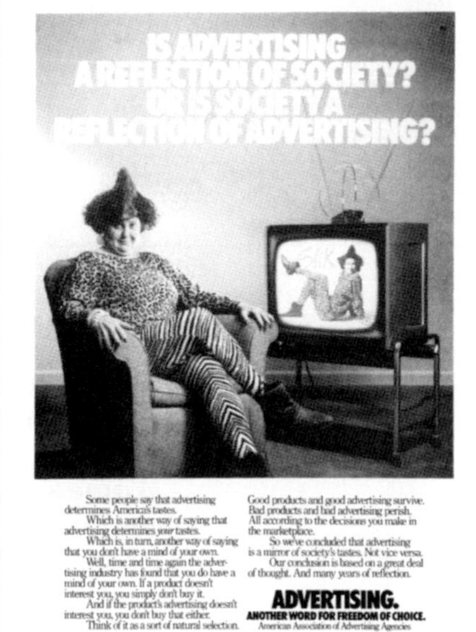

> To blame advertising now for those most basic tendencies in American history is to miss the point. It is too obvious, too easy, a matter of killing the messenger instead of dealing with the bad news. The people who have created modern advertising are not hidden persuaders pushing our buttons in the service of some malevolent purpose. They are just producing an especially visible manifestation, good and bad, of the American way of life.[36]

The ad shown in Exhibit 18–7 was developed by the American Association of Advertising Agencies and suggests that advertising is a reflection of society's tastes and values, not vice versa. The ad was part of a campaign that addressed criticisms of advertising.

Advertising does contribute to our materialism by portraying products and services as symbols of status, success, and achievement and by encouraging consumption. As Richard Pollay says, "While it may be true that advertising reflects cultural values, it does so on a very selective basis, echoing and reinforcing certain attitudes, behaviours, and values far more frequently than others."[37]

Advertising Makes People Buy Things They Don't Need

A common criticism of advertising is that it manipulates consumers into buying things they do not need. Many critics say advertising should just provide information useful in making purchase decisions and should not persuade. They view information advertising (which reports price, performance, and other objective criteria) as desirable but persuasive advertising (which plays on consumers' emotions, anxieties, and psychological needs and desires such as status, self-esteem, and attractiveness) as unacceptable. Persuasive advertising is criticized for fostering discontent among consumers and encouraging them to purchase products and services to solve deeper problems. Critics say advertising exploits consumers and persuades them to buy things they don't need.

Defenders of advertising offer a number of rebuttals to these criticisms. First, they point out that a substantial amount of advertising is essentially informational in nature.[38] Also, it is difficult to separate desirable informational advertising from undesirable persuasive advertising. Shelby Hunt, in examining the *information–persuasion dichotomy,* points out that even advertising that most observers would categorize as very informative is often very persuasive.[39] He says, "If advertising critics really believe that persuasive advertising should not be permitted, they are actually proposing that no advertising be allowed, since the purpose of all advertising is to persuade."[40]

Defenders of advertising also take issue with the argument that it should be limited to dealing with basic functional needs. In our society, most lower-level needs recognized in Maslow's hierarchy, such as the need for food, clothing, and shelter, are satisfied for most people. It is natural to move from basic needs to higher-order ones such as self-esteem and status or self-actualization. Consumers are free to choose the degree to which they attempt to satisfy their desires, and wise advertisers associate their products and services with the satisfaction of higher-order needs.

Exhibit 18–8 The AAAA responds to the claim that advertising makes consumers buy things they do not need

Proponents of advertising offer two other defences against the charge that advertising makes people buy things they do not really need. First, this criticism attributes too much power to advertising and assumes consumers have no ability to defend themselves against it. Second, it ignores the fact that consumers have the freedom to make their own choices when confronted with persuasive advertising. While they readily admit the persuasive intent of their business, advertisers are quick to note it is extremely difficult to make consumers purchase a product they do not want or for which they do not see a personal benefit. If advertising were as powerful as the critics claim, we would not see products with multimillion-dollar advertising budgets failing in the marketplace. The reality is that consumers do have a choice, and they are not being forced to buy. Consumers ignore ads for products and services they do not really need or that fail to interest them (see Exhibit 18–8).

Advertising and Stereotyping

Advertising is often accused of creating and perpetuating stereotypes through its portrayal of women and ethnic minorities.

Women The portrayal of women in advertising is an issue that has received a great deal of attention through the years.[41] Advertising has received much criticism for stereotyping women and failing to recognize the changing role of women in our society. Critics have argued that advertising often depicts women as preoccupied with beauty, household duties, and motherhood or shows them as decorative objects or sexually provocative figures. The various research studies conducted through the years show a consistent picture of gender stereotyping that has varied little over time. Portrayals of adult women in American television and print advertising have emphasized passivity, deference, lack of intelligence and credibility, and punishment for high levels of efforts. In contrast, men have been portrayed as constructive, powerful, autonomous, and achieving.[42]

Research on gender stereotyping in advertising targeted to children has found a pattern of results similar to that reported for adults. A recent study found sex-role stereotyping in television advertising targeted at children in the United States as well as in Australia.[43] Boys are generally shown as being more knowledgeable, active, aggressive, and instrumental than girls. Nonverbal behaviours involving dominance and control are associated more with boys than girls. Advertising directed toward children has also been shown to feature more boys than girls, to position boys in more dominant, active roles, and to use male voiceovers more frequently than female ones.[44]

Feminist groups such as MediaWatch argue that advertising that portrays women as sex objects contributes to violence against women. MediaWatch and its supporters often communicate to advertisers and their agencies about ads they find insulting to women and have even called for boycotts against offending advertisers. MediaWatch has also been critical of advertisers for the way they portray women in advertising for clothing, cosmetics, and other products. The organization feels that many of these ads contribute to the epidemic of eating disorders and smoking among women and girls who hope such means will help them control their weight.[45]

In a recent annual report, MediaWatch gave "thumbs-down awards" to Vichy, Browns Shoes, Calvin Klein, and Kahlúa Black Russian. Positive recognition went to "Cam's Breast Exam," a TV ad showing eager lads ready to do a breast exam for women to prevent cancer, and Body Shop for realistically portraying women. MediaWatch also effectively identifies advertisers who portray women inappropriately and offers tips for marketers to advertise more effectively and avoid controversy. For example, it noted that Terra Footwear stopped a national billboard campaign that showed "lingerie-clad female models holding construction tools in suggestive poses."[46]

While sexism and stereotyping still exist, advertising's portrayal of women is improving in many areas. Many advertisers have begun to recognize the importance of portraying women realistically. The increase in the number of working women has resulted not only in women having more influence in family decision making but also in more single-female households, which means more independent purchasers.

Exhibit 18–9 Many advertisers now portray women in powerful roles

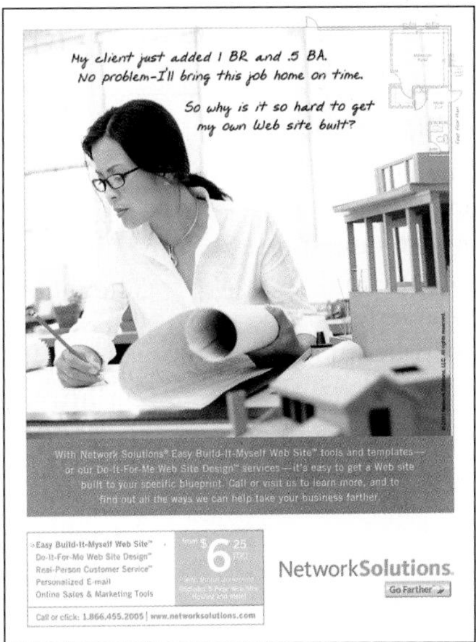

Researchers Steven Kates and Glenda Shaw-Garlock argue that the transformed social positioning of women in North American society is perhaps the most important social development of this century.[47] They note that as women have crossed the boundary from the domestic sphere to the professional arena, expectations and representations of women have changed as well. For example, a number of magazines, such as *Ms* and *Working Woman,* now incorporate and appeal to the sociocultural shifts in women's lives. Many advertisers are now depicting women in a diversity of roles that reflect their changing place in society. In many ads, the stereotypic character traits attributed to women have shifted from weak and dependent to strong and autonomous.[48]

The ad for Network Solutions shown in Exhibit 18–9 is an example of how advertisers are changing the way they portray women in their ads. One reason for the changes in the way women are portrayed in advertising is the emergence of females in key agency roles. Women advertising executives are likely to be more sensitive to the portrayal of their own gender and to strengthen the role of women beyond stereotypical housewives or a position of subservience to men.[49]

Visible Minorities Several U.S. academic studies in the late 1980s and early 90s examined the incidence of visible minorities in advertising. A study conducted in 1987 found that 11 percent of the people appearing in commercials were African-Americans.[50] Another study conducted two years later found that African-Americans appeared in 26 percent of all ads on network TV that used live models but Hispanics appeared in only 6 percent of the commercials with live models. The researchers also found that TV ads in which blacks appeared were overwhelmingly

Exhibit 18–10 Ikea broke new ground with this ad showing an interracial couple shopping for furniture

integrated (Exhibit 18–10) and the blacks were likely to have played either minor or background roles in the majority of the ads.[51] A study conducted in 1995 found that 17 percent of prime-time network TV ads featured African-Americans as dominant characters and the majority of commercials featured them in minor roles.[52] A recent study by Corliss L. Green found that ads targeting African-Americans through racially targeted media, especially with race-based products, benefit from featuring African-American models with a dominant presence in the ad.[53]

A recent study of U.S. prime-time TV commercials found that Asian male and female models are overrepresented in terms of their proportion of the U.S. population (3.6 percent), appearing in 8.4 percent of the commercials. However, Asian models were more likely than members of other minority groups to appear in background roles, and Asian women were rarely depicted in major roles. The study also found that portrayals of Asian-Americans put more emphasis on the work ethic and less on other aspects of their lives.[54]

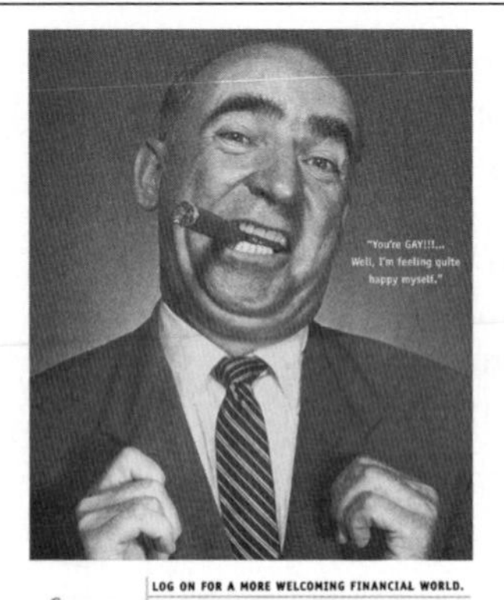

Exhibit 18–11 The Gay Financial Network broke barriers by becoming the first gay-oriented company to advertise in the mainstream media

It may be difficult to generalize these findings to Canada; however, we should keep in mind that Canadians are exposed to these ads when watching U.S. television programs that do not simulcast Canadian commercials or when reading American magazines. So to a degree, Canadian consumers will experience and perceive some amount of imbalance through this exposure.

Visible minorities comprise about 18 percent of Canada's population, of which 23 percent are Chinese, 19 percent are South Asians, and 19 percent are black. Recent Canadian trends and commentary by practitioners suggest that the portrayal of visible minorities can be improved in Canadian advertising, even though there has been significant improvement over the past 5 years. For example, a recent study suggests that 45 percent of all Canadians feel that advertising is directed to whites, and 48 percent feel that visible minorities are under-represented.[55] IMC Perspective 18–2 tells the story of how Wal-Mart reflects Canada's diversity in its advertising.

Advertising and the Media

The fact that advertising plays such an important role in financing the media has led to concern that advertisers may influence or even control the media (Exhibit 18–11). It is well documented that *economic censorship* occurs, whereby the media avoid certain topics or even present biased news coverage, in acquiescence to advertiser demands.[56] In fact, Professors Lawrence Soley and Robert Craig say, "The assertion that advertisers attempt to influence what the public sees, hears, and reads in the mass media is perhaps the most damning of all criticisms of advertising, but this criticism isn't acknowledged in most advertising textbooks."[57] We will address this important issue in this book by considering arguments on both sides.

Arguments Supporting Advertiser Control Some critics charge the media's dependence on advertisers' support makes them susceptible to various forms of influence, including exerting control over the editorial content of magazines and newspapers; biasing editorial opinions to favour the position of an advertiser; limiting coverage of a controversial story that might reflect negatively on a company; and influencing the program content of television.

Newspapers and magazines receive nearly 70 percent of their revenue from advertising; commercial TV and radio derive virtually all their income from advertisers. Small, financially insecure newspapers, magazines, or broadcast stations are the

IMC PERSPECTIVE 18–2

Wal-Mart's Diverse Advertising

Canada is said to be the most diverse nation in the world and Wal-Mart has been called Canada's mainstream retailer. But to accept that title, we feel we need to understand what it means and how the Canadian mainstream factors into every detail of our business, including marketing. In 1997, just three years after opening our doors in Canada, Wal-Mart initiated a multicultural advertising plan.

It had become clear that as Canadians flicked on the evening news or their favourite TV dramas, they weren't necessarily tuning into national networks and they weren't necessarily watching programs in either of Canada's official languages. Our English and French ads were largely irrelevant to many of our customers.

With the help of our advertising agency, Publicis—which identified the multicultural opportunity using Print Measurement Bureau and Census Canada data, as well as formulating production and media buying strategies—we were able to put numbers to our assumption that a large and growing segment of the population was missed by our traditional advertising. Intuitively, we also believed there was an issue of respect at play, and that we should be communicating to our customers in a language of their choice.

In that first year, we produced original TV creative for the four leading major-market ethnic groups: Italian, Portuguese, Cantonese and South Asian, all but the latter in their own language. Year after year we have reviewed the strategy, tweaking as we go (like altering market volumes or adding Mandarin and Spanish ads in 2003), but never once questioning the program's relevance. Our multicultural ads today are more relevant than ever, which brings us back to how Wal-Mart meets the Canadian mainstream.

Wal-Mart Canada governs its business with a philosophical approach called Store of the Community. Loosely, the philosophy suggests that if a store is to be part of a community it should stock merchandise, employ individuals, support philanthropic programs and operate in a way that is relevant to that community. The same is true of communications, and if you wish to communicate to the Canadian mainstream the list of relevant languages is growing.

Looking inward, our multicultural approach had unintended benefits in our stores. Associates working at Wal-Mart reported a sense of pride in our multicultural spots, and the feedback our multicultural associates received in their own homes and communities was resoundingly positive.

Reflecting on nearly a decade of multicultural ads, it's clear we could have overlooked a large and growing ethnic customer base. But data, intuition, anecdotes, customer relationships and a growing ethnic business tells us that wouldn't have been the right choice.

We could have approached the strategy half-heartedly. But, we decided that the only thing worse than not having a multicultural strategy would be to appear anything less than 100% authentic. Even today, we remain one of a handful of companies producing original creative for ethnic TV.

Similarly, we refuse to dub over English ads because the power of our ethnic spots is in the details-the dialect and the stories that truly reflect the customers with whom we're communicating. For example, one of our current ads features the story of Kelly, a Chinese-Canadian who shops at Wal-Mart for snacks to serve friends during mah-jong matches; in another spot is José, a Portuguese-Canadian whose drama group shops at Wal-Mart for props.

Just like our English and French advertising, our ethnic ads feature real people recruited while shopping in our stores. This requires an additional expense, lots of preparation and patience, and the talents of Publicis and Omni Television in Toronto, whose cultural and linguistic experts help refine our ads and the many cultural cues they contain.

We feel strongly that our business benefits when customers see us talking to them in their language, with the real-life stories of people who could easily be their neighbours. Though we hope this translates into sales, we know it has created a mutual sense of respect between our Wal-Mart stores and the multicultural customers in their communities.

Source: Lou Puim, "How Wal-Mart Learned Diversity, *Marketing Magazine,* January 23, 2006.

Questions

1. Prior to reading this perspective, had you noticed Wal-Mart had such diverse advertising?
2. What features of the strategy are very appropriate or inappropriate?

most susceptible to pressure from advertisers, particularly companies that account for a large amount of the media outlet's advertising revenue. A local newspaper may be reluctant to print an unfavourable story about a car dealer or supermarket chain on whose advertising it depends. A survey of 147 daily newspapers found that more than 90 percent of editors have been pressured by advertisers and more than one-third of them said advertisers had succeeded in influencing news at their papers.[58]

Individual TV stations and even the major networks also can be influenced by advertisers. Programming decisions are made largely on the basis of what shows will attract the most viewers and thus be most desirable to advertisers. Critics say this often results in lower-quality television as educational, cultural, and informative programming is usually sacrificed for shows that get high ratings and appeal to the mass markets.

Arguments Against Advertiser Control The commercial media's dependence on advertising means advertisers can exert influence on their character, content, and coverage of certain issues. However, media executives offer several reasons why advertisers do not exert undue influence over the media.

First, they point out it is in the best interest of the media not to be influenced too much by advertisers. To retain public confidence, they must report the news fairly and accurately without showing bias or attempting to avoid controversial issues. Media executives point to the vast array of topics they cover and the investigative reporting they often do as evidence of their objectivity. They want to build a large audience for their publications or stations so that they can charge more for advertising space and time.

Media executives also note that an advertiser needs the media more than they need any individual advertiser, particularly when the medium has a large audience or does a good job of reaching a specific market segment. Many publications and stations have a very broad base of advertising support and can afford to lose an advertiser that attempts to exert too much influence. This is particularly true for the larger, more established, financially secure media. For example, a consumer products company would find it difficult to reach its target audience without network TV and could not afford to boycott a network if it disagreed with a station's editorial policy or program content. Even the local advertiser in a small community may be dependent on the local newspaper, since it may be the most cost-effective media option available.

Exhibit 18–12 This ad points out how advertising lowers the cost of newspapers for consumers

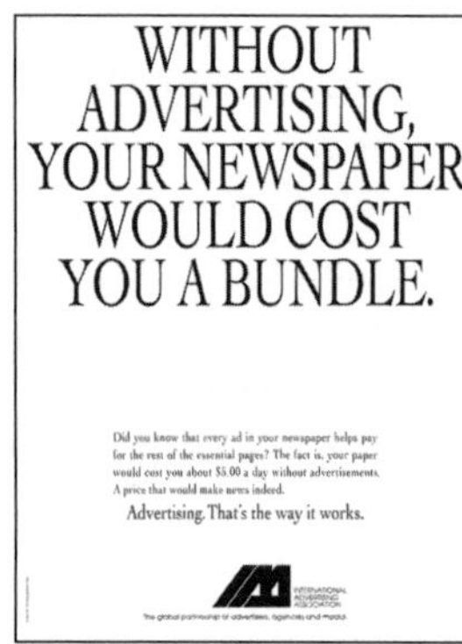

The media in Canada are basically supported by advertising; this means we can enjoy them for free or for a fraction of what they would cost without advertising. The alternative to an advertiser-supported media system is support by users through higher subscription costs for the print media and a fee or pay-per-view system with TV. The ad in Exhibit 18–12, part of a campaign by the International Advertising Association, explains how advertising lowers the cost of print media for consumers. Another alternative is government-supported media like those in many other countries, but this runs counter to most people's desire for freedom of the press. Although not perfect, our system of advertising-supported media provides the best option for receiving information and entertainment.

Summarizing Social Effects

We have examined a number of issues and have attempted to analyze the arguments for and against them. Many people have reservations about the impact of advertising and promotion on society. The numerous rules, regulations, policies, and guidelines marketers comply with do not cover every advertising and promotional situation. Moreover, what one individual views as distasteful or unethical may be acceptable to another.

Negative opinions regarding advertising and other forms of promotion have been around almost as long as the field itself, and it is unlikely they will ever disappear. However, the industry must address the various concerns about the effects of advertising and other forms of promotion on society. Advertising is a very powerful institution, but it will remain so only as long as consumers have faith in the ads they see and hear every day. Many of the problems discussed here can be avoided if individual decision makers make ethics an important element of the IMC planning process.

The primary focus of this discussion of social effects has been on the way advertising is used (or abused) in the marketing of products and services. It is important to note that advertising and other IMC tools, such as direct marketing and public relations, are also used to promote worthy causes and to deal with problems facing society (drunk driving, drug abuse, and the AIDS crisis, among others). Campaigns for nonprofit organizations and worthy causes are often developed pro bono by advertising agencies, and free advertising time and space are donated by the media.

Economic Effects of Advertising

Advertising plays an important role in a free-market system by making consumers aware of products and services and providing them with information for decision making. Advertising's economic role goes beyond this basic function, however. It is a powerful force that can affect the functioning of our entire economic system.

Advertising can encourage consumption and foster economic growth. It not only informs customers of available goods and services but also facilitates entry into markets for a firm or a new product or brand; leads to economies of scale in production, marketing, and distribution, which in turn lead to lower prices; and hastens the acceptance of new products and the rejection of inferior products.

Critics of advertising view it as a detrimental force that not only fails to perform its basic function of information provision adequately but also adds to the cost of products and services and discourages competition and market entry, leading to industrial concentration and higher prices for consumers.

In their analysis of advertising, economists generally take a macroeconomic perspective: they consider the economic impact of advertising on an entire industry or on the economy as a whole rather than its effect on an individual company or brand. Our examination of the economic impact of advertising focuses on these broader macro-level issues. We consider its effects on consumer choice, competition, and product costs and prices.

Effects on Consumer Choice

Some critics say advertising hampers consumer choice, as large advertisers use their power to limit our options to a few well-advertised brands. Economists argue that advertising is used to achieve (1) **differentiation**, whereby the products or services of large advertisers are perceived as unique or better than competitors', and (2) brand loyalty, which enables large national advertisers to gain control of the market, usually at the expense of smaller brands.

Larger companies often end up charging a higher price and achieve a more dominant position in the market than smaller firms that cannot compete against them and their large advertising budgets. When this occurs, advertising not only restricts the choice alternatives to a few well-known, heavily advertised brands but also becomes a substitute for competition based on price or product improvements.

Heavily advertised brands dominate the market in certain product categories, such as soft drinks, beer, and cereals.[59] But advertising generally does not create brand monopolies and reduce the opportunities for new products to be introduced to consumers. In most product categories, a number of different brands are on the store shelves and thousands of new products are introduced every year. The opportunity to advertise gives companies the incentive to develop new brands and improve their existing ones. When a successful new product such as a personal computer is introduced, competitors quickly follow and use advertising to inform consumers about their brand and attempt to convince them it is superior to the original. Companies like Virgin Atlantic Airways recognize that advertising has been an important part of their success (Exhibit 18–13 on page 546).

Effects on Competition

Exhibit 18–13 Virgin Atlantic Airways chair Richard Branson acknowledges the importance of advertising

One of the most common criticisms economists have about advertising concerns its effects on competition. They argue that power in the hands of large firms with huge advertising budgets creates a **barrier to entry**, which makes it difficult for other firms to enter the market. This results in less competition and higher prices. Economists note that smaller firms already in the market find it difficult to compete against the large advertising budgets of the industry leaders and are often driven out of business. For example, the Canadian beer industry is dominated by two national brewers, Molson and Labatt, which account for over 90 percent of the market. With their high advertising and promotion expenditures, these companies are spending much less per barrel than smaller firms, making it very difficult for the latter to compete.

Large advertisers clearly enjoy certain competitive advantages. First, there are **economies of scale** in advertising, particularly with respect to factors such as media costs. Firms such as Procter & Gamble, which spends millions of dollars per year on advertising and promotion, are able to make large media buys at a reduced rate and allocate them to their various products. Large advertisers usually sell more of a product or service, which means they may have lower production costs and can allocate more monies to advertising, so they can afford the costly but more efficient media like network television. Their large advertising outlays also give them more opportunity to differentiate their products and develop brand loyalty. To the extent that these factors occur, smaller competitors are at a disadvantage and new competitors are deterred from entering the market.

While advertising may have an anticompetitive effect on a market, there is no clear evidence that advertising alone reduces competition, creates barriers to entry, and thus increases market concentration. Lester Telser noted that high levels of advertising are not always found in industries where firms have a large market share. He found an inverse relationship between intensity of product class advertising and stability of market share for the leading brands.[60] These findings run contrary to many economists' belief that industries controlled by a few firms have high advertising expenditures, resulting in stable brand shares for market leaders.

Exhibit 18–14 LG has advertised heavily to penetrate the consumer electronics market

Defenders of advertising say it is unrealistic to attribute a firm's market dominance and barriers to entry solely to advertising. There are a number of other factors, such as price, product quality, distribution effectiveness, production efficiencies, and competitive strategies. For many years, Hershey was a dominant chocolate bar brand even though it spent little on advertising. Hershey did not advertise at all until 1970. For 66 years, the company relied on the quality of its products, its favourable reputation and image among consumers, and its extensive channels of distribution to market its brands. Industry leaders often tend to dominate markets because they have superior product quality and the best management and competitive strategies, not simply the biggest advertising budgets.[61]

While market entry against large, established competitors is difficult, companies with a quality product at a reasonable price often find a way to break in. Moreover, they usually find that advertising actually facilitates their market entry by making it possible to communicate the benefits and features of their new product or brand to consumers. For example, LG Electronics, which is a division of the South Korean conglomerate LG, began marketing products such as digital appliances, mobile phones, DVD players, and plasma TVs, and has become a formidable competitor. LG spends millions on advertising and other forms of marketing communication and has created a strong brand identity in the market[62] (Exhibit 18–14).

Effects on Product Costs and Prices

A major area of debate among economists, advertisers, consumer advocates, and policymakers concerns the effects of advertising on product costs and prices. Critics argue that advertising increases the prices consumers pay for products and services. First, they say the large sums of money spent advertising a brand constitute an expense that must be covered and the consumer ends up paying for it through higher prices. This is a common criticism from consumer advocates. Several studies show that firms with higher relative prices advertise their products more intensely than do those with lower relative prices.[63]

A second way advertising can result in higher prices is by increasing product differentiation and adding to the perceived value of the product in consumers' minds. Paul Farris and Mark Albion note that product differentiation occupies a central position in theories of advertising's economic effects.[64] The fundamental premise is that advertising increases the perceived differences between physically homogeneous products and enables advertised brands to command a premium price without an increase in quality.

Critics of advertising generally point to the differences in prices between national brands and private-label brands that are physically similar, such as cotton balls or tea bags, as evidence of the added value created by advertising. They see consumers' willingness to pay more for heavily advertised national brands rather than purchasing the lower-priced, nonadvertised brand as wasteful and irrational. However, consumers do not always buy for rational, functional reasons. The emotional, psychological, and social benefits derived from purchasing a national brand are important to many people. Moreover, say Albion and Farris,

> Unfortunately there seems to be no single way to measure product differentiation, let alone determine how much is excessive or attributable to the effects of advertising . . . Both price insensitivity and brand loyalty could be created by a number of factors such as higher product quality, better packaging, favorable use experience and market position. They are probably related to each other but need not be the result of advertising.[65]

Proponents of advertising offer several other counterarguments to the claim that advertising increases prices. They acknowledge that advertising costs are at least partly paid for by consumers. But advertising may help lower the overall cost of a product more than enough to offset them. For example, advertising may help firms achieve economies of scale in production and distribution by providing information to and stimulating demand among mass markets. These economies of scale help cut the cost of producing and marketing the product, which can lead to lower prices—if the advertiser chooses to pass the cost savings on to the consumer. The ad in Exhibit 18–15, from a campaign sponsored by the American Association of Advertising Agencies, emphasizes this point.

Advertising can also lower prices by making a market more competitive, which usually leads to greater price competition. A study by Lee Benham found that prices of eyeglasses were 25 to 30 percent higher in states that banned eyeglass advertising than in those that permitted it.[66] Robert Steiner analyzed the toy industry and concluded that advertising resulted in lower consumer prices. He argued that curtailment of TV advertising would drive up consumer prices for toys.[67] Finally, advertising is a means to market entry rather than a deterrent and helps stimulate product innovation, which makes markets more competitive and helps keep prices down.

Overall, it is difficult to reach any firm conclusions regarding the relationship between advertising and prices. After an extensive review of this area, Farris and Albion concluded, "The evidence connecting manufacturer advertising to prices is neither complete nor definitive . . . consequently, we cannot say whether advertising is a tool of market efficiency or market power without further research."[68]

Exhibit 18–15 This ad refutes the argument that reducing advertising expenditures will lead to lower prices

ADVERTISING MAKES THINGS COST MORE, RIGHT?
DRINKS 5¢ 4¢
DRINKS 5¢ 4¢ 3¢
We admit it. Advertising has a tremendous impact on prices. But you may be surprised by what *kind* of impact.
In addition to being informative, educational and sometimes entertaining, advertising can actually lower prices.
It works like this: Advertising spurs competition which holds down prices. And since advertising also creates a mass market for products, it can bring down the cost of producing each product, a savings that can be passed on to consumers.
Moreover, competition created by advertising provides an incentive for manufacturers to produce new and better products.
Which means advertising can not only reduce prices, but it can also help you avoid lemons.
ADVERTISING
ANOTHER WORD FOR FREEDOM OF CHOICE.
American Association of Advertising Agencies

Economist James Ferguson argues that advertising cannot increase the cost per unit of quality to consumers because if it did, consumers would not continue to respond positively to advertising.[69] He believes advertising lowers the costs of information about brand qualities, leads to increases in brand quality, and lowers the average price per unit of quality.

Summarizing Economic Effects

Albion and Farris suggest that economists' perspectives can be divided into two principal schools of thought that make different assumptions regarding the influence of advertising on the economy.[70] Figure 18–5 summarizes the main points of the "advertising equals market power" and "advertising equals information" perspectives.

Advertising Equals Market Power The belief that advertising equals market power reflects traditional economic thinking and views advertising as a way to change consumers' tastes, lower their sensitivity to price, and build brand loyalty among buyers of advertised brands. This results in higher profits and market power for large advertisers, reduces competition in the market, and leads to higher prices and fewer choices for consumers. Proponents of this viewpoint generally have negative attitudes regarding the economic impact of advertising.

FIGURE ***18–5*** Two schools of thought on advertising's role in the economy

Advertising = Market Power		Advertising = Information
Advertising affects consumer preferences and tastes, changes product attributes, and differentiates the product from competitive offerings.	Advertising	Advertising informs consumers about product attributes but does not change the way they value those attributes.
Consumers become brand loyal and less price sensitive and perceive fewer substitutes for advertised brands.	Consumer buying behaviour	Consumers become more price sensitive and buy best "value." Only the relationship between price and quality affects elasticity for a given product.
Potential entrants must overcome established brand loyalty and spend relatively more on advertising.	Barriers to entry	Advertising makes entry possible for new brands because it can communicate product attributes to consumers.
Firms are insulated from market competition and potential rivals; concentration increases, leaving firms with more discretionary power.	Industry structure and market power	Consumers can compare competitive offerings easily and competitive rivalry increases. Efficient firms remain, and as the inefficient leave, new entrants appear; the effect on concentration is ambiguous.
Firms can charge higher prices and are not as likely to compete on quality or price dimensions. Innovation may be reduced.	Market conduct	More informed consumers pressure firms to lower prices and improve quality; new entrants facilitate innovation.
High prices and excessive profits accrue to advertisers and give them even more incentive to advertise their products. Output is restricted compared with conditions of perfect competition.	Market performance	Industry prices decrease. The effect on profits due to increased competition and increased efficiency is ambiguous.

Advertising Equals Information The belief that advertising equals information takes a more positive view of advertising's economic effects. This model sees advertising as providing consumers with useful information, increasing their price sensitivity (which moves them toward lower-priced products), and increasing competition in the market. Advertising is viewed as a way to communicate with consumers and tell them about a product and its major features and attributes. More informed and knowledgeable consumers pressure companies to provide high-quality products at lower prices. Efficient firms remain in the market, whereas inefficient firms leave as new entrants appear. Proponents of this model believe the economic effects of advertising are favourable and think it contributes to more efficient and competitive markets.

It is unlikely the debate over the economic effects and value of advertising will be resolved soon. Many economists will continue to take a negative view of advertising and its effects on the functioning of the economy, while advertisers will continue to view it as an efficient way for companies to communicate with their customers and an essential component of our economic system. The International Advertising Association has been running a campaign for several years to convince consumers around the world of the economic value of advertising. Ads like the one shown in Exhibit 18–16 are used in countries such as China and Russia, where consumers are unfamiliar with the concept of advertising. The goal of the campaign is to get consumers in these countries to recognize the role advertising plays in contributing to their economic well-being.[71] A similar campaign in the United States featured famous brands and their ads (Exhibit 18–17).

Figure 18–6, excerpts from a speech given by famous adman Leo Burnett, summarizes the perspective of most advertising people on the economic effects of advertising. While many advertising and marketing experts agree that advertising and promotion play an important role in helping to expand consumer demand for new products, not everyone would agree that this is desirable.

WHEN ADVERTISING DOES ITS JOB, MILLIONS OF PEOPLE KEEP THEIRS.

Good advertising doesn't just inform. It sells. It helps move product and keep businesses in business. Every time an ad arouses a consumer's interest enough to result in a purchase, it keeps a company going strong. And it helps secure the jobs of the people who work there.

Advertising. That's the way it works.

INTERNATIONAL ADVERTISING ASSOCIATION

The global partnership of advertisers, agencies and media

Exhibit 18–16 This ad is part of a global campaign by the International Advertising Association to educate consumers about the economic value of advertising

Exhibit 18–17 This ad promotes the value of advertising in building strong brands

FIGURE *18–6* This message describes the positive economic effects of advertising

To me it means that if we believe to any degree whatsoever in the economic system under which we live, in a high standard of living and in high employment, advertising is the most efficient known way of moving goods in practically every product class.

My proof is that millions of businessmen have chosen advertising over and over again in the operations of their business. Some of their decisions may have been wrong, but they must have thought they were right or they wouldn't go back to be stung twice by the same kind of bee.

It's a pretty safe bet that in the next 10 years many Americans will be using products and devices that no one in this room has even heard of. Judging purely by past performance, American advertising can be relied on to make them known and accepted overnight at the lowest possible prices.

Advertising, of course, makes possible our unparalleled variety of magazines, newspapers, business publications, and radio and television stations.

It must be said that without advertising we would have a far different nation, and one that would be much the poorer—not merely in material commodities, but in the life of the spirit.

Leo Burnett

These excerpts are from a speech given by Leo Burnett on the American Association of Advertising Agencies' 50th anniversary, April 20, 1967.

SUMMARY

Various levels of government regulate different aspects of Canadian advertising; however, self-regulation of these laws is quite prominent in Canada. This self-regulation occurs through the Advertising Standards Council (ASC), a non-profit organization of advertising industry members. The ASC responds to all complaints with respect to advertising and publishes an annual report that summarizes the complaints it receives each year. The ASC is also responsible for clearing ads prior to their airing for a number of products. Some of the ASC's responsibilities have been given to it as the federal government has withdrawn services with the belief that industry is sufficiently responsible.

Even though there appears to be sufficient control of advertising, it is a very powerful institution that has been the target of considerable criticism regarding its ethical, social, and economic impact. The criticism of advertising concerns the specific techniques and methods used as well as its effect on societal values, tastes, lifestyles, and behaviour. Critics argue that advertising is deceptive and untruthful; that it is often offensive, irritating, or in poor taste; and that it exploits certain groups. Many people believe advertising should be informative only and advertisers should not use subjective claims, puffery, embellishment, or persuasive techniques.

Advertising often offends consumers by the type of appeal or manner of presentation used; sexually suggestive ads and nudity receive the most criticism. Advertisers say their ads are consistent with contemporary values and lifestyles and are appropriate for the target audiences they are attempting to reach. Advertising to children is an area of particular concern, since critics argue that children lack the experience, knowledge, and ability to process and evaluate persuasive advertising messages rationally.

The pervasiveness of advertising and its prevalence in the mass media have led critics to argue that it plays a major role in influencing and transmitting social values. Advertising has been charged with encouraging materialism, manipulating consumers to buy things they do not really want or need, perpetuating stereotypes through its portrayal of certain groups such as women and visible minorities.

Advertising has also been scrutinized with regard to its economic effects. The basic economic role of advertising is to give consumers information that helps them make consumption decisions. Some people view advertising as a detrimental force that has a negative effect on competition, product costs, and consumer prices. Economists' perspectives regarding the effects of advertising follow two basic schools of thought: the advertising equals market power model and the advertising equals information model. Arguments consistent with each perspective were considered in analyzing the economic effects of advertising.

KEY TERMS

barrier to entry, *546*
consumer complaints, *528*
consumer socialization process, *537*
differentiation, *545*
economies of scale, *546*
ethics, *531*
materialism, *538*
Protestant ethic, *538*
puffery, *533*
special interest group complaints, *528*
trade disputes, *528*

DISCUSSION QUESTIONS

1. Explain why you agree or disagree with the rulings of the ASC presented in this chapter regarding the Ford Focus and Kia automobile ads?

2. Discuss the role of ethics in advertising and promotion. How do ethical considerations differ from legal considerations?

3. What is meant by shock advertising? Evaluate the arguments for and against the use of shock advertising by marketers.

4. Evaluate the arguments for and against advertising to children. Do you feel restrictions are needed for advertising and other forms of promotion targeted to children?

5. A common criticism of advertising is that it stereotypes women. Discuss the ways this might occur. Do you think the Airwalk ad shown in Exhibit 18–4 is suggestive and symbolizes sexual submission?

6. Discuss how attitudes toward the use of sex in advertising differ between men and women. Discuss the implications of these attitudinal differences for marketers who are developing ads for each gender.

7. With which position do you agree: "Advertising determines Canadian consumers' tastes and values and is responsible for creating a materialistic society," or "Advertising is a reflection of society and mirrors its tastes and values"?

8. Discuss how advertising can impact consumer choice, as well as its impact on product costs and the prices paid for products and services.

9. Discuss the two major perspectives of the economic impact of advertising: "advertising equals market power" versus "advertising equals information."

ENDNOTES

CHAPTER ONE

1. "AMA Board Approves New Marketing Definition," *Marketing News,* March 1, 1985, p. 1.
2. Richard P. Bagozzi, "Marketing as Exchange," *Journal of Marketing, 39,* October 1975, pp. 32–39.
3. J. Paul Peter and Jerry C. Olson, *Consumer Behavior* (Burr Ridge, IL.: Richard D. Irwin, 1987), p. 505.
4. Michael R. Solomon, "The Role of Products as Social Stimuli: A Symbolic Interactionism Perspective," *Journal of Consumer Research,* December 1983, pp. 319–29.
5. Peter and Olson, *Consumer Behavior,* p. 571.
6. Paul W. Farris and David J. Reibstein, "How Prices, Ad Expenditures, and Profits Are Linked," *Harvard Business Review,* November–December 1979, pp. 172–84.
7. Roger A. Kerin, Steven W. Hartley, Eric N. Berkowitz, and William Rudelius, *Marketing,* 8th ed. (Burr Ridge, IL: Irwin/McGraw-Hill, 2006).
8. Michael L. Ray, *Advertising and Communication Management* (Englewood Cliffs, NJ: Prentice Hall, 1982).
9. Ralph S. Alexander, ed., *Marketing Definitions* (Chicago: American Marketing Association, 1965), p. 9.
10. Clarence Poirier, "Making the Most of Magazines," *Marketing Magazine,* October 15, 2001.
11. H. Frazier Moore and Bertrand R. Canfield, *Public Relations: Principles, Cases, and Problems,* 7th ed. (Burr Ridge, IL: Irwin, 1977), p. 5.
12. Karin Scott, "Beyond Press Coverage," *Marketing Magazine,* June 16, 2003.
13. Michelle Warren, "Pub Visits Lead Guinness Holiday Push," *Marketing Magazine,* January 27, 2003.
14. Adrienne Ward Fawcett, "Integrated Marketing—Marketers Convinced: Its Time Has Arrived," *Advertising Age,* November 6, 1993, pp. S1–2.
15. "Do Your Ads Need a SuperAgency?" *Fortune,* April 27, 1991, pp. 81–85; Faye Rice, "A Cure for What Ails Advertising?" *Fortune,* December 16, 1991, pp. 119–22.
16. Don E. Schultz, "Integrated Marketing Communications: Maybe Definition Is in the Point of View," *Marketing News,* January 18, 1993, p. 17.
17. Joep P. Cornelissen and Andrew R. Lock, "Theoretical Concept or Management Fashion? Examining the Significance of IMC," *Journal of Advertising Research,* September–October 2000, pp. 7–15.
18. Philip J. Kitchen, Joanne Brignell, Tao Li, and Graham Spickett Jones, "The Emergence of IMC: A Theoretical Perspective," *Journal of Advertising Research,* March 2004, pp. 19–30.
19. Don E. Schultz, "IMC Receives More Appropriate Definition," *Marketing News,* September 15, 2004, pp. 8–9.
20. Joep P. Cornelissen and Andrew R. Lock, "Theoretical Concept or Management Fashion? Examining the Significance of IMC," *Journal of Advertising Research,* September–October 2000, pp. 7–15.
21. Harlan E. Spotts, David R. Lambert, and Mary L. Joyce, "Marketing Déjà Vu: The Discovery of Integrated Marketing Communications," *Journal of Marketing Education, 20,* no. 3 (December 1998), pp. 210–18.
22. Tom Duncan and Sandra E. Moriarty, "A Communication-Based Model for Managing Relationships," *Journal of Marketing 62,* no. 2, (April 1998), pp. 1–13.
23. Philip J. Kitchen, Joanne Brignell, Tao Li, and Graham Spickett Jones, "The Emergence of IMC: A Theoretical Perspective," *Journal of Advertising Research,* March 2004, pp. 19–30.
24. Anthony J. Tortorici, "Maximizing Marketing Communications through Horizontal and Vertical Orchestration," *Public Relations Quarterly, 36*(1), 1991, pp. 20–22.
25. Sergio Zyman, *The End of Marketing As We Know It* (New York: HarperBusiness, 1999); Joe Cappo, "Agencies: Change or Die," *Advertising Age,* December 7, 1992, p. 26.
26. Chris Powell, "Idol Worship," *Marketing Magazine,* November 10, 2003; and Danny Kucharsky, "Because You're Worth It," *Marketing Magazine,* February 9, 2004.
27. Leonard L. Berry, "Relationship Marketing of Services—Growing Interest, Emerging Perspectives," *Journal of the Academy of Marketing Science, 23,* no. 4, 1995, pp. 236–45; Jonathan R. Capulsky and Michael J. Wolfe, "Relationship Marketing: Positioning for the Future," *Journal of Business Strategy,* July–August 1991, pp. 16–26.
28. B. Joseph Pine II, Don Peppers, and Martha Rogers, "Do You Want to Keep Your Customers Forever?" *Harvard Business Review,* March–April 1995, pp. 103–14.
29. Lisa M. Keefe, "What Is the Meaning of 'Marketing'?" *Marketing News,* September 15, 2004, pp. 17–18.
30. Paul-Mark Rendon, "Melitta Brews National Pormotions," *Marketing Magazine,* March 8, 2004.
31. Paul-Mark Rendon, "Where Above Meets Below," *Marketing Magazine,* May 8, 2006.

CHAPTER TWO

1. Jack Neff, "P&G Redefines the Brand Manager," *Advertising Age,* October 13, 1997, pp. 1, 18, 20.
2. Thomas J. Cosse and John E. Swan, "Strategic Marketing Planning by Product Managers—Room for Improvement?" *Journal of Marketing, 47* (Summer 1983), pp. 92–102.
3. "Behind the Tumult at P&G," *Fortune,* March 7, 1994, pp. 74–82; "Category Management: New Tools Changing Life for Manufacturers, Retailers," *Marketing News,* September 25, 1989, pp. 2, 19.
4. Cosse and Swan, "Strategic Marketing Planning by Product Managers—Room for Improvement?"
5. Timothy Dewhirst and Brad Davis, "Brand Strategy and Integrated Marketing Communications," *Journal of Advertising,* vol. 34, no. 4 (Winter 2005), pp. 81–92.
6. Victor P. Buell, *Organizing for Marketing/Advertising Success* (New York: Association of National Advertisers, 1982).
7. M. Louise Ripley, "What Kind of Companies Take Their Advertising In-House?" *Journal of Advertising Research,* October/November 1991, pp. 73–80.
8. Bruce Horovitz, "Some Companies Say the Best Ad Agency Is No Ad Agency at All," *Los Angeles Times,* July 19, 1989, Sec IV, p. 5.
9. Danny Kucharsky, "Survival of the Fittest," *Marketing,* May 15, 2006.
10. Sally Goll Beatty, "Global Needs Challenge Midsize Agencies," *The Wall Street Journal,* December 14, 1995, p. B9.
11. Gordon Fairclough, "Pace of Ad Mergers Is Expected to Continue," *The Wall Street Journal,* April 23, 1999, p. B2.
12. Bob Lammons, "A Good Account Exec Makes a Big Difference," *Marketing News,* June 3, 1996, p. 12.
13. "Call in the Specialists," *Marketing Magazine,* June 4, 2001.
14. Jeffery Thibodeau, "Better Ways to Get Paid," *Marketing Magazine,* March 22, 2004.
15. www.aca-online.com.
16. Paul-Mark Rendon, "Pay as You Play," *Marketing Magazine,* June 21, 2004.
17. "The Benefits of PBR," *Marketing Magazine,* July 9, 2001; "Executive Summary," *Marketing Magazine,* July 9, 2001; "Finding the Right PBR Performance Measures," *Marketing Magazine,* July 16, 2001.

18. Rob Gerlsbeck, "Creative Compensation," *Marketing Magazine,* April 17, 2006.
19. Chris Daniels, "Part-Time Partners," *Marketing Magazine,* June 23, 2003.
20. Michelle Warren, "Project Work," *Marketing Magazine,* April 19, 2004; Michelle Warren, "The Year of Treading Water," *Marketing Magazine,* November 24, 2003.
21. Prema Nakra, "The Changing Role of Public Relations in Marketing Communications," *Public Relations Quarterly, 1* (1991) pp. 42–45.
22. "A Potent New Tool for Selling: Database Marketing," *Business Week,* September 5, 1994, pp. 56–62.
23. "Ad Firms Falter on One-Stop Shopping," *The Wall Street Journal,* December 1, 1988, p. 81; and "Do Your Ads Need a Superagency?" *Fortune,* April 27, 1987, p. 81.
24. Hy Haberman, "Walking the Talk on Integration," *Marketing Magazine,* February 9, 2004.
25. Philip J. Kitchen and Don E. Schultz, "A Multi-Country Comparison of the Drive for IMC," *Journal of Advertising Research,* January/February 1999, pp. 21–38.
26. David N. McArthur and Tom Griffin, "A Marketing Management View of Integrated Marketing Communications," *Journal of Advertising Research, 37,* no. 5, September/October 1997, pp. 19–26; Adrienne Ward Fawcett, "Integrated Marketing—Marketers Convinced: Its Time Has Arrived," *Advertising Age,* November 6, 1993, pp. S1–2.
27. Michelle Warren, "What Marketers Want," *Marketing Magazine,* November 24, 2003.
28. Kevin Astle, "The Shaky State of Marketer–Agency Relations," *Marketing Magazine,* November 24, 2003.

CHAPTER THREE

1. Leon G. Schiffman and Leslie Lazar Kannuk, *Consumer Behavior,* 4th ed. (Englewood Cliffs, NJ: Prentice Hall, 1991), p. 192.
2. Eric N. Berkowitz, Roger A. Kerin, Steven W. Hartley, and William Rudelius, *Marketing,* 6th ed. (Burr Ridge, IL: Irwin/McGraw-Hill, 2000), p. 14.
3. A. H. Maslow, "'Higher' and 'Lower' Needs," *Journal of Psychology, 25* (1948), pp. 433–36.
4. For an excellent discussion of memory and consumer behaviour, see James R. Bettman, "Memory Factors in Consumer Choice: A Review," *Journal of Marketing, 43* (Spring 1979), pp. 37–53.
5. Danny Kucharsky, "World Wide Vacations," *Marketing Magazine,* June 12, 2006.
6. Gilbert Harrell, *Consumer Behavior* (San Diego: Harcourt Brace Jovanovich, 1986), p. 66.
7. Raymond A. Bauer and Stephen A. Greyser, *Advertising in America: The Consumer View* (Boston: Harvard Business School, 1968).
8. J. Paul Peter and Jerry C. Olson, *Consumer Behavior,* 2nd ed. (Burr Ridge, IL: Irwin/McGraw-Hill, 1990), p. 73.
9. Gordon W. Allport, "Attitudes," in *Handbook of Social Psychology,* ed. C. M. Murchison (Winchester, MA: Clark University Press, 1935), p. 810.
10. Robert B. Zajonc and Hazel Markus, "Affective and Cognitive Factors in Preferences," *Journal of Consumer Research, 9* (1982), pp. 123–31.
11. Alvin Achenbaum, "Advertising Doesn't Manipulate Consumers," *Journal of Advertising Research,* April 2, 1970, pp. 3–13.
12. William D. Wells, "Attitudes and Behavior: Lessons from the Needham Lifestyle Study," *Journal of Advertising Research,* February–March 1985, pp. 40–44; and Icek Ajzen and Martin Fishbein, "Attitude–Behavior Relations: A Theoretical Analysis and Review of Empirical Research," *Psychological Bulletin,* September 1977, pp. 888–918.
13. Joel B. Cohen, Paul W. Minniard, and Peter R. Dickson, "Information Integration: An Information Processing Perspective," in *Advances in Consumer Research,* vol. 7, ed. Jerry C. Olson (Ann Arbor, MI: Association for Consumer Research, 1980), pp. 161–70.
14. Peter and Olson, *Consumer Behavior,* p. 182.
15. Peter L. Wright and Fredric Barbour, "The Relevance of Decision Process Models in Structuring Persuasive Messages," *Communications Research,* July 1975, pp. 246–59.
16. James F. Engel, "The Psychological Consequences of a Major Purchase Decision," in *Marketing in Transition,* ed. William S. Decker (Chicago: American Marketing Association, 1963), pp. 462–75.
17. Richard L. Oliver, *Satisfaction: A Behavioral Perspective on the Consumer* (New York: McGraw-Hill, 1997).
18. John A. Howard and Jagdish N. Sheth, *The Theory of Consumer Behavior* (New York: John Wiley & Sons, 1969).
19. Lyman E. Ostlund, *Role Theory and Group Dynamics in Consumer Behavior: Theoretical Sources,* ed. Scott Ward and Thomas S. Robertson (Englewood Cliffs, NJ: Prentice Hall, 1973), pp. 230–75.
20. James Stafford and Benton Cocanougher, "Reference Group Theory," in *Perspective in Consumer Behavior,* ed. H. H. Kassarjian and T. S. Robertson (Glenview, IL: Scott, Foresman, 1981), pp. 329–43.
21. Jagdish N. Sheth, "A Theory of Family Buying Decisions," in *Models of Buying Behavior,* ed. Jagdish N. Sheth (New York: Harper & Row, 1974), pp. 17–33.
22. Larry Percy, John R. Rossiter, and Richard Elliot, *Strategic Advertising Management* (Oxford University Press, 2001).
23. John Rossiter and Larry Percy.
24. Norma Ramage, "Educating the Young," *Marketing Magazine,* March 22, 2004.
25. Edward M. Tauber, "Research on Food Consumption Values Finds Four Market Segments: Good Taste Still Tops," *Marketing News,* May 15, 1981, p. 17; Rebecca C. Quarles, "Shopping Centers Use Fashion Lifestyle Research to Make Marketing Decisions," *Marketing News,* January 22, 1982, p. 18; and "Our Auto, Ourselves," *Consumer Reports,* June 1985, p. 375.
26. Judith Graham, "New VALS 2 Takes Psychological Route," *Advertising Age,* February 13, 1989, p. 24.
27. Norma Ramage, "Chinese Theme Added to Bell Effort," *Marketing Magazine,* February 2, 2004.
28. Celine Wong, "Can't Knock the Hustle," *Marketing Magazine,* May 3, 2004.
29. For an excellent discussion of social class and consumer behaviour, see Richard P. Coleman, "The Continuing Significance of Social Class to Marketing," *Journal of Consumer Research, 10,* no. 3, December 1983, pp. 265–80.
30. Chris Daniels, "Almost Rich, *Marketing Magazine,* April 26, 2004.
31. Russell Belk, "Situational Variables and Consumer Behavior," *Journal of Consumer Research,* December 1975, pp. 157–64.
32. John Rossiter and Larry Percy, *Advertising Communications and Promotion Management* (New York: McGraw Hill, 1996).
33. Chris Powell, "TMN Puts Spotlight on Subscribers," *Marketing Magazine,* February 23, 2004.
34. Dave Scholz and Jean-Marc Leger, "The Fickle Beer Consumer," *Marketing Magazine,* May 10, 2004.
35. Ibid.
36. Sarah Dobson, "Coffee Crisp Targets Caffeine Crowd," *Marketing Magazine,* February 10, 2003.
37. Eve Lazarus, "Vancouver's Driving Force," *Marketing Magazine,* August 28, 2006.
38. Ace Alvarez, "How to Send Happiness," *Marketing Magazine,* August, 28, 2006.
39. Lisa D'Innocenzo, "Is Your Target a Man's Man? Then Reach Out to Women," *Strategy Magazine,* February 2006.

CHAPTER FOUR

1. Wilbur Schram, *The Process and Effects of Mass Communications* (Urbana: University of Illinois Press, 1955).

2. Ibid.
3. Joseph Ransdell, "Some Leading Ideas of Peirce's Semiotic," *Semiotica, 19* (1977), pp. 157–78.
4. Nina Munk, "Levi's Ongoing Quest for Street Cred," *Fortune,* February 1, 1999, p. 40.
5. For an excellent article on the application of semiotics to consumer behaviour and advertising, see David G. Mick, "Consumer Research and Semiotics: Exploring the Morphology of Signs, Symbols, and Significance," *Journal of Consumer Research, 13,* no. 2, September 1986, pp. 196–213; see also Edward F. McQuarrie and David Glen Mick, "Figures of Rhetoric in Advertising Language," *Journal of Consumer Research, 22,* March 1996, pp. 424–38.
6. Barry L. Bayus, "Word of Mouth: The Indirect Effect of Marketing Efforts," *Journal of Advertising Research,* June/July 1985, pp. 31–39; Robert E. Smith and Christine A. Vogt, "The Effects of Integrating Advertising and Negative Word-of-Mouth Communications on Message Processing and Response," *Journal of Consumer Psychology, 4,* no. 2, 1995, pp. 133–51.
7. Larry Yu, "How Companies Turn Buzz Into Sales," *MIT Sloan Management Review,* Winter 2005, pp. 5–6.
8. E. K. Strong, *The Psychology of Selling* (New York: McGraw-Hill, 1925), p. 9.
9. Robert J. Lavidge and Gary A. Steiner, "A Model for Predictive Measurements of Advertising Effectiveness," *Journal of Marketing, 24,* October 1961, pp. 59–62.
10. Everett M. Rogers, *Diffusion of Innovations* (New York: Free Press, 1962), pp. 79–86.
11. William J. McGuire, "An Information Processing Model of Advertising Effectiveness," in *Behavioral and Management Science in Marketing,* ed. Harry J. Davis and Alvin J. Silk (New York: Ronald Press, 1978), pp. 156–80.
12. Anthony G. Greenwald and Clark Leavitt, "Audience Involvement in Advertising: Four Levels," *Journal of Consumer Research, 11,* no. 1 (June 1984), pp. 581–92; and Judith L. Zaichkowsky, "Conceptualizing Involvement," *Journal of Advertising, 15,* no. 2 (1986), pp. 4–14.
13. Michael L. Ray, "Communication and the Hierarchy of Effects," in *New Models for Mass Communication Research,* ed. P. Clarke (Beverly Hills, CA: Sage, 1973), pp. 147–75.
14. Herbert E. Krugman, "The Impact of Television Advertising: Learning without Involvement," *Public Opinion Quarterly, 29* (Fall 1965), pp. 349–56.
15. Scott A. Hawkins and Stephen J. Hoch, "Low-Involvement Learning: Memory without Evaluation," *Journal of Consumer Research, 19,* no. 2 (September 1992), pp. 212–25.
16. Robert E. Smith, "Integrating Information from Advertising and Trial: Processes and Effects on Consumer Response to Product Information," *Journal of Marketing Research, 30.*
17. DeAnna S. Kempf and Russell N. Laczniak, "Advertising's Influence on Subsequent Product Trial Processing," *Journal of Advertising, 30,* no. 3, Fall 2001, pp. 27–38.
18. Jerry C. Olson, Daniel R. Toy, and Phillip A. Dover, "Mediating Effects of Cognitive Responses to Advertising on Cognitive Structure," in *Advances in Consumer Research, 5,* ed. H. Keith Hunt (Ann Arbor, MI: Association for Consumer Research, 1978), pp. 72–78.
19. Anthony A. Greenwald, "Cognitive Learning, Cognitive Response to Persuasion and Attitude Change," in *Psychological Foundations of Attitudes,* ed. A. G. Greenwald, T. C. Brock, and T. W. Ostrom (New York: Academic Press, 1968); Peter L. Wright, "The Cognitive Processes Mediating Acceptance of Advertising," *Journal of Marketing Research, 10* (February 1973), pp. 53–62; Brian Wansink, Michael L. Ray, and Rajeev Batra, "Increasing Cognitive Response Sensitivity," *Journal of Advertising, 23,* no. 2 (June 1994), pp. 65–76.
20. Peter Wright, "Message Evoked Thoughts, Persuasion Research Using Thought Verbalizations," *Journal of Consumer Research, 7,* no. 2 (September 1980), pp. 151–75.
21. Scott B. Mackenzie, Richard J. Lutz, and George E. Belch, "The Role of Attitude toward the Ad as a Mediator of Advertising Effectiveness: A Test of Competing Explanations," *Journal of Marketing Research, 23* (May 1986), pp. 130–43; and Rajeev Batra and Michael L. Ray, "Affective Responses Mediating Acceptance of Advertising," *Journal of Consumer Research, 13* (September 1986), pp. 234–49.
22. Tim Ambler and Tom Burne, "The Impact of Affect on Memory of Advertising," *Journal of Advertising Research, 29,* no. 3 (March/April 1999), pp. 25–34; Ronald Alsop, "TV Ads That Are Likeable Get Plus Rating for Persuasiveness," *The Wall Street Journal,* February 20, 1986, p. 23.
23. David J. Moore and William D. Harris, "Affect Intensity and the Consumer's Attitude toward High Impact Emotional Advertising Appeals," *Journal of Advertising, 25,* no. 2 (Summer 1996), pp. 37–50; Andrew A. Mitchell and Jerry C. Olson, "Are Product Attribute Beliefs the Only Mediator of Advertising Effects on Brand Attitude?" *Journal of Marketing Research, 18* (August 1981), pp. 318–32.
24. David J. Moore, William D. Harris, and Hong C. Chen, "Affect Intensity: An Individual Difference Response to Advertising Appeals," *Journal of Consumer Research, 22* (September 1995), pp. 154–64; Julie Edell and Marian C. Burke, "The Power of Feelings in Understanding Advertising Effects," *Journal of Consumer Research, 14* (December 1987), pp. 421–33.
25. Richard E. Petty and John T. Cacioppo, "Central and Peripheral Routes to Persuasion: Application to Advertising," in *Advertising and Consumer Psychology,* ed. Larry Percy and Arch Woodside (Lexington, MA: Lexington Books, 1983), pp. 3–23.
26. David A. Aaker, Rajeev Batra, and John G. Myers, *Advertising Management,* 5th ed. (Upper Saddle River, NJ: Prentice Hall, 1996).
27. Gerald J. Gorn, "The Effects of Music in Advertising on Choice: A Classical Conditioning Approach," *Journal of Marketing, 46* (Winter 1982), pp. 94–101.
28. James J. Kellaris, Anthony D. Cox, and Dena Cox, "The Effect of Background Music on Ad Processing: A Contingency Explanation," *Journal of Marketing, 57,* no. 4 (Fall 1993), p. 114.
29. Richard E. Petty, John T. Cacioppo, and David Schumann, "Central and Peripheral Routes to Advertising Effectiveness: The Moderating Role of Involvement," *Journal of Consumer Research, 10* (September 1983), pp. 135–46.
30. Demetrios Vakratsas and Tim Ambler, "How Advertising Works: What Do We Really Know?" *Journal of Marketing, 63* (January 1999), pp. 26–43.
31. Bruce F. Hall, "A New Model for Measuring Advertising Effects," *Journal of Advertising Research, 42,* no. 2, (March/April 2002), pp. 23–31.
32. William M. Weilbacher, "Point of View: Does Advertising Cause a 'Hierarchy of Effects'?" *Journal of Advertising Research, 41,* no. 6 (November/December 2001) pp. 19–26.
33. Thomas E. Barry, "In Defense of the Hierarchy of Effects: A Rejoinder to Weilbacher," *Journal of Advertising Research* (May/June 2002), pp. 44–47.

CHAPTER FIVE

1. Robert A. Kriegel, "How to Choose the Right Communications Objectives," *Business Marketing,* April 1986, pp. 94–106.
2. Donald S. Tull, "The Carry-Over Effect of Advertising," *Journal of Marketing,* April 1965, pp. 46–53.
3. Darral G. Clarke, "Econometric Measurement of the Duration of Advertising Effect on Sales," *Journal of Marketing Research, 23* (November 1976), pp. 345–57.
4. Philip Kotler, *Marketing Decision Making: A Model Building Approach* (New York: Holt, Rinehart & Winston, 1971), ch. 5.
5. For a more detailed discussion of this, see William M. Weilbacher,

Advertising, 2nd ed. (New York: Macmillan, 1984), p. 112.
6. Russell H. Colley, *Defining Advertising Goals for Measured Advertising Results* (New York: Association of National Advertisers, 1961).
7. Ibid., p. 21.
8. Don E. Schultz, Dennis Martin, and William Brown, *Strategic Advertising Campaigns,* 2nd ed. (Lincolnwood, IL: Crain Books, 1984).
9. Courtland I. Bovee and William F. Arens, *Advertising,* 3rd ed. (Burr Ridge, IL: Richard D. Irwin, 1989).
10. Stewart H. Britt, "Are So-Called Successful Advertising Campaigns Really Successful?" *Journal of Advertising Research, 9,* no. 2 (1969), pp. 3–9.
11. Steven W. Hartley and Charles H. Patti, "Evaluating Business-to-Business Advertising: A Comparison of Objectives and Results," *Journal of Advertising Research, 28* (April/May 1988), pp. 21–27.
12. Ibid., p. 25.
13. Study cited in Robert F. Lauterborn, "How to Know If Your Advertising Is Working," *Journal of Advertising Research, 25* (February/March 1985), pp. RC 9–11.
14. Chris Powell, "*Globe* Targets Circulation Gains," *Marketing Magazine,* February 2, 2004.
15. Angela Scardillo, "Making Milk COOL," *Marketing Magazine,* August 11, 2003.
16. Paul Ferris, "CTC Hits the Road with Toyota," *Marketing Magazine,* September 15, 2003.
17. Paul Ferris, "Ditching the Minivans," *Marketing Magazine,* March 15, 2004.
18. Danny Kucharsky, "French Transit Ads Tell Traffic Truths," *Marketing Magazine,* February 9, 2004.
19. Frank Dennis, "Selling Hidden Brands," *Marketing Magazine,* May 10, 2004.
20. Eve Lazarus, "Taking on Goliath," *Marketing Magazine,* March 22, 2002.
21. Brent Cuthbertson and Grant Stockwell, "That Rings a Bell," *Marketing Magazine,* October 20, 2003.
22. Dave Scholz and Gilbert Paquette, "The Impact of Auto Advertising," *Marketing Magazine,* June 30, 2003.
23. Lesley Young, "It Pays to Get Aggressive," *Marketing Magazine,* February 12, 2001.

CHAPTER SIX

1. *Ayer's Dictionary of Advertising Terms* (Philadelphia: Ayers Press, 1976).
2. "WestJet Fuels Up Advertising Effort," *Marketing Magazine,* March 2001; "Flying the Cluttered Skies," *Marketing Magazine,* April 9, 2001.
3. Davis A. Aaker and John G. Myers, *Advertising Management,* 3rd ed. (Englewood Cliffs, NJ: Prentice Hall, 1987), p. 125.
4. Jack Trout and Al Ries, "Positioning Cuts through Chaos in the Marketplace," *Advertising Age,* May 1, 1972, pp. 51–53.
5. "Sleeman Brings Out the Truth," *Marketing Magazine,* May 28, 2001; "Sleeman Shifts Its Target," *Marketing Magazine,* April 16, 2001; "Sleeman Ads Bow without Brewery Boss," *Marketing Magazine,* April 4, 2001; "Sleeman Touts Label-Free Brand," *Marketing Magazine,* April 15, 2002.
6. Larry Percy and Richard Elliot, *Strategic Advertising Managemet,* 2nd ed. (Oxford University Press, 2004); Orville Walker Jr., John Mullins, Harper Boyd Jr., and Jean-Claude Larreche, *Marketing Strategy: A Decision-Focused Approach,* 8th ed. (McGraw-Hill Irwin, 2006).
7. Lesley Young, "Harvey's Keeps an Eye on the Grill," *Marketing Magazine,* September 29, 2003.
8. Emily Spensieri, "A Slow, Soft Touch," *Marketing Magazine,* June 5, 2006.
9. For a review of multiattribute models, see William L. Wilkie and Edgar A. Pessemier, "Issues in Marketing's Use of Multiattribute Models," *Journal of Marketing Research, 10* (November 1983), pp. 428–41.
10. Lesley Young, "An Order of Fries, with Attitude," *Marketing Magazine,* November 17, 2003.
11. Lesley Young, "Wireless Marketers Unleash Hounds," *Marketing Magazine,* December 8, 2003.
12. Norma Ramage, "WestJet Finds a Competitive Niche," *Marketing Magazine,* July 28, 2003.
13. Jeff Robillard and Phil Copithorne, "Big Idea Fits in Small Space," *Marketing Magazine,* February 23, 2004.
14. George Walton, "Appealingly Local," *Marketing Magazine,* May 5, 2003.
15. Michelle Warren, "*Fubar* Guys Light Up Anti-Smoking Ads," *Marketing Magazine,* January 19, 2004.
16. Sarah Dobson, "Sub Culture," *Marketing Magazine,* May 10, 2004.

CHAPTER SEVEN

1. Elizabeth C. Hirschman, "Role-Based Models of Advertising Creation and Production," *Journal of Advertising, 18,* no. 4 (1989), pp. 42–53.
2. Ibid., p. 51.
3. Cyndee Miller, "Study Says 'Likability' Surfaces as Measure of TV Ad Success," *Marketing News,* January 7, 1991, pp. 6, 14; and Ronald Alsop, "TV Ads That Are Likeable Get Plus Rating for Persuasiveness," *The Wall Street Journal,* February 20, 1986, p. 23.
4. Nicolas Massey, "Answer a Higher Calling," *Marketing Magazine,* March 22, 2004.
5. For an interesting discussion on the embellishment of advertising messages, see William M. Weilbacher, *Advertising,* 2nd ed. (New York: Macmillan, 1984), pp. 180–82.
6. David Ogilvy, *Confessions of an Advertising Man* (New York: Atheneum, 1963); and Hanley Norins, *The Compleat Copywriter* (New York: McGraw-Hill, 1966).
7. Hank Sneiden, *Advertising Pure and Simple* (New York: ANACOM, 1977).
8. Jeff Jensen, "Marketer of the Year," *Advertising Age,* December 16, 1996, pp. 1, 16.
9. Cathy Taylor, "Risk Takers: Wieden & Kennedy," *Adweek's Marketing Week,* March 23, 1992, pp. 26, 27.
10. James Webb Young, *A Technique for Producing Ideas,* 3rd ed. (Chicago: Crain Books, 1975), p. 42.
11. Sandra E. Moriarty, *Creative Advertising: Theory and Practice* (Englewood Cliffs, NJ: Prentice Hall, 1986).
12. Brian Mills, "The Egg Man Cometh," *Marketing Magazine,* February 26, 2001.
13. Bruce MacDonald, "The Art of the Brief," *Marketing Magazine,* October 27, 2003.
14. John O'Toole, *The Trouble with Advertising,* 2nd ed. (New York: Random House, 1985), p. 131.
15. Rosser Reeves, *Reality in Advertising* (New York: Knopf, 1961), pp. 47, 48.
16. Michael McCarthy, "New Theme for Reebok," *USA TODAY,* February 10, 2005, p. 5B.
17. Martin Mayer, *Madison Avenue, U.S.A.* (New York: Pocket Books, 1958).
18. Pamela Parker, "IBM Campaign Introduces Company's 'Other Side,'" www.clickz.com/news, April 11, 2005.
19. Jack Trout and Al Ries, "The Positioning Era Cometh," *Advertising Age,* April 24, 1972, pp. 35–38; May 1, 1972, pp. 51–54; May 8, 1972, pp. 114–16.
20. Ingrid Button, "Turning the Export Ship Around," *Marketing Magazine,* August 27, 2001.
21. Lara Mills, "Campaigns with Legs," *Marketing Magazine,* May 15, 2000.
22. Danny Kucharsky, "Pepsi Guys Star in Quebec Ads," *Marketing Magazine,* March 17, 2003.
23. "Cows Cheer Olympic Athletes," *Marketing Magazine,* February 4, 2002.
24. Jean Halliday and Alice Z. Cuneo, "Nissan Reverses Course to Focus on the Product," *Advertising Age,* February 16, 1998, pp. 1, 39.
25. Jean Halliday, "Nissan Launches New Brand Campaign," August 21, 2002, http://www.adage.com/news.
26. Lara Mills, "Campaigns with Legs," *Marketing Magazine,* May 15, 2000.
27. Michael Adams, *Fire and Ice* (Penguin, 2003).
28. Nancy Evans and Bruce Maclellan, "The Risk of Frost Bite," *Marketing Magazine,* June 30, 2003.

29. David Macdonald and Michael Adams, "We Are What We Drive," *Marketing Magazine,* March 15, 2004.
30. Stan Sutter, "Canada's Ad Renascence," *Marketing Magazine,* March 29, 2004.
31. Stan Sutter, "Vive la Difference," *Marketing Magazine,* January 26, 2004.
32. Chris Daniels, "Canucks vs. Yanks," *Marketing Magazine,* May 22, 2000.
33. *Marketing Magazine,* "Cannes-ada," July 3, 2000; "Cannes 2001," July 2, 2001; "Cannes Ad Festival Can be a Real Eye-Opener for Marketers," July 2, 2001; "The Bashful Beaver," November 26, 2001; "More Canuck Work Entered at Cannes," May 29, 2002; Jim McElgunn, "Canucks at Cannes," July 1, 2002; Angela Kryhul, "Where Big Ideas Rule," June 30, 2003; "Canada Arrives at Cannes," July 12, 2004.
34. Sandra E. Moriarty, *Creative Advertising: Theory and Practice,* 2nd ed. (Englewoods Cliffs, NJ: Prentice Hall, 1991), p. 76.
35. William M. Weilbacher, *Advertising,* 2nd ed. (New York: Macmillan, 1984), p. 197.
36. William Wells, John Burnett, and Sandra Moriarty, *Advertising* (Englewood Cliffs, NJ: Prentice Hall, 1989), p. 330.
37. William L. Wilkie and Paul W. Farris, "Comparative Advertising: Problems and Potential," *Journal of Marketing, 39* (1975), pp. 7–15.

38. For a review of comparative advertising studies, see Cornelia Pechmann and David W. Stewart, "The Psychology of Comparative Advertising," in *Attention, Attitude and Affect in Response to Advertising,* ed. E. M. Clark, T. C. Brock, and D. W. Stewart (Hillsdale, NJ: Lawrence Erlbaum, 1994), pp. 79–96; and Thomas S. Barry, "Comparative Advertising: What Have We Learned in Two Decades?" *Journal of Advertising Research, 33,* no. 2 (1993), pp. 19–29.
39. Stuart J. Agres, "Emotion in Advertising: An Agency Point of View," in *Emotion in Advertising: Theoretical and Practical Explanations,* ed. Stuart J. Agres, Julie A. Edell, and Tony M. Dubitsky (Westport, CT: Quorom Books, 1991).
40. Francois Lacoursiere, "La Vie en Bleu," *Marketing Magazine,* February 2, 2004.
41. Edward Kamp and Deborah J. Macinnis, "Characteristics of Portrayed Emotions in Commercials: When Does What Is Shown in Ads Affect Viewers?" *Journal of Advertising Research,* November/December 1995, pp. 19–28.
42. For a review of research on the effect of mood states on consumer behaviour, see Meryl Paula Gardner, "Mood States and Consumer Behavior: A Critical Review," *Journal of Consumer Research, 12,* no. 3 (December 1985), pp. 281–300.
43. Cathy Madison, "Researchers Work Advertising into an Emotional State," *Adweek,* November 5, 1990, p. 30.
44. Joanne Caza, "From Destination to Journey," *Marketing Magazine,* September 8, 2003.
45. Michael L. Ray and William L. Wilkie, "Fear: The Potential of an Appeal Neglected by Marketing," *Journal of Marketing, 34* (January 1970), pp. 54–62.
46. Brian Sternthal and C. Samuel Craig, "Fear Appeals Revisited and Revised," *Journal of Consumer Research, 1* (December 1974), pp. 22–34.
47. Punam Anand Keller and Lauren Goldberg Block, "Increasing the Persuasiveness of Fear Appeals: The Effect of Arousal and Elaboration," *Journal of Consumer Research, 22,* no. 4 (March 1996), pp. 448–60.
48. John F. Tanner, Jr., James B. Hunt, and David R. Eppright, "The Protection Motivation Model: A Normative Mode of Fear Appeals," *Journal of Marketing, 55* (July 1991), pp. 36–45.
49. Ibid.
50. Sternthal and Craig, "Fear Appeals Revisited and Revised."
51. Herbert Jack Rotfeld, "The Textbook Effect: Conventional Wisdom, Myth and Error in Marketing," *Journal of Marketing, 64* (April 2000), pp. 122–27.
52. For a discussion of the use of humour in advertising, see C. Samuel Craig and Brian Sternthal, "Humor in Advertising," *Journal of Marketing, 37* (October 1973), pp. 12–18.
53. Yong Zhang, "Response to Humorous Advertising: The Moderating Effect of Need for Cognition," *Journal of Advertising, 25,* no. 1 (Spring 1996), pp. 15–32; Marc G. Weinberger and Charles S. Gulas, "The Impact of Humor in Advertising: A Review," *Journal of Advertising, 21* (December 1992), pp. 35–59.
54. Marc G. Weinberger and Leland Campbell, "The Use of Humor in Radio Advertising," *Journal of Advertising Research, 31* (December/January 1990–91), pp. 44–52.
55. Thomas J. Madden and Marc C. Weinberger, "Humor in Advertising: A Practitioner View," *Journal of Advertising Research, 24,* no. 4 (August/September 1984), pp. 23–26.
56. David Ogilvy and Joel Raphaelson, "Research on Advertising Techniques That Work and Don't Work," *Harvard Business Review,* July/August 1982, p. 18.
57. *Topline,* no. 4 (September 1989), McCann-Erickson, New York.
58. Media Innovation Awards, *Marketing Magazine,* November 5, 2003.
59. Herbert C. Kelman, "Processes of Opinion Change," *Public Opinion Quarterly, 25* (Spring 1961), pp. 57–78.
60. William J. McGuire, "The Nature of Attitudes and Attitude Change," in *Handbook of Social Psychology,* 2nd ed., ed. G. Lindzey and E. Aronson (Cambridge, MA: Addison-Wesley, 1969), pp. 135–214; Daniel J. O'Keefe, "The Persuasive Effects of Delaying Identification of High- and Low-Credibility Communicators: A Meta-Analytic Review," *Central States Speech Journal, 38* (1987), pp. 63–72.
61. Roobina Ohanian, "The Impact of Celebrity Spokespersons' Image on Consumers' Intention to Purchase," *Journal of Advertising Research,* February/March 1991, pp. 46–54.
62. Erick Reidenback and Robert Pitts, "Not All CEOs Are Created Equal as Advertising Spokespersons: Evaluating the Effective CEO Spokesperson," *Journal of Advertising, 20,* no. 3 (1986), pp. 35–50; Roger Kerin and Thomas E. Barry, "The CEO Spokesperson in Consumer Advertising: An Experimental Investigation," in *Current Issues in Research in Advertising,* ed. J. H. Leigh and C. R. Martin (Ann Arbor: University of Michigan, 1981), pp. 135–48; and J. Poindexter, "Voices of Authority," *Psychology Today,* August 1983.
63. A. Eagly and S. Chaiken, "An Attribution Analysis of the Effect of Communicator Characteristics on Opinion Change," *Journal of Personality and Social Psychology, 32* (1975), pp. 136–44.
64. For a review of these studies, see Brian Sternthal, Lynn Phillips, and Ruby Dholakia, "The Persuasive Effect of Source Credibility: A Situational Analysis," *Public Opinion Quarterly, 42* (Fall 1978), pp. 285–314.
65. Brian Sternthal, Ruby Dholakia, and Clark Leavitt, "The Persuasive Effects of Source Credibility: Tests of Cognitive Response," *Journal of Consumer Research, 4,* no. 4 (March 1978), pp. 252–60; and Robert R. Harmon and Kenneth A. Coney, "The Persuasive Effects of Source Credibility in Buy and Lease Situations," *Journal of Marketing Research, 19* (May 1982), pp. 255–60.
66. For a review, see Noel Capon and James Hulbert, "The Sleeper Effect: An Awakening," *Public Opinion Quarterly, 37* (1973), pp. 333–58.
67. Darlene B. Hannah and Brian Sternthal, "Detecting and Explaining the Sleeper Effect," *Journal of Consumer Research, 11,* no. 2 (September 1984), pp. 632–42.
68. H. C. Triandis, *Attitudes and Attitude Change* (New York: Wiley, 1971).
69. Lise Laguerre, "It's Respect in Either Language," *Marketing Magazine,* May 6, 2002.
70. J. Mills and J. Jellison, "Effect on Opinion Change Similarity between the Communicator and the Audience He Addresses," *Journal of Personality and Social Psychology, 9,* no. 2 (1969), pp. 153–56.
71. Louisa Flinn, "Kings of the Road," *Marketing Magazine,* February 16, 2004.

72. Jason Stein, "Inside Chrysler's Celine Dion Advertising Disaster," www.adage.com, November 24, 2003.
73. Valerie Folkes, "Recent Attribution Research in Consumer Behavior: A Review and New Directions," *Journal of Consumer Research, 14* (March 1988), pp. 548–65; John C. Mowen and Stephen W. Brown, "On Explaining and Predicting the Effectiveness of Celebrity Endorsers," in *Advances in Consumer Research,* vol. 8 (Ann Arbor, MI: Association for Consumer Research, 1981), pp. 437–41.
74. Charles Atkin and M. Block, "Effectiveness of Celebrity Endorsers," *Journal of Advertising Research, 23,* no. 1 (February/March 1983), pp. 57–61.
75. Michael A. Kamins, "An Investigation into the 'Match-Up' Hypothesis in Celebrity Advertising," *Journal of Advertising, 19,* no. 1 (1990), pp. 4–13.
76. Grant McCracken, "Who Is the Celebrity Endorser? Cultural Foundations of the Endorsement Process," *Journal of Consumer Research, 16,* no. 3 (December 1989), pp. 310–21.
77. Ibid., p. 315.
78. B. Zafer Erdogan, Michael J. Baker, and Stephen Tagg, "Selecting Celebrity Endorsers: The Practitioner's Perspective," *Journal of Advertising Research, 41,* no. 43 (May/June 2001), pp. 39–48.
79. For an excellent review of these studies, see Marilyn Y. Jones, Andrea J. S. Stanaland, and Betsy D. Gelb, "Beefcake and Cheesecake: Insights for Advertisers," *Journal of Advertising, 27,* no. 2 (Summer 1998), pp. 32–51; and W. B. Joseph, "The Credibility of Physically Attractive Communicators," *Journal of Advertising, 11,* no. 3 (1982), pp. 13–23.
80. Michael Solomon, Richard Ashmore, and Laura Longo, "The Beauty Match-Up Hypothesis: Congruence between Types of Beauty and Product Images in Advertising," *Journal of Advertising, 21,* no. 4, pp. 23–34; M. J. Baker and Gilbert A. Churchill, Jr., "The Impact of Physically Attractive Models on Advertising Evaluations," *Journal of Marketing Research, 14* (November 1977), pp. 538–55.
81. Robert W. Chestnut, C. C. La Chance, and A. Lubitz, "The Decorative Female Model: Sexual Stimuli and the Recognition of the Advertisements," *Journal of Advertising, 6* (Fall 1977), pp. 11–14; and Leonard N. Reid and Lawrence C. Soley, "Decorative Models and Readership of Magazine Ads," *Journal of Advertising Research, 23,* no. 2 (April/May 1983), pp. 27–32.
82. Amanda B. Bower, "Highly Attractive Models in Advertising and the Women Who Loathe Them: The Implications of Negative Affect for Spokesperson Effectiveness," *Journal of Advertising, 30,* no. 3 (Fall 2001), pp. 51–63; Amanda B. Bower and Stacy Landreth, "Is Beauty Best? Highly Versus Normally Attractive Models in Advertising," *Journal of Advertising, 30,* no. 1, pp. 1–12.
83. Jack Neff, "In Dove Ads, Normal Is the New Beautiful," *Advertising Age,* September 27, 2004, pp. 1, 80.
84. Michelle Jeffers, "Behind Dove's 'Real Beauty,'" *Adweek,* September 12, 2005, pp. 34–35.

CHAPTER EIGHT

1. "Dove Revives Soap Litmus Test," *Marketing Magazine,* January 15, 2001.
2. Norma Ramage, "Toyota Owners Drive Prairie Effort, *Marketing Magazine,* March 17, 2003.
3. Bob Garfield, "Listerine Eschews 'Creativity' for an Ad That Actually Works," *Advertising Age,* September 20, 2004, p. 57.
4. Jeff Chatterton, "A Whole New Ball Game," *Marketing Magazine,* November 10, 2003.
5. Angela Kryhul, "The Great Canadian Icon," *Marketing Magazine,* June 26, 2000.
6. Barbara B. Stern, "Classical and Vignette Television Advertising: Structural Models, Formal Analysis, and Consumer Effects," *Journal of Consumer Research, 20,* no. 4 (March 1994), pp. 601–15; and John Deighton, Daniel Romer, and Josh McQueen, "Using Drama to Persuade," *Journal of Consumer Research, 15,* no. 3 (December 1989), pp. 335–43.
7. Karen Howe and Ian Mcintosh, "A Clever Parody," *Marketing Magazine,* January 12, 2004.
8. Herbert E. Krugman, "On Application of Learning Theory to TV Copy Testing," *Public Opinion Quarterly, 26* (1962), pp. 626–39.
9. C. I. Hovland and W. Mandell, "An Experimental Comparison of Conclusion Drawing by the Communicator and by the Audience," *Journal of Abnormal and Social Psychology, 47* (July 1952), pp. 581–88.
10. Alan G. Sawyer and Daniel J. Howard, "Effects of Omitting Conclusions in Advertisements to Involved and Uninvolved Audiences," *Journal of Marketing Research, 28* (November 1991), pp. 467–74.
11. George E. Belch, "The Effects of Message Modality on One- and Two-Sided Advertising Messages," in *Advances in Consumer Research, 10,* ed. Richard P. Bagozzi and Alice M. Tybout (Ann Arbor, MI: Association for Consumer Research, 1983), pp. 21–26.
12. Robert E. Settle and Linda L. Golden, "Attribution Theory and Advertiser Credibility," *Journal of Marketing Research, 11* (May 1974), pp. 181–85; and Edmund J. Faison, "Effectiveness of One-Sided and Two-Sided Mass Communications in Advertising," *Public Opinion Quarterly, 25* (Fall 1961), pp. 468–69.
13. "Campaigns with Legs," *Marketing Magazine,* May 15, 2000.
14. Alan G. Sawyer, "The Effects of Repetition of Refutational and Supportive Advertising Appeals," *Journal of Marketing Research, 10* (February 1973), pp. 23–37; and George J. Szybillo and Richard Heslin, "Resistance to Persuasion: Inoculation Theory in a Marketing Context," *Journal of Marketing Research, 10* (November 1973), pp. 396–403.
15. Andrew A. Mitchell, "The Effect of Verbal and Visual Components of Advertisements on Brand Attitudes and Attitude toward the Advertisement," *Journal of Consumer Research, 13* (June 1986), pp. 12–24; and Julie A. Edell and Richard Staelin, "The Information Processing of Pictures in Advertisements," *Journal of Consumer Research, 10,* no. 1 (June 1983), pp. 45–60; Elizabeth C. Hirschmann, "The Effects of Verbal and Pictorial Advertising Stimuli on Aesthetic, Utilitarian and Familiarity Perceptions," *Journal of Advertising, 15,* no. 2 (1986), pp. 27–34.
16. Jolita Kisielius and Brian Sternthal, "Detecting and Explaining Vividness Effects in Attitudinal Judgments," *Journal of Marketing Research, 21,* no. 1 (1984), pp. 54–64.
17. H. Rao Unnava and Robert E. Burnkrant, "An Imagery-Processing View of the Role of Pictures in Print Advertisements," *Journal of Marketing Research, 28* (May 1991), pp. 226–31.
18. Susan E. Heckler and Terry L. Childers, "The Role of Expectancy and Relevancy in Memory for Verbal and Visual Information: What Is Incongruency?" *Journal of Consumer Research, 18,* no. 4 (March 1992), pp. 475–92.
19. Michael J. Houston, Terry L. Childers, and Susan E. Heckler, "Picture–Word Consistency and the Elaborative Processing of Advertisements," *Journal of Marketing Research,* November 1987, pp. 359–69.
20. William F. Arens, *Contemporary Advertising,* 6th ed. (Burr Ridge, IL: Irwin/McGraw-Hill, 1998), p. 284.
21. W. Keith Hafer and Gordon E. White, *Advertising Writing,* 3rd ed. (St. Paul, MN: West Publishing, 1989), p. 98.
22. Michelle Warren, "Press and Poster," *Marketing Magazine,* March 24, 2003.
23. Janet Kestin, "Reality Rules," *Marketing Magazine,* February 26, 2001.
24. Carol Marie Cooper, "Who Says Talk Is Cheap," *New York Times,* October 22, 1998, pp. C1, 5; and Wendy Brandes, "Star Power Leaves Some Voice-Over Artists Speechless," *The Wall Street Journal,* June 2, 1995, p. B6.
25. Linda M. Scott, "Understanding Jingles and Needledrop: A Rhetorical Approach to Music in Advertising," *Journal of Consumer Research, 17,* no. 2 (September 1990), pp. 223–36.
26. Ibid., p. 223.

27. Russell I. Haley, Jack Richardson, and Beth Baldwin, "The Effects of Nonverbal Communications in Television Advertising," *Journal of Advertising Research, 24,* no. 4, pp. 11–18.
28. Gerald J. Gorn, "The Effects of Music in Advertising on Choice Behavior: A Classical Conditioning Approach," *Journal of Marketing, 46* (Winter 1982), pp. 94–100.
29. "Bud Light Sells Spoof Soundtrack," *Marketing Magazine,* February 21, 2002.
30. "Follow the Bouncing Ball to P.E.I.," *Marketing Magazine,* March 22, 2004.
31. Angela Kryhul, "Name Your Tune," *Marketing Magazine,* October 14, 2002.
32. Ibid.
33. Richard Vaughn, "How Advertising Works: A Planning Model," *Journal of Advertising Research, 20,* no. 5 (October 1980), pp. 27–33.
34. Richard Vaughn, "How Advertising Works: A Planning Model Revisited," *Journal of Advertising Research, 26,* no. 1 (February/March 1986), pp. 57–66.
35. Christopher P. Puto and William D.Wells, "Informational and Transformational Advertising: The Different Effects of Time," in *Advances in Consumer Research, 11,* ed. Thomas C. Kinnear (Ann Arbor, MI: Association for Consumer Research, 1984), p. 638.
36. Eric LeBlanc and Kate Tutly, "The Heart of the Matter," *Marketing Magazine,* July 16, 2001.

CHAPTER NINE

1. Mary Tolan, "Holidays Are Here and So Is Ad Puzzle," *Advertising Age,* November 16, 1998, p. 36.
2. Ibid.
3. Laura Bird, "Loved the Ad. May (or May Not) Buy the Product," *The Wall Street Journal,* April 7, 1994, p. B1.
4. "What Is Good Creative?" *Topline,* no. 41 (New York: McCollum Spielman Worldwide, 1994), p. 4.
5. James R. Hagerty, "Tests Lead Lowe's to Revamp Strategy," *The Wall Street Journal,* March 11, 1999, p. B18.
6. John M. Caffyn, "Telepex Testing of TV Commercials," *Journal of Advertising Research, 5,* no. 2 (June 1965), pp. 29–37; Thomas J. Reynolds and Charles Gengler, "A Strategic Framework for Assessing Advertising: The Animatic vs. Finished Issue," *Journal of Advertising Research,* October/November 1991, pp. 61–71; Nigel A. Brown and Ronald Gatty, "Rough vs. Finished TV Commercials in Telepex Tests," *Journal of Advertising Research, 7,* no. 4 (December 1967), p. 21.
7. Charles H. Sandage, Vernon Fryburger, and Kim Rotzoll, *Advertising Theory and Practice,* 10th ed. (Burr Ridge, IL: Richard D. Irwin, 1979).
8. Lyman E. Ostlund, "Advertising Copy Testing: A Review of Current Practices, Problems and Prospects," *Current Issues and Research in Advertising,* 1978, pp. 87–105.
9. Jack B. Haskins, "Factual Recall as a Measure of Advertising Effectiveness," *Journal of Advertising Research, 4,* no. 1 (March 1964), pp. 2–7.
10. John Philip Jones and Margaret H. Blair, "Examining 'Conventional Wisdoms' about Advertising Effects with Evidence from Independent Sources," *Journal of Advertising Research,* November/December 1996, pp. 37–52.
11. Paul J. Watson and Robert J. Gatchel, "Autonomic Measures of Advertising," *Journal of Advertising Research, 19* (June 1979), pp. 15–26.
12. Priscilla A. LaBarbera and Joel D. Tucciarone, "GSR Reconsidered: A Behavior-based Approach to Evaluating and Improving the Sales Potency of Advertising," *Journal of Advertising Research,* September/October 1995, pp. 33–40.
13. Flemming Hansen, "Hemispheric Lateralization: Implications for Understanding Consumer Behavior," *Journal of Consumer Research, 8* (1988), pp. 23–36.
14. Kevin Lane Keller, Susan E. Heckler, and Michael J. Houston, "The Effects of Brand Name Suggestiveness on Advertising Recall," *Journal of Marketing,* January 1998, pp. 48–57.
15. Jan Stapel, "Recall and Recognition: A Very Close Relationship," *Journal of Advertising Research,* July/August 1998, pp. 41–45.
16. Hubert A. Zielske, "Does Day-after Recall Penalize 'Feeling Ads'?" *Journal of Advertising Research, 22,* no. 1 (1982), pp. 19–22.
17. Arthur J. Kover, "Why Copywriters Don't Like Advertising Research—And What Kind of Research Might They Accept," *Journal of Advertising Research,* March/April 1996, pp. RC8–RC10; Gary Levin, "Emotion Guides BBDO's Ad Tests," *Advertising Age,* January 29, 1990, p. 12.
18. Terry Haller, "Day-after Recall to Persist Despite JWT Study; Other Criteria Looming," *Marketing News,* May 18, 1979, p. 4.
19. Dave Kruegel, "Television Advertising Effectiveness and Research Innovations," *Journal of Consumer Marketing, 5,* no. 3 (Summer 1988), pp. 43–52.
20. Gary Levin, "Tracing Ads' Impact," *Advertising Age,* November 12, 1990, p. 49.
21. John Philip Jones, "Single-source Research Begins to Fulfill Its Promise," *Journal of Advertising Research,* May/June 1995, pp. 9–16.
22. Jeffrey L. Seglin, "The New Era of Ad Measurement," *Adweek's Marketing Week,* January 23, 1988, p. 24.
23. James F. Donius, "Marketing Tracking: A Strategic Reassessment and Planning Tool," *Journal of Advertising Research, 25,* no. 1 (February/March 1985), pp. 15–19.
24. "21 Ad Agencies Endorse Copy-Testing Principles," *Marketing News, 15,* no. 17 (February 19, 1982), p. 1.
25. Ibid.
26. Russell I. Haley and Allan L. Baldinger, "The ARF Copy Research Validity Project," *Journal of Advertising Research,* April/May 1991, pp. 11–32.

CHAPTER TEN

1. Bruce Grondin, "Building North–South Links," *Marketing Magazine,* March 15, 2004.
2. Chris Powell, "Youth Confound Traditional Media," *Marketing Magazine,* March 1, 2004.
3. Lesley Young, "Primus Takes Aim at Cable, Telcos," *Marketing Magazine,* January 19, 2004.
4. Chuck Ross, "Study Finds for Continuity vs. Flights," *Advertising Age,* April 19, 1999, p. 2.
5. Lesley Young, "Campbell Warms Up to Bad Weather," *Marketing Magazine,* February 16, 2004.
6. Michael J. Naples, *Effective Frequency: The Relationship between Frequency and Advertising Effectiveness* (New York: Association of National Advertisers, 1979).
7. Joseph W. Ostrow, "Setting Frequency Levels: An Art or a Science?" *Journal of Advertising Research, 24* (August/September 1984), pp. 9–11.
8. Naples, *Effective Frequency.*
9. Joseph W. Ostrow, "What Level Frequency?" *Advertising Age,* November 1981, pp. 13–18.
10. Jack Myers, "More Is Indeed Better," *Media Week,* September 6, 1993, pp. 14–18; Jim Surmanek, "One-Hit or Miss: Is a Frequency of One Frequently Wrong?" *Advertising Age,* November 27, 1995, p. 46.
11. Ostrow, "What Level Frequency?"
12. David A. Aaker and John G. Myers, *Advertising Management,* 3rd ed. (Englewood Cliffs, NJ: Prentice Hall, 1987), p. 474.
13. Joel N. Axelrod, "Induced Moods and Attitudes toward Products," *Journal of Advertising Research, 3* (June 1963), pp. 19–24; Lauren E. Crane, "How Product, Appeal, and Program Affect Attitudes toward Commercials," *Journal of Advertising Research, 4* (March 1964), p. 15.
14. *McGraw-Hill Lap Report* no. 3151 (New York: McGraw-Hill, 1988); Alan D. Fletcher, *Target Marketing through the Yellow Pages* (Troy, MI: Yellow Pages Publishers Association, 1991), p. 23.
15. Frank M. Bass, "A Simultaneous Equation Regression Study of Advertising and Sales of Cigarettes," *Journal of Marketing Research, 6,* no. 3 (August 1969), p. 291; David

A. Aaker and James M. Carman, "Are You Overadvertising?" *Journal of Advertising Research, 22,* no. 4 (August/September 1982), pp. 57–70.
16. Julian A. Simon and Johan Arndt, "The Shape of the Advertising Response Function," *Journal of Advertising Research, 20,* no. 4 (1980), pp. 11–28.
17. Paul B. Luchsinger, Vernan S. Mullen, and Paul T. Jannuzzo, "How Many Advertising Dollars Are Enough?" *Media Decisions, 12* (1977), p. 59.
18. Paul W. Farris, *Determinants of Advertising Intensity: A Review of the Marketing Literature* (Report no. 77–109, Marketing Science Institute, Cambridge, MA, 1977).
19. Melvin E. Salveson, "Management's Criteria for Advertising Effectiveness" (Proceedings 5th Annual Conference, Advertising Research Foundation, New York, 1959), p. 25.
20. Robert Settle and Pamela Alreck, "Positive Moves for Negative Times," *Marketing Communications,* January 1988, pp. 19–23.
21. Boonghee Yoo and Rujirutana Mandhachitara, "Estimating Advertising Effects on Sales in a Competitive Setting," *Journal of Advertising Research, 43*(3), 2003, pp. 310–320.
22. James O. Peckham, "Can We Relate Advertising Dollars to Market Share Objectives?" in *How Much to Spend for Advertising,* ed. M. A. McNiven (New York: Association of National Advertisers, 1969), p. 30.
23. George S. Low and Jakki Mohr, "Setting Advertising and Promotion Budgets in Multi-Brand Companies," *Journal of Advertising Research,* January/February 1999, pp. 667–78.
24. *Strategy Magazine*, April 2006.
25. John P. Jones, "Ad Spending: Maintaining Market Share," *Harvard Business Review,* January/February 1990, pp. 38–42; James C. Schroer, "Ad Spending: Growing Market Share," *Harvard Business Review,* January/February 1990, pp. 44–48.
26. Randall S. Brown, "Estimating Advantages to Large-Scale Advertising," *Review of Economics and Statistics, 60* (August 1978), pp. 428–37.
27. Kent M. Lancaster, "Are There Scale Economies in Advertising?" *Journal of Business, 59,* no. 3 (1986), pp. 509–26.
28. Johan Arndt and Julian Simon, "Advertising and Economics of Scale: Critical Comments on the Evidence," *Journal of Industrial Economics, 32,* no. 2 (December 1983), pp. 229–41; Aaker and Carman, "Are You Overadvertising?"
29. Mary Welch, "Upbeat Marketers Wield Bigger Budgets, Shift Marketing Mix," *Business Marketing,* February 1993, p. 23.
30. George S. Low and Jakki J. Mohr, "The Budget Allocation between Advertising and Sales Promotion: Understanding the Decision Process," 1991 AMA Educators' Proceedings, Chicago, Summer 1991, pp. 448–57.

CHAPTER ELEVEN

1. Television Bureau of Canada website (www.tvb.ca).
2. 2001 Fall Survey, BBM Canada.
3. "Making the Most of Magazines," *Marketing Magazine,* October 15, 2001.
4. Laura Petrecca, "4A's: Production Costs for TV Spots Up by 6%," *Advertising Age,* August 18, 1997, p. 30.
5. Joe Flint, "Commercial Clutter on TV Networks Rises to Record," *The Wall Street Journal,* March 2, 2000, p. B18.
6. Lex van Meurs, "Zapp! A Study on Switching Behavior during Commercial Breaks," *Journal of Advertising Research,* January/February 1998, pp. 43–53; John J. Cronin, "In-Home Observations of Commercial Zapping Behavior," *Journal of Current Issues and Research in Advertising, 17,* no. 2 (Fall 1995), pp. 69–75.
7. John J. Cronin and Nancy Menelly, "In-Home Observations of Commercial Zapping Behavior," *Journal of Advertising, 21,* no. 2 (June 1992), pp. 1–7.
8. Carrie Heeter and Bradley S. Greenberg, "Profiling the Zappers," *Journal of Advertising Research,* April/May 1985, pp. 9–12; Fred S. Zufryden, James H. Pedrick, and Avu Sandaralingham, "Zapping and Its Impact on Brand Purchase Behavior," *Journal of Advertising Research, 33* (January/February 1993), pp. 58–66; and Patricia Orsini, "Zapping: A Man's World," Spring Television Report, *Adweek's Marketing Week,* April 8, 1991, p. 3.
9. Lex van Meurs, "Zapp! A Study on Switching Behavior during Commercial Breaks," *Journal of Advertising Research,* January/February 1998, pp. 43–53.
10. Christopher Kelly, "What They Want, When They Want It," *Marketing Magazine,* May 5, 2003.
11. John J. Cronin and Nancy Menelly, "Discrimination vs. Avoidance: 'Zipping' of Television Commercials," *Journal of Advertising, 21,* no. 2 (June 1992), pp. 1–7.
12. Kirsten Chase, "Confessions of a PVR User," *Marketing Magazine,* March 26, 2007; Chris Powell, "PVRs: Canadians vs. Americans," *Marketing Magazine,* March 26, 2007; Pierre Delagrave, "Dawn of the Ad Zapper," *Marketing Magazine,* February 20, 2006.
13. Linda F. Alwitt and Parul R. Prabhaker, "Identifying Who Dislikes Television Advertising: Not by Demographics Alone," *Journal of Advertising Research, 32,* no. 5 (1992), pp. 30–42.
14. Banwari Mittal, "Public Assessment of TV Advertising: Faint Praise and Harsh Criticism," *Journal of Advertising Research* no. 34, 1 (1994), pp. 35–53; Ernest F. Larkin, "Consumer Perceptions of the Media and Their Advertising Content," *Journal of Advertising, 8* (1979), pp. 5–7.
15. Lucy L. Henke, "Young Children's Perceptions of Cigarette Brand Advertising Symbols: Awareness, Affect, and Target Market Identification," *Journal of Advertising, 24,* no. 4 (Winter 1995), pp. 13–28.
16. Susanne Boyce, "Cooking with Gas," *Marketing Magazine,* May 10, 2004.
17. Janet Eastwood, "Specialty Is Our Specialty" *Marketing Magazine,* November 10, 2003.
18. Rick White and Mary Kreuk, "Money Show Management," *Marketing Magazine,* May 3, 2004.
19. Tim Wilson, "Give Digital a Chance," *Marketing Magazine,* March 29, 2004.
20. Chris Powell, "Follow the Viewer," *Marketing Magazine,* May 17, 2004.
21. David Chilton, "The Meter Merge," *Marketing Magazine,* August 14, 2006.
22. "It's Make or Break Time in TV as More Viewers Skip the Ads," *Marketing Week,* May 24, 2007; and Stuart Elliott, "Live Plus Three," *National Post,* May 18, 2007.
23. Suein L. Hwang, "Old Media Get a Web Windfall," *The Wall Street Journal,* September 17, 1999, p. B1.
24. Verne Gay, "Image Transfer: Radio Ads Make Aural History," *Advertising Age,* January 24, 1985, p. 1.
25. Avery Abernethy, "Differences Between Advertising and Program Exposure for Car Radio Listening," *Journal of Advertising Research, 31,* no. 2 (April/May 1991), pp. 33–42.
26. Martin Peers, "Radio Produces Both Gains and Skeptics," *The Wall Street Journal,* January 1, 1999, p. B6.
27. Ibid.

CHAPTER TWELVE

1. Herbert E. Krugman, "The Measurement of Advertising Involvement," *Public Opinion Quarterly, 30* (Winter 1966–67), pp. 583–96.
2. Magazinescanada.ca.
3. Maureen Cavan, "Building Our Own," *Marketing Magazine,* April 14, 2003.
4. Chris Powell, "A Pro-Barf Buy," *Marketing Magazine,* April 5, 2004; Eve Lazarus, "The Luxe Approach," *Marketing Magazine,* March 29, 2004.
5. Barb Grant, "Getting the Right Balance," *Marketing Magazine,* September 22, 2003.
6. Chris Powell, "La Difference," *Marketing Magazine,* May 10, 2004.
7. *The Magazine Handbook.*
8. Ibid.

9. *A Study of Media Involvement,* Vol. 7 (New York: Magazine Publishers of America, 1996).
10. Mary Pompili and Janet Eger, "Power Tools," *Marketing Magazine,* April 19, 2004.
11. Study cited in Jim Surmanek, *Media Planning: A Practical Guide* (Lincolnwood, IL: Crain Books, 1985).
12. *How Advertising Readership Is Influenced by Ad Size,* Report no. 110.1, Cahners Advertising Research, Newton, MA; and *Larger Advertisements Get Higher Readership,* LAP Report no. 3102, McGraw-Hill Research, New York.
13. Effect of Size, Color and Position on Number of Responses to Recruitment Advertising, LAP Report no. 3116, McGraw-Hill Research, New York.
14. Paul-Mark Rendon, "Osprey Takes Flight," *Marketing Magazine,* August 11, 2003.
15. David Chilton, "The Daily News," *Marketing Magazine,* March 13, 2006.
16. Norma Ramage, "Frisky Business," *Marketing Magazine,* May 3, 2004.
17. Randy Stein, "The Intimate Medium," *Marketing Magazine,* August 11, 2003.
18. Chris Powell, "Cheery of Evolution," *Marketing Magazine,* November 20, 2006.
19. Chris Powell, "When Push Comes to Shove It," *Marketing Magazine,* March 15, 2004.

CHAPTER THIRTEEN

1. *Adweek,* August 25, 1997, p. 3.
2. Mukesh Bhargava and Naveen Donthu, "Sales Response to Outdoor Advertising," *Journal of Advertising Research,* August 1999, pp. 7–18.
3. Lynne Kilpatrick, "Taking a Retail Approach All the Way to the Bank," *Marketing Magazine,* September 22, 2003.
4. Chris Powell, "Hip to Be Square," *Marketing Magazine,* March 10, 2003.
5. Maritz AmeriPoll, August 1998.
6. Tom Shepansky, "The Exotic Tuna," *Marketing Magazine,* March 10, 2003.
7. Danny Kucharsky, "Outdoor's Measurement Challenge," *Marketing Magazine,* May 17, 2004.
8. Sally Basmajian, "Walking the Talk," *Marketing Magazine,* September 15, 2003.
9. "Cinema Advertising Comes of Age," *Marketing Magazine,* May 6, 2002.
10. Michael A. Belch and Don Sciglimpaglia, "Viewers' Evaluations of Cinema Advertising," Proceedings of the American Institute for Decision Sciences, March 1979, pp. 39–43.
11. Adam Snyder, "Are Spots on Home Video Badvertising?" *Brandweek,* January 29, 1996, p. 40.
12. Alice Cuneo, "Now Playing: Gap, Target Take Retail to the Movies," *Advertising Age,* June 9, 1997, p. 14.
13. Promotional Products Association International (Irving, TX), 1996.
14. 2003 Promotional Products Industry Sales Volume Study, Promotional Products Association of Canada, May 2003.
15. Mark Freed, "Trinkets to Treasure," *Marketing Magazine,* May 8, 2006; Norma Range, "Treasured Trinkets," *Marketing Magazine,* August 28, 2006.
16. George L. Herpel and Steve Slack, *Specialty Advertising: New Dimensions in Creative Marketing* (Irving, TX: Specialty Advertising Association, 1983), pp. 76, 79–80.
17. Ibid., p. 78.
18. M. J. Caballero and J. B. Hunt, *Smilin' Jack: Measuring Goodwill,* unpublished research report from the Center for Professional Selling, Baylor University, 1989; M. J. Cooper and J. B. Hunt, *How Specialty Advertising Affects Goodwill,* research report of Specialty Advertising Association International (now PPAI), Irving, TX, 1992.
19. Herpel and Slack, *Specialty Advertising,* p. 75.
20. Philip J. Hart, "Product Placement for Dummies," *Marketing Magazine,* May 5, 2003; Paul-Mark Rendon, "Casting Call," *Marketing Magazine,* May 5, 2003.
21. Eve Lazarus, "Keep It Real," *Marketing Magazine,* March 13, 2006.
22. Philip J. Hart, "Product Placement for Dummies," *Marketing Magazine,* May 5, 2003.
23. Hart; Danny Kucharsky, "A New Brand of Show," *Marketing Magazine,* May 5, 2003; Paul-Mark Rendon, "Casting Call," *Marketing Magazine,* May 5, 2003; Rosanne Caron, "On the Right Track," *Marketing Magazine,* July 14, 2003.
24. Philip J. Hart, "Product Placement for Dummies," *Marketing Magazine,* May 5, 2003.
25. Wahjudi Harsono and Elizabeth Kan, "Reaching the Target," *Marketing Magazine,* May 5, 2003.
26. Danny Kucharsky, "A New Brand of Show," *Marketing Magazine,* May 5, 2003.
27. Danny Kucharsky, "Rona Wants to Build a Stronger Image," *Marketing Magazine,* March 24, 2003.
28. Paul-Mark Rendon, "Casting Call," *Marketing Magazine,* May 5, 2003.
29. Pola Gupta and Kenneth Lord, "Product Placement in Movies: The Effect of Prominence and Mode on Audience Recall," *Journal of Current Issues and Research in Advertising, 20,* no. 1 (Spring 1998), pp. 1–29.
30. Pola B. Gupta and Stephen J. Gould, "Consumers' Perceptions of the Ethics and Acceptability of Product Placements in Movies: Product Category and Individual Differences," *Journal of Current Issues and Research in Advertising, 19,* no. 1 (Spring 1997), pp. 40–49.

CHAPTER FOURTEEN

1. Louis J. Haugh, "Defining and Redefining," *Advertising Age,* February 14, 1983, p. M44.
2. Scott A. Nielsen, John Quelch, and Caroline Henderson, "Consumer Promotions and the Acceleration of Product Purchases," in *Research on Sales Promotion: Collected Papers,* ed. Katherine E. Jocz (Cambridge, MA: Marketing Science Institute, 1984).
3. J. Jeffrey Inman and Leigh McAlister, "Do Coupon Expiration Dates Affect Consumer Behavior?" *Journal of Marketing Research, 31,* August 1994, pp. 423–28.
4. "Slow + Steady: Promo's Exclusive Annual Report of the U.S. Promotion Industry," *Promo,* April 2002.
5. Betsy Spethman, "Sudden Impact," *Promo,* April 1999, pp. 42–48; Betsy Spethman, "Is Advertising Dead?" *Promo,* September 1998, pp. 32–36.
6. "Promo's New Prominence," *Marketing Magazine,* September 3, 2001.
7. Brent Armstrong, "The First Meal's Not Enough," *Marketing Magazine,* September 10, 2001.
8. *The Effects of Promotion Stimuli on Consumer Purchase Behavior* (Glenview, IL: FSI Council, 1999).
9. "1996 Trend Report," *Actmedia, Inc.,* Anaheim, CA.
10. Richard Sale, "Evaluation in Evolution," *Promo,* September 1998, pp. 63–68.
11. "It's Elementary," *Marketing Magazine,* December 3, 2001.
12. R. M. Prentice, "How to Split Your Marketing Funds Between Advertising and Promotion Dollars," *Advertising Age,* January 10, 1977, pp. 41–42, 44.
13. Betsy Spethmann, "Money and Power," *Brandweek,* March 15, 1993, p. 21.
14. Adapted from Terrence A. Shimp, *Advertising, Promotion, and Supplemental Aspect of Integrated Marketing Communication,* 4th ed. (Fort Worth, TX: Dryden Press, 1997), p. 487.
15. Brian C. Deslauries and Peter B. Everett, "The Effects of Intermittent and Continuous Token Reinforcement on Bus Ridership," *Journal of Applied Psychology, 62* (August 1977), pp. 369–75.
16. Michael L. Rothschild and William C. Gaidis, "Behavioural Learning Theory: Its Relevance to Marketing and Promotions," *Journal of Marketing Research, 45,* no. 2 (Spring 1981), pp. 70–78.
17. "Hostess' Heroes," *Marketing Magazine,* August 6, 2001.
18. "Trial and Conversion VI: Consumers' Reactions to Samples and Demonstrations," Promotional Marketing Association, Inc. 2002.

19. Peter Breen, "Sophisticated Sampling," *Promo,* September 1999, pp. 63–68.
20. Lesley Young, "Marketing Direct Briefs," *Marketing Magazine,* November 3, 2003.
21. Couponing Facts, www.couponscanada.org.
22. J. Jeffrey Inman and Leigh McAlister, "Do Coupon Expiration Dates Affect Consumer Behavior?"
23. Wayne Mouland, "Choosing the Right Face Value," *Marketing Magazine,* May 10, 2004.
24. Redemption rates for all coupons provided by Wayne Mouland of Resolve Corporation.
25. Lesley Young, "Stores Remain Wary of Web Coupons," *Marketing Magazine,* September 29, 2003.
26. Survey by Oxtoby-Smith, Inc., cited in "Many Consumers View Rebates as a Bother," *The Wall Street Journal,* April 13, 1989, p. B1.
27. William R. Dean, "Irresistible But Not Free of Problems," *Advertising Age,* October 6, 1980, pp. S1–12.
28. Eric Schmuckler, "Two Action Figures to Go, Hold the Burger," *Brandweek,* April 1, 1996, pp. 38–39.
29. Michelle Halpern, "Labatt's Big PROMO! Score," *Marketing Magazine,* October 6, 2003.
30. "Cereal Killer," *Marketing Magazine,* May 14, 2001.
31. "Doughboy Promo Pops Off the Shelf," *Marketing Magazine,* January 14, 2002.
32. "Sweepstakes Fever," *Forbes,* October 3, 1988, pp. 164–66.
33. Wayne Mouland, "Sweeping Up Additional Sales," *Marketing Magazine,* October 6, 2003.
34. "P&G and MuchMusic Head to the Prom," *Marketing Magazine,* February 23, 2001; "Much, P&G Team Up to Target Teens," *Marketing Magazine,* March 5, 2001.
35. Paul-Mark Rendon, "Axe Seeks Best Mating Calls," *Marketing Magazine,* July 28, 2003.
36. Bob Woods, "Picking a Winner," *Promo,* August 1998, pp. 57–62.
37. Bruce Hawley, "More Than Just O.K.," *Marketing Magazine,* July 28, 2003.
38. Maxine S. Lans, "Legal Hurdles Big Part of Promotions Game," *Marketing News,* October 24, 1994, pp. 15–16.
39. Survey by Oxtoby-Smith, Inc., "Many Consumers View Rebates."
40. Peter Tat, William A. Cunningham III, and Emin Babakus, "Consumer Perceptions of Rebates," *Journal of Advertising Research,* August/September 1988, pp. 45–50.
41. Martha Graves, "Mail-In Rebates Stirring Shopper, Retailer Backlash," *Los Angeles Times,* January 11, 1989, Pt. IV, p. 1.
42. Edward A. Blair and E. Lair Landon, "The Effects of Reference Prices in Retail Advertisements," *Journal of Marketing, 45,* no. 2 (Spring 1981), pp. 61–69.
43. R. J. Igneizi, "WD-40@50," *The San Diego Union-Tribune,* November 10, 2003, pp. D1, 4.
44. Betsy Spethmann, "Switching Loyalty," *Promo,* July 2002, pp. 40–45.
45. Kathleen M. Joyce, "Keeping the Faith," *Promo's 12th Annual Source Book 2005,* p. 24.
46. Paul-Mark Rendon, "Aveeno Smoothes the Slopes," *Marketing Magazine,* February 16, 2004.
47. Paul-Mark Rendon, "Coffee-Mate Gets Street Smart," *Marketing Magazine,* February 23, 2004.
48. "Takin' It to the Streets," *Marketing Magazine,* September 10, 2001.
49. Michelle Warren, "P&G Celebrates Small Communities with Nice'n Easy Skating Tour," *Marketing Magazine,* February 2, 2004.
50. Frank Green, "Battling for Shelf Control," *San Diego Union,* November 19, 1996, pp. C1, 6, 7.
51. Paul N. Bloom, Gregory T. Gundlach, and Joseph P. Cannon, "Slotting Allowances and Fees: Schools of Thought and Views of Practicing Managers," *Journal of Marketing, 64,* April 2000, pp. 92–108.
52. Melissa Campanelli, "What's in Store for EDLP?" *Sales & Marketing Management,* August 1993, pp. 56–59; "Procter & Gamble Hits Back," *Business Week,* July 19, 1993, pp. 20–22; and Amy Barone and Laurel Wentz, "Artzt Steering Barilla into EDLP Strategy," *Advertising Age,* February 26, 1996, p. 10.
53. NCH Reporter, no. 1 (Nielsen Clearing House, 1983).
54. Srinath Gopalakrishna, Gary L. Lilien, Jerome D. Williams, and Ian K. Sequeria, "Do Trade Shows Pay Off?" *Journal of Marketing, 59,* July 1995, pp. 75–83.
55. Cynthia Rigg, "Hard Times Means Growth for Co-op Ads," *Advertising Age,* November 12, 1990, p. 24.
56. Edwin L. Artzt, "The Lifeblood of Brands," *Advertising Age,* November 4, 1991, p. 32.
57. "Everyone Is Bellying Up to This Bar," *Business Week,* January 27, 1992, p. 84.
58. Jack Neff, "The New Brand Management," *Advertising Age,* November 8, 1999, pp. S2, 18; Benson P. Shapiro, "Improved Distribution with Your Promotional Mix," *Harvard Business Review,* March/April 1977, p. 116; and Roger A. Strang, "Sales Promotion—Fast Growth, Faulty Management," *Harvard Business Review,* July/August 1976, p. 119.
59. Priya Raghubir and Kim Corfman, "When Do Price Promotions Affect Pretrial Brand Evaluations?" *Journal of Marketing Research, 36* (May 1999), pp. 211–22.
60. Alan G. Sawyer and Peter H. Dickson, "Psychological Perspectives on Consumer Response to Sales Promotion," in *Research on Sales Promotion: Collected Papers,* ed. Katherine E. Jocz (Cambridge, MA: Marketing Science Institute, 1984).
61. William E. Myers, "Trying to Get Out of the Discounting Box," *Adweek,* November 11, 1985, p. 2.
62. Leigh McAlister, "Managing the Dynamics of Promotional Change," in *Looking at the Retail Kaleidoscope,* Forum IX (Stamford, CT: Donnelley Marketing, April 1988).
63. "Promotions Blemish Cosmetic Industry," *Advertising Age,* May 10, 1984, pp. 22–23, 26.
64. Elizabeth Gardener and Minakshi Trivedi, "A Communications Framework to Evaluate Sales Promotion Strategies," *Journal of Advertising Research,* May/June 1998, pp. 67–71.

CHAPTER FIFTEEN

1. Raymond Simon, *Public Relations, Concept and Practices,* 2nd ed. (Columbus, OH: Grid Publishing, 1980), p. 8.
2. Scott M. Cutlip, Allen H. Center, and Glen M. Broom, *Effective Public Relations,* 8th ed. (Upper Saddle River, N.J.: Prentice Hall, 2000).
3. Richard E. Rotman, "When Worlds Combine," *Marketing Magazine,* September 29, 2003.
4. William N. Curry, "PR Isn't Marketing," *Advertising Age,* December 18, 1991, p. 18.
5. Martha M. Lauzen, "Imperialism and Encroachment in Public Relations," *Public Relations Review, 17*(3) (Fall 1991), pp. 245–55.
6. Cutlip, Center, and Broom, *Effective Public Relations.*
7. Simon, *Public Relations,* p. 164.
8. John E. Marston, *Modern Public Relations* (New York: McGraw-Hill, 1979).
9. Karin Scott, "Beyond Press Coverage," *Marketing Magazine,* June 16, 2003.
10. Thomas L. Harris, "How MPR Adds Value to Integrated Marketing Communications," *Public Relations Quarterly,* Summer 1993, pp. 13–18.
11. Raymond Simon, *Public Relations, Concepts and Practices,* 3rd ed. (New York: John Wiley & Sons, 1984), p. 291.
12. Walter K. Lindenmann, "An Effectiveness Yardstick to Measure Public Relations Success," *Public Relations Quarterly, 38,* no. 1 (Spring 1993), pp. 7–10.
13. Deborah Holloway, "How to Select a Measurement System That's Right for You," *Public Relations Quarterly, 37,* no. 3 (Fall 1992), pp. 15–18.
14. Julie Rusciolelli, "PR Discovers Metrics," *Marketing Magazine,* March 29, 2004.

15. Raymond Serafin, "Cars Squeeze Mileage from Awards," *Advertising Age,* June 4, 1990, p. 36.
16. Linda Smith, "When the Trust Begins to Rust," *Marketing Magazine,* March 1, 2004.
17. Dave Scholz, "It's Hard Out There for a Reputation," *Marketing Magazine,* May 14, 2007.
18. Norma Ramage, "Shell Builds a Worldwide Reputation," *Marketing Magazine,* September 15, 2003.
19. Lesley Young, "New Names, New Challenges," *Marketing Magazine,* March 19, 2001.
20. John Burnett, "Shopping for Sponsorships? Integration Is Paramount," *Brandweek,* February 14, 1994, p. 18.
21. Prakash Sethi, *Advertising and Large Corporations* (Lexington, MA: Lexington Books, 1977), pp. 7–8.
22. Harvey Meyer, "When the Cause Is Just," *Journal of Business Strategy,* November/December 1999, pp. 27–31.
23. Michelle Warren, "Cause Commotion," *Marketing Magazine,* October 6, 2003.
24. Natalia Williams, "All Heart—Becel," *Strategy Magazine,* August 2006.
25. Harvey Meyer, "When the Cause Is Just," p. 28.
26. Michelle Warren, "Cause Commotion."
27. Sarah Dobson, "The Hucksters Are Gone," *Marketing Magazine,* April 5, 2004.
28. David Brown, "Tackling Sponsorship," *Marketing Magazine,* May 22, 2006.
29. Michelle Warren, "The Sporting Life," *Marketing Magazine,* February 23, 2004.
30. Mark Harrison, "Own Alone," *Marketing Magazine,* February 23, 2004.
31. Dan Cimoroni, "Don't Just Wish Upon a Star," *Marketing Magazine,* February 23, 2004.
32. Sarah Dobson, "The Measurement Question," *Marketing Magazine,* December 4, 2006.
33. Chris Daniels, "Show Time," *Marketing Magazine,* January 16, 2006.
34. "Clairol Expands CFL Sponsor Roster," *Marketing Magazine,* July 30, 2001.
35. "The 'Bush Leagues,'" *Marketing Magazine,* May 14, 2001.
36. Bettina Cornwell and Isabelle Maignan, "An International Review of Sponsorship Research," *Journal of Advertising,* March 1998.
37. Michel Tuan Pham, "The Evaluation of Sponsorship Effectiveness: A Model and Some Methodological Considerations," *Gestion 2000,* pp. 47–65.
38. Sandra Iacobelli, "Harder-Working Sponsorships," *Marketing Magazine,* October 6, 2003.
39. Ian Malcolm, "Made to Measure," *Marketing Magazine,* February 23, 2004.
40. Sarah Dobson, "The Measurement Question," *Marketing Magazine,* December 4, 2006.
41. Karen Benezra, "Cause and Effects Marketing," *Brandweek,* April 22, 1996, p. 38.
42. Donath, "Corporate Communications," p. 52.
43. Jaye S. Niefeld, "Corporate Advertising," *Industrial Marketing,* July 1980, pp. 64–74.
44. Arlene Lebovic, "A Eureka Moment," *Marketing Magazine,* September 18, 2006.

CHAPTER SIXTEEN

1. Peter D. Bennett, ed., *Dictionary of Marketing Terms* (Chicago: American Marketing Association, 1988), p. 58.
2. Jagdish N. Sheth, "Marketing Megatrends," *Journal of Consumer Marketing, 1,* no. 1 (June 1983), pp. 5–13.
3. "A Potent New Tool for Selling: Database Marketing," *Business Week,* September 5, 1994, pp. 56–59.
4. Herbert Kanzenstein and William S. Sachs, *Direct Marketing,* 2nd ed. (New York: Macmillan, 1992).
5. Lesley Young, "Campbell Evolves from 'Soup to Food' with New Direct Campaigns," *Marketing Magazine,* November 3, 2003.
6. *Canadian Facts 2000,* Canada Post website, March 25, 2002.
7. Cleveland Horton, "Porsche 300,000: The New Elite," *Advertising Age,* February 5, 1990, p. 8.
8. Michelle Warren, "Counting on Catalogues," March 6, 2006.
9. Lesley Young, "Home Depot Unveils 'Dream Book'," *Marketing Magazine,* October 20, 2003.
10. Profiling study by Naveen Donthu and David Gilliland.
11. Lesley Young, "HBC Custom Magazine *Living Spree* to Track Readers' Shopping Habits," *Marketing Magazine,* August 11, 2003.
12. Tom Eisenhart, "Tele-media: Marketing's New Dimension," *Business Marketing,* February 1991, pp. 50–53.
13. Direct Marketing Association 2000.
14. *Canadian Marketing Association 2005 Fact Book,* 2005.
15. Michelle Warren, "Sprint Grows Up," *Marketing Magazine,* April 19, 2004.
16. "Bear Market," *Direct,* December 1999, p. 1+.

CHAPTER SEVENTEEN

1. http://www.statcan.ca, online data tables.
2. David A. Aaker, "Fast Brand Building in Slow-Growth Markets," *Strategy and Business,* third quarter 2002, pp. 48–57.
3. Karen Benezra, "Branding the Web," *Chief Executive,* January 2001, pp. 30–34.
4. Erwin Ephron, "Direct Response or Branding?" *Advertising Age,* November 5, 2001, p. 14.
5. Sean Callahan, "Branding: Is it Worth It?" *B to B,* August 20, 2001, pp. 1, 24.
6. Mike Sharma, "If Not Online, Where Are You?" *Marketing Magazine,* June 5, 2006.
7. Joe Plummer, Steve Rapparport, Taddy Hall, Robert Barocci, *The Online Advertising Playbook, 2007* (John Wiley & Sons, Hoboken, NJ).
8. Chris Gaither, "Yahoo to Sell 'Contextual' Website Ads," *Los Angeles Times,* August 3, 2005, p. C2.
9. Rob Gerlsbeck, "The Next Prime Time," *Marketing Magazine,* May 8, 2006.
10. Wendy Davis, "Web Ad Industry Facing Down Problems," 2002.
11. Wendy Davis, "Banner Ads Are Alive—Though Not Clicking," *Marketing Week,* January 29, 2004, p. 37.
12. Tessa Wegert, "The Ad Banner Turns 10," www.clickz.com, November 4, 2004, pp. 1–2.
13. Chris Daniels, "Off to a Flying Start," *Marketing Magazine,* February 3, 2003.
14. Tessa Wegert, "Consumers Unhappy with Web Site Simply Go Away," www.CenterforMediaResearch.com, August 23, 2005, pp. 1–2.
15. www.Wikipedia.com.
16. Ian Schafer, "What Is Rich Media, Really?" www.clickz.com, September 23, 2005, p. 1.
17. Danny Kucharsky, "Ads On Demand," *Marketing Magazine,* May 15, 2006.
18. Chris Powell, "Broadband or Bust," *Marketing Magazine,* June 19, 2006.
19. Jeff Leiper, "The Battle for Internet TV," *Marketing Magazine,* February 27, 2006.
20. Sam Whitmore, "Podcasting: Making Waves," www.Forbes.com, April 21, 2005, pp. 1–2.
21. Joel Gehman, "Podcasting Demystified," www.mediapost.com, June 6, 2005, pp. 1–2.
22. Jack Neff, "Durex Buys Condom Product Placements in Podcasts," www.AdAge.com, May 12, 2005, pp. 1–3.
23. Chris Sherman, "What Is RSS, and Why Should You Care?" www.search-enginewatch.com, August 30, 2005, pp. 1–4.
24. Shel Holtz, *Public Relations on the Internet* (New York: American Management Association, 1998).
25. Sarah Dobson, "Taking the High Road," *Marketing Magazine,* April 7, 2003.
26. Gary Schwartz, "Mobile Marketing 101," *Marketing Magazine,* July 14, 2003.
27. Ibid.
28. Sarah Dobson, "Mobile Matters," *Marketing Magazine,* October 9, 2006.
29. Michelle Halpern, "Friends and Their Phones," *Marketing Magazine,* January 30, 2006.

30. Sarah Dobson, "Mobile Matters," *Marketing Magazine,* October 9, 2006.
31. Paul-Mark Rendon, "Does Text Sell?" *Marketing Magazine,* April 26, 2004.
32. Michelle Halpern, "Shows On the Go," *Marketing Magazine,* February 6, 2006.
33. Chris Daniels, "Tiny Screen, Huge Potential," *Marketing Magazine,* May 15, 2006.
34. Michelle Halpern, "Shows On the Go."
35. Chris Daniels, "Tiny Screen, Huge Potential," *Marketing Magazine,* May 15, 2006.
36. Alexa Bezjian-Avery, "New Media Interactive Advertising vs. Traditional Advertising," *Journal of Advertising Research,* August 1998, pp. 23–32; Qimel Chen and William D. Wells, "Attitude toward the Site," *Journal of Advertising Research,* September 1999, pp. 27–38; Kim Bartel Sheehan and Sally J. McMillan, "Response Variation in E-Mail Surveys," *Journal of Advertising Research,* July 1999, pp. 45–54; and John Eighmey, "Profiling User Responses to Commercial Websites," *Journal of Advertising Research,* May 1997, pp. 59–66.
37. "Measurement Guidelines and Measurement Certification," www.iab.net, 2006.

CHAPTER EIGHTEEN

1. Robert L. Heilbroner, "Demand for the Supply Side," *New York Review of Books, 38* (June 11, 1981), p. 40.
2. Chris Powell, "Digital Dogfight," *Marketing Magazine,* September 8, 2003.
3. Chris Powell, "The Inventory Debate," *Marketing Magazine,* January 26, 2004.
4. Brenda Pritchard and Susan Vogt, *Advertising and Marketing Law in Canada* (LexisNexis, Butterworths, 2006).
5. "Fanning the Embers," *Marketing Magazine,* September 10, 2001.
6. Stan Sutter, "Common Sense Evolution," *Marketing Magazine,* June 9, 2003.
7. http://adstandards.com/en/standards/complaints_report/2001ascReportEn.pdf, accessed December 12, 2007.
8. http://www.adstandards.com/en/standards/adComplaintsReports.asp?periodquarter=1&periodyear=2007, accessed December 12, 2007.
9. Eric N. Berkowitz, Roger A. Kerin, Steven W. Hartley, William Rudedius, et al., *Marketing,* 5th ed. (Burr Ridge, IL: Irwin/McGraw-Hill, 1997), p. 102.
10. "Calvin's World," *Newsweek,* September 11, 1995, pp. 60–66.
11. Stephanie O'Donohoe, "Attitudes to Advertising: A Review of British and American Research," *International Journal of Advertising, 14* (1995), pp. 245–61.
12. Banwari Mittal, "Public Assessment of TV Advertising: Faint Praise and Harsh Criticism," *Journal of Advertising Research, 34,* no. 1 (1994), pp. 35–53.
13. Sharon Shavitt, Pamela Lowery, and James Haefner, "Public Attitudes toward Advertising; More Favorable Than You Might Think," *Journal of Advertising Research,* July/August 1998, pp. 7–22.
14. Gita Venkataramini Johar, "Consumer Involvement and Deception from Implied Advertising Claims," *Journal of Marketing Research, 32* (August 1995), pp. 267–79; J. Edward Russo, Barbara L. Metcalf, and Debra Stephens, "Identifying Misleading Advertising," *Journal of Consumer Research, 8* (September 1981), pp. 119–31.
15. Ivan L. Preston, *The Great American Blow-Up: Puffery in Advertising and Selling* (Madison: University of Wisconsin Press, 1975), p. 3.
16. David Menzies, "Carlsberg Conspiracy," *Marketing Magazine,* March 29, 2004.
17. Shelby D. Hunt, "Informational vs. Persuasive Advertising: An Appraisal," *Journal of Advertising,* Summer 1976, pp. 5–8.
18. Banwari Mittal, "Public Assessment of TV Advertising: Faint Praise and Harsh Criticism"; J. C. Andrews, "The Dimensionality of Beliefs toward Advertising in General," *Journal of Advertising, 18,* no. 1 (1989), pp. 26–35; Ron Alsop, "Advertisers Find the Climate Less Hostile Outside the U.S.," *The Wall Street Journal,* December 10, 1987, p. 29.
19. David A. Aaker and Donald E. Bruzzone, "Causes of Irritation in Advertising," *Journal of Marketing,* Spring 1985, p. 47–57.
20. Stephen A. Greyser, "Irritation in Advertising," *Journal of Advertising Research, 13* (February 1973), pp. 3–10.
21. Ron Alsop, "Personal Product Ads Abound as Public Gets More Tolerant," *The Wall Street Journal,* April 14, 1986, p. 19.
22. Joanne Lipman, "Censored Scenes: Why You Rarely See Some Things in Television Ads," *The Wall Street Journal,* August 17, 1987, p. 17.
23. For an interesting analysis of an interpretation of this ad from a literary theory perspective see Aaron C. Ahuvia, "Social Criticism of Advertising: On the Role of Literary Theory and the Use of Data," *Journal of Advertising, 27,* no. 1 (Spring 1998), pp. 143–62.
24. James B. Arndorfer, "Skyy Hit the Limit with Racy Ad: Critics," *Advertising Age,* February 7, 2005, p. 6.
25. Tim Nudd, "Does Sex Really Sell?" *Adweek,* October 17, 2005, pp. 14–17.
26. Scott Ward, Daniel B. Wackman, and Ellen Wartella, *How Children Learn to Buy: The Development of Consumer Information Processing Skills* (Beverly Hills, CA: Sage, 1979).
27. Thomas S. Robertson and John R. Rossiter, "Children and Commercial Persuasion: An Attribution Theory Analysis," *Journal of Consumer Research, 1,* no. 1 (June 1974), pp. 13–20; and Scott Ward and Daniel B. Wackman, "Children's Information Processing of Television Advertising," in *New Models for Communications Research,* ed. G. Kline and P. Clark (Beverly Hills, CA: Sage, 1974), pp. 81–119.
28. Merrie Brucks, Gary M. Armstrong, and Marvin E. Goldberg, "Children's Use of Cognitive Defenses against Television Advertising: A Cognitive Response Approach," *Journal of Consumer Research, 14,* no. 4 (March 1988), pp. 471–82.
29. For a discussion on consumer socialization, see Scott Ward, "Consumer Socialization," *Journal of Consumer Research, 1,* no. 2 (September 1974), pp. 1–14.
30. Tamara F. Mangleburg and Terry Bristol, "Socialization and Adolescents' Skepticism toward Advertising," *Journal of Advertising, 27,* no. 3 (Fall 1998), pp. 11–21.
31. Robert E. Hite and Randy Eck, "Advertising to Children: Attitudes of Business vs. Consumers," *Journal of Advertising Research,* October/November 1987, pp. 40–53; Ann D. Walsh, Russell N. Laczniak, and Les Carlson, "Mother's Preferences for Regulating Children's Television," *Journal of Advertising, 27,* no. 3 (Fall 1998), pp. 23–36.
32. Paul-Mark Rendon, "Cherry's Bubba's Out, Says ASC," *Marketing Magazine,* September 22, 2003.
33. John K. Galbraith, *The New Industrial State* (Boston: Houghton Mifflin, 1967), cited in Richard W. Pollay, "The Distorted Mirror: Reflections on the Unintended Consequences of Advertising," *Journal of Marketing,* August 1986, p. 25.
34. Raymond A. Bauer and Stephen A. Greyser, "The Dialogue That Never Happens," *Harvard Business Review,* January/February 1969, pp. 122–28.
35. Morris B. Holbrook, "Mirror Mirror On the Wall, What's Unfair in the Reflections on Advertising," *Journal of Marketing, 5* (July 1987), pp. 95–103; and Theodore Levitt, "The Morality of Advertising," *Harvard Business Review,* July/August 1970, pp. 84–92.
36. Stephen Fox, *The Mirror Makers: A History of American Advertising and Its Creators* (New York: Morrow, 1984), p. 330.
37. Richard W. Pollay, "The Distorted Mirror: Reflections on the Unintended Consequences of Advertising," *Journal of Marketing, 50* (April 1986), p. 33.
38. Jules Backman, "Is Advertising Wasteful?" *Journal of Marketing, 32* (January 1968), pp. 2–8.

39. Hunt, "Informational vs. Persuasive Advertising."
40. Ibid., p. 6.
41. Alice E. Courtney and Thomas W. Whipple, *Sex Stereotyping in Advertising* (Lexington, MA: Lexington Books, 1984).
42. Daniel J. Brett and Joanne Cantor, "The Portrayal of Men and Women in U.S. Television Commercials: A Recent Content Analysis and Trends of 15 Years," *Sex Roles, 18,* no. 9/10 (1998), pp. 595–608; John B. Ford and Michael La Tour, "Contemporary Perspectives of Female Role Portrayals in Advertising," *Journal of Current Issues and Research in Advertising, 28,* no. 1 (1996), pp. 81–93; "Body Shop, Zig Ad Lauded by Report," *Marketing Magazine,* March 18, 2002; "How Far Really?" *Marketing Magazine,* July 2, 2001.
43. Beverly A. Browne, "Gender Stereotypes in Advertising on Children's Television in the 1990s: A Cross-National Analysis," *Journal of Advertising, 27,* no. 1 (Spring 1998), pp. 83–96.
44. Richard H. Kolbe, "Gender Roles in Children's Advertising: A Longitudinal Content Analysis," in *Current Issues and Research in Advertising,* ed. James H. Leigh and Claude R. Martin, Jr. (Ann Arbor: University of Michigan, 1990), pp. 197–206.

45. "Body Shop, Zig Ad Lauded by Report," *Marketing Magazine,* March 18, 2002; "How Far Really?" *Marketing Magazine,* July 2, 2001.
46. Shari Graydon, "Putting the Boots to Terra," *Marketing Magazine,* November 17, 2003.
47. Steven M. Kates and Glenda Shaw-Garlock, "The Ever Entangling Web: A Study of Ideologies and Discourses in Advertising to Women," *Journal of Advertising, 28,* no. 2 (Summer 1999), pp. 33–49.
48. Basil Englis, Michael Solomon, and Richard Ashmore, "Beauty before the Eyes of Beholders: The Cultural Encoding of Beauty Types in Magazine Advertising and Music Television," *Journal of Advertising,* June 1994, pp. 49–64.
49. Suzanne Vranica, "Stereotypes of Women Persist in Ads," *The Wall Street Journal,* October 17, 2003, p. B4.
50. James Stearns, Lynette S. Unger, and Steven G. Luebkeman, "The Portrayal of Blacks in Magazine and Television Advertising," in *AMA Educator's Proceedings,* ed. Susan P. Douglas and Michael R. Solomon (Chicago: American Marketing Association, 1987).
51. Robert E. Wilkes and Humberto Valencia, "Hispanics and Blacks in Television Commercials," *Journal of Advertising, 18,* no. 1 (1989), pp. 19–26.
52. Julia Bristor, Renee Gravois Lee, and Michelle Hunt, "Race and Ideology: African American Images in Television Advertising," *Journal of Public Policy and Marketing, 14* (Spring 1995), pp. 48–59.
53. Corliss Green, "Ethnic Evaluations of Advertising: Interaction Effects of Strength of Ethnic Identification, Media Placement, and Degree of Racial Composition," *Journal of Advertising, 28,* no. 1 (Spring 1999), pp. 49–64.
54. Charles R. Taylor and Barbara B. Stern, "Asian-Americans: Television Advertising and the 'Model Minority' Stereotype," *Journal of Advertising, 26,* no. 2 (Summer 1997), pp. 47–61.
55. Jo Marney, "Counting Ethnic Canadians In," *Marketing Magazine,* June 4, 2001.
56. Jef I. Richards and John H. Murphy, II, "Economic Censorship and Free Speech: The Circle of Communication between Advertisers, Media and Consumers," *Journal of Current Issues and Research in Advertising, 18,* no. 1 (Spring 1996), pp. 21–33.
57. Lawrence C. Soley and Robert L. Craig, "Advertising Pressure on Newspapers: A Survey," *Journal of Advertising,* December 1992, pp. 1–10.
58. Soley and Craig, "Advertising Pressure on Newspapers."
59. For a discussion of monopolies in the cereal industry, see Paul N. Bloom, "The Cereal Industry: Monopolists or Super Marketers?" *MSU Business Topics,* Summer 1978, pp. 41–49.
60. Lester G. Telser, "Advertising and Competition," *Journal of Political Economy,* December 1964, pp. 537–62.
61. Robert D. Buzzell, Bradley T. Gale, and Ralph G. M. Sultan, "Market Share—A Key to Profitability," *Harvard Business Review,* January/February 1975, pp. 97–106.
62. Beth Snyder Bulik, "LG's $100-Mil Charge Apes Samsung Tack," *Advertising Age,* June 21, 2004, pp. 1, 33.
63. Robert D. Buzzell and Paul W. Farris, *Advertising Cost in Consumer Goods Industries,* Marketing Science Institute, Report no. 76, August 1976, p. 111; and Paul W. Farris and David J. Reibstein, "How Prices, Ad Expenditures, and Profits Are Linked," *Harvard Business Review,* November/ December 1979, pp. 173–84.
64. Paul W. Farris and Mark S. Albion, "The Impact of Advertising on the Price of Consumer Products," *Journal of Marketing* 44, no. 3 (Summer 1980), pp. 17–35.
65. Paul W. Farris and Mark S. Albion.
66. Lee Benham, "The Effect of Advertising on the Price of Eyeglasses," *Journal of Law and Economics, 15* (October 1972), pp. 337–52.
67. Robert L. Steiner, "Does Advertising Lower Consumer Price?" *Journal of Marketing, 37,* no. 4 (October 1973), pp. 19–26.
68. Farris and Albion, "The Impact of Advertising," p. 30.
69. James M. Ferguson, "Comments On 'The Impact of Advertising on the Price of Consumer Products,'" *Journal of Marketing, 46,* no. 1 (Winter 1982), pp. 102–5.
70. Farris and Albion, "The Impact of Advertising."
71. Cyndee Miller, "The Marketing of Advertising," *Marketing News,* December 7, 1992, pp. 1, 2.

CREDITS & ACKNOWLEDGEMENTS

CHAPTER 1

p. 3: Reprinted by permission of CV Technologies. **p. 5:** James Leynese/CORBIS SABA; **p. 6 (top):** Courtesy of Rolex Watch U.S.A., Inc.; **p. 6 (bottom):** M&M'S® and M&M'S MINIS® are registered trademarks of Mars, Incorporated and its affiliates. These trademarks are used with permission. Mars, Incorporated is not associated with the authors or publisher. Advertisement printed with permission of Mars, Incorporated. © Mars, Inc. 2006. Courtesy of Etón Corporation. **p. 7 (middle):** Courtesy of Pfizer Consumer Healthcare; **p. 7 (left):** Courtesy of P&G Prestige Products; **p. 7 (right):** Courtesy of Eton Corporation; **p. 10 (left):** Courtesy of the got milk? Campaign; **p. 10 (right):** Courtesy of Degussa Corporation; **p. 13 (top):** Courtesy of Energy Speaker Systems; **p. 13 (bottom):** Photo courtesy of Lee Valley Tools Ltd.; **p. 17:** Courtesy of The Procter & Gamble Company; **p. 18:** Courtesy of WestJet; **p. 19:** Courtesy of Facebook; **p. 20:** Canadian Blood Services. 1/800 Alta Vista. Ottawa, ON K1G 4J5; **p. 26:** © 2005 Starbucks Corporation. All rights reserved. Used with permission.

CHAPTER 2

p. 33: Reprinted by permission of Telus; **p. 36:** © The Proctor & Gamble Company; **p. 39:** © 2005 Benetton Group SpA. Photographer David Sims; **p. 46 (top):** Courtesy of Sobeys; **p. 46 (bottom):** Courtesy of Initiative; **p. 49:** Courtesy of International Business Machines Corporation; **p. 51:** DR PEPPER® is a registered trademark of Dr. Pepper/Seven Up, Inc. © 2000 Dr. Pepper/Seven Up, Inc.; **p. 53:** © Photodisc/Getty Images; **p. 54:** Courtesy of Protocol Integrated.

CHAPTER 3

p. 61: © 2007 Getty Images; **p. 63:** © Everready Battery Company, Inc. 1999. Reprinted with permission; **p. 64 (left):** Courtesy of Research in Motion; **p. 64 (right):** Advertisement reprinted with permission of Rogers Communications Inc. © 2007; **p. 65:** Kimberly-Clark Worldwide, Inc. Used with permission.; **p. 66:** Courtesy of DaimlerChrysler Corporation; **p. 67:** Courtesy of Tropicana Products, Inc.; **p. 69:** Courtesy of PING; **p. 71:** Reprinted with permission from Labatt Brewing Company Limited.; **p. 73:** Fidelity Investments. © 2002 FMR Corp. All rights Reserved. Used with permission.; **p. 74 (left):** Director General Public Affairs, Department of National Defence; **p. 74 (right):** Courtesy of MADD; **p. 75:** Courtesy of Unilever; **p. 79 (top):** Reproduced with the permission of McDonald's Restaurants of Canada Limited; **p. 79 (bottom):** Courtesy of Mountain Equipment Co-op; **p. 82:** CP/Steve White; **p. 83:** Courtesy of Novartis Consumer Health Canada Inc.; **p. 85 (middle):** Ian Campbell/Westside Studio/Cossette; **p. 85 (bottom):** Courtesy of Toyota Canada Inc. and Dentsu Canada; **p. 86:** CP/REX; **p. 87 (top):** Courtesy of Grolsch Canada; **p. 87 (bottom left):** Courtesy of Danone Canada; **p. (bottom right):** Courtesy of Porter Airlines and Tyler Brûlé of Winkreative.

CHAPTER 4

p. 93: Stuart Gregory/Photodisc/Getty Images; **p. 95:** Courtesy of Coast Forest and Lumber Association; **p. 97 (top):** Courtesy of Coach, Inc.; **p. 97 (bottom):** © 1999 Time inc. Reprinted by permission.; **p. 99:** CP/Steve White; **p. 102:** Courtesy of Johnson & Johnson Consumer Products, Inc.; **p. 103:** Courtesy of Zenith Electronics Corp.; **p. 104:** Courtesy of Subaru of America, Inc.; **p. 105:** Used with permission of VISA, USA. Photography © Karen Moscowitz/Getty Images; **p. 106:** © H.J. Heinz Company, L.P. Used with permission.; **p. 107:** Royalty-Free/CORBIS; **p. 109 (top):** Used with permission of The Procter & Gamble Company; **p. 109 (middle):** Courtesy of Alberto-Culver Company; **p. 111:** Courtesy of LG Electronics; **p. 112:** Courtesy of Maxfli Golf; **p. 113:** Courtesy of Lancôme, Paris.

CHAPTER 5

p. 121: Courtesy of Lenovo Canada.; **p. 123:** Courtesy of Ford; **p. 124:** Courtesy of Molson Canadian; **p. 128:** Reprint of the "Safety for Everyone" ad is courtesy of American Honda Motor Co., Inc.; **p. 129:** The McGraw-Hill Companies, Inc./John Flournoy; **p. 133:** Courtesy of Philips Electronics North America Corporation; **p. 137:** Courtesy of Nestlé Canada Inc.; **p. 139:** Courtesy of FPAC; **p. 140:** Saputo Cheese G.P.; **p. 141:** Courtesy of Philips.

CHAPTER 6

p. 147: CP/Adrian Brown; **p. 149:** © CHANEL Inc.; **p. 151:** Courtesy of Pepsi-Cola North America; **p. 155:** Courtesy of Taxi/Cara Foods Ltd.; **p. 156 (top):** © 2002 Lands' End, Inc. Used with permission.; **p. 156 (middle):** Courtesy of Church & Dwight Co., Inc.; **p. 157 (middle):** Courtesy of the Valvoline Company, a division of Ashland Inc.; **p. 157 (bottom):** Courtesy of the Proctor & Gamble Company; **p. 158:** Courtesy of Clearly Canadian Brands; **p. 160:** Courtesy of Panasonic; **p. 161 (top):** Reproduced with the permission of Malt-O-Meal Company, Minneapolis, Minnesota; **p. 161 (middle):** Courtesy of The Gillette Company; **p. 162:** Courtesy of ASICS America Corporation; **p. 165:** Courtesy of Stokely-Van Camp, Inc.; **p. 168:** Courtesy of Moores Clothing for Men… Well made. Well priced. Well dressed.

CHAPTER 7

p. 175: Courtesy of Bell Canada.; **p. 177:** © 2005 BMW of North America. Used with permission. The BMW name and logo are registered trademarks.; **p. 179:** Courtesy of NIKE, Inc.; **p. 180:** Courtesy of Taxi; **p. 183:** Courtesy of Skyy Spirits; **p. 185:** Courtesy of Pfizer Canada Inc.; **p. 186:** Courtesy of Reebok, Acamonchi, John Leguizamo; **p. 187 (top):** Courtesy of Leo Brunett Company7, Inc. as agent for Hallmark Cards, Incorporated; **p. 187 (bottom):** Courtesy of International Business Machines Corporation. Photography by Michele Asselin/Corbis Assignment & Representation.; **p. 189:** © 2004 Nissan. Nissan, Nissan 350Z, Nissan model names, and the Nissan logo are registered trademarks of Nissan.; **p. 193 (left):** Courtesy of Nordica; **p. 193 (right):** Courtesy of MacGregor Golf; **p. 194 (top):** Casey's is a registered trademark of PRC Trademarks Inc.; **p. 194 (bottom):** © 2005 The Boeing Company; **p. 195:** Courtesy of Neutrogena Corporation; **p. 199:** Courtesy of Wm. WRIGLEY Jr. Company; **p. 201 (left):** Courtesy of MasterCard International Incorporated; **p. 201 (right):** Courtesy of Porsche Cars North America, Inc.; **p. 202:** Courtesy of HEAD/Penn Racquet Sports; **p. 203:** Courtesy of Lever Brothers Company; **p. 205:** Photo: P. Demarchelier for TAG Heuer; **p. 206:** CP/Halifax Daily News/Jeff Harper; **p. 207:** Courtesy of PowerBar; **p. 209:** Courtesy of Unilever.

CHAPTER 8

p. 215: Used with permission of Intel and Cohn & Wolfe; **p. 216:** Courtesy of Hitachi America Ltd.; **p. 217 (top):** Courtesy of Eagle One Industries, an operating unit of Valvoline, a division of Ashland, Inc. Eagle One, Nanowax, and Valvoline are trademarks owned by Ashland, Inc.; **p. 217 (middle):** Courtesy of Church & Dwight Co., Inc.; **p. 218:** Courtesy of Pfizer Consumer Healthcare, Pfizer Inc.; **p. 219:** © 2007 Paul Spinelli/MLB Photos via Getty Images; **p. 220 (top):** Courtesy of DaimlerChrysler Corporation; **p. 220 (bottom):** Courtesy of bebe; **p. 221 (left):** Courtesy of BASF Corporation; **p. 221 (right):** Eaton Corporation. All rights reserved 2005; **p. 223:** Courtesy of White Wave, Inc.; **p. 224:** Courtesy of Novartis Consumer Health Canada Inc.; **p. 226 (top):** Courtesy of Team One Advertising for LEXUS. Photo by Martin Oort.; **p. 226 (bottom):** Courtesy of Cambridge SoundWorks; **p. 227:** Courtesy of Sims; **p. 234:** Courtesy of Skyy Spirits; **p. 235:** Courtesy of Skyy Spirits.

CHAPTER 9

p. 243: JFB/Stone+/Getty Images; **p. 245:** © Michael Newman/PhotoEdit; **p. 251:** Tetra Images/Getty Images; **p. 258:** Kieth Brofsky/ Photodisc/Getty Images; **p. 260:** Courtesy of Gfk NOP; **p. 263:** Courtesy of Ipsos-ASI, Inc.; **p. 264:** Decision Analyst.

CHAPTER 10

p. 271: © Getty Images; **p. 276:** McGraw-Hill Archive.

CHAPTER 11

p. 315: CP/LEHTIKUVA/MATTI BJORKMAN; **p. 317:** Courtesy of Porsche Cars North America, Inc.; **p. 328:** Steven Errico/Digital Vision/ Getty Images; **p. 334:** Courtesy of Nielsen; **p. 336:** CP/Fred Lummber; **p. 338:** 2000-2001 BBM Television Data Book. Television Summer Drop-off. Used with permission.

CHAPTER 12

p. 347: Infocus International/Getty Images; **p. 351:** Courtesy of Outpost Magazine; **p. 352:** Courtesy of Alberta Beef Magazine; **p. 354:** Courtesy of Elle Magazine; **p. 355 (top):** Courtesy of Newsweek, Inc. All rights reserved; **p. 355 (bottom):** Courtesy of Toronto Life Magazine; **p. 356:** Used with permission of WD-40 Company; **p. 358:** Harry magazine cover courtesy of Harry Rosen Inc.; **p. 369:** CP/ Steve White.

CHAPTER 13

p. 379: Dick Hemingway Editorial Photographs; **p. 381:** CP/Steve White; **p. 382:** Andrew Simpson; **p. 383:** Courtesy of Outdoor Advertising Association of America, Inc.; **p. 385:** Image reproduced with the permission of VisionTrack; **p. 387 (top):** Courtesy of Vert, Inc.; **p. 387 (middle):** Courtesy of Outdoor Advertising Association of America, Inc.; **p. 390:** Courtesy of WestJet; **p. 398:** Photofest; **p. 401:** AP Photo/Adam Butler.

CHAPTER 14

p. 407: CP/AP/Aijaz Rahi; **p. 411:** Kraft Canada Ltd.; **p. 413:** © 2006 Kellogg north America Company. The copyright in and to the image is and shall remain the sole property of Kellogg North American Company.; **p. 414:** Courtesy of DVC Worldwide; **p. 415:** Courtesy of Burson marstellar for Church & Dwight Company, Inc.; **p. 421:** ArmorAll Products Corporation; **p. 426:** Courtesy of Kellogg Company. Eggo®, Common Sense®, and Kellogg's® are registered trademarks of Kellog Company. All rights reserved.; **p. 427:** Courtesy of Valpak Direct marketing Systems, Inc.; **p. 428:** AP Images; **p. 429:** Used with permission of General Motors Corp.; **p. 430:** CP/Patrick Doyle; **p. 432:** ArmorAll Products Corporation; **p. 433:** Courtesy of Bristol-Myers Company; **p. 434:** Courtesy of WD-40 Company; **p. 435:** Logos courtesy of Volvo Cars of Canada Corp.; **p. 440:** Courtesy of Wilson Sporting Goods, Co. and Great Northern Corporation-Display Group; **p. 442 (top):** Courtesy of Intel Corporation; **p. 442 (middle):** Courtesy of Bridgestone Golf, Inc.; **p. 444 (top):** Courtesy of WD-40 Company; **p. 444 (bottom):** Courtesy of Lever Brothers Company.

CHAPTER 15

p. 451: Courtesy of Ethos JWT; **p. 453:** Courtesy of Bridgeston/ Firestone Americas Holding, Inc.; **p. 456:** McGraw-Hill Ryerson; **p. 457 (left):** Courtesy of BP; **p. 457 (right):** Courtesy of Syngenta; **p. 463:** Courtesy of Edward Jones; **p. 464:** Reprinted with the permission of General Mills; **p. 466:** Courtesy of Tyco International; **p. 467 (left):** Courtesy of Juno Awards **p. 467 (right):** Courtesy of Grant Thornton LLP, US member firm of Grant Thornton International; **p. 468:** WHIRLPOOL is a registered trademark of Whirlpool, U.S.A. © 2005 Whirlpool Corporation. All rights reserved. Habitat For Humanity is a registered trademark of Habitat For Humanity International, Inc.

CHAPTER 16

p. 479: PhotoLink/Getty Images; **p. 481:** Courtesy of Tourism Saskatchewan, www.sasktourism.com; **p. 483 (top):** BLOCKBUSTER name, design, and related marks are trademarks of Blockbuster, Inc. © 2003 Blockbuster, Inc. All rights reserved.; **p. 483 (middle):** © 2005 Hertz System, Inc. Hertz is a registered service mark and trademark of Hertz System, Inc. Photography © altrendo images/Getty Images; **p. 485 (top):** Courtesy of Porsche Cars North America, Inc.; **p. 485 (middle):** © Mercedes-Benz USA, LLC. Courtesy of DaimlerChrysler AG; **p. 485 (bottom):** Courtesy of Lee Valley Hardware; **p. 486:** Shoppers Optimum and Shoppers Optimum Card are trademarks of 911979 Alberta Ltd., used under license.; **p. 487:** Courtesy of Volvo Cars of North America; **p. 488 (top):** Andrew Simpson; **p. 488 (bottom):** Courtesy of Lenox; **p. 490:** Do Not Call logo courtesy of the Federal Trade Commission of the United States of America; **p. 493:** Courtesy of Costco.

CHAPTER 17

p. 497: Reproduced with the permission of Marketing Magazine; **p. 501:** The Procter & Gamble Company; **p. 502:** Courtesy of Snapple Beverage Corporation; **p. 503:** © Kimberly-Clark Worldwide, Inc. Used with permission; **p. 506:** Courtesy of Grantastic Designs, Inc.; **p. 508:** Reproduced with the permission Yahoo! Inc. © 2005 by Yahoo! Inc. YAHOO! And the YAHOO! Logo are trademarks of Yahoo! Inc.; **p. 510:** Habbo Hotel screenshot courtesy of Sulake Corporation; **p. 511 (middle):** Courtesy of DaimlerChrysler Corporation; **p. 511 (bottom):** Courtesy of Ben & Jerry's; **p. 512:** Virgin Mobile Canada.

CHAPTER 18

p. 523: Courtesy of Unilever; **p. 531:** Used with permission of Calvin Klein; **p. 532:** Concept: O. Toscani. Courtesy of United Colors of Benneton; **p. 535:** Reprinted with permission of Church & Dwight Virginia Co., Inc.; **p. 536 (left):** Courtesy of Airwalk; **p. 536 (right):** Courtesy of Skyy Spirits, LLC; **p. 538:** Reprinted with permission of Rolls Royce Motor Cars Inc.; **p. 539:** © American Association of Advertising Agencies; **p. 540:** © American Association of Advertising Agencies; **p. 541:** Courtesy of Network Solutions. © 2005 Network Solutions. All rights reserved; **p. 542 (top):** Courtesy of IKEA and Deutsch Inc.; **p. 542 (middle):** Courtesy of www.gfn.com, the Gay Financial network, Inc.; **p. 543:** Courtesy of Wal-Mart Canada and Publicis; **p. 544:** Courtesy of International Advertising Association; **p. 546 (top):** © American Association of Advertising Agencies; **p. 546 (bottom):** Courtesy of LG Electronics U.S.A., Inc.; **p. 547:** © American Association of Advertising Agencies; **p. 549 (top):** Courtesy of International Advertising Association; **p. 549 (middle):** Courtesy of American Advertising Federation.

NAME AND COMPANY INDEX

Name and Company Index

Name and Company Index

SUBJECT INDEX

Subject Index

D

J

L

M

Subject Index

N

O

Subject Index